P9-DES-025

George Washington and
Abraham Lincoln, Mount
Rushmore National Memorial,
South Dakota.

Thor's Hammer basking in the reflected light of a sunrise, Bryce Canyon National Park, Utah.

Volcanic dust in the atmosphere casts a warm glow on Delicate Arch, Arches National Park, Utah.

Morning in Badlands National Park, South Dakota.

Frommer's®

National Parks

of the

American West

2nd Edition

by Don and Barbara Laine

with Geoff O'Gara, Jack Olson,
Eric Peterson, Alex Wells, Stacey
Wells, Charles P. Wohlforth, and
Stephanie Avnet Yates

IDG Books Worldwide, Inc.
An International Data Group Company
Foster City, CA • Chicago, IL • Indianapolis, IN • New York, NY

IDG BOOKS WORLDWIDE, INC.

An International Data Group Company
919 E. Hillsdale Blvd.
Suite 400
Foster City, CA 94404

Find us online at **www.frommers.com**

Copyright © 2000 by IDG Books
  Worldwide, Inc.
Maps copyright © 2000 by IDG Books
  Worldwide, Inc.

All rights reserved. No part of this book
may be reproduced or transmitted in any
form or by any means, electronic or
mechanical, including photocopying,
recording, or by any information storage
and retrieval system, without permission in
writing from the Publisher.

FROMMER'S is a registered trademark of
Arthur Frommer. Used under license.

ISBN 0-02-863620-1
ISSN 1097-783X

Editors: Justin Lapatine and Margot Weiss
Production Editor: Tammy Ahrens
Production Team: Melissa Auciello-Brogan,
  Natalie Hollifield, Bob LaRoche, and
  Heather Pope
Design by Paul Costello
Digital Cartography by Barbara Laine
Photo Editor: Richard Fox
Front cover photo: Canoers on String Lake
in Grand Teton National Park.

Special Sales

For general information on IDG Books
Worldwide's books in the U.S., please call
our Consumer Customer Service department at 1-800-762-2974. For reseller information, including discounts, bulk sales,
customized editions, and premium sales,
please call our Reseller Customer Service
department at 1-800-434-3422.

Manufactured in the United States of
America

5 4 3 2 1

Note: Please be advised that travel information
is subject to change at any time. The publisher
and the authors have endeavored to provide
useful information in this publication, but we
suggest that you write or call ahead for confirmation when making your travel plans. The
publisher and authors cannot be held responsible for the experiences of readers while traveling. National parks are, by their very nature,
potentially hazardous places. In visiting any of
the places or doing any of the activities
described herein, readers assume all risk of
injury or loss that may accompany such activities. The publisher and the authors disavow all
responsibility for injury, death, loss, or property
damage that may arise from a reader's visit to
any of the places or participation in any of the
activities described herein, and the publisher
and the authors make no warranties regarding
the competence, safety, and reliability of outfitters, tour companies, or training centers
described in this publication.

Color insert photo credits:

Yosemite: © Cosmo Condina/Tony Stone Images
Crater Lake: © David Muench
*Arches, Badlands, Bryce Canyon, Canyon de Chelly,
Carlsbad Caverns, Death Valley, Denali, Devils Tower,
Grand Canyon, Mojave National Preserve, Mount
Rainier, Mount Rushmore, Petrified Forest:* © Fred
Hirschmann
Yellowstone: © Randi Hirschmann
Zion: © Scott T. Smith

Contents

List of Maps

Authors

Don and Barbara Laine have written about and traveled extensively throughout the Rocky Mountains and the Southwest. They are the authors of Frommer's guides to Utah, Colorado and Denver, Boulder & Colorado Springs, as well as *Frommer's Zion & Bryce Canyon National Parks* and *Frommer's Rocky Mountain National Park.*

A native of Los Angeles and an avid traveler, **Stephanie Avnet Yates** believes California is best seen from behind the wheel of a red convertible. She is the author of *Frommer's Los Angeles, Frommer's San Diego, Frommer's Wonderful Weekends from Los Angeles,* and coauthor of *Frommer's California.*

Geoff O'Gara writes travel guides, fiction, and books on natural resource issues from his home in Lander, Wyoming, where he also works for Wyoming Public Television. His next book is *What You See in Clear Water* (Knopf).

Jack Olson, a longtime resident of Denver, wanders the Rockies and the entire country as a freelance photographer and writer. He writes travel articles for AAA magazines and his photos may be seen in such publications as *Backpacker, Audubon, Sierra,* and *National Geographic Books.*

A Denver-based freelance writer, **Eric Peterson** has contributed to numerous travel publications about the American West. He also writes for several Denver-based business and entertainment magazines, makes a mean chicken chili, and enjoys indoor and outdoor activities of all kinds, including but not limited to watching movies, hiking, fishing, and Chia Head horticulture.

A resident of Park City, Utah, **Alex Wells** has written for magazines including *Condé Nast Traveller, Men's Journal,* and *Outside.* When not on assignment, he enjoys backcountry skiing and backpacking. His idea of heaven is an eternal hike through the Grand Canyon—with weekly breaks for pizza and showers. He is the author of *Frommer's Grand Canyon National Park.*

Stacey Wells is a native Californian who grew up in the foothills of the Sierra Nevada and now lives in Oakland, California, where she works for an Internet start-up. She survives city life by making weekend trips to the Sierra. Stacey is the author of *Frommer's Yosemite & Sequoia/Kings Canyon National Parks.*

Charles P. Wohlforth is a lifelong Alaskan who has been a writer and journalist since 1986. In 1992 he became a freelance writer for various regional and national magazines and for books such as *Frommer's Alaska* and *Frommer's Family Vacations in the National Parks,* which covers parks all over the United States based on insights from the Wohlforth family's own camping experiences.

Some of the chapters in this second edition are based on material from the first edition written by **T. D. Griffith, Ed Lawrence, Jim Moore, Matthew R. Poole,** and **Tom Wells.** Further information has been provided by **Karl Samson** and **Lesley King.**

Acknowledgments

THE FOLLOWING INDIVIDUALS HAVE REVIEWED CHAPTERS OR HELPED THE AUTHORS in their research:

Diane Allen, **Arches;** Peter Allen, **Rocky Mountain;** Jane Andersen, **Mesa Verde;** Terry Baldino, **Death Valley;** Doug Ballou, **Carlsbad Caverns;** Doug Buehler, **Guadalupe Mountains;** Doug Caldwell, **Rocky Mountain;** Malinee Crapsey, **Sequoia/Kings Canyon** and **Yosemite;** Tom Danton, **Saguaro;** Denny Davies, **Zion;** Anne Marie Fender, **Canyon de Chelly;** Sheri Forbes, **Mount Rainier;** Larry Frederick, **Glacier;** Paul Henderson, **Canyonlands;** Paula Hosking, **Petrified Forest;** Scott Isaacson, **Lassen Volcanic;** Beth Kaeding, **Yellowstone;** Bruce Kaye, **Theodore Roosevelt;** Peter Keller, **Redwood;** Rich McCamant, **Guadalupe Mountains;** Timothy Manns, **North Cascades;** Barbara Maynes, **Olympic;** Dave Mecham, **Bryce Canyon;** Marianne Mills, **Badlands;** Riley Ann Mitchell, **Devils Tower;** Will Morris, **Mesa Verde;** Valerie Naylor, **Big Bend;** Thea Nordling, **Capitol Reef;** Linda Olson, **Grand Teton;** Annie Hopkins Pfaff, **Great Basin;** Jim Popovich, **Mount Rushmore;** Dave Rachlis, **Zion;** Karen Rosga, **Jewel Cave;** Cheryl Schreier, **Bryce Canyon;** Ellen Seeley, **Grand Canyon;** Teresa Shirakawa, **Petrified Forest;** Carol Spears, **Channel Islands;** Kirsten Talken, **Mojave;** Kent Taylor, **Crater Lake;** Ron Terry, **Wind Cave;** Joe Zarki, **Joshua Tree;** Paul Zaenger, Phil Zichterman, **Black Canyon of the Gunnison.**

An Invitation to the Reader

In researching this book, we discovered many wonderful places. We're sure you'll find others. Please tell us about them, so we can share the information with your fellow travelers in upcoming editions. If you were disappointed with a recommendation, we'd love to know that, too. Please write to:

Frommer's National Parks of the American West, 2nd Edition
Frommer's Travel Guides
1633 Broadway
New York, NY 10019

The following abbreviations are used for credit cards:

AE	American Express	JCB	Japan Credit Bank
CB	Carte Blanche	MC	MasterCard
DC	Diners Club	V	Visa
DISC	Discover		

Introduction: Enjoying the Parks Without the Crowds

THE NATIONAL PARK SERVICE SEEMS TO BE WALKING A TIGHTROPE. THE service really has two missions, and they sometimes seem to run in opposition to each other. Its first mission is to preserve some of America's most unique and important natural areas for future generations; the second is to make these places available for the enjoyment of all Americans. Because the number of visitors to our national parks has grown tremendously over the years, some of the busiest parks, including the Grand Canyon, Yosemite, Zion, and Yellowstone, are now searching for ways to make both these goals reality.

Park service officials have often said that the real source of congestion in the most heavily visited parks is not the numbers of people but rather the numbers of cars. (You don't go to a national park hoping to get caught up in a traffic jam, do you?) As a result, those parks with yearly attendance in the millions are now putting together plans to limit vehicle traffic within their boundaries.

If all this leads you to despair that you can't have a true "wilderness" experience in one of the national parks of the American West, don't think that for a minute. Even in a park as crowded as Yosemite, there are places where you can completely escape the crowds, where you'll be able to walk among the trees and hear nothing but the sound of your own footsteps. All it takes is a little effort and planning, and that's where this book comes in handy.

Our authors have talked to the rangers, hiked the trails, and taken the tours, all the while asking, "How can our readers avoid the crowds?" In each of the following chapters, you'll find a section giving you straightforward, practical advice on just how to do this. Sure, if you're an outdoors iron man (or woman), you can avoid the crowds by taking off on the most strenuous backcountry hikes, but not everyone is made of iron. So we've searched for secluded trails that can be hiked by the average person (not just the ones you'll see on the covers of *Outside* magazine), scenic drives where you won't get caught in bumper-to-bumper traffic, and points where, with only a minimum of effort, you'll be afforded spectacular views without feeling as if you're packed into Times Square on New Year's Eve.

We've also discovered that *when* you go is as important as *where* you go. Since most of the West's national parks and monuments are busiest in July and August, you can avoid many of the people by coming in April or September, especially if you can come just before or just after the times when schools are generally out for summer vacation. Remember that most national parks are open year-round, though services are sometimes limited during the off-season. In fact, many are great places to go in winter for skiing and exploring, and these are also times when you're less likely to feel mobbed. The hoodoos of

Bryce Canyon, for example, are just as strikingly beautiful when they're snow-covered, and you won't be jostling with nearly as many people at the view points.

The last thing we've discovered (though it's not a very big secret) is that there are many hidden gems among the national parks and monuments of the American West. Everyone knows about Mount Rainier and Carlsbad Caverns but not always about the less-visited parks, such as Great Basin in Nevada, Canyon de Chelly in Arizona, the Channel Islands in California, Little Bighorn Battlefield in Montana, Jewel Cave in the Black Hills of South Dakota, and the Guadalupe Mountains in Texas. These are places of great beauty or historical significance, but they're often overlooked because of their remoteness or simply because they're relatively new to the national park system.

The most important thing to remember as you make your trip is that the parks and monuments discussed in the following chapters have been set aside and are maintained for future generations, not only our own.

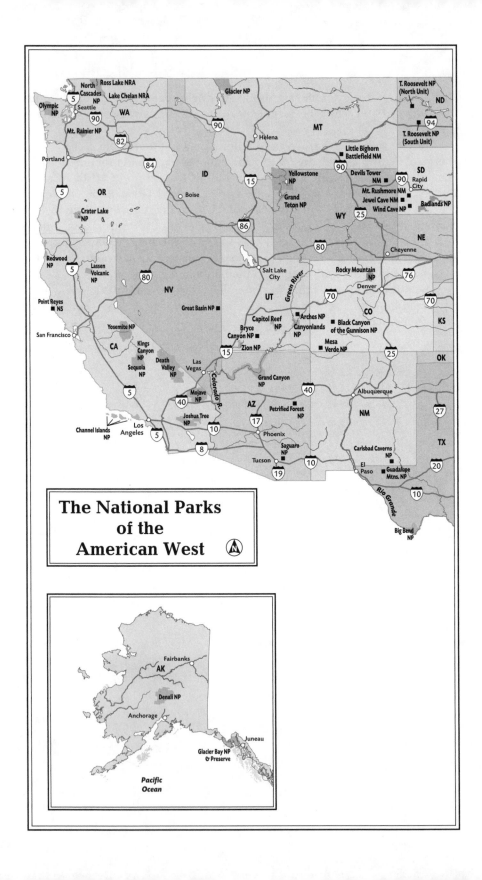

The National Parks
of the
American West

JUST THE FACTS:

Planning Your Trip to the National Parks of the American West

I N THIS CHAPTER, WE'VE TRIED TO GIVE YOU ALL THE GENERAL INFOR-mation you will need to help plan your trip to the national parks of the western United States. The individual park chapters that follow will be able to answer your more specific questions.

The Parks Without the Crowds—Some General Tips

It's not easy to commune with nature when you're surrounded by hordes of fellow visitors. For each park, we've discussed the best times of year to go and listed certain areas, trails, and sites less visited than the others. Beyond that, here are a few general guidelines.

◆ **Avoid the high season.** For most parks in the West, this especially means July and August, but any time schools are not in session, parks are crowded with families on vacation. Spring and fall in many of these national parks offer mild weather, vibrant plant and animal life, and relatively empty trails and roads.

◆ **Walk away if you find yourself in a crowd.** It sounds simple, but often, while a scenic overlook is crowded, you'll find an equally good view that is completely empty just a short stretch down the road or trail.

◆ **Visit popular attractions at off-peak hours,** especially early in the morning or late in the afternoon. You'll be surprised at how empty the park is before 9 or 10am. Dawn and dusk are also often the best times to see wildlife. You can also avoid waits and crowds at restaurants by

eating at off-peak hours—try lunch at 11 and dinner at 4—and campers using public showers will often find them jammed first thing in the morning and just before bedtime, but deserted the rest of the time.

◆ **Don't forget winter.** You may not see wildflowers and some roads and areas may be closed, but many national parks are wonderful places to ski, snowshoe, or snowmobile.

◆ Finally, **remember that some parks are rarely crowded,** and we've made a special effort to include information about many of them in this book. Generally, the more difficult a park is to get to, the fewer people you'll encounter there. And many of the smaller parks remain essentially undiscovered, while offering scenery and recreation opportunities that rival or even surpass the big name parks. Consider parks such as Big Bend and Great Basin, as well as America's newest national park: Black Canyon of the Gunnison.

Information

Doing your homework can help you make the most of your trip; it can also help you avoid the crowds. For park

Planning a Trip Online

For those with access to the Internet, there is a world of information available—in fact, sometimes it seems that there is almost too much information out there. In each of the following chapters we have included pertinent Web sites and e-mail addresses, but there are several Web sites that stand out.

The National Park Service's Web site, www.nps.gov, has general information on the national parks, monuments, and historic sites; as well as individual park maps that can be down-loaded in a variety of formats. The site also contains a link to every individual park's Web site, and those often contain links to nearby attractions and other useful information.

Another useful Web site for anyone interested in the outdoors is www.recreation.gov, a partnership among federal agencies that can take you to information on national parks, national forests, Bureau of Land Management sites, Bureau of Reclamation sites, Army Corps of Engineers sites, and National Wildlife Refuges.

Finally, anyone planning to travel with a dog or cat will want to check out www.petswelcome.com, a site that provides useful tips on traveling with pets, as well as lists of lodgings that accept pets, kennels for temporary pet boarding, and veterinarians you can call in an emergency.

brochures and general planning information, contact the **Department of the Interior, National Park Service, Office of Public Inquiries,** 1849 "C" St. NW, Room 1013, Washington, DC 20240 (☎ 202/208-4747), Monday to Friday, from 9am to 3pm.

However, it's usually best to contact each park directly, and that information is included in each of the following chapters.

A WORD ON NATURE ASSOCIATIONS

Throughout this book you'll read that a certain nature association or organization with a similar name operates the park bookstore. Practically every national park has a bookstore now—some have several—and they are excellent sources for maps, guidebooks, videos, postcards, posters, and the like. Most of these nature associations also offer memberships (usually $15 to $25 per year for individuals) that entitle the member to discounts of 15% to 20% on all purchases. You'll also usually get a quarterly newsletter. And for frequent travelers,

here's the really good news: Membership in one nature association almost always entitles you to a 15% to 20% discount at other nature association bookstores, at national parks, monuments, historic sites, and recreation areas. For those of us who like to collect books, topo maps, posters, and so on, the savings add up quickly. And we can also feel very smug about what a good deed we're doing in supporting these nonprofit groups.

Planning a National Park Itinerary

Even though distances seem vast in the western United States, it's possible to visit more than one of the national parks there in a single trip. In fact, people often combine visits to Yellowstone and Grand Teton, Yosemite and Sequoia, and Zion and Bryce Canyon.

The parks of the California desert (Death Valley, Joshua Tree, and Mojave Preserve) can be knitted into a nice itinerary that might even leave you time to stop off in the resort town of Palm Springs. A popular trip for families is a drive through Badlands National Park and Black Hills of South Dakota, all the way through Devils Tower to Yellowstone. It's not a small stretch, but doable if you have more than a week.

However, although it can be a lot of fun to combine several national parks in your vacation trip, try to not make the all-too-common mistake of attempting to see everything there is to see in too short a period of time. Be realistic about how much you want to see at each park, and create an itinerary that lets you thoroughly enjoy one or two aspects of a park rather than just glimpsing every corner as you speed by. And, especially for trips of more than a week, try to schedule a little relaxation time—perhaps loafing in the campground one afternoon, or lounging by the motel swimming pool.

Visitor Centers

Your first stop at any national park should be the visitor center. Not only will you learn the why of the park, but you'll also get timely information such as road and trail closures, safety issues, and the schedule for upcoming ranger programs. Visitor center hours usually vary by season; most are open daily from 8am until 6 or 7pm in summer, and closing earlier at other times.

Fees & Permits

Though fees have increased in the past few years, visiting a national park is still a bargain—a steal compared to a theme park. Entry fees, ranging from nothing at Guadalupe to $20 at Grand Canyon, are usually charged per vehicle regardless of how many visitors are stuffed inside. Those arriving on foot or by bicycle pay lower per-person fees. Some parks offer passes good for unlimited visits to the same park for 12 months.

Special Passes. There are several passes that offer discounts or completely free admission to as many different parks as you care to visit.

For anyone, the **Golden Eagle Passport** costs $50, lasts 1 year, and provides free entry to all national parks for the pass holder and any accompanying passengers in a personal vehicle. For those traveling in another manner, such as by bicycle or on foot, the pass admits free the pass holder, spouse, children, and parents. The only catch is that the pass covers entry fees to the parks, but not what the Park Service calls user fees, such as cave tours, camping, boat launching, and whatever. Unfortunately, in a grab for quick cash, some parks, such as Bryce Canyon, have instituted a mandatory user fee for shuttle bus service, whether you use the shuttle or not. The best way to buy the Golden Eagle Pass is to purchase it at the first national park entry station you get to (checks are accepted). You can also send a check for $50 to: Attention: Golden Eagle Passport, National Park Service, 1100 Ohio Dr. SW, Room 138, Washington, DC 20242.

The **Golden Age Passport** is a lifetime entrance pass available to those 62 years or older. It costs $10 and must be purchased in person at a National Park Service fee entry area. Be sure to bring proof of age and U.S. citizenship or permanent residency. Like the Golden Eagle, this pass admits for free the pass holder and any accompanying passengers in a personal vehicle. An additional advantage to the Golden Age Passport is that it provides a 50% discount on user fees for all park services and facilities, such as camping, swimming, parking, boat launching, or cave tours, but not what are called "special recreation fees" or fees charged by concessionaires.

The **Golden Access Passport** provides the same benefits as the Golden Age Passport, both free entry for the pass holder and companions and a 50% discount on park services and facilities fees. It costs nothing and is available to those who are blind or permanently disabled, regardless of age. To get one, go to any park entrance fee area and show proof of disability and eligibility for receiving benefits under federal law.

A New National Park?

As this book went to press, residents of southern Colorado were optimistic that their favorite sandbox, **Great Sand Dunes National Monument,** near Alamosa, would soon be given additional acreage and gain national park status. The park-to-be contains America's tallest sand dunes, rising over 700 feet, and offers hiking, wildlife viewing, nature programs, and camping. Contact Great Sand Dunes at 11500 Colo. 150, Mosca, CO 81146 (☎ 719/378-2312; www.nps.gov/grsa).

Other Fees. You may also be required to pay other recreational use fees, ranging from charges for guided cave tours to camping fees. Almost all park museums and exhibits are free, but there are many services operated by private concessionaires. So you will have to pay extra to go horseback riding in Theodore Roosevelt National Park (unless you bring our own horses) or to rent one of the audio driving tours at Yellowstone.

Backcountry Permits. At most national parks, it is necessary to obtain a backcountry permit to stay overnight in the park's undeveloped backcountry. In some parks, there are even more restrictions. To be safe, if you intend to do any backpacking, look in the individual park chapter or contact the park's backcountry office in advance. In some cases, it may be possible to obtain a permit by mail; in most cases, you must appear in person the day before your trip. Some parks charge for backcountry permits, while others are free; and some restrict the number of permits issued.

Other Permits. Hunting is not allowed in national parks, but fishing often is, and you will usually need a state fishing license. Licenses are generally available at local sporting goods stores and offices of states' game and fish departments. Fees vary for state residents and nonresidents, for various time periods, and sometimes by location within the state, but you can usually get a nonresident 1-day license for $5 to $10 and a 5- to 7-day nonresident license for $15 to $20.

In some parks (Yellowstone and Grand Teton, for example), you will need a special permit to go boating. In others you may need a special permit for cross-country skiing. Check the individual park chapters for details on these and other permits that might be required.

Getting a Campsite

Although a growing number of national park campgrounds accept campsite reservations, many still do not. If you plan to camp and are heading to a first-come, first-served campground, the first thing to do upon arrival is to make sure a site is available. Campsites at major park campgrounds fill up early in summer, on weekends, and during other peak times, such as school holidays. A reservation, or an early morning arrival at a campground (sometimes as early as 7 or 8am), is the best defense against disappointment. In each chapter, we've given an indication if a campground tends to fill up especially early, and whether or not reservations are accepted.

The **National Park Reservation Service** (☎ 800/365-2267; www.reservations. nps.gov) provides reservations for National Park Service campgrounds at many popular parks, including Channel Islands, Death Valley, Glacier, Grand Canyon, Joshua Tree, Mount Rainier, Rocky Mountain, Sequoia–Kings Canyon, Yosemite, and Zion. You can also make reservations in many **National Forest Service** campgrounds through its national reservations number (☎ 877/444-6777; www. reserveusa.com).

Maps

When you arrive at a national park site, you'll receive a large, four-color brochure that has a good map of the park on it; and of course, you'll also have the maps in this book. However, these won't be enough if you want to do some serious hiking, especially into backcountry and wilderness areas. What you'll really need are detailed topographic maps.

Particularly good are the maps from National Geographic Maps/Trails Illustrated, which publishes more than 60 maps of national park areas. Most retail for around $10 and are available in bookstores (including the national park bookstores), or directly from **National Geographic Maps/Trails Illustrated,** P.O. Box 4357, Evergreen, CO 80437-4357 (☎ 800/962-1643 or 303/670-3457; www.trailsillustrated.com). The company also offers CD-ROMS on many national parks.

Tips for RVers

Especially in the warm months, many people prefer to explore the national parks in an RV—a motor home, truck camper, or camper trailer. One advantage to this type of travel is that early morning and early evening are among the best times to be in the parks if you want to avoid crowds and do some wildlife watching. Needless to say, it's a lot more convenient to experience the parks at these times if you're already there, staying in one of the park campgrounds.

Carrying your house with you, like a turtle, also lets you stop for meals anytime and anywhere you choose; and it means you won't have to worry about sleeping on a lumpy mattress. Another added benefit is that you won't spend time searching for a rest room—almost all RVs have some sort of bathroom facilities, ranging from a full bathroom with tub/shower combination to a porta-potty that is stored under a seat.

There are disadvantages, of course. Number one, you probably won't save a lot of money. Renting a motor home will probably end up costing almost as much as driving a compact car, staying in mod-erately priced motels, and eating in family style restaurants and cafes. That's because the motor home will go only one-third as far on a gallon of gas as your compact car will, and they're expensive to rent. Some of the private campgrounds charge as much for an RV site with utility hookups as you'd expect to pay in a cheap motel.

Other disadvantages include the limited facilities in national park campgrounds (although they are being upgraded to the point where camping purists are starting to complain). Even in most commercial campgrounds the facilities are less than you'd expect in moderately priced motels. And parking is often limited in national parks, especially for motor homes and other large vehicles. However, since most people are driving in the parks between 10am and 5pm, the solution is to head out on the scenic drives either early or late in the day, when there's less traffic. It's nicer then, anyway.

If you'll be traveling in the park in your RV and want to make it obvious that your campsite is occupied, carry something worthless to leave in it, such as a cardboard box with "Site Taken" clearly written on it. You can usually find a rock to weigh it down.

Because many of the national park campsites are not level, carry four or five short boards, or leveling blocks, that can be placed under the RV's wheels. You can buy small, inexpensive levels at RV and hardware stores, and you'll discover that not only will you sleep better if your rig is level, but your food won't slide off the table and the refrigerator will run more efficiently.

Renting an RV for Your National Park Trek. If you're flying into the area and renting an RV when you arrive, choose your starting point carefully; not only do you want to keep your driving to a minimum—you'll be lucky to get 10 miles per gallon of gas—but rental rates vary depending on the city in which you pick up your RV. Rates are generally highest in midsummer, between $1,000 and $1,100 per week. The nation's largest rental company is **Cruise America** (☎ 800/327-7799; fax 602/464-7321; www.cruiseamerica.com), with outlets in most major Western cities. RV rentals are also available from **El Monte RV** (☎ 800/367-3687 or 562/483-4941; www.elmonte.com), with rental locations in California, Washington, Florida, and New Jersey. Information on additional rental agencies, as well as tips on renting, can be obtained from the **Recreation Vehicle Rental Association** (no phone), 3930 University Dr., Fairfax, VA 22030 (www.rvra.org).

Tips for Traveling with Kids

The **Junior Ranger Program** offered at most parks gives kids the chance to earn certificates, badges, and patches for completing certain projects, such as tree or animal identification, or answering questions in a workbook. It's a good way to learn about the national parks and the resources that the Park Service protects. Also, many parks offer special discussions, walks, and other ranger-led activities for children.

Tips for Travelers with Disabilities

The National Park Service has come a long way in the past dozen or so years in making the parks more accessible for visitors with disabilities. Most parks have accessible rest rooms, and many have at least one trail that is wheelchair accessible—the Rim Trail at Bryce Canyon is a prime example. In addition, as campgrounds, boat docks, and other facilities are being upgraded, improvements are being made to make them more accessible. Some parks now have campsites designed specifically for those in wheelchairs; and park amphitheaters can usually accommodate wheelchair users.

But perhaps just as important as upgrades in facilities is the prevailing attitude on the part of park rangers that these parks are for the public—the entire public—and they are going to do whatever it takes to help everyone enjoy his or her park experience. Those with special needs are encouraged to talk with park personnel, who can usually assist, such as by opening locked gates to get vehicles closer to scenic attractions, or simply by advising as to trails with the lowest grades or which portable toilets are accessible.

One note on service dogs: Seeing Eye and other service dogs are not considered pets, and are permitted anywhere in the parks. However, because of potential problems with wildlife or terrain (sharp rocks on some trails can cut dogs' paws), it's usually best for those taking service dogs into the parks to discuss their plans with rangers beforehand.

Among resources available for people with disabilities is *A World of Options,* a 658-page book for travelers with disabilities that covers everything from biking trips to scuba outfitters. It costs $45 and is available from **Mobility International USA,** P.O. Box 10767, Eugene, OR 97440 (☎ 541/343-1284, voice and TDD; www.miusa.org). **Wheelchair Getaways** (☎ 800/642-2042; www.blvd.com/wg.htm) rents specialized vans with wheelchair lifts and other features for the disabled in more than 100 U.S. cities.

And don't forget your **Golden Access Passport** (see "Fees & Permits," above). It is free and will grant you free admission to most national parks and a 50% discount on many park services and facilities.

Tips for Travelers with Pets

National parks as well as other federal lands administered by the National Park Service are not pet-friendly, and those planning to visit the parks should consider leaving their pets at home. Pets are almost always prohibited on hiking trails, in the backcountry, and in buildings, and must always be on a leash. Essentially, this means that if you take your dog or cat into the parks they can be with you in the campgrounds and inside your vehicle, and you can walk them in parking areas, but that's about it. It's no fun for either you or your pet.

Aside from regulations, though, you need to be concerned with your pet's well being. Pets should never be left in closed vehicles, where temperatures can soar to over 120°F in minutes, resulting in brain damage or death, and there is no punishment too severe for the human who subjects a dog or cat to that torture.

Those who do decide to take pets with them into these parks despite these warnings should take the pets' leashes, of course; carry plenty of water (pet shops sell clever little travel water bowls that won't spill in a moving vehicle); and proof that the dogs or cats have been vaccinated against rabies. Flea and tick spray or powder is also important, since fleas that may carry bubonic plague have been found on prairie dogs and other rodents in some parks.

Protecting Your Health & Safety

First of all, don't forget that motor vehicle accidents cause more deaths in the parks every year than anything else. Scenic drives are often winding and steep; take them slowly and carefully. And no matter how stunning the snow-capped peak you may glimpse off to the side—keep your eyes on the road.

When out on the trails, even for a day hike, keep safety in mind. The wild, untouched nature of these parks is what makes them so exciting and breathtakingly beautiful—but along with wildness comes risk. The national parks are not playgrounds, nor are they zoos. The animals here are truly untamed and sometimes dangerous. This doesn't mean that disaster could strike at any time, but it does mean that visitors should exercise basic caution and common sense at all times, respecting the wilderness around them and always following the rules of the park.

Never feed, bother, or approach animals. Even the smallest among them can carry harmful, sometimes deadly, diseases, and feeding them is dangerous

Special Tip for Pet Owners

Although pets are not permitted on the trails or backcountry in practically all national parks, those traveling with their dogs can hike with them over miles of trails administered by the U.S. Forest Service and Bureau of Land Management, adjacent to many parks.

not only to yourself, but to the animals too, which (like us) will happily eat what their bodies can't handle. In addition, wild animals' dependence on human handouts can lead to unpleasant confrontations, which often result in rangers having to relocate or kill the animal. As the park service reminds us, "A fed bear is a dead bear."

It's often a good idea to make noise as you hike, to make sure you don't accidentally stumble upon and frighten a large animal into aggression; and to follow park rules on food storage when in bear country. Photographers should always keep a safe distance when taking pictures of wildlife—the best photos are shot with a telephoto lens.

It's equally important for your safety to know your limitations, to understand the environment, and to take the proper equipment when exploring the park. The visitor center should always be your stop before you hike. Park staff there can offer you advice on your hiking plans and supply you with pamphlets, maps, and information on weather conditions or any dangers, such as bear activity or flash flood possibilities on canyon hikes. Once out on the trail, hikers should always carry sufficient water and, just as important, remember to drink it. Wear sturdy shoes with good ankle support and rock-gripping soles. Always keep a close eye on any children in your group, and never let them run ahead.

Since many park visitors live at or near sea level, one of the most common health hazards is **altitude sickness,** caused by the parks' high elevations. Symptoms include headache, fatigue, nausea, loss of appetite, muscle pain, and lightheadedness. Doctors recommend that, until you are acclimated, which can take several days, the best remedy is to consume light meals and drink lots of liquids, avoiding those with caffeine or alcohol. It's a good idea to take frequent sips of water, as well.

One proven method of minimizing the effects of high altitudes is to work up to them. For instance, on a visit to southern Utah, go to lower elevation Zion National Park for a day or two before heading to the higher mountains of Bryce Canyon.

A waterborne hazard is *Giardia,* a parasite that wreaks havoc on the human digestive system. If you pick up this pesky hanger-on, it may accompany you on your trip home. The best solution is to carry all the water you'll need (usually a gallon a day). If necessary, untreated water from the parks' lakes and streams should be boiled for 3 to 6 minutes before consumption.

Hiking Tips

Don't venture off on any extensive hike, even a day hike, without the following gear: a compass, a topographical map, bug repellent, a whistle, and a watch. In many Western parks, sunglasses, sunscreen, and wide-brimmed hats are also considered essential. To be on the safe side, you should keep a **first aid kit** in your car or luggage, and have it handy when hiking. At a minimum, it should contain butterfly bandages, sterile gauze pads, adhesive tape, an antibiotic ointment, pain relievers, alcohol pads, and a knife with scissors and tweezers.

Planning a Backcountry Trip

Here are some general things to keep in mind when planning a backcountry trip:

◆ **Permits** In many parks, overnight hiking and backcountry camping require a permit.

◆ **Camping Etiquette & Special Regulations** Follow the basic rules of camping etiquette: Pack out all your trash, including uneaten food and used toilet paper. Camp in obvious campsites. If pit toilets are not available, bury human waste in holes 6 inches deep, 6 inches across, and at least 200 feet from water and creek beds. When doing dishes, take water and dishes at least 200 feet from the water source, and scatter the waste water. Hang food and trash out of reach of wildlife.

◆ **Shoes** Be sure to wear comfortable, sturdy hiking shoes that will resist water if you're planning an early season hike.

◆ **Sleeping Bags** Your sleeping bag should be rated for the low temperatures found at high elevations. Most campers are happy to have a sleeping pad.

◆ **Water** If you're not carrying enough water for the entire trip, you'll also need a good water purifying system, since that seemingly clear stream is filled with a bacteria likely to cause intestinal disorders.

◆ **Your Pack** The argument rages about the merits of old fashioned external-frame packs and the newer, internal-frame models. Over the long run, the newer versions are more stable, and allow you to carry greater loads more comfortably; however, they also cost more. The key issue is finding a pack that fits well, has plenty of padding, a wide hip belt, and a good lumbar support pad.

Protecting the Environment

Many of the parks receive millions of visitors each year. Every visitor has an obligation to preserve the park for other visitors, now and in the future.

Stay on designated trails. Leave no garbage behind, even the smallest gum-wrapper. Don't disturb plants, wildlife, or archaeological resources. Don't pick flowers or collect rocks. Pay attention to trail-specific rules provided by the park rangers. Camp in designated areas only.

2

ARCHES NATIONAL PARK

by Don and Barbara Laine

NATURAL STONE ARCHES AND FANTASTIC ROCK FORMATIONS, SCULPT-ed as if by an artist's hand, are the defining feature of this park, and they exist in remarkable numbers and variety. Just as soon as you've seen the most beautiful, most colorful, most gigantic stone arch you can imagine, walk around the next bend and there's another—bigger, better, and more brilliant than the last. It would take forever to see them all, with more than 2,000 officially listed and more being discovered or "born" every day.

Just down the road from Canyonlands National Park, Arches is more visitor-friendly, with relatively short, well-maintained trails leading to most of the park's major attractions. It's also a place to let your imagination run wild. Is Delicate Arch really so delicate? Or would its other monikers (Old Maid's Bloomers or Cowboy Chaps) really be more appropriate? And what about those tall spires? You might imagine they're castles, giant stone sailing ships, or petrified skyscrapers of some ancient city.

Exploring the park is a great family adventure. The arches seem more accessible and less forbidding than the spires and pinnacles at Canyonlands and other Utah parks. Some think of arches as bridges, imagining the power of water that literally cuts a hole through a solid rock. Actually, to geologists there's a big difference. Bridges are formed when a river cuts a channel, while the often bizarre and beautiful contours of arches result from the erosive force of rain and snow, freezing and thawing, as it dissolves the "glue" that holds sand grains together, and chips away at the stone.

Although arches usually grow slowly—*very* slowly—occasionally something dramatic happens. Like that quiet day in 1940 when a sudden crash instantly doubled the size of the opening of Skyline Arch, leaving a huge boulder lying at its feet. Luckily, no one (at least no one we know of) was standing underneath at the time. The same thing happened to the magnificently delicate Landscape Arch in 1991, when a slab of rock about 60 feet long, 11 feet wide, and 4½ feet thick fell from the underside of the arch. Now there's such a thin ribbon of stone that it's hard to believe it can continue hanging on at all.

Spend a day or a week here, exploring the terrain, watching the rainbow of colors deepen and explode with the long rays of the setting sun, or the moonlight glistening on ribbons of desert varnish on tall sandstone cliffs. Watch for mule deer, cottontail rabbits, and the bright green collared lizard as they go about the task of desert living. And let your imagination run wild among the Three Gossips, the Spectacles, the Eye of the

9

Whale, the Penguins, the Tower of Babel, and the thousands of other statues, towers, arches, and bridges that await your discovery in this magical playground.

Avoiding the Crowds. This is a very popular park, and you should expect to find crowded parking areas and full campgrounds daily from March through October, with the peak month being August. The quietest months are December, January, and February, but it can be cold. Those wanting to avoid crowds might gamble on Mother Nature and visit in November or late February, when days might be delightfully sunny and just a bit cool; or bitterly cold, windy, and awful. As with most popular parks, avoid visiting during school vacations if possible.

Just the Facts

GETTING THERE & GATEWAYS

The entrance to the park is 5 miles north of Moab, Utah, on U.S. 191. To get there from Salt Lake City, about 230 miles away, follow I-15 south to Spanish Fork; then take U.S. 6 southeast to I-70; follow that east to Crescent Junction, where you'll pick up U.S. 191 south. From Grand Junction, Colorado, take U.S. 70 west until you reach Crescent Junction, and then go south on U.S. 191.

The Nearest Airport. Sunrise Airlines (☎ 800/842-8211) provides daily service between Salt Lake City and Moab's **Canyonlands Field Airport** (☎ 435/259-3422).

The closest major airport is **Walker Field** in Grand Junction, Colorado (☎ 970/244-9100; fax 970/241-9103; www.walkerfield.com), about 125 miles east of Moab. Located about a mile north of I-70 exit 31 (Horizon Drive), on the north side of Grand Junction, Walker Field has commercial flights connecting Grand Junction with most major cities, including **America West Express,** with daily service to Phoenix; **Delta/Skywest,** with daily service to Salt Lake City; and **United Express,** with daily service to Denver. A list of toll-free numbers is in the appendix.

GROUND TRANSPORTATION

The easiest way to get from Salt Lake City to Moab is with **Bighorn Express** (☎ 888/655-7433 or 801/328-9920; fax 801/328-4490; www.bighornexpress. com; e-mail: bighorn@prodigy.net). Rates are $45 one way or $85 round-trip.

Rentals, either standard passenger cars, vans, or four-wheel-drive vehicles, are available from **Thrifty** (☎ 435/259-7317) and **Farabee 4X4 Rentals** (☎ 888/806-5337 or 435/259-7494), which is also the local agent for **Budget.** Four-wheel-drive vehicles are also available from **Slickrock 4X4 Rentals** (☎ 888/238-5337 or 435/259-5678) and **Mike Young 4X4 Rentals** (☎ 435/259-5432). (See appendix for toll-free numbers.)

Local taxi service is provided by **West Tracks Taxi** (☎ 435/259-7317).

INFORMATION

Contact the **Superintendent, Arches National Park,** P.O. Box 907, Moab, UT 84532-0907 (☎ 435/259-8161; www.nps. gov/arch).

Books, maps, and videos on Arches as well as Canyonlands National Park and other southern Utah attractions can be purchased from the nonprofit **Canyonlands Natural History Association,** 3031 South U.S. 191, Moab, UT 84532 (☎ 800/840-8978; fax 435/259-8263; www.moabutah.com/cnha). Some publications are available in foreign languages, and a variety of videos can be purchased in either VHS or PAL formats. For more detailed descriptions of the park's hiking trails and backcountry roads, purchase *Exploring Canyonlands and Arches National Parks* (Falcon Press, 1997) by Bill Schneider, at the visitor center or by contacting the Canyonlands Natural History Association.

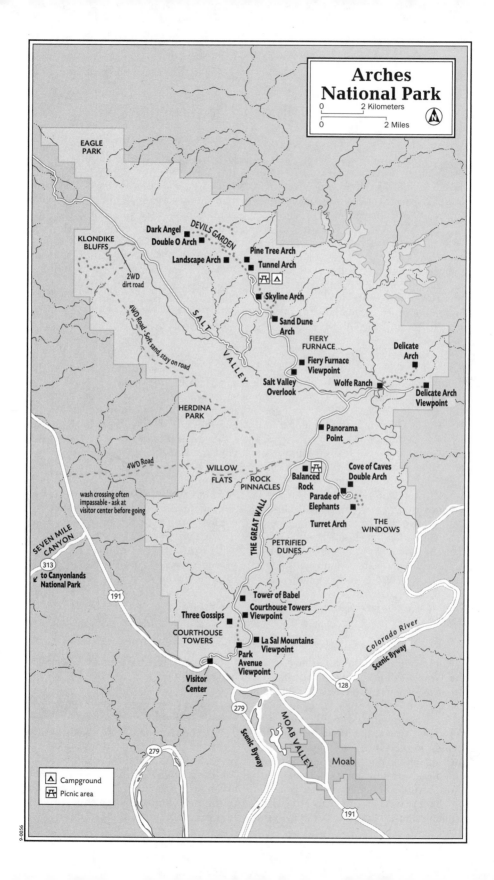

Arches National Park

0   2 Kilometers

0   2 Miles

EAGLE PARK

KLONDIKE BLUFFS

Dark Angel

Double O Arch

DEVILS GARDEN

Pine Tree Arch

Landscape Arch

Tunnel Arch

2WD dirt road

Skyline Arch

4WD Road - Soft sand, stay on road

Sand Dune Arch

SALT VALLEY

FIERY FURNACE

Delicate Arch

Fiery Furnace Viewpoint

Salt Valley Overlook

Wolfe Ranch

Delicate Arch Viewpoint

HERDINA PARK

Panorama Point

4WD Road

WILLOW FLATS

ROCK PINNACLES

Balanced Rock

Cove of Caves Double Arch

wash crossing often impassable - ask at visitor center before going

Parade of Elephants

SEVEN MILE CANYON

Turret Arch

THE WINDOWS

313

to Canyonlands National Park

THE GREAT WALL

PETRIFIED DUNES

191

Tower of Babel

Courthouse Towers Viewpoint

Three Gossips

Colorado River

COURTHOUSE TOWERS

La Sal Mountains Viewpoint

Scenic Byway

Park Avenue Viewpoint

128

Visitor Center

279

Scenic Byway

MOAB VALLEY

Moab

279

191

△ Campground

🛆 Picnic area

9-0056

Tips from a Park Ranger

A "good family park" is how Arches' chief of interpretation Diane Allen describes this national park. "What makes Arches special is its variety of rock formations and the ease of accessibility," she says. "You can see quite a bit even if you have only a few hours."

Allen says that 2 hours is about the minimum amount of time needed to tour the scenic drive, stopping at the viewpoints, and taking a few short walks, but 1 to 1½ days would give you a pretty good look at the park.

She suggests starting your park experience at the **visitor center,** to find out about guided hikes and other ranger-led activities, and then getting out on the trails early in the day, while it's still cool. **The Devils Garden Trail** provides a variety of experiences, Allen says, and is a fairly easy hike to scenic **Landscape Arch.** She says that hikers need to carry and drink plenty of water—rangers recommend a gallon per person each day—because in this extremely arid climate dehydration and heat problems can be fatal. She adds that if at the end of the day you have a slight headache and feel a bit lethargic and grouchy, it's likely because you didn't drink enough water.

Although park visitors will of course want to see the park's arches—**Delicate Arch** has practically become the symbol for the state of Utah—Allen says that Arches National Park has more than arches. "There are many other formations—spires, pinnacles, a few natural bridges, and great walls," she says, adding that the park is a prime example of Colorado Plateau vegetation.

"We've got a little bit of everything," she says, "wildflowers, cactus, piñon, juniper, a few riparian areas; and if you want to learn about geology, it's all exposed, easy to see."

The park is busiest between March and October, with August usually registering the most visitors. She says that summers are hot, and spring and fall are very pleasant. One way to avoid crowds, Allen says, is to visit in winter—"You can get fantastic hiking days in February, although you have to keep in mind that days are shorter then." The other proven way to avoid crowds, even at the height of the summer, is to get out onto the trails early in the day. "It's a much more pleasant time to be in the park," she says. "It's cooler, you have a better chance of seeing wildlife, and there are fewer people."

You can also ask rangers for suggestions on lesser-used trails. Allen says she likes the **Tower Arch Trail,** which is more of a primitive experience where you are less likely to see a lot of other hikers.

For advance area information, contact the **Grand County Travel Council,** P.O. Box 550, Moab, UT 84532 (☎ **800/635-6622** or 435/259-8825; fax 435/259-1376; www.canyonlands-utah.com).Once you arrive, stop at the **Moab Information Center,** located in the middle of town at the corner of Main and Center streets. Open 8am to 9pm in the summer, with shorter winter hours, the center is staffed by Park Service, Bureau of Land Management, Forest Service, and Canyonlands Natural History Association personnel.

VISITOR CENTER

The **Arches National Park Visitor Center,** located just inside the entrance gate, has maps, brochures, and other information. A museum tells you all you need to know about arch formation and other features of the park, and there is a short orientation program in the auditorium.

FEES & PERMITS

Entry for up to 7 days costs $10 per private vehicle or $5 per person on foot or bike. A $25 annual pass is also available; it's good for Arches and Canyonlands national parks as well as Natural Bridges and Hovenweep national monuments. Campsites are $10 per night when water is available, and $5 per night from November through mid-March when water is shut off. Required permits for overnight trips into the backcountry, available at the visitor center, are free.

SPECIAL REGULATIONS & WARNINGS

Wood fires are not permitted. Be aware that the desert terrain, although it appears hardy, is easily damaged. Rangers ask that hikers stay on trails, and be careful around the bases of arches and other rock formations.

SEASONS & CLIMATE

Summer days are hot, often reaching 100°F, and winters can be cool or cold, dropping below freezing at night, with snow possible. The best time to visit, especially for hikers, is in the spring or fall, when daytime temperatures are usually between 60° and 80°F and nights are cool. Spring winds, although not usually dangerous, can be gusty, particularly as they whip through an arch, so keep hold of your hat.

SEASONAL EVENTS

An Easter sunrise service takes place annually.

If You Only Have 1 Day

Arches is one of the easiest national parks to see in a day if that's all you can spare. A **scenic drive** offers splendid views of countless natural rock arches and other formations, and several easy hikes open up additional scenery. The drive is 18 miles one way, plus 5 miles for a side trip to the Windows and 4.5 miles for a side trip to Delicate Arch.

Start out by viewing the short slide show at the **visitor center,** and then ask rangers for their suggestions for a short hike, so you can get a close-up view of some of the arches. Possibilities include the short, easy hike to **Double Arch** and the longer and sometimes hot hike to **Delicate Arch.** If you're up for a more strenuous excursion, and the timing's right, join one of the ranger-guided hikes to **Fiery Furnace,** one of the most colorful areas of the park.

Exploring the Park by Car

You can see many of the park's most famous rock formations through your car windows, although we strongly urge you to get out and explore on foot. You have the option of walking short distances to a number of viewpoints, or stretching your legs on a variety of longer hikes (see "Day Hikes," below). The main road is easy to navigate, even for RVs, but parking at some viewpoints is limited. Please be considerate and leave trailers at the visitor center parking lot or in a campground.

After leaving the visitor center, drive north past the Moab Fault to the overlook parking for **Park Avenue,** a solid rock "fin" that reminded early visitors of the New York skyline. From here, your next stop is **La Sal Mountain Viewpoint,** where you look southeast to the La Sal Mountains, named by early Spanish explorers who thought the snow-covered mountains looked like huge piles of salt. In the overlook area is a "desert scrub" ecosystem, composed mostly of blackbrush, with some sagebrush, saltbush, yucca, and prickly pear cactus, all plants that can survive in sandy soil with little moisture. The area's wildlife includes the kangaroo rat, black-tailed jackrabbit, rock squirrel, coyote, and several species of lizards.

Continuing on the scenic drive, you begin to see some of the park's major formations at **Courthouse Towers,** where large monoliths such as Sheep Rock, the Organ, and the Three Gossips dominate the landscape. Leaving Courthouse Towers, watch for the **Tower of Babel** on the east (right) side of the road, then proceed past the "petrified" sand dunes to **Balanced Rock,** a huge boulder weighing about 3,600 tons, perched on a slowly eroding pedestal.

Continuing, you'll soon take a side road east (right) to **The Windows.** Created when erosion penetrated a sandstone fin, they can be seen via a short walk from the parking area. Also in this area are **Turret Arch** and the **Cove of Caves.** As erosion continues in the back of the largest cave it will probably eventually become an arch. A short walk from the parking lot takes you to **Double Arch,** which looks exactly like what the name implies. From the end of this trail you can also see the delightful **Parade of Elephants.**

Return to the main park road, turn north (right), and drive to **Panorama Point,** with an expansive view of Salt Valley and the Fiery Furnace, which can really live up to its name at sunset.

Next, turn east (right) off the main road onto the Wolfe Ranch Road and drive to the **Wolfe Ranch** parking area. A very short walk leads to what's left of this 100-year-old ranch. If you follow the trail a bit further, you'll see some Ute petroglyphs. More ambitious hikers can continue for a moderately difficult 3-mile round-trip excursion to **Delicate Arch,** with a spectacular view at trail's end. If you don't want to take this hike you can still see this lovely arch, albeit from a distance, by getting back in your car and continuing down the road for 1 mile and walking a short trail to the **Delicate Arch Viewpoint.**

Returning to the park's main road, turn north (right) and go to the next stop, the **Salt Valley Overlook.** The various shades and colors in this collapsed salt dome have been caused by varying amounts of iron in the rock, as well as other factors.

Continue now to the viewpoint for **Fiery Furnace,** which offers a dramatic view of colorful sandstone fins. From here, drive to a pullout for **Sand Dune Arch,** located down a short path from the road, where you'll find shade and sand, a good place for kids to play, along with the arch. The trail also leads across a meadow to **Broken Arch** (which isn't broken at all, it just looks that way from a distance).

Back on the road, continue to **Skyline Arch,** which doubled in size in 1940 when a huge boulder tumbled out of it. The next and final stop is the often crowded parking area for the **Devils Garden Trailhead.** From here you can hike to some of the most unique arches in the park, including **Landscape Arch,** among the longest natural rock spans in the world.

From the trailhead parking lot, it's 18 miles back to the visitor center.

Organized Tours & Ranger Programs

From March through October, rangers lead **guided hikes** on the Fiery Furnace Trail twice daily (see "Day Hikes," below), as well as daily nature walks from various park locations. **Evening campfire programs,** from April through October, cover topics such as rock art, geological processes, and wildlife. Check the schedule at the visitor center and on bulletin boards throughout the park.

Historic & Man-Made Attractions

Although not many have left their mark in this rugged area, a few intrepid Ute Indians and pioneers have spent time here. Just off the Delicate Arch Trail is a **Ute petroglyph panel** that includes etchings of horses and bighorn sheep. Also, near the beginning of the trail is **Wolfe Ranch.** Disabled Civil War veteran John

Wesley Wolfe and his son Fred moved here from Ohio in 1898, and in 1907 were joined by John's daughter Flora, her husband, and their two children. They left in 1910, after which John's cabin was destroyed by a flash flood. The cabin used by Flora's family survived and has been preserved by the Park Service. You'll see the cabin, a root cellar, and a corral.

Day Hikes

Most trails here are short and relatively easy, although because of the hot summer sun and lack of shade, it's wise to wear a hat and carry plenty of water on any jaunt expected to last more than 1 hour. Guided hikes in Arches National Park are offered by **Dreamrides** (see "Outfitter" chart, below), at rates of about $55 for a half day and $75 for a full day.

SHORTER TRAILS

Balanced Rock Trail

0.3 mi. RT. Easy. Access: Balanced Rock parking area on the east side of the main park road.

This short, easy walk is perfect for visitors who want to get out and stretch their legs and incidentally get a great close-up view of the huge and precariously perched Balanced Rock. The loop takes you around the formation.

Broken Arch

1 mi. RT. Easy. Access: At the end of Devils Garden Campground.

This is an easy hike with little elevation change traversing sand dunes and slickrock to the arch. Watch for the rock cairns, in some places poorly defined, marking the path through the arch. A little further along there's a connecting trail to **Sand Dune Arch,** about a half mile out and back. At the end of the loop you have a 0.25-mile walk along the

paved campground road back to your car.

Desert Nature Trail

0.2 mi. RT. Easy. Access: Bates Wilson Memorial in front of the visitor center.

A short and easy walk following numbered posts that's a terrific introduction to the plant life you'll be seeing throughout the park. Pick up a trail guide from the brochure box at the trailhead.

Double Arch

0.25 mi. one way. Easy. Access: Double Arch parking area, in Windows section of the park.

This easy walk, with very little elevation change, leads you to the third-largest arch opening in the park—don't be fooled by how small it looks from the parking area. Along your way look for the **Parade of Elephants,** off to the left. Once there, you can go a little further and climb right up under the arch, being very careful not to disturb the delicate desert vegetation or natural features. To the right of Double Arch are several **caves,** which one day may become arches. If you're visiting in spring, watch for the sego lily, Utah's state flower. It has three lovely cream-colored petals with a reddish-purple spot fading to yellow at the base.

Park Avenue

1 mi. one way. Easy. Access: Park Avenue or Courthouse Towers parking areas.

This easy downhill hike takes you into the canyon through groves of Utah juniper, single-leaf ash, black brush, and, in spring, wildflowers that sprinkle the sides of the trail with color. **Courthouse Towers, Tower of Babel, Three Gossips,** and **Organ Rock** can all be seen from the park road, but it's not nearly as awe-inspiring as actually walking among them. The names of several companies that offer hiker shuttle services along the park road are given at the beginning of the section "Other Sports & Activities," below. If you don't have a shuttle return, you might want to consider beginning the hike at the **Courthouse Towers** end and make the 320-foot climb first, so the return to your vehicle is downhill.

Sand Dune Arch

0.3 mi. one way. Easy. Access: Sand Dune Arch parking area.

This is an easy walk through low shrubs and grasses to the arch, which is hidden among and shaded by rock walls, with a naturally created giant sandbox below. By the way, please resist the temptation to climb onto the arch and jump down into the sand—not only is it dangerous, but it can damage the arch. Just before reaching **Sand Dune Arch** there's a trail cutting off to the left that leads to **Broken Arch,** adding 1.2 miles to your hike. Those who try this detour should watch for mule deer and kit foxes, which inhabit the grassland along the way.

Skyline Arch

0.2 mi. one way. Easy. Access: Skyline Arch parking area.

This is an easy walk along a flat, well-defined trail, with a view of Skyline Arch dominating the horizon. On a cold November night in 1940, a large boulder fell from the opening of this arch, doubling its size.

Windows Primitive Loop

1.25-mi. loop. Easy. Access: Windows parking area.

This easy, fairly flat hike leads to three massive arches, two of which appear to be almost perfectly round windows. It's a busy trail, but you'll find fewer people if you hike early or late in the day. On your way to **North Window,** take a short side trip to **Turret Arch.** Once you reach North and **South** Windows, take the loop around back and see for yourself why they are sometimes called Spectacles—it almost looks like a sea monster poking its large snout up into the air.

LONGER TRAILS

Delicate Arch

1.5 mi. one way. Moderate to strenuous. Access: Wolfe Ranch parking area.

Climbing about 480 feet, this hike is considered by many to be the park's best and most scenic, though complicated by slippery slickrock, no shade, and some steep drop-offs along a narrow cliff. Your efforts are rewarded with a dramatic, spectacular view of **Delicate Arch.** Along the way, you'll see the **John Wesley Wolfe Ranch** and have an opportunity to take a side trip to a **Ute petroglyph panel** that includes drawings of horses and what may represent a bighorn sheep hunt.

When you get back on the main trail, watch for **collared lizards,** bright green foot-long creatures with stripes of yellow or rust and a black collar. Feeding mostly in the daytime, they particularly enjoy insects and other lizards, and can stand and run on their large hind feet in pursuit of prey. Continuing along the trail, watch for **Frame Arch,** off to the right. Its main claim to fame is that numerous photographers have used it to "frame" a photo of Delicate Arch in the distance. Just past Frame Arch, the trail gets a little weird, having been blasted out from the cliff.

Should you opt to not take this hike, consider driving to the **Delicate Arch Viewpoint Trail,** which provides an ideal location for a photo, preferably with the arch highlighted by a clear blue sky. From the parking area it is about a 5-minute walk to the viewpoint.

Devils Garden

7.2 mi. RT. Easy to strenuous. Access: Devils Garden parking area.

The whole loop is a fairly long, strenuous, and difficult hike, from which you can see 15 to 20 arches and some exciting scenery. Be sure to take plenty of water, and not to hurry.

You don't have to go the entire way to see some unusual formations. Just 0.25

mile from the trailhead, a spur takes off to the right down a little hill. Here a left turn takes you to **Pine Tree Arch,** and turning right brings you to **Tunnel Arch.**

After returning to the main trail, stay to the left, and soon you'll reach the turnoff to **Landscape Arch,** a long (306 feet), thin ribbon of stone that is one of the most beautiful arches in the park. This is about a 2-mile round-trip, but is an absolute must-see for a visit to Arches National Park. Geologically speaking, Landscape Arch is quite mature and may collapse any day. Almost immediately after passing Landscape Arch, look to your right for **Wall Arch.** From here the trail is less well-defined but marked by cairns.

After another 0.25 mile, a side trip to the left has two spurs leading to **Partition Arch,** which you could see earlier behind Landscape Arch, and **Navajo Arch.** The spurs take you right up under the arches. Navajo Arch is shaded, providing a good spot to stop and take a breather while absorbing the view.

Once back on the main trail, which gets rougher and slicker as you hike, it's 0.5 mile to the strange **Double O Arch,** where one arch stands atop another. Now you've reached another junction, whose left spur leads to the **Dark Angel,** a dark sandstone spire reaching toward the heavens from the desert floor. The right spur takes you on to the **primitive loop,** a difficult trip through a dramatic desert environment with some drop-offs and narrow ledges. There is just one major arch along this part of the trail, **Private Arch,** located on a short spur to the right. You'll have the primitive loop almost to yourself, as most people turn back at Double O Arch rather than tackle this more difficult trail.

Fiery Furnace

2 mi. RT. Moderate to strenuous. Access: Fiery Furnace parking area.

This is a difficult and strenuous ranger-led hike to some of the most colorful formations in the park. By the way, the name comes not from the summer heat, but rather from the rich reddish glow the rocks take on at sunset, resembling that of a furnace. As you hike along, a ranger describes the desert plants, points out hard-to-find arches, and discusses the geology and natural history of the area. Guided hikes are given twice daily from March through October, by reservation ($6 per adult and $3 per child over 6). Reservations can be made up to 7 days in advance, but must be made in person.

You can choose to head out on your own (permits required, $2 per person) for an off-trail adventure, but special restrictions apply, so you must first talk with a ranger. Trails aren't marked, so unless you are experienced in the Fiery Furnace, it's best to join a guided hike.

Tower Arch

1.7 mi. one way. Strenuous. Access: Follow Salt Valley Rd. for 7.1 mi., turn left toward Klondike Bluffs, and go 1.5 mi. to the Tower Arch Trailhead. (Be careful not to take the left turn just before the Klondike Bluffs Rd. as it is a difficult four-wheel-drive rd.)

This is a short but rugged hike on a primitive trail. It starts with a steep incline to the top of the bluff and proceeds up and down, with great views of the Klondike Bluffs to the right. From here you can see the enormous **Tower Arch** among a maze of sandstone spires. Beware of the slickrock that makes up part of the trail, and watch for the cairns leading the way. The hardest part is near the end, where you struggle uphill through loose sand. Climb up under the arch for a soothing view while you take a much-deserved break. In spring, the majestic, snow-capped **La Sal Mountains** can be seen to the east through the arch opening.

Exploring the Backcountry

There are no designated backcountry trails or campsites, and very little of the park is open to overnight camping, but backcountry hiking is permitted. Ask park rangers to suggest routes. No fires are allowed, and hikers must carry their own water and practice low-impact hiking and camping techniques. Those planning to be out overnight need to get free backcountry permits, available at the visitor center.

Other Sports & Activities

Although Arches National Park and the surrounding public lands offer plenty for the do-it-yourselfer, some 50 local outfitters offer excursions of all kinds just outside the park, from rugged mountain-bike treks to relatively comfortable four-wheel-drive adventures. You can also rent a canoe or take a guided boat trip on the Colorado River, which follows the park's southeast boundary.

The chart below lists some of the major companies that can help you fully enjoy this beautiful country, including those that rent equipment and will shuttle you and/or your vehicle to or from trailheads. They are all located in Moab (zip code 84532). Advance reservations are often required, and it's best to check with several outfitters before deciding which best fits your needs. When making reservations, be sure to ask about the company's cancellation policy, just in case.

Biking. Bikes are prohibited on all trails and off-road in the backcountry. They are, however, permitted on the scenic drive, although the 18-mile dead-end road is narrow and winding in spots, and can be crowded with motor vehicles during the summer.

Mountain bikers also have the option of tackling one of several four-wheel-drive roads (see the "Four-Wheeling" section, below). Cyclists can get information, as well as rent or repair bikes, at **Rim Cyclery,** 94 W. 100 North (☎ 435/259-5333); and **Poison Spider Bicycle Shop,** 497 N. Main St. (☎ 800/635-1792 or 435/259-7882). Bike rentals start at about $30 per day. Bike shuttle services are available from **West Tracks Taxi and Shuttle** (☎ 435/259-7317), **Coyote Shuttle** (☎ 435/259-8656), and **Roadrunner**

Shuttle (☎ 435/259-9402). Several local companies (see the "Outfitter" chart) also offer guided mountain bike tours, with rates of about $70 for a half day and $90 for a full day, including bike rental. Multiday biking/camping trips are also available, starting at about $400 per person for a 3-day excursion.

Boating, Canoeing & Rafting. Although there are no bodies of water actually in Arches National Park, the Colorado River follows the park's boundary along its southeast edge, and river-running is a wonderful change of pace from hiking over the park's dry, rocky terrain. You can travel down the river in a canoe, kayak, large or small rubber raft (with or without a motor), or in a speedy, solid jet-boat.

Do-it-yourselfers can rent kayaks or canoes for $25 to $40 for a half day and $30 to $50 for a full day, or rafts from $50 to $65 per half day and $65 to $95 for a full day. Half-day **guided river trips** cost from $25 to $35 per person, and full-day trips are usually in the $40 to $70 range. Multiday **rafting expeditions,** which include meals and camping equipment, start at about $150 per person for 2 days, but can be much higher depending on location. **Jet-boat trips,** which cover a lot more river in a given amount of time, start at about $50 for a half-day trip, with full-day trips about $85 per person. Children's rates are usually about 20% less. Some companies also offer sunset or dinner trips.

Public boat-launching ramps are opposite Lion's Park, near the intersection of U.S. 191 and Utah 128; at Take-Out Beach, along Utah 128 about 10 miles east of its intersection with U.S. 191; and at Hittle Bottom, also along Utah 128, about 23.5 miles east of its intersection with U.S. 191. The **Colorado Basin River Forecast Center** (☎ 801/539-1311; www.cbrfc.gov/public/ for.html) provides information on river flows and reservoir conditions statewide.

Outfitter	4X4	Bike	Boat	Horse	Rent	Shuttle
Adrift Adventures 378 N. Main St., Box 577 ☎ 800/874-4483, 435/259-8594 www.adrift.net	Yes	No	Yes	Yes	No	Yes
Canyon Voyages 401 N. Main St., Box 416 ☎ 800/733-6007, 435/259-6007 www.canyonvoyages.com	Yes	No	Yes	No	Yes	No
Dreamrides 96 E. Center ☎ 888/662-2882, 435/259-6419 www.dreamride.com	No	No	Yes	No	Yes	No
Kaibab Adventure Outfitter & **Moab Cyclery** 391 S. Main St. ☎ 800/451-1133, 435/259-7423 www.utah.com/kaibab	No	Yes	No	No	Yes	No
Moab Rafting Co. Box 801 ☎ 435/259-7238 www.moab-rafting.com	No	No	Yes	No	No	No
Navtec Expeditions 321 N. Main St., Box 1267 ☎ 800/833-1278, 435/259-7983 www.navtec.com	Yes	No	Yes	No	No	No
Nichols Expeditions 497 N. Main St. ☎ 800/648-8488, 435/259-3999 www.nicholsexpeditions.com	No	Yes	Yes	No	No	No
North American River/ **Canyonlands Tours** 543 N. Main St. ☎ 800/342-5938, 435/259-5865 www.oars.com	Yes	Yes	Yes	No	No	No
Tag-A-Long Expeditions 452 N. Main St. ☎ 800/453-3292, 435/259-8946 www.tagalong.com	Yes	No	Yes	No	No	Yes
Western River Expeditions 1371 N. U.S. 191 ☎ 888/622-4097, 435/259-7019	No	No	Yes	No	Yes	No

Four-Wheeling. Although there aren't nearly as many four-wheel-drive opportunities here as in nearby **Canyonlands National Park,** there are a few—but check first with rangers on possible road closures and conditions that make the routes impassable. One possibility is the 17-mile road from Klondike Bluffs to Willow Flats, which is best driven from north to south because of soft sand on steep grades. Turn west off the main park road 1 mile south of Devils Garden Trailhead, and follow the road up through the Salt Valley about 7.7 miles to the turnoff for Klondike Bluffs. The next 17 miles, heading into high desert terrain, are strictly for four-wheelers, opening up panoramas of surrounding mountains and red rock formations. The route also passes Eye of the Whale Arch, views of Elephant Butte (the highest point in the park at 5,653 feet), and the imposing Courthouse Towers. Also seen along the route are drifting sand dunes and the red rock Marching Men formation. The road brings you out at the Balanced Rock Parking Area.

Rock Climbing. Technical climbing is permitted in some areas of the park, but only for experienced climbers. In addition, it is prohibited on many of the park's best-known arches, as well as Balanced Rock and a few other locations. Information is available from park rangers.

Camping

INSIDE THE PARK

Located at the north end of the park's scenic drive, **Devils Garden Campground**

Campground	Elev.	Total Sites	RV Hookups	Dump Station	Toilets	Drinking Water
Inside Arches						
Devils Garden	5,355	52	No	No	Yes	Yes
Inside Canyonlands						
Willow Flat	6,200	12	No	No	Yes	No
Squaw Flat	5,100	26	No	No	Yes	Yes
Near Canyonlands						
Dead Horse Point	5,600	21	21	Yes	Yes	Yes
Mountain View RV Park	7,000	35	29	Yes	Yes	Yes
Newspaper Rock	6,000	8	No	No	Yes	No
In and Near Moab						
Arch View Camp Park	5,000	85	54	No	Yes	Yes
Canyonlands Campark	4,000	144	113	Yes	Yes	Yes
Moab KOA	5,000	118	61	Yes	Yes	Yes
Moab Valley RV & Campark	4,000	130	92	Yes	Yes	Yes
Spanish Trail	4,200	73	60	No	Yes	Yes

is Arches' only developed campground. The sites are nestled among rocks, with plenty of piñon and juniper trees. In the summer, the campground fills early, so get to the visitor center by 7:30am to get your registration packet for camping. Campers will find water and flush toilets in the summer; but chemical toilets and no water from November through mid-March.

NEAR THE PARK

There are more than a dozen commercial campgrounds in and around Moab. Located at the junction of U.S. 191 and U.S. 313, **Arch View Camp Park,** U.S. 191 (P.O. Box 1496), Moab, UT 84532 (☎ 800/813-6622 or 435/259-7854; www.fulltiming-america.com/archview), offers all the usual RV hookups, showers, and other amenities you'd expect in a first-class commercial RV park, plus great views into the park. Arch View has a grassy tent area, trees throughout the park, a convenience store, a swimming pool, playground, and propane, gasoline, and diesel sales.

Canyonlands Campark, 555 S. Main St., Moab, UT 84532 (☎ 800/522-6848 outside Utah, or 435/259-6848; www.moab-utah.com/canyonlands/rv.html), is surprisingly shady and quiet given its in-town location, and is convenient to Moab's restaurants and shopping. On-site is a convenience store with food and some RV supplies.

The **Moab KOA,** 3225 S. U.S. 191, Moab, UT 84532 (☎ 800/562-0372 for reservations, or 435/259-6682; fax 435/259-8703), located about 3 miles south of Moab, has trees and all the usual KOA amenities, plus great views of the La Sal Mountains. Amenities

Showers	Fire Pits/ Grills	Laundry	Public Phone	Reserve	Fees	Open
No	Yes	No	Yes	No	$10	Year-round
No	Yes	No	No	No	$5	Year-round
No	Yes	No	No	No	$10	Year-round
No	Yes	No	Yes	Yes	$13	Year-round
Yes	Yes	Yes	Yes	Yes	$12–$16	Year-round
No	Yes	No	No	No	Free	Year-round
Yes	Yes	Yes	Yes	Yes	$15–$21	Mar–Nov
Yes	Yes	Yes	Yes	Yes	$15–$20	Year-round
Yes	Yes	Yes	Yes	Yes	$20–$26	Mar–Oct
Yes	Yes	Yes	Yes	Yes	$15–$22	Apr–Oct
Yes	No	No	Yes	Yes	$16–$22	Year-round

include a miniature golf course, game room, two playgrounds, cable TV hookups, and a convenience store with RV supplies and propane. About half of the sites are for tents only. There are also one- and two-room cabins ($38 to $45 double).

On the north side of Moab, near the intersection of U.S. 191 and Utah 128, is **Moab Valley RV & Campark,** 1773 N. U.S. 191, Moab, UT 84532 (☎ 435/259-4469). All sites offer great views of the surrounding rock formations. The park accommodates practically any size RV in its extralarge pull-through sites, and provides maximum entertainment with cable television connections on the full RV hookups. There are trees and patches of grass for both tenters and RVers. You can refuel at the convenience store that sells propane, groceries, and RV and camping supplies. Dogs are permitted in RV sites, but not in tent sites. The park also has six comfortable cabins ($35 double), which nonetheless require a walk to the bathhouse.

Just south of Moab is **Spanish Trail RV Park and Campground,** 2980 S. U.S. 191, Moab, UT 84532 (☎ 800/787-2751 or 435/259-2411; fax 435/259-2410; www.moab.net/spanishtrail/; e-mail: spanishtrail@moab-utah.com), with spacious sites accommodating big RVs, some shaded sites, and scenic views. It offers cable TV hookups, volleyball, and horse-shoes, and a convenience store with RV supplies.

You'll also find campgrounds at nearby Canyonlands National Park (see "Camping" in chapter 8) and in areas under the jurisdiction of the U.S. Forest Service, Bureau of Land Management, and Utah state parks. The **Mountain View RV Park** in Monticello (included in the campground chart here) is discussed in chapter 8. Also, check at the **Moab Information Center** or with the **Grand Country Travel Council** (see "Information," above).

Accommodations

There are no lodging facilities inside the park.

NEAR THE PARK

Moab is the nearest town to Arches (5 miles south). Room rates are generally highest from mid-March through October, and sometimes drop by up to half in the winter.

There are a variety of chain motels in Moab. Rates shown here are for two people in the high season. The town's largest lodging property is the **Super 8,** on the north edge of town at 889 N. Main St. (☎ 435/259-8868), charging $69 to $79. The **Days Inn,** 426 N. Main St. (☎ 435/259-4468), charges $77 to $89; **Comfort Suites,** 800 S. Main St. (☎ 435/259-5252), has rates of $80 to $110; and **Sleep Inn,** 1051 South U.S. 191 (☎ 435/259-4655), charges $70 to $95. The **Ramada Inn,** 182 S. Main St. (☎ 435/259-7141; fax 435/259-6299), charges $45 to $99. Moab has two Best Westerns: the **Best Western Canyonlands Inn,** 16 S. Main St. (☎ 435/259-2300), charges $99 to $149 double; and the **Best Western Greenwell Inn,** 105 S. Main St. (☎ 435/259-6151; fax 435/259-4397), has rates of $69 to $119. Chain motel toll-free phone numbers are listed in the appendix.

Archway Inn

1551 North U.S. 191, Moab, UT 84532. ☎ **800/341-9359** or 435/259-2599. Fax 435/259-2270. 97 units. A/C TV TEL. Mid-Mar to Oct $79–$97 double, $140–$150 suite; lower rates Nov to mid-Mar. Rates include continental breakfast. AE, DISC, MC, V.

This two-story property, just 2 miles from the entrance to Arches National Park on the north edge of Moab, has large rooms with great views, decorated in southwestern style. Most rooms contain two queen-size beds; eight family units also have a queen hide-a-bed; there are a variety of suites; and all have refrigerators and microwave ovens. Facilities include a large outdoor heated pool, a courtyard with barbecue grills, an indoor hot tub, exercise room, bike storage, coin-operated laundry, conference rooms, and gift shop. There are also two apartments, with full kitchens and 46-inch TVs (call for rates). The entire facility is no-smoking.

Bowen Motel

169 N. Main St., Moab, UT 84532. ☎ **800/ 874-5439** or 435/259-7132. Fax 435/259-6641. www.moab-utah.com/bowen/motel.htm. E-mail: bowenmotel@lasal.net. 40 units. A/C TV TEL. $65–$75 double; off-season 40% less. Rates include morning coffee and pastries. AE, DC, DISC, MC, V.

This family-owned and -operated motel offers fairly large, comfortable, clean, basic rooms with attractive wallpaper, one or two queen-size beds, and shower/ tub combos. Two family rooms sleep up to six each. The original structure was built in the 1940s, with an addition made in 1978; a major renovation was completed in 1993–94. Facilities include an outdoor heated swimming pool. Several restaurants are within easy walking distance.

The Lazy Lizard International Hostel

1213 South U.S. 191, Moab, UT 84532. ☎ **435/259-6057.** Fax 435/259-6105. E-mail: lazylzrd@lasal.net. 25 dorm beds, 6 private rms, 8 cabins, 1 teepee; total capacity 65 persons. $8 dorm bed; $20 private rm; $25 and up cabin; $6 per person teepee and camp space. Showers $2 for nonguests. Hostel membership not necessary. No credit cards.

Offering exceptionally clean, comfortable lodging at bargain rates, the Lazy Lizard is on the south side of town, behind the A-1 self-storage units. The main house, which is air-conditioned, has basic dorm rooms plus two private rooms. A separate building contains four additional private rooms, which look much like older motel units (with fans but no air-conditioning). The best facilities are the cabins, constructed of real logs and with beds for up to six. The teepee is, well, a teepee. Everyone shares the bathhouses, and there's a telephone in the main house. Guests also have use of a fully equipped kitchen; living room with television, VCR, and a collection of movies; whirlpool; self-service laundry; gas barbecue grill; and picnic tables. Groups should inquire about the nearby houses that can be rented by the night ($100 to $300, for 14 to 30 people).

Red Stone Inn

535 S. Main St., Moab, UT 84532. ☎ **800/ 772-1972** or 435/259-3500. Fax 435/259-2717. www.moabutah.com/redstoneinn. 50 units. A/C TV TEL. Winter $30–$35 double; summer $60–$65 double; slightly higher in Sept and during special events. AE, DISC, MC, V. Pets $5 extra.

This centrally located motel is comfortable, clean, and quiet. The exterior gives the impression that these are cabins, and the theme continues inside with attractive light-colored knotty pine walls, decorated with colorful posters and maps showing off the area's attractions. Rooms are a bit on the small side, although perfectly adequate and spotlessly maintained, and contain either one queen-size bed or two doubles. All but three rooms have kitchenettes with microwave ovens, with coffee and other supplies. Roll-away beds are available at $5 extra. Three handicapped-accessible rooms have shower/ tub combos, while the rest have showers only. There is no swimming pool, but a picnic area has gas barbecue grills.

Sunflower Hill Bed & Breakfast Inn

185 N. 300 East, Moab, UT 84532. ☎ **800/ 662-2786** or 435/259-2974. Fax 435/259-3065. www.sunflowerhill.com. E-mail: innkeeper@sunflowerhill.com. 11 units. A/C TV. Mar to mid-Nov and holidays $95–$160

double; mid-Nov to Feb $65–$125 double. Rates include full breakfast and evening refreshments. AE, DISC, MC, V. Children under 8 by prior arrangement only.

This country-style B&B, located 3 blocks off Main Street on a quiet dead-end road, offers elegant rooms and lovely outdoor areas. Guest rooms have handmade quilts with matching sham pillows and private bathrooms; some have jetted tubs and private balconies. The extremely popular French Bedroom includes a 200-year-old carved bedroom set from France, stained-glass window, vaulted ceiling, white lace curtains, and a large whirlpool tub and separate tiled shower. The Sun Porch has a flowered rock-wall mural in the bedroom, and sunflowers stenciled along the bottom of the walls in a separate sitting area, which overlooks the shady side yard.

The breakfast buffet is substantial, with homemade breads and pastries, honey-almond granola, fresh fruits, and a hot entree such as a Canadian bacon and leek quiche, or poached eggs with mushrooms and smoked turkey. The grounds are grassy and shady, with fruit trees and flowers in abundance. There's a year-round outdoor hot tub, a swing, picnic table, barbecue, and a guest laundry.

Dining

There are no restaurants inside the park.

NEAR THE PARK

Buck's Grill House

1393 North U.S. 191. ☎ **435/259-5201.** Main courses $5.95–$19.95. DC, DISC, MC, V. Daily 5:30pm–closing. Closed Dec–Jan. About 1½ mi. north of town. AMERICAN WESTERN.

This popular restaurant, a great place for steak, offers a number of choices to suit a variety of palates. The dining room's subdued Western decor is accented by exposed wood beams, and Western and

scenic paintings by local artist Pete Plastow. There is patio dining when the weather cooperates. Steak choices include a spicy cowboy-style; the adventurous will likely enjoy the buffalo meat loaf, with black onion gravy and mashed potatoes. Also popular are the prime rib and the zucchini pot pie—mushroom polenta stuffed with zucchini and topped with a tomato-garlic sauce. Southwestern dishes include grilled chicken tacos, shrimp tacos, and catfish Yucatán style— marinated in fruit juices, peppers, and onions, then sautéed. All breads and other baked items are made in-house. Buck's offers full liquor service and serves a variety of Utah microbrews.

Eddie McStiff's

57 S. Main St. (in McStiff's Plaza, just south of the information center). ☎ **435/259-2337.** Main courses $6.50–$20; pizza $5.50–$20. DISC, MC, V. Daily 6:30am–noon and 3pm–midnight. Check on possible closure Dec–Jan. ECLECTIC.

This bustling, somewhat noisy brew pub is half family restaurant and half tavern, plus an enclosed garden patio. In the restaurant dining room, you'll find Southwest decor and paintings by local artists, while the tavern looks just as a tavern should: long bar, low light, and lots of wood. The menu changes seasonally to accommodate sports enthusiasts in spring and fall, Europeans and families in summer. There's always a wide range of appetizers, salads, and burgers, plus grilled steaks, pasta, and Southwestern items. Among specialties are the grilled salmon fillet, served with an asparagus cream sauce, and the house-smoked St. Louis–style barbecued ribs. Breakfasts include the usuals plus create-your-own omelettes, a large breakfast burrito smothered in green chile sauce, and blue corn pancakes. At least a dozen fresh-brewed beers are on tap at any given time and can also be purchased to go. Mixed drinks, wine, and beer are sold in the dining room with food only, and beer can be purchased with or without food in the tavern. (You must be at least 21 to enter the tavern.)

Fat City Smokehouse

36 S. 100 West (1 block west of Main St. just south of Center St.). ☎ **435/259-4302.** Main courses $5.50–$16.50. MC, V. Daily 4–10pm. Closed Sun in Dec. Closed Jan. BARBECUE/VEGETARIAN.

Genuine Texas-style pit barbecue makes this a favorite of locals, who pile into the plain, cafe-style dining room for pork ribs, beef tips, chicken, and homemade sausage, all rubbed with a variety of seasonings, smoked from 12 to 14 hours, and served with the restaurant's own sauce. Flame-grilled dinners, cooked over apple and cherry hardwoods, include fresh catfish with sweet pepper seasoning; a popular summer special is the 24-ounce T-bone. For the nonbarbecue-lover, there are several vegetarian sandwiches. Service is fast and friendly, and beer is available with meals.

Honest Ozzie's Cafe & Desert Oasis

60 N. 100 West (1 block west of Main St. and just north of Center St.). ☎ **435/259-8442.** Breakfast $1.75–$6.75; lunch $3.75–$7.50. MC, V. Daily 8am–3pm. Closed Nov–Feb. INTERNATIONAL/HEALTH FOOD.

This cheery little cafe has both a comfortable dining room and a shaded garden patio with a waterfall and an abundance of hummingbirds. Inside, you'll find a cafe-style atmosphere with white walls, light-colored woods, and local artwork. Food is prepared fresh, with lots of baked items plus deli salads and sandwiches, daily specials, flat-bread pizzas, and wraps—a full meal all wrapped up in a large tortilla. Popular breakfasts include whole-grain waffles, breakfast burritos, and homemade granola. For lunch, try the Gobbler wrap—roast turkey breast, sage stuffing, cranberry sauce, country potatoes, and mushroom gravy; the Thai veggie with

tofu; or the Cajun catfish. The restaurant serves local microbrewery beer.

Moab Brewery

686 S. Main St. ☎ **435/259-6333.** Main courses $5.95–$18.95. AE, DISC, MC, V. Daily 11:30am–10pm summer; 11:30am–9pm winter. Check on possible winter closure of 2–4 weeks. ECLECTIC.

Fresh handcrafted ales brewed on-site, along with a wide variety of burgers, sandwiches, salads, soups, vegetarian dishes, and assorted house specialties, are served at this open, spacious micro-brewery/restaurant on the south side of town. You can sample the brews—from a German-style unfiltered wheat ale to a light-bodied easy-drinking American lager—at the separate bar. In all, the brewery produces some 16 different ales and about half a dozen are available on tap at any given time. The restaurant is popular with families, who gobble down basic American fare like half-pound burgers, steaks, and fresh fish. The adventuresome can choose from the more exotic selections, such as salmon-artichoke pasta, the mixed sausage grill plate, or the spicy chicken burrito. Hickory-smoked prime rib is available after 5pm. The huge dining room is decorated with light-colored woods, outdoor sports equipment—including a hang glider on the ceiling—and local artwork. Patio dining is available; there's a gift shop plus beer-to-go in half-gallon jugs in insulated carriers.

Moab Diner

189 S. Main St. (2 blocks south of Center St.). ☎ **435/259-4006.** Main courses $3.25–$15.95. MC, V. Daily 6am–10:30pm. Closes earlier in the winter. AMERICAN/SOUTHWESTERN.

Late risers can get breakfast—among the best in town—all day here, with all the usual egg dishes, biscuits and gravy, six kinds of omelettes, and a spicy breakfast burrito. The decor tells you that this is definitely a diner, but it does have lots of green plants (real, not plastic). Hamburgers, sandwiches, and salads are the offerings at lunch, of course, and for dinner there's steak, shrimp, and chicken, plus liver and onions. In addition to ice cream, you can get sherbet, frozen yogurt, malts, and shakes, plus sundaes with seven different toppings. No alcoholic beverages are served.

Poplar Place Restaurant & Pub

11 E. 100 North (just east of Main St., 1 block north of Center St.). ☎ **435/259-6018.** Main courses $4.95–$9.95; pizza $7–$16.75. MC, V. Daily 11:30am–11pm. Shorter hrs. in the winter. MEXICAN/ITALIAN.

This two-story corner pub has been a busy lunch and dinner stop for locals since it opened in 1972, serving lots of pizzas, pasta, sandwiches, soups, and Mexican dishes. The popular pizzas, with homemade crust and sauces, come with either a tomato or an Alfredo sauce and your choice of toppings. Pasta offerings include lasagna; linguine with a choice of pesto, Alfredo, or marinara sauces; shrimp scampi; and chicken Parmesan. Mexican dishes include crab or vegetable enchiladas, chicken or pork burritos with green chile sauce, and what the Poplar Place calls a "faco," a cross between a fajita and taco. Dine inside or in the fresh air on the patio. Full liquor service is available, in addition to Utah microbrews and Guinness Stout on tap.

Sunset Grill

900 N. U.S. 191. ☎ **435/259-7146.** Main courses $9.95–$17.95. AE, DISC, MC, V. Daily 5–10pm. AMERICAN.

Perched on a hill at the north edge of Moab, this fine restaurant offers the best sunset views in town. Once the home of Moab area miner Charles Steen, the Sunset Grill contains four tastefully decorated dining rooms and three patios. A favorite of locals celebrating special events, the restaurant serves aged USDA Choice steaks, hand cut in-house, plus fresh seafood such as Alaskan halibut—grilled and finished with a lime-caper sauce—and grilled Atlantic salmon fillet, prepared with an Oriental glaze and served in a light soy-sherry cream sauce. Texas-style prime rib sells out often, so arrive early. The menu also includes a number of chicken dishes, Colorado lamb, and several pasta selections. Utah microbrews, some 30 wines, and full liquor service are offered.

Picnic & Camping Supplies

The best grocery store in town is **City Market,** 425 S. Main St. (☎ **435/259-5181**). You can pick up sandwiches from the deli, assemble your own salad at the salad bar, or choose fresh-baked items from the bakery. The store also sells fishing licenses, money orders and stamps, offers photo finishing and Western Union services, and has a pharmacy. For camping supplies and equipment for hiking, biking, and other outdoor activities, try **Red Canyon Outfitters,** 23 N. Main St. (☎ **435/259-3353**); **Moab Outdoors General Store,** 702 S. Main St. (☎ **435/259-5731**); or **Gearheads,** 471 S. Main St. and 59 S. Main St. (☎ **888/740-4327** or 435/259-4327), which offers free filtered water—just bring your own containers.

Nearby Attractions

Many visitors to Arches also spend time at nearby Canyonlands National Park, which is discussed in chapter 8.

3

BADLANDS NATIONAL PARK

by Jack Olson

I T'S A STRANGE AND SEEMINGLY WICKED PLACE. FROM THE RAGGED RIDGES and sawtooth spires to the wind-ravaged desolation of Sage Creek Wilderness Area, Badlands National Park is an awe-inspiring sight and an unsettling experience. Few leave here unaffected by the

vastness of this geologic anomaly, spread across 381 square miles of moonscape in western South Dakota.

The Sioux Indians who once traversed this incredible landscape named it *mako sica* or "land bad." Early French-Canadian trappers labeled them *les mauvaises terres a traverser* or "bad lands to travel across."

Steep canyons, towering spires, and flat-topped tables are all found among Badlands buttes. Yet, despite their apparent complexity, the unusual formations of the Badlands are essentially the result of two basic geologic processes: deposition and erosion.

The layered look of the Badlands comes from sedimentary rocks composed of fine grains that have been cemented into a solid form. Layers with similar characteristics are grouped into units called formations. The bottom formation or "layer" is the **Pierre Shale,** deposited 68 million to 77 million years ago during the Cretaceous period, when a shallow, inland sea stretched across the present-day Great Plains. The black mud of the sea floor hardened into shale, leaving fossil clam shells and ammonites that today confirm a sea environment. The sea eventually drained away, and the

upper layers of shale were weathered into soil, now seen as yellow mounds.

The **Chadron Formation,** deposited 32 million to 37 million years ago during the Eocene epoch, sits above the Pierre Shale. By this time, a floodplain had replaced the sea and each time the rivers flooded, they deposited a new layer of sediment on the plain. Alligator fossils indicate a lush, subtropical forest covered the region. However, mammal fossils dominate. The Chadron is best known for its large, elephantlike mammals called titanotheres.

Some of the sediment carried by the rivers and by the wind was volcanic ash, the product of eruptions associated with the creation of the Rocky Mountains. The ash mixed with river and stream sediments to form clay stone, the main material from which Badlands buttes are constructed. After the Eocene epoch, the climate began to dry and cool and tropical forests gave way to open savanna. The **Brule and Sharps Formations** were deposited by rivers during the Oligocene epoch from 26 million to 32 million years ago, and today these formations contain the most rugged peaks and canyons of the Badlands.

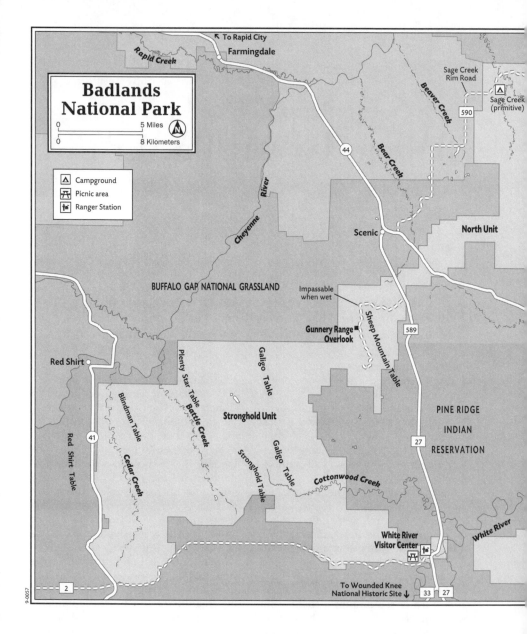

Badlands National Park

0 ——— 5 Miles

0 ——— 8 Kilometers

△ Campground
🎪 Picnic area
🏠 Ranger Station

To Rapid City
Farmingdale
Rapid Creek

Sage Creek
Rim Road
Sage Creek
(primitive)
590
Beaver Creek

44

Bear Creek

Cheyenne River

Scenic

North Unit

BUFFALO GAP NATIONAL GRASSLAND

Impassable
when wet

Gunnery Range
Overlook

Sheep Mountain Table

589

Red Shirt

Plenty Star Table

Galigo Table

PINE RIDGE

Blindman Table

Battle Creek

Stronghold Unit

INDIAN

Red Shirt Table

Cedar Creek

Stronghold Table

Galigo Table

27

RESERVATION

41

Cottonwood Creek

White River
Visitor Center

White River

2

To Wounded Knee
National Historic Site ↓

33 27

9-0057

The Badlands' serrated ridges and deep canyons did not exist until about 500,000 years ago when water began to cut through the layers of rock, carving fantastic shapes into what had been a flat floodplain. Once again, the ancient fossil soils, buried for millions of years, became exposed. That erosion is ongoing. Every time it rains or snow melts in spring, more sediments are washed from the buttes in this endless work of sculpting the earth. On average, the

buttes erode 1 inch each year, although change can occur much slower or faster, and scientists believe that the Badlands buttes will be gone in another 500,000 years.

Established as Badlands National Monument in 1939, it gained national park status in 1978. The Badlands are one of the richest Oligocene fossil beds known to exist. Remains of three-toed horses, dog-sized camels, saber-toothed cats, giant pigs, and other species have

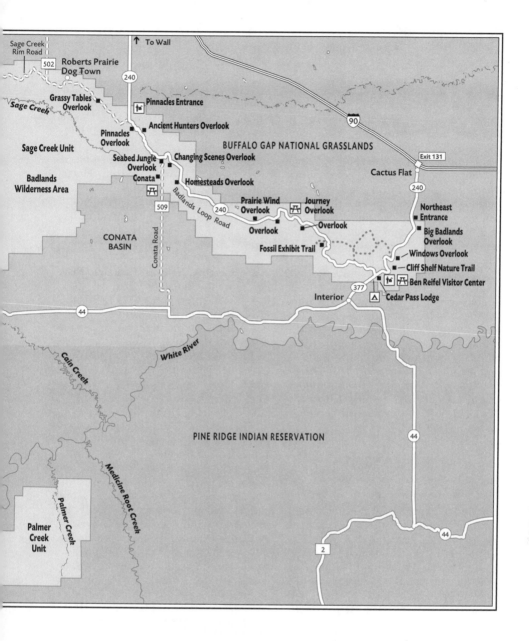

been found here, all dating from 25 million to 35 million years ago.

Flora & Fauna. Largely a mixed-grass prairie, the park contains 56 different types of grasses, most of which are native species, including green needlegrass and buffalo grass. What you won't find are many trees.

Wildflowers are an important part of the landscape, and you'll find such species as the curlycup gumweed and the pale purple coneflower. The best time to see wildflowers is June and July.

You're likely to see bison and Rocky Mountain bighorn sheep (the native Audubon's bighorn is now extinct), as well as pronghorns and mule deer. Darting in and out of the grass are desert and eastern cottontail rabbits. And prairie dogs thrive in the area; there's a prairie dog town just beyond the end of the Badlands Loop Road. You might also see a prairie rattlesnake slithering through the grass, not to mention several nonpoisonous snake species.

Avoiding the Crowds. The vastness of Badlands National Park means that overcrowding is usually not a problem. Entrance stations, visitor centers, park concessions, and the Loop Road can become busy during the height of the summer season, especially during July and August, but most roads, trails, and services are not overtaxed any time of the year.

As with most other national park units, those wishing to avoid crowds should visit during the shoulder seasons of April to May and September to October. If you must go during the summer season, visit early in the day when the numbers of people are lowest and the sun hasn't begun to scorch the earth. Dawn and dusk are ideal times to photograph the unearthly beauty of Badlands National Park, and are also the best times to see wildlife.

Just the Facts

GETTING THERE & GATEWAYS

Located in extreme southwestern South Dakota, Badlands National Park is easily accessed by car either on **S. Dak. 44** east of Rapid City, or off **Interstate 90** at Wall or Cactus Flat. Westbound I-90 travelers take Exit 131 south (Cactus Flat) onto S. Dak. 240, which leads to the park boundary and the **Ben Reifel Visitor Center** at Cedar Pass. This roadway becomes **Badlands Loop Road,** the park's primary scenic drive. After passing through the park, S. Dak. 240 rejoins I-90 at Exit 110 at Wall. Eastbound travelers do the reverse, beginning in Wall and ending back at I-90 at Exit 131.

The Nearest Airport. Rapid City Regional Airport (☎ 605/393-9924), located 10 miles southeast of Rapid City on S. Dak. 44, provides direct access to the Badlands, Black Hills, and Mount Rushmore. **Northwest, Delta/Skywest,** and **United Express** serve the airport with daily flights to Minneapolis, Salt Lake City, and Denver. Car-rental companies at the airport include **Avis, Budget, Hertz, National, Sears,** and **Thrifty.** You'll find a list of toll-free numbers for airlines and car-rental agencies in the appendix.

INFORMATION

For a **Badlands National Park Trip Planner**, contact Badlands National Park, P.O. Box 6, Interior, SD 57750 (☎ 605/433-5245; www.nps.gov/badl).

For information about the area, contact **South Dakota Tourism,** 711 E. Wells Ave., Pierre, SD 57501-3369 (☎ 605/773-3301; fax 605/773-3256); or the **Black Hills, Badlands & Lake Association,** 1931 Discovery Circle, Rapid City, SD 57702-2583 (☎ 605/341-1462).

The National Park Service makes available a wide variety of brochures on topics including geology, prairie grasses, backpacking, biking, wildlife, plants, and use of horses in the park, which are available at the park visitor centers and ranger stations. In addition, *The Prairie Preamble,* published by the nonprofit **Badlands Natural History Association,** P.O. Box 47, Interior, SD 57750, provides up-to-date information on visitor center hours, park programs, camping, and hiking trails.

VISITOR CENTERS

Visitor centers are located at Cedar Pass and White River. The **Ben Reifel Visitor Center** at Cedar Pass is open year-round (7am to 8pm from June 10 to August 15, and 9am to 4pm the rest of the year) and features exhibits on the park's natural and cultural history. The **White River Visitor Center** is open June through late August only (call for hours), and includes exhibits about Oglala Sioux history.

FEES

Park entry costs $10 per passenger vehicle (up to 7 days) or $5 per person on foot or bike. Members of the Oglala Sioux tribe pay half price. Camping costs $10 per site per night at the Cedar Pass Campground in summer; $8 in winter. Camping at Sage Creek Primitive Campground is free.

SPECIAL REGULATIONS & WARNINGS

Water in the Badlands is too full of silt for humans to drink and will quickly clog a water filter. When hiking or traveling in the park, always carry an adequate supply of water. Drinking water is only available at the Cedar Pass area, the White River Visitor Center, and the Pinnacles Ranger Station. No campfires are allowed. Climbing Badlands buttes and rock formations is allowed, but can be extremely dangerous due to loose, crumbly rock.

SEASONS & CLIMATE

Badlands weather is often unpredictable. Heavy rain, hail, and high, often damaging winds are possible, particularly during spring and summer. Lightning strikes are common. Summer temperatures often exceed 100°F, so sunscreen, a hat, and water are essential to avoid severe sunburn, dehydration, and heat stroke. Winter travelers should be aware of approaching storms and be prepared for sleet, ice, heavy snow, and blizzard conditions.

ROAD CONDITIONS

Park roads are winding and steep in places, but most are paved and driving is generally a straightforward affair. Accessibility to some areas of the park is limited in the off-season due to inclement weather and poor road conditions. Unpaved roads can become dangerous in winter and during thunderstorms, when surfaces may become extremely slippery.

If You Only Have 1 Day

It's relatively easy to explore the highlights of the North Unit of Badlands National Park in a day or less (most visitors spend an average of 3 to 5 hours in the park). A few miles south of the park's northeast entrance (the closest entrance to I-90), is the **park headquarters,** open year-round, which includes the Ben Reifel Visitor Center, Cedar Pass Lodge, and a campground, amphitheater, and dump station. After stopping at the visitor center exhibits, bookstore, information desk, and watching an orientation video (which we recommend), it's time to hit the trail.

The visitor center is located within 5 miles of several trailheads, scenic overlooks, and three self-guided nature trails. Each of the seven trails in the area offers an opportunity to view some of the formations for which the Badlands is famous. The **Fossil Exhibit Trail** is wheelchair accessible. The **Cliff Shelf Nature Trail** and the **Door Trail** are moderately strenuous and provide impressive glimpses of Badlands formations. But none is longer than 1 mile, and any one of them can be hiked comfortably in less than an hour. (See "Day Hikes," below.)

Leading directly from the visitor center is the 30-mile **Badlands Loop Road,** the park's most popular scenic roadway. Angling northwest toward the town of Wall, this road passes numerous overlooks and trailheads, each of which commands inspiring views of the Badlands and the prairies of the Buffalo Gap National Grassland. Binoculars will increase your chances of spotting bison, pronghorn, bighorn sheep, and coyote.

The paved portion of the Loop Road ends at the turnoff for the Pinnacles Entrance. Beyond this point the road becomes the **Sage Creek Rim Road,** a 30-mile gravel road, at the end of which is the **Sage Creek Campground.** Five miles west of the end of the pavement, a visit to the **Roberts Prairie Dog Town** gives you a chance to watch black-tailed prairie dogs "barking" their warnings and protecting their "town."

If You Have More Time

Those camping or staying overnight at Cedar Pass Lodge or in the area have more opportunities to explore the park at a leisurely pace, taking advantage of some of the other trails, such as the **Castle Trail,** which connects the Fossil Exhibit Trail and Window Fossil Exhibit Trail, and **Notch Trail.** You could also

> I've been about the world a lot and pretty much over our own country; but I was totally unprepared for that revolution called the Dakota Badlands . . . Let sculptors come to the Badlands. Let painters come. But first of all the true architect should come. He who could interpret this vast gift of nature in terms of human habitation so that Americans on their own continent might glimpse a new and higher civilization certainly, and touch it and feel it as they lived in it and deserved to call it their own. Yes, I say the aspects of the Dakota Badlands have more spiritual quality to impart to the mind of America than anything else in it made by man's God.
>
> —Frank Lloyd Wright, in a letter to a friend following his 1935 visit to the Badlands

take in some of the park's summer evening ranger programs.

Organized Tours & Ranger Programs

In addition to these suggestions, look at "Other Sports & Activities," below.

Motor Coach Tours. A number of charter bus park tours and "step-on" guide services throughout the area are available. **Gray Line of the Black Hills,** P.O. Box 1106, Rapid City, SD 57709 (☎ 800/456-4461 or 605/342-4461; fax 605/341-5152), offers bus tours of the area, with prices from $15 to $40. Tours are also available, at similar rates, from **America Tours West,** P.O. Box 867, Keystone, SD 57751-0167 (☎ 605/666-4545; fax 605/666-4996); and **Jack Rabbit Charter & Tours,** 301 N. Dakota Ave., Sioux Falls, SD 57104 (☎ 605/335-2290; fax 605/336-8731).

Ranger Programs. A limited schedule of naturalist-led walks and programs generally begins in mid-June, increasing as visitation increases. Times and topics vary. Check the activities board at the Ben Reifel Visitor Center or campground bulletin boards for locations and other details. Activities often include the following:

♦ **Evolving Prairie Walk.** Generally conducted in the early morning and early evening, this 90-minute, 1-mile stroll introduces visitors to the paleontology, prairie, and people of the Badlands. Participants meet at the Ben Reifel Visitor Center. Participants are encouraged to wear comfortable walking shoes and a hat, and to bring water and sunglasses.

♦ **Fossil Talk.** Generally slated for midmorning and late afternoon, this program allows participants to join a naturalist for a 20-minute discussion on the geological history and fossil resources of the White River Badlands. It's wheelchair

Tips from the Chief of Interpretation

Badlands National Park's 244,000 acres of stark scenery deserve special attention on any visitor's itinerary, according to the park's chief of interpretation Marianne Mills.

"This park is larger than all of the other National Park Service units in the Midwest combined," Mills notes. "We have a great diversity of stories that converge here—the fossils, the prairie grasses and wildlife, Lakota history, pioneer history, and homesteading. It's all here waiting to be explored."

Mills suggests no less than 2 days to fully experience the park. "Visitors to the Badlands should at least experience a night in the park. The air is so clear here that the stars shine."

She also advises visiting in the spring or fall. "The grasses are just greening in spring, the birds are migrating, and the prairie animals are giving birth to their young. In the fall, the canyons and the ravines are filled with beautiful golden colors, the birds are migrating . . . and you can enjoy an uncrowded hike, a bike ride, or just a solitary experience."

accessible and meets at the Fossil Exhibit Trail.

♦ **Evening Program.** Begins at 9pm in early summer, then 8:30pm starting in early August. Join a park ranger, intern, or researcher for a 45-minute in-depth examination of a topic relating to Badlands National Park. Topics include paleontology, geology, the prairie, human history, and wilderness. The program is wheelchair accessible and meets at the Cedar Pass Campground amphitheater.

Day Hikes

Numerous hiking trails provide a closer look at the Badlands for those adventurous enough to leave the comforting confines of their vehicles. All developed trails start from parking areas within 5 miles of the Ben Reifel Visitor Center at Cedar Pass.

Castle Trail

5 mi. RT. Moderate. Access: Trailheads are at the Fossil Exhibit Trail and at the Door Trail parking area.

Winding more than 5 miles through the mixed-grass prairie and badlands, this is the longest developed trail in the park.

The trail is fairly level and connects the Fossil Exhibit Trail and the Doors and Windows parking area. It's possible to make this a loop, if you follow the signs and turn off onto the well-marked Medicine Root Trail. The Castle Trail runs parallel to some interesting Badlands formations. Since this trail is not heavily used, it offers an ideal opportunity to escape the crowds, but it can be treacherous during and just after a heavy rain.

Cliff Shelf Nature Trail

0.5 mi. RT. Moderate. Access: 0.5 mi. north of the Ben Reifel Visitor Center.

A popular trail through a "slump" area where increased water retention supports an oasis of green surrounded by stark badlands formations. A self-guided brochure can be purchased on the trail. The trail has some steeper sections and boardwalk stairs. Its parking lot cannot accommodate RVs towing other vehicles.

Door Trail

0.6 mi. RT. Moderate. Access: 2 mi. northeast of the Ben Reifel Visitor Center.

This trail winds through some of the "baddest" of the Badlands. The first 100 yards to a beautiful view at "The Door" are mostly downhill and accessible to athletic or assisted people in wheelchairs. A self-guided brochure can be purchased 100 yards up the trail. The more rugged section takes off to the right of the viewing area; striped posts mark the way, indicating where to stop and read the trail brochure.

Fossil Exhibit Trail

0.25 mi. RT. Easy. Access: 5 mi. northwest of the Ben Reifel Visitor Center.

An easy boardwalk loop that will give you an idea of what animal life was like 30 million years ago. A self-guided brochure can be purchased at the trailhead. Wheelchair accessible.

Notch Trail

1.5 mi. RT. Moderate. The north end of the Door Trail parking area.

This trail takes you up a drainage, then up a 45° angle cable/wood ladder. This is definitely not for those afraid of heights. Follow the drainage to the "Notch"; the payoff is a striking view overlooking the Cliff Shelf area and the White River Valley.

Saddle Pass Trail

0.25 mi. RT. Moderate to strenuous. Access: This trail branches off the Castle Trail just west of its intersection with the Medicine Root Trail, and leads to the Badlands Loop Rd.

In less than 0.25 mile, this trail rises steeply 200 feet from the bottom of the Badlands Wall to the top, connecting with the Castle and Medicine Root trails. It's impassable after rains, however, so be sure to ask at the visitor center.

Window Trail

0.25 mi. RT. Easy to moderate. Access: The trailhead is at the center of the Door Trail parking area.

A 100-yard trail leads to a spectacular view through a "window" or opening in the Badlands Wall. Wheelchair accessible.

Exploring the Backcountry

The park encompasses the largest prairie wilderness in the United States, where expansive grasslands make cross-country travel unique. Vast ranges of classic badlands provide rugged, challenging terrain for even skilled hikers. Wildlife is close and abundant. Best of all, crowding is unknown in Badlands National Park. Few people explore the backcountry of this park, and hikers often have hundreds of acres to themselves.

Unlike many Western national parks, the Badlands has no formal system of backcountry permits or reservations. *Let friends and relatives know when you depart and when you expect to return.* Rangers at the Ben Reifel Visitor Center can assist in planning a safe, enjoyable excursion by offering directions, safety tips, maps, and information sheets.

When planning your backcountry hike, examine past, present, and forecasted weather carefully. With even a small amount of precipitation, some trails can become slick and impassable. Carry water if you think you could be out for as little as a half hour. Cross-country hikers are encouraged to carry a map, compass, and water, and to wear or carry appropriate clothing. No campfires are allowed. All overnight backcountry hikers should discuss their route with a park ranger before departure.

Spring and fall may be the best times to experience the Badlands backcountry. Days are often pleasant and nights are cool. In summer, temperatures often exceed 100° and pose health hazards. Avoid heat sickness by drinking plenty of water and avoiding the midday sun. Only the hardiest hikers attempt winter backpacking trips in the Badlands. Weather is unpredictable. Severe winter temperatures coupled with strong winds and sudden blizzards make backcountry survival difficult for those unprepared. Winter hikers should speak with a ranger at the

Ben Reifel Visitor Center before setting out.

Other Sports & Activities

Aerial Tours. If you want to see the Badlands from above, you have two options: helicopter or hot-air balloon. **Badger Helicopters** (☎ **605/433-5322** or 608/752-4001), takes off near the park's east entrance (take I-90, Exit 131) between mid-May and mid-September. Call for current rates.

If it's a hot-air balloon adventure you're looking for, contact **Black Hills Balloons,** P.O. Box 210, Custer, SD 57730-0210 (☎ **608/673-2520;** fax 608/673-5075), which offers flights over the Badlands and Black Hills year-round; expect to pay about $165 per person.

Biking. Off-road biking is not allowed in Badlands National Park, but the park's Loop Road is accessible to bikes (there are even bike racks at the Ben Reifel Visitor Center). Just be aware that the road can be steep. The 22-mile route from Pinnacles Overlook to the Ben Reifel Visitor Center is mostly downhill (though there are several steep passes to climb). Many bikers ride along Sage Creek Rim Road, past the prairie dog town, to spectacular views of the Badlands wilderness. During summer, though, car traffic is heavy and the temperatures hot. There are no bike rentals available in the park.

Horse-Packing Trips. Several companies offer guided trail rides through the backcountry of the Badlands (and the Black Hills), including family-run **Dakota Badland Outfitters,** P.O. Box 85, Custer, SD 57730 (☎ **608/673-5363;** fax 605/673-6010; www.wordpros.com/dakota; e-mail: dakota@wordpros.com). They conduct a 4-day Badlands Horse Camp for $680 per person (September and October), offer a Working Ranch Visit at $170 per day (June through September), or they can put together a custom Badlands trip.

Prices include all meals; sleeping bag rentals and airport transportation are available at additional charges.

Camping

A chart summarizing facilities at campgrounds in the Badlands and Black Hills area is in chapter 6.

INSIDE THE PARK

Camping is available inside Badlands National Park at either the Cedar Pass Campground or the Sage Creek Primitive Campground, on a first-come, first-served basis.

Cedar Pass Campground, located just off the Loop Road, has 96 sites suitable for tents or RVs, as well as an amphitheater, rest rooms, drinking water, shaded tables, trash containers, pay phone, campground host, dump station, and Night Sky Interpretive Area; however, there are no RV utility hookups, showers, or laundry. The campground is $10 per site per night in summer, with a 14-day maximum stay, and $8 per site per night in winter. Campfires are not allowed in the park.

Sage Creek Primitive Campground, which is also open year-round, has picnic tables and pit toilets. However, access may be limited in winter months due to impassable roads; the campground is located at the end of Sage Creek Rim Road, a gravel road that begins at the point where the park's Loop Road turns toward the Pinnacles Entrance. The campground is free, with a 14-day maximum stay (there are 15 sites). Water is not available.

Backcountry camping is also permitted (see "Exploring the Backcountry," above).

NEAR THE PARK

There is one commercial campground near Badlands National Park. Others are located closer to the Mount Rushmore area and are listed in chapter 6.

The Famous Wall Drug Store

You'll see the signs offering "free ice water" at the Wall Drug Store at 510 Main St. in Wall, which is about 8 miles north of Badlands National Park on S. Dak. 240 and I-90. And you'll see them almost everywhere you go throughout the Black Hills region, all of them telling you how many miles it is to the small town of Wall and the eponymous drugstore. In fact, there are now more than 3,000 of these signs, all over the world. The advertising gimmick saved what used to be a small-town drugstore in an isolated community from bankruptcy during the Great Depression. But Dorothy and Ted Hustead's gimmick also turned their little establishment into a block-long Old West emporium that now draws crowds from all over the United States and the world. You can buy pancakes or donuts (some of the best in the state, in fact), American Indian crafts, books, jewelry, Western apparel, and watch the animated "cowboy band" perform every 15 minutes. Do you want a "genuine" jackalope? Yes, they've got those too. Oh, and the ice water is still free.

Badlands Ranch Resort is much more than a campground. You'll find a barbecue area with gas grills, a pool, showers, whirlpool, laundry facilities, playground, good fishing, rock hunting, and trail rides. There are 35 sites with full RV hookups ($20 per night), or pitch a tent on the grounds for $12 a night. For more information, see the "Accommodations" section, below.

Accommodations

INSIDE THE PARK

Cedar Pass Lodge Cabins

Badlands National Park, P.O. Box 5, Interior, SD 57750. ☎ **605/433-5460.** Fax 605/433-5560. 24 cabins. A/C TEL. $42–$60 double. AE, DISC, MC, V. Closed late Oct to mid-Apr.

The Cedar Pass Lodge, adjacent to the Ben Reifel Visitor Center, offers air-conditioned cabins. The Badlands at dawn and dusk is an incredible experience. Visitors are encouraged to stay the night and see the best the Badlands has to offer.

NEAR THE PARK

The closest lodging outside the park is in the tiny community of Interior. Wall, north of the park, and Rapid City, 55 miles to the west on I-90, offer hundreds of hotel and motel rooms, as well as quaint bed-and-breakfasts. Reliable chains in Wall include **Best Western Plains Motel,** 712 Glenn St., Wall, SD 57790 (☎ **800/279-2145** or 605/279-2145), charging $45 to $95 double; **Econo Lodge,** 804 Glenn St., Wall, SD 57790 (☎ **605/279-2121**), charging $49 to $109 double; and **Super 8 Motel,** 711 Glenn St., Wall, SD 57790 (☎ **605/279-2688**), with rates of $39 to $75 double. A list of toll-free numbers appears in the appendix.

Accommodations in Rapid City and the Mount Rushmore area are listed in chapter 6.

Rates vary by season, with the highest rates in summer, and some properties close for several months in winter.

IN INTERIOR

Badlands Ranch Resort

S. Dak. 44, Interior, SD (HCR 53, P.O. Box 3, Interior, SD 57750). ☎ **605/433-5599.** Fax

605/433-5598. www.wall-badlands.com. 7 cabins, 4 motel units, B&B space for up to 25. A/C TV. $30–$68 cabin, $30–$50 motel rm, $68–$100 B&B rm; rates are negotiable during winter months. Breakfast is included in the B&B rates only. AE, DISC, MC, V. From the park, head west on S. Dak. 44 approximately 6 mi. toward Interior; when you go past the KOA Campground, look for the marked turnoff that leads to the resort's grounds.

This friendly, year-round resort, which opened in 1997, is located on 200 picturesque acres with views of the Badlands and plenty of wildlife for watching. In addition to the several accommodations options, there are also 35 complete RV hook-ups as well as tent camping sites (see "Camping," above). The resort offers a pool and hot tub, not to mention nightly bonfires and cookouts with entertainment, two fishing lakes, and horseback trails (moonlight trail rides can also be arranged). If you wish, the owners can also help arrange guided tours of the area's attractions and the adjoining Indian reservation. Cabins and motel units are comfortable and well maintained. Rooms in the B&B are more plush. Its top-floor honeymoon suite has a sunroom, whirlpool, and views of the Badlands.

Dining

INSIDE THE PARK

Cedar Pass Lodge Restaurant

In Badlands National Park. ☎ **605/433-5460.** Main courses $5–$9. AE, DISC, MC, V. Open daily for all meals, call for hours. Closed late Oct to mid-Apr.

Located near the Ben Reifel Visitor Center in the park's North Unit, the Lodge's restaurant (the only dining choice inside the park) has a full menu ranging from buffalo burgers to steaks and trout, as well as ice-cold soft drinks, beer, and wine for superb after-hike refreshments.

NEAR THE PARK

In Interior, the **Wooden Knife Cafe,** at the junction of S. Dak. 44 and S. Dak. 377, on Interior's east side (☎ **605/433-5463**), is home to the world-famous Wooden Knife Fry Bread, authentic American Indian dishes, burgers, chicken, old-fashioned scoop ice cream, and Indian tacos. It's an inexpensive place to stop for a quick meal.

There are other eating places in the communities surrounding Badlands National Park, including Wall and Interior. Establishments in Rapid City and the communities surrounding Mount Rushmore are listed in chapter 6.

PICNICKING IN THE PARK

Badlands National Park has two designated picnic areas, though you're likely to see people munching at nearly every overlook and trailhead in the park.

Conata Picnic Area is located on Conata Road, just south of Dillon Pass and the Badlands Loop Road in the North Unit. It has tables, trash cans, and pit toilets. Camping and fires are not allowed, and there is no drinking water.

Big Foot Picnic Area is located near Big Foot Pass on the Badlands Loop Road in the North Unit, about 7 miles northwest of the Ben Reifel Visitor Center. It also has tables, trash cans, and pit toilets but not drinking water. Camping and fires are not allowed.

Nearby Attractions

Beyond the boundaries of Badlands National Park are several other areas and sites that you may wish to visit, including Mount Rushmore National Memorial, Wind Cave National Park, Jewel Cave National Monument, Custer State Park, and Crazy Horse Memorial. All are discussed in chapter 6.

4

BIG BEND NATIONAL PARK

by Don and Barbara Laine

AST AND WILD, BIG BEND NATIONAL PARK IS A LAND OF EXTREMES, diversity, and a few contradictions. Its rugged terrain harbors thousands of species of plants and animals—some seen almost nowhere else on earth. A visit to the park can be a hike into the sun-baked desert, a float down a majestic river through the canyons, or a trek in high mountains where bears and mountain lions rule.

Geologists tell us that millions of years ago an inland sea covered this area. As it dried up, sediments of sand and mud turned to rock, and then came the creation of mountains and roar of volcanoes until, finally, millions of years of erosion produced the delightful canyons and rock formations we marvel at today. These rock formations—with their wonderful hues of red, orange, yellow, white, and brown—have created a unique and awe-inspiring world of immensity and rugged beauty. This is not a fantasyland of delicate shapes and intricate carvings, such as Bryce Canyon in Utah, but a powerful and dominating landscape. Although the greatest natural sculptures can be seen in the park's three major river canyons—the Santa Elena, Marsical, and Boquillas—throughout Big Bend you'll find spectacular and majestic examples of what nature can do with this mighty yet malleable building material we call rock.

Visitors to Big Bend National Park encounter not only a geologic wonder, but also a wild, rugged wilderness, populated by myriad desert and mountain plants and animals, ranging from box turtles and black-tailed jackrabbits to funny-looking javelina and powerful black bears and mountain lions. The park is considered a birders' paradise, with more species than at any other national park. It's also a wonderful spot to see wildflowers and the delightfully colorful display of cactus blooms.

For hikers, there's a tremendous variety of trails, from easy walks to rugged backcountry routes that barely qualify as trails at all. There are also opportunities to let the Rio Grande do the work, carrying water-sports enthusiasts on rafts, canoes, and kayaks through canyons carved in 1,500 feet of solid rock. Drivers of 4X4s enjoy exploring the backcountry roads, and history buffs find a number of historical attractions and cultural experiences.

Avoiding the Crowds. Average annual visitation is just over 300,000. Although the park is relatively uncrowded much of the year, there are several periods when lodging and campgrounds are full: spring break (usually the second and third weeks in March), Easter weekend, Thanksgiving weekend, and the week

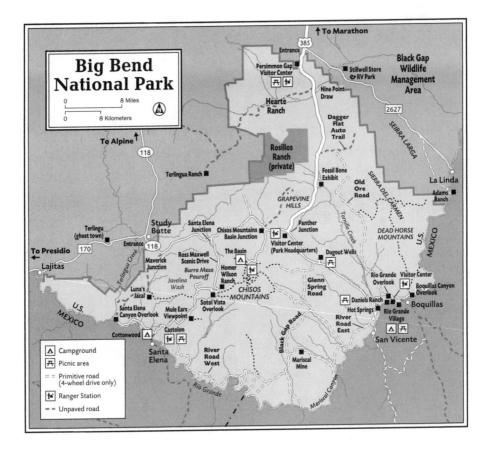

Big Bend National Park

Campground
Picnic area
Primitive road (4-wheel drive only)
Ranger Station
Unpaved road

between Christmas and New Year's Day. Park visitation is generally highest in March and April, and lowest in August and September.

But although the park's visitor centers, campgrounds, and other developed facilities may be taxed during the busier times, visitors can still be practically alone simply by seeking out lesser-used hiking trails. Discuss your hiking skills and expectations with rangers, who can offer advice on the best areas to get away from the crowd.

Just the Facts

Big Bend National Park is not really close to anything except the Rio Grande and Mexico. There is no public transportation to or through the park.

Park headquarters is 108 miles southeast of the town of Alpine via Tex. 118 and 69 miles south of Marathon via U.S. 385. There is train and bus service to Alpine, where the nearest hospital is located.

From El Paso, 323 miles northwest of the park, take I-10 east 121 miles to Exit 140, follow U.S. 90 southeast 99 miles to Alpine, then turn south on Tex. 118 for 108 miles to park headquarters.

The Nearest Airport. The nearest airport is **Midland International** (☎ 915/560-2200), 225 miles north, serviced by **American, America West Express, Continental,** and **Southwest Airlines.** From the airport, located between Midland and Odessa, take I-20 west about 50 miles to Exit 80 for Tex. 18, which you follow south about 50 miles to Fort Stockton. There, take U.S. 385 south 125 miles through Marathon to park headquarters.

Tips from a Park Ranger

"This park has something for everyone," says Valerie Naylor, Big Bend's chief of interpretation and visitor services. One of the park's assets, she says, is its variety of activities, including both easy day hikes and extended backpacking trips, great bird watching, wildlife viewing, and camping.

Big Bend is not a good choice for a quick visit, and Naylor recommends that people spend at least 3 days. "Be prepared for long distances, and don't expect all the amenities you might find in other places," she says.

Although Big Bend is one of America's lesser-used national parks, Naylor says that it does get busy occasionally, particularly during spring break time,

usually March and early April, when college students arrive en masse to hit the trails. The hottest months are May and June, she says, adding that the heat of July and August is usually tempered by afternoon thunderstorms. September is among the slowest times in the park, and it can be very nice, although still hot. "October is a great time, still quiet and a bit cooler," she says.

Naylor advises summer visitors to avoid hiking in the desert, but you can still get out on the trails by going up into the Chisos Mountains, where it can be 20° cooler than on the river. She also recommends hiking into the high country from October through December to see the beautiful fall colors.

Car rentals are available from **Advantage, Avis, Budget, Dollar, Hertz,** and **National.** Toll-free numbers for airlines and car-rental agencies are given in the appendix.

INFORMATION

For information, contact the **Superintendent,** P.O. Box 129, **Big Bend National Park,** TX 79834 (☎ 915/477-2251; www.nps.gov/bibe).

The free park newspaper, *The Big Bend Paisano,* published seasonally by the Park Service, is a great source of current information on seminars, new or special publications, suggested hikes, kids' activities, and local facilities, with telephone numbers inside and outside the park.

Books, maps, and videos are available from **Big Bend Natural History Association,** P.O. Box 196, Big Bend National Park, TX 79834 (☎ 915/477-2236). The *Official Big Bend National Park Handbook* (Washington, D.C.: Department of the Interior, 1983) by the Division of Publications, National Park

Service, is a good introduction to the what and why of the park, describing in detail the terrain, flora, fauna, and human history of the area. There are also several booklets detailing improved and unimproved roads and hiking trails, produced by the Park Service. A particularly good hiking guide is *Hiking Big Bend National Park* (Helena, Mont.: Falcon Press, 1996) by Laurence Parent. Those planning backpacking trips will also want to get the appropriate topo maps, which, along with the publications discussed above, are available at the park's visitor centers or by mail from the Big Bend Natural History Association.

For information on nearby attractions, as well as places to stay and eat, contact the **Brewster County Tourism Council** (☎ 877/244-2363; www.visitbigbend.com).

VISITOR CENTERS

There are four visitor centers in the park. **Panther Junction Visitor Center** (open daily year-round) is centrally located at park headquarters; **Persimmon Gap Visitor Center** (open most of the year) is at the North Entrance to the park on U.S. 385; **Rio Grande Village Visitor Center** (open November through April) is on the river in the eastern part of the park; and **Chisos Basin Visitor Center** (open year-round) is in the Chisos Mountains in the middle of the park, at 5,401 feet in elevation.

All visitor centers provide information, backcountry permits, books, and maps, and also have exhibits; there is a particularly impressive display on mountain lions at Chisos Basin. At **Castolon,** near the river in the southwest end of the park, there is a visitor contact station. Bulletin boards with schedules of ranger programs, notices of animal sightings, and other visitor information are located at each of the visitor centers and the contact station.

FEES & PERMITS

Entry into the park for up to a week costs $10 per passenger vehicle, and $5 per person on foot or bicycle. Camping costs $7 per night in the three developed campgrounds. There's a concession-operated RV campground at Rio Grande Village, with full hookups, costing $14.50. A free camping permit, available at any visitor center, is required for all backcountry camping; and free permits are also required for all river-float trips (see "Camping" and "River Running," below).

SPECIAL REGULATIONS & WARNINGS

Watch for wild animals along the roads, particularly javelina, deer, and rabbits, especially at night when they may be blinded by your vehicle's headlights and freeze in the middle of the road. Of course, feeding wildlife is prohibited, not only to minimize the risk of injuries to park visitors, but also because it's bad for the animals.

The Basin Road Scenic Drive into the Chisos Mountains has sharp curves and steep grades and is not recommended for trailers longer than 20 feet or RVs longer than 24 feet. The **Ross Maxwell Scenic Drive** to Castolon is okay for most RVs and trailers but can present a problem for those with insufficient power to handle the steep grade. These roads require extra caution by all users—drivers of motor vehicles, pedestrians, and bicyclists. Horses are not permitted on any paved roads in the park.

Desert heat can be dangerous. Hikers should carry at least 1 gallon of water per person per day; wear a hat, long pants, and long sleeves; and use a good sunscreen. Don't depend on springs as water sources, and avoid hiking in the middle of the day in summer. Early mornings and evenings are best for both comfort and sightseeing. Talk to rangers about your plans before heading out; they can help you plan a hike in accordance with your ability and time frame. They can also advise you on expected weather conditions—sudden summer thunderstorms are common and can cause flash flooding in usually dry washes and canyons.

Swimming is not recommended in the Rio Grande, even though it may look tantalizingly inviting on a hot summer day. Waste materials and waterborne microorganisms have been found in the river, and can cause serious illness. Also, strong undercurrents, deep holes, and sharp rocks in shallow water are common. Should you decide to swim in spite of these warnings, be sure to wear a life jacket.

Wood or ground fires are prohibited in the park, and caution is advised when using camp stoves, charcoal grills, and cigarettes. Smoking is prohibited on all trails. Check at the visitor centers for current drought conditions, and any special restrictions that may be in effect when you visit.

SEASONS & CLIMATE

Weather here is generally mild to hot, although because of the vast range of elevations—from about 1,800 feet at the

Keeping the Wild in Wildlife, or How to Avoid an Unpleasant Encounter

The signs and warnings are everywhere: "This is bear and mountain lion country," and although one of the thrills of visiting Big Bend National Park is the opportunity to see wildlife, for the safety of both the human visitors and the park's wildlife, these animals should always be viewed from a distance. Rangers say that since the 1950s there have been more than 1,000 sightings of mountain lions in the park, and numerous sightings of black bears. While the vast majority have been relatively uneventful—although definitely something to tell the neighbors about when you get home—three people have been attacked by mountain lions in the park. Fortunately, all recovered from their injuries; unfortunately, it was considered necessary to kill the mountain lions.

Hikers, especially in the Chisos Mountains, should be especially careful to minimize the danger of an encounter. First, discuss your hiking plans with park rangers to see if there have been any recent mountain lion sightings where you plan to hike. Don't hike alone, especially at dawn or dusk. Watch children carefully—never let them run ahead. If you do end up face-to-face with a mountain lion, rangers offer these tips: Don't run, but stand your ground, shout, wave your arms, and try to appear as large as possible. If you have children with you, pick them up. If the mountain lion acts aggressively, throw stones, and try to convince it that not only are you not prey, but that you may be dangerous. Then report the incident to a ranger as soon as possible.

The other animal you may see is one of the estimated 15 to 20 black bears that currently live in the Chisos Mountains.

Bears are attracted to food, and the best way to avoid an unwanted encounter with a bear is to keep a clean camp. Park rangers recommend that you store all foodstuffs, cooking utensils, and toiletries in a hard-sided vehicle. Food storage lockers are available for hikers and campers in the Chisos Mountains. Always dispose of garbage properly in the receptacles provided. If you do see a bear, keep a safe distance; do not approach or follow it, and of course, never attempt to feed a bear. If a bear approaches you, scare it away by shouting, waving your arms, or throwing rocks or sticks. Watch for cubs—you never want to be between a mother bear and her cubs. Report any sightings of bears to a ranger.

Bears and mountain lions aren't the only wild animals in the park. Many visitors see javelinas (officially known as collared peccaries), which look a bit like pigs and are very near-sighted. A group of 10 to 20 are often seen in and near Rio Grande Village Campground, and some of them have learned to recognize the crinkling sound of potato chip bags, and will run toward the sound in hopes of a snack. Although javelina are not aggressive, they are easily frightened, and could inflict some damage with their javelin-sharp tusks, from which they get their name.

Also deserving of mention are the park's poisonous snakes, scorpions, spiders, and centipedes, which are most active during the warmer months. Rangers advise that you watch carefully where you put your feet and hands, and use flashlights at night. Hikers may want to consider wearing high boots or protective leggings. It's also a good idea to check your shoes and bedding before use.

eastern end of Boquillas Canyon to 7,825 feet on Emory Peak in the Chisos Mountains—conditions can vary greatly throughout the park at any given time. Essentially, the higher you go, the cooler and wetter you can expect it to be, although no section of the park gets a lot of precipitation.

Summers here are hot, often well over 100°F in the desert in May and June, and afternoon thunderstorms are common from July through September. Winters are usually mild, although temperatures occasionally drop below freezing, and light snow is possible, especially in the Chisos Mountains. Fall and spring are usually warm and pleasant.

SEASONAL EVENTS

The **International Good Neighbor Day Fiesta,** annually on the third Saturday in October, is designed to promote international friendship and understanding with music, dancing, food, and cultural demonstrations.

If You Only Have 1 Day

Big Bend National Park is huge, and you can't hope to see all of it in 1 day or even 2. It's best to allow at least 3 days, essentially devoting 1 day each to the desert, river, and mountains. However, if you have a limited amount of time in the park, the best choice is to start with the **Chisos Basin** and see the mountains in the middle of the park. Take the short, easy **Window View Trail,** a self-guided nature trail (see "Day Hikes," below) that discusses the flora and fauna of the Chisos Mountains. Then head back down and drive the **Ross Maxwell Scenic Drive** (see "Exploring the Park by Car," below) through the Chihuahuan Desert to the Rio Grande. If time allows, hike into **Santa Elena Canyon** (see "Day Hikes," below), one of the most beautiful canyons in the park. Finally, take in a ranger program at one of the park amphitheaters.

Exploring the Park by Car

There are several paved roads in the park—one goes through and others take you to different sections. In addition, there are several unimproved roads requiring high clearance or 4X4 vehicles (see "Backcountry Driving," below).

There are two scenic drives in the park, both with sharp curves and steep inclines and not recommended for certain RVs and trailers (see "Special Regulations & Warnings," above).

The 7-mile **Chisos Basin Drive** climbs up Green Gulch to Panther Pass before dropping down into the Basin. Near the pass there are some sharp curves, and parts of the road are at a 10% grade. The views are wonderful any time of the year, and particularly when the wildflowers dot the meadows, hills, and roadsides. The best month for wildflowers is usually October, after the summer rains.

When you've breathed your fill of clear mountain air, head back down and turn west toward the **Ross Maxwell Scenic Drive** through the Chihuahuan Desert and finally to the Rio Grande. This drive winds through the desert on the west side of the Chisos Mountains, providing a different perspective. Afterwards, it passes through Castolon, and then continues along and above the river to **Santa Elena Canyon.** Here you should park and hike the trail, which climbs above the river, offering great views into the steep, narrow canyon (see "Day Hikes," below).

Another worthwhile drive, recommended for all vehicles, begins at **Panther Junction Visitor Center** and goes to Rio Grande Village, a distance of 20 miles. From the visitor center head southeast through the desert toward the high mountains that form the skyline in the distance. The first half of the drive passes through desert grasses, finally making a comeback after severe overgrazing in the decades before the establishment of the park in 1944. Recovery is slow in this harsh climate, but it is beginning to revegetate.

As the elevation gradually decreases, you progress further into the desert, and the grasses give way to lechugilla and ocotillo stalks, cacti, and other arid-climate survivors. Off to the south is the long, rather flat **Chilicotal Mountain,** named for the chilicote, or Mescal-bean bushes, growing near its base. The chilicote's poisonous red bean is used in Mexico to kill rats. Several miles further the River Road turns off and heads southwest toward Castolon, more than 50 miles away. This is a primitive road for high-clearance vehicles only.

If you feel adventurous, take the **Hot Springs** turnoff about a mile beyond the Tornillo Creek Bridge. It follows a rough wash to a point overlooking the confluence of Tornillo Creek and the Rio Grande. A trail along the riverbank leads to several springs. The foundation of a bathhouse is a remnant of the town of Hot Springs, which thrived here about 20 years before the park was established, and continued as a concession for another 10 years.

Back on the paved road, you'll soon pass through a short tunnel in the limestone cliff, after which is a parking area for a short trail to a viewpoint overlooking Rio Grande Village. It's just a short drive from here to **Rio Grande Village,** your destination, where you can take a 0.25-mile nature trail ending at a high point above the Rio Grande, offering terrific views up and down the river.

Organized Tours & Ranger Programs

Park naturalists offer a variety of programs year-round. Illustrated evening programs take place at the 5,400-foot **Chisos Basin amphitheater** in summer. From November through April, evening programs are offered regularly in the amphitheater at **Rio Grande Village** and occasionally at Cottonwood Campground. Subjects include the park's geology, plants, animals, and human history. Rangers also offer guided **nature walks,** and occasionally lead driving tours.

Workshops are also planned, on subjects such as adobe construction or photography. Look for weekly schedules on the bulletin boards scattered about the park.

The **Big Bend Natural History Association** (see "Information," above) offers a variety of seminars, ranging from 1-day workshops, starting at $40, to multiday programs starting at $80. Subjects could include black bears, archaeology, bats, birds, cacti, and wildflowers. A 1-day introductory overview covers the plants, animals, geology, and history of the park. In recent years there have also been multiday photography workshops by noted nature photographer Jim Bones.

Historic & Man-Made Attractions

There is evidence that both prehistoric Indians and later Apaches, Kiowas, and Comanches occupied this area. Throughout the park you can find **petroglyphs, pictographs,** and other signs of early human presence, including ruins of **stone shelters.** There are pictographs along the Hot Spring Trail (see "Day Hikes," below), and along the river. Watch for **mortar holes** scattered throughout the park, sometimes a foot deep, where American Indians would grind seeds or mesquite beans.

Also within the park boundaries are the remains of several early 20th-century communities, a mercury mine, and projects by the Civilian Conservation Corps.

The **Castolon Historic District,** located in the southwest section of the park just off the Ross Maxwell Scenic Drive, includes the remains of homes and other buildings, many stabilized by the Park Service, that were constructed in the early 1900s by Mexican American farmers, Anglo settlers, and the U.S. Army. The first is the **Alvino House,** the oldest surviving adobe structure in the park, dating from 1901. Nearby is **La Harmonia Store,** built in 1920 to house cavalry troops during the Mexican Revolution, but never actually used by soldiers because the war ended. Two civilians then purchased the building, converting it to a general store. The store continues to operate, selling snacks, groceries, and other necessities.

The village of **Glenn Springs,** located in the southeast section of the park and accessible by dirt road off the main park highway, owes its creation to having a reliable water source in an otherwise arid area. It was named for a rancher called H. E. Glenn, who grazed horses in the area until he was killed by Indians in the 1880s. By 1916 there were several ranches, a factory that produced wax from the candelilla plant, a store, a post office, and a residential village divided into two sections—one for the Anglos and the other for the Mexicans. But then Mexican bandit-revolutionaries crossed the border and attacked, killing and wounding a number of people, looting the store, and partially destroying the wax factory. Within 3 years the community was virtually deserted. Today, the spring still flows, and you can see the remains of several adobe buildings and other structures.

Remains of a small health resort can be seen at the **Hot Springs,** accessible by hiking trail or dirt road, along the Rio Grande west of Rio Grande Village in the park's southeast section. Construction of the resort was begun by J. O. Langford in 1909, who was forced to leave during the Mexican Revolution. However, Langford returned and completed the project in the 1920s, advertising the Hot Springs as "The Fountain of Youth that Ponce de León failed to find." Today you'll see the ruins of a general store/post office, other buildings, and a foundation that fills with natural mineral water, at about 105°F, creating an almost natural hot tub.

To get to the **Marsical Mine** you will likely need a four-wheel-drive or high-clearance vehicle. Located in the south-central part of the park, it is most easily accessed by River Road East, which begins 5 miles west of Rio Grande Village. The mine operated on and off between 1900 and 1943, producing 1,400 76-pound flasks of mercury, which was almost one-quarter of the total amount of mercury produced in the United States during that time. Mining buildings, homes, the company store, a kiln, foundations, and other structures remain, in what is now a National Historic District.

Also in the park you can see some excellent examples of the work done by the **Civilian Conservation Corps** in the 1930s and early 1940s. These include stone culverts along the Basin Road, the Lost Mine Trail, and several buildings, including some stone-and-adobe cottages that are still in use at the Chisos Mountain Lodge.

Day Hikes

SHORTER TRAILS

Boquillas Canyon Trail

1.4 mi. RT. Moderate. Access: End of Boquillas Canyon Rd.

This hike begins by climbing a low hill and then drops down to the Rio Grande, ending near a shallow cave and huge sand dune. There are good views of the scenic canyon and the Mexican village of Boquillas, across the Rio Grande.

Burro Mesa Pour-Off

1 mi. RT. Easy. Access: Parking area at the end of Burro Mesa spur road, about 11.5 mi. down the Ross Maxwell Scenic Drive on the west (right).

This short hike takes you to the bottom of a desert pour-off. The beginning of the trail is a well-marked path, but as you turn into Javelina Wash it becomes less obvious so watch for the lines of rocks pointing the way. The trail has an elevation gain of about 60 feet. The pour-off is a long, narrow chute that is usually dry, but the extensive cut gives testimony to the power of rushing water after a heavy summer rain. Don't attempt to climb to the top from here; it is quite hazardous. There is an easier way for those with good route-finding skills: See "Top of Burro Mesa Pour-Off," below.

Chihuahuan Desert Nature Trail

0.5 mi. RT. Easy. Access: Dugout Wells Picnic Area, 5.9 mi. east of Panther Junction.

A good introduction to the flora of the Chihuahuan Desert, this is an easy stroll along a relatively flat gravel path with signs describing the plants you see along the way.

Chisos Basin Loop Trail

1.6-mi. loop. Easy. Access: Chisos Basin Trailhead.

This fairly easy walk climbs about 350 feet into a pretty meadow and leads to an overlook that offers good views of the park's mountains, including Emory Peak, highest point in the park at 7,825 feet.

Hot Springs Trail

1 mi. RT. Easy. Access: End of improved dirt road to Hot Springs, off rd. to Rio Grande Village.

An interpretive booklet available at the trailhead describes the sights, including a historic health resort and homestead (see "Historic & Man-Made Attractions," above), along this easy loop. Fairly substantial ruins remain of a general store/post office, other buildings, and a foundation that fills with natural mineral water, at about 105°F, creating an inviting hot tub. Also along the trail are pictographs left by ancient Indians, and panoramic views of the Rio Grande and Mexico.

Panther Path

50 yd. RT. Easy. Access: Panther Junction Visitor Center.

This is a short walk through a garden of cacti and other desert plants. A booklet discussing the park's plant life is available at the trailhead.

Rio Grande Village Nature Trail

0.75 mi. RT. Easy. Access: Southeast corner of Rio Grande Village Campground, across from site 18.

A good choice for sunrise and sunset views, this self-guided loop nature trail (booklet available at the trailhead) climbs from the surprisingly lush river floodplain about 125 feet into desert terrain and up a hilltop that offers excellent panoramic views.

Santa Elena Canyon

0.8 mi. one way. Moderate. Access: End of Ross Maxwell Scenic Drive.

You may get your feet wet crossing a broad creek on this trail, which also takes you up a series of steep steps. But it's one of the most scenic short trails in the park, leading along the canyon wall, with good views of rafters on the Rio Grande, and down among the boulders along the river. Interpretive signs describe the canyon environment. Beware of flash flooding as you cross the Terlingua Creek, and skip this trail if the creek is running swiftly.

Top of Burro Mesa Pour-Off

1.8 mi. one way. Moderate. Access: Trailhead parking about 7 mi. down the Ross Maxwell Scenic Drive on the west (right).

This moderate hike takes you through some narrow rocky gorges to the top of the Burro Mesa Pour-Off. The trail may not be well marked, so it's a good idea to carry a topographical map and compass. As you hike along the now-dry washes you'll realize that the rock cairns marking the trail are quickly scattered when water floods through them. There is a gradual decline of about 525 feet to the top of this desert waterfall, where the drainage drops suddenly and precipitously from the wash where you stand to the one below. Do not chance this hike in stormy weather, as you might get washed away with the rock cairns.

Tuff Canyon

0.75 mi. RT. Easy. Access: Ross Maxwell Scenic Drive, 5 mi. south of Mule Ears Overlook access rd.

This easy trail leads into a narrow canyon, carved from soft volcanic rock called tuff, with several canyon overlooks.

Window View Trail

0.3 mi. RT. Easy. Access: Chisos Basin Trailhead.

Level, paved, and wheelchair accessible, this self-guided nature trail (a brochure is available at the trailhead) runs along a low hill and offers beautiful sunset views through the Window, a V-shaped opening in the mountains to the west.

LONGER TRAILS

Chimneys Trail

4.8 mi. RT. Moderate. Access: Ross Maxwell Scenic Drive, 1.2 mi. south of the Burro Mesa Pour-Off access rd.

This flat trail through the desert follows an old dirt road to a series of chimney-shaped rock formations. American Indian petroglyphs can be seen on the southernmost chimney, and nearby are ruins of rock shelters. Those who want to extend this hike can continue, although the trail is difficult to follow after the Chimneys and a topographical map is highly recommended.

Grapevine Hills Trail

2.2 mi. RT. Easy. Access: 6 mi. down the unpaved Grapevine Hills Rd.

An easy walk, this trail follows a sandy wash through the desert, among massive granite boulders, ending at a picturesque balancing rock. There is an elevation change of about 240 feet.

Lost Mine Trail

4.8 mi. RT. Moderate. Access: Chisos Basin Rd. at Panther Pass.

This self-guided nature trail (a booklet is available at the trailhead) is a popular mountain hike that climbs about 1,100 feet. It was built in the early 1940s by the Civilian Conservation Corps—evidence of their rock work can still be seen. Along the way, the trail climbs through forests of piñon, juniper, and oak, and offers splendid views. Those with limited time or ambition don't have to hike all the way—some of the trail's best views are about 1 mile from the trailhead, from a saddle where you can look out over a pretty canyon to the surrounding mountains and even deep into Mexico.

Mule Ears Spring Trail

3.8 mi. RT. Moderate. Access: Mule Ears Overlook parking area, along the Ross Maxwell Scenic Drive.

This relatively flat desert trail crosses several arroyos and then follows a wash most of the way to Mule Ears Spring. It offers great views of unusual rock formations, such as the Mule Ears, and ends at a historic ranch house and rock corral.

Pine Canyon Trail

4 mi. RT. Moderate. Access: End of unpaved Pine Canyon Rd. (check on road conditions before going).

With a 1,000-foot elevation gain, this trail takes you from desert grasslands, dotted with sotols, into a pretty canyon with dense stands of piñon, juniper, oak, and finally bigtooth maple and ponderosa pine. At the higher elevations you'll also see Texas madrones—evergreen trees with smooth reddish bark shed each summer. At the end of the trail is a 200-foot cliff, which becomes a picturesque waterfall after heavy rains. At the cliff's base you're likely to see columbine, a member of the buttercup family, with delicate yellow flowers.

Slickrock Canyon

10 mi. RT. Moderate. Access: Main Park Rd., about 12 mi. west of Panther Junction, at Oak Creek Bridge.

This hike follows Oak Creek northwest to a small, scenic canyon, passing along the south edge of Slickrock Mountain. This is not a marked trail, but rather a route through sand and gravel washes, and a topographical map is helpful. Hikers in this deep canyon will find desert plants such as mesquite and creosote bush, and possibly tracks of coyotes, javelinas, and mountain lions.

Window Trail

5.2 mi. RT. Moderate. Access: Chisos Basin Trailhead.

A scenic trail through Oak Creek Canyon, this hike involves descending about 800 feet to the base of the Window, a V-shaped opening in the mountains that frames panoramic desert scenes. Following the Oak Creek drainage, it provides a good chance to see deer, javelina, rock squirrels, and a variety of birds.

Exploring the Backcountry

There are numerous possibilities for backpacking in the park, both on established and marked hiking trails and on relatively unmarked hiking routes following washes, canyons, or abandoned rough dirt roads dating from the late 1800s. In all there are more than 150 miles of designated trails and routes. Cross-country hiking is also permitted. Because many trails and hiking routes are hard to follow, rangers advise that hikers carry detailed 7.5-minute topographical maps and compasses.

Campers can use numerous designated backcountry campsites, and are also allowed to camp in desert areas. The required free permits must be obtained in person, no more than 24 hours in advance. In the high Chisos Mountains, backcountry campers must stay at designated campsites and carry special permits, available on a first-come, first-served basis. These campsites are often difficult to obtain during the park's busiest times—Thanksgiving and Christmas holidays and college spring break season, usually in March or early April.

Ground fires are prohibited throughout the park. Rangers warn that backcountry water availability is spotty and changeable, and advise backpackers to carry enough water for their entire trip.

Other Sports & Activities

Desert Sports, P.O. Box 448, Terlingua, TX 79852 (☎ 888/989-6900 or 915/371-2727; fax 915/371-2726; www.desertsportstx.com), provides equipment rentals and a variety of guided adventures both in and around the park. It's on FM 170, 5 miles west of the junction of FM 170 and Tex. 118.

Backcountry Driving. There are a number of unimproved roads in Big Bend requiring high-clearance vehicles and sometimes a 4X4. Many have roadside campsites. Get details on current road conditions from rangers before setting out and pick up the useful backcountry road guide, available at visitor centers. All overnight trips require backcountry permits.

Horseback Riding. Horses are permitted on most dirt roads and many park trails (check with rangers for specifics), and may be kept overnight at many of the park's primitive road campsites, although not at the developed campgrounds. The **Government Springs Campsite,** located 3.5 miles from Panther Junction, is a primitive campsite with a corral that accommodates up to eight horses. It can be reserved up to 10 weeks in advance (☎ 915/477-2251, ext. 158). Those riding horses in the park must get free stock use permits, which should be obtained in person up to 24 hours in advance at any of the park's visitor centers.

Although there are no commercial outfitters offering guided rides in the park as of this writing, there are opportunities for rides just outside the park on private land, at nearby Big Bend Ranch State Park, and across the river in Mexico. **Big Bend Stables,** P.O. Box 6, Terlingua, TX 79852 (☎ **800/887-4331** or 915/371-2212), and **Lajitas Stables,** Star Route 70, Box 380, Terlingua, TX 79852 (☎ **888/508-7667** or 915/424-3238; www.lajitasstables.com), offer a variety of guided trail rides, lasting from 1 hour to all day to several days. Some trips follow canyon trails; others visit ancient Indian camps, ghost towns, or abandoned mines. They can also take you to see pictographs, fossils, and petrified wood. Both stables are under the same management. Rates are about $20 per hour for the first hour and $10 per hour after that; multiday trips are usually about $130 to $150 per day, and include all meals and camping equipment. Novice riders and children 4 and up are welcome.

Mountain Biking. Bikes are not permitted on hiking trails, but are allowed on the park's many established dirt roads. Mountain bikes are available for rent from **Desert Sports** (see above), at a cost of $25 per day, $125 for 5 to 7 days, and $15 for each additional day after 7. The company also offers multiday guided trips, including a combination mountain-biking and float trip in the park—3 days for $350.

River Running. The Rio Grande follows the southern edge of the park for 118 miles, and extends another 127 miles downstream as a designated Wild and Scenic River. The river offers mostly fairly calm float trips, but does have a few sections of rough white water during high-water times. It can usually be run in a raft, canoe, or kayak. You can either bring your own equipment, or rent equipment near the park (none is available in the park), or take a trip with one of several river guides approved by the National Park Service.

Those planning trips on their own must obtain free permits at a park visitor center, in person only, no more than 24 hours before the trip. Permits for the lower canyons of the Rio Grande Wild and Scenic River are available at the **Persimmon Gap Visitor Center,** when it's open, and a self-serve permit station located at **Stillwell Store and RV Park,** 7 miles from the park's north entrance on FM 2627. Permits for the section of river through Santa Elena Canyon can also be obtained at a self-serve permit station at the **Barton Warnock Environmental Education Center** in the community of Lajitas, Texas, west of the park. Park rangers, however, strongly advise that everyone planning a river trip check with them beforehand to get the latest river conditions. A river-running booklet, with additional information, is available at park visitor centers and from the **Big Bend Natural History Association** (see "Information," above).

Rafts, inflatable kayaks, and canoes can be rented from **Desert Sports** (see above). Rafts cost $20 per person per day (with a three-person minimum) with discounts for trips longer than 4 days; inflatable kayaks cost $30 per day for one person and $40 per day for two people; and canoes cost $40 per day, with discounts for multiday rentals. The company also provides shuttle services, and offers guided multiday canoe and raft trips, where you can either take an active role, or sit back and let your boatman and the river do the work. Typical prices are $240 per person for 2 days on the river through Santa Elena Canyon; and $395 per person for 3 days on the river through Marsical Canyon, considered the most remote canyon in the national park.

Desert Sports also offers trips that combine a float trip with hiking or mountain biking. Also see "Mountain Biking," above.

Another company that provides guided trips on the Rio Grande is **Big Bend River Tours,** P.O. Box 317, Lajitas, TX 79852 (☎ **800/545-4240** or 915/424-3219; fax 915/424-3411; www.bigbendrivertours.com), which has raft trips daily year-round. Trips range from a delightful half-day float for about $55 per person to 10-day excursions for about $1,200 per person.

Among the company's most popular trips is the 19-mile float through beautiful Santa Elena Canyon, which offers spectacular scenery and wonderful serenity, plus the excitement of a challenging section of rapids called the Rockslide. There are often opportunities to see javelinas, coyotes, beavers, wild burros, golden eagles, and peregrine falcons. The canyon can be explored on a day trip (about $115 per person), a 2-day trip (about $245 per person), or a 3-day trip (about $355 per person), with rates varying based on the number of people making the trip. The longer trips include a stop in a side canyon with waterfalls and peaceful swimming holes.

Big Bend River Tours also offers guided canoe and inflatable kayak trips, provides a shuttle service, and rents equipment.

Also offering raft trips year-round, at similar rates, is **Far Flung Adventures,** P.O. Box 31, Terlingua, TX 79852 (☎ **800/359-4138** or 915/371-2489; fax 915/371-2325; www.farflung.com), and **Texas River Expeditions,** P.O. Box 583, Terlingua, TX 79852 (☎ **800/839-7238** or 915/371-2633; www.texasriver.com).

Wildlife Viewing & Bird Watching. There is an absolutely phenomenal variety of wildlife at Big Bend National Park. About 450 species of birds will be found here over the course of the year—that's more than at any other national park and nearly half of all those found in North America. At latest count there are also about 75 species of mammals, close to 70 species of reptiles and amphibians, and more than three dozen species of fish.

This is the only place in the United States where you'll find the Mexican long-nosed bat, listed by the federal government as an endangered species. Other endangered species that make their homes in the park include the black-capped vireo, the peregrine falcon, and a tiny fish—the Big Bend gambusia, whose favorite food is mosquito larvae.

Birders consider Big Bend National Park a key bird-watching destination, especially for those looking for some of America's more unusual birds. Among the park's top bird-watching spots are Rio Grande Village and Cottonwood campgrounds, the Chisos Basin, and the Hot Springs. Species to watch for include the colorful golden-fronted woodpecker, which can often be seen year-round among the cottonwood trees along the Rio Grande; and the rare colima warbler, whose range in the United States consists solely of the Chisos Mountains at Big Bend National Park. Among the hundreds of other birds that call the park home, at least part of the year, are scaled quail, spotted sandpipers, white-winged doves, greater roadrunners, lesser nighthawks, white-throated swifts, black-chinned hummingbirds, broad-tailed hummingbirds, acorn woodpeckers, northern flickers, western wood-pewees, ash-throated flycatchers, tufted titmice, bushtits, cactus wrens, canyon wrens, loggerhead shrikes, Wilson's warblers, and Scott's orioles.

Mammals you may see in the park include desert cottontails, black-tailed jackrabbits, rock squirrels, Texas antelope squirrels, Merriam's kangaroo rats, coyotes, gray foxes, raccoons, striped skunks, mule deer, and white-tailed deer. There are occasional sightings of mountain lions, usually called panthers here, in the Green Gulch and Chisos Basin areas. Three attacks on humans have occurred (see the special section titled "Keeping the Wild in Wildlife, or How to Avoid an Unpleasant Encounter," above). Black bears, frequently seen in the area until about 1940, were mostly killed off by area ranchers who saw them as a threat to their livestock. However, with the protection provided by national park status, they began to return in the mid-1980s, and have established a small population.

There are a number of reptiles in the park, including some poisonous snakes, such as diamondback, Mojave, rock, and black-tailed rattlesnakes, plus the transpecos copperhead (see "Keeping the Wild in Wildlife, or How to Avoid an Unpleasant Encounter," above). Fortunately, it is unlikely you will see a rattler or copperhead, since they avoid both the heat of the day and busy areas. You are more apt to encounter nonpoisonous western coachwhips, which are often seen speeding across trails and roadways. They're reddish, sometimes bright red, and among America's fastest snakes, sometimes called "red racers." Other nonpoisonous snakes that inhabit the park include Texas whipsnakes, spotted night snakes, southwestern black-headed snakes, and black-necked garter snakes.

Among the lizards you may see scurrying along desert roads and trails is the southwestern earless lizard—adult males are green with black and white chevrons on their lower sides, and often curl their black-striped tails over their backs. You'll also see various whiptail lizards in the desert, but in the canyons and higher in the mountains, watch for the crevice spiny lizard, which is covered with scales and has a dark collar. Although rare, there are also western box turtles in the park, as well as several types of more common water turtles.

Camping

A free camping permit, available at any visitor center, is required for use of the primitive backcountry roadside and backpacking campsites.

INSIDE THE PARK

There are three developed campgrounds run by the Park Service plus an RV park run by a concessionaire.

Rio Grande Village Campground is the largest. It has numerous trees, many with prickly pear cacti growing up around them, and thorny bushes everywhere. Sites are either graveled or paved and are nicely spaced for privacy. They often fill up by 1pm in winter (the high season). One area is designated a "No Generator Zone." Separate but within walking distance is **Rio Grande Village**

Trailer Park, a concessionaire-operated RV park with full hookups. It looks like a parking lot in the midst of grass and trees, fully paved with curbs and back-in sites (no pull-throughs). Tents are not permitted. The small store has limited camping supplies and groceries, a coin-operated laundry, showers for a fee, propane, and gasoline.

Chisos Basin Campground, although not heavily wooded, has small piñon and juniper trees and well-spaced sites. The campground is nestled around a circular road in a bowl below the visitor center. The access road to the campground is steep and curved, so take it slowly.

Cottonwood Campground is named for the huge old cottonwood trees that dominate the scene. Sites in this rather rustic area are gravel and spacious, within walking distance of the river. There are pit toilets.

NEAR THE PARK

About 7 miles east of the park's North Entrance on FM 2627 is **Stillwell Store and RV Park,** HC 65, Box 430, Alpine, TX 79830 (☎ and fax **915/376-2244**), a casual RV park in desert terrain. There are two areas across the road from each other. The west side has full hookups, while the east has water and electric only, but the east side also features horse corrals and plenty of room for horse trailers. There is also almost unlimited space for tenters, who are charged $4 per person. The park office is at the Stillwell Store, where you can get groceries, limited camping supplies, and gasoline. There is also a small museum (donations accepted), with exhibits from the Stillwell family's pioneer days.

About 3 miles from the West Entrance to the park is **Terlingua Oasis RV Park,** part of the Big Bend Motor Inn complex at the junction of Tex. 118 and FM 170 (P.O. Box 336, Terlingua, TX 79852; ☎ **800/848-BEND** or 915/371-2218). This park offers pull-through and back-in sites, grassy tent areas, gas and diesel fuel, a restaurant (see "Dining," below), a convenience store, and a gift shop.

Campground	Elev.	Total Sites	RV Hookups	Dump Station	Toilets	Drinking Water
Inside the Park						
Chisos Basin	5,401	63	No	Yes	Yes	Yes
Cottonwood	2,169	31	No	No	Yes	Yes
Rio Grande Village	1,850	100	No	Yes	Yes	Yes
Rio Grande Village Trailer Park	1,850	25	25	No	Yes	Yes
Near the Park						
Terlingua Oasis	2,480	175	125	No	Yes	Yes
Stillwell Store and RV Park	2,600	80+	80	Yes	Yes	Yes

Accommodations

INSIDE THE PARK

Chisos Mountains Lodge

Chisos Basin, Big Bend National Park, TX 79834-9999. ☎ **915/477-2291.** Fax 915/477-2352. 72 units. $70–$80 double. AE, DC, DISC, MC, V. Pets accepted.

The lodge offers a variety of accommodations from simple motel rooms to historic stone cottages. Motel rooms are small and simply decorated but well maintained. They have two double beds, air-conditioning, tub/shower combo, and terrific views of the Chisos Mountains, but no telephones or TVs. The Casa Grande Motor Lodge, part of the Chisos Mountains Lodge, offers somewhat larger motel rooms, attractively furnished, with a tiled bathroom, tub/shower combo, and most have two beds. Each room has a private balcony and air-conditioning.

Built by the Civilian Conservation Corps in the 1930s, the six delightful stone cottages are very popular, with stone floors, front patio, wooden furniture, three double beds, and shower only. Book as far in advance as possible.

The lodge units are the least expensive accommodations and are a bit more rustic. They have one double and one single bed, a tiled bath, tub/shower combo, wood furnishings, painted brick walls with Western and/or Southwestern art, and good views.

NEAR THE PARK

Big Bend Motor Inn

Junction of Tex. 118 and FM 170 (P.O. Box 336), Terlingua, TX 79852. ☎ **800/848-BEND** or 915/371-2218. Fax 915/371-2555. 86 units. A/C TV TEL. $65–$72 double; $105–$125 duplex. AE, DC, DISC, MC, V.

About 3 miles from the west entrance to the park, this motel offers simple but comfortable rooms, most with one king bed or two queen-size beds. Some have kitchenettes, and two units each have a bedroom, a living room, and a kitchen. There are also a few smaller rooms with one queen bed.

Chisos Mining Co. Motel

On FM 170 about 0.75 mi. west of Tex. 118 (P.O. Box 228), Terlingua, TX 79852. ☎ **915/371-2254.** 28 units including 8 cabins. A/C. $35–$51 double. MC, V.

This is an attractive, homey, well-maintained motel. The motel units have tub/shower combos, and some have TVs.

Showers	Fire Pits/ Grills	Laundry	Public Phone	Reserve	Fees	Open
No	Yes	No	Yes	No	$7	Year-round
No	Yes	No	No	No	$7	Year-round
No	Yes	No	No	No	$7	Year-round
Yes	No	Yes	Yes	No	$14.50	Year-round
Yes	Yes	Yes	Yes	No	$9–$18	Year-round
Yes	Yes	Yes	Yes	Yes	$13–$14	Year-round

Cabins, also with shower/tub combos, have fully equipped kitchens but no TVs. There's a curio shop on the premises, and next door the Hungry Javelina offers speedy take-out for breakfast and lunch.

Mission Lodge

Junction of Tex. 118 and FM 170 (P.O. Box 336), Terlingua, TX 79852. ☎ **800/848-BEND** or 915/371-2218. Fax 915/371-2555. 36 units. A/C TV TEL. $55–$60 double. AE, DC, DISC, MC, V.

Located across the street from the Big Bend Motor Inn, and owned by the same people, the Mission Lodge is smaller, simpler, and less expensive, but still clean and well maintained. Rooms have one queen-size bed and a tub/shower combo. Phones are for outgoing calls only.

Dining

INSIDE THE PARK

Chisos Mountains Lodge Restaurant

Chisos Basin, Big Bend National Park. ☎ **915/477-2291.** Main courses $6.25–$16. AE, DC, DISC, MC, V. Daily 7am–8pm. AMERICAN.

The dining room is simply but attractively decorated, with good views from the large windows. The menu changes but generally includes steak, pork chops, roast turkey, baked trout, and sandwiches, plus specials such as chicken fajitas, lasagna, and a vegetarian dish. Hikers and others on the move can order a "traveler's lunch" to be picked up the next morning.

NEAR THE PARK

Big Bend Motor Inn Restaurant & Convenience Store

Junction of Tex. 118 and FM 170, Terlingua. ☎ **915/371-2483.** Main courses $4–$12. AE, DC, DISC, MC, V. Daily 6am–10pm. MEXICAN/ AMERICAN.

This cafe-style restaurant offers basic Mexican and American fare such as sandwiches and burgers, burritos and tacos, and one of the best breakfasts in the area—try the breakfast burrito or biscuits and gravy. You can also get full dinners such as chicken fried steak as well as Mexican combination plates.

Picnic & Camping Supplies

Inside the park there are limited groceries and camping supplies available at Chisos Basin, Rio Grande Village, Castolon, and Panther Junction; and there is a gift shop in the lodge at the Basin. Gasoline is available at Rio Grande Village and Panther Junction only, so check your gas gauge before heading out, as everything in this park is pretty far from everything else. Minor car repairs are available at Panther Junction.

Outside the North Entrance to the park, southeast about 7 miles on FM 2627, is **Stillwell Store and RV Park** (☎ 915/376-2244), where you'll find groceries, limited camping supplies, and gasoline. Just outside the west entrance to the park, in Study Butte/Terlingua, you'll find several gas stations, a convenience store, and liquor store. Also in the Study Butte/Terlingua area is **Desert Sports** (see above), with rental equipment, bike and boat parts and supplies, maps, and guidebooks.

Nearby Attractions

A QUICK TRIP TO MEXICO

You can turn your national park visit into an international excursion by visiting Santa Elena or Boquillas, two dusty little border towns just across the Rio Grande from the park. Many park visitors make the quick trip into Mexico for lunch and a walk around; for more information, pick up the Park Service pamphlet regarding visiting the two towns. The restaurants serve good Mexican dishes such as enchiladas and tacos, in the $3 to $5 range. U.S. dollars are welcome. The menus are in English, although few people in the villages speak English.

To reach either village you'll pay about $2 (round-trip) for a short trip across the river in the rowboat operating as a ferry. Though the trip is legal, these are not official ports of entry and you will usually see no border guards or customs officials. Those uncomfortable leaving the United States in such an informal manner may want to discuss the trip with Big Bend National Park rangers before going.

Boquillas is home to about 25 families. It has one restaurant (Falcon's), a bar, and several stores. The town has no electricity, telephone service, or medical facilities. The river crossing is located just downstream of Rio Grande Village. Once you cross the river you need to either walk, or rent a burro, or use the "truck taxi": a pickup truck that usually takes visitors into the village for a small fee. The village of **Santa Elena** is about the same size as Boquillas, but has electricity. There are three restaurants—Enadina's, Restaurante El Cañon, and Maria Elena's—plus a small museum containing fossils and other items, a small grocery store, and a curio shop. The river crossing is southwest of Cottonwood Campground.

A NEARBY STATE PARK

Perhaps even more remote and rugged than Big Bend National Park is **Big Bend Ranch State Park,** P.O. Box 2319, Presidio, TX 79845 (☎ 915/229-3416), which covers some 277,000 acres of Chihuahuan Desert wilderness along the Rio Grande west of the national park. Purchased by the state of Texas from private owners in 1988, this mostly undeveloped park contains two mountain ranges, extinct volcanoes, scenic canyons, and a wide variety of plants and animals. There is also a small herd of Texas longhorn cattle, a reminder of the property's ranching days. Several outfitters offer river trips as well as mountain-biking and hiking excursions in the state park. See "Other Sports & Activities," above.

A 35-mile well-maintained gravel road (FM 170) provides a wonderful scenic drive along the Rio Grande, and also offers access to several put-in and take-out points for rafts and canoes. The park has several miles of designated four-wheel-drive roads, and about 30 miles of hiking and backpacking trails, with trailheads along FM 170. There are also about 14 miles of unimproved roads open to four-wheel-drive vehicles, mountain bikes, and hikers. The park has a number of primitive camping areas. At the ranch headquarters there is a small interpretive center with displays on the region's ranching heritage, a gift shop and bookstore, and showers.

Those planning trips into the park can get permits and information at Barton Warnock Environmental Education Center (see below); **Fort Leaton State Historical Park,** 4 miles east of Presidio on FM 170 (☎ **915/229-3613**); or the **ranch administrative offices,** just west of Fort Leaton State Historical Park. Entrance fees are $3 for adults, $2 for senior citizens, and free for children under 13. There is also a $3 per person fee for some activities, such as camping, boat launching, and fishing.

While you're in the neighborhood, consider an hour or two at **Barton Warnock Environmental Education Center,** 1 mile east of Lajitas on FM 170 (☎ **915/424-3327**), with exhibits on the geology, archaeology, human history, and wildlife of the Big Bend area. There are also 2.5 acres of desert gardens with a self-guided walk among the various plants of the Chihuahuan Desert, and a gift shop and bookstore. Gates are open daily year-round from 8am to 4:30pm; admission costs $3 for adults, $1.50 for children 6 to 12 years old, and $2 for senior citizens.

5

BLACK CANYON OF THE GUNNISON NATIONAL PARK

By Don and Barbara Laine

EARLY AMERICAN INDIANS AND LATER UTES AND ANGLOS avoided the Black Canyon of the Gunnison, believing that no human could survive a trip to its depths. Now, the deepest and most spectacular 14 miles of this 53-mile canyon comprise America's newest national park.

The Black Canyon, which had been a national monument since 1933, became a national park on October 21, 1999. In a statement issued after the bill signing ceremony, Pres. Bill Clinton called it a "true natural treasure," adding, "Its nearly vertical walls, rising a half mile high, harbor one of the most spectacular stretches of wild river in America."

The Black Canyon ranges in depth from 1,730 to 2,700 feet. Its width at its narrowest point (cleverly called "The Narrows") is 1,100 feet at the rim and only 40 feet at the river. This deep slash in the earth was created by 2 million years of erosion, a process that's still going on—albeit slowed by the damming of the Gunnison River above the park.

At 30,300 acres, the Black Canyon is the third smallest of America's 55 national parks, larger only than Hot Springs and Wind Cave.

Most visitors view the canyon from the South Rim Road, site of the Visitor Center, or the lesser-used North Rim Road.

Short paths branching off both roads lead to splendid viewpoints with signs explaining the canyon's unique geology.

The park also has hiking trails along both rims, backcountry hiking routes down into the canyon, and offers excellent trout fishing for ambitious anglers willing to make the trek to the canyon floor. It also provides an abundance of thrills for the experienced rock climbers who challenge its sheer canyon walls. In winter, much of the park is closed to motor vehicles, but a delight for cross-country skiers and snowshoers.

The Black Canyon shares its eastern boundary with Curecanti National recreation Area, which offers boating and fishing on three reservoirs, as well as hiking and camping.

Avoiding the Crowds. Although overcrowding has not been much of a problem in the past, with an average of 230,000 visitors per year, visitation is expected to increase now that the Black Canyon has gained national park status. Summer will remain the busiest time,

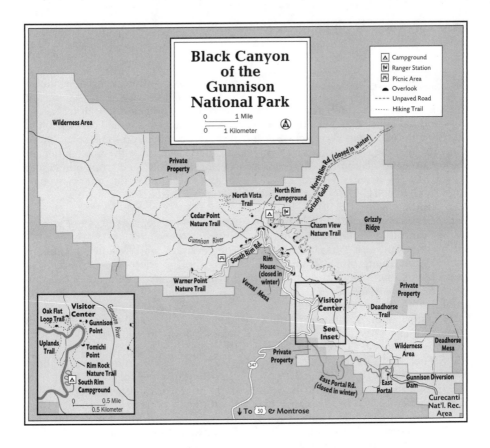

Black Canyon
of the
Gunnison
National Park

0   1 Mile

0   1 Kilometer

△ Campground
🏠 Ranger Station
🏕 Picnic Area
⏺ Overlook
---- Unpaved Road
····· Hiking Trail

Wilderness Area

Private
Property

North Rim Rd. (closed in winter)

North Vista
Trail

North Rim
Campground

Grizzly Gulch

Cedar Point
Nature Trail

Chasm View
Nature Trail

Grizzly
Ridge

Gunnison River

South Rim Rd.

Rim
House
(closed in
winter)

Warner Point
Nature Trail

Vernal Mesa

Visitor
Center

Deadhorse
Trail

Private
Property

See
Inset

Private
Property

Wilderness
Area

Deadhorse
Mesa

East Portal Rd.
(closed in winter)

East
Portal

Gunnison Diversion
Dam

Curecanti
Nat'l. Rec.
Area

347

↓ To 50 & Montrose

Oak Flat
Loop Trail

Visitor
Center

Gunnison River

Gunnison
Point

Uplands
Trail

Tomichi
Point

Rim Rock
Nature Trail

South Rim
Campground

0   0.5 Mile

0.5 Kilometer

with more than half the park visitors arriving between Memorial Day and Labor Day. December through February will be the quietest. Those seeking solitude should visit before Memorial Day and after Labor Day. Although winter can be beautiful, park access is limited.

Just the Facts

GETTING THERE & GATEWAYS

The park is located on Colo. 347, 6 miles north of U.S. 50. To reach the south rim, travel east 8 miles from Montrose on U.S. 50 to the well-marked turnoff. To reach the north rim from Montrose, drive north 21 miles on U.S. 50 to Delta, east 31 miles on Colo. 92 to Crawford, then south on an 11-mile access road.

The Nearest Airports. The **Montrose Regional Airport,** 2100 Airport Rd. (☎ 970/249-3203), off U.S. 50, 2 miles

northwest of Montrose, is served by **America West** and **United Express,** with rental cars from **Budget, Dollar, Enterprise, Hertz, National,** and **Thrifty.**

A bigger airport is **Walker Field** in Grand Junction (☎ 970/244-9100; www. walkerfield.com), about 75 miles northwest of the park. Located about a mile north of I-70 Exit 31 (Horizon Drive), on the north side of Grand Junction, Walker Field has commercial flights connecting Grand Junction with most major cities. Airlines operating at Walker Field include **America West Express,** with daily service to Phoenix; **Delta/Skywest,** with daily service to Salt Lake City; and **United Express,** with daily service to Denver. Rental cars are available from **Avis, Budget, Enterprise, Hertz, National,** and **Thrifty.**

Toll-free reservation numbers for airlines and car rental companies are listed in the appendix.

INFORMATION

For information on both the national park and the adjacent Curecanti National Recreation Area, contact **Black Canyon of the Gunnison National Park/Curecanti National Recreation Area,** 102 Elk Creek, Gunnison, CO 81230 (☎ **970/641-2337**) or the **South Rim Visitor Center** (☎ **970/249-1914,** ext. 23; www.nps.gov/blca). A bookstore at the South Rim Visitor Center, operated by the Southwest Parks and Monuments Association, offers a variety of publications, including the very useful *South Rim Driving Tour Guide,* which was published by the association.

For information on other area attractions, lodging, and dining, contact the **Montrose Visitors & Convention Bureau,** 433 S. First St. (P.O. Box 335), Montrose, CO 81402 (☎ **800/873-0244** or 970/240-1413; www.visitmontrose.net). Information on federal lands in the area is also available at the **Public Lands Center,** 2505 S. Townsend Ave., Montrose, CO 81401 (☎ **970/240-5300**), which is open year-round Monday through Friday.

VISITOR CENTER

The **South Rim Visitor Center** is open year-round, except winter federal holidays; the **North Rim Ranger Station** is open intermittently in summer but closed at other times.

FEES & PERMITS

Admission for up to 7 days costs $7 per vehicle or $4 per person on foot or bike. Camping costs $8 per night. Required backcountry permits are free.

SPECIAL REGULATIONS & WARNINGS

Visitors are warned to not throw anything from the rim into the canyon, since even a single small stone thrown or kicked from the rim could be fatal to people below; and to supervise children very carefully because many sections of the rim have no guard rails or fences.

Unlike at most national parks, leashed pets are permitted on some of the shorter rim trails (check with rangers), but are specifically prohibited from others and are not permitted in the inner canyon or wilderness areas.

SEASONS & CLIMATE

Temperatures and weather conditions often vary greatly between the canyon rim and the canyon floor, and it gets progressively hotter as you descend into the canyon. Average summer temperatures range from highs of 60° to 100°F, with summer lows dropping to 30° to 50°F. During winter, highs range from 20° to 40°F, with lows from 20° to 10°F. Brief afternoon thunderstorms are fairly common in the summer. The South Rim Road usually remains open to the Visitor Center through the winter, but the North Rim Road is often closed by snow between December and March.

If You Only Have 1 Day

It's fairly easy to see a great deal here in a short amount of time, especially if you stick to the South Rim. First, stop at the Visitor Center to see the exhibits and get an understanding of how this phenomenal canyon was created. Then, drive the 7-mile (one-way) South Rim Drive, stopping at the overlooks. Finally, take off on one of the rim hiking trails, such as the easy Cedar Point Nature Trail or the somewhat more challenging Warner Point Nature Trail (see "Day Hikes," below. If you'll be camping in the park or staying nearby, you might plan to attend the evening ranger program.

Exploring the Park by Car

The park's 7-mile (one-way) **South Rim Drive** provides an excellent and fairly easy way to see much of the park. There are about a dozen overlooks along the drive, and in most cases you'll be walking from 140 to about 700 feet to reach the viewpoints from your vehicle.

Among the not-to-be-missed overlooks are **Gunnison Point,** behind the Visitor Center, which offers stunning views of the seemingly endless walls of dark rock, capped by a pinkish rock layer; and the **Pulpit Rock Overlook,** which provides a splendid view of the rock walls and about 1.5 miles of the Gunnison River, some 1,770 feet down. Further along the drive is **Chasm View,** where you can see the incredible power of water, which here cut through more than 1,800 feet of solid rock. Near the end of the drive, be sure to stop at **Sunset View,** where there's a picnic area and a short (140 ft.) walk to a view point, which offers distant views beyond the canyon as well as of the river, now 2,430 feet below your feet. And, if your timing is right, you might be treated to a classic Western sunset, in all its red and orange glory.

Organized Tours & Ranger Programs

Ranger-conducted **nature walks, geology talks, and evening campfire programs** are presented daily from Memorial Day through late September on the South Rim (a schedule is posted at the Visitor Center).

During the winter, guided **snowshoe walks** and **moonlight cross-country ski tours** are offered on the South Rim when snow conditions are right (stop at the Visitor Center or call ahead for information and reservations).

Day Hikes

Trails on the monument's rims range from short, easy walks to moderate-to-strenuous hikes of several miles; and hiking below the rim is mostly difficult and not recommended for those with a fear of heights. Permits are not needed for

hiking rim trails, but are required for all treks below the rim.

SOUTH RIM TRAILS

Cedar Point Nature Trail

0.7 mi. RT. Easy. Access: Cedar Point Trailhead, along South Rim Rd.

With signs along the way describing the plants you'll see, this sunny trail not only offers a painless botany lesson, but at the end provides breathtaking views of the Gunnison River, 2,000 feet down, as well as the Painted Wall, considered the tallest cliff in Colorado at 2,250 feet.

Oak Flat Loop Trail

2 mi. RT. Moderate to strenuous. Access: Near the Visitor Center.

Dropping slightly below the rim, this trail offers excellent views into the canyon, while also taking you through a grove of aspen, past Gambel oak, and finally through a forest of aspen, Gambel oak, and Douglas fir. Be aware that the trail is narrow in spots, and a bit close to steep drop-offs.

Rim Rock Nature Trail

1 mi. RT. Moderate. Access: Near the entrance to the campground's Loop C.

Following the rim along a relatively flat path, this trail leads to an overlook, providing good views of the Gunnison River and the canyon's sheer rock walls. A pamphlet available at the trailhead describes plant life and other points of interest.

Warner Point Nature Trail

1.5 mi. RT. Moderate. Access: High Point Overlook at the end of South Rim Rd.

Offering a multitude of things to see, from this trail you can view mountain mahogany, piñon pine, Utah juniper, and other area flora; distant mountains and valleys; as well as the Black Canyon and its creator, the Gunnison River. A trail guide is available at the trailhead.

NORTH RIM TRAILS

Chasm View Nature Trail

0.3 mi. RT. Moderate. Access: End of the North Rim campground loop.

Staring in a piñon-juniper forest, this trail heads to the rim for good views of the canyon and the river, and where you'll also have a good chance of seeing swallows, swifts, and raptors.

Deadhorse Trail

5 mi. RT. Easy to moderate. Access: Kneeling Camel Overlook.

Actually an old service road, this trail offers a good chance of seeing various birds, plus views of Deadhorse Gulch and the East Portal area at the southeast end of the park.

North Vista Trail

7 mi. RT. Moderate to strenuous. Access: North Rim Ranger Station.

Offering some of the best scenic views in the Black Canyon, this trail also provides hikers with a good chance of seeing red-tailed hawks, white-throated swifts, Clark's nutcrackers, and ravens. You might also be lucky enough to see the rare peregrine falcon. The trail goes through a piñon-juniper forest along the canyon's rim about 1½ miles to Exclamation Point, which offers one of the best views into the canyon. Up to this point the trail is rated moderate, but it continues another 2 miles (rated strenuous) to Green Mountain, where you'll find broad, panoramic vistas.

Exploring the Backcountry

Experienced hikers in excellent physical condition may want to hike down into the canyon. Although there are no maintained or marked trails, there are several routes that rangers can help you find. Free permits are required. There are also a limited number of campsites available for backpackers.

The most popular inner canyon hike is the strenuous **Gunnison Route,** which branches off the South Rim's Oak Flat Trail (see above) and heads down to the river. Eighty feet of chain help keep you from falling on a stretch about a third of the way down. This hike has a vertical drop of 1,800 feet and takes 4 to 5 hours.

Other Summer Sports & Activities

Biking. Although bikes are not permitted on any park trails, this is still a popular destination for bikers, who travel the **South Rim Road** to the various overlooks and trailheads, some of which have bicycle racks.

Climbing. The sheer vertical walls and scenic beauty of the Black Canyon make it an ideal and popular destination for rock climbers, but, and we cannot emphasize this too strongly, this is no place for on-the-job training. These cliffs require a great deal of experience and the best equipment. Free permits are required, and prospective climbers should discuss their plans first with park rangers.

Fishing. Dedicated anglers can make their way to the Gunnison River at the bottom of the canyon in a quest for brown and rainbow trout. The Gunnison within the park has been designated as Gold Medal Waters. Only artificial lures are permitted, and other special rules apply (check with park rangers). A Colorado fishing license is required.

Water Sports. Mostly, don't do it! The Gunnison River through the park is *extremely dangerous,* for both swimmers and rafters (it's considered unraftable). There are sections of river west of the park that are more suitable; information is available from the Public Lands Center office in Montrose (see "Information," above). The only exception is for experienced kayakers, who find the river an exhilarating challenge. Free permits are required.

Wildlife Viewing. The monument is home to a variety of wildlife, and you're likely to see chipmunks, ground squirrels, badgers, marmots, and mule deer. Although not frequently seen, there are also black bear, cougars, and bobcats; and you'll probably hear the lonesome high-pitched call of coyotes at night. The peregrine falcon can sometimes be spotted along the cliffs, and you may also see red-tailed hawks, turkey vultures, golden eagles, and white-throated swifts.

Winter Sports

When the South Rim Road is closed by winter snows, the Park Service plows only to the South Rim Visitor Center, leaving the rest of the park the domain of cross-country skiers and snowshoers.

Camping

There are campgrounds on both rims, usually open from May through October, with a limited water supply hauled in by truck. They have pit toilets, but no showers or RV hookups. Sites are available on a first-come, first-served basis, and cost is $8 per site. The **South Rim Campground,** which rarely fills, has 102 sites, but the **North Rim Campground,** with only 13 sites, does occasionally fill up.

Campgrounds with hot showers and RV hookups are available in Montrose. **The Hangin' Tree R.V. Park,** 17250 U.S. 550 S., Montrose (☎ **970/249-9966**), is open year-round. It has tent sites and large pull-through RV sites, a playground, horseshoe pits, a self-service laundry, convenience store, and 24-hour

Ed Nelson, the first man to boat through the Black Canyon of the Gunnison, accomplished what practically everyone considered impossible in September 1949 in a 5-pound collapsible boat, and using Ping-Pong paddles for oars!

gas station. Its 25 sites run $15 to $22 a night and credit cards are accepted.

Accommodations

NEAR THE PARK

There is no lodging in the park; the nearest facilities are in Montrose. In addition to the properties discussed below, Montrose has a **Comfort Inn,** 2100 E. Main St. (☎ **970/240-8000**), $45 to $75 double; **Days Inn,** 1655 E. Main St. (☎ **970/249-3411**), $40 to $65 double; **Holiday Inn Express Hotel & Suites,** 1391 S. Townsend Ave. (☎ **970/240-1800**), with rates for two from $79 to $149; and **Super 8,** 1705 E. Main St. (☎ **970/249-9294**), with double rates from $42 to $61. National toll-free reservation numbers are listed in the appendix. Rates here are usually highest in July and August, and lowest from November through April.

Best Western Red Arrow Motor Inn

1702 E. Main St. (P.O. Box 236), Montrose, CO 81402. ☎ **800/468-9323** or 970/249-9641. Fax 970/249-8380. E-mail: redarrow@gwe.net. 60 units. A/C TV TEL. $76–$115 double. Rates include continental breakfast. AE, CB, DC, DISC, MC, V.

The Red Arrow is a large two-story building near the east end of town. Spacious rooms, most with firm queen beds, have coffeemakers, bathrobes, and hair dryers. A handful of "spa rooms" have large whirlpool tubs. Amenities include a solarium with a hot tub and fitness center, a heated outdoor pool, a playground and picnic area, and guest laundry.

Western Motel

1200 E. Main St. (at Stough Ave.), Montrose, CO 81401. ☎ **800/445-7301** or 970/249-3481. Fax 970/249-3471. 28 units. A/C TV TEL. Memorial Day to Labor Day, $48–$58 double; Labor Day to mid-Nov, $40–$46 double; mid-Nov to Memorial Day, $36–$45 double. Family units $52–$90. AE, DC, DISC, MC, V.

A one-story white stucco building with a two-story annex, this attractive motel, renovated in late 1999, offers clean, comfortable rooms, a tad larger than average, with some homey touches, bed sizes from full to king, and good-size desks. A few family rooms are available, and most units have door-front parking. VCRs are available to rent, and there's free coffee in the lobby. Facilities include a heated outdoor swimming pool, plus a hot tub and sauna.

Dining

NEAR THE PARK

The only food available in the park is at **Rim House,** at Pulpit Rock on the South Rim, a snack bar and gift shop that's open daily from mid-May to late September. You'll find several good restaurants in Montrose, including the following:

Glenn Eyrie Restaurant

2351 S. Townsend Ave. ☎ **970/249-9263.** Reservations recommended. Main courses $9.75–$24. AE, CB, DC, DISC, MC, V. Tues–Sat 5–9pm. CONTINENTAL/AMERICAN.

This small, cozy restaurant is lodged in a colonial farmhouse on the south end of town. In summer, guests can dine inside or outdoors in the garden; in winter, folks seek tables near the cozy central fireplace. Just about everything is made in-house, including rolls, jams, and sauces; and many items are grown on the grounds—fruits, herbs, and greens. Owner-chef Steve Schwathe changes the menu frequently to reflect the seasons and availability of fresh ingredients, but choices might include whole rack of lamb, which is grilled, then slow-baked, and served with a sauce of tomato, rosemary, and garlic; or steak Diane, a butterflied beef tenderloin steak that is flamed table-side in a mustard, applejack brandy, and cream sauce, with mushrooms and artichoke hearts. There are also fresh seafood selections and vegetarian dishes; and there's a full bar.

The Whole Enchilada

44 S. Grand Ave., near W. Main St. ☎ **970/249-1881.** Main courses $3.75–$6.50 at lunch, $4.75–$9.25 at dinner. AE, DISC, MC, V. Mon–Thurs 11am–9pm, Fri–Sat 11am–10pm. MEXICAN.

Come to this local favorite for well-prepared Mexican fare, such as burritos, tostadas, fajitas, and tacos. Those seeking a bit more adventure might opt for enchiladas Acapulco (corn tortillas stuffed with chicken, black olives, almonds, and cheese); or from the "Not for Gringos" section of the menu, the El Paso chimichanga (a fried flour tortilla filled with beef and jalapeños, and smothered in green chile sauce). A variety of burgers are also available. The restaurant is locally famous for its margaritas, and a delightful outdoor patio is open in summer.

Picnic & Camping Supplies

A good bet for those seeking groceries, deli sandwiches, a bakery, or a salad bar is one of the two **City Market** grocery stores in Montrose. There's one at 128 S. Townsend Ave. and another at 16400 S. Townsend Ave. For information call ☎ 970/249-3405.

THE BLACK HILLS:
Mount Rushmore National Memorial, Wind Cave National Park, Jewel Cave National Monument & Custer State Park

by Jack Olson

CHISELED IN GRANITE HIGH ON A PINE-CLAD CLIFF IN SOUTH DAKOTA'S fabled Black Hills are the portraits of four of America's greatest leaders. Since 1941, George Washington, Thomas Jefferson, Abraham Lincoln, and Theodore Roosevelt have gazed quietly across the Great Plains and a land they did so much to mold, drawing 2.7 million visitors a year.

Most people spend but a short hour or two gazing at the memorial, maybe eating a sandwich, then going on their way to Yellowstone or their next destination. Those with the time and inclination will find much to occupy their time. Within an hour's drive of Mount Rushmore, you will find not only Wind Cave National Park and Jewel Cave National Monument, but also Custer State Park, one of the best and largest state parks in the country, as well as the Crazy Horse Memorial, a work in progress that will be far larger than Mount Rushmore. And if you are willing to get off the beaten path—something that relatively few visitors do—you will find a backcountry dotted with trails through the region's pine forests, a virtually untrammeled wilderness where you can escape the crowds for days, or perhaps just an hour.

Geologists predict the presidents will continue their earthly vigil at **Mount Rushmore National Memorial** for many centuries, eroding less than 1 inch every 5,000 years. But while major changes aren't predicted for the giant faces anytime soon, visitors to the base of the mountain will discover greatly improved facilities.

Thanks to the Mount Rushmore Preservation Fund—one of the most successful public-private fundraising partnerships for the National Park Service to date—$56 million in improvements await travelers at the base of the sculpture, including new theaters, viewing terraces, interpretive exhibits, walking trails, and concession facilities.

As the "crown jewel" of South Dakota's state park system, **Custer State Park** offers 73,000 acres of prime Black Hills real estate, the largest and most diverse population of wildlife, the best accommodations and facilities, and the most

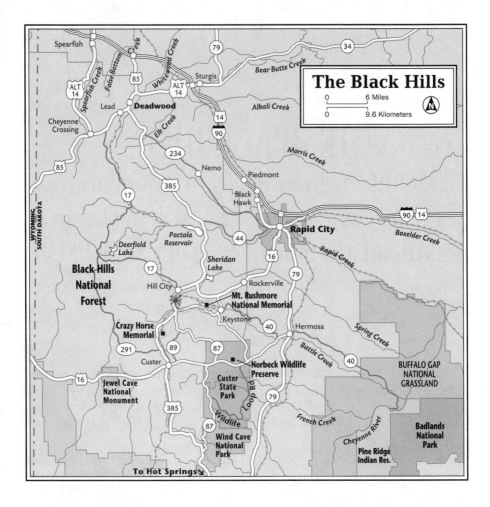

The Black Hills

| 0 | 6 Miles |
| 0 | 9.6 Kilometers |

memorable natural resources of any park in the state.

Located east of the town of Custer, the park is home to four resorts, four fishing lakes, wildlife loops, campgrounds, scenic drives, and granite spires so impressive that they make you want to get out of the car and walk the forest floor. Alternating between rolling meadows and foothills, pine forests, and the giant fingerlike granite spires of the Needles, Custer State Park is a must on any Black Hills itinerary.

Even after more than 100 years, there is still something to discover in the darkened depths of **Wind Cave National Park.** With 83 miles of mapped passageway, Wind Cave is one of the longest caves in the world. And, with each succeeding expedition, the interconnecting network of known passages continues to grow, sometimes by a few paces, other times by several hundred feet. Barometric wind studies conducted by the U.S. Geological Survey estimate that approximately 5% of the total cave has been discovered.

But there's a great deal more to Wind Cave than just its underground geological wonders. Aboveground, 28,295 acres of rolling prairie and ponderosa pine forests are littered with wildflowers and teeming with wildlife. Bison and antelope graze on the park's lush grasslands while prairie dogs watch from the relative safety of their "towns." In the fall, elk can be herd "bugling" throughout the confines of the park, and overhead, watch for hawks, eagles, and vultures that float on the thermal currents that rise from the rocky ridges of the Black Hills.

In the limestone labyrinth that rests below the Black Hills, **Jewel Cave National Monument** offers a mysterious maze-like network of caverns and passageways, filled with rare specimens and beautiful jewel-like crystals, that have yet to be fully explored.

Just the Facts

GETTING THERE & GATEWAYS

Rapid City is the most popular gateway to the Black Hills and its bountiful selection of national and state parks, monuments, and memorials.

The most direct route to the Black Hills by car is I-90. To reach **Mount Rushmore,** take Exit 57 to U.S. 16 (Mount Rushmore Road) and continue approximately 23 miles southwest of Rapid City to the memorial entrance.

Custer State Park, between Mount Rushmore and Wind Cave National Park, is accessible via S. Dak. 79 and S. Dak. 36 from the east, U.S. 16A from the north and west, and S. Dak. 87 from the north and south.

Wind Cave National Park is best accessed via U.S. 385 north of Hot Springs, South Dakota, or S. Dak. 87 from Custer State Park, which shares its southern boundary with Wind Cave's northern perimeter. It's about an hour's drive south from Mount Rushmore.

The Crazy Horse Memorial is 5 miles north of Custer on U.S. 16/385.

Jewel Cave National Monument is just off U.S. 16, 13 miles west of Custer. It's almost equidistant from Mount Rushmore or Wind Cave.

The Nearest Airport. Rapid City Regional Airport (☎ 605/393-9924), located 10 miles southeast of Rapid City on U.S. 44, provides direct access to the Black Hills and Mount Rushmore. **Northwest Airlines, Delta/Skywest,** and **United Express** serve the airport with daily flights to Minneapolis, Salt Lake City,

and Denver. Car-rental agencies at the airport include **Avis, Budget, Hertz, National, Sears,** and **Thrifty.** You'll find a list of toll-free numbers in the appendix.

INFORMATION

For information on Mount Rushmore, contact the **Superintendent, Mount Rushmore National Memorial,** P.O. Box 268, Keystone, SD 57751-0268 (☎ 605/574-2523; www.nps.gov/moru). For information about **Custer State Park,** contact the park at HC83, Box 70, Custer, SD 57730-9705 (☎ 605/255-4515; www.state.sd.us/state/executive/tourism/sdparks/custer/custer. htm.) or the **Division of Parks and Recreation,** Department of Game, Fish and Parks, 523 E. Capitol Ave., Pierre, SD 57501-3182 (☎ 605/773-3391). To get information about Wind Cave, contact the **Superintendent, Wind Cave National Park,** RR1, P.O. Box 190-WCNP, Hot Springs, SD 57747-9430 (☎ 605/745-4600; www.nps.gov/wica). For details on Jewel Cave, contact the **Superintendent, Jewel Cave National Monument,** RR1, Box 60 AA, Custer, SD 57730 (☎ 605/673-2288; www.nps.gov/jeca). To get information about Crazy Horse, contact the **Crazy Horse Memorial,** Avenue of the Chiefs, Crazy Horse, SD 57730-9506 (☎ 605/673-4681; www.crazyhorse.org).

For information about the entire area, contact **South Dakota Tourism,** Capitol Lake Plaza, 711 E. Wells Ave., Pierre, SD 57501-3369 (☎ 800/SDAKOTA or 605/773-3301; e-mail: SDINFO@ goed.state.sd.us); or the **Black Hills, Badlands & Lake Association,** 1851 Discovery Circle, Rapid City, SD 57701 (☎ 605/355-3600; www. blackhillsattractions. com).

SEASONS & CLIMATE

Summer daytime temperatures in the Black Hills average around 80°F and higher, so comfortable clothing, a hat, and sunscreen are advised.

Temperatures often drop rapidly after sunset, particularly in the mountains. In the fall, sunny skies and crisp temperatures can make for pleasant traveling conditions, though snowstorms may occur as early as September in higher elevations.

Winter temperatures average 40° to 20°F. Beware of icy road conditions and limited services during winter. Even in spring, weather can often be cold and wet.

Visiting Mount Rushmore National Memorial

Widely regarded as one of the man-made wonders of the world, Mount Rushmore is as much a work of art as it is an engineering marvel. Its creator, Gutzon Borglum, wanted to symbolize in stone the very spirit of a nation and, through four of its most revered leaders, its birth, growth, preservation, and development. A half century after its completion, Mount Rushmore remains one of America's most enduring icons.

In 1924, sculptor Gutzon Borglum visited the Black Hills, looking for a place to carve a lasting legacy for himself and the nation. The artist hoped to locate a mountain with a suitable mass of stone, as well as a southeasterly exposure, which would take advantage of the sun's rays for the greatest portion of the day. He decided on a rock outcropping named Mount Rushmore.

Inclement weather and lack of funds frequently stalled progress on the memorial. All told, the monument was completed at a cost of about $1 million during 6½ years of work over a 14-year period.

Plaster Portraits. Having studied under master sculptor Auguste Rodin in Paris, Borglum understood art. When he arrived at Rushmore ready to create his life's work in 1925, Borglum was 58 years old and already had created a full roster of memorials to famous Americans, including Gen. Philip Sheridan, Gen. Robert E. Lee, and Abraham Lincoln. Relying on his independent study of the four presidents, as well as life masks, paintings, photographs, and descriptions of others, Borglum created plaster sketches of the four presidents. These sketches became the models for the memorial, and copies of each president's likeness were always on display on the mountain as a guide for the workmen.

Using a method of measurement called "pointing," Borglum taught his crews to measure the models, multiply by 12, and transfer the calibrations to the mountain carving. Using a simple ratio of 1:12, 1 inch on the model would equal 1 foot on the mountain.

Borglum and his dedicated crew used dynamite to carve more than 90% of the memorial. Powdermen became so skilled in the use of dynamite that they could grade the contours of the cheeks, chin, nose, and eyebrows to within inches of the finished surface. Skilled drillers used bumper bits and pneumatic drills to complete each portrait, leaving the surfaces of the presidents' faces as smooth as a concrete sidewalk. Up close, the pupils of each of the presidents' eyes are actually shallow recessions with projecting shafts of granite. From a distance, this unlikely shape makes the eyes sparkle. Several men were injured while working at Mount Rushmore, but miraculously, no one was killed during its construction.

As work neared completion in March 1941, Borglum died in a Chicago hospital at age 74. His son, Lincoln, carried on the work for another 6 months, but that work was soon interrupted by the winds of war. On October 31, as war clouds rumbled over Europe, the younger Borglum and his crew turned off the drills and removed the last scaffolding from the sculpture, returning the mountain to the eternal silence from which they had awakened it in 1927.

The untiring effort of the Borglums and their determined cadre of influential supporters resulted in a work of art for the ages. Washington, the most prominent figure in the group, symbolizes the birth of a republic founded on the principle of individual liberty; Jefferson, who managed to fund the Louisiana Purchase and balance the federal budget, signifies the growth of the United States; Lincoln, the Great Emancipator, imparts the strength of character responsible for preserving the union in the throes of the bloody Civil War; and Theodore Roosevelt, the "Trust Buster" and friend of the common man, who completed the Panama Canal and asserted America's role in the world.

Avoiding the Crowds. Peak visitation at Mount Rushmore is during June, July, and August. When travel patterns and weather are considered, the best time to visit Mount Rushmore is September and October, with April and May as alternatives. Although spring months can be wet and cold, fall visits can be ideal due to the Hills' dry weather patterns. The varied mix of trees and plant life found in the alpine meadows and creek-carved canyons also makes the Black Hills a popular destination for avid "leaf-peepers."

If possible, view the sculpture at daybreak, when the golden orb of the sun crawls out of the morning mist of the badlands. Few vacationers are awake at sunrise, making it among the best times to enjoy a more contemplative and less crowded experience. And there may be no finer setting for breakfast than the park's Buffalo Dining Room, which affords a commanding view of the presidents.

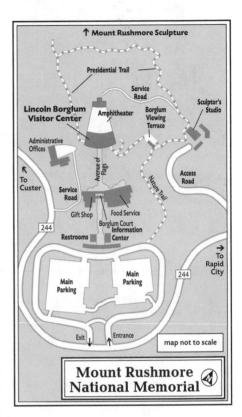

ESSENTIALS

Visitor Center. Mount Rushmore is open 24 hours a day, year-round. The **Information Center,** located just inside the entrance to the memorial, is open daily (except Christmas) from 8am to 5pm in winter, and 8am to 10pm in the summer. The new **Lincoln Borglum Visitor Center and Museum** maintains the same hours. This outstanding visitor center contains 5,200 square feet of exhibits, a bookstore, and two 125-seat theaters. One interactive display features the dynamite blasting used to carve the mountain. This is an educational experience not to be missed, and the visitor center also features some of the best views of the sculptures.

Fees. Mount Rushmore remains one of the few popular parks that's managed to avoid an entrance fee. However, there is an $8 fee for parking, which is funding the parking structure at the memorial. Golden Eagle, Golden Age, and Golden Access passes are not accepted for the parking fee. Limited free parking is available near the sculptor studio as you arrive at Rushmore from Keystone. Expect a short walk if you park here.

Special Regulations & Warnings. Visitor access is prohibited within a restricted area around the Mount Rushmore sculpture. In other areas of the park, rock climbing and hiking are permitted.

Tips from the Park Superintendent

Mount Rushmore has undergone a great many changes recently, according to Superintendent Dan Wenk, who says, "The new Lincoln Borglum Visitor Center provides an interpretive experience unequaled in western national park areas." Wenk says that interactive displays depict sculptor Gutzon Borglum and his crew at work, plus a large mural on the history of the United States that helps visitors understand why these four presidents were selected for the monument.

The Presidential Trail is a favorite of visitors, according to Wenk, who adds, "This trail allows visitors to get close to the carving to better understand the scale of the sculpture." He adds that it also offers extraordinary views. "Our ranger program in the evening, with the lighting of the memorial, is a popular, patriotic experience," Wenk says.

Useful Publications. The National Park Service has a number of informational pamphlets and other materials at the Information Center as you enter the memorial. A variety of books, maps, and videos are sold in the bookstore located in the Lincoln Borglum Visitor Center. All proceeds from the bookstore—operated by the nonprofit Mount Rushmore History Association—are dedicated to the Park Service's interpretive programs at the memorial.

IF YOU HAVE ONLY 1 DAY

Unlike many of the larger national park units in the country, a complete visit to Rushmore may be accomplished in 2 to 3 hours. Even with its new repertoire of interpretive exhibits, trails, and theaters, the park can be fully explored and appreciated in a fraction of the time of many of its Western counterparts.

Particularly in the high-visitation summer months, the park is best placed at the beginning or end of a visitor's daily itinerary. Excellent light at daybreak, coupled with its scenic setting and great breakfasts in the Buffalo Dining Room, makes Mount Rushmore hard to beat for the first stop of the day. The patriotic ranger program and dramatic lighting ceremony, held nightly at 9pm from mid-May through September, also make the memorial memorable at night.

EXPLORING THE PARK BY CAR

While Mount Rushmore is best enjoyed on foot, many visitors overlook an impressive view of the sculpture that is best reached by car. After leaving the park's parking lot, turn right on S. Dak. 244 and proceed west then northwest around the memorial. Less than a mile from the parking lot you'll discover the proud profile of George Washington in the upper-right corner of your windshield. While surveying the scene, keep an eye out for Rocky Mountain goats that frequent the memorial and the Black Elk Wilderness Area to the west.

ORGANIZED TOURS & RANGER PROGRAMS

Mount Rushmore offers a variety of excellent interpretive programs, including:

◆ A 30-minute **Nature Walk** leads to the Sculptor's Studio, with frequent stops to discuss the area's flora, fauna, and geology. The walking tour ends at the historic studio in time for the Studio Talk.

◆ The 15-minute **Studio Talk** (summer only) at the 1939 Sculptor's Studio examines techniques used by the artist to carve the memorial, as well as the original tools and plaster models employed in its construction.

◆ **Amphitheater Programs** are extremely popular and often patriotic. Depending on the timing of your visit, you could be treated to a solemn ceremony, a full-fledged celebration, or a musical presentation.

◆ There is **a regular 30-minute program** at the amphitheater that includes a talk and a movie about the memorial, which coincides with its dramatic lighting ceremony. The program begins at 9pm from mid-May through September and at 8pm in the spring and fall months.

◆ The sculpture is **illuminated** nightly for 1 to 2 hours all year long.

◆ A 13-minute **film** narrated by noted reporter and South Dakotan Tom Brokaw is shown continuously at the Visitor Center and Museum. Painting a broad overview of the memorial's history, construction, and subjects, the movie gives visitors a greater understanding of the colossal carving.

HISTORIC BUILDINGS & OTHER ATTRACTIONS

The 1939 **Sculptor's Studio** played an important role in the final years of the construction of Mount Rushmore. Today, the spacious studio and the artist's models it houses are integral to understanding how Borglum and his drill-dusty crew carved the sculpture from Black Hills granite.

Located on the walkway between the Concession Building and the Lincoln Borglum Visitor Center and Museum, the **Avenue of Flags** features the official flags of all U.S. states, territories, districts, and commonwealths, arranged in alphabetical order. The flags serve as a patriotic, colorful frame to Mount Rushmore.

DAY HIKES

The **Presidential Trail** begins near the main viewing terrace, then proceeds west through the ponderosa pines to the talus slope at the base of the sculpture. The trail is 0.6 mile long and a large portion of it is accessible to travelers with disabilities. The other portion of the trail consists of many steps, and depending on which direction a visitor walks, the trail can be a climb. The boardwalk circles the southeastern slope of the mountain before arriving at the Sculptor's Studio. In addition to decreasing crowding on the memorial's viewing terraces, this new trail takes visitors into the woods and affords new vantage points from which to view the four presidents.

ROCK CLIMBING

Although climbing on the Mount Rushmore sculpture and within the restricted zone adjacent to the sculpture is prohibited, much of the park is open to climbing. The park is known internationally as a world class sports climbing area, with its massive spires and large rock faces nestled amid tall ponderosa pines.

Visiting Custer State Park

Despite its size (it's one of the largest state parks in the Lower 48), Custer State Park can become crowded. Its unique historical, cultural, and natural resources attract throngs of visitors in the summer months, who tend to crowd scenic drives, lakeshores, campgrounds, stores, and resorts.

The best times to visit are from May to mid-June and September to October. Spring offers a reawakening of the grasslands and the birth of cinnamon-colored bison calves, as well as elk, deer,

Crazy Horse Memorial

Known by locals as the "Fifth Face" in the Black Hills, the sculpture of the legendary Lakota leader Crazy Horse began with the dedication of the work on June 3, 1948. A half century later, work continues on what will be the world's largest sculpture.

Begun by the late sculptor Korczak Ziolkowski (pronounced Jewel-*cuff*ski), and carried on by his widow, sons, and daughters, the mountain sculpture memorial is dedicated to all American Indians.

"My fellow chiefs and I would like the white man to know the red man has great heroes, too," Sioux Chief Henry Standing Bear wrote Ziolkowski in 1939, inviting him to create the mountain memorial. Seven years later, the sculptor agreed and began carving the colossal work.

When completed, Crazy Horse will sit astride his mount, pointing over his stallion's head to the sacred Black Hills. So large is the sculpture (563 ft. high) that all four presidents on Mount Rushmore would fit in Crazy Horse's head.

Visitors driving by the site on U.S. 16/385, 5 miles north of the town of Custer, often hear dynamite blasts, a surefire signal that work on the mountain carving is progressing. When night blasts are detonated, they tend to be among the most impressive events in the Black Hills.

In addition to viewing the carving in progress and watching an audiovisual display about the work, visitors may stop at the **Indian Museum of North America** at Crazy Horse, which is home to one of the most extensive collections of American Indian artifacts in the country. The museum's gift shop features authentic Indian crafts.

antelope, and other wildlife. Fall beckons the change of colors in every canyon and ravine, as well as the bugling of bull elk as they search for mates.

ESSENTIALS

Visitor Centers. The **Peter Norbeck Visitor Center,** located between the State Game Lodge and the Coolidge Inn Store on U.S. 16A, offers brochures, interpretive exhibits, and a variety of educational items.

The **Wildlife Station Visitor Center,** located on the southeast part of the Wildlife Loop, has shade, information, and exhibits.

Fees. Contact the park for current **entrance fees.** Modern **campsites** cost $14 per unit per night; semimodern campsites are $11; basic campsites are $6; and firewood may be purchased at park concessions.

Special Regulations & Warnings. The park's biggest attraction may be its 1,500 head of bison. Remember that all animals in the park are wild and can be dangerous. Bison are extremely fast and can be lethal if provoked, so give them plenty of space.

Campers and hikers should never drink water from lakes, streams, or springs.

Useful Publications. The **South Dakota Game, Fish and Parks Department** provides a number of helpful brochures for the park, available at the Peter Norbeck Visitor Center and at park headquarters. The park's newspaper, *Tatanka,* provides information on the park's resorts and activities. The newspaper is available at each park entrance station, the visitor center, and park headquarters.

Of all the state and federal parks in South Dakota, Custer State Park may be the most difficult to see in a day. Three scenic drives, numerous hiking trails and nature walks, historic sites, wildlife loops, resorts, and some of the most spectacular scenery in the West tend to slow you down.

If you only have a day, try the 18-mile **Wildlife Loop** (described below); and then stop at the observation deck of the **Mount Coolidge Fire Tower** and the historic **Gordon Stockade.** If time permits, take a hike, perhaps on the popular trail to the **Cathedral Spires.**

EXPLORING THE PARK BY CAR

For a first-class sightseeing excursion, pick any of the park's three scenic drives: the Needles Highway, the Wildlife Loop Road, or the Iron Mountain Road. When driving through the park, however, it's important to keep an eye on the road and not your watch. Winding roads generally keep travel at 25 miles per hour or less.

Needles Highway. This is a 14-mile mesmerizing journey through pine and spruce forests, meadows surrounded by birch and quaking aspen, and giant granite spires that reach to the sky. Visitors pass the picturesque waters of Sylvan Lake, through tunnels, and near a unique rock formation called the "Needle's Eye."

Wildlife Loop Road. This 18-mile drive takes you through open grasslands and pine-clad hills—an area that is home to most of the park's wildlife. Count pronghorn, bison, white-tailed deer and mule deer, elk, coyote, begging wild burros, prairie dogs, eagles, hawks, and other

birds. The best wildlife viewing time is early morning and evening, when animals are most active. Stop by the Wildlife Station Visitor Center on the southeast part of the loop for information and exhibits.

Iron Mountain Road. Although only a portion of this scenic roadway rests in Custer State Park, it ranks as a must-see on any South Dakota visit. The winding road runs between Mount Rushmore and the junction of U.S. 16A and S. Dak. 36. Along the route are wildfire exhibits, wooden "pig-tail" bridges, pullouts with wonderful views, and tunnels that frame the four presidents at Mount Rushmore.

Be Aware: Tunnels on Iron Mountain Road (U.S. 16A) are 12 feet, 6 inches high and 13 feet, 6 inches wide. Tunnels on the Needles Highway/Sylvan Lake Road (S. Dak. 87) are as low as 10 feet, 8 inches and as narrow as 8 feet, 7 inches.

Custer State Park is home to a wide variety of hiking experiences ranging from short nature walks to backcountry treks. A 22-mile segment of the South Dakota Centennial Trail, the **Harney Peak Summit Trail,** extends through the park. The **Cathedral Spires Trail** is also a popular choice. Be aware that some trails are also open to mountain bikers.

Visiting Wind Cave National Park

For several centuries, American Indians have told stories of holes in the Black Hills through which the wind would blow and howl. But the first recorded discovery of Wind Cave came in 1881 when brothers Jesse and Tom Bingham were lured to the cave by a whistling noise. As the legend goes, the wind was rushing from the cave entrance with such force that it blew Tom's hat right off his head.

Tips from the Park Superintendent

Wind Cave National Park Superintendent Jimmy Taylor loves where he works.

"This is truly an amazing park," says Taylor. "You can see and hear wildlife here. We have 300 to 400 head of elk, 300 bison, 125 antelope, two highways, and two all-weather gravel roads that make this park very accessible and suitable to the family sedan."

Wind Cave is "an intimate park" where road-weary travelers can put the brakes on and enjoy plant and animal life at its best, Taylor says. Visitors often settle back and just watch prairie dogs build their colonylike "towns" or bison graze on the prairie grasses. In fall, Taylor says there's nothing quite like the sound of a lonely bull elk bugling from a rocky ridge in the park.

And beneath this remarkable place, says Taylor, is an underground wilderness whose depths have only been guessed at, and whose complexity we are only beginning to understand.

"Imagine," the superintendent says, "that only a few hundred feet underground there are spaces people have never seen, and perhaps, may never see. Think, that every time someone crawls through a hole or peeks into the next opening, they may literally be the first person in the history of mankind who has ever seen it."

A few days later, when Jesse returned to the cave to show this phenomena to friends, he was surprised to find that the wind had shifted directions and his hat was sucked into the cave. A hundred years later, we know that the direction of the wind is related to the difference in atmospheric pressure between the cave and the surface.

J. D. McDonald was the first person to attempt to establish a tourist attraction at Wind Cave, complete with stagecoach transportation, a hotel, and gift shop. He did this primarily because there were no valuable mineral deposits in the cave to mine. But "ownership" of the cave came into question, and the matter soon entered a courtroom. The controversy caught the attention of the Department of the Interior, which decided in December 1899 that no party had a claim to Wind Cave. In 1901, the department withdrew all the land around the cave from homesteading.

On January 9, 1903, Pres. Theodore Roosevelt signed the bill that established Wind Cave as America's seventh national park, and the first one created to protect the underground resources of a cave. In 1913 and 1914, the American Bison Society assisted in reestablishing a bison herd at Wind Cave, through the donation of 14 head from the New York Zoological Society. Also arriving in the park were 21 elk from Wyoming and 13 pronghorn antelope from Alberta, Canada. Today, Wind Cave is home to 350 bison, as well as large herds of elk and antelope.

Avoiding the Crowds. With more than 28,000 acres, two paved highways, two all-weather gravel roads, eight excellent trails, backcountry camping, and plenty of room to roam, avoiding the crowds in Wind Cave National Park is a cinch.

July and August are the busiest months. Annual visitation averages 800,000, while about 100,000 people participate in a cave tour each year. When planning daily itineraries, include Wind Cave in either the early morning or late afternoon, when visitation is lowest and wildlife is most active. Buy your cave tour tickets early in the day.

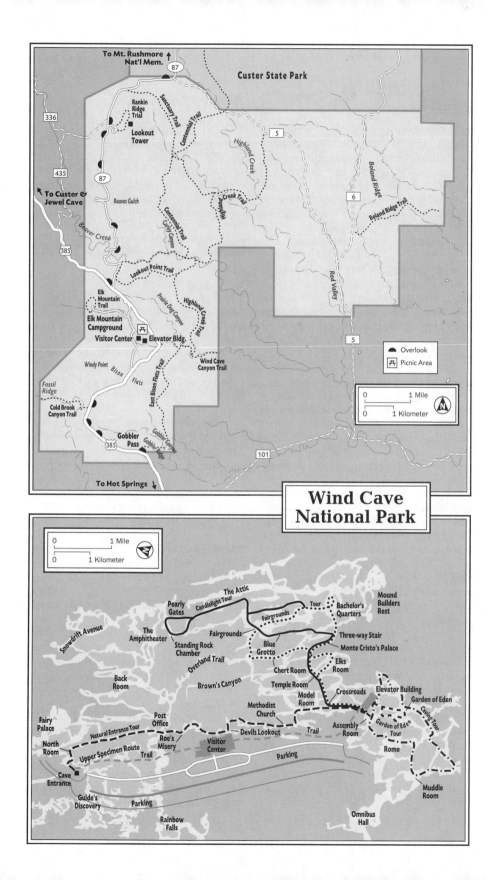

Wind Cave
National Park

Upper map — surface

To Mt. Rushmore Nat'l Mem. ↑
87

Custer State Park

336

Rankin Ridge Trail
Sanctuary Trail
Centennial Trail
Lookout Tower

Highland Creek

5

Boland Ridge
6
Boland Ridge Trail

435

To Custer & Jewel Cave →

Beaver Creek

87

Reaves Gulch

Centennial Trail
Cuny Canyon

Highland Creek Trail

Red Valley

Lookout Point Trail

Elk Mountain Trail
Elk Mountain Campground
Visitor Center
Elevator Bldg.

Prairie Dog Canyon

Highland Creek Trail

Wind Cave Canyon Trail

5

385

Windy Point

Bison Flats

East Bison Flats Trail

Fossil Ridge

Cold Brook Canyon Trail

Gobbler Pass
385

Gobbler Ridge
Gobbler Canyon

101

To Hot Springs ↓

Legend:
- 🦪 Overlook
- 🪧 Picnic Area

0 — 1 Mile
0 — 1 Kilometer

Lower map — cave

0 — 1 Mile
0 — 1 Kilometer

Snowdrift Avenue

Pearly Gates
Candlelight Tour
The Attic
Tour
Bachelor's Quarters
Mound Builders Rest

The Amphitheater
Standing Rock Chamber
Fairgrounds
Fairgrounds
Three-way Stair
Monte Cristo's Palace

Overland Trail
Blue Grotto
Chert Room
Elks Room

Back Room
Brown's Canyon
Temple Room
Crossroads
Elevator Building
Garden of Eden

Model Room

Fairy Palace

Post Office
Methodist Church
Assembly Room
Garden of Eden Tour
Caving Tour

North Room
Natural Entrance Tour
Roe's Misery
Devils Lookout
Trail

Rome

Cave Entrance
Upper Specimen Route Trail
Visitor Center
Parking

Guide's Discovery
Parking

Muddle Room

Rainbow Falls
Omnibus Hall

ESSENTIALS

Visitor Center. The visitor center (located right off U.S. 385), which is open daily year-round (except Thanksgiving and Christmas), has books, brochures, exhibits, and slide programs about the cave and other park resources. Cave tour information and tickets are available, and schedules of activities, including talks and nature walks, are posted.

Fees & Permits. Wind Cave National Park does not charge an entrance fee. It does, however, charge a fee for cave tours, ranging from $4 ($2 with a Golden Age Passport) for a simple guided tour to $18 for a 4-hour introduction to basic caving techniques.

Camping in Elk Mountain Campground costs $10 per night from mid-May through mid-September, and $5 per night during the rest of its season; all camping is on a first-come, first-served basis. Backcountry camping is allowed at Wind Cave; a free permit is required and must be picked up in person at the park visitor center.

Special Regulations & Warnings. The danger of wildfire is usually high year-round. Build fires only in the campground and only in fire grills or camp stoves. Never leave a fire unattended. Off-road driving is prohibited in the park. Watch for rattlesnakes and black widow spiders, which favor prairie dog burrows and may strike without warning.

Cave tour pathways may be uneven or wet and slippery. Watch your step and wear low-heeled, nonslip shoes. A jacket, sweater, or sweatshirt is recommended for protection from the cave's 53°F temperature. If you have breathing, heart, or walking problems, or are claustrophobic, consult with a ranger before taking a tour. The cave's delicate formations are easily broken or discolored by skin oils, so please don't touch them. Smoking, food, and drink are prohibited in the cave.

Useful Publications. The National Park Service publishes a variety of informational handouts on topics such as park history, hiking, camping, geology, wildlife, bird life, prairie grasses and ecosystems, and environmental concerns. In addition, the park produces *Passages,* a free visitor guide to Wind Cave that is available at the visitor center.

IF YOU ONLY HAVE 1 DAY

Even with more than 44 square miles of forest, grasslands, and quiet canyons, visitors can appreciate most of the highlights of Wind Cave National Park in a day or less. You'll have time for a cave tour, most of which take less than 2 hours, and a drive through the park to view the bison and elk. If you have time, then get out on one of the park's hiking trails.

ORGANIZED CAVE TOURS

The park offers five cave tours during the summer season and one tour the remainder of the year. Adventurous cavers should consider the two tours that are limited to 10 people each; these will definitely take them away from the crowds.

The Garden of Eden Tour. Entering and leaving Wind Cave by an elevator, this 1-hour tour takes participants past representative cave features. It's the park's least strenuous tour, climbing 150 stairs.

Natural Entrance Tour. Beginning at the walk-in entrance to the cave and leaving by elevator, this moderately strenuous 75-minute tour has 300 stairs (though most of these are down) and leads visitors through the middle of the cave, with an abundance of "box work"—thin blades of calcite that project from the cave's walls and ceiling in a honeycomb pattern.

Fairgrounds Tour. This includes some of the larger rooms found in the developed area of the cave. Participants view many

Deadwood: The Wildest & Woolliest Town in the West

There was a time when it wasn't safe to walk the cobblestone streets of the Black Hills' original sin city. But that was a thousand gunfights and barroom brawls ago, when Deadwood was known as the wildest, wickedest, woolliest town in the West, where Wild Bill Hickok was gunned down and where Calamity Jane Canary claimed she could outdrink, outswear, and outspit any man.

Today, the sounds of slot machines and street-side barkers have replaced the sporadic gunshots, crunching blows, and general rowdiness of a century ago, where miners, gamblers, and painted ladies all searched for their pot of gold. They found gold, of course, but seldom did they retain it.

The city's merchants, bankers, and saloon-keepers, however, cleverly invested their money in beautiful Victorian buildings and residences that today stand as testament to a richer time.

Although Deadwood was labeled "a disaster" by historic preservation officials a decade ago, it's alive and kicking today. This is due to a great extent to limited stakes gaming, approved by South Dakota voters in 1989 to generate revenues that would then be dedicated to restoring and preserving this mile-high community.

Now, state and national historic preservation officials call Deadwood's metamorphosis "a miracle." Brick streets, period lighting, and colorful trolleys greet visitors, who spend hours ducking in doorways and trying their luck in the town's 80—yes 80—gambling halls. In addition to gambling, Deadwood has some of the finest restaurants and hotels in the state.

For more information on accommodations, walking tours, museums, attractions, special events, and gambling packages, contact the **Deadwood Chamber of Commerce & Visitor Bureau** (☎ 800/999-1876; www.deadwood.org), or stop by the History and Information Center in the classic train depot at 3 Siever St.

---

cave formations, including box work. The tour enters and exits by elevator. This moderately strenuous excursion has 450 stairs and lasts 90 minutes.

Candlelight Tour. This is one of the most popular tours, especially for children 8 and over. Trekking through a less-developed, unlighted section of the cave, tour participants each carry a candle bucket and experience the cave by candlelight. Shoes with nonslip soles are required; no sandals are allowed. This tour is limited to 10 people (minimum age is 8). This strenuous tour covers 1 mile of rugged trail and lasts 2 hours. Reservations, available no more than 1 month before the tour, are strongly advised.

Caving Tour. You can also explore Wind Cave away from the established trails. On this 4-hour adventure, visitors are introduced to basic, safe caving practices. You need to wear old clothes and gloves, since much of the tour is spent crawling. Long pants, long-sleeve shirts, and sturdy, lace-up boots or shoes with nonslip soles are a must. The park provides hard hats, lights, and kneepads. Do not bring jewelry, watches, or other valuables. This tour is limited to 10 people and the minimum age is 16. (Signed consent forms from a parent or guardian are required for 16- and 17-year-olds.) Reservations, which are available 1 month before the tour, are required.

Tours for People with Disabilities. The visitor center and the cave are accessible to people with limited mobility. Call ahead (☎ 605/745-4600) to make special arrangements or inquire about a special tour at the information desk. Some areas of the cave are accessible to wheelchairs. Fees are charged for special services.

EXPLORING THE PARK BY CAR

The rolling prairies of western South Dakota run smack into the ponderosa pine forests of the Black Hills in Wind Cave National Park, and the park's roadways provide the scenic backdrop for some of the best wildlife viewing opportunities in the region. Bison, pronghorn, elk, and other wildlife abound in this rugged preserve, and you'll be able to see many of them as you drive down through Custer State Park on S. Dak. 87 to Wind Cave. Several scenic roadways lead through the Black Hills to Wind Cave. Roadside sightseers will find the Wildlife Loop Road, Iron Mountain Road, and the Needles Highway particularly enjoyable. All of these are in Custer State Park, just north of Wind Cave National Park, and are described in the preceding section.

Warning: Tunnels on Iron Mountain Road (U.S. 16A) are 12 feet, 6 inches high and 13 feet, 6 inches wide. Tunnels on the Needles Highway/Sylvan Lake Road (S. Dak. 87) are as low as 10 feet, 8 inches and as narrow as 8 feet, 7 inches.

RANGER PROGRAMS

Park rangers provide a number of **talks** and programs at Wind Cave. Topics range from local wildlife, plants and geology to area history and spelunking and cave surveying. **Campfire programs** are conducted most evenings during the summer months. There is a ranger-guided **prairie hike** conducted at 9am daily during the summer, which lasts about 2 hours. Check with the visitor center for times and locations.

DAY HIKES

More than 30 miles of trails crisscross the park's backcountry. Several can be combined to create round-trip hikes, or you may want to leave the trails and hike a ridgeline, through a canyon, or across an open prairie bordered by ponderosa pine. Backcountry camping is permitted in the northwestern portion of the park with a free permit available at the visitor center or either of the Centennial trailheads.

Park handouts also provide information on more than a half-dozen other trails ranging from 1.4 miles to 8.6 miles.

Centennial Trail

6 mi. one way. Moderate. Access: Along S. Dak. 87, 0.7 mi. north of its intersection with U.S. 385.

Wind Cave provides the southern terminus for the 110-mile-long Centennial Trail, built in honor of South Dakota's centennial in 1989. The trail leads through the heart of the Black Hills before ending at Bear Butte State Park near Sturgis. Wind Cave hosts a 6-mile section of the Centennial Trail, where hikers can explore the diversity of the park. The trail crosses the prairie, climbs the foothills and forested ridges, then examines the wetter, riparian habitat of Beaver Creek.

Elk Mountain Nature Trail

0.5 mi. one way. Easy. Access: Elk Mountain Campground.

This interpretive trail explores an ecotone, or meeting zone, where prairie and forest converge. Booklets are available at the trailhead.

Rankin Ridge Nature Trail

0.75 mi. RT. Moderate. Access: Rankin Ridge parking lot.

This loop trail leads to the highest point in the park, and is one of Wind Cave's most popular. You can stop at the lookout tower, about halfway around the loop. Booklets are available at the trailhead.

Visiting Jewel Cave National Monument

The exploration of Jewel Cave began about 1900 when two South Dakota prospectors, Frank and Albert Michaud, and a companion, Charles Bush, happened to hear wind rushing through a hole in the rocks in Hell Canyon. After enlarging the hole, they discovered a cave full of sparkling crystals. The entrepreneurs filed a mining claim on the "Jewel Lode," but they uncovered no valuable minerals, so they attempted to turn the cave into a tourist attraction instead. The business was never a success, but the cave's uniqueness did attract attention, and in 1908 Pres. Theodore Roosevelt established Jewel Cave National Monument to protect this remarkable natural wonder.

A half-century later, exploration of the cave intensified. Led by the husband and wife team of Herb and Jan Conn, spelunkers discovered new wonders and explored and mapped miles of passageways.

When first asked to consider a trek below the surface, the Conns were reluctant. But after their first excursion into the underworld, the couple could not be turned away. In more than 2 decades of spelunking in Jewel Cave, the Conns logged 708 trips into the cave and 6,000 hours of exploration and mapping. Their efforts proved that Jewel Cave was among the most extensive and complex cave ecosystems in the world, filled with scenic and scientific wonders.

The explorers discovered chambers with exquisite calcite crystals and other rare specimens. One room mapped by the Conns, the Formation Room, is now a highlight of the park service tours. They also found rooms as large as 150 by 200 feet, passageways as long as 3,200 feet, and a place where the cave wind blows at speeds of 32 miles per hour. In 1980, after discovering more than 65 miles of passageways, the Conns retired, and a new generation of spelunkers have pushed the known boundaries of the cave to well over 118 miles.

When the Conns said, "We are still just standing on the threshold," they could not have known how accurate they were. Studies by the U.S. Geological Survey have since attempted to determine the amount of passageway in the cave by measuring the volume of air leaving or entering the cave, depending on the barometric pressure outside. Conclusions of those studies indicate that known passageways at Jewel Cave constitutes less than 5% of what actually exists in the quiet darkness below the Black Hills.

Only Mammoth Cave in Kentucky and Optimisticeskaja in the Ukraine are longer than Jewel Cave. Explorations of Jewel Cave in 1997 moved the cave from fourth- to third-longest, surpassing Holloch Cave in Switzerland.

Known for its calcite nailhead and dogtooth spar crystal, Jewel Cave also is home to some extremely rare and unusual specimens. The Cave's hydromagnesite "balloons," fragile silvery bubbles that look as if they might pop any minute, have been found in just a handful of other caves. Scintillites, reddish rocks coated with sparkling clear quartz crystals, were unknown until they were discovered in Jewel Cave. One particularly intriguing mineral, gypsum, combines with time and the ceaseless presence of seeping water to assume the shapes of flowers, needles, spiders, and cottony beards that sway from the heat of an explorer's lamp.

Avoiding the Crowds. The highest visitation at Jewel Cave occurs in June, July, and August. With 1,274 acres above the surface and annual visitation of approximately 140,000, Jewel Cave is rarely overcrowded, even at the height of the tourist season. However, because space on some scenic tours is limited and 92,000 park

Tips from the Chief of Interpretation

Fall, winter, and spring are ideal times to visit Jewel Cave National Monument, according to Chief of Interpretation Karen Rosga. Even with arctic blasts on the surface, temperatures within the cave are constant at 49°F, with humidity averaging 98%. "In the middle of winter, it can actually be quite pleasant in the cave," says Rosga.

"Jewel Cave is one of the most structurally complex caves in the world and it is still being explored. This is not a cave that has been fully mapped and it's probable that it will not be fully explored in any of our lifetimes." She adds, "To this point, we have been very successful in developing a visitor experience that allows people to enjoy the cave in a relatively pristine state."

For travelers with children over 6, Rosga recommends the "adventurous experience" of a candlelight tour into the cave, the park's Junior Ranger Program, and the variety of surface programs that augment the cave tours.

interpretive programs, and answering questions about the park's cultural, historical, and geologic resources. Up-to-date cave information and tour tickets also are available at the visitor center, which is open daily year-round.

Fees. There is no entry fee for the national monument, but you'll pay for cave tours. The Scenic and Candlelight tours cost $6 ($3 for children under 17); the Spelunking tour is $18. Golden Age and Golden Access Passport-holders pay reduced tour fees.

Special Regulations & Warnings. Low-heeled, rubber-soled shoes are highly recommended because trails can be slippery; some stair-climbing is required on each tour. A jacket, sweater, or sweatshirt will keep you comfortable in the 49°F year-round temperature of the cave. Persons with respiratory or heart problems, who have been recently hospitalized, or have a fear of heights or confined spaces should talk with a park ranger before selecting a tour. Damaging or even touching cave formations is prohibited due to the fragile and irreplaceable nature of the formations. Pets and smoking are not allowed in the cave. Cameras are permitted on cave tours, but tripods are not.

Useful Publications. The Park Service publishes brochures covering a variety of topics, such as bats, birds, wildflowers, surface trails, spelunking tours, and the history and exploration of the cave.

visitors participate in a cave tour annually, visitors should anticipate a wait as long as 90 minutes to be able to enter the cave. If you want to keep your wait to a minimum, arrive early in the morning or late in the day.

ESSENTIALS

Visitor Center. The park visitor center has books and brochures, and park rangers can assist travelers with planning their visit, pointing out special

IF YOU ONLY HAVE 1 DAY

There are only 2 square miles of aboveground real estate at Jewel Cave National Monument, so exploring the highlights is possible in a fraction of a day. Allocate 2 to 3 hours for a trip to the visitor center, a scenic cave tour, and a walk on one of the monument's surface trails.

CAVE TOURS

Visitors can have an adventure in Jewel Cave by taking any of the park's ranger-guided tours. Tickets for the Scenic Tour or Candlelight Tour must be purchased at the visitor center on the day of the tour. Reservations for the Spelunking Tour are strongly encouraged. It's also a good idea to contact the monument before visiting to determine whether special hours, activities, or tour schedules are being observed.

Scenic Tour. This 0.5-mile, 80-minute tour visits chambers decorated with calcite crystals and colorful stalactites, stalagmites, and draperies. The loop tour begins at the visitor center with an elevator ride into the cave. Tour participants take a paved, lighted path and climb up and down more than 700 stairs on this moderately strenuous journey into the underground wilderness. The tour, which is offered year-round, is conducted several times daily from May to September and is limited to 30 persons.

Candlelight Tour. This 0.5-mile, 105-minute tour follows in the footsteps of early Jewel Cave explorers. Tour participants see the cave's calcite-coated passageways lighted by old-style candle lanterns. This round-trip tour starts at the cave's historic entrance in Hell Canyon, is moderately strenuous with many steep stairs, and requires much bending and stooping. Long pants and sturdy, closed-toe shoes are highly recommended. The tour is offered several times daily from mid-June through late August and is limited to 25 persons (definitely call ahead to find out if it will be offered when you are in the area). Children under age 6 are not allowed.

Spelunking Tour. This physically and mentally challenging 0.5-mile, 3- to 4-hour tour gives participants a taste of modern-day cave crawling in a wild, undeveloped portion of Jewel Cave. The round-trip tour begins at the visitor center with an elevator ride into the cave. Old clothes, knee pads, and gloves are recommended; ankle-high laced boots with lug soles are required. The park supplies hard hats and headlamps. To qualify for the tour, participants are required to crawl through an 8½-by-24-inch concrete block tunnel. This tour is offered daily (12:30pm) from mid-June through mid-August; the limit is five persons (here's your chance to avoid the crowds). Children 15 years of age and younger are not allowed; 16- and 17-year-olds must have a parent or guardian's written permission. You can (and should) reserve your place on a tour up to 30 days in advance).

RANGER PROGRAMS

During the summer season, a number of special interpretive programs take place at the visitor center, including ranger talks, demonstrations, and guided walks. Check at the visitor center for specifics.

DAY HIKES

Travelers to Jewel Cave should also take time to experience life in the world aboveground, such as by taking a nature hike (there are two hiking trails), enjoying a picnic, or searching out the plants and animals that inhabit the rugged hills and canyon country of the Black Hills.

In the stillness of the ponderosa pine forest that blankets the park live mule deer, white-tailed deer, elk, porcupines, coyote, squirrels and chipmunks, and several species of birds, including golden eagles and hawks. Plants of both the prairie and the hills grow here, and in summer, wildflowers paint the landscape.

Canyons Trail

3.5 mi. RT. Easy to moderate. Access: Visitor center.

This loop trail provides the opportunity to become more familiar with surface resources and geologic features of the monument. The trail winds past several natural attractions entrusted to the National Park Service, including the limestone palisades of Hell Canyon and Lithograph Canyon, as well as the deer, birds, and wildflowers that live in the ponderosa pine forest through which the trail winds. If you want to experience a part of the Canyon Trail without going the entire distance, you might try the 1.5-mile round-trip between the visitor center and the historic area of the cave.

Walk on the Roof

0.25 mi. RT. Easy. Access: Visitor center.

While visiting the "roof" of Jewel Cave on this self-guided interpretive walk, you'll learn how the monument's surface and subsurface resources interact. Interpretive trail guides for this walk are available at the information desk in the visitor center.

Guided Tours

A number of charter bus park tours and guide services throughout the area are available. **Gray Line of the Black Hills,** P.O. Box 1106, Rapid City, SD 57709 (☎ 800/456-4461 or 605/342-4461; www.blackhillsgrayline.com) offers bus tours of the area; as does **America Tours West,** P.O. Box 867, Keystone, SD 57751-0167 (☎ 605/666-4545). **Jack Rabbit Charters & Tours,** 301 N. Dakota Ave., Sioux Falls, SD 57104 (☎ 800/678-6543 or 605/335-2290; www.jackrabbitlines.com) offers one day and extended tours. **Golden Circle Tours,** P.O. Box 454, Custer, SD 57730 (☎ 877/811-4349 or 605/673-4349), offers guided van tours of the area. Its office is located on U.S. 16A, 1 mile east of Custer. The company rents cars and vans as well.

Sports & Activities

Aerial Tours. If you want to see the Black Hills from above, contact **Black Hills** Balloons, P.O. Box 210, Custer, SD 57730-0210 (☎ 605/673-2520; e-mail: balloons@rapidnet.com), which offers flights over the Black Hills, as well as Badlands National Park and Devils Tower National Monument, year-round; expect to pay $165 per person for a flight.

Biking. There are more than 6,000 miles of fire trails, logging roads, and other undeveloped roads throughout the Black Hills region, so this is quickly becoming a top spot for mountain biking. **Custer State Park** is a prime spot for mountain biking since most park trails and roads are open to bikers. (The Legion Lake Resort in Custer State Park rents mountain bikes; see the complete listing under "Accommodations," below.

Fishing. **Horsethief Lake,** below Mount Rushmore, where there is a Forest Service campground (see "Camping," below), is stocked with rainbow trout. **Center** and **Stockade lakes** in Custer State Park are also good fishing spots. Many streams in this area, including **Grizzly Bear Creek,** behind Mount Rushmore, have good fishing for brook trout. You'll need a fishing license, available at sporting-goods stores and at many convenience stores.

Horse-Packing Trips. Several companies offer guided trail rides through the backcountry of the Black Hills. One family-run company, **Dakota Badland Outfitters,** P.O. Box 85, Custer, SD 57730 (☎ 605/673-5363; www.wordpros.com/dakota), conducts a 4-day Badlands Horse Camp for $680 per person (September and October), a Working Ranch Visit at $170 per day (June through September), or they can put together a custom trip. Fees include all meals. The company also rents sleeping bags and provides airport shuttle services for additional charges.

Snowmobiling. There are hundreds of miles of groomed snowmobile trails in the upper Black Hills, and many guest ranches and resorts, such as **Deadwood Gulch Resort** (see "Accommodations," below), rent snowmobiles to their guests. You can get more information on trails and companies that rent snowmobiles from South Dakota Tourism (see "Information," above).

Camping

While there are no campgrounds within the boundaries of Mount Rushmore National Memorial or Jewel Cave National Monument, there are several campgrounds in Custer State Park and another campground in Wind Cave National Park, plus those in the Black Hills National Forest and privately operated campgrounds. Many commercial campgrounds offer free shuttle services, nightly entertainment, pools, convenience stores, and horseback riding. Reservations are recommended. Choice spots are often filled by midmorning, so arriving at popular campgrounds early in the day is advised.

For more information on camping opportunities, contact South Dakota Tourism (see "Information," above). For information on National Forest Service campgrounds, contact the Forest Supervisor, Black Hills National Forest, RR2, P.O. Box 200, Custer, SD 57730 (☎ 605/673-2251; www.fs.fed.us/bhnf).

INSIDE WIND CAVE NATIONAL PARK

Located in the pine forests 1 mile north of the park visitor center, **Elk Mountain Campground** has shady sites for tents and recreational vehicles. The campground fee is $10 per night per site mid-May through mid-September and $5 per night per site the remainder of its season, when water is turned off. Park rangers give campfire programs at the amphitheater in the summer. **Backcountry campers** are encouraged to practice low-impact camping and hiking techniques.

INSIDE CUSTER STATE PARK

Campgrounds here require park entrance fees as well as camping fees.

Each campsite at Custer State Park has a gravel or paved camping pad and a picnic table, and all campgrounds but Center Lake have flush toilets. About 200 campsites throughout the park may be reserved beginning in January for the entire season, while other sites are available on a first-come, first-served basis.

Campsites range from modern and semimodern to primitive campsites located in natural areas of the park. Group camping is available at two campgrounds and the French Creek Horse Camp is designated specifically for campers with horses.

For information and reservations contact **Custer State Park,** HC 83, Box 70, Custer, SD 57730 (☎ **800/710-2267** or 605/255-4515).

Blue Bell Campground is located in a mature stand of ponderosa pine near French Creek, not far from the site where Lt. Col. George Armstrong Custer and his 7th Cavalry discovered gold in 1874. It offers easy access to the Wildlife Loop Road, horseback riding, stream fishing, and fabulous hiking.

Game Lodge Campground is another of Custer State Park's fine campgrounds. This one was designed for larger RVs, but tenters will find cool, shady sites and an occasional bison along the banks of Grace Coolidge Creek. It's located near the park's Peter Norbeck Visitor Center and the State Game Lodge.

Legion Lake Campground is centrally located in Custer State Park, with fishing, boating, and hiking opportunities right at your doorstep. Historic sites are within walking distance, as is the Legion Lake Resort across the highway.

You'd probably have to camp in Yosemite Valley to get a better view than the one at **Sylvan Lake Campground.** This mountain retreat is located just off the incredible Needles Highway, near 7,242-foot Harney Peak, the highest

Campground	Total Sites	RV Hookups	Dump Station	Toilets	Drinking Water
Inside Badlands National Park					
Cedar Pass	110	No	Yes	Yes	Yes
Sage Creek	15	No	No	Yes	No
Near Badlands National Park					
Badlands Ranch Resort	35	Yes	No	Yes	Yes
Inside Wind Cave National Park					
Elk Mountain	75	No	No	Yes	Yes
Inside Custer State Park					
Blue Bell	35	No	No	Yes	Yes
Center Lake	70	No	No	Yes	Yes
Game Lodge	55	No	Yes	Yes	Yes
Grace Coolidge	26	No	No	Yes	Yes
Legion Lake	25	No	No	Yes	Yes
Stockade Lake	85	No	No	Yes	Yes
Sylvan Lake	40	No	No	Yes	Yes
Inside Black Hills National Forest					
Horsethief Lake	36	No	No	Yes	Yes
Roubaix Lake	56	No	No	Yes	Yes
Private Campgrounds in the Black Hills					
American Presidents	40	Yes	No	Yes	Yes
Berry Patch	130	Yes	Yes	Yes	Yes
Big Pine	85	Yes	No	Yes	Yes
Miners	28	Yes	No	Yes	Yes
Mount Rushmore KOA	500	Yes	Yes	Yes	Yes
Rapid City KOA	200	Yes	Yes	Yes	Yes
Whistler Gulch	107	Yes	Yes	Yes	Yes

point between the Rockies and the Swiss Alps, and affords visitors the best in Black Hills hiking and mountain climbing. Its campsites fill quickly, so make your reservations early, as all sites are reservable.

The park's other three campgrounds are **Center Lake,** 5 miles northeast of the junction of U.S. 16A and S. Dak. 87; **Grace Coolidge,** 13 miles east of Custer on U.S. 16A; and **Stockade Lake,** located just inside the park's western boundary on U.S. 16A.

Reservations are accepted at Game Lodge, Legion Lake, Blue Bell, Stockade North, Sylvan Lake, and French Creek Horse Camp. It's first-come, first-served

Showers	Fire Pits/ Grills	Laundry	Public Phone	Reserve	Fees	Open
No	No	No	Yes	No	$10	Year-round
No	No	No	No	No	Free	Year-round
Yes	Yes	Yes	Yes	Yes	$12–$20	May 1–Sept 20
No	Yes	No	Yes	No	$5–$10	Apr–Oct
Yes	Yes	Yes	Yes	Yes	$14	May 1–Sept 15
No	Yes	No	No	Yes	$11	May 1–Sept 15
Yes	Yes	Yes	Yes	Yes	$14	May 1–Sept 15
No	Yes	No	No	Yes	$14	May 1–Sept 15
Yes	Yes	No	Yes	Yes	$14	May 1–Sept 15
No	Yes	No	No	Yes	$14	May 1–Sept 15
Yes	Yes	Yes	Yes	Yes	$14	May 1–Sept 15
No	Yes	No	No	Yes	$15–$17	Year-round
No	Yes	No	Yes	Yes	$14–$16	Year-round
Yes	Yes	Yes	Yes	Yes	$19–$26.50	May 15–Oct 1
Yes	Yes	Yes	Yes	Yes	$20.95–$28.95	Apr 1–Nov 1
Yes	Yes	Yes	Yes	Yes	$15.50–$20	May 10–Oct 1
Yes	Yes	Yes	Yes	Yes	$21.50	Apr 15–Oct 1
Yes	Yes	Yes	Yes	Yes	$22.95–$318.95	May 1–Oct 1
Yes	Yes	Yes	Yes	Yes	$20.95–$28.95	Apr 15–Oct 15
Yes	Yes	Yes	Yes	Yes	$17–$27	May 1–Oct 31

at Grace Coolidge, Center Lake, and Stockade South.

INSIDE THE BLACK HILLS NATIONAL FOREST

National Forest camping reservations can be made by calling ☎ 877/444-6777 or online at www.reserveusa.com. A reservation fee of $8.65 is charged for single-site camping.

Horsethief Lake Campground, only a mile west of Mount Rushmore, offers scenic sites adjacent to picturesque Horsethief Lake. At a 5,000-foot elevation, 28 sites are for tents, travel trailers, and RVs, while eight sites are for tents only. Sites not reserved (up to 50% can be reserved) fill quickly, so you need to claim yours early in the day.

Roubaix Lake Campground, off U.S. 385 on FDR 255, is nestled in a ponderosa pine forest next to scenic Roubaix Lake, which offers great fishing and swimming at a 5,500-foot elevation. Spaces fill fast and some can be reserved.

COMMERCIAL CAMPGROUNDS

A variety of privately operated campgrounds provide all the usual RV hookups and other services.

American Presidents Cabins & Camp, 1 mile east of Custer on Highway 16A, P.O. Box 446, Custer, SD 57730 (☎ 605/673-3373; www.presidentsresort.com), is a perfect home base for touring the southern Black Hills. The campground's 40-by-60-foot heated pool is popular, as are its free miniature golf and horseshoes. The campground also has a store and fishing nearby. A 10% discount is offered on reservations made before May 15. Also available are 45 full-service cabins, some with kitchens, that sleep from 2 to 12 people (call for rates).

Berry Patch Campground, 1860 E. North St. (I-90 at Exit 60), Rapid City, SD 57701 (☎ 800/658-4566 or 605/341-5588; e-mail: berrypat@rapidnet.com), is the easiest campground to reach on and off I-90; it's also clean and friendly. Full hookups and drive-throughs complement its heated pool, store, and game room.

Big Pine Campground, R.R. 1, P.O. Box 52, Custer, SD 57730 (☎ 800/235-3981 for reservations, or 605/673-4054), secluded from traffic noises, offers level, naturally shaded sites, fireplaces and wood, as well as a store, game room, playground, hiking, and horseshoes.

Miners RV Park, P.O. Box 157, Keystone, SD 57751 (☎ 800/727-2421 or 605/666-4638), in the heart of the former mining town of Keystone, is close to numerous attractions and only a stone's

throw from Mount Rushmore National Memorial. The campground and its adjacent motel offer cool shade and a gurgling brook, as well as a store, gas, ice, gifts, restaurant, heated pool and hot tub, and a fun walk down Keystone's Main Street.

Mount Rushmore KOA, P.O. Box 295, Hill City, SD 57745 (☎ 800/562-8503; e-mail: palmerkoa.aol.com), part of the Palmer Gulch Resort, is among the best in the region, if not the largest. With 450 sites and 55 Kamping Kabins, two pools and spas, water slide, Indian dancers, movies, miniature golf, fishing, hayrides, restaurant, tours, and car rentals, this is what many campgrounds want to be when they grow up.

Rapid City KOA, P.O. Box 2592, Rapid City, SD 57709 (☎ 800/KOA-8504 or 605/348-2111; e-mail: RPDCityKOA@ aol.com), is conveniently located on Rapid City's eastern flank. This KOA also is large with 200 sites and cabins. It offers a free pancake breakfast, and a grand pool and spa. Bus tours and car rentals are available, and great shopping, sightseeing, and Rushmore Plaza Civic Center are nearby.

Whistler Gulch Campground, 235 Cliff St., Highway 85 South, Deadwood, SD 57732 (☎ 800/704-7139 or 605/578-2094), is nestled in one of Deadwood's famous mining gulches. The campground offers more than 100 full-service RV sites and secluded tent sites. Facilities include a heated swimming pool, sport court, and small store. The town trolley takes visitors to Deadwood's casinos and historic sites.

Accommodations

There are no accommodations at Mount Rushmore, Wind Cave, or Jewel Cave, but inns, hotels, motels, lodges, and bed-and-breakfasts are plentiful in nearby Black Hills communities and parks. However, there are four popular lodges in Custer State Park. Reservations are strongly recommended, especially in summer months. For some popular destinations such as Custer State Park, it's best to call 6 months to a year in advance of your visit. In addition to the properties listed below in Rapid City, Nemo, and Deadwood, you'll find accommodations in Keystone and Hill City (especially convenient to Mount Rushmore), as well as in Custer and Hot Springs (more convenient to Jewel Cave and Wind Cave, respectively). If you're continuing west, you might also consider lodging in Newcastle, Wyoming, 25 miles west of Jewel Cave National Monument.

For information on accommodations in the Black Hills, contact the South Dakota Department of Tourism or the Black Hills, Badlands and Lakes Association (see "Information," above). Rates below may be higher during special events.

IN RAPID CITY

Abend Haus Cottages and Audrie's B&B

23029 Thunderhead Falls Rd., Rapid City, SD 57702-8524. ☎ **605/342-7788.** www.audriesbb.com. 9 units. TV. $95–$145 double. Rates include full breakfast. No credit cards. Couples only. Located 6 mi. west of town on U.S. 44.

Set on the banks of a rippling trout stream, Audrie's is ideally situated to explore the wonders of the national parks, monuments, and memorials in the Black Hills. Antiques, fireplaces, and hot tubs grace every suite and cottage. And you won't go away hungry. This is a no-smoking establishment.

Hotel Alex Johnson

523 Sixth St., Rapid City, SD 57701. (☎ **800/888-2539** or 605/342-1210. Fax 605/342-7436. www.alexjohnson.com. E-mail: info@alexjohnson.com. 143 units. A/C TV TEL. Apr to mid-Oct $101–$145 double, $123–$400 suite; mid-Oct to Mar $69–$79 double, $85–$395 suite. AE, DC, DISC, MC, V.

This finely restored hotel, listed on the National Historic Register, has a Germanic Tudor mixed with Lakota Sioux atmosphere on the inside, with a Germanic Tudor exterior. The furniture was handcrafted in Rapid City to replicate the hotel's original furnishings in 1928. It contains an Irish pub, gift shop, and a highly recommended restaurant, The Landmark, that is open for breakfast, lunch, and dinner.

Rushmore Plaza Holiday Inn

505 N. Fifth St., Rapid City, SD 57701. ☎ **605/348-4000.** Fax 605/348-9777. 205 units. A/C TV TEL. Jan 4–June 6 $79–$99 double; June 7–Jan 3 $108–$147 double. AE, DC, DISC, MC, V.

This eight-story atrium hotel with a pool and waterfall also has a relaxing piano lounge and exercise facilities. It's a great place to stay when you don't feel the need to go outdoors, and is close to downtown shopping, dining, and entertainment.

IN NEMO

Twin Peaks Ranch

17 mi. west of Sturgis Rd. on Nemo Rd., 2 mi. before Nemo in Paradise Valley (P.O. Box 80, Nemo, SD 57759). ☎ **888/627-9928** or 605/578-2771. www.twinpeaksresort.com. Ranch House (accommodates up to 14 persons) plus 3 cabins. Ranch House: May 15–Sept 15 $395; Sept 16–May 14 $375. Cabin: May 15–Sept 15 $98; Sept 16–May 14 $80. AE, DISC, MC, V.

Nestled in the scenic valley carved by Box Elder Creek and surrounded by the grandeur of Black Hills National Forest, Twin Peaks' 6,700-square-foot log house is ideal for group gatherings and family reunions, while the cabins are good for quiet hideaways. Favored activities include fly-fishing, hiking, rock climbing, mountain biking, horseback riding, and star gazing. Horse boarding is available.

IN CUSTER

Bavarian Inn Motel

U.S. 16/385 North, Custer, SD 57730.
☎ **800/657-4312** or 605/673-2802. Fax
605/673-4777. 64 units. A/C TV TEL.
$38–$83 double; $55–$125 suite. AE, DISC,
MC, V.

One mile north of downtown, the Bavarian Inn is well located to visit many of the Black Hills' most popular attractions, including Mount Rushmore, Crazy Horse Memorial, and Custer State Park. There's a restaurant and lounge on site, outdoor pool, heated indoor pool, tennis court, sauna and hot tub, and game room.

IN DEADWOOD

The Bullock Hotel

633 Historic Main St., Deadwood, SD 57732.
☎ **800/336-1876** or 605/578-1745. Fax
605/578-1382. www.bullockhotel.com. E-mail:
hub@mato.com. 36 units. A/C TV TEL.
$35–$155 double. AE, DISC, MC, V.

This is the finest hotel in South Dakota. You'll find turn-of-the-century surroundings complemented by modern amenities, a perfect combination. There's also 24-hour gambling, a full-service bar, and a quaint restaurant called Bully's. For a special treat, try one of the Jacuzzi suites. Keep an eye out for the hotel's namesake, legendary lawman Seth Bullock, whose ghost has a habit of reappearing here.

Deadwood Gulch Resort

U.S. 85 S., 1 mi. from Historic Main St. (P.O.
Box 643, Deadwood, SD 57732). ☎
800/695-1876 or 605/578-1294. Fax
605/578-2505. 100 units. A/C TV TEL.
Oct–June 15 $62–$75 double; June 16–Sept 5
$99 double; Sept 6–30 $65–$75 double. AE,
DISC, MC, V.

With a comfortable hotel, three casinos, a convention center, bars, creek-side restaurant, convenience store and gas station, amusement park, arcade, spa, and heated pools, this ranks as South Dakota's only true resort. There's trolley service to historic Main Street. In the summer, the resort has mountain-bike rentals; in the winter, you can rent snowmobiles, and there are special events year-round.

INSIDE CUSTER STATE PARK

Custer State Park is home to four rustic resorts that offer lodging, dining, and a wealth of recreational opportunities in the heart of the Black Hills.

The **State Game Lodge & Resort,** located on U.S. 16A near the park's main visitor center, served as the "Summer White House" for Pres. Calvin Coolidge in 1927. The stone and wood lodge features stately rooms, motel units, and pine-shaded cabins, as well as meeting and banquet facilities. The Lodge offers an excellent Buffalo Jeep Safari Ride into the backcountry and a Safari Ride cookout dinner tour.

The **Sylvan Lake Resort,** on S. Dak. 87 in the northeast corner of Custer State Park, overlooking scenic Sylvan Lake and the Harney Range, features cozy lodge rooms and rustic family cabins. The lodge also is close to a number of outdoor activities, including hiking, swimming, fishing, boating, and rock climbing.

The **Blue Bell Lodge & Resort,** located on S. Dak. 87, just before the turnoff for the Wildlife Loop Road (if you are traveling south), is among western South Dakota's best-kept secrets. The retreat has a Western guest ranch flavor, with handcrafted log cabins scattered around a lodge with dining room, lounge, and meeting room. A general store, gift shop, and gasoline station are located on-site, and fishing is available nearby. The Blue Bell also offers hayrides, chuck-wagon cookouts, and trail rides.

The **Legion Lake Resort,** located near the junction of the Needles Highway (S. Dak. 87 and U.S. 16A), dates from 1913 and features cottages nestled in the pines near the lakeshore. A dining room, store, paddleboats, and mountain bikes are available at the resort, and the 110-mile Centennial Trail passes through the Legion Lake area.

Rates at these lodges range from around $65 for a sleeping cabin at Legion Lake in the high season, to $300 for a four-bedroom cabin at the State Game Resort. The more facilities and amenities, the more you pay. Most of the resorts open in late April or May and close down in September or late October; a few cabins are kept open for winter visitors. These fill up quickly, and some people call 6 months in advance for reservations. For more information or to make reservations at any of Custer State Park's resorts, call ☎ 800/658-3530.

DINING

Dining in the Black Hills tends to be a casual affair, but the selection can be excellent, ranging from homemade pies and ranch-raised buffalo to hearty steaks and succulent pheasant. "Summer" means Memorial Day through Labor Day.

Inside the Parks. The only national park in the Black Hills with full-service dining for all meals is at Mount Rushmore (the Buffalo Dining Room is described below). At Wind Cave, you'll find only vending machines. At Jewel Cave, you'll find only snack and soda vending machines in the foyer of the rest room building in the visitor center area. The resorts at Custer State Park offer dining facilities, which nonguests may enjoy as well (see the individual resort descriptions under "Accommodations," above).

In addition to the restaurants listed below, you might consider two establishments in Custer, which is east of Jewel Cave National Monument, west of Custer State Park, and northwest of Wind Cave National Park. The **Bavarian Inn,** at the junction U.S. 385 and U.S. 16 (☎ 605/673-4412), serves American and German dishes at reasonable prices, with musical entertainment most nights. The **Chief**

Restaurant, 140 Mount Rushmore Rd. (☎ 605/673-4402), offers family style dining, with choices ranging from prime rib and steaks to pizza and buffalo burgers.

AT MOUNT RUSHMORE NATIONAL MEMORIAL

Buffalo Dining Room

At Mount Rushmore National Memorial. ☎ 605/574-2515. Breakfast items $3–$6.50; lunch and dinner entrees $6–$8. AE, DISC, MC, V. Summer daily 7am–8pm; other times of the year daily 8am–4pm (though hrs. may vary during the off-season). AMERICAN.

Every day, visitors to the Black Hills dine with presidents at Mount Rushmore's fabled Buffalo Dining Room. Operated by AmFac Parks and Resorts, the memorial's concessionaire, the dining room serves a wide array of fare year-round in one of the world's most famous settings. Scrambled eggs, hash browns, homemade biscuits and sausage gravy, country-fried steak with coffee, tea, or milk are a deal at $2.99. What's especially nice about the place is that most choices retain a homemade taste, not something you can say about all national park fare. Buffalo stew is excellent; you'll also find burgers, hot dogs, chicken dishes, pot roast, spaghetti, baked fish, ham steaks, great pies and fudge, and monumental scoops of ice cream.

IN KEYSTONE

The Ruby House Restaurant and Red Garter Saloon

126 Winter St., Keystone. ☎ 605/666-4404. Lunch entrees $5–$9; dinner entrees $7–$20. DISC, MC, V. Summer daily for 3 meals (hours vary, so call ahead). STEAK/SEAFOOD.

Steaks, seafood, and other specialties are served in a richly appointed Victorian dining room. This is a quiet stop in a tumultuous town.

IN HILL CITY

The Alpine Inn

225 Main St., Hill City. ☎ **605/574-2749.** Lunch entrees $2–$6; dinner entrees $6–$8. No credit cards. Summer Mon–Sat 11am–2:30pm and 5–10pm; other times Mon–Sat 11am–2:30pm and 5–9:30pm. STEAK.

The Alpine Inn remains a favorite among most locals and all carnivores. If you're a vegetarian, this might not be the ideal spot for you. Lack of wide selection on entrees is mitigated by a choice of more than 30 desserts, most of which are homemade and all of which are delectable.

IN RAPID CITY

Botticelli Ristorante Italiano

523 Main St., Rapid City. ☎ **605/348-0089.** Lunch entrees $4.25–$9; dinner entrees $8.50–$15.50. MC, V. Mon–Fri 11am–3pm; Mon–Thurs 5–10pm; Fri–Sat 5–11pm; and Sun 5–9pm. ITALIAN.

One of the region's newest restaurants, Botticelli has quickly become a culinary hot spot. Featuring a wide selection of creamy pastas and delightful chicken and veal dishes, the fare smacks of northern Italy. Even though they set up shop in the middle of cattle country, seafood specials are featured on the menu, and owners/chefs Luigi Turletti and Dino Faryat may have struck a gold mine.

Firehouse Brewing Co.

610 Main St., Rapid City. ☎ **605/348-1915.** Lunch entrees $5–$8; dinner entrees $5–$16. AE, DC, DISC, MC, V. Summer Sun–Thurs 11am–10pm, Fri–Sat until midnight; other times of the year Sun–Thurs 11am–9pm, Fri–Sat until 10pm. CONTINENTAL/PUB FARE.

The entire brewing process is visible behind glass in this classic, renovated fire station. Bratwurst, burgers, buffalo, and chicken wings round out the selection. Among the most popular choices are the Reuben sandwich, the bean soup offered in fall, and the desserts, such as the Big Cookie—a freshly baked white and dark chocolate mix that fills a dinner plate, then is topped with two large scoops of French vanilla ice cream and served with melba sauce on the side. Live entertainment is offered on a large, heated patio Friday and Saturday nights in summer.

Fireside Inn

On S. Dak. 44, 7 mi. west of Rapid City. ☎ **605/342-3900.** Dinner entrees $12–$35. AE, DISC, MC, V. Daily 5–9pm. ITALIAN/STEAKS.

Bean soup is a greater starter, but this place has made a name for itself with its excellent prime rib and intimate fireside setting. Relax with refreshments on a spacious new patio before checking out the 20-ounce Cattlemen's Cut. Or you might want to sample the fresh salmon or the indescribable Chicken Wellington. The New York steak is among the best in the business.

Golden Phoenix

2421 W. Main St., Rapid City. ☎ **605/348-4195.** Lunch entrees $4.50–$4.75; dinner entrees $5–$9. AE, DC, DISC, MC, V. Daily 11am–10pm. CHINESE.

A relaxed atmosphere with great prices, quick service, and convenient parking make this a good choice in Rapid City. There is a wide selection of Chinese dishes, but it's hard to beat the Mongolian beef, the sesame chicken, or the Hunan shrimp.

IN ROCKERVILLE

The Gaslight Restaurant

Main St., Rockerville, 12 mi. south of Rapid City on U.S. 16. ☎ **605/343-9276.** Lunch entrees $4–$9; dinner entrees $7–$17. AE, DISC, MC, V. Summer daily 11am–10pm; other times of the year Wed–Sun 11am–9pm. STEAK/PASTA.

The Gaslight brings fun to family dining in a casual Old West saloon setting with an antique soda fountain, great steaks, a candy counter, and homemade ice cream. The hand-cut steaks are lean and tasty, and the restaurant also offers seafood and pasta dishes in a relaxed setting.

IN PIEDMONT

Elk Creek Steakhouse & Lounge

I-90 at Exit 46, north of Rapid City. ☎ **605/787-6349.** Dinner entrees $4.50–$29. AE, DISC, MC, V. Mon–Thurs 5–10pm, Fri–Sat 5–11pm, Sun 4:30–10pm. STEAKS.

Steak's the thing at Elk Creek, and its buffalo cuts are excellent. The special duchess potatoes are wonderful, and the chef's special—a rib eye served on an English muffin, topped with broccoli, mock crab, and a hollandaise-cheese sauce—is wicked. The lounge features a live band on Saturday night and homegrown country music talent Sunday afternoons.

NEAR HOT SPRINGS

Dakota Rose Restaurant

Jct. U.S. 18/385 and S. Dak. 79, 5 mi. southeast of Hot Springs. ☎ **605/745-6447.** Lunch entrees $4–$8; dinner entrees $5–$15. MC, V. Mon–Thurs 11am–9pm, Fri–Sat 11am–10pm, Sun 11am–3pm. AMERICAN.

Here you'll find family style dining, plus a soup-and-salad bar in a covered wagon. Chicken-fried steaks, prime rib, and homemade soups are the most popular dishes. There is a bar and lounge.

IN DEADWOOD

Deadwood Social Club

On the 2nd floor of Saloon No. 10, 657 Main St. ☎ **800/952-9398.** Reservations appreciated but not required. Lunch entrees $4–$7; dinner entrees $5.50–$14. AE, MC, V. Summer daily 11am–10pm; other times of the year Tues–Sun 11am–9pm. STEAKS/PASTA.

A warm atmosphere is made even cozier with light jazz and blues in the background, and one of South Dakota's largest wine selections in the cellar. Pasta dishes, such as the popular rigatoni con pollo, are exquisite. The tenderloin and rib eye are each served with grilled vegetables and roasted New England potatoes, then topped with a special demiglace. On the lighter side, Mother's Enchiladas are a favorite. After lunch or dinner, you can browse through the only museum in the world with a bar.

Jakes

Atop the Midnight Star, 677 Main St., Deadwood. ☎ **800/999-6482** or 605/578-3656. Reservations recommended. Dinner entrees $16–$29. AE, DC, DISC, MC, V. Summer Sun–Fri 5–10pm, Sat 5–11pm; other times of the year Sun–Thurs 5:30–9:30pm, Fri 5–10pm, Sat 5–11pm. NEW AMERICAN.

Before dining, browse handsomely displayed costumes worn by Kevin Costner in his feature films like *The Postman, Dances with Wolves,* and *Tin Cup.* Kevin and his brother Dan own the place, which features some of the most unique food in the region. Sample seasonal dishes including salmon, elk, chicken, duck, lamb, and buffalo. A different chef's feature item is part of the menu every night. Appetizers can range from escargot to buffalo carpaccio. There is also an excellent wine list.

7

BRYCE CANYON NATIONAL PARK & GRAND STAIRCASE – ESCALANTE NATIONAL MONUMENT

by Don and Barbara Laine

WELCOME TO A MAGICAL LAND, A PLACE OF INSPIRATION AND spectacular beauty where thousands of intricately shaped hoodoos stir the imagination as they stand together in silent watch.

Hoodoos, geologists tell us, are simply pinnacles of rock, often oddly shaped, left standing by the force of millions of years of water and wind erosion. But perhaps the truth really lies in a Paiute legend. These American Indians, who lived in the area for several hundred years before being forced out by Anglo pioneers, told of a "Legend People" who lived here in the old days; for their evil ways they were turned to stone by the powerful Coyote, and even today they remain frozen in time.

Whatever the cause, Bryce Canyon is unique. Its intricate and often whimsical formations are smaller and on a more human scale than the impressive rocks seen at Zion and Canyonlands national parks. And it's far easier to explore than the huge and sometimes intimidating Grand Canyon. Bryce is comfortable and inviting in its beauty; we feel we know it simply by gazing over the rim.

Although the colorful hoodoos grab your attention first, it isn't long before you notice the deep amphitheaters that enfold them, with their cliffs, windows, and arches—all colored in shades of red, brown, orange, yellow, and white—that change and glow with the rising and setting sun. Beyond the rocks and light are the other faces of the park: three separate life zones, each with its own unique vegetation, changing with elevation; and a kingdom of animals, from the busy chipmunks and ground squirrels to stately mule deer and their archenemy, the mountain lion.

Human exploration of the Bryce area likely began with the Paiutes, and it's possible that trappers, prospectors, and early Mormon scouts may have visited here in the early to mid-1800s, before Maj. John Wesley Powell conducted the first thorough survey of the region in the early 1870s. Shortly after Powell's exploration,

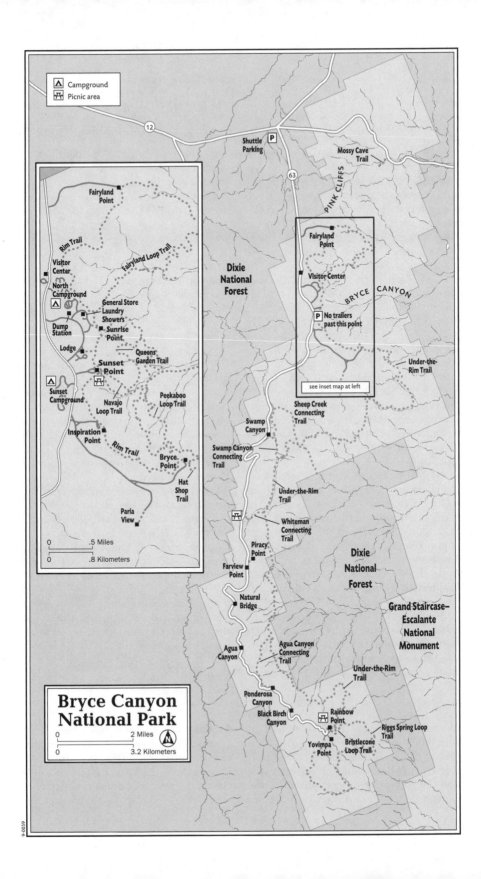

Bryce Canyon National Park

Campground
Picnic area

Fairyland Point
Rim Trail
Visitor Center
North Campground
General Store
Laundry
Showers
Dump Station
Sunrise Point
Lodge
Queens Garden Trail
Sunset Point
Fairyland Loop Trail
Sunset Campground
Navajo Loop Trail
Peekaboo Loop Trail
Inspiration Point
Rim Trail
Bryce Point
Hat Shop Trail
Paria View

0   .5 Miles
0   .8 Kilometers

12

Shuttle Parking
P

63

PINK CLIFFS

Mossy Cave Trail

Fairyland Point
Visitor Center
BRYCE CANYON
P No trailers past this point

Under-the-Rim Trail

see inset map at left

Dixie National Forest

Sheep Creek Connecting Trail

Swamp Canyon
Swamp Canyon Connecting Trail

Under-the-Rim Trail

Whiteman Connecting Trail

Piracy Point

Farview Point

Dixie National Forest

Natural Bridge

Grand Staircase–Escalante National Monument

Agua Canyon
Agua Canyon Connecting Trail

Under-the-Rim Trail

Ponderosa Canyon

Black Birch Canyon
Rainbow Point
Riggs Spring Loop Trail

Yovimpa Point
Bristlecone Loop Trail

Bryce Canyon National Park

0   2 Miles
0   3.2 Kilometers

9-0059

Tips from a Park Insider

"A lot of people think this is one of America's prettiest parks," says Dave Mecham, who has spent more than a dozen years at Bryce Canyon National Park working in a variety of capacities. "The hoodoos are what people come to see—that's what made Bryce famous—and it's the most popular thing."

"But living here, it's not my favorite aspect of the park," Mecham says. "I enjoy the long-distance views from the rim; that's what really inspires me." He adds, "Looking out from the rim of Bryce, across the hoodoos, it seems you can see forever. The atmospheric conditions are almost ideal, and you get the feeling that you're looking at a piece of America that's still pretty wild, and just hasn't changed much through time."

Bryce Amphitheater has the best scenery in the park, in Mecham's opinion.

"It's the place in the park where everything's coming together geologically to carve hoodoos at their best," he says. He particularly enjoys the **Rim Trail** that runs along the edge of the canyon, and highly recommends the section between Inspiration and Bryce points, with perhaps the very best view from **Upper Inspiration Point,** which is 300 to 400 yards south of Inspiration Point.

Mecham calls Bryce Canyon a "morning park," because the views are much better illuminated by early morning light than at any other time of day. He recommends spending at least 1 night at or near the park. "If you're spending the night close by, I think it would be a big mistake to miss sunrise."

Getting up early is also the best way to avoid crowds, according to Mecham, since most people don't get to the view points or out onto the trails until about 10am. The other way to avoid crowds is to walk away from them. Mecham says that you're likely to not see anyone at all on the park's two backcountry trails at the south end of the park, but avoiding crowds even in the park's most popular areas often takes only a short walk.

"Sunset Point is the busiest place in the park, especially in midsummer at midday," he says. "You finally get a parking spot, then walk out to a very crowded view point, where you're standing shoulder to shoulder—it's real hectic—but if you take a 5-minute walk south along the rim trail towards Inspiration Point, you'll leave the people immediately—they just cluster at those views."

Mecham says September and October are probably the best times to visit. "It's still busy," he says, "but less crowded on trails." However, if you really want to avoid people, you'll feel you have the park all to yourself if you visit midweek in the middle of the winter. "We plow the roads so people can drive to the view points and photograph the canyon with snow on it, and the people that ski or snowshoe will enjoy it the most," he says, adding, "Skiing is at its best in January and February, when it's really cold."

Mormon pioneer Ebenezer Bryce and his wife, Mary, moved to the area and tried raising cattle. Although they stayed only a few years, Bryce left behind his name and his oft-quoted description of the canyon as "a helluva place to lose a cow."

Avoiding the Crowds. Although Bryce Canyon receives only two-thirds the number of annual visitors that pour into nearby Zion National Park, Bryce can still be crowded, especially during its peak season from mid-June to mid-September, when the campgrounds are often full by 2pm. If you have to visit then, try to hike some of the lesser-used trails (ask rangers for recommendations), and get out onto the trails as soon after sunrise as possible.

A better time to visit, if your schedule allows, is spring or fall. If you don't mind a bit of cold and snow, the park is practically deserted in the winter—a typical January sees some 22,000 to 25,000 visitors, while in August there are well over 10 times that number—and the sight of bright red hoodoos capped with fresh white snow is something you won't soon forget.

Just the Facts

GETTING THERE & GATEWAYS

Situated in the mountains of southern Utah, the park is crossed from east to west by Utah 12, with the bulk of the park, including the visitor center, accessed by Utah 63, which turns south off Utah 12 into the main portions of the park. U.S. 89 runs north to south, west of the park, and Utah 12 heads east to Tropic and eventually Escalante.

From Salt Lake City, it's about 250 miles to the park. Take I-15 south about 200 miles to Exit 95, head east 13 miles on Utah 20, south on U.S. 89 for 17 miles to Utah 12, and east 17 miles to the park entrance road. The entrance station and visitor center are 3 miles south of Utah 12.

From St. George, about 135 miles southwest of the park, travel north on I-15 10 miles to Exit 16, then head east on Utah 9 for 63 miles to U.S. 89, north 44 miles to Utah 12, and east 17 miles to the park entrance road.

From Cedar City (I-15 exits 57, 59, and 62), about 80 miles west of the park, take Utah 14 west 41 miles to its intersection with U.S. 89 and follow that north 21 miles to Utah 12, then east 17 miles to the park entrance road.

A couple of other handy driving distances: Bryce is 83 miles east of Zion National Park, 160 miles north of the North Rim of the Grand Canyon, and 245 miles northeast of Las Vegas, Nevada.

The Nearest Airport. Bryce Canyon Airport (☎ 435/834-5239), several miles from the park entrance on Utah 12, has charter service from **Bryce Canyon Airlines** (☎ 435/834-5341) and car rentals from **Speedy** (☎ 435/834-5341) and **Bryce Canyon Car Rental** (☎ 800/432-5383 or 435/834-5200), which also has a desk in the lobby of **Ruby's Inn.**

You could also fly into St. George or Cedar City and rent a car at either of their airports.

INFORMATION

Contact **Superintendent, Bryce Canyon National Park,** P.O. Box 170001, Bryce Canyon, UT 84717 (☎ 435/834-5322; www.nps.gov/brca.). It's best to write at least a month before your planned visit, and ask for a copy of the national park newspaper *Hoodoo,* which contains a map of the park, plus information on hiking, weather, ranger-conducted activities, and current issues.

If you want more details, you can order books, maps, and videos from the nonprofit **Bryce Canyon Natural History Association,** Bryce Canyon, UT 84717 (☎ 888/362-2642). The association does not offer memberships, but does give a discount to current members of other national park natural history associations. A particularly useful book for serious hikers is *Hiking Zion & Bryce Canyon National Parks* (Helena, Mont.: Falcon Publishing Co., 1997) by Erik Molvar and Tamara Martin.

VISITOR CENTER

Located at the north end as you enter the park, the visitor center has exhibits on the geology and history of the area and presents a short introductory slide show. Rangers can answer your questions and provide backcountry permits. You can also pick up free brochures, and buy books, maps, videos, postcards, and posters. The visitor center is open daily year-round except Thanksgiving, Christmas, and New Year's days.

FEES & PERMITS

Entry into the park (for up to 7 days) costs $10 per family group or $5 per single person. In addition, from late spring through early fall, a mandatory $5 fee for shuttle use for each family unit will be charged, plus an additional $5 user fee for those who want to take their motor vehicles into the park. These extra user fees are not covered by the Golden Eagle, Access, or Age passports. Campsites cost $10 per night.

Permits, which cost $5 and are available at the visitor center daily until 8pm, are required for all overnight trips into the backcountry.

SPECIAL REGULATIONS & WARNINGS

While most visitors to Bryce Canyon enjoy an exciting vacation without serious mishap, accidents can occur. The most common injuries are sprained, twisted, and broken ankles. Park rangers strongly recommend that hikers, even those just out for short day hikes, wear sturdy hiking boots with good traction and ankle support.

Another concern in the park in recent years has been **bubonic plague,** which, contrary to popular belief, is treatable with antibiotics if caught early. The bacteria that causes bubonic plague has been found on fleas in prairie dog colonies in the park, so you should avoid contact with wild animals, especially prairie dogs, squirrels, and other rodents. Those taking pets into the park should dust them with flea powder. Avoiding contact with infected animals will greatly minimize the chances of contracting this holdover from the Dark Ages, but caution is still necessary. Symptoms, which generally

occur from 2 to 6 days after exposure, may include high fever, headache, vomiting, diarrhea, and swollen glands. Anyone showing these symptoms after visiting the park should get medical attention immediately—the plague can be fatal if not treated promptly.

Backcountry hikers should carry water; fires are not permitted.

SEASONS & CLIMATE

With elevations ranging from 6,000 to 9,000 feet, Bryce Canyon is cooler than southern Utah's other, lower elevation parks. From May through October, daytime temperatures are pleasant—usually from the low 60s to the upper 80s—while nights are cool, dropping into the 40s even at the height of summer. Afternoon thunderstorms are common in July and August. During winter, days are generally clear and crisp, with high temperatures often reaching the 40s, while nights are cold, usually in the single digits or teens, or even dipping well below zero. Snow is common in winter, but park staff plows the roads to the viewpoints.

SEASONAL EVENTS

In addition to the nightly campfire/ amphitheater programs, once each month astronomers from Hansen Planetarium in Salt Lake City present a **star-watching program.** Check at the visitor center for the current schedule.

If You Only Have 1 Day

It would be easy to spend a week in Bryce Canyon, starting with the visitor center, then moving along to the scenic drive, a few short walks, and then advancing to more serious hikes. But what makes this park so attractive is that there are ways to see a good deal of Bryce in a short amount of time.

Start at the **visitor center** and watch the short slide show that explains some of the area's geology. Then drive the 18-mile (each way) dead-end **park road,** stopping at view points to gaze down into the canyon (see "Exploring the Park by Car," below); visit the most popular view points on the **Bryce Canyon Shuttle;** or hop on the **Bryce Tours van** for a 2-hour guided tour, complete with lively commentary (see "Organized Tours & Ranger Programs," below).

Whichever way you choose to get around, make sure you spend at least a little time at **Inspiration Point,** which offers a splendid (and yes, inspirational) view into **Bryce Amphitheater** and its hundreds of statuesque pink, red, orange, and brown hoodoo stone sculptures. After seeing the canyon from the top down, it's time to get some exercise, so walk at least partway down the **Queen's Garden Trail.** If you can spare 3 hours, hike down the Navajo Loop and return to the rim via Queen's Garden Trail (see "Day Hikes," below). Those not willing or physically able to hike into the canyon can enjoy a leisurely walk along the **Rim Trail,** which provides spectacularly views down into the canyon, especially about an hour before sunset. That evening, try to take in the **campground amphitheater program.**

Exploring the Park by Car

The park's **18-mile scenic drive** (one way) follows the rim of Bryce Canyon, offering easy access to a variety of views into the fanciful fairyland of stone sculptures below. Trailers, not allowed on the road, must be left at several parking lots. Because all overlooks are on your left as you begin your drive, it's best to avoid crossing traffic by driving all the way to the end of the road and stopping at the overlooks on your return. Allow 1 to 2 hours.

After leaving the visitor center, drive the length of the 18-mile road to **Yovimpa and Rainbow Point overlooks,** which offer expansive views of southern Utah, Arizona, and sometimes even New Mexico. From these pink cliffs you can look down on a colorful platoon of stone soldiers, standing at eternal attention. A short loop trail from Rainbow Point leads to an **1,800-year-old bristlecone pine,** believed to be the oldest living thing at Bryce Canyon.

From here, drive back north to **Ponderosa Canyon Overlook,** where you can gaze down from a dense forest of spruce and fir at multicolored hoodoos, and then continue to **Agua Canyon Overlook,** with some of the best color contrasts in the park. Looking almost straight down, watch for a hoodoo known as **The Hunter,** with a hat of green trees.

Now continue on to **Natural Bridge,** actually an arch carved by rain and wind, spanning 85 feet. From here, continue to **Farview Point,** where there's a panoramic view to the distant horizon and the Kaibab Plateau at the Grand Canyon's North Rim. Next, pass through **Swamp Canyon,** and continue until you hit a turnoff from the main road on the right.

This turnoff leads to three viewpoints, the first of which is **Paria View,** looking off to the south of the White Cliffs, carved into light-colored sandstone by the Paria River. To the north of Paria View, you'll find **Bryce Point,** a splendid stop for seeing the awesome **Bryce Amphitheater,** the largest natural amphitheater in the park, as well as distant views of the Black Mountains to the northeast and Navajo Mountain to the south. From here it's just a short drive to **Inspiration Point,** which offers views similar to those at Bryce Point plus the best view in the park of the **Silent City,** a sleeping metropolis of stone.

Now return to the main road and head north to **Sunset Point,** where you can see practically all of Bryce Amphitheater, including the aptly named **Thor's Hammer** and the 200-foot-tall cliffs of **Wall Street.**

Continue north to a turnoff for your final stop at **Sunrise Point,** where there's an inspiring view into Bryce Amphitheater. This is the beginning of the **Queen's Garden Trail,** an excellent choice for even a quick walk below the canyon's rim.

Organized Tours & Ranger Programs

Park rangers present a variety of free programs and activities. **Evening programs,** which may include a slide show, take place most nights at campground amphitheaters. Topics vary, but could include such subjects as the animals and plants of the park, geology, and man's role in the park's early days. Rangers also give **half-hour talks** on similar subjects several times daily at various locations in the park, and lead **hikes and walks,** including a moonlight hike (reservations required) and a wheelchair-accessible 1-hour canyon rim walk. Schedules are posted on bulletin boards at the visitor center, general store, campgrounds, and Bryce Canyon Lodge.

Once or twice a week spring through fall, usually in the evening, a **talk** is given on the patio of Bryce Canyon Lodge. Topics include lodge history, the geology of the area, and discussion of some trails. These talks are free of charge. Check at the lodge for the current schedule.

Bryce Canyon Scenic Tours & Shuttles (☎ 800/432-5383; www.brycetours.com) offers 1½- to 2-hour tours year-round, leaving from Ruby's Inn just outside the park entrance. A general tour, stopping at several viewpoints, costs $24 for adults, $12 for children aged 5 to 15, and free for those under 5. The sunrise/sunset tours cost $26. Combination and other specialized tours can be arranged.

Getting a Bird's-Eye View of the Park. For an unforgettable view of the canyon and its numerous formations, contact **Bryce Canyon Helicopter Scenic Flights** (ask for the flight desk at Ruby's Inn, ☎ 435/834-5341). Tours last from less than 20 minutes to more than an hour, and the longer trips include surrounding attractions. Prices range from $55 to $225, and passengers weighing less than 100 pounds are charged half. Go in the morning for the clearest air and best lighting, and try to make reservations a day ahead.

Historic & Man-Made Attractions

Although early Indians and 19th-century pioneers spent some time in what is now Bryce Canyon National Park, they left little evidence. The park's main historic site is the handsome sandstone and ponderosa pine **Bryce Canyon Lodge,** built by the Union Pacific Railroad and opened in 1924. Much of it has been faithfully restored to its 1920s appearance.

Day Hikes

One of the wonderful things about Bryce Canyon is that you don't have to be an advanced backpacker to really get to know the park.

All trails below the rim have at least some steep grades, so you should wear hiking boots with a traction tread and good ankle support to avoid ankle injuries, the most common accidents in the park. During the hot summer months you'll want to hike either early or late in the day, always keeping in mind that it gets hotter the deeper you go into the canyon. Bryce's rangers do not rate hiking trails as to their difficulty, saying that what is easy for one person may be difficult for another. Ratings here are provided by the authors and other experienced hikers, and are entirely subjective.

SHORTER TRAILS

Bristlecone Loop

1 mi. RT. Easy. Access: Rainbow Point parking area at the end of the scenic drive.

An easy walk entirely above the canyon rim, the trail traverses a subalpine fir forest. Here you'll find more Bristlecone pines than along the other park trails. It takes just ³/₄ to 1 hour to complete the loop, which has an elevation change of 100 feet.

Hat Shop Trail

3.8 mi. RT. Strenuous. Access: Bryce Point Overlook.

This is a strenuous hike with a 900-foot elevation change. Leaving the rim, you'll drop quickly to the Hat Shop, so-named because it consists of hard gray "hats" perched on narrow reddish brown pedestals. The trail offers close-up views of gnarled ponderosa pine and Douglas fir, as well as distant panoramas across the Aquarius Plateau toward the Grand Staircase–Escalante National Monument. This trail is also the beginning of the Under the Rim Trail (see "Exploring the Backcountry," below).

Mossy Cave Trail

0.8 mi. RT. Easy. Access: Along Utah 12, about 3.5 mi. east of the highway's intersection with Utah 63.

This often-overlooked trail located outside the main part of the park offers an easy and picturesque 45-minute walk. The trail follows an old irrigation ditch up a short hill to a shallow cave, where seeping water nurtures the cave's moss. Just off the trail you'll also see a small waterfall. Elevation gain is 150 feet. Hikers will usually get their feet wet, and should be careful when crossing the ditch.

Navajo Loop Trail

1.4 mi. RT. Moderate. Access: Trailhead sign-post at the central overlook point at Sunset Point.

This trail descends from the rim 521 feet to the bottom of the canyon floor and back up again, and is considered moderately strenuous. It crosses graveled switchbacks and affords terrific views of several impressive formations.

A great choice for getting down into the canyon and seeing the most with the least amount of sweat is to combine Navajo Loop with the **Queen's Garden Trail** (see below). The total distance is just under 3 miles, with a 521-foot

elevation change. Most hikers take 2 to 3 hours. It's best to start at the Navajo Loop Trailhead at Sunset Point and leave the canyon on the less steep Queen's Garden Trail, returning to the rim at Sunrise Point, 0.5 mile to the north. Along the Navajo Loop section you'll pass Thor's Hammer (why hasn't it fallen?), view the awesome Twin Bridges, and gaze at the towering skyscrapers of Wall Street. Turning onto the Queen's Garden Trail, you'll see some of the park's most fanciful formations, including majestic Queen Victoria herself, for whom the trail was named, as well as the Queen's Castle and Gulliver's Castle.

Queen's Garden Trail

0.9 mi. one way. Easy to moderate. Access: South side of Sunrise Point.

This short, moderately easy trail takes you down into Bryce Amphitheater, with rest benches near the formation called Queen Victoria. It drops 320 feet below the rim. Combining the Queen's Garden Trail with the Navajo Loop Trail (see above) is a great way to see some magnificent hoodoos.

LONGER TRAILS

Fairyland Loop

8 mi. RT. Strenuous. Access: Fairyland Point Overlook, off the park access road north of the visitor center; also accessible from Sunrise Point.

From Fairyland Point this strenuous but little-traveled trail descends into Fairyland Canyon, then meanders up, down, and around Boat Mesa, crosses Campbell Canyon, passes Tower Bridge junction—a short 200-yard side trail takes you to the base of Tower Bridge—and begins a steady climb to the Chinese Wall. About halfway along the wall, the trail begins the serious ascent back to the top of the canyon, finally reaching it near Sunrise Point. To complete the loop follow the Rim Trail back through juniper, manzanita, and Douglas fir to Fairyland Point. The loop has an elevation change of 900 feet.

Peekaboo Loop

6.8 mi. RT. Strenuous. Access: Bryce Point Overlook parking area.

Open to hikers, mules, and horses, the Peekaboo Loop winds among hoodoos below Bryce and Inspiration points and has an elevation change of 800 feet. There are several fairly steep inclines and descents, but the views make all the effort worthwhile. You can see far to the east beyond Bryce Canyon toward the Aquarius Plateau, Canaan Mountain, and the Kaiparowits Plateau; or enjoy the closer prospect of the Wall of Windows, the Three Wisemen, the Organ, or the Cathedral. Various connecting trails make Peekaboo easily adaptable. However, be aware that horse use is heavy from spring to fall, and hikers should step aside as horseback riders pass them on the trail.

Rim Trail

5.5 mi. one way. Easy to moderate. Access: North trailhead is at Fairyland Point, south trailhead is at Bryce Point; also accessible from Sunrise, Sunset, and Inspiration points, and numerous other locations in between.

The Rim Trail, which does not drop into the canyon but offers splendid views from above, meanders along the rim for more than 5 miles, with a total elevation change of 550 feet. It includes a 0.5-mile section between two overlooks—Sunrise and Sunset—that is suitable for wheelchairs. Overlooking Bryce Amphitheater, the trail offers excellent views almost everywhere and is a good choice for an early morning or evening walk, when you can watch the changing light on the rosy rocks below.

Sheep Creek Trail

3–5 mi. one way. Easy to moderate. Access: Trailhead sign and parking area 5 mi. south of the visitor center.

This trail takes you down into the canyon bottom, and if you try the extension, right out of the park into the Dixie National Forest. The first mile is on the rim, but then the trail descends the Sheep Creek draw below pink limestone cliffs toward the canyon bottom, traversing part of the Under the Rim Trail along its way. Watch signs carefully; the route can be confusing. The trail has up to a 1,250-foot elevation change.

Exploring the Backcountry

For die-hard hikers who don't mind rough terrain, Bryce has two backcountry trails, usually open in the summer only. The truly ambitious can combine the two trails for a weeklong excursion. Permits, which cost $5 and are available at the visitor center, are required for all overnight trips into the backcountry.

Riggs Spring Loop

8.8-mi. loop. Moderate to strenuous. Access: South side of parking area for Rainbow Point.

This hike can be completed in 4 or 5 hours, or can be more comfortably done as a relaxing overnight backpacking trip. The trail goes through a deep forest, but also provides breath-taking views of the huge Pink Cliffs at the southern end of the plateau. It has an elevation change of 1,675 feet.

Under the Rim Trail

22.6 mi. one way. Moderate. Access: East side of the parking area for Bryce Point Overlook.

This moderately strenuous trail runs between Bryce and Rainbow points, and offers the full spectrum of views of Bryce Canyon's scenery. Since the trail runs below the rim, it is full of steep inclines and descents, with an overall elevation change of 1,500 feet. Allow 2 to 3 days to hike the entire length. There are five camping areas along the trail, plus a group camp area.

Other Summer Sports & Activities

Biking & Mountain Biking. Bikes are permitted only on the park's established roads, which are generally narrow, winding, and crowded with motor vehicles during the summer. However, there are mountain biking opportunities just outside the park in the Dixie National Forest. For information, stop at the national forest's **Red Canyon Visitor Center** (usually open from early May through mid-October) along Utah 12 about 10.5 miles west of the Bryce Canyon National Park entrance road (☎ **435/676-2676**); or contact the **Dixie National Forest,** 82 North 100 E., Cedar City, UT 84720 (☎ **435/865-3700**).

Mountain bikes can be rented across the street from **Ruby's Inn** (☎ **435/834-5341**) for $5 an hour, $15 for up to 4 hours, or $25 for a full day. They also do repairs.

Horseback Riding. To see Bryce Canyon the way early pioneers did, you need to look down from a horse or a mule. **Canyon Trail Rides,** P.O. Box 128, Tropic, UT 84776 (☎ **435/679-8665;** fax 435/679-8709; www.onpages.com/canyonrides), offers a close-up view of Bryce's spectacular rock formations from the relative comfort of a saddle, and welcomes first-time riders. They have a desk inside Bryce Lodge. A 2-hour ride to the canyon floor and back costs $26.50, including tax, per person, and a half-day trip farther into the canyon costs $40 per person. Rides are offered, weather permitting, from April through November.

Guided rides are also provided by **Ruby's Scenic Rim and Outlaw Trail Rides** (☎ **800/679-5859** or 435/834-5280), at Ruby's Inn, at similar rates; in addition, Ruby's offers a full-day ride with lunch for $75. There are age and weight limits, and reservations are recommended for both companies. Ruby's will also board your horse, starting at $8 per day.

Wildlife Watching. The park has a variety of wildlife, ranging from mule deer, which seem to be almost everywhere, to the often seen golden-mantled ground squirrel and Uinta chipmunk. Also in the park are black-tailed jackrabbits, coyotes, striped skunks, and deer mice. Occasionally visitors catch a glimpse of a mountain lion, most likely on the prowl in search of a mule deer dinner; elk and pronghorn may also be seen at higher elevations.

The Utah prairie dog, now listed as a threatened species, is actually a rodent. It inhabits park meadows in busy colonies, and can be fascinating to watch. However, be sure to keep your distance, because its fleas may carry disease (see "Special Regulations & Warnings," earlier in this chapter).

Of the many birds in the park, you're bound to hear the rather obnoxious call of the Steller's jay. Other birds often seen include violet-green swallows, common ravens, Clark's nutcrackers, American robins, red-shafted flickers, dark-eyes juncos, and chipping sparrows. Watch for white-throated swifts as they perform their exotic acrobatics along cliff faces. The park is also home, at least part of the year, to peregrine falcons, red-tailed hawks, golden eagles, bald eagles, and great horned owls.

The Great Basin rattlesnake, although pretty, should be given a wide berth. Sometimes growing to more than 5 feet long, this rattler is the park's only poisonous reptile. Fortunately, like most rattlesnakes, it is just as anxious as you are to avoid a confrontation. Other reptiles you may see in the park are the mountain short-horned lizard, the tree lizard, the side-blotched lizard, and the northern sagebrush lizard.

Winter Sports & Activities

Bryce is beautiful in the winter, when the white snow settles over the red, pink, orange, and brown statues standing proudly against the cold winds.

Snowshoes may be used anywhere in the park except on cross-country ski tracks. **Cross-country skiers,** meanwhile, will find several marked, ungroomed trails (all above the rim), including **The Fairyland Trail,** which leads 1 mile through a pine and juniper forest to the Fairyland Point Overlook. From here you can take the 1-mile **Forest Trail** back to the road, or continue north along the rim for another 1.2 miles to the park boundary. There are also connections to ski trails in the adjacent national forest.

Although the entire park is open to cross-country skiers, rangers warn that it's impossible to ski the steep trails leading down into the canyon. Stop at the visitor center for additional trail information, and go to **Ruby's Inn,** just north of the park entrance (☎ 435/834-5341), for information on cross-country ski trails and snowmobiling opportunities outside the park. Ruby's grooms over 50 kilometers of ski trails, and also rents cross-country ski equipment. Prices start at $7.

Camping

INSIDE THE PARK

Typical of the West's national park campgrounds, the two facilities at Bryce offer plenty of trees with a genuine "forest camping" experience and easy access to trails, but limited facilities. **North**

Campground is closer to the Rim Trail, making it easier to rush over to catch those amazing sunrise and sunset colors, but we wouldn't turn down a site at **Sunset Campground.** Try to get to the park early to claim a site (usually by 2pm in the summer). Showers ($2) are located at a general store in the park, although it's a healthy walk from either campground. The Park Service also operates an RV dump station ($2 fee) in the summer.

The general store near the Sunrise Point parking area has a coin-operated laundry and a snack bar, plus bundles of firewood, food and camping supplies, and souvenirs. There are tables on a covered porch along one side of the building.

NEAR THE PARK

Just outside the park is **Ruby's Inn RV Park & Campground,** Utah 63 (P.O. Box 22), Bryce, UT 84764 (☎ 435/834-5301 or 435/834-5341; fax 435/834-5481; www.rubysinn.com; credit cards accepted), along the park's shuttle route. It has shaded campsites, an adjacent lake and horse pasture, a swimming pool, game room, horseshoes, and a store with groceries and RV supplies.

Bryce Pioneer Village, 80 S. Main St. (Utah 12) (P.O. Box 119), Tropic, UT 84776 (☎ 800/222-0381 or 435/

Campground	Elev.	Total Sites	RV Hookups	Dump Station	Toilets	Drinking Water
North	7,700	105	No	No	Yes	Yes
Sunset	8,000	111	No	No	Yes	Yes
Bryce Pioneer Village	7,600	15	15	Yes	Yes	Yes
King's Creek (USFS)	8,000	34	No	Yes	Yes	Yes
Red Canyon (USFS)	7,400	36	No	Yes	Yes	Yes
Ruby's Inn RV Park	7,600	227	127	Yes	Yes	Yes
Kodachrome Basin SP	5,800	24	No	Yes	Yes	Yes

679-8546; fax 435/679-8607; www. bpvillage.com; credit cards accepted), is a small motel/cabins/campground combination in nearby Tropic, with easy access to several restaurants. Showers are available to noncampers for $2, and there's a dump station charging $3.

King's Creek Campground, in the Dixie National Forest (mailing address: 82 N. 100 E., Cedar City, UT 84720; ☎ 435/865-3700) is located above Tropic Reservoir, with graded gravel roads and sites nestled among tall ponderosa pines. The reservoir has two boat ramps and good trout fishing. From the park, head west on Utah 12 about 2.5 miles to the access road, turn south (left) and follow signs to Tropic Reservoir for about 7 miles to the campground.

About 9.5 miles west of the park is another Dixie National Forest campground, **Red Canyon Campground** (contact the Dixie National Forest, 82 N. 100 E., Cedar City, UT 84720; ☎ 435/865-3700, or direct to the campground 435/676-8608). Set among the trees along the south side of Utah 12, it offers terrific views of the red rock formations across the highway, although there is a bit of road noise.

Kodachrome Basin State Park, about 22 miles southeast of Bryce park, has an attractive campground with sites scattered among unusual rock "chimneys" and piñon and juniper trees.

Accommodations

INSIDE THE PARK

Bryce Canyon Lodge

Bryce Canyon National Park, UT. ☎ 435/834-5361. Information and reservations: AmFac Parks & Resorts, 14001 E. Iliff Ave., Suite 600, Aurora, CO 80014. ☎ 303/297-2757. Fax 303/338-2045. www.amfac.com. 114 units in motel rms and cabins; 3 suites and 1 studio in lodge. TEL. $85–$95 motel double; $95–$105 cabin; $119–$129 lodge unit. AE, DISC, MC, V. Closed Nov–Mar.

This is the perfect place to stay while exploring Bryce Canyon National Park, allowing you to watch the play of changing light on the rock formations throughout the day. The handsome sandstone and ponderosa pine lodge, which opened in 1924, contains desks in the lobby for horseback riding and other activities, and a gift shop that offers everything from postcards and souvenirs to a fine selection of Indian pawn jewelry. The luxurious lodge suites are wonderful, with white wicker furniture, ceiling fans, and separate sitting rooms. The guest units, on the other hand, are simply pleasant, modern motel rooms, with two queen-size beds and either a balcony or a patio. The best choice is one of the cabins. They're not large, but have two double beds, high ceilings, stone

Showers	Fire Pits/ Grills	Laundry	Public Phone	Reserve	Fees	Open
No	Yes	No	No	No	$10	Year-round
No	Yes	No	No	No	$10	May–Sept
Yes	Yes	No	Yes	Yes	$10–$15	Mid-Apr to Oct
No	Yes	No	No	No	$8	Memorial Day–Labor Day
Yes	Yes	No	No	No	$9	Apr–Oct
Yes	Yes	Yes	Yes	Yes	$14–$23	Apr–Oct
No	Yes	No	Yes	Yes	$13	Year-round

(gas-burning) fireplaces, and log beams—you might call the ambience "rustic luxury." There is no swimming pool. Try to reserve 4 to 6 months in advance.

NEAR THE PARK

Best Western Ruby's Inn

Utah 63 at the entrance to Bryce Canyon (P.O. Box 1), Bryce, UT 84764. ☎ **800/528-1234** or 435/834-5341. Fax 435/834-5265. www. rubysinn.com. 371 units, including 2 suites. A/C TV TEL. June–Sept $90–$115 double; $120–$130 suite. Apr–May and Oct $63–$95 double; $100–$120 suite. Nov–Mar $46–$73 double; $83–85 suite. AE, CB, DC, DISC, MC, V. Pets accepted.

This large Best Western provides most of the beds for tired hikers and canyon gazers visiting the park. The lobby is among the busiest places in the area, with an ATM, a small liquor store, car rentals, a beauty salon, a 1-hour film processor, and tour desks where you can arrange excursions of all sorts, from horseback and all-terrain vehicle rides to helicopter tours. Near the lobby is a restaurant; a Western art gallery; a huge general store that sells souvenirs, cowboy hats, camping supplies, and groceries; and a U.S. post office. Outside there are two gas stations.

Spread among nine separate buildings, the modern motel rooms contain art depicting scenes of the area, wood furnishings, and shower/tub combos. Some even have whirlpools. Services include a concierge and courtesy transportation from the Bryce Airport; facilities include two indoor pools, one indoor and one outdoor whirlpool, a sundeck, bike rental, nature and cross-country ski trails, a game room, and two coin-operated laundries.

Bryce Canyon Resorts

13500 E. Utah 12 (P.O. Box 640006), Bryce, UT 84764. ☎ **800/834-0043** or 435/834-5351. Fax 435/834-5256. 50 units. A/C TV TEL. Summer $69–$85 double; lower rates at other times. DISC, MC, V. Pets accepted for a fee plus deposit.

This complex, which includes a motel, restaurant, and campground, is located adjacent to the main parking area for the new Bryce Canyon shuttle at the intersection of Utah 12 and Utah 63. Under new ownership in 1999, a massive renovation was underway during our visit, but from what had already been completed it appeared that this will be a very attractive property, and a somewhat elegant change-of-pace from the Western and Southwestern decor found in most other area lodgings.

Rooms are Victorian, with drapes and bed coverings in royal purples and reds, and solid wood furniture stained a rich mahogany. Each of the spacious rooms contains one king or two queen-size beds, a table with two upholstered chairs, two sinks, a shower-tub combo, a TV in an armoire, an ample closet, and better-than-average lighting. There are two suites (one with a fireplace) and an indoor pool and sauna.

Bryce Country Cabins

320 N. Utah 12 (P.O. Box 141), Tropic, UT 84776. ☎ **888/679-8643** or 435/679-8643. Fax 435/679-8989. www.brycecountrycabins. com. 8 units. A/C TV. Summer $65–$75 double; lower rates rest of year. DC, MC, V.

There are six new log-style cabins and a two-room pioneer cottage on this 20-acre farm. The grounds surrounding the cabins and cottage are nicely landscaped, and you get views out over the national park. But the intriguing part is the farm behind the buildings, where cattle graze in the fields and the chickens think they own the place.

The comfortable cabins have knotty pine walls and ceilings, exposed beams, and ceiling fans. Each has two queen-size beds, a table with two chairs, a coffeemaker, and a private porch. Bathrooms have showers only. The cottage, built in 1905, has two spacious rooms with country-style decor, each with its own entrance. Both have shower/tub combos; one room has a king-size bed while the other has two queens. The two rooms can be rented together or individually. Room telephones for both the cottage and the cabins were planned for 2000.

Bryce Pioneer Village

80 S. Main St. (Utah 12; P.O. Box 119), Tropic, UT 84776. ☎ **800/222-0381** or 435/679-8546. Fax 435/679-8607. www.bpvillage.com. E-mail: info@bpvillage.com. 69 units. A/C TV TEL. $60–$85 double; $39–$85 cabins. DISC, MC, V. Pets accepted.

This is a good choice for those seeking a comfortable night's rest at a reasonable rate. The small, no-frills motel rooms in a modular building have showers only, but they're clean, comfortable, and have walk-in closets. Cabins, which were relocated from inside the national park, are more interesting. Most are small but cute, with one queen bed plus a twin bed, a chair, and a small bathroom with a corner shower but no tub. Several others, which have been renovated within the past few years, are much larger, with two queen beds and average-size bathrooms with shower/tub combinations. There are also two rooms with three queen beds each. There's an indoor heated swimming pool, whirlpool, two hot tubs, a picnic area, and a small curio shop. Just outside the motel office you can see the cabin where Ebenezer and Mary Bryce, for whom the national park is named, lived in the late 1870s.

Bryce Point Bed & Breakfast

61 N. 400 W. (P.O. Box 96), Tropic, UT 84776-0096. ☎ **435/679-8629.** 6 units. TV. $70 double; $90–$120 honeymoon cottage. Rates include full breakfast. MC, V.

Each room in Lamar and Ethel LeFevre's bed-and-breakfast is named for and decorated in the style of one of the couple's children. For instance, son Les is a firefighter, so the Les and Dela room contains fire-fighting memorabilia and photos; son Lynn is in the airline industry, so

you'll find airplane mementos in Lynn and Karen's room. In addition to memorabilia, most rooms offer beautiful views of Bryce Point through large picture windows. All rooms have queen beds and private bathrooms (showers only), TV/VCR combos, and free use of the LeFevre's video collection. The honeymoon cottage is beautifully furnished in country style, with a gas fireplace in the living room, full kitchen, washer and dryer, and king bed in the spacious bedroom. All guests have use of the enclosed hot tub. Breakfasts are full and satisfying. The B&B is entirely no-smoking.

Bryce View Lodge

Utah 63 across from Best Western Ruby's Inn (P.O. Box 64002), Bryce, UT 84764. ☎ **888/ 279-2304** or 435/834-5180. Fax 435/ 834-5181. www.bryceviewlodge.com. 160 units. A/C TV TEL. $44–$55 double. AE, CB, DC, DISC, MC, V. Pets accepted.

This basic modern American motel consists of four two-story buildings set back from the road. Rooms are simple but comfortable, with an occasional western touch, and are quite quiet. All have the vanity outside the toilet and tub/shower room; most have one or two double beds, some have a queen; plus a table and two chairs. Guests have access to the amenities across the street at Ruby's (see above).

Canyon Livery Bed & Breakfast

50 S. 660 W. (P.O. Box 24), Tropic, UT 84776-0024. ☎ **888/889-8910** or 435/679-8780; call for fax. www.canyonlivery.com. E-mail: tclbnb@color-country.net. 5 units. A/C. Apr–Oct $75–$95 double; Nov–Mar $65–$75 double. Rates include full breakfast. MC, V.

The simply decorated rooms in this delightful bed-and-breakfast have beautiful handmade quilts on the queen beds. Two are dedicated to women pioneers and have brass beds, two have handmade wooden beds and are dedicated to male pioneers, and the fifth is Western, with a wonderful high arched window providing terrific views of the night sky. Breakfasts include a hot dish, homemade breads, and fresh fruits (often from the B&B's own trees). All rooms have windows facing the national park, and the three upstairs rooms have private balconies. Each has its own entrance, and there is a corral if you happen to bring your horse. Smoking is not permitted.

Foster's

Utah 12 (mailing address: Star Route, Panguitch, UT 84759), Bryce, UT. ☎ **800/475-4318** or 435/834-5227. Fax 435/834-5304. E-mail: fosters@color-country.net. 52 units. A/C TV TEL. Winter $50 double; summer $60 double. AE, DISC, MC, V.

You'll find clean, quiet, and economical lodging at Foster's, located 1.5 miles west of the Bryce Canyon National Park access road turnoff. Also on the grounds is a restaurant (see "Dining," below) and a grocery store (open 7am to 8pm, closed December and January) with a decent bakery. The small rooms in this modular unit are decorated with posters showing scenery of the area and contain either one queen-size or two double beds. Bathrooms have showers only.

World Host Bryce Valley Inn

200 N. Main St., Tropic, UT 84776. ☎ **800/442-1890** or 435/679-8811. Fax 435/679-8846. www.brycevalleyinn.com. E-mail: bvi@color-country.net. 65 units. A/C TV TEL. Apr–Oct $60–$75 double; Nov–Mar $30–$45 double. AE, DISC, MC, V. Pets accepted for a fee.

Located 8 miles east of the park entrance road, these basic motel rooms are a clean, economical choice. Rooms, all of which have shower/tub combos, are furnished with either one or two queen beds. There's one suite with two queens and a hide-a-bed, and one handicapped-accessible room. The motel has an outdoor whirlpool tub and a 24-hour coin-operated laundry. The Hungry Coyote Restaurant & Saloon (see "Dining,"

below) serves basic American grub, and a gift shop offers a large selection of American Indian arts and crafts, handmade gifts, rocks, and fossils.

Dining

INSIDE THE PARK

Bryce Canyon Lodge

Bryce Canyon National Park. ☎ **435/834-5361.** Reservations required for dinner. Breakfast $3.75–$6.25; lunch $4.95–$8.95; dinner $11.50–$19.95. AE, DC, DISC, MC, V. Daily 6:30am–4:30pm and 5:30–9:30pm. Closed Nov–Mar. AMERICAN.

It's worth coming here just for the delightful mountain lodge atmosphere, with two large stone fireplaces, American Indian weavings and baskets, a huge 45-star 1897 American flag, and large windows looking out on the park. But the food's good, too, and reasonably priced considering that this is the only real restaurant actually in the park. House specialties at dinner include an excellent slow-roasted prime rib au jus and broiled chicken breast. We also recommend the fresh mountain trout. Vegetarians should try the black bean stuffed pepper or the vegetarian lasagna. Afterwards, ask about the lodge's specialty desserts, such as the exotic and very tasty wild "Bryceberry" crumb cake. At lunch you'll find the trout, plus burgers, sandwiches, and salads; breakfasts offer all the usual American selections. Service is attentive and friendly. The restaurant will pack lunches to go for hikers, and offers full liquor service.

NEAR THE PARK

Bryce Canyon Pines

Utah 12 (3 mi. west of intersection with park entrance rd.). ☎ **435/834-5441.** Sandwiches $3.75–$6.95; full dinners $9.95–$16.50. AE, CB, DC, DISC, MC, V. Daily 6:30am–10pm (may close slightly earlier in spring and fall). Closed Dec–Feb. AMERICAN.

A country cottage-style dining room, with an old wood stove and white eyelet-trimmed curtains, is a good setting for the wholesome American food served here. Especially popular for its traditional breakfasts, the restaurant is also known for its homemade soups and pies. Both sandwiches and full dinners are available at lunch and dinner. Recommended are the hot sandwiches, the Utah trout, and the 8-ounce tenderloin steak. Beer and wine are available.

Canyon Diner

Just north of the park entrance on Utah 63, in the Ruby's Inn complex, Bryce Canyon. ☎ 435/834-5341. Breakfast, lunch, and dinner items $2–$7.90. AE, DISC, MC, V. Daily 6:30am–10pm. AMERICAN.

This fast-food restaurant adjacent to the Best Western Ruby's Inn is a great place to fill up the kids without going broke. Breakfasts include several egg croissants; for lunch and dinner you can get hoagies, burgers, hot dogs, stuffed potatoes, pizza, fried chicken, and salads. Specialties include the mesquite-smoked half-chicken and a fish-and-chips basket. No alcohol is served.

Foster's Family Steak House

Utah 12 about 1.5 mi. west of the park entrance rd. ☎ 435/834-5227. Reservations not accepted. Breakfast and lunch items $1.75–$6; main dinner courses $9–$19. AE, DISC, MC, V. Mar–Nov daily 7am–10pm; Dec–Feb daily 5–10pm. STEAK/SEAFOOD.

The simple Western decor here provides the appropriate atmosphere for a family steak house, popular for its slow-roasted prime rib and steamed Utah trout. Foster's also offers several steaks (including a 14-ounce T-bone), sandwiches, a soup of the day, and homemade western-style chili with beans. All the pastries, pies, and breads are baked on the premises. Bottled beer is available.

Hungry Coyote Restaurant & Saloon

199 N. Main St. (Utah 12; 8 mi. east of the park entrance rd.), at the World Host Bryce Valley Inn, Tropic. ☎ 435/679-8822. Main breakfast courses $3.95–$6.95; dinner $6–$21. AE, DISC, MC, V. Daily 6–11am and 5–11pm; shorter hrs. in winter. AMERICAN.

The Old West is still king here; look around at the rough wood walls, old ranch tools, kerosene lanterns, and warnings that patrons must "check your gun with the waitress." Beef eaters will savor the thick 20-ounce T-bone, the most expensive item on the menu. You can also get pork chops, grilled chicken breast, or trout. The restaurant has full liquor service as well.

Ruby's Inn Cowboy's Buffet and Steak Room

Ruby's Inn complex, Bryce. ☎ 435/834-5341. Breakfast buffet $7.50 adults, $6 children 3–12; lunch buffet $8.50 adults, $7 children 3–12; main courses breakfast and lunch $3–$13.50; dinner buffet $14.50 adults, $7 children 3–12; main dinner courses $5.50–$19.50. AE, CB, DC, DISC, MC, V. Summer daily 6:30am–9:30pm; winter daily 6:30am–8:30pm. STEAK/SEAFOOD.

The busiest restaurant in the Bryce Canyon area, Ruby's moves 'em through with buffets at every meal plus a well-rounded menu and friendly service. The breakfast buffet offers more choices than the usual family restaurant buffet, with scrambled eggs, fresh fruit, several breakfast meats, potatoes, pastries, and cereals; and as part of the buffet you can also get omelets and eggs cooked to order. The lunch buffet offers country-style ribs, fresh fruit, salads, soups, vegetables, and breads. The dinner buffet features slow-roasted beef and other meats, pastas, potatoes, and salads. Regular menu dinner entrees include prime rib, southern Utah rainbow trout, broiled chicken breast, burgers, and salads. Full liquor service is available.

Picnic & Camping Supplies

A small store inside the national park has groceries and camping supplies, plus snacks, and all at surprisingly low prices. Just outside the park, the huge general store in Ruby's Inn (see "Accommodations," above) offers camping supplies, groceries, Western clothing, and souvenirs.

Nearby Attractions

For other diversions, the **Best Western Ruby's Inn** (☎ 435/834-5341), on Utah 63 just north of the Bryce Canyon National Park entrance (see "Accommodations," above), is practically a one-stop entertainment center.

Directly across Utah 63 from the motel are **Old Bryce Town Shops,** open from mid-May to September, where you'll find a rock shop, souvenir shops, a Christmas store, and an opportunity to buy that genuine cowboy hat you've been wanting. Next to the shops is a children's petting farm (free admission), with performing horses and a cowboy poet; you can also try your hand at gold-panning ($4 pan rental).

Nearby, **Bryce Canyon Country Rodeo** has bucking broncos, bull riding, calf roping, and all sorts of rodeo fun in a 1-hour program from Memorial Day to August, Monday to Saturday evenings at 7:30pm. Admission is $7 for adults and $4 for children under 12.

Grand Staircase–Escalante National Monument

Covering almost 2 million acres, this vast area of red-orange canyons, mesas, plateaus, and river valleys became a national monument by presidential proclamation in 1996. Known for its rugged beauty, it contains a combination of geological, biological, paleontological, archaeological, and historical resources. In announcing the creation of the monument, President Clinton proclaimed, "This high, rugged, and remote region was the last place in the continental United States to be mapped; even today, this unspoiled natural area remains a frontier, a quality that greatly enhances the monument's value for scientific study."

Unlike most other national monuments, almost all of this vast area is undeveloped—there are few all-weather roads, only one maintained hiking trail, and two small campgrounds. But for the adventurous there are miles upon miles of dirt roads and practically unlimited opportunities for hiking, horseback riding, mountain biking, and camping.

The national monument can be divided into three distinct sections: The Grand Staircase of sandstone cliffs—including five life zones from Sonoran Desert to coniferous forests—is the southwest section; the Kaiparowits Plateau, a vast, wild region of rugged mesas and steep canyons, is the center section; and the Escalante River Canyons, a delightfully scenic area containing miles of interconnecting river canyons, is the northern section.

JUST THE FACTS

Getting There. The national monument takes in a large region of southern Utah, covering an area almost as big as the states of Delaware and Rhode Island combined. Bryce Canyon National Park is to the west; Capitol Reef National Park is on the northeast edge; and Glen Canyon National Recreation Area lies along the east and part of the south sides.

Access is via Utah 12 along the monument's northwest edge, from Kodachrome Basin State Park and the communities of Escalante and Boulder; and via U.S. 89 to the southern section of the monument, east of the town of Kanab.

Information & Visitor Centers. Contact the **Escalante Interagency Office** on the west side of Escalante at 755 W. Main St. (Utah 12), P.O. Box 246, Escalante, UT 84726 (☎ **435/826-5499**); or the **Bureau of Land Management/Monument Office** at 318 N. 100 East St., Kanab, UT 84741 (☎ **435/644-2672**). Information is also available on the web at www.ut.blm.gov/monument.

Fees, Regulations & Safety. There is no charge to enter most of the monument; those planning overnight trips into the backcountry should obtain permits (free at press time) at either of the offices listed above. **Calf Creek Recreation Area** charges $2 for day use and $7 for camping. Regulations are similar to those on other public lands, and particularly forbid damaging or disturbing archaeological and historic sites.

The main safety concern is water, either too little or too much. This is generally very dry country, so those going into the monument should carry plenty of drinking water. However, thunderstorms can turn the monument's dirt roads into impassable mud bogs in minutes, stranding motorists. Potentially fatal flash floods through narrow canyons can catch hikers by surprise. Everyone planning trips into the monument should check first with one of the offices listed above on current and anticipated weather and travel conditions.

SPORTS & ACTIVITIES

Hiking, Mountain Biking & Horseback Riding. Located about 15 miles northeast of Escalante via Utah 12, the **Calf Creek Recreation Area** has a campground (see "Camping," below) and a picnic area with fire grates, tables, trees, drinking water, and flush toilets. Well shaded, it lies along a creek at the bottom of a narrow, high-walled rock canyon.

The best part of the recreation area is the moderately strenuous 5.5-mile round-trip hike to **Lower Calf Creek**

Falls. A sandy trail leads along **Calf Creek,** past beaver ponds and wetlands, to a beautiful waterfall cascading 126 feet down a rock wall into a tree-shaded pool. You can pick up an interpretive brochure at the trailhead.

Even though the Calf Creek Trail is the monument's only officially marked and maintained trail, there are numerous unmarked cross-country routes ideal for hiking, mountain biking, and horseback riding. We strongly recommend that hikers stop at the Interagency Office in Escalante or the Bureau of Land Management office in Kanab to get recommendations on hiking routes and to purchase topographical maps.

Among the popular and relatively easy-to-follow hiking routes is the footpath to **Escalante Natural Bridge,** which repeatedly crosses the river, so be prepared to get wet up to your knees. The easy 2-mile (one way) hike begins at a parking area at the bridge that crosses the Escalante River near Calf Creek Recreation Area, 15 miles northeast of the town of Escalante. From the parking area, hike upstream to Escalante Natural Bridge, on the south side of the river. The bridge is 130 feet high and spans 100 feet. From here you can continue upstream, exploring the side canyons, or turn around and head back to the parking lot.

Also starting at the Utah 12 bridge parking area is a hike downstream to **Phipps Wash.** Mostly moderate, this hike goes about 1.5 miles to the mouth of Phipps Wash, which enters the river from the west. On a north side drainage of Phipps Wash you'll find Maverick Natural Bridge; by climbing up the south side you can get to Phipps Arch.

Hiking the national monument's **slot canyons** is very popular, but we can't stress too strongly that you need to check on flood potentials before starting out. One challenging and very strenuous slot canyon hike is through **Peek-a-boo and Spooky canyons,** which are accessed from the Hole-in-the-Rock Road (see

"Sightseeing & Four-Wheeling," below). Stop at the Escalante Interagency Office for precise directions.

Sightseeing & Four-Wheeling. Since this is one of America's least-developed large sections of public land, it offers a wonderful opportunity for exploration by the adventurous. Be aware, though, that roads inside the monument are dirt that becomes mud, and impassable, when it rains.

One particularly popular road is the **Hole-in-the-Rock Scenic Backway,** which is partly in the national monument and partly in the adjacent Glen Canyon National Recreation Area. Like most roads in the monument, this should be attempted in dry weather only. Starting about 5 miles northeast of Escalante off Utah 12, this clearly marked dirt road travels 57 miles (one way) to the Hole-in-the-Rock, where Mormon settlers in 1880 cut a passage through solid rock to get their wagons down a 1,200-foot cliff to the canyon floor and Colorado River below.

About 12 miles in, the road passes by the sign to **Devil's Rock Garden,** an area of classic red rock formations and arches, where you'll also find a picnic area (about 1 mile off the main road). The road continues across a plateau of typical desert terrain, ending at a spectacular scenic overlook of Lake Powell. The first 35 miles of the scenic byway are relatively easy (in dry weather) in a standard passenger car, but then it gets a bit steeper and sandier, and the last 6 miles of the road require a high-clearance 4X4 vehicle. Allow about 6 hours round-trip, and make sure you have plenty of fuel and water.

Another recommended drive in the national monument is the **Cottonwood Canyon Road,** which runs from Kodachrome Basin State Park south to U.S. 89, along the monument's southern edge, a distance of about 46 miles. The road is sandy and narrow, and washboard in places, but usually passable for passenger cars in dry weather. It mostly follows Cottonwood Wash, with good views of red rock formations plus distant panoramas from hilltops. Unfortunately, views through the canyon are marred by two power lines, which make photography a challenge—though in all fairness, we should acknowledge that the road would not exist at all if not for the power lines.

About 10 miles east of Kodachrome Basin State Park is a short turnoff from Cottonwood Canyon Road that leads to **Grosvenor Arch.** This magnificent stone arch, with an opening 99 feet wide, was named for National Geographic Society founder and editor Gilbert H. Grosvenor, and is well worth the trip.

Wildlife Viewing & Bird Watching. The isolated and rugged terrain offers good habitat for a number of species, such as desert bighorn sheep and mountain lions. As for birds, more than 200 species have been spotted, including bald eagles, golden eagles, Swainson's hawks, and peregrine falcons. The best areas for seeing wildlife are along the Escalante and Paria Rivers and Johnson Creek.

CAMPING

Backcountry camping is permitted in most areas of the monument with a permit (free at press time), available at the Interagency office in Escalante and BLM office in Kanab. There are also two designated campgrounds. **Calf Creek Recreation Area,** about 15 miles northeast of the town of Escalante via Utah 12, has about a dozen sites and a picnic area. Open year-round, the tree-shaded campground often fills by 10am in summer. Located in a scenic, steep canyon along Calf Creek, surrounded by high rock walls, the campground has a volleyball court and offers access to an interpretive hiking trail (see "Hiking, Mountain Biking & Horseback Riding," above). There's drinking water and rest rooms with flush toilets, but no showers, RV hookups or dump station, or garbage removal. In addition, from November through March water is turned off and only vault toilets are available. To reach the campground vehicles ford a shallow creek. The campground is not recommended for vehicles over 25 feet long. Campsites cost $7 per night; day use is $2 per vehicle.

The national monument's other designated campground is **Deer Creek,** located 6 miles east of the town of Boulder along the scenic Burr Trail Road. Here there are four primitive sites and no drinking water or other facilities—but at least the camping is free.

8

CANYONLANDS NATIONAL PARK

by Don and Barbara Laine

U TAH'S LARGEST NATIONAL PARK, CANYONLANDS IS A RUGGED HIGH desert of rock, with spectacular formations and gorges carved over the centuries by the park's primary architects, the Colorado and Green rivers. This is a land of extremes: vast panoramas, dizzyingly deep canyons, dramatically steep cliffs, broad mesas, and towering red spires.

The most accessible part of Canyonlands is the Island in the Sky District, in the northern section of the park between the Colorado and Green rivers, where a paved road leads to sites such as Grand View Point, overlooking some 10,000 square miles of rugged wilderness. Island in the Sky also has several easy to moderate trails offering sweeping vistas of the park. A short walk provides views of Upheaval Dome, which resembles a large volcanic crater but may actually have been created by the crash of a meteorite. For the more adventurous, the 100-mile White Rim Road takes experienced mountain bikers and those with high-clearance four-wheel-drive vehicles on a winding loop tour through a vast array of scenery.

The Needles District, in the park's southeast corner, offers only a few viewpoints along the paved road, but numerous possibilities for hikers, backpackers, and those with high-clearance 4X4s.

Named for its tall, red-and-white striped rock pinnacles, this diverse district is home to impressive arches, including the 150-foot-tall Angel Arch, as well as grassy meadows and the confluence of the Green and Colorado rivers. Backcountry visitors to the Needles District will also find ruins and rock art left by prehistoric Indians some 800 years ago.

Most park visitors don't get a close-up view of the Maze District, but instead see it off in the distance from Grand View Point at Island in the Sky, or Confluence Overlook in the Needles District. That's because it's inhospitable and practically inaccessible, lying on the west side of the Green and Colorado rivers. You'll need a lot of endurance and at least several days to see even a few of its sites. Hardy hikers can visit Horseshoe Canyon in 1 day, where they can see the Great Gallery, an 80-foot-long rock art panel.

The park is also accessible by boat, which is how explorer Maj. John Wesley Powell first saw the canyons in 1869, when he made his first trip down the Green to its confluence with the

Tips from a Park Ranger

"A wilderness of rock," is how Paul Henderson, Canyonlands' chief of interpretation, describes the park, adding that it contains some of the most remote country left in the Lower 48. "There's some wonderful opportunities here to find solitude that don't exist in too many other places," Henderson says.

"Island in the Sky District receives the highest visitation and has the most extensive front-country road system, so it's a place where folks that aren't equipped for a backcountry adventure can still get a good feeling for what this park is all about," he says. "There's a paved road system, and you can have a really good experience in half a day."

However, Henderson says that Island in the Sky is not only for the pavement-bound. "The premier opportunity at Island in the Sky is the White Rim Road," he says, "a network of old mining roads and cowboy trails that make about a 100-mile trip—it's one of the premier mountain-biking trips in the country."

The Needles District, he says, is not a good place to cycle, but it has absolutely first rate options for hiking, backpacking, and four-wheeling. "Needles is pretty rough country, with some classic four-wheel-drive roads that for the most part are not for novice four-wheel-drivers," Henderson says. He adds, "I cringe when I see somebody in a brand-new $35,000 rig and it's probably the first time they've locked it into four-wheel drive."

The park's third district, the Maze, is very rough backcountry, Henderson says, and certainly not for everyone. It is, however, a good place to go if you don't want to see many people. "In August 1997, we had about 40,000 people at Island in the Sky, about 20,000 at Needles, and we had 546 at the Maze."

Colorado, and then even further downstream, eventually to the Grand Canyon. River access is from the towns of Moab and Green River; local companies offer boat trips of various duration.

You'll find a fascinating mixture of mountain and desert animals in Canyonlands, depending on the time of year and particular location within the park. The best times to see most wildlife are early and late in the day, especially in the summer when the midday sun drives all Canyonlands residents in search of shade. Throughout the park you'll probably hear, if not see, coyotes, and it's likely you'll spot white-tailed antelope squirrels and other rodents scampering among the rocks as well. Watch for the elusive and rather antisocial bighorn sheep along isolated cliffs, where you might also see a golden eagle or turkey vulture soaring above the rocks in search of food. In the little pools of water that appear in the slickrock after rainstorms, you're likely to see tadpole shrimp—1-inch-long crustaceans that look as though they would be more at home in the ocean. Among the cottonwoods and willows along the rivers you'll find a variety of wildlife: deer, beaver, an occasional bobcat, and various migratory birds.

Avoiding the Crowds. Although Canyonlands does not get nearly as crowded as most other national parks, the more popular trails can be busy at certain times. Spring and fall see the most visitors, but summer too has recently become more popular, despite scorching temperatures. Those who seriously want to avoid humanity should visit from November through mid-March, when the park is

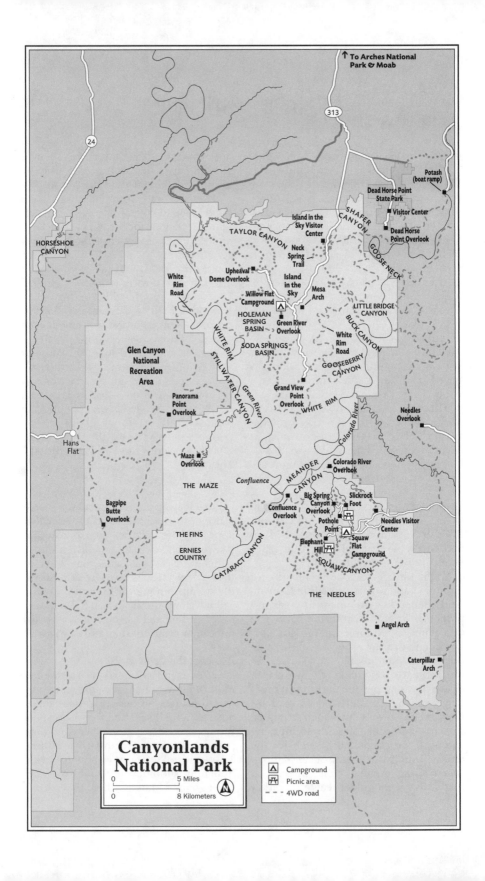

To Arches National Park & Moab

313

24

Potash
(boat ramp)

Dead Horse Point
State Park

Visitor Center

SHAFER CANYON

Island in the
Sky Visitor
Center

Dead Horse
Point Overlook

HORSESHOE
CANYON

TAYLOR CANYON

Neck
Spring
Trail

GOOSE NECK

White
Rim
Road

Upheaval
Dome Overlook

Island
in the
Sky

Mesa
Arch

LITTLE BRIDGE
CANYON

Willow Flat
Campground

Green River
Overlook

White
Rim
Road

BUCK CANYON

HOLEMAN
SPRING
BASIN

Glen Canyon
National
Recreation
Area

SODA SPRINGS
BASIN

GOOSEBERRY
CANYON

WHITE RIM

STILLWATER CANYON

Green River

Grand View
Point
Overlook

Panorama
Point
Overlook

WHITE RIM

Needles
Overlook

Hans
Flat

Maze
Overlook

Colorado River

MEANDER
CANYON

Colorado River
Overlook

THE MAZE

Confluence

Big Spring
Canyon
Overlook

Slickrock
Foot

Bagpipe
Butte
Overlook

Confluence
Overlook

Pothole
Point

Needles Visitor
Center

THE FINS

ERNIES
COUNTRY

Elephant
Hill

Squaw
Flat
Campground

CATARACT CANYON

SQUAW CANYON

THE NEEDLES

Angel Arch

Caterpillar
Arch

Canyonlands
National Park

0   5 Miles

0   8 Kilometers

N

△ Campground

🅿 Picnic area

– – – 4WD road

practically deserted, though some trails and 4X4 roads may be inaccessible. College spring-break time—usually mid-March and April—can be especially busy, and any other school vacation usually brings more visitors as well. But even in the high season, hiking in the early morning—often the best time to hike anyway—is a good way to beat the crowds.

One thing that makes the backcountry experience here especially pleasant, even during the park's busiest times, is that the number of permits for overnight trips is limited (and often sold out well in advance). If you're willing to hike, bike, or drive far enough you're guaranteed that you won't be sharing the trail or road with a lot of other people.

Just the Facts

There are no lodgings, restaurants, or stores inside the park. Most visitors use Moab as a base camp.

GETTING THERE & GATEWAYS

For directions to Moab, see "Getting There & Gateways" in chapter 2.

To get to the Island in the Sky Visitor Center from Moab (about 34 miles away), take U.S. 191 (which runs north-south through eastern Utah from Wyoming to Arizona) north to Utah 313, which you follow south into the park.

To reach the Needles Visitor Center from Moab, leave U.S. 191 at Utah 211 south of Moab, and head west into the park. It's about 75 miles.

Getting to the Maze District is a bit more interesting. From Moab take U.S. 191 north, then go west for about 11 miles on I-70, crossing Green River, and then take Utah 24 south. Watch for signs and follow two- and four-wheel-drive dirt roads east into the park.

The detached Horseshoe Canyon area of the park is about 120 miles from Island in the Sky. To get there by two-wheel-drive vehicle, again follow I-70

west from Green River to U.S. 24, and then go south about 24 miles to the Horseshoe Canyon turnoff (near the WATCH FOR SAND DRIFTS sign), where you turn left. Follow this maintained dirt road for about 30 miles to the canyon's west rim, where you can park. This is the trailhead for the hike to the Great Gallery (see "Day Hikes," below).

The Nearest Airport & Renting a Car. See the "The Nearest Airport" and "Ground Transportation" sections in chapter 2.

INFORMATION

Contact the **Superintendent, Canyonlands National Park,** 2282 SW Resource Blvd., Moab, UT 84532-8000 (☎ 435/259-7164; www.nps.gov/cany). You can get additional information from the **Moab Information Center** (see "Information" in chapter 2).

Canyonlands Natural History Association offers a number of helpful books and maps for sale (see the "Information" section of chapter 2). A couple of very good guides to hiking and off-roading are *Exploring Canyonlands and Arches National Parks* (Helena, Mont.: Falcon Press, 1997) by Bill Schneider, and *Canyon Country Off-Road Vehicle Trails, Canyon Rims and Needles Areas* (Moab, Utah: Canyon Country Publications, 1990) by F. A. Barnes.

VISITOR CENTERS

Canyonlands National Park operates two visitor centers: **Island in the Sky Visitor Center,** in the northern part of the park, and **Needles Visitor Center,** in the southern section. In both, you can get advice from rangers as well as maps and free brochures on hiking trails.

FEES & PERMITS

From late February through October, entry into the park (for up to 7 days) costs $10 per private vehicle or $5 per person on foot or bike. Entry is free the rest of the year. The camping fee at Squaw Flat Campground in the Needles District is $10; camping at Willow Flat Campground in the Island in the Sky District costs $5.

Backcountry permits, available at either visitor center, are required for all overnight stays in the park, except at the two established campgrounds. Permit reservations can be made in advance (☎ 435/259-4351). Permits for overnight four-wheel-drive and mountain-bike trips are $25, while those for overnight backpacking trips are $10. The permit for white-water boating through Cataract Canyon is $25; flat-water boating costs $10.

There is also a $5 day-use fee for those visitors bringing motor vehicles, horses, or mountain bikes on roads into Salt Creek/Horse Canyon and Lavender Canyon in the Needles District.

SPECIAL REGULATIONS & WARNINGS

Backcountry hikers must pack out all trash, and wood fires are prohibited. Canyonlands National Park is not a good place to take pets. Dogs, which must be leashed at all times, are prohibited in public buildings, on all trails, and in the backcountry. This includes four-wheel-drive roads—dogs are not permitted even inside your vehicle.

It cannot be stressed too strongly that the terrain at Canyonlands can be brutal, and it's important that you know not only your own limitations, but also the limitations of your vehicle and other equipment. Due to the extreme variety of terrain, the main safety problem at Canyonlands is that people underestimate the hazards. Rangers warn hikers to carry at least 1 gallon of water per person per day, to be especially careful near cliff edges, to avoid overexposure to the intense sun, and to carry maps when

going off into the backcountry. During lightning storms, avoid lone trees, high ridges, and cliff edges. Four-wheel-drive vehicle operators should be aware of their vehicles' limitations and carry extra food and emergency equipment. Also, everyone going into the backcountry should let someone know where they're going and when they plan to return. Traveling alone in Canyonlands is not a good idea.

SEASONS & CLIMATE

Summers here are hot, with temperatures sometimes exceeding 100°F. Winters can be cool or cold, dropping well below freezing at night. The best time to visit, especially for hikers, is in the spring or fall, when daytime temperatures are usually from 60° to 80°F, and nights are cool. Late summer and early fall visitors should be prepared for afternoon thunderstorms.

If You Only Have 1 Day

Canyonlands is not an easy place to see in a short period of time. In fact, if your schedule permits only a day, skip the Needles and Maze districts entirely, and drive directly to the **Island in the Sky Visitor Center.** After looking at the exhibits, drive to several of the overlooks, stopping along the way for a short hike or two. Make sure you get to the **Grand View Point Overlook,** at the south end of the paved road. Among the best trails for this quick trip is the **Grand View Trail,** which starts at the overlook and is especially scenic in late afternoon. Allow about 1½ hours for this easy 2-mile walk. Also recommended is the **Upheaval Dome Overlook Trail,** which should take about a half hour, and brings you to a mile-wide crater of mysterious origins.

Perhaps a better choice for a quick visit to the park, especially for those with a bit of extra cash, is to take a guided trip by four-wheel-drive vehicle or raft. See the "Organized Tours & Ranger Programs" and "Outfitters Based in Moab" sections, below.

Exploring the Park by Car

No driving tour has yet been designed to show off Canyonlands National Park. The Island in the Sky District has about 20 miles of paved highway, some gravel roads accessible to two-wheel-drive vehicles, and several viewpoints. The Needles District only has 8 miles of paved roads. Many (but not all) of Needles' viewpoints and trailheads are accessible only by high-clearance 4X4 vehicles or plain old foot power. The Maze District has only two main roads, neither of them paved. Both lead to trailheads.

Of course, if you happen to have a serious 4X4, and if you are equally serious about doing some hard-core four-wheeling, this is the park for you. See the "Other Sports & Activities" section, below. Due to constantly changing conditions of dirt roads, we strongly suggest that you discuss your plans with rangers before setting out.

Organized Tours & Ranger Programs

In summer, rangers offer evening **campfire programs** at Squaw Flat Campground in the Needles District and short morning talks frequently at the Island in the Sky Visitor Center.

Canyonlands by Night (☎ 800/394-9978 or 435/259-5261) is an evening river trip, operating spring through fall, that combines a sunset boat ride with stories of outlaws, rock formations, and a sound-and-light show against the backdrop of the canyon walls. The office and dock are just north of Moab at the Colorado River Bridge. Dutch oven dinners in a covered patio with live country western entertainment, precedes the boat trip. Cost for the boat trip alone is $25

for adults, $15 for children ages 6 to 12, and $5 for kids 2 to 5; the dinner alone is $14, $6, and $2.50, respectively; and combo tickets for both cost $35, $21, and $7.50, respectively. Reservations are recommended.

FLYING TOURS

Many of Canyonlands' most spectacular sections are difficult to get to, to say the least. One solution is to take to the air. **Redtail Aviation,** P.O. Box 515, Moab, UT 84532 (☎ **800/842-9251** or 435/259-7421; fax 435/259-4032; www.moab-utah.com/redtail/aviation.html; e-mail: redtail@lasal.net), based at Moab's Canyonlands Field Airport, offers several easy ways to see the most of Canyonlands and surrounding areas. A 1-hour flight covers all three of the park's districts, plus Dead Horse Point State Park (described later in this chapter), at about $75 per person. A 2-hour flight explores the same areas plus Lake Powell, Robber's Roost (where outlaw Butch Cassidy is said to have hidden out), and either Capitol Reef National Park or Monument Valley Navajo Tribal Park; cost is about $150 per person.

Slickrock Air Guides of Moab (☎ **800/332-2439** or 435/259-6216; fax 435/259-2226; www.slickrockairguides.com; e-mail: slickair@hotmail.com) offers a 1-hour scenic flight over Canyonlands National Park and Dead Horse State Park for about $80 per person. A 2½-hour flight that takes in Canyonlands and Monument Valley costs about $160 per person.

Historic & Man-Made Attractions

This land was once the domain of prehistoric Indians, who constructed their buildings out of the region's rock, hunted deer and bighorn sheep, and left numerous drawings on rock walls. Most of the park's archaeological sites are in the Needles District. They include the well-preserved cliff dwelling called **Tower Ruin,** high on a cliff ledge in Horse Canyon; and an easy-to-reach **ancient granary,** near the Needles Visitor Center, accessible on the short self-guided Roadside Ruin Trail. Throughout the park you'll also find evidence of more modern peoples—the trappers, explorers, and cowboys of the 19th century.

In Horseshoe Canyon, a separate and remote section of the park on the west side of the Green River, you'll find the **Great Gallery,** one of the most fantastic rock art panels in the Southwest. More than 80 feet long, the panel contains many red-and-white paintings of what appear to be larger-than-life human figures. The paintings are believed to be at least 2,000 years old.

Day Hikes

On these trails with little shade, no reliable water sources, and temperatures soaring to over 100°F in the summer, rangers strongly advise that hikers carry at least 1 gallon of water per person per day, along with sunscreen, a hat, and all the usual hiking and emergency equipment. Ideally, if you expect to do some serious hiking, try to plan your trip for the spring or fall, when conditions are much more hospitable.

All hikers should be careful on the many trails that cross slickrock, a general term for any bare rock surface. As the name implies, it can be slippery, especially when wet. Also, because some of the trails may be confusing, hikers attempting the longer ones should take good topographical maps, available at park visitor centers and at stores in Moab.

Guided hikes in the park are available from **Dreamrides** (see "Outfitters Based in Moab," below), with full-day trips ranging from $95 to $115.

The following are some of the park's many hiking possibilities, arranged by

district; check with rangers for other suggestions.

ISLAND IN THE SKY DISTRICT

SHORTER TRAILS

Grand View Trail

1 mi. one way. Easy. Access: Grand View Point Overlook at south end of paved rd.

At the trailhead, stop and read the sign that points out all the prominent features you can see, such as the Totem Pole, the confluence of the Colorado and Green rivers, and the White Rim Trail. Although this is a fairly flat and easy trail to hike, you should watch carefully for the cairns, since some are on the small side. And remember to stay back from the cliff edge. This trail is especially beautiful at sunset, when the panorama seems to change constantly with the diminishing angle of sunlight.

Mesa Arch Trail

0.5 mi. RT. Easy. Access: The trailhead is along a paved rd. about 6 mi. south of the visitor center.

This is an easy self-guided nature walk through an area of piñon and juniper trees, mountain mahogany, cactus, and a plant called Mormon Tea, from which Mormon pioneers made their hot drinks. The trail's main scenic attraction is the Mesa Arch, made of Navajo sandstone. It hangs precariously on the edge of a 500-foot cliff, framing a spectacular view of nearby mountains.

Upheaval Dome Overlook

0.5 mi. one way. Moderate. Access: The trailhead is at the end of the Upheaval Dome Rd.

This hike to the overlook has a few steep inclines. Upheaval Dome doesn't fit with the rest of the Canyonlands' terrain—it's the result not of gradual erosion like the rest of the park, but rather of a dramatic deformity in which rocks have been pushed into a domelike structure. At one time it was theorized that the dome was formed by a hidden volcano, but now experts say the cause may have been a meteorite that struck the earth some 60 million years ago. Hiking another 0.5 mile takes you to a second overlook, closer to the Dome, but with a less panoramic view.

Whale Rock Trail

0.5 mi. one way. Moderate. Access: The trailhead is about 4 mi. down the Upheaval Dome Rd.

This trail provides breathtaking 360° views of the Island in the Sky District. It's a climb of 300 feet up a slickrock trail with handrails. Wander around on top a bit and study the varied formations; to those with some imagination, the outcrop you just climbed resembles a whale.

LONGER TRAILS

Gooseberry Trail

3 mi. one way. Moderate. Access: Island in the Sky Picnic Area, about 11 mi. south of the visitor center.

Although the beginning of this trail is so steep it looks like a cliff, don't be deterred. True, it drops 1,400 feet over the course of the hike, and most of that (1,300 ft.) in the first 1.5 miles. But the trail is well made, and with a little care is quite safe. As you gingerly hike down the switchbacks—be careful of the loose sand—you get superb views of the White Rim Country. Once down in Gooseberry Canyon, it's nearly a level walk out to the road. When you decide you're ready to face the climb back to the top, remember you can take lots of rest stops to admire the varying scenery.

Lathrop Trail

5 mi. one way. Strenuous. Access: The trailhead is about 1.5 mi. south of the visitor center along paved rd.

The first 2.5 miles of this trail are on top of the mesa, but then it meanders down into the canyon, descending about 1,600 feet to the White Rim Road. This strenuous hike traverses steep terrain and loose rock—and remember, you have to climb back up to your car, unless you have been able to arrange for someone to meet you at the road. As you hike down the slope, you get grand views of Lathrop Canyon, and occasional glimpses of the Colorado River. It is possible to continue down to the river from the road (another 4 mi. each way), but check with rangers about the feasibility of this overnight trip before attempting it.

Neck Spring Trail

5 mi. RT. Moderate to strenuous. Access: The trailhead is about 0.5 mi. south of the visitor center along paved rd.

This fairly strenuous hike follows the paths that animals and early ranchers created to reach water at two springs. You'll see water troughs, hitching posts, rusty cans, and the ruins of an old cabin. Because of the water source, you'll encounter types of vegetation not usually seen in the park, such as maidenhair ferns and gamble oak. The water also draws wildlife, including mule deer, bighorn sheep, ground squirrels, and hummingbirds. Climbing to the top of the rim, you get a beautiful view of the canyons and even the Henry Mountains, some 60 miles away.

Syncline Loop Trail

8 mi. RT. Strenuous. Access: Upheaval Dome Picnic Area at the end of Upheaval Dome Rd.

This is a long, hot day hike over one of the only three loop trails in the Island in the Sky District. Be sure to start early and carry plenty of water. The trail drops 1,300 feet, and is best hiked clockwise so you take the steepest part going down, into Upheaval Canyon. Along the way, you'll follow dry washes, climb small hills and steep canyon sides, cross part of the

Syncline Valley, pass Upheaval Dome, traverse some slickrock, and finally hit an area of lush vegetation.

NEEDLES DISTRICT

Hiking trails here are generally not too tough, but keep in mind that slickrock can live up to its name and that there is generally little shade.

SHORTER TRAILS

Roadside Ruin Trail

0.3 mi. RT. Easy. Access: The trailhead is just over 0.5 mi. west of the visitor center along paved road.

This self-guided nature walk leads to an ancient granary, probably used by the Ancestral Puebloans some 700 to 1,000 years ago to store corn, nuts, and other foods. For 25¢ you can get a brochure at the trailhead that discusses the plants along the trail. Although flat, this trail can be muddy when wet.

Slickrock Foot Trail

2.4 mi. RT. Moderate. Access: The trailhead is about 6.5 mi. from the visitor center, almost at the end of the road.

Viewpoints along this trail show off the stair-step topography of the area, from its colorful canyons and cliffs to its flat mesas and striped needles.

LONGER TRAILS

Confluence Overlook Trail

5.5 mi. one way. Moderate to strenuous. Access: Big Spring Canyon Overlook.

This hike has steep drop-offs and little shade, but the hard work is worthwhile—it shows off splendidly the many colors of the Needles District, and also offers excellent views into the Maze District of the park. The climax is a spectacular view overlooking the confluence of the Green and Colorado Rivers in a 1,000-foot-deep gorge. This hike can be done as a day

hike (allow 4 to 6 hrs.) or quite pleasantly as an overnight hike.

Elephant Hill–Druid Arch Trail

5.4 mi. one way. Moderate. Access: Elephant Hill Trailhead at end of graded gravel rd., drivable in most 2-wheel-drive passenger cars, although those in large vehicles such as motor homes will want to avoid it.

A number of interconnecting trails lead into the backcountry from this trailhead. The hike to Druid Arch, though not difficult, challenges hikers with steep drop-offs, quite a bit of slickrock, and a 1,000-foot increase in elevation. But the effort is worth the views, as you hike through narrow rock canyons, past colorful spires and pinnacles, and up the steep climb to the bench just below the huge Druid Arch, its dark rock somewhat resembling the stone structures of Stonehenge.

Squaw Canyon– Big Spring Canyon Loop

7.5-mi. loop. Strenuous. Access: Squaw Flat Campground.

This hike over steep slickrock winds through woodlands of piñon and juniper, offering views along the way of the Needles rock formations for which the district is named, plus nearby cliffs and mesas as well as distant mountains. Watch for wildflowers from late spring through summer. The hike can be completed in about half a day, but there are also several backcountry campsites making it available to overnighters.

MAZE DISTRICT

Getting to the trailheads in the Maze District involves serious four-wheel-drive roads.

The 3-mile **Maze Overlook Trail** is not for beginning hikers or anyone with a fear of heights, and is quite steep in places, requiring the use of your hands for safety. At the trailhead you get a fine view of the many narrow canyons that inspired this district's name; then the trail descends 600 feet to the canyon bottom.

The 12-mile **Harvest Scene Loop** (12-mile loop, difficult, 7 to 10 hr. or overnight) leads over slickrock and along canyon washes—watch for the cairns to be sure you don't wander off the trail—to a magnificent example of rock art.

Other trailheads lie in what is known as the **Doll House Area.** Check with a ranger for current trail conditions and difficulty.

HORSESHOE CANYON

This detached section of the park was added to Canyonlands in 1971 mainly because of its **Great Gallery,** an 80-foot-long rock art panel with larger-than-life human figures, believed to be at least several thousand years old. Horseshoe Canyon Unit is some 120 miles (one way) from Island in the Sky, and there's only one road in (see "Getting There & Gateways," above). From the parking area it's a 6.5-mile round-trip hike to see the rock art. The hike begins with a 1.5-mile section down an 800-foot slope to the canyon floor, where you then turn right and go 1.75 miles to the Great Gallery. There is no camping in Horseshoe Canyon, but just outside the park boundary primitive camping is available on Bureau of Land Management property on the rim.

Exploring the Backcountry

There are many opportunities for backpacking in Canyonlands National Park, although hikers will often be sharing trail/road combinations with four-wheel-drive vehicles and mountain bikes. Additional information is provided below.

OTHER SPORTS & ACTIVITIES

Canyonlands is a park that begs to be explored—if you've come to Utah for mountain biking, hiking, four-wheeling,

or rafting, this is the place. The region holds a few surprises, too, from ancient American Indian dwellings and rock art to dinosaur bones.

Unlike most national parks, the backcountry at Canyonlands is not only the domain of backpackers. Here, rugged four-wheel-drive and mountain-bike roads, as well as rivers navigable by boat, journey to some of the park's most scenic areas. Primitive campsites, strategically located throughout the backcountry, are available to all visitors, regardless of their mode of transport. Just be sure to make your backcountry campsite reservations well in advance—up to a year ahead for the more popular areas. You can get reservation forms and detailed information by mail, phone, or from the park's Web site (see "Information," above).

OUTFITTERS BASED IN MOAB

Although this area offers plenty for the do-it-yourselfer, some 50 local outfitters offer excursions of all kinds, from lazy canoe rides to hair-raising jet-boat and four-wheel-drive adventures. The chart below lists some of the major companies that want to help you fully enjoy this beautiful country. They are all located in Moab (zip code is 84532). Advance reservations are often required, and it's best to check with several outfitters before deciding on one. In addition to asking about what you'll see and do and what it will cost, it doesn't hurt to make sure the company is insured and has the proper permits with the various federal agencies. Also ask about its cancellation policy, just in case.

Boating, Canoeing & Rafting. After spending hours in the blazing sun looking at mile upon mile of huge red sandstone rock formations, it's easy to get the idea that Canyonlands National Park is a baking, dry, rock-hard desert. Well, it is. But both the Colorado and Green rivers run through the park, and one of the most exciting ways to see the park and surrounding country is from river level.

Outfitter	4X4	Bike	Boat	Horse	Rent	Shuttle
Adrift Adventures 378 N. Main St., Box 577 ☎ 800/874-4483, 435/259-8594 www.adrift.net	Yes	No	Yes	Yes	No	Yes
Canyon Voyages 401 N. Main St., Box 416 ☎ 800/733-6007, 435/259-6007 www.canyonvoyages.com	Yes	No	Yes	No	Yes	No
Dreamrides 96 E. Center ☎ 888/662-2882, 435/259-6419 www.dreamride.com	No	No	Yes	No	Yes	No
Kaibab Adventure Outfitter & Moab Cyclery 391 S. Main St. ☎ 800/451-1133, 435/259-7423 www.utah.com/kaibab	No	Yes	No	No	Yes	No
Lin Ottinger Tours 600 N. Main St. ☎ 435/259-7312	Yes	No	No	No	No	No
Moab Rafting Co. Box 801 ☎ 435/259-7238 www.moab-rafting.com	No	No	Yes	No	No	No
Navtec Expeditions 321 N. Main St., Box 1267 ☎ 800/833-1278, 435/259-7983 www.navtec.com	Yes	No	Yes	No	No	No
Nichols Expeditions 497 N. Main St. ☎ 800/648-8488, 435/259-3999 www.nicholsexpeditions.com	No	Yes	Yes	No	No	No
North American River/ Canyonlands Tours 543 N. Main St. ☎ 800/342-5938, 435/259-5865 www.oars.com	Yes	Yes	Yes	No	No	No
Pack Creek Ranch U.S. 191, south of Moab P.O. Box 1270 ☎ 435/259-5505	No	No	No	Yes	No	No

Outfitter	4X4	Bike	Boat	Horse	Rent	Shuttle
Red River Canoe Co. 702 S. Main St. ☎ 800/753-8216, 435/259-7722 www.redrivercanoe.com	No	No	Yes	No	Yes	Yes
Rim Tours 1233 S. U.S. 191 ☎ 800/626-7335, 435/259-5223	Yes	No	No	No	No	No
Sheri Griffith Expeditions 2231 S. U.S. 191 Box 1324 ☎ 800/332-2439, 435/259-8229 www.griffithexp.com	No	No	Yes	No	No	No
Tag-A-Long Expeditions 452 N. Main St. ☎ 800/453-3292, 435/259-8946 www.tagalong.com	Yes	No	Yes	No	No	Yes
Tex's Riverways 691 N. 500 W. Box 67No ☎ 435/259-5101	No	No	Yes	No	Yes	Yes
Western River Expeditions 1371 N. U.S. 191 ☎ 888/622-4097, 435/259-7019	No	No	Yes	No	Yes	No

You can travel into the park in a canoe, kayak, large or small rubber raft (with or without motor), or speedy, solid jet-boat. Do-it-yourselfers can rent kayaks or canoes for $25 to $40 for a half day and $30 to $50 for a full day, or rafts from $50 to $65 per half day and $65 to $95 for a full day. Half-day guided river trips cost from $25 to $35 per person, and full-day trips are usually in the $40 to $70 range. Multi-day rafting expeditions, which include meals and camping equipment, start at about $150 per person for two days, but can be much higher depending on location. Jet-boat trips, which cover a lot more river in a given amount of time, start at about $50 for a half-day trip, with full-day trips about $85 per person. Children's rates are usually about 20% less. Some companies also offer sunset or dinner trips. **Sheri Griffith Expeditions** even offers a 4-day, 3-night "Expedition in Luxury," at $1,825 per person, offering live chamber music plus gourmet food served with white tablecloths, wine glasses, and candles, and your every need anticipated.

The Colorado and Green rivers meet in the park, and both are fairly calm before the confluence. However, after the confluence the Colorado becomes serious white water, where you will most likely want to be on a guided raft trip.

One fantastic canoe trip is along the Green River. Canoeists usually start in or near the town of Green River (put in at Green River State Park or at Mineral Bottom, just downstream) and spend about 2 days to get to the Green's confluence with the Colorado, where they can arrange to be picked up by a local outfitter.

Public boat-launching ramps in the Moab area are opposite Lion's Park, near the intersection of U.S. 191 and Utah 128; at Take-Out Beach, along Utah 128 about 10 miles east of its intersection with U.S. 191; and at Hittle Bottom, also along Utah 128, about 23.5 miles east of its intersection with U.S. 191. Information on river flows and reservoir conditions statewide can be obtained from the **Colorado Basin River Forecast Center** (☎ **801/539-1311;** www.cbrfc. gov/public/for.html).

Four-Wheeling. Unlike most national parks, where all motor vehicles and mountain bikes must stay on paved roads, Canyonlands has miles of rough, four-wheel-drive roads where mechanized transport is king. Keep in mind that we're talking serious four-wheeling here, where most roads require high-clearance short-wheelbase vehicles. Many of these roads also require the skill that comes only from experience, so it's usually a good idea to discuss your plans with rangers before putting your high-priced vehicle on the line. Four-wheelers must stay on designated 4X4 roads, but here the term *road* can mean anything from a graded, well-marked two-lane gravel byway to a pile of loose rocks with a sign that says "that-a-way." Many of the park's Jeep roads are impassable during heavy rains and for a day or two after.

Local companies offering four-wheel-drive rentals include **Thrifty** (☎ 800/367-2277 or 435/259-7317); and **Farabee 4X4 Rentals** (☎ 888/806-5337 or 435/259-7494), which is also the local agent for **Budget; Slickrock 4X4 Rentals** (☎ 888/238-5337 or 435/259-5678); and **Mike Young 4X4 Rentals** (☎ 435/259-5432). Rates are usually $80 to $90 per day, with some mileage included.

The best four-wheel-drive adventure in Canyonlands' Island in the Sky District is the **White Rim Road,** which runs some 100 winding miles and affords spectacular and ever-changing views, from broad panoramas of rock and canyon to close-ups of red and orange towers and buttes. A high-clearance 4X4 is essential. Expect the journey to be slow, lasting 2 to 3 days, although with the appropriate vehicle it isn't really difficult. There are primitive campgrounds along the way, but reservations on this popular route should be made well in advance.

Four-wheeling on one of many exciting routes in the Needles District can be an end in itself or simply a means to get to some of the more interesting and remote hiking trails and camping spots. Four-wheelers will find one of their ultimate challenges on the **Elephant Hill Jeep Road,** which begins at a well-marked turnoff near Squaw Flat Campground. Although most of the 10-mile trail is only moderately difficult, the stretch over Elephant Hill itself near the beginning can be a nightmare, with steep, rough slickrock, drifting sand, loose rock, and treacherous ledges. Coming down the hill there is one switchback that requires you to back to the edge of a steep cliff before continuing ahead. This is also a favorite of mountain bikers, although bikes will have to be walked on some stretches over an abundance of sand and rocks. The route offers views of numerous rock formations, from striped needles to balanced rocks, plus steep cliffs and rock "stairs." Side trips can add another 30 miles. Allow from 8 hours to 3 days.

For a spectacular view of the Colorado River, the **Colorado River Overlook Road** can't be beat. This 14-mile round-trip is popular with four-wheelers, backpackers, and mountain bikers. Considered among the park's easiest 4X4 roads, the first part is very easy indeed, accessible by high-clearance two-wheel-drives, but the second half has a few rough and rocky sections that require four-wheel-drive. Starting at the Needles Visitor Center parking lot, the trail takes you past numerous panoramic vistas to a spectacular 360° view of the park and the Colorado River some 1,000 feet below.

Biking. Road bikes are of little use in Canyonlands, except for getting to and from trailheads, viewpoints, visitor centers, and campgrounds in the Island in the Sky and Needles districts. Although bikes of any kind are prohibited on hiking trails and cross country in the backcountry, they are permitted on designated two- and four-wheel-drive roads. This means that mountain bikers have many possibilities here, although they will find themselves sharing dirt roads with motor vehicles and hikers. Since some of the four-wheel-drive roads have deep sand in spots, which can turn into quicksand when wet, mountain biking, while certainly a challenge, may not be as much fun as you'd expect. It's wise to talk with rangers about conditions on specific roads before setting out.

Among popular rides are the Elephant Hill and Colorado River Overlook Jeep roads, both in the Needles District. The 100-mile White Rim Road, in the Island in the Sky District, also makes a great mountain-bike trip (allow at least 4 days), especially for bikers who can arrange for an accompanying 4X4 vehicle to carry water, food, and camping gear. See the "Four-Wheeling" section, above. For information on where to get advice, bike rentals and repairs, equipment, and bike shuttle services, see the "Biking" section in chapter 2.

Camping

INSIDE THE PARK

The park has two developed campgrounds. In the Island in the Sky District, **Willow Flat Campground** has no water; in the Needles District, **Squaw Flat Campground** offers a year-round water supply. Primitive campsites are also available throughout the park for four-wheelers, boaters, mountain bikers, and backpackers (see "Exploring the Backcountry," above).

NEAR THE PARK

Near Island in the Sky, the campground at **Dead Horse Point State Park** (☎ 435/259-2614) has electric hookups; while the BLM's **Newspaper Rock Campground** (☎ 435/587-1500), along the road to the Needles District, offers primitive camping. Additional camping facilities are available on nearby public lands administered by the Bureau of Land Management and U.S. Forest Service; check at the **Moab Information Center,** located in Moab at the corner of Main and Center streets (☎ 435/259-8825). Those heading north to the community of Green River will find additional camping at two state parks. There are also over a dozen commercial campgrounds in and around Moab.

Near the Needles District of the park are several commercial campgrounds in the town of Monticello, along U.S. 191, about 15 miles south of the intersection of U.S. 191 and the park entry road. These include **Mountain View RV Park,** along the north edge on Monticello at 632 N. Main St. (P.O. Box 910), Monticello, UT 84535 (☎ 435/587-2974), a well-maintained campground with grassy sites, some trees, and cable TV hookups.

For details on all these campgrounds, see the campground chart in chapter 2.

Accommodations, Dining, & Picnic & Camping Supplies

There are no facilities for lodging, dining, or buying supplies inside Canyonlands National Park. The nearest town to the park is Moab. For information on restaurants, hotels, and supply stores in Moab, see the "Accommodations," "Dining," and "Picnic & Camping Supplies" sections in chapter 2.

9

CAPITOL REEF NATIONAL PARK

by Don and Barbara Laine

APITOL REEF NATIONAL PARK IS ONE OF THOSE UNDISCOVERED GEMS, quietly going about its business of protecting and interpreting its natural wonders and historic sites, and drawing fewer visitors than its more famous neighbors, Bryce Canyon and Zion.

But when people do stumble across this park, they are often amazed—Capitol Reef not only offers spectacular southern Utah scenery, but also has a unique twist and a personality all its own.

The geologic formations here are incredible, if not downright peculiar. This is a place to let your imagination run wild, where you'll see the commanding Castle; the tall, rust-red Chimney Rock; the silent and eerie Temple of the Moon; and the appropriately named Hamburger Rocks, sitting atop a white sandstone table. The colors of Capitol Reef's canyon walls come from a spectacular palette, which is why the Navajos called the area "The Land of the Sleeping Rainbow."

Unlike some of southern Utah's other parks, Capitol Reef is more than brilliant rocks and barren desert. Here the Fremont River has helped create a lush oasis in an otherwise unforgiving land. Cottonwood, willow, and other trees fill its banks. In fact, 19th-century pioneers found the land so inviting that they established the community of Fruita,

planting orchards that have been preserved by the National Park Service.

Because of differences in geologic strata, elevation, and water availability in different sections of the park, you'll find a variety of ecosystems and terrain, along with a variety of possible activities. There are trails for hiking; roads for mountain biking and four-wheeling; lush fruit orchards; rich, green cottonwood groves and desert wildflowers; an abundance of songbirds; and a surprising amount of wildlife, from lizards and snakes to the bashful ring-tailed cat (which isn't a cat at all, but a member of the raccoon family). You'll also find thousand-year-old petroglyphs left behind by the ancient Fremont and Ancestral Puebloan peoples, and other traces of the past left by the more recent Utes and Southern Paiutes. This was both a favorite hideout for Wild West outlaws and a home for industrious Mormon pioneers, who planted orchards while their children learned the three R's and studied the Bible and the Book of Mormon in the one-room Fruita Schoolhouse.

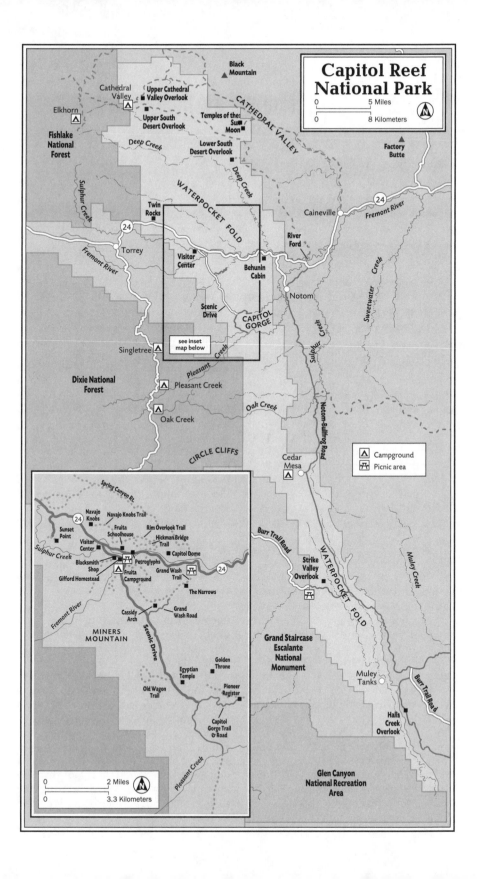

Capitol Reef National Park

0 ——— 5 Miles
0 ——— 8 Kilometers

Black Mountain

Cathedral Valley
Upper Cathedral Valley Overlook

Elkhorn

Fishlake National Forest

Upper South Desert Overlook

Temples of the Sun Moon

Lower South Desert Overlook

Deep Creek

Deep Creek

CATHEDRAL VALLEY

Factory Butte

WATERPOCKET FOLD

Twin Rocks

Caineville

24

Fremont River

Sulphur Creek

24

Torrey

Fremont River

Visitor Center

Behunin Cabin

River Ford

Notom

Sweetwater Creek

Scenic Drive

CAPITOL GORGE

see inset map below

Singletree

Pleasant Creek

Sulphur Creek

Dixie National Forest

Pleasant Creek

Oak Creek

Oak Creek

Notom-Bullfrog Road

Cedar Mesa

CIRCLE CLIFFS

⛺ Campground
🏕 Picnic area

Spring Canyon Rt

Navajo Knobs
Navajo Knobs Trail

24

Sunset Point

Fruita Schoolhouse

Rim Overlook Trail

Hickman Bridge Trail

Burr Trail Road

Visitor Center

Capitol Dome

Blacksmith Shop

Petroglyphs

Fruita Campground

Gifford Homestead

Grand Wash Trail

24

Strike Valley Overlook

Muley Creek

Sulphur Creek

The Narrows

Fremont River

Cassidy Arch

Grand Wash Road

WATERPOCKET FOLD

MINERS MOUNTAIN

Scenic Drive

Golden Throne

Egyptian Temple

Pioneer Register

Grand Staircase Escalante National Monument

Old Wagon Trail

Muley Tanks

Burr Trail Road

Capitol Gorge Trail & Road

Halls Creek Overlook

0 ——— 2 Miles
0 ——— 3.3 Kilometers

Pleasant Creek

Glen Canyon National Recreation Area

Tips from a Park Ranger

Thanks to the geology of the Waterpocket Fold, there's a lot of variety in the park—in elevation, landscape, and terrain, according to Thea Nordling, Capitol Reef's chief of interpretation.

"This tilted layer cake of geologic strata formed a variety of different micro-habitats as it eroded," she says. "There's an immense desert wilderness, but within that you've got perennial streams that have created a very rich riparian habitat, where prehistoric and historic people settled."

Capitol Reef is still relatively unknown, she says, and hasn't changed much since *Outside* magazine sang its praises as one of America's eight under-visited national parks—"parks as they were meant to be." Nordling says, "When people stop at Capitol Reef on their way to one of Utah's better-known national parks, they're usually pleasantly surprised."

The park is known for its wonderful colors, and Nordling says you can see them practically everywhere. "At sunset along Utah 24 and along the Scenic Drive you'll find a brilliant spectrum of colors—you can see them right from your car."

"The Frying Pan Trail is one of my favorite hikes," she says. "It's well marked, easy to get to, and you get wonderful views from the top as you hike along the crest of the Waterpocket Fold." Nordling adds that an added benefit to the trail is that it provides access to the spectacular spur trail to Cassidy Arch.

The dirt roads in the park can be a bit rugged, but most are accessible by two-wheel-drive, high-clearance vehicles, she says. However, Nordling advises that a four-wheel drive vehicle makes exploring the remote areas of the park easier and less worrisome in bad weather.

Given a choice, Nordling would probably visit in the spring or fall, because it's a bit cooler. But, she adds, "summer's beautiful too, because wildflowers are in bloom and the orchards are open for fruit picking."

The name Capitol Reef conjures up images of a tropical shoreline—it seems odd for a park composed of cliffs and canyons in landlocked Utah. But many of the pioneers who settled the West were former seafaring men, and they extended the traditional meaning of the word *reef* to include these seemingly impassable rock barriers. They added *Capitol* to the name because the huge white rounded domes of sandstone reminded them of the domes of capitol buildings.

Actually, to be accurate, the park should probably be called The Big Fold. When the earth's crust uplifted some 60 million years ago, creating the Rocky Mountains, most of this uplifting was relatively even. But here, through one of those fascinating quirks of nature, the crust wrinkled into a huge fold. Extending 100 miles, almost all within the national park, it's known as the Waterpocket Fold.

Avoiding the Crowds. Although Capitol Reef receives only about 750,000 visitors annually it can still be busy, especially during its peak season, which lasts from April through September. For this reason, the best time to visit is fall; particularly in October and November, when temperatures are usually warm enough for comfortable hiking and camping, but not so high as to send you constantly in search of shade. You also don't have to be as worried about flash floods through narrow canyons as you do during the July-through-September thunderstorm season.

Just the Facts

The park is about 121 miles northeast of Bryce Canyon National Park, 204 miles northeast of Zion National Park, 224 miles south of Salt Lake City, and 366 miles northeast of Las Vegas, Nevada.

It straddles Utah 24, which connects with I-70 to both the northeast and the northwest. Coming from the east along I-70, take Exit 147 and follow Utah 24 southwest to the park. Traveling from the west along I-70, there are two options: Exit 48 for Sigurd and follow Utah 24 east to the park; or Exit 85 for Fremont Junction, take Utah 72 south to Loa, where you pick up Utah 24 east to the park.

Those coming from Bryce Canyon National Park can follow Utah 12 northeast to its intersection with Utah 24 at the small town of Torrey, and turn right (east) to Capitol Reef. If you're approaching the park from Glen Canyon National Recreation Area, take Utah 276 (from Bullfrog Basin Marina) or Utah 95 (from Hite Crossing) north to the intersection with Utah 24, and follow that west to the park.

The Nearest Airport. The closest major airport is **Walker Field** in Grand Junction, Colorado (☎ **970/244-9100;** fax 970/241-9103; www.walkerfield.com), which has direct flights or connections from most major cities on **America West Express, Delta/Skywest,** and **United Express.**

Renting a Car. Car rentals are available at the Grand Junction airport from **Avis, Budget, Enterprise, Hertz, National, and Thrifty.** Toll-free reservations numbers are given in the appendix.

Contact **Capitol Reef National Park,** HCR 70 Box 15, Torrey, UT 84775 (☎ 435/425-3791; www.nps.gov/care).

Books and maps are available from the nonprofit **Capitol Reef Natural History Association,** Capitol Reef National Park, HC 70, Box 15, Torrey, UT 84775-9602 (☎ **435/425-3791,** ext. 106 or 113).

The visitor center is located on the Scenic Drive at its intersection with Utah 24. A path connects it to the campground, passing the historic blacksmith shop, orchards, and a lovely shaded picnic ground. There are exhibits on the geology and history of the area, and a 10-minute slide show on the park. Rangers can answer questions and provide backcountry permits. You can also pick up free brochures, and buy books, maps, videos, postcards, and posters.

Entry into the park (for up to 7 days) costs $4 per vehicle or $2 per person on foot or bike. Camping in the main campground costs $10 per night; the two primitive campgrounds are free. The **backcountry permits** (available at the visitor center) required for all overnight hikes are free.

Because skunks refuse to follow park rules regarding wildlife diet, campers should be especially careful of where and how they store food and dispose of garbage promptly.

While most visitors to the park enjoy a wonderful vacation without mishap, problems can occur. Hikers need to carry plenty of water, especially in summer. A major concern is weather: Afternoon thunderstorms during July, August, and September can bring flash floods, which fill narrow canyons suddenly and without warning. Steep-walled Grand Wash and Capitol Gorge can be particularly hazardous, and should be avoided whenever storms are threatening.

Because of its higher elevation, Capitol Reef doesn't get as hot as some of the other Southwestern parks, but summer temperatures can be uncomfortably warm on the trail. Winters can be very pleasant—snow falls occasionally, but doesn't usually last, and temperatures are often in the 50s. Late winter and spring can be windy.

Depending on weather, the Scenic Drive sometimes closes, most frequently in late summer during flash flood season, but occasionally in winter due to snow. When closed, you can still access a network of trails from Utah 24 and also get to the picnic area and campground.

Usually scheduled the third Friday in September, **Harvest Homecoming** celebrates the annual fruit harvest and the area's pioneer legacy. Activities include demonstrations of pioneer crafts and skills, such as candle making, quilting, soap making, and sheep shearing.

If You Only Have 1 Day

Because Capitol Reef is such a compact park, it's fairly easy to see a lot in a short amount of time. Although the ideal situation would be to have 2 or 3 days in the park, it is quite possible to have an enjoyable time with just half a day or so. Because there are no food services in the park (except fruit in season), you'll want to pack a picnic lunch.

Start at the **visitor center,** and watch the short slide show explaining the park's geology and early history. Then head out on the paved 25-mile round-trip **Scenic Drive** (described below), stopping along the way for a short hike, perhaps the easy walk up the Grand Wash. In the historic pioneer community of **Fruita,** near the beginning of the Scenic Drive, you can wander through orchards, where you're likely to see deer.

Then visit the historic **Gifford Farmhouse,** where you can get a taste of the daily life of Fruita's Mormon settlers and purchase replicas of pioneer era household items and crafts. Then hike one of the shorter trails in the Fruita area before going to see the Fruita Schoolhouse and some of the park's **petroglyphs.** In the evening, try to take in a ranger program at the amphitheater.

Exploring the Park by Car

Capitol Reef is relatively easy to see from the comfort of your automobile. From the visitor center, the **Scenic Drive** leads about 12.5 miles south into the park. Pick up a copy of the free Scenic Drive brochure at the entrance station, then set out, stopping at viewpoints to gaze up and out at the array of colorful cliffs, monoliths, and commanding rock formations.

If the weather is dry, drive down the gravel **Capitol Gorge Road** at the end of the paved Scenic Drive for a look at what many consider the park's best scenery. It's a 5-mile round-trip drive. If you're up for a short walk, the relatively flat 2-mile (round-trip) **Capitol Gorge Trail,** which starts at the end of Capitol Gorge Road, takes you to the historic **Pioneer Register,** a rock wall where traveling pioneers "signed in" (see "Day Hikes," below).

Another dry-weather driving option is the **Grand Wash Road,** a maintained dirt road that is subject to flash floods, but in good weather offers an easy route into a spectacular canyon. Along the 2-mile round-trip you'll see Cassidy Arch, named for famed outlaw Butch Cassidy, who, at least by some accounts, hid out in this area.

Utah 24, which crosses Capitol Reef from east to west, also has several viewpoints offering a good look at some of the park's best features, such as the monumental **Capitol Dome,** which resembles the dome of a capitol building; the striking **Chimney Rock;** the aptly named **Castle;** the historic **Fruita Schoolhouse;** and some **petroglyphs** left by the prehistoric Fremont people (see "Historic & Man-Made Attractions," below).

Organized Tours & Ranger Programs

Park rangers present a variety of free programs and activities from the spring through fall. **Campfire programs** take place most evenings at the outdoor amphitheater at Fruita Campground. Topics vary, but could include the animals and plants, geology, and human history of the area. Rangers also lead walks, and give short talks on a variety of subjects, such as the history of the pioneer Fruita Schoolhouse and the Gifford Farmhouse. Schedules are posted on bulletin boards at the visitor center and campground.

Historic & Man-Made Attractions

Throughout the park you'll find evidence of human presence. The Fremont people lived along the river as early as A.D. 700, staying until about A.D. 1300. Primarily hunters and gatherers, the Fremonts also grew corn, beans, and squash to supplement their diet. Their dwellings were pit houses, which were dug into the ground; the remains of one can be seen from the **Hickman Bridge Trail.** Many Fremont petroglyphs (images carved into rock) and pictographs (images painted on rock) are still visible on the canyon walls. If we could understand them, they might tell us why these early Americans left the area, a puzzle that continues to baffle archaeologists. One easily accessible site is located 1.5 miles east of the visitor center along Utah 24. There is a sign near the parking area and a short path to the petroglyph panels, which contains some of the most interesting images in the park.

Prospectors and other travelers passed through the **Capitol Gorge** section of the park in the late 1800s, leaving their names on the **Pioneer Register,** reached via a 2-mile round-trip walk (see "Day Hikes," below).

Mormon pioneers established the community of **Junction** (later named Fruita) in 1880. Now an historic district listed on the National Register of Historic Places, the orchards those settlers planted continue to flourish, tended by park workers who invite you to sample the "fruits" of their labor. Nearby is an historic blacksmith shop. The tiny **Fruita Schoolhouse,** built in 1896, was a church, social hall, and community meeting hall in addition to a one-room schoolhouse. The school closed in 1941, and was restored in 1984. It's furnished with old wood and wrought-iron desks, a wood stove, chalkboard, and textbooks. A handbell used to call students to class still rests on the corner of the teacher's desk.

Also in the Fruita district, the **Gifford Farmhouse,** built in 1908, is typical of rural Utah farmhouses of the early 1900s. Renovated and furnished by the Capitol Reef Natural History Association, the home is located off the Scenic Drive about 1 mile south of the visitor center, and is open from April through September. The home's former kitchen is a gift shop, selling reproductions of the household tools, toys, and utensils used by Mormon pioneers, plus crafts, jams and jellies, dried fruits, historic postcards, and books.

> The colors are such as no pigments can portray. They are deep, rich, and variegated; and so luminous are they, that light seems to flow or shine out of the rock.
>
> —Geologist C. E. Dutton, 1880

Day Hikes

Trails through the park offer sweeping panoramic views of colorful cliffs and domes, eerie journeys through desolate, steep-walled canyons, and cool walks along the tree-shaded Fremont River. Watch carefully for petroglyphs and other reminders of this area's first inhabitants. This is also the real Wild West, little changed from the way cowboys, bank robbers, settlers, and gold miners found it in the late 1800s. One of the best things about hiking here is the combination of scenic beauty, American Indian art, and Western history you'll discover.

Among the last areas in the continental United States to be explored, many parts of Capitol Reef are still practically unknown, perfect for those who want to see this rugged country in its natural state. Several local companies offer guide and shuttle services, including **Wild Hare Expeditions,** P.O. Box 750194, Torrey, UT 84775 (☎ **888/304-HARE** (4273) or 435/425-3999; www.color-country.net/~thehare; e-mail: thehare@color-country.net). In addition to the treks discussed below, Wild Hare offers photo tours, cross-country ski tours, and snowshoe tours, and also rents snowshoes ($7 per day). Located in the Best Western Capitol Reef Resort complex, a mile west of the park entrance, Wild Hare Expeditions' shop, called **"The Hare Lair,"** rents bikes (see below), bike racks, tents, sleeping bags, and backpacks; repairs bikes; and sells bike accessories, climbing equipment, backcountry clothing and gear, and maps. The shop is usually open from March through mid-November, daily from 8 to 10am and 4 to 9pm.

SHORTER TRAILS

Capitol Gorge Trail

1 mi. one way. Easy. Access: End of the Capitol Gorge dirt road.

This is a mostly level walk along the bottom of a narrow canyon. Looking up at the tall, smooth walls of rock conveys a strong sense of what the pioneers must have seen and felt 100 years ago when they moved rocks and debris to drive their wagons through this canyon. The trail leads past the Pioneer Register, where early travelers carved their names.

Fremont River Trail

1.25 mi. one way. Easy to moderate. Access: Fruita Campground.

This self-guided nature trail is quite easy (and wheelchair accessible) for the first 0.5 mile as it meanders past the orchards along the river, but becomes increasingly strenuous thereafter. The path climbs up to an overlook of the lovely valley. A part of the trail is steep, with long drop-offs.

Goosenecks Trail

0.1 mi. one way. Easy. Access: Panorama Point Turnoff on Utah 24, 3 mi. west of the visitor center, then 1 mi. on a gravel access rd.

This short walk affords great views of Sulphur Creek Canyon. It's a good trail for those with little time because it offers both sweeping panoramic views of the geology of Waterpocket Fold and close-ups of interesting rock formations.

Hickman Bridge Trail

1 mi. one way. Moderate. Access: Hickman Bridge parking area on Utah 24, 2 mi. east of the visitor center.

Starting at the Fremont River, this self-guided nature trail heads into the desert, ascending several short steep hills to Hickman Natural Bridge, which has an opening 133 feet wide and 125 feet high. The trail has a 400-foot elevation gain.

Sunset Point Trail

0.3 mi. one way. Easy. Access: Panorama Point Turnoff on Utah 24, 3 mi. west of the visitor center, then 1 mi. on a gravel access rd.

This hike affords panoramic views of cliffs and domes, which are most dramatic around sunset.

LONGER TRAILS

Cassidy Arch Trail

1.75 mi. one way. Strenuous. Access: Grand Wash Trailhead, via Scenic Drive and Grand Wash Rd.

This trail offers spectacular views as it climbs steeply from the floor of Grand Wash to high cliffs overlooking the park. From the trail you'll also get several perspectives of Cassidy Arch, a natural stone arch named for outlaw Butch Cassidy, who is believed to have occasionally used the Grand Wash as a hideout.

Chimney Rock Trail

3.5 mi. RT. Moderate to strenuous. Access: Chimney Rock parking area on Utah 24, 2 mi. west of the visitor center.

This trail begins with a strenuous climb up switchbacks to the more moderate loop trail on top. It affords views of Chimney Rock from both below and above, plus panoramic views of the Waterpocket Fold and surrounding areas.

Cohab Canyon Trail

1.75 mi. one way. Moderate to strenuous. Access: Across from Fruita Campground.

After the first 0.25 mile, which is rather strenuous, this trail levels out a bit and has fewer steep grades. It climbs to a hidden canyon above the campground, and has two short side trails leading to overlooks. From the overlooks you get good views of the Fremont River, historic Fruita, and the campground.

Fremont Gorge Overlook Trail

2.25 mi. one way. Strenuous. Access: Blacksmith shop.

A strenuous climb to 1,000 feet above the Fremont River, this trail rewards you with a great view into the Fremont Gorge at the end. The middle of the hike, across Johnson Mesa, is fairly easy. The trail also affords good views of Fruita and the escarpment of the Waterpocket Fold.

Frying Pan Trail

3 mi. one way. Strenuous. Access: Across from the Fruita Campground or Grand Wash parking area.

This strenuous but scenic trail links Cohab and Cassidy Arch trails on the summit. It follows the ridge of the Waterpocket Fold escarpment, with a number of climbs up and down canyons and over slickrock. You'll get good views of Miners Mountain to the southwest, rugged canyons to the side, and the Grand Wash below near the end of the trail.

Golden Throne Trail

2 mi. one way. Strenuous. Access: Capitol Gorge parking area.

A strenuous climb from the bottom of the gorge to the top of the cliffs at the base of the Golden Throne, this trail provides several panoramic vistas, good spots to stop to catch your breath. The Golden Throne is a large formation of Navajo sandstone that glows golden-yellow in the light of the setting sun.

Grand Wash Trail

2.25 mi. one way. Easy. Access: Grand Wash parking area, or on Utah 24 east of the visitor center.

This is a relatively easy hike along a narrow wash bottom with sheer rock walls on both sides. The trail shows the phenomenal power of water, as it winds between tall polished walls of stone, scoured smooth by the force of flash floods.

Old Wagon Trail

3.5 mi. RT. Strenuous. Access: West side of Scenic Drive near end.

This 1,000-foot climb up the east flank of Miners Mountain is certainly strenuous, but it affords spectacular and unusual views of the Waterpocket Fold escarpment. This hike is best done late in the day when the cliffs are lit by the setting sun.

Rim Overlook Trail

2.25 mi. one way. Strenuous. Access: Hickman Bridge parking area on Utah 24 east of the visitor center.

After a strenuous 1,000-foot climb, hikers are rewarded with good views of Fruita and vistas to the south.

Exploring the Backcountry

The park offers a variety of backpacking opportunities, including the 15-mile round trip **Upper Muley Twist** route, which follows a canyon through the Waterpocket Fold and offers views of arches and narrows, and panoramic vistas from the top of the fold; and the 22-mile round-trip **Halls Creek Narrows,** which follows Halls Creek through a beautiful slot canyon (where you may have to wade or swim). **Free backcountry permits** (available at the visitor center) are required for all overnight hikes. Backcountry hikers should discuss their plans with rangers before setting out, since many of these routes are prone to flash floods.

Other Sports & Activities

Four-Wheeling & Mountain Biking. As in most national parks, bikes and 4X4s are restricted to established roads, but Capitol Reef has several such "established" roads—actually little more than dirt trails—that provide exciting opportunities for those using 4X4s or pedal-power.

The only route appropriate for road bikes is the **Scenic Drive,** described above, but both the Grand Wash and Capitol Gorge roads (see "Exploring the Park by Car," above), plus three longer backcountry roads, are open to mountain bikes as well as four-wheel-drive vehicles. Be aware that rain can make the roads impassable, so it's best to check on current conditions before setting out.

One recommended trip is the **Cathedral Valley Loop.** It covers about 60 miles on a variety of road surfaces, including dirt, sand, and rock, and requires the fording of the Fremont River, where water is usually 1 to 1.5 feet deep. The rewards are beautiful, unspoiled scenery, including bizarre sandstone monoliths and majestic cliffs, in one of the park's more remote areas. There's a small primitive campground (see "Camping," below). Access to this loop is from Utah 24, just outside the park, 11.7 miles east of the visitor center via the river ford road, or 18.6 miles east of the visitor center on the Caineville Wash Road.

Mountain-bike and four-wheel-drive **tours** into the national park and surrounding areas are provided by **Wild Hare Expeditions** (see above). Full-day tours, including lunch, cost $60 to $75; a variety of other guided trips, including multiday excursions, are offered as well. The company rents mountain bikes at $20 for a half day and $30 for a full day, with discounts for those taking guided tours and for multiday rentals. Four-wheel-drive tours are also available from **Hondoo Rivers and Trails** (see "Horseback Riding" below), including multiday trips to petroglyph and pictograph sites in the area. Those wanting to go four-wheeling on their own can rent a 4X4 for about $75 per day, at **Thousand Lakes RV Park & Campground** (see "Camping," below).

Horseback Riding. Horses are welcome in some areas of the park but prohibited in others; check at the visitor center. **Capitol Reef Trail Rides,** at the Best Western in Torrey (see below), P.O. Box 375, Bicknell, UT 84715 (☎ 435/425-3761), offers a variety of rides in the area, ranging from 1 hour to all day. A 1-hour ride costs $15 and a 4-hour ride costs $50. First-time riders are welcome, minimum age is 8, and maximum weight is 230 pounds. Several cookout rides and other special activities are available, call for information.

Horseback trips are also run by **Hondoo Rivers and Trails** (P.O. Box 98, Torrey, UT 84775; ☎ 800/332-2696 or

435/425-3519; fax 435/425-3548; www.
hondoo.com). Their goal is to provide
comfortable and informative backcountry experiences for small groups using
low-impact camping techniques. Scheduled trips include 5-day excursions into
the backcountry of Capitol Reef National Park, nearby Boulder Mountain, and
the canyons of Grand Staircase–
Escalante National Monument. Trail
rides aimed at wildflower or wildlife viewing and fall colors are also scheduled;
plus shorter photographic safaris ($55 to
$90 per person), and cattle roundups.
Cost for multiday trips ranges from $700
to $825 per person.

Wildlife Viewing. Summer in Capitol
Reef is hot and sometimes stormy, but it's
a good season for wildlife viewing. In particular, many species of lizards make
their home in the park; you will probably
catch a glimpse of one warming itself on
a rock. The western whiptail, eastern
fence, and side-blotched lizards are the
most common, but the loveliest is the
collared lizard, dark in color but with
light speckles that allow it to blend easily
with lava rocks and become almost invis-
ible to its foes.

Watch for deer and marmots in Fruita, especially along the path between the
visitor center and Fruita Campground.
This area is also where you're likely to see
chipmunks and antelope ground squirrels. Although they're somewhat shy and
only emerge from their dens at night, the
ring-tailed cat, a member of the raccoon
family, also calls the park home; as do
bighorn sheep, bobcat, cougar, fox, and
coyote.

If you keep your eyes to the sky you
may see a golden eagle, Cooper's hawk,
raven, or any of the many other types of
birds attracted by the park's variety of
habitats. Year-round residents include
chukars, common flickers, yellow-bellied
sapsuckers, horned larks, canyon wrens,
rock wrens, American robins, ruby-
crowned kinglets, starlings, and American kestrels. In warmer months you're

Especially for Kids

In addition to the **Junior Ranger
Program** (see chapter 1), kids
from third through eighth grades
can become **Junior Geologists** by
joining a ranger on a field trip (usually held once each week in summer). Families are invited to borrow
a **Family Fun Pack** at the visitor center. The pack contains park-related
games and activities.

also likely to see yellow warblers, red-
winged blackbirds, western tanagers,
northern orioles, violet-green swallows,
white-throated swifts, and black-chinned
hummingbirds. Bird watching is particularly good along the Fremont River Trail
in the spring and early summer.

Camping

INSIDE THE PARK

The pleasant **Fruita Campground,** located along the Scenic Drive, 1 mile south
of the visitor center, has shade trees,
modern rest rooms, and is within walking distance of the Fruita School and
other historic attractions.

Capitol Reef also has two primitive
campgrounds. **Cedar Mesa Campground,** in the southern part of the park,
is reached by going east of Utah 24 about
9 miles to the unpaved Notom-Bullfrog
Road, which you take about 23 miles
south to the campground. The road may
be impassable in wet weather. **Cathedral
Valley Campground** is in the northern
part of the park, about 35 miles from the
visitor center (get directions at the visitor
center). *Note:* Access roads to Cathedral
Valley Campground require a high-
clearance or four-wheel-drive vehicle at
all times and may be completely inaccessible in bad weather.

Backcountry camping is permitted in much of the park with a free permit, available at the visitor center.

WEST OF THE PARK

There are several commercial campgrounds in the community of Torrey about 5 miles west of the park entrance, and an attractive U.S. Forest Service campground not too far away.

At **Sandcreek RV Park & Hostel,** 540 Utah 24 (P.O. Box 750276), Torrey, UT 84775 (☎ 877/425-3578 or 435/425-3577), you'll find RV sites with full hookups, plus grassy tent sites, not to mention great views in all directions. Trees have been planted and will provide shade as they grow, and a swimming pool is also planned. There is already a gift shop and espresso bar.

Also in Torrey is **Thousand Lakes RV Park & Campground,** Utah 24 (P.O. Box 750070), Torrey, UT 84775 (☎ 800/355-8995 for reservations, or 435/425-3500). In addition to the usual amenities, this campground offers good views of surrounding rock formations, plus some shade trees. RV sites are gravel; tent sites are grass. The campground also has four cabins ($26 to $55). Campers can rent 4X4s for $75 a day, and can feast on Western dinners Tuesday through Saturday. There is also a convenience store, horseshoes, and barbecues.

Wonderland RV Park, at the junction of Utah 24 and 12 (P.O. Box 67), Torrey, UT 84775 (☎ 435/425-3345), is a new campground with some nice shade trees. The area is mostly open, with gravel roads and grassy sites, including about 50 tent sites.

In addition to the commercial campgrounds discussed above, **Austin's Chuck Wagon Lodge and General Store** in Torrey has a half dozen RV sites. See the "Accommodations" section, below.

Those looking for a forest camping experience on the west side of the national park will like **Singletree Campground,** on Utah 12 about 16 miles south of Torrey (Teasdale Ranger District of the Dixie National Forest, Box 90, Teasdale, UT 84773; ☎ 435/425-3702; reservations 877/444-6777; www.reserveusa.com). Located in a forest of tall pines, this campground has standard individual campsites plus five multiple-family sites. All sites are paved, and many offer distant panoramic views of the national park. Near two of the large multiple-family sites ($20 to $25), you'll find a horseshoe pit and volleyball court.

EAST OF THE PARK

Located along Utah 24 about 15 miles east of the park is **Sleepy Hollow Campground,** HC 70, Box 40, Caineville, UT 84775 (☎ 435/456-9130). Although the terrain is generally desert, the tent sites

Campground	Elev.	Total Sites	RV Hookups	Dump Station	Toilets	Drinking Water
Fruita	5,500	70	0	Yes	Yes	Yes
Cedar Mesa	5,400	5	0	No	Yes	No
Cathedral Valley	7,000	6	0	No	Yes	No
Sandcreek	6,840	24	12	Yes	Yes	Yes
Singletree	8,200	31	31	Yes	Yes	Yes
Sleepy Hollow	4,600	35	16	Yes	Yes	Yes
Thousand Lakes	6,840	67	58	Yes	Yes	Yes
Wonderland	6,980	83	33	Yes	Yes	Yes

are nicely shaded, and there are also a few trees in the RV area. Hookups are electric only. Reservations are recommended. There's a convenience store with beverages, snack items, film, ice, and souvenirs.

Accommodations

There are no lodging facilities in the park itself, but the town of Torrey, just west of the park entrance where Utah 12 meets Utah 24, can take care of most needs.

NEAR THE PARK

In addition to the properties discussed below, Torrey has a **Days Inn,** 675 E. Utah 24, at its intersection with Utah 12 (☎ 435/425-3111), doubles $39 to $69 in summer; and a **Super 8,** 600 E. Utah 24, near the intersection of Utah 24 and Utah 12 (☎ 435/425-3688), doubles $58 to $72 in summer. Both have lower rates the rest of the year. Also see the Sleepy Hollow Campground listing in the "Camping" section, above. Chain's toll-free reservation numbers are listed in the appendix.

Austin's Chuck Wagon Lodge & General Store

12 W. Main St. (P.O. Box 750180), Torrey, UT 84775. ☎ **800/863-3288** or 435/425-3335.

Fax 435/425-3434. 21 units. A/C TV. New units $58 double, older units $39 double; family suite $100 double plus $5 for each additional person. AE, MC, V. Closed Dec–Feb.

This attractive, nicely landscaped motel has two sections—the newer, modern motel rooms, with Southwest decor, telephones, satellite TV, free in-room movies, and two queen-size beds; and the older, slightly rustic units, which have knotty pine walls, one queen bed, and no phones. Also available is a newly remodeled family suite, with large living room, fully equipped kitchen, and three bedrooms that sleep six. The grounds are nicely landscaped, with a lawn and large trees, and facilities include an outdoor pool and whirlpool. On the property are a grocery store/bakery, coin-operated laundry, and hair salon. An attached RV park has six sites with full hookups, at $15 per night.

Best Western Capitol Reef Resort

2600 E. Utah 24 (P.O. Box 750160), Torrey, UT 84775. ☎ **435/425-3761.** Fax 435/425-3300. www.bwcapitolreef.com. E-mail: jacksonhole@compuserve.com. 50 units. A/C TV TEL. June–Sept $75–$85 double; Oct–May $47–$75 double; $90–$125 suite. AE, CB, DC, DISC, MC, V.

Located a mile west of the national park entrance, this attractive Best Western provides an excellent location for park visits. Try to get a room on the back side

Showers	Fire Pits/ Grills	Laundry	Public Phone	Reserve	Fees	Open
No	Yes	No	Yes	No	$10	Year-round
No	Yes	No	No	No	Free	Year-round
No	Yes	No	No	No	Free	Year-round
Yes	No	Yes	Yes	Yes	$9–$18	Mid-Mar to mid-Oct
No	Yes	No	No	Yes	$10	Memorial Day to mid-Sept
Yes	No	No	Yes	Yes	$12–$15	May–Sept
Yes	Yes	Yes	Yes	Yes	$9–$17	Apr–Oct
Yes	Yes	Yes	Yes	Yes	$13	Apr–Oct

of the motel; you'll be rewarded with fantastic views of the area's red rock formations. Standard rooms have two queen-size beds, white stucco walls, and Southwestern-style scenic prints. A restaurant serves three meals daily year-round. The outdoor heated pool, whirlpool, and sundeck are a plus; all are situated out back, away from road noise, with glass wind barriers and spectacular views.

Boulder View Inn

385 W. Main St. (Utah 24), Torrey, UT 84775. ☎ **800/444-3980** or 435/425-3800. 12 units. A/C TV TEL. $52 double. Rates include continental breakfast. AE, DISC, MC, V.

This is an attractive, well-maintained modern motel with a Southwestern motif. Rooms are large and comfortable, containing tub/shower combos, queen or king beds, and a table with two chairs. Swimmers and smokers are out of luck—there is no swimming pool and no smoking permitted in any of the rooms.

Capitol Reef Inn & Cafe

360 W. Main St. (Utah 24), Torrey, UT 84775. ☎ **435/425-3270.** www.capitolreefinn.com. E-mail: cri@capitolreefinn.com. 10 units. A/C TV TEL. $44 double. AE, DISC, MC, V. Closed Nov–Mar.

An older Western-style motel—small, beautifully landscaped, and adequately maintained—rooms here are homey and comfortable, with one queen-size bed, two queens, or one queen and a double. Only one room has a tub/shower combo; the others have showers only. Furniture is handmade solid wood. Facilities include a playground, trampoline, and 10-person whirlpool tub. Adjacent, under the same ownership, are an excellent restaurant (see "Dining," below) and a gift shop with American Indian crafts, guide books, and maps.

Cockscomb Inn

97 S. State St. (P.O. Box 18), Teasdale, UT 84773. ☎ **800/530-1038** or 435/

425-3511. www.go-utah.com/cockscombinn. E-mail: coxcomb@color-country.net. 4 units. $55–$80 double; cottage $100 double, 2-night minimum. Rates (except cottage) include full breakfast. AE, DISC, MC, V. No children under 8. From Torrey head west on Utah 24 about 2 mi. to the green sign for Teasdale and turn left a short distance to the inn (on your left).

This 100-year-old adobe farmhouse is comfortably furnished with Victorian antiques and collectibles, plus family photos and memorabilia. Elissa Stevens has named the three rooms in the house after herself, her mother Mary, and granddaughter Rachel. None are large, but all have queen beds, and the Elissa room has a TV and direct access to the lovely backyard patio. Bathrooms have showers only. There's a TV in the common living room. Breakfast includes coffee, juice, granola, fresh fruit, yogurt, a homemade bread such as banana bread or muffins, plus a main hot dish, which might be pecan waffles or croissant French toast with homemade fruit spreads.

The modern cottage is large and can sleep 5. It has a fully equipped kitchen with dishwasher and microwave, full bathroom, stereo, TV, wood stove, and private deck with gas barbecue. There's a queen bed in the bedroom plus a futon and a queen hide-a-bed in the living room. Breakfast is available at an extra charge ($5).

The entire property is no-smoking.

Skyridge Bed & Breakfast Inn

On Utah 24, just east of its intersection with Utah 12 (P.O. Box 750220), Torrey, UT 84775. ☎ **435/425-3222.** www.bbiu.org/skyridge. E-mail: skyridge@color-country.net. 6 units. TV TEL. $92–$138 double. Rates include breakfast and evening hors d'oeuvres. MC, V.

This combination bed-and-breakfast and art gallery is housed in a three-story contemporary inn, with territorial-style appearance. There are six distinctive rooms, each with VCR. Rooms are decorated with an eclectic mix of antiques, collectibles, folk sculpture, and contemporary art. Two rooms have private decks with hot tubs, while another features a two-person whirlpool tub. An impressive fireplace, decorated with more than 30 pounds of roofing nails, sits in the shared gallery/living room, which also contains books, games, and a collection of classic and contemporary movies available for guest use. A new outdoor hot tub has been added. The inn is located on 75 acres, with its own hiking and biking trails and spectacular views of the national park and Boulder Mountain. Smoking is not permitted inside.

Wonderland Inn

At the junction of Utah 24 and 12 (P.O. Box 67), Torrey, UT 84775. ☎ **800/458-0216** or 435/425-3775. Fax 435/425-3212. 52 units. A/C TV TEL. $40–$80 double. AE, CB, DC, DISC, MC, V.

Built in 1990, this modern motel is perched on a hill set back from the highway, making it very quiet and peaceful. Built, owned, and managed by Ray and Diane Potter and family, the property is especially well kept. Standard motel rooms have two queen-size beds or one king, and typical modern motel decor with some genuine wood touches. Facilities include a combination indoor/outdoor heated swimming pool with tanning room, whirlpool, sauna, beauty salon, and gift shop. A restaurant serves three meals daily year-round, with a popular breakfast buffet in the summer.

Dining

There are no dining facilities in the park.

NEAR THE PARK

Brink's Burgers Drive-In

165 E. Main St., Torrey. ☎ **435/425-3710.** Most items $1.50–$4.50. MC, V. Daily 11am–9pm. Closed in winter. BURGERS/SANDWICHES.

This nonfranchise fast-food restaurant serves good burgers in a cafelike decor, or you can take your food outside to picnic tables. In addition to better than average burgers, choices include a garden burger, chicken and fish selections, cheese sticks, onion rings, zucchini slices, and spicy potato wedges. Milk shakes and ice-cream cones are also available; no alcohol is served.

Cafe Diablo

599 W. Main St., Torrey. ☎ **435/425-3070.** Main courses $12.95–$16.95. MC, V. May–Oct 15, daily 4–10pm. Closed Oct 16–Apr. SOUTHWESTERN.

Looks are deceiving. What appears to be a simple small-town cafe in a converted home is in fact a very fine restaurant, offering innovative beef, pork, chicken, and seafood selections, many created with a southwestern flair. The menu varies, but could include pumpkinseed-crusted local trout, served with cilantro-lime sauce and rice pancakes; lime and honey painted chicken breast, chargrilled and served with tomatillo salsa; or baby back pork ribs slow roasted in a chipotle, molasses, and rum glaze. Pastries, all made on the premises, are spectacular, and beer—both microbrewed and regular—is available.

Capitol Reef Inn & Cafe

360 W. Main St. ☎ **435/425-3271.** Main courses lunch $5.50–$8.50; dinner $5–$16. AE, DISC, MC, V. Daily 7–9pm. Closed Nov–Mar.

A local favorite, this restaurant offers fine, fresh, and healthy dining that is among the best you'll find in Utah. Famous for its locally raised trout, it is equally well known for its 10-vegetable salad served with all dinner entrees. Vegetables are grown locally, and several dishes, such as spaghetti, an excellent fettuccine primavera, and shish kebabs, can be ordered vegetarian or with various meats or fish. Steaks and chicken are also served. Portions are large and prices reasonable. The atmosphere is casual with comfortable seating, American Indian rugs and crafts, and large windows. The restaurant offers an extensive wine list, plus domestic and imported beers.

Rabbit Valley Bakery & Cafe

37 Utah 24, Bicknell. ☎ **435/425-3953.** Main courses lunch $5.95–$8.95; dinner $6.95–$15.95; pizzas start at $8.95. AE, MC, V. Tues–Sat 11am–9pm; Fri–Sat 11am–10pm. From Torrey head west on Utah 24 about 8 mi., the restaurant is on the left at the east edge of Bicknell. AMERICAN.

This large modern log building of post and beam construction is light and airy, and there's also a lovely outdoor patio. The lunch menu includes cold deli sandwiches and a half-dozen hot sandwiches ranging from burgers to chicken to a delicious hot veggie—sautéed squash, onions, and peppers served on a sourdough roll. After 5, dinner offerings include charbroiled steaks, broiled halibut or baked trout, tortellini Alfredo, and fried chicken. Deli meats and cheeses are sold by the pound. The fresh baked breads, pastries, fruit pies, specialty cakes, and cinnamon rolls round out your meal. Beer and wine, including Utah microbrews, are served.

Picnic & Camping Supplies

In addition to groceries, **Austin's Chuck Wagon Lodge & General Store,** at 12 W. Main St. in Torrey (☎ 435/425-3335), has a bakery, a coin-operated laundry, and a hair salon. Austin's is closed December through February.

10

CARLSBAD CAVERNS NATIONAL PARK

by Don and Barbara Laine

O NE OF THE LARGEST AND MOST SPECTACULAR CAVE SYSTEMS IN THE world, Carlsbad Caverns National Park comprises some 80 known caves that snake through the porous limestone reef of the Guadalupe Mountains. Fantastic and grotesque formations

fascinate visitors, who find every shape imaginable (and unimaginable) naturally sculpted in the underground— from frozen waterfalls to strands of pearls, soda straws to miniature castles, draperies to ice-cream cones.

Formation of the caverns began some 250 million years ago, when a huge inland sea covered this region. A reef formed, and then the sea disappeared, leaving the reef covered with deposits of salts and gypsum. Eventually uplifting and erosion brought the reef back to the surface, and then the actual cave building began. Rainwater seeped through cracks in the earth's surface, dissolving the limestone and leaving hollows behind. With the help of sulfuric acid, created by gases released from oil and gas deposits further below ground, the cavern passageways grew, sometimes becoming huge rooms.

Once the caves were hollowed out, nature became artistic, decorating the rooms with a vast variety of fanciful formations. Very slowly, water dripped down through the rock into the caves,

dissolving more limestone and absorbing the mineral calcite and other materials on its journey. Each drop of water then deposited its tiny load of calcite, gradually creating the cave formations that lure visitors to Carlsbad Caverns each year.

Although American Indians had known of Carlsbad Cavern for centuries, it was not discovered by settlers until ranchers in the 1880s were attracted by sunset flights of bats emerging from the cave. The first reported trip into the cave was in 1883, when a man supposedly lowered his 12-year-old son into the cave entrance. A cowboy named Jim White, who worked for mining companies that collected bat droppings for use as a fertilizer, began to explore the main cave in the early 1900s. Fascinated by the formations, White shared his discovery with others, and soon word of this magical underground world spread.

Carlsbad Cave National Monument was created in October 1923. In 1926, the first electric lights were installed, and in 1930 Carlsbad Caverns gained national park status.

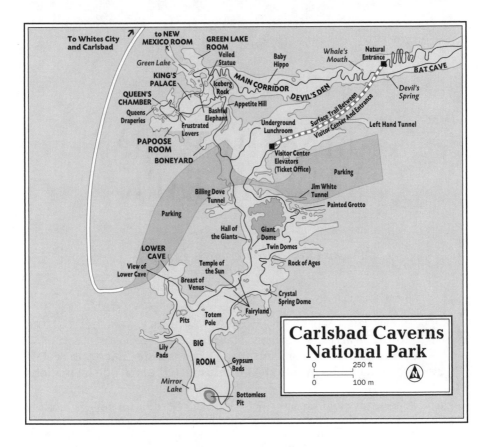

Carlsbad Caverns National Park

Underground development at the park has been confined to the famous Big Room, one of the largest and most easily accessible of the caverns, with a ceiling 25 stories high and a floor large enough to hold 14 football fields. Visitors can tour parts of it on their own, aided by a new state-of-the-art CD-ROM portable audio guide, and explore other sections and several other caves on guided tours. The cave is also a summer home to about 1 million Mexican free-tailed bats, which hang from the ceiling of Bat Cave during the day, but put on a spectacular show each evening as they leave the cave in search of food, and again in the morning when they return.

In addition to the fascinating underground world, the national park has a scenic drive, interpretive nature trail, and backcountry hiking trails through the Chihuahuan Desert.

Avoiding the Crowds. The park is open year-round. Crowds are thickest in summer, and on weekends and holidays year-round, so visiting on weekdays between Labor Day and Memorial Day is the best way to avoid them. January is the quietest month.

Visiting during the park's off-season is especially attractive because the climate in the caves doesn't vary regardless of the weather above. The only downside to an off-peak visit is that you won't be able to see the bat flights. The bats head to Mexico when the weather starts to get chilly, usually by late October, and don't return until May. There are also fewer guided cave tours off-season. The best time to see the park might well be September, when you can still see the bat flights but there are fewer visitors than during the peak summer season.

Tips from a Park Ranger

"**C**aves are not familiar to the human experience—they're unknown, scary," says Douglas Ballou, the park's cave supervisor. "Here, under the guise of an adventure, we're helping people gain a greater appreciation of caves and the world of caving."

Visitors actually see only a few of the many caves that are in the park, according to Ballou, who says that of the park's 80-plus caves only 10 are open for wild caving, and then only to experienced cavers. Most people, of course, visit the park's namesake, Carlsbad Cavern, and some also take ranger-guided tours of nearby Slaughter Canyon Cave and Spider Cave.

"If you can only see one thing here, see the Big Room in Carlsbad Cavern," advises Ballou. "Allow an hour, and if you have more time and are in good physical condition, take the Natural Entrance Route into the cave, which has a 750-foot descent and is a bit strenuous."

The scientific potential from caves is tremendous, Ballou says, adding that research is underway in one of the park's caves that may eventually provide a cure for certain types of cancer. "They're collecting microscopic life forms—bacteria that survive without sunlight and secrete an enzyme that appears to be able to kill breast cancer cells without harming healthy human cells." While park visitors usually don't have the opportunity to see scientists at work, they can get a feel for what it's like to explore caves, and to see the pools of water and other isolated environments that allow these microscopic life forms to exist.

Ballou says that many park visitors miss out on the aboveground attractions, and he particularly recommends the 9.5-mile scenic drive, which provides panoramic views of the surrounding desert. "Late afternoon or early evening is best, when it's not so hot," Ballou says. He also suggests a picnic at Rattlesnake Springs, a "birders' paradise," he calls it, and adds that those who want to experience the Chihuahuan Desert without any crowds should consider hiking the park's backcountry, which is done by less than 1% of the park's visitors.

Just the Facts

GETTING THERE & GATEWAYS

The main section of the national park, with the visitor center and entrance to Carlsbad Cavern, is about 30 miles southwest of the city of Carlsbad via U.S. 62/180 and N. Mex. 7. From Albuquerque drive east on I-40 for 59 miles to Clines Corners, and turn south on U.S. 285 for 216 miles to the city of Carlsbad. For the caverns, continue southwest 23 miles on U.S. 62/180 to White's City, and go about 7 miles on N. Mex. 7, the park access road, to the visitor center. From El Paso drive east 150 miles on U.S. 62/180 to White's City, and then 7 miles on N. Mex. 7 to the visitor center.

The Nearest Airport. Air travelers can fly to **Cavern City Air Terminal** (☎ 505/887-1500), at the south edge of the city of Carlsbad, which has commercial service from Albuquerque with Mesa Airlines (☎ 800/637-2247), plus Hertz car rentals and taxi service.

The nearest major airport is **El Paso International** (☎ 915/780-4749) in central El Paso just north of I-10, with service from **American, America West, Continental, Delta, TWA, Southwest, Frontier,** and

Aero Litoral (☎ 800/237-6639); and car rentals from **Advantage, Alamo, Avis, Budget, Dollar, Hertz,** and **National.** Toll-free numbers are given in the appendix.

INFORMATION

Contact the **Superintendent, Carlsbad Caverns National Park,** 3225 National Parks Hwy., Carlsbad, NM 88220 (☎ 505/785-2232, or 505/785-2107 for recorded information; www.nps.gov/cave). Those arriving in the city of Carlsbad before going to the park can get brochures, maps, and other information at the **National Park Service's Administrative Office and Bookstore,** at 3225 National Parks Hwy. (at the intersection with West Pecan Street). It's open Monday through Friday from 8am to 4:30pm.

Because the park's backcountry trails may be hard to follow, rangers strongly recommend that those planning any serious aboveground hiking obtain topographical maps. An excellent book for hikers is *Hiking Carlsbad Caverns and Guadalupe Mountains National Parks* (Helena, Mont.: Falcon Press, 1996) by Bill Schneider, which was published in partnership with the Carlsbad Caverns–Guadalupe Mountains Association and is keyed to the Trails Illustrated topographical map of the park. These and other books and maps are available at the visitor center's bookstore or from the **Carlsbad Caverns–Guadalupe Mountains Association** (see "Visitor Center," below).

VISITOR CENTER

The visitor center at the park is open daily 8am to 7pm from Memorial Day to mid-August; and self-guided cave tours can be started from 8:30am to 3:30pm. The rest of the year the visitor center is open from 8am to 5:30pm, with self-guided cave tours from 8:30am to 2pm. Tour times and schedules may be modified during slower times in the winter. The park is closed on Christmas Day.

At the visitor center are displays depicting the geology and history of the caverns, bats and other wildlife, and a three-dimensional model of Carlsbad Cavern. You can also get information about the tours available and other park activities, both below- and aboveground. There is a well-stocked bookstore, operated by the **Carlsbad Caverns–Guadalupe Mountains Association,** 727 Carlsbad Caverns Hwy., Carlsbad, NM 88220 (☎ 505/785-2232, ext. 480; www.caverns.org). An annual family membership in the nonprofit association costs $25, and provides a 15% discount at this and many other national park bookstores.

Attached to the visitor center is a family-style restaurant (see "Dining," below) and a gift shop (☎ 505/785-2281) that offers the usual souvenir items such as postcards and sweatshirts, plus film and a variety of gift items including handmade American Indian crafts. Another gift shop is located in the Underground Rest Area (see "Dining," below).

FEES & RESERVATIONS

Admission to the visitor center and aboveground sections of the park is free. The basic cavern entry fee, which is good for 3 days and includes self-guided tours of the Natural Entrance and Big Room, is $6 for adults and $3 for children 6 to 15. The entrance fee for Golden Age and Golden Access cardholders is $3; Golden Eagle Passports are not valid for cave entrance or tours. An excellent audio tour of the two self-guided routes is available for a $3 rental fee.

A general cave admission ticket is required in addition to tour fees for all guided cave tours except those to Slaughter Canyon Cave and Spider Cave. Reservations are required for all guided tours. Holders of Golden Age and Golden Access passports receive 50% discounts on tours. The King's Palace guided tour costs $8 for adults, $4 for children 6 to 15, and is free for children aged 4 and 5 with an adult—younger children are not permitted. Guided tours of Left Hand Tunnel, limited to those 6 and older, cost $7 for adults and $3.50 for children 6 to 15. Guided tours of Spider Cave, Lower Cave, and Hall of the White Giant are limited to those 12 and older, and cost $20 for adults and $10 for youths 12 to 15. Slaughter Canyon Cave tours, for those 6 and older, cost $15 for adults and $7.50 for children 6 to 15.

You can make reservations for cave tours up to 3 months in advance by phone or via the Internet (☎ **800/ 967-CAVE** (2283) or 301/722-1257; www. nps.gov/cave).

SPECIAL REGULATIONS & WARNINGS

As you would expect, damaging the cave formations in any way is prohibited. What some people do not understand is that they should not even touch the formations, walls, or ceilings. This is not only because many of the features are delicate and easily broken, but also because skin oils will both discolor the rock and disturb the mineral deposits that are necessary for growth.

All tobacco use is prohibited underground. In addition, food, drinks, candy, and chewing gum are not allowed on the underground trails. Those making wishes should not throw coins or other objects into the underground pools.

Cave explorers should wear flat shoes with rubber soles and heels, because of the slippery paths. Children under 16 must remain with an adult at all times while in the caves. Although strollers are not allowed for younger children, child backpacks are a good idea, but beware of low ceilings and doorways along the pathways.

Flash photography is not permitted at the evening Bat Flight programs.

Pets are not permitted in the caverns, on park trails, or in the backcountry, and because of the hot summer temperatures pets should not be left unattended in vehicles. There is a kennel (☎ 505/ 785-2281) available at the visitor center.

It has cages in an air-conditioned room, but no runs, and is primarily used by pet owners for periods of 3 hours or so while they are on cave tours. Pets are given water, but not food, and there are no grooming or overnight facilities. Reservations are not necessary; cost is $4 per pet.

SEASONS & CLIMATE

The climate aboveground is warm in the summer, with highs often in the 90s and sometimes exceeding 100°F, and evening lows in the mid-60s. Winters are mild, with highs in the 50s and 60s in the day and nighttime lows usually in the 20s and 30s. Summers are known for sudden intense afternoon and evening thunderstorms; August and September see the most rain. Underground it's another story entirely, with a year-round temperature that varies little from its average temperature of 56°F, making a jacket or sweater a welcome companion.

SEASONAL EVENTS

On the second Thursday in August (usually), a "bat flight breakfast" from 5 to 7am encourages visitors to watch the bats return to the cavern after their night of insect-hunting. Park rangers prepare breakfast for early morning visitors for a small fee and then join them to watch the early morning return flight. Call the park for details.

If You Only Have 1 Day

Those with only 1 day to spend at Carlsbad Caverns National Park can see quite a bit if they organize their time well. First, stop at the **visitor center** to look at the exhibits and check out that day's tours and programs. If you would like to take any guided tours later in the day, it's best to buy tickets now. Then head into the main cave through the steep **Natural Entrance Route,** and continue on a self-guided tour of the **Big Room.** For those not wishing to follow the steep switchback trail into the Natural Entrance, and anyone with health concerns, an elevator is also available in the visitor center that will deliver you easily and safely to the Big Room.

You'll finish your Big Room tour at the elevators near the **Underground Rest Area,** so pick up a sandwich there or take the elevator up to the surface, where you can dine in the restaurant at the visitor center or drive out to **Rattlesnake Springs** for a picnic lunch. After lunch, take the **King's Palace Guided Tour** (for which you wisely purchased tickets earlier). Then walk the nature trail outside the visitor center and drive the 9.5-mile **Walnut Canyon Desert Drive.** If possible, try to get back to the amphitheater at the cave's Natural Entrance by dusk to see the nightly **bat flight** (mid-May through October only), when thousands of bats leave the cave for a night of insect-hunting.

Exploring the Park by Car

No, you can't take your car into the caves, but it won't be totally useless here, either. For a close-up as well as panoramic view of the Chihuahuan Desert, head out on the **Walnut Canyon Desert Drive,** a 9.5-mile loop. You'll want to drive slowly on the one-way gravel road, both for safety and to thoroughly appreciate the dramatic scenery. Passenger cars can easily handle the tight turns and narrow passage, but the road is not recommended for motor homes and cars pulling trailers. Pick up an interpretive brochure for the drive at the visitor center bookstore.

Organized Tours & Ranger Programs

In addition to the cave tours, which are discussed below, rangers give a talk on bats at sunset each evening from mid-May through October at the cavern's Natural Entrance (times change; check at the visitor center). They also offer a variety of demonstrations, talks, guided nature walks, and other programs daily. Especially popular are the climbing programs, where rangers demonstrate caving techniques. In recent years there have also been a series of stargazing programs presented by graduate students from New Mexico State University. A schedule of ranger-led activities is posted at the visitor center.

Historic & Man-Made Attractions

While this park is devoted primarily to the work of nature, observing human activities in the caves is also part of the Carlsbad Caverns National Park experience. Throughout the main cavern you'll see evidence of human use (and misuse) of the caves. Those taking the guided Lower Cave tour will see historical artifacts left by early cave explorers, including members of a 1924 National Geographic Society expedition.

Cave Exploration

Carlsbad Cavern (the park's main cave), Slaughter Canyon Cave, and Spider Cave are open to the general public. Experienced cavers with professional-level equipment can request permission to explore ten of the park's other caves.

Most park visitors head first to Carlsbad Cavern, which has elevators, a paved walkway, and an Underground Rest Area. A 1-mile section of the Big Room self-guided tour is accessible to those in wheelchairs (no wheelchairs are available at the park), though it's best to have another person to assist. Pick up a free accessibility guide at the visitor center.

MAIN CARLSBAD CAVERN ROUTES

Most visitors see Carlsbad Cavern by taking the following three trails, all of which are lighted, paved, and have handrails. However, the Big Room is the only one of the three that's considered easy.

The formations along these trails are strategically lit to display them at their most dramatic. The odd tints of green and yellow that may appear in your photos are caused by the various types of electric lighting used, and not by your film processor.

Big Room Self-Guided Tour

1.25-mi. loop. Easy. Access: Visitor center elevator to Underground Rest Area or via the Natural Entrance Route (see below).

Considered the one essential of a visit to Carlsbad Caverns National Park, this easy trail meanders through a massive chamber—it isn't called the Big Room for nothing—where you'll see some of the park's most spectacular formations and likely be overwhelmed by the enormity of it all. Allow about 1½ hours.

King's Palace Guided Tour

0.75-mi. loop. Moderate. Access: Visitor center elevator to Underground Rest Area.

This ranger-led walk wanders through some of the cave's most scenic chambers, where you'll see wonderfully fanciful formations in the King's Palace, Queen's Chamber, and Green Lake Room. Watch for the delightful Bashful Elephant formation between the King's Palace and Green Lake Room. Along the way, rangers discuss the geology of the cave and early explorers' experiences. Although the path is paved, there is an 80-foot elevation change.

Natural Entrance Route

1.25 mi. Moderate to strenuous. Access: Outside the visitor center.

This fairly strenuous hike takes you into Carlsbad Cavern on the same basic route used by its early explorers. You leave the daylight to enter a big hole, and then descend more than 750 feet into the cavern on a steep and narrow switchback trail, moving from the "twilight zone" of semidarkness to the depths of the cave, which would be totally black without the

electric lights conveniently provided by the Park Service. The self-guided tour takes about 1 hour and ends near the elevators, which can take you back to the visitor center. However, it is strongly recommended that from here you proceed on the Big Room Self-Guided Tour, which is described above, if you have not already been there.

CAVING TOUR PROGRAMS IN CARLSBAD CAVERN

Ranger-led tours to these less-developed sections of Carlsbad Cavern provide more of the experience of exploration and genuine caving than the above routes over well-trodden trails. These caving tours vary in difficulty, but all include a period of absolute darkness or "blackout," which can make some people uncomfortable. Because some tours involve walking or crawling through tight spaces, people who suffer from claustrophobia or who have other health concerns should discuss specifics with rangers before purchasing tickets.

See below for age requirements and required equipment. Rangers provide headlamps and helmets on some tours. All tours must be reserved and have individual fees in addition to the general cave entry fee. Tours are popular and are sometimes fully booked weeks in advance, so reserve early.

Hall of the White Giant

0.5 mi. one way. Strenuous. Access: Starts at the visitor center.

If you want a strenuous, 3- to 4-hour trip where you crawl through narrow, dirty passageways and climb up slippery rocks, this tour is for you. The highlight is, of course, the huge formation called the White Giant. Only those in excellent physical condition should consider this tour; children must be at least 12. Four AA batteries for the provided headlamp and sturdy hiking boots are required; and knee pads, gloves, and long pants are strongly recommended.

Left Hand Tunnel

0.5 mi. one way. Easy. Access: Starts at the visitor center near the elevator.

The easiest of the caving tours, in this one you actually get to walk (rather than crawl) the entire time! Hand-carried lanterns (provided by the Park Service) light the way, and the trail is dirt but relatively level. You'll see a variety of formations, fossils from Permian times, and pools of water. Ages 6 and up. The tour takes about 2 hours.

Lower Cave

1 mi. RT. Moderate. Access: Starts at the visitor center near the elevator.

This 3-hour trek involves descending or climbing over 50 feet of ladders, and an optional crawl. It takes you through an area that was explored by a National Geographic Society expedition in the 1920s, and you'll see artifacts from that and other explorations. In addition, you'll encounter a variety of formations, including cave pearls, which look a lot like the pearls created by oysters and can be as big as golf balls. Ages 12 and up. Four AA batteries are required for the provided headlamp; sturdy hiking boots and gloves are recommended.

OTHER CAVING TOURS

It takes some hiking to reach the other caves in the park, so carry drinking water, especially on hot summer days. Children under 16 must be accompanied by an adult; other age restrictions apply as well. Each tour includes a period of true and total darkness or "blackout." There are tour fees for both, but a general cave admission ticket is not required. Tours are popular and are frequently fully booked, so call a few months ahead for reservations.

Slaughter Canyon Cave

1.25 mi. RT (plus 0.5-mi. hike to and from cave). Moderate. Access: The cave is about a

45-min. drive from Carlsbad and is reached via U.S. 62/180, going south 5 mi. from White's City, to a marked turnoff that leads 11 mi. to a parking lot. Tours meet and depart from the cave entrance located 0.5 mi. west of the parking lot.

Discovered in 1937, this cave was mined for bat guano (used as fertilizer) until the 1950s. It consists of a corridor 1,140 feet long with many side passageways. This highly recommended guided tour lasts about 2½ hours, plus at least another half hour to hike up the steep trail to the cave entrance. No crawling is involved, although the smooth flowstone and old bat guano on the floor can be slippery, so good hiking boots are recommended. You'll see a number of wonderful cave formations, including the crystal-decorated Christmas Tree, the Teardrop, the 89-foot-high Monarch, and the menacing Klansman. Ages 6 and up. Participants must take D battery flashlights.

Spider Cave

1-mi. loop (plus 0.5-mi. hike to and from cave). Strenuous. Access: Meet at the visitor center and follow a ranger to the cave.

Very strenuous, this tour is ideal for those who want the experience of a rugged caving adventure as well as some great underground scenery. Highlights include climbing down a 15-foot ladder, squeezing through very tight passageways, and climbing on slippery surfaces. All this after a fairly tough 0.5-mile hike to the cave entrance. But it's worth it. The cave has numerous beautiful formations—most much smaller than those in the Big Room—and picturesque pools of water. Ages 12 and up. Participants need four AA batteries for the provided headlamps, and good hiking boots. Kneepads, gloves, and long pants are strongly recommended.

WILD CAVING

Experienced cavers with the proper gear can request permits from the park's **Cave**

Resources Office (☎ 505/785-2232, ext. 363 or 368) to enter one of several undeveloped caves in the park on their own. In addition, Ogle Cave is open to experienced vertical cavers on ranger-led trips. Applications should be submitted at least 1 month ahead of time. There is a $12 fee for entry into Ogle Cave; permits for other caves are free. Further information is available from the Cave Resources Office.

Other Sports & Activities

Hiking & Backpacking. Most of the hiking here is done underground, but there are opportunities for hiking on the earth's surface as well. The park's busiest trail is the **Nature Trail,** a fairly easy, 1-mile paved loop that begins just outside the visitor center and has interpretive signs describing the various plants of the Chihuahuan desert.

About a half dozen other trails wander through the park's 30,000 acres of designated wilderness. These **backcountry trails** are generally poorly marked—rangers strongly recommend that hikers carry topographical maps, which can be purchased at the visitor center. Be careful of rattlesnakes, especially in warmer months. Lighting fires and entering backcountry caves without permits are prohibited. Free permits, available at the visitor center, are required for all overnight hikes.

Backcountry trails include the 3.5-mile (one way) Guano Road Trail, with an elevation change of 710 feet; the 6-mile (round-trip) Rattlesnake Canyon Trail, with an elevation change of 670 feet; the 6-mile (one way) Slaughter Canyon Trail, which has an elevation change of 1,850 feet; the 11-mile (one way) Yucca Canyon Trail, with a 1,520-foot elevation change; the 11.8-mile (one way) Guadalupe Ridge Trail, with an elevation change of 2,050 feet; the 3.5-mile (one way) Juniper Ridge Trail, with an 800-foot elevation change; and the 1.5-mile (one way) Ussery Trail, which has an elevation change of 2,500 feet.

Backcountry camping is permitted (with a free permit) on all of the above trails except Guano Road. Additional trail information is available from park rangers.

Horseback Riding. Most of the backcountry trails are open to those on horseback. A small corral is available, with advance arrangements. Contact the park **Resource Management Office** (☎ 505/785-2232, ext. 363 or 368).

Wildlife Viewing & Bird Watching. At sunset, from mid-May through October, a crowd gathers at the Carlsbad Cavern Natural Entrance to watch hundreds of thousands of bats take off for the night. All day long the **Mexican free-tailed bats,** which spend their winters in Mexico, sleep in the cavern, and then strike out on an insect hunt each night. An amphitheater in front of the Natural Entrance provides seating, and ranger programs are held each evening (exact times vary, check at the visitor center) during the bat's residence at the park. The most bats will be seen in August and September, when baby bats born earlier in the summer join their parents, along with migrating bats from the north, on the nightly forays. Early risers can also see the return of the bats just before dawn. Flash photography is not permitted, as it may disturb the bats.

However, bats aren't the only wildlife at Carlsbad Caverns. The park has a surprising number of **birds**—more than 300 species—many of which are seen in the Rattlesnake Springs area. Among species you're likely to see are turkey vultures, red-tailed hawks, scaled quail, killdeer, mourning doves, lesser night-hawks, black-chinned hummingbirds, vermilion flycatchers, canyon wrens, northern mockingbirds, black-throated sparrows, and western meadowlarks. In addition, each summer several thousand cave swallows usually build their mud nests on the ceiling just inside the Carlsbad Cavern Natural Entrance (the bats make their home further back in the cave).

Especially for Kids

Children usually love the self-guided walk through the main cavern's **Big Room,** with its many bizarre and beautiful shapes, especially when they're encouraged to let their imaginations run wild. Younger children, however, are often bored on the **King's Palace Guided Tour** because it has several stops, and everyone must remain with the group. (Children under 4 are not permitted on the King's Palace tour.) Families with children at least 6 years old (and preferably a bit older) usually enjoy the **Slaughter Canyon Cave** tour, which has some spectacular formations and gives the feeling of exploring a wild cave.

Among the park's **larger animals** are mule deer and raccoons, which are sometimes spotted near the Natural Entrance at the time of the evening bat flights. The park is also home to porcupines, hog-nosed skunks, desert cottontails, black-tailed jackrabbits, rock squirrels, and the more elusive ringtails, coyotes, and gray fox. These are sometimes seen in the late evenings along the park entrance road and the Walnut Canyon Desert Drive. In recent years there have also been a few sightings of mountain lions and bobcats.

Camping

There are no developed campgrounds or vehicle camping of any kind inside the national park. Backcountry camping, however, is permitted in some areas (see "Backcountry Trails" under "Hiking & Backpacking," above). Pick up free permits at the visitor center.

NEAR THE PARK

The closest camping is **White's City RV Park,** 17 Carlsbad Cavern Hwy. at N. Mex. 7 (P.O. Box 128), White's City, NM 88268 (☎ **800/228-3767** or 505/785-2291; fax 505/785-2283), located in the White's City complex at the east edge of the park boundary, about 7 miles east of the visitor center. In addition to RV sites with hookups and shade shelters, the campground has practically unlimited tent camping in a grassy area with picnic tables and some trees. Because the campground is part of the White's City complex, with its motels, restaurants, and other services, campers have access to the motel pool, an ATM, convenience store, liquor store, post office, and gift shop.

A good choice in the city of Carlsbad is **Carlsbad RV Park & Campground,** 4301 National Parks Hwy., Carlsbad, NM 88220 (☎ **888/878-7275** or 505/885-6333; www.carlsbadrvpark.com). This tree-filled campground offers pull-through sites large enough to accommodate big rigs with slide-outs, as well as tent sites and sites for everything in between. Some sites have cable TV

Campground	Elev.	Total Sites	RV Hookups	Dump Station	Toilets	Drinking Water
Carlsbad RV Park & Campground	3,110	136	95	Yes	Yes	Yes
Brantley Lake State Park	3,300	51+	51	Yes	Yes	Yes
White's City RV Park	3,630	150	80	Yes	Yes	Yes

hookups. There's an indoor heated pool, a game room, a playground, and a meeting room with kitchen. A convenience store sells groceries, gifts, and RV supplies.

Those who will be exploring the city of Carlsbad and other area attractions may want to use as a base camp **Brantley Lake State Park,** P.O. Box 2288, Carlsbad, NM 88221 (☎ **505/457-2384**). Located 12 miles north of the city of Carlsbad via U.S. 285, and then 4.5 miles northeast on Eddy County Road 30, this quiet and relaxing park is almost 40 miles from the Carlsbad Caverns Visitor Center. Activities include boating, swimming, and fishing on the 2,800-acre lake, as well as bird watching. In addition to the developed campsites, there is primitive camping along the lakeshore for 20 to 50 RVs or tents, depending on the lake level. The park also has boat ramps, picnic tables, two playgrounds, and exhibits on the 19th-century community of Seven Rivers, once considered one of the West's wildest towns, which now lies at the bottom of the lake.

Accommodations

There are no accommodations within the park. The closest are at White's City, which contains a variety of businesses under one management, including lodging, dining, shops, a museum, gas station, and an RV park.

The next closest services are in and near the city of Carlsbad (zip code 88220). Here you'll find several chain and franchise motels. Those located on the southwest edge of the city, on the road to Carlsbad Caverns, include **Days Inn of Carlsbad,** 3910 National Parks Hwy. (☎ **505/887-7800**), $60 to $80 double; **Motel 6,** 3824 National Parks Hwy. (☎ **505/885-0011**), $34 double; **Quality Inn,** 3706 National Parks Hwy. (☎ **505/ 887-2861**), $59 to $69 double; and **Super 8 Motel,** 3817 National Parks Hwy. (☎ **505/887-8888**), $46 to $58 double. Toll-free reservation numbers are given in the appendix.

For additional information on area lodging contact the **Carlsbad Chamber of Commerce,** P.O. Box 910, Carlsbad, NM 88220 (☎ **800/221-1224** or 505/ 887-6516; fax 505/885-1455; www. chamber.caverns.com).

Best Western Cavern Inn

17 Carlsbad Cavern Hwy. at N. Mex. 7, White's City, NM 88268. ☎ **800/228-3767** (direct) or 505/785-2291. Fax 505/785-2283. E-mail: bestwest@cavern.com. 105 units. A/C TV TEL. May 15–Sept 15 $60–$85 double; Sept 16– May 14 $55–$75 double. AE, DC, DISC, MC, V. Small pets accepted.

This motel and its associated properties are the most convenient places to stay while visiting Carlsbad Caverns. Rooms are spacious, with Southwestern decor and either two queen-size beds or one king. About half have whirlpool tubs. Most folks dine and drink at the complex's Velvet Garter Saloon and Restaurant or pick up a quick meal at nearby Fast Jack's (see "Dining," below). The White's City arcade contains a post office, a small grocery store, a gift shop,

Showers	Fire Pits/ Grills	Laundry	Public Phone	Reserve	Fees	Open
Yes	Yes	Yes	Yes	Yes	$15–$23	Year-round
Yes	Yes	No	Yes	No	$8–$14	Year-round
Yes	Yes	Yes	Yes	Yes	$16–$20	Year-round

a museum, and a theater. Between the Cavern Inn and its neighbor properties, there are two swimming pools, two hot tubs, and a tennis court.

Best Western Stevens Inn

1829 S. Canal St., Carlsbad, NM 88220. ☎ **800/730-2851** (direct), 800/528-1234, or 505/887-2851. Fax 505/887-6338. www.carlsbadnm.com/stevens. E-mail: bwstevensinn@carlsbadnm.com. 217 units. A/C TV TEL. $55–$65 double; $65 and up suite. AE, DC, DISC, MC, V. Small pets accepted.

Well-landscaped gardens surround this handsome property, composed of several buildings spread across spacious grounds. All the rooms have Southwestern decor and coffeemakers, and most have two queen beds. Some units, with peaked ceilings to make them feel even larger, also have back-door patios. You can save money on dining by renting a microwave/refrigerator combo ($5), or by using the kitchenettes in the suites. There are some wheelchair-accessible rooms with roll-in showers. The motel has a restaurant (see "Dining," below), room service, courtesy airport transportation, guest laundry, 24-hour front desk, a swimming pool, and a playground.

Holiday Inn

601 S. Canal St. (P.O. Box 128), Carlsbad, NM 88220. ☎ **800/742-9586** (direct) or 505/885-8500. Fax 505/887-5999. E-mail: holidayinn@carlsbadnm.com. 100 units. A/C TV TEL. $73–$95 double. Rates include breakfast. AE, DC, DISC, MC, V. Pets accepted.

A handsome New Mexico Territorial–style building houses this first-rate full-service hotel in downtown Carlsbad, where guests can frolic in an attractive outdoor heated swimming pool, sauna, and whirlpool. There's also an exercise room and playground, a self-service laundry, and courtesy transportation. The large rooms are decorated in southwestern motif, and have coffeemakers. Some

wheelchair-accessible rooms have roll-in showers. Ventana's Restaurant offers fine dining and serves steaks, prime rib, seafood, and pastas.

Dining

INSIDE THE PARK

There are two concessionaire-operated restaurants at the park (☎ 505/785-2281). A family style full-service restaurant at the **visitor center** serves three meals daily. It offers standard breakfasts such as bacon and eggs, hot cakes, sweet rolls, and Spanish omelettes. For lunch and dinner you'll find a variety of sandwiches, beef burgers, a veggie burger, and a few Mexican items. The menu also includes chicken-fried steak, a garden salad with chicken breast, and daily specials. Prices are in the $2 to $7 range. The restaurant is open 8:30am to 4:30pm most of the year, with extended hours from Memorial Day through mid-August.

The **Underground Rest Area,** located inside the cavern 750 feet belowground, contains a cafeteria-style eatery offering fast food such as sandwiches, pizza, and burritos. Prices range from $2.50 to $6. There is also a gift shop, with a variety of items including postcards, sweatshirts, and film. Concession hours are coordinated with cave hours.

NEAR THE PARK

The Flume

Best Western Stevens Inn, 1829 S. Canal St., Carlsbad. ☎ **505/887-2851.** Lunch $4–$8; dinner $7–$18. AE, DC, DISC, MC, V. Mon–Sat 6am–10pm, Sun 6am–9pm. AMERICAN.

This relatively elegant restaurant has comfortable seating, candlelight, wall sconces, and chandeliers. For breakfast and lunch you can choose from a good selection of American favorites. The dinner menu includes a variety of steaks, seafood such as the New Orleans shrimp plate, and chicken, including a house specialty, teriyaki chicken breast. Dinners for light eaters are also available.

Larez Restaurant

1524 S. Canal St., Carlsbad. ☎ **505/885-5113.** Main courses $3–$10. AE, DISC, MC, V. Mon–Fri 11am–2pm and 4–9pm. MEXICAN.

Real Mexican food prepared personally by restaurant owner Dora Larez is what you'll get here, and be prepared to wait a little for it, since items are prepared from scratch. Decor is unpretentious—cafelike, simple, and clean. The food is tasty, but not excessively spicy. Try the guacamole salad with homemade chips for an excellent appetizer. A good main choice is the Larez deluxe plate, which includes an enchilada, a tamale, a taco, rice, beans, a chile relleno, green chile, and a guacamole salad. American dishes include a chicken strip plate and a green chile cheeseburger. Take-out is available.

Velvet Garter Saloon and Restaurant

26 Carlsbad Hwy., White's City. ☎ **505/785-2291.** Main courses $8–$14. AE, DC, MC, V. Daily 4–9pm. AMERICAN.

This comfortable family-style restaurant, with a separate saloon, has two beautiful stained-glass windows portraying the caverns and the Guadalupe Mountains, as well as other works of western art and assorted Old West touches. The menu includes steaks, chicken, and fish; there's also a salad bar. Nearby, Fast Jack's (same address and phone as above) serves three meals daily, with various breakfast items, burgers, sandwiches, and a few full meals, with prices from $2 to $6.

Picnic & Camping Supplies

The closest grocery store to the national park is the convenience store at the **Texaco gas station** in the White's City complex, at the intersection of U.S. 62/180 and N. Mex. 7, about 7 miles from the visitor center. You'll find a good variety of stores in the city of Carlsbad, including an **Albertson's grocery store** at 808 N. Canal St., at its intersection with West Church Street (☎ 505/885-2161). It has a well-stocked deli and bakery, and is open daily 6am to 11pm.

11

CHANNEL ISLANDS NATIONAL PARK

by Eric Peterson

A RUSTED WINDMILL WATCHES OVER SCORPION RANCH ON THE eastern end of Santa Cruz Island, a reminder of man's impact on even our wildest places. But the Channel Islands are still places defined more by the wind and the sea. On land, the dry

grasses and shrubs remain constantly in motion, mimicking the whitecapped water of the Santa Barbara Channel separating the islands from the mainland. In the waters surrounding the islands lives a diversity of life matched by few places on earth.

Even though it is among America's less-visited national parks, without the awe-inspiring scenery of Yosemite or Grand Teton, there is plenty to keep visitors coming back to the Channel Islands. Opportunities for sea kayaking and hiking are many; you'll find plants and animals that live nowhere else, as well as archaeological remains of long-vanished cultures. It's also a draw for underwater explorers from all over—five times as many people come here to explore the waters around the islands than ever set foot on the shore.

Channel Islands National Park encompasses the five northernmost islands of an eight-island chain: Santa Barbara, Anacapa, Santa Cruz, Santa Rosa, and San Miguel. (Santa Catalina,

San Clemente, and San Nicolas are not included in the park.) Not limited to the islands themselves, the park also encompasses 1 nautical mile of ocean around each island, and the 6 nautical miles around each island have been designated a national marine sanctuary. The smallest of the park's islands, tiny Santa Barbara, lives a solitary existence. The four northern islands are clustered in a 40-mile-long chain—though during the last ice age, before the continental ice sheets melted, raising the level of the seas, these islands were actually connected, forming one huge island geologists call Santarosae.

The four northern islands in the park are actually an extension of the Santa Monica Mountains; fossil records indicate that Santa Cruz, Santa Rosa, and San Miguel were connected to the mainland at one point, but massive geological turmoil pushed them seaward some 600,000 years ago. Only Anacapa and Santa Barbara began their existence as islands (though some geologists argue

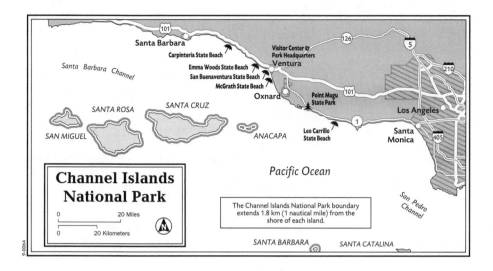

9-0064

Channel Islands National Park

0 ——— 20 Miles

0 ——— 20 Kilometers

The Channel Islands National Park boundary extends 1.8 km (1 nautical mile) from the shore of each island.

Pacific Ocean

that Santa Cruz was also never attached to the mainland)—both were formed by underwater volcanic activity.

Flora & Fauna. The isolation of the Channel Islands, which have been separated from the mainland for thousands of years, has allowed a diverse array of life to develop and evolve, prompting some biologists to dub them the "North American Galapagos." Most of the differences from mainland species are in size, shape, or color variation. Perhaps the most curious of the islands' inhabitants was the pygmy mammoth, only 4 to 6 feet tall, that roamed over Santarosae during the Pleistocene era—fossilized remains have been found on San Miguel and Santa Rosa.

Other island species, however, have survived. Like the mammoth, the Santa Cruz gopher snake, island spotted skunk, and island fox have all evolved to be smaller than their mainland relatives. Weighing just 4 pounds, the island fox is actually the smallest fox species in North America. Like Darwin's finches in the Galapagos, the islands' native birds also show marked adaptation: The Santa Cruz Island scrub jay displays "gigantism"—it is one-third larger and deeper blue than mainland jays, and the orange-crowned warbler and rufous-sided towhee have oversize body parts.

The diversity of animal life on the islands is outdone only by the vast array of native plant life. One of the most spectacular of the islands' plants is the yellow coreopsis, or "tree sunflower," which can be found on all five islands as well as the mainland. Other species of plants live nowhere else on earth—the islands support 43 endemic varieties of plants. Some are prehistoric species that vanished from the mainland thousands of years ago—the ironwood has lived only on these islands for the past 3 million years. Like the pygmy mammoth, Santa Rosa's endemic Torrey pine population dates from the Pleistocene era, though a remnant mainland subspecies survives at Torrey Pines State Reserve north of La Jolla, California.

Marine life around the islands, however, easily wins the diversity award. The islands are the meeting point of two distinct marine ecosystems: The cold, nutrient-rich waters of Northern California swirl together with the warmer, clearer currents of Baja California. Everything from microscopic plankton to the largest creature ever to live on earth, the blue whale, calls these waters home. Orcas and great white sharks, anemone and abalone, lobsters and starfish, plus dozens of varieties of fish, live in the tide pools, kelp forests, and waters surrounding the islands. Six varieties of seal and sea lions beach themselves on San Miguel, five of which breed here, making it the largest seal and sea lion breeding colony in the United States. The islands are also the most important seabird nesting area in California.

Avoiding the Crowds. Unlike many of the more popular (and more easily accessible) national parks, crowds are rarely a problem on any of the islands. (In a given year, about 320,000 people stop in at the park visitor center; 300,000 go into the park waters, but only about 60,000 actually travel to the islands themselves.) While visitors rarely number above 80 a day to any given island, the open section of Anacapa (the closest and most heavily visited island) is so small that it may be difficult, though still possible, to completely separate yourself from the flock. As for the other four islands in the park, you should have no trouble finding a secluded picnic spot or overlook. Santa Barbara Island is the most distant and least crowded; San Miguel is the wildest and offers wonderful, solitary backcountry hiking possibilities.

Just the Facts

GETTING THERE & GATEWAYS

Most people travel to the islands by boat from **Ventura,** but even though there are no park fees, getting there is expensive—anywhere from $32 to $120 per person, the higher price being for a trip by air to Santa Rosa. If you fly, you may leave from the **Camarillo** airport. Anacapa, 14 miles out, is closest to the mainland, about a 1-hour boat ride.

The Nearest Airport. The closest major airport to the Channel Islands is **Los Angeles International Airport (LAX)** (☎ 310/646-5252). It's served frequently by all major airlines, with connections to almost anywhere you want to go. Los Angeles is 96 miles southeast of Santa Barbara, Ventura is 30 miles southeast of Santa Barbara. All major **car-rental** companies have vehicles at LAX. Toll-free numbers for airlines and car rentals are listed in the appendix.

Getting to the Islands by Boat. Island Packers, next to the visitor center at 1867 Spinnaker Dr. (☎ 805/642-7688 recorded information, or 805/642-1393 for reservations; www.islandpackers.com), is one of the park's two concessionaires for boat transportation to and from the islands. They will take you on a range of regularly scheduled excursions, from 3½-hour nonlanding tours of the islands to 2-day excursions to two islands. Prices start at $22 per person for the nonlanding tours to $32–$62 for the 2-day excursions. Island Packers also arranges specialty trips to the islands—diving, sea kayaking, and so on. Private yachts and commercial dive and tour boats also visit the park on a regular basis. The new, second boat concessionaire, leaving from Santa Barbara Harbor is **Truth Aquatics** (☎ 805/962-1127). They charge $75 for a 1-day round-trip to either San Miguel or Santa Rosa. The trips take 3 hours each way.

If You Have Your Own Boat. If you want to take your own boat, check with the mainland visitor center. Access to the islands is prohibited in some places and difficult in others—going ashore often requires a skiff, raft, or small boat:

♦ You may land without a permit on east Anacapa, Santa Barbara, and east Santa Cruz between Chinese Harbor and Sandstone Point.

♦ West Anacapa, except the beach at Frenchy's Cove, is closed to the public to protect nesting brown pelicans.

♦ Access to Middle Anacapa requires a ranger escort.

♦ Landings, beach use, and inland excursions on Santa Rosa and San Miguel do not require a permit.

♦ To land on the private western portion of Santa Cruz, boaters must obtain a permit from **The Nature Conservancy, Santa Cruz Island Preserve,** P.O. Box 23259, Santa Barbara, CA 93121 (☎ **805/694-7839**). A fee is charged, no overnight stays are permitted, and it may take 10 or 12 days to process the request. Applications are available from the mainland visitor center or by contacting the Nature Conservancy directly.

Getting to the Islands by Air. If you want to get to Santa Rosa in a hurry, **Channel Islands Aviation,** 305 Durley Ave., Camarillo, CA 93010 (☎ **805/987-1678**), will fly you there in one of its small, fixed-wing aircraft.

INFORMATION

Contact the **Superintendent, Channel Islands National Park,** 1901 Spinnaker Dr., Ventura, CA 93001 (☎ **805/ 658-5730;** fax 805/658-5799; www.nps. gov/chis).

For information on Ventura, try the **Ventura Visitors & Convention Bureau,** 89-C S. California St., Ventura, CA 93001 (☎ **800/333-2989** or 805/648-2075; www.ventura-usa.com).

VISITOR CENTERS

The main visitor center for the islands is actually on the mainland, in Ventura Harbor, where you'll also find the park headquarters. Visit the **Channel Islands National Park Headquarters and Visitor Center,** 1901 Spinnaker Dr., Ventura, CA 93001 (☎ **805/658-5730**), to get acquainted with the various programs and individual personalities of the islands through maps and displays. While a wide variety of publications is available, among the most helpful are the free handouts focusing on the individual islands. The center is open from 8:30am to 4:30pm weekdays, 8am to 5pm weekends; hours are slightly extended (a half hour on each end) during the "busier" summer season between Memorial Day and Labor Day.

Anacapa and **Santa Barbara** also have smaller visitor centers, and rangers run interpretive programs both on the islands and at the mainland visitor center year-round.

FEES

There are neither entrance nor camping fees for the islands, but you should consider the cost of getting to the islands when planning your budget. There is a nightly $2.50 per site charge for camping on all five islands; you must make reservations by calling the park visitor center permits line (☎ **800/365-2267**).

SPECIAL REGULATIONS & WARNINGS

The relative inaccessibility of these islands makes preplanning a must. The boat concessionaires are often booked a month or so in advance, so be sure to make reservations. Also, remember that once on the islands, you can't go back to your car, so be sure to bring anything you might need (including water, food, and equipment if you're camping). If you're camping, bring a good tent—if you don't know the difference between a good and a bad tent, the island wind will gladly demonstrate.

SEASONS & CLIMATE

While the climate is mild with little variation in temperature year-round, the weather on the islands is always unpredictable. Thirty-mile-an-hour winds can blow for days, or sometimes a fog bank will settle in and smother the islands for weeks at a time. Winter rains can turn island trails into mud baths. In general, plan on wind, lots of sun (bring sunscreen), cool nights, and the possibility of hot days. Water temperatures are in the 50s and 60s year-round. Also be aware that inclement weather or sea conditions can cause concessionaires to cancel trips on the day of the excursion, so

Which Island Should You Visit?

Since you will probably only make it to one or two of the islands during your visit, figuring out which islands to devote your time to is probably a more important question than how to avoid the crowds. The answer is simply: It depends on what you want to do.

ANACAPA. Families with children will probably want to start with Anacapa. There are more **organized activities** here than on the other islands, and the crossing to Anacapa is the shortest—an important consideration when dealing with potentially seasick youngsters. If you're interested in **sea kayaking,** Anacapa's scores of sea caves also make it your best bet. Though much smaller than its huge neighbor Santa Cruz, Anacapa has several times more caves, many of which can be entered by kayak.

SANTA CRUZ. Even with fewer caves than Anacapa, Santa Cruz is still a good choice for sea kayakers—the island's **Painted Cave** is the largest and deepest sea cave in the world. This is the largest of the islands, but most of it is owned by **The Nature Conservancy,** and you must apply for permission to visit the portions of the island they manage.

SANTA ROSA. This is probably your best bet if you want to visit one of the islands for more than a day (it's relatively big, so there's more to explore). Those interested in **ranching history** and

vaquero (Mexican cowboy) **culture** will probably want to visit Santa Rosa. Santa Rosa's hundreds of undisturbed **archaeological sites** (please leave them undisturbed) also may attract anthropology buffs and others interested in Chumash culture (the Chumash were the Native Americans who inhabited all four of the islands). Those interested in **endemic plant life** will probably also enjoy a visit. Though a century of ranching has wreaked havoc on the island's traditional landscape, the prehistoric stand of Torrey pines is spectacular—this particular species grows in only one other spot on earth (near San Diego).

SAN MIGUEL. If **backcountry hiking** is what you're after, the choice is pretty simple: The 15-mile trek to Point Bennet offers the most visible wildlife and greatest diversity of scenery among the park's hikes. San Miguel is also your best choice if you want to **observe wildlife**—as many as 35,000 seals and sea lions can gather at Point Bennet; Prince Island in the mouth of Cuyler Harbor is an important seabird nesting area, and the park's largest land mammal, the diminutive island fox, roams the island.

SANTA BARBARA. This is the smallest of the island chain, not to mention the most **distant and solitary.** After a 3-hour boat trip, you'll be completely free to hike this tiny island as alone as you might ever care to be.

it's a good idea to have a plan B just in case.

From January through March, **gray whales** can be viewed as they pass by on their annual 10,000-mile migration from their warmer breeding grounds off the coast of Baja California to their cold water feeding grounds in the Arctic

Ocean. **Blue and humpback whales** can be seen in the waters off the islands between June and October.

Exploring the Islands

Each of the islands is distinct. **If you only have a day,** Anacapa and east Santa Cruz are the closest to the mainland and the easiest to get to. The bad side: They're the most crowded (though *crowded* is a

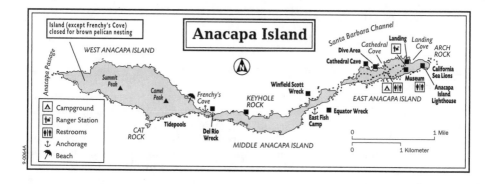

Anacapa Island

Santa Barbara Channel

Island (except Frenchy's Cove) closed for brown pelican nesting

WEST ANACAPA ISLAND

Anacapa Passage

Summit Peak

Camel Peak

Frenchy's Cove

Tidepools

Del Rio Wreck

CAT ROCK

Winfield Scott Wreck

KEYHOLE ROCK

MIDDLE ANACAPA ISLAND

East Fish Camp

Equator Wreck

Dive Area

Cathedral Cove

Cathedral Cave

Landing

Landing Cove

ARCH ROCK

California Sea Lions

Museum

EAST ANACAPA ISLAND

Anacapa Island Lighthouse

△ Campground
★ Ranger Station
†|† Restrooms
⚓ Anchorage
⚘ Beach

0 — 1 Mile
0 — 1 Kilometer

relative term here). Even if you have a few days to visit the Channel Islands, odds are you're only going to visit one or two islands on a given trip, so it's a good idea to study your options before going.

EXPLORING ANACAPA

Sitting only 14.5 nautical miles off the Ventura coast, tiny Anacapa is easily the most visited of the park's islands. Referring to Anacapa as an island, however, is somewhat misleading—it is actually a chain of three small islets—East, Middle, and West Anacapa—inaccessible to each other except by boat. Seen from shore, the flat landscapes of East and Middle Anacapa stand out in sharp contrast to West Anacapa's twin peaks.

Anacapa is the only island in the chain to keep anything resembling its original name—Anacapa is actually a corruption of the Chumash word *Eneepah,* meaning island of deception or mirage, and on a foggy or hot day it is easy to see why: Tricks of light make the island's cliff walls seem enormous at times or almost nonexistent at other times; 40-foot-high **Arch Rock,** a natural offshore bridge, can seem to dominate the eastern end of the island or barely emerge from the water.

At only 1.1 square miles, Anacapa is probably not the best choice for people who need a lot of room to roam. To cramp things even more, only East Anacapa is completely open to the public. Visitors to Middle Anacapa must be accompanied by a park ranger.

Visitors interested in seeing the island's marine life up close may want to opt for a trip to **Frenchy's Cove** on West Anacapa instead of visiting East Anacapa. Unlike most of the tide pools on the mainland, the island's tide pools remain in pristine condition, housing thriving marine communities. Only the beach at Frenchy's Cove is open to visitors, though. The rest of West Anacapa is closed to protect the nesting areas of the endangered brown pelican—the islet houses the largest breeding rookery for the bird on the West Coast.

Seabirds are easily the island's most abundant wildlife. Because of the island's relative lack of predators, thousands of birds nest on the island, including the endangered brown pelican and western gulls. Cormorants, scoter ducks, and black oystercatchers can also be seen plying the air and waters above and around the island.

The island also harbors a community of California sea lions and harbor seals. The animals rest and breed on Anacapa's rocky shores and feed in the kelp forests surrounding the island. Overlooks at **Cathedral Cove, Pinniped Point,** and **Inspiration Point** offer visitors excellent views of the animals.

While most of the year the island is covered with scrubby brownish vegetation, winter rains bring the island's vegetation to vibrant life—the bright blossoms of the yellow coreopsis, or "tree sunflower," are often so numerous that they can be seen from the mainland.

Organized Tours & Ranger Programs. Despite its confines, Anacapa is the most visitor-friendly island in the park: Rangers lead guided nature walks daily during the summer, and self-guided trail booklets are available at the visitor center on the island.

Every Tuesday and Thursday from Memorial Day through Labor Day, rangers plunge into the kelp forest off the island with a video camera. The rangers allow visitors to view the undersea world in the monitor on the island's landing dock (or on a large screen in the mainland visitor center).

Historic & Man-Made Attractions. In 1853, the steamer *Winfield Scott* grounded and sank off the coast of Middle Anacapa (remains of the wreck can still be seen off the north coast of the islet), prompting the government to build a 50-foot tower supporting an acetylene beacon.

In 1932, the U.S. Lighthouse Service replaced the tower with the present **lighthouse** and facilities on East Anacapa. The fully automated lighthouse still used the original handmade Fresnel lens until 1990, when a more modern lighting system was installed—the original lead crystal lens is now on display in the island's visitor center. The lighthouse is still operated by the U.S. Coast Guard, but visitors are warned not to approach the building—the foghorn can leave permanent hearing damage. Special ranger-led tours are available.

Today the other lighthouse service buildings house the visitor center and ranger residences. The churchlike building actually houses two 55,000-gallon water tanks that supply fresh water for the residences and fire fighting. The building was designed to resemble a Spanish mission to discourage snipers who used to take pot shots at the wooden tanks.

Day Hikes. The 2-mile, figure-eight **Loop Trail** on East Anacapa serves up plenty of great views and is a good introduction to the island's natural history. A pamphlet describing the island's most significant features is available in the small visitor center. Rangers also lead guided nature walks daily during the summer.

Camping. Camping is allowed on East Anacapa year-round, but don't bring more than you can carry up the 154-stair, half-mile trail from the landing cove. The campground has seven sites and a capacity of 30 people. The campsites are primitive; there is no shade, and food and water are not available. Pit toilets are provided. No fires are allowed, but cooking is permitted on enclosed, backpack-type stoves. Bring earplugs and steer clear of the foghorn. There is a nightly $2.50 per campsite charge, and a reservation is required; call ☎ 800/365-CAMP (2267). Campground reservations fill quickly, so be sure to call in advance.

EXPLORING SANTA CRUZ

By far the biggest of the islands—nearly 100 square miles—Santa Cruz is also the most diverse. It has huge canyons, year-round streams, beaches, cliffs, the highest mountain in the Channel Islands (2,400 ft.), abandoned cattle and sheep ranches, and American Indian Chumash village sites.

The pastoral **central valley** that separates the island's two mountains is still being created by a major earthquake fault. The island also hosts seemingly endless displays of flora and fauna, including 650 species of plants, nine of which are endemic; 140 land bird species; and a small group of other land animals, including the island fox. Lying directly between cold northern and warm southern waters, the waters off the island host a marine community representing 1,000 miles of coastline.

Originally called *Limuw* by the Chumash, the island gained its present moniker after a priest's staff was accidentally left on the island during the Portola expedition of 1769. A resident Chumash found the cross-tipped staff and returned it to the priest, inspiring the Spaniards to dub the island *La Isla de Santa Cruz,* or the Island of the Sacred Cross.

Most of the island is still privately owned: **The Nature Conservancy** holds the western nine-tenths. In 1997 the Park

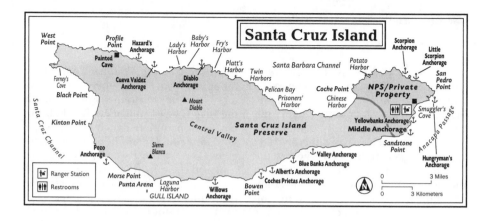

Service took over the eastern end from the Gherini family, which had operated a sheep ranch here. Most visitors come to **Scorpion Ranch** and **Smuggler's Ranch** on the Park Service's land. Unfortunately, the island's ranching heritage has left its mark on the land—the island has been badly overgrazed by feral sheep. At press time, nearly all of the feral sheep had been shipped off the island to spend the rest of their years at an Oregon conservancy. Much of the most beautiful land is on The Nature Conservancy property, which includes Santa Cruz's lush Central Valley and the islands' highest peaks.

On December 5, 1997, the island was doused with more than 12 inches of rain. Floodwaters crested at nearly 4 feet, effectively destroying the campground—it has since been restored. However, there was still a great deal of restoration underway at the Scorpion Ranch area as of press time.

It's difficult, but not impossible, to get access to the more pristine Conservancy land; Island Packers runs occasional trips to **Prisoner's Harbor.** At one point, it was possible to arrange stays at Christy Ranch on the windswept west end of the island and visits to the Main Ranch in the Central Valley, but at press time the ranches were under restoration, and access needed to be arranged before arrival. Contact **The Nature Conservancy** (☎ 805/962-9111) for up-to-date information.

Valdez Cave (also known as Painted Cave for its colorful rock types, lichens, and algae) is the largest and deepest known sea cave in the world. The huge cave stretches nearly a quarter of a mile into the island and is nearly 100 feet wide. The entrance ceiling rises 160 feet, and in the spring, a waterfall tumbles over the opening. Located on the northwest end of the island, the cave can only be entered via dinghy or kayak. See "The Extra Mile: Exploring the Coastline & Waters Off the Channel Islands," below.

Historic & Man-Made Attractions. After more than a century of ranching, Santa Cruz has acquired its fair share of historic buildings, including adobe ranch houses, barns, blacksmith and saddle shops, wineries, and a chapel. The ranch house and adobe bunkhouse at **Scorpion Ranch** are now used as the ranger residence and headquarters. All around Scorpion Ranch fascinating ranch and farm implements, some dating back decades, speckle the landscape. The Park Service has plans to include some in a visitor center on the island. Also planned is an interpretive center in the historic buildings.

Day Hikes. Most hikes in the national parkland of Santa Cruz begin at Scorpion Ranch. The easiest and shortest is the **Historic Ranch Walk.** The ranch area is visible from the beach. This hike is basically the beginning leg of all the hikes described below, so if you are planning to take one of those, you don't really need to allocate much additional time for this hike.

The hike up to **Cavern Point** leads you to the bluffs northwest of Scorpion Harbor, providing spectacular views of the north coast of the island. Between December and February, this is an excellent vantage from which to spot migrating gray whales. Follow the main trail from the beach through the ranch area. Just past the ranch look for the first side canyon on your right (west). Follow the trail through the cypress grove and up the side of the canyon to Cavern Point. Avoid the unstable cliff ledges at the top and return the way you came. At 2 miles round-trip, the hike is ranked moderate to difficult due to a 200-yard uphill climb, uneven terrain, and loose rock.

A little longer than the Cavern Point Hike, the hike up to the **Potato Harbor Overlook** also provides magnificent coastal views. Head past the ranch about 0.75 mile until you come to a big break in the eucalyptus trees. A trail sign marks the spot. Follow the old road on the right (west) up to the dirt airstrip. Walk around the airstrip (be aware of aircraft operations) to the northwest side until you reach the bluff trail to Potato Harbor Overlook. Avoid cliff edges, and return the way you came. The trip is 4 miles round-trip and is ranked moderate due to a 1-mile uphill climb.

For another coastal view, you can head up to **Scorpion Bluffs.** Approximately 100 feet past the ranch area, before the eucalyptus grove, head left (east) on the road/trail across the streambed to the base of Smugglers Road. At the top of the road, follow the trail that goes along the bluffs. Avoid cliff ledges, and return the way you came. The round-trip is 2 miles and is ranked moderate for its 300-foot elevation gain.

Your best chance to see the endemic island jay is to head up **Scorpion Canyon.** Follow the main road/trail though the ranch area and into the eucalyptus grove. The trail will eventually wind in and out of an old streambed before reaching the first oak tree after approximately 1.5 miles. You may continue up the streambed, but the terrain is rocky and uneven.

For those with a little more time, the hike to **Smugglers Cove** is a nice way to spend a day. At 7 miles round-trip, though, it is not recommended for visitors with time constraints. Easy to follow, the hike follows Smugglers Road all the way from Scorpion Ranch to the white sand and cobblestone beaches of Smugglers Cove. If the Park Service has not removed them by your visit, you may see groups of feral sheep or horses left over from the island's ranching days. Due to the 600-foot elevation gain over many uphill sections, the hike is ranked strenuous.

There are also numerous hikes through The Nature Conservancy property, many beginning at Pelican Bay. Often the hikes are led by a Nature Conservancy naturalist who points out natural and historical highlights. For information contact **The Nature Conservancy** at ☎ 805/962-9111.

Camping. Camping is allowed at the Scorpion Ranch Campground on the east end of Santa Cruz year-round. All gear must be carried 0.5 mile to the numerous sites, curiously littered with rusted, abandoned ranch implements and vehicles. At press time the Park Service was planning to haul most away for possible inclusion in a planned ranch implement museum. The campsites are primitive; there is plenty of shade, but food and water are not available. Pit toilets are provided. Cooking is permitted on enclosed backpack-type stoves, and open fires are allowed in specified locations. There is a nightly $2.50 per campsite charge. A reservation is required and can be obtained at the park visitor center or by calling ☎ 800/365-CAMP (2267). There is no camping allowed on Nature Conservancy land (the western 90% of the island).

EXPLORING SANTA ROSA

Windy Santa Rosa was California's only singly owned, private island until it was purchased by the Park Service for $30 million in the 1980s from the Vail and Vickers ranching company. In 1998, the

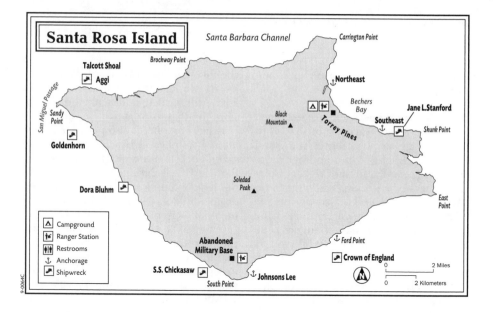

9-0064C

Santa Rosa Island

Santa Barbara Channel

Carrington Point

Brockway Point

Talcott Shoal

⚓ Aggi

Northeast

San Miguel Passage

Sandy Point

Black Mountain ▲

Bechers Bay

Jane L.Stanford

Torrey Pines

Southeast

Skunk Point

Goldenhorn

Dora Bluhm

Soledad Peak ▲

East Point

△ Campground
†•† Ranger Station
†|† Restrooms
⚓ Anchorage
⚑ Shipwreck

Abandoned Military Base

Ford Point

Crown of England

0   2 Miles

S.S. Chickasaw

Johnsons Lee

0   2 Kilometers

South Point

---

company ceased all cattle operations, ending nearly 2 centuries of ranching on the islands that now form the national park.

The second largest island in the park, Santa Rosa displays widely different landscapes: After decades of ranching, rolling nonnative grasslands cover about 85% of the island, but columnar volcanic formations and high mountains with deep canyons are also present. A unique **coastal marsh** on the east end of the island is among the most extensive freshwater habitat found on any of the Channel Islands.

As with Santa Cruz, the island's size allows for a fantastic variety of life. While the impact of ranching has been severe, native plant species still survive, primarily in the rocky canyons and upper slopes. Santa Rosa is home to a large concentration of endangered plant species, 34 of which occur only on the islands. **Torrey pines** grow only in two places. One is on Santa Rosa, in two ancient groves near Bechers Bay. (They also grow on the mainland near San Diego.) The island's vast grasslands provide prime habitat for 195 bird species; shore birds and waterfowl prefer the marshy terrain on the island's eastern tip.

Santa Rosa is also home to the diminutive island fox, a tiny cousin of the gray

fox that has become nearly fearless as it has evolved in the predator-free island environment. They'll walk right through your camp if you let them. In all the world, the rarely seen spotted skunk lives only here and on Santa Cruz.

The **kelp beds** that surround the island function as an invaluable nursery for the sea life that feeds the Channel Islands' marine mammals and seabirds.

The Chumash lived on *Wima* (their name for the island) until they were moved to mainland Missions in approximately 1820. Through radiocarbon dating, scientists have been able to date human use of the island back 13,000 years, making Santa Rosa an invaluable archaeological resource. More than 500 largely undisturbed **archaeological sites** have been recorded. In 1959 archaeologist Philip Orr discovered an individual we now refer to as Arlington Woman. Lacking evidence of a traditional burial site, scientists believe she was killed accidentally some 13,000 years ago, possibly while gathering food. The bones of the Arlington Woman may be the oldest human remains found in the United States.

The island also provides an important fossil record. A fossilized pygmy mammoth skeleton carbon-dated at 12,000 years old was discovered on the island in

1994. It is the most complete specimen ever discovered.

Historic & Man-Made Attractions. While visitors are warned not to disturb Chumash archaeological sites, the island does provide insight into another more modern culture: Vail and Vickers Company operated a working cattle ranch on the island until 1998. Except for the addition of modern-day vehicles, the ranch's operation has changed little since its beginning in 1902. While visitors are not allowed into the main ranch areas out of respect for the ranch personnel's privacy, the flavor of traditional *vaquero* (Mexican cowboy) lifestyle is still evident.

Day Hikes. Because of its large size, Santa Rosa offers a diverse array of possible hikes. The shortest and easiest is probably the **East Point Trail.** At only 1-mile round-trip the hike provides rare glimpses of the island's endemic stand of Torrey pines, as well as the brackish marsh on the island's east end.

The **Cherry Canyon Trail** provides excellent opportunities to see inland island wildlife. There are also sweeping views of the interior of the island. The trail is 4 miles round-trip and is ranked moderate.

The **Lobo Canyon Trail** descends through Lobo Canyon to a Chumash Village site—be sure not to disturb this or any of the island's other archaeological sites—and then on to an excellent tide-pooling area. Unlike most mainland tide pools, the Channel Islands' intertidal zones have not been destroyed by human impact on their fragile habitats. The hike is 5 miles round-trip and is ranked moderate.

Camping. Camping is allowed in the old ranch compound in Water Canyon on Santa Rosa's northeast end year-round. All gear must be carried 1½ miles from the pier on Bechers Bay. The campground is provided with water,

chemical toilets, and each of the 15 sites has its own picnic table and windbreak. Foxes will sneak in and steal food scraps; store food appropriately.

Beach camping is also permitted on a limited number of beaches around the island at certain times of the year. While the winds will definitely test your tent, this is a good option for sea kayakers and divers who don't want to lug their equipment all the way into Water Canyon.

There is a nightly $2.50 charge per campsite for camping anywhere on the island, but a reservation is required. Reservations can be obtained at the park visitor center or by calling ☎ 805/658-CAMP (2267).

EXPLORING SAN MIGUEL

People often argue about what's the wildest place left in the Lower 48. They bat around names like Montana, Colorado, and Idaho. Curiously, no one ever thinks to consider San Miguel, the farthest west of the Channel Islands. They should, for this 9,500-acre island is a wild, wild place. Lying west of the influence of Point Conception, the wind blows constantly here, and the island can be shrouded in fog for days at a time. Human presence is definitely not the status quo.

Visitors land at **Cuyler Harbor,** a half moon–shaped cove on the island's east end. Arriving here is like arriving on earth the day it was made: perfect sand, outrageously blue water; seals basking on the offshore rocks. The island's caliche forest appears otherworldly. Created by caliche (calcium carbonate) sand castings of a once-living forest, today all that remains are these natural stone sculptures.

As it did on most of the other islands in this chain, a rich history of ranching nearly destroyed native vegetation. The removal of the imported grazing animals, though, has given the island's recovery a major boost. Today many native species are reclaiming their ancestral lands.

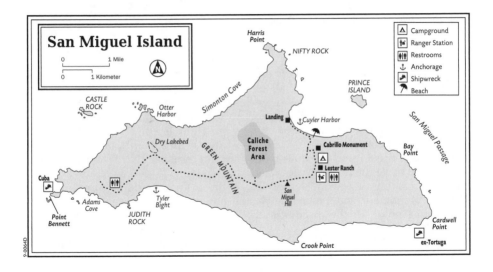

Though widely hunted during the 19th century, the island's pinniped (seals and sea lions) population has clearly recovered. At certain times of the year 35,000 animals, including California sea lions, northern elephant seals, and northern fur seals, occupy the beach at **Point Bennet,** making it one of the largest concentrations of wildlife in the world. The Guadalupe fur seal and Stellar sea lion, former island residents, are also occasionally spotted. Harbor seals haul out on other island beaches.

Prince Island, just outside the mouth of Cuyler Harbor, is an important nesting area for western gulls, brown pelicans, cormorants, and Cassin's auklets. And San Miguel's inland bird species can once again count the peregrine falcon among their number. After years of decimation by the pesticide DDT, the falcon has been reintroduced to the island and is now nesting successfully.

The waters around San Miguel are the richest yet most dangerous of all the islands, as it is exposed to wave action from all sides. Harsh sea conditions have resulted in a fair number of shipwrecks in the surrounding waters. Among the most scenic wrecks is the *Cuba,* which went under on September 8, 1923. (Everyone on board the luxury liner was rescued, along with $2.5 million in gold and silver bullion.)

Swimming among the wrecks are a wide variety of sea mammals: In addition to the pinnipeds, dolphins, porpoises, gray whales, orcas, and even blue whales can sometimes be seen off the island's shore.

The boat concessionaires' schedule to San Miguel is sporadic in summer and almost nonexistent in winter, so call ahead.

Historic & Man-Made Attractions. Like Santa Rosa, San Miguel has more than 500 **Chumash archaeological sites—** visitors are warned not to disturb them.

The island also holds the remains of the earliest modern structure on any of the islands. In the 1850s Capt. George Nedever established a sheep, cattle, and horse ranch on the island. The **adobe** he built is barely visible today.

In the 1930s, Herbert and Elizabeth Lester became the island's caretakers. During his time on the island Herbert became known as "the King of San Miguel." After being asked to leave the island during World War II by the navy, which owned San Miguel, Herbert committed suicide in 1942. Both he and Elizabeth are buried on San Miguel. Today only a few fence posts and small piles of rubble near the trail mark the **Lester Ranch Complex.** Technically the navy still owns San Miguel, though the Park Service manages it.

Day Hikes. Outside of the Cuyler Harbor/Lester Ranch Area, hikes on San

Miguel must be led by a ranger. There are three trails on San Miguel, all of which meet at Lester Ranch. Due to terrain, length, and the tiring effects of walking in all that wind, all three are ranked moderately strenuous.

If you don't feel up to a serious trek, you can still make the relatively easy walk from the landing at Cuyler Harbor to Cabrillo Monument and Lester Ranch, the starting point for the three official hikes.

The first trail heads north to **Harris Point,** allowing marvelous views of Prince Island to the east and Simonton Cove to the west. Taking the trail southeast from Lester Ranch will lead you to **Cardwell Point.**

San Miguel's most popular hike, though, is the 7-mile round-trip trek along the **Point Bennet Trail** to the aforementioned caliche forest.

For those with more time, consider following the trail all the way to Point Bennet, a 15-mile round-trip. You cannot camp along the trail! The diversity of scenery and wildlife on view is seemingly endless for those hikers hardy enough to endure the wind and weather. After crossing San Miguel Hill, the trail passes the caliche forest. From the caliche forest, the trail heads west to Point Bennet, passing south of the island's other peak, Green Mountain. At the end of the trek, the barking of sea lions will signal your arrival at Point Bennet, where as many as 35,000 pinnipeds can congregate.

Note: San Miguel Island was used as a bombing range for the U.S. Navy between 1948 and 1970. Live ordnance is still occasionally uncovered by shifting sand, so it is extremely important to stay on established trails.

Camping. Camping is allowed on San Miguel year-round, though camping dates are subject to the availability of the San Miguel Island ranger. Located 1 mile south of Cuyler Harbor, between Cabrillo Monument and the old Lester Ranch complex, the campground has nine primitive sites and a capacity of 30 people. The second half of the hike-in is a steep climb up Nidever Canyon—keep this in mind before packing your accordion. There is a pit toilet and basic wind shelter at each site, but food and water are not available. No fires are allowed, but cooking is permitted on enclosed backpack-type stoves. Be sure to bring a strong tent, sleeping bag, and waterproof clothes—the wind is often fierce and damp fog can set in for days.

There is a nightly $2.50 charge per site for camping, and a reservation is required. Reservations can be obtained at the park visitor center or by calling ☎ 800/365-CAMP (2267); campground reservations fill up quickly, so be sure to call in advance.

EXPLORING SANTA BARBARA

Lonely, lonely Santa Barbara. As you come upon Santa Barbara Island after a typical 3-hour crossing, you'll think that someone took a single, medium-size grassy hill, ringed it with cliffs, and plunked it down in the middle of the ocean. In terms of land, there's just not a lot here. Even the Chumash eschewed residing on the island because of its lack of fresh water. But the upside is that, of all the islands, Santa Barbara gives you the best sense of what it's like to be stranded on a desert isle, surrounded by the immense Pacific Ocean.

The island's deserted appearance is somewhat misleading, though. During the 1920s, farming, overgrazing, intentional burning by island residents, and the introduction of rabbits all but destroyed the island's native vegetation. To survive the island conditions, plants must be tolerant of salt water and wind—and unfortunately, perfectly suited to this type of environment is the Santa Barbara ice plant.

Originally imported from South Africa in the early 1900s, the nonnative ice plant survives by capturing moisture from sea breezes and subsequently leaches salt into the soil, raising the soil's salt concentration and making it difficult for native species to survive. Like the infamous story of Australia's imported rabbits (or the not-so-famous story of Santa Barbara's imported rabbits), the ice plant has wreaked havoc on the natural ecosystem, virtually taking over much of the island. Through their resource management program, however, the Park Service is taking steps to eradicate nonnative species from the islands. With the rabbits now removed, the giant coreopsis is once again thriving, blanketing the island in gold every spring.

Other than the **landing cove,** there's no access to the water's edge. (The snorkeling in the chilly cove is great.) You can hike the entire 640-acre island in a few hours; then it's time to stare out to sea. You won't be let down. The cliffs and rocks are home to elephant seals and sea lions that feed in the kelp forests surrounding the island. Weighing up to 6,000 pounds, the once threatened elephant seal is appropriately named; and because of the island's small size, the barking of sea lions can be heard almost everywhere. The **Sea Lion Rookery, Webster Point,** and **Elephant Seal Cove** all provide excellent overlooks from which to observe the animals. Be sure to stay at least 100 yards away, particularly from January through July during pupping time—young animals may become separated from their mothers if disturbed.

Santa Barbara's cliffs and rocks are also home to swarms of seabirds such as you'll never see on the mainland, including western gulls, endangered brown pelicans, and the world's largest colony of xantus murrelets. Inland species include the horned lark, orange-crowned warbler, and house finch, all endemic subspecies found only on Santa Barbara Island.

There's also a tiny **museum** chronicling island history. Island Packers and Truth Aquatics only schedule boats to

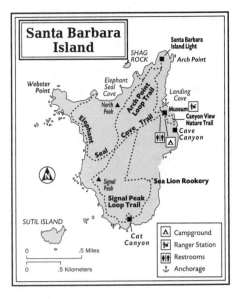

Santa Barbara between April and November. (See "Getting to the Islands by Boat," above, for more information.)

Day Hikes. Hiking the short **Canyon View Nature Trail** is a good introduction to Santa Barbara, but since it's the smallest of the Channel Islands, it's not all that difficult to hike all three of the island's main trails (they only come to 5.5 miles combined). All trails begin and end at the campground and visitor center.

The **Elephant Seal Cove Trail** heads southwest from the visitor center to the west coast of the island, and then heads up by Webster Point, a favorite beach for sea lions and elephant seals, and then up to Elephant Seal Cove.

The **Arch Point Loop Trail** heads north from the visitor center to Arch Point, the northernmost tip of the island. It then turns south, following the island's northwestern bluffs before turning inland and crossing the Elephant Seal Cove Trail. Once across the Elephant Seal Cove Trail, the trail becomes the **Signal Peak Loop Trail** and continues southwest and up Signal Peak. It then follows the bluffs around the southern portion of the island, cutting inland briefly to bypass Cat Canyon. Once on the southeastern side of the island, the trail heads up to Sea Lion Rookery where it heads inland to the middle of the island and then north back to the visitor center.

Camping. Camping is allowed on Santa Barbara year-round. Note, though, that all gear must be carried up the 131 steps to the campground, located approximately 0.25 mile inland. The eight campsites are primitive; there are pit toilets, but food, water, and shade are not available. No fires are allowed, but cooking is permitted on enclosed backpack-type stoves. There is a nightly $2.50 per site charge for camping, and a reservation is required. Permits can be obtained at the park visitor center or by calling ☎ 800/365-CAMP (2267); campground reservations fill up quickly, so be sure to call in advance.

The Extra Mile: Exploring the Coastline & Waters Off the Channel Islands

Sea Kayaking. One of the best ways to explore the fascinating coastline of the islands is by kayak. Warren Glaser of **OAARS** (Outdoor and Aquatic Recreation Specialists), 1215 Anchors Way, no. 279, Ventura, CA 93001 (☎ 805/642-2912), leads small group tours by sea kayak to all five Channel Islands. The trips allow you to explore sea caves and rock gardens. Channel crossing by charter boat, brief lessons, and lunch are included. Fares generally run $135 per person. Three-day adventures to Santa Rosa, with meals, campsite, and guide included are offered for $295.

Aqua Sports (☎ 800/773-2309 or 805/968-7231) and **Paddle Sports** (☎ 805/899-4925), both headquartered in Ventura, also lead similar trips, or trips can be arranged through Island Packers or Truth Aquatics (see "Diving," below).

Diving. Half of Channel Islands National Park is underwater. In fact, twice as many visitors come annually to dive the waters than ever set foot on the islands. Scuba divers come here from all over the globe for the chance to explore stunning kelp forests, shipwrecks, and underwater caves, all with the best visibility in California. Everything from sea snails and urchins to orcas and great white sharks call these waters home.

Truth Aquatics in Santa Barbara (☎ 805/962-1127) is the best provider of single- and multiday dive trips to all the islands.

Ventura Dive & Sport (☎ 805/650-6500) also leads trips, including their "Discover Program," which allows novice and uncertified divers to explore the waters accompanied by an instructor. They also have a well-stocked rental department that delivers to Ventura-harbored boats free of charge.

Channel Islands Scuba (☎ 805/644-3483) and **Pacific Scuba** (☎ 805/984-2566) also lead regular trips, as do boats from San Pedro and other Southern California ports.

Accommodations in Ventura

While there are no accommodations other than camping available on any of the islands, there are lots of options in Ventura, the launching point for most island trips. The Nature Conservancy used to allow stays at Christy Ranch on the windswept west end of Santa Cruz, but at press time the ranch was under restoration and access was restricted. Contact **The Nature Conservancy** (☎ 805/962-9111) for up-to-date information.

In addition to the lodgings discussed below, chain motels in the area include the **Best Western,** 708 E. Thompson Blvd. (☎ 805/648-3101) $60 to $89 double; and **Motel 6,** 2145 E. Harbor Blvd. (☎ 805/643-5100), $48 to $58 double. Toll-free reservation numbers are given in the appendix.

Bella Maggiore Inn

67 S. California St. (½ block south of Main St.), Ventura, CA 93001. ☎ **800/523-8479** or

805/652-0277. 24 units. TV TEL. $75–$150 double; $100–$130 suite. Rates include full breakfast and afternoon refreshments. AE, DISC, MC, V.

The Bella Maggiore is an intimate Italian-style inn whose simply furnished rooms (some with fireplaces, balconies, or bay window seats) overlook a romantic courtyard or roof garden. Breakfast is served each morning around the patio fountain, an intimate spot known to nonguests as Nona's Courtyard Cafe. Nona's also serves lunch and dinner daily. A kind of European elegance pervades here; be sure to ask about midweek specials.

The Country Inn & Suites By Carlson

298 Chestnut St. (½ block south of Thompson), Ventura, CA 93001. ☎ **805/653-1434.** 122 units. $99–$109 double; $309–$329 suite. Rates include full breakfast and afternoon cocktails and appetizers. AE, DISC, MC, V.

Set within walking distance of the beach and Ventura pier, the Country Inn is a good choice for families. It pleasantly blends the convenience of a chain hotel with the perks of a bed-and-breakfast. All rooms come with a 25-inch color TV and pay-per-view movies, and for an additional $10, you can upgrade to a fireplace minisuite. Try to get a room facing away from the highway—the traffic can get pretty loud.

La Mer European Bed & Breakfast

411 Poli St. (west of City Hall), Ventura, CA 93001. ☎ **805/643-3600.** Fax 805/653-7329. www.vcol.net/lamer. 5 units. $95–$185 double. Rates include full breakfast and complimentary wine in room. AE, MC, V. No children.

Perfect for a romantic getaway, La Mer is an 1890 Victorian Cape Cod–style home with a spectacular view of the ocean from the parlor, breakfast room, and two of the five units, each of which is furnished in a different international

style. Whether you choose the "Madame Pompadour" French chamber with wood-burning stove, the "Vienna Woods" Austrian hideaway with sunken bathtub, or one of the others, you'll love these cozy little cottages. They offer generous midweek packages for couples, which can include gourmet candlelit dinners, cruises to Anacapa Island, country carriage rides, therapeutic massages, or all of the above.

Dining in Ventura

There is no food available on any of the islands in the national park; however, there are several recommendable places in Ventura.

Andria's Seafood Restaurant and Market

1449 Spinnaker Dr. (in Ventura Harbor Village). ☎ **805/654-0546.** Main courses $6–$15. Sun–Thurs 11am–9pm; Fri–Sat 11am–10pm. No credit cards; ATM cards accepted. SEAFOOD.

Set aside your inevitable reservations at seeing the fast-food decor here and proceed to the counter to place your order—Andria's has been voted Ventura County's best seafood restaurant for over a decade. Doubling as a fresh seafood market and restaurant, the fish goes directly from the ocean into the deep-fat fryer (charbroiled selections are also available) and onto your plate, with only a short stint on the boat in between. The food isn't fancy, but it's fresh, and the outdoor harborside seating is pleasant.

Rosarito Beach Cafe

692 E. Main St. (at Fir St.). ☎ **805/653-7343.** Main courses $10–$19. Tues–Sat 11:30am–2pm; Tues–Thurs and Sun 5:30–9pm, Fri–Sat 5–10pm. AE, DISC, MC, V. MEXICAN.

This cafe really packs them into this 1938 Aztec-revival moderne building and its welcoming outdoor patio. The superb Baja-style cuisine borrows tangy elements from the Caribbean. It has a culinary sophistication rare in modest Ventura. Make sure to try the delicious handmade tortillas.

The Sportsman

53 California St. (½ block south of Main). ☎ **805/643-2851.** Main courses $4–$14. Mon–Fri 11am–10pm, Sat 9am–2pm and 5–10pm, Sun 9am–2pm and 4–10pm. AE, MC, V. AMERICAN.

You might walk right by the inconspicuous facade of Ventura's oldest (since 1950) restaurant. Like the intriguingly retro lettering on its awning, the interior hasn't changed a lick since then: plush leather booths, brass lamps, wood-paneled bar, giant trophy swordfish on the back wall, and light kept at dimness levels normally reserved for planetariums. The Sportsman looks "fancy"but is quite affordable (especially at breakfast and lunch), and they serve up fine hearty breakfasts, burgers, steaks, and other grilled items. Or you can wet your whistle with $2.50 well drinks from the bar.

Yolie's Fresh Mex Grill

26 S. Garden St. (corner of Main, west of Mission). ☎ **805/652-0338.** Main courses $5–$13. Mon–Thurs 11am–9pm, Fri–Sat 11am–10pm, Sun 10am–9pm. AE, DISC, MC, V. MEXICAN.

This colorful cantina's funny moniker is a nickname of the proprietor, Yolanda, and the place is better than its nondescript business-park exterior leads you to believe. Yolie's offers an impressive fresh salsa bar (authentic and delicious) as well as an admirable beer, margarita, and tequila menu. The patio and dining room are festooned with rainbow serapes and sombreros; the kitchen quickly sends out traditional combination plates (as well as lighter and/or vegetarian adaptations).

Picnic & Camping Supplies

Since there is no food available on any of the islands, make sure to bring a picnic lunch and water for day trips and enough food and water (1 gallon a day per person) if you are camping. Picnic supplies can be bought at the **Von's** grocery store at 2433 E. Harbor Blvd. (☎ 805/642-6761) in Ventura; the **Village Market** (☎ 805/644-2970) in Ventura Harbor Village is another source.

The **Sports Chalet** in Oxnard, 1885 Ventura Blvd. (☎ 805/485-5222), is the best area choice for picking up any camping essentials you forgot to pack.

12

CRATER LAKE NATIONAL PARK

by Jack Olson

TO MANY PEOPLE, SOUTHERN OREGON MEANS ONE THING: CRATER Lake. Even if it weren't the deepest lake in the country, its astounding beauty would be undeniable. Visitors to the area have not even the slightest hint of the awesome grandeur that lies ahead as they approach the rim of the caldera, which makes the lake's stunning appearance 1,000 feet below all the more astounding.

"I came, I saw, I left," might be the motto of most of the 500,000 visitors each year, who, from mid-July to mid-September, ride dutifully around the Rim Road and then move on. If you're looking to interact with the landscape on a more personal level, however, there are options, such as road biking around the Rim Road, and day hiking to the summits of several peaks, including that of 764-foot Wizard Island in the middle of the lake, not to mention superb cross-country skiing and snowshoeing.

Southern Oregon has some of the most complex geography in the state. It is here that the Cascade Range, Coast Range, and Siskyou Mountains combine in a jumble of peaks and valleys. However, the lack of high peaks deceives many into thinking this region is not as wild as more mountainous areas to the north and south. It is partly this perception that kept the region relatively unexplored by Europeans until the late 1800s.

With Mount Shasta, Mount Lassen, the Trinity Alps, and the Marble Mountains just to the south of the border in California, it's hard to get excited about the low peaks of southern Oregon. Here, signs of past volcanic activity are less vertical, yet more dramatic. Mount Mazama, in which Crater Lake is located, once stood as tall as its neighbors to the south, but 7,700 years ago it erupted with almost unimaginable violence. When it had finished erupting, this volcano collapsed in on itself, forming a vast caldera 6 miles wide and almost 4,000 feet deep. Within 500 years, the caldera filled with water to become today's Crater Lake. The sapphire-blue lake's surface is at the base of 1,000- to 2,300-foot cliffs that rise to a total elevation of more than 8,000 feet.

Rising from the middle of the lake is 764-foot high Wizard Island, which can be visited on boat tours from the Cleetwood Cove on the Lake's north shore. The high elevation of the caldera rim and heavy winter snowfalls mean that the busy summer season here is short.

The lake was first encountered by whites when, in 1853, gold prospectors searching for a lost gold mine stumbled upon the lake's rim. The American Indian tribes of the region, which held the lake as sacred, had never mentioned its existence to the first explorers and settlers. But, by 1886, explorers had made soundings and established its depth at 1,996 feet, making it the deepest lake in the United States. Sonar soundings later set the depth at 1,932 feet. In 1902, the lake was designated a national park.

The lake has no inlet or outlet streams and is fed solely by springs, snowmelt, and rainfall. Evaporation and ground seepage keep the lake at a nearly constant level. Because it is so deep, it rarely freezes over entirely, despite long, cold winters.

The Pacific Crest Trail passes through the park, with a 6-mile stretch on the west side of the lake. There are even fish to be caught in the lake. Wildlife is mostly limited to the lowlands surrounding the caldera, although at the summit you can see hawks, eagles, and many types of birds and small mammals. In addition, the spotted owl has been found nesting within the park boundaries. The forested slopes provide refuge for deer, elk, porcupine, and rabbit.

Avoiding the Crowds. It's hard to avoid crowds here. Given the area's harsh winters, most visitors come during the relatively short "summer" season between late-June and the end of September. Since many day visitors drive from cities some distance from the park, the Rim Road is not crowded early in the morning. Circle the lake before 10am and you can easily pick your viewpoint. The best advice is to stay longer than the single day that 90% of the visitors allot to the park. Once you've seen and appreciated the lake (take the lake cruise early before the crowds form), go off and hike some of the less-trampled paths. Several of the longer trails will lead you to fabulous and relatively uninhabited viewpoints. Especially recommended are the Dutton

Creek, Garfield Peak, and Mount Scott trails (see "Day Hikes," below).

Just the Facts

GETTING THERE & GATEWAYS

There are three ways into Crater Lake National Park, the most convenient being from the west and south on Ore. 62, which runs through the southwest corner of the park.

To get to the park's west entrance, drive northeast from Medford 75 miles on Ore. 62.

To get to the park's south entrance from Klamath Falls, travel north on U.S. 97, then northwest on Ore. 62; the total distance is 60 miles.

To get to the park's north entrance from Roseburg, take Ore. 138 east; the total distance to Rim Drive is approximately 92 miles (this entrance is open only during summer).

If you're arriving in winter call the Crater Lake National Park Headquarters for road information (☎ 541/594-2211, ext. 402). From October to May, access to the park by the northern route is frequently limited by snow, so expect delays.

The Nearest Airports. Area airports include **Rogue Valley International** (☎ 541/772-8068), in Medford, which is served by **Horizon Air, United,** and **United Express** airlines with car rentals from **Avis, Budget, Hertz,** and **National.** The **Klamath Falls International Airport** (☎ 541/883-5372) is served by **Horizon Airlines,** with autos from **Budget, Harvest,** and **Hertz.** The toll-free reservation numbers are given in the appendix.

INFORMATION

Contact **Crater Lake National Park,** P.O. Box 7, Crater Lake, OR 97604 (☎ 541/594-2211, ext. 400; www.nps.gov/crla). The park publishes a free park guide, *Crater Lake Reflections,* which has a good summary of most of the park's trails, accommodations, and seasons. You can obtain a catalog of books

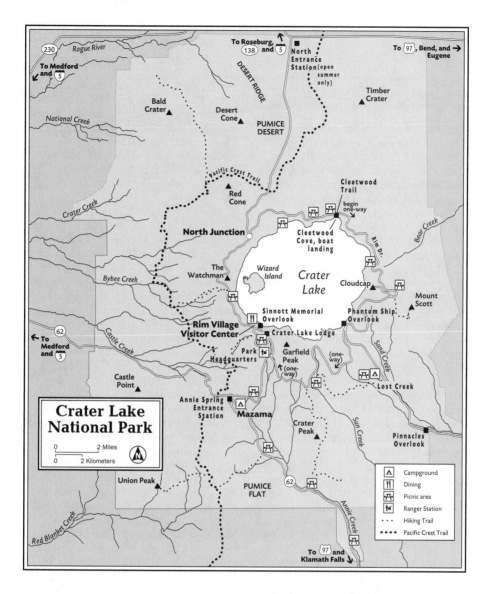

Crater Lake National Park

and maps about the park from the **Crater Lake Natural History Association,** P.O. Box 157, Crater Lake, OR 97604.

VISITOR CENTERS

The park has two visitor centers. **Steel Information Center,** south of the lake off Ore. 62, is open daily year-round and contains park headquarters. You can talk to a ranger and find out about local weather forecasts and general park information, purchase books and maps, as well as watch an 18-minute film. The **Rim Village Visitor Center,** along the southern edge of the caldera rim, is open daily from June through September. Here you can obtain general park information, and books, videos, and maps. In addition, there is a short, paved trail leading from the visitor center to the Sinnot Overlook, which offers a fine view of the lake and several interpretive exhibits.

FEES

Entrance into the park costs $10 per vehicle. Camping in Mazama Campground is $13 per tent site, and $14 per RV site. Camping in the Lost Creek Campground is $10 per site. Backcountry camping requires registration, but no fee.

SPECIAL REGULATIONS & WARNINGS

No, you may not climb into the caldera. The only access to the lake is through the Cleetwood Cove Trail. And after getting a view at some of the steep and sharp-looking volcanic boulders lining the trip down, you won't want to try.

Fire prevention is of such a concern in this park that smoking on the trails is prohibited, much less building a fire anywhere other than in the pits at the designated camping sites.

SEASONS & CLIMATE

At Crater Lake there are basically two seasons. The main tourist season lasts from mid-June, when most of the park's facilities open, through September. The busiest months are July and August. Summer temperatures in southern Oregon can get pretty scorching in the lower elevations, sometimes hovering near the 100°F mark. The upper elevations (including most of the park) remain slightly cooler, but even the lake's rim can get pretty hot and dusty in summer.

In the winter, snowfall up to 44 feet deep buries the park, making it virtually impassable to everyone save skiers and snowshoers. Roads along the lake rim are left unplowed and are open to the non-car travelers exclusively. The winter season generally includes fall and spring, stretching from late October to mid-June or even early July.

If You Only Have 1 Day

Most people enter the park's West and South entrances on Ore. 62. Bypass the Mazama Village area unless you need to load up on snacks, and stop at the **Steel Information Center** for a preview of what lies ahead.

At this point, provided you have the stamina to hike down to the lakeshore, it might be a good idea to head for the requisite boat trip to Wizard Island before it gets too late in the day, and

consequently, too crowded at the boat dock. The first boat leaves at 10am.

Drive north, clockwise around the rim from the Rim Village entrance, to the **Cleetwood Cove Trailhead** (the only trail in the park that leads to the lakeshore), approximately 5 miles past the junction of the northern route to the Pumice Desert.

The trip down Cleetwood Cove Trail to the cove is for the muscles in the front of your thighs, and the trip back is for your calves. It's a steep, strenuous trail, equal to a climb of 65 flights of stairs, or an elevation change of about 700 feet over 1 mile's distance. Consider carefully whether you are in good enough shape to make the 1-mile climb back up before you head down to the boat dock. There are benches along the way, if you have to rest (you will). At the trailhead is a concessionaire who sells tickets for the guided boat ride. The tour takes approximately 1³/₄ hours before you arrive back on shore, provided that you don't layover on Wizard Island when the boat stops there during the tour.

It's perfectly fine to explore **Wizard Island** for a while, climbing the 700 feet to its summit on the Wizard Island Trail, and then catching the next boat back. You might want to eat lunch on the beach at Cleetwood Cove before you head back up the trail. After all, this is the only area of the park where you can get next to the water, so why not take advantage?

After the boat trip, it's time for the **Rim Drive.** Go clockwise toward the **Cloudcap Overlook** turnoff, for a brief drive to the 2,000-foot views of the lake and, farther off on the horizon to the south, Mt. Scott and Mt. Shasta. Make a short stop to admire pretty **Vidae Falls;** there may be lovely wildflowers blooming along the cascade. Then, keep heading clockwise. You'll eventually approach a turnoff to view **The Pinnacles,** an area of unique rock formations. These spires are the remnants of fumaroles that formed in hot volcanic debris from the great eruption of Mount Mazama.

The Crater Lake Rim Drive

Exploring the park by car is *de rigueur* for most people. There are 33 miles of the famous Rim Drive, with more than 30 overlooks lining this summertime-only two-lane road, and a couple of spur roads that lead to spectacular spots in the southeastern section of the park. Allow 2 hours to complete the drive, and allow even more time to enjoy any of the many trails and overlooks that are accessible from the Rim Drive. Gasoline is available only at Mazama, and then only from late May to mid-October. Otherwise, gasoline should be purchased in Medford, Roseburg, or any of the other outlying communities.

It's best to travel clockwise on Rim Drive because all the lake view points are located on the inside, or right, side of the road as you drive that way, so entering and exiting the view points is easier. There are also some viewpoints on the other side of the road that give vistas of mountain scenery away from the lake.

The road back to the rim terminates at a junction with another great viewpoint, the **Phantom Ship Overlook.** The "ship" is an ornate piece of eroded basalt jutting up from the lake that sometimes seems to be sailing when the wind is whipping up the water just right. Then again, you might want to skip this if you got the up-close look on your boat ride.

Return to the Rim Village for the last stop of the day, a little walk to the **Rim Village Visitor Center** and down the path to the **Sinnott Overlook,** which has exhibits that tell you about the names and histories of the many peaks that may now be lit by the late-day sun.

You can get a cup of coffee at the Rim Village Cafeteria, or sit back and watch the sun go down with a meal at the Crater Lake Lodge (see "Accommodations," below), just east of the visitor center. (Be sure to call ahead for reservations. Way ahead.)

If you skipped the boat ride, you'll have time for a short hike. Two of the easy, short trails in the park are the Annie Creek Canyon and Godfrey Glen trails, which begin around Mazama Village. A third is the Castle Crest Wildflower Trail, which begins at the Steel Information Center. None .of these trails are over 2 miles (see "Day Hikes," below).

If You Have More Time

Even though most summer visitors come into the park's west or south entrances, you can still access Crater Lake from the north. And it's a shame to miss these northern perimeter lands, as the sands of the Pumice Desert are otherworldly when wildflowers are scattered across its flat canvas. If you have the time, it might be worthwhile to detour north when driving in from the south, just to see this area. From the south entrance, it adds only an extra 15 miles or so, depending on how far out toward the north entrance station you want to drive.

If you're out for something a little more strenuous, try the Pacific Crest Trail listed under "Longer Trails," below.

Organized Tours & Ranger Programs

There are numerous ranger-led programs and tours in the summer. From the Rim Village, 15-minute talks are given daily at the Sinnott Memorial Overlook (below the visitor center) from 10am to 5pm, on the hour. There is also a guided afternoon hike up Garfield Peak that meets at the flagpole in front of the visitor center.

At Mazama Campground, there are evening programs at an outdoor amphitheater on a variety of topics posted daily at the visitor centers. The talks start at 9pm from late June through July, and at 8:30pm from August to Labor Day.

Of course, the most famous Crater Lake tour is the guided boat tour that leaves the Cleetwood Cove every 45 minutes or so, daily from late June through mid-September, from 10am to the last shove-off at 4:30pm. Remember, there is a steep trail down to the boat landing. The tour docks briefly at Wizard Island and glides past the Phantom Ship before heading back to the Cleetwood Dock. Take a jacket because weather here can be changeable. Tickets, available at the trailhead, cost $12.50 for adults, $7.50 for children.

Sometimes the wait for the boat ride can be as long as 1½ hours. Purchase your ticket and then go off and do some hiking. Come back, and your boat will be waiting when you make it to the dock. Also, keep in mind that if you do get off the boat on Wizard Island, you might have to wait until somebody gets off the next boat arriving, so you can get on for the return trip. Boat capacity is limited, and people have on occasion been stuck on the island for several hours.

Historic & Man-Made Attractions

In addition to the Crater Lake Lodge, which you might want to take a look at even if you don't spend the night, there is the Sinnott Memorial Overlook. There is evidence of past travels through, and visits to, this area by numerous people over the last 150 years. If you're lucky, you might find some wagon tracks, whose faint impressions can be found here and there throughout the outer perimeters of the park. Ask the rangers at the visitor center to suggest trails where you might be able to see them.

Day Hikes

SHORTER TRAILS

Annie Creek Canyon

1.7 mi. RT. Easy. Access: Reach the trailhead via the Mazama Campground Trailhead, between the D and E loops of the campground.

This is a scenic walk through old-growth forest and wildflower meadows, which serves as a nice little breather to all the ancient volcanic starkness going on up at the rim. There is an elevation gain of about 200 feet.

Castle Crest Wildflower Trail

0.4 mi. RT. Easy. 100-ft. elevation gains. Access: The trailhead is at park headquarters in Mazama Village.

Summer is short on the rim of Crater Lake, so when the snow finally melts, wildflowers burst forth with nearly unrivaled abandon. This trail meanders through one of the best displays of wildflowers in the park. Late July and early August are the best wildflower periods. Although this trail is judged "easy," be careful of slick rocks, which must be traversed along the way. Hiking boots, or shoes with good tread, are helpful.

Cleetwood Trail

2.2 mi. RT. Moderate. Access: North side of the lake, 4.5 mi. east of the North Junction.

This is the only trail down to the shore of Crater Lake, and it stays busy with those who just want to get to the water and those who are headed to Cleetwood Cove to take the boat tour. Because the trail leads downhill, many visitors are lured into thinking that this is an easy trail. It's not! The climb 675 feet back up from the water to the rim is strenuous and steep.

Godfrey Glen

1 mi. RT. Easy. Access: 1.5 mi. past the Mazama Village Entrance, on the right side of the rd.

This trail is a very easy walk through old-growth forest and alpine meadows overlooking the Annie Creek Valley. You'll cross Munson Creek at Duwee Falls before you head back to the car. It's a good walk for the kids, with lots of possibilities to see deer, elk, rabbits, or grouse.

The Watchman

1.4 mi. RT. Moderate. Access: 3.7 mi. northwest of Rim Village on West Rim Dr.

With a historic fire lookout perched on its summit, the Watchman is one of the high points on the rim of the caldera. A short but steep (655-ft. elevation gain) hike leads to the top for an outstanding view of the lake with the conical Wizard Island rising from the deep blue of the foreground. This is the shortest climb you can do along the rim of the caldera.

Wizard Island

2 mi. RT. Easy to moderate. Access: Take the Cleetwood Trail (see above) and then a boat tour around the lake, disembarking on the island.

Though it is small, Wizard Island is a great temptation to many Crater Lake visitors. The island, with its steep volcanic cone rising from the deep, is fun to explore for a few hours, and this trail climbs 765 feet up to the island's summit. To spend some time here, take an early boat tour, get off on the island, and return on a later boat. Because most of the hiking is on jagged lava rock, be sure to wear sturdy boots.

LONGER TRAILS

Bald Crater/Boundary Springs

20 mi. RT. Easy to moderate. Access: Via the Rim Dr. to northwest of the Rim Village area; continue to the Northern Park Junction of the Rim Dr. and the northern access rd.; from here, it's 3 mi. down the northern access rd. to the trailhead on the left.

The ashy, flat, and rolling Pumice Desert stretches to the north along the trail as you travel some 3-odd miles toward the 8,763-foot summit of the Red Cone, a miniature Mount Mazama before it collapsed and created the caldera that holds the lake. The plains give way to ancient forests interspersed with fields of wildflowers. At the junction of the Pacific Crest Trail and the Bald Crater Trail, turn right to head for another miniature Mount Mazama experience: Bald Crater Peak. The peak is about 2 miles south of some fine campsites at the end of the Bald Crater Trail, along Boundary Springs, near the headwaters of the beautiful Rogue River.

Crater Peak

5 mi. RT. Easy to moderate. Access: From park headquarters, head east around the Rim Dr. The trailhead is approximately 1.5–2 mi. east from the Steel Information Center.

This beautiful little walk takes you to a peak that is both a peak and a crater. How? The summit of this hike is the rim of yet another little volcanic cone to the south of the once huge Mount Mazama.

The trail begins with an uphill stroll through 2 miles of alpine forest and meadow, before reaching the steep final 0.5 mile to the summit of Crater Peak, with its full panoramic vistas of Sun Mountain, Maklaks, and Scoria to the south, and the rim of Crater Lake to the north. To the west lies Arant Point, near Mazama, and to the east the Grayback Ridge. All of them combine to form an incredible view. Early in the morning or late in the evening, you may see deer or elk.

Discovery Point

2.6 mi. RT. Easy to moderate. Access: Get to the trailhead from the west end of the Rim Village parking area.

This trail, like most trails around the rim, provides brilliant views of the vast lake and Wizard Island below, ending after a short climb at an overlook where John Hillman, one of the first European explorers of the area, first witnessed the beauty of Crater Lake in 1853.

Dutton Creek

4.8 mi. RT. Easy to moderate. Access: Via the trailhead at the west end of the Rim Village parking area.

If you think the whole volcano experience is about ash and pumice, check out the old-growth forest of hemlocks, fir, and pine located on the sometimes-vertiginous Dutton Creek Trail. This is also the section of the Pacific Crest Trail that leads the long-distance hiker up to the rim. But for short-timers heading south, it provides an opportunity to get away from the crowds and see something besides a volcano's mouth. That something might be a deer or an elk as you hike down this narrow, heavily forested valley along Dutton Creek, before reaching the junction with the Pacific Crest Trail and getting ready for the climb back the way you came.

Garfield Peak

3.4 mi. RT. Moderate. 1,010-ft. elevation gain. Access: East end of Rim Village parking area.

Sure the view from the Rim Village borders on sublime, but this is even better. You'll leave most of the crowds behind, get in a good hike, and treat yourself to an even more breathtaking (literally, since the hike starts above 7,000 ft.) view of the lake by hiking to the summit of 8,054-foot Garfield Peak, which lies just east of the Rim Village. The route gains all its elevation in a short 1.5 miles of nearly constant switchbacks. From the summit, the entire lake is visible below, including the island called Phantom Ship, which is hard to see from the Rim Village. To the south, Mount Shasta can be seen.

Mount Scott

5 mi. RT. Strenuous. 1,480-ft. elevation gains. Access: 14 mi. east of park headquarters on East Rim Dr. and across the road from Cloud-cap Junction.

If the trail to Garfield Peak had a few too many other hikers on it for your tastes, try this trail to the top of 8,929-foot Mount Scott. This is the highest point within Crater Lake National Park, and the trail is longer, steeper, and entails more elevation gain than the trail up Garfield Peak. The views from the summit are the most far-reaching in the park, encompassing not only the entire lake but such surrounding peaks as Mount Thielsen, Mount Shasta, and Mount McLoughlin, as well as the vast expanse of Klamath Lake to the south.

Pacific Crest Trail Section

33 mi. one way. Moderate to strenuous. Access: Via Mazama Village. Approximately 0.1 mi. west of the village, the trailhead is on the left.

For those who want to chalk up this particular section of the Pacific Crest Trail, there's a lot to chalk up. The trail essentially bisects the park, with only one section that follows the rim for views of the lake. Otherwise, you're pretty much out there in the flatlands.

From the trailhead, the path follows the base of the mountain's curve to the west for views of the mountain's slow climb to its rim to your right, and the rolling high desert plains to your left. At the northern end of the walk, before crossing into the vast Pumice Desert, there is an opportunity to circle back to the rim at North Junction.

Pumice Flat

6 mi. RT. Easy to moderate. Access: 3 mi. south of Mazama Village on Ore. 62.

This is the southern equivalent of the park's northern Pumice Desert area. This dusty trail takes you through gently rolling pumice and ash plains littered with sharp volcanic rocks, before intersecting the Pacific Crest Trail for the loop to Mazama. You can also simply return on the shorter route back to the trailhead where you started.

Stuart Falls

11 mi. RT. Easy to moderate. Access: 3 mi. south of the Mazama Village park entrance on Ore. 62.

Stuart Falls is really outside the park's boundaries, but the trailhead isn't. There's a nice contrast as you climb down to the dusty and volcanically beautiful Pumice Flats before heading into the Red Blanket Valley after the junction with the Pacific Crest Trail. You'll begin to notice a bare trickle of water turning into a creek turning into a much bigger creek that ends up as a fine crashing mist of spray known as Stuart Falls. Folks have been known to take a rest in Stuart Fall's fine white spray before heading back up the steep and often parched trail.

Other Summer Sports & Activities

Biking. The 33-mile circuit of Crater Lake is one of the most popular road-bike trips in the state, despite the heavy car traffic. Although it would seem at first that this would be an easy trip, numerous ups and downs (especially on the east side of the lake) turn it into a demanding ride. Keep in mind that there are more hills on the east side, but there are also more views. An alternative is to do the 21-mile out and back ride from the Rim Village to the Cleetwood Cove Trailhead (and maybe add on a boat tour of the lake). There are no bike rentals available in the park, but Diamond Lake Resort rents them in the summer. (See "Accommodations," below).

Swimming. Although Crater Lake is too deep to ever reach a truly comfortable temperature (even in the summer), plenty of people take the plunge and do a few quick strokes to cool down after hiking the Cleetwood Cove Trail or after exploring Wizard Island. But there are no facilities for swimmers, as this is an informal activity.

Winter Sports & Activities

Cross-Country Skiing. The **Diamond Lake Nordic Center,** 4 miles north of the park on Ore. 138 (☎ **800/733-7593**), offers Crater Lake ski tours that include a snowcat ride to the North Rim Ski Trail. Cost is $35 per person, with a minimum of 10 participants. They also rent cross-country skis. Maps of ski areas are available at the Steel Information Center at park headquarters.

Without a doubt, the **rim** of Crater Lake National Park offers some of the best cross-country skiing in the country. Not only are there numerous views of sapphire-blue Crater Lake 1,000 feet below you, but the views to the west and south take in Mount McLoughlin, Mount Shasta, and countless ridges and seemingly endless forest vistas as well.

The **ultimate ski tour** is the 30- to 33-mile circuit of the lake. Although this route has been done in a single day by racers, most skiers take 3 days and enjoy the views along the way. Because the weather is better and there's still plenty of snow, March and April are the most popular months. The route is very straightforward, although you may have to do some route finding on the northeast side of the lake.

The **West Rim Trail,** which follows Rim Drive, is the most popular day skiing area. By mid-October the road is unplowed and the snow cover turns it into an excellent trail, which requires a little climbing. It's best done in good weather and good snow conditions. Consult a park ranger for snow conditions before heading out.

The **East Rim Trail** is not nearly as popular as the West Rim Trail for the simple reason that it is between 4.25 and 5.4 miles to the first view of the lake (depending on where you start). This trail also has a lot more ups and downs. So, why would you want to start on this section at all? To stay out of the wind, that's why. If, after driving all the way up here there's a gale-force wind blowing up the west slopes, you really don't have much choice. Never set out, though, without checking with the rangers at park headquarters to find out about avalanche conditions and other dangers.

Snowmobiling. During winter months snowmobiling is allowed, but only on the north entrance road up to its junction with Rim Drive (snowmobiles are not allowed on Rim Drive). You cannot drive snowmobiles on any park trails, either. Snowmobile rentals are available from Diamond Lake Resort at up to $125 per day per person, depending on whether you're just renting or going on a resort-led snowmobile tour. See "Accommodations," below.

Snowshoeing. With its jewel of a lake for a centerpiece and views that extend all the way to Mount Shasta in California, Crater Lake National Park is a natural magnet for snowshoers. The **West Rim Trail** is the most popular route (just as it is for cross-country skiing), but snowshoers have the advantage of being able to go where few skiers can. Before you head out, discuss possible routes with the rangers and ask about avalanches and other potential dangers.

If you've never snowshoed before, you can give it a try at Rim Village, where 90-minute guided snowshoe hikes are offered weekends at 1pm from late November 25 through March.

Camping

Within Crater Lake National Park, there are only two campgrounds, one large and one small. No reservations are taken.

Mazama Village Campground ($13 per tent and $14 per RV per night) has 198 sites available, with drinking water, disposal station, rest rooms, a public phone, and fire pits. It's at Mazama Village off Ore. 62. There is also a general store and an adjacent post office. It's open from June through mid-October.

Lost Creek Campground ($10 per night) has 16 sites for tents only. It is located on the southeastern section of the park, on the spur road to The Pinnacles. It's open from mid-July to mid-September.

Accommodations & Dining

INSIDE THE PARK

Aside from the Crater Lake Lodge Dining Room, places to eat in the park are limited to the snack bar at the Rim Village Cafeteria and Gift Shop, as well as the grocery store in the Mazama Village.

Crater Lake Lodge

Mailing address: 1211 Ave. C, White City, OR 97503. ☎ **541/830-8700.** Fax 541/830-8514. www.crater-lake.com. E-mail: info@crater-lake.com. 71 units. $110–$150 double. MC, V. Closed mid-Oct to mid-May.

Perched on the edge of the rim overlooking Crater Lake, this lodge was completely rebuilt in 1995 and has since become the finest national park lodge in the Northwest. Not only are the views breathtaking, but the amenities are modern without sacrificing the rustic atmosphere that visitors expect in a mountain lodge. Among the lodge's few original features are the stone fireplace and ponderosa pine–bark walls in the Great Hall. Slightly more than half the guestrooms overlook the lake, and although most of the rooms have modern bathrooms, there are eight rooms with claw-foot bathtubs. The very best rooms are the corner ones on the lake side of the lodge. As at other national park lodges, reservations should be made as far in advance as possible.

The lodge's dining room serves creative Northwest cuisine and provides views of both Crater Lake and the Klamath River basin.

Mazama Village Motor Inn

Mailing address: 1211 Ave. C, White City, OR 97503. ☎ **541/830-8700.** Fax 541/830-8514. www.crater-lake.com E-mail: info@crater-lake.com. 40 units. $84 double. MC, V. Closed Nov–May.

Though the Mazama Village Motor Inn isn't on the rim of the caldera, it's just a short drive away. The modern motel-style guest rooms are housed in 10 steep-roofed buildings that look much like traditional mountain cabins. A laundry, gas station, and general store make Mazama Village a busy spot in the summer.

NEAR THE PARK

Since the park is so isolated, there are few options in the small, surrounding communities for dining outside of the following.

Diamond Lake Resort

Diamond Lake, OR 97731. ☎ **800/733-7593** or 541/793-3333. Fax 541/793-3309. 92 units. TV. $69 double; $76 studio for 2; $129–$185 cabin. MC, V.

Located on the shores of Diamond Lake near the park's north entrance, this resort has long been a popular family vacation spot, and with Mounts Thielsen and Bailey flanking the lake, it's one of the most picturesque settings in the Oregon Cascades. The variety of accommodations provides plenty of choices, but our favorites are the lakefront cabins, which are large enough for a family or two couples, with great views of the lake and mountains. If you want to do your own cooking, you'll find kitchenettes in both the cabins and the studios. Lodge guests and campers can dine at the resort's two dining rooms and one pizza parlor. Boat, mountain-bike, and horse rentals are available, and there's a small sandy beach and a bumper-boat area. In winter the resort is most popular with snow-mobilers but also attracts a few cross-country skiers.

Prospect Historical Hotel and Motel

391 Mill Creek Dr., Prospect, OR 97536. ☎ **800/944-6490** or 541/560-3664. Fax 503/560-3825. www.prospecthotel.com. E-mail: prospect@internetcds.com. 22 units. $50–$85 double. DC, DISC, MC, V.

This hotel, located in the tiny hamlet of Prospect, 30 miles from Crater Lake's Rim Village, is a combination vintage/modern hotel. The old (1889) hotel is a big white building with a wraparound porch on which are set several bent-willow couches. The small rooms are furnished with antiques and have a country styling that gives them a bit of charm. The motel rooms are modern and clean and have TVs and telephones, and some also have kitchenettes. The elegant dining room is well known for its excellent meals, ranging from $7 to $22. Sunday brunch is particularly popular.

Steamboat Inn

42705 N. Umpqua Hwy., Steamboat, OR 97447-9703. ☎ **800/840-8825** or 541/ 498-2230. Fax 541/498-2411. www. thesteamboatinn.com. E-mail: stmbtinn@ rosenet. net. 19 units. $130 double; $165 cottages and houses; $245 suite. MC, V.

Located roughly midway between Roseburg and Crater Lake, this inn on the bank of the North Umpqua River is by far the finest lodging on the North Umpqua. While the lodge appeals primarily to anglers, the beautiful gardens, luxurious guest rooms, and gourmet meals also attract a fair number of people looking for a quiet getaway in the forest and a base for hiking and biking. If you aren't springing for one of the suites, which have their own soaking tubs overlooking the river, your best bet will be stream-side rooms, which are referred to as cabins but really aren't. These have all been recently renovated, have gas fireplaces, and open onto a long deck that overlooks the river. The hideaway cottages are more spacious but don't have river views and are 0.5 mile from the lodge (and the dining room). Dinners are multicourse affairs served in a cozy dining room, and breakfast is available all day. There's also a fly-fishing shop on the premises.

Union Creek Resort

56484 Ore. 62, Prospect, OR 97536.
☎ **541/560-3565.** 23 units. $38–$48 double; $50–$90 cabin for 2 to 6 people. MC, V.

Located almost across the road from the Rogue River Gorge, this rustic resort has been catering to Crater Lake visitors since the early 1900s and is listed on the National Register of Historic Places. Tall trees shade the grounds of the resort, which is right on Ore. 62 about 23 miles from Rim Village. Accommodations include both lodge rooms and very basic cabins (many of which have kitchenettes), and most have been updated in recent years. Across the road from the cabins and lodge building is Beckie's Café, which serves home-style meals and is best known for its pies. This is your best and closest option outside the Crater Lake National Park on the west side.

13

DEATH VALLEY NATIONAL PARK & MOJAVE NATIONAL PRESERVE

by Eric Peterson and Stephanie Avnet Yates

N 1994, DEATH VALLEY NATIONAL MONUMENT BECAME DEATH VALLEY National Park. The forty-niners, whose suffering gave the valley its name, would've howled at the notion. Death Valley National *Park* seems a contradiction in terms, an oxymoron of the great outdoors.

To them, other four-letter words would've come to mind: gold, mine, heat, lost, dead. And the four-letter words shouted by the teamsters who drove the 20-mule-team borax wagons need not be repeated.

Americans looking for gold in California's mountains in 1849 were forced to cross the burning sands here to avoid the severe snowstorms in the nearby Sierra Nevada. One person perished along the way, and the land became known as Death Valley. Not much about the valley's essence has changed. Its mountains stand naked, unadorned. The bitter waters of saline lakes evaporate into bizarre razor-sharp crystal formations. Jagged canyons jab deep into the earth. The ovenlike heat, the frigid cold, and the driest air imaginable combine to make this one of the world's most inhospitable locations.

Death Valley is raw, bare earth, the way things must've looked before life began.

Here, earth's forces are exposed to view with dramatic clarity; just looking out on the landscape, you'll find it impossible to know what year, or century, it is. It's no coincidence that many of Death Valley's topographical features are associated with hellish images: Funeral Mountains, Furnace Creek, Dante's View, Coffin Peak, and Devil's Golf Course. But the valley can be a place of serenity as well.

Human nature being what it is, it's not surprising that people have long been drawn to challenge the power of Mother Nature, even in this, her "home court." The area's first foray into tourism was in 1925, a scant 76 years after the forty-niners' harrowing experiences. It probably would've begun sooner, but the valley had been consumed by lucrative borax mining since the late 1880s.

In one of his last official acts, Pres. Herbert Hoover signed a proclamation designating Death Valley a national monument in February 1933. With the stroke of a pen he not only authorized the protection of a vast and wondrous land but also helped to transform one of the earth's least hospitable spots into a popular tourist destination.

The naming of Death Valley National Monument came at a time when Americans were discovering the romance of the desert. Land that had previously been considered hideously devoid of life was now being celebrated for its spare beauty; places that had once been feared for their harshness were now being admired for their uniqueness.

In 1994, when President Clinton signed the California Desert Protection Act, Death Valley National Park became the largest national park outside Alaska, with more than 3.3 million acres. Though remote, it's one of the most heavily visited, and you're likely to hear less English spoken than German, French, and Japanese.

Flora & Fauna. Most of Death Valley's climate zones are harshly limiting to plants and animals, but they're nevertheless diverse. Within the park, elevations range from 282 feet below sea level (Badwater, the lowest point in the Western Hemisphere) to 11,049 feet above sea level (Telescope Peak, blanketed by snow during winter and early spring). At the lowest elevations is little sign of life; any groundwater is highly saline and supports only algae and bacteria. One notable exception is the unique and endangered **desert pupfish,** an ancient species that's slowly adapted to Death Valley's increasingly harsh conditions. You can see the tiny fish in the marshes of Salt Creek, halfway between Furnace Creek and Stovepipe Wells, where a boardwalk lined with interpretive plaques allows you an up-close look.

Hardy desert shrubs like **mesquite, creosote,** and **arrowweed** flourish at the mouths of canyons, where enough fresh water is channeled from the mountains to support these miserly plants. You have to look closely to discern the surprising number of small mammals and birds that live at the lower elevations (sea level to 4,000 ft.); **rabbits, rodents, bats, snakes, roadrunners,** and even **coyotes** all get by on very little water. At the higher elevations, where **piñon** and **juniper** woodlands blanket the slopes, animals are more plentiful and can also include **bobcats** and the elusive **bighorn sheep.** Over 10,000 feet, look for small stands of **bristlecone pine,** the planet's longest-lived tree; some specimens on Telescope Peak are more than 3,000 years old.

Avoiding the Crowds. You may think that no one would plan their vacation in a 120°F–plus remote desert, but Death Valley is full year-round. Summer is when primarily Europeans visit, and many are disappointed when the thermometer doesn't soar to record-breaking heat. North Americans tend to avoid the hottest season and crowd Death Valley on weekends and school holidays the rest of the year. December and January are the quietest months (with the exception of Christmas week and Martin Luther King Day weekend). The following advice will help ease the crush during your visit.

◆ Make all accommodations reservations as far in advance as you can, at least 2 or 3 months. Facilities are limited inside the park, and Death Valley's isolation makes it time-consuming to locate elsewhere. Of Death Valley's campgrounds, only Furnace Creek is currently accepting reservations (☎ 800/365-2267), from October 15 to April 15. Those planning to set up in one of the "first-come, first-served" camping areas should try to claim a site between 9am and noon.

◆ Avoid visiting on weekends and during school vacation periods, and plan to enjoy the most popular activities early in the day, since crowds start building up around 10am. An alternative, particularly on summer days, is to wait until crowds dissipate around 4pm. Remember, the sun doesn't set until after 7pm between June and September and it stays hot well past midnight.

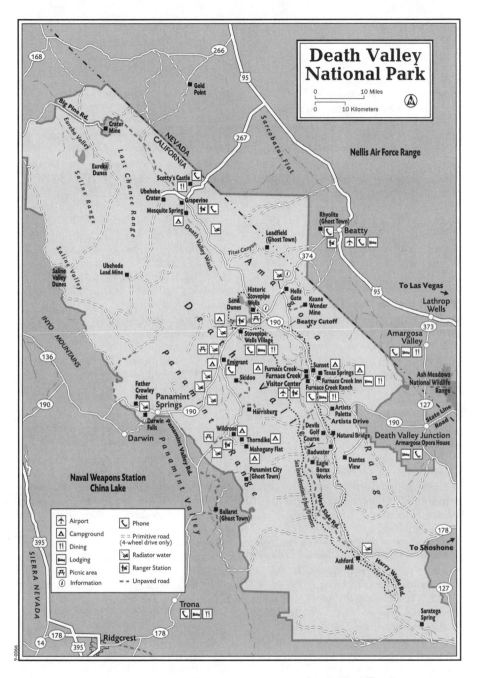

Death Valley National Park

0   10 Miles
0   10 Kilometers

Legend:
- ✈ Airport
- △ Campground
- ⛽ Dining (!!)
- 🛏 Lodging
- ⛱ Picnic area
- ⓘ Information
- 📞 Phone
- = = Primitive road (4-wheel drive only)
- Radiator water
- Ranger Station
- - - Unpaved road

Map labels:
168 · 266 · Gold Point · 95 · Big Pine Rd. · Eureka Valley · Crater Mine · NEVADA CALIFORNIA · 267 · Sarcobatus Flat · Eureka Dunes · Last Chance Range · Saline Range · Scotty's Castle · Ubehebe Crater · Grapevine · Mesquite Spring · Nellis Air Force Range · Rhyolite (Ghost Town) · Beatty · Saline Valley · Saline Valley Dunes · Ubehede Lead Mine · Death Valley Wash · Titus Canyon · Leadfield (Ghost Town) · 374 · To Las Vegas · 95 · Lathrop Wells · INYO MOUNTAINS · Amargosa · Historic Stovepipe Wells · Hells Gate · Keane Wonder Mine · Sand Dunes · 190 · Beatty Cutoff · Amargosa Valley · 373 · 136 · Stovepipe Wells Village · Emigrant · Skidoo · Furnace Creek · Furnace Creek Visitor Center · Sunset · Texas Springs · Furnace Creek Inn · Furnace Creek Ranch · Ash Meadows National Wildlife Range · 127 · Father Crowley Point · Panamint Springs · 190 · Harrisburg · Artists Palette · Artists Drive · State Line Road · 190 · Darwin Falls · Darwin · Panamint Range · Wildrose · Thorndike · Mahogany Flat · Devils Golf Course · Natural Bridge · Death Valley Junction · Armargosa Opera House · Naval Weapons Station China Lake · Panamint City (Ghost Town) · Badwater · Eagle Borax Works · Dantes View · 395 · SIERRA NEVADA · Ballarat (Ghost Town) · West Side Rd. · Ashford Mill · Harry Wade Rd. · 178 · To Shoshone · 127 · 14 · 178 · 395 · Ridgrest · 178 · Trona · Saratoga Spring

9-0066

Just the Facts

GETTING THERE & GATEWAYS

◆ With the help of a high-clearance 4X4 you'll find a whole world of hidden valleys and ghost towns, mountainous sand dunes, and remote canyons that are inaccessible to most of Death Valley's visitors. Check the Park Service's official map, where roads are clearly marked according to degree of passability.

There are several routes into the park—all involve crossing one of the steep mountain ranges that isolate Death Valley. The most common access route from Los Angeles and points south is via Calif.

127 from I-15 at the town of Baker; from Death Valley Junction, Calif. 190 leads to the park's center. From Las Vegas, Nev. 160 and 372 lead to Shoshone at the intersection of Calif. 178 and 127, which is just 27 miles south of Calif. 190. Perhaps the most scenic entry is via Calif. 190 from the west, reached from Calif. 14 and U.S. 395 by taking Calif. 178 from Ridgecrest. To access the same route from the north, pick up Calif. 190 directly from U.S. 395 at Olancha. You can also approach the park from Nevada, by taking Nev. 374 from Beatty, located on U.S. 95.

The Nearest Airport. The nearest airport is Las Vegas's **McCarran International Airport,** 5757 Wayne Newton Blvd. (☎ 702/261-5743), with regularly scheduled flights from practically all major airlines, and vehicles from all major rental agencies. See the appendix for toll-free phone numbers. In addition, **Allstate** (☎ 800/634-6186 or 702/736-6147) is a local company that rents standard cars plus four-wheel-drive vehicles.

It's a 2.5-hour drive from Vegas to Death Valley. A four-wheel-drive vehicle is recommended for backcountry travel, and you'll need one to access 2 of the 10 campgrounds (see "Fees," below).

INFORMATION

Contact the **Superintendent, Death Valley National Park,** Death Valley, CA 92328 (☎ 760/786-2331; www.nps.gov/deva). Be sure to pick up the official *Guide for the Visitor,* a newspaper-style free handout listing most of the park basics. It's available at ranger stations and the Furnace Creek Visitor Center (see below). Also see if they're still distributing a little orange folder called *Hot Weather Hints.* In addition to providing a wealth of information on avoiding heat exhaustion and on high-temperature auto care, the pamphlet has amusing circa-1960 illustrations.

The **Death Valley Natural History Association,** P.O. Box 188, Death Valley, CA 92328 (☎ 760/786-3285; fax 760/786-2236), operates the park bookstores; contact them for their latest publications list and catalog.

VISITOR CENTERS

Park headquarters are at the **Furnace Creek Visitor Center** (☎ 760/786-2331), open daily year-round in Furnace Creek, 15 miles inside the eastern park boundary on Calif. 190. You'll find well-done interpretive exhibits and an hourly slide program as well as an extensive bookstore. There's also a museum, a bookshop, and an information center at **Scotty's Castle** (☎ 760/786-2313), also open daily year-round (see "Historic & Man-Made Attractions," below).

There are ranger stations that collect fees and can provide you with information at **Stovepipe Wells** (☎ 760/786-2342) and **Grapevine** (☎ 760/786-2313), as well as in Beatty, Nevada (☎ 702/553-2200).

FEES

Entry into the park for up to 7 days costs $10 per car (or $5 per person on foot or bike). Be sure to keep the receipt handy for the duration of your stay, since you'll be required to show it when passing the entry checkpoint near Scotty's Castle (Grapevine).

There are 10 campgrounds within park boundaries. Four are free; overnight fees elsewhere range from $10 to $16.

SPECIAL REGULATIONS & WARNINGS

It isn't called Death Valley for nothing, but there's little chance that you'll encounter any life-threatening situations, especially if you carefully follow some common-sense safety tips. You'll find these and many more hints in brochures available at the park's visitor centers.

♦ **Always carry a supply of water for everyone,** including your car. Dehydration is your most urgent concern, particularly in summer, when temperatures routinely reach 120°F and higher at the arid lower elevations. Recommended minimum amounts are 1 gallon per person per day and twice that if you're planning strenuous activity. Drink often, whether you feel thirsty or not, and be alert for the signs of dehydration: dizziness, headache, and cold, clammy skin. It's a good idea to stow several gallons for the car, even though radiator water is available from tanks placed at strategic points (uphill climbs) along the main roads.

◆ **Always carry sunscreen and protective clothing,** including a wide-brimmed hat and sunglasses.

◆ **When driving, turn off your air-conditioning** on uphill grades to lessen engine strain and prevent overheating. In the event that your car does overheat, keep the engine running and turn the car into the breeze. While the car idles, pour sufficient water over the radiator to cool it before removing the cap and refilling the radiator water.

◆ **Be alert for wildlife on the road** and don't let yourself be distracted by the scenery. Single-car accidents are the number-one cause of death in Death Valley, and they can occur summer or winter, daylight or nighttime. There are many long miles of roads through the park; though well paved, they often have sharp curves, dips, and steep downhill grades. If your tires wander off the edge of the pavement at high speed, don't jerk the wheel, which can cause you to skid out of control. Instead, gradually slow down until it's safe to bring all four tires back onto the road.

SEASONS & CLIMATE

Although Death Valley is undeniably one of the world's driest deserts, altitudes range from 282 feet below sea level to over 11,000 feet above; therefore, *desert* doesn't always equal *hot*. From June to September, temperatures in the valley can soar above 120°F, making the mountain sections of the park a welcome relief with temperatures in the 70s and 80s. But from November to February, when valley temperatures are comfortable in the 60s and 70s, many higher areas are frigid and snowy.

SEASONAL EVENTS

The weeklong **Death Valley 49'ers Encampment** is held the second week in November. It features a fiddlers' contest, a burro flapjack race, square dancing, tours, a Western art show, and a golf tournament.

If You Only Have 1 Day

The distances inside Death Valley National Park are prohibitive, so the following is merely a guideline. If there's a destination you don't want to miss, you'll have to pass up some of the other sites in the interest of time.

If you have only 1 day and want to get a sampling of the park's best-loved spots, start at the **Furnace Creek Visitor Center,** located at the center of the action in Furnace Creek (see "Visitor Centers," above). View either the **slide show** or the **short film** (shown continuously) for an overview of the park and a taste of the things you won't get a chance to see. This advice holds even for visitors with several days; there's *always* something you'll have to miss. Step over to the center's museum for a look at the 10-by-20-foot **relief map** of the entire park, which will give you a feel for where your destinations are in the context of the whole region, including the all-important elevation factor. If you have time, check out the tiny **Borax Museum,** housed in an old miners' boardinghouse at nearby Furnace Creek Ranch. Admission is free.

Scotty's Castle is a must-see for most people, but you need to plan ahead due to the popularity of ranger-guided house tours. Even if you want to explore only the grounds, remember that the castle is 53 miles north of Furnace Creek, an hour's drive each way. A good plan is to make the castle your first activity after breakfast, avoiding the crowds and freeing up the afternoon for seeing other sites or squeezing in an easy half-hour hike. Easily reached spots are **Artists Palette, Harmony Borax Works, Badwater, Devil's Golf Course, Zabriskie Point,** and **Dante's View.**

If the weather is fine, replace one or two of these attractions with a short hike (like **Mosaic Canyon, Sand Dunes,** or the **Salt Creek Nature Trail**)—for details, see "Day Hikes," below. Just after the junction where Calif. 190 turns west toward the Sand Dunes and Stovepipe Wells, you'll pass the **Devil's Cornfield,** where arrowweed bushes grow in unusual clumps resembling corn stalks. There's a turnout where you can park to explore this strange landscape and plant, which was named for the way American Indians fashioned arrow shafts from the stalks.

Because each gateway to Death Valley has its own features, visitors with time limitations can maximize their experience by choosing a different entrance and exit route. If you drove in on Calif. 127 through Death Valley Junction, try leaving via the scenic route west through the Panamint Valley. If you entered from the Panamint side, try following Calif. 178 south from Furnace Creek, across the Black Mountains and Greenwater Valley, to pick up Calif. 127 at Shoshone.

Exploring the Park by Car

Death Valley National Park is crisscrossed by a network of roads, ranging from washboard remnants of old mining days to well-maintained highways built during the 1930s. You'll find that most of the popular destinations, as well as the five major entry routes, have superior-quality roads suitable for all passenger vehicles as well as trailers and motor homes. One exception is the Emigrant/Wildrose Canyon pass between Calif. 190 and Calif. 178, sections of which are rough, narrow, and winding; vehicles over 25 feet are prohibited at all times, and other drivers may want to consult the ranger about current road conditions before attempting the unpaved section south of Wildrose.

The park is ideal for viewing by car. Conservationists are adamant that the parade of vehicles detracts from the valley's natural beauty and preservation, but this feature does help make the park more accessible to those with limited time to traverse the vast distances involved (and limited ability to withstand the often grueling weather). Some of the most beautiful sites have handy access roads, vista turn-outs, or loop drives to facilitate viewing. These include **Artists Palette,** where the 8-mile one-way Artists Drive takes you through a colorful display hidden from the main road. Over millions of years, mineral deposits have created brilliant swaths of color across the low, rocky hills. There's a scenic overlook at the beginning of the drive as well as a parking area farther ahead in case you want to stop and scramble amid the pink, blue, red, orange, and green patches.

South of Artists Drive, Calif. 178 takes you past several of Death Valley's highlights, which best illustrate this environment of low-elevation extremes. **Devil's Golf Course,** accessible by a short spur of graded dirt road, sets your car right in the middle of a forbidding landscape created by salt and erosion on a lake bed that dried up about 2,000 years ago. The results are spikes, pits, craters, and jagged ridges stained brown and smoothed by human feet near the parking area; walk just 2 minutes in any direction and you'll see the salty white surface in its natural state.

About 5 miles south of this is **Badwater,** whose simple name indicates the lowest, hottest, and (curiously) wettest spot on the valley floor. At 279 feet below sea level, Badwater is the lowest spot in the park accessible by auto and marked by permanent spring-fed pools. The water at first seemed like relief to early travelers—until they tasted the amounts of chloride, sodium, and sulfate. It isn't poisonous, however, and is home to beetles, soldier fly larvae, and a soft-bodied saltwater snail that slowly adapted to these conditions.

A similar site is 25 miles north on Calif. 190: **Salt Creek,** home to the **Salt Creek pupfish,** found nowhere else on earth. You can glimpse this little fish, which has made some amazing adaptations to survive in this arid land, from a wooden boardwalk nature trail. In spring, a million pupfish might be wriggling in the creek; but by summer's end only a few thousand remain.

Your car will also take you all the way to two of the best lookout points around, both along Calif. 190 southeast of Furnace Creek. Before sunrise, photographers set up their tripods at **Zabriskie Point,** 5 miles southeast of Furnace Creek off Calif. 190, and aim their cameras down at the pale mudstone hills of Golden Canyon and the great valley beyond. The panoramic view is magnificent.

Another grand park vista is at **Dante's View,** located 25 miles south of Furnace Creek via Calif. 190 and Dante's View Road, a 5,475-foot point looking out over the shimmering Death Valley floor backed by the high Panamint Mountains.

Nearly everyone takes the scenic drive up Scotty's Castle Road to visit the park's major man-made attraction, **Scotty's Castle** (see below). While you're there it's worth taking the 15-minute drive to **Ubehebe Crater,** 9 miles west of the Castle, the otherworldly pockmark from a volcanic explosion 3,000 years ago. You'll know that you're close when the landscape begins to darken from layers of cinders spewn from the half-mile crater. A convenient loop road takes you up to the most scenic lip. A few explanatory signs grace the parking area, and there's a hiking path (for those willing to brave the often-gusting winds) to an even more dramatic overlook and a field of smaller craters.

Organized Tours & Ranger Programs

In addition to providing hourly **Scotty's Castle** "Living History" tours (see below), Death Valley rangers keep busy giving lectures, group discussions, and film presentations. The topics are varied, and for those eager to get their shoes dusty, several hikes and guided walks are conducted seasonally, with themes like Moonlight Meander and Canyon Secrets. Contact park headquarters for a seasonal schedule of day and evening events; nearly all programs (except for year-round Scotty's Castle tours) cease between mid-May and early October.

Historic & Man-Made Attractions

Scotty's Castle, the Mediterranean hacienda in the northern part of the park, is unabashedly Death Valley's premier attraction. Visitors are wowed by the elaborate Spanish tiles, well-crafted furnishings, and innovative construction that includes solar water heating. Even more compelling is the colorful history of this villa in remote Grapevine Canyon, brought to life by park rangers dressed in 1930s clothing. Construction of the "castle"—more officially, Death Valley Ranch—began in 1922. It was to be a winter retreat for devout Chicago millionaire Albert Johnson. The insurance tycoon's unlikely friendship with prospector/cowboy/spinner-of-tall-tales Walter Scott put the $2.3 million structure on the map and captured the public's imagination. Scotty greeted visitors and told them fanciful stories from the early hard-rock-mining days of Death Valley.

The 50-minute guided tour of Scotty's Castle is excellent, both for its inside look at the mansion and for what it reveals about the eccentricities of Johnson and Scotty. Tours depart about every 20 minutes from 9am to 5pm; they fill up quickly, so arrive early for the first available spots (there's an $8 fee). During busy periods, you may have to wait an hour or more, perusing the gift shop or relaxing in the snack bar. There's also a self-guided walking tour (excluding the interiors); the pamphlet *A Walking Tour of Scotty's Castle* leads you on an exploration from stable to pool, from bunkhouse to powerhouse. **Organized groups** (only) can reserve tour times by calling ☎ **760/786-2392.**

For another side of the human experience here, visit the **Harmony Borax Works,** located 2 miles south of Furnace Creek off Calif. 190 and then a short spur road—a rock-salt landscape as tortured as you'll ever find. Death Valley prospectors called borax "white gold," and though it wasn't exactly a glamorous substance, it was a profitable one. From 1883 to 1888, more than 20 million pounds of it were transported from the Harmony Borax Works, and borax mining continued in Death Valley until 1928. A short trail with interpretive signs leads past the ruins of the old borax refinery and some outlying buildings.

Transport of the borax was the stuff of legends, too. The famous 20-mule teams hauled the huge loaded wagons 165 miles to the rail station at Mojave. (To learn more about this colorful era, visit the Borax Museum at Furnace Creek Ranch, near the park visitor center). Other remnants of human industry are the **Eagle Borax Works** ruins, 20 miles south of Furnace Creek via Badwater Road and the unpaved dirt West Side Road, and the **Wildrose Charcoal Kilns,** 39 miles south of Stovepipe Wells off Emigrant Canyon Road, where vast amounts of charcoal were manufactured for use on the lucrative silver mining in neighboring Panamint Valley. Located near the Wildrose Ranger Station and campground, the road to the kilns is paved but precariously twisted, and vehicles over 25 feet are prohibited.

Day Hikes

There are trails to suit all levels of expertise and at varying elevations. Wherever you hike, never forget to bring enough water; even in seemingly mild weather conditions, hikers can become dehydrated quickly. Park rangers can provide topographical maps, current weather conditions, and detailed directions to each trailhead.

SHORTER TRAILS

Borax Flats

1 mi. RT. Easy. Access: Parking area for the Harmony Borax Works, 2 mi. north of Furnace Creek off Calif. 190, then down a short spur road.

At the borax works, an old boiler, tanks, and mule-drawn wagons preserve the early history of lucrative borax refining in Death Valley. At the parking area, a paved trail with interpretive signs encircles the relics; leaving the paved loop, it descends to the dry lake bed and crusty salt marshes where Chinese laborers once gathered the precious substance. The salt flats can be muddy and very hot, so watch your footing.

Eureka Dunes

1 mi. RT. Easy. Access: The trailhead is well marked in the Eureka Sand Dunes National Natural Landmark Area, at the end of South Eureka Rd.

This area is approachable only from the remote north end of the park and by rutted dirt and gravel roads subject to washout, so travel to this area requires a sturdy vehicle in good condition. The dunes, however, are magnificent, the tallest and oldest in North America. The whole family will enjoy romping here, spotting dune grass and wildflowers or the tracks of lizards and rodents. The view from atop the highest dune (700 ft.) takes in the splendid contrast of creamy sand against the layer-cake band of nearby rock, and small avalanches of sand create the trademark "singing" peculiar to such dunes.

Keane Wonder Mine

2 mi. RT. Strenuous. Access: The trailhead, which is marked, is located past the parking area and the old mill site; the mine is 20 mi. north of Furnace Creek via Daylight Pass Cutoff and then after 3 mi. of graded dirt rd.

A rocky mountainous trail climbs steeply to the site of this successful gold mine, passing along the way the solid, efficient wooden tramway that carried ore out of the mountain. The trail obeys an old miner's adage that the best way up a mountainside is the straightest, even if the most strenuous—but you'll be rewarded with spectacular views of the park and substantial artifacts from the mining operation. The many mine tunnels and shafts are fascinating though potentially deadly; cave-ins, rattlesnakes, poisonous gases, and abandoned explosives lead the list of reasons to keep your distance. If this hike seems too challenging, try the Keane Wonder Spring, below.

Keane Wonder Spring

2 mi. RT. Easy. Access: The trailhead leads away from the Keane Wonder parking area in a northerly direction, away from the steeper mine hike.

This trail undulates gently across an alluvial fan and follows the pipeline from the spring that supplied water for the gold-mining operation. The smell of sulfur and piping calls of birds signal your arrival at the spring, which lies slightly uphill of the trail. A short walk beyond leads to cabin ruins and a mine shaft.

Mosaic Canyon

2.4 mi. RT. Easy. Access: The trailhead is located at the end of a short, graded dirt rd. just east of Stovepipe Wells via Calif. 190.

This easy stroll requires a bit of rock scrambling into a canyon where water has polished the marble rock into white, gray, and black mosaics. The first mile is very easy, suitable for every skill level, and children will love running their hands over the water-smoothed rock walls. More adventurous climbers can continue up a series of chutes and dry waterfalls in the latter half of the hike.

Natural Bridge

1 mi. RT. Moderate. Access: Located 15 mi. south of Furnace Creek via Badwater Rd. and a 2-mi. unpaved spur rd. suitable for passenger vehicles.

This short walk takes you into a colorful narrow canyon. The loose gravel underfoot makes for a tiring walk, but it's less than half a mile to the distinctive formation that gives the canyon its name: a rock bridge overhead, formed when rushing waters cut through the softer underlayer of rock.

Salt Creek Nature Trail

0.5 mi. RT. Easy. Access: Salt Creek is located 14 mi. north of Furnace Creek via Calif. 190 or 13 mi. east of Stovepipe Wells, then down a 1-mi. graded dirt spur rd. Closed in summer.

A leisurely hike on a wooden boardwalk leads you along the unique salt marshes, passing a myriad of unusual plants along the way. Watch also for the amazingly adaptive Salt Creek pupfish flashing about in the shallow water.

Sand Dunes

2 mi. RT. Easy. Access: 3 mi. west of the Calif. 190 junction; it's indicated with a signed turnoff and has picnic tables and a rest room.

While not as majestic as the remote Eureka Dunes in northern Death Valley, these golden mounds off Scotty's Castle Road are easy to reach and fun to romp around on. There's no formal trail—simply explore to your heart's content; kids especially will enjoy a barefoot romp on the fine sand dotted with stands of mesquite. Don't forget an adequate supply of water; in the midday sun, the dunes get very hot.

Titus Canyon

3 mi. RT. Easy. Access: The trailhead is up a signed dirt rd. off Scotty's Canyon Rd. (about 15 mi. north of Calif. 190) that leads to the mouth of Titus Canyon, where a rd. for four-wheel-drive vehicles continues through to Nev. 374; the trail begins at the point where the rd. becomes one way coming toward you (from Nevada). Closed in summer.

As you hike, watch for vehicle traffic coming one way from the other direction. The canyon's rock walls are an amateur geologist's dream—layers of orange and black volcanic sediment streaked with threads of gleaming white calcite. Though you can augment this easy hike by continuing through the canyon, there's a broad pullout from the road at 1.5 miles; it's a good place to enjoy the view, and perhaps a picnic, before returning the way you came.

Ubehebe Crater

1.5 mi. RT. Moderate. Access: The trailhead leads up from the parking area for Ubehebe Crater, which is 7 mi. northwest of the Grapevine Ranger Station.

You get to the crater via a steep but plain trail that leads from the parking area, up to the crater's lip, around some of the contours, and past to several lesser craters. Black cinders and volcanic fragments cover the desolate countryside surrounding Ubehebe Crater, which erupted as recently as 1,000 years ago. Fierce winds can hamper your progress, but you'll get an exhilarating feeling, as though you're visiting another planet. High-top boots or shoes are recommended for the pebbly path.

LONGER TRAILS

Golden Canyon

4.6 mi. RT. Easy to moderate. Access: The parking lot for Golden Canyon along Calif. 178, about 2 mi. south of the Furnace Creek Inn.

This trail's proximity to Furnace Creek, plus its varying degrees of difficulty, make it popular. Start by hiking along the once-paved route that allowed cars to drive into the canyon but was destroyed by flash flooding. Soon you'll be scrambling around the "badlands," yellowed hills of mud and silt deposited by ancient lakes. Those with more stamina can continue past towering Manly Beacon (a sandstone formation), across gullies and washes, and then steeply up to Zabriskie Point for panoramic views of the forbidding badlands.

Grotto Canyon

4 mi. RT. Moderate to strenuous. Access: 2.5 mi. east of Stovepipe Wells on Calif. 190.

This trail is marked by deep "grottoes" in the rocks (smooth hollows formed by erosive floodwaters). The first mile follows a rugged gravel road up the canyon's alluvial fan; if you have an off-road vehicle, drive this portion as far as the wash. Continue on foot from there, as the canyon narrows and you begin to encounter the grottos, beyond which waterfalls trickle. The cool hidden grottos are a nice place to stop for a snack, sheltered from the sun.

Jayhawker Canyon

4.2 mi. RT. Moderate. Access: Off Calif. 190, just west of the Emigrant Ranger Station.

This route follows the path of a desperate group of pioneers attempting to find a way out of Death Valley in 1849. The footing is treacherous in this debris-filled canyon, and several forks and tributaries can distract you from staying in the main wash. At the end of the trail lies a spring marking the Jayhawkers' camp, also a popular stopping place for the native Shoshone. Boulders in the area are marked with petroglyphs depicting bighorn sheep, along with the initials of several pioneers scratched into the rocks.

Telescope Peak

14 mi. RT. 8,130 ft. to 11,049 ft. Strenuous. Access: Mahogany Flat Campground, past the Wildrose Charcoal Kilns (only experienced drivers with high-clearance 4-wheel-drive vehicles should attempt the road).

A grueling 3,000-foot climb ultimately leads to the 11,049-foot summit, where you'll be rewarded with the view described thusly by one pioneer; "You can see so far, it's just like looking through a telescope." Snow-covered in winter, the peak is best climbed from May to November. Consult park rangers for current conditions and detailed advice—and *never attempt this climb alone.*

Wildrose Peak

8.4 mi. RT. 6,890 ft. to 9,060 ft. Strenuous. Access: Wildrose Charcoal Kilns, usually accessible by passenger vehicles (check with park rangers for road conditions).

Mostly comprised of steady and unrelenting ascents, this steep hike has several level portions for rest stops. And you'll need them since you'll be climbing over 2,000 feet on the way to the 9,060-foot summit. Marvelous views along the way take in the Panamint and Death Valleys as far as the Sierra. It's unwise to attempt this hike in winter or without obtaining a topographical map from the ranger station.

Other Sports & Activities

Biking. Because 94% of the park is federally designated wilderness, cycling is allowed only on roads used by autos and not on hiking trails. Weather conditions between May and October make bicycling at the lower elevations ill-advised at times other than early morning.

There are no bike rentals available in the park, and given the park's isolation, the only practical option is to bring your own. You'll need a pretty rugged mountain bike to do most of these routes.

Good choices are **Racetrack** (28 mi., mainly level), **Greenwater Valley** (30 mi., mainly level), **Cottonwood Canyon** (20 mi.), and **West Side Road** (40 mi., fairly level with some washboard sections). **Artists Drive** is 8 miles long, paved, with some steep uphills. A favorite is **Titus Canyon** (28 mi. on a one-way hilly road— it has some very difficult uphill and downhill stretches).

Camping

Death Valley offers little variety to those seeking conventional accommodations, but campers (tent, trailer, and RV) can expect to find similar comforts to most other desert parks. You should take special care, however, when selecting a campground. While most locations are closed seasonally to protect visitors from the harshest elements (only five campgrounds are open year-round), there's always a risk of unseasonably hot temperatures at the largely unshaded campgrounds on the valley floor, as well as early or late snow at remote mountain sites. Always inquire with the park ranger about current conditions before setting up camp.

Emigrant Campground is located 9 miles southwest of Stovepipe Wells on Calif. 190. **Furnace Creek Campground,** located just north of the Furnace Creek Visitor Center, has 133 sites, has showers nearby, for a fee, from a limited water supply. **Mahogany Flats Campground,** 38 miles south of Stovepipe Wells, off Trona-Wildrose Road, can only be reached by four-wheel-drive vehicle. It has pit toilets but no other facilities. **Mesquite Spring Campground** is 5 miles south of Scotty's Castle on Grapevine Road. The **Panamint Springs Resort** (☎ **702/482-7680**), located 30 miles west of Stovepipe Wells on Calif. 190, operates a commercial campground with 40 spaces (12 with RV utility hookups) for $15 per night for the RV hookups, $8 for just a tent campsite. **Stovepipe Wells Campground** has 200 spaces with 15 RV hookups, and charges $10 for a campsite, $15 if you want an RV utility hookup.

The huge **Sunset Campground,** located just 0.25 mile east of the Furnace Creek Ranch, has nearby showers (from a limited supply, for a fee). **Texas Spring,** in the same area as Sunset Campground, has 92 sites and 2 group sites. The fee is $12 per site for an individual site, $40 for group sites, which can be reserved. **Thorndike Campground,** which is 37 miles south of Stovepipe Wells and one mile from Mahogany Flats Campground, off the Trona-Wildrose Road, is accessible only by four-wheel-drive vehicle. It has eight primitive campsites with pit toilets but no other facilities. **Wildrose Campground,** located 30 miles south of Stovepipe Wells off the Trona-Wildrose

Road, has pit toilets. Drinking water is available only from April through November.

Campsite **Reservations** for Furnace Creek and the group sites at Texas Spring are available from the **National Park Reservation Service** at ☎ 800/ 365-2267. Payment can be made by DISC, MC, V, check, or money order. For reservations at privately owned **Panamint Springs,** call ☎ 702/482-7680. For RV reservations at Stovepipe Wells, call ☎ 760/786-2337.

Accommodations

INSIDE THE PARK

Furnace Creek Inn

Calif. 190, 1 mi. south of Furnace Creek Visitor Center (P.O. Box 1, Death Valley, CA 92328). ☎ **760/786-2345.** www. furnacecreekresort. com. 66 units. A/C TV TEL. Oct–May $230–$325 double; May–Oct $155–$210 double. AE, DC, DISC, MC, V.

The Furnace Creek Inn is exceptional and exceptionally expensive, a 1930s resort whose charm has been successfully preserved. Like an oasis in the middle of stark Death Valley, the inn's red-tiled roofs and sparkling, spring-fed pool hint at the elegance within, where the deluxe rooms and suites have every modern amenity. Stroll the lush palm-shaded gardens before sitting down to a meal in the elegant dining room, where the food is excellent but the formality a bit out of place. Tennis on lighted courts and nearby golf and horseback riding are available; there's even a shuttle from the Furnace Creek private airstrip. *Reserve early:* The inn is booked solid year-round.

Furnace Creek Ranch

On Calif. 190, adjacent to the Furnace Creek Visitor Center (P.O. Box 1, Death Valley, CA 92328). ☎ **760/786-2345.** Fax 760/686-9945. 224 units. A/C TEL. $99–$139 per unit. AE, DC, DISC, MC, V.

Though the Furnace Creek Ranch is run by the same folks who maintain the elegant Furnace Creek Inn, the ranch is more down to earth, with rustic cottages that are great for families. Amenities include a spring-fed pool, an 18-hole golf

Campground	Elev.	Total Sites	RV Hookups	Dump Station	Toilets	Drinking Water
Emigrant	2,100	10	No	No	Yes	Yes
Furnace Creek	−196	133	No	Yes	Yes	Yes
*Mahogany Flat**	8,200	10	No	No	Yes	No
Mesquite Spring	1,800	30	No	Yes	Yes	Yes
Panamint Springs Resort	N/A	40	12	No	Yes	Yes
Stovepipe Wells	sea level	200	15	Yes	Yes	Yes
Sunset	−190	1,000	No	Yes	Yes	Yes
Texas Spring	sea level	94	No	Yes	Yes	Yes
*Thorndike**	7,800	8	No	No	Yes	No
Wildrose	4,100	30	No	No	Yes	Yes[†]

* Road not passable for trailers, campers, or motor homes. Passenger cars not advised; four-wheel-drive vehicle may be necessary.

course, lighted tennis courts, and a selection of dining options (see below).

Panamint Springs Resort

Calif. 190, 30 mi. west of Stovepipe Wells (P.O. Box 395, Ridgecrest, CA 93556). ☎ **702/482-7680.** www.deathvalley.com. 14 units, 1 cottage. A/C. $50–$95. AE, DISC, MC, V.

The only lodging within the park not operated by the official concessionaire is the Panamint Springs Resort, across the Panamint Range and about a 45- to 60-minute drive west from Furnace Creek. A welcome change from the furious consumerism of Death Valley, this truly charming rustic motel has plain but clean rooms as well as a full-service restaurant that serves breakfast, lunch, and dinner. Featuring traditional American fare, dinner is priced at $10 to $20.

Stovepipe Wells Village

On Calif. 190 at Stovepipe Wells (Calif. 190, Death Valley, CA 92328). ☎ **760/786-2387.** Fax 760/786-2389. 83 units. A/C. $55–$78 double. AE, DC, DISC, MC, V.

The truly budget-conscious opt for Stovepipe Wells Village, where 83

modest air-conditioned motel rooms surround a small pool. About 23 miles northwest of Furnace Creek, Stovepipe Wells has a general store, saloon, and dining room (see below). The rates are the same year-round, and all have two twin beds, two double beds, or one king.

NEAR THE PARK

Because accommodations in Death Valley are limited, you might consider the money-saving (but inconvenient) option of spending a night in one of the two gateway towns: **Lone Pine** on the west side of the park, and **Baker** on the south. **Beatty, Nevada,** and **Shoshone, California,** which both have inexpensive lodgings, are each slightly more than an hour's drive from the park's center. Accommodations are limited to unremarkable motels. In Death Valley Junction, the restored **Amargosa Hotel** (☎ 760/852-4441) offers 14 air-conditioned rooms in a historic out-of-the-way place, 40 minutes from Furnace Creek. Credit cards (MC, V) are accepted, and room rates are $35 to $55 double.

Showers	Fire Pits/ Grills	Laundry	Public Phone	Reserve	Fees	Open
No	No	No	Yes	No	Free	Year-round
Nearby (fee)	Yes	Nearby	Yes	Yes***	$16	Year-round
No	Yes	No	No	No	No	Mar–Nov
No	Yes	No	No	No	$10	Year-round
Yes	Yes	No	Nearby	Yes	$8/$15	Year-round
Nearby (fee)	Yes	No	Yes	No	$10/$15	Oct–Apr
Nearby (fee)	No	No	No	No	$10	Oct–Apr
Nearby (fee)	Yes	No	Yes	No**	$12/$40	Oct–Apr
No	Yes	No	No	No	No	Mar–Nov
No	Yes	No	No	No	No	Year-round

** Groups (only) may make reservations.
*** Reservations can be made October 15 to April 15 only.
† April–November only.

Dining

There aren't many dining options inside the park, and most are run by the same concessionaire anyway. Here's a run-down.

There are three dining options at the **Furnace Creek Ranch,** all are relatively informal. The best and most economical is the **49'er Cafe,** a diner with better-than-average food and a widely varied menu. It's open daily from 7am to 9pm. The adjacent **Wrangler Steakhouse** offers an all-you-can-eat buffet for breakfast (6 to 9am), lunch (11am to 2pm), and dinner (3:30 to 5:30pm). The prices are higher than average, but the buffet is a good choice for families with hearty eaters. From 6:30 to 9:30pm, the Wrangler reverts to table service, grilling steaks, ribs, and other satisfying specialties; the servings are generous, but the dinners pricey. All these places accept major credit cards (AE, DC, DISC, MC, V).

The dining room at the **Furnace Creek Inn** (☎ 760/786-2345) is formal and the menu features elements of several continental and regional cuisines. The peaceful setting and attentive service can be a welcome (though pricey) treat during otherwise exhausting travels through the park: Breakfast, lunch, and dinner are served. The Sunday buffet brunch, served from mid-May to mid-October, is truly decadent. Reservations are necessary. The dining room serves breakfast and dinner year-round, but closes from 2:30 to 5:30pm daily and does not serve lunch from mid-May to mid-October. Major credit cards (AE, DC, DISC, MC, V) are accepted.

There's a restaurant at **Stovepipe Wells** (☎ 760/786-2604), kind of a cross between a camp dining room and a casual cafe. It's open daily 7am to 2pm and 6:30 to 10pm and accepts major credit cards (AE, DC, DISC, MC, V). Other choices are a **snack bar** at **Scotty's Castle** and a rustic (and affordable) burgers-and-beer **cafe** at **Panamint Springs.**

Helpful hint: Meals and groceries are exceptionally costly inside the park due to the remote location. If possible, consider bringing a cooler with some snacks, sandwiches, and beverages to last the duration of your visit. Ice is easily obtainable, and you'll also be able to keep water chilled.

Too far away for a round-trip excursion once you're in Death Valley, **The Mad Greek** (☎ 760/733-4354) in Baker is simply a must on the way there or home. Literally at the junction of I-15 and Calif. 127, this roadside treasure is an ethnic surprise beloved by many. White tiles and Aegean-blue accents complement a menu of traditional Greek specialties like souvlaki, spinach-and-feta spanikopita, stuffed grape leaves, green salad with tangy feta, exquisite pastries, and even Greek beer. The mile-long menu also includes traditional road fare, like hamburgers and hot sandwiches.

Picnic & Camping Supplies

Within park boundaries **Furnace Creek Ranch** has a market carrying a fairly wide selection of groceries and ice; propane gas is available at the adjacent service station. **Stovepipe Wells** offers ice, limited groceries, propane gas, and white gas.

Outside the park, if you want to stock up before entering, groceries and supplies are available in the towns of **Baker, Beatty, Shoshone, Pahrump,** and **Ridgecrest.** For visitors approaching on U.S. 395 from the south, Ridgecrest is your best choice—it's a sizable city with chain grocery stores, fast-food restaurants, and a selection of gas stations.

A Nearby Desert Preserve: Mojave National Preserve

To most Americans, the eastern Mojave is that vast, bleak, interminable stretch of desert to be crossed as quickly as possible along California's I-15 and I-40. But just southeast of Death Valley National Park, this national preserve is what many consider the crown jewel of the California desert.

This is a hard land to get to know—it has no lodgings or restaurants, few campgrounds, and only a handful of roads suitable for the average passenger vehicle. But hidden within this natural fortress are some true gems—its 1.6 million acres include the world's largest Joshua tree forest; abundant wildlife; spectacular canyons, caverns, and volcanic formations; tabletop mesas; and a dozen mountain ranges.

It's ironic that the eastern Mojave owes much of its appearance to water—canyons carved by streams, mineral-encrusted dry lake beds, mountains whose colorful layers represent sandstone deposited in ancient oceans—for today the landscape is distinguished primarily by its extreme dryness. The climate changed dramatically following the end of the last ice age, about 10,000 years ago; around this time the first humans are believed to have migrated into the area. Lakes fed by glacial runoff supported fish, large animals, and diverse vegetation. When traditional food like bison and antelope diminished, the inhabitants adapted a lifestyle better suited to the arid climate, ultimately relying on small game and plants.

The European invasion started in the 18th century, when Spanish missionaries and explorers ventured north from Mexico, but in the 19th century American pioneers arrived, crossing the Mojave on their way west to the coast. Then in 1883 the railroad arrived, boosting existing mining and ranching operations.

By the 1970s, environmentalists had become gravely concerned with the region's protection. Destructive off-road use, the theft of rare desert plants, the plunder of archaeological sites, and the killing of threatened desert tortoises all endangered the delicate ecological balance. Then in 1994 President Clinton signed the California Desert Protection Act, creating Mojave National Preserve.

Thus far, the Mojave's elevated status hasn't attracted hordes of sightseers, and devoted visitors are happy to keep it that way. Unlike with a fully protected national park, the national preserve designation allows hunting, and continued grazing and mining within the preserve's boundaries are a sore spot for ardent preservationists.

Flora & Fauna. There's much more life in the Mojave Desert than the human eye can immediately discern. Many animals are well camouflaged and/or nocturnal, but if you stay still and keep a sharp eye, the experience is rewarding. Wildlife includes the hopping **kangaroo rat, ground squirrels, cottontails** and **jackrabbits, bobcats, coyotes, lizards, snakes,** and the threatened **desert tortoise.** Consider yourself lucky to spot elusive **bighorn sheep** or shy **mule deer.** Migrating birds that stop off in the Mojave are met by permanent residents like **quail, piñon jays, sparrows,** noisy **cactus wrens,** and the distinctive **roadrunner.**

You're certain to see familiar desert plants like the fragrant **creosote bush,** several varieties of **cacti** (including the deceptively fluffy looking **cholla "teddy bear"**), and several strains of **yucca,** all relatives to the trademark high desert plant, the **Joshua tree.** On and around Cima Dome grows the world's largest and densest **Joshua tree forest.** Botanists say that Cima's Joshuas are more symmetrical than their cousins elsewhere in the Mojave. The dramatic colors of the sky at sunset provide a breathtaking backdrop for Cima's Joshua trees, some more than 25 feet tall and several hundred years old.

Other desert flora include therapeutic **Mormon tea, cliff rose, aromatic blue sage, desert primrose,** and **catsclaw;** these flowering plants are among many that make the spring wildflower season a popular time to visit. **Junipers,** seed-bearing **piñons,** and **scrub oaks** are found in the preserve's higher elevations.

Getting There. I-15, the major route between Los Angeles and Las Vegas, extends along the northern boundary of the preserve. I-40, the major route between southern California and Arizona, is the southern access route.

Common entry points include **Kelbaker Road,** which bisects the preserve from Baker at the north, through Kelso in the south. There are Kelbaker exits from both I-15 and I-40. The **Essex Road** exit from I-40, 25 miles east of Kelbaker Road, is the access point for **Providence Mountains State Recreation Area** (Mit- chell Caverns) and two other campgrounds. The **Cima Road** exit from I-15 in Mountain Pass leads into the center of the preserve.

The town of **Nipton,** technically outside preserve boundaries but a common destination for Mojave travelers, is reached via Nipton Road from I-15, within visual range of the Nevada border.

The nearest airport is Las Vegas's **McCarran International,** discussed earlier in this chapter.

Information & Visitor Centers. Contact the **Superintendent, Mojave National Preserve,** 222 E. Main St., Suite 202, Barstow, CA 92311 (☎ 760/255-8801; www.nps.gov/moja).

The best source for up-to-date weather conditions and a free map is the **Mojave National Preserve-Baker Information Center,** 72157 Baker Blvd. (under the "World's Tallest Thermometer"), Baker, CA 92309 (☎ 760/733-4040), which offers a superior selection of books. Those approaching the preserve from I-40 can stop in **Needles** at the **Information Center,** 707 W. Broadway (☎ 760/326-6322), which is open Wednesday to Sunday only.

Additional information and maps are available inside the preserve at the **Hole-in-the-Wall Ranger Station** (☎ 760/928-2572), which is open seasonally (as staffing allows).

Fees & Warnings. Entry into the preserve is free. Campsites cost $10 to $12. A constant threat in the desert is **dehydration.** Rangers recommended drinking 1 gallon of water per person per day, or twice that if you're planning strenuous activity.

Seasons & Climate. Mojave National Preserve's 1.5 million acres lie in the high desert, with elevations from 1,000 feet to 5,000 feet. While December to February can be windy and cold with a dusting of snow, summers often see blistering temperatures exceeding 100°F. The best time to visit is between March and May, when temperatures are mild and wildflowers are in bloom. October and November have comfortable weather and very few visitors. The area gets precious little rainfall, but what does occur (usually during winter) can begin suddenly and cause flash flooding.

Seasonal Events. Best between February and May, the **wildflower viewing** is dependent on weather conditions like rainfall, sunshine, and temperatures, but you can bet on seeing the brilliant blooms somewhere in the preserve each year. The information centers can help direct you to the flowers currently in bloom, and 24-hour recorded information on prime viewing sites is available from the **Payne Foundation Wildflower Hotline** at ☎ 818/768-3533 or the **Living Desert Wildflower Hotline** at ☎ 760/340-4954.

EXPLORING THE PARK BY CAR

At the risk of discouraging you from leaving your car to really experience the Mojave, we must admit that **Kelbaker Road** provides an excellent opportunity to sample the preserve with a minimal expenditure of time or trouble. The well-paved two-lane road, bisecting the preserve north to south, between I-15 and I-40, takes about 1 hour one way without stops.

You'll drive through the eerie blackened landscape of **lava beds** and **cinder**

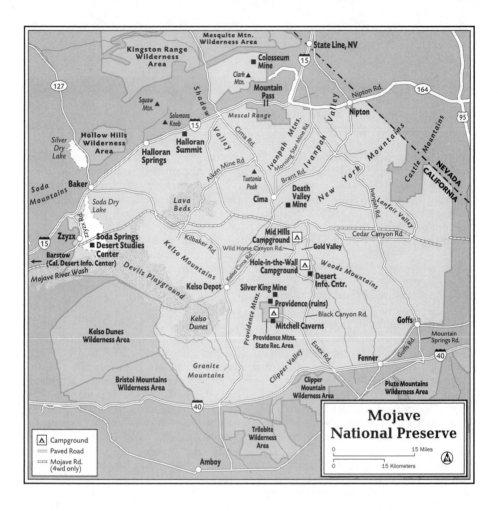

Campground
Paved Road
Mojave Rd.
(4wd only)

Mojave National Preserve

0   15 Miles

0   15 Kilometers

cones, visit the elegant but empty **Kelso Depot,** and see the towering golden mounds of **Kelso Dunes.** This 45-square-mile formation of magnificently sculpted sand dunes is famous for its "booming," a low rumble emitted when small avalanches or blowing sands pass over the underlying layer. Geologists speculate that the extreme dryness of the East Mojave Desert, combined with the wind-polished, rounded nature of the sand grains, has something to do with the musicality. Sometimes the low rumbling resembles a Tibetan gong; other times it sounds like a 1950s doo-wop musical group. After the Kelso Dunes you'll end your trip with views of the **Granite Mountains,** where erosion has removed all but resilient chunks of extraordinarily hard rock, leaving piles of rosy-hued boulders that are alternately smooth and jagged.

Leading northeast from Kelso Depot, the **Kelso-Cima Road** provides another scenic diversion, running alongside railroad tracks to the tiny town of **Cima** (Spanish for "summit"), at the foot of a geological oddity called **Cima Dome,** an almost perfectly rounded landform rising 1,500 feet above the desert. The dome is a batholith, created by molten rock that, unlike its volcano cousin, stopped rising below the surface. This unusual formation is blanketed by majestic Joshua trees. The community of Cima consists of a tiny U.S. Post Office and a ramshackle market (don't be fooled by its boarded-up appearance). Be prepared for the many heart-stopping dips in the Kelso-Cima Road; they're a favorite with young backseat passengers.

Visitors with four-wheel-drive vehicles or especially rugged two-wheel drives can explore the **Wildhorse Canyon Road,** looping from Mid Hills to Hole-in-the-Wall, at the preserve's heart. In 1989, this short route was declared the nation's first official "Backcountry Byway," an honor that federal agencies bestow on America's most scenic back roads. The 11-mile horseshoe-shaped route crosses wide-open country dotted with cholla and, in season, delicate purple, yellow, and red wildflowers. Dramatic volcanic slopes and flattop mesas tower over the low desert.

ORGANIZED TOURS & RANGER PROGRAMS

Park Service ranger programs operate only when requested, but they're worth planning a trip around. Ranging from 30 minutes to 3 hours, programs might include talks on the endangered desert tortoise or the area's violent geological history; guided hikes to Kelso Dunes or the Hole-in-the-Wall petroglyph sites; and evening excursions to stargaze. Contact one of the information centers listed above.

The only organized attraction is **Mitchell Caverns,** contained in a State Recreation Area in the National Preserve. Rangers lead regular tours of these rock rooms, where you'll see marvelous stalactites, stalagmites, and other limestone formations, plus archaeological artifacts from the area's early human inhabitants. The caves, which maintain an almost constant temperature of 65°F, provide a welcome respite during hot weather. Tours are given daily between Labor Day and Memorial Day weekdays at 1:30pm and weekends/holidays at 10am and 1:30 and 3pm. In summer tours are Saturday and Sunday only at 1:30pm. Cost is $6 for adults, $3 for kids 6 to 17, and free for those under 6. Tours are limited to 25 people and fill quickly, so arrive early to ensure a spot. For information, call ☎ 805/942-0662. *Note:* Additional tours are often added without notice during periods of high demand. To check last-minute schedules or find out whether a particular tour is sold out, call the visitor center (☎ 760/928-2586).

HISTORIC & MAN-MADE ATTRACTIONS

In the days of steam trains, the town of Kelso was a critical watering spot for locomotives. Built in 1924, the elegant **Kelso Depot** is Spanish Revival style, with a red-tile roof, graceful arches, and a brick platform. At its peak, during World War II, the town supported 2,000 residents, and the depot's diner, the Beanery, served customers 24 hours a day. Once slated for demolition, Kelso Depot is boarded up now, but the National Park Service is considering refurbishing the building for use as the preserve's visitor center.

Skirting the preserve's northern boundary is the charming whistle-stop town of **Nipton.** Founded in 1885, Nipton was a true ghost town nearly a century later, when Los Angeles transplants Jerry and Roxanne Freeman began restoring its dilapidated buildings. At its height, Nipton was at the center of Mojave industry, providing railroad access for miners and ranchers, and silent film star Clara Bow was a frequent visitor.

At the preserve's western boundary, on the shores of the stark white Soda Dry Lake, is **Soda Springs/Zzyzx.** Reached by taking the Zzyzx Road (a cryptic name that's puzzled generations of motorists) exit from I-15 and carefully negotiating a 4-mile rocky dirt road, the springs have a colorful history. In addition to being an important watering hole for those crossing the desert, the site was an Indian camp, a military outpost, a wagon station, the headquarters of a Hollywood radio evangelist, and a once-trendy health resort (sporting the fanciful name of Zzyzx Mineral Springs). The springs are still active, feeding the elegant pools left over from the resort's heyday and supporting an entire ecosystem of wildlife at the lakebed's edge. You can stroll among the buildings, now used by the California State University's Desert Studies Center, and learn more about the area's history at an unstaffed visitor center.

Throughout the preserve are remnants of the historic **Mojave Road,** a popular 19th-century wagon route to the West Coast. Check with preserve rangers for tips on where to find sections of the old road.

DAY HIKES

In addition to the preserve's marked and maintained hiking trails, many hikers create their own routes using the abundant dirt roads crisscrossing the area. Some are so poor that they're passable only by high-clearance off-road vehicles, so there's little or no traffic.

There are several good hiking areas along **New York Mountains Road,** west of Ivanpah Road (itself unpaved and rough), an area of mine ruins, ranch structures, and cool pine-studded canyons. Several sections of the historic **Mojave Road** are also great for hiking but can be reached only by four-wheel-drive vehicles; remains of a wagon route stretch from Piute Wash beyond the eastern boundary of the preserve, through Cedar Canyon and past the lava beds, all the way to Zzyzx Springs on Soda Dry Lake at the western edge. When you're hiking in the backcountry, please respect private lands, which are not always well marked.

SHORTER TRAILS

Kelso Dunes

3 mi. RT (to the dunes). Moderate. Access: A parking area 8 mi. south of the Kelso Depot.

These are the second-highest dunes in California, covering 45 square miles and reaching 700 feet high. The dunes are visible from Kelbaker Road, and 3 miles of graded dirt road lead to a parking area, where several interpretive signs give information on dunes ecology. Follow the trail out past the vegetation, then ramble to your heart's content, trying to spot examples of the many plants and animals that live in the seemingly barren dunes. Among them are rodents, kit foxes, lizards, sand verbena, and desert

primrose, which color the dunes with brilliant blooms of yellow, white, and pink in springtime. *Note:* Climbing the soft dunes requires time and exertion, but tumbling back down is the fun reward.

Mary Beal Nature Trail

0.5 mi. Easy. Access: Providence Mountains State Recreation Area Visitor Center, on Essex Rd., 16 mi. from I-40.

Suitable for all ages, the path winds past examples of the diverse plant and animal life found in the Mojave. Named for a prominent naturalist who spent 50 years exploring this desert, the trail has numbered posts keyed to a brochure (25¢) from the visitor center.

LONGER TRAILS

Mid Hills/Hole-in-the-Wall

2 mi. RT to 8 mi. one way. Easy to strenuous. Access: Hole-in-the-Wall Picnic Area.

Stretching between the two campgrounds, this maintained trail can be hiked in part or full. The entire hike is a grand tour of canyons and tabletop mesas, large piñon trees, and colorful cacti; it's an all-day, one-way undertaking if you can arrange a car shuttle, and is much more enjoyable in the downhill direction from Mid Hills to Hole-in-the-Wall. If you're not up for a long day hike, the 2-mile hike from Hole-in-the-Wall Campground to Banshee Canyon offers an easier alternative. From Hole-in-the-Wall, the initial segment of the trail offers the most adventure; climbers descend through a vertical chute in the rock using a series of metal rings. Even with handholds, the climb requires agility and concentration—don't try it if you have any doubts.

Teutonia Peak

4 mi. RT. Moderate. Access: On Cima Rd. between I-15 and the town of Cima.

The well-maintained trail leads to a view of Cima Dome, an unusual volcanic

Especially for Kids

There's a lot for kids to enjoy in Mojave, from scrambling on sandy Kelso Dunes to exploring Mitchell Caverns, which resemble an Indiana Jones movie set. You can show them lava beds so similar to the moon's surface that U.S. astronauts once trained here, or make a contest of finding familiar shapes and profiles in the jagged Granite Mountains.

formation, from the top of Teutonia Peak (600 ft. higher than the trailhead) and panoramic views of the surrounding desert. You'll walk among Joshua trees, Mojave yucca, and cholla "teddy bear" cactus. Near the summit, the trail is faint but marked with cairns—small piles of stones. This land is leased for grazing, and the hiking trail encounters two ranch gates: Be sure to close them as you pass through.

BIKING

Opportunities are as extensive as the preserve's hundreds of miles of lonesome dirt roads. The 140-mile-long historic **Mojave Road,** a rough four-wheel-drive route, bisects the preserve east to west and visits many of the most scenic areas in the East Mojave; sections of this road make excellent bike tours, but you'll definitely need a mountain bike. Prepare well—the Mojave's dirt roads are rugged routes surrounded by miles of desert wilderness. There are no bike rentals in the park.

CAMPING

There are three established campgrounds in the preserve, all open year-round on a first-come, first-served basis. None have showers, laundry facilities, or RV hookups, though the Hole-in-the-Wall Campground has a dump station.

The **Mid Hills Campground,** with 26 sites, is in a woodland of piñon and juniper and offers outstanding views. It is located 35.5 miles northwest of Essex, off Black Canyon Road. This mile-high camp is the coolest in the East Mojave. Pit toilets, fire grates, and drinking water are provided, but there are no public telephones. Cost is $10 per night.

Nearby **Hole-in-the-Wall Campground** is perched above two dramatic canyons, 25.5 miles northwest of Essex, on Black Canyon Road, near the Mid Hills Campground. There are 37 sites for $10 per site per night. You'll find pit toilets, drinking water, public phones, fire grates, and a dump station.

Warning: The washboard dirt road between the Mid Hills and Hole-in-the-Wall campgrounds might be too jarring for many two-wheel-drive passenger cars.

The sites at **Providence Mountain State Recreation Area** (☎ 805/932-0662) are adjacent to the Mitchell Caverns Visitor Center. There are only six sites, for $12 each per night. You'll find pit toilets, drinking water, public telephones, and fire grates.

A highlight of the East Mojave is camping in the open desert all by your lonesome; at press time **backcountry camping** was fairly unregulated, requiring no registration. Campfires are prohibited outside of designated fire grates; backcountry campers need to pack out all trash; and take care not to set up in a gully or dry wash subject to flash flooding. It's advisable to contact an information center before establishing camp. And please respect private lands.

In addition to the campgrounds in the preserve, there are 30 acres of camping space available in a privately owned campground in Nipton, in the open desert beyond the town's historic B&B inn. Amenities include hot showers, drinking water, two cabin tents, and four RV hookups. For information call ☎ 760/856-2335.

14

DENALI NATIONAL PARK

by Charles P. Wohlforth

DENALI (DEN-*AL*-EE) NATIONAL PARK STANDS ALONE AMONG PARKS IN the United States: It gives regular people easy access to real wilderness. It's also got sweeping tundra vistas, abundant wildlife, and North America's tallest mountain. But what

makes Denali unique is that you can get there, and that your ability to do so hasn't spoiled the natural experience as it has at so many other parks.

At Denali you can see the heart of the park for little more than it would cost you at Yellowstone. And when you get there, it's a pristine natural environment with truly wild animals living in a complete ecosystem pretty much without human interference. A single National Park Service decision makes this possible: The only road through the park is closed to the public. This means that to get into the park, you must ride a crowded bus over a dusty gravel road hour after hour, but it also means that the animals are still there to watch, and their behavior remains essentially normal. It may be the only $20 safari in the world.

What's even more unique is that you can get off the bus pretty much whenever you want. Simply walk away from the road across the tundra, and you'll be alone in this primeval wilderness. Unfortunately, many Denali visitors never take advantage of the opportunity. But that's the essence of Alaska—learning, deep down, how big nature is and how small

are you, one more mammal on the tundra under the broad sky. And when you're ready to return to civilization, just walk to the road and catch the next bus—they come every half hour.

The Denali experience spreads beyond the park. After all, the park boundary is an artificial line—the wildlife and the scenery of the Alaska Range don't observe its significance. To the east, the Denali Highway runs through the same extraordinary terrain, with opportunities for hikes and canoeing on tundra and lakes managed by the Bureau of Land Management. To the south, Denali State Park and the town of **Talkeetna** provide another vantage on Mount McKinley, plus salmon fishing in the rivers and remote lake recreation. The construction of comfortable new lodges and a variety of good outdoor guides have helped make Talkeetna a popular alternative gateway to Denali. Even though it's 150 miles from the park entrance by car, Talkeetna is physically closer to the mountain than is the park headquarters.

Visitors often skip all that, and the area's other attractions, focusing instead

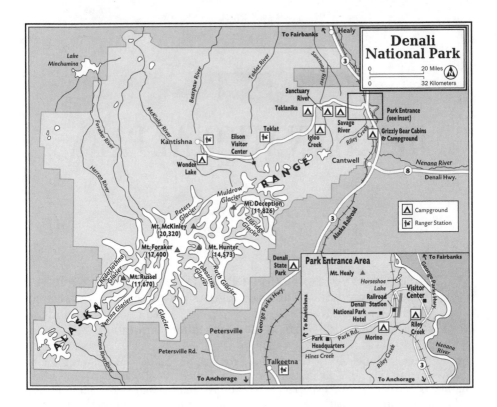

on **Mount McKinley,** which, at 20,320 feet, is the tallest mountain in North America. It is an impressive peak, but you don't need to go to the park to see the mountain, and most people who do go don't see it. Summer weather patterns usually sock in the mountain by midafternoon, at least as seen from the ground in the park. Unfortunately, Denali has become a thing people feel they must do, and seeing Mount McKinley is a thing they must do when they visit Denali. Many package tours rush through the park so quickly it becomes a blur outside a window rather than an experience. A friend swears she overheard a tourist ask, as she boarded the train leaving Denali, "Why did they put the park way out here in the boondocks?"

The answer is there for you to find, at the bottom of the steps of the shuttle bus door.

Avoiding the Crowds. Crowding is relative. Once you're out in the park, Denali is never crowded. A transportation bottleneck, the shuttle system, protects the park from overuse. What makes the busy season difficult is getting through that bottleneck from the crowded park entrance into the wilderness. For that, planning to avoid the busy season, from mid-May to mid-September, may help.

During the visitor season, you can improve your chances of getting away by avoiding the peak month of July. The season really gets into high gear in mid-June and starts to wind down in mid-August, providing a month of relative quiet and often reduced prices at the beginning of the season and another at the end.

Another way to avoid the crowds is to book a stay in a wilderness lodge. Three lodges in Kantishna, listed below, have the right to carry clients to their businesses over the park road in buses and vans. Outside the park, several other lodges fly in clients. Either way, you bypass the bottleneck at the park entrance.

Just the Facts

GETTING THERE & GATEWAYS

The total of Denali National Park and Preserve is 6 million acres, a roughly triangular polygon about 20 percent larger than Massachusetts. The only park entrance is 230 miles north of Anchorage and 120 miles south of Fairbanks on the paved **George Parks Highway** or the **Alaska Railroad.** Although Mount McKinley is visible from as far away as Anchorage, you can't see it at all from the park entrance, where you will find the railroad depot and all services accessible by private vehicle. A mile north on the Parks Highway, along a cliff-sided canyon of the Nenana River, hotels and restaurants have developed a kind of seasonal town on private land in the immediate area of the park entrance. Other services are at **Carlo Creek,** 13 miles south of the Parks; at another roadside development 7 miles south of the park entrance; and in the year-round town of **Healy,** 10 miles north of the park entrance. From the park entrance, a road accessible only by shuttle bus leads west 89 miles through the park, past a series of campgrounds and a visitor center, and ending at the Kantishna district, a collection of inholdings with wilderness lodges.

The Nearest Airports. Anchorage is the main entry hub for Alaska. It's served by several major carriers, primarily with connections through Seattle, including **United, Delta,** and **Alaska** airlines. You can also fly into **Fairbanks** with the same carriers. All the major **car-rental companies** have outlets at the **Anchorage Airport** (☎ 907/266-2525). **Avis** has an outlet at the **Fairbanks Airport** (☎ 907/474-2500). You'll find toll-free numbers for airlines and car rentals in the appendix.

By Car. Renting a car and driving from Anchorage will usually prove cheaper than taking the train. The drive is about 4½ hours from Anchorage, 2½ hours from Fairbanks, on a good two-lane highway. Many of the views along the **Parks Highway** are equal to the views on the train, but large stretches, especially in the Matanuska and Susitna valleys, near Anchorage, have been spoiled by ugly roadside development, which you don't see on the train. A long but spectacular detour around the mess leads through **Hatcher Pass** on a mountainous gravel road open only in the summer.

By Rail. The most popular way to get to Denali National Park is by train. The **Alaska Railroad,** P.O. Box 107500, Anchorage, AK 99510-7500 (☎ **800/544-0552** or 907/265-2494; www.akrr.com), which pioneered tourism to the park before the George Parks Highway was built in 1972, has daily service in the summer from Anchorage and Fairbanks. Trains leave both cities at 8:15am, arriving at the park from Anchorage at 3:45pm and from Fairbanks at noon, crossing and going on to the opposite city for arrival at 8:15pm in each. The fare from Anchorage to Denali is $102 one way. The full train runs only from mid-May to mid-September, with slightly lower fares in May and September than during the summer. During the winter, the Alaska Railroad runs a single passenger car from Anchorage to Fairbanks and back once a week. If you're here, ride it one way—it's a truly spectacular, truly Alaskan experience.

The advantages of taking the train to Denali are that it's a historic, unspoiled route through beautiful countryside; there's a good chance of seeing moose and caribou; it's fun and relaxing; there's commentary along the way; and the food is good. There are disadvantages, too. The train is more expensive. You can rent a car for 4 days and drive up for the same price as one round trip on the train. It's slow, adding 3 hours to a trip from Anchorage to the park, and when it's late, it can be very late. And, once you arrive, you have to rely on shuttles and courtesy vans to get around outside the park—not a big drawback, since shuttles are frequent.

The Alaska Railroad's locomotives also pull two sets of cars with full domes owned by **Princess Cruises and Tours,** 2815 Second Ave., Suite 400, Seattle, WA 98121-1299 (☎ **800/835-8907**); and **Holland America–Westours/Gray Line of Alaska,** 300 Elliot Ave. West, Seattle, WA 98119 (☎ **800/544-2206** or 907/277-5581). Each provides separate, distinct service and operates independently, as described below. Fares on these two operations run about 25% above the railroad's fares, but they're mainly sold, and much more advantageously priced, as lodging packages in the company's Denali hotels, for around $300 for a 1-night stay.

The Princess and Holland America–Westours cars offer a luxurious but controlled experience wherein each passenger has his or her own dome-car seat on a beautifully appointed railroad car. You're expected to stay in your assigned seat and eat during a scheduled dining seating, and you may have to ride backward or sideways in cars designed with tables and living room–style furniture. The Alaska Railroad cars are traditional railroad cars, with seats facing forward, and you can sit anywhere you want, move between cars and stand in the breezeway between cars, and eat when you want to. The food is served in an old-fashioned dining car with tablecloths and flowers. A couple of dozen dome-car seats are available, with a 20-minute limit on staying in them. Well-trained guides provide intermittent commentary and answer questions in each car. Children will enjoy the Alaska Railroad cars more.

Between the two cruise-line car offerings, I preferred Princess's Midnight Sun Express Ultra Dome Rail Cars, with more headroom in the upstairs dome area and rear platforms that allowed passengers to get out of their seats and enjoy the fresh air. However, my personal preference would be for the Alaska Railroad cars.

By Bus. Several van and bus services inexpensively connect Anchorage and Fairbanks to Denali. Most will carry bikes and other gear for an additional fee. The **Alaska Backpacker Shuttle** (☎ 800/266-8625 or 907/344-8775; www.alaska.net/~backpack) carries passengers in comfortable small buses that leave Anchorage from the Voyager Hotel, at Fifth Avenue and K Street, and from the courtesy car lane at the airport. The fare is $40 one way, $70 round-trip; from Fairbanks $20 one way, $35 round-trip.

INFORMATION

Contact **Superintendent, Denali National Park,** P.O. Box 9, Denali Park, AK 99755 (☎ 907/683-2294; www.nps.gov/dena). You may want a copy of Kim Heacox's worthwhile booklet *Denali Road Guide,* available for $5 at the visitor center bookstore, published by the **Alaska Natural History Association,** Denali Branch, P.O. Box 230, Denali National Park, AK 99755 (☎ 907/683-1272; www.alaskanha.org). It provides a milepost commentary you can follow as you ride the shuttle bus. The same nonprofit association publishes guides to Denali birds, mammals, geology, and trails. Also see "Exploring the Backcountry," below.

For general information on travel in Alaska, contact the **Alaska Division of Tourism,** P.O. Box 110801, Juneau, AK 99811-0801 (☎ 907/465-2010; www.commerce.state.ak.us/tourism).

VISITOR CENTERS

The **Denali National Park Visitor Center,** half a mile right of the Parks Highway intersection, is the place to pick up bus tickets and campground permits. The center also has an auditorium showing a slide show and a small bookstore. Rangers staff a backcountry permit desk and an information desk, and rove the center, answering questions. The visitor center is open from 7am to 8pm daily in the high season, 10am to 4pm May and late September, and is closed October to April.

Inside the park, there is a visitor center at **Eielson** (at 66 mi.) and ranger stations at **Toklat** (53 mi.) and **Wonder Lake** (95 mi.).

You can also get questions answered, see fascinating displays about Alaska's outdoors, and gather maps and books at interagency **Alaska Public Lands Information Center** (☎ **907/271-2737** in Anchorage, or 907/456-0527 in Fairbanks).

FEES

The park entrance fee is $10 per family or $5 per person, good for 7 days. There is no entrance station to collect the fee, but it is automatically added to your bill when you make shuttle or campground reservations. In addition, a reservation fee of $4 is charged for each reservation session, regardless of how many different reservations you make when you call. Camping fees range from $6 to $12 for individual sites.

Fees for the various bus trips are described in "Regular Shuttles: A Summary," below.

WHO CAN DRIVE THE PARK ROAD

Lodges in Kantishna can use the park road to bring in customers, but everyone else is under strict controls. You can drive past **mile 14** on the park road only under certain circumstances: (1) You have a 3-day camping permit at Teklanika Campground (you must remain parked at the campground for the entire 3 days); (2) you are a credentialed professional photographer or researcher with a special permit; or (3) it is the last few days in September and you have won a permit in a lottery that allows some cars free passage on the road. After the days of permit driving are over, the road is open to anyone as far as mile 30 until the snow flies; then it's maintained only as far as the headquarters, 3 miles from the entrance.

SEASONS & CLIMATE

The park is populated by people beginning in mid-May, when there still is some snow; the humans migrate south again in mid- to late September, when winter closes in. In the off-season only a few dozen residents remain—caretakers who watch over the hotels and other buildings and sled-dog-driving rangers who patrol the backcountry.

May is iffy at Denali, but fall is a wonderful time to go. The weather gets frigid at night and there can be surprise snowfalls, but rain is less likely and the trees and tundra turn wonderful colors. By early September, visitors are so few that the park no longer takes telephone reservations. Summer highs can reach the 80s, with lows in the low 40s.

PLANNING A VISIT TO DENALI

For the busy season, you must plan a trip to Denali well in advance, reserving all accommodations, campsites, and trips into the park by May for mid-July peak travel. The park hotel is sometimes booked up by December for midsummer. Travelers who just show up at the visitor center without any reservations may have to spend a day, and often two, outside the park before they can get a seat on a shuttle bus, a campground site, or a backcountry permit.

Your park experience, and how you plan it, depends on the level of comfort you demand. Generally, the more you're willing to rough it, the closer you get to the real Denali—there are no hotels in the heart of the park. If you intend to do backcountry camping and exploring on your own, be sure to check out "Exploring the Backcountry," below.

Hotel Stays. Arrive by train at the park, checking into accommodations nearby—shuttles and courtesy vans will get you around. Use the shuttle bus to get into the park, see some wildlife and possibly the mountain, and do a day hike.

First to the Top

You can see Mount McKinley from Anchorage, more than 100 miles away. On a flight across Alaska, the mountain stands out grandly over waves of other mountains. It's more than a mile taller than the tallest peak in the other 49 states.

The Athabascans of Interior Alaska named it Denali, translated as "the high one," or "the great one." The first white men to wander into the area were looking for gold; in 1896 a prospector named the mountain after William McKinley of Ohio, who was elected president that year. Alaskans prefer the Athabascan name, and since 1975 they have petitioned to change it officially back to Denali. Ohio won't allow it. In 1980, Congressmen from Alaska and Ohio compromised on the issue, changing the name of the national park to Denali but leaving the mountain named McKinley.

In 1903, Judge James Wickersham's group became the first to try to climb Mount McKinley. They made it less than halfway up, but on the trip they found gold in the Kantishna Hills, setting off a small gold rush that led to the first permanent human settlement in the park area.

On September 27, 1906, renowned world explorer Dr. Frederick Cook announced to the world that he had reached the summit of Mount McKinley after a lightning-fast climb, covering more than 85 miles and 19,000 vertical feet in 13 days with one other man by his side. On his return to New York, Cook was lionized as a conquering explorer and published a popular book of his summit diary and photographs.

In 1909, Cook again made history, announcing that he had beat Robert Peary to the North Pole. Again Cook was the toast of the world. Then his Eskimo companions mentioned that he'd never been out of sight of land, and his story began to fall apart. After being paid by

Peary to come forward, Cook's McKinley companion also recanted. (As it turns out, Peary probably also faked his pole discovery.) A year later, Cook's famous summit photograph was re-created on a peak 19 miles away and 15,000 feet lower than the real summit.

In 1910, four prospectors from Fairbanks took a more Alaskan approach to the task. Without fanfare or special supplies they marched up the mountain carrying a large wooden flagpole to plant on top as proof of arrival. But on arriving at the summit, they realized that they'd climbed the slightly shorter north peak. Weather closed in, so they set up the pole there and descended without attempting the south peak. When they got back to Fairbanks, no one could see the pole, and they were accused of trying to pull off another hoax.

In 1913, Episcopal Archdeacon Hudson Stuck organized the first successful climb to reach the real summit—and reported seeing the pole on the other peak. Harry Karstens led the climb (he would become the park's first superintendent in 1917) and the first person to stand at the summit was an Alaska Native, Walter Harper.

Although McKinley remains one of the world's most difficult climbs, the number of attempts has boomed since 1980. It's become crowded at the top, and littering is a problem. Over 1,000 people try to climb the peak each year, and about half make it to the summit. Approximately 10,000 people have made it to the top since Hudson Stuck's party.

During the season, the Park Service keeps rescue rangers and an emergency medical clinic at the 14,200-foot level of the mountain, and has a special high-altitude helicopter for climbers who get in trouble. They and the military spend about half a million dollars a year rescuing climbers. Over the years, 91 people have perished on McKinley.

Family Camping. Arrive at the park entrance by car with your camping gear and food for a couple of nights. Reserve a camp site well ahead of time. Catch a shuttle bus or camper bus well into the park for sightseeing and hiking. If staying three nights, you can drive your car to the Teklanika Campground, with good hiking on the Teklanika riverbed, and the advantage of having your home base well within the park.

Backcountry Camping. Arrive with your backpack, camping gear, and food for at least several days' hiking. Go immediately to the visitor center to orient yourself to the backcountry-permit process and choose the unit area that looks most promising. Backcountry permits cannot be reserved in advance, only in person for the next day, and they go fast. If you're lucky, permits will be left for the day after you arrive; more likely, you'll need to camp at the Morino Backpacker's Campground, 1.9 miles on the park road from the highway, and arrive at the visitor center by the 7am opening to get your permit for the following day.

Wilderness Lodges. For those who can afford it, this may be the best way to see Denali. The lodge will fly you out—or, if it's in Kantishna, drive you through the park—and you'll immediately be away from the crowds in remote territory. The lodges all have activities and guides to get you out into the wilderness.

The Talkeetna Option. Drive only as far as Talkeetna, about 110 miles north of Anchorage, and board a flightseeing plane from there to the park, perhaps landing on a glacier on Mount McKinley itself. You'll stand a better chance of seeing the mountain than anyone else. You'll also save yourself hours of driving, and you'll have the pleasure of staying in a town with some character, unlike the park entrance area. But you'll miss the wildlife-viewing opportunities that can be

had only on the ground in the park. Details on Talkeetna are at the end of the chapter.

Climbing Mount McKinley. McKinley, because of its altitude and weather, is among the world's most challenging climbs. If you're looking here for advice, you're certainly not up to an unguided climb. A guided climb is a challenging and expensive endeavor requiring months of conditioning and about a month on the mountain. Get names of guides from the Park Service's **Talkeetna Ranger Station,** P.O. Box 588, Talkeetna, AK 99676 (☎ 907/733-2231). The climbing season lasts from late April or early May until the snow gets too soft, in late June or early July. About 1,000 climbers attempt the mountain annually in about 300 parties; about half typically make it to the top each year, and usually several die trying.

THE RESERVATION SYSTEM

Here's the system for reserving shuttle bus tickets and the developed campgrounds, at it existed at the writing. Changes happen every year, so ask when you call. The backcountry permit system is covered under "Backpacking," below. This section may look long, but paying attention to the details of the reservation system greatly improves your chances of a good visit to the park.

FOR ADVANCE RESERVATIONS

Sixty-five percent of shuttle-bus seats and 100% of campground sites (except Morino, Sanctuary, and Igloo) are offered for booking by telephone, fax, or mail, with the balance held back for walk-ins. Full payment is due within 10 days of your reservation if you don't use a credit card. Reservations by mail or fax open for the whole summer on November 1 of the preceding year. Reservations by phone open sometime in February. After that date, lines are answered Monday through Friday 7am to 6pm, Saturday and Sunday 7am to 5pm, Alaska time (4 hours behind eastern standard time), but at times it has been impossible to get through. By faxing, you bypass this problem and can get in before the phone lines open. Reservation forms to fax or mail are available on the Denali Web site (**www.nps.gov/dena**), or you can just use a blank piece of paper, making sure to include the dates, times, and campgrounds you want, plus alternate dates; the names and ages of the people in your party; and entrance and reservation fees (see "Fees," below) along with a Visa, MasterCard, American Express, or Discover card number, with expiration and signature. You don't have to figure out the total. You can also pay by check if reserving by mail. Don't use the mail unless you're writing well ahead of the time of your trip—more than a month, certainly.

FOR WALK-INS

Reservations for shuttle bus seats and campsites are available by phone, mail, and fax up to the day before you want them. Walk-in reservations for the remaining 35% of the shuttle bus seats and any leftover car camping campsites, and all sites in two primitive backcountry campgrounds begin two days before your bus trip or arrival at the campground, offering. If it's a busy time of year, desirable shuttle reservations are snapped up early in the day. That means you may not get a good reservation for the day of your arrival or even the day after. That's why it's so critical to reserve in advance.

On the other hand, don't despair if you arrive without reservations, as the flow of visitors rises and falls unpredictably, and it's perfectly possible you'll walk into the visitor center and get a shuttle seat on the same day.

On (& Off) the Bus

Your visit to Denali will likely revolve around your ride on the shuttle bus into the park to see the wildlife and get out for a walk in the wilderness. Some planning will make it a more comfortable ride.

ABOUT THE SHUTTLES

If you drive to the park, you'll still need to take the shuttle bus to get into its heart. If you take the train or bus, you'll find that virtually all accommodations have arrangements to get you around, although this becomes less convenient as you get farther from the park entrance. If your hotel doesn't have a courtesy van of its own, there usually is a scheduled shuttle. ARAMARK operates a bus that carries guests from its Denali Park Resort hotels, a mile north and 7 miles south of the park, to the park entrance. You can use the bus even if you're not staying at an ARAMARK hotel—have the desk at your hotel call for a pickup. You can also get around on a rented bike. See "Other Sports & Activities," below.

For a summary of bus trips and fares, see "Regular Shuttles: A Summary," below.

CHOOSING YOUR DESTINATION

You can buy shuttle tickets to the Toklat (*toe*-klat) River, 53 miles into the park; the Eielson (*aisle*-son) Visitor Center at 66 miles; Wonder Lake at 85 miles; or Kantishna, at 89 miles (fares are on the chart, "Denali Park Road Bus Facts"). On any day trip, you have to go both ways, so you're in for a long drive. If you don't get off the bus along the way, the round-trip takes 6½ hours to Toklat, 8 hours to Eielson, 11 hours to Wonder Lake, and 12 hours to Kantishna. In choosing your destination, you need to balance your stamina, your desire to save time for a day hike, and your desire to see wildlife. There are no firm rules about where wildlife show up, but in the early morning, you can often see **moose** on the first part of the road; in mid-summer, **brown (grizzly) bear** seem to appear most in the higher country, beyond Toklat, which also is the best area for **caribou;** and in the fall berry season, the grizzlies show up all along the drive. The best **views of Mount McKinley** show up after mile 61, also beyond Toklat. The mountain is most likely to be visible in the morning, as clouds often pile up during the day. Going beyond Eielson to Wonder Lake provides more amazing views, including the land-covered **Muldrow Glacier** and many classic images of Mount McKinley. There's really no reason to go as far as Kantishna unless you are headed to a lodge there. In general, I think Eielson is the best destination for most people, offering both the chance to see the mountain and some wildlife while leaving some time to get out and walk.

You won't be able to time your trip for good weather, as you need to book ahead, but don't despair if it rains—the sun may be out at the other end of the park. The best weather for wildlife sightings is cool overcast skies without rain. One trick of the system that allows visitors to wait for sun is to stay at Teklanika Campground. If you drive to a campsite there, agreeing to stay for at least three days, you're eligible to buy a special shuttle ticket for $21 that is good for rides deeper into the park the entire time you're staying at the campground. Or you can buy a three-trip pass from the Park Service for the price of two.

Denali can be a challenge for families. Young children will go nuts on an 8-hour bus ride, and often can't pick out the wildlife—this isn't a zoo, and most animals blend into their surroundings. Older children also have a hard time keeping their patience on these trips, as do many adults. The only solution is to get off the bus and turn your trip into a romp in the heather. When you've had a chance to revive, catch the next bus. Also, if your child normally needs a car seat, you must bring it along on the bus, or borrow one from the park service.

ARAMARK also operates narrated bus tours, booked mostly with package visitors. The **Natural History Tour** provides just a taste of the park, going 17 miles down the park road. The **Wildlife Tour** goes to Toklat when the mountain is hidden by clouds, and 8 miles farther, to Highway Pass, when it is visible. Food is provided, but you can't get off the bus along the way, and the route skips the beautiful grizzly and caribou habitat toward the Eielson Visitor Center. The **Kantishna Roadhouse** (listed below under "Wilderness Lodges") offers a 190-mile, 13-hour marathon with lunch and a dog sled or gold panning program at the halfway mark, at the lodge. It's well done, with commentary, but you can't get off the bus along the way, and the return trip may be too rushed to stop for all wildlife sightings.

SHUTTLE ADVICE

Reserve your shuttle ticket for as early as you can stand to get up in the morning. This will give you more time for day hikes and increase your chances of seeing the mountain and wildlife. Many animals are more active in the morning, especially on hot days. The first bus leaves the visitor center at 5:15am, the next at 6am, and then every half hour until the 2:30pm bus, which gets back at 10:30pm. By taking an early bus, you can get off along the way for a hike, then walk back to the road and get the next bus that comes along with a spare seat. If you were to take the 5am bus, you'd have $9\frac{1}{2}$ hours of slack time before you'd have to catch the last bus heading east. (To be on the safe side, don't push it to the very last bus.) The sun won't set until after 11pm May to July, so there'll be plenty of light. If you need to get back to the park entrance at a certain hour, leave yourself plenty of time, because you can't reserve seats going back, and you may have to wait for a bus with room to take you.

Before you leave for the visitor center to get on your shuttle bus, you need a packed lunch and plenty of water; you should be wearing sturdy walking shoes and layers of warm and cooler clothing with rain gear packed; and you should have binoculars or a spotting scope and insect repellent.

There are no reserved seats on the bus, but if you arrive early find a place on the left side, which has the best views on the way out. Shuttle-bus etiquette is to yell out when you see wildlife. The driver will stop, and everyone will rush to your side of the bus. After you've had a look, give someone else a chance. Try to be quiet and don't stick anything out of the bus, as that can scare away the animals. Of course, you have to stay on the bus when animals are present. Most buses will see grizzly bears, caribou, Dall sheep, and moose, and occasionally wolves, but it's possible that you won't see any at all.

The shuttle bus drivers generally offer commentary about the sights on the road, but they don't have to and haven't specifically been trained to teach about natural history. Some do a great job, some pass on inaccurate information, and some don't say much. The tour bus drivers are trained to give commentary.

A ROAD LOG

Here are some of the highlights along the road (check the visitor center or the park service information handouts to confirm times of the guided walks):

Mile 9. In clear weather, this is the closest spot to the park entrance with a view of Mount McKinley. This section also is a likely place to see moose, especially in the fall rutting season.

Mile 14. The end of the paved road at the Savage River Bridge. This generally is as far as private vehicles can go. A park service checkpoint stops anyone who doesn't have a proper permit. From the parking lot by the bridge, a simple climb over dry tundra leads to Primrose Ridge, also known as Mount Wright.

Mile 17. The portable toilets here are as far as the Natural History Tour bus goes.

Mile 29. An hour and 10 minutes into the drive, a large rest stop overlooks the Teklanika River, with flush toilets, the last

plumbing until the Eielson Visitor Center. The Teklanika, like many other rivers on Alaska's glacier-carved terrain, is a braided river—a stream wandering in a massive gravel stream bed that's much too big for it. The braided riverbeds, sometimes miles wide, were created by water from fast-melting glaciers at the end of the last ice age.

Mile 34. Craggy Igloo Mountain is a likely place to see Dall sheep. Without binoculars, they'll just look like white dots. Manageable climbs on Igloo, Cathedral, and Sable mountains take off along the road in the section from Igloo Creek to Sable Pass.

Miles 38–43. Sable Pass, a critical habitat area for bears, is closed to people. A half-eaten sign helps explain why. Bears show up here mostly in the fall. This is the start of the road's broad alpine vistas.

Mile 46. The top of 5-mile-wide Polychrome Pass, the most scenic point on the ride, and a toilet break, two hours, 25 minutes into the trip. Caribou look like specks when they pass in the great valley below you, known as the Plain of Murie. Note how the mountains of colored rock on either side of the plain match up— they once connected before glacial ice carved this valley. Huge rocks on its floor are glacial erratics, plucked from the bedrock by moving ice and left behind when it melted.

Mile 53. The Toklat River, another braided river, is a flat plain of gravel with easy walking. The glaciers that feed the river are 10 miles upstream; without going that far, the river bottom is habitat for bears, caribou, and wolves, and a good place for picnics. A ranger leads a hike here of up to 2 hours, the Toklat Trek— check the visitor center for times.

Mile 58. Highway Pass, the highest point on the road. In good weather, dramatic views of Mount McKinley start here. The alpine tundra from here to the Eielson

Regular Shuttles: A Summary

Note: *Shuttle fares were under negotiation between the Park Service and concessionaires at press time and were expected to change.*

◆ The **ARAMARK courtesy shuttle** links hotels (1 mi. north, 7 mi. south, and within the park) to the park entrance. It operates on a continuous loop and is free. It requires no ticket or reservations.

◆ The **Riley Creek Loop** links facilities within the park entrance area. The route includes the main visitor center, Riley Creek Campground, train depot, and Park Hotel. It operates on a continuous loop and is free, requiring no ticket or reservations.

◆ The **Camper shuttle** provides access to campgrounds beyond the park entrance. The route operates from the main visitor center to Wonder Lake Campground, 85 miles into the park. It runs several times a day, but check with the park for an exact schedule. The cost is $15.50 adults, $7.75 children 13 to 16, free children 12 and under.

◆ The **Backcountry shuttle** (or just "the shuttle") provides general access to the park and wildlife viewing; there is limited commentary, depending on the driver; no food service is available. The route goes from the main visitor center as far as Kantishna, 89 miles away through the park. The shuttle runs every 30 minutes to Eielson Visitor Center, every hour to Wonder Lake, less frequently to Kantishna. The fare is $21 to Eielson, $27 to Wonder Lake, $31 to Kantishna; children 13 to 16 half price, children 12 and under free.

Visitor Center is inviting for walking, but beware, tundra is soft underfoot and can conceal holes and declivities that can twist an ankle.

Mile 64. Thorofare Pass, where the road becomes narrow and winding, is a good area to look for bear and caribou. Bus drivers know best where the animals are on any particular day; they exchange information among themselves.

Mile 66. The Eielson Visitor Center, the end of most bus trips, has flush toilets, a covered picnic area, and a small area of displays where rangers answer questions. Among the exhibits is one explaining why you probably can't see the mountain from this best of vantage points, just 33 miles from its summit. Mount McKinley creates its own weather and is visible about a third of the time in the summer. There's also a seismograph on display, registering the frequent small earthquakes that accompany McKinley's prodigious growth—about an inch every

3 years. Starting late in June, a ranger-guided tundra walk occurs daily at 1:30pm, lasting no more than an hour. If you leave the bus here for a hike, you can get a ride back later by signing up on the standby list kept by a ranger.

Mile 68.5. The incredibly rugged terrain to the north is the earth and vegetation covering Muldrow Glacier. The ice extends to McKinley's peak, and was the early and arduous route for climbers; these days, they fly to a base camp at 7,200-feet elevation on the Kahiltna Glacier, on the south side. McKinley's glaciers, falling 15,000 vertical feet and extending up to 45 miles in length, are among the world's greatest. The Ruth Glacier has carved the Great Gorge on the south side, which is almost 6,000 feet deep above the ice and another 4,000 below—almost twice the depth of the Grand Canyon. The park road comes within a mile of the Muldrow's face, then continues through wet, rolling terrain past beaver ponds, and finally descends into a small spruce patch near mile 82.

Mile 86. Wonder Lake campground is the closest road point to Mount McKinley, 27 miles away. Some buses continue another half hour to Kantishna. The fact that McKinley looks so massive from this considerable distance, dominating the sky, is a testament to its stupendous size. From its base (your elevation here is only 2,000 ft.) to its top is an elevation gain greater than any other mountain on earth. Other mountains are taller over all, but they stand on higher ground.

Organized Tours & Hikes

FLIGHTSEEING

Getting a good, close look at Mount McKinley itself is best accomplished by air. Frequently, when you can't see McKinley from the ground, you can see it from above the clouds. Best of all, some Talkeetna operators that fly mountaineers also land visitors on the mountain itself, a unique and unforgettable experience (see the Talkeetna section at the end of the chapter for an air excursion from there). Small planes and helicopters fly from the park airstrip, private heliports and airstrips along the Parks Highway, and the Healy airstrip. **Denali Air** (☎ **907/683-2261**) has an office in the Nenana Canyon area, and flight operations at mile 229.5 of the Parks Highway. An hour-long flight going within a mile of the mountain costs $165 for adults, $135 for children age 12 and under. **Era Helicopters** (☎ **800/843-1947** or 907/683-2574; www.era-aviation.com) has hourly flights for $195, including van pickup from the hotels. Their heli-hikes land for a 3-hour hike, for $285, and their 75-minute glacier landing flights are $295.

GUIDED HIKES

For a first foray beyond the trails, consider joining one of the park service guided hikes. Two daily **Discovery Hikes** last about 4 hours (5 to 11 hrs. including the bus ride), with one going somewhere near the Eielson Visitor Center and another nearer the entrance end of the park. A ranger takes only 15 hikers, leading them into wilderness while teaching about the nature of the places they visit. Most of the hikes are not too strenuous for families with school age children, and they cost no more than the price of your shuttle ticket. You need to wear waterproof hiking shoes or boots and bring food, water, and rain gear, including pants. Reserve a place in advance, as the hikes fill up during July and you'll need to know when and where to catch the special bus. The **Toklat Trek** is an irregularly scheduled ranger-led walk in the Toklat River stream bed. The **Eielson Stroll,** at 1:30pm daily starting in early June, is a short guided stroll from the Eielson Visitor Center, at mile 66 on the park road. Check in at the visitor center for late word on all the hikes before heading out on a long bus trip.

Ranger Programs & Activities

Check the park newspaper, *The Alpenglow* for ranger talks and slide shows that happen as often as several times a day at the Park Hotel auditorium, at the visitor center, and at the Riley Creek, Savage River, and Teklanika campgrounds. The most noteworthy of these is the **Sled Dog Demonstration.** In the winter, rangers patrol the park by sled dog, as they have for decades. In the summer, to keep the dogs active and amuse the tourists, they run a sled on wheels around the kennel, and give a talk two to three times a day. This was the highlight of my son's trip to Denali when he was 3 years old. There's a shortage of parking at the kennels, near the headquarters at mile 3.4 on the park road, so take a free bus from the visitor center a half hour before each show. Times are listed in the Alpenglow park newspaper.

Day Hikes

IN THE BACKCOUNTRY

One of the unique aspects of Denali is the lack of developed trails—you really can take off in any direction. I've covered some of the best hiking areas above, in the "Road Log," including **Primrose Ridge, Teklanika River, Igloo and Sable mountains,** and the **Toklat River.** A 2-mile path leads from the **Wonder Lake Campground to the McKinley River Bar,** which extends far to the east and west.

The broad, hard gravel flats of the braided riverbeds, such as the McKinley, Toklat, Teklanika, and Savage, are among the best routes for hiking in the park. **Stony Creek,** leading up a gorge to the north from the road at mile 60, is an excellent walk into the mountains. You can also hike on the **tundra;** there are two varieties. The wet tundra lies on top of permanently frozen ground called permafrost; it's mushy at best, like hiking on foam rubber laid over bowling balls. At worst, it's swamp. Dry tundra clothes the mountainsides and generally makes for firmer footing and easier walking. The brush and stunted forest of the region are virtually impenetrable.

The major risks of hiking here relate to the weather and rivers. It can get cold and wet in the middle of summer, and if you're not prepared with warm, waterproof clothing, you could suffer the spiraling chill of hypothermia. The rivers are dangerous because of their fast flow and icy cold water. Avoid crossing any sizable rivers unless you've learned how to do it safely. Bears, which most people worry most about, have never killed a Denali visitor. Tips on avoiding them are widely distributed at the park. No permit is needed for day hiking.

AT THE PARK ENTRANCE

There are six short trails at the park entrance, weaving through the boreal forest around small lakes, and one steep and spectacular hike to the **Mount Healy overlook,** a 5-mile round trip. That trail breaks through treeline to slopes of tundra and rock outcroppings, where you can see just how small the pocket of human infestation is at the park entrance area: The Alaska Range and its foothills extend far into the distance. If you were to continue on an all-day hike right to the top of Mount Healy, you could see all the way to McKinley on a clear day. The Alpenglow park newspaper contains a brief guide for these trails, and you can get a natural history guide, *The Nature of Denali,* at the visitor center.

Exploring the Backcountry

Imagine backpacking over your own area of wilderness, without trails, limits, or the chance of seeing other people. There's no need to retrace your route: Anywhere you meet the 89-mile Denali Park Road you can catch a bus back to the world of people. Any experienced backpacker should consider a backcountry trek at Denali. Yes, it can be challenging. Hiking on tundra, broken rock mountainsides, and braided rivers is tiring and it's easy to fall or turn an ankle. You must be prepared for river crossings and cold weather, know how to find your way with a map and compass, and how to avoid attracting bears. But if you've done a backpacking trip in a less challenging area, you surely can manage it here, so long as you prepare and don't underestimate the additional time you'll need in trailless terrain. Nor do you need to trek far—you could camp just a few miles off the road and still be in a place that looks like no one has ever been there before.

You must be flexible about where you're going and be prepared for any kind of terrain, because you can't choose the backcountry unit you will explore until arriving at the backcountry desk at the visitor center and finding out what's available. This information, and a map of the units, is posted on a board behind the desk. Groups of four or more may have a hard time finding a place to hike, but there's almost always somewhere to go. You can reserve permits only 1 day in advance; you're unlikely to get one for the day you arrive, but you can reserve permits for up to 14 days at the same time. The first night of a trip is the hard one to get—you can only reserve units that are contiguous to the park road for the first night—but after that, each night gets progressively easier. A couple of rangers are there to help you through the process. Buy the **Denali National Park and Preserve topographical map,** published by Trails Illustrated, available for $9.95 from the Alaska Natural History Association, listed above under "Information." Printed on plastic, the map includes the boundaries of the 43 backcountry units and other valuable information. Also, you'll want a copy of *Backcountry Companion,* by Jon Nierenberg, a book selling for $8.95 that describes conditions and routes in each area, published and sold by ANHA. It's for sale at the visitor center, or you can look at a well-thumbed copy kept at the backcountry desk.

The alpine units from the Toklat River to Eielson Visitor Center are most popular. That's where you get broad views and can cross heathery dry tundra, walking in any direction. But to go far, you'll also have to be ready to climb over some rugged, rocky terrain, and the tundra itself is deceptively difficult walking—it's soft and hides ankle-turning holes. The wooded units are the least popular, since bushwhacking through overgrown land is anything but fun. The best routes for making time here and anywhere in the Alaska Bush are along the braided river valleys and stream beds. You need to be ready for stream crossings.

Before venturing into the backcountry, everyone is required to watch an orientation film called *The Backcountry Simulator.* It's intended to teach you how not to attract bears, but it's intimidating enough to scare you out of the park— don't let it. The park service provides bear-resistant food containers in which you are required to carry all your food. Guns are not permitted in the park; a pepper spray for self-defense from bears is allowed. You'll have to take the camper bus to get to your backcountry unit, at a cost of $15.50 for each adult.

Other Sports & Activities

Biking. A bicycle provides special freedom in the park. Bikers can ride past the mile 14 checkpoint where cars have to turn back. Park campgrounds have bike stands, and you can take a bike on the shuttle or camper bus. The longest stretch on the park road between campgrounds is 52 miles. On the downside, the buses kick up a lot of dust, and bikes may not go off-road. But if you ride in the evening, after most buses stop running, or even at night under the midnight sun, you can have the park all to yourself. Pick up a copy of the bike rules from the backcountry desk before you start. **Denali Outdoor Center** (☎ **888/303-1925** or 907/683-1925; www.denalioutdoorcenter.com) rents front-suspension bikes for $40 for 24 hours, with discounts for longer rentals. Or shop for a better price in Anchorage and bring it up with you.

Rafting & Boating. Rafting on the Nenana River, bordering the park along the Parks Highway, is fun and popular. Several commercial guides float two stretches of the river: an upper portion, where the water is smoother and the guides explain passing scenery; and the lower portion, where the river roars through the rock-walled Nenana Canyon, and rafts shoot through class III and IV rapids. Guides take children as young as 5 on the slow trip (although I don't know if I'd let my kid go at that age); the youngest accepted for the fast portion is age 12. White-water rafting carries risk you shouldn't discount just because a lot of people do it, as a fatal accident confirmed in 1999, on the supposedly easy tour. Each session takes 2 to 2½ hours, including safety briefings, suiting up, and rides to the put-in and take-out points. Prices are around $55 for adults, with discounted rates for children. **Denali Outdoor Center** (☎ 888/303-1925 or 907/683-1925; www.denalioutdoorcenter. com) is a professional operation, offering rafting trips and instruction in river techniques. There are five firms in competition, however, so you may be able to save by shopping around. When reserving, make sure to ask what kind of gear is provided: Dry suits will keep you comfortable; you're likely to get drenched if all they give you is rain gear or Mustang floatation suits. If you're camping, plan a shower afterward, as the silt in the river water will stick to your skin and hair.

Horseback Riding. There is no riding in the park itself, but there are several opportunities in similar terrain outside its boundaries. Various companies offer rides, although the line-up of firms seems to change every year. Sixty- to 90-minute rides cost from $55 to $70, and pack trips and extended journeys are available, too. Among the operators are **Tumbling B Ranch** (☎ 970/683-6002), and **Denali Saddle Safaris** (☎ 907/683-1200). Both are in Healy, just outside the northeast corner of the park.

Camping

The park has eight campgrounds. There are spots for RVs, as well as tent campers who want to be away from people out in the wilderness. For private campgrounds see "Accommodations," later in this chapter.

Each Park Service campground has different fees, regulations, and access limitations. All sites must be reserved, except the Morino Backpacker Campground, which has a self-registration system and is only for people without vehicles. The Sanctuary and Igloo campgrounds can be reserved only in person and sites may not be available when you arrive, so it's wise to at least start your stay with reservations at another campground.

When you make your reservation, you'll receive a confirmation in the mail or by fax. Take that document to the "will

call" desk at the visitor center to pick up your camping permit. The visitor center is open 7am to 8pm. If you won't make it by 8pm you must call ☎ 907/683-1266 to avoid losing your site. Canceling or changing camping reservations carries a fee of $6 per site and is possible only up to 2 days before the reservation.

To get to campgrounds beyond mile 14 on the park road, you have to take the $15.50 camper bus (unless you're staying 3 days or more at Teklanika). If it seems expensive, consider this: The ticket is a free pass to travel all over the park, which would cost as much as $11 more if bought for the shuttle.

Riley Creek is the traditional family campground in the woods, right at the entrance to the park. With its paved roads and other amenities it's certainly not the wilderness; but it is readily accessible, easy to get a permit, and young children won't care if it's not exactly the backcountry. For more ambitious campers, Riley Creek is a good stop for your first night in the park. The front-country shuttle bus stops in the parking lot. Riley Creek is a roaring tributary of the Nenana, running just below the campground; the best sites back onto the creek. Riley is the only campground open year-round, although the water is off in the winter.

Morino Backpacker Campground, set aside for walk-in campers, is intended for backcountry travelers waiting for their permits. It is simply a wooded area about a mile from the visitor center where backpackers can put up their tents and use portable outhouses. Sites are designated by stakes, are self-registered, and are limited to two people. There is no parking area.

Savage River, just a mile short of the park road checkpoint beyond which vehicles cannot go, is both easily accessible and relatively remote, 13 miles from the park entrance. It's the best choice for car or RV campers who want to get away from the park entrance but don't have 3 days to spend camping at Teklanika. Savage Group is the nearby group camping area. The Savage River's broad bed and nearby rounded mountain shoulders are good for exploring, and there's a decent chance of seeing moose and possibly bear.

Sanctuary River is a small, primitive tent camping area 9 miles beyond the road checkpoint, located in the woods near a ranger station.

Teklanika River, at mile 29 on the park road, is the only campground for car or RV camping beyond the checkpoint. You can drive in if you agree not to move your vehicle for at least 3 days. You'll also need a special $20 shuttle pass, good for the duration of your stay, which allows free exploration of the park. It's a large campground, but the sites are adequately separated by trees.

Igloo Creek, the last campground for 52 miles, is a primitive tent camp near a ranger station. It's the closest campground to the open terrain of alpine tundra.

The tent-camping sites at **Wonder Lake,** near the end of the park road, are in high demand, next to placid Wonder Lake and with spectacular views of Mount McKinley. A ranger station is 2 miles away. Winter stays late at this end of the park, and the campground doesn't open until sometime in June.

Campground Programs. The Riley Creek, Savage River, Teklanika, and Wonder Lake campgrounds have ranger programs almost nightly.

Supplies. Convenience stores with limited camping supplies are located near the park hotel and at the gas station near the large hotels a mile north of the park entrance.

Accommodations

Patterns of land ownership and the furious pace of development around Denali have led to a hodgepodge of roadside hotels, cabins, lodges, campgrounds, and restaurants in pockets along more than 20 miles of the Parks Highway. There are decent rooms in each of the pockets, but the going rates vary widely. The most expensive rooms, and the first booked, are in the immediate area of the park entrance. Next are the hotels south of the park. Both these areas are entirely seasonal. The best deals are in Healy, 10 miles north of the park, where you can find a room for $50 less than a comparable room near the park entrance. Of course, if you don't have a car, it's most convenient to stay in or near the park. The other choices are to stay in Talkeetna,

Campground	Total Sites	RV Hookups	Dump Station	Toilets	Drinking Water
Riley Creek	150	No	Yes	Flush	Yes*
*Morino Backpacker***	60	No	No	Chemical	Yes
Savage River	33 sites	No	No	Flush	Yes
Savage Group	3	No	No	Flush	Yes
*Sanctuary River***	7	No	No	Chemical	No
Teklanika River	53	No	No	Flush	Yes
*Igloo Creek***	7	No	No	Chemical	No
*Wonder Lake***	28	No	No	Flush	Yes

  * No water in winter.
 ** Tent sites only.
 † Reservations must be made in person (not in advance of your park trip).

the back door to the park, described in the next section; at a lodge in the Kantishna inholding within the park; or at a remote wilderness lodge (covered below). I've listed each of the choices separately. Despite their high prices, rooms can be hard to find in the high season, and it's wise to book well ahead. If you don't mind gambling, however, you can often get great last-minute deals from hotels that have had large cancellations from their package tour clients.

NEAR THE PARK

This area, sometimes known as Denali or Nenana Canyon, extends about a mile north of the park entrance on the Parks Highway, including the park hotel, which is 1½ miles within the park. Two huge hotels dominate the area, the **Denali Princess Lodge,** mile 238.5, Parks Hwy. (P.O. Box 110), Denali National Park, AK 997555 (☎ **800/426-0500;** fax 206/336-6100), and the **McKinley Resorts Chalets,** mile 238.5, Parks Hwy. (mailing address: 241 W. Ship Creek Ave., Anchorage, AK 99501; ☎ **800/276-7234** or 907/276-7234; fax 907/258-3668). Rates for two at both hotels range from $179 to $279. The McKinley Resorts Chalets also is a good place to book activities.

Among smaller lodgings, you'll find good standard rooms at **Denali River View Inn,** mile 238.4 Parks Hwy. (P.O. Box 49), Denali National Park, AK 99755 (☎ **907/683-2663;** fax 907/683-7433), for $134 double. **Sourdough Cabins,** mile 238.5 Parks Hwy. (P.O. Box 118), Denali, AK 99755 (☎ **907/683-2773**), which has comfortable little cabins in the woods below the highway for similar prices. All of the hotels in this area are open only during the tourist season, roughly May 15 to September 15.

Denali Bluffs Hotel

Mile 238.4 Parks Hwy. (P.O. Box 72460, Fairbanks, AK 99707). ☎ **907/683-7000.** Fax 907/683-7500. www.denalibluffs.com. 112 units. TV TEL. High season $179 double. Low season $126 double. AE, DISC, MC, V.

A series of 12 buildings on a steep mountainside look down on the Nenana Canyon area from above the highway. The light, tastefully decorated rooms have two double beds, coffeemakers, and small refrigerators, and those on the upper floor have vaulted ceilings and balconies with great views. A courtesy van will take you anywhere in the area, and a token-operated laundry is available. A

Showers	Fire Pits/ Grills	Laundry	Public Phone	Reserve	Fees	Open
Nearby	Yes	No	Yes	Yes	$12	Year-round
Nearby	No	No	Yes	No	$6	Late May to Sept
No	Yes	No	No	Yes	$12	Late May to Sept
No	Yes	No	No	Yes	$40	Late May to Sept
No	No	No	No	Yes†	$6	Late May to Sept
No	Yes	No	No	Yes	$12	Late May to Sept
No	No	No	No	Yes†	$6	Late May to Sept
No	No	No	No	Yes	$12	June–Sept

dining room serves simple meals for breakfast and lunch.

Denali Crow's Nest Cabins

Mile 238.5, Parks Hwy. (P.O. Box 70), Denali National Park, AK 99755. ☎ **907/683-2723.** Fax 907/683-2323. www.denalicrowsnest. com. 39 cabins. High season $154 cabin for 2. Low season $109 cabin for 2. MC, V.

Perched in five tiers on the side of a mountain above the Nenana Canyon area, looking down on Horseshoe Lake and the other, larger hotels, the cabins are roomy and comfortable, especially those on the 100 and 200 level. A log cabin and the warmth of the Crofoot family create more of an appropriate, Alaskan feeling than the modern, standard rooms that have filled the canyon. You spend a lot of time climbing stairs, however, and despite the great views and the price, the cabins are simple, not luxurious; the rooms have shower enclosures, not tubs. They book tours and offer a courtesy van, free coffee, and an outdoor Jacuzzi. The restaurant, The Overlook, is recommended separately under "Dining," below.

Denali National Park Hotel

Mile 1.5, Denali National Park Rd. (P.O. Box 87), Denali Park, AK 99755. (For reservations, contact Denali Park Resorts, 241 W. Ship Creek Ave., Anchorage, AK 99501.) ☎ **800/276-7234.** Fax 907/258-3668. www. denalinationalpark.com. 100 units. High season $152 double. Low season $111 double. AE, DISC, MC, V.

The original park hotel burned down in 1972, replaced by this "temporary" structure, cobbled together from old railroad cars and modular housing units. It will close for good in September 2001 as part of a long-term park plan. Despite its flawed pedigree, the doomed structure has quirky, oddly historic character beyond most of the bland, standard places outside the park. Staying here puts you at the center of park activities, with the front-country hiking trails leaving out the back door. The rooms need remodeling, however, and have no views. There's a courtesy shuttle, coffee in the rooms, and a tour desk.

The attractive dining room serves large portions. The lounge, in a pair of railroad cars, has a good, campy feel. Smoking is permitted in one of the two rail cars. For fast food, the snack bar is quite adequate and probably the best place for take-out in the area. The gift shop has reasonable prices, regulated by the park service.

IN HEALY

Healy is 10 miles north of the park entrance, but a world away. It's a year-round community with an economy based primarily on a large coal mine and only secondarily on the park. It sits in a large, windy valley with a few patches of stunted trees and big, open spaces of tundra. There are many hotels and bed-and-breakfasts with rooms that cost from $20 to $90 less than those near the park. They say the water tastes better, too. On the downside, you need a car to stay in Healy.

Besides my two favorites listed below, you'll find hundreds of small, serviceable rooms with twin beds at a converted pipeline camp, the **Denali North Star Inn,** mile 248.5, Parks Hwy. (P.O. Box 240), Healy, AK 99743 (☎ **800/684-1560** or 907/683-1560; fax 907/683-4026; www.alaskan.com/denalinorthstar), for $110 double. Across the highway, the **Stampede Lodge,** mile 248.8, Parks Hwy. (P.O. Box 380), Healy, AK 99743 (☎ **907/683-2242;** fax 907/683-2243; www.alaskaone.com/stampede/index. htm), has attractively decorated rooms, on the small side, in a renovated 1946 railroad building. They charge $89 double in the summer. There's a reasonably priced restaurant inside serving three meals a day.

Motel Nord Haven

Mile 249.5, Parks Hwy. (P.O. Box 458), Healy, AK 99743. ☎ **800/683-4501** or

907/683-4500. Fax 907/683-4503. www. motelnordhaven.com. 24 units. TV TEL. High season $108–$117 double. Low season $70 double. AE, MC, V.

This fresh little gray hotel with a red roof has large, immaculate rooms with one or two queen-size beds. They're equal to the best standard rooms in the Denali Park area and a lot less expensive. Bill and Patsy Nordmark offer free newspapers, coffee, tea, and hot chocolate, free laundry machines, and a sitting room with a collection of Alaskan books. The rooms, decorated with Alaskan art and oak trim, all have interior entrances and have been nonsmoking since construction. Up to four people can stay in the rooms with two beds for the price of a double. They'll pack a sack lunch for $8, or you can eat breakfast or lunch from a menu of soup, salad, or sandwiches.

White Moose Lodge

Mile 248, Parks Hwy. (P.O. Box 68), Healy, AK 99743. ☎ 800/481-1232 or 907/683-1231. Fax 907/683-1232. www.mtaonline.net/ ~mooseinn. 12 units. TV. $90 double. Rates include continental breakfast. AE, DC, DISC, MC, V. Closed Oct to mid-May.

This old, low-slung building among stunted black spruce contains some unlikely finds—comfortable, cheerfully decorated rooms with flower boxes, and a small greenhouse. The breakfast consists of coffee, tea, orange juice, and pastries in the small lobby.

SOUTH OF THE PARK

There are several groups of accommodations south of the park.

Denali Cabins

Mile 229, Parks Hwy. (P.O. Box 229), Denali National Park, AK 99755. ☎ 907/683-2643. Fax 907/683-2595. www.alaskan.com/ denalicabins. (In winter, 200 W. 34th Ave., Suite 362, Anchorage, AK 99503; ☎ 907/ 258-0134; fax 907/243-2062.) 43 units. High season $128 cabin for 2; $159 suite. Low

season $84 cabin for up to 4 people. MC, V. Closed mid-Sept to mid-May.

These roomy cedar cabins, arranged around a grassy compound with a pair of hot tubs, are a good choice for families. The kids may well find someone their own age to play with, and, with a cabin you don't have to worry as much about noise. The prices are high, however, for rooms that are quite basic, lacking TVs or telephones and with shower stalls instead of tubs.

Denali River Cabins

Mile 231, Parks Hwy. (P.O. Box 81250, Fairbanks, AK 99708). ☎ 800/230-7275 or 907/683-2500. Fax 907/683-2502. www. denalirivercabins.com. (Winter ☎ 907/ 456-5200; fax 907/456-5212.) 54 cabins. High season $149–$159 cabin for 2. Low season, $95–$105 cabin for 2. AE, DISC, MC, V.

These cedar cabins along boardwalks above the Nenana River feel fresh and luxurious. They have showers only, and lack closets. Those on the river, with decks over the water, are $10 more. The sauna has a picture window on the river and there's a Jacuzzi and a comfortable lobby.

The Perch

Mile 224, Parks Hwy. (P.O. Box 53) Denali National Park, AK 99755. ☎ 888/322-2523, or phone/fax 907/683-2523. www.alaskaone. com/perchrest. 21 cabins, 14 with bathrooms. $65–$95 cabin for 2. AE, DISC, MC, V.

In the trees along rushing Carlo Creek, 13 miles south of the park entrance, a variety of cabins range from large, modern units with private bathrooms to adorable if Spartan little A-frames with lofts and shared bathhouse. There's a sense of privacy and of being out in the woods along the wooden and gravel walkways. It's an exceptional value, open year round. Atop a steep hill, the restaurant and bar, is one of my favorites in the area, described below under "Dining."

PRIVATE CAMPGROUNDS

There are two commercial campgrounds in the area. **Denali Grizzly Bear Cabins and Campground** is about 7 miles south of the park entrance (P.O. Box 7), Denali National Park, AK 99755 (☎ 907/683-2696; fax 907/683-2697; www.AlaskaOne.com/dengrzly), with some exposed sites and others on a hillside among small trees. Small cabins and tent cabins dot the property, too. There is a coin-operated shower. Tent sites are $17 for up to four people, with electrical and water hookups $6 more. A more-developed campground is 10 miles north of the park, in Healy. **McKinley RV and Campground,** at mile 248.5 on Parks Hwy. (P.O. Box 340) Healy, AK 99743 (☎ 800/478-2562 in Alaska, or 907/683-2379), has a token-operated laundry, hot showers, and a small playground. Basic tent sites are $17.50 to $20.25, full hookups $28.75.

WILDERNESS LODGES

For those who can afford it, a lodge allows you to experience real wilderness in complete comfort. Below are the three lodges in the Kantishna district, an old gold mining inholding at the heart of the peak, near McKinley, plus one fly-in lodge east of the park. All are open only in the summer. You get to Kantishna on a private bus or van over the 89-mile park road, guided by your host. Once there, you can explore the park using a special pass for shuttle rides starting in Kantishna, which costs $15.50. See the Talkeetna section, below, for other choices.

Camp Denali/North Face Lodge

Kantishna District (P.O. Box 67), Denali National Park, AK 99755. ☎ 907/683-2290 or 907/683-1568. www.gorp.com/dnpwild. 17 cabins, none with bathroom (Camp Denali); 15 units with bathroom (North Face Lodge). $325 per person per night, double occupancy, all inclusive. Minimum stay 3 nights. No credit cards.

Uniquely at this pioneering ecotourism establishment, you can wake to the white monolith of Mount McKinley filling your window. Also uniquely, the naturalist guides here have the right to use the park road free of the shuttle system for hikes, biking, lake canoeing, bird watching, photography sessions, and other outdoor learning activities. During some sessions, nationally reputed academics and other experts lead the program. All arrivals and departures are on fixed session dates. The Camp Denali cabins each have their own outhouse and share a central bath house and wonderful shared lodge rooms—it would be my first choice for anyone who can stand not having their own flush toilet. North Face Lodge has smallish traditional rooms with private bathrooms. A conservation ethic pervades the operation.

Denali Backcountry Lodge

Kantishna District (P.O. Box 189), Denali National Park, AK 99755. ☎ 800/841-0692 or 907/683-2594. Fax 907/683-1341. www.denalilodge.com. (In winter P.O. Box 810, Girdwood, AK 99587; ☎ 907/783-1342; fax 907/783-1308). 30 cabins. $315 per person per night, double occupancy, all inclusive. 3-night minimum recommended. MC, V.

Comfortable, modern, cedar cabins sit in rows on a deck next to babbling Moose Creek and a two-story lodge building. Guests sit in a screened porch away from the mosquitoes and watch the day go by, or join a guided hike, natural history program, or other activity around the lodge. To go into the park, you're on your own, either on a lodge mountain bike or the shuttle, although the ride in from the entrance is treated as a safari.

Denali Wilderness Lodge

Wood River (P.O. Box 50, Denali National Park, AK 99755). ☎ 800/541-9779, or 907/683-1287 summer only. Fax 907/479-4410. www.DenaliWildernessLodge.com. (In winter P.O. Box 71784, Fairbanks, AK 99707; ☎ 907/479-4000.) 23 units and cabins. $290 per person per night, double occupancy, all inclusive; plane fare to lodge $100 round-trip. AE, DISC, MC, V.

The extraordinary log buildings were built by the late big-game guide Lynn Castle along the Wood River, and his amazing collection of mounted exotic animals is in a sort of museum room. They don't kill the animals anymore—now they're more valuable to look at alive, and the lodge has become an ecoestablishment, flying guests in for as little as a half day for flightseeing, horseback riding, rafting, hiking, and talks by naturalists. Stay at least a couple of days to really experience the place. This is the best place for riders, with a sizable stable and one ride included in the price. The cabins, while not luxurious, are quite comfortable and have private bathrooms. The food is terrific. The location is distant from Mount McKinley, in a remote valley 30 miles east of the park entrance.

Kantishna Roadhouse

Kantishna District, Denali National Park (P.O. Box 81670, Fairbanks, AK 99708). ☎ **800/ 942-7420** or 907/683-1475. Fax 907/683-1449. www.kantishnaroadhouse.com. (Winter ☎ 907/479-2436; fax 907/479-2611.) 27 units. $295 per person per night, double occupancy, all inclusive. 2-night minimum. AE, DC, DISC, MC, V.

This well-kept property along Moose Creek in the old Kantishna Mining District trades on both the mining history and outdoor opportunities of the area. Some rooms are large and luxurious, while others are in smaller single cabins with lofts. The log central lodge has an attractive lobby with people coming and going—it's got more of a hotel feel and might be more attractive to an older, less active set or to families than the other lodges in the Kantishna District. It's also less expensive and accommodates two night stays. Daily activities include guided hikes, wagon rides, horseback riding, biking, and gold panning, and there's an excellent sled-dog demonstration.

Dining

The large hotels all have fine dining and casual restaurants. The restaurants at the **Denali Princess Lodge** have beautiful dining rooms with great views. The **Chalet Center Cafe** at the McKinley Resorts Chalets serves casual meals in a large, light room. You can't miss the tacky highway frontage of the **McKinley Denali Salmon Bake** in the Nenana Canyon area. Although casual to the point of indifference, it can be a fun place to eat, and the food is fine. A full-service restaurant, **The Denali Roadhouse** (☎ 907/683-2500) was planned to open in 2000 at the Denali River Cabins.

Lynx Creek Pizza

Mile 238.6, Parks Hwy. ☎ **907/683-2547.** All items $3.25–$22.95. AE, DISC, MC, V. Daily 11am–11:30pm. Closed late Sept to early May. PIZZERIA.

This ARAMARK-managed pizza restaurant is a center of activity, as its the only place to get a slice and a beer. The food isn't anything special, and there often are lines to order, but the dining room is a relatively nontouristy place to meet young people.

The Overlook Bar and Grill

Mile 238.5, Parks Hwy., up the hill above the Denali Canyon area. ☎ **907/683-2641.** Lunch main courses $9–$15; dinner $16–$30. MC, V. 11am–11pm. Closed mid-Sept to mid-May. BURGERS/STEAK/SEAFOOD.

This fun, noisy place has the feeling of a classic bar and grill, with a vaulted ceiling of rough-cut lumber and a spectacular view of the Nenana Canyon. There are two dining rooms, one with the bar, and another, behind a glass partition, which is quieter and has table cloths. A huge variety of craft beers is available, with several on tap. At times I've gotten superb fare here, but the last time I visited, I found the meal prices too high and the food no better than acceptable—my halibut obviously had been long frozen. All the steaks on the menu are $30.

The Perch

Mile 224 Park Hwy. ☎ **907/683-2523.** Main courses $7.50–$8.50 lunch, $14–$40 dinner. Summer daily 6am–10pm. Winter hours vary. AE, DISC, MC, V. STEAK/SEAFOOD

The odd, knoblike hill the restaurant stands on provides reason for the name (the attractive cabins, described above, are down below). It's a friendly, family run place serving a simple steak and seafood menu—they don't try anything fancy, but they do what they do right. The dining room is light, with well-spaced tables, and makes up for a certain coldness with big picture windows on three sides. It's located 13 miles south of the park.

Denali in the Evening

The main evening event is the concessionaire's **Cabin Nite Dinner Theater,** at the McKinley Resorts Chalets (☎ **800/276-7234** or 907/683-8200), a professionally produced musical revue about a gold rush–era woman who ran a roadhouse in Kantishna. You can buy the $39 tickets, half price under age 11, virtually anywhere in the area. The actors, singing throughout the evening, stay in character to serve big platters of food to diners sitting at long tables, doing a good job of building a rowdy, happy atmosphere for adults and kids. You go for the show, not the all-you-can-eat salmon and ribs, which were plentiful but less than memorable when we visited. Princess Cruises and Tours puts on a similar evening show, **Mt. McK's Roadhouse Review,** in a big wall tent at the Denali Princess Lodge. The local rap says: better food, worse show. Tickets are for sale at the hotel's tour desk (☎ **800/426-0500** or 907/683-2282) for $35 (half price 12 and younger), or $14 for the show without the meal.

Talkeetna: Back Door to Denali

Talkeetna, a historic and funky little town with a sense of humor but not much happening, slept soundly from its decline around World War I until just a few years ago. Now there are paved streets (both of them), a new National Park Service building of stone, a new railroad depot, and two large new luxury lodges. It seems that while Talkeetna slumbered in a time capsule, an explosion of visitors was happening at Denali National Park. Now, not entirely voluntarily, Talkeetna finds itself enveloped in that boom.

As a threshold to the park, Talkeetna has significant pros and cons. On the positive side, it's closer to Anchorage; the development is much more interesting and authentic than at the park entrance; and there's lots to do in the outdoors and great views of the mountain, less frequently obscured by clouds. On the negative side, a big minus: You can't get into the park from here. That means you miss the dramatic scenery, easy backcountry access, and unique wildlife viewing on the park road.

The town itself dates from the gold rush, and there are many charming log and clapboard buildings. The entire downtown area has been listed on the National Register of Historic Places. You can spend several hours looking at two small museums and meeting people in the 2-block main street, then go out on the Talkeetna or Susitna river for rafting, a jet boat ride, or fishing, or take a flightseeing trip to the national park.

GETTING THERE

By Car. Talkeetna lies on a 13-mile spur road that branches from the Parks Highway 99 miles north of Anchorage and 138 miles south of the park entrance.

By Train. The Alaska Railroad serves Talkeetna daily on its runs to Denali

National Park during the summer, and weekly in the winter. See the listing earlier in this chapter. The summer fare from Anchorage to Talkeetna is $60 one way for adults, half price for children.

By Van. The **Talkeetna Shuttle Service,** P.O. Box 468, Talkeetna, AK 99676 (☎ **907/733-1725** office, or 907/355-1725 cellular), runs back and forth to Anchorage for $42 one way, $80 roundtrip.

ESSENTIALS

Visitor Information. The **Denali National Park Talkeetna Ranger Station,** downtown Talkeetna (P.O. Box 588), Talkeetna, AK 99676 (☎ **907/733-2231;** www.nps.gov/dena), is open in summer daily 8am to 6pm, winter Monday to Friday 8am to 4:30pm. Built to serve people who aim to climb Mount McKinley, the station makes a fascinating stop for anyone curious about mountaineering. Inside the handsome river rock structure you'll find a large sitting room with a fireplace, climbing books and pictures of the mountain—it's like an old-fashioned explorers' club. Records open for inspection cover the history of McKinley climbs. Rangers are on hand to answer questions, too.

The **Denali/Talkeetna Visitor Center,** at the intersection of the Parks Highway and Talkeetna Spur Road (P.O. Box 688), Talkeetna, AK 99676 (☎ **800/ 660-2688** or 907/733-2688 summer, or 907/733-2499 winter; www.alaskan. com/talkeetnadenali), is open in summer daily 8am to 8pm; call for hours at other times. This commercial center in a tiny cabin on the highway provides brochures and information while trying to snag bookings for the sponsoring businesses. It's the handiest commercial information stop in the region.

Orientation. This unincorporated town of 350 doesn't take long to figure out.

Just drive the 13-mile spur road till you hit the historic area on Main Street, then explore on foot. Turn right across the railroad tracks as you get into town for the **Talkeetna State Airport,** campground, boat launch, and some businesses.

Getting Around. You can walk everywhere in Talkeetna, but there are good **mountain-biking** routes, too. **CGS Bicycles,** on Main Street (P.O. Box 431), Talkeetna, AK 99676 (☎ **907/733-1279**), is a full-service bike shop that rents mountain bikes for $15 a day and leads trail tours starting at $20 per person.

A Fun Festival. The big event of the year is the **Talkeetna Moose Dropping Festival,** over a weekend in mid-July, a community fair finishing its third decade as a fundraiser for the Talkeetna Historical Society (☎ **907/733-2487;** www.moosedrop.com). The main event does not involve dropping moose, as an aggrieved animal lover once complained, but dropping moose droppings. There's also a parade and many other events.

IN TOWN

Talkeetna is famous for its laid-back atmosphere and outdoors, but there are several places to stop in to get the sense of the place. One is the **ranger station** mentioned above under "Visitor Information." If you come in May or June, you're sure to meet many international mountain climbers; you'll have no difficulty picking them out. The **Fairview Inn** is a historic bar with the rough edges still in place. Along **Main Street,** artists and craftspeople have shops where you can often find them at work. The **Talkeetna Historical Society Museum,** on the Village Airstrip a half block south of Main Street (☎ 907/733-2487), contains artifacts and displays on the local mining history, including photographs and biographies. It's also a good place to get community information. Open daily in summer, 10:30am to 5:30pm. Admission is $1. The **Museum of Northern Adventure** is a wax museum of Alaska scenes and memorabilia, on the east end of Main Street (☎ **907/733-3999**). It's funny and corny, and great for children. Admission is $2 for adults, $1 for children.

The most affecting site in town is the **mountain climbers' memorial** at the town cemetery, near the airstrip on the east side of the railroad tracks. Besides a granite memorial of plaques for lost mountaineers, there is a small garden of monuments to many individual climbers, some in Japanese. The bodies of 34 climbers who died on the mountain have never been recovered.

GETTING OUTSIDE

Flightseeing. The only way you'll get into the park from Talkeetna is by flying with one of the glacier pilots who support McKinley climbs, which typically begin with a flight from here to the 7,200-foot level of the Kahiltna Glacier. There are several operators with long experience. The least expensive flights are around $75 per person, if the plane is full, and either cruise through the Talkeetna mountains for wildlife watching or approach McKinley's south face. Rates often depend on how many are going, so if you can put together a group of four or five, or the operator can add you to a group, you save as much as half. If you have the money and the weather is good, consider an extended tour that circles the mountain and flies over its glaciers, for $120 to $200 per person with a full plane. Best of all, in May and June you can arrange a landing on the mountain itself, just as the climbers do (the snow is too soft starting in July). These landings are usually treated as add-ons to the tours mentioned above, for an additional price of $20 to $40 per person. Try any of these companies, all operating out of the Talkeetna airport, and all with complete Web sites for comparison shopping: **K2 Aviation,** (P.O. Box 545-B), Talkeetna, AK 99676 (☎ **800/764-2291** or 907/733-2291; www.alaska.net/~flyk2); **Doug Geeting Aviation,** (P.O. Box 42), Talkeetna, AK 99676 (☎ **800/770-2366** or 907/733-2366; www.airtours.com); or **Talkeetna Air Taxi,** (P.O. Box 73), Talkeetna, AK 99676 (☎ **800/533-2219** or 907/733-2218; www.gorp.com/flytat).

Fishing and Jet Boat Tours. Talkeetna is at the confluence of the wild Talkeetna and Susitna rivers. **Mahay's Riverboat Service,** P.O. Box 705, Talkeetna, AK 99676 (☎ **800/736-2210** or 907/733-2223; www.fish-world.com/mahays), is a top guide, with 2-hour tours on a unique, 51-foot jet-boat for $45 per person, operating several times a day from a dock near the public boat launch on the Talkeetna River. Owner Steve Mahay is legendary, the only person ever to shoot Devil's Canyon in a jet boat. Mahay offers fishing charters as well.

Rafting. Talkeetna River Guides, on Main Street (P.O. Box 563), Talkeetna, AK 99676 (☎ **800/353-2677** or 907/733-2677; www.alaska.net/~trg/trg_dir/), offers a 2-hour wildlife river rafting tour, without white water, on the Talkeetna three times a day for $39 adults, $15 children under 12. They also offer longer trips and guided fishing.

ACCOMMODATIONS & DINING

Besides the hotels described below, good budget rooms are available at the **Talkeetna Motel,** at the west end of Main Street (P.O. Box 115) Talkeetna, AK 99676 (☎ **907/733-2323**). The clean, basic rooms go for $62 to $95 double. In a small A-frame they operate the TeePee restaurant, with three hearty, inexpensive meals a day in an eight-table dining room that's a slice of old Talkeetna.

Swiss-Alaska Inn

F Street, near the boat launch (P.O. Box 565), Talkeetna, AK 99676. ☎ **907/733-2424.** 20 units. $100 double. AE, DISC, MC, V.

This is more the essence of old Talkeetna than the flashy new lodge discussed above. It's a friendly family business with a small restaurant serving good, familiar American meals, plus a few German dishes. There are large, attractive rooms with oak furniture and Jacuzzis in the newer of the two buildings. The smoking rooms in the old building are clean but quite small.

Talkeetna Alaskan Lodge

Mile 12.5 Talkeetna Spur Rd. (P.O. Box 93330, Anchorage, AK 99509-3330). ☎ **877/258-6877** or 907/265-4500. Fax 907/263-5559. www.talkeetnalodge.com. 98 units. TV TEL. Summer $179 double; winter $79 double. AE, MC, V.

Built of big timbers and river rock, this grand hotel was opened in 1999 by Cook Inlet Region, a Native corporation. Off the Talkeetna Spur Highway, it stands just 2 miles from the town but feels like it's out in the wilderness. The view from on top of a high river bluff is a broad-canvas masterpiece of the Alaska Range, with McKinley towering in the center. Rooms are thoughtfully crafted with regional birch trim and understated stylish touches. Those in the main building are somewhat larger and have queen-sized beds. There's a good restaurant, sharing the stupendous view, and a small bar. Unlike other large hotels in the area, they are open year round and employ mainly local people.

15

DEVILS TOWER NATIONAL MONUMENT

by Jack Olson

RISING 1,270 FEET ABOVE THE FOREST FLOOR AND THE VALLEY OF the Belle Fourche River, the stone stump of Devils Tower greets visitors miles before they arrive at the nation's first national monument. Established in 1906 by Pres. Theodore Roosevelt in the first use of the new Antiquities Act, Devils Tower may rest off the beaten path in extreme northeast Wyoming, but it's well worth an excursion. It is probably best remembered as the site of an alien spaceship landing in the 1977 film *Close Encounters of the Third Kind*.

Col. Richard I. Dodge, who commanded a military escort to a U.S. Geological Survey party that visited the Black Hills in 1875, is credited with giving the formation its name. In his book *The Black Hills*, written the year after his journey, Dodge described Devils Tower as "one of the most remarkable peaks in this or any other country."

The steep-sided mass of igneous rock rises abruptly from the grasslands and pine forests, and remains one of the Black Hills most conspicuous geologic features. Devils Tower National Monument covers an area of about 2 square miles (1,347 acres).

Geology. While the 60 million-year-old tower itself is composed of hard igneous rock, much of the remaining exposed rock within the monument boundaries is composed of soft sediments from the warm shallow seas of the Mesozoic era. These colorful bands of rock encircling the igneous core include layers of sandstone, shale, mudstone, siltstone, gypsum, and limestone.

The story of Devils Tower's geology is but one chapter in the geologic history of the Black Hills. Unfortunately, even after extensive studies and detailed geologic mapping, the definitive chapter explaining the origins of Devils Tower has yet to be written.

There are several theories that attempt to explain the formation of Devils Tower. The most popular suggests that the tower is the result of volcanic activity in the early Tertiary period some 60 million years ago. Scientists believe that a mass of molten rock forced its way upward through miles of rock, forming an inverted, cone-shaped structure under layers of sedimentary rock that form what is now northeastern Wyoming. As the molten rock slowly cooled, it cracked and fractured, creating one of the most striking features of

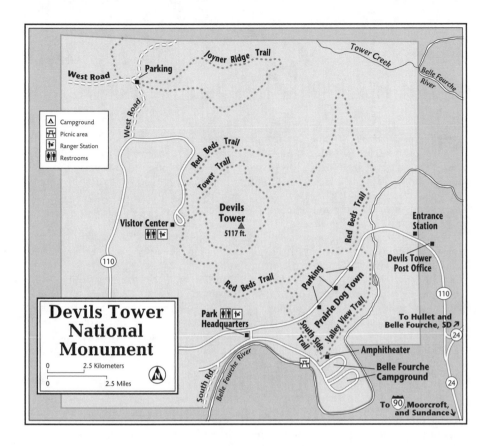

Devils Tower National Monument

0 — 2.5 Kilometers
0 — 2.5 Miles

Legend:
- Campground
- Picnic area
- Ranger Station
- Restrooms

the monument, its polygonal columns. Most of the columns are five-sided, but some are four- and six-sided. The largest columns measure 6 feet to 8 feet in diameter at their base and taper gradually upward to about 4 feet in diameter at the summit.

Over centuries, the gentle waters of the Belle Fourche River carried away sedimentary layers, leaving the more erosion-resistant igneous rock behind. Today the tower appears to sit quietly on the crest of a wooded hill. But the tower base is actually the top of the unexposed magma, which is covered with fallen columns and soil.

Indian Legend. American Indians have their own name for Devils Tower. They call it *Mato Tipila,* or Grizzly Bear Lodge. Descendants of several of the Indian nations of the Great Plains share similar legends of how the prominent butte was formed.

According to one version of the legend, seven sisters watch with horror as their brother is turned into a bear. The sisters run from him, to the stump of a large tree, which beckons them to climb on. (In other versions, they run to a large, flat stone.) When they do, the stump rises up into the sky, and the bear, unable to climb up the stump to reach the sisters, scores it with its claws. The sisters are then raised into the sky, becoming the seven stars of the Big Dipper.

What inspired the imagination of American Indians more than 100 years ago also attracts their reverence. In deference to the religious significance of the tower to many tribes, the National Park Service has requested that climbing of the tower be voluntarily suspended during June so that ceremonies may be conducted without interference.

First Ascent. As a battle to preserve the monument from commercial

Tips from the Park Superintendent

Former Devils Tower National Monument superintendent Deb Liggett has seen much of what the National Park Service has to offer. After a stint at Everglades National Park, she moved to the superintendent's post in northeastern Wyoming. Then in late 1997, the career Park Service employee transferred to Alaska. She says her $3\frac{1}{2}$ years at Devils Tower will always stay with her: "I have a friend who says that Devils Tower is like a piece of sculpture—perfect in every light and from every angle. I think that's really true. The tower can be quite dramatic."

In 1998, 403,000 travelers visited this national monument—almost as many people as live in the state of Wyoming. Liggett says visitors, particularly photo buffs, prefer the light in early morning or at dusk. With the surrounding forest and decreased crowds, she notes that fall can be a perfect time to visit. Whenever you choose to stop at Devils Tower, she says you'll probably be pleased.

"The tower often creates its own shadows and its own weather, with terrific thunder and lightning storms in the summer," she says. "People often come to Devils Tower as a lark—as a quick trip between Rushmore and Yellowstone. I think they have a classic park experience. They are definitely pleasantly surprised by their discovery."

encroachment was being waged in 1893, two local ranchers decided it was time someone made the first recorded climb to its summit.

William Rogers and Willard Ripley planned for months before making their first attempt on the southeast face on July 4, 1893. As the date approached, the pair began distributing handbills offering such amenities as ample food and drink, daily and nightly dancing, and plenty of grain for horses. The flyers also touted the feat as the "rarest sight of a lifetime."

Rogers and Ripley used a wooden stake ladder for the first 350 feet of the climb. As more than 1,000 spectators watched, the pair made the harrowing climb in about an hour, raised Old Glory, then sold pieces of it as mementos of the occasion. Thereafter, the tower became a popular place for Independence Day family gatherings. At the annual affair in 1895, Mrs. Rogers used her husband's ladder to become the first woman to reach the summit.

On Top of the Tower. From its base, most visitors would surmise that the top of

Devils Tower is a flat, barren pinnacle. As more than 5,000 climbers who made it to the peak in 1997 will attest, the top of the tower isn't that much different than the countryside that surrounds it—except, perhaps, that five states can be seen.

The summit is actually slightly domed with a few small outcroppings and covered with prairie grasses, prickly pear cactus, currant and gooseberry bushes, and native big sage, thanks to prairie falcons and turkey vultures that nest in the tower's columns and deposit seeds on top. A number of animals also have been spotted on the crown of Devils Tower, including rattlesnakes, pack rats, and red squirrels that have slithe red and scampered up the cracks and fissures.

At the top, climbers may sign a register and record any unusual aspect or oddity of their adventure. More than 28,000 signatures have been gathered since records of tower climbs were first kept in 1937. In that time, climbers have used more than 220 routes to the top; in 1941 world-record holding parachutist George Hopkins jumped from an airplane to the cap of the tower, then lost his escape rope and was stranded on top for 6 days.

Avoiding the Crowds. Traffic patterns at the monument are similar to those of national park areas throughout the West. Expect the highest visitation from June through August, with lower visitation in the shoulder months of April to May and September to October; the lowest visitation is during winter. Parking is limited in summer.

If you visit during the summer, stop at the tower early in the day, or take in a fireside ranger talk when crowds have thinned in the evening. Be advised that during the second week in August a motorcycle rally takes place in nearby Sturgis, South Dakota. Attendance may significantly increase during that period.

Just the Facts

GETTING THERE & GATEWAYS

Because of its remote location, Devils Tower is best accessed by private vehicle. The monument entrance is 33 miles northeast of Moorcroft, Wyoming, and 27 miles northwest of Sundance, Wyoming, via U.S. 14 (you travel to the immediate area on I-90). Scheduled airlines service Gillette, Wyoming (regional commuter service), and Rapid City, South Dakota, where cars may be rented. For information on the Rapid City airport and rental car options, see chapter 3.

INFORMATION

Contact **Devils Tower National Monument,** P.O. Box 10, Devils Tower, WY 82714 (☎ 307/467-5283; www.nps. gov/deto). The **Devils Tower Natural History Association,** P.O. Box 37, Devils Tower, WY 97214-0037, operates a bookstore at the monument's Visitor Center and offers a variety of publications, including *Devils Tower National Monument: A Climber's Guide,* by Steven Gardiner and Dick Guilmette (Seattle: The Mountaineers, 1986).

VISITOR CENTER

Open April through October only, the Visitor Center is located 3 miles from the monument's entrance, with exhibits about the tower's history and geology.

FEES

There is an entrance fee of $8 per vehicle or $3 per person on foot or bike. Camping costs $12 per night.

SPECIAL REGULATIONS & WARNINGS

Do not feed, chase, or disturb prairie dogs; they bite and may carry diseases. Abandoned prairie dog holes are often homes to black widow spiders and rattlesnakes. Disturbing any wildlife or gathering items such as rocks or flowers is prohibited. Also see "Climbing the Tower," below.

SEASONS & CLIMATE

The monument is open year-round. The climate and seasons at Devils Tower echo those in the Black Hills region. Summer

---

"A dark mist lay over the Black Hills, and the land was like iron. At the top of the ridge I caught sight of Devils Tower upthrust against the gray sky as if in the birth of time the core of the earth had broken through its crust and the motion of the world was begun. There are things in nature that engender an awful quiet in the heart of man; Devils Tower is one of them."

—N. Scott Momaday, Pulitzer Prize-winning author of *House Made of Dawn* days can be hot and dry; evenings and early mornings damp and cool. Spring weather is often chilly and wet, while fall storms are common. Winters are usually cold, but snow and sunlight can combine to create incredible pictures of the land-mark.

If You Only Have 1 Day

It's easy to experience all that Devils Tower has to offer in less than a day. Rangers recommend that you allow 2 to 4 hours to walk a trail, stop at the visitor center, and view the prairie dogs.

Surrounded by ponderosa pines and bathed in blue sky, the towering rock obelisk is visible for miles, and it's easy to imagine the reaction of the first lonely Indian scouts and French fur trappers who stumbled upon this stunning geo-logic anomaly a few centuries ago.

Home to the feisty black-tailed **prairie dog,** the grounds of Devils Tower Nation-al Monument are perfect for picnicking and viewing wildlife. You can watch the sociable prairie dogs in their colony, or "town," just inside the park's east entrance station. The critters excavate elaborate networks of underground pas-sageways, then guard their burrows with warning "barks" when predators such as hawks, eagles, bullsnakes, coyote, red fox, and mink come too close. Walk the leisurely **Valley View Trail,** or savor a pic-nic lunch among the wildflowers at the monument's picnic area on the banks of the sleepy Belle Fourche River.

Climbing the Tower

Climbers must register with a ranger before starting their climb and on their return, otherwise there are no permits or requirements for climbing the tower. Be prepared for sudden storms; carry rain gear and a flashlight. Rockfall is common, so climbing helmets are advised. Ask a ranger for additional safe-ty and climbing information. A volun-tary climbing ban is observed each June out of respect for American Indian beliefs.

Organized Tours & Ranger Programs

A variety of activities are scheduled, most-ly in summer. Check at the Visitor Center for locations and times.

Interpretive Talks. Meet a park ranger in front of the Visitor Center for bear tales and interpretive talks about the region's geology and Tower trivia. Pro-grams last about 15 minutes and are wheelchair accessible.

Tower Walk. Meet a park ranger in front of the Visitor Center and enjoy a lively walk as the sun rises above the tower. Good walking shoes and water are rec-ommended. These guided walks last about an hour and end on the Tower Trail (see "Day Hikes," below).

Climbing Demonstrations. Join a park ranger at the climbing kiosk, located in the middle of the Visitor Center parking lot, for a climbing demonstration and to learn about technical rock climbing dur-ing a 30-minute program.

Evening Programs. Learn more about America's first national monument by the glow of a campfire. Join a park ranger in the monument's amphitheater each evening from Memorial Day through Labor Day. During inclement weather, programs may be moved to the picnic shelter.

Cultural Program Series. During the summer, Devils Tower plays host to cul-tural demonstrators who bring their expertise to the monument, including American Indian storytellers, musicians, historians, impersonators, photogra-phers, poets, and astronomers.

Day Hikes

Devils Tower will announce itself (through your windshield) miles before you arrive. In fact, you may drive to with-in a few hundred yards of the tower. But the real highlight of any visit to Devils Tower is the park's trails; get out and enjoy them. Pets are not allowed on trails.

The paved 1.3-mile **Tower Trail,** rated easy, goes all the way around the tower, offering close-up views of the tower on fairly level ground. Wayside exhibits tell the Devils Tower story.

There are several other trails: **Red Beds Trail,** 3 miles; **Southside Trail,** 0.6 mile; **Joyner Ridge Trail,** 1.5 miles; **Valley View Trail,** 0.6 mile (combine Southside and Valley View for 1.2 mi.). Since none of the trails get very crowded, these are a good way to examine the terrain around the monument, including the pine forest and the prairie dog town, and avoid some of the summer crowds.

Camping

Located a mile from the monument's headquarters, **Belle Fourche Campground** is open from April through October. Its 55 sites accommodate RVs and tents on a first-come, first-served basis. Each campsite has a cooking grill, table, and nearby drinking water. There are no showers, RV hookups, or dump station. Sites costs $12 per night, and there are three group sites, which cost $3 per person per night, for up to 20 persons each. Rest rooms are accessible for persons with disabilities. The adjacent Valley View Trail skirts a giant prairie dog town, and the campground's amphitheater offers excellent interpretive ranger programs.

Those looking for a commercial campground with RV hookups, hot showers, and all the usual amenities, will find the **Devils Tower KOA,** P.O. Box 100, Devils Tower, WY 82714 (☎ 800/KOA-5785 or 307/467-5395; e-mail: dtkoa@trib.com), just outside the monument entrance. Open from mid-May to late September, it offers 45 campsites and 5 cabins. Rates for two adults are $21 to $24 in hookup sites, $18 for tents, and $35 for cabins (major credit cards accepted). Amenities include a heated swimming pool, self-service laundry, game room, cafe, gift shop, hayrides, and a nightly showing of *Close Encounters of the Third Kind,* filmed at Devils Tower.

Accommodations & Dining

There are no accommodations or dining within the monument boundaries; however, there are options in the surrounding communities of Sundance and Hulett.

NEAR THE PARK

Recommended in Sundance is the **Bear Lodge Motel,** 218 Cleveland St., on Wyo. 14 at Business Loop I-90 (P.O. Box 912), Sundance, WY 82729 (☎ 800/341-8000 or 307/283-1611); fax 307/283-2537; www.sundancewyoming.com; e-mail: bearlodge@vcn.com). A double room costs around $60 per night during the summer and fall, less during the winter and spring; major credit cards (AE, DISC, MC, V) are accepted. A 32-ton native stone fireplace greets guests in the Western-style lobby, where you can have free coffee. Its location in the center of town, across the street from two restaurants and the community's museum, is convenient.

There are two moderately priced restaurants, open year-round, across the street from the Bear Lodge Motel: **Aro Restaurant** (☎ 307/283-2000) serves three meals daily, while **Higbee's Café** (☎ 307/283-2165) serves breakfast and lunch Monday through Friday plus dinner on Wednesdays. There's also a grocery store nearby.

In Hulett, try the **Motel Pioneer,** 3 blocks north of downtown on Wyo. 24 (P.O. Box 389), Hulett, WY 82720 (☎ 800/231-6335 or 307/467-5656; fax 307/467-5650). Several units have kitchenettes or refrigerators. Rates for two are $49 from May through November and $39 from December through April; major credit cards (AE, DISC, MC, V) are accepted. Rooms are clean and well maintained, and there are two large family units. Public tennis courts are next door, and there's a golf course across the highway. It's 9 miles to the national monument entrance from here. There's a grocery store about 3 blocks from the motel.

16

GLACIER NATIONAL PARK & WATERTON LAKES NATIONAL PARK

by Jack Olson

NAMED TO DESCRIBE THE 30 TO 40 SLOW-MOVING GLACIERS THAT carved awe-inspiring valleys throughout this expanse of nearly 1 million acres, Glacier National Park exists because of the efforts of George Bird Grinnell, a 19th-century magazine publisher and cofounder of the Audubon Society. Following a pattern established with Yellowstone and Grand Teton, Grinnell lobbied for a national park to be set aside in the St. Mary region of Montana, and in May 1910 his efforts were rewarded. Just over 20 years later, it became, with its northern neighbor Waterton Lakes National Park in Canada, Glacier-Waterton International Peace Park—a gesture of goodwill and friendship between the governments of two countries.

Majestic and wild, this vast preserve overwhelms visitors, beckoning with stunning mountain peaks (many covered year-round with glaciers), verdant mountain trails that cry out for hikers, and the sheer diversity of its plant and animal life. Every spring, Glacier is a postcard come to life: Wildflowers carpet its meadows; bears emerge from months of hibernation; and moose, elk, and deer again play out the drama of birth, life, and death. The unofficial mascot in these parts is the grizzly, a refugee from the high plains.

Here you'll see that nature is at work as well: The glaciers are receding (the result of global warming, some say) and avalanches have periodically ravaged Going-to-the-Sun Road, the curving, scenic 50-mile road that bisects the park. For the time being, the park is intact and very much alive, a treasure in a vault that opens to visitors.

If your time is limited, simply motor across Going-to-the-Sun Road, viewing the dramatic mountain scenery. Visitors with more time will find diversions for both families and hard-core adventurers; while some hiking trails are suitable for tykes, many more will challenge those determined to conquer and scale the park's tallest peaks. Glacier's lakes, streams, ponds, and waterfalls are equally engaging. Travelers board cruise boats to explore the history of the area; recreational types can fish, row, and kayak.

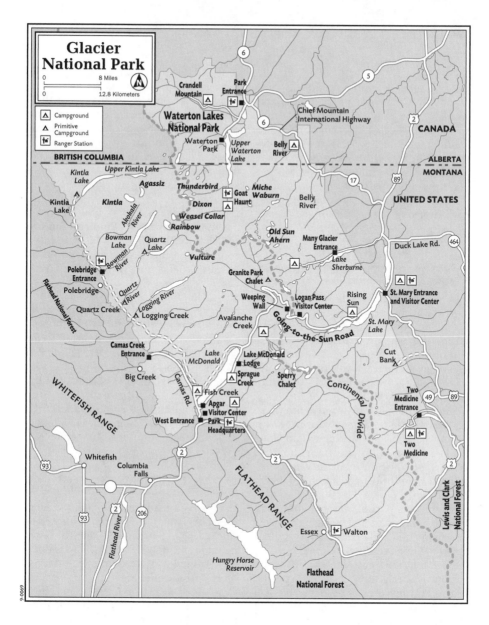

Glacier National Park

0 — 8 Miles
0 — 12.8 Kilometers

△ Campground
▲ Primitive Campground
🚹 Ranger Station

BRITISH COLUMBIA

Crandell Mountain

Park Entrance

Waterton Lakes National Park

Chief Mountain International Highway

CANADA

Waterton Park

Upper Waterton Lake

Belly River

ALBERTA
MONTANA

Kintla Lake

Upper Kintla Lake

Agassiz

Thunderbird

Goat Haunt

Miche Waburn

Belly River

UNITED STATES

Kintla Lake

Kintla

Akokala River

Dixon

Weasel Collar

Rainbow

Old Sun Ahern

Many Glacier Entrance

Duck Lake Rd.

464

Bowman Lake

Quartz Lake

Bowman River

Vulture

Lake Sherburne

Polebridge Entrance

Polebridge

Quartz River

Logging River

Granite Park Chalet

Weeping Wall

Logan Pass Visitor Center

Rising Sun

St. Mary Entrance and Visitor Center

Flathead National Forest

Quartz Creek

Logging Creek

Avalanche Creek

Going-to-the-Sun Road

St. Mary Lake

Camas Creek Entrance

Lake McDonald

Lake McDonald Lodge

Sperry Chalet

Continental Divide

Cut Bank

Big Creek

Camas Rd.

Sprague Creek

Two Medicine Entrance

49

89

WHITEFISH RANGE

Fish Creek

Apgar Visitor Center

West Entrance

Park Headquarters

Two Medicine

Whitefish

93

Columbia Falls

2

FLATHEAD RANGE

2

Lewis and Clark National Forest

93

2

206

Flathead River

Essex

Walton

2

Hungry Horse Reservoir

Flathead National Forest

9-0069

However, to truly experience Glacier requires slightly more effort, interest, and spunk than a drive through, but abandon the pavement for even the easiest and shortest hiking trail, and you'll find a window into Glacier's soul.

Avoiding the Crowds. The simplest way to do this is to travel in the off-season, before mid-June, when the park begins to fill, and after Labor Day, when families traveling with youngsters have returned

home. (August is the busiest month.) Late September and October, when the fall colors highlight the park, are excellent months to visit. A highlight is the display put on by the larch trees throughout the western portions of the park. Entire hillsides turn a bright yellow, fading to a dull orange glow as the month of October wanes.

If visiting in the off-season isn't possible, consider the following: Since most people congregate in close proximity to the major hotels, find a trailhead that is equidistant from two major points and head for the woods. If you must drive, to make the trip more enjoyable (and traffic-free), journey across the Going-to-the-Sun Road before 8:30am; you'll be astounded at the masterful job Mother Nature does of painting her mountains. You can always see more wildlife in the early morning (or just before dark).

Just the Facts

GETTING THERE & GATEWAYS

Glacier National Park is located in the northwest corner of Montana, on the Canadian border. The closest cities with airline service are **Kalispell,** 29 miles southwest of the park, and **Great Falls,** 143 miles southeast. If you're driving, the easiest ways to reach the park are from **U.S. 2** and **U.S. 89.**

Among the park's entrances are those at West Glacier; Camas Road; St. Mary; Many Glacier; Two Medicine; and Polebridge. Access is primarily at either end of Going-to-the-Sun Road: at West Glacier on the southwest side and St. Mary on the east.

From the park's western boundary, you may enter at Polebridge to access Bowman and Kintla Lakes or take Camas Road to Going-to-the-Sun Road.

The following east-side entrances are primarily designed to access specific places and may not necessarily take you into the heart of the park: Essex, East Glacier, Two Medicine, Cut Bank, and Many Glacier.

Visitor entrance passes are sold at the West Glacier, Two Medicine, Many Glacier, Polebridge, and St. Mary Park entrances. Entrance is severely restricted during winter months when most of Going-to-the-Sun Road is closed. (See "Seasons & Climate," below.)

The Nearest Airports. Glacier Park International Airport, north of Kalispell at 4170 U.S. 2 (☎ 406/257-5994), is serviced by **Northwest, Delta,** and **Horizon;**

these airlines also serve **Great Falls International Airport** (☎ 406/727-3404). **Avis, Budget, Hertz,** and **National** have counters at Kalispell's airport; **Hertz, Avis,** and **National** have counters at Great Falls International Airport. Toll-free reservations numbers for airlines and car-rental companies are given in the appendix.

By Rail. Amtrak's **Empire Builder** (☎ 800/872-7245), a Chicago-Seattle round-trip route, makes stops seasonally at East Glacier and year-round at West Glacier and Essex.

INFORMATION

Contact the **Superintendent, Glacier National Park,** West Glacier, MT 59936 (☎ 406/888-7800; fax 406/888-7808; www.nps.gov/glac). A vast array of publications can be obtained from the **Glacier Natural History Association,** P.O. Box 428, West Glacier, MT 59936 (☎ 406/888-5756; fax 406/888-5271; www.nps.gov/glac/gnha.htm).

VISITOR CENTERS

For up-to-date information on park activities, check in at visitor centers located at Apgar, Logan Pass, and St. Mary; a center manned by info-givers from Travel Alberta is located at **West Glacier. St. Mary** is open from mid-May through mid-October; **Logan Pass,** from mid-June through mid-October; and **Apgar,** from late April through October (and weekends during the winter). Park information may also be obtained from the **Two Medicine, Polebridge,** and **Many Glacier Ranger Station** or park headquarters.

ESSENTIAL SERVICES

East Glacier. The **Glacier Park Trading Company** (☎ 406/226-4433), on U.S. 2, has a limited supply of fresh and canned goods. There's a shop in the back where you can purchase freshly made deli sandwiches. Also in East Glacier is a gas station, post office, several gift shops, a small market with a limited supply of fresh meats and produce as well as beer and wine, and a modest supply of fishing and camping accessories.

West Glacier. A gas station, general store, Laundromat, photo shop, rafting companies, post office, and gift shop are located in this compound, as is the **West Glacier Bar,** a dimly lit four-seater that doubles as a retail liquor store. The **West Glacier Restaurant** serves ho-hum food from 7am to 10pm.

St. Mary. The **St. Mary Supermart** (☎ 406/732-4431) will never be confused with a metropolitan area supermarket, but it's the closest thing you will find in any of the park gateway cities except Kalispell, which is 80 miles due west. Fresh produce, canned goods, and beverages, including beer and wine, will be found here, but you can expect to pay tourist-town prices. There's also a post office.

FEES

A vehicle pass good for 7 days costs $10. An individual pass for walk-ins and bike riders, also good for 7 days, is available for $5. A separate entrance fee is charged for visitors to Waterton Lakes National Park.

Camping fees are $10 to $15 per night at the regular park campgrounds.

SPECIAL REGULATIONS & WARNINGS

Biking. Bikes are restricted to established roads, bike routes, or parking areas, and are not allowed on trails. Restrictions apply to the most hazardous portions of Going-to-the-Sun Road during peak travel times from around mid-June to Labor Day; call ahead to find out when the road will be closed to bikers. During low-visibility periods of fog or darkness, a white front light and a back red reflector are required.

Boating. While boating is permitted on some of Glacier's lakes, motor size is restricted to 10 horsepower on most. A detailed list of other regulations is available at park headquarters and staffed ranger stations. Park rangers may inspect or board any boat to determine regulation compliance.

Camping. Camping is permitted only at designated locations, even in the back-country, and is strictly prohibited on the roadside.

Fishing. A fishing license is not required within the park's boundaries; however, there are guidelines, so check with rangers at visitor centers or ranger stations for regulations. Also, keep in mind since the eastern boundary of the park abuts the Blackfeet Indian Reservation, you may find yourself fishing in their territorial waters. To avoid a problem, purchase a $10 use permit from businesses in the gateway towns; the permit covers fishing, hiking, and biking in the reservation. Fishing outside the park in Montana waters requires a state license; check in at a local fishing shop to make certain you're within the laws.

Horses. While visitors may bring their own horses and pack animals into the park, restrictions apply to private stock. A free brochure detailing regulations regarding horseback riding is available from the Park Service.

Vehicles. RVs and other vehicles longer than 21 feet or wider than 8 feet are prohibited on the 24-mile stretch of Going-to-the-Sun Road between Avalanche Campground and Sun Point on St. Mary Lake. Snowmobiling is prohibited in the park.

SEASONS & CLIMATE

Glacier is magnificent at any time of the year, but some roads are closed and park access is limited in the winter. By far the most popular time to visit is during the

Picnicking Tips

The best picnicking spot on the Going-to-the-Sun Road is at **Sun Point,** which is also the trailhead for the 1.6-mile round-trip to Baring Falls, a trail that follows the shoreline of the lake. From the picnic area the views across the lake to the mountains are unrivaled. Even better: Be there at sunrise.

summer, when Going-to-the-Sun Road is fully open; during summer months sunrise is around 5am, and sunset at nearly 10pm, so there's plenty of time for exploring. The shoulder seasons of spring and fall are equally magnificent with budding wildflowers and variegated leaves and trees, but these sights can only be viewed from the park's outer boundaries and a limited stretch of the scenic highway.

In winter, Glacier shuts itself off from much of the motorized world. The Going-to-the-Sun Road is usually plowed from West Glacier to the head of Lake McDonald. U.S. 89 provides access to the St. Mary area. The North Fork Road from Columbia Falls is open for winter travel to the North Fork area and the Polebridge Ranger Station. Temperatures sometimes plummet to −30°F, so appropriate dress for those conditions is essential.

If You Only Have 1 Day

If you have a limited amount of time to spend in Glacier, the best way to experience the park's full beauty is to drive **Going-to-the-Sun Road,** the 50-mile road that bisects the park between West Glacier and St. Mary. Points of interest are clearly marked and correspond to the park brochure *Points of Interest Along the Going to the Sun Road,* available at visitor centers.

Remember that the road gains more than 3,400 feet in 32 miles, and is very narrow in places. Visitors with a fear of heights might consider a guided coach tour (see "Organized Tours & Ranger Programs," below).

Just a short drive from West Glacier is **Lake McDonald,** the largest body of water in the park; numerous turnouts along the way present opportunities to photograph the panoramic views of the lake with its mountainous backdrop. **Sacred Dancing Cascade** and **Johns Lake** are visible by taking an easy 0.5-mile hike from the roadside through a red cedar/hemlock forest. You'll often see moose and waterfowl. The **Trail of the Cedars** is a short, wheelchair-accessible boardwalk trail thickly carpeted in vibrant, verdant hues. All hiking trails mentioned below are described in the "Day Hikes" section.

Almost exactly halfway along Going-to-the-Sun is the **Loop,** an excellent vantage point for views of **Heaven's Peak.** Just 2 miles farther is the **Bird Woman Falls Overlook,** an outlook for falls located across the valley. **The Weeping Wall,** a wall of rock that does, in fact, weep groundwater profusely in the summer, is a popular subject for photographers.

At the 32-mile mark from West Glacier is **Logan Pass,** one of the park's most highly trafficked areas and the starting point for the hike to **Hidden Lake,** one of the park's most popular. There's a visitor center here, atop the Continental Divide.

As you head downhill, you'll reach the turnout for **Jackson Glacier,** the most easily recognizable glacier in the entire park; followed by **Sunrift Gorge** and **Sun Point,** which are accessible via two short trails that present opportunities to view wildlife.

Exploring the Park by Car

Because of the massive mountains that surround visitors to Glacier National Park, it is impossible to drive through the park without drawing comparisons to

Grand Teton. Perhaps the most significant difference is that here one drives among the mountain peaks; at Teton the mountains are viewed from a distance, unless you're willing to head for the hiking trails.

Going-to-the-Sun Road is by far the most driver-friendly avenue in which to enjoy the park and see some of the more spectacular views. Consult the previous section, "If You Only Have 1 Day," for an idea of what you'll see along this road.

You can easily **circumnavigate the lower half of the park** in 1 long day, without traveling at warp speed. Along the way, you'll experience Glacier's splendor and get a bird's-eye view of Big Sky country in the process. After a leisurely breakfast in West Glacier, you'll be in East Glacier in plenty of time for lunch at the Glacier Park Lodge (see "Accommodations," below) and at St. Mary or Many Glacier for dinner. To complete a counterclockwise loop from West Glacier, take U.S. 2 along the park's southern boundary to Essex and East Glacier, then north to St. Mary.

The **road between West Glacier and East Glacier,** which is approximately 57 miles, is a well-paved, two-lane affair that winds circuitously around the western and southern edges of the park and follows the Middle Fork of the Flathead River. In the summertime, the fluorescent orange blobs you'll see on the river below are inner tubes and white-water rafts filled with the hordes who travel the river every summer. As you descend to the valley floor, you'll drive through beautiful, privately owned Montana ranch- and farmland. Shortly after entering the valley, look to the north and admire the park's massive peaks—spires as beautiful as any on the planet. The Goat Lick parking lot, on U.S. 2 just east of Essex, gets you off the beaten path and provides a view into a canyon carved by the Flathead River; if you have time, take the short hike down to the stream.

Beyond East Glacier, as you head northwest on Mont. 49 and west toward Two Medicine, you'll notice that the earth appears to fall off. The contrast is inescapable—mountains tower in the west, but to the east the Hi-Line begins, sporting a horizon that extends so far and so flat as to seemingly lend credence and legitimacy to the Flat Earth Society. But round a corner on the Two Medicine Road and suddenly you'll find yourself faced with three mountains (Appistocki Peak, Mount Henry, and Bison Mountain) bare of vegetation but as red as their Southwest counterparts. The difference here is that the crevasses are filled with snow, even in mid-August. Ten miles later, continuing the route northward on U.S. 89, you'll come across a wide panorama of mountain peaks, valleys, ridges, and forested mountains that truly characterize Glacier's personality. Conclude the bottom half of your long loop by winding downward from these high elevations to the village of St. Mary. Not a bad day's drive!

There are two ways to see the park's western boundary and to access the Polebridge area, in the north; one is slow and uncomfortable, the other slightly faster and less uncomfortable. The **North Fork Road** (Mont. 486) from Columbia Falls takes about an hour to negotiate. It's a sometimes-paved (mostly gravel and pothole-filled) stretch that follows the North Fork of the Flathead River; spectacular views ameliorate the condition of the drive. Not much is there besides water and scenery, but the area around Polebridge is a popular spot for the outdoor crowd—an excellent location to experience Montana's natural beauty without modern-day distractions like telephones and TVs.

The **Inside North Fork Road,** just north of Apgar, also runs to Polebridge. However, it's totally unpaved, takes an hour longer, and is much harder on driver, passenger, and equipment. Unless you are a glutton for punishment, take the faster route and spend that extra hour relaxing on a riverbank.

Photo Tips

The adventurous shutterbug will find that the best photo ops occur early in the morning, regardless of location. Near bodies of water, the sunrise provides an unrivaled multitude of oranges, blues, and yellows. Then, as the earth warms, lakes are transformed to fog-covered valleys, creating a mystical photographic opportunity.

One of the most picturesque spots is the west end of St. Mary Lake; not only does it paint the lake orange and yellow, it paints the mountains red and orange. A close runner-up is the view west from an overlook across St. Mary Lake to Wild Goose Island in the foreground and the peaks and glaciers at the west end of the lake.

Organized Tours & Ranger Programs

Ranger-guided activities and evening campfire and slide-show programs are offered daily throughout the park. The park's *Nature with a Naturalist* publication—free upon entering the park and also available at visitor centers—is a thorough source for days, times, and locations of various educational programs. Local tribal members provide programs highlighting **American Indian culture and history.** Most programs are free, although those including boat trips may include a minimal charge.

Narrated **boat tours** from Lake McDonald, St. Mary, Two Medicine, and Many Glacier are offered daily from mid-June to mid-September by Glacier Park Boat Co. These "scenicruises" combine the comfort of an hour-long lake cruise with a short hike or picnic to create an unforgettable Glacier experience.

Spectacular views of Lake McDonald sunsets, the awe-inspiring Grinnell Glacier, and the panoramic rugged cliffs ringing St. Mary Lake are just a few of the possible photo opportunities you may have while enjoying a cruise. The boats typically depart every other hour, usually five times each day, although schedules are subject to change in late season or if the weather is inclement. For a complete listing of departure times and dates, contact **Glacier Park Boat Co.,** P.O. Box 5262, Kalispell, MT 59903 (☎ 406/257-2426). Listed below are seasonal phone numbers for cruises at the following locations: **Lake McDonald** (☎ 406/888-5727), **Many Glacier and Two Medicine** (☎ 406/732-4480), and **St. Mary** (☎ 406/732-4430).

Unique **coach tours** are given aboard a scarlet 1936 "Jammer" coach—so-named because of its standard transmission—along Going-to-the-Sun Road and north to Waterton. These coaches, with their roll-back tops, are an ideal means of transportation along this scenic route: their drivers provide insightful commentary about the park and its history and you don't have to worry about how close you may be to the edge of the often-precipitous road! For schedules contact **VIAD Corp. Center,** Phoenix, AZ 85077-0928 (☎ 602/207-6000).

Van tours of the Going-to-the-Sun Road conducted by American Indian guides originate from East Glacier, Browning, and St. Mary. Contact **Sun Tours** (☎ 800/786-9220 or 406/226-9220).

Scenic **helicopter tours** of Glacier are offered by **Eagle Aviation** (☎ 406/755-2612), **Glacier Heli Tours** (☎ 800/879-9310), and **Kruger Helicopters** (☎ 406/387-4565). Prices range from $60 to $90 for 1- to 2-hour tours, depending on your destination. All are located within 2 miles of West Glacier off U.S. 2.

The **Glacier Institute** conducts field classes each summer that examine Glacier's cultural and natural resources.

These 1- to 8-day courses are open to anyone and include instruction, transportation, park fees, and college credit. Instructors are highly skilled in their area of expertise, bringing to each course an intimate knowledge of the region and subject matter. The classroom is Glacier National Park and the Flathead National Forest. Previous courses have covered alpine wildflowers, Glacier's grizzlies, weather systems, and nature photography. Contact the institute for a copy of their current catalog at 137 Main St., P.O. Box 7457, Kalispell, MT 59904 (☎ **406/755-1211;** www.digisys.net/glacinst; e-mail: glacinst@digisys.net). Prices range from $35 to $650 per session.

Finally, **Glacier Wilderness Guides,** P.O. Box 330, West Glacier, MT 59936 (☎ **800/521-7238** for reservations, or 406/387-5555; fax 406/387-5656; www.glacierguides.com; e-mail: glguides@cyberport.net), organizes backpacking trips into the Glacier National Park backcountry. They have been the exclusive backpacking guide service in the park since 1983. See "Exploring the Backcountry," below.

Day Hikes

With more than 700 miles of maintained trails, the park is best explored by hiking. Clearly, the joy is in getting from point A to point B, since accommodations are pretty sparse once you arrive. As most of these trails are rather short, you might also wish to look in "Exploring the Backcountry," below. Many of the longer trails described there can be done fully (or at least partially) in a day, and are likely to take you farther off the beaten path and away from the crowds.

Trail maps are available at outdoor stores in Whitefish and Kalispell as well as at visitor centers and the major ranger stations at each entry point. Before striking off into the wilderness, however, check with the nearest visitor center or ranger station to determine the accessibility of your destination, trail conditions, and recent bear sightings. This may save you a lot of headache (even in the summer months) if you're planning a high-country hike and 10 miles into the trip a ranger turns you back.

The Park Service asks you to stay on trails to keep from eroding the fragile components of the park. Also, snowbanks shouldn't be traversed, especially the steeper ones. You should have proper footwear and rain gear, enough food, and, most important, enough water, before approaching any trailhead. A can of **pepper spray** can also come in handy when you're in grizzly habitat. Note: If you're planning on hiking in Canada, be sure to purchase the pepper spray that can be transported across the border; there is a difference. Contact **Canadian Customs** (☎ **800/320-0063**) for regulations. See "Exploring the Backcountry," below, for further relevant information.

LAKE MCDONALD AREA

Trail of the Cedars Nature Trail

0.25 mi. RT. Easy. Access: Across from the Avalanche Campground Ranger Station.

This level trail, consisting of a wheelchair-accessible boardwalk, offers a respite from the crowds in a forested area. There are interpretive signs along the way.

> Give a month to this precious reserve. The time will not be taken from the sum of your life. Instead of shortening, it will indefinitely lengthen it and make you truly immortal.
>
> —John Muir, naturalist and conservationist

Trout Lake

8.4 mi. RT. Moderate. Access: North end of Lake McDonald, 1.5 mi. west on Lake McDonald Rd.

This is a good workout if you're moping around Lake McDonald Lodge sipping coffee and skipping rocks off the lake. This hike is straight up and straight down. The trail to the foot of Trout Lake and back is a little more than 8 miles and begins from the north end of Lake McDonald.

LOGAN PASS AREA

Hidden Lake Nature Trail

1.5 mi. one way. Easy to moderate. Access: Logan Pass Visitor Center.

This trail climbs 460 feet and requires more spunk than others in the area, yet it's still not too hard. It's a popular trail, but if you hike all the way to the lake, you'll be able to avoid some of the crowds. This is an interpretive nature trail, with several signs along the way that point out what you are seeing.

The Loop

7 mi. RT. Moderate. Access: Along Going-to-the-Sun Rd., about halfway between Avalanche Campground and Logan Pass Visitor Center.

Not considered easy mainly on account of its altitude gain, The Loop is a popular hiking trail that winds up to Granite Park Chalet and back. Many people use it as a continuation of the Highline Trail, but this is the section to do if you're not quite so adventurous (the Highline Trail is almost 12 miles long). If you want to spend the night in the chalet, contact **Glacier Wilderness Guides** for reservations (☎ **800/521-7238**). (See the descriptions of the chalets under "Camping," below.)

Sun Point Nature Trail

1.4 mi. RT. Easy. Access: 9 mi. west of St. Mary at Sun Point parking area.

This walk on gentle slopes away from the road presents commanding views of Baring Falls.

MANY GLACIER AREA

Iceberg Lake

9.5 mi. RT. Moderate. Access: Starts at a trailhead in a cabin area east of the Swiftcurrent Coffee Shop and Campstore.

This beautiful hike traverses flower-filled meadows to a jewel of a high lake backed against a mountain wall. Even in summer, there may be snow on the ground and ice floating in the lake. Look for mountain goats or bighorn sheep on the cliffs above. And, as in many Glacier backcountry areas, keep an eye out for the grizzlies.

Swiftcurrent Lake Nature Trail

2.4 mi. RT. Easy. Access: Picnic area 0.5 mi. west of the hotel turnoff.

This is a fun hike along the shore, through the woods, and near a marsh, so you may see deer and birds. Keep an eye out for blue grouse, too. If you have time, continue on the trail as it circles Lake Josephine, another easy hike, adding 2.8 miles to the trip. Dramatic Mount Gould towers above the far end of the lake. Midsummer wildflowers can be spectacular. A longer, 10.4-mile round-trip trail to Grinnell Glacier, the park's largest, is also accessed from this area.

TWO MEDICINE AREA

Appistoki Falls

1.2 mi. RT. Easy. Access: The trailhead is the same as the Mt. Henry Trailhead.

This trail, with an elevation gain of only 260 feet, is an ideal spot for an early morning cup of coffee or midday repast.

Running Eagle Falls

0.3 mi. one way. Easy. Access: 1 mi. west of the Two Medicine entrance.

Hardly even a hike, the easiest trail in the area is to Running Eagle Falls along a path that winds through a heavily forested area to a large, noisy waterfall.

Twin Falls Trail

3.8 mi. one way. Easy. Access: Two Medicine Campground.

The most popular hiking path in this area is the one to Twin Falls, which originates at the campground. Hikers may walk the entire distance to Twin Falls on a clearly identified trail, or boat across Two Medicine Lake to the foot of the trailhead, and hike the last mile.

Exploring the Backcountry

Depending upon your point of view, negotiating the backcountry may translate to a leisurely stroll, or a tortuous experience in the high country. Choices range from 4-mile day hikes to multiday treks, so you'll need to consider your experience and fitness level before heading into the underbrush. Then, locate a park map that presents trails and campsites in the area you want to explore.

Backcountry campgrounds have maps at the entrance to show you the location of each campground, the pit toilet, food preparation areas, and, perhaps most important, food storage areas. If you fish while camping, it's recommended you exercise catch-and-release to avoid attracting wildlife in search of food. If you eat the catch, be certain to puncture the air bladder and throw the entrails into deep water at least 200 feet from the nearest campsite or trail. When backpacking in Glacier, especially in the high country, it's important to remember to pack as lightly as possible and make sure you're aware of the trail's degree of the ascent. And remember the cardinal rule: Pack it in, pack it out. No exceptions.

Wherever you decide to go, remember that you must secure a backcountry permit before your trip. Advance reservations can be made (☎ 406/888-7800).

A Guided Backcountry Trip. Many folks like to stand back and let someone else make all the arrangements, leaving themselves free to concentrate on the hiking experience itself. If this seems like your kind of trip, then you may wish to consider the services of **Glacier Wilderness Guides,** the exclusive backpacking guide service in Glacier National Park. For a price, they will put together any kind of trip; they have several regularly scheduled throughout the season, from the end of June through the beginning of September. These include a 3-day "taste" of the park for $315 per person, and an entire week in the wilderness for $630 per person. Add $10 per day if you want them to provide a backpack, tent, sleeping bag, and pad. Custom trips run $130 a day per person, with a four-person minimum. They'll even organize a trip where you spend the day hiking and the night cuddled in a comfy inn inside the park or in the Granite Park Chalet (see "Camping," below).

Their main office is located 1.5 miles west of West Glacier on U.S. 2 (a second office is in West Glacier itself, behind the Glacier Highland Motel, across from the Amtrak depot). For information and reservations, contact the company at P.O. Box 535, West Glacier, MT 59936 (☎ **800/521-7238** for reservations, or 406/387-5555; fax 406/387-5656; www.glacierguides.com; e-mail: glguides@cyberport.net).

KINTLA LAKE AREA

Kintla Lake to Upper Kintla Lake

12 mi. one way. Moderate. Access: Kintla Lake Campground.

Skirting the north shore of Kintla Lake above Polebridge for about 7 miles, before climbing a couple hundred feet, this stretch of the Boulder Pass hike is a breeze. However, once you hit Kintla Creek you may want to reconsider going any farther. With 12 miles under your belt at this point, climbing 3,000 feet may not seem like a great idea. The trail, once it breaks into the clear, offers views of several peaks, including Kinnerly Peak to the south of Upper Kintla Lake.

POLEBRIDGE AREA

Bowman Lake

7.1 mi. one way. Moderate. Access: Bowman Lake Campground; follow Glacier Rte. 7 to Bowman Lake Rd., just north of Polebridge, then follow the signs to Bowman Lake Campground.

This trail (14 miles to Brown Pass) is similar to the Kintla Lake hike in difficulty, and, like the Kintla Lake Trail, passes the lake on the north. After a hike through the foliage, the trail climbs out of reach for anyone in bad shape, ascending 2,000 feet in less than 3 miles to join the Kintla Lake Trail at Brown Pass. A left turn takes you back to Kintla Lake (23 mi.), a right takes you to Goat Haunt at the foot of Waterton Lake (9 mi.).

Quartz Lake

12 mi. RT. Moderate. Access: Bowman Lake Picnic Area; cross the bridge over Bowman Creek and you're on your way.

The loop runs up and over a ridge and down to the south end of Lower Quartz Lake. From there it's a level 3-mile hike to the west end of Quartz Lake, then it's 6 miles back over the ridge farther north (and higher up) before dropping back to Bowman Lake. An interesting aspect of this trail is evidence of the Red Bench Fire of 1988, which took a chunk out of the North Fork area.

LOGAN PASS AREA

Highline Trail

11.9 mi. one way (including The Loop). Moderate. Access: Granite Park Chalet.

This relatively easy hike gains a mere 200 feet in elevation over 7.6 miles. It begins at the Logan Pass Visitor Center and skirts the Garden Wall at heights of over 6,000 feet to Granite Park Chalet. Give yourself plenty of time for the return hike to Logan Pass. Or, rather than retracing your steps, continue on from the chalet to the Loop, the aptly named section of Going-to-the-Sun Road. The trail actually terminates here (an additional 3.5 mi.), although you'll need to plan for a shuttle back to your car. (It's also possible to continue all the way to Upper Waterton Lake, but if you do this, you should allow 3 days for the trip.)

TWO MEDICINE AREA

Pitamakan Pass Trail

8.8 mi. one way. Moderate. Access: Two Medicine Campground.

This trail presents several options: 1 or 2 long day hikes, or you can use it as the jumping-off point for an extended trip. From the trailhead, the path winds to Old Man Lake and a campground, and then on to Pitamakan Pass. At this point, your options are to return via the same trail or to continue to Dawson Pass, through Twin Falls, then back to the campground, which adds 10 miles to the trip and completes the 18.8-mile loop. Alternately, you could head north on the Cut Bank or Nyack Creek trails, which will add days to your trip.

Other Summer Sports & Activities

Boating. With all of this water around, it only makes sense that boat rentals would also be available, as they are. At Apgar and Lake McDonald you will find kayaks, canoes, rowboats, and motorboats; gas-powered outboard motors of 10 horsepower or less are permitted at Two Medicine Lake and Bowman Lake. You can also rent kayaks, canoes, rowboats, and electric motorboats at Two Medicine. At Many Glacier you can rent kayaks, canoes and rowboats. For details call **Glacier Park** (GPI) at ☎ 406/257-2426.

Fishing. The crystal-clear mountain streams and lakes of Glacier are home to many native species of trout. Anglers looking to hook a big one should try the North Fork of the Flathead for cutthroat and any of the three larger lakes in the park (Bowman Lake, St. Mary Lake, and Lake McDonald) for lake trout and cutthroat. For sound equipment, sage advice, or to schedule a guided foray, contact **Lakestream Flyshop** in Whitefish (☎ 406/862-1298).

Horseback Riding. One alternative to overstressing your muscles on hiking trails is to saddle up Old Paint and take an Old West approach to transportation. Horseback riding at East Glacier is provided by **Two Medicine River Outfitters** (☎ 406/226-4408), located a stone's throw from the front door of the lodge; they offer hourly and half-day rides into the nearby wilderness. **Mule Shoe Outfitters** (☎ 406/888-5121) offers similar rides from corrals at Lake McDonald, Apgar, and the Many Glacier Corral.

Kayaking. Most kayaking in the park involves passages across lakes; the most popular are Bowman Lake and Lake McDonald. Inquire at any ranger station for details and conditions (for rentals, see "Boating," above).

Mountain Climbing. The peaks of Glacier Park rarely exceed elevations of 10,000 feet, but don't let the surveyors' measurements fool you. Glacier has some incredibly difficult climbs, and you must inquire at a visitor center or ranger station regarding climbing conditions and closures. In general, the peaks are unsuitable, except for experienced climbers or those traveling with experienced guides.

Rafting & Float Trips. Though the waters that are actually in the park don't lend themselves to white-water rafting, the boundary forks of the Flathead River are some of the best in the northwest corner of the state. For just taking it easy and floating on your back in the summer sun, the North Fork of the Flathead River stretching from Polebridge to Columbia Falls and into Flathead Lake is ideal. Portaging in Polebridge can be difficult if there's not a good sport waiting for you downstream, however. The same may be said for the Middle Fork of the Flathead, which forms the southern border of the park.

For white-water voyagers, the North Fork of the Flathead River (classes II and III) and the Middle Fork (class III) are the best bets. Inquire at any ranger station for details and conditions, since flow rates change dramatically as snow melts or storms move through the area.

The Middle Fork is a little more severe and isn't the sort of river you enjoy with an umbrella drink in hand. The names of certain stretches of the Middle Fork are terror-inspiring in themselves (the Narrows, Jaws, Bonecrusher) and to assuage that terror, several outfitters offer expert, sanctioned guides.

Several outfitters based in Whitefish and Kalispell organize such trips, including **Rising Sun Outdoor Adventures,** 501 S. Karrow, Whitefish, MT 59937 (☎ 406/862-5934). The company organizes sailing adventures on Flathead Lake, custom horseback and float trips on nearby rivers, and mountain-biking and hiking tours.

Montana Raft Company, P.O. Box 535, West Glacier, MT 59936 (☎ 800/521-7238 for reservations, or 406/387-5555; fax 406/387-5656; www.glacierguides.com; e-mail: glguides@cyberport.net), part of Glacier Wilderness Guides, also offers rafting trips through Glacier and the area. They offer trips throughout the season ranging from 2-day trips for $260 per person, to 3½-day trips for $430 per person; all trips include a day hike in Glacier National Park. Their prices include all necessary equipment and food. They also offer daily raft trips, inflatable kayaks, and fly-fishing from drift boats. See "Exploring the Backcountry," above.

Winter Sports & Activities

All unplowed roads become trails for snowshoers and cross-country skiers, who rave about the vast powdered wonderland that exists here. Guided trips into the backcountry are a great way to experience the park in winter, or you can strap on a pair of snowshoes and explore it on your own.

Snowshoeing & Cross-Country Skiing. Glacier has an abundance of cross-country ski trails, the most popular of which is the **Upper Lake McDonald Trail** to the Avalanche picnic area. This 8-mile trail offers a relatively flat route up Going-to-the-Sun Road with views of McDonald Creek and the mountains looming above the McDonald Valley.

For the advanced skier, the same area presents a more intense trip that heads northwest in a roundabout fashion to the Apgar Lookout. This 10.5-mile trip may be a little more than the beginner bargains for.

The most popular trail on the east side is the **Autumn Creek Trail** near Marias Pass. However, avalanche paths cross this area, so the prudent skier will inquire about current weather conditions.

Yet another popular spot is in Essex along the southern boundary of the park at the **Izaak Walton Inn.**

Winter Road Conditions. Going-to-the-Sun Road is open seasonally, usually from early June to mid-October, although it may be open earlier or later, depending upon weather conditions. Call the park to find out when tentative openings and closings are scheduled. During the winter, you may drive Going-to-the-Sun Road for 10 miles from West Glacier along Lake McDonald to the road closure; this is a popular destination for cross-country skiers.

Camping

INSIDE THE PARK

Two of the ways to spend your evenings at the park are from inside the hotel lounge looking across a martini at the folks in the campground, and vice versa. For those who prefer the latter, Glacier offers 13 campgrounds, 8 of which are accessible by paved road.

Most campgrounds are available on a first-come, first-served basis. Fish Creek and St. Mary campgrounds may be reserved through the **National Park Service Reservation System** (☎ 800/365-CAMP). Most campgrounds have rest rooms with flush toilets and cold running water.

Fish Creek is on the west side of Lake McDonald; **Many Glacier** is in the northeast part of the park; **Rising Sun** is on the north side of St. Mary Lake; **St. Mary** is on the east side of the park; and **Two Medicine** is at the southeast part of the park near East Glacier. **Sprague Creek,** near the West Glacier entrance, offers a paved road but does not allow towed vehicles or vehicles longer than 21 feet.

Despite its proximity to the center of the hotel and motel activity, the **Many Glacier Campground** is a well-forested, almost secluded campground that provides as much privacy in a public area as you'll see anywhere. The campground has adequate space for recreational vehicles and truck/camper combinations, but space for trucks pulling trailers is limited. It is a veritable mecca for tent campers.

Apgar Campground is located at the bottom of Lake McDonald, near the West Glacier Entrance and the Apgar Visitor Center. The **Avalanche Campground** may be the nicest of all because it is situated in the bottom of the valley, 4 miles north of Lake McDonald on Going-to-the-Sun Road in a heavily treed area that is also immediately adjacent to the creek. Of its 87 sites, 50 are suitable for RVs.

Bowman Lake Campground is located at the end of a primitive dirt road in the northwest section of the park (accessed through the Polebridge entrance). It's not recommended for RVs. The bad news about the Cut Bank Campground road is that it's not paved. The good news is it's only 5 miles from the pavement of U.S. 89 to the ranger station and campground, which are located in the southeast portion of the park between St. Mary and Two Medicine. Still more good news is that the unpaved road deters many from heading into the outback to this campground, which sits in the shadow of Bad Marriage and Medicine Wolf mountains. The campground was only recently reopened after being rebuilt, so is still relatively undiscovered; the road, and campground, are best suited to recreational vehicles 21 feet or shorter.

Fish Creek Campground is located 2 miles from Apgar, on the western shore of Lake McDonald. Kintla Lake Campground is located in the northwest section of the park, reached by primitive dirt roads through the Polebridge entrance station, so it is not recommended for RVs. Logging Creek is a primitive campground reached by dirt roads, just beyond Quartz Creek; and Quartz Creek is another primitive campground, accessed by dirt roads through the Polebridge entrance.

Sprague Creek Campground is located on the eastern shore of Lake McDonald. No towed trailers or vehicles longer than 21 feet are allowed. St. Mary Campground is located just outside the town of St. Mary. Rising Sun Campground, located 6 miles west of St. Mary, is close to the public showers at Rising Sun Motor Inn.

The Two Medicine Campground is situated in the shadows of major mountains near three lakes and a stream. It is a forested area that has beautiful sites, plenty of shade, and opportunities to wet a fishing line or dangle your feet in cool mountain water.

Backcountry Camping. If it's the backcountry you're bent on seeing, Glacier has 66 backcountry campgrounds. Fortunately, many are at lower elevation, so inexperienced backpackers have an opportunity to take advantage of them. For an accurate depiction of your itinerary's difficulty, and advice on what may be needed, check with rangers in the area you are contemplating visiting. One of the main dangers is running into a bear. Visitors planning to camp overnight in Glacier's backcountry must stop at a visitor center or ranger station and obtain a **Backcountry Use Permit.** Backcountry permits may be reserved in advance. Permits are limited to 6 nights, with no more than 3 nights allowed at each campground. Certain campgrounds have a 1-night limit. There are separate fees for advance reservations and backcountry camping.

Backcountry camping permits may be obtained in person from the visitor centers at Apgar, Waterton Townsite, and St. Mary, or the ranger stations at Many Glacier, Two Medicine, and Polebridge. During summer months permits may be obtained no earlier than 24 hours before your trip.

Winter Backcountry Camping. Though snow camping isn't for everyone, it's a great way to see the park in winter, and to complement a winter excursion. Permits are required for all overnight trips but, due to lower demand, there is no fee to reserve one up to 7 days in advance. There are a few rules that do take effect beginning each November 20, so double-check at visitor centers for details.

Chalets. Two of the park's most popular destinations, Granite Park and Sperry Chalets, are National Historic Landmarks built by the Great Northern Railway between 1912 and 1914. Each has been the subject of an extensive restoration project; they have been reopened, but as a hiker's shelter only.

Guests must bring their own food, water, cooking and eating utensils, flashlights, and sleeping bags. Rooms and beds are provided, as are a kitchen with a cooking stove and dining room. No public water is available, so bring your own.

Sperry Chalet, a rustic backcountry chalet, is accessible by trail only. It operates from July through mid-September. Services include overnight accommodations and full meal service. Reservations are required. For information and reservations ☎ **888/345-2649** or 406/387-5555, or write: **Belton Chalets,** P.O. Box 188, West Glacier, MT 59936.

For information on **Granite Park Chalet** contact **Glacier Wilderness Guides/Montana Raft Company** (☎ **800/521-7238** or 406/387-5555; www.glacierguides.com). This company handles the reservations for Granite Park Chalet, a backcountry hikers hut, and operates guided hikes into the Glacier backcountry (see "Exploring the Backcountry," above). The chalet has 12 rooms (all single bunk beds), and sleeps two to six per room. The chalet is pricey if you just stay overnight ($60 per person per night, with an additional $10 per person linen charge; there's no running water or other facilities); you may get better value by going on an organized trip.

Campground	Total Sites	RV Hookups	Dump Station	Toilets	Drinking Water
Inside the Park					
Apgar	196	No	Yes	Yes	Yes
Avalanche	87	No	Yes	Yes	Yes
Bowman Lake*	48	No	No	Yes	Yes
Cut Bank*	19	No	No	Yes	Yes
Fish Creek	180	No	Yes	Yes	Yes
Kintla Lake*	13	No	No	Yes	Yes
Logging Creek*	8	No	No	Yes	Yes
Many Glacier	110	No	Yes	Yes	Yes
Quartz Creek*	7	No	No	Yes	Yes
Rising Sun	83	No	Yes	Yes	Yes
Sprague Creek	25	No	No	Yes	Yes
St. Mary	148	No	Yes	Yes	Yes
Two Medicine	99	No	Yes	Yes	Yes
Near the Park					
Y Lazy R	40	Yes	Yes	Yes	Yes
Johnson's of St. Mary	115	Yes	Yes	Yes	Yes
Glacier Campground	160	Yes	Yes	Yes	Yes
Lake Five Resort	35	Yes	Yes	Yes	Yes

* Campground accessible only by narrow dirt roads. RVs not recommended.
** Public showers located nearby, for a fee.

NEAR THE PARK

IN EAST GLACIER

Y Lazy R

P.O. Box 146, East Glacier, MT 59434. ☎ **406/226-5573.** 10 tent sites, 30 RV sites. $10 tent, $15 full hookup.

Situated just off U.S. 2, this campground is conveniently located within walking distance of East Glacier and is the closest to town with laundry facilities. Plan to arrive early if you want to snag one of the few sites with trees. This place is a great value and an ideal place to plant the RV before heading off to explore the region.

The same owners also operate Firebrand Campground 3 miles west of East Glacier with 10 tent and 20 RV sites at the same prices.

IN ST. MARY

Johnson's of St. Mary

St. Mary, MT 59417. ☎ **406/732-4207** (campground), or 406/732-5565 (cafe). www. babbmt.com/johnsons. 50 tent sites, 65 RV sites. $14 tent; $18 RV with electricity and water only, $20 full hookup; $16 motor home, no hookup.

From April through September (depending on the weather) this is

Showers	Fire Pits/ Grills	Laundry	Public Phone	Reserve	Fees	Open
No	Yes	No	Yes	No	$12	Early-May to Mid-Oct
No	Yes	No	No	No	$12	Mid-June to Labor Day
No	Yes	No	No	No	$10	Mid-May to Mid-Sept
No	Yes	No	No	No	$10	Early May to Mid-Sept
No	Yes	No	Yes	Yes	$15	Early June to Labor Day
No	Yes	No	No	No	$10	Mid-May to Mid-Sept
No	Yes	No	No	No	$10	July–Labor Day
Yes**	Yes	No	Yes	No	$12	Late May to Mid-Sept
No	Yes	No	No	No	$10	July–Labor Day
Yes**	Yes	No	Yes	No	$12	Late May to Late Sept
No	Yes	No	No	No	$12	Mid-May to Late Sept
No	Yes	No	Yes	Yes	$15	Late May to Mid-Sept
No	Yes	No	Yes	No	$12	Late May to Mid-Sept
Yes	Yes	Yes	Yes	Yes	$10/$15	June to Mid-Sept
Yes	Yes	Yes	Yes	Yes	$12/$15/$16	Apr–Oct
Yes	Yes	Yes	Yes	Yes	$15/$18	Mid-May to Sept
Yes	Yes	Yes	Yes	Yes	$16/$20	Mid-May to Sept

where you want to camp if you can get a spot. With showers ($2) and a Laundromat, campers both inside the park and out come to St. Mary for ablutions and a good meal.

IN WEST GLACIER

Glacier Campground

P.O. Box 447, 12070 U.S. 2, West Glacier, MT 59936. ☎ **406/387-5689.** 80 tent sites, 80 RV sites, 5 cabins. $17 tent; $20 RV; $30–$40 cabin.

One mile west of West Glacier on U.S. 2 is the closest campground outside the park. Set amid a forested area overgrown with evergreens, it's a quiet, comfortable place to retreat under the shade of the trees, especially on hot summer days. Most sites have water and electric hookups; the balance are perfect for tent camping. Five rather primitive cabins are also available, but furnishings are modest: sleeping beds with mattresses, electricity, but no plumbing or kitchen facilities. Recreational facilities include volleyball, horseshoes, and a basketball court; also on the premises are a Laundromat and teensy general store that has little to offer except a fresh quart of milk or a T-shirt.

Lake Five Resort

540 Belton Stage Rd., West Glacier, MT 59936. ☎ **406/387-5601.** E-mail: lakefive@ digisys.net. 9 cabins, 6 tepee lodges, 45 sites with electricity and water (14 of which have sewer hookups). $45–$115 cabin; $40 tepee; $16–$22 site.

Located 3 miles west of West Glacier and ³/₄ mile from U.S. 2 is this cabin and campground arrangement, an alternative to potentially crowded park campgrounds. Situated on a 235-acre lake surrounded by private homes and summer cottages, the resort is far from the maddening crowd (though still close to the park itself). Seven of the nine cabins are on the lakefront, all of them equipped with bathrooms and showers.

Accommodations

INSIDE THE PARK

With only one exception, Glacier Park (GPI) operates all of the hostelries in Glacier National Park, which fall into two different categories. Lake McDonald Lodge, Glacier Park Lodge, and Many Glacier Hotel are first-tier properties that have been popular destinations since early in the century; Swiftcurrent Motor Inn is typical of the casual motel-style properties at the other end of the spectrum that provide good accommodations for less money. Although the lodges have a certain stately charm, don't expect in-room hot tubs or even air conditioning. For example, the structures may have been constructed to withstand natural disasters, but little thought was given to interior soundproofing. So if you're an eavesdropper, you'll be in heaven; if you're a light sleeper, bring earplugs. While all of the lodges are adequately comfortable, their greatest attribute, aside from the architecture, may be their location in one of the most stunning natural settings in the world.

Reserve well in advance; July and August dates may fill before the spring thaw. For more information on the following properties or to make reservations contact **Glacier Park,** VIAD Corp. Center, Phoenix, AZ 85077-0928 (☎ 602/207-6000; www. glacierparkinc. com).

Apgar Village Lodge

Apgar Village, Box 398, West Glacier, MT 59936. ☎ **406/888-5484.** Fax 406/888-5273. 28 cabins, 20 motel rms. TV. $72–$210 cabin; $57–$90 motel rm. DISC, MC, V. Closed mid-Oct to Apr.

The Apgar Village Lodge is located on the south end of Lake McDonald and is one of two lodgings located in Apgar Village. A less expensive alternative to the park's GPI-owned properties, the log-and-frame cabins have a rustic charm but lack in-room amenities.

Glacier Park Lodge

Glacier National Park, MT 59936. ☎ **602/207-6000.** Fax 602/207-5589. www.glacierparklodge.com. 154 units. TEL. $130–$160 double; $235 suite. AE, DISC, MC.

Conveniently located just inside the Southeast Entrance at East Glacier, this is the flagship inn of the park, an imposing timbered lodge that stands as a stately tribute to the Great Northern Railroad and its early attempts to lure tourists to Glacier. The carefully manicured lawn and ever-blooming wildflowers frame the grounds in colors spectacular enough to rival the mountain backdrop. The interior features massive Douglas fir pillars, some 40 inches in diameter and 40 feet tall. In fact, stand in the middle of the lobby and look up—you'll discover beams carved from massive trees that are the structural supports for the entire building. Skylights, wrought iron chandeliers, and a desk hewn from a 36-inch-diameter log add to the Old West flavor.

Rooms are well furnished, but showers are elbow-banging small, and sinks are significantly smaller than those found in today's modern hotels and motels. A wooden deck outside the lounge provides an excellent spot for cocktails, reading, or a late-afternoon snooze. A glass-enclosed breezeway connects the main building to the annex; the oak chaise lounges found there are the ideal spot from which to watch sunrise. There's even an immaculately groomed executive-style 9-hole golf course. The Trading Post offers traditional souvenirs, as well as nicely crafted American Indian artwork and clothing.

While here, plan to spend an evening around the fireplace as members of the Blackfeet tribe recount their history and culture.

Lake McDonald Lodge

Glacier National Park, MT 59936. ☎ **602/ 207-6000.** Fax 602/207-5589. www. glacierparkinc.com. 62 units in lodge and motel, 38 cottage units (some without private bathroom). TEL. $130 lodge rm; $81 motel unit; $87–$130 cottage. DISC, MC, V.

The Lake McDonald Lodge feels like a lodge, perhaps because that's how it began. This two-story building doesn't have the same towering ceilings and open spaces as other park hotels, but it has a warm, cozy feel inspired by its construction. Situated on the shore of the park's largest lake, it provides a marvelous central base for exploring the western part of the park. The lodge is a center for boating activity; scenic cruises depart daily and canoe rentals are popular. Rooms in the Stewart Annex and well-preserved cabins are comfortable, but less desirable; be sure to inquire as to whether yours has a private bathroom. Common lounging areas are furnished with heavy couches, sofas, and chairs that surround a stone fireplace. The lodge houses a dining room, gift shop, and lounge; a coffee shop, post office, and sundries store are also on the grounds.

Many Glacier Hotel

Glacier National Park, MT 59936. ☎ **602/207-6000.** www.glacierparkinc.com. 208 units. TEL. $103–$130 double; $190 suite. DISC, MC, V.

This alpine-style hotel may be the most photographed building in the park. When you arrive at Many Glacier after driving along the park's interior road from Babb, it comes slowly into view, as picturesque as a Swiss chalet and almost as inviting as the turquoise blue waters of Swiftcurrent Lake. Built in 1915 by the Great Northern Railway, this is the largest lodging in the park and among the most popular. Its chalet-style architecture fits right in with the alpine environment that surrounds it. In August, after the huckleberries ripen, you can almost count on seeing grizzly bears on the slopes of the mountain across the road from the hotel.

Rooms are located in the main lodge around the balconies overlooking the lobby or in the adjoining annex. A dining room, coffee shop, gift shop, and lounge are all located in the hotel; nightly cabaret performances begin midsummer.

Rising Sun Motor Inn

Glacier National Park, MT 59936. ☎ **602/207-6000.** Fax 602/207-5589. www. glacierparkinc.com. 63 units. TEL. $72–$75 double; $64 cottage. AE, DISC, MC, V.

Located 6.5 miles from St. Mary, just off Going-to-the-Sun Road, the Rising Sun is a complex made up of a restaurant, a motor inn, cottages, a camp store, a gift shop, and a service station. While the rooms are comfortable enough, the lake is across the street, and you'll be ideally located to explore the eastern side of the park from Going-to-the-Sun, the Rising Sun is considerably lacking in appeal. There's a lot of asphalt and rustic cabins here, along with 28 motel rooms, 9 of which are located in the same building as the camp store, and 35 rooms in duplex cottages. It's still a convenient place to be, though, especially if you plan to take a scenic cruise or rent a boat.

Swiftcurrent Motor Inn

Glacier National Park, MT 59936. ☎ **602/207-6000.** Fax 602/207-5589. www. glacierparkinc.com. 88 units and cabins (most cabins without private bathroom). TEL. $75–$87 double in motor inn; $40–$65 double in cabin. DISC, MC, V.

The appeal here is for those satisfied with modest prices and decor—primarily active types interested in spending lots of time exploring the backcountry trails. Like Many Glacier, which is just up the street, the inn is set against a mountain backdrop in what is considered a hiker's paradise. There are 42 motor inn rooms, 20 motel rooms, and 26 cabins. Each of the motel units includes a private bathroom; cabins are outfitted with kitchenettes, one or two bedrooms, and perhaps a bathroom (public facilities are nearby). There's also a coffee shop/ restaurant on the premises. Actually, with the money you'll save by staying here

instead of in the more posh Many Glacier, you might just be able to afford dinner in the hotel dining room.

Village Inn

Glacier National Park, MT 59936. ☎ **602/207-6000.** Fax 602/207-5589. www. glacierparkinc.com. 36 units. $90–$140 double; $124 suite. DISC, MC, V.

Not to be confused with Apgar Village Lodge (see above), the Village Inn is the smallest of the properties operated by GPI in Glacier. Located in Apgar Village, the inn is near the general store, cafes, and boat docks. Like its counterparts throughout the park, the Village Inn is comfortably outfitted with modest furnishings, making it a cozy and convenient place to set up camp: All 36 rooms are located on 2 floors of the inn and 12 of them have kitchenettes. Second-level rooms have the same lake views as those downstairs, but have less people traffic. Though you won't find a dining room on the property, the restaurants of Lake McDonald and Apgar are all close by. Close to the Apgar corral and the docks of Lake McDonald, not to a plethora of hiking trails, Apgar Village bustles with activity during the summer and is a great choice for families.

NEAR THE PARK

If the convenience of staying on Glacier's back porch is important to you, the following are your best bets. However, in surrounding communities not necessarily classified as gateway towns, you'll find a greater variety of accommodations, especially if you're willing to travel as far as Whitefish, Kalispell, or Columbia Falls. These places might be more in line with your needs if the park is merely a 1- or 2-day part of your vacation.

IN EAST GLACIER

Backpacker's Inn

P.O. Box 94, East Glacier, MT 59434. ☎ **406/226-9392.** 3 cabins, sleeping 20 people. $10 per person. DISC, MC, V. Closed mid-Oct to Apr.

This dorm-style hostel consists of three cabins—one for men, one for women, and one coed—each sleeping up to six people (the coed cabin sleeps eight). At $10 per person, the price is right, but don't expect the rooms to include much more than a bed.

Brownies Grocery and AYH Hostel

P.O. Box 229, East Glacier, MT 59434. ☎ **406/226-4426** or 406/226-4456. http://grizzlyadventures.com/brownies. 12 units (all with shared bathroom). AYH members $10–$15 or $35 family rm; nonmembers $13–$23 or $35 family rm. Family rooms sleep 2–6. MC, V. Closed Oct to early May, depending on the weather.

Reservations are recommended at this popular combination grocery store/hostel, which offers comfortable rooms at extremely affordable prices. Dorm and family rooms are located on the second floor of a rustic, older log building with several common rooms for guests to share, including a porch, kitchen, bathrooms, and laundry. A bakery and deli have been added to the grocery; there's a restaurant next door.

Jacobson's Cottages

P.O. Box 216, East Glacier, MT 59434. ☎ **406/226-4422.** 12 cottages. $50–$75 double. AE, DISC, MC, V. Closed Nov to Apr.

Located in a nicely wooded area, these quaint cottages are small but comfortable. And while they aren't equipped with either TVs or kitchens (with one exception), entertainment and good food are short walks away with the Restaurant Thimbleberry a half block down the street and Two Medicine a mere 4-mile drive. The cottages are available seasonally, and reservations are recommended.

Mountain Pine Motel

Mont. 49, East Glacier, MT 59434. ☎ **406/226-4403.** 25 units and 2 houses. TV TEL. $50–$66 double. AE, DC, DISC, MC, V.

This property is a one-story, 1950s-type motel that provides clean, well-furnished rooms equipped with cable TV, in a shaded, timbered area on the main highway. Most standard rooms have two queen-size beds, reading chairs and table, chest, and bathrooms with tub-shower combinations. Considering the fact that rooms here are about a third as expensive as at the park hotels, this is an excellent alternative.

IN ESSEX

Izaak Walton Inn

P.O. Box 653, Essex, MT 59916. ☎ **406/888-5700.** Fax 406/888-5200. E-mail: izaakw@digisys.net. 33 units plus 4 caboose cottages. $98 double, $150 suite, $475 caboose (3-night minimum). MC, V.

Built in 1939 by the railway, this historic Tudor lodge once served as living quarters for rail crews who serviced the railroad. Located just off U.S. 2 on the southern boundary of Glacier Park, the Izaak Walton is now extremely popular with tourists and locals alike, many of whom choose to travel via train, which arrives a mere 50 feet from the front door of the lodge. During winter months this inn is a popular jumping-off spot for cross-country skiers.

Paola Creek Bed & Breakfast

HC 36 Box 4C, Essex, MT 59916. ☎ **888/311-5061** or 406/888-5061. Fax 406/888-5063. www.wtp.net/go/paola. E-mail: paola@in-tch.com. 4 units. $120 double. MC, V.

This hand-crafted log home, nestled between Glacier National park and the Great Bear Wilderness, features a relaxing Great Room with river rock fireplace, a library, and a large dining room with a stunning view. In addition to breakfast, Paola Creek offers five-course family style gourmet dinners, and even lunches on request. It's open year-round, for nearby summer hiking, biking and river activities, and winter snowshoeing and ski touring.

IN POLEBRIDGE

North Fork Hostel and Square Peg Ranch

P.O. Box 1, Polebridge, MT 59928. ☎ **406/ 888-5241.** www.nfhostel.com. E-mail: nfhotel@ nfhostel.com. 12 bunks, 2 log homes, 2 cabins. $13 bunk, $50 log home, $25 cabin. AE.

Formerly called the Quarter Circle MC Ranch and located inside the park, this lodge was moved to its present location near Polebridge in the late 1960s, and is probably best suited to the back-to-nature traveler. It now sits within a stone's throw of the North Fork of the Flathead River. The lodge features complete kitchen facilities, as do the log homes, each with three double beds, a fireplace, and a refrigerator.

Polebridge Mercantile and Cabins

P.O. Box 280042, Polebridge, MT 59928. ☎ **406/888-5105.** www.members.tripod. com/polebridge. E-mail: montana@excite.com. 4 cabins, 1 tepee. $30–$55 cabin, $20 tepee. MC, V.

If you can make the trek up the gravelly North Fork Road, then give these bare-bones cabins a try. There is no electricity and no running water in the lower-priced cabins, let alone bedding—it's bring your own sleeping bag at the Merc. The $55 cabin has a bathroom and running water in the kitchenette. Each cabin has propane cooking stoves and lights, and the views out over the west side of Glacier National Park make the price tag a steal, especially if you brought the kids. This may sound like an adventure in hell, but Polebridge is a happening spot in the summer when all the river rats and seasonal residents converge for whopping good times and tall tales about running rapids and climbing peaks.

IN ST. MARY

St. Mary Lodge

U.S. 89 and Going-to-the-Sun Rd., St. Mary, MT 59417. ☎ **800/368-3689** or 406/732-4431.

Fax 406/732-9265. www.glcpark.com. E-mail: stmary@glcpark.com. 57 units, 19 cabins and cottages. $93 double, $285 cottage. AE, DISC, MC, V.

Situated at the St. Mary end of Going-to-the-Sun Road, this lodge is another member of the minority of properties that aren't managed by GPI. The main lodge and attendant rooms are standard Montana fare, with tasteful western lodgepole furnishings. Lodging is in three different areas in close proximity to the center of the complex; lodge and motel rooms are nicely done motel-style units that may have two single beds or a queen. Rooms are tiny but are furnished with stylish lodgepole pine beds, tables, and brass reading lamps. Bathrooms are small, self-contained units with showers. Nicer units are in the Glacier cabins, which boast living areas with dining tables, kitchenettes with microwaves and minifridges, and queen beds in a separate sleeping area. The most expensive units here are the Pinnacle Cottages, newly constructed cabins perched on a bluff across the highway from the main complex that afford views of Going-to-the-Sun Road and St. Mary Lake.

IN WEST GLACIER

Glacier Wilderness Resort

P.O. Box 295, West Glacier, MT 59936. ☎ **406/888-5664.** 10 lodges. TEL. $150–$170 per lodge per night. 5-night minimum stay. MC, V.

Surrounded by Forest Service lands, the lodges at this year-round resort are as private as you can get. Each lodge is a "home," complete with a stereo, VCR, and a hot tub on the front porch. Families will find the two-bedroom lodges to their liking, and kids can play outdoors during the day (there are 23 undeveloped acres) and at the Recreation Center, with diversions like foosball, pool, and video games. Hiking trails abound and some even come up on some surprising waterfalls. For a summer stay, reservations should be made before March.

Great Northern Chalets

12127 U.S. 2, West Glacier, MT 59936.
☎ **800/387-5340.** www.gnwhitewater.com.
E-mail: whiteh2o@digisys.net. 5 units. $120–
$260 double. DISC, MC, V.

This small, family-oriented resort located near West Glacier offers log chalets that have balconies facing landscaped flower gardens and a pond, with mountain views in the distance. A 16-foot indoor hot tub spa is on the property, as are a volleyball court that doubles as a sandbox for children, and a pond that is used for fly-fishing instruction. Two types of chalets are offered, the largest being a beautifully furnished two-story, two-bedroom unit with three queen beds, a full bathroom upstairs, and half bathroom downstairs. Smaller chalets have one large upstairs bedroom with two queen beds, and a downstairs level with a full-size sleeper sofa and a kitchen with service for six.

Mountain Timbers

P.O. Box 94, West Glacier, MT 59936.
☎ **800/841-3835** or 406/387-5830.
Fax 406/387-5835. 6 units (4 with private bathroom). $75–$95 double with shared bathroom; $95–$125 double with private bathroom. AE, MC, V.

Tucked away on the other side of the Flathead River near the south side of the park is this cozy B&B. Situated on 240 acres, the beautiful 5,000-square-foot lodge offers easy access to West Glacier and Camas Creek entrances to the park and more than 10 miles of gorgeous hiking and biking trails of its own. It's an excellent spot for avoiding park crowds. After a day in the outdoors, evenings may be spent soaking in the hot tub or lounging in the library. During winter months the lodge is transformed into an excellent base for cross-county skiers, with more than 10 miles of well-groomed trails that are even good enough for the locals.

Vista Motel

P.O. Box 90, West Glacier, MT 59936.
☎ **406/888-5311.** 27 units. TV. $60–$180 double. AE, DISC, MC, V. Closed Nov–Feb.

Perched atop a hill at the West Entrance to Glacier National Park, the Vista boasts tremendous views of the mountains. Accommodations are not memorable, but rooms are clean and comfortable, and there's an outdoor heated pool.

West Glacier Motel

200 Going-to-the-Sun Rd., West Glacier, MT 59936. ☎ **406/888-5662.** 32 units. Motel $68 double, cabins $99–116. DISC, MC, V.

Formerly the River Bend Motel, this property has two locations. Half of the units are in West Glacier on the Going-to-the-Sun Road, about 1 mile from the park entrance, and a second set of units is 1 mile away on forested grounds with panoramic views of the park. This 1950s-style motel is equipped with TV sets despite the fact that there is virtually no reception unless it happens to be your lucky day. However, the prices can't be beat during peak season, and rates drop dramatically the week before Labor Day. Cabins are better suited for families; they come with two or three queen beds, and fully equipped kitchens.

Dining

INSIDE THE PARK

Food options inside the park are primarily limited to dining rooms operated by GPI. They're convenient, however, and you're almost always assured of friendly service from a staff of 20-something college students from around the country. Credit cards accepted at all GPI properties include Discover, MasterCard, and Visa. Most lunch entrees are $7 to $10; most dinner entrees $10 to $25.

You'll find above-average food served at above-average prices in the dining rooms at the major properties. Glacier Park Lodge has the **Goatlick Steak & Rib**

House and the **Teepee Room;** Lake McDonald Lodge has the **Cedar Dining Room and Lounge;** and Many Glacier Hotel has the **Ptarmigan Dining Room.** The dining rooms open with the park and close sometime in September, depending on the facility. At each dining room, breakfast is served from 6:30 to 9:30am; lunch from 11:30am to 2pm; and dinner from 5:30 to 9:30pm. Coffee and snack shops open either at 7 or 8am and close at 9pm.

The alternatives include second-tier restaurants in close proximity to the hotels, most of which are comparable to chain restaurants. The **coffee shop** at the Rising Sun Motor Inn serves "hearty American fare"; the Swiftcurrent Motor Inn restaurant is the **Italian Garden,** which serves meals from 6am to 10pm. Breakfast prices range from $4 to $7; lunch and dinner feature combinations of salads, sandwiches, pasta dishes, and "create your own" pizzas. At Apgar you'll find the **Cedar Tree Deli,** which specializes in sandwiches, ice cream, and cold drinks, and **Eddie's Cafe,** a family dining arrangement. The restaurant at Lake McDonald is **Trail's End,** where you'll find Continental breakfast ($5) and a full buffet breakfast ($8.25). Lunch is sandwiches and soup ($6 to $9); among items on the dinner menu are beef tenderloin, roast duckling, seared mountain trout, roast turkey, Alaskan salmon, pasta, chicken, and steaks ($12 to $20).

NEAR THE PARK

The gateway cities aren't exactly a culinary wasteland, but for really good food head for Whitefish or Kalispell.

IN EAST GLACIER

Whistle Stop, 1020 Mont. 49 (☎ 406/226-9292), may serve up the very best breakfasts in the area. Omelettes and French toast are a specialty; they come in seven different styles, including a Spanish omelette with chorizo, lots of peppers, tomatoes, onions, and spinach. Definitely an eye-opener.

The **Snowgoose Grille,** located in St. Mary Lodge Resort, is the high-priced alternative. Breakfasts start at $4.75 for a stack of flapjacks and run to $9.25 for steak and eggs. The ambience is upscale for these parts—a glass-enclosed dining room with views of the mountains and the creek. Lunch entrees include typical restaurant sandwiches with fancy names like the "Garden Wall," filled with such diverse items as turkey and buffalo steak; prices range from $6 to $9. The dinner menu features Montana ground buffalo steak ($28), lake whitefish ($12), and prime rib ($22).

The **Park Cafe** (☎ 406/732-4482), only 1½ blocks away on U.S. 89, is a cozier, less-pretentious, home-style restaurant in an old house that presents an excellent alternative to resort and patio dining. The food's good, prices are moderate, and it's not as crowded. Homemade pies are the specialties. They're open from 7am to 10pm. Dinner prices range from $8 to $13.

Glacier Village Restaurant

304–308 Mont. 2, East Glacier. ☎ 406/226-4464. Breakfast items $3–$7; main courses $5–$8 lunch, $8–$15 dinner. MC, V. Daily 6am–10pm. Closed Oct–Apr. AMERICAN.

This family-owned, seasonal restaurant is one of the few full-service joints in the area that serves three meals, starting with breakfast at 6am. Portions are healthy and prices are moderate, with standards like yummy waffles and pancakes made from homemade batter. The restaurant's impressive menu includes pork chops with huckleberry sauce, plus jams and syrups to go.

Restaurant Thimbleberry

1112 Park Dr., East Glacier. ☎ 406/226-5523. Breakfast items $5–$6; main courses $5–$7 lunch, $9–$15 dinner. AE, DC, DISC,

MC, V. Daily 7am–9:30pm. Closed Oct–Apr. AMERICAN.

Locally famous for their incredible pies— the lemon meringue and raspberry are both excellent choices—the Thimbleberry also serves a great veggie omelette for breakfast, sandwiches and salads for lunch, and an excellent cornmeal-dusted St. Mary's Lake whitefish for dinner. This is a good choice for vegetarians or those looking for something other than a Montana steak or hamburger, and the calorie-conscious will find several fat-free choices. If you've never had fry bread, then this is the place to try it.

Serrano's

29 Dawson Ave., East Glacier. ☎ **406/ 226-9392.** Main courses $8–$10. DISC, MC, V. May to mid-Oct daily 5–10pm; closed mid-Oct to Apr. MEXICAN.

Perhaps the area's best restaurant, except for the hotels, Serrano's is just off the highway at the center of town. Serrano's has an outstanding local reputation, so don't be surprised if you encounter masses of people during the height of summer. You can expect hearty portions of Mexican food, plus an ample selection of imported beers and microbrews, and a full bar featuring margaritas.

IN POLEBRIDGE

Northern Lights Saloon

Polebridge. ☎ **406/888-5669.** Reservations not accepted. Main courses $7–$9. MC, V. May–Sept, daily 11am–2pm and 4–9pm (most summer evenings until midnight); Oct–Feb, weekends only. Closed Mar–Apr. AMERICAN.

When people don't mind traveling over 30 miles of bumpy gravel road, when they don't blink an eye as they hit yet another gaping pothole and lose a hubcap or bend a rim, they must know something you don't about wherever it is they're going: in this case, the Northern Lights Saloon. This small

restaurant, located squarely in the middle of nowhere, attracts summer crowds that often have to wait patiently outside for a table to clear. Picnic tables, a volleyball net, and the peaks of Glacier Park are there to make the wait as painless as possible. Seating choices are uncomplicated: Take a seat at one of the five tables, or find a spot at the bar. You won't find a place with more character or with friendlier staff and customers, and you don't need a tie.

IN WEST GLACIER

Glacier Highlander Restaurant

U.S. 2, West Glacier. ☎ **406/888-5427.** Breakfast items $3–$5; lunch $5–$7; dinner main courses $7–$14. DISC, MC, V. Daily 7am–9pm (midsummer hours 6:30am–10pm). Closed Nov 2–Mar. AMERICAN.

This may be the spot to satisfy the sweet tooth; a baker is on hand, so the pies are well worth the stop, and the cinnamon rolls are breakfast giants. The Highland Burger is, by any standard, a great hunk of beef, and the fresh trout is a dinner specialty.

Heaven's Peak Dining and Spirits

12130 U.S. 2, West Glacier. ☎ **406/ 387-4754.** Lunch $6–$8, main dinner courses $9–$15. AE, DISC, MC, V. Daily 11am–3pm and 5–10pm. AMERICAN.

West Glacier's newest eating facility is in a massive log building right off the highway within footsteps of town. A huge deck overlooks a beautiful sculpted rock garden and manicured lawns and provides comfortable seating but, alas, also provides road noise. The chef proudly uses only fresh ingredients; nothing is deep-fried here. The lunch menu includes several salads as well as various sandwiches; dinners include fresh fish as well as pasta, chicken, buffalo, beef, and roast duck.

A Side Trip to Waterton Lakes National Park

It's worth finding the time to explore the upper regions of this area. From St. Mary, head north to visit Waterton Lakes National Park, Glacier's northern, Canadian counterpart. You'll be rewarded with different yet equally beautiful scenery and a touch of European culture.

Located in Alberta, Canada, Waterton is considered the place where the Canadian mountains meet the rolling prairies; hence, there's an incredible variety of flowers and animals here. As you travel along the high ridge you'll see meadows and boggy areas that are ideal habitat for moose; later, you'll find yourself surrounded by lakes, as the Canadian Rockies fill the horizon. The area is also a haven for elk, mule deer, and bighorn sheep, and both grizzly and black bears are found in the park.

JUST THE FACTS

Getting There. From the eastern entrance of Glacier National Park at St. Mary, drive north through Babb, which is barely a whistle-stop, until you reach the intersection of Mont. 17—it's very well marked. Head northwest to the Canadian border, where Mont. 17 becomes Alberta Highway 6 (**remember, you need proof of citizenship—and a driver's license doesn't always work**). Head down into the valley until you reach the park entrance on your left.

Visitor Information. The park's **Visitor Reception Centre** is just inside the park, on the same road you used coming in (☎ 403/859-5133).

Fees & Permits. Park entrance costs Can$4 (US$2.80) per person, at a maximum of Can$8 (US$5.60) per vehicle. Day hiking does not require a permit, but backcountry overnight trips do, at a cost of Can$6 (US$4.20) per person per day, with a maximum

per person for multiday trips of Can$30 (US$21).

A BRIEF HISTORY

Compared to its counterparts in the Lower 48, Waterton is a tiny park; the total size is only 203 square miles. However, the park has great historical significance: Based on more than 200 identified archaeological sites, historians think that Aborigines first populated the area 11,000 years ago.

In modern times, Waterton Lakes became a national park about 6 years before oil was discovered here. (Oil and mineral exploration was allowed in Canada's national parks during the system's infancy.) It was set aside as a national park, thanks to the efforts of a local rancher. Then in 1932, following an initiative by the Rotary Clubs of Alberta and Montana, Waterton Lakes and Glacier National Parks were designated the world's first **International Peace Park,** and have since come to represent the need for cooperation between nations where sharing resources and ecosystems is possible. The areas were designated Bio-Sphere Reserves by the UNESCO Man and Bio-Sphere Program, in order to provide information about the relationships between people and the environment. The two parks were jointly designated a UNESCO World Heritage Site in 1995.

EXPLORING THE PARK

Unlike most "park centers"—essentially a smattering of restaurants, souvenir shops, and gas stations clustered around the primary lodging—Waterton Village actually is a village. As you cruise the perimeter of the lake headed for Waterton Village, you'll pass three large lakes, the habitat of bald eagles that are often seen perched atop the snags of dead trees. The park bears a striking resemblance to Teton in that its attractions spread out across a narrow valley floor; however, the valley is narrower and three-fourths of it is surrounded by peaks, so the overall effect is cozier but equally dramatic.

By most standards, it's also windier here, though locals say that they don't acknowledge the wind unless there are whitecaps in the rest room toilets at the Prince of Wales Hotel (see "Accommodations," below).

Hiking, cruising the lake, or just doing nothing are ideal pastimes in this neck of the woods. Most of the 191 miles of trails are easily accessible from town and range in difficulty from short strolls to steep treks for overnight backcountry enthusiasts.

DAY HIKES

The park is a popular destination for European, Canadian, and American hiking fanatics. For nearly 20 years, the 10.8-mile **Crypt Lake Trail** has been rated as one of Canada's best hikes—except for those prone to seasickness, since the trailhead is reached by taking a 2-mile boat ride across Upper Waterton Lake. After that, the trail leads past Hellroaring Falls, Twin Falls, and Burnt Rock Falls before reaching Crypt Falls, and a passage through a 60-foot rock tunnel. The elevation gain is 2,300 feet, but veterans say the hike is doable in 3 hours, one way.

A second extended tour starts at the marina and heads south across the international boundary to **Goat Haunt,** Montana, an especially popular trip because of the sightings of bald eagles, bear, bighorn sheep, deer, and moose, as well as numerous unusual geologic formations. For details regarding the boat shuttle, contact **Waterton InterNation Shoreline Cruises** (☎ 403/859-2362).

The **International Peace Park Hike** is a free guided trip held on Saturdays from the end of June through the end of August. Participants meet at the Bertha Trailhead at 10am and spend the day on an 8.5-mile trail that follows Upper Waterton Lake. At the end of the trail, hikers return via boat to the main dock. Adult fare is Can$10 (US$7); children's fare Can$5 (US$3.50).

CAMPING

At the west end of the village is **Townsite Campground,** a Parks Canada–operated facility with 235 sites that's an especially popular jumping-off spot for campers headed into the park's backcountry. Prices range from Can$15 to Can$21 (US$10.50 to US$14.70); half of the sites have electricity and sewage disposal; also available on the premises are kitchen shelters, washrooms, and shower facilities. The site is perched right on the lake, so views are excellent and trails await evening strollers.

There are 13 designated **wilderness campgrounds** with dry toilets and surface water, some of which have shelters.

ACCOMMODATIONS

For complete lodging information contact **central reservations** for the Waterton area (☎ 800/215-2395).

While the Prince of Wales Hotel (see below) is clearly the flagship in these woods, alternate arrangements can be made at **Kilmorey Lodge** (☎ 888/859-8669). This cozy country inn on Emerald Bay, at the north end of the lake, has an antique decor. Bedrooms have down comforters and the dining room and lounge are on premises. Waterton's newest property is the **Lodge at Waterton Lake** (☎ 888/985-6343 or 403/859-2150), which opened in July 1997. In the heart of Waterton Village, the lodge offers lake and mountain views; some rooms have fireplaces, whirlpool tubs, and kitchenettes. Other facilities include a health center spa and indoor pool.

The Prince of Wales Hotel

Waterton Lakes National Park, AB T0K 2M0. ☎ **403/859-2231,** or 602/207-6000 in the off-season. Fax 403/859-2630. www. glacierparkinc.com. 87 units. TEL. Can$210–Can$345 (US$147–US$242) double, Can$699 (US$490) suite. MC, V. Closed Oct–Apr.

The Prince of Wales compares to the finest park hostelries in Montana and

Wyoming. Built in 1927 by the Great Northern Railway, the hotel boasts soaring roofs, gables, and balconies that convey the appearance of a giant alpine chalet. The lobby, like many of the old railroad hotels, is wood, wood, and more wood—in this case accented by tufted furniture and carpeting. Two-story-tall windows overlook the lake and village, only minutes away by footpath. Rooms, though small, have aged well, with dark-stained high-paneled wainscoting and heavily upholstered chairs. Bathrooms are European-style tubs with wraparound curtains; one look at the size of the wash basins, and you'd surmise guests were Lilliputian-size when the hotel was first constructed.

If you don't spend the night at the Prince of Wales, at least stop in for a traditional British high tea, served afternoons at 3pm for Can$14 (US$10). All in all, the experience is very European—the gift shop even sells china and crystal.

DINING

All of the village's restaurants and retail outlets are within a 4-block area on Waterton Avenue (which the locals call Main Street). So despite the fact that many buildings aren't numbered, you'll have no problem finding places to eat or shop.

Little Italian Cafe (no phone) has indoor dining on plastic chairs and tables and is organized for the family looking for a modestly priced meal. Just up the street, **Zum's** (☎ 403/859-2388) is another family-oriented restaurant with a comparable menu but lower prices. You'll find more luxurious surroundings, and slightly higher prices, at **Kootenai Brown Dining Room** (☎ 403/859-2211) at the Bayshore Inn, considered the luxury spot on the lake. The order of the day is steaks, chicken, rack of lamb, and the occasional seafood entree; prices range from Can$13 to Can$20 (US$9 to US$15).

Frank's Restaurant (☎ 403/859-2240) serves both conventional Western fare that includes beef, chicken, and spaghetti—with prices ranging from Can$6 to Can$15 (US$4 to US$10.50)—as well as a Chinese menu that includes an all-you-can-eat evening buffet for Can$10 (US$7).

17

GLACIER BAY NATIONAL PARK

by Charles P. Wohlforth

GLACIER BAY IS A WORK IN PROGRESS; THE BOAT RIDE TO ITS HEAD IS a chance to see creation fresh. The bay John Muir discovered in a canoe in 1879 didn't exist a century earlier. Eighteenth-century explorers had found instead a wall of ice a mile thick where the entrance to the branching, 65-mile-long fjord now opens to the sea. Receding faster than any other glacier on earth, the ice melted into the ocean and opened a spectacular and still-unfinished land. The land itself is rising 1½ inches a year as it rebounds from the weight of now-melted glaciers. As your vessel retraces Muir's path—and then probes northward in deep water where ice stood in his day—the story of this new world unravels in reverse. The trees on the shore get smaller, then disappear, then all vegetation disappears, and finally, at the head of the bay, the ice stands at the water's edge surrounded by barren rock, rounded and scored by the passage of the ice, but not yet marked by the water-falls cascading from above. It's often windy and cold at the head of the bay, near the glaciers. Be prepared, and try to enjoy the beauty of the mist and rain—at times the smooth, silver water, barren rock, white clouds, and ice create an ethereal study in white.

Set aside by Pres. Calvin Coolidge in 1925, Glacier Bay is a rugged park the size of Connecticut that can be seen only by boat or plane, but the presence of too many boats threatens the park. The whales appear to be sensitive to the noise of vessels and since the 1970s the Park Service has used a permit system to limit the number of ships that can enter the bay. After a bitter controversy, the Park Service recently increased the number of cruise ships entering the bay, and whale sightings, including humpback whales breaching—leaping all the way out of the water—have continued to be quite frequent.

Avoiding the Crowds. There are no crowds in this huge wilderness park, but the lone tour boat into the bay can feel crowded. Large cruise ships bring most visitors to the park, viewing the scenery without getting close to shore or wildlife, and missing the shore-based attractions. Smaller ships see more, and have fewer people and more chances to get outdoors. Independent travelers can spend a few days in some of Alaska's most attractive wilderness accommodations, with great fishing, hiking, sea kayaking, and tour boat rides. The only way to see the heart of the park in true solitude, however, is on a boat you charter for yourself (out of range of most budgets) or on a rugged overnight sea kayaking adventure.

Just the Facts

GETTING THERE & GATEWAYS

Unless you're on a cruise ship, you'll fly or take a passenger ferry to **Gustavus,** then take a van to the park headquarters. The vans meet the planes and boats and cost $10 to make the 10-mile trip to the park, plus $2 for baggage. Most Gustavus inns and lodges offer free transfers to the park.

By Boat. The *Auk Nu* passenger ferry, a high-speed catamaran (☎ 800/820-2628 or 907/586-8687; www.auknutours.com) leaves Juneau's Auke Bay harbor from 11789 Glacier Highway, next to the ferry terminal, at 11am daily May through September. The adult fare is $45 one way, $85 round-trip; children 3 to 12 $30 and $60. The *Auk Nu* lands at Gustavus at 1:15pm, goes on an afternoon whale-watching cruise in Icy Strait, then leaves for Juneau at 5:45pm, arriving at 8pm. Adding the highly recommended whale watch brings the adult round trip fare to $139. The boat also carries kayaks and bikes, for an added fee.

A **multiday boat excursion** into the park from Juneau is described under "Seeing the Park," below.

By Air. During the summer, **Alaska Airlines** (☎ 800/426-0333; www.alaskaair.com) flies once a day from Juneau to Gustavus and back. Various commuter carriers serve Gustavus from Juneau and other nearby towns, including **L.A.B. Flying Service** (☎ 800/426-0543 or 907/766-2222). Daily flights from Juneau are $70 one way.

It's possible to take a flightseeing trip to Glacier Bay from Haines; details are given under "Seeing the Park," below.

INFORMATION

Contact **Glacier Bay National Park and Preserve,** P.O. Box 140, Gustavus, AK 99826 (☎ 907/697-2230; www.nps.gov/glba). For most information, contact the concessionaire, **Glacier Bay Tours,** 520 Pike St., Suite 1400, Seattle, WA 98101 (☎ 800/451-5952 or 206/623-2417; fax 206/623-7809; www.glacierbaytours.com) or, locally, in the summer only, at P.O. Box 199, Gustavus, AK 99826 (☎ 907/697-2226; fax 907/697-2408). This well-run company operates the lodge at Bartlett Cove and most of the activities in the park.

Books on the natural and cultural history of Glacier Bay and of Alaska are available from the **Alaska Natural History Association,** 750 W. Second Ave., Suite 100, Anchorage, AK 99501-2167 (☎ 907/274-8440; fax 907/274-8443; www.alaskanha.org).

VISITOR CENTER

The park service interprets the park mainly by placing well-prepared rangers on board all cruise and tour vessels entering the bay. The park also maintains a modest Visitor Information Center with exhibits on the second floor of the lodge at wooded Bartlett Cove.

FEES & PERMITS

There are no fees to visit or camp in Glacier Bay National Park and Preserve other than those included in the price of any paid activity, such as boat trips or rooms. Campers should obtain permits at the Visitor Information Station, but these are not limited and need not be reserved. Backcountry permits are required for overnight backcountry travel.

Entrance into the park and preserve by private boat requires a permit from June through August. Permits are limited and may be reserved (call the park office).

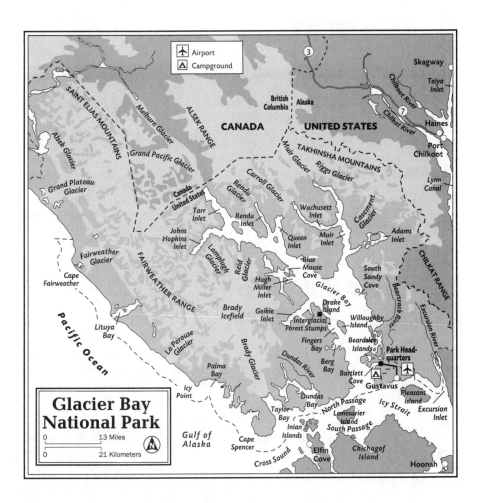

Map legend:
- ✈ Airport
- ⛺ Campground

Glacier Bay National Park

0 — 13 Miles
0 — 21 Kilometers

Do not gather mussels and clams from Glacier Bay without an OK from the park service or other authority: a naturally occurring neurotoxin that causes paralytic shellfish poisoning sometimes shows up in the area's shellfish.

Firearms are prohibited in Glacier Bay National Park and must be secured at the Visitor Information Center for the duration of your stay if you bring them into the park boundaries.

The travel season to Glacier Bay generally lasts from mid-May through September, when most of the area's accommodations shut down for the winter and the Visitor Information Center closes. Rain and long periods of cool, overcast weather are common in the summer, with daytime temperatures ranging from 45° to 65°F. Bring a hat, gloves, rain gear, and waterproof footwear. Boat service to Gustavus or into the park runs only during summer, making off-season visits impractical. You can fly to Gustavus year-round, but weather conditions can cause cancellations in any season—try to leave some time in your schedule to accommodate a delay.

If You Only Have 1 Day

Because of its isolation, Glacier Bay cannot be seen easily in a day trip (except by cruise ship passengers), but it is possible. **Glacier Bay Tours and Cruises** (see "Information," above) offers a one-day trip from Juneau, Haines, or Skagway, which begins with a very early flight to Gustavus, then a boat tour and a return flight in the evening. *Warning:* This makes for a very long day and leaves no time in Glacier Bay for anything but the boat trip. The package fare from Juneau is $346.50, about $100 more from the other towns. A better choice is to spend the night before the boat trip at one of the inns in Gustavus, or at the park lodge. The overnight lodge package is $481 to $639, depending on your starting point.

Seeing the Park

BY BOAT

The *Spirit of Adventure* tour boat is the main way for independent travelers to see the park. It is operated by park concessionaire **Glacier Bay Tours and Cruises** (see "Information," above). The boat is fast and quiet, carrying up to 250 passengers in upper and lower lounges. Its shortcomings are inadequate outdoor deck space and a tendency for the windows to fog up. Some find the table-oriented seating arrangements a bit confining, and the 9-hour voyage is too long for most children. There's a snack bar and a simple lunch is provided. Bring good rain gear. Binoculars, a necessity, are available for use. A Park Service ranger does the commentary, so you can count on accuracy and a didactic approach missing from most commercial tours. The fare is $175 for adults, half price for children.

If your budget allows, one of the best ways to see Glacier Bay is on a small cruise ship on an excursion of a couple of days or more. **Glacier Bay Tours and Cruises** has developed a small-ship cruise fleet around this idea. The four vessels provide a choice of itineraries and activities, including the standard **Inside Passage** cruise, which is offered on a smaller boat that can go closer to shore and into less visited towns. More relevant for national park visitors, the *Wilderness Explorer* and the larger *Wilderness*

Adventurer carry racks of sea kayaks, and include time to get off and experience the outdoors paddling and hiking. They don't spend time in towns, instead visiting beautiful and remote places. Back on board, you're still comfortable and even pampered. Tours leave Juneau or Glacier Bay, and last 5 to 7 nights; the *Wilderness Explorer,* with only 36 passengers, spends 4 days of a 5-night cruise in the bay and the exceptional whale watching waters of Icy Strait. Prices range from $1,480 to $2,675 per person.

Smaller operators based in Gustavus also offer trips. If you have a large group, you can have a boat and guide to yourself. Mike Nigro, a former backcountry ranger and 25-year resident, takes groups of four to six for $1,400 to $1,650 per day on a 42-foot yacht. **Gustavus Marine Charters** is reached at P.O. Box 81, Gustavus, AK 99826 (☎ **907/697-2233;** fax 907/697-2414; www.gustavusmarinecharters.com).

BY AIR

The other common way to explore the park is by **flightseeing. Frontier Air,** P.O. Box 1, Gustavus, AK 99826 (☎ **907/697-2386**), offers flights from the Bartlett Cove visitor center. Other companies offer tours from various towns, Haines being the closest, served by **L.A.B. Flying Service** (☎ **800/426-0543** or 907/766-2222), for one. Cost for a 1-hour flight, with a two-person minimum, is about $105 per person.

Exploring the Backcountry

This vast, undeveloped park offers **sea kayakers** an opportunity to explore a true wilderness, far from the support of civilization; however, going on an extended trip without a guide is only for those who already have learned their skills and limitations in more forgiving waters.

Most backcountry kayakers go to see the glaciers up the protected eastern fjords after being carried part of the way by the concessionaire-operated *Crystal*

Fjord, or stay in the islands near the Bartlett Cove lodge, where there are no glaciers. Make sure you calibrate the length of your trip to your experience—this is remote territory, and you can't just leave once you're out there. Also, everyone going into the backcountry is required to get a backcountry permit at the ranger station and attend an orientation. There is a limit on the number of permits issued, but it has never been reached, so at present you can count on getting one through the first-come, first-served process. **Glacier Bay Sea Kayaks,** P.O. Box 26, Gustavus, AK 99826 (☎ **907/697-2257;** fax 907/ 697-3002; www.he.net/~kayakak), operating May through September, offers instruction and rentals for $50 a day, and drop-offs up the bay are $167.50 round-trip.

See "Sea Kayaking," below, for guided options.

Ranger Programs

Programs, scheduled only in summer, take place at the lodge. Videos show in the auditorium at various times daily. In the morning, rangers lead short nature walks; in the afternoon a ranger-led hike covers the 1-mile Forest Loop Trail (see below). Two slide shows take place each evening.

Day Hikes

Three short hiking trails wind through the rain forest of Sitka spruce and western hemlock at Bartlett Cove. Each weaves through the cool, damp quiet that these huge trees and the moss create on the forest floor, and wet spots often are crossed by boardwalks with railings. A free trail guide is available at the visitor center.

The **Forest Loop** is an easy 1-mile one-way trail that begins at the lodge and travels through the woods and past some park buildings to the cove's pebble beach, with its dock and sea kayak racks. The best months for wildflower-viewing are June and July; the best months for

bird watching are May and June (when the bird migration is at its peak).

The **Bartlett River Trail,** 4 miles round-trip, is an easy to moderate hike with a few muddy spots that ends at the Bartlett River Estuary, a good bird-watching spot, especially during migrations.

The **Bartlett Lake Trail** branches off the Bartlett River Trail after about 0.25 mile. The 6-mile moderate round-trip weaves through the forest to the lake, where you must double back to return.

Other Sports & Activities

Hiking & Biking in Gustavus. Gustavus offers some of Alaska's most enjoyable hiking and biking. There are few cars in and around the town because they have to be hauled here on a barge. Most inns in Gustavus provide bikes. The roads are fun to explore, and the sandy beaches, accessed from the town dock, are a great place for a walk and a picnic. It's 14 miles from Good River Road along the shore around Point Gustavus to the Bartlett Cove National Park Center, 7 miles from the town dock along the beach to the airport. Most will find no need to walk so far, traveling just far enough to be totally alone, where its possible to see eagles and orcas, and built sand castles.

Sea Kayaking. The great majority of people see the park on cruise ships or tour boats, but a sea kayak is the outdoors way. You won't forget the sight of a breaching humpback whale from a kayak, just inches off the water, and feeling the waves from its stupendous splash passing under your hull.

Inexperienced paddlers should choose a guided trip. **Alaska Discovery,** 5449 Shaune Dr., Suite 4, Juneau, AK 99801 (☎ **800/586-1911** or 907/ 780-6226; fax 907/780-4220; www. akdiscovery.com), is Alaska's best large sea kayak guide organization. They offer trips ranging from 6 hours to 8 days in Glacier Bay. A 6-hour guided paddle around Bartlett Cove and the Beardslee Islands is a good choice for beginners. Although the trip goes nowhere near the glaciers, the paddlers stand a good chance of seeing whales, sometimes quite close up. The guides are well trained and know how to teach and make the trip an adventure. Any fit person could enjoy the trip. It costs $119, including a tasty lunch and transport from your lodgings or the airport.

The longer tours also are well guided and outfitted, but not recommended for those who haven't tried sea kayaking before. If you're up to it, this is the most intimate and authentic way to experience this wilderness, with almost unlimited time to see the glaciers and wildlife. The 5-day trip to the bay's more visited west arm is $1,675; 8 days in the spectacular but forgotten east arm is $1,975. The company also operates a simple bed-and-breakfast in Gustavus, convenient at the end or beginning of a sea-kayaking excursion.

It's also possible to paddle around Bartlett Cove or near Gustavus without a guide. Raw beginners can try it, but a safer course is to take a guided outing first. **Glacier Bay Sea Kayaks** (see "Exploring the Backcountry," above) offers an instructional briefing before sending visitors out in kayaks that rent for $50 a day for a double.

Whale Watching. Whales keep their own schedule, and you may or may not see them in Glacier Bay National Park proper. But you're almost certain to see them on a whale watching excursion from nearby Gustavus, where the swirling current of Icy Strait creates such a rich feeding ground that humpbacks come back every summer. Whale-watching trips aboard the *Auk Nu,* a large, comfortable catamaran, leave the town dock for Point Adolphus every day at 2pm. The commentary is first rate, and a good, light meal is included. The fare for the 3-hour cruise is $78, and you get your money back if you don't see whales—which virtually never happens.

Other, smaller operators will provide a more intimate experience on smaller boats, usually getting you closer to the whales. They'll also combine the trip

with superb halibut and salmon fishing. Your inn host in Gustavus can make the arrangements. A boat typically charters for $200 or more per person for a full day.

Camping

A primitive **free campground** is located about 0.25 mile by trail from the main dock and ranger station, with bear-resistant food caches, firewood, pit toilets, and a warming hut. There is no running water. Showers are available at the lodge. You must do all your cooking and eating in the intertidal zone, where there is a designated fire ring, and observe other bear-country camping techniques that the rangers explain at a required orientation. You cannot reserve, but the campground is virtually never full. Obtain a free camping permit at the ranger station on arrival.

Accommodations & Dining

INSIDE THE PARK

Glacier Bay Lodge

Bartlett Cove (P.O. Box 199), Gustavus, AK 99826. ☎ **800/451-5952** or 907/697-2226. Fax 206/623-7809 or 907/697-2408. www. glacierbaytours.com. 56 units. TEL. $165 double. Hostel bunks $28 per person. AE, DC, DISC, MC, V. Closed mid-Sept to mid-May.

Operated by park concessionaire Glacier Bay Tours and Cruises, this is the only place to stay in the park. The lodge rooms are comfortable and well maintained, but for the price, nothing special. However, the setting is among the soothing quiet of large rain forest trees. For those on a budget, there are bunk rooms with six beds each for men and women. The lodge restaurant, looking out on Bartlett Cove, offers a few inexpensive main courses on the dinner menu, but mainly it's a fine-dining establishment with white tablecloths and dishes in the $20 range. Breakfast is available as early as 5:30am and dinner as late as

10pm. The lodge also provides showers for the free park service campground. Laundry facilities and bike rentals are available.

Gustavus contains many of Alaska's best remote accommodations, but unfortunately, it is short on restaurants. Each of the full-service inns serves meals by prior arrangement, and there is the restaurant at the lodge at Bartlett Cove. You might also enjoy the moderately priced **A Bear's Nest Cafe,** on Rink Creek Road (☎ **907/697-2440**), where Lynne Morrow serves organic dishes, homemade bread, seafood specials, soup and sandwiches in a dining room that's also the ground floor of her house. Hours are 1 to 8pm daily in the summer, and Discover, MasterCard and Visa are accepted.

Lodgings below operate in "Gustavus style," which means charging a single daily price for comfortable, unique rooms, breakfast and dinner served family style, brown bag lunches, bicycles and other equipment, transportation around the area, and someone to make all the arrangements for fishing, sea kayaking, hiking, and Glacier Bay tours.

Glacier Bay's Bear Track Inn

255 Rink Rd, Gustavus, AK 99826. ☎ **888/ 697-2284** or 907/697-3017. Fax 907/ 697-2284. www.BearTrackInn.com. 14 units. $393 per person, double occupancy. Rates include round-trip air from Juneau and all meals. AE, DISC, MC, V. Closed Nov–Jan.

Six miles from Gustavus, this extraordinary log building faces its own field of wildflowers, which, if you walk half a mile across it, leads to the sea. You look out on this scene from a lobby with a huge fireplace, a ceiling 28 feet high, and a wall of windows. The immense logs of the walls and the isolation give the inn the feeling of a wilderness lodge, and the rooms' large dormer windows offer sweeping views. Unlike other accommodations in Gustavus, meals are cooked to order from a varied menu. Most entrees come from a grill that stands on one side of the dining room. Nonguests can buy dinner for $30.

Gustavus Inn at Glacier Bay

Gustavus Rd. (P.O. Box 60), Gustavus, AK 99826 (in winter, 7920 Outlook, Prairie Village, KS 66208). ☎ **800/649-5220** or 907/697-2254. Fax 907/697-2255 in summer, 913/649-5220 in winter. 11 units. $270 double. AE, MC, V. Closed Sept 16–May 15.

This is the original and still the best of the Gustavus full-service inns. By objective standards of modern luxury, imitators have surpassed the old homestead farmhouse, but no one could duplicate the extraordinary hospitality of the Lesh family, honed over 35 years of running the inn. The site is unsurpassed, too, standing at the center of the community, amid blowing grass and with a huge vegetable garden that provides much of the dining room's wonderful food. Dave is the chef, and the seasonings he uses on seafood are a real revelation. There's also a beer and wine bar. Talk over what you want to do with Dave or his father, Jack, and let them book everything. They drive guests around and offer free bikes and fishing rods (bring your own tackle) and laundry service.

Meadow's Glacier Bay Guest House

Off Dock Rd. (P.O. 93), Gustavus, AK 99826. ☎ **907/697-2348**. Fax 907/697-2454; www. glacier-bay-alaska.com. 5 units, 4 with bathroom. $139–$179 double with private bathroom, $119 with shared bathroom. MC, V.

At high tide the sea comes to the base of the lawn by the grassy meadow and estuary where this house stands, a rich foreground for stunning views in every direction. If any house could live up to such a setting, this is it. Its cool, airy spaces interpret those outside with big geometric shapes, shining wood floors, and white walls hung with some of the best of Alaska's contemporary art. Each guest room is fashionable, immaculate, and perhaps a bit too good for mere mortals.

18

GRAND CANYON NATIONAL PARK

by Alex Wells

THE FIRST THING YOU MAY NOTICE ABOUT THE GRAND CANYON IS ITS size. At 277 river miles long, roughly 5,000 feet deep, and an average of 10 miles across, it's so big that even the breezes seem to draw a deep breath at the rims. In the past 6 million years, while river or rivers that would eventually become the Colorado River were carving the main canyon, runoff from the rims cut hundreds of side canyons draining into the larger one. Separating these side canyons, buttes and mesas rise thousands of feet from the floor. Early cartographers and geologists noticed similarities between these terraced buttes and some of the greatest works of human hands. They began calling them temples, and named them after Far Eastern deities such as Brahma, Vishnu, and Shiva.

The canyon not only inspires reverence but tells the grandest of stories. Half the earth's history is represented in its rocks. The oldest and deepest rock layer, the Vishnu Formation, began forming 2 billion years ago, before aerobic life forms even existed. The different layers of sedimentary rock that piled up atop the Vishnu Formation tell of landscapes that changed like dreams. They speak of mountains that really did move, eroding away into nothingness; of oceans that poured forth across the land before receding; of deserts, swamps, and rivers the size of the Mississippi—all where the canyon now lies. The very evolution of life is illustrated by the fossils in these layers.

Many of the latest products of evolution—more than 1,500 plant and 400 animal species—still survive at the canyon today. If you include the upper reaches of the Kaibab Plateau (on the canyon's North Rim), this small area of northern Arizona includes zones of biological life comparable to ones found as far south as Mexico and as far north as Alaska. The species come in every shape, size, and temperament, ranging from tiny ant lions dwelling on the canyon floor to 1,000-pound elk roaming the rims. And for every species there is a story within the story. Take the Douglas fir, for example. Once part of a forest that covered both rims and much of the canyon, this tree has endured since the last ice age on shady, north-facing slopes beneath the South Rim—long after the sun-baked rim itself became too hot and inhospitable.

A number of different tribes have lived in or around the canyon, and the Navajo, Havasupai, Kaibab Paiute, Hopi, Zuni, and Hualapai tribes still live in this area. The Hopi still regard the canyon as their place of emergence and the place to which their dead return. Their predecessors left behind more than 3,000 archaeological sites and artifacts as old as 10,000 years.

In the 1500s Spanish missionaries and gold-greedy explorers passed through the area, but it wasn't until the 1800s that white people began settling here. Prospectors clambered through the canyon in search of precious minerals, and some of them stayed after their mines, plagued by high overhead, shut down. The first tourists followed, and began flooding the area after the railroad linked Grand Canyon Village to Williams, Arizona, in 1901.

When Theodore Roosevelt visited here in 1903, the canyon moved him to say, "Leave it as it is. You cannot improve on it. The ages have been at work on it, and man can only mar it. What you can do is to keep it for your children, your children's children . . . as the one great sight which every American . . . should see." Roosevelt did his part to back up his words, using the Antiquities Act to declare Grand Canyon a national monument in 1908. Congress established Grand Canyon National Park in 1919.

Although designated a "park," Grand Canyon still has a daunting, even ominous side. Visitors, no matter how many times they enter it, must negotiate with it for survival. One look at the clenched jaw of a boater as he or she rows into Lava Rapids will remind you that the canyon exacts a heavy price for mistakes, the most common of which is to underestimate it. Try to escape, and it becomes a prison, with walls 4,000 feet high. The canyon's menace reminds us that we still haven't completely conquered nature. It even has its own symbols: the rattlesnake's warning; the elegant symmetry of the black widow; the seductive, lilylike flower of the deadly sacred datura.

Clearly, you can suffer here, but reward is everywhere. It's in the spectrum of colors: The Colorado River, filled with runoff from a recent rain, runs blood red beneath slopes of orange Hakatai shale; cactus flowers explode in pink, yellow, and red; and lichens paint rocks orange, green, and gray, creating art more striking than the works in any gallery. It's in the shapes, too—the spires, amphitheaters, temples, ramps, and cliffs—and in the shadows that bend across them before lifting like mist. It's in the myriad organisms and their individual struggles for survival. Perhaps most of all, it's in the constancy of the river, which, even as it cuts closer to a beginning, reminds us that all things break down, wash away, and return to the earth in time.

Avoiding the Crowds. Maureen Oltrogge, the public affairs officer for Grand Canyon, offers this straightforward advice for people wanting to avoid the crowds at the park: "Prime season is July and August. Try to visit at another time. If you can't come during the off-season, we recommend that you come before 10am or after 2pm, so that you can avoid both the lines at the entrance gates and the parking problems inside the park."

The advice holds true for both rims. Oltrogge points out that because the North Rim lacks facilities for large numbers of people, it sometimes feels as crowded as the South Rim, in spite of having roughly one-eighth the visitation.

Although mass transit won't help you avoid the crowds, it might make those crowds more bearable, says Oltrogge. "We recommend alternate transportation. There's a shuttle [to the South Rim] from Tusayan, and there's also a train into the park from Williams. We recommend that you park your vehicle and use these."

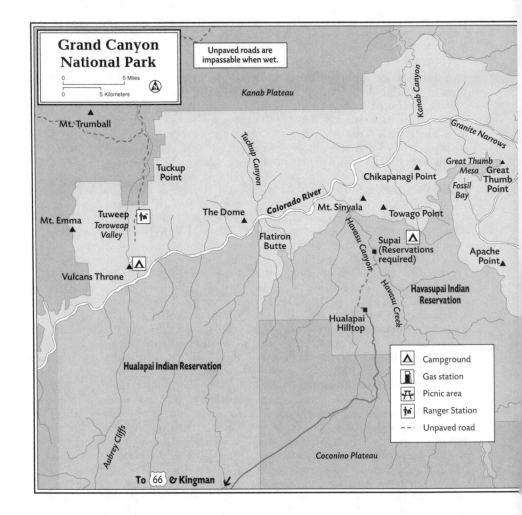

Grand Canyon National Park

0 — 5 Miles
0 — 5 Kilometers

Unpaved roads are impassable when wet.

Kanab Plateau

Kanab Canyon

Mt. Trumball

Tuckup Canyon

Granite Narrows

Tuckup Point

Chikapanagi Point

Great Thumb Mesa

Great Thumb Point

Fossil Bay

Mt. Emma

Tuweep

Toroweap Valley

The Dome

Colorado River

Mt. Sinyala

Towago Point

Flatiron Butte

Havasu Canyon

Supai (Reservations required)

Apache Point

Vulcans Throne

Havasupai Indian Reservation

Hualapai Indian Reservation

Havasu Creek

Hualapai Hilltop

	Campground
	Gas station
	Picnic area
	Ranger Station
---	Unpaved road

Aubrey Cliffs

Coconino Plateau

To 66 & Kingman

Just the Facts

GETTING THERE & GATEWAYS

The nearest cities to the Grand Canyon are Flagstaff, Arizona, 78 miles south of Grand Canyon Village on U.S. 180; and Williams, Arizona, 59 miles south on Ariz. 64.

The closest town to the park is Tusayan, Arizona, 1 mile south of the South Entrance gates on Ariz. 64. The closest substantial town to the North Rim is Kanab, Utah, 78 miles northwest of Grand Canyon National Park on U.S. 89A.

The Nearest Airports. Many travelers fly to **Phoenix/Sky Harbor International**

Airport (☎ 602/273-3300), 220 miles from the South Rim, or to **McCarron International Airport** (☎ 702/261-5743) in Las Vegas, 263 miles from the North Rim. Both these airports are served by the major airlines and car-rental companies. See the appendix for toll-free numbers.

For those who would like to fly closer than Phoenix or Las Vegas, **America West Express** (☎ 800-235-9292) has daily jet service connecting Phoenix/ Sky Harbor International Airport and **Flagstaff Pulliam Airport.** Closer still is **Grand Canyon National Park Airport** (☎ 520/638-2446) in Tusayan, 1.5 miles outside the park entrance. **Arizona Professional Air Travel** (☎ 800/933-7590; www.fly-in-america.

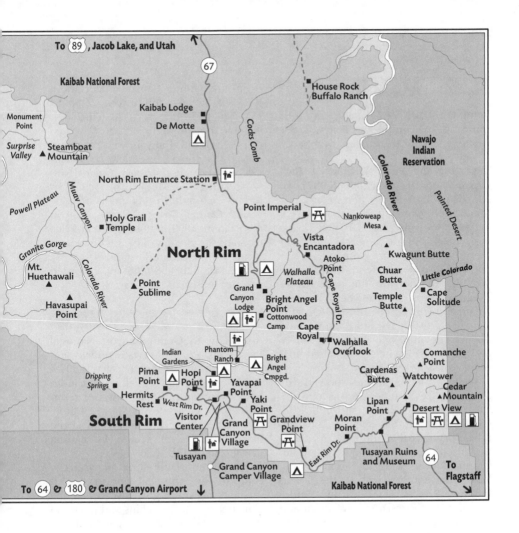

To ⑧⑨ , Jacob Lake, and Utah

Kaibab National Forest

⑥⑦

Monument
Point

*Surprise
Valley* ▲ Steamboat
   Mountain

Kaibab Lodge

De Motte

House Rock
Buffalo Ranch

North Rim Entrance Station

**Navajo
Indian
Reservation**

Powell Plateau

Cochs Comb

Point Imperial

Nankoweap
Mesa ▲

Painted Desert

Muav Canyon

Holy Grail
▪ Temple

North Rim

Vista
Encantadora

Atoko
Point

Kwagunt Butte

Granite Gorge

Mt.
Huethawali ▲

Point
Sublime

*Walhalla
Plateau*

Chuar
Butte ▲

Little Colorado

Colorado River

Grand
Canyon
Lodge

Bright Angel
Point

Temple
Butte ▲

▪ Cape
Solitude

▲
Havasupai
Point

Cottonwood
Camp

Cape
Royal

Cape Royal Dr.

Indian
Gardens

Phantom
Ranch

Bright
Angel
Cmpgd.

Walhalla
Overlook

Comanche
▲ Point

*Dripping
Springs* ▪

Pima
Point

Hopi
Point

Yavapai
Point

Cardenas
Butte ▪

Watchtower

Hermits
Rest ▪ *West Rim Dr.*

Yaki
Point

Lipan
Point

Cedar
▲ Mountain

South Rim

Visitor
Center

Grand
Canyon
Village

Grandview
Point

Moran
Point

Desert View

Tusayan

Grand Canyon
Camper Village

East Rim Dr.

Tusayan Ruins
and Museum

⑥④

**To
Flagstaff**

To ⑥④ & ⑱⓪ & Grand Canyon Airport ↓

Kaibab National Forest

com) offers commercial service between Flagstaff and Tusayan on tiny four- or six-passenger aircraft. **Air Vegas** (☎ 800/255-7474 or 702/736-3599) and **Scenic Airlines** (☎ 800/634-6801 or 702/638-3300) both offer daily service between Las Vegas and Grand Canyon National Park Airport. Air Vegas departs from Henderson Executive Airport; Scenic leaves from Tropicana Airport, and North Las Vegas Air and Las Vegas Executive Terminals.

By Rail. Amtrak (☎ 800/872-7245 or 520/774-8679) regularly stops in downtown Flagstaff, where lodging, rental cars, and connecting bus service are available, and in Williams, where lodging, connecting bus and rail service

(on the historic Grand Canyon Railway) are available. The Williams stop is unmanned, but a free shuttle bus transports passengers to town.

The **Historic Grand Canyon Railway** (☎ 800/843-8724) offers daily service linking Williams and Grand Canyon Village. The train leaves Williams in the morning and returns in late afternoon.

By Bus. Nava-Hopi Tours (☎ 800/892-8687) has bus service linking Grand Canyon National Park with Williams and Flagstaff. To reach those cities by bus, call **Greyhound** (☎ 800/231-2222). Daily bus service between the North and South rims is available on the **Trans-Canyon Shuttle** (☎ 520/638-2820).

GROUND TRANSPORTATION

Renting a Car. Most major car-rental companies have offices in Flagstaff. See the appendix for the toll-free numbers.

Exploring the Park Without a Car. CASSI Tours (☎ 520/638-0871 or 520/638-0821) offers a regular year-round service linking five Tusayan stops to Grand Canyon Village. To avoid parking problems inside the park, leave your car at Grand Canyon National Park Airport (or at your hotel) in Tusayan and take the shuttle into the park. Other Tusayan stops include Best Western Grand Canyon Squire Inn, IMAX Theater, Babbitt's Village Store, and Moqui Lodge. The adult one-way fare is $4 (16 and under free). The shuttle schedule is posted at each stop.

Once at the South Rim, you can ride the park's **free shuttles** during high season. From mid-March through Mid-October, the shuttles operate daily running every 15 to 20 minutes from 7:30am to sunset. They serve marked stops in Grand Canyon Village, Yavapai Point, Yaki Point, South Kaibab trailhead, and the West Rim Drive. When the shuttles run, the West Rim Drive, Yaki Point and the South Kaibab Trailhead are closed to most private vehicles. During months when the shuttles are running, early morning hiker shuttles go to the South Kaibab Trailhead. Call the **Bright Angel Transportation Desk** (☎ 303/297-2757) for the schedule.

When the shuttles aren't running, you may need to take advantage of **Fred Harvey's 24-hour taxi service** (☎ 520/638-2631).

INFORMATION

Contact **Grand Canyon National Park,** P.O. Box 129, Grand Canyon, AZ 86023 (☎ 520/638-7888; www.nps.gov/grca), for a copy of the *Grand Canyon Trip Planner.* Those who want more in-depth information can buy books, maps, and videos

from the Grand Canyon Association, P.O. Box 399, Grand Canyon, AZ 86023 (☎ 520/638-2481; fax 520/638-2484). Among the hundreds of books written on the Grand Canyon, several stand out. For a general overview, try *Grand Canyon: A Natural History Guide* (New York: Houghton Mifflin Co., 1993), by Jeremy Schmidt. In *An Introduction to Grand Canyon Geology* (Grand Canyon Association, 1999) author L. Greer Price explains the geology of Grand Canyon in terms anyone can understand.

Call ☎ 520/638-7888 for recorded weather information.

FEES & PERMITS

Admission to Grand Canyon National Park costs $20 per private vehicle and $10 for those on foot or bicycle. The receipt is good for a week and includes both rims. You can make advance reservations for campsites at Mather Campground (on the South Rim) and at the North Rim Campground by calling ☎ 800/365-CAMP (2267).

Permits are required for all overnight camping in the backcountry. This includes all overnight stays below the rims (except in the cabins and dorms at Phantom Ranch) and on parkland outside of designated campgrounds.

Permits for the month desired go on sale on the first of the month, 4 months earlier. For example, permits for all of May go on sale January 1; permits for June go on sale February 1, and so on. You can get a **Backcountry Permit Request Form** by ordering the free Backcountry Trip Planner from the park. To do this, call the park's main extension at ☎ 520/638-7888 and choose the "backcountry information" option, or write to Grand Canyon National Park, P.O. Box 129, Grand Canyon, AZ 86023.

You can fax in your Permit Request Form to 520/638-2125 no earlier than the date the permits become available; or mail it with a postmark no earlier than the date the permits become available.

No requests are taken by phone. However, the **Backcountry Office** (☎ 520/638-7875) does answer questions over the telephone Monday through Friday from 1 to 5pm Arizona time.

VISITOR CENTERS

At press time, the park's largest visitor center is the **South Rim Visitor Center,** located in Grand Canyon Village. It has displays, a free slide show on the park, and an information desk staffed by rangers. Perhaps as early as fall 2000, however, this building will be converted to administrative space, to be replaced by a new state-of-the-art orientation center—**the Canyon View Information Plaza**—inside the park near Mather Point. This center will eventually be served by a light rail system linking it with Tusayan.

There are three other visitor centers. The **Yavapai Observation Station,** 1 mile east of the South Rim Visitor Center on Yavapai Point, has an observation room where you can see and identify many of the monuments in the central canyon. Rangers here frequently lead interpretive programs.

The **Desert View Contact Station,** 26 miles east of Grand Canyon Village, is small and staffed by volunteers. It sells books and provides information on the canyon.

The **North Rim Visitor Center** has a small bookstore and information desk staffed by rangers and employees of the **Grand Canyon Association.**

SPECIAL REGULATIONS & WARNINGS

It's illegal to remove any resources from the park. These can be anything from flowers to potsherds. Even seemingly useless articles such as bits of metal from the canyon's old mining operations have historical value and are protected by law.

Fires are strictly prohibited except at North Rim, Desert View, and Mather campgrounds. In the backcountry, use a small camp stove for cooking.

SEASONS & CLIMATE

The climate at Grand Canyon varies greatly not only from season to season but from point to point. At 8,000 feet in elevation, the North Rim is by far the coldest, dampest part of the park. Its temperatures run about 30° cooler than at the canyon-bottom Phantom Ranch more than 5,000 feet below, and 7° cooler than the South Rim, roughly 1,000 feet below. It averages 25 inches of precipitation per year, compared to just 8 inches at Phantom Ranch and 16 inches on the South Rim.

The North Rim doesn't open until mid-May, so your only choice in early spring is the South Rim, where daily highs average 60°F and 70°F in April and May, respectively. Travelers should be prepared for late-winter storms, which occasionally bring snow to the rim. This is an ideal time to hike the inner canyon, with highs in April averaging 82°F.

In summer, the rims seldom become unbearably hot. Summer highs are usually in the 80s on the South Rim and in the 70s on the North Rim. The Inner Gorge, on the other hand, can be torrid, with highs in July averaging 106°F. Localized thunderstorms frequently drench the park in late July and August, the wettest month of the year, when nearly 2.25 inches of rain falls on the South Rim. On the North Rim, nights can be nippy even during July, when low temperatures average a chilly 46°F.

After the thunderstorms taper off in mid-September, fall is a great time to be anywhere in the park. Highs on the South Rim average 76° in September, 65° in October, and 52°F in November. The North Rim has highs of 69° in September and 59°F in October. (It closes in mid-October.) The Inner Gorge remains hot in September, but cools off considerably, to an average high of 84°F, in October.

The first winter storms can hit the North Rim as early as mid-October.

In winter, the North Rim is closed, and drivers to the South Rim should be prepared for icy roads and occasional closures as well. When the snow isn't falling, the South Rim warms up nicely, with average highs of 41°F in January.

SEASONAL EVENTS

For 3 weeks every September, world-renowned musicians gather for the **Grand Canyon Music Festival.** Most of the offerings are chamber-music concerts, and all are at the acoustically superb Shrine of the Ages Auditorium next to the South Rim Visitor Center. Tickets for the 7:30pm concerts are available in advance through **Grand Canyon Chamber Music Festival,** P.O. Box 1332, Grand Canyon, AZ 86023 (☎ 800/997-8285 or 520/638-9215).

Kolb Studio houses special arts exhibits relating to the area. Also, actors occasionally stage historical dramas at the Shrine of the Ages Auditorium. For up-to-date information on special events, consult the park's newspaper, *The Guide.*

If You Only Have 1 Day

After stopping at one of the **visitor centers** to get your bearings, hike a short distance down the **Bright Angel** or **North Kaibab trails** in the morning. (If the weather is hot or if your condition is not top-notch, a rim trail may be preferable.) At midday, attend a ranger presentation, for which times and locations are posted at the visitor centers. Later in the day, go on a scenic drive. On the South Rim, your best choice on the first day would be the **East Rim Drive,** which is open to cars year-round and has expansive views of the central and eastern canyon. On the North Rim, drive down the **Cape Royal Road.** To complete your scenic drive, watch sunset from **Lipan Point** on the South Rim or from **Cape Royal** on the North Rim.

Exploring the Park by Car

West Rim Drive

This 8-mi.-long road from Grand Canyon Village to Hermit's Rest is open to private cars only when the shuttles aren't running, from mid-Oct to mid-Mar. Allow a half day.

Your first stops are at **Trailview 1 and 2.** From these viewpoints, you can look back at Grand Canyon Village. Looking north across the canyon, you can see down the Bright Angel fault all the way to the North Rim. Below, you may spot lush vegetation growing around a spring. This area is Indian Gardens, where Havasupai Indians once farmed.

The next stop, **Maricopa Point,** overlooks the old Orphan Mine, which produced some of the richest uranium ore anywhere during the 1950s. Below and to the west, you can see the metal framework from the tramway used to move ore to the rim from 1956 to 1959.

At the **Powell Memorial,** you'll find a memorial to John Wesley Powell, the one-armed Civil War veteran thought to be the first white person to float through the canyon. From atop the memorial, you can get an especially fine view 60 miles southeast to the San Francisco peaks, including Humphreys Peak, which at 12,643 feet is the highest point in Arizona.

Because the next stop, **Hopi Point,** projects far into the canyon, its tip is the best place on the West Rim Drive to watch the sunset. As the sun drops, its light will play across four of the canyon's loveliest temples. The flat mesa almost due north of the point is Shiva Temple. The temple southwest of it is Osiris; the one southeast of it is Isis. East of Isis is Buddha Temple.

The next stop, **Mohave Point,** is a great place to observe some of the Colorado River's most furious rapids. Furthest downstream (to your left) is Hermit Rapids. Above it, you can make out the top of the dangerous Granite Rapids. Just above Granite Rapids, you can make

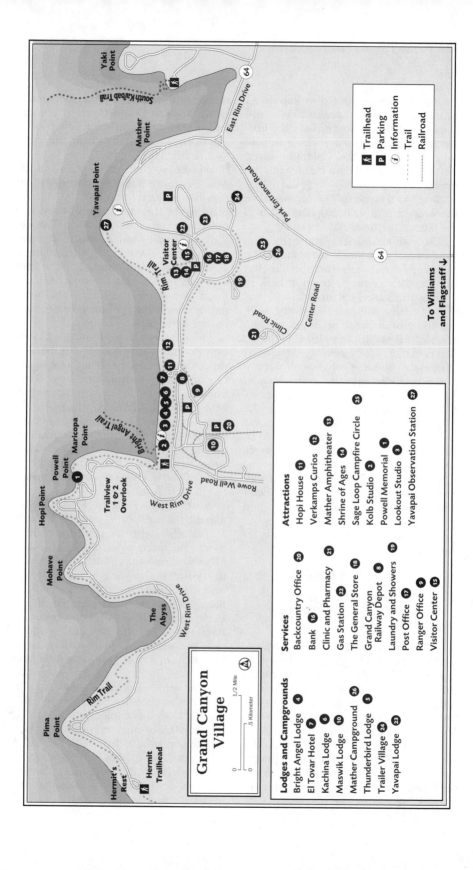

Grand Canyon Village

0 ___ .5 Kilometer
0 ___ 1/2 Mile

Lodges and Campgrounds

Bright Angel Lodge ④
El Tovar Hotel ⑦
Kachina Lodge ⑥
Maswik Lodge ⑩
Mather Campground ㉖
Thunderbird Lodge ⑤
Trailer Village ㉔
Yavapai Lodge ㉓

Services

Backcountry Office ⑳
Bank ⑯
Clinic and Pharmacy ㉑
Gas Station ㉒
The General Store ⑱
Grand Canyon Railway Depot ⑧
Laundry and Showers ⑰
Post Office ⑨
Ranger Office ⑨
Visitor Center ⑮

Attractions

Hopi House ⑪
Verkamps Curios ⑫
Mather Amphitheater ⑬
Shrine of Ages ⑭
Sage Loop Campfire Circle ㉕
Kolb Studio ②
Powell Memorial ①
Lookout Studio ③
Yavapai Observation Station ㉗

Legend

🚶 Trailhead
🅿 Parking
ⓘ Information
····· Trail
┼┼┼ Railroad

Yaki Point
Mather Point
Yavapai Point
Powell Point
Hopi Point
Mohave Point
The Abyss
Pima Point
Maricopa Point
Hermit's Rest

South Kaibab Trail
Bright Angel Trail
Rim Trail
West Rim Drive
East Rim Drive
Park Entrance Road
Center Road
Clinic Road
Rowe Well Road
Trailview 1 & 2 Overlook
Hermit Trailhead

To Williams and Flagstaff ↓

out the bottom of Salt Creek Rapids. As you look at Hermit Creek Canyon and the rapids below it, you can easily visualize how floods washed rocks from the side canyon into the Colorado River, forming the natural dam that creates the rapids.

Next you'll come to **The Abyss,** where the steep canyon walls drop 2,600 feet to the base of the Redwall Limestone.

Three thousand feet below the next stop, **Pima Point,** you'll see some of the foundations and walls from the old Hermit Camp, a tourist destination built in 1912 by the Santa Fe Railroad.

Before descending to Hermit Camp, tourists took a break at the next stop, **Hermit's Rest.** In this 1914 building, Mary Colter celebrated the "hermit" theme, by building what resembled a crude rock shelter, with stones heaped highest around the chimney. Inside, Colter covered the ceiling above the large fireplace with soot, so that the room had the look of a cave warmed by fire. Nearby are rest rooms and a snack bar selling sweets, chips, and soda.

Highlights: Closed to cars during high season; the overlooks are much quieter than those on the East Rim drive and afford excellent river views.

Drawbacks: Occasional long waits for buses.

East Rim Drive

Allow a half-day for this 25-mi.-long scenic drive on Ariz. 64, which connects Grand Canyon Village with Desert View.

The first stop, **Yavapai Point,** features some of the most expansive views both up and down the canyon. A historic observation station here has huge plate glass windows overlooking the canyon, along with interpretive panels identifying virtually all the major landmarks.

People entering the park from the south generally catch their first glimpse of the canyon from the next stop, **Mather Point.** It's a clamorous place with one redeeming feature, its panoramic vista,

similar to the one at the Yavapai Observation Station. Grand Canyon National Park hopes to finish construction on a large orientation center near this overlook in fall 2000.

Yaki Point, the first stop located off Ariz. 64, is accessible by car only when the shuttles aren't running. It's a great place to see the monuments of the central canyon, including Wotans Throne, Vishnu Temple, and Zoroaster Temple. Two trails are also easy to spot from here. To the north, the South Kaibab Trail descends in switchbacks below Skeleton Point. Meanwhile, the Tonto Trail meanders across the broad blue-green terrace known as the Tonto Platform.

The next stop, 7,406-foot-high **Grandview Point,** is one of the highest spots on the South Rim. In the 1890s, one of the canyon's early prospectors, Pete Barry built, and in some cases hung, a trail from Grandview Point to nearby Horseshoe Mesa, where he had a mining claim. He then built cabins and a dining hall on the mesa, and a hotel a short distance from Grandview Point. Today only a trace of the hotel's foundation remains, but the trail is still used.

Next you'll come to **Moran Point,** named for landscape painter Thomas Moran. This is the best place from which to view the tilting block of rock known as "The Sinking Ship." Stand at the end of the point and look southwest at the rocks level with the rim. The "Sinking Ship" appears to be "submerged" in the horizontal layers of Coronado Butte (in the foreground). It's part of the Grandview Monocline, a place where rocks have bent in a single fold around a fault line.

Next comes **Tusayan Pueblo,** built in 1185 by the ancestral Pueblo people. It's the last known occupied pueblo among the 3,500 documented archaeological sites in and around the Grand Canyon. A self-guided tour takes you through it. Built in 1932, the adjoining Tusayan Museum celebrates the traditions of the area's Native American tribes.

Don't miss the next stop, **Lipan Point.** With views far down the canyon to the west, it's a great place to catch the sunset. It also overlooks the Colorado River where the river makes two sweeping curves to form an enormous S. Just downstream of the S, the river begins cutting through the Vishnu Formation, and the steep-walled Inner Gorge begins.

Like Lipan Point, the next stop, **Navajo Point,** offers fine views of the Grand Canyon Supergroup, a formation of igneous and sedimentary rocks that have eroded altogether in many other parts of the canyon. The long, thin streaks of maroon, gray, and black, which tilt at an angle of about 20°, are layers of this formation.

The last stop on the East Rim Drive is **Desert View,** where you'll find the Watchtower, a 70-foot-high stone building designed by Mary Colter. Colter modeled it after towers found at ancient pueblos such as Mesa Verde and Hovenweep. Atop the Watchtower is an enclosed observation deck, which at 7,522 feet is the highest point on the South Rim. The rim at Desert View offers spectacular views of the eastern canyon.

Highlights: Spectacular views of both the central and the eastern canyon.

Drawbacks: Packed parking lots in summer.

North Rim: Cape Royal Drive

From the Grand Canyon Lodge on the North Rim, it's best to go the length of the scenic drive 23 mi. directly to Cape Royal, on the Walhalla Plateau, then make your stops on the way back to the lodge. That way, you can do the short hikes near Cape Royal while your legs are fresh, then stop at the picnic areas, closer to the lodge, on your way back. Allow a half day to a day for this drive.

Start your driving tour at **Cape Royal,** where a gentle, paved 0.3-mile (each way) trail passes a natural bridge, Angel's Window, carved into a rock peninsula along the rim. The trail ends at the tip of Cape Royal, with views of the looming temple known as Wotan's Throne.

Your next stop may be at the **Cliff Springs Trail,** a 0.5-mile walk that ends at a small spring. (See "Day Hikes," below.)

From the next stop, **Walhalla Overlook and Walhalla Glades,** you can follow with your eyes the tan line of Unkar Creek as it snakes down toward Unkar Delta. The soil and abundant water at the delta made for excellent farming for the ancestral Pueblo people, who occupied the canyon through about A.D. 1175. Many of these people migrated seasonally to dwellings such as the two small pueblos across the street from this overlook.

The next stop, **Roosevelt Point,** is one of the best places in the Canyon to see the confluence of the gorge of the Little Colorado River with the Grand Canyon. They meet at nearly a right angle, unusual in that most tributaries enter at close to the same direction as the larger rivers.

By starting your driving tour of the Walhalla Plateau early in the day, you can reach the next stop, **Vista Encantadora,** in time for a late picnic. You'll find several tables with views of the canyon.

From there you can finish your driving tour by taking the 3-mile spur from the Cape Royal Road to **Point Imperial,** which at 8,803 feet is the highest point on the North Rim. It's also the best place on either rim to view the northeastern end of the park.

Highlights: Sparse crowds and lovely views of the eastern canyon.

Drawbacks: Has only one view point (Cape Royal) from which to see the central canyon; the Colorado River is not visible as often on this drive as on the South Rim drives.

Organized Tours & Ranger Programs

The park offers a host of ranger programs whose schedule changes seasonally. A typical schedule includes guided hikes and walks, kids' programs, and discussions of geology, native species, and natural and cultural history. Evening programs are scheduled nightly. In winter, the South Rim cuts back on its programs and the North Rim is closed. For an up-to-date schedule, consult the park newspaper, *The Guide.*

Guided Hikes & Trips. The nonprofit **Grand Canyon Field Institute** schedules dozens of backpacking trips and outings ranging in length from 2 to 9 days. Some explore broad subjects such as ecology; others hone narrow skills such as orienteering or drawing. Each is guided by an expert on the topics covered. Because the courses vary greatly, the Field Institute assigns a difficulty level to each and attempts to ensure that participants find ones suited to their skill levels and interests. For more information, call ☎ **520/ 638-2485;** write to P.O. Box 399, Grand Canyon, AZ 86023; or check out the Web site at **www.thecanyon.com/fieldinstitute.**

Bus Tours. **Fred Harvey** schedules East Rim and West Rim tours ($24.50 and $13.50, respectively), sunset tours to Hopi or Mojave Point ($10), and all-day outings ($29.50) that combine two of the shorter tours. Unlike the drivers on the park's free shuttles, Fred Harvey drivers narrate the tours. Kids 16 and under ride free. Once at the canyon, visit the Fred Harvey desks at Yavapai, Maswick, or Bright Angel lodges, or call ☎ **520/638-2631,** ext. 6015.

Nava-Hopi Tours (☎ **520/774-5003**) offers 1-day guided canyon tours that depart from Flagstaff at 8:30am and return by 5:30pm. Total cost for adults is $46. For kids ages 5 to 15, it's $19.

Historic & Man-Made Attractions

Most of the historic buildings on the South Rim are concentrated in **Grand Canyon Village,** a National Historic District. Hermit's Rest, on the West Rim Drive, and The Watchtower, on the East Rim Drive, are also of historical significance (see "Exploring the Park by Car," above).

More than a half dozen of these historic buildings were designed by Mary Colter, a Minneapolis schoolteacher who began decorating the shops that sold Indian art along the Santa Fe Railroad line in 1902. As both a decorator and a self-trained architect, Colter later designed these Grand Canyon landmarks: Hopi House (1905), The Lookout (1914), Hermit's Rest (1914), Phantom Ranch (1922), Watchtower (1932), and Bright Angel Lodge (1935). Colter's work drew heavily on the architectural styles of Native Americans and Spanish settlers in the Southwest. Another historic building, The El Tovar Hotel (1905), was designed by Charles Whittlesey in a style reminiscent of a northern European hunting lodge.

On the North Rim, Grand Canyon Lodge, built in 1928, is included on the National Register of Historic Places.

Day Hikes

There's no better way to enjoy the canyon than by actually walking down into it, watching the vegetation and rock layers change as you descend. The experience is far more rewarding than merely looking down from the rims.

Unfortunately, hiking below the rims is not always a smart idea, especially at midday during summer. Changes in temperature and elevation can make hiking extremely difficult even in ideal conditions. The jarring descent can strain your knees; the climb back out will test your lungs and heart. If it's hot out or you aren't up to climbing, consider walking on one of the rim trails, which can often be as pleasant as walks inside the canyon. They're especially nice in the forests on the North Rim.

First-time hikers in the canyon should consider one of the **corridor trails:** North Kaibab, South Kaibab, and Bright Angel. Well maintained and clearly marked, these are regularly patrolled by park rangers. Each has at least one emergency phone and pit toilet. Drinking water is available at several sources along both the Bright Angel and North Kaibab trails, but not on the South Kaibab. Wherever you hike, carry plenty of water, and check with the rangers about the availability of additional water along the trail. Eat and drink regularly. Wear sunscreen, sunglasses, and protective clothing. If you hike into the canyon, allow yourself twice as much time for the trip out as for the descent.

RIM TRAILS: SOUTH RIM

West Rim Trail and South Rim Trail

8 mi. on West Rim Trail to Hermit's Rest, 1.5 mi. on South Rim Trail to Yavapai Point. Easy to moderate. Access: Grand Canyon Village, along the rim behind the El Tovar Hotel. Water sources at Grand Canyon Village, Hermit's Rest, South Rim Visitor Center, Yavapai Point.

From Grand Canyon Village, you can follow the rim trail 8 miles west to Hermit's Rest or 1.5 miles northeast to Yavapai Point.

West Rim Trail. Walking instead of driving along this trail is a great way to see the canyon without the crowds. It travels near the West Rim Drive and passes through all the same scenic overlooks, described in the driving tour. The 1.3-mile stretch from the Village to Maricopa Point is paved with one 200-vertical-foot climb. Past Maricopa Point, it planes off somewhat and the pavement ends. For the rest of the way to Hermit's Rest, the trail meanders through piñon-juniper woodland along the rim (when not crossing overlooks). Sagebrush roots and loose rocks make for tricky footing, but the scenery is lovely, and the crowds thin as you move farther west.

As 16 miles might be too much hiking for 1 day, I recommend hiking out on this trail from Grand Canyon Village and taking the shuttle back (mid-March through mid-October). By hiking out, you can avoid revisiting the same overlooks on the shuttle ride back—the shuttles stop at every turnout while en route to Hermit's Rest, but only stop at Mohave Point and Hopi Point on their way back to Grand Canyon Village.

South Rim Trail. This smooth, paved trail connects Grand Canyon Village and Yavapai Point. Around the lodges, the path is a flat sidewalk teeming with people. The crowds dissipate somewhat between the east edge of the village and Yavapai Point. Near Yavapai Point you'll find many smooth flat rocks along the rim—great places from which to contemplate the canyon. Located 5 miles north of the park's south entrance, **Yavapai Point** has a historic observation station overlooking the canyon. From here, you can take a shuttle back to near your starting point.

RIM TRAILS: NORTH RIM

Cape Final Trail

1.5 mi. one way. Easy. Access: An unmarked dirt parking area off the Cape Royal Rd., 4.9 mi. south of Roosevelt Point.

This relatively flat, boulder-free trail is a good choice for a first hike in the backcountry. It meanders through ponderosa pine forest on an old Jeep trail, ending on the north side of Cape Final, where you'll have partial views of the northern canyon and Juno Temple.

Cliff Springs Trail

0.5 mi. one way. Moderate. Access: A small pullout 0.3 mi. north of Cape Royal on the Cape Royal Rd.

Both scenic and fairly short, this hike is perfect for relatively active families. This dirt trail first seems to head into forest away from the canyon, then quickly descends into a narrow, rocky side canyon that drains into the larger one—a reminder that the Walhalla Plateau is a peninsula. It hugs the north wall of the side canyon, passing under limestone overhangs, in light colored green by the canopies of box elder trees. The springs drip from one of these overhangs, where mosses carpet fissures in the rock. A waist-high boulder marks the end of the trail.

Ken Patrick Trail

10 mi. one way. Strenuous. Access: From the south side of the parking area for Point Imperial or from the parking area for the North Kaibab Trail (on the North Rim entrance rd., 2 mi. north of Grand Canyon Lodge).

This steeply rolling trail travels through ponderosa pine and spruce-fir forest between the head of Roaring Springs Canyon and Point Imperial. Starting at the North Kaibab end, the first mile of the trail has been pounded into dust by mules. It becomes very faint about 4 miles in, after passing the trailhead for the old Bright Angel Trail. Past the Cape Royal Road, the trail descends into, then climbs out of, a very steep drainage overgrown with thorn-covered New Mexican locust. While challenging, the 3-mile section between the Cape Royal Road and Point Imperial is also the prettiest stretch, skirting the rim of the canyon above upper drainages of Nankoweap Creek. In these areas you'll see plenty of scarlet bugler, identifiable by tubular red flowers with flared lower petals, as well as a number of Douglas firs interspersed among the ubiquitous ponderosa pines.

The Transept Trail & Bright Angel Point Trail

Bright Angel Point Trail 0.25 mi. each way. Transept Trail 1.5 mi. Easy. Access: Behind North Rim General Store (near the campground), or by descending the back steps off the patios at Grand Canyon Lodge.

To familiarize yourself with the North Rim, start with these trails, which are different sections of the same pathway. At the bottom of the stairs behind Grand Canyon Lodge, the Bright Angel Point Trail goes to the left, while the Transept Trail goes right.

The **Bright Angel Point Trail,** which is paved, travels along a narrow peninsula dividing Roaring Springs and Transept canyons. It passes a number of craggy outcroppings of Kaibab Limestone, around which the roots of wind-whipped juniper trees cling like arthritic hands. The trail ends at 8,148-foot-high Bright Angel Point.

The **Transept Trail** travels northeast along the rim of Transept Canyon, connecting the lodge and the North Rim Campground. Passing through old-growth ponderosa pine and quaking aspen, it descends into, then climbs out of, three shallow side drainages, with ascents steep enough to take the breath away from people unaccustomed to the altitude.

Widforss Trail

5 mi. one way. Moderate. Access: A dirt road 0.25 mi. south of the Cape Royal Rd. Follow this rd. about .7 mi. to the parking area, which is well marked.

Named for landscape painter Gunnar Widforss, this trail skirts the head of Transept Canyon before venturing south to Widforss Point. For the first 2 miles, the trail undulates through ponderosa pine and spruce-fir forest, with spruce-fir on the shady side of each drainage. Past the head of Transept Canyon, the trail heads south through a stand of old-growth ponderosa. You'll also note a number of badly singed pines. The trail reaches the rim again at Widforss Point, where you'll have a nice view of five temples. Near the rim are a picnic table and several good campsites.

CANYON TRAILS

Because of the huge elevation changes on the canyon trails, none should be called easy. (More people are rescued off the Bright Angel Trail, generally considered the "easiest" trail into the canyon than off any other trail.) In general, please note that rating a trail easy, moderate, or difficult oversimplifies the situation. For example, among the wilderness trails, the **Hermit Trail** is fine for many day hikers going to Santa Maria Spring, but it's much more rugged beyond that point; the **Tonto Trail** is often easy to walk on, but has almost no water. It's always a good idea to discuss your plans and your experience with a ranger before setting out on a hike.

SOUTH RIM CORRIDOR TRAILS

Bright Angel Trail

4.6 mi. to Indian Garden, 7.8 mi. to Colorado River, 9.3 mi. to Bright Angel Campground. Access: Just west of Kolb Studio, near Grand Canyon Village. 6,860 ft. at trailhead; 3,800 ft. at Indian Garden; 2,450 ft. at Colorado River. Water sources at Mile-and-a-Half Rest House (seasonal), Three-Mile Rest House (seasonal), Indian Garden, Colorado River, Bright Angel Campground.

Both Native Americans and early settlers recognized this as a choice location for a trail. First, there's an enormous fault line, creating a natural break in the cliffs. Then there's the water—more of it than anywhere on the South Rim.

On a day hike, follow the switchbacks below Grand Canyon Village to One-and-a-Half Mile House or Three-Mile House, each of which has shade, an emergency phone, and seasonal drinking water. The Park Service, which responds to hundreds of emergency calls on this trail every year, discourages many day-hikers from going past Mile-and-a-Half house.

If you continue on the trail past Three-Mile House, you begin a long descent to the picnic area near the spring at Indian Garden, where lush vegetation will surround you and large cottonwood trees provide shade. At 4.6 miles and more than 3,000 vertical feet

from the rim, Indian Garden is dangerously deep for many people. However, a few well-prepared day-hikers may wish to hike an additional 1.5 miles past Indian Garden on the relatively flat (in this area) Tonto and Plateau Point trails. The Plateau Point Trail eventually dead ends at an overlook of the Colorado River 1,300 feet below.

South Kaibab Trail

6.3 mi. to Colorado River, 7.3 mi. to Bright Angel Campground. Access: At Yaki Point (Ariz. 64, East Rim Dr., 5 mi. east of Grand Canyon Village). 7,260 ft. at trailhead; 2,450 ft. at Colorado River. Water sources at Colorado River and Bright Angel Campground.

The South Kaibab trail travels on ridge lines with expansive views; as it has no water and little shade, the Bright Angel Trail is a safer trail for most hikers.

For a good day hike, follow the trail as it makes a series of switchbacks through the upper rock layers, down the west side of Yaki Point. Below the Coconino Sandstone, the trail heads north to Cedar Ridge, a platform that has pit toilets and a hitching post for mules. Shaded by piñon and juniper trees, it affords expansive views down side canyons to the east and west. This is an excellent place for day-hikers to picnic and rest before hiking the 1.5 miles and 1,500 vertical feet back out.

NORTH RIM CORRIDOR TRAIL

North Kaibab Trail

2.7 mi. to Supai Tunnel, 4.7 mi. to Roaring Springs, 6.8 mi. to Cottonwood Campground, 14.4 mi. to the Colorado. Moderate. Access: On North Rim entrance rd., 2 mi. north of Grand Canyon Lodge. 8,250 ft. at North Kaibab Trailhead; 5,200 ft. at Roaring Springs; 4,080 ft. at Cottonwood Campground; 2,400 ft. at Colorado River. Water sources at Roaring Springs (seasonal), Bright Angel Creek, Cottonwood Campground (seasonal), Phantom Ranch, Bright Angel Campground.

Less crowded than the South Rim corridor trails, this one begins at a parking area off the North Rim entrance road, 2 miles north of Grand Canyon Village. It starts with a long series of switchbacks through thickly forested terrain at the head of Roaring Springs Canyon. The first major landmark is Supai Tunnel. At 2.7 miles from the trailhead, and with seasonal water, shade, and rest rooms available, this is an excellent turnaround point for day-hikers. Beyond the tunnel, the trail descends in relatively gradual switchbacks through the bright red Supai Group rocks, then crosses a bridge over a creek bed. Past the bridge, the creek plummets. The trail travels along the south wall of Roaring Springs Canyon, on ledges above Redwall Cliffs.

A spire of Redwall Limestone known as "The Needle" marks the point where the trail begins its descent of the Redwall. Roaring Springs, the water source for both rims, becomes audible just above the confluence of Bright Angel and Roaring Springs canyons. A 0.2-mile-long spur trail descends to the springs. In the lush vegetation around it, you'll find drinking (seasonal) water, shade, and picnic tables. Roughly 5 miles and 3,000 vertical feet below the rim, this is the farthest a day-hiker will probably want to go.

WILDERNESS TRAILS

Rangers are seldom encountered on the boulder-strewn and sometimes confusing wilderness trails, which are not maintained by the park. These trails have washed away in some places; in others, they descend steeply through cliffs.

Two South Rim wilderness trails, the Grandview and Hermit trails, work well for day hikes. Day-hikers often descend 2,600 vertical feet on the **Grandview Trail** to Horseshoe Mesa (avoid when wet or icy), or follow the **Hermit Trail** to Santa Maria or Dripping Springs (via a spur on the Dripping Springs Trail). Other South Rim wilderness trails, poorly suited for day hikes, include the Tanner, New Hance, Boucher, and South Bass. North Rim wilderness trails include the Bill Hall, Thunder River, Deer Creek, North Bass, and Nankoweap.

Other Sports & Activities

Fishing. You're welcome to fish in the Colorado River inside the park (the hard part is reaching the canyon bottom), provided you have an Arizona Fishing Permit and trout stamp, available at the South Rim's **General Store** (☎ 520/638-2262) in Grand Canyon Village. The trout fishing is best at the eastern end of the canyon, upstream of Phantom Ranch. It's better still—and more easily accessible—just upstream up the park, above Lees Ferry. For advice on fishing this area, contact **Lee's Ferry Anglers Guides and Fly Shop** (☎ 800/962-9755 or 520/355-2261), next to Lee's Ferry Lodge, about 2½ hours north of Flagstaff on U.S. 89A.

Biking. Inside the park, cyclists are required to stay on roads, many of them narrow and crowded. The best riding is on the West Rim Drive when the road is closed to most cars. At these times, you'll still have to watch out for tour buses, shuttles and an occasional private vehicle.

Cross-Country Skiing. When snow sticks on the South Rim, you can cross-country ski at the **Grandview Nordic Center** in the Kaibab National Forest near Grandview Point. To get there, drive east toward Desert View on Ariz. 64. About 1.7 miles past the Grandview Point turn-off, turn right on the road to the Arizona Trail. The forest service has marked three loops in this area, each meandering through meadows and ponderosa pine forest. For more information call the **Kaibab National Forest Tusayan Ranger District Office** at ☎ 520/638-2443.

White-Water Rafting. White-water raft trips inside the park generally last from 3 to 14 days and must be booked well ahead of time. While most trips begin at

Lee's Ferry, Arizona, the end points vary. Some companies allow for partial trips by picking up or dropping off passengers at various points in the Canyon (most often at Phantom Ranch).

All the companies operating in the Grand Canyon are experienced and run excellent trips, though subject to the whims of the Colorado River and the storms that move through the canyon. For about $200 per day, all provide food, portable toilets, and some camping equipment, as well as access to parts of the Inner Canyon that are difficult, if not impossible, to reach on foot. Among them are some of the most beautiful places on earth.

For a list of companies offering both motorized and oar-powered river trips through the canyon contact the park directly or log on to www.thecanyon.com/nps/.

Tamer Alternatives. Aramark-Wilderness River Adventures, 50 S. Lake Powell Blvd., Page, AZ (☎ **800/528-6154** or 520/645-3279), offers half-day and full-day smooth-water raft trips from the base of Glen Canyon Dam to Lee's Ferry, where the companies floating into Grand Canyon *begin* their trips. Cost for the half-day trip is for $51 for adults, $44 for 11 and under. The full day trip costs $71 for adults, $64 for 11 and under.

AmFac offers the half-day trip, plus round-trip transportation (totaling 290 miles) from Moqui Lodge, just south of the Park's south entrance. Cost for this 12-hour tour is $96 ($48 for 11 and under). For advance reservations call ☎ **303/297-2757.** Within 4 days, call ☎ **520/638-2631,** ext. 6015.

One- and 2-day trips through the westernmost part of Grand Canyon are available through **Hualapai River Runners** (☎ **800/622-4409** or 520/769-2210), P.O. Box 246, Peach Springs, AZ 86434. These motorized trips begin with rapids in the lower Granite Gorge of Grand Canyon and end on Lake Mead. Costs range from $221 to $321 per person. A 15% family discount is also offered.

Overflights. Ten companies at Grand Canyon National Park Airport in Tusayan currently offer scenic airplane or helicopter rides over the canyon. With more than 250,000 people flying out of Tusayan alone every year, the flights, which generate a great deal of noise in parts of the park, have become a politically charged issue. Besides the noise pollution in what should be a pristine wilderness area, there have been a few crashes over the years.

The following companies offer air tours originating from Tusayan:

Papillon Grand Canyon Helicopters (☎ 800/528-2418 or 520/638-2419, www.papillon.com); **Air Grand Canyon** (☎ 520/638-2686); **AirStar Airlines** (☎ 520/638-2139); **AirStar Helicopters** (☎ 520/638-2622); **Grand Canyon Airlines** (☎ 800/528-2413 or 520/638-2407, www.grandcanyonairlines.com); **Kenai Helicopters** (☎ 520/638-2764).

Mule Rides. The prospect of descending narrow trails above steep cliffs on animals hardly famous for their intelligence might make you nervous. Once on the trail, however, you'll soon discover that the mules are no more enthralled by the idea of falling than you are. Although the mules walk close to the edges, accidents are rare.

From the South Rim, you can take a 12-mile round-trip day ride to Plateau Point, or purchase 1- or 2-night packages that go to the bottom of the canyon and include lodging and meals at Phantom Ranch. Because the rides are strenuous for both riders and mules, the wranglers strictly adhere to the following requirements: you must weigh less than 200 pounds, be at least 4 feet, 7 inches tall, speak fluent English, and not be pregnant.

Costs range from $100 for the Plateau Point trip to $385 for the 2-night package. Trips to Phantom Ranch fill up months in advance, so make your reservations early. Starting on the first of the month you can make reservations for the next 23 months. For **advance reservations** call ☎ 303/297-2757. For reservations in the next 4 days, call the **Bright Angel Transportation Desk** at ☎ 520/638-2631, ext. 6015.

On the North Rim, mule rides are through a small, family run outfit, **Grand Canyon Trail Rides.** The company offers two types of rim rides and two canyon rides (none of which go to Phantom Ranch), at prices ranging from $15 to $85. Riders must be at least 12 to go on the all-day ride. No one over 200 pounds is allowed on the canyon rides; for the rim rides, the limit is 220 pounds. All riders must speak English.

The mule rides on the North Rim tend to fill up later than those on the South Rim. To sign up, visit the **Grand Canyon Trail Rides** desk (open daily 7am to 6pm) at Grand Canyon Lodge, or call

☎ 520/638-9875. The off-season number is ☎ 801/679-8665.

Horseback Riding. The only horseback riding near the South Rim is at **Apache Stables** (☎ 520/638-2891), which operates at Moqui Lodge, just outside the park's South Entrance. This is a great family activity. Children as young as 6 are allowed on the 1-hour trail rides, which, like the 2-hour ones, loop through the Kaibab National Forest near the stables. Apache Stables also offers a 4-hour ride east through the forest to near Grandview Point. Prices for the rides, running mid-March through the end of November, range from $25 to $65.

On the North Rim, **Allen's Guided Tours** (☎ 801/644-8150) offers horseback rides from 8am to 6pm Monday through Saturday. Departing from a

Campground	Rim	Total Sites	RV Hookups	Dump Station	Toilets	Drinking Water
Cameron Trading Post RV Park	South	48	48	Yes	No	Yes
Demotte Park Campground	North	23	No	No	Yes	Yes
Desert View Campground	South	50	No	No	Yes	No
Diamond Creek Campground	South	open tent camping	No	No	Yes	No
Flintstone Bedrock City	South	unlimited tent sites	27	Yes	Yes	Yes
Grand Canyon Camper Village	South	300	250	Yes	Yes	Yes
Jacob Lake Campground	North	53	No	No	Yes	Yes
Kaibab Lake Campground	South	74	No	No	Yes	Yes
Kaibab Camper Village	North	130	70	Yes	Yes	Yes
Mather Campground	South	323	No	Yes	Yes	Yes
North Rim Campground	North	87	No	Yes	Yes	Yes
Ten X Campground	South	70	No	No	Yes	Yes
Trailer Village	South	84	84	Nearby	Yes	Yes
Tuweep	North	11	No	No	No	No

    * $12 two-person tent, $14 electric hookup, $16 water/electric, $1.50 each additional person

  ** $23 full hookup, $21 water/electric, $19 electric, $15 tent sites, $19 teepees

*** $22 hookups, $12 dry sites, $12 tent sites

corral 0.25 mile south of Jacob Lake on Ariz. 67, the tours travel on gentle terrain in the Kaibab National Forest. Prices range from $20 to $85.

Camping

INSIDE THE PARK

You can make reservations for campsites in the Mather and North Rim campgrounds by calling ☎ 800/365-2267.

Inside the park on the South Rim, 26 miles east of Grand Canyon Village on Ariz. 64, you'll find **Desert View Campground** (no phone). At dusk, the yips of coyotes drift over this campground in piñon-juniper woodland at the eastern edge of the park. Elevated, cool and breezy, the peaceful surroundings offer no clue that the

bustling Desert View Overlook is within walking distance. The floor of the woodland makes for smooth tent sites, the most secluded being on the outside of the loop drive. The only drawback: The nearest showers are 26 miles away at Camper Services. During high season, this campground usually fills up by noon.

Near Grand Canyon Village on the South Rim is **Mather Campground** (☎ 520/638-7851). Despite its relatively small area, this remains a pleasant place. Piñon and juniper trees shade the sites, spaced far enough apart to afford privacy to most campers. However avoid sites 150 to 171 on the Juniper Loop, which lie unpleasantly close to the entrance road. Also, don't stay too near the showers, located in the Camper Services building next to the campground. If

Showers	Fire Pits/ Grills	Laundry	Public Phone	Reserve	Fees	Open
No	No	No	Yes	Yes	$15	Year-round
No	Yes	No	No	No	$10	mid-May to mid-Oct
Yes	No	No	No	No	$12 per site	mid-May to mid-Oct
No	Yes	No	No	No	$10 per person	Year-round
Yes	No	Yes	Yes	Yes	*16	Feb–Nov
Yes	Yes	No	Yes	Yes	**	Year-round
No	Yes	No	No	No	$10	Year-round
No	Yes	No	No	No	$10	Apr–Oct
No	No	No	Yes	Yes	***	May 15–Oct 15
Yes	Yes	Yes	No	Mar–Nov	†	Mar–Nov
Nearby	Yes	Nearby	Yes	Yes	‡	May 15–Oct 15
No	Yes	No	No	No	$10	Apr–Oct
Nearby	Yes	No	Nearby	Yes	$20	Year-round
No	Yes	No	No	No	No charge	when roads are passable

† $12 Mar–May and Sept–Nov, $15 June–Aug
‡ $15–$20 site, $4 tent only, no car

you're too close, hundreds of campers tramp past.

For RV drivers on the South Rim, there's **Trailer Village** in Grand Canyon Village (P.O. Box 699), Grand Canyon, AZ 86023. Advance reservations: ☎ 303/ 297-2757; same-day reservations, campground questions ☎ 520/638-2631, ext. 6035; fax 520/638-9247.

The neighbors are close, the showers far (0.4 mile) away, and the vegetation sparse. A few sites at the end of the numbered drives have grass, shade trees, and one neighbor-free side. You can catch a shuttle bus at a stop near the campground.

Inside the park on the North Rim, the **North Rim Campground** (☎ 800/365-2267 for advance reservations) is 44 miles south of Jacob Lake on Ariz. 67. Shaded by old-growth ponderosa pines and situated alongside Transept Canyon (part of Grand Canyon), this is a delightful place to spend a few days. The 1.5-mile-long Transept Trail links the campground to Grand Canyon Lodge, and the North Rim General Store is within walking distance. The nicest sites are the rim sites, which open onto the canyon. These cost an extra $5 but are worth it, being some of the prettiest anywhere. Showers (cost: $1.25 for 5 min.) are within walking distance.

With only 83 sites, the North Rim Campground fills up for much of the summer. If you show up without a reservation only to find the SORRY, CAMPGROUND FULL sign on the entry booth, don't be afraid to ask if there have been any cancellations—you might just end up with a campsite. The best time to ask about openings is 8am, when sites made available by the previous night's cancellations go up for sale. The campground sometimes stays open on a limited basis after October 15.

NEAR THE PARK: SOUTH RIM

Just outside the park is **Grand Canyon Camper Village** in Tusayan, 1 mile south of the park entrance on Ariz. 64 (P.O. Box 490, Grand Canyon, AZ 86023-0490, ☎ 520/638-2887). This campground's advantage is its location, within easy walking distance of stores and restaurants on one side and of Kaibab National Forest on the other. Its disadvantages are its relatively narrow (average width: 27 ft.) campsites and the noise from the nearby Grand Canyon National Park Airport.

The tent sites are best. Shaded by ponderosa pines, they sit above the rest of the campground and border the national forest. The rest rooms are clean, and showers cost 25¢ for 2 minutes. There's also a playground and a gravel basketball court.

Ten X Campground (☎ 520/638-2443) is 2 miles south of Tusayan on Ariz. 64. Large, wooded campsites make this the nicest campground within 20 miles of the South Rim. With plenty of distance between you and your neighbors, it's a great place to linger over a fire. All sites have fire pits and grills, and the campground host sells wood. Later, you'll find the soft, needle-covered floor perfect for sleeping. This campground does sell out. If you're driving up from Flagstaff or Williams, consider snagging a site before going to the canyon for the day.

NEAR THE PARK: NORTH RIM

Kaibab Camper Village is 0.5 mile west of Ariz. 67, just south of Jacob Lake. Mailing address only: P.O. Box 3331, Flagstaff, AZ 86003 (☎ 520/643-7804 when open, 800/525-0924 or 520/526-0924 when closed). Compared to most South Rim RV parks, where sagebrush is often the largest plant in sight, this is like a fairy tale. The setting makes this easily the prettiest RV park in the Grand Canyon area. Tent campers will also be comfortable here, especially if they pay the extra $3 for one of the improved sites, which have sand rings and views of tiny Jacob Lake. The use of generators is forbidden, so everyone can enjoy the quiet.

DeMotte Park Campground (☎ 520/643-7298) is a Forest Service campground 5 miles north of the park boundary on Ariz. 67. If you come here, bundle up for the night. It's 8,760 feet high, in spruce-fir forest, so you're sure to be cool. The road through the campground curves sharply and some of the spaces are small, so this place may not work for large RVs.

Just north of Jacob Lake on U.S. 89A and nestled into rolling hills covered with ponderosa pine forest, **Jacob Lake Campground** (☎ **520/643-7298** or 520/ 643-7395) is a beauty of a Forest Service campground. Towering pines shade sites only a short drive from Jacob Lake (where you'll find a gas station, store, restaurant and motel). This campground has regular naturalist programs. Although it is open year-round, water is seasonal and during the winter un-plowed roads pose a major obstacle.

Accommodations

INSIDE THE PARK

Lodging inside the park is handled by **AmFac Parks and Resorts,** 14001 E. Iliff, Aurora, CO 80014 (☎ **303/297-2757,** fax 303/297-3175). Beginning the first of the month, you can reserve a room for the next 23 months. For example, on January 1, 2000, you can reserve rooms through the end of December 2002. For reservations, only MasterCard and Visa are accepted. American Express, Diners Club, and Discover are acceptable upon arrival. AmFac can take reservations up to the minute of your arrival. Pets are not allowed in accommodations inside the park.

The hotels themselves can be contacted through the same switchboard (☎ **520/638-2631;** fax 520/638-9247) and mailing address (P.O. Box 699, Grand Canyon, AZ 86023). The phone number for the **Grand Canyon Lodge** is ☎ 520/638-2611. The hotels do not have specific street addresses. When you enter the park, you will receive a map locating all the hotels.

SOUTH RIM

Bright Angel Lodge & Cabins

☎ **520/638-2631** (main switchboard) or 303/297-2757 (reservations only). Fax 303/297-3175. 34 units (10 with sink only, 10 with sink and toilet, 14 with bathroom), 55 cabin rms. $44 double (with sink only); $50 (with sink and toilet only); $60 (standard, with bathroom); $70 (historic cabins with queen beds); $96 (rim cabins); $225 (Bucky O'Neill Cabin). AE, DC, DISC, MC, V.

Guests of Bright Angel Lodge stay in tightly clustered buildings west of the main lodge. These buildings, which vary widely in both age and design, cover the site of the old Bright Angel Camp, whose tents and cabins served as lodging in the early 1900s. Low-end accommodations start with dormitory-style rooms in two long buildings adjacent to Bright Angel Lodge. At $44 a night, the "hiker rooms" are the least expensive in the park. Each has a bed and desk but no television or private bathroom. Other rooms have double beds and toilets but no showers. Still others are appointed like standard motel rooms, only with showers instead of tubs.

Rooms in the historic cabins cost only $10 more than the nicest lodge rooms and are worth the extra money. Most of these freestanding cabins house two guest rooms and are bright inside. Those away from the rim are fairly quiet. At the high end of the price range are the four rim-side cabins, which have partial views of the canyon and cost $96. The luxurious Bucky O'Neill Cabin, one of the oldest structures in the park, boasts a fireplace and canyon views. The rim-side cabins tend to fill up far in advance.

El Tovar Hotel

☎ **520/638-2631** (main switchboard) or 303/297-2757 (reservations only). Fax 303/297-3175. 75 units. A/C TV TEL. $114–$171 double; $194–$279 suite. AE, DC, DISC, MC, V.

Designed as a cross between a Swiss chalet and a Norwegian villa, the El Tovar is a dark, cool counterpoint to the warm, pueblo-style buildings of Mary Colter. Completed in 1905 to accommodate the influx of tourists on the Santa Fe Railroad, the El Tovar, situated a few yards from the rim, casts a long shadow over Grand Canyon Village. A pointed cupola sits like a witch's cap above its three stories of Oregon pine and stone, and spires rise above an upstairs deck. The building's interior is as unforgettable as the outside. Moose and elk heads hang on varnished walls, dimly lit by copper chandeliers. Take away the modern-day tourists and the El Tovar probably looks much as it did at its inception.

The hotel is the most luxurious at the canyon and the only one to offer room service and a nightly turndown. You'll find a pleasant upstairs sitting area (reserved for guests) and rooms with classic American furnishings. If the hotel isn't busy, ask to see a few rooms before settling in, as they vary in size and shape. The El Tovar Dining Room, the best restaurant in the village, serves Continental cuisine.

Maswik Lodge

☎ **520/638-2631** (main switchboard) or 303/297-2757 (reservations only). Fax 303/297-3175. 278 units. TV TEL. Maswik South $63–73; Maswik North $63–$113. AE, DC, DISC, MC, V.

Built in the 1960s, Maswik Lodge is in a wooded area, a 10-minute walk from the rim. If you're not up to walking, the Maswik Transportation Center, the hub for the canyon shuttles, is opposite the lodge. The lodge has a restaurant, sports bar, and gift shop.

Most of the guest rooms are in the two-story wood-and-stone buildings known as Maswik North and South. The rooms in Maswik North have new carpeting, drapes, and bathroom tile—not to mention queen beds. The upstairs rooms in Building 12, which have private balconies and high ceilings, are among the

nicest in the park. Rooms in Maswik South are 5 years older, a bit smaller, and have less pristine views. But during high season they cost $40 less.

Thunderbird and Kachina Lodges

☎ **520/638-2631** (main switchboard) or 303/297-2757 (reservations only). Fax 303/297-3175. 55 units at Thunderbird, 49 at Kachina. A/C TV TEL. Park side $109, canyon side $119. AE, DC, DISC, MC, V.

The newest lodges inside the park, these are already slated for demolition in the new Grand Canyon master plan. It won't be any tragedy to see these buildings, which resemble 1960s-era college dormitories, get razed. Outside, they have flat roofs, decorative concrete panels, and metal staircases; inside are concrete steps, tile floors, and brick walls. The rooms are pleasant enough, with Southwestern-style furnishings and windows as wide as the rooms themselves. Although AmFac refuses to guarantee a canyon view, most of the upstairs units on the more expensive "canyon side" have at least a partial view of the canyon. Check-in for the Thunderbird is at the Bright Angel Lodge; for the Kachina, it's at the El Tovar.

Yavapai Lodge

☎ **520/638-2631** (main switchboard) or 303/297-2757 (reservations only). Fax 303/297-3175. 348 units. TV TEL. $63–$84 Yavapai West; $63–$99 Yavapai East. AE, DC, DISC, MC, V.

The largest lodge at the canyon, Yavapai is a mile from the historic district but close to Bank One, The South Rim's General Store, and the South Rim visitor center. Built between 1970 and 1972, the A-frame lodge has a large cafeteria and gift shop. The rooms are in 10 single-story buildings known as Yavapai West and six two-story wood buildings known as Yavapai East. Most rooms in Yavapai West have cinder-block walls, and all are compact. Little has been done to improve its rooms in recent years. It's worth the extra $15 for Yavapai East's larger units, many of which have nice views of the forest.

CANYON BOTTOM

Phantom Ranch

Located at the bottom of the canyon, $1/2$ mi. north of the Colorado River on the North Kaibab Trail. ☎ **520/638-2631** (main switchboard) or 303/297-2757 (reservations only). Fax 303/297-3175. 7 four-person cabins, 2 cabins for up to 10 people, 4 dorms of 10 people each. $22.85 dorm bed; $65.95 cabins (for 2). $11.70 for each additional person. AE, DC, DISC, MC, V.

The only park lodging below the canyon rims, the cabins at Phantom Ranch often sell out on the first day of availability—more than 23 months ahead. To reserve a spot, call as early as possible. (See directions for AmFac lodges, above.) If you arrive at the canyon without a reservation, contact the **Bright Angel Transportation Desk** (☎ **520/638-2631**, ext. 6015) for information about openings in the next 4 days.

The reason for the booked slate? Clean sheets never felt better than at the bottom of the Grand Canyon, beer never tasted this good (not even close), and a hot shower never felt so, well, miraculous. Phantom Ranch is the only place below the rims inside the park that has these amenities.

The ranch's nine evaporatively cooled cabins are a simple pleasure. Famous Grand Canyon architect Mary Colter designed four of them using rocks from the nearby Bright Angel Creek. Connected by dirt footpaths, they sit, natural and elegant, alongside picnic tables and under the shade of cottonwood trees. Inside each cabin, there's a desk, concrete floor, and 4 to 10 bunk beds, as well as a toilet and sink. A shower house for guests is nearby.

While most of Phantom Ranch was completed in the 1920s and '30s, four 10-person dorms, each with its own bathing facilities, were added in the early 1980s. Used mostly by hikers, these are ideal for individuals and small groups looking for a place to bed down; larger groups are better served by reserving cabins, which provide both privacy and a lower per-person price than the dorms.

In the late afternoon, many guests and hikers from the nearby Bright Angel Campground gravitate to the canteen, which sells snacks when not serving meals.

NORTH RIM

Grand Canyon Lodge

☎ **520/638-2611** (main switchboard) or 303/297-2757 (reservations only). Fax 303/297-3175. 208 cabin and motel units. TEL. $74 Frontier Cabin; $80 motel rm.; $88 Pioneer Cabin; $94 Western Cabin; $104 Rim Cabin. AE, DC, DISC, MC, V.

Like the North Rim itself, Grand Canyon Lodge attracts little attention. Although Union Pacific Railroad built the lodge in 1928, the train never came closer than Cedar City, Utah. After burning in 1932, the lodge reopened in 1937 and now blends almost seamlessly with the landscape. In its expansive lobby, a 50-foot-high ceiling absorbs sound like the forest floor. Beyond it, the octagonal "Sun Room" has three enormous picture windows opening onto the canyon. Two long decks with rocking chairs flank the sun-room, overlooking the canyon. The lodge also houses a saloon, a snack bar, a meeting room, and a full-service restaurant.

The 140 cabins come in four types, all with private bathrooms. With wicker furniture, bathtubs, and small vanity rooms, the Western Cabins and Rim Cabins are the most luxurious. The Western Cabins cost $10 less than the four Rim Cabins, which overlook the Bright Angel Canyon. The Rim Cabins generally fill up on their first day of availability, nearly 2 years in advance.

The two other types—Pioneer and Frontier—are more rustic. Tightly clustered along the rim of Transept Canyon, they have walls and ceilings of exposed logs, electric heaters, and showers instead of bathtubs. The Frontier Cabins have one guest room while the Pioneer Cabins have two. For $95 ($21 more than the price of a Frontier Cabin), a family of five can stay in comfort in one of the Pioneer Cabins. If your reservations are for a Frontier or Pioneer cabin, ask at check-in for one that overlooks Transept Canyon. The lodge may be able to accommodate you, and there's no extra charge for the view.

A few motel rooms are also available. Although they're well maintained and were remodeled in 1999, their atmosphere doesn't compare to the cabins.

NEAR THE PARK

TUSAYAN

A chain hotel with doubles ranging from $56 to $99 in Tusayan is **Grand Canyon Rodeway Inn Red Feather Lodge** (☎ **800/538-2345** or 520/638-2414), on Highway 64 one mile south of the Park.

Best Western Grand Canyon Squire Inn

P.O. Box 130 (1.5 mi. south of the park on Hwy. 64), Grand Canyon, AZ 86023-0130. ☎ **800/622-6966** or 520/638-2681. Fax 520/638-0162. 250 units. A/C TV TEL. Apr 1–Oct 17, $135 double; Oct 18–Mar 30 $85 double. AE, DC, DISC, MC, V.

There's a lot to do at this hotel, which prides itself on being the only full-service resort at Grand Canyon. You'll find two restaurants (including the town's best, The Coronado Room), two bars, tennis courts, a beauty shop, an exercise room, and an outdoor swimming pool. The kids will love the family recreation center, which features bowling and video games.

At $15 extra, the deluxe rooms are spacious, thick-walled, and quiet;

they're among the nicest in town. The standard rooms are no larger than the rooms at the other area motels, but they do offer hair dryers and coffeemakers.

Grand Canyon Quality Inn and Suites

P.O. Box 520 (on Hwy. 64, 1 mi. south of the park entrance), Grand Canyon, AZ 86023. ☎ **800/221-2222** (reservations only) or 520/638-2673. Fax 520/638-9537. www.grandcanyonqualityinn.com. E-mail: gcqi@aol.com. 288 units. A/C TV TEL. High season $118 double; low season, $68 double. AE, DC, DISC, MC, V.

In summer, guests here sun themselves around the large outdoor swimming pool and hot tub. In winter, they head for the hotel's atrium, where tropical plants and palm trees shade an 18-foot-long spa with a waterfall. As the area's hot tubs go, this one is grandest, with jets to massage every aching joint. When the guests finally finish soaking, they find themselves occupying some of the nicest accommodations in town, including a number of rooms with private decks and refrigerators.

Grand Hotel

P.O. Box 331 (on Highway 64, 1.5 mi. south of the park entrance), Grand Canyon, AZ 86023. ☎ **888/634-7263** or 520/638-3333. Fax 520/638-3131. www.canyon.com. E-mail: thegrand@canyon.com. 122 units. A/C TV TEL. High season $138 double; low-season $89 double. AE, DISC, MC, V.

Tusayan's newest hotel is also its most stylish. Modeled after a lodge of the Old West, the hotel's lobby features an enormous fireplace, hand-woven carpets, and hand-oiled, hand-painted goatskin lanterns. The rooms are also pleasant, though perhaps not large enough to justify their high prices. The nicest rooms have balconies facing away from the highway and cost an extra $10. The hotel also has an indoor heated pool, a restaurant, and a bar.

Holiday Inn Express

P.O. Box 3245 (on Hwy. 64, 1.5 mi. south of the park entrance), Grand Canyon, AZ 86023. ☎ **520/638-3000.** Fax 520/638-0123. www.gcanyon.com. 197 units. A/C TV TEL. Mar 15–May 30 $89–$109; June 1–Oct 15 $99–$139. Oct 15–Mar 14 $69–$89. Rates include continental breakfast. AE, DC, DISC, MC, V.

Decorated in a Southwestern motif, the rooms at this 1995 motel feel crisp and new. In the morning, enjoy complimentary coffee, juice, and pastries in the newly expanded breakfast area. The Holiday Inn Express also operates 32 suites, each with a different theme, in a building adjacent to the larger property.

7-Mile Lodge

P.O. Box 56 (1.5 mi. south of park entrance on Hwy. 64), Grand Canyon, AZ 86023. ☎ **520/638-2291.** 20 units. A/C TV. High season $80 double; low season $48 double. AE, DISC, MC, V.

Instead of taking reservations, the owners of this motel start selling spaces at around 9am and usually sell out by early afternoon. If you need a place to stay, think about stopping here on your way into the park. Don't be put off by the motel's cramped office, the rooms are actually quite nice and large enough to hold two queen beds. Built in 1984, they have 2-inch doors and walls thick enough to muffle the noise of planes from the nearby airport.

WILLIAMS

Two good midprice chain hotels in Williams are **Quality Inn Mountain Ranch** (☎ 520/635-2693), 8 miles east of Williams on Route 1 (near I-40, Exit 171); and **Holiday Inn** (☎ 520/635-4114), 950 N. Grand Canyon Blvd., off I-40, Exit 163. Others include **Days Inn** (☎ 520/635-4051), 2488 W. Rte. 66; **Fairfield Inn by Marriott** (☎ 520/635-9888), 1029 N. Grand Canyon Blvd., off

I-40 exit 163. Doubles at these hotels usually run about $45 to $99.

Inexpensive chain hotels include the **Travelodge** (☎ 520/635-2651), 430 E. Rte. 66; **Motel 6** (☎ 520/635-9000), 831 W. Rte. 66; **Howard Johnson Express** (☎ 800/720-6614 or 520/635-9561), 511 N. Grand Canyon Blvd., off I-40 exit 163; and **Super 8 West** (☎ 520/635-4045), 911 W. Rte. 66. Doubles average about $30 to $60.

Best Western Inn of Williams

2600 Rte. 66, Williams, AZ 86046. ☎ **520/635-4400.** Fax 520/635-4488. 79 units. A/C TV TEL. $79–$135 double. Rates include breakfast. AE, DC, DISC, MC, V.

Some of the nicest rooms in Williams are at this hotel, atop a forested hill west of town. In addition to sofas, glass-topped coffee tables, and classic American furniture, the rooms offer smaller amenities such as coffeemakers and hair dryers. Outside, the pines grow to near the edge of the swimming pool. A free hot breakfast is served in a small dining area, and a nearby Denny's delivers room-service meals.

Fray Marcos Hotel

235 N. Grand Canyon Blvd., Williams, AZ 86046. ☎ **800/843-8724** or 520/635-4010. Fax 520/635-2180. 89 units. A/C TV TEL. $69–$119 double. AE, DISC, MC, V.

Named for a Franciscan monk, this sprawling, luxurious hotel replaces the original Fray Marcos Hotel, which now houses a gift shop and the museum for the Grand Canyon Railway. In the lobby of the new hotel, oil paintings of the Grand Canyon adorn the walls, and cushy chairs surround a large flagstone fireplace. Next to the lobby, Spenser's Lounge offers simple dining and drinks from behind a 100-year-old bar.

Thanks to the success of the Grand Canyon Railway, the hotel grew rapidly in the late '90s. A new 300-seat restaurant, Max and Thelma's, was built nearby, and the hotel more than doubled the number of guest units. Although this is a nice hotel providing good service, it does feel less intimate and more commercial than other area lodges.

Norris Motel

1001 W. Rte. 66 (P.O. Box 388), Williams, AZ 86046. ☎ **800/341-8000** (reservations only) or 520/635-2202. Fax 520/635-9202. www.thegrandcanyon.com/norris. E-mail: ukgolf@primenet.com. 33 units. A/C TV TEL. $30–$59 double. AE, DISC, MC, V.

The sign at the Norris Motel heralds its "British Hospitality," and indeed, Brian and Kathleen James, the English managers, do everything possible to make guests feel at home. While all three buildings are pleasant, the newest, built in 1990, has the best view of the surrounding hills and is closest to the outdoor pool and spa. The oversized rooms in the new building easily house two double beds (or one queen), a desk, table, and refrigerator, all for a price lower than at most chain motels.

Red Garter Bed and Bakery

137 W. Railroad Ave. (P.O. Box 95), Williams, AZ 86046. ☎ **800/328-1484** or 520/635-1484. www.redgarter.com. E-mail: redgarter@thegrandcanyon.com. 4 units. A/C TV. $65–$105 double. Rates include continental breakfast. AE, DISC, MC, V. Closed Dec–Jan.

In the early 1900s this Victorian Romanesque building had a brothel upstairs, a saloon downstairs, and an opium den in the back. The innkeeper, John Holst, has worked hard to preserve both the building, built in 1897, and its colorful history. Each of the four rooms has custom-made moldings, a 12-foot-high ceiling, a ceiling fan, and antique furnishings. The Best Gals' Room, overlooks Route 66 and is the largest and most luxurious of the four. Its two adjoining rooms were once reserved for the brothel's "best gals," who would lean out of the Pullman windows to flag down customers.

Sheridan House Inn

460 E. Sheridan Ave., Williams, AZ 86046. ☎ **888/635-9345** or 520/635-9441. Fax 520/635-1005. www.thegrandcanyon.com/sheridan. E-mail: egardner@primenet.com. 10 units. A/C TV TEL. $110–$225 double. AE, DISC, MC, V. Ask about pets in advance.

This inn bristles with bronze sculptures and shimmers with original paintings. Guest rooms are ultraluxurious, with brass beds, glass-topped coffee tables, TVs, stereos, VCRs, and refrigerators stocked with cold drinks. Outside, under the ponderosa pines at the end of a quiet, dead-end street (a short walk from downtown Williams), the hot tub awaits. Making the setting all the more enjoyable are the friendly innkeepers, Steve and Evelyn Gardner.

FLAGSTAFF

In addition to the properties described below, a recommended B & B in Flagstaff is **Jeanette's Bed and Breakfast** (☎ **800/752-1912** or 520/527-1912), 3380 E. Lockett Rd., Flagstaff, AZ 86004-4043; double $99.

One good, expensive chain hotel in Flagstaff is **Residence Inn by Marriott** (☎ **520/526-5555**), 3440 Country Club, Flagstaff, AZ 86004; $160 suite with kitchen. Other options are **AmeriSuites,** 2455 S. Beulah (north of I-40 Exit 195B), ☎ **520/774-8042**, $99 double; and **Little America Hotel,** 2515 E. Butler (off I-40 Exit 198), ☎ **520/779-2741**, $119-$129 double.

Midprice chain hotels include: **Quality Inn Flagstaff,** 2000 S. Milton (near I-40 Exit 195B), ☎ **520/774-8771; Best Western Kings House Motel,** 1560 E. Rte. 66, ☎ **520/774-7186; Best Western Pony Soldier Motel,** 3030 E. Rte. 66, ☎ **520/526-2388; Comfort Inn,** 914 S. Milton Rd. (near I-40 Exit 195B), ☎ **520/774-7326; Days Inn Route 66,** 1000 W. Rte. 66, ☎ **520/774-5221; Days Inn East,** 3601 E. Lockett (near I-40 Exit 201), ☎ **520/527-1477; Days Inn I-40,** 2735 S. Woodlands Village Blvd. (near I-40 Exit

195B), ☎ 520/779-1575; **Fairfield Inn by Marriott,** 2005 S. Milton (near I-40 Exit 195B), ☎ 520/773-1300; **Holiday Inn Flagstaff Grand Canyon,** 2320 E. Lucky Lane (off I-40 Exit 198), ☎ 520/526-1150; **Howard Johnson,** 2200 E. Butler (off I-40 Exit 198), ☎ 520/779-6944; **Ramada Limited,** 2755 S. Woodlands (near I-40 Exit 195B), ☎ 520/773-1111.

One good, inexpensive chain hotel is **Super 8,** ☎ 888/324-9131 or 520/526-0818, 3725 N. Kasper Ave. (on Rte. 66, 1 mi. west of I-40 Exit 201), Flagstaff, AZ 86004. Others include **Howard Johnson Inn,** 3300 E. Rte. 66, ☎ 520/526-1826; **Motel 6,** 2010 E. Butler (off I-40 Exit 198), ☎ 520/774-1801; **Motel 6,** 2440 E. Lucky Lane (off I-40 Exit 198), ☎ 520/774-8756; **Motel 6,** 2500 E. Lucky Lane (off I-40 Exit 198), ☎ 520/779-6184; **Motel 6,** 2745 S. Woodlands Village Blvd. (near I-40 Exit 195B), ☎ 520/779-3757; **Ramada Limited,** 2350 E. Lucky Lane (off I-40 Exit 198), ☎ 520/779-3614; **Econo Lodge Lucky Lane,** 2480 E. Lucky Lane (off I-40 Exit 198), ☎ 520/774-7701; **Rodeway Inn East,** 2650 E. Rte. 66, ☎ 520/526-2200; **Rodeway Inn West,** 913 S. Milton (near I-40 Exit 195B), ☎ 520/774-5038; **Travelodge Flagstaff University Grand Canyon,** 801 W. Rte. 66, ☎ 888/259-4404; **Travelodge Flagstaff,** 2610 E. Route 66, ☎ 520/526-1399.

For toll-free numbers, see the appendix.

Comfi Cottages

1612 N. Aztec St., Flagstaff, AZ 86001. ☎ **888/774-0731** or 520/774-0731. Fax 520/773-7286. www.comficottages.com. E-mail: pat@comficottages.com. TV TEL. 6 cottages, accommodating 2–6 people, in different locations in Flagstaff. $105–$210 double. Rates include breakfast foods inside cottages. AE, DISC, MC, V. Ask about pets.

In the 1970s Pat Wiebe, a nurse at the local hospital, began purchasing and renovating small homes in Flagstaff. Today she rents out six of these quaint cottages. Most were built in the 1920s and '30s; they're old but not ancient, the type of places that have laundry chutes, flour bins, ironing boards that fold into the walls, see-through cupboard doors, and hardwood floors. Wiebe has modernized them somewhat, adding thermostat-controlled fireplaces, televisions, VCRs, and washer/dryers. Two of the cottages have air-conditioning. And she goes out of her way to make them comfortable. In every unit you'll find fresh-cut flowers, antiques, cupboards stocked with breakfast foods, and rag dolls from her personal collection.

The Inn at 410 Bed & Breakfast

410 N. Leroux St., Flagstaff, AZ 86001. ☎ **800/774-2008** or 520/774-0088. Fax 520/774-6354. www.inn410.com. E-mail: info@inn410.com. 9 units. A/C. $125–$175. MC V.

Peering into each of the rooms at this inn is like flipping the pages in an issue of *House And Garden.* Each expertly decorated room is daringly different, yet tasteful. Collectively, they make this 1894 home owned by Sally and Howard Krueger one of the most stunning B&Bs anywhere. One room, "Monet's Garden," is reminiscent of a French country garden, complete with impressionist paintings brushed upon the walls. My favorite, "The Dakota Room," has barn wood on one wall, wallpaper with a cowpoke motif on others, and lamps made partly of horseshoes—not to mention a cowboy hat that once belonged to Sally Krueger's grandfather.

Radisson Woodlands Hotel Flagstaff

1175 W. Rte. 66, Flagstaff, AZ 86001. ☎ **800/333-3333** (reservations only) or 520/773-8888. Fax 520/773-0597. 183 units. A/C TV TEL. $69–$119 double. AE, DC, DISC, MC, V.

Built in 1990, this four-story hotel has the look and feel of a luxury resort. A pianist often plays in the lobby, where crystal chandeliers hang above a polished marble floor. The decor in the common areas reflects Far Eastern influences. Asian-style vases sit alongside ornately carved teak doors, and one of the restaurants serves sushi. The rooms, with traditional European styling, are almost as opulent as the lobby, and they're quiet too.

OUTSIDE THE PARK

NORTH RIM

Jacob Lake Inn

Junction of Hwy. 67 and 89A, Jacob Lake, AZ 86022. ☎ **520/643-7232.** Fax 520/643-7235. E-mail: jacob@jacoblake.com. 12 motel units, 27 cabins. May 14–Nov, $69 double; Dec–May 13, $49 double. AE, DC, DISC, MC, V. Small pets only, $5 extra.

In 1922, Harold and Nina Bowman bought a barrel of gas and opened a gas "stand" near the present-day site of the Jacob Lake Inn. Seven years later they built this inn at the junction of highways 67 and 89A. Today Jacob Lake Inn is the main hub of activity between the North Rim and Kanab, Utah, and encompasses a bakery, soda fountain, gift shop, restaurant, and gas station.

Lodgers can choose between motel units and cabins. The rooms in the front building are not nearly as peaceful as the rooms and cabins behind the lodge. Built in 1958, the motel rooms in back are solid and clean, if a bit threadbare in spots. Most people prefer the rustic cabins, even though they cost more. The cabin floors creak, the guest rooms (from one to three per cabin) are cramped, and most smell like soggy pine needles. In other words, they're exactly how cabins should be. Unfortunately, two have been nicely restored and therefore ruined.

Kaibab Lodge

HC 64, Box 30 (26 mi. south of Jacob Lake on Hwy. 67), Fredonia, AZ 86022. ☎ **520/638-2389** (May 15–Oct 30), 800/525-0924 or 520/526-0924 (rest of year). Fax 520/527-9398. www.canyoneers.com. E-mail: answers@canyoneers.com. 29 units. $70 double. DISC, MC, V. Leashed pets accepted.

The main lodge here feels as warm and comfortable as a beloved summer camp. It has an upright piano, plastic trees, Christmas lights, wagon wheels, Indian rugs, watercolor paintings, board games, and portable heaters, all under an open-framed ceiling and enormous pine beams that date from its construction in the 1920s. Guests tend to congregate in the Adirondack-style chairs in front of the 5-foot-wide fireplace, in the small television room, or at the tables across from the counter that doubles as front desk and beer bar. There's also a small gift shop and a restaurant that serves breakfast and dinner.

Each cabinlike building houses two or more of the 24 guest rooms, which sleep from two to five people. The rooms are spare but clean, with paneling of rough-hewn pine. Most have showers but not tubs. One luxury room, added in 1999, has a queen bed, microwave, refrigerator, and coffeemaker. Because the walls of the older units are thin, it's best to share a cabin with friends. Located roughly a quarter-mile from the highway, the rooms open onto the broad expanse of DeMotte Park, one of the large, naturally occurring meadows on the Kaibab Plateau.

KANAB & FREDONIA

Kanab has two pleasant, moderately priced chain hotels: **Holiday Inn Express** (☎ 801/644-8888), 815 E. Hwy. 89, and **Best Western Red Hills** (☎ 435/644-2675), 125 W. Center St. There's also a delightful chain hotel 19 miles north of Kanab, en route to Zion National Park: **Best Western Thunderbird Resort** (☎ 888/848-6358 or 435/648-2203), located at junction of highways 89 and 9 (P.O. Box 5536), Mt. Carmel Junction, Utah 84755. Rates range from about $80 to $100 double.

Clean, inexpensive rooms can be found at **Crazy Jug Motel** (☎ 520/643-7752), 465 S. Main St. (Hwy. 89A),

Fredonia, and at the **Blue Sage Motel and RV Park** (☎ 520/643-7125), 330 S. Main St. (Hwy. 89A), Fredonia. Prices for doubles run about $25 to $45.

Aiken's Lodge

79 W. Center St., Kanab, UT 84171. ☎ **800/524-9999** (reservations only) or 435/644-2625. Fax 435/644-8827. 31 units. A/C TV TEL. Double-occupancy $29–$36 Nov–Apr 30; $49–$54 May–Oct; family units $59–$69. AE, DISC, MC, V. Pets $10 per stay. Limit 1 pet per room.

This motor lodge has aged nicely during its 50 years. Its large, clean rooms have huge windows, solid walls, and showers instead of bathrooms. My favorite ones, upstairs in the two-story section of the motel, have views over the shade trees to the surrounding red-rock cliffs as well as down to the small outdoor swimming pool. The quietest rooms, however, are in the single-story building farthest from Center Street. Large families can stay in the motel's two-bedroom, two-bathroom or three-bedroom, three-bathroom units for a fraction of what they'd pay for separate rooms.

Grand Canyon Motel and Old Travelers Inn

175 Main St. (Box 456), Fredonia, AZ 86022-0456. ☎ **520/643-7646.** Fax 520/643-7287. E-mail: gcmotel@xpressweb.com. 15 units, 8 with showers only. A/C TV. Grand Canyon Motel $32.50 May 15–Oct; $27 Nov–May 14. Old Travelers Inn $30. AE, MC, V. Small pets accepted.

Low prices make this motel popular even in winter. Four rooms with high ceilings, original trim, and ceiling fans are in the historic Old Travelers Inn, built in 1886. The other units are in cabin-type buildings, built between 1936 and 1948. The cabin rooms, each with cable television, refrigerator, and pine furniture, are a tad dark, but they surround a grassy courtyard shaded by elm and spruce trees. Some of these rooms also have kitchenettes.

Nine Gables Inn Bed & Breakfast

106 W. 100 North, Kanab, UT 84741. ☎ **435/644-5079.** 3 units (showers only). A/C. $80–$110 double. Open Apr–Oct. May be open at other times (call to check). MC, V. Older kids only.

This B&B occupies a home built in 1872 by the town's first Mormon bishop, Levi Stewart. The oldest building in Kanab, the home has always had an extra room for guests. Famous travelers such as Buffalo Bill Cody, Zane Gray, and Brigham Young all used it to take refuge from the rugged landscape around town.

Today, guests take refuge in three upstairs rooms, two of which still have decks where people slept outside on hot nights before air-conditioning existed. All have pedestal sinks in the bathrooms and are decorated with the heirlooms of the owners. These furnishings make the place resemble a home, and the amiable hosts make it feel like one.

Parry Lodge

89 E. Center St., Kanab, UT 84741. ☎ **800/748-4104** or 801/644-2601. Fax 801/644-2605. www.infowest.com/parry/index.html. E-mail: bpalmer@xpressweb.com. 89 units. A/C TV TEL. High season $67 double; low season $30 double. AE, DISC, MC, V. Pet rooms $5 extra.

Many of the older rooms in this 1929 Colonial-style lodge display plaques bearing the names of stars who stayed here while filming Westerns. Room 131, for example, was built to house Frank Sinatra's mother-in-law while the famed crooner starred in *Sergeants Three*. (Sinatra stayed in an adjoining room.) Maple trees shade the older one-story buildings, making them look as if they really were in the original colonies. If you want to spread out, though, bypass these historic buildings in favor of the two-story building. Completed in 1985, it has expansive (if somewhat drab) rooms. Open for all three meals, the lodge's restaurant serves good breakfasts.

EAST OF THE PARK

Cameron Trading Post Motel

Hwy. 89 (P.O. Box 339), Cameron, AZ 86020. ☎ **800/338-7385** or 520/679-2231. Fax 520/679-2350. 66 units. A/C TV TEL. $59–$74 double. AE, DC, MC, V. Pets accepted.

Renovated in the early '90s, the rooms in this motel are some of the nicest in the Grand Canyon area. Each features its own unique Southwestern-style furnishings, many of them handmade by the motel's staff. Some rooms open onto the gorge of the Little Colorado River, and a few afford views all the way down to the river. The motel's Hopi building borders a small terraced garden with stone picnic tables, a fountain, and a large grill. There's a restaurant and an enormous trading post on the premises.

Lee's Ferry Lodge

4 mi. west of Navajo Bridge on Hwy. 89A (HC 67-Box 1), Marble Canyon, AZ 86036. (Located in the tiny "Arizona designated place" of Vermilion Cliffs.) ☎ **520/355-2230** or 520/355-2231. Fax 520/355-2301. 11 units, including 3 two-rm units. A/C. $53 double. MC, V. Pets accepted.

Some of the best porch-sitting anywhere can be enjoyed outside the low sandstone buildings of this sleepy roadside lodge, a popular stopping place for trout fishers. Although the hotel sits close to the road, traffic is slow at night, and the overall effect is restful. Paintings of wildfowl, trout, and flowers grace the small, rustic rooms. The only thing not relaxing are the showers, which erupt like Old Faithful, only less faithfully.

Dining

INSIDE THE PARK

SOUTH RIM

Arizona Steakhouse

At Bright Angel Lodge. ☎ **520/638-2631.** Reservations not accepted. Dinner entrees $12.75–$20.70. AE, DC, DISC, MC, V. 5–10pm daily. AMERICAN.

Lining up before this restaurant's 5pm opening isn't a bad idea. Instead of arriving after sunset to find an hour's wait, you can watch the sunset's colors through the long, canyon-facing windows. Or, when the days are longer, finish the meal in time to step outside for the evening's show of changing colors.

The service generally runs at a sluggish pace, which (ideally) creates a relaxing atmosphere. You'll have plenty of time to choose from the restaurant's wine list or order an appetizer—the sautéed mushroom caps are one good choice. Entrees include hand-cut steaks and prime rib; marinated chicken breast, broiled halibut, grilled Atlantic salmon; and a daily vegetarian special. The food here tends to be inconsistent, but on a good night, a tasty meal can be had by all.

Bright Angel Coffee Shop

Bright Angel Lodge. ☎ **520/638-2631.** Reservations not accepted. Breakfast $1.95–$6.60; lunch $6.10–$8.55; dinner $6.10–$17.55. AE, DC, DISC, MC, V. 6:30–10:45am and 11:15am–10pm daily. AMERICAN.

The burgers and patty melts here are tasty, as are some of the Southwestern dishes. This is also a good place for families, who can dine here without worrying too much about the children's behavior. The games on the kid's menu should distract the young ones until the french fries arrive.

Still, this restaurant doesn't merit high marks. It gets soiled from the throngs that tramp through it, and it seems to serve as a training camp for new AmFac employees destined either to be fired or promoted to the fancy El Tovar Hotel. Besides, equally good food is available for less money at the Maswick and Yavapai cafeterias.

El Tovar Restaurant

In the El Tovar Lodge. ☎ **520/638-2631,** ext. 6432. Reservations for dinner only. Breakfast

$2.50–$9.70; lunch $5.95–$17.50; dinner $15.75–$24.75. AE, DC, DISC, MC, V. 6:30–11am, 11:30am–2pm, and 5–10pm daily. CONTINENTAL.

More than 90 years after opening its doors, this restaurant remains a pleasant dining experience. It starts with a lovely room—walls of Oregon pine graced with murals depicting the ritual dances of four Indian tribes and banks of windows at the north and south ends. Atop the restaurant's linen tablecloths, fresh flowers catch light from those windows, as do the clean white shirts of the wait staff, a group professional enough to do justice to the room.

At dinner, a Southwestern influence spices the Continental cuisine. A tasty appetizer is the baked portobello mushroom with artichoke, roasted peppers, and Jack cheese on smoked tomato coulis. For an entree, meat eaters will enjoy the broiled filet mignon with roasted garlic demiglace, or the baked blue cornmeal–crusted Atlantic salmon. Meanwhile, vegetarians can munch on the blue corn tamales filled with black beans, guacamole, and fire-roasted corn salsa.

In 1999 some locals maintained that the food at the El Tovar had slipped, and my experiences seemed to validate this opinion. But the restaurant seems likely to rebound, as it no doubt has in the past, and the atmosphere remains as enticing as ever.

The General Store Delicatessen.

In the South Rim's General Store (at Mather Business Center). ☎ **520/638-2262.** $2–$5. No credit cards. 8am–6pm daily. DELI.

Many Park Service employees duck into this delicatessen for lunch. Here, you can sit in a corner booth, read the paper, and watch the tourists pass. The deli serves sandwiches, salads, and fried chicken, but the best offerings are often the specials.

Maswick and Yavapai Cafeterias

At Maswik and Yavapai lodges, respectively. ☎ **520/638-2631.** No reservations.

Breakfast $1.40–$5.25; lunch and dinner $3.75–$6.75. AE, DC, DISC, MC, V. Maswik 6am–10pm daily; Yavapai 6:30am–10pm daily (may change seasonally). AMERICAN.

For the price of a burger, fries, and a soft drink at the Tusayan McDonald's, you can eat a full meal at either Maswik or Yavapai cafeterias. While the food at both usually tastes like dormitory fare, there are some key differences. Maswik serves full-dinner plates from a Mexican station, pasta station, burger station, and a station with fish and daily specials. At Yavapai you can mix and match from a variety of stations, picking up a chicken leg from one, a slice of pizza from another, a dish of mashed potatoes from another. At the salad bar, you can assemble a dinner salad for under $2. When business slows in the winter, Yavapai sometimes closes; Maswik doesn't.

INSIDE THE CANYON

Phantom Ranch

Inside the canyon 0.5 mi. north of the Colorado River on the North Kaibab Trail. To order meals more than 4 days in advance, call ☎ **303/297-2757;** to order meals in the next 4 days, contact the Bright Angel Transportation Desk at ☎ **520/638-2631,** ext. 6015. Steak $28.15; stew $17.60; sack lunch $7.95; breakfast $12.65. AE, DC, DISC, MC, V (for advance reservations: MC, V only). AMERICAN.

At the bottom of the Grand Canyon, whether you get there by mule or on foot, pretty much anything tastes good. Every evening two options are offered: a steak dinner at 5pm and a hearty beef stew at 6:30pm. The vegetarian plate consists of the side dishes to the steak dinner: vegetables, cornbread, and salad. Dessert is usually chocolate cake.

The family style, all-you-can-eat breakfasts are also excellent, as heaping platters of eggs, bacon, and pancakes are laid out on the long, blue tables. The only disappointment is the sack lunch, whose meager offerings (summer sausage, bagel with cream cheese, apple, peanuts, raisins, and juice) don't seem worth the price.

Because the number of meals is fixed, hikers and mule riders must reserve them ahead of time through AmFac (see number above) or at the Bright Angel Transportation Desk. As a last resort, inquire upon arrival at Phantom Ranch to see whether any meals remain. Between 8am and 4pm and from 8 to 10pm, anyone is allowed in the canteen, which has snacks, soda, beer (sold only after dinner), and wine.

NORTH RIM

Grand Canyon Lodge Dining Room

At Grand Canyon Lodge. ☎ **520/638-2611,** ext. 160. Reservations required for dinner, not accepted for breakfast and lunch. Breakfast $1.85–$6.75; lunch $5.70–$7.45; dinner $12.25–$17.75. AE, DC, DISC, MC, V. 6:30–10am, 11:30am–2:30pm, and 4:45–9:30pm daily. CONTINENTAL.

Long banks of west- and south-facing windows afford views of Transept Canyon and help warm this room, where the high ceiling absorbs the clamor of diners. While it's unreasonable to expect gourmet dining in a place as remote as the North Rim, the food here is nearly as satisfying as the surroundings.

Served by waiters in black slacks, white shirts, and bolo ties, the broiled stuffed mushrooms are a delectable starter at dinnertime. One tasty main course is the Pasta Lydia—fresh asparagus and potatoes tossed in pesto sauce with bow-tie pasta. Also recommended is the New York strip steak with three-pepper glaze. Other choices include prime rib, steak, pork medallions, and dishes with fish or poultry. Lunch offerings include a variety of salads, sandwiches, and burgers. At breakfast, a full buffet costs under $8.

Grand Snack Shop

In the west wing of Grand Canyon Lodge. ☎ **520/638-2611.** Breakfast $1.95–$4.25; lunch and dinner $1.30–$3.80; 14-in. supreme pizza $15.50. 7am–9pm daily. AMERICAN/PIZZA.

The snack bar serves the best pizza on the North Rim, or so the joke goes. That speaks well for the pizza, which could just as easily—and no less truthfully—be called the worst. At any rate, at $2.25 a slice, it's an economical alternative to firing up the camp stove. The snack bar also serves calzones, burgers, premade salads, and breakfasts. If all you desire is a cup of coffee and a muffin, stop by the saloon, where an espresso bar operates from 5 to 9:30am daily.

EAST OF THE PARK

Lee's Ferry Lodge Vermilion Cliffs Bar & Grill

4 mi. west of Navajo Bridge on Hwy. 89A, Marble Canyon, AZ. ☎ **520/355-2231.** Breakfast $2–$6.50; lunch $4.25–$7.95; dinner $5.95–$16.95. 6am–9pm daily. AMERICAN.

After rigging boats for trips down the Colorado, many river guides come here, and not just for the 150 types of bottled beer. They also come for nicely prepared steaks, chicken, and fish, and for imaginative sandwiches such as the "Turkey in a Straw"—sliced turkey breast, sauerkraut, and Swiss cheese grilled on sourdough bread and served with Thousand Island dressing. It's easily the best food near Lee's Ferry and arguably the best within two hours of the North Rim. The staff is low-key and friendly.

TUSAYAN

Cafe Tusayan

Next to the Rodeway Inn, 1.5 mi. south of the park on Hwy.64, Tusayan. ☎ **520/638-2151.** Breakfast $1.95–$9.25; lunch $4.50–$8.95; dinner $4.50–$18.95. MC, V. Call for hours. AMERICAN/ SOUTHWESTERN.

This restaurant, which opened in spring 1999 in a space formerly occupied by Denny's, serves a few varieties of salads; appetizers such as jalapeño poppers and sautéed mushrooms; and a handful of entrees, including salmon with herb butter, top sirloin steak, baked chicken, and stroganoff. Perhaps because the chefs are able to focus on just a few dishes, the food is some of the best in Tusayan. Alas, the decor still reflects the Denny's influence. The restaurant's booths, hanging lamps, display cases, and counter all scream "chain restaurant."

Canyon Star Restaurant

At Grand Hotel on Hwy. 64 (1.5 mi. from the park's south entrance, Tusayan. ☎ **888/ 634-7263** or 520/638-3333. Breakfast $3.50–$7.50; lunch $7.95; dinner $14.95–$21.95. Summer daily 6:30am–10pm; winter daily 7am–9:30pm. AE, DISC, MC, V. REGIONAL.

The entertainment at this sprawling restaurant seems designed to give tourists exactly what they hope to find in the American West. Each night during summer, lonesome cowboy balladeers and spiritual Native American drummers take turns performing for the visitors. In case anyone gets bored with this sanitized Western show, video clips of the canyon play constantly on monitors above the dance floor. The distractions are more than enough to make a person forget the food, even the mesquite smoked barbecue.

Coronado Dining Room

Located at Best Western Grand Canyon Squire Inn (1.5 mi. south of the park on Hwy. 64), Tusayan. ☎ **520/638-2681,** ext. 4419. Breakfast buffet $8.95; dinner $10.95–$19.95. AE, DISC, MC, V. 6:30–11am (high season only) and 5–10pm (year-round). SOUTHWESTERN/AMERICAN.

This restaurant, which is the best in Tusayan, serves the usual mix of Southwestern and American food. The difference is that everything here is prepared with more expertise than in other area restaurants. Of the Southwestern dishes, the *pollo asada* (charbroiled chicken breast with tomatoes and scallions) rates

high marks. On summer nights, the most cost-effective time to eat here is between 5 and 7pm, when some entrees are discounted by $2 or more.

Moqui Lodge Dining Room

At Moqui Lodge on Hwy. 64 (0.25 mi. from the park's south entrance), Tusayan. ☎ **520/638-2424.** Reservations not accepted. Breakfast $6.35; dinner $4.95–$18. Daily 6–10am and 5–10pm. AE, DC, DISC, MC, V. Lodge closed Nov 1–Apr 1. MEXICAN.

Occupying a wide wood-paneled room with a high ceiling, this restaurant calls to mind a country church. Electric candles and metal chandeliers flush the darkness from every corner, giving the room an open, inviting feel. Moqui attracts both locals and tourists with its appetizing, albeit cheese-heavy Mexican fare, including tostadas, enchiladas, and tacos. The fajitas—chicken or beef served with peppers and onions along with warm flour tortilla—make a trip here worthwhile.

FLAGSTAFF

The Black Bean Burrito Bar and Salsa Company

12 E. Rte. 66, Gateway Plaza Suite 104, Flagstaff. ☎ **520/779-9905.** All items $1–$6. No credit cards. Summer hours Sun noon–8pm; Mon–Thurs 11am–10pm; Fri–Sat 11am–11pm. Call for winter hours. MEXICAN.

The best burritos seem to turn up in the plainest environments. At the Black Bean, you'll eat out of plastic drive-in baskets while sitting at a counter that opens onto a pedestrian walkway. Sure enough, the burritos, which come with a choice of eight different salsas, are delicious. A favorite among Northern Arizona University students, the Black Bean offers 14 house specialty wraps (steamed or stir-fried food wrapped in tortillas), including exotic flavors such as peanut tofu and hummus, as well as traditional bean, chicken, and steak burritos. The burritos may have the heft of hand weights, but their price won't burden you financially.

Cafe Express

16 N. San Francisco St., Flagstaff. ☎ **520/774-0541.** Breakfast $2.50–$6.25; lunch and dinner $4.50–$8.95. M, V. Daily 7am–9pm. VEGETARIAN/NEW AMERICAN.

Like Macy's (see below), Cafe Express serves great vegetarian fare and displays paintings by local artists. But Cafe Express's food is slightly more refined, in terms of both preparation and ingredients. It may not be as healthful as the food at Macy's, but it sure tastes good.

Breakfast features delicious omelettes, huevos rancheros, and pancakes, with tofu available as a substitute for eggs. The lunch and dinner menu includes soups, sandwiches, enormous salads, and Southwestern fare. The tastiest items, however, are house specials like the tofu mushroom stroganoff and spanakopita. Don't forget to order one of the desserts, which are among the best in town.

Charly's

In the historic Hotel Weatherford, 23 N. Leroux, Flagstaff. ☎ **520/779-1919.** Lunch $2.95–$8.95; dinner $6.50–$16.95. AE, DC, DISC, MC, V. Daily 11am–11pm (10pm in winter). SOUTHWESTERN/AMERICAN.

Charly's is spacious and cool, both inside, where the 12-foot-high ceilings of the Hotel Weatherford provide breathing room, and on the sidewalk, a favorite place for summertime dining. Besides steaks and burgers, the restaurant offers a number of vegetarian dishes and salads that make for perfect light dining. It also has more than 20 beers on tap.

Chez Marc Bistro

503 Humphreys St., Flagstaff. ☎ **520/774-1343.** Lunch $11.95–$16.95; dinner $19.95–$29.95. AE, CB, DC, DISC, MC, V. Reservations recommended. Thurs–Sun 11:30am–2:30pm, 5–9pm; Mon–Wed 5–9pm. COUNTRY FRENCH.

This restaurant's talented chef, Marc Balocco, has cooked for luminaries such as Margaret Thatcher and Queen Elizabeth II, but he seems to take nearly as much pride in feeding everyday tourists and Flagstaff locals. Attended by waiters in formal attire, you can dine in the bistro's brick-walled, wooden-floored interior, where magnums of champagne line the walls, or, during warm weather, on its outside terrace, surrounded by lovely gardens. You'll savor food that's superb not only in taste, but also in texture and appearance. For an entree, try *Le Thon aux Epices* (seared ahi tuna with spicy crust laid over a puree of butternut squash laced by a Pinot Noir sauce).

Dara Thai

14 S. San Francisco St., Flagstaff. ☎ **520/774-0047** or 520/774-8390. Main courses $6.95–$14.95. AE, DISC, MC, V. Mon–Sat 11am–10pm. THAI.

Among the 80-some entrees served at Dara Thai are many fine curry, vegetarian, and fish dishes. Everything I've had here has been terrific, but you should order cautiously nonetheless. Your server will ask you to select the spiciness level for many sauces, and if you choose the highest level you may soon find your tongue hotter than Phantom Ranch in July.

Macy's European Coffee House Bakery & Vegetarian Restaurante

14 S. Beaver St., Flagstaff. ☎ **520/774-2243.** Reservations not accepted. Main courses $3.50–$6.25. No credit cards. Mon–Wed 6am–8pm, Thurs–Sat 6am–9pm, Sun 6am–6pm. VEGETARIAN/BAKED GOODS.

Macy's may not be able to save the world, but its fine vegetarian food, fresh pastries, and great coffee encourage people to slow down and smell the latte. It's a place where vegans are welcomed, where bikes lean against the building, and where the bathroom graffiti is life-affirming. A cashier here earnestly told me that she loves everything on the menu. In addition to the standard menu items such as hummus sandwiches and breakfast couscous, Macy's serves daily specials, including a pasta of the day.

Pasto

19 E. Aspen Ave., Flagstaff. ☎ **520/779-1937.** Dinner $7.95–$15.95. AE, MC, V. Reservations recommended. Daily 5pm–9pm. ITALIAN.

This restaurant bills itself as "fun Italian dining," perhaps referring to the crayons on the tables. Still, the dining is more delicious than fun. The Southwestern black-bean ravioli, which comes with a choice of sauces, is outstanding, as is the tortellini Florentine (garlic-lemon pasta with spinach and cream sauce). The atmosphere is also pleasant. The dining room has a stamped tin ceiling, and old horns and trombones hang from a brick wall.

WILLIAMS

Cruisers Cafe 66

233 W. Rte. 66, Williams. ☎ **520/635-2445.** $4.25–$14.95. AE, MC, V. Summer daily noon–10pm; winter usually 3–10pm. AMERICAN.

Built in an old Route 66 gas station, this restaurant (formerly Tiffany's), is jammed with gas-station memorabilia, including stamped glass, filling-station signs, "Sky Chief" gas pumps, and photos of classic stations. Served up with plenty of napkins as well as drinks in unbreakable plastic mugs, the roadhouse-style food will fuel you for days to come. Start with the sampler of appetizers—wings, chicken strips, mozzarella sticks, and fried mushrooms—served on a real automobile hubcap. The burgers are delicious, but the best choice, if you really want to fill up, is the baby back ribs. Check on the daily specials in the bar, which attract many locals.

Grand Canyon Coffee and Café

125 W. Rte. 66, Williams. ☎ **520/635-1255.** Reservations not accepted. $3.50–$4.50. AE,

MC, V. Summer Mon–Sat 7am–4:30pm, 7–8:30pm. SANDWICHES.

For a quick lunch, try this restaurant, which prominently displays Harley-Davidson T-shirts and traffics in food and drink like Mocha Espresso Frappes, fruit smoothies, bottled waters, and Panini sandwiches served on focaccia bread. Cooked on a cast-iron grill imported from Switzerland, the Panini sandwiches are delicious—and relatively inexpensive.

Old Smoky's Restaurant.

624 W. Route 66. ☎ **520/635-2091.** Reservations not accepted. Breakfast $2–$6; lunch $3–$7. AE, DISC, MC, V. Daily 6am–1:30pm. AMERICAN.

Built in 1946, this tiny Route 66 restaurant pays homage to the mountain-man lifestyle of the town's namesake, Bill Williams. On its walls of varnished wood hang logging saws, a muzzle loader gun, and coonskin caps. The breakfasts, which are the best in town, could easily satisfy a hungry logger. Every meal comes with a slice of homemade sweet bread.

Pancho McGillicuddy's Mexican Cantina

141 Railroad Ave., Williams. ☎ **520/635-4150.** $3.75–$13.50. AE, DISC, MC, V. Summer daily noon–10pm. Hours vary in winter. MEXICAN/AMERICAN.

The first tough decision at this restaurant is where to eat. Your choices are the outside deck, which receives some nice late-afternoon sun and features live entertainment in summer; the main dining room, done up like a courtyard in a Mexican villa; and the historic barroom, site of the (1893) Cabinet Saloon. The next tough choice is which of the heavy but zesty Mexican dishes to order. The chicken *mole* (chicken breast served with a sweetened red chile sauce) is one good option. Others include a *carne asada* (rib-eye steak broiled over a flame and topped with green chilies, tomatoes, onion, and cheese) and red snapper in tomato and olive sauce.

Rod's Steak House

301 E. Rte. 66, Williams. ☎ **520/635-2671.** $7–$24. MC, V. Daily 11:30am–9:30pm. STEAKS.

If you're a steak lover, brake for the cow-shaped sign on Route 66 as you would for real livestock. This landmark restaurant, sprawling across a city block between the highway's east- and west-bound lanes, has hardly changed since opening in 1946. Printed on a paper cutout of a cow, the menu is still only about 6 inches across—more than enough space for its laconic descriptions of the restaurant's offerings. You can choose nonsteak items such as "beef liver grilled onions and bacon" and "jumbo fantail shrimp tempura battered"; or prime rib in three sizes, from the 9-ounce "ladies lite cut" to the 16-ounce "cattleman's hefty cut." The corn-fed mesquite-broiled steaks that have made this place a hit for a half century are also available.

KANAB & FREDONIA

Houston's Trails End Restaurant

32 E. Center St., Kanab. ☎ **435/644-2488.** Breakfast $3–$7; lunch $4–$7.75; dinner $5.25–17.25. AE, DISC, MC, V. 6am–10:30pm daily. Closed Dec–Feb. STEAK/SEAFOOD/MEXICAN.

For a taste of Kanab's traditional fare, head for Houston's. While country music plays, waitresses wearing toy (we hope) sidearms serve up meaty courses. The house special is a chicken-fried steak. Other specialties include baby back ribs and a chicken breast slathered in barbecue sauce. The soup is made fresh daily, as are the enormous yeast rolls that come with each dinner. Breakfast includes a choice of omelettes, and lunch consists primarily of burgers and sandwiches.

Nedra's Cafe

Hwy. 89A, Fredonia. ☎ **520/643-7591.** $2.75–$15.95. AE, DC, MC, V. May 15–Oct 7am–10pm daily; Nov–May 14 11am–8pm Thurs–Sun. MEXICAN.

Because this restaurant serves tasty Mexican food at moderate prices, it's a great place to fill up after completing a North Rim backpacking trip. In addition to enchiladas, tostadas, burritos, and tacos, Nedra's serves less-common Mexican dishes such as *carnitas* (seasoned roast pork topped with fresh cilantro and green onions) and *machaca* (shredded beef cooked with tomatoes, onion, green chilies, cilantro, and egg). A few American dishes, including hamburgers, sandwiches, and steaks, are on the menu.

In Kanab you'll find a similar restaurant, **Nedra's Too.** But the tastiest Mexican fare in that community is at **Escobar's Mexican Restaurant** (☎ 435/ **644-3739**), 373 E. 300 South.

Wildflower Health Food

18 E. Center St., Kanab. ☎ **435/644-3200.** $3–$3.95. MC, V. Mon–Sat 10am–6pm. HEALTH FOOD.

When you absolutely cannot eat another bite of red meat or white flour, head to this tiny eight-table restaurant and store for a light lunch. Offerings include sandwiches made with fresh vegetables and a choice of tempeh, tofu, hummus, turkey or pastrami; fresh salads; daily soup specials (served with fresh baked bread); and baked goods. The restaurant also has smoothies injected with supplements and pick-me-ups guaranteed to cleanse you of that maple roll you had for breakfast.

Picnic & Camping Supplies

If possible, stock up on your camping items at a grocery store in a large city such as Flagstaff. In general, prices are lowest in Flagstaff and rise steadily as you near the canyon, peaking at The General Store inside the park. Inside the park, on the South Rim, you'll find **General Store,** in Grand Canyon Village (☎ 520/638-2262); and **Desert View Store,** at Desert View off Ariz. 64 (☎ 520/638-2393). On the North Rim is the **North Rim General Store,** adjacent to North Rim Campground (☎ 520/638-2611, ext. 270).

Outside the park, in Tusayan, is **Babbitt's Supermarket,** 1 mile south of park entrance on U.S. 89 and Ariz. 64 (☎ 520/638-2854). In Williams: **Safeway,** 637 Rte. 66 (☎ 520/635-0500). In Cameron: **Simpson's Market,** at the junction of U.S. 89 and Ariz. 64, next to the Chevron (☎ 520/679-2340). In Kanab: **Glazier's Food Town,** 264 S. 100 E. (☎ 801/644-5029); and **Honey's IGA Food and Drug,** 260 E. 300 South (☎ 435/644-5877). There are three large supermarkets in Flagstaff: **Albertson's,** 1416 E. Rte. 66 (☎ 520/773-7955); **Basha's,** 2700 Woodlands Village Blvd. (☎ 520/774-3882); and **Fry's,** 201 N. Switzer Canyon Dr. (☎ 520/774-2719).

19

GRAND TETON NATIONAL PARK

by Geoff O'Gara

THOUGH SMALLER AND MORE UNDERSTATED THAN NEIGHBORING Yellowstone, Grand Teton is just as impressive. Except for the towering mountains that made it famous, it's not as brassy as its cousin. You'll see wildlife—eagles and osprey along the

Snake River, moose and, if you're lucky, a black bear in the vicinity of the Jackson Lake Junction, and pronghorn on the valley floor—but it is the landscape that makes this park.

Contrasted to the undulations of Yellowstone, Grand Teton presents two vistas: a long, wide valley and straight-up peaks. If possible, once you enter the park, make a beeline for the summit of Signal Mountain, near Jackson Lake. There you will have a commanding 360° view that will put the park and surrounding areas in perspective. It's also the spot that inspired the most famous photos of the park.

From the Jackson Point Overlook on Signal Mountain, you'll see a valley floor that was once covered with thousands of tons of ice and a freshwater sea; to the west are views of a mountain formation towering more than a mile overhead.

Consider this: The tops of the Tetons, which sit on a 40-mile-long fault, were uplifted more than 30,000 feet from beneath the surface. The canyons and

valleys that punctuate the mountains were carved during the Ice Age; glaciers also gouged out hundreds of lakes in the park.

One advantage of Grand Teton is that it's significantly easier to get around in than Yellowstone, in part because the park is smaller and activity centers are closer to each other. Jackson Lake and the Snake River, prime recreational areas for fishers and boaters, are only short distances from the hiking trails and campsites. And though less imposing than the more famous Old Faithful Inn, Jackson Lake Lodge is every bit as appealing and comfortable.

The first homesteaders began arriving in the area in the 1880s. Many discovered, though, that the frigid winters and short growing season made it difficult—indeed, virtually impossible—to eke out a living, so they abandoned the area. However, by 1903 cattle ranchers discovered that wealthy Eastern hunters were attracted to the area as a vacation site, and the dude-ranching industry secured its first foothold in the area.

When cattle interests learned of a movement to convert privately owned grazing land on the valley floor to a national park, a rancorous tug-of-war began. Congress had designated the area outside Yellowstone Park the Teton Forest Reserve in 1897 and attempted to create a larger sanctuary in 1917; however, local opposition defeated the measure. In 1923, a more well-reasoned and successful attempt was made to preserve the area for future generations when Maude Noble, a local environmentalist, and a group of other locals, aided by Yellowstone Superintendent Horace Albright, prepared a plan for setting aside a portion of the Jackson Hole (the great valley that runs the length of the Tetons on the east side) as a national recreation area. Congress first set aside 96,000 acres of mountains and forests (excluding Jackson Lake) as a national park in 1929.

John D. Rockefeller Jr. got into the act by establishing the Snake River Land Company, which became the vehicle through which he accumulated more than 35,000 acres of land between 1927 and 1943. His goal was to donate the property for an enlarged park, but opponents in Congress prevented the government from accepting his gift.

Finally, in 1950, the feds and the locals reached a compromise: The government agreed to reimburse Teton County for revenue that would have been generated by property taxes, and to honor existing leaseholds. Grand Teton National Park was born.

Avoiding the Crowds. The bulk of the travelers who visit Grand Teton are visiting both Yellowstone and Grand Teton—and this means that when winter closes in on Yellowstone, the crowds abandon both parks. Since Grand Teton usually holds out against winter a bit longer than the higher plateau to the north, you may enjoy a wonderfully uncrowded visit in early June and late October at Grand Teton. But I emphasize the word *may:* Snow can fall as early as September.

The risks, in addition to unseasonal snowfall, are that it's sometimes harder to get around. In the spring, higher trails are still blocked by snow, or the mud that follows it. That can last well into June. In the fall, temperatures can drop at night, and chill winds sometimes blow.

However, wildflowers are particularly riotous in spring, filling the meadows and hillsides with vast arrays of color. In the fall, golden aspens rustle amidst the evergreens, and both you and the wildlife are less distracted by crowds. In some streams, this is the best time for angling. It's cheaper, too: Motels drop their rates during the off season.

If crowds make you claustrophobic, the key months to avoid are July and August. But most of the people who come through the gates in midsummer go only to the developed campgrounds and lodges at Colter Bay, Jenny Lake, and Moose; to the lakes and views accessible by car; and to the short paths that stay within view of the visitors center. If you have the energy to hike up into Cascade Canyon and beyond, it's not so bad. And, of course, summer is a beautiful time of year, with wildflowers blooming well into July, and wildlife always in evidence.

Just the Facts

GETTING THERE & GATEWAYS

The park is essentially the east slope of the Tetons and the valley below, so if you drive to it, you enter from the south, east, or north. From the north, you can enter the park from Yellowstone National Park, which is linked to Grand Teton by the John D. Rockefeller Jr. Memorial Parkway (U.S. Highways 89/191/287). When you come this way, you will already have paid your entrance to both parks, so there is no entrance station, but you can stop at Flagg Ranch, approximately 5 miles north of the park boundary, and get park information. From December to March, Yellowstone's south entrance is open only to snowmobiles and snowcoaches.

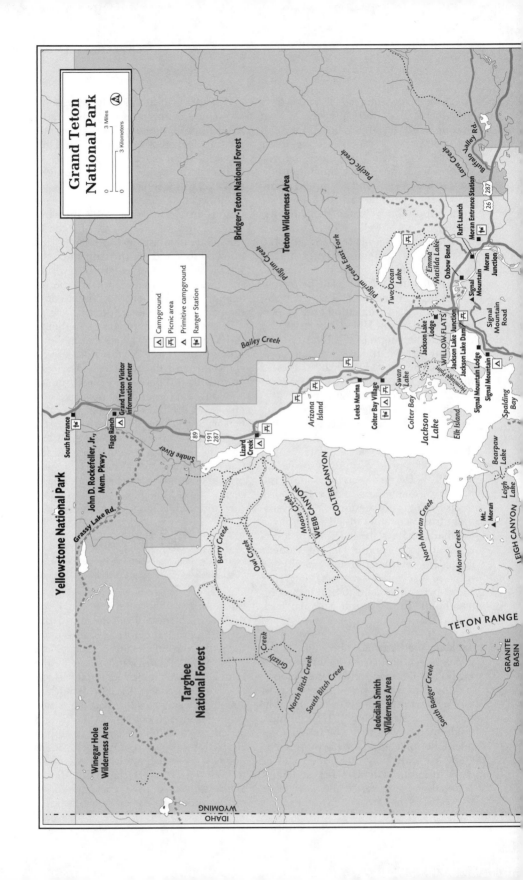

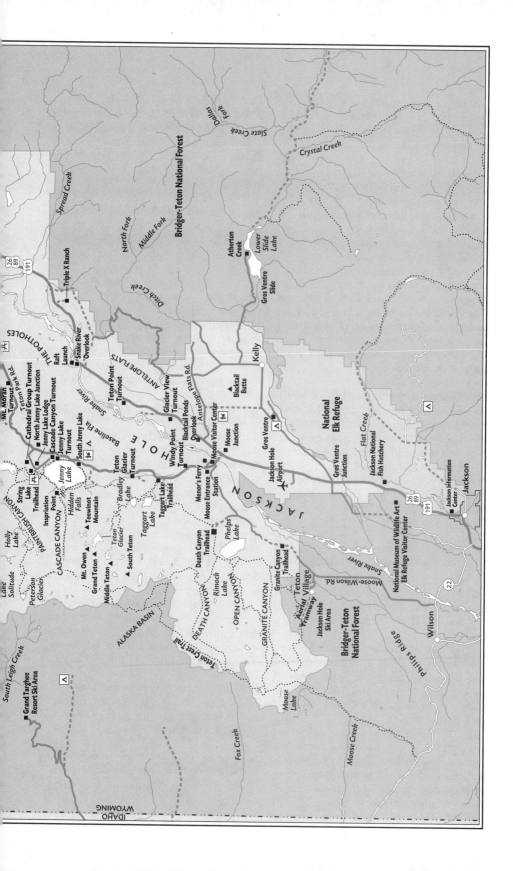

You can also approach the park from the east, via U.S. Highways 26/287. This route comes from Dubois, 55 miles east on the other side of the Absaroka and Wind River Mountains, and crosses Togwotee Pass, where you'll get your first and one of the best views of the Tetons from above the valley. Travelers who come this way can continue south on U.S. 26/89/191 to Jackson without paying an entrance fee, though they are within the park boundaries.

Finally, you can enter Grand Teton from Jackson in the south, driving about 12 miles north on U.S. Highways 26/89/191 to the Moose turnoff and the park's south entrance. Here you'll find the park headquarters and visitor center, and a small community that includes dining and shops.

The Nearest Airport. Inside the southern boundary of Grand Teton National Park, **Jackson Hole Airport** (☎ 307/733-7682) is clearly the most convenient airport. It is served by American, Continental Express, Delta, Skywest (Delta Connection), and United Express. Most of the major car-rental companies have outlets here. For toll-free numbers, see the appendix.

INFORMATION

To receive park maps and information before your arrival, contact **Grand Teton National Park,** P.O. Drawer 170, Moose, WY 83012 (☎ 307/739-3300; www.nps. gov/grte).

The **Grand Teton Natural History Association** provides information about the park through retail book sales at park visitor centers; you can also buy these books by mail. Contact them at P.O. Drawer 170, Moose, WY 83012 (☎ 307/739-3403; www.grandteton. com/gtnha/). The following books are recommended. *Teton Trails* by Katy Duffy and Darwin Wile and *Grand Teton National Park,* both available from the Grand Teton Natural History Association; *A Guide to Exploring Grand Teton National*

Park, Linda Olson and Tim Bywater, RNM Press, Box 8531, Salt Lake City, UT 84108; and *An Outdoor Family Guide to Yellowstone and Grand Teton National Parks,* Lisa Gollin Evans, The Mountaineers, 1001 SW Klickitat Way, Seattle, WA 98134.

The **Jackson Hole Chamber of Commerce** (☎ 307/733-3316) provides information on just about everything in and around Jackson. Along with the U.S. Forest Service and National Park Service, representatives of the chamber can be found at the informative **Visitors Center,** 532 N. Cache, about 3 blocks north of the town square with a view of the National Elk Refuge. For information on lodging, events, and activities, contact the chamber at P.O. Box E, Jackson, WY 83001; www.jacksonholechamber.com; e-mail: info@jacksonholechamber.com.

VISITOR CENTERS

There are three visitor centers in Grand Teton National Park. The **Moose Visitor Center** is a half mile west of Moose Junction at the southern end of the park. It's the park headquarters, and offers exhibits on geology and natural history, a bookstore, as well as audiovisual programs. You can pick up maps and permits for boating and backcountry trips.

The **Jenny Lake Visitor Center** at South Jenny lake has maps, publications, and a geology exhibit.

The **Colter Bay Visitor Center,** the northernmost of the park's visitor centers, provides permits, information audiovisual programs, and a bookstore. This is also the home of the **Indian Arts Museum.**

Finally, there is an information station at the **Flagg Ranch** complex (no phone), which is approximately 5 miles north of the park's northern boundary.

FEES & PERMITS

There are no park gates on U.S. Highways 26/89/191, so the views are free as you pass through the park on that route, but if you want to get off the highway and explore, you'll pay $20 per automobile for a 7-day pass. If you expect to visit Yellowstone and Grand Teton (admission is good for both) more than once a year, buy a $40 annual permit.

Fees for **camping** in Grand Teton are $12 per night at all the park campgrounds. You must have a permit to sleep in the backcountry. See "Exploring the Backcountry" for more information.

SPECIAL REGULATIONS & WARNINGS

It is unlawful to approach within 100 yards of a bear or within 25 yards of other wildlife. Feeding any wildlife is illegal.

SEASONS & CLIMATE

A popular song once romanticized "Springtime in the Rockies," but what the rest of the world calls **spring** is likely to be chilly and spitting snow or rain here. Trails are still clogged with snow and mud. Cold and snow may linger into April and May, though temperatures are generally warming. The average daytime readings are in the 40s and 50s, gradually increasing into the 60s and 70s by early June. A warm jacket, rain gear, and water-resistant walking shoes are advisable.

Summer is finally underway in mid-June, with wildflowers blooming beginning in May in the lower valleys and plains, and in July in the higher elevations. Temperatures are typically 70° to 80°F in the lower elevations and are especially comfortable because of the lack of humidity. Nights, however, even during the warmest months, will be cool, with temperatures dropping into the low 40s, so you'll want to include a light jacket in your wardrobe. Summer thunderstorms are common.

As **fall** approaches you'll want to have an additional layer of clothing, since temperatures remain mild but begin to cool. The first heavy snows typically fall by November 1 and continue through March or April.

Winter is a glorious season here, though not for everyone. It can be very cold. But the air is crystalline, the snow is powdery, the skiing is fantastic. You'll want long johns, heavy shirts, vests and coats, warm gloves, and thick socks since temperatures hover in single digits, and subzero overnight temperatures are common. If you drive in the parks' vicinity in the winter always carry sleeping bags, extra food, flashlights and other safety gear.

If you're planning on visiting Yellowstone as well as Grand Teton, and are considering making your trip to the parks prior to the middle of June, think about beginning your exploration in Grand Teton before working north to Yellowstone. Elevations here are slightly lower and snow melts earlier so accumulations on trails are reduced, and temperatures are more moderate.

ROAD OPENINGS

Teton Park Road opens to conventional vehicles and RVs around May 1. The **Moose-Wilson Road** opens to vehicles about the same time. Roads close to vehicles on November 1 and open for snowmobiles in mid-December, though they never close for nonmotorized use.

If You Only Have 1 Day

A 1-day trip around this park is not unreasonable, given its size, and you can complete a loop that encompasses many major attractions without having to retrace your steps. Although this 1-day itinerary assumes you are entering Grand Teton from the north, after visiting Yellowstone, you could just as easily begin your itinerary in Jackson, which is 8 miles south of the Moose Entrance Station.

Begin at the south entrance of Yellowstone National Park, driving the **John D. Rockefeller, Jr., Memorial Parkway** (U.S. 89/181/287) south past the **Flagg Ranch Information Station.** As you drive south, you'll find yourself skirting the northern shore of Jackson Lake, with a view of **Mt. Moran** to the west, and, further south, the towering **Cathedral Group.**

Colter Bay Village on the northeast shore of Jackson Lake is one of the park's busiest spots. Several popular hiking trails start here. If you turn right at Colter Bay Junction and go another 0.5 mile, you'll be at the **Colter Bay Visitor Center;** stop here only if you wish to take in the **Indian Arts Museum** (☎ 307/543-2467).

The **Lakeshore Trail** begins at the marina entrance and runs along the harbor for an easy 2-mile round-trip. It's level, paved, shady and wheelchair-accessible, offering you your best opportunity for a hike in this area if you don't have much time. The Douglas firs and pine trees here are greener and healthier than the lodgepole pines you see at higher elevations in Yellowstone.

A few minutes' drive south of Colter Bay you'll pass Jackson Lake Lodge and then **Jackson Lake Junction,** where a right turn puts you on **Teton Park Road,** the beginning of a 43-mile loop tour. You'll be driving parallel to the mountain range, with Grand Teton the 13,770-foot centerpiece. You'll see lakes created by glaciers thousands of years ago, bordering a sagebrush valley inhabited by pronghorn and elk.

Just 5 miles down the road along Jackson Lake, a left-hand (east) turn will take you up **Signal Mountain,** where you'll have a 360° view of the valley. You might want to grab a quick lunch at Signal Mountain Lodge, a friendly place where you eat lakeside with a beautiful view. Then continue down Teton Park Road to **South Jenny Lake.** If you have time, go to the other side (it's a 2-mile hike) and make the short climb to **Hidden Falls.** Otherwise, your best bet for a day hike in this area is the **Moose Ponds Trail** (see "Day Hikes," below).

When you leave South Jenny Lake, you'll drive a flat, sagebrush stretch to Moose, the southernmost of the park's service centers. One-half mile before Moose Junction is the **Moose Visitor Center.** While you're in Moose, you might wish to visit the **Menor/Noble Historic District** and the **Chapel of the Transfiguration.**

Coming out of Moose, take a left (north) on U.S. 26/89/191, which crosses the open flats above the Snake River to Moran Junction. The best views along this road are the **Glacier View Turnout** and the **Snake River Overlook,** both of which are right off the road and well-marked. At Moran Junction, turn left for a final 5-mile drive back to Jackson Lake Junction, past **Oxbow Bend,** a great spot for wildlife-viewing.

If You Have More Time

A 1-day whirlwind tour of Grand Teton is not for everyone. A better idea is to allow at least 2 days. That leaves time for some relaxed hikes, picnics, touring the visitor centers, and getting a real feel for the park and the history and culture of the area.

As with the short tour in the previous section, we begin at the northern end of the park. But you could just as easily start exploring from the southern end near Jackson. From Jackson, it's 13 miles to the Moose Entrance Station, another 8 miles to the Jenny Lake Visitor Center, another 12 miles to the Jackson Lake Junction, and 5 more miles to Colter Bay.

JACKSON LAKE & THE NORTH END OF THE PARK

A great many people enter Grand Teton National Park from the north end, emerging from Yellowstone's south entrance with a 7-day park pass that gets them into Grand Teton as well. Yellowstone is connected to Grand Teton by a wilderness corridor through which the **John D. Rockefeller Jr. Memorial Parkway** runs for 56 miles, past meadows sometimes dotted with elk, over the Snake River above Jackson Lake, and through forests.

Along the parkway, not far from Yellowstone, you'll come to the recently modernized **Flagg Ranch** (see "Accommodations," below), with gas, restaurants, lodging and other services. In the winter this is a busy staging area for the snowcoach and snowmobiling crowd.

Giant **Jackson Lake,** a huge expanse of water filling a deep gouge left 10,000 years ago by retreating glaciers, dominates the north end of the park. Though it empties east into the Snake River, curving around in the languid **Oxbow Bend**—a favorite wildlife-viewing float for canoeists—the water from Jackson Lake eventually turns south and then west through Snake River Canyon and into Idaho. Streamflow from the dam is regulated both for potato farmers downstream in Idaho and for rafters in the canyon, and, for better or ill, we have an irrigation dam in a national park. Elsewhere on the lake, things look quite natural, except when water gets low in the fall.

As the road follows the east shore of the lake from the north, the first development that travelers encounter is **Leeks Marina,** where boats can launch, gas up, and moor from mid-May to mid-September. There are numerous scenic pullouts along the lake, some good for picnics.

Just south of Leeks is **Colter Bay,** a busy outpost of park services including a visitor center, a general store, a laundry, two restaurants, a boat launch, and boat rentals, and tours. Colter Bay has lots of overnight options, from cabins to old-fashioned tent camps to a trailer park. You can take pleasant short hikes in this area, including a walk around the bay or out to **Hermitage Point** (see "Day Hikes," below).

The **Indian Arts Museum** (☎ **307/ 543-2467**) at the Colter Bay Visitors Center is worth a visit, though it is not strictly about the Native American cultures of this area. The artifacts are mostly from Plains Indian tribes, but there are also some Navajo items from the Southwest. The collection was assembled by David T. Vernon, and includes pipes, shields, dolls, and war clubs sometimes called "skull crackers." There are large historic photos in the exhibit area.

From Colter Bay the road swerves east and then south again past Jackson Lake Lodge. Numerous trails emanate from here, both to the lakeshore and east to **Emma Matilda Lake.** The road then comes to **Jackson Lake Junction,** where you can either continue west along the lakeshore or go east to the park's Moran Entrance Station. Here the park's odd entrance configuration comes into play. If you go out through the Moran entrance you are still in the park, and may turn south on U.S. Highway 26/89/191 and drive along the Snake River to Jackson, making most of your journey within the park's borders.

But if you're here to enjoy the park, you should turn right (west) on **Teton Park Road** at Jackson Lake Junction. After only 5 miles, you will arrive at **Signal Mountain.** Like its counterpart at Colter Bay, this developed recreation area, on Jackson Lake's southeast shore, offers camping sites, accommodations in cabins and multiplex units, two restaurants, and a lounge with one of the few live televisions in the park. If you need to stock up with gas or food, do so at the small convenience store here. Boat rentals and scenic cruises of the lake are also available.

If you turn east instead of west off Teton Park Road at Signal Mountain, you can drive up a narrow, twisty road to the **top of the mountain,** 1,000 feet above the valley, where you'll have a fine view of the ring of mountains—Absarokas, Gros Ventres, Tetons, and Yellowstone Plateau—that create the Jackson "Hole." Note also the potholes created in the valley's hilly moraines left by retreating glaciers. Below the summit, about 3 miles from the base of the hill, is **Jackson Point Overlook,** a paved path 100 yards long leading to the spot where the Hayden Expedition's photographer William Henry Jackson shot his famous wet plate photographs of Jackson lake and the Tetons more than a century ago—proof to the world that such spectacular places really existed.

Looking for a hideaway? On the right (west) side of the road between Signal Mountain and North Jenny Lake Junction, approximately 2 miles south of the Mt. Moran Turnout, is an unmarked, unpaved road leading to **Spalding Bay.** It's a sheltered little campsite and boat launch area with a primitive rest room. There isn't much space if others have beaten you there, but it's a great place to be alone with great views of the lake and mountains. An automobile or SUV will have no problem with this road, taking it slowly. You'll pass through brush and forest and might spot a moose.

JENNY LAKE & THE SOUTH END OF THE PARK

Continuing south along Teton Park Road you move into the park's southern half, where the tallest peaks rise abruptly above a string of smaller lakes strung together in the foothills—**Leigh Lake,** the appropriately named **String Lake,** and **Jenny Lake,** many visitors' favorite. At North Jenny Lake Junction you can take a turnoff west to Jenny Lake Lodge. The road then continues as a one-way scenic loop along the lakeshore before rejoining Teton Park Road about four miles later.

Beautiful **Jenny Lake** gets a lot of traffic throughout the summer, both from hikers who circumnavigate the lake on a 6-mile trail and from more sedentary folks who pay for a boat ride across the lake to Hidden Falls and the short steep climb to **Inspiration Point** (see "Day Hikes," below). The parking lot at **South Jenny Lake** is often jammed, and there can be a long wait for the boat ride, so you might want to get there early in the day. Or you can save your money by taking the 2-mile hike around the lake—it's level and easy. There is also a tents-only campground, a visitor center, and a general store. You'll have to buy a ticket and wait in line for the trip across the lake in a powerboat that holds about 30

people. Contact **Teton Boating Company** (☎ **307/733-2703**).

South of the lake, Teton Park Road crosses open sagebrush plains with never-ending views of the mountains. You'll pass the Climbers' Ranch and some trailheads for enjoyable **hikes to Taggart Lake** and elsewhere. Look closely in the sagebrush for the shy pronghorn, more commonly called antelope. This handsome animal, with tan cheeks and black accent stripes, can spring up to 60 miles an hour. If you wander in the sagebrush here, you may encounter a badger, a shy but mean-spirited creature that sometimes comes out of its hole in the morning or at twilight.

The **Teton Glacier Turnout** presents a view of a glacier that grew for several hundred years until, pressured by the hotter summer temperatures in the past century, it reversed direction, and began retreating.

The road arrives at the park's south entrance—again, actually well within the park's boundaries—and the sprawling **Moose Visitor Center,** which is also park headquarters.

Just behind the visitor center is **Menor's Ferry.** Bill Menor had a country store and operated a ferry across the Snake River at Moose back in the late 1800s. The ferry and store have been reconstructed, and you can buy items like those once sold here. Also in the area is the **Chapel of the Transfiguration.** In 1925 this chapel was built in Moose so that settlers wouldn't have to make the long buckboard ride into Jackson. It's still in use for Episcopal services from spring to fall, and it's a popular place to get hitched, with a view of the Tetons through a window behind the alter.

Dornan's is a small village area just south of the visitor center on an inholding of private land owned by one of the area's earliest homesteading families. There are a few shops and a semi-gourmet grocery store, a post office, a bar with occasional live music, and a first-rate wine shop, of all things.

THE EAST SIDE OF THE PARK

At Moose Junction, just east of the visitor center, drivers can rejoin the highway and either turn south to Jackson and the Gros Ventre turn, or cruise north up U.S. Highway 89/26/191 to Moran Junction. This 18-mile trip is the fastest route through Grand Teton National Park, and, being further from the mountains, offers views of a broader mountain tableau.

The junction of U.S. 89 with **Antelope Flats Road** is 1.2 miles north of the Moose Junction. The 20-mile route beginning here is an acceptable biking route. It's all on level terrain, passing by the town of Kelly and the Gros Ventre campground before looping back to U.S. 26/89/191 at the Gros Ventre Junction to the south. If you continue straight on Antelope Flats Road, you'll reach the **Teton Science School** at the road's end, about a 5-mile trip.

Less than a mile further along U.S. 26/89/191, on the left, **Blacktail Ponds Overlook** offers an opportunity to see how beavers build dams and the effect these hard-working creatures have on the flow of the streams. The area is marshy early in summer, but it's still worth the 0.25-mile hike down to the streams where the beaver activity can be viewed more closely.

Two miles further along U.S. 89 brings you to the **Glacier View Turnout,** which offers views of an area that 140,000 to 160,000 years ago was filled with a 4,000-foot-thick glacier. The view of the gulch between the peaks offers vivid testimony of the power of the glaciers that carved this landscape. Lower **Schwabacher Landing** is at the end of a 1-mile, fairly well maintained dirt road that leads down to the Snake River; you'll see the turnoff 4.5 miles north of the Moose Junction. The road winds through an area filled with glacial moraine (the rocks, sand, gravel, and so forth, that were left behind as glaciers passed through the area), the leftovers of the Ice Age. At the end of the road is a popular launch site for float trips and for fly-fishing. It's also an ideal place to retreat from the crowds. Don't be surprised to see bald eagles, osprey, moose, river otter, and beaver, which regularly patrol the area.

The **Snake River Overlook,** approximately 4 miles down the road beyond the Glacier View Turnout, is the most famous view of the Teton Range and the Snake River, immortalized by Ansel Adams. From this overlook you'll also see at least three separate, distinctive, 200-foot-high plateaus that roll from the riverbed to the valley floor, a vivid example of the power of the glaciers and ice floes as they sculpted this area.

Half a mile north of the Snake River Overlook, signs warn that the road to **Deadman's Bar Overlook,** which leads to a clearing on the river bank, should only be negotiated by four-wheel-drive vehicles. Though the 1-mile road is unpaved and bumpy, it is maintained well enough to be handled by most cars if there's no snow on the road and if it has not been raining.

Cunningham Cabin, 1.75 miles north of Deadman's Bar Overlook, is a nondescript historic site at which the first homesteaders, Pierce and Margaret Cunningham, built their ranch in 1890. By 1928 they had been defeated by the elements and sold out to Rockefeller's Snake River Land Co. You can visit it at any time.

If you head down the highway in the other direction (south) from Moose Junction, on U.S. Highway 26/89/191 you can turn east on the **Gros Ventre River Road** 5 miles before you reach Jackson and follow the river east into its steep canyon—a few miles past the little town of Kelly you'll leave the park and be in **Bridger-Teton National Forest.** In 1925, a huge slab of mountain broke off of the north end of the Gros Ventre Range on the east side of Jackson Hole, a reminder of nature's violent and unpredictable side.

The slide left a gaping open gash in the side of Sheep Mountain, sloughing off nearly 50 million cubic yards of rock and forming a natural dam across the Gros Ventre River half a mile wide. Two years later, the dam broke, and a cascade of water rushed down the canyon and through the little town of Kelly, taking several lives. The town of **Kelly** is a quaint and eccentric community with a large number of yurts. Up in the canyon formed by the Gros Ventre River, there is a roadside display with photographs of the slide area and a short nature walk from the road down to the residue of the slide and **Lower Slide Lake.** Here, signs identify the trees and plants that survived or grew in the slide's aftermath.

Organized Tours & Ranger Programs

The **Grand Teton Lodge Company** (☎ 307/543-2811) runs bus tours of both Grand Teton and Yellowstone from mid-May to mid-October.

Winter and summer, wildlife biologists lead tours of Grand Teton, Yellowstone and forest lands through the **Great Plains Wildlife Institute**, P.O. Box 7580, Jackson Hole, WY 83002 (☎ 307/773-2623; www.wildlifesafari.com). With open-roofed vans, rafts, sleighs and on foot, these tours bring visitors closer to the wildlife than they're likely to get on their own, and guests sometimes participate in radio tracking and other research projects. The **Teton Science School**, P.O. Box 68, Kelly, WY 83011 (☎ 307/733-4765; e-mail tss@wyoming.com), offers summer programs for students and adults that discuss the ecology, geology, and wildlife of the park, as well as workshops in photography and tracking.

Within the park, there are several interesting ranger programs. These range from a ranger-led, 3-mile hike from the Colter Bay Visitor Center to Swan Lake, to a relaxed evening chatting with a ranger on the back deck of the Jackson Lake Lodge, with the Tetons as a dramatic backdrop and spotting scope for watching moose and birds. There are numerous events during the summer at Colter Bay, South Jenny Lake, and the Moose Visitors Center. Check the daily schedules in the park's paper, the *Teewinot,* which you can pick up at any visitor center.

At Jenny Lake, there are **wildflower walks** led by rangers who can tell you the difference between lupine and larkspur, daily in June and July, and morning and twilight hikes to Hidden Falls (you take the boat across the lake), among other activities.

At Colter Bay you can climb aboard a boat for an afternoon **"fire and ice" cruise,** during which a ranger will talk about the volcanics, the glaciers, and the fires that have shaped and colored the landscape. There are programs on Indian art and culture, lakeshore strolls with rangers, and evening gatherings at the Colter Bay amphitheater in which rangers teach about park wildlife.

Youngsters 8 to 12 can join **Young Naturalist programs** at Colter Bay or Jenny Lake and learn about the natural world for 2 hours while hiking with a ranger. Signups are at the visitor centers, and the kids will need basic hiking gear.

There are evening campfire gatherings at the Gros Ventre, Signal Mountain, Lizard Creek, and Colter Bay campground amphitheaters. Topics vary.

Day Hikes

COLTER BAY AREA

Lakeshore Trail

2 mi. RT. Easy. Access: Marina entrance.

This short hike leads out to pebble beaches on the west side of a point with views across Jackson Lake of the entire Teton range. It's wide and shady, and at the end of the trail the views across Jackson Lake of the entire Teton range leap out at you.

TRAILS FROM THE HERMITAGE POINT TRAILHEAD

The Hermitage Point Trailhead near the marina is the starting point for an interesting variety of trips. With careful planning, it's possible to start the day with a hike beginning at Colter Bay that leads past **Cygnet Lake** across **Willow Flats** to Jackson Lake Lodge (for lunch). Then, after a break, take the path that returns back to Colter Bay in time for the evening outdoor barbecue—all told, that's 9.3 miles round-trip.

When choosing your route, keep in mind that the three trails running through this same forested part of the Colter Bay area—Heron Pond Trail, Swan Lake Trail, and Hermitage Point Trail—have virtually identical foliage and terrain. The numerous options can be confusing, so carry a map.

Hermitage Point Trail—A Loop

6.5 mi. RT. Moderate. Access: Swan Lake/ Heron Pond trail intersection.

This trails goes through a thickly forested area to the isolated Hermitage Point, a peninsula jutting into Jackson Lake, from which you can look across the bay to the Signal Mountain Lodge. If you're seeking solitude, this is an excellent place to find it, though you should check with rangers before leaving since this is bear country.

Heron Pond Trail

3 mi. RT. Easy. Access: Hermitage Point trailhead.

If you take this trail in the early morning, you will be more likely to see the beavers that live in the pond. This is bear territory, as well as a home for Canada geese, trumpeter swans, and moose. Wildflowers are part of the show in the early summer—look for lupine, gilia, heart leaf arnicas, and Indian paintbrush. Don't be put off by the fact that the first 200 yards of the trail are steep; after

reaching the top of a rise, it levels out and has only moderate elevation gains from that point on.

Swan Lake Trail

3.9 mi. RT. Easy. Access: Hermitage Point trailhead.

Finding swans at Swan Lake requires a trip to the south end where a small island offers them isolation and shelter for nests. The distance from Swan Lake through a densely forested area to a sign at the Heron Pond intersection is 0.3 mile. Hermitage Point is 3 miles from this junction along a gentle path that winds through a wooded area that is a popular bear hangout.

Willow Flats

5 mi. one way. Easy. Access: Horse corrals at Colter Bay.

An alternative to mountainous, forested trails, this trip from Colter Bay to Jackson Lake Lodge takes you across marshy flats where you'll have an excellent view of the Tetons and a good chance of seeing moose and other wildlife. You begin by skirting the sewage ponds at Colter Bay (sorry), then pick up a trail east to Cygnet Lake. Instead of looping back to Colter Bay, you take a spur that crosses Pilgrim Creek going east across the flats. You can hike in either direction, but drop a car at each end so you don't have to double back on foot.

JACKSON LAKE LODGE AREA

Christian Pond Trail

1 mi. RT. Easy. Access: 200 yd. south of the entrance to Jackson Lake Lodge. It's unmarked, so look carefully.

This trail begins with a half-mile walk through a grassy, wet area to a pond with nesting trumpeter swans and other waterfowl. You can circle the pond, adding another 3 miles to the trip. In

May and June this a great wildflower walk, but also prime habitat for bears, so check with rangers first. The south end of the pond is covered with little grassy knolls upon which the birds build their nests and roost, and beavers have constructed a lodge here too. It's a restful sanctuary but one often infested by gnats and mosquitoes.

Signal Summit Mountain Trail

6 mi. RT. Moderate. Access: Near the entrance to the Signal Mountain Lodge, or 1 mi. (by car) up Signal Mountain Rd. to a pond on the right.

This up-and-down trail gives you a few fine hours of solitude with views of the mountains, wildflowers, and, at the end, a grand panorama of the glacially carved valley. After negotiating a steep climb at the beginning of the trail, you'll come upon a broad plateau covered with lodgepole pines, grassy areas, and seasonal wildflowers. Cross a paved road to a lily-covered pond, and just beyond you'll choose from two different trails—take the right one up (ponds, wildlife, maybe moose and bear) and the left one down (open ridges with views).

TWO OCEAN & EMMA MATILDA LAKE TRAILS

You can come to these lakes from the east or west: From the west you'd begin at the Grand View Point Trailhead; 1 mile north of Jackson Lake Lodge; or at the Christian Pond Trailhead, just east of Jackson Lake Lodge. From the east, you'd go up Pacific Creek Road, 4 miles east of Jackson Lake Junction on the road to the Moran entrance. There is a pullout for Emma Matilda Lake two miles up this road, or you can go 0.5 mile further, take a left on Two Ocean Lake Road, and go to the Two Ocean Lake trailhead parking lot, with trails leading to both lakes.

Emma Matilda Lake Trail

11.7 mi. RT. Easy to moderate. Access: Emma Matilda Lake Trailhead on Pacific Creek Rd. or trailhead off Two Ocean Lake Rd. north of Jackson Lake–Moran Rd.

Circumnavigating this lake is a pleasant, up-and-down journey with great views of the mountains and a good chance of seeing wildlife. The hike winds uphill for 0.5 mile from the parking area to a large, meadowed area favored by mule deer. The trail follows the northern side of the lake through a pine forest 400 feet above the lake, then descends to an overlook where you'll have panoramic views of the Tetons, Christian Pond, and Jackson Lake. The trail on the south side of the lake goes through a densely forested area populated by Englemann spruce and subalpine fir. Be watchful and noisy, because this is bear country. It's possible to branch off onto the Two Ocean Lake Trail along the northern shore of the lake.

Two Ocean Lake Trail

5.7 mi. RT. Easy. Access: Two Ocean Lake Trailhead on Two Ocean Lake Rd., or Grand View Point trailhead.

Take your time and take a picnic on this delightful, underused trail around Two Ocean Lake. You can start at either end, but I recommend a side trip up Grand View Point, which will add about 2.5 miles. You'll be rested for this climb because the walk around the lake is fairly level. The variety of habitat—marshes, lakes, woodlands, and meadows—means you'll see birds, wildflowers, butterflies, and possibly beaver, elk, deer, and moose. There are great views of the Tetons, too, but for the best views you need to take the trip up to Grand View Point, a climb that will take you from lodgepole to fir to a hilltop of arrowleaf balsamroot, with its large, orange flowers. You'll look down on lakes, meadows, and volcanic outcrops, and in the distance you'll gaze at the Tetons, the Mount Leidy Highlands and Jackson Lake. It's possible to branch off onto the Emma Matilda Lake Trail at the east end of Two Ocean Lake.

JENNY LAKE AREA

Amphitheater Lake Trail

9.6 mi. Strenuous. Access: Lupine Meadows trailhead. From the Moose entrance station on Teton Park Rd., drive 6.6 mi. to the Lupine Meadows Junction and follow signs to the trailhead; if you're coming from Jenny Lake, the trailhead is at the end of a rd. less than 1 mi. south of South Jenny Lake.

Here's a trail that can get you up into the high mountains and out in a day, if you're in good shape and acclimated to the altitude (you'll climb 3,000 ft.). You'll cross glacial moraines and meadows quilted with flowers, and enter forests of fir and lodgepole and whitebark pine (a bear food—be alert!). Finally you clear the trees and come into an amphitheater of monstrous rock walls topped by Disappointment Peak, with the Grand and Teewinot in view. Surprise Lake and Amphitheater Lake sit in this dramatic setting, with a few gnarled trees struggling to survive on the slopes.

Cascade Canyon Trail

4.5 mi. one way. Moderate to strenuous. Access: Inspiration Point.

For those who have time to go a little further, Cascade Canyon Trail is the most popular in the park. You can begin the hike from South Jenny Lake, but you can also shave 2 miles off each way by riding the boat service across the lake and beginning your hike at the Boat Dock. At this point, you're only a steep 1-mile hike from Inspiration Point (see the "Hidden Falls & Inspiration Point Trail," below), which is as far as many visitors go. From here, you make a brief steep climb to the glacially rounded canyon, where the trail levels out and you're in a wonderland of wildflowers and waterfowl and busy pikas. On a nice day the warblers will be singing and you may see moose and bear. If you want to go further once you reach forks of North and South Cascade Canyon, follow either the South Fork to Hurricane Pass, or the North Fork to Lake Solitude. These are overnight trips.

A less taxing alternative to the Cascade Canyon trip mentioned above is a detour to **Moose Ponds,** which begins on the Inspiration Point trail. The ponds, located 2 miles from either west or east boat docks, are near the south end of the lake, and are alive with birds. The area near the base of Teewinot Mountain, which towers over the area, is populated with elk, mule deer, black bears, and moose. The trail is flat (at lake level), short, and easy to negotiate in 1 to 1½ hours. The best times to venture forth are in early morning and evening.

Hidden Falls & Inspiration Point Trail

1.8–5.8 mi. RT. Moderate. Access: East or West Shore Boat Dock.

Many people cross Jenny Lake, either by boat or on foot around the south end, and then make the short, forest-shaded uphill slog to Hidden Falls (less than 1 mile of hiking if you take the boat; 5 miles RT if you walk around), which tumbles down a broad cascade. Some think that's enough, and don't go another steep half mile to Inspiration Point. Up there you get a great view of Jenny Lake below, and you can see the glacial moraine that formed it. If you're only going to these two overlooks we recommend a relaxed and easy hike around the south end of the lake.

Jenny Lake Loop Trail

7 mi. Easy to moderate. Access: Trailhead at East Shore Boat Dock.

Another lake to circumnavigate, following the shore. You can cut it in half by taking the Jenny Lake Boat Shuttle from the East Shore Boat Dock to the West Shore Boat Dock. The lake has a pastoral setting at the foot of the mountain range, providing excellent views throughout the summer. *Warning:* This is one of the most popular spots in the park; to avoid crowds travel early or late in the day. The trails to Hidden Falls, Inspiration Point, and the Moose Ponds branch off of this trail on the southwest shore of the lake. The trails to String and Leigh lakes branch off this trail on the north shore of Jenny Lake.

A less taxing alternative to the Cascade Canyon trip mentioned above is a detour to Moose Ponds, which begins on the Inspiration Point trail. The ponds, located 2 miles from either west or east boat docks, are near the south end of the lake, and are alive with birds. The area near the base of Teewinot Mountain, which towers over the area, is populated with elk, mule deer, black bears, and moose. The trail is flat (at lake level), short, and easy to negotiate in 1 to 1½ hours. The best times to go are early morning and evening.

Exploring the Backcountry

Grand Teton may seem small compared to Yellowstone, but there are over 200 miles of trails in the backcountry, and good opportunities for solitude and adventure. You must have a permit from the Park Service to sleep in the backcountry—the permits are free, but reservations are not. The permit is valid only on the dates for which it is issued. There are two methods of securing permits: They may be picked up the day before you commence your trip at park visitor centers, or you can make a reservation for a permit in advance of your arrival, for a $15 fee. Reservations are only accepted from January 1 to June 1, by writing the **Permits Office,** Grand Teton National Park, P.O. Drawer 170, Moose, WY, 83012, or faxing 307/739-3438.

Remember that this region has a short summer, and virtually no spring. While the lower elevation areas of the park are open in May, some of the high country trails may not be clear of snow or high water before late June. Look in the "Backcountry Trip Planner" for approximate dates when specific campsites will be habitable.

Perhaps the most popular backcountry trail in Grand Teton is the 19.2-mile

Cascade Canyon Loop, which starts on the west side of Jenny Lake, winds northwest 7.2 miles on the **Cascade Canyon Trail** to Lake Solitude and the Paintbrush Divide, then returns on the 10.3-mile-long **Paintbrush Trail** past Holly Lake. It is one of the most rigorous hikes in either park because of gains in elevation—more than 2,600 feet—rocky trails, and switchbacks through scree that can become slippery, especially in years when snow remains until the middle of summer on the north-facing side of Paintbrush Divide.

Rangers recommend the hike for several reasons, the most noteworthy of which is unsurpassed scenery. Moose and black bears inhabit this part of the park, so hikers are cautioned to be diligent about making noise. There's also the possibility of sighting harlequin ducks, since they nest near the trail in Cascade Creek. You'll see many types of wildflowers, large stands of whitebark pine trees, and an almost unimaginable array of bird life.

Though it adds 5.1 miles to the trip (one way), a detour west from the Cascade Canyon Trail to **Hurricane Pass** will reward you with a view from the foot of **Schoolroom Glacier.** If you're feeling spunky, head west into the Jedediah Smith Wilderness on a trail that eventually crosses into Idaho. If you're feeling *particularly* spunky, you can actually continue this trek to Alaska.

If you're unable to complete the hike in 1 day, you can trek 7.2 miles on the Cascade Canyon Trail to **Solitude Lake** and return via the same trail. If you can afford a 2-day trip, camping zones are 6 miles west of the trailhead on the Cascade Canyon Trail and 8.7 miles northwest on the Paintbrush Canyon Trail at Holly Lake. Be sure and get a reservation.

Perhaps the quickest way to get up high in these mountains for a backcountry foray is to hitch a ride up **Rendezvous Mountain** on the Jackson Hole Ski Resort Tram. This puts you at 10,450 feet in **Bridger-Teton National Forest,** just south of the park, and ready to embark north toward the park's Middle Fork Cutoff. From here you can head down into Granite Canyon to Phelps Lake, or go north along the **Teton Crest Trail** to Fox Creek Pass (over 8 difficult mi. from the tram) and **Death Canyon** and beyond. If you are hardy enough to make it to **Death Canyon Shelf,** a wildflower-strewn limestone ledge that runs above Death Canyon toward **Alaska Basin,** you'll have an extraordinary high-altitude view of the west side of the Tetons' biggest peaks. If you are on an extended backcountry trip, you can continue north to Hurricane Pass, where you can come back down to the valley floor by way of Cascade Canyon.

This kind of backcountry trip is really an expedition, and requires skill and experience. Go over any such plans with park rangers, who can help you evaluate your ability to take on such a challenge.

Other Summer Sports & Activities

Biking. This is no bicyclist's paradise; bikes are banned from hiking trails in the park, and on the paved roads below the problem is safety—there are huge RVs careening about, and some roads have only narrow shoulders. Teton Park Road has been widened somewhat, but traffic is heavy here; road bikers should try **Antelope Flats,** beginning at a trailhead 1 mile north of Moose Junction and going east. Sometimes called **Mormon Road,** this paved route crosses the flats below the Gros Ventre Mountains, past old ranch homesteads and the small town of Kelly. It connects to the unpaved **Shadow Mountain Road,** which actually goes outside the park into national forest, climbing through the trees to the summit. Total distance is 7 miles and the elevation gain is 1,370 feet; you'll be looking at Mt. Moran and the Tetons across the valley.

Mountain bikers have a few more options: Try **Two-Ocean Lake Road** (reached from the Pacific Creek Road just north of Moran Junction) or the **River Road,** a 15-mile dirt path along the Snake River's western bank (bison use it, too, and you'd be smart to yield). Ambitious mountain bikers may want to load their overnight gear and take the **Grassy Lake Road,** once used by Indians, west from Flagg Ranch on a 50-mile journey to Ashton, Idaho.

A map that shows bicycle route, *Grand Teton Bicycling,* is available from the Park Service at visitor centers, or at **Adventure Sports,** at Dornan's in the town of Moose (☎ **307/733-3307**), which is inside the boundaries of Grand Teton National Park. You can also rent mountain bikes here.

Boating. If you bring your own boat, you must register it: For nonmotorized craft, it's $5 for 7 days, or $10 for a year permit; motorized skippers pay $10 for 7 days and $20 for an annual permit, which you can buy at any visitor center. Boat and canoe rentals, tackle, and fishing licenses are available at Colter and **Signal Mountain** (rental fees of $16 per hour for motorboats include permits). Shuttles to the west side of Jenny Lake, as well as cruises, are conducted by **Teton Boating Company** (☎ **307/733-2703**).

Motorized boats are allowed on Phelps, Jackson, and Jenny Lakes, but on Jenny Lake the motor can't be over 8 horsepower. Only human-powered vessels are permitted on Phelps, Emma Matilda, Two Ocean, Taggard, Bradley, Bearpaw, Leigh, and String lakes. Rafts, canoes, dories, and kayaks are allowed on the Snake River within the park. No boats are allowed on Pacific Creek or the Gros Ventre River.

Scenic cruises of Jackson Lake are conducted daily, and floating steak-fry cruises are twice weekly; both leave from the **Colter Bay Marina** from May through September. Cruises cost $11 for adults, $6 for children; dinner cruises are $35 for adults, $23 for children.

Additionally, you can rent kayaks and canoes at **Adventure Sports** at Dornan's in the town of Moose (☎ 307/733-3307), which is in the boundaries of Grand Teton National Park.

Climbing. The Tetons have a strong allure for climbers, even inexperienced ones, perhaps because you can reach the tops of even the highest in a single day. The terrain is mixed, with snow and ice year-round—knowing how to self-arrest with an ice axe is a must—and the weather can change suddenly. The key is to get good advice, know your limitations, and if you're not already skilled, take some lessons and hire a guide at the local climbing schools. Try **Exum Mountain Guides,** P.O. Box 56, Moose, WY 83012 (☎ 307/733-2297), and **Jackson Hole Mountain Guides and Climbing School,** 165 N. Glenwood St., Jackson, WY 83001 (☎ 307/733-4979). Those who want to practice their moves indoors should try the **Teton Rock Gym,** 1116 Maple (☎ 307/733-0707). The **Jenny Lake Ranger Station** (☎ 307/739-3343) is the center for climbing information (open only in summer); climbers are encouraged to stop in and obtain information on routes, conditions, and regulations.

Fishing. The lakes and streams of Grand Teton are popular fishing destinations, loaded with lively cutthroat trout, whitefish, and mackinaw (lake) trout in Jackson, Jenny, and Phelps lakes. Jackson has produced some monsters weighing as much as 50 pounds, but you're more likely to catch fish under 20 inches, fishing deep with trolling gear from a boat during hot summer months.

The Snake River runs for about 27 miles in the park, and has cutthroat and whitefish up to about 18 inches. It's a popular drift boat river for fly-fishers. If you'd like a guide who knows the holes, try **Jack Dennis Fishing Trips** (☎ 307/733-3270) or **Solitude Float Trips** (☎ 307/733-2871). **Westbank Anglers** (☎ 307/733-6483) is another full-service fly shop that sells gear and

organizes trips in Jackson Hole. As an alternative, stake out a position on the banks below the dam at **Jackson Lake,** where you'll have plenty of company and just might snag something. You'll need a Wyoming state fishing license and you'll have to check creel limits, which vary from year to year and place to place.

Float Trips. One of the most effective and environmentally sound methods of viewing wildlife in Grand Teton is aboard a floating watercraft that silently moves downstream without disturbing the animals. The park's 27-mile stretch of river is wonderful for wildlife, with moose, eagles, and other animals coming, like you, to the water's edge. There are many commercial float operators in the park who will allow you to relax more and look around. They mostly run from mid-May to mid-September (depending on weather and river flow conditions). These companies offer 5- to 10-mile scenic floats, some with early-morning and evening wildlife trips. Try **Triangle X-Osprey Float Trips** (☎ 307/733-5500), **Barker-Ewing Float Trips** (☎ 800/365-1800), **Grand Teton Lodge Company** (☎ 307/543-2811); **Signal Mountain Lodge,** in Grand Teton National Park, P.O. Box 50, Moran, WY 83013 (☎ 307/543-2831); and **Flagg Ranch Float Trips** (☎ 307/543-2861).

Horseback Riding. The **Grand Teton Lodge Company** offers tours from stables next to popular visitor centers at Colter Bay and Jackson Lake Lodge. Choices are 1- and 2-hour guided trail rides daily aboard well-broken, tame animals. An experienced rider may find these tours too tame; wranglers refer to them as "nose-and-tail" tours. In Jackson, try **Bridger-Teton Outfitters** (☎ 307/739-4314 or 307/733-7745), **Green River Outfitters** in Pinedale (☎ 307/733-1044 or 307/367-2416), **Jackson Hole Trail Rides** (☎ 307/733-6992), **Snow King Stables** (☎ 307/733-5781), and the **Mill Iron Ranch** (☎ 307/733-6390).

Winter Sports & Activities

Park facilities pretty much shut down during the winter, except for a skeleton staff at the Moose Visitor Center, and the park shows no signs of becoming the winter magnet for snowmobilers or backcountry skiers that Yellowstone is. That may be just as well—you can enjoy some quiet, fun times in the park without the crowds.

Skiing. You can ski flat or you can ski steep in Grand Teton. The two things to watch out for are hypothermia and avalanche. As with climbing, know your limitations, and make sure you're properly equipped. Check with local rangers and guides for trails that match your ability. Among your options are the relatively easy **Jenny Lake Trail,** starting at the Taggart Lake Parking Area, about 8 miles of flat and scenic trail that follows Cottonwood Creek. A more difficult ski is the **Taggart Lake-Beaver Creek Loop,** about a 3-mile route that has some steep and icy pitches coming back. About 4 miles of the **Moose-Wilson Road**—the back way to Teton Village from Moose—is unplowed in the winter, and is an easy trip through the woods. You can climb the windy unplowed road to the top of **Signal Mountain**—you may encounter snowmobiles—and have some fun skiing down. There is an easy ski trail from the Colter Bay Ranger Station area to Heron Pond; it's about 2.6 miles, with a great view of the Tetons and Jackson Lake. Get a ski trail map from the visitor centers.

Skiers who come to Jackson Hole are usually after the hard, steep stuff at the Jackson Hole Ski Resort, but there's a growing contingent of backcountry telemark skiers, who ski off Teton Pass and out of the ski resort boundaries.

Snowmobiling. Snowmobiling is another popular winter option. The main roads in Grand Teton are groomed, providing access to trails in the nearby Bridger-

Teton National Forest, the area to the immediate east of Grand Teton National Park, and to the **Continental Divide Trail,** which runs 320 miles through the Rockies.

For snowmobile rentals in Jackson, contact **Leisure Sports** (☎ 307/733-3040), **BEST Adventures** (☎ 307/733-4845), and **Wyoming Adventures** (☎ 800/637-7147).

During winter, **Flagg Ranch Resort** (see "Accommodations") is a base for snowmobiling in the southern reaches of Yellowstone, but given its isolation from the rest of Grand Teton during these months, we don't recommend you consider basing yourself there.

Camping

INSIDE THE PARK

The campground chart below lists amenities for each campground in the park. All the park-run campgrounds but Jenny Lake can accommodate tents, RVs and trailers, but there are no utility hookups at any of them. **Jenny Lake Campground,** a tents-only area with 49 sites, is situated in a quiet, wooded area near the lake. You have to be here first thing in the morning to get a site.

The largest campground, **Gros Ventre,** is the last to fill, if it fills at all—probably because it's located on the east side of the park, a few miles from Kelly on the Gros Ventre River Road. It has 360 sites, a trailer dump station, a tents-only section, and no showers. If you arrive late in the day and you have no place to stay, go here first.

Signal Mountain Campground, with views of the lake and access to the beach, is another popular spot that fills first thing in the morning. It has 86 sites overlooking Jackson Lake and Mt. Moran, as well as a pleasant picnic and boat launch. No showers or laundry, but there's a store and service station nearby.

Colter Bay Campground and Trailer Village has 310 sites, some with RV hookups, showers, and a launderette. The area has access to the lake but is far enough from the hubbub of the village to offer a modicum of solitude; spaces are usually gone by noon.

Lizard Creek Campground, at the north end of Grand Teton National Park near Jackson Lake, offers an aesthetically pleasing wooded area near the lake with views of the Tetons, bird watching, and fishing (and mosquitoes; bring your repellent). It's only 8 miles from facilities at Colter Bay and has 60 sites that fill by 2pm.

A final concessionaire-operated campground is located at the **Flagg Ranch Resort** complex on the John D. Rockefeller, Jr., Memorial Parkway. The area, situated in a wooded area next to the parkway, has 121 sites for RVs and campers, showers, and a launderette.

<hr>

NEAR THE PARK

There are several places to park the RV or pitch a tent around Jackson Hole, and a few of them are reasonably priced and not too far away from the park. Some of your best bets are either out of Jackson or way out of Jackson. Most campgrounds are open from late spring to early fall.

In Jackson, the **Wagon Wheel Campground** (☎ 307/733-4588) is about 5 blocks north of Town Square at the Wagon Wheel Motel. The **Teton Village KOA** (☎ 307/733-5354), 12 miles northwest of Jackson, has 148 sites. Also away from the crowds, the **Snake River Park KOA Campground** is also on U.S. 89, 10 miles south of town (☎ 307/733-7078) and has 80 sites.

Accommodations

INSIDE THE PARK

There aren't a lot of lodging options in Grand Teton, but they are varied. You can get information about or make reservations for Jackson Lake Lodge, Jenny Lake Lodge, and Colter Bay Village through the **Grand Teton Lodge Company,** Box 240, Moran, WY 83013 (☎ 307/

Campground	Total Sites	RV Hookups	Dump Station	Toilets	Drinking Water
Inside the Park					
Colter Bay	350	No	Yes	Yes	Yes
Colter Bay Trailer Village	112	Yes	Yes	Yes	Yes
Gros Ventre	360	No	Yes	Yes	Yes
Jenny Lake*	49	No	No	Yes	Yes
Lizard Creek	60	No	No	Yes	Yes
Signal Mountain	86	No	Yes	Yes	Yes
Near the Park					
Flagg Ranch	165	Yes	Yes	Yes	Yes
Snake River Park KOA	80	Yes	Yes	Yes	Yes
Teton Village KOA	148	Yes	Yes	Yes	Yes
Wagon Wheel	12	Yes	Yes	Yes	Yes

* Tents only are allowed here.

543-2811; www.gtlc.com). For Signal
Mountain Lodge, contact **Signal
Mountain Lodge Co.,** Box 50, Moran,
WY 83013 (☎ **307/543-2831;** www.
signalmtnlodge.com). Reservations at
Flagg Ranch are made though Flagg
Ranch, Box 187, Moran, WY 83013
(☎ **800/443-2311**).

Grand Teton National Park properties
have in-room telephones, but none have
in-room televisions or air-conditioning.
You'll find televisions in the lounge areas
at the Jackson Lodge, Signal Mountain
Resort, and Flagg Ranch.

FLAGG RANCH VILLAGE AREA

Like Grant Village in Yellowstone, Flagg
Ranch offers travelers the full gamut of
services: cabins, tent and RV sites, an
above-average restaurant, and gas station. It's also a popular jumping-off spot
for snowmobilers during winter months.
However, since it's situated in a stand of
pines in the middle of nowhere, there's
not much to do in the immediate vicinity except watch the Snake River pass by.

Flagg Ranch Resort

P.O. Box 187, Moran, WY 83013. ☎ **800/
443-2311** or 307/543-2861. www.flaggranch.
com. 92 units. TEL. $131 double ($89 spring
and fall, $99 winter). AE, DISC, MC, V.

A few years ago this resort just outside
Yellowstone National Park was showing
its age—the sort of place a hunter would
rent a drafty room to collapse in after a
few days in the woods. Not anymore: It's
all fixed up, transformed into an all-
seasons resort on the Snake River with
log-and-luxury ambience. The newest
accommodations are duplex and fourplex log cabins constructed in 1994 that
feature king-size beds, spacious sitting
areas with writing desks and chests of
drawers, wall-to-wall carpeting, and bathrooms with tub-shower combinations
and separate vanities.

The only livestock on the ranch these
days are the herds of snowmobiles that
gather here in the winter to warm up
before entering Yellowstone. In the summer, there are float trips, horseback
rides, and excellent fishing in Polecat

Showers	Fire Pits/ Grills	Laundry	Public Phone	Reserve	Fees	Open
Yes	Yes	Yes	Yes	No	$12	Mid-May to Late Sept
No	Yes	Yes	Yes	Yes	$29	Mid-May to Late Sept
No	Yes	No	Yes	No	$12	Early May to Oct
No	Yes	No	Yes	No	$12	Late May to Late Sept
No	Yes	No	Yes	No	$12	Early June to Early Sept
No	Yes	No	Yes	No	$12	Mid-May to Oct
Yes	Yes	Yes	Yes	Yes	$19/$25	Mid-May to Late Sept
Yes	Yes	Yes	Yes	Yes	$27/$35	Mid-Apr to Mid-Oct
Yes	Yes	Yes	Yes	Yes	$26/$34	May to Mid-Oct
Yes	Yes	Yes	Yes	Yes	$15	Mar to Oct

Creek or the Snake River. The new lodge is a locus of activity, with its fireplace, dining room, gift shop, espresso bar and pub, convenience store, and gas station.

COLTER BAY VILLAGE AREA

Colter Bay Village

P.O. Box 240, Moran, WY 83013. ☎ **800/628-9988** or 307/543-2855. www.gtlc.com. 166 units. $31–$116 log cabin; $30 tent cabin. Open mid-May to late Sept. AE, DC, MC, V.

You might call this the people's resort of Grand Teton. Its simpler lodgings, lower prices and a lively, inclusive atmosphere seem particularly suited to families. Situated on the eastern shore of Jackson Lake, 35 miles north of Jackson, Colter Bay Village is a full-fledged recreation center. Guest accommodations are in roughly built log cabins perched on a wooded hillside; they are clean and simply furnished with area rugs on tile floors, beamed ceilings, and copies of pioneer furnishings—chests, oval mirrors, and extralong bedsteads with painted headboards. The simple bathrooms have stall showers, and some singles share bathrooms. If you want to take a trip back to the early days of American auto travel, when car-camping involved unwieldy canvas tents on slabs by the roadside, you can spend an inexpensive night in "tent cabins." Bring your sleeping bags and sleep on squeaky bunks, and stop that giggling because there's another tent nearby with equally thin walls and small children trying to settle down. The shared shower/bathroom is just down the road.

Jackson Lake Lodge

P.O. Box 240, Moran, WY 83013. ☎ **800/628-9988** or 307/543-2811. www.gtlc.com. 385 units. TEL. $110–$190 single or double; $126–$136 cottage. Open mid-May to mid-Oct. AE, DC, MC, V.

Much the way Old Faithful Inn or the Lake Hotel capture historic eras of Yellowstone tourism, Jackson Lake Lodge epitomizes the architectural milieu of the period when Grand Teton became a park. Unfortunately, that era was the 1950s, an era of right angles, flat roofs, and big windows. Still, the lodge is popular, particularly for its wonderful setting overlooking Willow Flats, the lake in the distance, and towering over it, without a stick in the way, the Grand Teton and Mount Moran. You don't even have to go outside to see this impressive view—the lobby has 60-foot tall windows. Add to that a good restaurant, comfortable rooms, and easy access from Jackson, only 35 miles away. Guestrooms are in the three-story main lodge and in cottages scattered about the property, some of which have large balconies and mountain views. Lodge rooms are spacious and cheery, and most offer double beds, electric heat, and newly tiled bathrooms. There is a large outdoor swimming pool, a cocktail lounge, full-course dining in the Mural Room, and lighter fare at the Pioneer Grill.

SIGNAL MOUNTAIN AREA

Signal Mountain Lodge

P.O. Box 50, Moran, WY 83013. ☎ **307/543-2831.** www.signalmtnlodge.com. Open May–Oct. 80 units. TEL. $85–$180 double. AE, DISC, MC, V.

Signal Mountain has a different feel, and different owners, from the other lodgings in Grand Teton. What they all have in common is the Teton view, and this lodge, located right on the banks of Jackson Lake, may have the best. For one, it's got lakefront retreats that you can really inhabit, with stoves, refrigerators, and fold-out sofa beds for the kids. Other accommodations, mostly free-standing cabins, come in a variety of flavors, from motel-style rooms in four-unit buildings set amidst the trees to family bungalows with decks, some enjoying beach frontage. The carpeted cabins feature handmade pine furniture, electric heat, covered porches, and tiled bathrooms; some have fireplaces.

The registration building has a small TV viewing area, a gift shop, and outdoor seating on a deck overlooking the lake. A restaurant and coffee shop that serve average food share a separate building with a small lounge and gift shop. Recreational options include cycling, rafting, waterskiing, and fishing, but note that boat rentals are expensive here. A convenience store and gas station are on the property.

JENNY LAKE AREA

Jenny Lake Lodge

Box 240, Moran, WY 83013. ☎ **800/628-9988** or 307/543-3300. www.gtlc.com. 37 units. $380 double. Rates include breakfast and dinner and activities. Open June to mid-Oct. AE, DC, MC, V.

Though it's located 20 miles from Jackson Airport, this small resort prides itself on its seclusion and tranquility. It also has an award-winning restaurant. The Lodge is a hybrid of mountain lake resort and dude ranch, with activities like horseback- and bike-riding. Accommodations are in rustic, pitched-roof log cabins fronted by a long, pillared porch. Each cabin has been named for a resident flower and most have forest views; some can see the lake. The luxurious interiors contain bright braided rugs, dark wood floors, beamed ceilings, log furniture with cowhide upholstery, and tiled combination bathrooms. Rooms have one queen, one king, or two double beds.

The lodge functions primarily as a dining establishment. Catering to an older, affluent clientele, the style here is an odd mixture of peaceful rusticity and occasional reminders of class and formality (jackets for men are "appreciated").

NEAR THE PARK

IN JACKSON

Clustered together near the junction west of downtown where Highway 22

leaves U.S. Highway 26/89 and heads north to Teton Village is a colony of chain franchises **Motel 6** (600 S. Hwy. 89; ☎ 800/466-8356 or 307/733-1620) and the not-just-numerically superior **Super 8** (750 S. Hwy. 89; ☎ 800/800-8000 or 307/733-6833). Also in the vicinity is the more expensive **Days Inn,** at 350 S. Hwy. 89 (☎ 800/329-7466 or 307/733-0033), with private hot tubs and fireplaces, and the **Red Lion Inn,** at 90 W. Broadway (☎ 307/734-0035). High season prices for the motels range from $85 to $160. Rooms at the Red Lion start at $500 a night.

Jackson Hole Lodge

420 W. Broadway, Jackson, WY 83001. ☎ **307/733-2992.** 59 units. A/C TV TEL. $80–$130 double; $150–$280 condo. AE, DC, DISC, MC, V.

Though it sits near one of the busiest intersections in Jackson, and is packed into a small space, this lodge is quiet and well designed. The pool is not just for splashing—you can swim its 40-foot length, sit in one of the whirlpools, take a sauna, or lounge on your own sundeck. If you're traveling with kids, your best bet is the condo lodgings, with two upstairs bedrooms, a full kitchen, and a living room with foldout couch.

Rusty Parrot Lodge

175 N. Jackson, Jackson, WY 83001. ☎ **307/733-2000.** www.rustyparrot.com. 32 units. TV TEL. $108–$275 double. Rates include full breakfast. AE, CB, DC, DISC, MC, V.

The name sounds like an out-of-tune jungle bird, but since 1990 the Rusty Parrot has shown excellent pitch, cultivating a country lodge and spa right in the heart of busy Jackson. Located across from Miller Park, the Parrot is decorated in the new-Western style of peeled log, with an interior appointed with pine furniture and river rock fireplaces. The breakfast that comes with your room includes omelets, fresh pastries, fruits, cereals, and freshly ground coffee.

Trapper Inn

235 N. Cache, Jackson, WY 83001. ☎ **800/ 341-8000,** or 307/733-2648 for reservations. 50 units. A/C TV TEL. $98–$178 double, reduced rates in winter. AE, DC, DISC, MC, V.

The employees here are among the most helpful in Jackson. Just 2 short blocks from town square, the Trapper is hard to miss if you're walking north on Cache from the Town Square. On the left side of Cache you'll notice the crazy Trapper guy on the sign. Though the decor of the rooms is undistinguished, their spaciousness is luxurious. In the newest building, erected in 1991, many rooms come with miniature refrigerators; laundry facilities and an indoor/outdoor hot tub are also on hand.

Virginian Lodge

750 W. Broadway, Jackson, WY 83001. ☎ **800/262-4999** or 307/733-2792. 181 units. A/C TV TEL. $95–$109 double. AE, DC, DISC, MC, V.

It's not brand-new; it's not a resort; it doesn't have a golf course; and the highway is right outside the door, but since its overhaul in 1995, the Virginian is attempting to earn its spurs as one of the better motels in Jackson. Given its location on the busy Broadway strip, that's not likely to happen, but the prices remain reasonable, and it's a busy, cheerful place to stay. There is a large outdoor pool during warm weather, and you can get a room with a private Jacuzzi. Kids can romp in the arcade, families can eat in the Carriage House, and parents can relax in the Virginian Saloon.

Wort Hotel

50 N. Glenwood, Jackson, WY 83001. ☎ **307/ 733-2190.** www.worthotel.com. 60 units. A/C TV TEL. $125–$174 double. AE, DISC, MC, V.

Located on Broadway just off the town square, an area constantly in flux with new buildings and new shops, the Wort's Tudor-style two-story building was largely rebuilt after a 1980 fire. Opened in the early 1940s by the wife and son of Charles Wort, an early 20th-century homesteader, it has an older style, both in the noisy and relaxed **Silver Dollar Bar** and the quiet, formal dining room (there's a more bustling coffee shop next to it). The comfortable rooms feature lodgepole pine furniture, thick carpeting, and a modern decor with Western artwork.

A warm, romantic fireplace graces the lobby; another fireplace and a huge hand-carved mural accent a mezzanine sitting area, providing a second hideaway. In the famous bar, the bar itself is inlaid with 2,032 silver dollars, the most precious piece of furniture rescued during the fire.

NEAR JACKSON

Amangani

1535 North East Butte Rd., Jackson, WY 83002 (on top of East Gros Ventre Butte). ☎ **877/734-7333** or 307/734-7333. 40 suites. A/C TV TEL. Summer $600–$800; winter $500–$700. AE, DC, DISC, MC, V.

Chopped into the side of East Gros Ventre Butte, Amangani's rough rock exterior blends in so well that the lights from its windows and pool appear to be glowing from within the mountain. The style is understated and rustic, but every detail is expensively done. Owner Adrianne Zecha has resorts like this around the world, from Bali to Hong Kong, and while the designs are tailored to the landscape, the approach is the same: personal service, luxury, and all the little touches. Like CDs in every bedroom, cashmere throws on the day beds, and slate and redwood walls. There's an outdoor pool, a health center, and an on-site restaurant.

Spring Creek Resort

P.O. Box 4780 (on top of the East Gros Ventre Butte), Jackson, WY 83001. ☎ **800/**

443-6139 or 307/733-8833. 106 units. A/C TV TEL. $210 double; $375–$1,200 condo. AE, MC, V.

Atop East Gros Ventre Butte, 1,000 feet above the Snake River and minutes from the airport and downtown Jackson, this resort commands a panoramic view of the Grand Tetons and 1,500 acres of land populated by deer, moose, and the horses at its riding facility in the valley below. Though it seems a little less exclusive now that Amangani has opened next door, Spring Creek still has much going for it. The rooms are divided among four buildings with cabinlike exteriors and have fireplaces, Native American floor and wall coverings, refrigerators, coffeemakers, and balconies with views of the Tetons. Most rooms have king- or queen-size beds, and the studio units boast kitchenettes. In addition to its own rooms, the resort arranges accommodations in the privately owned condominiums that dot the butte—large, lavishly furnished and featuring completely equipped kitchens. There is a pool, two tennis courts, and a concierge.

IN TETON VILLAGE

While lodging in the town of Jackson tends to be a little cheaper in the winter than the summer, at Teton Village the ratio is reversed—rooms by the ski hill get more expensive after the snow falls.

Alpenhof Hotel

3255 W. McCollister Dr., Teton Village, WY 83025. ☎ **800/732-3244** or 307/733-3242. Fax 307/739-1516. www.alpenhof.com. E-mail: gm@alpenhoflodge.com. 42 units. A/C TV TEL. Dec–Apr $108–$408, May–Sept $78–$324 double. AE, DC, DISC, MC, V. Closed Nov.

This chaletlike hostelry has a prize location only 50 yards from the ski resort tram. Four stories tall, with a pitched roof and flower boxes on the balconies, the hotel combines an old-world atmosphere with excellent service. Recent upgrades include redoing the dining room and deluxe accommodations with brightly colored alpine fabrics, newly constructed handcrafted European furnishings, and tiled bathrooms with big, soft towels. Two junior suites with kitchenettes, five rooms with fireplaces and four rooms with a shared deck—which you get to by an outside staircase—are among the outstanding features of the rooms. Economy rooms offer double or queen beds, while deluxe units are larger. Your choices for dinner include award-winning and expensive Continental fare that is served in The Alpenhof dining room, or pork, game, and pasta, which are staples in Dietrich's Bar and Bistro.

Jackson Hole Resort Lodging

3200 McCollister Dr., P.O. Box 51087, Teton Village, WY 83025. ☎ **800/443-8613** or 307/733-3990. Fax 307/733-0244. E-mail: info@jhresortlodging.com. 125 units. A/C TV TEL. Winter $90–$100 double; $340 2-bedroom loft; $635–$1,440 3–5 bedroom homes. Off season $52–$64, $126 2-bedroom loft, $190–$606 3–5 bedroom homes. Call for shoulder season rates. AE, DISC, MC, V.

The wide range of prices above is indicative of the variety of properties now under the wing of this management group. Most of them are in the Teton Village area, and they range from rooms in the relatively inexpensive and simple Crystal Springs Inn to deluxe private homes. Also available are condos at the Jackson Hole Racquet Club, 4 miles south of the ski resort at Teton Village on 550 acres along the Moose-Wilson Road. The condos are fully equipped with balconies, fireplaces, washer/dryers, and kitchens. You can comfortably fit a family in many of these loft-style condos, and the resort has amenities (some for a fee) like tennis courts, a health club, and an indoor pool. Don't expect coddling from the staff, which checks you in and lets you be.

The Resort Hotel

Box 348, Teton Village, WY 83025. ☎ **800/445-4655** or 307/733-3657. Fax 307/733-9543. www.ResortHotelatJH.com. 101 units. A/C TV TEL. $99–$299 double. AE, DC, DISC, MC, V.

Major renovations were completed in 1998, and this hotel was reborn as a better facility, with prices that compare favorably to surrounding resorts. Wooden walls, stone floors, overstuffed furniture, and stone fireplaces accent the main reception area. Standard guest rooms in the main lodge provide a comfortable place to hang your hat, especially in rooms with views of either the mountains or the valley floor. Larger rooms in the mountain lodge have living areas with sofa beds and tiled combination baths. Four have kitchenettes. Two restaurants are on the mezzanine level: The J. Hennesey Steak House serves steak and chicken meals family style, and the Irish Pub and Grill offers a place to unwind with simple fare, and any beer you can think of. Summer visitors can enjoy the outdoor pool and whirlpools; winter visitors can ski directly to a locker room with whirlpool or sauna, and drop their skis off for an overnight tune-up.

Teton Pines Resort

3450 N. Clubhouse Dr., Jackson, WY 83001. ☎ **800/238-2223** or 307/733-1005. 16 suites, 2 town homes. A/C TV TEL. Summer $350–$695 suite; rest of year $125–$485 suite. AE, MC, V.

Arnold Palmer and Ed Seay designed the challenging 18-hole golf course attached to this luxury resort. Don't expect to improve your handicap, but you can expect to sooth your frustrations in the comfortable rooms, which feature his-and-her bathrooms, one with tub, one with shower. The resort offers a range of activities, some for a fee, including tennis, diving, and fly-fishing. The Jackson Hole Ski Resort is 5 minutes away. The dining room, The Grille at the Pines, is one of the better places to eat in Jackson, though pricey.

Dining

INSIDE THE PARK

NEAR THE NORTHERN BOUNDARY

Flagg Ranch

John D. Rockefeller, Jr., Pkwy., Moran. ☎ **800/443-2311.** Breakfast $2–$6; lunch $4–$9; dinner $10–$20. AE, DISC, MC, V. Summer hours daily 7am–1:30pm, 5–9:30pm. TRADITIONAL AMERICAN.

The food at this oasis is better than what is typically found in what most refer to as a "family restaurant," and servings are generous. The dinner menu includes fish, chicken, and beef dishes, as well as home-style entrees like ranch beef stew and chicken pot pie. The ambience is nice as well; during both winter and summer months wooden chairs and tables with colorful upholstery liven up this newly constructed log building.

COLTER BAY

John Colter Chuckwagon/ Cafe Court Pizza and Deli

Across from the visitor center and marina in Colter Bay Village. ☎ **307/543-2811.** Breakfast $3–$6; lunch $5–$8; dinner $6–$14. DISC, MC, V. Daily 6am–10pm. Closed Oct–Apr. DELI/COMFORT FOOD.

These are the two sit-down restaurants in the village (though there's also a snack shop in the grocery store). Three meals are served daily during the summer months. The **Deli** serves sandwiches, chicken, pizzas, salads, and soup, with prices that range from $4.50 for an individual pizza to $12.99 for a chicken dinner. The **Chuckwagon's** breakfast menu features a huge and quite wonderful all-you-can-eat buffet. Lunch is soup, salad, and hot sandwiches; dinner is a buffet with a nightly special each evening. Among the dinner entrees are trout, lasagna, pork chops, beef stew, and New York strip steaks. The ambience is very casual.

JACKSON LAKE JUNCTION

The casual dining choice at the Jackson Lake Lodge is the **Pioneer Grill,** entrees are light and less expensive than those at the Mural Room (see below). The **Blue Heron** cocktail lounge is one of the nicest spots in either park to enjoy a cocktail.

Aspens Dining Room

Signal Mountain Resort. ☎ **307/543-2831.** Breakfast $4–$6; lunch $6–$8; dinner $8–$21. AE, DISC, MC, V. Summer daily 7–10am, 11:30am–2:30pm, and 5:30–10pm. COMFORT FOOD.

There are actually two restaurants here, both serving delicious food in the friendliest style in the park. The fine dining room and lounge is **Aspens,** whose top-notch fare is supplemented by the Cottonwood Café's sandwiches and Mexican entrees. Dishes at Aspen's include chicken pot pie, pasta, and veal saltimbocca. When the bargain-hunting folks who work for the park's concessionaires head out for dinner, though, chances are good they'll land here and order Nachos Supreme from Cottonwood Café's bar menu. This nutritionist's nightmare— melted cheddar and Jack cheese with spicy beef or chicken served on a bed of corn chips topped with sour cream—will satisfy the appetite of two adults. Since the bar has one of three televisions in the park and is equipped with cable for sports nuts, the crowd tends to be young and noisy. As an alternative, snacks are served on the deck overlooking the lake.

The Mural Room

Jackson Lake Lodge. ☎ **800/628-9988.** Breakfast buffet $8, lunch $6–$9, dinner $16–$22. AE, MC, V. Summer daily 7–9:30am, noon–1:30pm, 6–9:30pm. BEEF/WILD GAME.

Jackson Lake's main dining room is quiet and fairly formal, catering to a more sedate crowd as well as corporate groups; it's also more expensive than other park restaurants. The floor-to-ceiling windows provide stellar views across a meadow that is moose habitat, to the lake and the Cathedral Group. Walls are adorned with hand-painted Western murals. Dinner may be a grand, five-course event that includes a shrimp cocktail, French onion soup, and Caesar salad, followed by an entree of Idaho trout, buffalo strip loin, vegetable lasagna, or rack of lamb.

JENNY LAKE

Jenny Lake Lodge Dining Room

Jenny Lake Lodge. ☎ **307/543-3300.** Fixed-price dinner $41.50, not including alcoholic beverage. AE, MC, V. Summer daily 7:30–9am, noon–1:30pm, and 6–9pm. CONTINENTAL.

The finest meals in either park are served here, where a cordon bleu chef creates culinary delights for guests (who have included on occasion a president of the United States). All three daily meals are appetizing, but the six-course dinner is the bell-ringer. Guests choose from appetizers like chilled lobster salad, smoked sturgeon ravioli, or buffalo mozzarella and plum tomato salads; and entrees such as grilled salmon, rack of lamb, or prime rib of buffalo. Desserts are equally decadent. Price is no object, at least for guests, since meals are included in the room charge.

NEAR THE PARK

IN TETON VILLAGE

The Granary at Spring Creek

P.O. Box 3154 (on top of the East Gros Ventre Butte), Jackson, WY 83001. ☎ **800/ 443-6139** or 307/733-8833. Reservations suggested. Lunch $8–$15; dinner $15–$28.

AE, DC, MC, V. Daily 11:30am–2pm and 5:50–8pm. AMERICAN.

In this restaurant perched atop Gros Ventre Butte 15 minutes from downtown Jackson, you can enjoy a fantastic view over a plate of roasted monkfish and Tuscan bean and lobster ragout. Across the valley lie the Tetons and below is the Spring Creek equestrian center. Lunch is especially pleasant when weather allows dining outside on a wood deck. The menu changes, but you may find elk flank fajitas at lunch and potato encrusted red snapper at dinner.

Mangy Moose

Teton Village. ☎ **307/733-4913.** Reservations for larger parties recommended. Main dinner courses $11–$20. AE, MC, V. Open daily 5:30–10pm. AMERICAN

Coming off the slopes at the end of a hard day of skiing or snowboarding, you can slide right to the porch of this ski area institution. Good luck getting a seat inside, but if you like a lot of noise and laughter and tasty dishes like buffalo meatloaf, be patient—it beats getting into your car and driving elsewhere. The decor matches the pandemonium: It looks like an upscale junk shop, with bicycles, old signs and, naturally, a moose head or two hanging from the walls and rafters. They have typical Wyoming fare (steak, seafood, and pasta), a good salad bar, and a smattering of Mexican dishes. Try the hot spinach and artichoke heart dip as an appetizer.

Nora's Fish Creek Inn

5600 W. WY 22, Wilson. ☎ **307/733-8288.** DISC, MC, V. Daily 6am–9:30pm. AMERICAN.

If you want to hang with the locals and if you like to eat a lot, Nora's is the place to go—especially at breakfast, when they have all-you-can-eat pancakes and huevos rancheros that barely stay on the huge plates. Prices are inexpensive compared to those at any of the other restaurants in town. You still get as many coffee refills as you like. Dinner is fish, fish, and more fish, like fresh Idaho trout.

Stiegler's

Teton Village Rd. at the Aspens. ☎ **307/733-1071.** Reservations recommended. Main courses $14–$24. AE, MC, V. Tues–Sun 5:30–10pm. AUSTRIAN/CONTINENTAL.

Austrian cuisine isn't exactly lurking beyond every street corner waiting to be summoned with a Julie Andrews yodel, but in Jackson, there are two options: Stiegler's Restaurant or Stiegler's Bar. Since 1983, Stiegler's has been confusing, astonishing, and delighting customers with such favorites as the Bauern Schmaus (a "farmer's feast" that includes pork and bratwurst) and the less-perplexing venison St. Hubertus. You'll recognize the desserts, at least: Apfelstrudel and Sacher torte. Tyrolean leather breeches are, of course, optional.

IN JACKSON

Acadian House

170 N. Millward. ☎ **307/739-1269.** Reservations recommended. Dinner entrees $9–$17. AE, DC, MC, V. Daily 5:30–10pm. CAJUN.

Taking over a building next to the Blue Lion puts the Acadian House in snazzy culinary company, and its Cajun dishes seem to be holding their own. The spice doesn't burn the way it does in Louisiana, but there's plenty of cayenne for Rocky Mountain taste buds. Traditional dishes like *boudin*—sausage served with red beans and rice—and crawfish etouffée make appearances with continental-style creations like Cajun pasta. If you've never treated yourself to the South's most delicious bottom-feeder, try the catfish, a delicious, blackened-to-perfection delicacy topped with almonds, pecans, and white wine.

Billy's Giant Hamburgers

West side of town square. ☎ **307/733-3279.** Lunch and dinner entrees $4–$6. AE, MC, V.

Open daily 11:30am–10pm. Closed Nov to mid-Dec. BURGERS.

If you take a wrong turn while entering the posh Cadillac Grill (right instead of left) you find yourself in this cramped '50s-style lunch booth and counter shop—and you might just stay. Big, juicy burgers are what you'll get, cooked right in front of you. You can actually sit in here and order from the Cadillac Grill, perhaps a Maine lobster and a fine Sauvignon Blanc, or go easy on your wallet and order a giant cheeseburger with a pile of fries on the side.

The Blue Lion

160 N. Millward. ☎ **307/733-3912.** Reservations recommended. Main courses $15–$28. AE, DC, MC, V. Daily 5:30–10pm; closed Tues. CONTINENTAL.

In the fast-moving, high-rent world of Jackson dining, the Blue Lion stays in the forefront by staying the same. On the outside, it's a two-story blue clapboard building across from the town park—it looks like a comfy family home. On the inside, it's soft light in intimate rooms and unhurried meals of elegant food. The menu features rack of lamb and the usual (in Jackson) wild game specialties, like grilled elk loin in a peppercorn sauce. Fresh fish is flown in for dishes like the wine-basted trout stuffed with Canadian snow crab. Summer diners can eat outside on the patio deck just north of the entrance.

The Bunnery

130 N. Cache St. ☎ **307/733-5474.** Breakfast $4–$7; lunch $5–$7; dinner $8–$15. MC, V. Open daily 7am–3pm year-round, also open daily 5–9:30pm in summer. BREAKFAST/BAKERY/SANDWICHES.

A Jackson mainstay, this bakery and restaurant is a great place to have one of the famous Bunnery breakfasts—perhaps a big soft spinach omelette with sour cream and Swiss cheese, or eggs Benedict. These are cramped quarters,

though, and you'll often find yourself waiting in a line that stretches down the boardwalk of the Hole-In-The-Wall Mall just off the square—that's not bad in the summer, but you won't want to wait long on a cold winter morning. Sandwiches like the grilled tuna and cheddar are reasonably priced and the portions are large. The coffee is good. You might want to pick up a baguette or some other baked goodie on your way out.

The Cadillac Grille

55 N. Cache. ☎ **307/733-3279.** Reservations recommended. Lunch $5–$8; dinner $15–$25. AE, MC, V. Daily 11am–3pm and 5:30–9:30pm. Closed Nov to mid-Dec. CONTINENTAL.

Neon and an eclectic menu give this restaurant a trendy air that attracts see-and-be-seen visitors more than locals. The chefs work hard on presentation, but they also know how to cook a wide-ranging variety of dishes, from fire roasted elk tenderloins to garlic-painted Chilean sea bass. The wine list is equally long and varied. The menu in this art deco restaurant changes regularly, but the place itself is one of Jackson's longer-lived establishments.

Jedediah's House of Sourdough

135 E. Broadway. ☎ **307/733-5671.** Reservations not accepted. Breakfast $4–$6; lunch $5–$6. AE, DC, MC, V. Daily 7am–2pm. AMERICAN.

You feel like you've walked into the kitchen of some sodbuster's log cabin home when you enter Jedediah's. Bring a big appetite for breakfast, and a little patience—you may have to wait for a table, then you may have to wait for food, staring at the interesting old photos on the wall. But it's worth it, especially for the rich flavor of the sourjacks, a stack of sourdough pancakes served with blueberries. The 'Diah's omelette is a big three-egg concoction stuffed with bacon, onions, and cheddar cheese and served with a side of potatoes. In summer months, meals are also served outside on a patio.

Lame Duck

680 E. Broadway. ☎ **307/733-4311.** Dinner $8–$17. AE, MC, V. Daily 5:30–10pm. CHI-NESE/JAPANESE.

While Italian food seems to travel well to the Northern Rockies, to find a good Asian meal you have to search far and wide—or at least up Broadway toward the elk refuge. You may start worrying when you see the drinks menu—yes, they come with parasols—or the mix of Japanese and Chinese (and even Indonesian) items among the dinner fare, but don't be concerned: This is decent, middle-of-the-road cooking, and the sushi and sashimi are quite good. The menu includes dishes like Six Delicacies, (duck, lobster, shrimp, snow peas, and mushrooms served with a secret sauce) and the spicy Fireworks Shrimp (shrimp, snow peas, and bamboo shoots in a hot sauce that warrants a beware sign).

Nani's Genuine Pasta House

240 N. Glenwood. ☎ **307/733-3888.** Reservations suggested. Dinner entrees $10–$17. Open Tues–Sat 5–10pm. MC, V. ITALIAN.

At Nani's, the setting is simple but the food is extraordinary. There are 2 menus: a *carta classico* featuring pasta favorites like *puttanesca* (tomato, anchovy, garlic, and Kalamata olives) and mussels in wine broth; and a menu that features a region of Italy, with dishes like roasted pheasant or Fontina cheese melted with eggs and cream. Your only problem with this restaurant might be finding it—it's tucked away behind a rather run-down motel.

Snake River Brewing Company

265 S. Millward St. ☎ **307/739-2337.** Main dishes $7–$11. Open daily noon–11pm. PIZZA/PASTA.

Microbreweries are sprouting (and spouting) all over the country, but this one is a cut above the others, judging from the prizes it's won for lines like its pale ale and zonker stout. In a roomy, high-ceilinged new building, the brewery serves up excellent pizza cooked in a wood-fired oven—try the P.S.T. (Prosciutto, spinach, and tomato). They also have pastas, calzones, and various sandwiches. The 15 brewing vats are all around and above you, sometimes humming a bit too loudly, and you can play foozball and pool on the mezzanine. Beer lovers will appreciate the happy hour from 4 to 6pm, and occasionally there's live music.

Snake River Grill

Town Square, Jackson. ☎ **307/733-0557.** Reservations recommended. Dinner $15–$30. AE, MC, V. Daily 5:30–9pm. Closed Nov and Apr. ECLECTIC.

This is a popular drop-in spot for locals, including some of the glitterati who sojourn in the area—Harrison Ford and Uma Thurman have been spotted. It's an award-winning restaurant for both its wine list and its menu, which features regular fresh fish dishes (ahi tuna is a favorite), bourbon-marinated pork chops, and some game entrees like venison chops and Idaho trout. From a wood-burning oven come pizzas with exotic ingredients like duck sausage or eggplant with portobello mushrooms. The front-room dining area overlooks the busy Town Square, but there's a more private, romantic room in the back.

Sweetwater Restaurant

At the corner of King and Pearl. ☎ **307/733-3553.** Reservations recommended. Lunch $5–$7; dinner $13–$18. DC, MC, V. Daily 11am–3pm and 5:30–10pm, shorter hours in winter. AMERICAN.

Though this little log restaurant serves American fare, it does so in a decidedly offbeat way. The eclectic menu includes, for example, a Greek salad, a Baja chicken salad, and a cowboy grilled roast beef sandwich. An outside table is a great spot at which to enjoy a summer lunch. The dinner menu is just as quirky, and livened by nightly specials; try the unique smoked buffalo carpaccio before diving into the giant salmon fillet smoked on the Sweetwater's mesquite grill. Vegetarians will want to sample the spinach-and-feta casserole that is topped with a cheese soufflé.

Nearby Attractions

It's not exactly nature's way, but the U.S. Fish & Wildlife Service makes sure that the elk at the **National Elk Refuge** (☎ **307/733-9212**), U.S. Hwy. 26/89, P.O. Box 510, eat well during the winter by feeding them alfalfa pellets. It keeps them out of the haystacks of area ranchers, and creates a beautiful tableau on the meadowy flats along the Gros Ventre River: Thousands of elk, some with huge antler racks, dotting the snow for miles. Though the elk are absent in the summer, there is still plenty of life on the refuge, including in a recent year a quite visible mountain lion and cubs.

Each winter from mid-December until March, the Fish and Wildlife Service offers **horse-drawn sleigh rides** that weave among the refuge elk. Rides early in the winter will find young, energetic bulls playing and banging heads, while late-winter visits (when the Fish and Wildlife Service begins feeding the animals) wander through a more placid scene. Rides embark from the museum between 10am and 4pm on a first-come, first-served basis. Tickets for the 45-minute rides cost $10 for adults and $6 for children 6 to 12, and can be purchased at the National Museum of Wildlife Art. Ask about a combination pass for the sleigh ride and the museum.

20

GREAT BASIN NATIONAL PARK

by Don and Barbara Laine

AVAST AREA OF DESERT, VALLEYS, MOUNTAINS, LAKES, AND STREAMS, North America's Great Basin includes Nevada, Utah, and parts of California, Oregon, and Idaho. It received its name because the rainwater that falls here has no outlet to the sea.

Located along the Utah-Nevada border, Great Basin National Park provides an intimate glimpse into this vast, rugged section of America. Founded in 1986, the park not only looks out at the Great Basin's expanse of desert and mountains from the summit of 13,063-foot Wheeler Peak, but descends beneath the earth's surface for a fascinating tour among the intricately and delicately formed stalactites, stalagmites, and other exotic formations in the unreal world of Lehman Caves.

Hiking trails abound, through rugged pine and aspen forests, or above the tree line to a moonlike world of barren, windswept rocks. Camping in the park is a delight, with quiet campgrounds, plenty of trees, and splendid scenery. The park contains forests of bristlecone pine—a species that scientists believe are the oldest living trees on earth—as well as piñon, juniper, spruce, fir, pine, and aspen. You'll see wildflowers such as yellow aster and Parry's primrose during the summer, and watch for mule deer, bighorn sheep, squirrels, and golden eagles.

Like most of the West's national parks, Great Basin offers ample activities to keep you busy for at least a week, and it is strongly suggested that you plan to spend a minimum of 1 full day in the park. But for the best park experience, try to allow at least 3 full days, to provide enough time not only to tour Lehman Cave and explore the scenic drive, but also to hike to the delightful bristlecone pine forest and perhaps to one of the park's high-mountain lakes.

Because of its remoteness—Great Basin isn't near any other popular tourist destinations or even along a route to one—you'll find it relatively quiet and uncrowded, similar to what you would have found 30 or 40 years ago in America's loved-to-death parks such as Yosemite and Grand Canyon. Although Great Basin National Park is in Nevada, many visitors are Utah residents, on long-weekend excursions from Salt Lake City. Visitors to the national parks of Arizona and Utah who start their trips in Las Vegas, Nevada, can easily add Great Basin to their driving loop, either at the beginning or end.

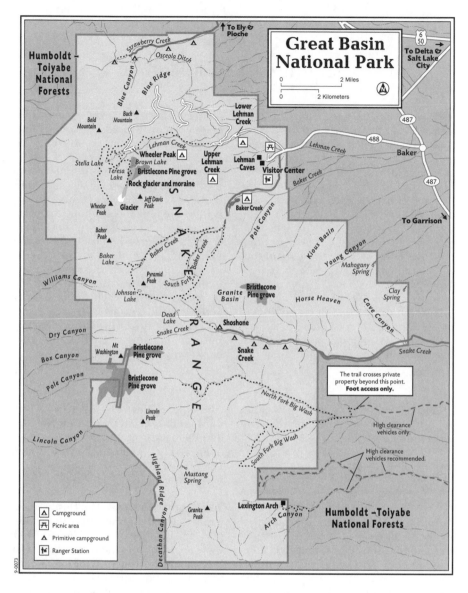

Great Basin National Park

↑ To Ely &
Pioche

To Delta &
Salt Lake
City

Humboldt –
Toiyabe
National
Forests

0   2 Miles

0   2 Kilometers

Strawberry Creek
Osceola Ditch

Bald
Mountain

Buck
Mountain

Blue Canyon

Blue Ridge

Lehman Creek

Wheeler Peak
Brown Lake
Bristlecone Pine grove
Rock glacier and moraine

Stella Lake
Teresa
Lake

Upper
Lehman
Creek

Lower
Lehman
Creek

Lehman
Caves

Visitor Center

Lehman Creek

Baker

488

487

Baker Creek

487

Wheeler
Peak

Glacier

Jeff Davis
Peak

Baker Creek

Baker Creek Canyon

Pole Canyon

To Garrison

Baker
Peak

Baker Creek

Kious Basin

Young Canyon

Mahogany &
Spring

Clay &
Spring

Baker
Lake

Pyramid
Peak

South Fork

Williams Canyon

Johnson
Lake

Granite
Basin

Bristlecone
Pine grove

Horse Heaven

Cave Canyon

Dead
Lake

Shoshone

Dry Canyon

Snake Creek

S N A K E   R A N G E

Mt
Washington

Bristlecone
Pine grove

Box Canyon

Snake
Creek

Snake Creek

Pole Canyon

Bristlecone
Pine grove

The trail crosses private
property beyond this point.
Foot access only.

Lincoln
Peak

North Fork Big Wash

High clearance
vehicles only.

Lincoln Canyon

South Fork Big Wash

High clearance
vehicles recommended.

Highland Ridge

Decathon Canyon

Mustang
Spring

Granite
Peak

Lexington Arch

Arch Canyon

Humboldt –Toiyabe
National Forests

△ Campground
🏕 Picnic area
▲ Primitive campground
👤 Ranger Station

9-0073

Avoiding the Crowds. Because Great Basin National Park is seemingly in the middle of nowhere, it receives far fewer visitors than most other national parks. However, it isn't deserted. During the relatively busy summer season you'll need to arrive at the visitor center early for your cave tour tickets (or purchase them in advance), and don't count on finding a campsite if you arrive late in the day, especially on weekends. The busiest times are Memorial Day weekend and from July through Labor Day, and although the park is quieter in spring, weather can be a problem, with snow in the higher elevations. The park has its lowest visitation in January and February, but that is also when it will be the coldest and snowiest. For those who can arrange it, the best time to visit is from the day after Labor Day through the end of September, when there are fewer people and the weather is beautiful—with warm days and crisp, cool nights. Early October is

Tips from a Park Ranger

Park ranger Anne Hopkins Pfaff, who has worked at Great Basin National Park on and off since 1988, enjoys both the park and the surrounding desert. "It's a gorgeous area," she says, "I like the remoteness."

Asked what she especially likes about the 77,100-acre park, Pfaff replies, "The variety of vegetation and habitats, and the views—especially the views that include both Wheeler Peak and out across the Great Basin, such as you get from Mather Overlook." This park, she says, "is one of America's real treasures, where you can get out on the trails and not see another human being." Pfaff says that as far as national parks go, Great Basin's campgrounds offer minimal services, and while many visitors thoroughly enjoy this aspect, others miss their creature comforts, such as hot showers and RV hookups.

Pfaff says she's impressed by the bristlecone pines—their age and their beauty—and considers a hike to the bristlecone pine forest among the park's top experiences. Also on her list of things all visitors should do are touring Lehman Caves and taking the Wheeler Peak Scenic Drive. If she were to come to the park as a visitor it would be in September, she says, "when the crowds are gone and the weather is usually beautiful—not too hot at the lower elevations but not yet snow-covered in the upper elevations."

also usually nice, but check the weather reports—you could find yourself in an early winter snowstorm.

Just the Facts

GETTING THERE & GATEWAYS

Great Basin National Park is 5 miles west of the small town of Baker, Nevada; 70 miles southeast of Ely, Nevada; 385 miles east of Reno, Nevada; 286 miles north of Las Vegas, Nevada; 200 miles north of St. George, Utah; and 234 miles southwest of Salt Lake City, Utah.

From points in west-central Utah, take U.S. 50 west just across the state line into Nevada, go south on Nev. 487 to the village of Baker, and then west on Nev. 488 into the park. From St. George, take I-15 north to Cedar City, continue north on Utah 130 to Minersville, take Utah 21 west through Milford to the Nevada state line, where it becomes Nev. 487, which you follow to Baker, and then take Nev. 488 west to the park.

If coming from Las Vegas, Nevada, follow U.S. 93 north to U.S. 50, which you take east to Nev. 487, where you turn south to Baker, and then follow Nev. 488 into the park.

From Ely and Reno, Nevada, follow U.S. 50 east to Nev. 487, and follow directions above.

The Nearest Airports. The closest major airports are **McCarran International Airport** in Las Vegas (☎ 775/261-5743; www.mccarran.com) and **Salt Lake City International Airport** (☎ 801/575-2400; www.ci.slc.ut.us/airport) in Salt Lake City, Utah. Both are served by most major airlines and national car rental agencies, whose toll-free numbers are included in the appendix.

INFORMATION

Contact the **Superintendent, Great Basin National Park,** Baker, NV 89311-9702 (☎ 775/234-7331; www.nps.gov/grba). Be sure to ask for a copy of the park's excellent newspaper-style guide, *Bristlecone,* which includes a map, current activities and costs, and nearby services.

Those who want to buy maps and books can contact the **Great Basin Natural History Association** (☎ 775/234-7270) at the park address above.

VISITOR CENTER

The visitor center, located on Nev. 488 at the northeast corner of the park, is where you'll buy tickets for cave tours. It contains the natural history association's bookstore, brochures and other free information, and exhibits on the park's geology, history, flora, and fauna. In addition, a slide show provides an introduction to the park.

The park is open every day of the year, but the visitor center and cave are closed Thanksgiving, Christmas, and New Year's Day.

FEES

Park entry is free. The 90-minute cave tour costs $6 adults, $3 for those under 12; the 60-minute tour costs $4 adults, $2 for those under 12; and the 30-minute tour fee is $2 adults and free for kids under 12. Golden Age and Golden Access card holders pay half the adult rates. Cave tour tickets can be purchased by phone (☎ 775/234-7331, ext. 242) from 24 hours to 30 days in advance. Camping costs $7 per night; use of the dump station costs $2.

SPECIAL REGULATIONS & WARNINGS

Lehman Caves is 50° year-round, so a jacket or sweater is recommended. Also, because the path is often wet, good traction shoes with rubber soles are strongly recommended. Because some passageways are narrow, items such as fanny packs, purses, backpacks, and the like are prohibited; although handheld cameras are permitted. Children under 5 are not permitted on the 90-minute cave tour.

Although backcountry permits are not required, those planning to go into the backcountry are encouraged to register at the visitor center, where they will also receive information on the latest backcountry conditions and regulations. Hikers going to the top of 13,063-foot Wheeler Peak may develop symptoms of altitude sickness (headache, nausea), in which case they should turn back immediately. Vehicles are also sometimes affected by the elevation and steep roads, and the Wheeler Peak Scenic Drive, which leads to several trailheads, is not recommended for motor homes over 24 feet long and vehicles pulling trailers.

SEASONS & CLIMATE

Although open year-round, aboveground activities are limited during the winter by deep snow and bitter cold. The cave can be visited at any time. Year-round temperature inside the cave is 50° and humidity is 90%, so a sweater or light jacket is advised. Outdoors, conditions are tied to elevation, which ranges from 6,825 feet at the visitor center to 13,063 feet at Wheeler Peak. Hiking trails at lower elevations are usually free of snow from late spring through early fall, but snow is possible at any time above 10,000 feet. Summer thunderstorms are common during the afternoon but can occur any time.

If You Only Have 1 Day

In some ways, this is two parks: the caverns and the mountains. Because of the frequency of afternoon thunderstorms in the summer, it is usually best to do outdoor activities early in the day. Therefore, those with only 1 day at the park should spend the morning on the **Wheeler Peak Scenic Drive,** possibly allowing time to hike at least part of one of the trails. Then, after a picnic lunch or sandwich from the cafe, take a **cave tour** (it's best to purchase tickets in advance; see "Fees," above), see the exhibits and programs in the **visitor center,** and take a walk along the **Mountain View Nature Trail.**

Exploring the Park by Car

The **Wheeler Peak Scenic Drive** runs 12 miles one way. The road is paved, but steep (about an 8% grade) and winding, as it ascends over 3,000 feet from the visitor center, at 6,825 feet elevation, to the base of Wheeler Peak, at almost 10,000 feet. Along the way there are pullouts where you can stop for views of the Great Basin and Wheeler Peak. At the first pullout, a short walk brings you to the remnants of an 18-mile aqueduct built in 1890 to carry water from Lehman Creek to a gold mining operation. The road ends at Wheeler Peak Campground, where several hiking trails begin. The road is not recommended for motor homes over 24 feet or vehicles pulling trailers, and it is usually closed by snow (except for the first 3 miles) from fall through spring.

Organized Tours & Ranger Programs

The only way to see **Lehman Caves** is on a guided tour led by a park naturalist, who points out the intricately decorated stalactites, stalagmites, draperies, and shields that have been formed by the oozing and dripping of water. Although Lehman lacks the vastness of Carlsbad, it makes up for that in the number of beautiful cave formations it squeezes into this small space, and can be seen easily and fairly quickly. In addition, Lehman Cave possesses formations called shields, rarely seen in other caves. These consist of two roughly circular halves that look like flattened clam shells. Scientists have yet to agree on how the shields are formed.

Cave tours begin near the visitor center and are given daily year-round (call for schedules), except on Thanksgiving, Christmas, and New Year's Day. A part of the tour is accessible to those in wheelchairs, with assistance. All children under 16 must be accompanied by adults; and because the cave temperature averages 50° year-round, warm clothing is suggested.

Although the park's main ranger-led activity is the Lehman Cave tour, during the summer rangers also lead guided nature walks and hikes and present other programs. These change each year, but recent programs have included a 1.4-mile hike (one way) to the bristlecone pine grove. Rangers usually present short talks several times daily at the visitor center, and evening campfire programs at Wheeler Peak and Upper Lehman campgrounds, with subjects such as the night sky, gold prospecting, and the area's bat population. One-hour programs for children, who must be accompanied by adults, have also been scheduled in recent years.

Historic & Man-Made Attractions

Throughout the park are reminders of the region's mining days, and along several of the trails you will see the ruins of miners' cabins, mining equipment, and mine shafts and tunnels (which are dangerous and should not be entered). Just outside the visitor center is the historic **Rhodes Cabin,** which dates from the period 1920 to 1932 when Clarence Rhodes and his wife owned the property. The cabin, constructed of Englemann spruce and white fir, was one of nine tourist cabins built in the 1920s, along with a log lodge, a dining room, dance hall, and a swimming tank. This particular cabin was rented to tourists until 1933, and from then until 1936 was used as the home of the national monument custodian and his family. It was then used for storage before being restored by the Park Service.

Day Hikes

There's a wide variety of trails here, ranging from easy walks to challenging, high-altitude hikes. Higher-elevation areas may be closed by snow from late October until mid-June, and afternoon thunderstorms are common during July and August. Exposed ridges should be avoided during lightning storms. Hikers should also be aware that they may be sharing trails with rattlesnakes, which have the right-of-way.

Because of loose rock and steep grades on some trails, sturdy hiking boots with good ankle support are recommended. Hikers also need to carry plenty of water—usually 1 gallon per person per day. Park rangers emphasize that although the rocky alpine sections of the park at its highest elevations may appear rugged, they are actually quite fragile. Plants grow slowly and even under the best of conditions their survival rate is low. Therefore, hikers should be diligent about staying on trails, and having the least impact possible on the land.

SHORTER TRAILS

Alpine Lakes Loop

3 mi. RT. Easy to moderate. Access: Just north of Wheeler Peak Campground.

With an elevation gain of only about 400 feet, this is a relatively easy and accessible trail, especially popular with families. However, keep in mind that those not accustomed to the 10,000-foot elevation may find any activity tiring. The loop can be hiked in either direction, passing through forests of spruce and pine trees, as well as meadows dotted with colorful wildflowers. Teresa and Stella lakes are shallow and clear, and the reflections of snowcapped peaks are often seen in their smooth surfaces.

Bristlecone Pine Trail

4.6 mi. RT. Easy to moderate. Access: Near the Wheeler Peak parking area.

Those who want to take a relatively easy hike through a unique forest will enjoy this trail. It goes through a grove of bristlecone pines and then on to a view of an ice field and what is believed to

be a rock glacier—a rock-covered permanent mass of ice moving very slowly downhill. Distance to the bristlecone pine grove is 1.4 miles one way, and the ice field is another 0.9 mile. During summer, rangers often lead hikes to the bristlecone grove. Elevation is about 10,000 feet.

Lexington Arch

1.7 mi. one way. Moderate. Access: About 18 mi. south of the visitor center off a dirt rd.; ask park rangers for specific directions and current road conditions.

This six-story arch is a bit out of the way, but the splendidly framed views through the arch's 75-by-120-foot opening prove an ample reward. After driving into Utah and then following a dirt road, you will find yourself hiking a sunny, moderately rated trail that takes you past wildflowers, mountain mahogany, fir, and piñon. The easy-to-follow trail ends at the arch, unique because it has been carved from limestone, not sandstone as is usually the case in the American West. Some geologists believe it is not really an arch at all, but a natural bridge; the difference being that arches are formed by wind, rain, and ice; while bridges are created by the erosional forces of streams and rivers.

Mountain View Nature Trail

0.4 mi. RT. Easy. Access: Outside the visitor center.

This is an easy self-guided loop, with a brochure available at the visitor center that provides information on plants, animals, and geology. The short trail is popular among those with 20 to 30 minutes to wait before their guided cave tour.

LONGER TRAILS

Baker Creek Trail

6 mi. one way. Moderate to strenuous. Access: End of Baker Creek Rd.

Following Baker Creek, this trail leads to Baker Lake, climbing from about 8,000 feet elevation to over 10,500 feet. It passes through meadows and forests, past piñon, juniper, aspen, and pine, changing with the elevation. It's a good choice for wildlife viewing; you are likely to see mule deer, rock squirrels, and a variety of birds. Anglers often stop to catch a trout or two in the creek, and the trail provides excellent views of the surrounding mountain peaks. Along the way you pass the remains of a miner's log cabin, before reaching picturesque Baker Lake.

Johnson Lake Trail

3.6 mi. one way. Moderate to strenuous. Access: End of Snake Creek Rd.

This rugged trail follows an old mining road, with an elevation gain of about 1,000 feet, before arriving at Johnson Lake, named for Alfred Johnson, who mined and processed tungsten here in the early part of the 20th century. The Johnson Lake Trail can be combined with the Baker Creek Trail to produce a loop, starting with the Baker Creek Trail and descending along Snake Creek. Parts of this loop are difficult to follow, and topographical maps and good mountaineering skills are needed.

Lehman Creek Trail

3.4 mi. one way. Easy. Access: Connects Upper Lehman Creek Campground with Wheeler Peak Campground.

Although there is a 2,100-foot elevation change along this trail, it's an easy downhill walk for those who start at Wheeler Peak Campground and have a vehicle waiting at Lehman Creek Campground. The trail mostly follows a bluff above Lehman Creek, crossing through several separate life zones and offering views of a wide variety of plant life, from sagebrush and cactus to forests of aspen, spruce, piñon, and tall Douglas fir. Along the way you will also see mountain mahogany, and if your timing's right, an abundance of wildflowers.

Wheeler Peak Summit Trail

8.6 mi. RT (from campground). Strenuous. Access: Begins at Summit Trailhead, about 0.5 mi. from Wheeler Peak Campground, or from the campground via Alpine Lakes Loop Trail, which intersects with Summit Trail.

Those looking for absolutely stupendous panoramic vistas should consider this strenuous trail, which begins as a relatively gentle walk through a forest of pine, becoming considerably steeper as it reaches the tree line. Eventually you find yourself on the summit, at an elevation of 13,063 feet, the second-highest point in Nevada. During its 3,000-foot ascent, the trail passes through several plant communities, including forests of Englemann spruce and pine, before climbing above the tree line. This is generally an all-day hike, and rangers advise starting early so you're off the summit by the time afternoon thunderstorms appear. Hikers are also advised to carry plenty of drinking water, extra clothing, and rain gear.

Exploring the Backcountry

There are numerous opportunities for backcountry hiking in the park, but few maintained trails. The most commonly used routes follow river valleys or ridgelines. Topographical maps, available at the visitor center, are essential, and although backcountry permits are not required, rangers strongly recommend that those planning to go into the backcountry register and discuss their plans with park staff before setting out.

Backcountry camping is permitted in most areas, although not within 0.25 mile of most trails, in bristlecone pine forests, in Wheeler Peak and Lexington Day Use Areas, or within 100 feet of a water source. Backcountry campers are encouraged to use backpacking stoves; campfires are permitted below 10,000 feet elevation only, and you are not allowed to burn any bristlecone pine. Trash, including toilet paper, should be packed out, and human waste should be buried at least a half-foot deep and no less than 100 feet from water sources.

Other Summer Sports & Activities

Biking. Although biking is permitted only on designated motor vehicle roads, the park has miles of dirt roads, many of which receive little traffic. Bikers should check with rangers about which roads are open and their current condition.

Educational Programs. The Great Basin Natural History Association (see "Information," above) presents a series of programs for both adults and children, such as field trips to sketch wildlife, spot and identify raptors and other birds, learn about the park's plants, or explore the area's human history. Kids' activities in recent years have included a Saturday afternoon nature and drawing adventure at a park campground. Most of the adult programs last 1 day and cost $25 to $40, while the children's activities last several hours and cost about $10.

Fishing. The park's small, clear mountain streams provide good but somewhat challenging fishing for rainbow, brook, and brown trout. Anglers over 11 will need a Nevada fishing license and trout stamp, available in Baker.

Horseback Riding. Some of the maintained trails plus the backcountry trails are open to horseback riding; check with park rangers.

Wildlife Viewing. Almost every visitor to Great Basin National Park will see wildlife, whether it be some of the many mule deer that frequent the campgrounds, meadows, and creek sides; or birds such as the piñon jays, western tanagers, and Clark's nutcrackers. Park visitors should also watch for golden eagles, bighorn sheep, bobcats, and small

Especially for Kids

In addition to **The Great Basin Junior Ranger Program,** (see chapter 1), families are invited to stop at the visitor center and borrow a **Family Adventure Pack,** which offers activity ideas and equipment, such as a hand lens, compass, string, and pencils. Rangers also lead various walks, hikes, and other activities that are suitable for children, including some specifically geared to kids.

mammals including rock squirrels and wood rats.

Winter Sports

Although there are no designated cross-country ski trails, once snow falls—sometimes as early as October—the park becomes a winter playground, especially at higher elevations. You can use cross-country skis or snowshoes on many of the trails and several roads, although it's best to talk with rangers about your plans before setting out so you can avoid trails that might be too steep for your ability. In lean snow years you may have to hike a bit from parking areas to skiable snow, but there's almost always plenty of snow at the higher elevations.

One favorite cross-country ski trip is up **Baker Creek Road,** which leads to Baker Creek Campground, and then on up the Baker Creek Trail for a while before heading back. Those particularly skilled and in good physical condition might ski the 4-mile trail from **Upper Lehman Creek Campground** up to **Wheeler Peak Campground.** The trail climbs about 2,100 feet. Although Wheeler Peak Campground is technically closed from about mid-October through mid-June, skiers are welcome to spend the night.

There are no snowshoe or cross-country ski rentals available in the park or nearby.

Camping

The park has four developed campgrounds—Lower Lehman Creek, Upper Lehman Creek, Baker Creek, and Wheeler Peak—with a total of just over 100 sites. They have lots of trees, pit toilets, and picnic tables. Those with large RVs will want to arrive as early in the day as possible, since there are only a limited number of sites that can easily accommodate rigs over 25 feet.

One campground is open year-round, while the others are open from spring through fall, weather permitting. There are also some primitive campsites available along **Strawberry Creek** in the far northern reaches of the park, and along **Snake Creek** in the southern half of the park. These sites have tables and fire grates, but no drinking water. There are a few pit toilets along Snake Creek, but no toilets along Strawberry Creek.

Backcountry camping is also permitted; see the section "Exploring the Backcountry," above. The park has an RV dump station (near the visitor center) but no hookups or showers (see "Accommodations," below). The park's only public telephone is at the visitor center, which is not within walking distance of any campgrounds. All campsites are on a first-come, first-served basis.

The **Whispering Elms,** Nev. 487, Baker, NV 89311 (☎ 775/234-7343; credit cards accepted), located on the northwest edge of the village of Baker, has shady tent and RV sites and all the usual amenities. There is also a small motel (see below).

Accommodations

There are no hotels inside the park, but the tiny community of Baker, 5 miles east of the park entrance, has several places to stay. Otherwise, park visitors will find services in Ely, Nevada, 70 miles west; and Delta, Utah, about 100 miles east. Among franchise properties in Ely is the **Ramada Inn–Copper Queen Casino,** 805 Great Basin Blvd., Ely, NV 89301 (☎ 775/289-4884), $60 to $83 double. Motels in Delta include the **Best Western Motor Inn,** 527 E. Topaz Blvd., Delta, UT 84624 (☎ 800/354-9378 or 435/864-3882), $52 to $65 double. Both Ely and Delta also have a variety of restaurants, plus fuel, groceries, and camping supplies.

The Border Inn

U.S. 50/6 at the Nevada–Utah border, 13 mi. northeast of the national park (P.O. Box 30, Baker, NV 89311). ☎ 775/234-7300. 29 units. A/C TV TEL. $30–$40 double. AE, DISC, MC, V. Pets accepted.

Campground	Elev.	Total Sites	RV Hookups	Dump Station	Toilets	Drinking Water
Lower Lehman Creek	7,500	11	No	No	Yes	Yes
Upper Lehman Creek	7,800	24	No	No	Yes	Yes
Baker Creek	8,000	32	No	No	Yes	Yes
Wheeler Peak	9,950	37	No	No	Yes	Yes
Whispering Elms	5,300	35	15	No	Yes	Yes

This comfortable motel has basic rooms and 12 kitchenette units in Utah, and a restaurant with a bar and slot machines a few feet away in Nevada. The wood-paneled rooms are simply but attractively furnished. There is a coin-operated laundry, VCRs and videotape rentals, and gasoline and diesel fuel are available. Campers can also come here for hot showers. Also see "Dining," below.

Silver Jack Motel and Gift Shop

Downtown Baker, 5 mi. east of the national park (P.O. Box 166, Baker, NV 89311). ☎ **775/234-7323.** 7 units, 1 mobile home. A/C TV. $36–$45 double; mobile home $60 double. DISC, MC, V. Closed mid-Nov to mid-Mar. Pets accepted.

This well-maintained family-owned and operated motel is the closest lodging to the national park. Basic motel rooms have either one or two double beds, and one unit has two double beds plus a twin bed in a separate room. Some units have shower-tub combinations, while others have showers only. There is an attractive patio with a fountain where guests sit, chat, and watch the hummingbirds. The attached gift shop offers local art and high-quality crafts, and the town's two restaurants (see below) are across the street. The separate mobile home, which has two bedrooms, a fully equipped kitchen, and a living room, is several blocks away.

Whispering Elms

Nev. 487, Baker, NV 89311. ☎ **775/234-7343.** 6 units. A/C TV. $40 double. MC, V.

Among shade trees on the northwest edge of Baker, the Whispering Elms has pleasant rooms with wood paneling and a few western touches. Each room has one double bed, a tub/shower combo, refrigerator, microwave, desk, and a table with two chairs.

Dining

INSIDE THE PARK

The only services in the park are the visitor center's cafe and gift shop, which are open from early April through October. Your choices here include light breakfasts, lunches, and snack items.

NEAR THE PARK

The Border Inn

U.S. 50/6 at the Nevada-Utah border, 13 mi. northeast of the national park. ☎ **775/234-7300.** Lunch $2.25–$5.95; dinner $6.45–$10.95. AE, DISC, MC, V. Kitchen open daily 6am–10pm; bar and store open daily 24 hrs. Closed Christmas Day. AMERICAN.

Good burgers and chicken-fried steak are served at this roadside restaurant, which also specializes in homemade soups and baked items. Mexican food specials are featured Friday night. The room is large and open, with a bar along

Showers	Fire Pits/ Grills	Laundry	Public Phone	Reserve	Fees	Open
No	Yes	No	No	No	$7	Year-round
No	Yes	No	No	No	$7	May 15–Oct 15
No	Yes	No	No	No	$7	May 15–Sept 15
No	Yes	No	No	No	$7	June 15–Sept 15
No	Yes	Yes	No	Yes	$10–$17	Year-round

one side. There are also slot machines, video games, a pool table, a gift shop, a convenience store, an ATM, and a gas station with diesel fuel.

The Outlaw

Downtown Baker. ☎ **775/234-7302.** Lunch $3.95–$6.95; dinner $4.75–$18.95. AE, DISC, MC, V. Summer daily 7am–8:30pm; bar usually open later. Call for winter hours. AMERICAN.

The name conjures up an image of a rough Western bar, and the bar and pool table add to the decidedly Wild West saloon atmosphere. But this is actually a friendly family place, considered "Baker's living room," where locals come to sip coffee or beer and discuss the events of the day. Known for its hand-cut charbroiled steaks, The Outlaw has vegetarian dishes as well, including a garden burger. It also serves pastas, ground buffalo steaks, baby back ribs, and homemade burritos—and during the summer offers prime rib Friday and Saturday evenings. A popular breakfast dish is The Scramble (fried potatoes, onions, mild green chile, scrambled eggs, and cheddar cheese, with salsa on the side). In addition to the pool table, you can try your luck on the slot machines.

T&D's Country Store, Restaurant & Bar

Corner of Elko and Main, downtown Baker. ☎ **775/234-7264.** Sandwiches and meals $2.75–$6.85; large pizzas $9.95–$15.25. DISC, MC, V. Restaurant Sun–Thurs 11:30am–9pm, Fri–Sat 11:30am–10pm; store daily 8am–7pm in summer, shorter hours in winter. AMERICAN/ MEXICAN.

The restaurant is located in a bright and cheery sunroom attached to the small grocery store. It's known for its pizzas, deli sandwiches, and big steak and chicken burritos, but also serves burgers, steak sandwiches, pita sandwiches, and several more elaborate meals, including barbecued ribs and an Oriental chicken salad. There is a full bar, with several beers on tap, and a surprisingly good stock of wines available by the glass. There is also a large-screen TV in a separate sports lounge. You can get your food items to go, and there is a full liquor store, gasoline and propane, videotape rentals, camping and fishing gear, plus Nevada hunting and fishing licenses.

Picnic & Camping Supplies

In addition to the snacks available at the cafe and gift shop in the park, you can find take-out food, ice, and packaged liquor at **The Outlaw** and **T&D's Country Store & Restaurant.** At **The Border Inn,** along U.S. 50/6 at the Nevada-Utah border, there's a small convenience store. All three properties are listed above.

21

GUADALUPE MOUNTAINS NATIONAL PARK

by Don and Barbara Laine

ONCE A LONG REEF POKING UP THROUGH THE OCEAN, THEN A DENSE forest, Guadalupe Mountains National Park is today a rugged wilderness of tall Douglas firs and lush vegetation rising out of a vast desert. Here you will find varied hiking trails,

panoramic vistas, the highest peak in Texas, plant and animal life unique in the Southwest, and a canyon that many believe is the prettiest spot in all of Texas.

As you approach from the north, the mountains seem to rise gradually from the landscape, but seen from the south they stand tall and dignified. El Capitan, the southern tip of the reef escarpment, watches over the landscape like a sentinel. In the south-central section of the park, Guadalupe Peak, at 8,749 feet the highest mountain in Texas, provides hikers with incredible views of the surrounding mountains and desert.

The 96,416-acre park has several separate sections. Park headquarters and the visitor center are at Pine Springs, along the park's southeast edge, where you'll also find a campground and several trailheads, including one with access to the Guadalupe Peak Trail, the park's premier mountain hike. Nearby, a short dirt road leads to historic Frijole Ranch, with a museum and more trailheads. A horse corral is nearby. The McKittrick Canyon section of the park, near its northeast corner, may be the most beautiful spot in

Texas, especially in fall, when its oaks, maples, and other trees produce a spectacular show of color. A day-use area only, McKittrick Canyon has a delightful although intermittent stream, a wide variety of plant and animal life, several trailheads, and historic buildings. Along the park's northern boundary, practically in New Mexico, is the secluded and forested Dog Canyon.

Particularly impressive is Guadalupe Mountains National Park's vast variety of flora and fauna. You'll find species here that don't seem to belong in west Texas, such as the maple and oak that produce the wonderful fall colors in McKittrick Canyon. Scientists say these seemingly out-of-place plants and animals are leftovers from a time when this region was cooler and wetter. As the climate changed and the desert spread, some species were able to survive in these mountains, where conditions remained somewhat cooler and more moist. At the base of the mountains, at lower elevations, you'll find desert plants such as sotol, agave, and prickly pear cactus; but as you start to climb, especially in

343

Tips from a Park Ranger

"**T**his is essentially a hiking park," says Rich McCamant, the park's former chief of interpretation. He says the park's two main attractions, which he recommends to all visitors, are the hike to the top of Guadalupe Peak and the colors in McKittrick Canyon, either the trees in fall or the wildflowers in spring.

McCamant says that those without the time or desire to hike the strenuous Guadalupe Peak Trail should consider the moderately rated Smith Springs Loop Trail or Devil's Hall Trail.

"This is a park you can visit almost any time of year and have a good experience," McCamant says, although he adds that many consider October to have the best weather, while spring can be windy.

McCamant says there are five species of rattlesnakes in the park, but visitors probably won't see any, and in the history of the park there have been no reported rattlesnake bites. "The biggest threat here is the sun," he says. "Hikers really need to carry a gallon of water per day, and drink it."

He also warns that because many of the trails have a lot of loose rock, good hiking boots are essential. The other thing he wants park visitors to keep in mind is that there is no gasoline or other services close to the park, so they should bring plenty of fuel and everything else they might want.

---

stream-nurtured canyons, expect to encounter ponderosa pine, ash, walnut, oak, and ferns. Wildlife abounds, including mule deer, elk, and all sorts of birds and snakes.

Avoiding the Crowds. Overall, Guadalupe Mountains National Park is one of America's lesser-visited national parks, with attendance of only about 225,000 each year. This is partly because it is primarily a wilderness park, where you'll have to tackle rugged hiking trails to get to the best vistas. But it's also out of the way and somewhat inconvenient—the closest lodging is 35 miles away from the park's main section. In fact, about the only time the park might be considered even slightly crowded is during spring break time at Texas and New Mexico colleges, usually in March, when students bring their backpacks and hit the trails. There are also quite a few families visiting during summer, although the park is not usually crowded even then, and visitation drops considerably once schools open in late August.

An exception is McKittrick Canyon, renowned throughout the Southwest for its beautiful fall colors, at their best in late October and early November. The one road into McKittrick Canyon will be a bit busy then, but once you get on the trails you can usually walk away from the people.

Just the Facts

GETTING THERE & GATEWAYS

Located on the border of New Mexico and Texas, the park is 55 miles southwest of Carlsbad, New Mexico, along U.S. 62/180. From Albuquerque drive east on I-40 for 59 miles to Clines Corners, and turn south on U.S. 285 for 216 miles to the city of Carlsbad, then head southwest 55 miles on U.S. 62/180 to the park entrance at Pine Springs. From El Paso drive northeast 110 miles on U.S. 62/180 to Pine Springs.

The Nearest Airport. Air travelers can fly to **Cavern City Air Terminal**

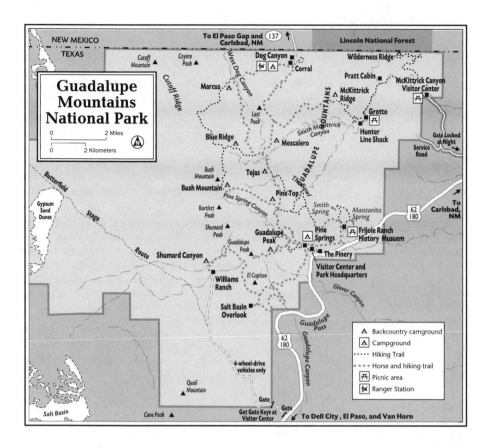

Guadalupe Mountains National Park

NEW MEXICO
TEXAS

To El Paso Gap and Carlsbad, NM — 137

Lincoln National Forest

Cutoff Mountain ▲
Coyote Peak ▲
Dog Canyon
Corral
Wilderness Ridge
Pratt Cabin ■
McKittrick Canyon Visitor Center
Marcus △
West Dog Canyon
Cutoff Ridge
McKittrick Ridge
Lost Peak ▲
South McKittrick Canyon
Grotto
Blue Ridge △
Mescalero △
Hunter Line Shack
Gate Locked at Night
Service Road
Butterfield
Bush Mountain ▲
Tejas △
Bush Mountain △
GUADALUPE MOUNTAINS
The Bowl
Pine Top △
Gypsum Sand Dunes
Bartlett Peak ▲
Pine Spring Canyon
Smith Spring
Manzanita Spring
To Carlsbad, NM — 62 180
Stage
Shumard Peak ▲
Guadalupe Peak ▲
Pine Springs
Frijole Ranch History Musuem
Route
Shumard Canyon △
(Guadalupe Peak) △
The Pinery
Williams Ranch ■
El Capitan
Visitor Center and Park Headquarters
Glover Canyon
Salt Basin Overlook ■
Guadalupe Pass
62 180
Guadalupe Canyon
4-wheel-drive vehicles only
Quail Mountain ▲
Gate
Salt Basin
Cone Peak ▲
Get Gate Keys at Visitor Center
Gate
To Dell City, El Paso, and Van Horn

0   2 Miles
0   2 Kilometers

△ Backcountry camground
Ⓐ Campground
····· Hiking Trail
•••• Horse and hiking trail
🏕 Picnic area
Ⓡ Ranger Station

(☎ 505/887-1500), at the south edge of the city of Carlsbad, which has commercial service from Albuquerque with **Mesa Airlines** (☎ 800/637-2247), plus Hertz car rentals.

The nearest major airport is **El Paso International** (☎ 915/780-4749) in central El Paso just north of I-10, with service from **American, America West, Continental, Delta, TWA, Southwest, Frontier,** and **Aero Litoral** (☎ 800/237-6639); and car rentals from **Advantage, Alamo, Avis, Budget, Dollar, Hertz,** and **National.** Reservations numbers for major airlines and car-rental agencies are given in the appendix.

INFORMATION

Contact the **Superintendent, Guadalupe Mountains National Park,** HC 60, Box 400, Salt Flat, TX 79847 (☎ 915/828-3251; www.nps.gov/gumo. Books and maps can be ordered from the **Carlsbad**

Caverns–Guadalupe Mountains Association, 727 Carlsbad Caverns Hwy., Carlsbad, NM 88220 (☎ 505/785-2232, ext. 480; www.caverns.org).

Those arriving in the city of Carlsbad before going to the park can get a variety of brochures, maps, and other information at the **National Park Service's Administrative Office and Bookstore,** at 3225 National Parks Hwy. (at its intersection with West Pecan Street). It's open Monday to Friday year-round, plus weekends in the summer.

Because the park's backcountry trails often crisscross each other and can be confusing, rangers strongly recommend that those planning any serious hiking carry topographical maps. An excellent book for hikers is *Hiking Carlsbad Caverns and Guadalupe Mountains National Parks* (Helena, Mont.: Falcon Press, 1996) by Bill Schneider, which was published in partnership with the Carlsbad Caverns–Guadalupe Mountains

Association and is keyed to the Trails Illustrated topographical map of the park. Also very useful is a shorter and less expensive trail guide, *Trails of the Guadalupes* (Champagne, Ill.: Environmental Associates, 1992), by Don Kurtz and William D. Goran. These are available at the visitor center's bookstore or from the Carlsbad Caverns–Guadalupe Mountains Association.

A small seasonal publication, *The Capitan Reef,* contains pertinent up-to-the-minute information for visitors. It is available free at the visitor center.

VISITOR CENTERS

Park headquarters and the main visitor center are located at Pine Springs just off U.S. 62/180. There are three other access points along this side of the park: Frijole Ranch, about 1.5 miles east of Pine Springs and a mile north of the highway; McKittrick Canyon (day use only), about 7 miles east and 4 miles north of the highway; and Williams Ranch, about 8 miles south of Pine Springs and 8 miles north of the highway on a four-wheel-drive road.

The **Pine Springs Visitor Center,** open daily year-round except Christmas, has natural history exhibits, a bookstore, and an introductory slide program. **McKittrick Canyon** has a visitor contact station with outdoor exhibits and an outdoor slide program on the history, geology, and natural history of the canyon.

On the north side of the park is **Dog Canyon Ranger Station,** at the end of N. Mex. 137, about 70 miles from Carlsbad and 110 miles from park headquarters. Information, rest rooms, and drinking water are available.

Fees & Permits

Entry into the park is free. Camping costs $7 per individual site; group sites cost $2 per person with a 10-person minimum. Backcountry camping is free, but a permit is required. Corrals are available for those who bring their horses to ride in the park; although use is free, permits

are required. All permits are available at the Pine Springs Visitor Center and Dog Canyon Ranger Station, and must be requested in person, either the day before or the day of use.

SPECIAL REGULATIONS & WARNINGS

Visitors to McKittrick Canyon, a day-use area, must stay on the trail; entering the stream is not permitted. The McKittrick Canyon **entrance gate** opens at 8am daily, and closes at 4:30pm mountain standard time and at 6pm mountain daylight time.

Neither wood nor charcoal fires are allowed anywhere in the park. Horses are prohibited in the backcountry overnight.

SEASONS & CLIMATE

In general, summers in the Guadalupe Mountains are hot (highs in the 80s and 90s and lows in the 60s) and winters are mild (highs in the 50s and 60s and lows in the upper 20s and 30s). However, sudden and extreme changes can occur at any time. In spring and early summer, high winds can whip down the mountain slopes, sometimes reaching 100 miles per hour; on hot summer days, thunderstorms can blow up quickly. The sun is warm even in winter, and summer nights are generally cool no matter how hot the afternoon. Clothing that can be layered is best, comfortable and sturdy walking/hiking shoes are a must, a hat and sunscreen are highly recommended, and plenty of drinking water is essential for hikers.

SEASONAL EVENTS

McKittrick Canyon's beautiful display of fall colors usually takes place between early October and mid-November. It varies, however, so call before going.

If You Only Have 1 Day

This park is best explored over a period of 2 or 3 days, with at least 1 day devoted to the visitor center, historic attractions, and trails in the Pine Springs section; and another full day allotted to McKittrick Canyon. Those with additional time could then head over to the park's third section, Dog Canyon.

Those who have only 1 day, however, can still see quite a bit, but they need to decide on either Pine Springs or McKittrick Canyon. There won't be time for both. If it's fall and the colors are right, drive to the **McKittrick Canyon Visitor Contact Station,** look at the exhibits, and hike the **McKittrick Canyon Trail** to the historic **Pratt Lodge.** If it's not fall, or if you don't care about fall colors, drive directly to the **Pine Springs Visitor Center,** see the exhibits, and hike one of the trails—the **Guadalupe Peak Trail** for the ambitious or the **Devil's Hall Trail** for those who prefer less physical exertion.

Exploring the Park by Car

Guadalupe Mountains is not a good park for the vehicle-bound. There are no paved scenic drives traversing the park; roads here are simply means of getting to historical sites and trailheads.

Organized Tours & Ranger Programs

On summer evenings, rangers offer programs at the campground amphitheater. There are also frequent showings of an orientation video at the visitor center.

Historic & Man-Made Attractions

The Pinery was one of 200 stations along the 2,800-mile Butterfield Overland Mail Coach Route. The stations provided fresh mules every 20 miles and a new coach every 300 miles, in order to maintain the grueling speed of 5 miles per hour 24 hours a day. John Butterfield had seen the need for overland mail delivery between the eastern states and the West Coast, so he designed a route and the coaches, and acquired a federal

contract to deliver the St. Louis mail to San Francisco in 25 days. In March 1857 this was a real feat. The Pinery commemorates his achievement.

Named for nearby stands of pine, the Pinery had abundant water and good grazing. It was a high-walled rock enclosure with a wagon repair shop, blacksmith shop, and three mud-roofed rooms where passengers could get a warm meal, if they had time. The first mail coach came through on September 28, 1858. Use continued for 11 months until August 1859, when this route was abandoned for a new road that better served the West's military forts.

Located in McKittrick Canyon, **Pratt Lodge** was built by Wallace E. Pratt in 1931–32, of stone quarried from the base of the Guadalupe Mountains, using heart-of-pine from east Texas for rafters, collar beams, and roof supports. Pratt, a geologist for the Humble Oil Co. (now Exxon), and his family came for summer vacations when the heat in Houston became unbearable. He finally retired here in 1945. Soon after, he and his family built a second house, Ship on the Desert, outside the canyon. In 1957, the Pratts donated 5,632 acres of their 16,000-acre ranch to the federal government to begin the national park. In addition to the grand stone lodge, there are several outbuildings, stone picnic tables, and a wonderful stone fence.

Williams Ranch house rests at the base of a 3,000-foot rock cliff on the west face of the Guadalupe Mountains. The 7.3-mile access road, navigable only by high-clearance 4X4s, follows part of the old Butterfield Overland Mail Route for about 2 miles. The road crosses private land and has two locked metal gates, for which you must sign out keys at the visitor center.

History is unclear on exactly who built the house and when, but it's believed to have been built around 1908, and it is fairly certain that the first inhabitants for any significant period of time were Henry and Rena Belcher. For almost 10 years, they maintained a substantial ranch here, at times with close to 3,000 head of longhorn cattle. Water was piped from Bone Spring down the canyon to holding tanks in the lowlands. James Adolphus Williams acquired the property around 1917, and with the help of an Indian friend, ranched and farmed the land until moving to New Mexico in 1941. After Williams' death in 1942, Judge J. C. Hunter bought the property, adding it to his already large holdings in the Guadalupes.

Another historic site is **Frijole Ranch,** which was a working ranch from the 1870s until 1972. Inside the ranch house is a museum with exhibits on the cultural history of the Guadalupe Mountains, including prehistoric Indians, the later Mescalero Apaches, Spanish conquistadors, and ranchers of the 19th and 20th centuries. On the grounds are several historic buildings, including a schoolhouse.

Day Hikes

This is a prime hiker's park, with more than 80 miles of trails that range from easy walks to steep, strenuous, and sometimes treacherous adventures.

SHORTER TRAILS

Indian Meadow Nature Trail

0.6 mi. RT. Easy. Access: Dog Canyon Campground, walk south from the water fountain.

This exceptionally easy stroll follows a series of numbered stops keyed to a free brochure, available at the trailhead. You'll learn about the native vegetation and cultural history of the area as you ramble along a virtually level dirt trail in a lovely meadow.

McKittrick Canyon Nature Trail

0.9 mi. RT. Easy to moderate. Access: McKittrick Canyon Visitor Center.

An ideal way to discover the variety of plants and animals that inhabit the canyon, this trail has some steep climbs.

Read the numerous interpretive signs along the path, telling you all you wanted to know about, for example, why rattlesnakes are underappreciated and how cacti supply food and water for wildlife.

Pinery Trail

0.75 mi. RT. Easy. Access: The trailhead is by the Pine Springs Visitor Center; or from the parking area on U.S. 62/180, located 1 mi. north of the visitor center entrance road.

A paved trail, accessible by wheelchair, the Pinery Trail gives visitors a brief introduction to the low-elevation environment at the park. The interpretive signs discuss both the plants along the trail and the history of the area. About 0.25 mile from the visitor center the trail makes a loop around the ruins of an old horse-changing station, left over from the Butterfield Stage Route (see "Historic & Man-Made Attractions," above).

Smith Spring Loop

2.3 mi. RT. Easy to moderate. Access: The north edge of the Frijole Ranch and Museum.

The Smith Spring Loop begins in the dry desert and climbs 440 feet to the lush oasis of Smith Spring. The first part of the trail, which takes you to Manzanita Spring, is very easy and navigable by people with mobility impairments. If you take this walk in the evening, you might catch a glimpse of an elk, deer, or other wildlife coming to the spring for water. After Manzanita Spring, the trail begins the climb to Smith Spring, following a good example of a desert riparian zone along Smith Canyon. Look for the damage caused by a lightning fire in 1990, and how the desert environment has recovered, even improved. Smith Spring itself is a magnificent oasis, with enough water seeping out to form a small waterfall and stream. Here you'll find maidenhair fern, bigtooth maple, chinquapin oak, and Texas madrone—all in the middle of the Chihuahuan Desert. Although lush, the area is fragile, so please remain in the designated area to preserve the ecosystem.

LONGER TRAILS

El Capitan Trail

9.4 mi. one way. Moderate to strenuous. Access: Williams Ranch.

This trail, which offers little shade, climbs over 1,500 feet and takes a full day to complete, plus the drive to Williams Ranch (requiring a four-wheel-drive vehicle; see "Historic & Man-Made Attractions," above). This is the only trail into the remote western part of the Guadalupe Mountains. The incredible scenery along the first 2 miles more than makes up for the long, slow, and usually hot climb up Shumard Canyon, an elevation gain of over 1,300 feet. Stop occasionally to look back down the canyon to the west, and ahead toward Shumard Peak and the impressive escarpment of the Guadalupes. After Shumard Canyon the hike takes you 3 miles around El Capitan, keeping in the shadow of the escarpment and climbing another 200 feet. After about 5 miles, the Salt Basin Overlook loop takes off to the right, and you stay to the left, gradually dropping down into Guadalupe Canyon, where you meet the other end of the lower Salt Basin Overlook loop. From here the last 3.4 miles of the trail is fairly easy, level walking to Pine Springs. The trail can also be hiked out and back from Pine Springs, an arduous 18.8-mile overnight hike, which is why many hikers get lifts from friends to the ranch and hike back to Pine Springs. An alternative is to hike from Pine Springs to the Salt Basin Overlook Trail, hike around it, and then back to Pine Springs, a trip of 11.3 miles.

Guadalupe Peak Trail

4.2 mi. one way. Strenuous. Access: Pine Springs Campground.

This trail is strenuous, climbing almost 3,000 feet, but the views from the 8,749-foot high Guadalupe Peak are magnificent. The peak is the highest in the park and the state of Texas. If you have only 1 day to explore this park, and you are an average or better hiker, this is the hike you should choose. Start early, take plenty of water, and be prepared to work. When you've gone about halfway, you'll see what seems to be the top not too far ahead, but beware: This is a false summit. Study the changing life zones as you climb from the desert into the higher-elevation pine forests—this will take your mind off your straining muscles and aching lungs. A mile short of the summit, a campground lies in one of the rare level spots on the mountain. If you plan to spend the night, anchor your tent strongly since the winds can be ferocious up here, especially in spring.

From the summit, the views are stupendous. To the north are Bush Mountain and Shumard Peak, the next two highest points in Texas, with respective elevations of 8,631 and 8,615 feet. The Chihuahuan Desert stretches to the south, interrupted only by the Delaware and Sierra Diablo mountains. This is one of those "On a clear day you can see forever" spots—sometimes all the way to 12,003-foot-high Sierra Blanca, near Ruidoso, New Mexico, 100 miles north.

Lost Peak

3 mi. one way. Moderate. Access: Dog Canyon Trailhead.

A moderate hike you can probably complete in a half day, Lost Peak is especially good near dawn or dusk when wild turkey, deer, and other wildlife are often seen. A lightning-caused fire scorched the area in 1994, and although many plants have been diligently recovering, the loss of the tall trees will be felt for a long time. After leaving the trailhead, follow the Tejas Trail up Dog Canyon on a gradual climb for about 1.5 miles. Just before reaching Dog Canyon Springs, the trail starts switchbacking up the west side of the canyon to a ridgeline, offering great views back to the campground. If you continue all the way to the peak, the next 1.5 miles climbs about 1,100 feet, the steepest section of the trail. There's no sign for the peak and it's easy to hike on by, so watch your topographical map carefully—the peak is just a bit to the right of the trail. After scrambling up to the summit for a panoramic view, head back down the trail. The total elevation change is 1,420 feet.

McKittrick Canyon

5.1 mi. one way. Moderate to strenuous. Access: McKittrick Canyon Trailhead.

McKittrick Canyon is one of the most famous scenic areas in Texas, and this trail explores the length of it. The first 2.3 miles to the Pratt Lodge are easy; the following 1.2 miles to the Grotto gain 340 feet in elevation and are considered moderate; and the strenuous climb to the Notch rises 1300 feet in 1.6 miles. Even so, this is one of the most popular hikes in the park, though not everyone makes it to the Notch.

The canyon is forested with conifers and deciduous trees. In fall the maples, oaks, and other hardwoods burst into color, painting the world in bright colors set off by the rich variety of the evergreens. The stream in the canyon, which appears and disappears several times in the first 3 miles of the trail, is a unique, permanent desert stream, with reproducing trout. Hikers may not drink from, wade in, or disturb the stream in any way.

The first part of the trail is wide and seems quite flat, crossing the stream twice on its way to Pratt Lodge, which is wonderfully situated at the convergence of North and South McKittrick canyons. About a mile from the lodge a short spur veers off to the left to the Grotto, a recess with odd formations that look like they belong underground in a cave. This is a great spot for lunch at one of the stone picnic tables. Continuing down the spur trail to its end, you reach the Hunter Line Cabin, which served as temporary quarters for ranch hands of the Hunter family. Beyond the cabin, South McKittrick Canyon has been preserved as a Research Natural Area with no entry. Return to the main trail and continue toward the Notch, or head back down the canyon to your car. In another 0.5 mile, the trail begins switchbacking up the side of South McKittrick Canyon for the steepest ascent in the park, until it slips through the Notch, a distinctive narrow spot in the cliff. Sit down and rest while you absorb the incredible scenery. The view down the canyon is magnificent, and quite dazzling in autumn. You can see both Hunter Line Cabin and Pratt Lodge in the distance. Remember to start down in time to reach your car well before the gate closes.

Exploring the Backcountry

A variety of possibilities exist for backpacking. It's always best to discuss your plans with rangers before heading out into the backcountry, to find out about current trail conditions and to decide on the trail or trails you want to take. The free backcountry campsite permits can be obtained no more than 24 hours in advance at the Pine Springs Visitor Center or Dog Canyon Ranger Station. Also, see "Camping," below.

Campground	Elev.	Total Sites	RV Hookups	Dump Station	Toilets
Pine Springs	5,840	39	0	No	Yes
Dog Canyon	6,320	13	0	No	Yes
Carlsbad RV Park & Campground	3,110	136	95	Yes	Yes
Brantley Lake State Park	3,300	51+	51	Yes	Yes
White's City RV Park	3630	80+	80	No	Yes

The Bowl

13-mi. loop. Strenuous. Access: Pine Springs Campground.

This hike climbs 2,546 feet in elevation if you go to the top of Hunter Peak. As this is primarily an overnight hike, you'll camp either at Pine Top, about 4.2 miles down the trail and a bit off it to the left, or at Tejas Campsite about 5.5 miles along. The trail crosses a dry wash, follows the Tejas Trail up a hill, has a fairly level stretch, and then starts the climb up to Pine Top, rising 2,000 feet over 3 miles of switchbacks. The view from the top of the escarpment is breathtaking. The trail then continues through a magnificent pine forest—watch for elk along the way. There are some old water tanks and a pipe running along the trail in spots, left over from a water system used by ranchers years ago. You can take a side trip to the top of Hunter Peak for another incredible view before heading back down.

Other Sports & Activities

Horseback Riding. About 60% of the park's trails are open to horses for day trips, although horses are not permitted in the backcountry overnight. There are **corrals** at Frijole Ranch (near Pine Springs) and Dog Canyon (see "Fees & Permits," above). Each set of corrals contains four pens that can accommodate up to 10 horses. There are no horses or other pack animals available for hire in or near the park. Park rangers warn that horses brought into the park should be accustomed to steep, rocky trails.

Wildlife Viewing & Bird Watching. Because of the variety of habitats here, and also because these canyons offer some of the few water sources in west Texas, Guadalupe Mountains National Park offers excellent wildlife viewing and bird-watching possibilities. **McKittrick Canyon** and **Frijole Ranch** are considered among the best wildlife viewing spots, but a variety of species can be seen throughout the park. Those spending more than a few hours will likely see mule deer, and the park is also home to a herd of some 50 to 70 elk, which are sometimes seen in the higher elevations or along the highway in winter. Other **mammals** include raccoons, striped and hog-nosed skunks, gray foxes, coyotes, gray-footed chipmunks, Texas antelope squirrels, black-tailed jackrabbits, and desert cottontails. Black bears and mountain lions are also known to live in the park, but are seldom seen.

About two dozen varieties of **snakes** make their home in the park, including five species of rattlesnakes. There are also numerous **lizards,** which are usually seen in the mornings and early evenings. These include the collared, crevice spiny, tree, side-blotched, Texas horned, mountain short-horned, and marbled whiptail. The most commonly seen is the prairie lizard, which is identified by the light-colored stripes down its back.

More than 200 species of **birds** are known to spend time in the park,

Drinking Water	Showers	Fire Pits/ Grills	Laundry	Public Phone	Reserve	Fees	Open
Yes	No	No	No	Yes	No	$7	Year-round
Yes	No	No	No	Yes	No	$7	Year-round
Yes	Yes	Yes	Yes	Yes	Yes	$15–$19	Year-round
Yes	Yes	Yes	No	Yes	No	$7–$11	Year-round
Yes	Yes	Yes	Yes	Yes	Yes	$15–$20	Year-round

including peregrine falcons, golden eagles, turkey vultures, and wild turkeys. You are also likely to encounter rock wrens, canyon wrens, black-throated sparrows, common nighthawks, mourning doves, rufous-crowned sparrows, mountain chickadees, ladder-backed woodpeckers, solitary vireos, and western scrub jays.

Camping

There are two developed vehicle-accessible campgrounds in the park. **Pine Springs Campground** is near the visitor center and park headquarters just off U.S. 62/180. There are 18 spaces for RVs, 20 very attractive tent sites, and two group campsites. There is usually a campground host on duty. About 0.5 mile inside the north boundary of the park is **Dog Canyon Campground,** accessible from N. Mex. 137. Here there are nine tent sites and four RV sites. Although reservations are not accepted, you can call ahead to check on availability of sites (☎ 915/828-3251). Camp stoves are allowed, but wood and charcoal fires are prohibited.

The park also has 10 designated backcountry campgrounds, with from two to eight sites each. Be sure to pick up free permits at the Pine Springs Visitor Center or Dog Canyon Ranger Station the day of or the day before your backpacking trip. There is no drinking water available in the backcountry, and all trash, including toilet paper, must be packed out. Fires are strictly prohibited; use cookstoves only. You can only camp in designated campgrounds.

Nearby, you'll find commercial camping at **White's City RV Park** in White's City, and **Carlsbad RV Park** and **Brantley Lake State Park** in Carlsbad. For descriptions and information on these campgrounds, see "Camping" in chapter 10.

Accommodations

There are no accommodations within the park. The nearest are 35 miles northeast at **White's City,** New Mexico, and 55 miles northeast in **Carlsbad,** New Mexico. For information, see "Accommodations" in chapter 10.

Dining

There are no restaurants within the park, although about 5 miles northeast of Pine Springs on U.S. 62/180 the **Nickel Creek Cafe** (☎ 915/828-3295) serves breakfast and lunch from Monday through Saturday, with prices from $1.30 to $5.95.

The next closest dining possibilities are in **White's City,** New Mexico, 35 miles from the park, and in the city of **Carlsbad,** New Mexico, 55 miles from the park. See "Dining" in chapter 10.

Picnic & Camping Supplies

The closest grocery store to the national park is the convenience store located at the Texaco gas station in the **White's City complex,** at the intersection of U.S. 62/180 and N. Mex. 7, about 35 miles from the visitor center. You'll find a good variety of stores in the city of Carlsbad, including an **Albertson's** grocery store at 808 N. Canal St., at its intersection with West Church Street (☎ 505/885-2161), which has a well-stocked deli and bakery.

22

JOSHUA TREE NATIONAL PARK

by Eric Peterson and Stephanie Avnet Yates

AT JOSHUA TREE NATIONAL PARK, THE TREES THEMSELVES ARE merely the starting point for exploring the seemingly barren desert. Viewed from the roadside, the dry land only hints at hidden vitality, but closer examination reveals a giant mosaic

of intense beauty and complexity. From lush oases teeming with life to rusted-out relics of man's attempts to tame the wilderness, from low plains of tufted cacti to mountains of exposed, twisted rock, the park is much more than a tableau of the curious tree for which it's named.

The Joshua tree is said to have been given its name by early Mormon settlers traveling west, for its upraised limbs and bearded appearance reminded them of the prophet Joshua leading them to the promised land. It's not really a tree, though, but a variety of yucca, a member of the lily family.

Joshua Tree National Park's name is fitting, for here the peculiar tree reaches the southernmost boundary of its range. The park straddles two desert environments: The mountainous, Joshua tree–studded Mojave Desert forms the northwestern part of the park. Hotter, drier, lower, and characterized by a wide variety of desert flora like cacti, cottonwood, and native California fan palms, the Colorado Desert comprises the

park's southern and eastern sections. Between them runs the "transition zone," displaying characteristics of each.

The area's geological timeline is fascinating, stretching back 8 million years to a time when the Mojave landscape was one of rolling hills and flourishing grasslands; horses, camels, and mastodons abounded, preyed on by saber-toothed tigers and wild dogs. Displays at the Oasis Visitor Center show how resulting climatic, volcanic, and tectonic activity have created the park's signature cliffs and boulders and turned Joshua Tree into the arid desert you see today. Human presence has been traced back nearly 10,000 years with the discovery of Pinto Man, and you can see evidence of more recent habitation in the form of American Indian pictographs carved into rock faces throughout the park. Miners and ranchers began coming in the 1860s, but the boom went bust by the turn of the 20th century. Then a Pasadena doctor, treating World War I veterans suffering from respiratory and heart ailments caused by mustard gas, prescribed the

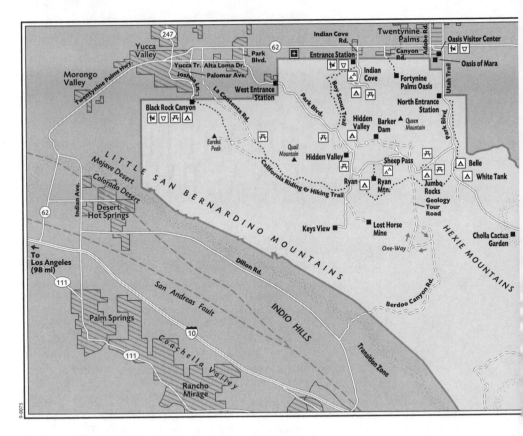

desert's clean, dry air—and modern interest in the area was born.

During the 1920s, a worldwide fascination with the desert emerged, and cactus gardens were much in vogue. Entrepreneurs hauled truckloads of desert plants into Los Angeles for quick sale or export, and souvenir hunters removed archaeological treasures. Incensed that the beautiful Mojave was in danger of being picked clean, Los Angeles socialite Minerva Hoyt organized the desert conservation movement and successfully lobbied for the establishment of Joshua Tree National Monument in 1936.

In 1994, under provisions of the federal California Desert Protection Act, Joshua Tree was "upgraded" to national park status and expanded to nearly 800,000 acres.

Flora. The eastern half of the park is mainly the lower Colorado Desert, dominated by the abundant and fragrant **creosote** bush, a drought-resistant survivor

that even releases secretions into the surrounding soil to kill competing seedlings. Adding interest to the arid land are small stands of spidery, tenacious **ocotillo,** a split personality that drops its leaves in times of drought, appearing dry and spindly. But the ocotillo can sprout bushy leaves in a few days when the rains come, and its flaming blooms atop leafy green branches bear little resemblance to its dormant alter ego.

Most people associate desert plants with cacti, which are indeed here in abundance. One of the more unusual members of the cactus family is the **Bigelow cholla cactus** ("teddy bear" and "jumping" cactus). Cholla's fine needles appear soft and fluffy from afar, but anyone who has accidentally gotten a clump stuck to his or her skin or clothing knows the truth about those deceptive barbed spines. Most of the park's points of interest lie in the higher, slightly cooler and wetter Mojave desert, the special habitat of the burly **Joshua tree,** which displays

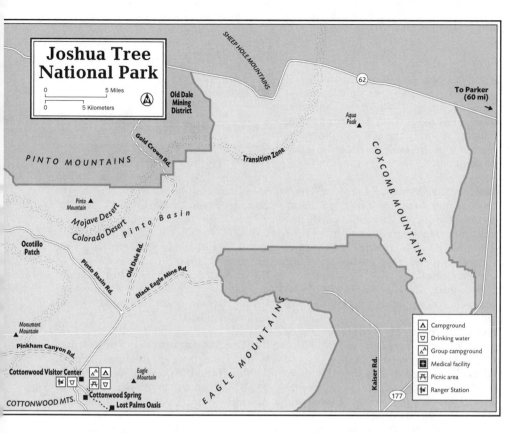

**Joshua Tree
National Park**

| 0 | 5 Miles |
| 0 | 5 Kilometers |

Old Dale
Mining
District

To Parker
(60 mi)

62

Aqua
Peak ▲

SHEEP HOLE MOUNTAINS

Gold Crown Rd.

PINTO MOUNTAINS

Transition Zone

C O X C O M B   M O U N T A I N S

Pinto ▲
Mountain

Mojave Desert
Colorado Desert

P i n t o   B a s i n

Ocotillo
Patch

Pinto Basin Rd.

Old Dale Rd.

Black Eagle Mine Rd.

Monument
▲ Mountain

Pinkham Canyon Rd.

E A G L E   M O U N T A I N S

Kaiser Rd.

177

Cottonwood Visitor Center

Eagle
▲ Mountain

Cottonwood Spring

COTTONWOOD MTS.

Lost Palms Oasis

△	Campground
▽	Drinking water
△	Group campground
⊞	Medical facility
⊼	Picnic area
⸙	Ranger Station

huge white flowers following a good rainy season. Early pioneers (and many ignorant modern campers) tried to chop down the "trees" for firewood, only to discover that what resembled trunks were just toughened stalks that won't burn. Five **fan palm** oases (in both climate zones) flourish in areas where water occurs naturally at or near the surface.

Wildflower lovers, take note: The Joshua Tree area has traditionally been an excellent place to view nature's springtime bonanza. In addition to the flowering plants discussed above, the desert is home to sand verbena, desert dandelion, evening primrose, and dozens more varieties, some so tiny that you must crouch down to make out their brightly colored petals—veteran viewers call these "belly flowers."

Fauna. One of the more wonderful aspects of the Joshua Tree desert is the way this seemingly harsh and barren

landscape slowly reveals itself to be richly inhabited. From the white-tailed **jackrabbits** abundant at the Oasis of Mara and throughout the park, to startling **bobcats** and **cougars** prowling around higher, less traveled elevations, the desert teems with life.

Some other frequently spotted residents: the **roadrunner,** a member of the cuckoo family with long, spindly legs and that telltale gait; the **coyote,** a fearless scavenger who'll openly trot along the road in search of food (*Beware:* They'll eat tennis shoes or picnic trash as eagerly as they eat rabbits or young tortoises); and **bighorn sheep,** most often seen atop the rocky hills they climb with sharp cloven hooves. Perhaps the most unusual animal is the **desert tortoise,** a slow-moving burrow dweller not often seen by casual visitors. The tortoises, which can live more than 50 years, are a protected endangered species, and you're prohibited from touching or interfering with them in any way. A poignant exception to this is if you encounter a tortoise on the road in danger of being hit—you're permitted to pick it up gently with two hands and, holding it level, carry it off the road, placing it in the same direction as it was traveling.

Avoiding the Crowds. As Joshua Tree's chief of interpretation, Joe Zarki is usually consulted for advice on the park's natural flora and fauna. But he offers the following valuable tips for maximizing your enjoyment even during the most crowded months:

♦ Joshua Tree's greatest volume occurs in spring, when temperatures are moderate and wildflowers blooming. From March to May, the number of monthly visitors ranges from 150,000 up (the unofficial record is 233,000 in April 1995). Compared to summer, which sees 60,000 to 70,000 people each month, these figures are staggering. October and November are also popular, with numbers around 100,000. If you can, time your visit outside of these crowded periods—if not, try to visit during the week to avoid the crush of weekenders from nearby Los Angeles, and stay away during spring break.

♦ Choose to enjoy the more popular activities (like designated nature trails and easy hiking routes) before 9 or 10am. Most people see the park between 10am and 4pm, so the evening hours can also offer some respite from crowds, and the sun sets after 7pm from May to September. In addition, you'll enjoy cooler temperatures during the morning and evening hours.

♦ Campers eager to stake their claim in the campground of their choice need to be diligent during springtime crowding, since it's first come, first served at all but one (Black Rock Canyon) of the park's campgrounds. Generally, it's best to arrive between 9am and noon to snatch an available space. The campsites near popular rock-climbing areas (Hidden Valley, Jumbo Rocks, Indian Cove) fill first. If you're staying over a weekend in peak season, try to claim your site Friday morning, before weekenders arrive.

Just the Facts

GETTING THERE & GATEWAYS

There are three roads into the park. The most commonly used is the **North Entrance Station** at the end of Utah Trail in the town of Twentynine Palms, on Calif. 62, 40 miles north of its junction with I-10. Also along Calif. 62 is the **West Entrance Station**, on Park Boulevard in the town of Joshua Tree. On the southern side of the park is the **Cottonwood Visitor Center**, about 25 miles east of Indio along I-10.

The Nearest Airport. The closest airport is the **Palm Springs Regional Airport**, 3400 E. Tahquitz Canyon Way (☎ 619/ 323-8161), served by **Alaska, American, America West, Delta/Skywest, United,** and **US Airways;** with car rentals from **Avis, Budget, Dollar, Hertz,** and **National.** See the appendix for their toll-free phone numbers.

INFORMATION

Contact the **Superintendent, Joshua Tree National Park,** 74485 National Park Dr., Twentynine Palms, CA 92277 (☎ 760/ 367-5500; www.nps.gov/jotr). A terrific Web site with abundant info on the park and surrounding communities is **www. desertgold.com**.

In addition to the complimentary newspaper-style *Joshua Tree Guide*, published by the Joshua Tree National Park Association, the following publications might prove helpful: Robert Cates's *Joshua Tree National Monument: A Visitors Guide* (Chatsworth, Calif.: Live Oak Press, 1984), and John Krist's *50 Best Short Hikes in California Deserts* (Berkeley: Wilderness Press, 1995). Order them from the **Joshua Tree National Park Association,** 74485 National Park Dr., Twentynine Palms, CA 92277 (☎ 619/367-5525).

VISITOR CENTERS

Your best source of information in the park is the large and well stocked Park Service's **Oasis Visitor Center,** 74485 National Park Dr., Twentynine Palms, CA 92277, on the road to the North Entrance Station. The **Cottonwood Visitor Center,** at the south end of the park, houses a gift shop/bookstore and an interpretive exhibit on the area's wildlife. The privately run **Park Center,** 6554 Park Blvd., Joshua Tree, CA 92252, is near the West Entrance Station in Joshua Tree. In addition to providing official visitor materials and information, this center has a supply/gift shop, a deli, and an art gallery.

FEES

Admission to the park is $10 per car (valid for 7 days). Four of the nine developed campgrounds charge fees, ranging from $8 to $10 for individual sites. Backcountry camping is free, although registration is required.

SPECIAL REGULATIONS & WARNINGS

In addition to the standard national park regulations designed to protect the fragile ecosystem, keep these in mind while enjoying Joshua Tree:

◆ Dehydration is a constant threat in the desert; even in winter, carry plenty of drinking water and drink regularly even if you don't feel thirsty. Recommended minimum supplies are 1 gallon per person per day or twice that if planning strenuous activity. Water is available only at five park locations: Cottonwood Springs, the Black Rock Canyon Campground, the Indian Cove Ranger Station, West Entrance, and the Oasis Visitor Center. Some of the water is dispensed via a coin-operated fountain—bring plenty of quarters.

◆ Sections of the park (identified on the official map) contain abandoned mines and associated structures. Use extreme caution in the vicinity, watching for open shafts and prospect holes. Supervise children closely and never enter abandoned mines.

◆ There's potential flash flooding following even brief rain showers, so avoid drainage areas and be especially observant of road conditions at those times.

SEASONS & CLIMATE

Joshua Tree National Park's nearly 800,000 acres straddle two distinct desert climates—the eastern half of the park is hot, dry, lower Colorado Desert, while most points of interest lie in the higher, slightly cooler and wetter Mojave Desert. The Mojave will occasionally get a dusting of snow in winter, but neither section sees more than 3 to 6 inches of annual rainfall. Winter temperatures are in the comfortable 50s or 60s during the day and often approach freezing overnight; summer days can blaze past 100°F at noon and even nighttime offers little relief in August and September, when lows are still in the 80s.

SEASONAL EVENTS

Best between February and May, the **springtime wildflower viewing** is dependent on rainfall, sunshine, and temperatures, but you can depend on seeing the brilliant blooms somewhere in the park each year. Rangers lead interpretive walks to the best displays, and 24-hour recorded information on prime viewing sites (updated at least weekly during the season) is available from the **Payne Foundation Wildflower Hotline** at ☎ 818/768-3533 or the **Living Desert Wildflower Hotline** at ☎ 760/340-4954.

If You Only Have 1 Day

An excellent first stop is the main **Oasis Visitor Center,** located alongside the Oasis of Mara, also known as the Twentynine Palms Oasis. For many generations the native Serrano tribe lived at this "place of little springs and much grass."

Get maps, books, and the latest in road, trail, and weather conditions before beginning your tour and stroll the short, paved nature trail through the oasis behind the center—it provides an introduction to the park's flora, wildlife, and geology.

From the Oasis Center, drive south to **Jumbo Rocks,** which captures the complete essence of the park: a vast array of rock formations, a Joshua tree forest, and the yucca-dotted desert open and wide. Check out the many boulders that appear to resemble humans, dinosaurs, monsters, cathedrals, and castles; if you're visiting with kids, it's a great way to put their imaginations to work. Stroll among the giant rock piles and observe the rock climbers who travel from around the world to practice their craft here—they're one of the park's most distinctive features.

At Cap Rock Junction, the main park road swings north toward the **Wonderland of Rocks,** 12 square miles of massive jumbled granite. This curious maze of stone hides groves of Joshua trees, trackless washes, and several small pools of water. To the south is the road that deadends at mile-high **Keys View.** You get a panoramic view of the park from this wind-whipped overlook; several informative plaques explain the topography you're seeing and provide some insight into the delicate desert ecosystems found in the park.

Don't miss the contrasting Colorado Desert terrain found along Pinto Basin Road—to conserve time, simply plan to exit the park via this route, which ends up at I-10. You'll pass both the **Cholla Cactus Garden** and spindly **Ocotillo Patch** on your way to vast Pinto Basin, a barren lowland surrounded by austere mountains and punctuated by trackless sand dunes. Then continue to **Cottonwood Springs,** which has a cool, palm-shaded oasis and groves of mature cottonwood trees.

Try to participate in a ranger-led tour or hike (see below). You'll learn to appreciate the park in a short amount of time, for the rangers here are as exuberant about their patch of wilderness as they are well informed.

Exploring the Park by Car

There are two main roads through the park, and by driving them both you'll be able to see virtually every feature that distinguishes Joshua Tree; there are even a couple of easy opportunities to stop and stretch your legs.

Park Boulevard loops through the high northern section between the North Entrance Station in Twentynine Palms and the West Entrance Station in Joshua Tree. Along the drive, which takes about 45 minutes one way, you'll get an eyeful of the spectacular rock formations and oddly shaped Joshua trees. Stop at one of the well-marked interpretive trails along the way (see "Day Hikes," below), but don't miss the detour to **Keys View,** the most visited spot in the park. A paved road leads to this mile-high mountain crest, where a series of plaques describe the land below and a panoramic view that encompasses both the highest (Mt. San Gorgonio) and the lowest (Salton Sea) points in Southern California.

Pinto Basin Road bisects the park from top to bottom, forking away from Park Boulevard near the North Entrance Station and winding down to the Cottonwood Entrance off I-10. Driving it, you'll pass from the higher Mojave Desert into the lower Colorado Desert, across the "Transition Zone" snaking through the middle of the park; it's a fascinating melting pot where the two climates are both represented. Stop to marvel at the Cholla Cactus Garden (see "Day Hikes," below) or the Ocotillo Patch, where this spidery, tenacious desert shrub sports flaming red blooms following spring rains. At the park's southern end you can explore the lush Cottonwood Spring or see relics of World War II training maneuvers (see "Historic & Man-Made Attractions," below). Driving from end to end takes between 45 and 60 minutes.

Organized Tours & Ranger Programs

A multitude of ranger-led seminars and guided hikes are offered. They include such topics as Photographing the Boulders, Birding for Beginners, Stars Over Joshua Tree (evening), and Wildlife Walk, as well as guided hikes on many of the park's popular trails. Throughout the wildflower blooming season, and especially during Easter week, special walks visit the most abundantly flowering areas.

The Park Service also conducts guided tours of the historic **Desert Queen Ranch** (see below). From approximately November to May, tours are given several times daily. Contact the visitor center for a seasonal schedule; tours are given much less frequently during the hot summer. Plan to arrive early, as these events are popular and groups are limited to 20.

Historic & Man-Made Attractions

Miners and ranchers began coming in the 1860s, including the McHaney brothers, who established the **Desert Queen Ranch.** It was later acquired by former Rough Rider Bill Keys, who lived there until his death in 1969. Though many of the ranch structures are now decrepit and overgrown, it's compelling to see how one hardy family made a home in the unforgiving desert. Admittance is limited to official Park Service tours (see above).

You can find petroglyphs near **Barker Dam,** where an easy 1.1-mile loop hiking trail leads to a small artificial lake framed by the Wonderland of Rocks. After scrambling a bit to get atop the dam, you'll find a sandy path leading to the "Disneyland Petroglyph" site. Its wry name stems from the fact that a movie crew once retraced the ancient rock carvings to make them more visible to the camera, thus defacing them forever. If you investigate the cliffs along the remainder of the trail, however, you're likely to find some untouched drawings depicting animals, humans, and other aspects of desert life as interpreted by long-ago dwellers. You'll see additional petroglyphs along the 18-mile **Geology Tour Road,** a sandy and lumpy dirt road accessible only by four-wheel-drive vehicles or hardy mountain bikers.

During World War II, George S. Patton trained over a million soldiers in desert combat at several sites throughout the Mojave and Colorado deserts. Tank tracks are still visible in the wilderness around the former Camp Young, near Cottonwood Springs. The **Camp Young Memorial** marker is 1 mile east of Cottonwood Springs Road, just before the park entrance; an informational kiosk there gives details of the training maneuvers and daily camp life. To learn more, you can visit the **General Patton Memorial Museum** (☎ 760/227-3483) in Chiriaco Summit, on I-10 about 5 miles east of the Cottonwood Entrance. The museum contains an assortment of memorabilia from World War II and other military glory days, as well as displays of tanks and artillery; it's open daily from 9am to 4:30pm (except Thanksgiving and Christmas).

Day Hikes

The good news about Joshua Tree: Its natural wonders are accessible to everyone, not just to the extreme outdoor adventurer. Nowhere is this more apparent than in the diversity of hiking and nature trails, which range from a 0.5-mile paved nature trail (ideal for even strollers and wheelchairs) to trails of 15-plus miles requiring strenuous hiking and backcountry camping.

SHORTER TRAILS

Barker Dam Nature Trail

1.1 mi. RT. Easy. Access: Barker Dam parking area.

This sandy path leads to a small lake—formed in a natural rock basin by an artificial dam—a relic of the ranchers who used such "tanks" to water their stock. Signs along the way describe some of the plant and animal life found here, including migratory wildfowl who use this as a watering hole on their journeys. After scrambling up the dam, you'll come to some petroglyph sites (see "Historic & Man-Made Attractions," above).

Cap Rock Nature Trail

0.4 mi. RT. Easy (paved). Access: Cap Rock parking area.

Climbers gather here, and they're as interesting to watch as the short, informative trail leading from the parking lot. In between identifying different desert plants along the path, test your footing on some of the rocks to get a feel for the climbing experience.

Cholla Cactus Garden Nature Trail

0.25 mi. RT. Easy. Access: Middle of the park, about halfway between the north and south entrances.

This trail winds through an unusually dense concentration of Bigelow cholla, one of the desert's more fascinating residents. Often called "teddy bear cactus" for its deceptively fluffy appearance, cholla is also nicknamed "jumping cactus" for the ease with which its barbed spines stick to the clothing and skin of anyone who passes too close. Any ranger can tell you horror stories of people who've tripped into a cholla bush and emerged porcupinelike and suffering—but please don't let that stop you from enjoying this pretty roadside diversion.

Cottonwood Springs Nature Trail

2 mi. RT. Easy. Access: Cottonwood Campground.

The trail leads through rolling desert hills long inhabited by Cahuilla Indians. Signs along the way relate how they used native plants in their everyday lives; the trail culminates at lush Cottonwood Springs. The prolific underground water source supports thick groves of cottonwood and palm trees, plus the birds and animals who make them home.

Desert Queen Mine

1.5 mi. RT. Easy to moderate. Access: Reached via a dirt road leading from Park Blvd., opposite the Geology Tour Rd.

The "trail" meanders and forks through the ruins of a gold mine that yielded several million dollars' worth of ore between 1895 and 1961. Building ruins, steel machinery parts, and sealed mine shafts dot the hillsides and ravine; there's a signboard at the overlook with more information about mine operations.

Fortynine Palms Oasis

3 mi. RT. Strenuous. Access: End of Canyon Rd. in Twentynine Palms (outside the park, down Canyon Rd.).

This hike begins with a steep harsh ascent to a ridge fringed with red-spined barrel cacti. Down the other side, a rocky canyon contains the spectacular oasis whose fan palm and cottonwood tree canopy shades clear pools of green water. Plants, birds, and other wildlife are abundant in this miniature ecosystem, and the scorched trunks of trees bear witness to past fires that have nourished rather than destroyed the life here. Beware of rattlesnakes in the shaded brush around the oasis.

Hidden Valley Nature Trail

1 mi. loop RT. Easy. Access: A paved spur near the Hidden Valley picnic area.

This trail is fun for kids and adults who like rock climbing and intrigue. You can see sport climbers surrounding the small valley, which is reputed to have been a hideout for 19th-century cattle rustlers. Signs posted along the trail talk about the area's geology and history. The trail is relatively level, though there's some easy boulder scrambling along the route.

High View Nature Trail

1.3 mi. RT. Moderate. Access: Dirt rd. turnoff immediately before the entrance to Black Rock Campground at the northwestern edge of the park.

This well-maintained and popular trail involves a steady, moderately steep climb to one of Joshua Tree's many spectacular vistas. Alternately rocky and sandy, the trail is marked by numbered signposts keyed to a leaflet often unavailable at the Black Rock Ranger Station. Benches are found at intervals and also at the summit.

Oasis of Mara Nature Trail

0.5 mi. RT. Easy (paved). Access: Behind the Oasis Visitor Center.

Leading into a miniature ecosystem of palm trees, small ponds, and abundant animal life, this supereasy path is lined with interpretive signs. It's a great place to start your first visit to Joshua Tree and an excellent introduction to the centuries of human inhabitants who used the oasis to sustain life.

Pine City

3 mi. RT. Easy. Access: Begin at the same trailhead for Desert Queen Mine.

This path takes you to a cluster of boulder formations and sandy washes. Piñons thrive in the moisture provided by these natural drainage courses—the tree was exploited for food (pine nuts) by early inhabitants. Today birds gather in the trees and bighorn sheep are occasionally found among the rocks.

Ryan Mountain

3 mi. RT. Strenuous. Access: A marked parking area along Park Blvd.

A constant, steep climb (almost 1,000 ft.) leads to the best panoramic views in the park, encompassing snowcapped mountain peaks, broad tree-dotted valleys, and dark volcanic mounds. Ascending through a juniper and piñon pine woodland, the trail is mostly rocky, well

maintained, and easy to follow—you'll likely spot rock climbers to the west of the mountain.

Skull Rock Nature Trail

1.7 mi. RT. Easy. Access: Jumbo Rocks Campground (Loop E).

Leading to another unusually anthropomorphic rock formation, the trail meanders through boulders, desert washes, and a rocky alleyway. Watch for the "ducks" (small stacks of rocks) that mark the pathway.

LONGER TRAILS

Boy Scout Trail

16 mi. RT. Moderate. Access: Wonderland of Rocks backcountry board, 6.4 mi. east of the West Entrance Station.

From the trailhead, you progress downhill, through picturesque, sandy washes lined with oak and pine trees. Traveling through a variety of terrain, this trail can also be taken one way, either direction. The latter portion skirts a rocky mountainside, then finishes through open desert, ending up at the Indian Cove Ranger Station and backcountry board.

California Riding and Hiking Trail

35 mi. RT. Easy to strenuous. Access: There are 6 access points along the trail's path; your best bet is to consult with park rangers and obtain a topographical map to help you stay on track.

In general, it's easier to travel from west to east since the western sections are at higher elevations. Marked by distinctive brown posts stenciled with "CRH," the many miles of this statewide trail pass through distinct areas of the park, from piñon/juniper forests to flat, lower desert terrain. It takes 2 to 4 days to hike the trail in its entirety, but you can also hike it in sections ranging from 4.4 to 11 miles.

Lost Horse Mine

4 mi. RT. Moderate. Access: End of a dirt rd. leading from Keys View Rd., 2.5 mi. south of its junction with Park Blvd.

This trail leads to the ruins of the area's most successful mining operation. Well-preserved remnants include the steam engine that powered the machinery, a winch for lowering equipment into the mine, settling tanks, and stone building foundations. The trail, actually an old wagon road, winds up gradually through rolling hills; once there, you can take an additional short, steep hike to the hilltop behind the ruins for a fine view into the heart of the park. Hikers with children should keep a watchful eye around the mine ruins.

Lost Palms Oasis

7.5 mi. RT. Moderate. Access: Park at Cottonwood Spring, accessible by paved rd. just beyond the Cottonwood Campground.

This long trail leads through sandy washes and rolling hills to the oasis overlook, then a steep, rugged, and strenuous trail continues on to the canyon bottom. Whether or not you're up to the entire challenge, the beauty of birdsong and rustling palms echoing through the canyon make this a special hike. Lost Palms is the park's largest oasis; look closely for elusive bighorn sheep in the remote canyon bottom.

Other Sports & Activities

Biking. Because most of Joshua Tree National Park is designated wilderness, special care must be taken not to damage the fragile ecosystem. That means bicycles are restricted to roads, none of which have bike lanes. This effectively puts biking out of reach for most casual pedalers. If you're into mountain biking, though, and up to a challenge, there are miles of unpaved roads ripe for exploration. Distraction from cars is rare, particularly on four-wheel-drive roads like the 18-mile **Geology Tour Road,** which

begins 2 miles west of Jumbo Rocks. Dry lake beds contrast with towering boulders along this downhill, sandy and lumpy dirt road; you can stop to see a Joshua tree woodland, abandoned mines, and American Indian petroglyphs.

A short but rewarding ride starts at **Covington Flats,** accessible only by unpaved (two-wheel-drive OK) La Contentata Road in the town of Joshua Tree. From the picnic area, ride west to Eureka Peak, 4 miles away through lush high desert vegetation like extralarge Joshua trees, junipers, and piñons. The road is steep near the end, but your reward will be a panoramic view of Palm Springs to the south, the Morongo Basin to the north, and the jagged mountain ranges of the park in between. For other bike-friendly unpaved and four-wheel-drive roads, consult the park map available at all visitor centers. There are no bike rentals available in the park, so you'll have to bring your own.

Rock Climbing. During most of the year, visitors to the park can observe rock climbers scurrying up, down, and across the many geological formations in the northwestern quadrant. Joshua Tree is one of the sport's premier destinations, with more than 4,000 individually rated climbs.

Spectacular geological formations have irresistible names like **Wonderland of Rocks** and **Jumbo Rocks**—lovers of Stonehenge and Easter Island will delight in bizarre stacks with names like **Cap Rock** (for the single flat rock perched atop a haphazard pile) or **Skull Rock** (where the elements have worn an almost-human countenance into a boulder arrangement). But human hands had nothing to do with nature's sculptural artistry here; these fantastic formations are made of quartz monzonite, once a molten liquid forced upward that cooled before reaching the surface. Groundwater seeped in and fractured the rocks, and as floods eventually washed away the ground cover and

Especially for Kids

Joshua Tree National Park is a great place for the kids—they'll see unusual plants and animals, learning just enough to stimulate their imaginations but not so much they zone out. From identifying familiar everyday shapes in rock formations to investigating the mysterious "teddy bear" cactus, the possibilities are endless. Parents must exercise caution, with regard to the weather and other dangers. Bring plenty of water, sunscreen, and protective clothing for children, and keep a close eye (if not grip) on them at all times to avoid their straying into perilous desert terrain (prickly cacti, steep rocks, or abandoned mine shafts).

Start by taking the kids on a designated nature trail (listed in the free *Joshua Tree Guide* and indicated by roadside signs). The park's 11 nature trails have numerous plaques along the way to help your family interpret the rocks, plants, and other characteristics you'll see in the context of their geological history and significance to animal and human desert dwellers. They're all short (0.25- to 2-mi. loops) and relatively flat, making them ideal for most visitors. Two of these (**Oasis of Mara** and **Cap Rock**) are even paved and wheelchair-accessible.

The Park Service is eager for younger visitors to learn nature appreciation and conservation. Inside the complimentary *Joshua Tree Guide* are several "games" (thinly veiled educational activities) for kids, ranging from sketching rock formations and plants to quizzes on the park's facilities. If your youngster is interested enough to complete five of the activities, rangers at the Oasis Visitor Center will reward him or her with an official Junior Ranger badge.

exposed the monzonite, natural erosion wore away the weakened sections, creating the bizarre shapes and piles you see today. Climbers of every skill level travel here from around the world, drawn by the otherworldly splendor of rock piles worn smooth by the elements.

Hidden Valley is another good place to watch enthusiasts from as far away as Europe and Japan scaling sheer rock faces with impossible grace. Climbers sometimes practice bouldering—working on strength and agility on smaller boulders within jumping distance to the ground. You can try some bouldering to sample the high-friction quartz monzonite; even tennis shoes seem to grip the rock surface.

If you'd like to learn the sport of rock climbing from scratch, it's easier than you think. The folks at (aptly named) **First Ascent** (☎ 800/325-5462) have licensed, experienced climbing guides who'll orchestrate your entire excursion, starting with detailed instruction on rock-climbing basics. Later, the teacher will lead each climb, setting up ropes for belay and rappelling, then guiding students every step of the way. All-day excursions range from $85 per person in groups of three or larger, $105 each for two people, or $175 for private instruction. The Oregon-based climbing school operates from October to May, and the prices include all necessary gear except special climbing shoes, which you must rent for $6 per day.

Camping

There are nine developed campgrounds in the park, as well as backcountry camping in the wilderness areas. Regulations are stringent for backcountry camping, including mandatory registration at 1 of 12 boards (see the Park Service map for locations). There are no showers or laundry facilities. You can only make fires in the fire pits provided at each campsite.

At present, you can only make reservations at Black Rock Canyon and Indian Cove for individual sites. Call ☎ 800/365-CAMP. You can also make group camping reservations (sites accommodate from 10 to 70 people) at the same number. **Belle Campground,** located on Pinto Basin Road 9 miles south of Twentynine Palms, has chemical toilets. **Black Rock Canyon Campground** is in the northwest corner, at the head of the 35-mile California Riding and Hiking Trail (to reach it you have to leave the park boundaries), and is the most developed campground. There is also a visitor center here. **Cottonwood Campground** is in the southern portion of the park, near the Cottonwood Visitor Center. **Hidden Valley Campground,** located 14 miles south of Joshua Tree, California, is on the main park road. **Indian Cove** is just inside park boundaries west of Twentynine Palms; like at Black Rock, there are many hiking trails leading farther into Joshua Tree but no roads. **Jumbo Rocks Campground** is 11 miles south of Twentynine Palms on Utah Trace. **Ryan Campground,** 16 miles southeast of Joshua Tree, California, is reached via Park Boulevard. **Sheep Pass group camp,** a few miles east of Ryan Campground, has group sites only. **White Tank Campground** is 2 miles beyond the Belle Campground on Utah Trace.

Accommodations

Aside from camping, there are no overnight accommodations available within the boundaries of Joshua Tree National Park.

NEAR THE PARK

Best Western Gardens Motel

71487 Twentynine Palms Hwy., Twentynine Palms, CA 92277. ☎ **800/528-1234** or 760/367-9141. Fax 760/367-2584. 96 units. A/C TV TEL. $79–$95 double. Rates include continental breakfast. AE, DC, DISC, MC, V.

Located on the main highway at the western end of town, the Best Western Gardens might be a predictable representative of this motel chain, but it's also more reliable than many of the funky roadside places you'll pass. Kept sparkling clean and recently refurbished, the Best Western even has some one-bedroom efficiencies whose extra sleeping area and kitchenette are perfect for families. Many rooms have hot tubs, plus

Campground	Total Sites	RV Hookups	Dump Station	Toilets	Drinking Water
Belle	18	No	No	Yes	No
Black Rock Canyon	100	No	Yes	Yes	Yes
Cottonwood	62 individual, 3 group	No	Yes	Yes	Yes
Hidden Valley	39	No	No	Yes	No
Indian Cove	101 individual, 13 group	No	No	Yes	No
Jumbo Rocks	125	No	No	Yes	No
Ryan	31	No	No	Yes	No
Sheep Pass	No individual, 6 group	No	No	Yes	No
White Tank	15	No	No	Yes	No

* Reservations can be made (by mail) for group sites

the motel has a heated outdoor pool and whirlpool.

Joshua Tree Inn Bed & Breakfast

61259 Twentynine Palms Hwy., Joshua Tree, CA 92252. ☎ **800/366-1444** or 760/366-1188. Fax 760/366-3805. 12 units. A/C. $95–$150 double; $210 cottages. Rates include full breakfast. AE, DC, DISC, MC, V.

Not all local lore has to do with pioneering miners and ranchers—and one former motel, now a gracious B&B, boasts of a more recent rock 'n' roll history. Built in the 1950s, the Joshua Tree Inn has been the choice of the Rolling Stones, the Flying Burrito Brothers, and the cast of Saturday Night Live. The lobby is decorated with posters of folk singer/songwriter Gram Parsons, who died of a drug overdose here in 1973. Legends aside, the low-slung adobe-style inn and cottages are charming and near the West Entrance of Joshua Tree National Park, though set back far enough from the main highway to escape most of the traffic noise. Furnished in countrified florals and rustic antiques, all nine rooms have private baths, and many open onto a serene Japanese-style center courtyard. Full gourmet breakfast is served each morning, and the chef will also prepare

(advance arrangements required) box lunches for the outdoor adventurer. If you visit midweek or during summer, the inn is likely to discount rates—it never hurts to ask.

Mojave Rock Ranch

P.O. Box 552, Joshua Tree, CA 92252. ☎ **760/366-8445**. Fax 760/366-1996. www.mojaverockranch.com. 4 cabins. A/C TV TEL. $175–$250 cabin (1–4 guest occupancy). MC, V.

Proprietors Troy Williams and Gino Dreese built these one-of-a-kind cabins north of the town of Joshua Tree beginning in 1997, renovating a quartet of abandoned shacks into very different (and very isolated) accommodations. The decor is kitschy yet organic—African masks, light fixtures sculpted from rusted cans, Hollywood prints, and antique ranching implements somehow mesh into a tasteful whole. All of the cabins have enclosed pet areas with lavish doghouses, an outdoor "cowboy spa," and incredible views of the mountains and city lights below. Satellite stereo and kitchens stocked with all the necessities (except the food) add to the aura, which, in William's mind, is "really all about relaxation."

Showers	Fire Pits/ Grills	Laundry	Public Phone	Reserve	Fees	Open
No	Yes	No	No	No	No	Year-round
No	Yes	No	No	Yes	$10	Year-round
No	Yes	No	No	No*	$8–$25	Year-round
No	Yes	No	No	No	No	Year-round
No	Yes	No	No	Yes*	$10–$35	Year-round
No	Yes	No	No	No	No	Year-round
No	Yes	No	No	No	No	Year-round
No	Yes	No	No	No*	$25	Year-round
No	Yes	No	No	No	No	Year-round

Oasis of Eden

56377 Twentynine Palms Hwy., Yucca Valley, CA 92284. ☎ **760/365-6321**. Fax 760/ 365-9592. 52 units. A/C TV TEL. Feb–Apr $59–$180 double; May–Jan $59–$130 (higher costs are for "theme" rms). AE, DC, DISC, MC, V.

It may look like a plain motel on the outside, but the Oasis of Eden has surprises waiting behind its doors. If you think the name makes it sound like a good place for illicit liaisons, wait till you see one of the 13 "theme rooms," each with a whirlpool and VCR. The Oasis of Eden is a less-grand cousin to San Luis Obispo's famous Madonna Inn; here you can relive *The English Patient* in the white linen and khaki Safari Suite, revisit Caesar's Palace in the marble-pillared Roman Suite, or return to your club-wielding roots in the Cave Room; ask about their special romance packages. There are also 39 standard motel rooms, all with air-conditioning and some with kitchenettes. As motels go, this one's a cut above, offering 24-hour complimentary coffee and tea, a heated outdoor pool and spa, free local phone calls, and juice and breakfast breads at no extra charge.

29 Palms Inn

73950 Inn Ave., Twentynine Palms, CA 92277. ☎ **760/367-3505**. Fax 760/367-4425. www. 29palmsinn.com. E-mail: 29palmsinn@eee. org. 19 units. A/C TV. Sept–June $83–$115 double; July–Aug $60–$110 double. Midweek discounts sometimes apply. AE, DC, DISC, MC, V.

The closest you can stay to the Joshua Tree National Park entrance is the 29 Palms Inn. This rustic, family-run inn dates from the 1920s and consists of adobe cottages and old frame cabins scattered among 70 acres of the Oasis of Mara, the other side of which holds the main visitor center for the park. It has gradually been discovered by Hollywood celebrities in need of a low-key resort dedicated to the art of relaxation. The grounds are quite lovely, including lawns strolled by geese from the nearby pond and shaded by the namesake 29 original palms. Behind the simple pool is the inn's restaurant, one of the best in town (see "Dining," below). Included with the room is morning coffee and fresh-baked muffins around the pool patio. The cottages are all unique; most have a fireplace or wood stove and patio or deck, but all have evaporative coolers for the sweltering summer—the perfect time for stargazing. There's also a three-bedroom, two-bathroom guest house available at $185 ($165 low season).

Dining

There are no restaurants in the park.

NEAR THE PARK

You can't be anywhere in the Southwest without seeing a Mexican restaurant, and the Morongo Basin is no exception. While none can compare to true south-of-the-border authenticity, you'll find tasty, traditional fare like saucy enchiladas, bulging burritos, layered tostadas, and plenty of crispy chips and salsa. The locals favor **Edchada's,** 56805 Twentynine Palms Hwy. in Yucca Valley (☎ **760/ 365-7655**), so well that they recently opened up a second restaurant in 29 Palms, at 73502 Twentynine Palms Hwy. (☎ **760/367-2131**). Both Edchada's are open daily from 11am to 9pm and have a full cocktail bar; they take credit cards (AE, DISC, MC, V) and vegetarian dishes are available. Also in 29 Palms is **Ramona's,** 72115 Twentynine Palms Hwy. (☎ **760/367-1929**), a tiny family run place with vinyl tablecloths, piñatas, and its own local following. Ramona's serves beer and wine only and is open Monday to Saturday from 11am to 8:30pm; credit cards are accepted (DISC, MC, V).

Don's American BBQ

72183 Twentynine Palms Hwy., Twentynine Palms, 92277. ☎ **760/367-0301**. Sandwiches/burgers $3–$4; full dinners

$6–$23 (most under $15). AE, DISC, MC, V. Mon–Thurs 4–10pm, Fri–Sun noon–10pm. BARBECUE.

Local folks drive up from Palm Springs just to get down 'n' dirty here. The tempting smell of tangy barbecue spices wafts through town from the giant grill outside the front door of this tiny shack decorated with beer-logo and military-insignia mirrors. Say hello to the grill master on your way in, then seat yourself at a wooden picnic table and roll up your sleeves. Regular- and oversized steaks, beef and pork ribs, chicken, and seafood are available, as well as some "exotic" fare like buffalo, kangaroo, alligator, and rattlesnake; every meal comes with a Paul Bunyan–size baked potato. The overhead must be low, because the prices are too. Don's is a fun choice if you've built up a hearty appetite with a day of hiking or rock climbing.

29 Palms Inn

73950 Inn Ave., Twentynine Palms. ☎ **760/367-3505.** Reservations recommended for dinner. Lunch entrees under $6; full dinners $8–$15. AE, DC, DISC, MC, V. Daily 11am–2pm and 5–9pm (until 9:30pm Fri–Sat). AMERICAN.

This restaurant is tucked away behind its namesake hotel's postage stamp–size pool and consists of a paneled dining room whose long, wide, hospitable bar sports a vaguely nautical Polynesian theme. Meals here enjoy their own fame, separate from the hotel's, and deservedly so. Starting with fresh vegetables from the inn's garden (which flourishes in this fertile oasis) and quality meat, poultry, and fresh fish, the kitchen sends out simple meals accented with zesty condiment inventions (like their citrusy mustard/herb salad dressing). Lunch choices include fluffy quiche du jour, creamy soups, crunchy salads, and tostadas, plus a variety of hot and cold sandwiches—call ahead if you'd like to have a sack lunch prepared for a day in the park. Dinner is more robust, featuring grilled meats and fish, seafood sautéed in butter

and garlic, and whimsical specials like Cat Ballou Drunk Steak. The evening ambience is further enhanced by the white-plumed barn owls cavorting among the palm canopy. And the prices are very reasonable.

CAFES

Whether you crave the jolt of a cup of java or a fix of bohemian coffeehouse culture, you won't find the Morongo Basin lacking. In the heart of Twentynine Palms, **Casa de Java y Musica,** 73554 Twentynine Palms Hwy. (☎ **760/361-6169**), offers every imaginable variation on espresso, plus several pleasant indoor diversions—books, chess sets, and table tennis as well as live music, poetry readings, and performance art on Friday and Saturday nights. In addition to scattered comfy couches and armchairs, there's a shady back patio and a kid's room stocked with toys and games. They do not accept credit cards. Down the road in Joshua Tree is well-stocked **Jeremy's Cyber Cafe,** 61597 Twentynine Palms Hwy. (☎ **760/366-9799**), where coffee drinks are only the beginning. They've got more than 70 varieties of imported and domestic beers; teetotalers can choose from around 35 teas, including yogi herbal blends, fruit infusions, and traditional English black teas. Deli snacks and baked treats are here for the noshing, and Jeremy's can even whip up a Häagen-Dazs milkshake. Internet access is also available to patrons for a very reasonable 13¢ per minute. While inside walls boast a changing display of local art, the front windows are taped over with flyers, usually heralding live bands that play Friday and Saturday nights. They accept credit cards (MC, V).

Picnic & Camping Supplies

General Stores. If there's camping (or climbing or hiking) gear that you left behind or suddenly decide you need, visit **Benton Bros. Family Center,** 73544 Twentynine Palms Hwy., Twentynine

Palms (☎ 760/367-7814), a general store carrying a limited selection of gear, including boots, cookstoves and fuel, ice chests, and hiking socks and hats. Or check out the **Park Center,** 6554 Park Blvd., Joshua Tree (☎ 760/366-3448), near the west entrance to the park; in addition to gift items and work by local artisans, it carries a limited selection of common items like water bottles and clothing. A more comprehensive outfitter is 15 minutes away: **Jernigan's Sporting Goods,** 56867 Twentynine Palms Hwy., Yucca Valley (☎ 760/365-1828), is in a shopping mall behind Denny's and can help you with everything from tents and lanterns to serious climbing gear and a dozen brands of heavy-duty hiking boots.

Serious Gear. Experienced climbers needing backpack or climbing equipment might want to step into **Nomad Ventures,** 61795 Twentynine Palms Hwy. (☎ 760/366-4684), an outfitter conveniently located on the way to the park's West Entrance. Open daily, it rents and sells climbing shoes, and sells packs, harnesses, and other necessities of the sport.

Picnic Supplies. Need provisions for picnicking or camping? You can stock up on the way in Yucca Valley, where **Kmart, Wal-Mart, Von's,** and **Stater Brothers** loom large on Highway 62, along with every fast-food joint you can imagine. Once you're in Twentynine Palms, though, try the **Plaza Market** (☎ 760/367-3464), across from the chamber of commerce in the Historic Plaza on the northwest corner of Adobe and Two Mile roads. This friendly local market is convenient to the park's North Entrance. A good place to pick up sandwiches, salads, and other prepared lunch foods (including tempting brownies, muffins, and baked treats) is the **Finicky Coyote,** 73511 Twentynine Palms Hwy. (☎ 760/367-2429), a downtown coffeehouse, deli, and gourmet food emporium popular among locals as a community hangout and purveyor of ultrarich fudge and truffles. You might also try the **Park Center** in the town of Joshua Tree. In addition to being the visitor center for the West Entrance Station, the Park Center has a deli/bakery/coffee bar ready to pack up easy lunchables.

23

LASSEN VOLCANIC NATIONAL PARK

by Eric Peterson

STASHED IN THE FAR NORTHEASTERN CORNER OF CALIFORNIA, LASSEN Volcanic National Park is a remarkable reminder that North America is still forming and that the ground below is alive with the forces of creation and sometimes destruction. Lassen Peak

is near the southern end of the Cascade Mountain Range, which includes a chain of volcanoes that stretches all the way north to British Columbia.

Though it's dormant, 10,457-foot Lassen Peak is still very much alive. It last awakened in May 1914, beginning a cycle of eruptions that spit lava, steam, and ash until 1921. The eruption climaxed in 1915 when Lassen blew its top, sending up a 6-mile-high mushroom cloud of ash that was seen from hundreds of miles away. The peak itself has been dormant for more than three quarters of a century, but the park's geothermal features still boil with ferocious intensity; hot springs, fumaroles, and mud pots are all still very active to this day. Volcanologists, however, cannot predict when (or if) Lassen or any of the volcanoes in the area will erupt again.

Until then, the park gives you an interesting chance to watch a landscape recover from the massive destruction brought on by an eruption. To the north of Lassen Peak is the aptly named Devastated Area, a huge swath of volcanic

destruction steadily repopulating with conifer forests. Forest botanists have revised their earlier theories that forests must be preceded by herbaceous growth after watching the Devastated Area immediately revegetate with a diverse mix of eight conifer species, four more than were present before the blast.

The Lassen area was inhabited by four groups of American Indians before the arrival of Europeans. The Atsugewi, Maidu, Yana, and Yahi all used portions of the park as their summer hunting grounds. The white man's diseases and encroachment into their territory quickly decimated their population. By the turn of the 20th century, they were thought to be gone from the wilds of the Lassen area. In 1911, however, a nearly naked American Indian man was discovered by butchers at a slaughterhouse in Oroville. When they couldn't communicate with him, the sheriff locked the man in a cell.

News of the "Wild Man" found a receptive audience among anthropologists at the University of California at

Berkeley, who quickly rescued the man. Ishi, as he came to be known, turned out to be the last of the Yahi tribe and lived at the university's Museum of Anthropology for 5 years before succumbing to tuberculosis. Ishi, through sharing his knowledge with anthropologist Alfred Kroeber and others, is responsible for much of what's known about American Indian culture in California.

The 108,000-acre park is a place of great beauty. The flora and fauna are an interesting mix of species from the Cascade Range, stretching north from Lassen, and species from the Sierra Nevada, stretching south. The resulting blend accounts for an enormous diversity of plants: 715 distinct species have been identified in the park. Though it's snowbound in winter, Lassen is an important summer feeding ground for transient herds of mule deer and numerous black bears.

In addition to the volcano and all its geothermal features, Lassen Volcanic National Park includes miles of hiking trails, more than 50 beautiful lakes, large meadows, cinder cones, lush forests, cross-country skiing, and great backcountry camping. In fact, three quarters of the park is designated wilderness.

Avoiding the Crowds. Crowds? Forget it. Lassen is one of the least-visited national parks in the contiguous 48 states. Unless you're here on July 4 or Labor Day weekend, you won't encounter anything that could rightly be called a crowd. Even then you can escape simply by skipping the popular sites, like Bumpass Hell and the Sulphur Works, and heading a few miles down any of the backcountry trails.

Just the Facts

GETTING THERE & GATEWAYS

Part of the reason Lassen Volcanic National Park is one of the least visited national parks is its remoteness. The most foolproof route is to take Calif. 44 east from Redding (via I-5), which leads

directly to the northwest entrance to the park. A shortcut if you're coming from the south along I-5 is Calif. 36 in Red Bluff, which leads to the park's Southwest Entrance.

If you're arriving from the east via I-80, take the U.S. 395 turnoff at Reno and head to Susanville. Depending on which end of the park you're shooting for, take either Calif. 44 (to the northwest entrance) or Calif. 36 (to the southwest entrance) from Susanville.

Only one major road, Calif. 89 (the Park Road), crosses the park in a 29-mile half-circle with entrances and visitor centers at either end.

Most visitors enter the park at the **Southwest Entrance Station,** drive through the park, and leave through the North Entrance, or vice versa. Two other entrances lead to remote portions of the park. **Warner Valley** and **Juniper Lake** are reached from the south on the road from Chester. **Butte Lake** entrance is reached by a cutoff road from Calif. 44 between Calif. 89 and Susanville.

The Nearest Airport. The closest airport is **Redding Municipal Airport,** 6751 Airport Rd. (☎ 530/224-4331), serviced by **United Express** (see the appendix for the phone number).

INFORMATION

Contact the **Superintendent, Lassen Volcanic National Park,** P.O. Box 100, Mineral, CA 96063-0100 (☎ 530/595-4444; www.nps.gov/lavo). *Lassen National Park Guide* is a free, handy little newspaper listing activities, hikes, and points of interest. Also useful is Ellis Richard's *Story Behind the Scenery* (K.C. Dendoven Press, 1997), which provides a general orientation to the park as well as insight into its natural and human history; and Robert and Barbara Decker's *Road Guide to Lassen Volcanic National Park* (Decker Press, 1997), which gives a tour of Lassen Volcanic National Park from a motorist's viewpoint.

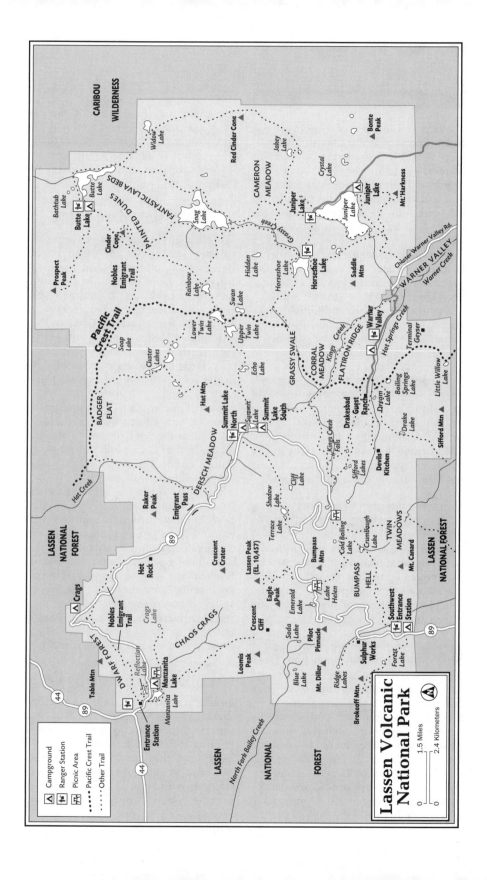

Lassen Volcanic
National Park

Legend
- △ Campground
- ⛺ Ranger Station
- ⛱ Picnic Area
- ⋯⋯⋯ Pacific Crest Trail
- ········ Other Trail

CARIBOU WILDERNESS

LASSEN NATIONAL FOREST

LASSEN NATIONAL FOREST

LASSEN NATIONAL FOREST

DWARF FOREST

Bonte Peak

Mt. Harkness

WARNER VALLEY

Chester Warner Valley Rd.

Warner Creek

Widow Lake

Red Cinder Cone

CAMERON MEADOW

Crystal Lake

Jakey Lake

Juniper Lake

Saddle Mtn

Hot Springs Creek

Terminal Geyser

Little Willow Lake

Boiling Springs Lake

Sifford Mtn

Drake Lake

Dream Lake

Guest Ranch

Drakesbad

Devils Kitchen

Warner Valley

Bathtub Lake

Butte Lake

Cinder Cone

Prospect Peak

Nobles Emigrant Trail

PAINTED DUNES

FANTASTIC LAVA BEDS

Snag Lake

Hidden Lake

Grassy Creek

Horseshoe Lake

Horseshoe Lake

Pacific Crest Trail

BADGER FLAT

Rainbow Lake

Swan Lake

Lower Twin Lake

Upper Twin Lake

Soap Lake

Cluster Lakes

GRASSY SWALE

CORRAL MEADOW

FLATIRON RIDGE

Kings Creek

Echo Lake

Hat Creek

Hat Mtn

Summit Lake North

Summit Lake

Summit Lake South

DERSCH MEADOW

Kings Creek Falls

Sifford Lakes

Raker Peak

Emigrant Pass

Cliff Lake

Shadow Lake

Cold Boiling Lake

Crumbaugh Lake

TWIN MEADOWS

Mt. Canard

Hot Rock

Crescent Crater

Lassen Peak (EL. 10,457)

Terrace Lake

Bumpass Mtn

Lake Helen

BUMPASS HELL

Eagle Peak

Emerald Lake

Crescent Cliff

Soda Lake

Pilot Pinnacle

Sulphur Works

Forest Lake

Southwest Entrance Station

Crags

Crags Lake

CHAOS CRAGS

Nobles Emigrant Trail

Loomis Peak

Reflection Lake

Manzanita Lake

Table Mtn

Manzanita Lake

Blue Lake

Mt. Diller

Ridge Lakes

Brokeoff Mtn

North Fork Bailey Creek

LASSEN NATIONAL FOREST

Entrance Station

0 — 1.5 Miles

0 — 2.4 Kilometers

VISITOR CENTERS

The largest visitor center is just inside the **North Entrance** at the Loomis Museum; there is also the **Southwest Information Station,** just inside the Southwest Entrance. Both are open daily from late May to late September, and provide the full spectrum of interpretive displays, ranger-led walks, and informational leaflets.

The **park headquarters** in Mineral, located on Calif. 36, southwest of the park, offers information and publications Monday to Friday (except holidays) year-round. There are additional ranger stations at Summit Lake, and also in the more isolated reaches of the park in the Warner Valley and at Butte Lake.

FEES & PERMITS

Entry into the park for up to a week costs $10 per vehicle or $5 per person on foot or bike. Camping fees range from $8 to $14. Anyone spending the night in the backcountry must have a wilderness permit issued free at the ranger stations.

SPECIAL REGULATIONS & WARNINGS

Because of the dangers posed by the park's thermal features, rangers ask that you remain on trails in active areas. Fires are allowed in campgrounds only. And don't forget to bring plenty of water, sunscreen, and warm clothing.

SEASONS & CLIMATE

The park is in one of the coldest places in California. Winter begins in late October and doesn't release its grip until June. Even in summer, you should be prepared for the possibility of rain and snow. Temperatures at night can drop below freezing at any time. Winter, however, shows a different and beautiful side of Lassen that more people are starting to appreciate. Since most of the park is over a mile high and the highest point is 10,457 feet, snow accumulates in incredible quantities (it's also a good thing to think about if you intend to stay in the area—some medical conditions can be affected by this high elevation). Don't be surprised to find snowbanks lining the Park Road into July.

If You Only Have 1 Day

The highlight of Lassen is, of course, the **volcano** and all its offshoots: boiling springs, fumaroles, mud pots, and so on. You can see many of the most interesting sites in a day, making it possible to visit Lassen as a short detour from I-5 or U.S. 395 on the way to or from Oregon.

Bumpass Hell, a 1.5-mile walk off the Park Road in the southern part of the park, is the largest single geothermal site in the park—16 acres of bubbling mud pots cloaked in a stench of rotten egg–smelling sulfur. The name comes from an early Lassen traveler, Bumpass, who lost a leg after he took a shortcut through the area while hunting and plunged into a boiling pool. Don't make the same error.

Sulphur Works is another stinky, steamy example of Lassen's residual heat. Two miles from the southwest park entrance, the ground hisses with seething gases escaping from the ground.

Boiling Springs Lake and **Devil's Kitchen** are two of the more remote geothermal sites; they're in the Warner Valley section of the park, which you can reach by hiking from the main road or entering the park through Warner Valley Road from the small town of Chester.

Exploring the Park by Car

Only one major road, **Calif. 89** (the Park Road), crosses the park in a half-circle with entrances and visitor stations at either end, and it is usually open from early June through much of October. Most visitors enter the park at the Southwest Entrance Station, drive through the park, and leave through the Northwest Entrance, or vice versa.

The 29-mile tour through this rugged yet captivating region should take no more than a few hours, though it's a good idea to factor in a few more hours to venture up Lassen Peak and explore the largest single geothermal site in the park, Bumpass Hell. If there's still time left, make an effort to stop at Sulphur Works near Mineral (about 2 miles from the southwest entrance), an acrid, noisy cauldron of steam vents that let off a mighty pungent odor.

Organized Tours & Ranger Programs

Free interpretive programs are offered daily in summer, highlighting everything from flora and fauna to geologic history and volcanic processes.

From January to March, a park ranger leads free 1.5- to 2-hour ecoadventure snowshoe hikes across Lassen's snow-packed hills. The tours take place on Saturday afternoon at 1:30pm at the Lassen Chalet, located at the park's southwest entrance. You must be at least 8 years old, warmly dressed, and wearing boots. Snowshoes are provided free of charge on a first-come, first-served basis, though a $1 donation is requested for upkeep. For more details, call park headquarters at ☎ **530/595-4444**, ext. 5133.

Day Hikes

Most Lassen visitors drive through in a day or two, see the geothermal hot spots, and move on. That leaves 150 miles of trails and expanses of backcountry to the few who take the time to get off-road.

Bumpass Hell Trail

1.5 mi. one way. Easy. Access: The well-marked trailhead is just off the Park Rd. in the southern part of the park.

This walk leads you to the middle of the largest geothermal site in the park—16 acres of bubbling mud pots cloaked in a stench of sulfur. Stay on the wooden boardwalks that safely guide you past the pyrite pools, steam vents, and noisy fumaroles.

Cinder Cone Trail

4 mi. RT. Moderate. Access: Butte Lake Campground.

If 4 miles seems too short, you can extend this hike (and shorten the drive) by walking in about 8 miles from Summit Lake on the Park Road. Black and charred, Cinder Cone is bare of any sort of life and surrounded by dunes of multihued volcanic ash.

Lassen Peak Trail

2.5 mi. one way. Moderate. Access: 7 mi. from the Southwest Entrance on the Park Rd.

This is probably the most popular hike in the park, a climb to the top of the peak. The trail may sound short, but it's steep and generally covered with snow until late summer. At 10,457 feet in elevation, though, you'll get a view of the surrounding wilderness that's worth every step of the way. On clear days you can see south all the way to Sutter Buttes near Yuba City and north into the Cascades. The round-trip takes about 4 to 5 hours.

Manzanita Lake Trail

1.5 mi. RT. Easy. Access: Northwest Entrance Station.

This trek runs along the shoreline of pretty Manzanita Lake, which is at the Northwest Entrance to the park. It's easy to get to by car, and an easy hike for almost anyone. (If you want to do a bit more distance, you can hike around Reflection Lake as well.)

Nobles Emigrant Trail

10 mi. RT. Easy. Access: northwest entrance.

One of the park's easiest longer hikes is this scenic trail that passes though an old-growth forest, past Choas Crags (pink-hued rocks from an old weathered volcano), and into Lassen's Dwarf Forest, a bizarre region of stunted trees.

Pacific Crest Trail

17 mi. one way. Moderate. Access: Via the Warner Valley Rd. or by a long hike from Hat Lake.

The most interesting section of the trail for hikers who aren't trying to hike all the way through the park is the 5-mile segment south of Drakesbad that leads toward the park's boundary via Boiling Springs Lake.

Paradise Meadow

3.5 mi. RT. Moderate. Access: Hat Lake parking area, off Calif. 89 between Emigrant Pass and the Summit Lake Campgrounds.

This hike rises at a steady grade along a creek, eventually coming to a series of small waterfalls and a postcard-perfect meadow with outstanding wildflower displays during midsummer.

Summit Lake Trail

1.5 mi. RT. Easy. Access: Accessible from either Summit Lake Campground.

This is another walk around a pristine alpine lake that's often frequented by deer in the evening.

Summit Lake Trailhead

8 mi. RT. Moderate. Access: The longer version of the trail breaks off from the midpoint of the Summit Lake Trail (described above).

A popular day hike for campers at Summit Lake, this trek passes a myriad of lakes and wildflower-filled meadows on the way to Lower Twin Lake. After you pass the first moderately steep crest, the rest of the hike is less strenuous.

Other Summer Sports & Activities

Biking. No mountain biking is allowed in Lassen. However, road bikers can test their stamina by tackling Lassen Volcanic National Park's Metric Century (100km/ 62 miles). Starting at the Lassen Chalet, you'll tour through beautiful wood countryside with occasional views of Lassen Peak. In the first 10 miles you'll climb almost 2,000 feet to crest the 8,512-foot summit. Eventually you'll reach

Campground	Elev.	Total Sites	RV Hookups	Dump Station	Toilets
Butte Lake	6,100	48	No	No	Yes
Crags	5,700	45	No	No	Yes
*Juniper Lake***	6,792	18	No	No	Yes
Manzanita Lake	5,890	179	No	Yes	Yes
Southwest	6,700	21	No	No	Yes
Summit Lake (North)	6,695	46	No	No	Yes
Summit Lake (South)	6,695	48	No	No	No
Warner Valley	5,650	18	No	No	Yes

  * Campgrounds usually open in June or July and close in September, but weather can affect these dates; call park headquarters for actual dates.

 ** Not recommended for trailers since approach is via a dirt road.

Manzanita Lake, a good place to rest because from here you have to climb almost 3,000 feet back up to the Park Road summit before you can coast back to the chalet and your car.

Canoeing & Kayaking. Paddlers can take canoes, rowboats, and kayaks on any of the park lakes except Reflection, Emerald, Helen, and Boiling Springs. Motors, including electric motors, are strictly prohibited on all park waters. Lakes accessible from the Park Road include Manzanita and Summit. You can get to Butte Lake in the northeast section of the park on a gravel road from Calif. 44. Juniper Lake can be reached from a gravel road in the southeast section of the park.

Winter Sports & Activities

Cross-Country Skiing. The park road usually closes to cars in November due to snow, and most years it doesn't open until June, so cross-country skiers have their run of the area. Snowmobiles are forbidden. Trails of all skill levels leave from Manzanita Lake at the north end of the park and Lassen Chalet at the south. There are heated bathrooms and

running water at the chalet. Popular trips are the trails to Sulphur Works. More advanced skiers can make the trek to Lake Helen.

You can also ski the popular 30-mile course of the Park Road in an overnight trek, but doing this involves a long car shuttle. For safety reasons, the park requires all skiers to register at the ranger stations before heading into the backcountry whether for an overnight or just the day.

Sledding. During winter, heavy snows close Calif. 89 (the Park Road), but the Southwest Entrance is kept open up to the chalet. On weekends, you can bring snow toys, kids, and picnic baskets and enjoy the gentle slopes in the area.

Camping

Car campers have their choice of eight park campgrounds with 423 sites total. There's no reservation system except group campgrounds. Sites do fill up on weekends, so your best bet is to get to the park early Friday to secure a spot. If the park is packed, myriad campgrounds are available in surrounding Lassen National

Drinking Water	Showers	Fire Pits/ Grills	Laundry	Public Phone	Reserve	Fees	Open
No	No	Yes	No	No	No	$10	June–Sept*
Yes	No	Yes	No	No	No	$8	June–Sept*
No	No	Yes	No	No	No	$8	June–Sept*
Yes	Yes	Yes	No	Yes	No	$14	June–Sept*
Yes	No	Yes	No	No	No	$10	June–Sept*
Yes	No	Yes	No	No	No	$12	June–Sept
Yes	No	Yes	No	No	No	$10	June–Sept
Yes	No	Yes	No	No	No	$10	June–Sept

Forest, so you'll find a site somewhere. There are no RV hookups at the park, but you'll find them at nearby private campgrounds, as well as Adam's Hat Creek Resort (see "Accommodations," below).

For information on how to make group camping reservations, call ☎ 530/595-4444, ext. 5155.

By far the most "civilized" camp-ground in the park is at **Manzanita Lake,** where you'll find flush toilets and a camper store. There is also the **Crags Campground,** about 5 miles away, which is much more basic, with vault toilets. Farther in the park along Calif. 89 are the **Summit Lake Campgrounds,** on the north and south ends of Summit Lake, where you'll find flush toilets (in the north campground only). It's a pretty spot, often frequented by deer, and is a launching point for some excellent day hikes. In the southern end of the park you'll find **Southwest Campground,** a walk-in camp directly adjacent to the Lassen Chalet parking lot.

The remote entrances to Lassen have their own campgrounds: **Warner Valley, Butte Lake,** and **Juniper Lake** camp-grounds. All three are reached via dirt roads, and Warner Valley and Juniper Lake are not recommended for trailers.

Backcountry camping is allowed almost everywhere, and traffic is light. Ask about closed areas when you get your wilderness permit, which is issued at the visitor stations for free and required for anyone spending the night in the back-country.

Accommodations

INSIDE THE PARK

Drakesbad Guest Ranch

At the end of the Warner Valley Rd. from Chester, in the southern part of the park. (California Guest Services, 2150 N. Main St., Suite 5, Red Bluff, CA 96080.) ☎ **530/529-9820** or 530/529-1512. E-mail: msilvalane@ snowcrest.net. 19 units. $215–$245 double. Rates include all meals. DISC, MC, V. Open 1st week June to mid-Oct, weather permitting.

The only lodge operating in Lassen Park is Drakesbad, hidden in a high mountain valley and surrounded by meadows, lakes, and streams. The 100-year-old Drakesbad is famous for its rustic cabins, lodge, and steaming thermal swimming pool, fed by a natural hot spring and open 24 hours. The horseback riding and stables are also a big draw. The place is as deluxe as only a place with very little electricity and no phones can be, with rustic quilts on every bed and kerosene lamps to read by. Full meal service is available and very good sack lunches are available. Since the lodge is extremely popular and open only for 5 months, reservations are booked as far as 2 years in advance (February is a good time to call to take advantage of cancellations).

NEAR THE PARK

The Bidwell House

1 Main St., P.O. Box 1790, Chester, CA 96020. ☎ **530/258-3338.** www.bidwellhouse.com. E-mail: bidwellhouse@thegrid.net. 14 units (12 with bathroom), 1 cottage. $75 double without bathroom, $95–$150 double with bathroom; $153 cottage for 6. Rates include full break-fast. MC, V.

In 1901, Gen. John Bidwell, a California senator who made three unsuccessful bids for the presidency, built a country retreat and summer home for his beloved young wife, Annie. After her death, when Chester had developed into a prosperous logging hamlet, the build-ing, with its farmhouse-style design and spacious veranda, was converted into the headquarters for a local ranch.

Today, the house sits at the extreme eastern end of Chester, adjacent to a rolling meadow. The lake is visible across the road, and inside, Ian and Kim James maintain one of the most charming B&B inns in the region. Seven of the rooms have Jacuzzi tubs, and three offer wood-burning stoves; the cottage comes with a kitchenette. Breakfast incorporates many gourmet omelettes. Dinner is served Thursday to Saturday.

Hat Creek Resort

On Calif. 89, P.O. Box 73, Old Station, CA 96071. ☎ **530/335-7121.** E-mail: hatcreekresort@juno.com. 17 units. $55–$95 double. AE, MC, V. Motel open year-round; cabins open May–Oct.

A haven for hunters and fishers (many of whom make their reservations years in advance), this small resort, 11 miles northeast of Lassen Volcanic National Park, features small housekeeping cabins and motel rooms situated alongside Hat Creek. The cabins come with kitchens where you can cook your catch. Otherwise, your main dining options are two nearby restaurants: Uncle Runt's Place and Indian John's Café. Also in the resort is an RV area with full hookups and accommodations for horses.

Lassen Mineral Lodge

On Calif. 36, P.O. Box 160, Mineral, CA 96063. ☎ **530/595-4422.** www.minerallodge.com. E-mail: cr72@snowcrest.net. 20 units. Summer and holidays $65–$95 double; winter $49 double. AE, DISC, MC, V.

A mere 9 miles south of the park's southern entrance, the Lassen Mineral Lodge offers motel-style rooms in a forested setting. In summer, the lodge is almost always bustling with guests and customers who venture into the gift shop, ski shop, general store, and full-service restaurant and bar. Also nearby is a tennis court, available during the summer. For families, this is probably the best option in the Lassen area.

Mill Creek Resort

On Calif. 172 (3 mi. south of Calif. 36), Mill Creek, CA 96061. ☎ **530/595-4449.** 9 cabins. $50–$70 cabin. No credit cards. Pets accepted.

Set deep in the forest, the Mill Creek is that rustic mountain retreat you've always dreamed of. A homey country general store and coffee shop serve as the resort's center, a good place to stock up on food while exploring Lassen Volcanic National Park. The housekeeping cabins, available on a daily or weekly basis, are clean, cute, and furnished with rustic wooden lodgepole beds. All of the cabins house kitchens (a good thing, since restaurants are scarce in this region).

The Weston House

2 mi. south of Calif. 44 off of Shingletown Ridge Rd. (19 mi. west of Lassen's northwest entrance), P.O. Box 276, Shingletown, CA 96088. ☎ **530/258-3382.** 5 units (2 share a bathroom). $85–$145 double. Rates include full breakfast. MC, V.

The only place to stay between Redding and the park's northwest entrance, The Weston House derives its namesake from its builder, the grandson of famed nature photographer Edward Weston. Sumptuous views of the upper Sacramento Valley abound at this out-of-the-way B&B, from each room as well as from an enchanting redwood deck that features a lap pool and Jacuzzi. The gourmet breakfast menu includes frittatas on some days, croissant French toast on others, but is always accompanied by fresh fruit and coffee. The suite has a sitting room with a wet bar, television, and VCR. Above it is Helen's Room, a small room with a kitchenette and a balcony with views of the breathtaking scenery and the inn's meticulously maintained perennial gardens.

Dining

INSIDE THE PARK

The only restaurant in the park (besides the Drakesbad Guest Ranch) is the **Chalet Food and Gifts** (☎ 530/595-3376), which serves inexpensive, basic breakfasts, and sandwiches and burgers for lunch. At the park's Southwest Entrance, it's open late May to mid-October, daily from 8am to 6pm (the grill usually closes at 4pm, however).

NEAR THE PARK

When you're this far into the wilderness, the question isn't *which* restaurant to choose, but *if* there is a restaurant. If bacon and eggs, sandwiches, steaks, chicken, burgers, pizza, and salads aren't part of your diet, you're in big trouble if you didn't pack your own grub. The best approach, is to either stay at a B&B or lodge that offers meals—such as the **Weston House, The Bidwell House,** or **Drakesbad Guest Ranch**—or at least provides a kitchen to cook your own, such as the **Hat Creek Resort** or **Mill Creek Resort.**

But if you're not staying at a lodge or B&B, deciding where you're going to eat depends mostly on whether you're on the north or south side of the park. Near the Northwest Entrance to the park in the town of Old Station (on Calif. 89; the town is small enough that street addresses aren't necessary) is **Uncle Runt's Place** (☎ 530/335-7177), which serves your standard steaks, chicken, burgers, sandwiches, and such for lunch and dinner, and **Indian John's Café** (☎ 530/335-7177), which serves basically the same

stuff as Uncle Runt's, as well as pizza and your standard American breakfast.

At the South Entrance, the closest restaurant is the **Lassen Mineral Lodge** (see "Accommodations," above) in the town of Mineral, which serves the usual uninspired mountain fare. A better bet is to head southeast along Calif. 36 to Chester and dine at the **St. Bernard Lodge,** which has one of the better restaurants in the Lassen region, and is open for breakfast, lunch, and dinner Thursday to Monday in summer and Friday to Monday in winter. For breakfast, try the large, fluffy pancakes with a side of honey ham. Top choice for dinner is steak with a side of fresh sweet corn.

Picnic & Camping Supplies

The **Manzanita Lake Camper Service Store** (☎ 530/335-7557), at the park's north entrance, is a good place to stock up on groceries and basic outdoor gear. At the southern end of the park, you'll find just about every outdoor toy you'd ever want at the **Lassen Mineral Lodge,** on Calif. 36 in Mineral (☎ 530/595-4422), including fishing and hunting supplies (this is big-time deer country) and the only cross-country ski rental in the area.

24

MESA VERDE, CANYON DE CHELLY, CHACO & OTHER ARCHAEOLOGICAL SITES OF THE FOUR CORNERS REGION

by Don and Barbara Laine

WITH MORE THAN 4,000 ARCHAEOLOGICAL SITES, MESA VERDE National Park is the largest archaeological preserve in the United States. Among the sites are some of the largest cliff dwellings in the world as well as mesa-top pueblos, pit houses, and kivas (subterranean rooms used for meetings and religious ceremonies)—all of which were built by the Ancestral Puebloans (also called the Anasazi). The sites here tell the story of a 1,000-year period (A.D. 300–1300) during which these people shifted from a semi-nomadic hunter-gatherer lifestyle to a largely agrarian way of life centered around large communities in cliff dwellings. To protect these archaeological treasures, Congress established Mesa Verde National Park in 1906.

Mesa Verde must have looked inviting to the Ancestral Puebloans, whose descendants are such modern Pueblo tribes as the Hopi, Zuni, and Acoma. On the mesa's north side, 2,000-foot-high cliffs form a natural barrier to invaders. The mesa slopes gently to the south, and erosion has carved numerous canyons, most of which receive abundant sunlight and have natural overhangs for shelter.

The Ancestral Puebloans became especially adept at surviving here. The mesa tops were covered with loess, a red, wind-blown soil good for farming. And while water was scarce, it could seep into the sandstone overhangs where they eventually made their homes. For food, they farmed beans, corn, and squash; raised turkeys; foraged in the piñon-juniper woodland; and hunted for game such as cottontail rabbits and deer. They wove sandals and clothing from yucca fibers, and traded for precious stones and shells, which they used to make jewelry.

To the visitor today, however, their most impressive accomplishments are the multistoried cliff dwellings, which had been largely ignored until they were discovered by two ranchers, Richard and Charles Wetherill, in the 1880s.

The **Cliff Palace,** the park's largest and best-known site, is a four-story apartment complex with stepped-back roofs forming porches for the dwellings above. Accessible by guided tour only, it is reached by a quarter-mile downhill path. Its towers, walls, and kivas are all set back beneath the rim of a cliff. Another ranger-led tour takes visitors up a 32-foot ladder to explore the interior of **Balcony House.** Each of these tours is given only in summer and into fall.

Two more important sites—**Step House** and **Long House,** both on Wetherill Mesa—can be visited in summer only. Rangers lead tours to **Spruce Tree House,** another of the major cliff-dwelling complexes, only in winter, when other park facilities are closed.

For reasons as yet not understood, these homes were only occupied for about a century; their residents left about 1300.

Although Mesa Verde is the largest and probably the most impressive archaeological site in the Four Corners region, it is not the only one. In fact, archeologists say that from about 700 to 1,000 years ago this area was teeming with busy communities, essentially the prehistoric equivalent of "Bos-Wash"—that mass of humanity that today inhabits the United States from Boston to Washington, D.C. Following the discussion of Mesa Verde is a quick look at some of the other important archaeological attractions in the region.

Mesa Verde National Park was rated the world's top monument in 1998 by readers of Condé Nast Traveller, but that same year it also made another list, giving it the worrisome distinction of being one of the National Trust for Historic Preservation's "Most Endangered Sites."

Avoiding the Crowds. With 650,000 visitors annually, Mesa Verde seems packed at times. But John Sheek, a district ranger, points out that the numbers are much lower just before and after the summer rush. "June 15th to August 15th is our high summer visitation period," he says. "If people can come the first 2 weeks of June or the last 2 weeks of August, they'll hit [fewer] crowds."

Another way to beat the crowds, says Sheek, is to make the 12-mile drive to Wetherill Mesa. In 1996, only 8% of the park's visitors—just over 50,000 people—ventured to the mesa, which has some of the park's most interesting archaeological sites. The third and perhaps best way to beat the crowds, according to Sheek, is to hike one of the backcountry trails. "With our backcountry closed to camping, our hiking trails aren't used very much," he says. "These are great ways for people to get away."

Just the Facts

GETTING THERE & GATEWAYS

Mesa Verde National Park is in southwestern Colorado, about 200 miles southwest of Denver and 252 miles northwest of Albuquerque. The park entrance is located on U.S. 160, 10 miles east of the town of Cortez and 6 miles west of Mancos,

From Cortez, U.S. 666 runs north to Monticello, Utah (and on to Salt Lake City), and south to Gallup, New Mexico (on I-40). U.S. 160 runs east through Durango to Walsenburg and I-25, and west through the Four Corners area into Arizona. Colo. 145, north to Telluride and Grand Junction, intersects U.S. 160 at the east end of town.

The Nearest Airport. Cortez Municipal Airport (☎ 970/565-7458), southwest of town off U.S. 666 and U.S. 160, is served by **United Express Airlines,** which offers daily service between Cortez and Denver; and has rental cars from **Budget** and

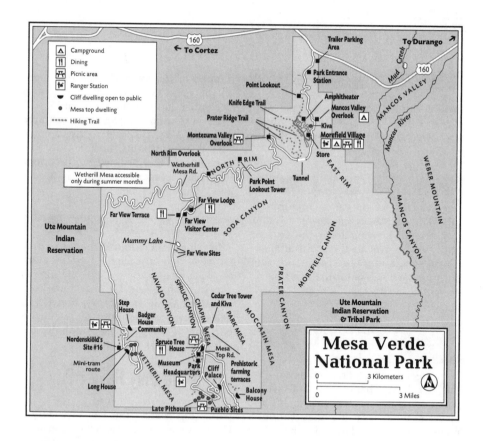

Map legend:
- ⛺ Campground
- 🍴 Dining
- 🎪 Picnic area
- 🚻 Ranger Station
- ▼ Cliff dwelling open to public
- ● Mesa top dwelling
- ••••• Hiking Trail

Map labels:
160 · ← To Cortez · To Durango · 160 · Trailer Parking Area · Mud Creek · MANCOS VALLEY · Park Entrance Station · Point Lookout · Amphitheater · Knife Edge Trail · Mancos Valley Overlook · Mancos River · Prater Ridge Trail · Kiva · Morefield Village · Montezuma Valley Overlook · WEBER MOUNTAIN · North Rim Overlook · Store · Wetherill Mesa Rd. · NORTH RIM · EAST RIM · Wetherill Mesa accessible only during summer months · Park Point Lookout Tower · Tunnel · MANCOS CANYON · Far View Lodge · Far View Terrace · Far View Visitor Center · SODA CANYON · Ute Mountain Indian Reservation · Mummy Lake · Far View Sites · MOREFIELD CANYON · PRATER CANYON · NAVAJO CANYON · SPRUCE CANYON · CHAPIN MESA · Cedar Tree Tower and Kiva · PARK MESA · MOCCASIN MESA · Ute Mountain Indian Reservation & Tribal Park · Step House · Badger House Community · Spruce Tree House · Mesa Top Rd. · Nordenskiöld's Site #16 · Museum · Park Headquarters · Cliff Palace · Prehistoric farming terraces · Mini-tram route · WETHERILL MESA · Long House · Balcony House · Late Pithouses · Pueblo Sites

Mesa Verde National Park

0 · 3 Kilometers
0 · 3 Miles

U-Save (☎ 970/565-9168). Toll-free reservations numbers are in the appendix.

INFORMATION

Contact **Mesa Verde National Park,** P.O. Box 8, Mesa Verde N.P., CO 81330 (☎ **970/529-4461;** www.nps.gov/meve). For advance information on the area, contact the **Mesa Verde Country Visitor Information Bureau,** P.O. Box HH, Cortez, CO 81321 (☎ **800/253-1616;** www.swcolo.org).

For more in-depth background, *The Story of Mesa Verde* (1980, Mesa Verde Museum Association) written by Gil Wenger, a former chief archaeologist at the park, summarizes the natural and human histories of this area, tracing developments in the Ancestral Puebloan culture. In *Indians of the Mesa Verde* (Mesa Verde Museum Association), author Don Watson attempts to re-create a year (1268) in the life of the Ancestral

Puebloans at Cliff Palace. These books and others are available from the **Mesa Verde Museum Association** (☎ **800/305-6053** or 970/529-4445).

VISITOR CENTERS

The **Far View Visitor Center,** 14 miles southwest of the Park entrance, is the only place that sells tickets for the ranger-guided hikes. There's an information desk, an impressive display of American Indian art, and a small bookstore. It's open only during the summer.

The staff at the small **Morefield Ranger Station** in Morefield Village also provide park information. It's open in summer only, usually during the afternoon and early evening.

The **Chapin Mesa Archaeological Museum** (open year-round) has dioramas and interpretive displays on Pueblo culture, a ranger-staffed information desk, and a bookstore.

FEES

Entry for up to 7 days costs $10 per vehicle, and there are also fees for guided tours (see "Organized Tours & Ranger Programs," below).

GETTING AROUND

The Park Service operates a **minitram** in the Wetherill Mesa area during the summer season. Leaving from the parking area, it takes you to the main archaeological sites, a real time-saver since your only other choice is to hike; cars aren't permitted in this area beyond the parking area.

SPECIAL REGULATIONS & WARNINGS

To protect the many archaeological sites, the Park Service has outlawed backcountry camping and off-trail hiking. It's also illegal to enter cliff dwellings without a ranger present. Similarly, all artifacts and archaeological sites are protected by federal law.

The Wetherill Mesa Road cannot accommodate vehicles longer than 25 feet. Cyclists must have lights to pedal through the tunnel on the entrance road.

SEASONS & CLIMATE

With an average annual precipitation of just 18 inches, Mesa Verde remains dry despite being between 6,000 feet and 8,572 feet high. June is the driest month, with .64 inches of rain, and August is the wettest, with 2.08 inches. The park typically receives 80 inches of snow in a season. Summer temperatures tend to be about 10° cooler than in the nearby Montezuma Valley. Even during July, the hottest month, highs average an easily bearable 87° and nighttime lows dip into the mid-50s. In winter, temperatures on the mesa can sometimes be 10° *warmer* than in the valley. This happens during calm, clear periods when cold air is trapped in the lowlands. Daytime highs on the mesa average in the low 40s in December, January, and February.

Because winter storms often continue well into March, spring tends to come late. Warm autumns, however, are not uncommon. In April, average temperatures are 5° cooler (60s for highs, 30s for lows) than in October.

SEASONAL EVENTS

Throughout the summer, American Indian artists demonstrate their crafts at various locations in the park. For 3 days in late July, Morefield Campground hosts the **Mesa Verde Indian Arts and Crafts Sales Show,** and in August, Hopi dancers perform at **Chapin Mesa Amphitheater.** Contact the park for exact dates.

If You Only Have 1 Day

If you have only a day to spend at the park, stop first at the Far View Visitor Center to buy tickets for a late-afternoon tour of either **Cliff House** or **Balcony House**—visitors are not allowed to tour both on the same day. Then travel to the **Chapin Mesa Museum** for a look at the history behind the sites you're about to see. From here, walk down the trail behind the museum to **Spruce Tree House.** Lunch at Spruce Tree Terrace, then take the **Mesa Top Loop Road.** Cap your day with the guided tour. If time permits, you may wish to stop at **Far View Sites** or the **Cedar Tree Tower** on your way out of the park.

Exploring the Park by Car

The main scenic drive in the park is the **Mesa Top Loop Road.** Each of the 10 stops along this 6-mile loop either overlooks cliff dwellings or is a short walk from mesa-top dwellings. The sites date from A.D. 675 to A.D. 1275 and include structures from the Basket Maker and three Pueblo periods. By reading the interpretive panels at each site, you can learn about the developments in architecture and the changes in Pueblo culture during those periods. Highlights include the **Square Tower House Viewpoint,** where binoculars are handy to hunt for some of the 60 cliff dwellings in this canyon; **Sun Point Pueblo,** where a tunnel links a kiva—a subterranean room used in ceremonies—to a lookout tower; and the mysterious **Sun Temple,** a D-shaped structure that may have been a shrine.

On your way back to the Far View Visitor Center, consider stopping at **Cedar Tree Tower,** the first right after the four-way stop. There, you'll find another tower connected to a kiva by a subterranean tunnel. Southwest of this tower is the trailhead to the **Farming Terrace Trail.** (See "Day Hikes," below.) At the **Far View Sites Complex,** located 1 mile south of the Far View Visitor Center, six sites are within walking distance, including what seems to be the remains of an ancient reservoir.

Organized Tours & Ranger Programs

Three of the park's spectacular cliff dwellings—Cliff Palace, Balcony House, and Long House—can only be visited during ranger-guided tours. Tickets ($1.75) go on sale daily at 8am at the Far View Visitor Center. Visitors may tour Long House and either Cliff Palace or Balcony House on the same day, but may not tour both Cliff Palace and Balcony House in 1 day.

Departing every half-hour between 9am and 6pm, the **Cliff Palace** tour involves a 100-vertical-foot descent to the dwelling and a same-height climb to exit. In between, you'll have to scale a single 10-foot-high ladder. The effort is well worth it. With 151 rooms and 23 kivas, Cliff Palace is the largest cliff dwelling in the Southwest and one of the largest in the world. Especially striking is the original red-and-white wall painting that remains inside a four-story tower.

Merely reaching the 45-room **Balcony House,** the most fortresslike of the Mesa Verde dwellings, will make you appreciate the agility of the Ancestral Puebloans, who used hand and footholds and log ladders to scale the cliffs. During the tour, you'll descend 90 vertical feet of stairs, climb 32- and 20-foot-long ladders, and slip through a narrow 30-foot-long crawl space. When you do reach the dwelling, you'll be standing on a level stone floor 700 feet above the creek bed of Soda Canyon. The Puebloans dumped tons of fill inside 15-foot-high stone retaining walls below this floor, creating a level surface on which to build. Tours run every half-hour between 9am and 5pm.

Some people remember the **Long House** tour for its 0.5-mile walk, the flight of 52 stairs, and the two 15-foot-high ladders they had to negotiate. Others will recall the dwelling itself, with its 21 kivas and 150 rooms stretching across a long alcove in Rock Canyon. At its center is a large plaza where the community gathered and danced. Granaries are tucked like mud dauber nests into two smaller alcoves (one above the other) to the rear of the large one. Tours meet at the minitrain depot on Wetherill Mesa and run every half-hour from 10am to 5pm.

The Cliff Palace tours run from mid-April to mid-November, a few weeks longer than the season for Balcony House. Wetherill Mesa, site of Long House, is open only from Memorial Day weekend through Labor Day. To replace these attractions during the off-season, the park offers ranger-guided tours of Spruce Tree House, a self-guided area in summer. Call the park to find out the exact opening and closing dates for its tours.

Day Hikes

Although none of the trails to the Mesa Verde sites are strenuous, the 7,000-foot elevation can make the treks tiring for visitors who aren't used to the altitude.

ON CHAPIN MESA

Spruce Tree House

0.25 mi. one way. Easy. Access: Chapin Mesa Museum.

Open from 8:30am to 6:30pm daily during summer, this paved trail descends from behind Chapin Mesa Museum to Spruce Tree House, a dwelling with 114 rooms and eight kivas. Because Spruce Tree House sits in an 89-foot-deep alcove, this is the best-preserved dwelling at Mesa Verde. Rangers are here to answer questions during high season. Off-season, they guide tours here. The trail is accessible to the mobility-impaired, although they may require assistance on some of its grades.

Farming Terrace Trail

0.25 mi. RT. Moderate. Access: Southwest of the Cedar Tree Tower parking area.

This trail crosses over to a wash (dry riverbed) in which the Ancestral Puebloans built a series of check dams used to trap water and soil for farming. It goes a short distance down the wash before looping back to the trailhead.

ON WETHERILL MESA

Badger House Community Trail

0.75 mi. RT. Easy. Access: Wetherill Mesa parking area.

This handicapped-accessible tour visits mesa-top sites on Wetherill Mesa. Usually uncrowded, the paved trail is accessible from one of three minitram stops or by making a longer walk from the parking area. The 12-stop self-guided tour details 600 years of history.

Nordenskiold's Site no. 16 Trail

2 mi. RT. Easy. Access: Wetherill Mesa parking area.

Begin this quiet hike by taking the minitram to its trailhead, or by making a longer walk from the parking area. Mostly flat, the dirt trail descends over rocks for the last few yards before it reaches an overlook of Site no. 16, a 50-room cliff dwelling that was occupied for most of the 13th century. On the way, the self-guided tour identifies many of the plants in the area.

Step House

0.5 mi. RT. Moderate. Access: Wetherill Mesa parking area.

This loop descends roughly 75 feet of stairs and switchbacks to Step House, a cliff dwelling that dates from A.D. 1226. Three Modified Basket Maker pit houses dating from A.D. 626 are found to the left of Step House (as you look toward it). A set of prehistoric stone stairs climbs from these dwellings toward a break in the cliffs.

NEAR MOREFIELD CAMPGROUND

Knife Edge Trail

1.5 mi. RT. Easy. Access: Near Morefield Village.

This trail follows the old Knife Edge Road, the only automobile route into the park until a tunnel was blasted between Prater and Morefield canyons in 1957. Now, during wet years, wildflowers brighten the old roadbed, which hugs the side of Prater Ridge on one side and drops off all the way to the Montezuma Valley on the other. A self-guided tour identifies many of the plant species along the trail. From the end of this trail, you can watch the sun set behind Sleeping Ute Mountain.

Point Lookout Trail

2.3 mi. RT. Moderate. Access: Near Morefield Village.

This trail rises in tight switchbacks from the northeast corner of the campground to the top of Point Lookout, a monument conspicuous from near the park's entrance. It then traverses the top of this butte to a stunning overlook of the Montezuma Valley. Sheer drops in several places make this trail unsuitable for small children.

Prater Ridge Trail

7.8 mi. RT. Moderate. Access: Near Morefield Village.

This loop rises 700 feet from the campground's west side to the top of Prater Ridge. Once atop the ridge, the trail forks, looping around the top of the mesa and opening onto views of the Montezuma and Mancos Valleys and the La Plata Mountains. A cutoff trail halves the mesa-top loop, which zigzags around a number of side canyons. Because the trail is faint in places where it crosses the sandstone, some route-finding skills may be necessary here.

LONGER TRAILS
ON CHAPIN MESA

Three backcountry trails on Chapin Mesa are open to day hikers. Before hiking the Petroglyph Point and Spruce Canyon trails, register at the trailhead ranger station, where a booklet for the self-guided tour on the Petroglyph Point Trail can be borrowed or purchased for 50¢. No registration is required for the third one, the Soda Canyon Overlook Trail.

Petroglyph Point Trail

2.8 mi. RT. Moderate. Access: A short distance down the paved trail to Spruce Tree House Ruin, just below the Chapin Mesa Museum and Chief Ranger Station.

This loop trail travels just below the rim of a side canyon of Spruce Canyon. It eventually reaches Petroglyph Point, one of the park's most impressive panels of rock art. Just past the petroglyphs, the trail climbs to the rim. It stays on the

relatively flat rimrock on its return to Chapin Mesa Museum.

Soda Canyon Overlook Trail

1.5 mi. RT. Easy. Access: A pull-off on the Cliff Palace Loop Rd.

This trail crosses the rim from a parking area on the Cliff Palace Loop Road to overlooks of Soda Canyon and Balcony House. To view Balcony House, go right when the trail forks.

Spruce Canyon Trail

2.1 mi. RT. Moderate. Access: Same as Petroglyph Point Trail.

This loop descends 500 feet into a tributary of Spruce Canyon. Turning to the north, it travels up the bed of Spruce Canyon before climbing in steep switchbacks to the rim. It reaches the rim near the park's picnic area, a short walk from Chapin Mesa Museum. The vegetation along the bottom of the canyon includes Douglas firs and ponderosa pines, which flourish in the moist, cool canyon-bottom soil.

Camping

The impressive **Morefield Campground,** c/o Aramark, P.O. Box 277, Mancos, CO 81328 (☎ **970/565-2133** in summer, or 800/449-2288 or 970/533-7731 in winter), located 4 miles past the entrance station on the park's entrance road, is among the largest in the national park system. Its 450 sites line four loop roads on the gently sloping floor of Morefield Canyon. For tent campers, the sites on Navajo Loop afford extra privacy. Though lower than the others, this loop is free of RVs and cuts into dense clusters of gambel oak.

If you prefer panoramic vistas, head for Hopi Loop, where the campsites are higher and less wooded than the others, affording views down the canyon. At dusk every night, mule deer browse in the bushes around many campsites. RV drivers will find 15 water-electric hookups. Showers cost $1 at Morefield Village, just outside the campground entrance, where laundry service is also available. The campground itself has toilets, drinking water, and public phones. The fee is $23 for RV hookups, $16 for other sites. The campground is closed from mid-October until late April (call ahead for exact dates). Reservations are not accepted, but don't worry: This mammoth campground practically never fills.

Accommodations

INSIDE THE PARK

Far View Lodge

C/o Aramark, P.O. Box 277, Mancos, CO 81328. ☎ **800/449-2288** or 970/533-7731. Fax 970/533-7831. www.visitmesaverde.com. 150 units. Late May to Sept $98 double; mid-Apr to late May and the first 3 weeks of Oct $88. Closed late Oct to mid-Apr. AE, DISC, MC, V.

You can save nearly 2 hours each day by staying here and not commuting to the park. This should free up time for relaxing in the captain's chairs on the private deck of your room, from which you'll see as far as New Mexico on a clear day. Located in 17 buildings scattered across the hilltop, the rooms don't have phones or TVs, so there's little in the way of distractions. Each has a convex ceiling, Southwestern decor, and two double beds. Surprisingly, this lodge often has openings during high season.

NEAR THE PARK

Among reliable franchise motels in nearby Cortez are the **Best Western Turquoise Motor Inn & Suites,** 535 E. Main St. (☎ 800/547-3376 or 970/565-3778), $59 to $159 double; **Comfort Inn,** 2308 E. Main St. (☎ 970/565-3400), $59 to $96 double; **Days Inn,** 430 N. Colo. 145 (☎ 970/565-8577), $46 to $89 double; **Super 8,** 505 E. Main St.

(☎ 970/565-8888), $40 to $76 double; and **Econo Lodge,** 2020 E. Main St., (☎ 970/565-3474), $36 to $99 double. See the appendix for a list of the national chain toll-free numbers.

Anasazi Motor Inn

640 S. Broadway, Cortez, CO 81231. ☎ **800/972-6232** or 970/565-3773. Fax 970/565-1027. http://iyp.uswestdex.com:80/anasazimotorinn. E-mail: amitrail@fone.net. 87 units. A/C TV TEL. June–Sept $62 double; Oct–May $48 double. AE, DC, DISC, MC, V.

This motel offers spacious Southwest-decorated rooms with either one king-sized bed or two queens, plus a swimming pool, hot tub, volleyball court, restaurant, and lounge. Large murals—one of pueblo sites, the other of American Indian dances—add color to cinder-block buildings. Many of the ground-floor rooms have patios.

A Bed & Breakfast on Maple Street

102 S. Maple (P.O. Box 327), Cortez, CO 81321. ☎ **800/665-3906** or 970/565-3906. Fax 970/565-2090. www.cortezbb.com. E-mail: maple@fone.net. 4 units. Apr–Oct $69–$129 double; lower rates Nov–Mar. Rates include full breakfast. DISC, MC, V.

Those who enjoy being spoiled and pampered will love this B&B. When not serving afternoon lemonade or a behemoth breakfast, hostess Nonnie Fahsholtz sews quilts for the beds, curtains for the windows, and napkins for the tables. Like her husband, Roy, she seems to love the work. One group of guests felt so much at home here that they returned after checking out to see whether Nonnie had leftovers. Altered repeatedly since its construction in 1901, the house has the idiosyncrasies of a home. In the Pine Room, the ceiling barely clears 6 feet, and the adjoining kid's room is even lower. A vine-festooned spiral staircase leads to a loft room above the parlor. Guests have use of the patio, a water garden, and a gazebo-enclosed hot tub.

Holiday Inn Express Cortez

2121 E. Main, Cortez, CO 81321. ☎ **800/ 626-5652** or 970/565-6000. Fax 970/ 565-3438. www.coloradoholiday.com. 100 units. A/C TV TEL. Summer $96 double; other times $78 double; $137 suite year-round. Rates include continental breakfast. AE, DC, DISC, MC, V.

The 4,000 flowering plants on the grounds of this family-owned and -operated hotel draw travelers like nectar draws hummingbirds. Once on the hotel grounds, guests flit between luxuries—a 15-station fitness center, an indoor swimming pool, a hot tub, and the margaritas and Foster's drafts at Ko Ko's Friendly Pub—or they simply relax in one of the comfortable and spotlessly clean Southwest-decor guest rooms, most of which have views of Mesa Verde or Sleeping Ute Mountain. Standard rooms have two queen-size beds or one king; several suites have been specially designed for kids—in addition to having a king-size bed for the parents, each comes with a partitioned area modeled after a Western fort, with bunk beds and a separate TV.

Rio Grande Southern Bed & Breakfast

101 S. Fifth St. (P.O. Box 516), Dolores, CO 81323. ☎ **800/258-0434** or 970/882-7527. E-mail: riograndesouthern@hubwest.com. 8 units (3 with bathroom). $50–$75 double; $140 suite. Rates include full breakfast. DISC, MC, V. Closed Dec–Feb.

Although the Rio Grande Southern Railroad folded in 1893 after just 2 years in business, the hotel built for its customers has endured to become a National Historic Landmark. You'll check in at the old front desk, climb carpeted stairs to the second floor, then drift down the hallway, passing Norman Rockwell prints, a tiny library, and the guest rooms themselves. Filled with antiques, they seem barely large enough to contain their own stories. If you're lucky, you'll be in Room 4, where Zane Gray is said to have stayed while writing "Riders of the Purple Sage." Breakfast is downstairs in a small cafe.

Travelodge

440 S. Broadway, Cortez, CO 81321. ☎ **800/ 578-7878** or 970/565-7778. Fax 970/ 565-7214. 42 units. A/C TV TEL. Memorial Day to Labor Day $49–$69 double; Labor Day to Memorial Day $36–$59 double. Rates include continental breakfast. AE, DISC, MC, V. Small pets accepted with $25 deposit.

Flower boxes decorate the buildings, and facilities here include a heated outdoor swimming pool, whirlpool, and guest laundry. Most of the attractive rooms have good quality queen beds, and a few have kings. You'll find tub/shower combos in 31 rooms, showers only in the rest. There's also in-room coffee.

Dining

INSIDE THE PARK

Reservations are not accepted at any of the restaurants within the park.

Far View Terrace

Across from the Far View Visitor Center. Main courses $4.50–$7.95. Daily 6:30am–9pm late Apr to late Oct. AE, DISC, MC, V. CAFETERIA.

This cafe serves a variety of foods, cafeteria-style, at stations with cryptic names such as "Easy Goes," "Cafe Features," and "Changing Scenes." The wide-ranging menu includes pancakes and eggs at breakfast; and salads, sandwiches, burgers, pizzas, and Southwestern dishes at lunch and dinner. While dining, you can see as far as New Mexico through a long bank of windows.

Knife Edge Café

Morefield Village. Main courses $3.50–$5. AE, DISC, MC, V. Daily 7:30am–10am late May to Labor Day. BREAKFAST.

This cafe near Morefield Campground serves all-you-can-eat pancake breakfasts, with tables outdoors in a sheltered porch, bordered on one side by a colorful mural.

Metate Room

Far View Lodge, across from Far View Visitor Center, 17 mi. down the park entrance rd. ☎ **970/529-4421.** Main courses $9.95–$23.95. AE, DISC, MC, V. Daily 5–9:30pm late Apr to late Oct. AMERICAN/ SOUTHWESTERN.

The best and by far the most expensive restaurant in the park, the Metate Room serves American dishes such as roast turkey, leg of lamb, and steaks, as well as Southwestern meals like enchiladas, carne asada, and chicken stuffed with green chiles. The restaurant displays high-quality Indian rugs and pottery, which you might not notice, given the breathtaking views from the windows.

Spruce Tree Terrace

Across from Chapin Mesa Museum. Most items $3–$6. AE, DISC, MC, V. Daily 8am–6pm mid-Apr to Oct; daily 10am–5pm Nov to mid-Apr. CAFETERIA.

Although hamburgers, cheeseburgers, and hot dogs dominate the menu, tossed salads, yogurt, and ice cream are also available. Sit in the Southwestern-style dining area, or take your food out onto the deck.

NEAR THE PARK

The Dry Dock Restaurant and Pub

200 W. Main, Cortez. ☎ **970/564-9404.** Main courses $5.25–$26.95. AE, DISC, MC, V. Daily 5–10pm. SEAFOOD.

Miles from the nearest reservoir, this restaurant still manages to serve fish that tastes like today's catch. Perhaps to compensate for the lack of water, parts of a fishing boat have been nailed to the restaurant walls. Although chicken, veal, and steak dishes are offered, this is the place to order seafood, whether it has legs (lobster), whiskers (blackened catfish), or size issues (beer-batter shrimp). If you're hankering for something Southwestern, try the fish burrito. The outdoor patio has live music on summer weekends.

Dusty Rose Café

200 W. Grand, Mancos. ☎ **970/533-9042.** Lunch entrees $4.25–$6.50; dinner entrees $7.95–$17.50. Wed–Mon 8:30am–2pm and 4:30pm–closing. MC, V. ITALIAN.

Sun-catchers in the windows, a friendly staff, and reasonable prices will remind you that you're in rural Colorado, while the handmade pastas and a number of delicious veal, chicken, and shrimp dishes seem to belong in northern Italy. For starters, you'll receive a hard Italian bread served with butter and cloves of juicy roasted garlic. Appetizers include deep-fried calamari, and grilled herb polenta with sherried mushrooms. If you're in the mood for pasta, try the Pasta Bella Vista—fettucine with shallots, bacon bits, sun-dried tomatoes, Parmesan cheese, and cream. A champagne brunch is served Sundays from 8am to 2pm.

Main St. Brewery and Restaurant

21 E. Main, Cortez. ☎ **970/564-9112.** Reservations not accepted. Main courses $6.25–$13.95. AE, MC, V. Mon–Sun 4pm–closing. AMERICAN.

Modern thin-bladed fans mince the air under a stamped-tin ceiling, and fanciful murals splash color above subdued wood paneling. The pleasant contrasts found in the decor carry over to the menu. In addition to pub grub like fish-and-chips, pizza, and bratwurst, there's delicious light dining, including a vegetarian skewer plate and pasta primavera. The beers here go well with everything. Two especially fine choices are the hoppy, slightly bitter "Pale Export," and the Porter, perfected through a collaboration between the restaurant's owner, Rudi Baeumel, and several world-class brew masters in Milwaukee.

Nero's

303 W. Main St., Cortez. ☎ **970/565-7366.** Main courses $6.95–$17.95. AE, MC, V. Summer daily 5–10pm, winter Mon–Sat 5–9pm. ITALIAN.

A county named Montezuma doesn't sound like a place where you'd expect to find two great Italian restaurants. But the Dusty Rose is one, and Nero's, with food prepared by chef Richard Gurd, a graduate of the Culinary Institute of America, makes two. With just 11 tables in winter (twice that when the deck opens in summer), Nero's is so small that even the six bar stools seem to jostle for space. The area that isn't crammed with furniture is dominated by American Indian pottery, paintings, and sculptures. On a menu that features pasta, chicken, veal, seafood, and steaks, the most popular item is the lasagna, made with spicy Italian sausage, hamburger, and four cheeses. If you can find room for an ultrarich desert, try the Bailey's Irish Cream Cheese Mousse.

Old Germany Restaurant

200 S. 8th St., Dolores. ☎ **970/882-7549.** Main courses $5.50–$16.95. MC, V. Tues–Sat 4–9pm. GERMAN/AMERICAN.

Come to this 1908 Victorian house when you're ready to trade "heart smart" for "hearty." Rita Blount, a native German, cooks up a dozen rich, flavorful entrees, including cordon bleu (breaded butterflied pork loin steak filled with ham and cheese); Hungarian chicken (a chicken breast covered with sliced bell peppers and onions in paprika sauce); and pork roast with purple cabbage. The menu does have at least one item that's said to be good for the heart: beer. Thirty-eight-ounce steins of Paulaner Oktoberfest go for $7.50.

Picnic & Camping Supplies

Inside the park, a general store in Morefield Village sells camping supplies and groceries from late April through mid-October. In nearby Cortez, **City Market,** 508 E. Main (☎ **970/565-6504**), with a deli, bakery, and excellent salad bar, sells everything you might want for a picnic or family outing.

Nearby National Monuments & Archaeological Sites

The major archaeological center of the United States, the Four Corners area—where the states of Colorado, New Mexico, Arizona, and Utah meet—is surrounded by a vast complex of ancient villages that dominated this entire region a thousand years ago. Here among the reddish-brown rocks, abandoned canyons, and flat mesas, you'll discover another world, once ruled by the Ancestral Puebloans (Anasazi), and today largely the domain of the Navajo.

HOVENWEEP NATIONAL MONUMENT

Preserving some of the most striking and isolated archaeological sites in the Four Corners area, *Hovenweep* is the Ute word for "deserted valley." Its inhabitants apparently left the area around 1300, and even today it's often overlooked by tourists, who instead flock to its more famous neighbor, Mesa Verde. Hovenweep contains six separate sites, and is noted for mysterious, 20-foot-high sandstone towers, some of them square, others oval, circular, or D-shaped. The towers have small windows up and down their masonry sides, and remain solid today. Archaeologists have suggested their possible function as everything from guard or signal towers, celestial observatories, ceremonial structures, to water towers or granaries.

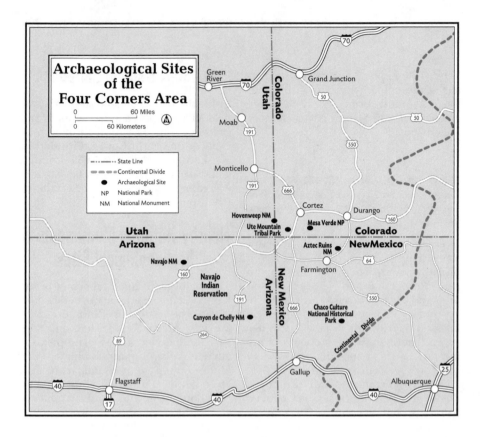

Archaeological Sites of the Four Corners Area

0 _____ 60 Miles

0 _____ 60 Kilometers

- - - - State Line
- ■ - ■ Continental Divide
● Archaeological Site
NP National Park
NM National Monument

A ranger station, with exhibits, rest rooms, and drinking water, is located at the **Square Tower Site,** the most impressive and best preserved of the sites. The **Tower Point Loop Trail** winds among the stone structures and identifies desert plants used for food, clothing, medicine, and other purposes. The other five sites are difficult to find, and you'll need to obtain detailed driving directions and check on current road conditions before setting out.

The **Hovenweep Campground,** with 30 sites, is open year-round. It has flush toilets, drinking water, picnic tables, and fire pits, but no showers or RV hookups. Cost is $10 per night. Reservations are not accepted, although the campground rarely fills, even during the peak summer season.

Regulations are much the same here as at most National Park Service properties, with an emphasis on being careful to not damage archaeological sites. Dogs must be leashed but are permitted on

trails. Summer temperatures can reach over 100°F, and water supplies are limited; so take your own and carry a canteen even on short walks. Gnats can be a nuisance in late May and June, and bug repellent is advised.

The ranger station is open daily from 8am to 4:30pm year-round, but may be closed for short periods while the ranger is on patrol. Admission costs $6 per vehicle. The monument straddles the Colorado-Utah border, 40 miles west of Cortez. From Cortez, take U.S. 160 south about 4 miles to County Rd. G, and go 41 miles into Utah and to the monument.

For information, contact **Hovenweep National Monument,** McElmo Route, Cortez, CO 81321 (☎ **970/749-0510** or 435/459-4344; www.nps.gov/hove).

UTE MOUNTAIN TRIBAL PARK

If you liked Mesa Verde, but would have enjoyed it more without the company of so many fellow tourists, you'll love the

Ute Mountain Tribal Park, P.O. Box 109, Towaoc, CO 81334 (☎ **800/847-5485** or 970/565-3751, ext. 330). Set aside by the Ute Mountain tribe to preserve its heritage, the 125,000-acre park—which abuts Mesa Verde National Park—includes hundreds of surface sites and cliff dwellings that compare in size and complexity with those in Mesa Verde, as well as wall paintings and ancient petroglyphs.

Accessibility to the park is strictly limited to **guided tours,** offered from April through October. Full- and half-day tours begin at the **Ute Mountain Museum and Visitor Center** at the junction of U.S. 666 and U.S. 160, 19 miles south of Cortez. Some climbing is necessary. Mountainbiking and backpacking trips are also offered. No food, lodging, gasoline, or other services are available within the park. There's one primitive **campground** ($10 per vehicle).

Charges for tours in your vehicle start at $17 per person for a half day, $30 for a full day; it's $5 extra to go in the tour guide's vehicle. Reservations are required.

CANYON DE CHELLY NATIONAL MONUMENT

It's hard to imagine narrow canyons less than 1,000 feet deep being more spectacular than the Grand Canyon, but in some ways Canyon de Chelly is just that. Gaze down from the rim at an ancient cliff dwelling as the whinnying of horses and clanging of goat bells drifts up from below, and you will be struck by the continuity of human existence. For more than 2,000 years people have called these canyons home, and today there are more than 100 prehistoric dwelling sites in the area.

The monument consists of two major canyons—Canyon de Chelly (which is pronounced canyon de *shay* and is derived from the Navajo word *tségi,* meaning "rock canyon") and *Canyon del Muerto* (Spanish for "Canyon of the Dead")—and several smaller canyons.

The canyons extend for more than 100 miles through the rugged slickrock landscape of northeastern Arizona, draining the seasonal runoff from the snowmelt of the Chuska Mountains.

Canyon de Chelly's smooth sandstone walls of rich reds and yellows contrast sharply with the deep greens of corn, pasture, and cottonwood on the canyon floor. Vast stone amphitheaters form the caves in which the Ancestral Puebloans built their homes, and as you watch shadows and light paint an ever-changing canyon panorama, it's easy to see why the Navajo consider these canyons sacred ground.

Your first stop should be the **visitor center,** which is open daily May through September from 8am to 6pm (on daylight saving time) and October through April from 8am to 5pm. In front of the visitor center is an example of a traditional crib-style hogan, a hexagonal structure of logs and earth that Navajo use as both home and ceremonial center. Inside, a small museum acquaints visitors with the history of Canyon de Chelly, and there's often a silversmith demonstrating Navajo jewelry-making.

From here most people tour the canyon by car. Each of the rim drives is around 20 miles in each direction, and with stops each can easily take 3 hours.

The **North Rim Drive** overlooks Canyon del Muerto. From overlooks you'll see **Ledge Ruin,** which was occupied between A.D. 1050 and 1275, and nearby, a lone kiva (circular ceremonial building) that was reached by means of toeholds cut into the soft sandstone cliff wall. **Antelope House,** once home to from 20 to 40 people, takes its name from the Navajo paintings of antelopes on a nearby cliff wall, believed to have been done in the 1830s. Further along the drive you'll see the most spectacular archeological site in the canyon: Named for two mummies found in burial urns, **Mummy Cave** is actually a giant amphitheater consisting of two caves, believed to have been occupied from A.D. 300 to 1300. There's a three-story structure

> Photo Tip—The best time to see and photograph the ruins along the North Rim Drive is in the morning, when they're bathed in sunlight.

similar to dwellings at Mesa Verde, and altogether there are 80 rooms. The final stop on the North Rim Drive is at the **Massacre Cave Overlook,** where Spanish troops in 1804 killed about 120 Navajo.

The **South Rim Drive** climbs slowly but steadily along the South Rim of Canyon de Chelly, and at each stop you're a bit higher above the canyon floor. From overlooks you'll see rugged canyons, the junction of Canyon del Muerto and Canyon de Chelly, and the **Junction Ruin,** with 10 rooms and one kiva. It was occupied from around 1100 until the Ancestral Puebloans disappeared shortly before 1300. Also visible is **First Ruin,** perched precariously on a long narrow ledge, with 22 rooms and two kivas. Further along is the **White House Overlook,** which provides the only opportunity for descending into Canyon de Chelly without a guide or ranger (see below). The next stop is at **Sliding House Overlook,** offering a view of ruins built on a narrow shelf that appear to be sliding down into the canyon. Inhabited from about 900 until 1200, Sliding House contained between 30 and 50 rooms. The final stop on the South Rim is one of the most spectacular, providing a view of monumental **Spider Rock,** twin towers that rise 800 feet from the canyon floor.

The **White House Ruins Trail,** the only trail into the canyon you can take without a guide, descends 600 feet to the canyon floor, crosses Chinle Wash, and approaches the White House Ruins. These buildings were constructed both on the canyon floor and 50 feet up the cliff wall in a small cave. One of the largest ruins in the canyon, it contains 80 rooms and was inhabited between 1040 and 1275. Notice the black streaks on the sandstone walls above the White House Ruins. These streaks were formed by seeping water that reacted with the iron in the sandstone. Iron is what gives the walls their reddish hue. Ancestral Puebloan artists chipped away at this black patina to create petroglyphs. Though you cannot enter the ruins, you can get close enough for a good look. You're not allowed to wander off this trail, and please respect the privacy of those Navajo living here. It's a 2½-mile round-trip hike and takes about 2 hours. Be sure to carry water.

Access to the floor of Canyon de Chelly is restricted, and in order to enter the canyon *you must be accompanied by either a park ranger or an authorized guide* (unless you're on the White House Ruins trail). **Navajo guides** will lead you into the canyon on foot or in your own or their four-wheel-drive vehicle, and there are also guided horseback tours. Check at the visitor center for details.

The cottonwood-shaded **Cottonwood Campground,** near the Visitor Center, has 96 sites, a dump station, toilets, fire pits, and no fee. There is water in summer but not in winter. Reservations are not accepted.

From Cortez, follow U.S. 160 south and west 76 miles into Arizona to U.S. 191, which you take south 62 miles to Chinle, where you turn east to enter the park.

The park is open daily year-round; admission is free.

For information contact **Canyon de Chelly National Monument,** P.O. Box 588, Chinle, AZ 86503 (☎ 520/674-5500).

NAVAJO NATIONAL MONUMENT

Located 30 miles west of Kayenta and 110 miles northwest of Canyon de Chelly, Navajo National Monument encompasses three of the best-preserved Ancestral Puebloan cliff dwellings in the region: Betatakin, Keet Seel, and

Inscription House. It's possible to visit both Betatakin and Keet Seel, but fragile Inscription House is closed to the public.

The name Navajo National Monument is a bit misleading. Although the Navajo people inhabit the area now, it was the Ancestral Puebloans who built the cliff dwellings. The Navajo arrived centuries later. The Ancestral Puebloan who lived here, in Tsegi Canyon, are considered the ancestors of today's Hopi and other Pueblo peoples.

They began abandoning their well-constructed homes around the middle of the 13th century for reasons unknown. Tree rings suggest that a drought in the latter part of the 13th century prevented the Ancestral Puebloans from growing sufficient crops. However, in Tsegi Canyon there's another theory for the abandonment. The canyon floors were usually flooded each year by spring and summer snowmelt, which made farming quite productive, but in the mid-1200s weather patterns changed and streams running through the canyons began cutting deep into the soil, forming deep, narrow canyons, which lowered the water table and made farming much more difficult.

Your first stop should be the **visitor center,** which has informative displays on the Ancestral Puebloan and Navajo cultures, including numerous artifacts from Tsegi Canyon. You can also watch several short films or a slide show. The center is open daily from 8am to 5pm (daylight saving time), and closed on New Years, Christmas, and Thanksgiving.

Betatakin, which means "ledge house" in Navajo, is the only one of the three ruins that can be seen easily. Built in a huge amphitheater-like alcove in the canyon wall, Betatakin was occupied only from 1250 to 1300, and at its peak may have housed 125 people.

The 1-mile round-trip paved **Sandal Trail** from the visitor center leads to overlooks of Betatakin. The strenuous 5-mile round-trip hike to Betatakin itself is led by a ranger, takes about 6 hours, and involves descending more than 700 feet

to the floor of Tsegi Canyon, and later hiking back up to the rim. This hike is conducted from early May through October and leaves from the visitor center. Hikers should carry 2 quarts of water. This popular hike is limited to 25 people per tour; many people line up at the visitor center an hour or more before the center opens.

Keet Seel, which means "broken pieces of pottery" in Navajo, has a much longer history than Betatakin, with occupation beginning as early as A.D. 950 and continuing until 1300. At one point Keet Seel may have housed 150 people.

The 17-mile round-trip hike to Keet Seel is quite strenuous. Hikers may stay overnight at a primitive campground near the ruins. You must carry enough water for your trip, since none is available along the trail. Only 20 people a day are given permits, and the trail is open only from Memorial Day to Labor Day. Permits are available in advance (call the park office).

The monument has a free, shady **campground** with 31 sites available on a first-come, first-served basis, plus an overflow area containing about a dozen more (summer only).

From Cortez, follow U.S. 160 south and west 137 miles into New Mexico and Arizona, to Ariz. 564, which leads north 9 miles to the monument.

For information, contact **Navajo National Monument,** HC-71, Box 3, Tonalea, AZ 86044-9704 (☎ 520/ 672-2366; www.nps.gov/nava). The park is open daily year-round. Admission is free.

CHACO CULTURE NATIONAL HISTORICAL PARK

A combination of a stunning setting and well-preserved ruins makes the dusty drive to Chaco Canyon worth the trip. Whether you come from the north or south, you drive in on a graded (and sometimes muddy) dirt road that seems to add to the authenticity and adventure of this remote New Mexico experience.

When you finally arrive, you walk through stark desert country that seems perhaps ill-suited as a center of culture. However, the ancient Ancestral Puebloan people successfully farmed the lowlands and built great masonry towns, which connected with other towns over a wide-ranging network of roads crossing this desolate place.

What's particularly interesting is how changes in architecture chart the area's cultural progress. These changes began in the mid-800s, when the Ancestral Puebloan started building on a larger scale than they had previously. They used the same masonry techniques that tribes had used in smaller villages in the region, walls one stone thick with generous use of mud mortar, but they built stone villages of multiple stories with rooms several times larger than in the previous stage of their culture. Within a century, six large pueblos were underway. This pattern of a single large pueblo with oversized rooms, surrounded by conventional villages, caught on throughout the region. New communities built along these lines sprang up. Old villages built similarly large pueblos. Eventually there were more than 75 such towns, most of them closely tied to Chaco by an extensive system of roads.

This progress led to Chaco becoming the economic center of the San Juan Basin by A.D. 1000. As many as 5,000 people may have lived in some 400 settlements in and around Chaco. As masonry techniques advanced through the years, walls rose more than four stories high. Some of these are still visible today.

Chaco's decline after 1½ centuries of success coincided with a drought in the San Juan Basin between A.D. 1130 and 1180. Scientists still argue vehemently over why the site was abandoned and where the Chacoans went. Many believe that an influx of outsiders may have brought new rituals to the region, causing a schism among tribal members. Most agree, however, that the people drifted away to more hospitable places in the region and that their descendants live among the Pueblo people today.

Exploring the ruins and hiking are the most popular activities here. A series of pueblo ruins stand within 5 or 6 miles of each other on the broad, flat, treeless canyon floor. Plan to spend at least 3 or 4 hours here, driving to and exploring the different pueblos. A one-way road from the visitor center loops up one side of the canyon and down the other.

You may want to focus your energy on **Pueblo Bonito,** the largest pre-historic dwelling ever excavated in the Southwest. It contains giant kivas and 800 rooms covering more than 3 acres. The **Pueblo Alto Trail** is a pleasant hike that takes you up on the canyon rim so you can see the ruins from above—in the afternoon, with thunderheads building, the views are spectacular. For cyclers, there's a map with ridable trails outlined, an excellent way to traverse the vast expanse while experiencing the quiet of these ancient dwellings.

Other ruins accessible directly from the auto road or via short walks are Chetro Ketl, Pueblo del Arroyo, Kin Kletso, Casa Chiquita, Casa Rinconada, Hungo Pavi, and Una Vida. Backcountry hikes (from 2 to 5 hrs.) are required to reach some ruins; they include Penasco Blanco, Tsin Kletsin, and Wijiji.

Most ruins are on the north side of the canyon. **Chetro Ketl** had some 500 rooms, 16 kivas, and an impressive enclosed plaza. **Pueblo del Arroyo** was a four-story, D-shaped structure, with about 280 rooms and 20 kivas; **Kin Kletso** had three stories, 100 rooms, and 5 kivas. **Una Vida,** a short walk from the visitor center, was one of the first pueblos built and has been left only partially excavated; it had 150 rooms and five kivas. **Casa Rinconada,** on the south side of the canyon, is the largest "great kiva" in the park, and is astronomically aligned to the cardinal directions and the summer solstice. It may have been a center for the community at large, used for major spiritual observances.

Aerial photos show hundreds of miles of roads connecting these towns with the Chaco pueblos, one of the longest running 42 miles straight north to Salmon Ruin and Aztec Ruins (see below). Settlements were spaced along the road at travel intervals of 1 day. They were not simple trails worn into the stone by foot travel, but engineered roadways 30 feet wide with a berm of rock to contain the fill. Where the road went over flat rock, walls were built along the sides of it. It is this road network that leads some scholars to believe Chaco was the center of a widespread, unified society.

The Chacoans' trade network, as suggested by artifacts found here, stretched from California to Texas and south into Mexico. Seashell necklaces, copper bells, and the remains of macaws or parrots were found among Chaco artifacts. Some of these items are displayed in the museum at the visitor center.

Ranger-guided walks and campfire talks are available in the summer at the visitor center (where you can get self-guiding trail brochures.

Gallo Campground, located within the park, is quite popular with hikers. It's located about 1 mile east of the visitor center; fees are $10 per night. The campground has 64 sites (group sites are also available), with fire grates (bring your own wood or charcoal), central toilets, and nonpotable water. Drinking water is available only at the visitor center. The campground cannot accommodate trailers over 30 feet.

This is an isolated area, and there are **no services** available within or close to the park—no food, gas, auto repairs, firewood, lodging (besides the campground), or drinking water (other than at the visitor center) are available.

There are two entrances, one on N. Mex. 57 and the other on San Juan County Road 7900. To get to Chaco from Santa Fe, take I-25 south to Bernalillo, then U.S. 550 northwest through Cuba to Nageezi. Turn left onto a dirt road that runs almost 30 miles south to the

park's boundary. The trip takes about 3½ to 4 hours. Farmington is the nearest population center, and it's still a 75-mile, 2-hour drive to these ruins. U.S. 550 takes you as far as the Nageezi Trading Post (the last stop for food, gas, or lodging), but the final 26 miles are graded dirt—fine in dry weather but dangerous when it rains, and often flooded where arroyos cross it. (A turnoff at Blanco Trading Post, 8 miles before Nageezi, cuts 5 miles off the trip, but the road is more subject to hazardous conditions.) The park can also be reached from Grants via I-40 west to N. Mex. 371, then north on N. Mex. 57 (with the final 19 miles graded dirt).

Whichever way you come, call ahead to inquire about **road conditions** (☎ **505/786-7014**) before leaving the paved highways. The dirt roads can get extremely muddy after rain or snow, and afternoon thunderstorms are common in late summer. There's also a 24-hour emergency assistance line at ☎ **505/786-7060,** which connects directly to the homes of law-enforcement rangers in the park.

For information, contact **Superintendent, Chaco Culture National Historical Park,** Star NM 4 (P.O. Box 6500), Bloomfield, NM 87413 (☎ **505/786-7014;** www. nps.gov/chca).

Admission is $8 per car. The visitor center, with a bookstore and a museum showing films on Ancestral Puebloan culture, is open daily year-round.

AZTEC RUINS NATIONAL MONUMENT

What's most striking about these ruins is the central kiva, which visitors can enter. The ruins of this 450-room pueblo, left by the Ancestral Puebloan 7 centuries ago, are located 14 miles northeast of Farmington in the town of Aztec on the Animas River. Early Anglo settlers, convinced that the ruins were of Aztec origin, misnamed the site. Despite the fact that this pueblo was built long before the

Aztecs of central Mexico lived, the name persisted.

The influence of the Chaco culture is strong at Aztec, as evidenced in the pre-planned architecture, the open plaza, and the fine stone masonry. But a later occupation shows signs of Mesa Verde influence. This second group of settlers, who lived here from about 1200 to 1275, remodeled the old pueblo and built others nearby, using techniques less elaborate and decorative than the Chacoans.

Aztec is best known for its **Great Kiva,** the only completely reconstructed great kiva in existence. About 50 feet in diameter, with a main floor sunken 8 feet below the surface of the surrounding ground, this circular ceremonial room rivets the imagination.

Visiting Aztec Ruins National Monument will take you approximately 1 hour, even if you take the ¼-mile self-guided trail and spend some time in the visitor center. This center displays some outstanding examples of Ancestral Puebloan ceramics and basketry, as well as such finds as an intact Pueblo ladder, turkey feather woven cloth bound with yucca cordage, and an empty case where a warrior's remains were once displayed. (They were subsequently removed out of deference to the Pueblo people's sensibilities). Add another half hour if you plan to watch the video imaginatively documenting the history of native cultures in the area.

There is no camping at the monument.

Aztec Ruins is approximately ½ mile north of U.S. 550 on Ruins Road (County Road 2900) on the north edge of the city of Aztec. Ruins Road is the first street immediately west of the Animas River bridge on U.S. 550.

For information, contact **Aztec Ruins National Monument,** P.O. Box 640, Aztec, NM 87410-0640 (☎ **505/334-6174,** ext. 30; www.nps.gov/azru). Admission is $4 per person and children under 17 are admitted free. The monument is open year-round; closed Thanksgiving, Christmas, and New Year's Day.

25

MOUNT RAINIER NATIONAL PARK

by Jack Olson

O

N SUMMER WEEKENDS, WHEN "THE MOUNTAIN IS OUT," AS THE LOCALS say, busloads of noisy tourists descend on Mount Rainier, camcorders whirring and cameras clicking. But for anyone willing to expend a little bit of energy to get away from the roadside

crowds, this mountain, which dominates the Puget Sound and western Washington skyline for miles around, has many secrets to share: mountain goats and marmots, streaming waterfalls, ominous walls of ice deep in the rain forest, and thousand-year-old trees set against subalpine meadows teeming with summer wildflowers.

Should you visit on a dreary October day, despite what you may think, Mount Rainier was not named for its climatological proclivities. Rather, it was named in 1792 by Capt. George Vancouver for his friend Rear Adm. Peter Rainier (who never laid eyes on the mountain). The region's native people had been calling it Tahoma for centuries, however, and the name remained (and some might say still remains) contentious up until the early 19th century. Nevertheless, the mountain remains Rainier to most people, while a sprawling city to the south, Tacoma, wound up with the American Indian name for some reason.

Although the early peoples stayed away from the glacial peaks out of a mixture of respect and fear, they hunted deer, elk, and mountain goats and gathered huckleberries on its lower slopes. Today, Mount Rainier is a symbol of the wild Northwest, providing constant reassurance of the beauty that lies beyond the sprawl of suburbia.

While most of the mountains in the West were seen as obstacles by the early pioneers, 14,410-foot Mt. Rainier so captivated early settlers that as early as the 1850s, less than a decade after Seattle was founded, aspiring mountaineers were heading for its snowcapped slopes. In 1857, an army lieutenant, August Valentine Kautz, climbed to within 400 feet of the summit, and in 1870, Gen. Hazard Stevens and Philemon Van Trump made the first recorded complete ascent of the mountain (trapped near the summit at dark, they survived the night huddled in ice caves formed by sulfurous steam vents that kept the air temperature in the caves near 170°F). In 1884, James and Virinda Longmire opened the mountain's first hotel, at a spot that now bears their name. In 1899, Mount Rainier became

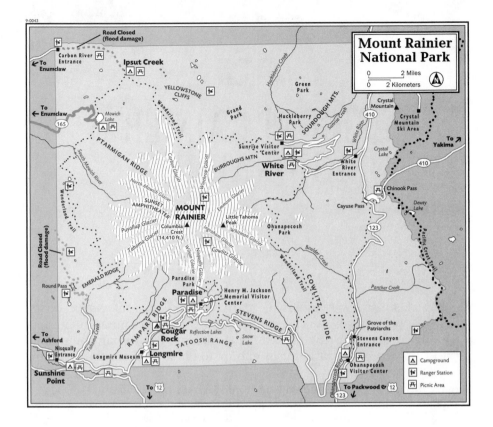

9-0043

Mount Rainier National Park

0   2 Miles
0   2 Kilometers

Road Closed (flood damage)

Carbon River Entrance
To Enumclaw
Ipsut Creek
Yellowstone Cliffs
Green Park
Huckleberry Creek
Crystal Mountain
Crystal Mountain Ski Area
To Enumclaw
Mowich Lake
165
Grand Park
Huckleberry Park
Sourdough Mts.
Sunrise Creek
White River
410
To Yakima
Ptarmigan Ridge
Wonderland Trail
Carbon Glacier
Winthrop Glacier
Burroughs Mtn
Sunrise Visitor Center
White River Entrance
Crystal Lake
410
South Mowich River
North Mowich Glacier
Sunset Amphitheater
MOUNT RAINIER
Columbia Crest (14,410 ft.)
Emmons Glacier
Little Tahoma Peak
Ohanapecosh Park
Cayuse Pass
123
Chinook Pass
Dewey Lake
Wonderland Trail
Puyallup Glacier
Tahoma Glacier
Ingraham Glacier
Whitman Glacier
Nisqually Glacier
Wilson Glacier
Cowlitz Glacier
Boulder Creek
Cowlitz Divide
Pacific Crest Trail
Road Closed (flood damage)
Emerald Ridge
Round Pass
Paradise Park
Paradise
Henry M. Jackson Memorial Visitor Center
Stevens Ridge
Panther Creek
Grove of the Patriarchs
To Ashford
Rampart Ridge
Tahoma Creek
Cougar Rock
Reflection Lakes
Tatoosh Range
Snow Lake
Stevens Canyon Entrance
Nisqually Entrance
Longmire Museum
Longmire
Ohanapecosh Visitor Center
Sunshine Point
To 12
To Packwood & 12
123

Campground
Ranger Station
Picnic Area

the nation's fifth national park, and by 1916, the trail system now known as the Wonderland Trail was completed, forming a loop nearly 100 miles long around the mountain.

Because of its massive system of glaciers and unpredictable weather, Mount Rainier is an unforgiving peak. Climbers throughout the years have died on its slopes, yet each year about 10,000 climbers set out for the summit of this dozing volcano. However, only approximately 4,500 of them ever reach the top. The rest are turned back by bad weather, altitude sickness, exhaustion, and hazardous glacial crossings. This is not a mountain to be treated lightly.

Although the mountain is a magnet for climbers, these adventurers make up only a tiny fraction of the 2 million visitors who come to the park each year. This mountain is really all about hiking through alpine meadows, and that is the main activity pursued by the vast majority of park visitors, most of whom

visit during the short summer season (from July to September in the higher elevations).

The Cascades are not dead, they're just sleeping. This fact was driven home with the eruption of Mount St. Helens on May 18, 1980. But what of Mount Rainier?

Snow and glaciers notwithstanding, Rainier has a heart of fire. Steam vents at the mountain's summit are evidence of that. Though this volcanic peak has been inactive for more than 150 years, it could erupt again at any time. Some scientists believe that Rainier's volcanic activity occurs in 3,000-year cycles, and luckily we have another 500 years (give or take) to go before there's another big eruption. So go ahead and plan that trip. Probably, only the scenery will blow you away. There are some risks the Park Service would like visitors to be aware of: Mud flows, glacial outburst floods, or rockfall are geohazards that may be encountered at Mount Rainier.

Terrain. According to local legend, Martha Longmire, who helped found the first hotel in the area, was supposed to have exclaimed, "This must be called paradise," upon her first visit to the subalpine meadows that now bear that name. It is these meadows, now the site of the seasonal Paradise Lodge and the Henry H. Jackson Memorial Visitor Center, that are the most popular spots in the park. Wildflowers cover the slopes here, and the vast bulk of the mountain rises so steeply overhead that it is necessary to strain one's neck to gaze up at the summit.

Mt. Rainier lies toward the southern end of the Washington Cascades. Here, the crags of the North Cascades are replaced by a volcanic landscape of rolling hills punctuated by Mount Rainier, Mount St. Helens, and to the east, Mount Adams and Goat Rocks, the latter but a remnant of an ancient volcano, the former, a snow cone as impressive as Mount Rainier.

It is said that Rainier makes its own weather, and more often than not, it isn't what people consider good weather. Rising more than 2 miles above the surrounding landscape, Mount Rainier interrupts the eastward flow of moisture-laden air that comes in off the Pacific Ocean. Forced upward into the colder altitudes, this moist air drops its load of water on the mountain. At lower elevations on the west side this moisture falls as rain, which creates a **rain forest** in the Carbon River Valley. However, at higher elevations, the mountain's precipitation falls as **snow.** On average, about 680 inches of snow falls each winter at Paradise on Mount Rainier, but in the winter of 1971–72, 1,122 inches (93.5 ft.) of snow was recorded at Paradise, setting a world annual snowfall record.

Mount Rainier is the single most glaciated mountain in the contiguous 48 states. So much snow falls here each winter that it can't melt over the short summer months. Each year the snow accumulates, eventually compressing into ice that adds to the mountain's **glaciers.** There are 26 named glaciers on Mount Rainier and another 50 unnamed ones. Among these are the largest (Emmons) and the lowest (Carbon) in the Lower 48.

These glaciers in turn feed a half dozen rivers. The Muddy Fork of the **Cowlitz River** and the **White River** take their names from the color that the glacial flour (silt) imparts to them. Fortunately, the **Carbon River** is not as black as its name implies. The river instead takes its name from the coal deposits found in the area. The **Nisqually,** the **Puyallup,** and the Cowlitz all retain names given to them centuries ago by the region's American Indian tribes. All of these rivers eventually flow westward to the Puget Sound, with the exception of the Cowlitz, which flows into the Columbia River.

Surrounding the national park are four different **national forests:** Mount Baker, Snoqualmie, Wenatchee, and Gifford Pinchot. Within these national forests are seven wilderness areas and thousands of miles of logging roads and trails.

Flora & Fauna. In a national park, where animals need not fear death from humans, you often get unexpected chances to encounter wildlife up close and personal, sometimes whether you want to or not. Yes, **cougars** live in this park, as do **black bears,** but neither is seen very often. Much more commonly spotted large mammals are the park's deer, elk, and mountain goats. **Deer,** mostly black-tailed, are the most frequently spotted. **Elk,** much larger and more majestic in stature, are in less evidence than the deer, but can sometimes be seen in the Sunrise area in the summer and throughout the eastern regions of the park during the autumn. **Mountain goats,** which are actually not goats but rather a long-haired relative of the antelope, keep to the rocky slopes of alpine and subalpine meadows during the summer.

Perhaps the most entertaining and enviable of the park's wild residents are its **marmots.** These largest members of the squirrel family spend their days nibbling wildflowers in subalpine meadows, and stretching out on rocks to bask in the sun. In meadows throughout the park, these chubby creatures seem oblivious to human presence, contentedly grazing only steps away from hikers.

Marmots share these subalpine zones with **pikas,** tiny relatives of the rabbits, that are more often heard than seen. Living among the jumbled rocks of talus slopes, pikas skitter about their rocky domains calling out warnings with a high pitched beep that is surprisingly electronic in tone.

Monkeyflowers, elephant's heads, parrot's beaks, bear grass; they represent just a small fraction of the variety of **wildflowers** to be found on the slopes of Mount Rainier. This mountain's subalpine meadows are among the most celebrated in the Northwest and the world. Although not as colorfully named as the flowers mentioned above, lupines, asters, gentians, avalanche lilies, phlox, heather, and Indian paintbrush all add their own distinctive splashes of color to these slopes in summer.

The meadows at Paradise are much wetter than those at Sunrise, which lies in a rain-shadow zone and consequently is relatively dry. In the northwest corner of the park, the **Carbon River Valley** opens out to the Pacific Ocean and channels moisture-laden air into its valleys. As a result, this valley is a rain forest where tree limbs are draped with mosses and lichens, and where Douglas firs and western red cedars grow to enormous proportions. However, it is in the southeast corner of the park, in the **Grove of the Patriarchs** near the Stevens Canyon Park Entrance, that some of the oldest trees stand—Douglas firs more than 1,000 years old and western cedars more than 25 feet in circumference.

Avoiding the Crowds. On a sunny summer weekend it is sometimes necessary to park more than a mile away from Paradise and walk on forest trails and the road to the meadows. Consequently, the best advice on how to avoid the crowds is to **visit in the spring or fall.** May and October are probably the best months; before and after these months, respectively, the weather can be somewhat dicey and affect road conditions. Keep in mind that in May Paradise will still be snow covered and most park roads will be closed; in June, Paradise may be snow covered and some park roads may be closed. Also, the rainy season starts in mid- to late October and keeps going until early summer.

Perhaps the best tip, if you're traveling in busy months, is to **visit on weekdays** rather than weekends. You might also consider avoiding the Sunrise and Paradise areas altogether, heading instead to the **more remote sections** of the park, such as the Carbon River area in the northwest section, or the Denman Falls/Gobblers Knob area in the southwest. Both are accessible by car and provide the same sorts of stunning vistas you get at Sunrise and Paradise. The Carbon River Road is subject to flood closures; check with park staff. The Westside Road, which leads to the Denman Falls area, is closed due to flood damage 3 miles up (open summer only), so you will have to do some hiking (be sure and check at the ranger station for the latest info).

Otherwise, a good plan is to arrive at either Sunrise or Paradise early in the day—before 10am—spend an hour checking out the visitor center, and then hightail it out to your favorite hiking spot. Likewise, people generally leave the park between 4 and 6pm, so if you can arrange to arrive at a visitor center around 5pm (with the idea of staying put for an hour or so), you can avoid a lot of the unpleasant traffic.

Finally, you might try reversing this advice, hitting Sunrise at sundown. Most park visitors are leaving via the Nisqually Entrance in the park's southwest corner late in the day; you'll be heading in the opposite direction.

Just the Facts

GETTING THERE & GATEWAYS

Unlike its cousin across the Puget Sound, Olympic National Park, no roads completely encircle Rainier; the northwest corner of the park, for example, is only accessible through one entrance.

The **Nisqually Entrance** (also known as the Nisqually-Longmire Road) in the southwest corner of the park is the park's main entrance. Just to the west on Wash. 706 is **Ashford,** where most of the area's accommodations and services are to be found. A few miles further west is **Elbe,** where a few more choices can be located.

However, at the park's northeast corner, the **White River Entrance,** off Wash. 410, provides easier access from Seattle and points north if your goal is only the Sunrise area. The town closest to this entrance is **Greenwater,** which also provides some overnight options.

In the northwest corner, the **Carbon River Entrance** is off Wash. 165. **Enumclaw** offers motels, restaurants, and fuel.

At the southeast corner, the **Stevens Canyon Entrance,** off Wash. 123 from U.S. 12, provides access from Yakima. **Packwood** and **Randle,** both located south of the park on U.S. 12, are two of the largest towns in the nearby area. You'll find some recommendable accommodations in Packwood.

During the summer it is also possible to enter the park from the east on Wash. 410, which also leads to Yakima by way of Chinook Pass. Entering this way gives you the option of heading north to the White River Entrance and Sunrise or south to Stevens Canyon.

In winter, only the Nisqually Entrance is open.

The Nearest Airport. The nearest airport is the **Seattle-Tacoma International Airport** (☎ 206/431-4444), 70 miles northwest of the park (allow about 2 hr. on I-5, Wash. 7, and Wash. 706 to the Nisqually Entrance). The airport is served by practically all major airlines and car-rental companies, whose toll-free numbers are in the appendix.

INFORMATION

Contact the **Superintendent, Mount Rainier National Park,** Tahoma Woods, Star Route, Ashford, WA 98304 (☎ 360/569-2211; www.nps.gov/mora). Mount Rainier National Park publishes a free newspaper, the *Tahoma,* available at all visitor centers, which gives concise information about all activities at the park on a seasonal basis.

VISITOR CENTERS

When you arrive, stop at one of the park's four visitor centers. The **Longmire Museum** (☎ 360/569-2211, ext. 3314) is located just inside the park beyond the Nisqually Entrance and is the welcoming center for the park. The **Henry M. Jackson Memorial Visitor Center** (☎ 360/569-2211, ext. 2328), near Paradise Meadows, is the park's main visitor center. The **Ohanepecosh Visitor Center** (☎ 360/569-2211, ext. 2352), off of Wash. 123 in the southeast corner of the park, is near the Stevens Canyon Entrance. (Open summer only.)

The **Sunrise Visitor Center,** off Wash. 410, past the White River Entrance (☎ 360/569-2211, ext. 2357), is in the northeast section of the park. (Open summer only.)

FEES

Entry into the parks for up to 7 days costs $10 per vehicle. Camping costs $10 to $12 per night.

SPECIAL REGULATIONS & WARNINGS

The main thing to remember in the heavily touristed spots in the subalpine portions of the park is to stay on the trails and stay off the wildflowers. Off-trail tramping erodes the thin, loam topsoil that supports the fragile vegetation.

Be sure to boil any water taken from the park's rivers, as it has been known to carry *Giardia*, the little bug of the mighty intestinal disorder.

Don't even think about heading for a day climb anywhere near the upper altitudes of Rainier without checking in at a ranger station, or employing a guide. Steep snowfields can become slippery in the sun, and there are unstable ice bridges in others. Remember, people die in the high altitudes every year.

SEASONS & CLIMATE

Summer is the warmest and driest time of the year, with frequent fog banks rolling in late and early in the day, and temperatures ranging from the upper 40s to the low 80s. The spring and fall are cool and drizzly, with occasional days of warm weather late in the spring and early in the fall. The greatest rainfall comes in January and December, with daytime temperatures in the 40s. Weather is generally going to get colder and nastier the higher up you go, and of course, there is lots of snow in the higher elevations. This snow can linger well into the summer, even at popular Paradise, as it did in the summer of 1999.

It's important that you dress in layers for a day visit, as you may encounter any type of weather. It can go from warm to cool very quickly as you climb in altitude. Rain can come in suddenly, so rain gear is a good precaution.

Park Highlights

Longmire, just inside the Nisqually Entrance, serves as welcoming center for the park. This is the park's oldest developed area, the site of the historic hotel which opened in 1899. Here you'll find the old Mount Rainier National Park Headquarters, The National Park Inn, a museum, general store, hiker information center, post office, and a year-round lodge and restaurant. Although it sounds as if this must be a small city, it is actually quite compact and rarely very crowded.

Paradise, in the south-central portion of the park, is a subalpine meadow and one of the most popular areas for visitors. Nearby you'll find the Henry M. Jackson Memorial Visitor Center, the park's main visitor center, a gracefully curving stone and concrete structure which houses a snack bar and the only public showers in the park. Interesting exhibits on geology, glaciers, and the local flora and fauna are here. Paradise is also the site of the seasonal (May to October) Paradise Inn, a historic mountain lodge. Rainier Mountaineering Inc., which offers mountaineering classes and leads summit climbs, also has its summer facilities at Paradise.

Ohanepecosh, off Wash. 123 in the park's southeast corner, offers scenic views of the Ohanepecosh River near the small visitor center located here. Inside, look for exhibits focusing primarily on the old-growth forest ecosystem that surrounds this particular area of the park. The 205-site Ohanepecosh Campground is here, as well as several good, short hikes.

At 6,400 feet, **Sunrise,** in the northeast part of the park, is the highest point to which you can drive in the park. Next to the Henry Jackson Visitor Center, this is the second most popular spot. You'll find displays and naturalist-led walks here, a snack bar/restaurant, and interpretive programs on the subalpine and alpine ecosystems. You can also look at the glaciers up close with free telescopes. The visitor center here is open daily from July through mid-September, when the roadway is open.

The **Carbon River area,** in the northwest corner, provides access to the most heavily forested area in the park. The jury is still out as to whether the terrain is actually lowland forest or temperate rain forest. Trails here lead into the backcountry and connect with the **Wonderland Trail.** The **Mowich Lake area** is reached by a separate road (Wash. 165), but they are in close proximity.

If You Only Have 1 Day

Most folks who make Mount Rainier a day trip are coming from the **Seattle** area, and they work their way around to Sunrise from the southwest corner of the park, driving first through **Longmire** to **Paradise,** then **Ohanepecosh,** and on to **Sunrise.** But, Sunrise being named what it is, you might want to go the other way around to get the best daylight, in which case you'll want to enter on Wash. 410 at the park's northeast corner. If you're coming from the south or from Yakima, you'll want to adjust your entry point and itinerary accordingly. The single-day-tripper will probably not be able to visit the Carbon River area in the northwest.

It might be a bit pedestrian, but if you want to get the whole flavor of what Mount Rainier is about, you will probably want to do the normal route and head into the park via the Longmire Entrance in late summer. You get old-growth forests, alpine meadows blooming with flowers, and a look at the rocky scree underneath the Emmons and Winthrop glaciers. Even if you can't see the Carbon River Rain Forest, you can at least read about it at one of the visitor centers. If you'd rather avoid lines of cars later in the day (and who doesn't?), get a jump on things early in the morning. By noon, Rainier is going to be packed, especially on weekends.

For an 80-mile trip, start out at the **Nisqually Entrance** on Wash. 706, and check out the **Longmire Museum** for exhibits on American Indian culture, European exploration, and the area's natural history, as well as the local flora and fauna. If you've already been driving a bit, take a walk on the excellent 0.8-mile **Trail of Shadows** across from the National Park Inn. The trail passes by the mineral springs which once hosted the early hotel, as well as the cabin (reconstructed) built by one of the Longmires in 1888.

Next is an up-close-and-personal look at the fantastic burst of colors in **Paradise's** fields of brilliant paintbrush,

anemones, and gentians. But first, visit the **Henry M. Jackson Memorial Visitor Center** and figure out what you're looking at. It might be the Nisqually or Wilson glacier hanging over your head. For a more up close view of the Nisqually Glacier, take the 1.2-mile (1-hr. round-trip) **Nisqually Vista Trail** from the visitor center. Otherwise, there are numerous trails leading from the parking lot that will allow you to create your own designer wildflower stroll. Please stay on the trails to protect those wildflowers.

From Paradise, head east toward the **Stevens Canyon Entrance,** with your next goal a short hike along the **Grove of the Patriarchs** at Ohanepecosh. This 1.5-mile walk, one of the most popular in the park, is famous for its absolutely huge Douglas firs and cedars, located on a small island accessible by a bridge across the beautiful Ohanepecosh River. If you have time, take the **Ohanepecosh Nature Trail,** which begins at the Visitor Center, a quick 0.5-mile jaunt that will allow you to dip your feet in a shallow hot spring alongside the trail as you gaze down at a meadow of lush grass.

Finally, wind your way through forests of fir, cedar, and hemlock on the way to **Sunrise.** The big, whitecapped mountain in your rearview mirror to the south is Mt. Adams, equal in beauty, but more remote than Mount Rainier. This side of the mountain is glacier-packed, so check out **Emmons Vista** for excellent views of Little Tahoma and the Emmons glacier, or take the 1.5-mile **Sunrise Rim Trail,** which also leads away from the day lodge. For a close-up view, use the telescopes at the visitor center.

If You Have More Time

The best way to explore the park is on foot, and with additional time you'll be able to get out on the trails. And the mother of all park trails is the **Wonderland Trail,** which, as it winds its labyrinthine route around the entire mountain (most folks plan 10 days to 2 weeks to do this one), takes you through any section of the park you might be interested in. There's no law that says you can't do a small portion of the Wonderland Trail, though. Since it's accessible from all the major park centers, you can do a piece as a day hike (see "Day Hikes," below).

The least visited sections of the park are really some of the best, including the incredibly beautiful **Carbon River** area northwest of the mountain. But, like many things in life, the good things take a little more effort to get to. Still, if you have the time, go here. The Carbon River basin, depending on which biologist you talk to, contains either a very wet forest or a temperate rain forest. Either way, the only other temperate rain forest in the United States is on the Olympic Peninsula, making the Carbon River area a unique jewel of an ecosystem. The Carbon River Road is very susceptible to flood damage and may not be passable to vehicles. Check with park staff before driving out.

Organized Tours & Ranger Programs

Gray Line Tours of Seattle (☎ 800/426-7532 or 206/626-5208) offers regularly scheduled bus tours into the park from midspring through midfall, departing daily at 8am from the Convention Center in downtown Seattle. Cost for a 1-day tour is $48.85 per person; an overnight tour, including a night at the Longmire Inn (meals not included), costs $137.90 per person.

Ranger-led tours, discussions, and seminars take place or begin at Longmire, Ohanepecosh, Paradise, and Sunrise visitor centers.

At **Longmire,** there is a daily hike to Carter Falls, a Sunday-morning walk through Longmire Meadow, and an evening stroll on Fridays and Saturdays that focuses on the area's cultural history. Other walks and discussions are frequently scheduled.

At **Ohanepecosh,** there are several ranger-led hikes and walks along popular trails almost daily, as well as evening programs during July and August devoted to Mount Rainier's history.

From **Paradise,** there are daily walks to view wildflowers and glaciers, as well as more strenuous ranger-led hikes on the weekends. Park naturalists also roam the area answering questions daily.

From the **Sunrise** area, there are daily ranger-led walks, weekend wildlife walks, and, on Saturday, a walk to the Emmons Glacier. During July and August there are evening campfire programs at White River Campground.

Day Hikes

Some trails, especially those near Sunrise and Paradise, are packed throughout the summer. However, many forest trails offer significant solitude. Trails in the northwest corner, near the Carbon River Entrance, are relatively quiet, though this road has been closed to motor vehicles since 1996 due to flood damage. Mowich Lake, however, sees more weekend foot traffic since the road there is open in the summer.

For information on trail availability or closures, call the **Wilderness Information Center** (☎ 360/569-2211, ext. 3317).

ALL THE WAY AROUND MOUNT RAINIER

Wonderland Trail

93 mi. RT. Allow 10 to 14 days. Strenuous. Approximate 7,000-ft. elevation gain possible in a day. Access: This hike can be started form Longmire, Paradise, Sunrise, Mowich Lake, or Carbon River.

With varying degrees of difficulty, this 93-mile loop circles Mount Rainier, with numerous connecting trailheads, and is the mother of all trails in the park. To some, it's a northwest rite of passage to make this loop through some of the most stunning vistas in the continental United

States. Think hard and plan ahead before you try to take it all at once. You'll probably want to leave yourself about 2 weeks' time to make the whole loop, and you might want to cache some chow at various points along the path that you can pick up along the way. There are more things to see on this trail than you can name. But, of course, expect to find yourself traveling through alpine meadows, glacial streams, mountain passes, valley forests, and an ultimate summit point of 6,500 feet at Panhandle Gap. There are many backcountry camping spots along the way that provide water in the summer, but be sure to purify every drop. In the interest of planning shorter trips, keep in mind that you can connect with this trail from any of the spokelike trails that crisscross and touch the trail throughout the park, allowing you to set up a hiking mileage and time schedule all your own.

LONGMIRE AREA

Although the Westside Road is closed 3 miles up, the **Lake George and Gobblers Knob Lookout Trail** is open.

SHORT HIKES

Carter Falls Trail

2 mi. one way. Easy. Access: 100 yd. downhill from the Cougar Park Campground on the road to Paradise.

This trail passes a wooden pipeline that once carried water which generated electricity for Longmire. Go past Carter Falls about 50 yards for a look at the second falls, the zany Madcap Falls. This trail is part of the Wonderland Trail and takes you to Paradise to the east, or Indian Henry's to the west.

Rampart Ridge Trail

4.6 mi. RT. Easy to moderate. 1,339-ft. elevation gain. Access: Across the road from the Longmire Museum.

This is a somewhat steep trail at first, before you arrive at the top of an ancient lava flow called the Ramparts, which offers panoramic views of the Nisqually Valley to the south, Mount Rainier to the north, and, to the west, the site of the massive Kautz Creek Mudflow of 1947. It's also your connection with many of the other trails in the area, including the Van Trump, Comet, and Christine Falls trails.

Trail of Shadows Nature Trail

0.7 mi. RT. Easy. Access: Across the road from the Longmire Museum.

This short, level loop trail is a highly enjoyable walk through the forest around Longmire Meadow. It takes you past the former site of the Longmire Springs Hotel, as well as an old log cabin that's the oldest man-made structure in the park. Don't drink out of the springs.

Van Trump Park & Comet Falls Trail

5 mi. RT. Moderate. Access: Near Christine Falls Bridge on the road to Paradise.

This steep (total elevation gain of 2,200 ft.) trail leads through beautiful old-growth forest to scenic Comet Falls, the second highest falls in the park at 320 feet. Another mile uphill takes you to beautiful views of the Nisqually, Van Trump, and Kautz glaciers. This is a popular trail in the summer, but can be dangerous in early summer due to flooding; stop in at the ranger station and ask for information on trail conditions before heading up.

PARADISE AREA

Alta Vista Summit

1.5 mi. RT. Easy. Access: Jackson Visitor Center parking lot.

This popular day hike meanders through alpine meadows along a trail that leads to the top of an overlook of Paradise

Meadows, Mount Adams, and Mount St. Helens to the south.

Bench & Snow Lakes Trail

2.5 mi. RT. Easy to moderate. Access: Stevens Canyon Rd., 1.5 mi. east of Reflection Lakes.

You can catch both lakes on this trail of gradual ups and downs over low ridges before reaching Bench Lake after 0.75 mile, then continuing another 0.5 mile to Snow Lake, with beautiful views of beargrass and meadow flowers. The round-trip takes about an hour, with a 700-foot elevation gain.

Dead Horse Creek Trail

3 mi. RT. Easy to moderate. Access: The northern end of the Jackson Visitor Center parking lot.

The Dead Horse Trail serves as a conduit to the Moraine and Glacier Vista trails, as well as providing beautiful views of the Nisqually Glacier to your left as you head up the ridge. You will be rewarded with especially dramatic views if you take the Moraine Trail spur to the left, 0.75 mile up the path.

Nisqually Vista Trail

1.2 mi. RT. Easy. Access: Henry M. Jackson Memorial Visitor Center.

This interpretive trail leads across rolling terrain to explore the high country flowers, with views of the Nisqually Glacier.

A LONGER HIKE

Skyline Loop Trails

5.8 to 6.5 mi. RT. Moderate. Access: To the left of the Paradise Ranger Station, next to the rest rooms.

Most hikers don't get much higher on Mount Rainier without going to the top, at least on a day hike. These trails are sort of the extended versions of all the trails that surround Paradise, offering lots of beautiful subalpine meadows and close-up views of the Nisqually Glacier, one of the most visible and beautiful glaciers in the park. At Panorama Point, there is a pit toilet for a quick stop before the trail begins to loop back around to the southeast. At the top of this loop, you may have to traverse some snow. There's a 1,700-foot elevation gain. On the way back, check out the views of Mount Adams and Mount St. Helens.

SUNRISE & NORTHEASTERN AREAS

Berkeley Park/Grand Park Trail

13 mi. RT. Strenuous. Access: Branches off the Sourdough Ridge Trail (described below).

Head for the high tableland meadows and wildflower and green field bonanza at Grand Park. You can even hike across these, should you so choose, and picnic under the trees. But bring plenty of water—there's none up here. Head out of the Sunrise parking lot to the Sourdough Ridge Trail, where the view is the most scenic and the road the easiest. At 6,700-foot Frozen Lake, descend toward Berkeley Park, keeping right with the trail to Mystic Lake. Berkeley Camp is 4 miles from Sunrise, and it's another 2.5 miles, mostly uphill, to the Plateau of Grand Park.

Burroughs Mountain Trail

7 mi. RT. Moderate to strenuous. Access: Branches off the Sunrise Rim Trail (described below).

If you can't handle the snow, you might not want to take this trail. It's ice-ax territory, sometimes until early August, so come prepared. Follow the Sunrise Rim Trail, which begins on the south side of the Sunrise Visitor Center parking lot, to Shadow Lake and Sunrise Campground, and to a sharp upturn toward the First Burroughs Peak at 7,000 feet. Beyond this point, you're in a delicate tundra climate, one of the few in the Lower 48. It's possible to take the Frozen Lake Trail at

First Burroughs and make a loop back to Sunrise, if you don't feel like climbing anymore. However, should you decide to head up the remaining 400 vertical feet, you'll be treated to fantastic views of Mount Rainier and the Emmons and Winthrop glaciers.

Glacier Basin Trail

7 mi. RT. Moderate to strenuous. Access: Past the White River Campground Entrance Station, in the upper area of the White River Campground.

Watch for rusting artifacts on this journey through a part of the park that wasn't always so protected. You'll see remnants of an old mining operation from the late 1800s in this glacial valley. Follow an old road up past the headwaters of the White River. After 1 mile, veer to the left for beautiful views of the Emmons Glacier. Beyond the junction of the trail with the Burroughs Mountain Trail, you'll arrive at Glacier Basin Camp. From here it's not far to Camp Schurman, in the crook of the Emmons and Winthrop glaciers. It does, however, involve crossing a glacier and is not for casual hikers. Look for climbers making the ascent to the summit here, along a secondary route.

Mt. Fremont Trail

5.5 mi. RT. Moderate. Access: The north end of the Sunrise Visitor Center parking lot.

From the trailhead you climb for about 0.33 mile along this popular trail through the surrounding meadows, then follow Sourdough Ridge to the left toward Frozen Lake. At the end of the lake, take the fork to the right for the easy 1.3-mile hike to the Fremont Lookout, from where you can get excellent glimpses of the surrounding Cascades and distant Olympics. You might even be able to see Seattle, on a clear day. The round-trip has a 1,200-foot elevation gain.

Naches Peak Trail

3.5 mi. RT. Easy. Access: Take the Pacific Crest Trailhead located near Tipsoo Lake for a junction with the Naches Peak Loop Trail (there is also a wheelchair-accessible path at Tipsoo Lake, near the Pacific Crest Trailhead junction).

This is another popular one, with stunning views from the top of Naches Peak of the meadows and lakes stretching toward Rainier's icy summit. From the Pacific Crest Trailhead, head south, traversing the east side of the Naches Peak. There's the junction with the loop that can be taken back to Tipsoo Lake, or continue ahead 0.5 mile to Dewey Lake, where there are good campsites.

Palisades Lake Trail

7 mi. RT. Easy to moderate. Access: Sunrise Visitor Center.

This is a pretty popular trail, so don't expect to get away from other hikers. However, if you're out for a fairly invigorating stroll through forest and meadowlands, this is a good one, with only small rises and falls in elevation as you wander past small alpine lakes towards a rock outcropping called, appropriately enough, the Palisades. There are also good wilderness campsites a little farther on at Dick's Lake and the Upper Palisades Lake, although they tend to be crowded in the summertime.

Sourdough Ridge Nature Trail

1.5 mi. RT. Easy. Access: Sunrise Visitor Center parking lot.

This loop provides you with a brief glimpse of what's on the larger path. It's a self-guided tour of the summer wildflowers and alpine meadows that's quite popular, and good for kids.

Sourdough Ridge/Dege Peak Trail

4 mi. RT. Easy to moderate. Access: Sunrise Visitor Center.

From the trailhead, climb to a ridge top and turn east beneath the gaze of Antler Peak, after which you'll cruise along the ridge for wonderful views of Rainier to the south and the brilliant greens of the Yakima parklands below.

At the top of Dege Peak, look south for close-up views of the Cowlitz Chimneys and farther-off views of whitecapped Mt. Adams.

Summerland Trail

8.5 mi. RT. Easy to moderate. Access: Past the White River Entrance, on the way to the Sunrise or the White River areas.

If you're into mountain goats, go ahead to Panhandle Gap, about 1.5 miles past the end of the 4-mile, one-way, entrance into the Frying Pan Glacier area. This trail can host hundreds of hikers on a peak summer day, so beware. And please stay on the trails to avoid trampling the wildflowers. It's a 3.5-mile graded walk through mature forests before entering the Frying Pan Creek area, where the scenery opens up into the brushy upper Frying Pan Valley. From there it's a 0.5-mile steep climb to the spectacular Summerland Meadows. The total elevation gain is 1,500 feet.

Sunrise Rim Trail

3 mi. RT. Easy. Access: Sunrise Visitor Center.

This is another nature trail with many interpretive signs to tell you what to look for as you gaze up at Mount Rainier to the north. About 1.5 miles into the trail, you'll arrive at Shadow Lake, and just beyond, the walk-in Sunrise Campground. With a little more effort, you can hike south to the glacier overlook and be awed by the blue-white overhangs of Emmons Glacier.

OHANEPECOSH AREA

Grove of the Patriarchs Trail

1.5 mi. RT. Easy. Access: Just west of the Stevens Canyon Entrance on Stevens Canyon Rd.

This short and incredibly popular trail follows the Ohanepecosh River before crossing over a bridge to an island of incredibly huge, thousand-year-old Douglas firs and western red cedars. Even though it's well traveled, it's still a pretty awe-inspiring place, if you can manage to find a little silence in which to meditate on the grandeur of the trees.

Silver Falls Trail

3 mi. RT. Easy. Access: Ohanepecosh Visitor Center.

This trail, a fairly level one, is popular with families as it winds its way through old-growth forests and over a bridge above the almost achingly pristine waters of the Ohanepecosh River facing the falls that give the area its name. The misty falls themselves drop 75 feet. Across the bridge below the falls is the return trail to the Ohanepecosh Campground.

NORTHWESTERN RAINIER

In 1999, the Carbon River Road reopened after years of storm damage. This is a very flood-prone area. For all trails listed below, remember that the road may end at the park boundary 5 miles from the Ipsut Creek Campground. Be sure to call the **Park Information Line** (☎ 360/569-2211) for information before taking any of the northwest Rainier trips.

Storm damage notwithstanding, all trails in the northwestern section of the park can best be reached by driving to the end of the Ipsut Creek Campground Road (or as close as possible) and connecting with the Wonderland Trail, or driving in on the Mowich River Road (Wash. 165). Access to the Wonderland Trail along this corner of the park by car, unlike those on the southern and northeastern side, is limited. The Carbon Glacier and Rainforest, Mystic Lake, Moraine Park, Mowich Lake, and Tolmie Peak trails can all be reached via the Carbon River Road and the Mowich Lake Road by car, or by the Wonderland Trail on an extended hike.

Carbon Glacier & Moraine Park Trails

7 to 11 mi. RT (depending on route). Moderate to strenuous. Access: The end of the road at the Ipsut Creek Campground.

You begin this hike toward Moraine Park on the Wonderland Trail, the first 3 miles of which are a gentle uphill grade as they parallel the beautiful glacial waters of the Carbon River. Subsequently, the trail crosses the river on a suspension bridge just below the lower edge of the Carbon Glacier. Take a right turn on the Wonderland Trail at its junction with the Northern Loop, and the trail will lead you to the edge of this, the lowest and seemingly most monstrous glacier in the Lower 48. The trail then becomes a series of steep switchbacks that lead you through the neighboring forest to Moraine Park. Along the way, you'll pass several campsites (Carbon River, Dick Creek, and further along, Mystic Lake).

Mystic Lake Trail

15.8 mi. Moderate to strenuous. Access: First, take the trail to Moraine Park, then continue to Mystic Lake.

To reach Mystic Lake, you must first hike to the narrow, subalpine valley of Moraine Park, a moderate to strenuous trip. When Mystic Lake is included in the hike, the entire round-trip distance becomes 15.8 miles with elevation gains of 3,900 feet. Beyond the park, the trail goes over two small, wooded ridges, and then descends a short distance to Mystic Lake. The trail was named by two early naturalists who claimed to have seen a mysterious whirlpool near the lake's outlet. Many people use the campsites around Mystic Lake as base camps for exploring the Curtis Ridge area, and for spectacular views of the Winthrop and Carbon glaciers.

Spray Park Trail

6 mi. RT. Moderate. Access: The southeast side of the Mowich Lake Walk-in Campground at the end of Mowich Lake Rd.

They say you should see Spray Falls at sunset if you want to see the light hit the spray action. Set amid subalpine meadows, Spray Falls is a spectacular sight in the summer when the flowers are blooming, although most of the hike proceeds through forested terrain. The trailhead intersects the Wonderland Trail after a 0.25-mile descent. Follow the Spray Park Trail east for 2 miles, through the woods, across Lee Creek, and eventually to a junction with a spur trail to overlook the falls. The next 0.5 mile to the Spray Park Meadows is a steep climb up a series of switchbacks. Even more extensive meadows are found in another 0.5 mile. The whole trip has an elevation gain of 1,300 feet.

Tolmie Peak

6.5 mi. RT. Moderate. Access: The end of Mowich Lake Rd. on the left side of the lake.

This is a hugely popular day hike, with lots of traffic from weekenders and kids, but you know you can't really go that wrong anywhere around here. The trail proceeds gently through 1.25 miles of forested woodland to the junction at Ipsut Pass (elevation 5,100 ft.). Stay left and proceed uphill another 1.75 miles to the subalpine meadows at Eunice Lake for a look at how far you're going to have to climb to Tolmie Peak. From this point on, the trail becomes moderate in difficulty as it gains elevation. *Note:* Tolmie Peak is closed to overnight backpackers. The entire hike has a 1,010-foot elevation gain.

Other Summer Sports & Activities

Biking. It seems that wildflowers and bike tires don't mix. There currently aren't any trails open to mountain bikers in Mount Rainier National Park. However, there are plenty of trails to ride at nearby **Crystal Mountain** and **White Pass ski areas** during the summer months.

Crystal Mountain is by far the most popular and is known for its grueling climbs and brake-turning downhills. Luckily, you can avoid much of the climbing by riding the lifts up. The lifts generally operate only on weekends. A good gravel road for great biking is Westside Road, which you can access through the Nisqually Entrance of Mount Rainier National Park. It is completely closed to motorized vehicles after three miles. One of the best reasons to ride this road is the chance to get on some of the little-used west-side hiking trails (closed to bikes). Try strapping some hiking boots on your bike; this is a great way to get away from the crowds and access some of the rare, less crowded areas of the park. However, you might want to call ahead for information on the usage of Westside Road.

Boating & Canoeing. Located in the northwest corner of the park, Mowich Lake is a pristine little lake with a peek-aboo view of the mountain from its west side. The water is incredibly clear, and it's fun to paddle around gazing down into the deep at the large logs and boulders lying on the bottom. Early morning and late afternoon are particularly good times. You might catch a glimpse of an otter, and in the evening, deer often feed in the meadows by the lake's edge. A walk-in campground beside the lake makes this a great spot for a weekend camping and paddling trip. Yes, there are even a few fish in the lake if you want to try your luck.

Fishing. One of the best things about fishing in Mount Rainier National Park is that no fishing license is required. The bad thing is that the fishing isn't very good. However there are some fish out there, and you're welcome to try your hand at catching a few. Lots of people do. Just remember that only artificial lures and flies can be used within the park, and some posted waters are closed to fishing. Ask for details.

For the most part, glacial silt keeps Mount Rainier's rivers too cloudy for fishing in the summer. The Ohanepecosh River is one exception. This river in the southeast corner of the park flows clear throughout the summer and is designated fly-fishing only. Anglers are also encouraged to release the trout they catch. Most of the park's many lakes are home to one or another species of trout, but in most cases you're going to have to hike in to do your fishing. Some shorter hikes include Sunrise Lake below Sunrise Point; and Louise, Bench, and Snow lakes, east of Paradise off the road to the Stevens Canyon Park Entrance.

Horseback Riding. If you'd like to do some horseback riding, you've got a couple of choices in the area. In Elbe, you'll find **EZ Times Outfitters,** 18703 Wash. 706 (☎ 360/569-2449), which leads rides into the Elbe State Forest. Over on the east side of the park, 19 miles east of Chinook Pass on Wash. 410, you'll find **Susee's Skyline Packers,** 90 Bumping River Rd. (☎ 509/653-2633). East of White Pass on U.S. 12, you'll find **Indian Creek Corral** (☎ 509/672-2400) near the shore of Rimrock Lake. Horse rental rates start around $16 per hour.

Mountaineering. Each year, more than 9,000 people set out to climb the 14,410-foot summit of Mount Rainier. That only slightly more than half make it to the top is a testament to how difficult this climb is. Although the ascent does not require rock-climbing skills, the glacier crossings require basic mountaineering knowledge, and the 9,000-foot climb from Paradise is physically demanding. Also, the elevation often causes altitude sickness. This is not a mountain to be attempted by the unprepared or the untrained. Over the years, dozens of people have died attempting the summit. Because of the many difficulties presented by summit ascents at Mount Rainier, this mountain often serves as a training ground for expeditions headed to peaks all over the world.

The easiest and most popular route starts at Paradise at 5,400 feet and climbs to the stone climbers' shelter at 10,188-foot Camp Muir. From here, climbers, roped together for safety, set out in the middle of the night to reach Columbia Crest, the mountain's highest point. From the summit on a clear day, seemingly all of Washington and much of Oregon stretches below.

The best way for most people to climb Mount Rainier is with **Rainier Mountaineering,** 535 Dock St., Suite 209, Tacoma, WA 98402 (☎ 253/627-6242; fax 253/627-1280; www.rmiguides.com), in winter, or Paradise, WA 98398 (☎ 360/569-2227), in summer, which offers a variety of mountaineering classes as well as guided summer climbs. A 1-day basic climbing class combined with the 2-day summit climb costs a little more than $500.

White-Water Rafting. The Tieton River, which flows down the eastern slopes of the Cascades to the east of the national park is one of the state's most popular rafting rivers. The rafting season lasts for the month of September during the annual drawdown of water from Rimrock Reservoir, and the rapids are class III. Rafting companies offering trips on this river include **All Rivers Adventures** (☎ 800/74-FLOAT or 509/782-2254), **Alpine Adventures** (☎ 800/926-RAFT), and **River Riders** (☎ 800/448-RAFT).

Wildlife Viewing. Hunting is prohibited in the Mount Rainier National Park, and consequently deer, elk, and mountain goats within the park have lost their fear of humans. Anyone hiking the park's trails in the summer can expect to encounter some of these large mammals. Deer are the most commonly spotted, although it is the park's mountain goats that seem to command the greatest interest. Look for goats on Goat Island Mountain across the White River valley from Sunrise (use binoculars) on the Summerland Trail, on Mount Fremont (5.5-mile round-trip hike from Sunrise), and at Skyscraper Pass (7-mile round-trip hike from Sunrise).

Undoubtedly, the most seen mammals in the park are the marmots, which resemble beavers, but have round tails and live in the subalpine meadows. These big, shaggy squirrels are often seen lying on rocks and soaking up the sun. They often allow people to approach quite close, but when alarmed, will let loose with a shrill whistle.

Winter Sports & Activities

Cross-Country Skiing. There are several ungroomed cross-country trails around the Paradise and Longmire areas. Perhaps what's equally satisfying is the absence of crowds and cars that haunt these regions during the summer months. Peace and quiet abound here when snow covers the landscape. There is often a threat of avalanches in this area (check at the Jackson Visitor Center or Paradise Ranger Station). The slopes above the Paradise Lodge usually stay covered with snow well into June. You can rent cross-country skis at **Longmire** at the National Park Inn (☎ 360/569-2411). Skis, poles, and shoes will cost you $15 per day.

West of the park, the Mount Tahoma Trails Association Trail System maintains almost 90 miles of easy to difficult trails, which are accessed from Ashford (just follow the signs to the sno-parks). For information, maps, or hut reservations, contact the **Tahoma Trails Association,** P.O. Box 206, Ashford, WA 98304 (☎ 360/569-2451; www.mashell.com/~mtta), or stop by their headquarters in Ashford, which is usually open on winter weekends.

There are 10 miles of trails at **White Pass** (☎ 509/672-3100, or 509/672-3101 for a snow report), which is located about 20 miles southeast of the park.

Outside the Northeast Entrance of the park, **Crystal Mountain** (☎ 360/663-2265; www.crystalmt.com) offers good backcountry skiing, though there are no maintained trails. Only experienced skiers should attempt backcountry skiing here due to the difficult conditions and danger of avalanches.

Downhill Skiing. There are no downhill ski possibilities within Mount Rainier National Park, however, the nearby **White Pass** and **Crystal Mountain ski areas** (see "Cross-Country Skiing," above) are highly recommended.

Snowmobiling. Snowmobiles are permitted on designated roadways only, when such roadways are closed by snow to normal traffic. Do not attempt to travel cross-country, on trails, or on undesignated roads. Obtain a copy of the park's snowmobile regulations.

Snowshoeing. If you've never tried snowshoeing and want to, visit Mount Rainier National Park on a winter weekend or holiday when free, ranger-led snowshoe walks lasting about 90 minutes are offered. If, after getting a taste for snowshoeing you want to do more, you can rent snowshoes by the day in Longmire at the **gift shop** beside the National Park Inn (☎ **360/569-2411**) for $12 per day.

One of the better snowshoeing routes in the park is the marked route from the Paradise parking lot behind the Jackson Visitor Information Center to the Nisqually Glacier Overlook. The Nisqually Vista Trail is only 1.25 miles long and twists and turns as it meanders up and down hills. At the turnaround, you're treated to a great view of the glacier and the rest of the mountain.

Lower down on the mountain, at Longmire, snowshoers can make a 4.6-mile loop up Rampart Ridge. This steep trail requires some route finding and the snow level is not always reliable, but if conditions are right, it makes for an enjoyable and rigorous hike. Another good snowshoeing trail in this same area is the trail to Carter Falls, which starts above Longmire just before the Cougar Rock Campground. This 2.2-mile round-trip trail follows a section of the Wonderland Trail. It's all uphill to Carter Falls and it crosses several avalanche chutes.

Camping

There are almost 600 campsites in Mount Rainier in five drive-in campgrounds. Only one of these, Sunshine Point, is open year-round; all others are open seasonally (all are open by the end of June until mid-September, though specific opening and closing dates are dependent on weather). There is a 14-day limit on camping during July and August. None of the campgrounds in the

Campground	Total Sites	RV Hookups	Dump Station	Toilets	Drinking Water
Cougar Rock	200	No	Yes	Yes	Yes
*Ipsut Creek**	29	No	No	No	No
La Wis Wis	105	No	No	Yes	Yes
*Mowich Lake**	10	No	No	No	No
Ohanepecosh	208	No	Yes	Yes	Yes
*Sunrise**	8	No	No	No	No
Sunshine Point	18	No	No	Yes	Yes
White River	117	No	No	Yes	Yes

* Camping here requires a Mount Rainier National Park backcountry permit.
** Currently closed to car campers due to road washout; camping possible year-round with backcountry permit.

park have RV utility hookups, nor are there laundry or shower facilities.

You must make reservations at Cougar Rock and Ohanapecosh Campgrounds between June 28 and Labor Day. Other campgrounds are on a first-come, first-served basis. You can make reservations for one of the five group sites at Cougar Rock Campground up to 90 days before your stay by contacting **Group Camping Reservations,** Mount Rainier National Park, Tahoma Woods, Star Route, Ashford, WA 98304 (☎ **360/569-2211,** ext. 3301).

Backcountry camping is free with a permit obtained at any of the ranger stations. Reservations, which cost $20 per permit, may be requested up to 60 days in advance of your hike or climb. Call ☎ **360/569/2211,** ext. 3317).

Cougar Rock Campground is located 2.3 miles northwest of Longmire and has an amphitheater for ranger programs. **Ohanepecosh Campground,** 11 miles north of Packwood, Washington, on Wash. 123, also has an amphitheater. **Sunshine Point Campground** is located 0.33 mile from the Nisqually Entrance, and **White River Campground** is 5 miles west of the White River Entrance. **Ipsut Creek Camp Campground,** 5.3 miles east of the park's Carbon River Entrance, is currently closed to vehicular traffic due

to storm damage, but is open to backcountry campers.

There are two walk-in campgrounds that often have spaces available even on weekends. **Mowich Lake Campground** is in the northwest corner of the park, not far from Ipsut Creek Campground, and the sites are only 100 yards from a parking lot. If you're prepared for a longer walk in, consider the **Sunrise Campground,** which is about a mile from the Sunrise parking lot.

When the park campgrounds are full, try **La Wis Wis,** a national forest campground on U.S. 12 and the Cowlitz River, near the Ohanepecosh Entrance to the park. There are also numerous unremarkable National Forest Service campgrounds along U.S. 12 east of White Pass and along Wash. 310 east of the park. These campgrounds will be your best chance of finding a campsite on a Friday or Saturday night in summer. The campgrounds along Wash. 410 tend to be less crowded since they are harder to reach and are not near any fishing lakes.

Accommodations

For information or reservations at the lodgings inside the park, contact **Mount Rainier Guest Services,** P.O. Box 108, Ashford, WA 98304 (☎ **360/569-2275;**

Showers	Fire Pits/ Grills	Laundry	Public Phone	Reserve	Fees	Open
No	Yes	No	Yes	No	$12	Late May to Mid-Oct
Yes	No	No	No	No	Free	**
No	Yes	No	No	No	$9–$12	Mid-May to Mid-Sept
No	Yes	No	No	No	Free	Year-round
No	Yes	No	Yes	No	$12	Late May to Late Oct
No	Yes	No	No	No	Free	Year-round
No	Yes	No	No	No	$10	Year-round
No	Yes	No	No	No	$10	Late June to Late Sept

fax 360/569-2770; www.guestservices.com/rainier).

There are a number of places to stay in the surrounding communities in addition to those reviewed here. For a list, contact the **Seattle Visitor's Bureau** (☎ **206/461-5800**) or the **Enumclaw Area Chamber of Commerce** (☎ **360/825-7666**).

INSIDE THE PARK

National Park Inn

Located at the Longmire Entrance, off Wash. 706 (P.O. Box 108, Ashford, WA 98304). ☎ **360/569-2275.** 25 units, 18 with bathroom. $73 double without bathroom, $101–$136 double with bathroom. AE, DC, DISC, MC, V.

Located in Longmire in the southwest corner of the park, this rustic lodge was opened in 1920 and fully renovated in 1990. With only 25 rooms and open year-round, the National Park Inn makes a great little getaway or base for exploring the mountain. The inn's front veranda has a view of Mount Rainier, and inside there's a guest lounge with a river-rock fireplace that's perfect for winter-night relaxing. The guest rooms vary in size, but come with rustic furniture, new carpeting, and coffeemakers. In winter this lodge is popular with cross-country skiers; skis and snowshoes can be rented here. The inn's restaurant has a limited menu that nevertheless manages to have something for everyone. There's also a small bar. This is a nonsmoking establishment. You'll need to book reservations well in advance during the summer months. If at first you don't succeed, keep trying because there are often plenty of cancellations.

Paradise Inn

Located just east of the Henry M. Jackson Memorial Visitor Center (P.O. Box 108, Ashford, WA 98304). ☎ **360/569-2275.** 119 units, 86 with bathroom. $73 double without bathroom, $100–$140 double with bathroom; $145 suite. AE, DC, DISC, MC, V. Closed early Oct to mid-May.

Built in 1917 high on the flanks of Mount Rainier in an area aptly known as Paradise, this rustic lodge offers breathtaking views of the mountain and the nearby Nisqually Glacier. Miles of trails and meadows make this the perfect spot for some relatively easy alpine exploring. Cedar-shake siding, huge exposed beams, cathedral ceilings, and a gigantic stone fireplace all add up to a quintessential mountain retreat. A warm and cozy atmosphere prevails. The guest rooms vary in size and amenities, so be sure to specify which type you'd like. The inn's large dining room serves three meals a day, and the Sunday brunch, served from 11am to 2:30pm, is legendary. There's also a snack bar and a lounge. The lodge is entirely nonsmoking.

OUTSIDE THE SOUTHWEST (NISQUALLY) ENTRANCE

Alexander's Country Inn

37515 Wash. 706 E., Ashford, WA 98304. ☎ **800/654-7615** or 360/569-2300. Fax 360/569-2323. 12 units, 2 houses. May 1–Oct 31 $89–$95 double; $115–$135 suite. Nov 1–Apr 30 $75 double; $85–$95 suite. Rates include full breakfast. MC, V.

Located just outside the park's Nisqually Entrance, this large bed-and-breakfast first opened as an inn back in 1912. Today, as then, it is one of the preferred places to stay in the area, offering not only comfortable rooms but some of the best food around. Much care went into the interior restoration. The first floor is taken up by the dining room, but on the second floor you'll find a big lounge where you can sit by the fire on a cold night. By far the best room in the house is the tower suite, which is in a turret and has plenty of windows looking out on the woods. After a hard day of playing on the mountain, there's no better place to relax than in the hot tub overlooking the inn's trout pond. The inn also rents two three-bedroom houses.

The Hobo Inn

Wash. 7 (P.O. Box 921), Elbe, WA 98330. ☎ **360/569-2500**. E-mail: mrrdc@mashell. com. 7 units. May–Sept $70–$85 double. Oct–Apr $50–$60 double. AE, DISC, DC, MC, V.

If you're a railroad buff, you won't want to pass up the opportunity to spend the night in a remodeled caboose. Each of the eight cabooses is a little different (one even has its own private hot tub). Though the oldest of the cars dates from 1916, they have all been outfitted with comfortable beds and bathrooms. Some have bay windows while others have cupolas. For the total railroad experience, you can dine in the adjacent Mount Rainier Dining Co. dining car restaurant and go for a ride on the Mount Rainier Scenic Railroad.

Mountain Meadows Inn Bed & Breakfast

28912 Wash. 706 E., Ashford, WA 98304. ☎ **360/569-2788**. 6 units (all with private bathroom). $85–$135 double. Rates include breakfast. MC, V.

Set beneath tall trees beside a small creek, this B&B was built in 1910 as the home of the superintendent for the lumber mill in the town of National, which was the site of the largest sawmill west of the Mississippi. This impressive old home still stands and is today filled with unique collections. There is an outstanding display of memorabilia of John Muir and the national parks, authentic Northwest Coast Indian basketry, and a 1,000-volume nature library. The big front porch overlooks the creek, and there is room to roam on nearby trails through the National town site.

Nisqually Lodge

31609 Wash. 706, Ashford, WA 98304. ☎ **360/569-8804**. Fax 360/569-2435. www. escapetothemountains.com. 24 units. TV. $73–$80 double. AE, DC, MC, V.

This modern lodge is well located near the Nisqually Entrance to Mount Rainier National Park, and with a popular restaurant, the Rainier Overland, next door. They offer guest laundry, an outdoor hot tub, and satellite TV. You can read or relax by the fireplace in their Great Room.

Stone Creek Lodge

38624 Wash. 706 E., Ashford, WA 98304. ☎ **800/678-3942** or 360/569-2355. 10 cabins. $50–$120 double. AE, DISC, MC, V.

Located only 200 yards from the park's Nisqually Entrance, these cabins are set amid green lawns that attract deer throughout the year. These are not the most atmospheric of the cabins right outside the park entrance, but they are the cleanest and most up-to-date (aside from those at Wellspring and Stormking, which are both several miles farther down the road). Big picture windows let in plenty of light. Larger cabins have kitchens and fireplaces and sleep up to six people; smaller ones have microwaves and refrigerators; and one (no. 10) has a fireplace. Hot tubs have been added. You might even get in on a marshmallow toast over an evening campfire.

Stormking

P.O. Box 126, Ashford, WA 98304. ☎ **360/ 569-2964**. Fax 360/569-2964. www.mashell. com/~strmking. 1 cabin. $110 double. Rate includes breakfast in winter. MC, V.

Stormking started out as another hot tub and massage facility similar to the long-established Wellspring, and people enjoyed the setting and experience so much that they kept telling co-owner Deborah Sample that she should build a cabin and take overnight guests. That's just what she and co-owner Steven Brown did, and it's a gorgeous cabin. Set on the far side of a footbridge over a tiny pond, the modern cabin has a slate-floored entry hall, parquet floors, a woodstove, stereo system with plenty of relaxing music, and a high ceiling. In the big bathroom, with flagstone floor and plants, you'll find a double shower amid the greenery. Out on the back deck you'll find the hot tub. Spa treatments are now offered. This place appeals primarily to young, active travelers and others without children.

Wellspring

54922 Kernahan Rd., Ashford, WA 98304. ☎ **360/569-2514.** Fax 360/569-2285. 4 units, 3 log cabins, 1 cottage, 1 tree house. $95–$145 double. MC, V.

Billing itself a woodland spa, this rustic and relaxing hideaway more than lives up to its name and is an excellent choice for anyone who enjoys being pampered. Private hot tubs and wood-fired saunas will take the chill out of even the coldest night, while sore muscles will benefit from a massage by owner Sunny Thompson-Ward. Accommodations are an eclectic and fanciful mix. In the modern log cabins, tucked up against the edge of the forest, you'll find feather beds, woodstoves, and vaulted ceilings. In The Nest, you'll find a queen-size bed suspended from the skylight ceiling by ropes. In the Three Bears Cottage, you'll find rustic log furniture and a full kitchen; kids are allowed in this cottage only. In the Tatoosh Room, there's a large stone fireplace, a whirlpool tub, and a waterfall shower. Want to sleep in a greenhouse with a cedar hot tub and wood-fired sauna? (You can, but you can't have the room to yourself until 9pm.) Several of the rooms and the cabins come with a breakfast basket. Hot tubs and saunas are an additional $5 per person per hour for guests. No smoking allowed. Three deluxe tent cabins are scheduled to be completed by 2000.

OUTSIDE THE NORTHEAST (WHITE RIVER) ENTRANCE

Alta Crystal Resort at Mount Rainier

68317 Wash. 410 E., Greenwater, WA 98022. ☎ **800/277-6475** or 360/663-0728. Fax 360/663-2500. www.altacrystalresort.com.

E-mail: altacrystalresort@msn.com. 24 units. $99–$179 (1–4 people). AE, MC, V.

This is the closest lodging to the northeast (White River) park entrance and the Sunrise area. This resort with wooded grounds is popular in winter when skiers flock to Crystal Mountain's slopes (just minutes away), but is most popular in late spring through early fall. The resort features chalets and cabins, and a new log honeymoon cabin is available. There is a rustic log lodge for recreation and groups, an outdoor pool, and horseback riding and hiking trails nearby. A hot tub is set in the woods. There are nightly bonfires, barbecues, and picnic tables. Accommodations are in one-bedroom and loft chalets. The former sleep up to two adults and two children and the latter have bed space for up to six people. No matter what size condo you choose, you'll find a full kitchen and fireplace.

OUTSIDE THE SOUTHEAST (STEVENS CANYON) ENTRANCE

Cowlitz River Lodge

13069 U.S. 12 (P.O. Box 488), Packwood, WA 98361. ☎ **360/494-4444.** Fax 360/494-2075. www.escapetothemountains.com. 32 units. TV. $50–$75 double. AE, DC, MC, V.

With easy access to Mount Rainier, Mount St. Helens, and White Pass skiing, this modern lodge offers many amenities. There's an outdoor hot tub, guest laundry, and a waxing room for cross-country skiers. They also offer a conference room accommodating 60. You may see deer or elk on the lawn, and you can laze by the lobby fireplace.

Hotel Packwood

104 Main St., Packwood, WA 98361. ☎ **360/494-5431.** Fax 360/494-4884. 9 units, 2 with bathroom. TV. $33 double without bathroom, $42 double with bathroom. MC, V.

Two stories tall with a wraparound porch and weathered siding, this renovated 1912 hotel looks like a classic mountain lodge even though it's right in the middle of this small town. The tiny rooms aren't for the finicky, but most guests spend their days traipsing around on park trails and come back to the hotel thoroughly exhausted. There are iron bed frames in some rooms, a fireplace in the lobby, and a hot tub. Packwood is about 10 miles from the Southeast Entrance to the park.

Dining

INSIDE THE PARK

In the park there are dining rooms at **Paradise Inn** (seasonal) and the **National Park Inn** (year-round). As the only formal dining options within the park, these restaurants tend to stay busy (the two inns are described in the preceding section). For quick meals, there are snack bars at the **Henry M. Jackson Memorial Visitor Center,** at **Paradise,** and at **Sunrise Lodge.**

In Ashford you'll find a place that bakes great pies, the **Copper Creek Restaurant,** Wash. 706 East (☎ 360/569-2326), which is one of the closest restaurants to the park's southwest (Nisqually) entrance. Just down the road another popular spot, **Rainier Overland Restaurant,** 31811 Wash. 706, (☎ 360/569-0851), is known for its fresh seafood, trout, and homemade pies. Another interesting dining option in the area is the **Mount Rainier Railroad Dinner Train** (☎ 888/RRDINER), which leaves from the town of Elbe, west of the park's Nisqually Entrance, and spends 4 hours meandering through the foothills. A

vintage steam locomotive pulls the restored passenger cars, which include an observation lounge car. The dinner train costs $70 per person, and passengers have the option of prime rib, salmon, or ground ostrich steak.

Alexander's

37515 Wash. 706 E., Ashford. ☎ **360/569-2300.** Reservations recommended. Full dinners $16–$19; à la carte $11–$14. MC, V. AMERICAN.

Alexander's, which is also a popular B&B, is the best place to dine outside the Nisqually Entrance to the park. Dining is now offered outside during the summer beside the pond and waterfall. Fresh trout from the inn's pond is the dinner of choice here, but you'll also find beef stew, bourbon T-bones, fresh salmon, pork ribs, and pasta. Whatever you order, just be sure to save room for the wild blackberry pie.

Mount Rainier Railroad Dining Co.

Wash. 7, Elbe. ☎ **360/569-2505.** Lunch $6–$17; main dinner courses $10–$17. AE, DC, DISC, MC, V. Mon–Fri 11am–9pm, Sat–Sun 8am–9pm. AMERICAN.

You can't miss this unusual restaurant in Elbe—just watch for all the cabooses of the adjacent Hobo Inn. Meals are basic, with steaks and fried seafood the staples of the dinner menu, but the surroundings make this place worth a stop. You'll be dining in an old railroad dining car. Your car won't go anywhere while you dine, but you'll get a sense of being on a rail journey.

26

NORTH CASCADES NATIONAL PARK

by Jack Olson

VAST AND INACCESSIBLE ARE NOT WORDS OFTEN USED TO DESCRIBE the Cascade Range, but here in the northern reaches they are the only ones appropriate for a landscape that contains the largest wilderness in the state of Washington. Here gray

wolves and grizzly bears still roam, and human encroachment on their dominion is limited for the most part to the edges of the wilderness.

The North Cascades National Park Service Complex is at the heart of this region. Note the name; this is not just a park but a complex, which includes not only the national park itself but also Ross Lake and Lake Chelan National Recreation Areas. In 1988, by act of Congress, about 93% of the acreage of the entire complex was designated the "Stephen Mather Wilderness." Unlike many national recreation areas, both Ross Lake and Lake Chelan are wild and remote, with minimal development or signs of human habitation outside a few areas.

A trip into this region is a true wilderness experience. Hiking here takes time and preparation. Although there are several shorter trails, most have been designed for the rugged few to take a few days or weeks to get reacquainted with the natural state of things. If you're prepared, though, there's nothing else like it in the continental United States.

Geologically speaking, the North Cascades are some of the most complex and least understood mountains in North America. These peaks were formed over millions of years as a tectonic plate drifting northward from the South Pacific slammed into the North American coast, causing the area's sedimentary rocks to buckle, fold, and transform. In some areas, the rock in the North Cascades is obviously the result of this collision and subsequent metamorphosis. However, in other areas, there is rock that predates the tectonic collision—one upthrust of mountain is believed to be 10 million years old.

Geologic complexity has been further augmented in the North Cascades by glaciation both past and present. In past ice ages both alpine glaciers and the continental ice sheet covered this region. The visual legacy of this intense activity today can be seen in the wide U-shaped valleys carved out by the ice sheet. The single most fascinating legacy of this glaciation is Lake Chelan, which lies in the heart of the North Cascades southern section.

Avoiding the Crowds. Actually, it's not hard at all to avoid the crowds in the North Cascades. The lack of roads, the weather, and the ruggedness of the terrain all work in concert to keep this one of the best-kept secrets in the national park system.

If it's true isolation you're looking for, head north. The Northern Unit of the national park has the least number of tourists (Lake Chelan, Ross Lake, and Diablo Lake are all tourist-heavy spots). But, considering that Stehekin (the cosmopolitan unit of the southern park section) has a permanent, year-round population of around 70, it's a matter of avoiding the crowds or being absolutely alone. At least for the fall and winter.

In the summer, this park can be like many of the others in the system, and you're more likely to run into folks on the Big Beaver Trail, or on your way to Hozomeen, than in the fall, which is about the last part of the year in which you can easily get anywhere in the park. Ross Lake is thicker with boaters on summer holiday weekends, and the heaviest load of visitors all year can be found in Stehekin and the Cascade Pass area during July and August. Of course, the deeper into the backcountry you go, the fewer people you are likely to encounter. Winter is not to be underestimated in this park, and remember Wash. 20 will almost certainly be closed.

Just the Facts

GETTING THERE & GATEWAYS

There's only one paved road that goes through the park complex, **Wash. 20.** There are a few unpaved alternatives, though. The **Cascade River Road,** which leaves Wash. 20 at Marblemount, enters the national park proper as an unpaved road. And the unpaved (and very rough) **Stehekin Valley Road** above High Bridge

enters the national park proper. This road, however, does not connect with the outside world; to use it, vehicles must be barged up Lake Chelan from Chelan, Washington.

From **Seattle** on the west side, take the Wash. 20 exit off I-5 and head east, toward Rockport and Marblemount, into the park. From **Spokane** (the major metropolitan area on the east side) it's U.S. 2 West, linking up with U.S. 97 North, to Wash. 153 and finally, Wash. 20. And remember, in the winter, these roads could be closed any time from late October to early May. Be sure to call ahead.

The Nearest Airport. The Seattle-Tacoma International Airport (☎ 206/431-4444) is located 15 miles south of Seattle on I-5. The airport is served by practically all major airlines and car rental companies, whose toll-free numbers are in the appendix.

INFORMATION

Contact **North Cascades National Park Service Complex,** 2105 Wash. 20, Sedro-Woolley, WA 98284 (☎ 360/856-5700; www.nps.gov/noca). The park publishes a newspaper, the *North Cascades Challenger,* which contains much useful information, such as road closures.

VISITOR CENTERS

The **North Cascades Visitor Center** (mile marker 120, Wash. 20, Newhalem; ☎ 206/386-4495), is open daily in the summer, weekends only during winter. It focuses primarily on preservation, with good exhibits, featuring slide shows and a walk-through environmental tour with placards and videos. There is also a wheelchair-accessible trail leading from the back of the building that affords excellent views of the surrounding mountains.

The **Golden West Visitor Center,** P.O. Box 7, Stehekin (☎ 360/856-5700, ext. 340, then ext. 14), located on the banks

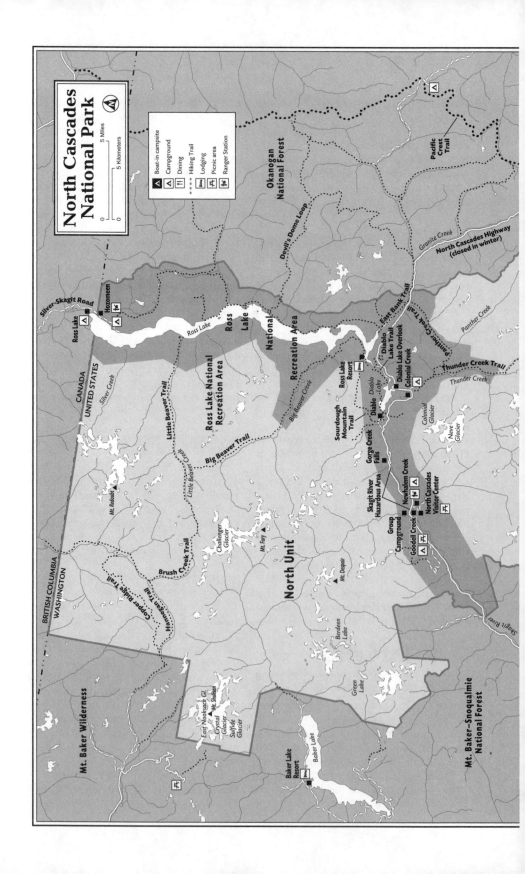

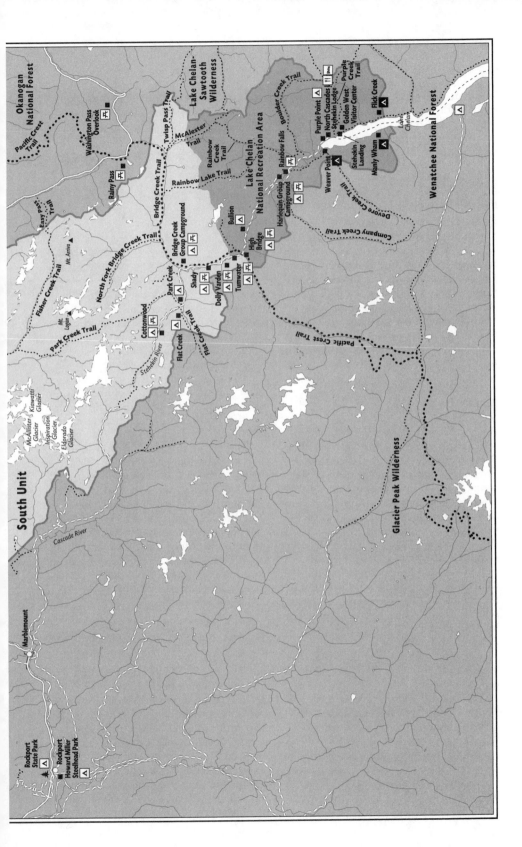

of the northern tip of Lake Chelan, provides information on camping, hiking, and the local environs in general, plus interpretive exhibits. Nearby, you can rent bikes.

GETTING AROUND INSIDE THE PARK

By Boat. On Lake Chelan in the spring and summer, the *Lady Express,* the *Lady II,* and the *Lady Cat* (a high-speed catamaran) run to and from the Lake Chelan boat landing, but in the fall and winter, there's only the Lady Express. Rides cost $22 round-trip. Contact **Lake Chelan Boat Company** (☎ 509/682-4584). The **Ross Lake Resort** (☎ 206/386-4437) operates water taxis to trailheads and campgrounds on Ross Lake.

By Shuttle Bus. Transportation up the Stehekin Valley Road is provided by two different shuttle buses.

One, operated by the National Park Service, costs either $5 or $10 depending on how far up the valley you go (currently Glory Mountain is the end of the bus route). Reservations should be made at least 2 days ahead of time (preferably much farther in advance) by calling the **Golden West Visitor Center** (☎ 360/856-5700, ext. 340, then 14).

Between mid-June and the end of September, another shuttle bus, operated by the **Stehekin Adventure Company,** runs several times a day between Stehekin Landing and High Bridge. No reservations are required, and the cost is $5. If you just want to ride as far as the Stehekin Pastry Company, the fare is only $1.

Taxi service is also available from the North Cascades Stehekin Lodge at the boat landing.

By Air. If you want to get to Stehekin in a hurry, you can make the trip by floatplane on **Chelan Airways** (☎ 509/682-5065 or 509/682-5555), which leaves from the dock next to the ferries. The

fare is $120 round-trip. This company also offers flightseeing trips for between $80 and $150.

FEES & PERMITS

There are currently no entrance fees for the park itself, though there are fees for camping. Backcountry permits are required but free.

SPECIAL REGULATIONS & WARNINGS

Beware of the wintertime! Wash. 20 is usually closed from mid-November through mid-April. Call ahead to the park complex headquarters in Sedro-Woolley (☎ 360/856-5700).

Check in at a visitor center for full details on trail info before you head in. Since this is bear and mountain lion country, you might want to pick up the free handout on hiking and camping safety.

Other than the general precautions that anyone would take when camping in a wilderness area, keep in mind that the North Cascades National Park Service Complex can be extremely remote for both the backcountry hiker and the mid-park driver. Even when day hiking, remember to carry enough water. Don't forget bug spray—there's a lot of water (not necessarily to drink), and consequently, lots of insects during some seasons at some locations.

SEASONS & CLIMATE

The most pernicious of seasons for people visiting the North Cascades area is the winter, which begins creeping up in October in the upper elevations and mid-November in most other parts. It lasts until mid- to late April, and is accompanied by the regular closure of Wash. 20. The first snow at the upper elevations is often in September.

After the thaw, from April to September, things get pretty temperate, with daytime temperatures ranging from 50°

to 70°F, depending on the elevation. However, this is a land of extremes: Trails at higher elevations are usually snow-covered into early July (though this varies considerably from year to year), and summer temperatures of 100°F are not unusual at Ross Lake and Lake Chelan. As can usually be expected in the northwest, rains arrive westerly from the Pacific in the spring and fall, with summer being the most pleasant all around. At any time, though, expect rain; it's always best to pack rain gear. The eastern side of the mountains is somewhat less wet than the western, though this is nothing to bank on.

In addition, with the extremes in altitude here, it's always good to bring something warm, even in the summer months.

SEASONAL EVENTS

There are several seasonal **art exhibits** at the Golden West Visitor Center in the summertime. Contact park headquarters for dates.

If You Only Have 1 Day

Considering that this is one of the most rugged wilderness areas in the United States, any attempt to see the park in a day must be made with the understanding that you're not going to see it all. For most folks with limited time, the choice is a **summer drive** across the park via Wash. 20 (described in the next section).

If You Have More Time

The road into the park is a beautiful drive along the banks of the Skagit River, past the Mount Baker–Snoqualmie National Forest. Your last real connection with civilization, and the last chance to stock up on groceries, is Marblemount, the oldest town in the region. From here, you can head south or east. South is the Cascade River Road, and east is Wash. 20.

The **Cascade River Road** is a 23-mile stretch of unpaved road that leads to the

Ten Essential Items

The Park Service considers the following 10 items absolute essentials for even the day-hiker in the North Cascades National Park Service Complex. Hikers should carry them and know how to use them.

♦ Navigation (a topographical map and compass)

♦ Food and water (boiling water can kill *Giardia*, but some treatment pills can't)

♦ Clothing (including rain gear, wool socks, a sweater, gloves, and hat)

♦ Light (a flashlight with spare bulb and batteries)

♦ Fire (waterproof matches and a fire starter, such as a candle)

♦ Sun protection (sunglasses and sunscreen)

♦ First aid (a kit including any special medications you might need)

♦ Knife (a folding pocket knife is best)

♦ Signals (both audible and visual: whistle and metal mirror)

♦ Emergency shelter (a plastic tube shelter or waterproof bivouac sack)

Cascade Pass Trailhead, at the southern end of North Cascades National Park. The road passes near a fish hatchery and crosses the Skagit River before terminating at the **Cascade Pass Trailhead.** Many folks take the 3.7-mile trip to the top of the pass, which takes the hiker up a relatively modest set of switchbacks to beautiful views of glaciers and subalpine meadows.

If you're not up to the unpaved twistiness of the Cascade River Road, continue on **Wash. 20 to Newhalem,** where the North Cascades Visitor Center has good exhibits and regularly scheduled ranger-led walks and talks. This is a good place to get information about the many short walks and hikes that are in the immediate vicinity. You'll find a short, boardwalk trail beginning behind the visitor center that affords beautiful views of the surrounding mountains. In addition, if you're there late enough in the day, check out the trail to **Ladder Creek Falls** (which is not on National Park Service property but rather owned by Seattle City Light), which is fun in a most decidedly touristy manner. There's a hydroelectric dam at the end of the trail that creates a miniature light show on the falls at night, created by James Ross, the master dam builder of the area. It's worth the hike.

Next up on the route is the little town of **Diablo,** located at the foot of 389-foot-high Diablo Dam, which holds in the blue-green waters of Diablo Lake. There's a boat landing here, and several tours operated by **Skagit Tours** (☎ 206/684-3030) that take you around Diablo Lake. One particularly cheap ride takes you up the **Incline Railway,** a steep elevator-like trip up the hillside. There you can take walks across the top of Diablo Dam and the surrounding area. As the road loops south from Diablo, look for fantastic views of **Neve Glacier.** In fact, there are beautiful views to be had from a plethora of turnouts along the road.

At the **Ross Lake Dam,** the lake begins its 24-mile dogleg up the eastern side of the park complex to the Canadian border. For views of the lake from the dam, stop the car and take the steep, 1-mile walk down the **Ross Dam Trail,** which leads over the top of the dam, eventually winding its way to the Ross Lake Resort and the North Cascades backcountry. Further along Wash. 20, take the turnout at the **Ross Lake Overlook,** where you can see the Ruby Arm (leading to Ruby Creek) as well as Ross Lake proper, heading north toward Canada.

The **Stehekin Area,** at the head of Lake Chelan, is not accessible by car. To get there, you have to either hike in, take a passenger ferry or floatplane up from the southern resort town of Chelan, or take the Cascade River Road from Marblemount to its southern terminus at the **Cascade Pass Trailhead.** From there, you can hike 12 miles over Cascade Pass to Glory Mountain, along the Stehekin Valley Road, where you may be able to catch a shuttle bus to the Stehekin area, if the road is open (from approximately July 1 to mid-October). (Flood damage has closed the road from Glory Mountain to its terminus 2.7 miles further at Cottonwood Camp.) Be sure to call ahead for up-to-date information and to reserve a seat on the **shuttle bus** (☎ 360/856-5700, ext. 340, then ext. 14). A ferry ride up the lake from Chelan is the only quick way to the Stehekin Area. (A floatplane is actually the quickest, though most expensive, option.)

Once you make it to Stehekin, you can rent a bike to ride the roads in the area, but bikes are not permitted on trails. Give yourself enough time and strength for the hike out, though.

If you wish to visit the **northern sections of the park,** there are a couple of options. From the Ross Dam area, park the car and hike the trail in to the **Ross Lake Resort.** You can hike around the general area, or, better yet, catch a water taxi up the shores of the lake (arrange this at the resort). The taxis will drop you off at any of the trailheads that intersect both sides of the shores of this lake all the way to Hozomeen, the northernmost part of the lake in U.S. territory. Ross Lake Resort offers boat rentals (small outboards, canoes, and kayaks) for those who want to create their own itinerary along the lake.

The only practical way to get near the **northwest section of the park** by vehicle is to head east from the Mount Baker Wilderness Area, which is popular and easily accessible because of the Mount Baker Ski Area. Beyond the Mount Baker area, take the **Hannegan Road,** which is accessible by four-wheel-drive regularly, and other vehicles semiregularly. As usual, it's a good idea to call ahead for road conditions. Beyond the end of the road lie the popular **Hannegan Pass, Copper Ridge,** and **Chilliwack trails.** These are popular trails in the summer season, but they are multiday hikes and require a permit for camping overnight. There are beautiful views all along the trails of glaciers spreading southward through the park, especially the Nooksack Glacier along the ridges overhanging the Nooksack River.

Organized Tours & Ranger Programs

For tours of Lake Diablo and Ross Dam, call **Seattle City Light, Skagit Tours** (☎ 206/684-3030). There's even a deluxe package that offers a fried chicken dinner after a cruise. The 4-hour boat tours start with a trip up an incline railway to the top of 389-foot-tall Diablo Dam. From there you board a boat for the 5-mile cruise to Ross Lake Dam, where you get a tour of the powerhouse. At the end of all this is a chicken or vegetarian spaghetti dinner. Tours are offered Thursday through Monday between mid-June through August, weekends only in September, and cost $25 for adults, $22 for seniors, $12.50 for children 6 to 11. Reservations are required. There are also 1½-hour tours of Diablo Dam, for $5, not including the boat ride or dinner. No reservations are needed for the shorter tour.

Want to track radio-collared mountain caribou? Stalk newts, frogs, and salamanders in Heather Meadows? Learn about Lummi Indian basketry? Delve into the mysteries of mycology? Hang with some bats? You can do any of these things if you sign up for the right class through the North Cascades Institute. Offering around 60 natural history field seminars each year, **North Cascades Institute,** 2105 Wash. 20, Sedro-Woolley, WA 98284-9394 (☎ 360/856-5700, ext. 213) is a nonprofit educational organization that offers a wide range of courses each year. While these seminars, many of which

involve camping out, focus on the North Cascades region, there are programs throughout the state. The Institute has plans to open a North Cascades Environmental Education Center in 2001.

A variety of day trips are operated in conjunction with the two passenger ferries of the **Lake Chelan Boat Company** (☎ 509/682-4584). Tours include a popular bus ride to 312-foot Rainbow Falls ($6 adults, $4 children ages 6 to 11), a bus ride up the valley and a bike ride back down ($12), and a narrated bus trip up the valley to High Bridge and then a picnic lunch ($20 adults, $10 children ages 6 to 11).

There are a limited number of ranger-led hikes in the park. These tours often start from the North Cascades Visitor Center or the Colonial Creek Campground, but this varies from year to year. Check at the visitor center for a schedule of daily events.

Day Hikes

Camping in the backcountry is free, but campers must obtain a free permit at one of the visitor centers, the National Park Service Complex headquarters in Sedro-Woolley, or the Wilderness Information Center in Marblemount. Day hikes do not require a permit.

ROSS LAKE NATIONAL RECREATION AREA

Desolation Peak

9.4 mi. RT. Moderate to strenuous. Access: Desolation Landing on Ross Lake via the Ross Lake Resort water taxi, or hike north along the East Bank Ross Lake Trail.

Calling all Kerouac fans! This is the peak that inspired Jack Kerouac's *Desolation Angels,* and it's no wonder that people (and in the middle of summer there are often quite a few of them) would be inspired to meditate on desolation after hiking up this steep hillside through alpine meadows. On the way to the top there are spectacular views of Hozomeen Mountain, Jack Mountain, and below, beautiful Ross Lake. This can be a very hot and dry hike in the summer, however, and the full round-trip takes several days. Carry plenty of water.

Diablo Lake Trail

7.6 mi. RT. Easy. Access: At the end of the road, across from Diablo Dam.

This is the Grand Central of the Diablo Lake area. You get views of Ross Dam and of the power lines, which the trail intersects, but you'll also see some larger old-growth trees and varied forests. The trail starts at Seattle City Light's power project dock, from where you can also pick up the tug for a ride to the base of upstream Ross Dam. Better to follow the trail as it winds along what was once the Skagit River, but is now Diablo Lake. In front of Ross Dam, however, you get a good idea of how well the dams really work. Check out the view as you cross the suspension bridge, which once traversed the Skagit River Gorge but now is part of the system of dams that make the Ross and Diablo lake areas.

East Bank Trail

0.5 to 31 mi. one way. Easy to strenuous. Access: Several points along the shore of Ross Lake via the Ross Lake Resort water taxi, or from the trailhead on Wash. 20 to the terminus of the trail at Hozomeen Campground.

During the summer, this is one of the most popular trails in the whole park because of its plentiful and well-maintained campsites, the easy grade of its path, and its proximity to Wash. 20. To avoid crowds, you might want to wait until late in the season. The path, part of the eastern perimeter of the park, borders the Pasayten Wilderness and the Okanogan National Forest, from which several trails intersect the East Bank Trail. The highest point along the trail is the Desolation Peak Trail, to the north.

Along the way, be prepared for black bears, beautiful fall foliage, and on the northern section of the trail, the possibility of sighting a member of one of the few remaining wolf packs in the Lower 48.

Fourth of July Pass/Panther Creek

10 mi. RT. Moderate. Access: Hike 1.8 mi. up the Thunder Creek Trail to the junction with the trailhead.

For a day hike through some of the most astonishing country in the Lower 48, this section of trail isn't too shabby. It's a popular summer hike to the top of Fourth of July Pass, which offers views of the ever-majestic Neve Glacier and Colonial Peak to the west. It ain't easy, though. It's a switchback-cursed climb from Thunder Creek up to the 3,500-foot top of the pass. But that's the hardest part. You get to return downhill via the beautiful Panther Creek Valley for 5 miles to the junction with Wash. 20 at the Panther Creek Bridge and the East Bank Trailhead.

Pyramid Lake

4 mi. RT. Moderate. Access: 1 mi. east of Diablo, on the south side of the highway near the creek, close to mile marker 127.

This trail is like many in the park—steep. But it's not so steep as to be avoided. The hike is a beautiful but relatively sharp climb, passing through pine and fir forests. It ends at a pond, fed by the Colonial Glaciers looming above you along the southeast side of Pyramid Peak. You're liable to see climbers descending from the peaks at the end of the day, looking tired but happy after having ascended the 7,000 feet to the top of Pyramid.

Sourdough Mountain

10.4 mi. RT. Moderate to strenuous. Access: In the town of Diablo, or via water taxi on the West Bank Trail to the Pierce Mountain Trailhead.

From the west, the trail is easily accessible by car. But rest assured, either way, you're going to be doing some serious climbing: Try a 3,000-foot climb from the Diablo direction, and in just 2 miles, too. And then there's the remaining 2,000 feet or so along the next 4 miles. It's a densely forested walk over the first couple of miles. Be sure to take the right fork at the 3-mile mark to get to the summit for spectacular views of the lake and the glaciers that dot the horizon to the north. This area is hot and dry in the summer, so take extra water.

Stetattle Creek

8 mi. RT. Easy. Access: Take the exit before the green bridge on Wash. 20, just before you reach the town of Diablo along Gorge Lake.

This is a good hike for fans of Diablo's power plant (there are more than you think), who hike along this gentle, scenic path in the summertime along the creek. The trail meanders north for some 3-odd miles before hitting a stretch of giant, moss-hung trees, and finally petering out in the middle of the forest. The waters of Stetattle Creek often flow milky blue-white from the glacial silt that comes down from McMillan Spire and Mount Terror.

Thornton Lakes Trail

10.6 mi. RT. Moderate. Access: Take Wash. 20 to Thornton Lakes Rd., 3 mi. west of Newhalem. The gravel road climbs steeply to the trailhead.

Despite the fact that the first part of the trail is basically an old logging road that might remind you of resource-stripping, this trip is not to be missed. It's a moderately steep walk to the lakes, where the trail cuts to the right (north), for sublime views of the Picket Range at the top of Trappers Peak. Even if you don't take the side route, the sight of Mount Triumph's glaciers to the north, from the nestled valleys in which the lakes sit, is worth the hike.

Thunder Creek Trail

1.6 to 38 mi. RT. Difficulty varies. Access: The two trailheads are south of Diablo Lake; one is at the Colonial Creek Campground parking lot, the other at the amphitheater, though the two trails shortly join.

There are plenty of things to do if you decide to take the Thunder Creek Trail. You could amble past the Thunder Creek Arm of Diablo Lake to the intersection with the Fourth of July Pass Trail (also called the Panther Creek Trail), then head to the left and make a loop around the hub of ever-looming (and it goes without saying, snowcapped and gorgeous) Ruby Peak. Or you could make a weekend trek through the rugged wilderness that lines the trail north to south on its way to its terminus in the Park Creek Area along the Stehekin River. Along the way, you can intersect with the Fisher Creek Trail, sloping left along the creek toward an intersection with a possible terminus over Easy Pass at Wash. 20.

From Diablo Lake, it's a broad and easy path for the first couple of miles, which then begins to slope upward for the next several miles, through the Panther Creek junction on the way to McAlester Creek Camp. This is the 6-mile mark, and a lot of day hikers head back the way they came at this point. Otherwise, it's off for the weekend in some of the most gorgeous country in the continental United States, through the rugged and lush valleys in the southern part of the North Cascades.

LAKE CHELAN NATIONAL RECREATION AREA

Agnes Gorge Trail

5 mi. RT. Easy. Access: High Bridge Campground; it can be reached via the park's shuttle bus.

This is an easy hike along the west-side cliffs of Agnes Gorge, with beautiful views of looming Mount Agnes above you. This is a good walk for a day visitor to the Stehekin area.

Coon Lake Trail

2.5 mi. RT. Moderate. Access: High Bridge, a stop on the shuttle bus up the valley.

This trail leads to a pretty little lake created by beavers. Wildlife, especially waterfowl, is plentiful on and around the 15-acre lake. On the far side, a waterfall on Coon Creek can be seen. Though forests surround the lake, there are views southwest to Agnes Mountain.

Rainbow Falls

7 mi. RT. Easy. Access: Stehekin Landing.

At 312 feet high, Rainbow Falls is among the most impressive falls in Washington and a popular destination for day-trippers who visit Stehekin by boat (see "Getting Around Inside the Park," above). The falls were created when a glacier scraped out the walls of the Stehekin Valley, leaving Rainbow Creek hanging high above the valley floor. The falls are 3.5 miles from Stehekin landing by road and make a good day-hike destination if you are staying at the North Cascades Stehekin Lodge; you get there by walking along the road. The lodge also offers a bus tour of the falls (although it's open to anyone and timed for the convenience of the "day-tripper"). Alternatively, if the shuttle bus is running, you can take it to and from the falls or just one way.

Rainbow Loop Trail

6 mi. RT. Moderate to strenuous. Access: Rainbow Creek Trailhead, 5.5 mi. from Stehekin.

While trails in the Stehekin area tend to be flat valley-bottom hikes or grueling climbs straight up steep walls, this hike makes a good in-between choice. Views of the Stehekin Valley and Lake Chelan are the payoff. Start the hike from the Rainbow Creek Trailhead, which can be reached from the shuttle bus. From here

climb 1,000 feet in 2.5 miles—along the way passing a bluff with a view of the valley—to a bridge over Rainbow Creek. Just before reaching the creek there is a trail junction. If you turn left here and hike up this trail 0.5 mile, you'll find views even more stunning than the ones along the main trail. The creek marks the midpoint of the trail. The lower trailhead is 2.5 miles down a steep trail with more great views.

NORTH CASCADES NATIONAL PARK—SOUTHERN UNIT

The interior of the southern unit of the North Cascades National Park is remote. Most of the trails are concentrated on the northern or southern end. The northern trails are accessed via Wash. 20. The southern trails are accessed via the Cascade River Road, a winding, sometimes rugged stretch of unpaved craziness which will get you to the Cascade Pass trail. Call ahead to Marblemount for road conditions; sometimes this is not easily accessible to the average vehicle. Hikers can take Thunder Creek Trail, an artery through the interior, for access to the Chelan/Stehekin area, but it's not a day hike.

Bridge Creek Trail

29 mi. RT. Moderate. Access: The trailhead is at the Bridge Creek Bridge on the Stehekin Valley Rd.; the other end of the trail is at Rainy Pass on Wash. 20.

This backcountry hike steadily ascends to Wash. 20 (never too steeply) through some beautiful valleys, after a short hike along a section of the Pacific Crest Trail. There are beautiful views of Goode Mountain and Mount Logan, as well as the massive ice-hangs below Memaloose Ridge.

Cascade Pass/Sahale Arm Trail

11 mi. RT. Strenuous. Access: From Marblemount on Wash. 20, cross the bridge and drive

east for 23.1 mi. on the Cascade River Rd. to the trailhead.

This is one of the most popular hikes in the park. Starting high above the valley of the North Fork Cascade River, the trail follows an ancient Indian trading route over the Cascades to Lake Chelan. Today the trail is popular as a day trip, an overnight trip, a climber's route to some challenging North Cascades rock, and as a through trail to Stehekin. For a spectacular day hike, climb to the top of Cascade Pass, then continue to ascend on a trail to the left until you cross a ridge. Soon, you will be traversing a slope far above jewel-like Doubtful Lake. From here, there are sweeping views of the North Cascades.

Park Creek Pass

8 mi. one way. Moderate to strenuous. Access: Park Creek Campground on the Stehekin Valley Rd.

Though this hike is often crowded in the summer with people passing through Stehekin, it's still worth it. Make your way up the steep, forested slopes towards the alpine meadows beyond the logistically named Five Mile Camp. From here on up it's glacier lilies and the cracking of calving glacier ice on the slopes of Goode Mountain. Huge chunks of ice have been known to crash into the valley below the slopes. Look for slabs as big as your average house. Beyond the 6,000-foot Park Creek Pass, you can connect with the Thunder Creek Trail for a much longer hike to the Ross Lake Area.

NORTH CASCADES NATIONAL PARK—NORTHERN UNIT

The backcountry trails in this region, such as **Hannegan Trail, Chilliwack Trail,** and **Big Beaver Trail,** aren't easy to get to, but they're worth the effort. Here you'll find the most stupendous mountain views in the park complex. This is the most remote wilderness area in the state and may still be home to both wolves and grizzly bears. From virgin forests in glacial valleys to high meadows with head-on views of the park's jagged Picket Range, these hikes have everything.

Start at the Mount Baker Wilderness trailhead in the Mount Baker–Snoqualmie National Forest, near the northwestern section of the North Cascades National Park Northern Unit. From the town of Glacier drive 13 miles to F.S. 32 (Hannegan Road), and continue to the trailhead at the Hannegan Camp at the road's end. You can also take a water taxi up Ross Lake and start your hike from the Big Beaver Landing. This ride will cost you $20 and must be arranged in advance.

Other Sports & Activities

Biking. Riding off the road is not allowed in the park, but there are still several good biking routes. Keep in mind that biking is usually best in late July and August, but even then, bad weather can descend suddenly to ruin the views and soak the riders.

The trip along Wash. 20 through the park and also west of the park between Rockport and Marblemount is strenuous but beautiful. The road has a wide shoulder in many (though not all) places and developed campgrounds. There are some extremely steep stretches.

Mountain bikers will want to try the Stehekin Valley Road route, a 21-mile stretch from the community of Stehekin to Flat Creek, on Lake Chelan. The road parallels the glacier-fed Stehekin River and provides plenty of great views of the North Cascades peaks. The 312-foot-high Rainbow Falls is a required stop along the way.

Cross-Country Skiing. West of the park complex, the **Mount Baker Ski Area** is where most skiers end up. But if you're looking to do some cross-country skiing away from the crowds, consider **Stehekin.**

The chance to ski past 312-foot-tall Rainbow Falls should not be missed.

Fishing. Anglers must have Washington state fishing licenses; these can be obtained at sporting goods stores.

Ross Lake contains populations of both native rainbow and cutthroat trout, as well as eastern brook trout and a few bull trout (which must be released). Fishing boats can be rented at the **Ross Lake Resort** (☎ 206/386-4437).

Lake Chelan, although it looks like an awesome fishing hole, is so large, so deep, and so cold that it doesn't support a large fish population. However it does have quite a variety, including kokanee; land-locked chinook salmon; cutthroat, rainbow, and Mackinaw trout; and freshwater ling cod (burbot). The **Stehekin River** and its tributary streams offer excellent fly-fishing.

If you want to hire a guide to take you where the fish are biting, try **Fish'n Lake Chelan** (☎ 509/682-2802) or **Graybill's Guide Service** (☎ 509/682-4294).

Hang Gliding and Paragliding. In recent years, Lake Chelan has become one of the nation's hang gliding and paragliding meccas. Strong winds and thermals allow flyers to sail for a hundred miles or more from the Chelan Sky Park atop Chelan Butte, which is located on the outskirts of town. Paragliding lessons are available here through **Chelan Paragliding School**

(☎ 509/682-7777 or 425/432-8900). A 2-day weekend session, including equipment, costs $300 per person.

Kayaking & Canoeing. Diablo Lake and Ross Lake both offer excellent flat-water paddling and are among the few inland waters in the Northwest with extensive boat-in campsites. However, there is no road access to **Ross Lake** in the U.S. (the unpaved Silver Skagit Road enters the park from British Columbia, leading to the north end of the lake). **Ross Lake Resort** (☎ 206/386-4437) offers a canoe and kayak shuttle service from Diablo Lake (which is accessible by car) around Ross Dam to Ross Lake. The resort charges from $15 to $25 per canoe or kayak. You can also rent outboard motorboats, kayaks, and canoes at the resort.

You'll need a backcountry permit to overnight on Ross Lake. These permits are available at the Wilderness Information Center in Marblemount. The permits allow you to stay at the many campsites along the shores of Ross Lake. Backcountry permits are also available at the Hozomeen Ranger Station. Here you can explore the Narrow Ruby Arm using Green Point Campground (1 mile above the dam) as a base camp. Farther north are the Cougar Island (2 miles above the dam), Roland Point (4 miles above the dam), McMillan (5.5 miles above the dam), and Spencer's (6 miles above the dam) campgrounds.

Campground	Elev.	Total Sites	RV Hookups	Dump Station	Toilets
Goodell Creek	500	22	0	No	Yes
Newhalem Creek	500	129	0	Yes	Yes
Colonial Creek	1,200	164	0	Yes	Yes
Hozomeen	1,600	122	0	No	Yes
Rockport State Park	500	90	50	Yes	Yes
Howard Miller Steekhead Park	400	59	49	Yes	Yes
Marble Creek	1,000	24	0	No	Yes

Because of the length of the lake and the strong winds that often blow in the afternoon, many paddlers stick to the lower end (unless they enter at Hozomeen at the lake's north end).

If you aren't inclined to spend the money for the shuttle, you can have a similar experience paddling on **Diablo Lake,** which is an amazing turquoise due to the amounts of glacial flour suspended in the water. Diablo also has three boat-in campsites (Thunder Point, Hidden Cove, and Buster Brown) as well as a couple of small islands to explore. Backcountry permits are needed for boat-in campgrounds on Diablo Lake. Alternatively, you can explore the lake from the drive-in Colonial Creek Campground on the Thunder Arm of the lake.

Snowshoeing. The **Stehekin Valley** makes an ideal snowshoeing destination, with various trails that offer opportunities for exploring the mountain slopes surrounding the valley. The road is plowed to a point 9 miles north of Stehekin Landing. You can rent snowshoes at the North Cascades Stehekin Lodge.

Camping

Camping in the national park and recreation areas is on a first-come, first-served basis, except for groups of 10 or more, who can call ☎ 360/873-4590, ext. 16 for reservations. Camping in

the backcountry requires a free backcountry permit, available at visitor centers or the Wilderness Information Center in Marblemount. The only drive-in campsites are located along Wash. 20 through the Ross Lake area, except Hozomeen, which is accessible by car only through the Silver Skagit Road, 40 miles south of Hope, in British Columbia, Canada.

IN ROSS LAKE NATIONAL RECREATION AREA

For information contact national park offices (☎ 360/856-5700).

Goodell Creek, just west of Newhalem, is popular with paddlers and anglers. It has a good view of the Picket Range from just across the highway. Drinking water is not available from late fall through winter.

Newhalem Creek, one of the area's busiest campgrounds, is at the center of the action near the North Cascades Visitor Center. It's wheelchair accessible and has many short hiking trails nearby.

Colonial Creek, on the banks of the Thunder Arm part of Diablo Lake, is the largest campground on the highway and also the busiest. It has pleasant sites on the water and access to boat ramps.

Hozomeen is a more primitive campground, with no garbage facilities, at the northern tip of Ross Lake.

Drinking Water	Showers	Fire Pits/ Grills	Laundry	Public Phone	Reserve	Fees	Open
Yes	No	Yes	No	No	No	$7	Year-round
Yes	No	Yes	No	No	No	$10	Late May to Oct
Yes	No	Yes	No	No	No	$10	Mid-May to Oct
Yes	No	Yes	No	No	No	Free	Late May to Oct
Yes	Yes	Yes	No	Yes	No	$15	Apr–Oct
Yes	Yes	No	No	Yes	Yes	$18	Year-round
No	No	Yes	No	No	No	$7	May 15–Oct 15

At the north end of the lake, near Stehekin, there are eleven campgrounds, most of which are served by the shuttle bus from Stehekin. Purple Point Campground is right in Stehekin and is the most convenient to the boat landing.

For information on campgrounds in the Stehekin Valley, contact the **Golden West Visitor Center,** P.O. Box 7, Stehekin, WA 98852 (☎ 360/856-5700, ext. 340, then ext. 14).

ALONG THE NORTH CASCADES HIGHWAY

Heading over the North Cascades Highway from the west side, you'll find a very nice campground at **Rockport State Park** (☎ 360/853-8461), just west of Rockport. This campground is set amid large old-growth trees. Right in Rockport itself, there are campsites in a large open field at the country-run **Howard Miller Steelhead Park** (☎ 360/853-8808).

East of Marblemount, there are a couple of small National Forest Service campgrounds on the Cascade River Road, which leads to the trailhead for the popular hike to Cascade Pass. Among them, **Marble Creek** is 8 miles east of Marblemount

Accommodations

There aren't a lot of choices for lodging in the park. To the west, along Wash. 20, you can find places in and near Marblemount and Rockport; to the east there's Mazama and Winthrop, also on Wash. 20.

INSIDE THE PARK

North Cascades Stehekin Lodge

P.O. Box 457, Chelan, WA 98816. ☎ **509/682-4494** or 509/682-8206 (reservation office). Fax 509/682-5872. www. stehekin. com. 28 units. $79–$110 double. DISC, MC, V.

Located right at Stehekin Landing, the North Cascades Stehekin Lodge is shaded by tall trees and overlooks the lake. There are a variety of different rooms ranging from basic ones with no lake view to spacious apartments. The studio apartments, which have kitchens and lake views, are the best deal. Fishing boat and bike rentals are available. Snowshoeing has become popular; Saturday moonlight snowshoe walks are held January to March. Narrated bus tours are also offered.

Ross Lake Resort

Rockport, WA 98283. ☎ **206/386-4437.** www.osslakeresort.com. 15 cabins. $62–$164 double. MC, V.

There may not be another lodging of this type in the United States. All 15 of the resort's cabins are built on logs that are floating on Ross Lake. If you're looking to get away from it all, this place comes pretty close. There is no road to the resort. To reach it, you first drive to the Diablo Dam on Wash. 20, and then take a tugboat to the end of Diablo Lake, where a truck carries you around the Ross Dam to the lodge. Alternatively you can hike in on a 2-mile trail from mile marker 134 on Wash. 20. There is no restaurant or grocery store here, so be sure to bring enough supplies for your stay. All cabins have some cooking facilities, ranging from stovetops to full kitchens. Most cabins have private bathrooms; some share with one other cabin. What do you do once you get here? Rent a boat and go fishing, rent a kayak or canoe, do some hiking, or simply sit and relax.

Stehekin Valley Ranch

P.O. Box 36, Stehekin, WA 98852. ☎ **800/ 536-0745** or 509/682-4677. www.courtney country.com. E-mail: info@courtneycountry. com. 5 cabins, 7 tent cabins. Cabins: $75 per adult, $65 per child 7–12, $50 per child 4–6, $10 per child 3 and under. Tent cabins: $10 less. Rates include all meals and transportation in lower valley. $5 off if you bring own bedding and towels. MC, V, if payment made in advance by phone. At the ranch, only cash or checks are accepted.

If you're a camper at heart, then the tent cabins at the Stehekin Valley Ranch should be just fine. With canvas roofs, screen windows, and no electricity or plumbing, these "cabins" are little more than permanent tents. Bathroom facilities are in the nearby main building. For slightly more comfortable accommodations, opt for one of the permanent cabins. Activities available at additional cost include horseback riding, river rafting, and mountain biking.

IN ROCKPORT

Clark's Skagit River Cabins & Resort

58468 Clark Cabin Rd., Rockport, WA 98283. ☎ **800/273-2606** or 360/873-2250. Fax 360/873-4077. www.northcascades.com. 23 cabins. TV. Summer $52–$109 double; winter $49–$98 double. AE, DISC, MC, V.

The first thing you notice when you turn into the driveway is the rabbits. They're everywhere—hundreds of them in all shapes and sizes, contentedly munching the lawn or just sitting quietly. Today the bunnies are one of the main attractions at Clark's, but it's the theme cabins that keep people coming back. Western, nautical, Victorian, American Indian, Adirondack, hacienda, and mill are the current choices for interior decor in these cabins. Other cabins on the property are equally comfortable, but the theme cabins are what make Clark's just a bit different. They're especially popular in winter, when folks flock to the area to watch the bald eagles congregate on the Skagit River. There's also a restaurant on the property.

IN MAZAMA

Freestone Inn

17798 Hwy. 20, Mazama, WA 98833. ☎ **800/ 639-3809** or 509/996-3906. Fax 509/

996-3907. 38 units. TEL. Summer $145–$215 double, $130–$265 cabin, $275–$440 lodge. Winter $130–$195 double, $120–$175 cabin, $250–$400 lodge. Lower rates in spring and fall. AE, DC, DISC, MC, V.

Located at the upper end of the Methow Valley outside the community of Mazama, the Freestone Inn is an up-and-comer. The inn's main building is a huge new log structure complete with massive stone fireplace in a cathedral-ceilinged great room that serves as lobby and dining room. The lodge sits on the shore of small Freestone Lake and has a superb view of the mountains rising beyond the far shore. Guest rooms are thoughtfully designed with gas fireplaces and sunken tubs that open to the bedroom. All in all, these are some of the most memorable rooms in the state. For more privacy, you can opt for one of the renovated Early Winters Cabins or one of the newly constructed cabins. Families may want to go all the way and rent one of the large lakeside lodges. Meals here are every bit as nice as the rooms. Northwest cuisine is the focus with prices in the $13 to $20 range.

The inn also offers tour arrangements, cross-country ski lessons, ski rentals, mountain-bike rentals, and sleigh rides. Nearby, there are ski trails and a lake for swimming or ice skating.

The Mazama Country Inn

42 Lost River Rd., Mazama, WA 98833. ☎ **800/843-7951** or 509/996-2681. Fax 509/996-2646. www.mazama-inn.com. 14 units. Summer $60–$95 double. Winter (including all meals) $150–$195 double. DISC, MC, V.

Set on the flat valley floor but surrounded by rugged towering peaks and tall pine trees, this modern mountain lodge is secluded and peaceful and offers an escape from the crowds in Winthrop. If you're out here to hike, mountain bike, cross-country ski, or horseback ride, the Mazama Country Inn makes an excellent base of operations. They also have a newly built private tennis court. After a hard day of outdoor fun, you can come back and soak in the hot tub and have dinner in the rustic dining room with its massive freestanding fireplace and high ceiling. The medium-size guest rooms are simply furnished, but modern and clean. The inn also rents out six cabins ranging in size from one to five bedrooms.

IN WINTHROP

Hotel Rio Vista

P.O. Box 815, Winthrop, WA 98862. ☎ 800/398-0911. www.methow.com/~riovista. 16 units. A/C TV TEL. $68–$100 double. MC, V.

As with all the other buildings in downtown Winthrop, the Rio Vista looks as if it had been built for a Hollywood Western movie set. Behind the false front you'll find modern rooms, with pine furnishings and an understated country decor; some have refrigerators. Step out onto your balcony for a view of the confluence of the Chewuch and Methow rivers. Guests often see deer, bald eagles, and many other species of birds. A hot tub overlooks the river. There's a riverside picnic area.

Sun Mountain Lodge

P.O. Box 1000, Winthrop, WA 98862. ☎ 800/572-0493 or 509/996-2211. Fax 509/996-3133. www.sunmountainlodge.com. E-mail: sunmtn@methow.com. 102 units, 13 cabins. Summer $155–$265 double, $155–$300 cabin. Winter $115–$215 double, $115–$250 cabin. Spring/fall $115–$230 double, $115–$280 cabin. AE, DC, MC, V.

If you're looking for resort luxuries and proximity to hiking, cross-country skiing, and mountain-biking trails, the Sun Mountain Lodge should be your first choice in the region. Perched on a mountaintop with grand views of the Methow Valley and the North Cascades, this luxurious lodge captures the spirit of the West in both its breathtaking setting and its rustic design. In the lobby,

flagstone floors, stone fireplaces, and wagon-wheel tables combine in a classically western style. Most guest rooms feature rustic Western furnishings and views of the surrounding mountains. The rooms in the Gardner wing have balconies and slightly better views than those in the main lodge. The newest rooms are in the Mount Robinson wing. If seclusion is what you're after, opt for one of the less luxurious cabins down on Patterson Lake.

A superb menu that focuses on Northwest cuisine makes the lodge's dining room the region's best restaurant, and the views will definitely take your breath away. Prices range from $18 to $25 for entrees.

The lodge offers ski rentals and ski school, horseback and sleigh rides, guided hikes, and boat, mountain-bike, and ice-skate rentals. Guests can also use the outdoor heated pools, two whirlpools, tennis courts, exercise room, ski shop, children's playground, spa services, and ice-skating pond.

The Virginian

808 N. Cascades Hwy. (P.O. Box 237), Winthrop, WA 98862. ☎ 800/854-2834 or 509/996-2535. www.methow.com/~virginian. E-mail: virginian@methow.com. 37 units, 7 cabins. A/C TV. $65–$80 double; $80 cabin. DISC, MC, V. Pets accepted.

Located just south of downtown Winthrop, the Virginian is a collection of small cabins and motel rooms on the banks of the Methow River. The deluxe rooms overlooking the river are our favorites. These have high ceilings, balconies, and lots of space. The cabins, though quaint, don't have river views. The rooms and cabins are all lined with cedar, which gives them a rustic feel. There's a heated swimming pool, hot tub, horseshoe pit, and volleyball court. An on-site restaurant provides family breakfasts and dinners. There's a cross-country ski and mountain bike trail out the front door.

Dining

Better stock up on the chow before you head into the park, Marblemount, or Winthrop. In most places, including Ross Lake Resort, there's just no food to be had.

IN STEHEKIN

There are several dining options in Stehekin, but if you plan to stay in a cabin or camp out, be sure to bring all the food you'll need. Otherwise, simple meals are available at **North Cascades Stehekin Lodge** (☎ 509/682-4494), which is located right at the boat dock in Stehekin. If you just have to have something sweet, you're in luck—the **Stehekin Pastry Company,** which is located 2 miles up valley from the boat landing, serves pastries and ice cream, as well as pizza and espresso.

IN MARBLEMOUNT

Buffalo Run Restaurant

60084 Wash. 20 (mi. marker 106), Marblemount. ☎ **360/873-2461.** Main dishes $2.50–$33. AE, DISC, MC, V. Sun–Thurs 8am–9pm, Fri–Sat 8am–10pm. AMERICAN.

From the outside this looks like any other roadside diner, but once you see the menu, it's obvious this place is a little bit more. The owners have a buffalo ranch, so it's no surprise that the menu includes buffalo burgers, buffalo chili, and buffalo T-bones. They also serve venison and ostrich, as well as salmon and mussels, plus vegetarian items. After a day of hiking, enjoy a pleasant meal on their garden patio. Of course there's a buffalo head (and hide) on the wall. By the way, they have a furnished bunkhouse in their barn which they rent

out in the summer for $55 per night for two.

IN THE WINTHROP AREA

The best meals in the Winthrop area are to be had at the dining rooms of **Sun Mountain Lodge,** where you'll also enjoy one of the most spectacular views in the state. See "Accommodations," above.

The Duck Brand

Wash. 20 (Riverside Ave.). ☎ **509/996-2192.** Main courses $6–$17. AE, DC, MC, V. Daily 7am–9:30pm (shorter hrs in winter). MEXICAN.

Located across the street from the gas station and partially hidden by trees, the Duck Brand is a casual restaurant with a big, multilevel deck that's a great spot for a meal on a warm summer day. In cold or rainy weather, you can grab a table in the small dining room and order a plate of fajitas or ribs and a microbrew to wash it all down. The Duck Brand's muffins and cinnamon rolls make great trailside snacks.

Winthrop Brewing Company

155 Riverside Ave. ☎ **509/996-3183.** Main courses $5–$17. MC, V. Daily 11:30am–midnight (shorter hrs in winter). AMERICAN.

Located in a tiny, wedge-shaped building in downtown Winthrop, this local watering hole is by far the liveliest restaurant/bar in town. The walls are covered with the owner's cigarette lighter collection, as well as old rifles and beer coasters from around the world. There's a deck out back overlooking the river and in summer, a beer garden. On weekends there's usually some kind of live music going on. The menu is typical pub fare—burgers, fish-and-chips, steaks, sandwiches, chicken, fish, and ribs.

27

OLYMPIC NATIONAL PARK

by Jack Olson

GET READY FOR SENSORY OVERLOAD. OLYMPIC NATIONAL PARK IS AN area of such variety in climate and terrain that it's hard to believe it's just one park. Here you can view white, chilled alpine glaciers; wander through a sopping-wet, green rain

forest; or sooth your muscles with a soak in heated springs. Or perhaps you'd prefer to ponder the setting sun from the sandy Pacific coastline, or disappear from the outside world altogether in the deep green forests of its largely untouched mountains.

In the mountains, remnants of 2-million-year-old glaciers that once crept northeast toward what is now the Strait of Juan de Fuca and the Hood Canal can still be seen. The 60 glaciers inside the park continue to grind and sculpt the Olympic Mountains now as they did then, if only a bit more slowly. Farther down some of the steep coastal valleys traversing the peninsula lie the major temperate rain forests in the contiguous United States. In addition, Olympic National Park contains the longest stretch of uninterrupted coastal wilderness area of any park south of Alaska.

Water is serious business here. Precipitation is measured in feet, not inches, with some areas receiving up to 20 feet in a single season. Contrast this with some parts of the drier eastern side of the peninsula, which receive a comparatively paltry 20 inches on average. Again, variety is the rule. If the crystalline, jade

waters of the glacier-fed lakes feel a little too cold for comfort, there's always the opportunity to warm your bones in hot springs in the northern section of the park.

Despite its inherent ruggedness, raininess, and mysterious nature, the interior of the park began yielding its secrets in the mid- to late 1800s. Unbridled curiosity and the inevitable desire for timber, mineral, and tourism dollars played a part in its exploration. Homesteads had been established by westward-moving pioneers on the peripheries of the peninsula as early as the mid-1800s. However, the first documented exploration of the interior didn't occur until 1885, and then it was no easy feat. It took one group of explorers a grueling month of hacking through dense brush to get from Port Angeles to Hurricane Ridge. Today, it takes approximately 45 minutes by car.

On the advice of these adventuresome explorers, Congress declared most of the peninsula a national forest. Then, in 1909, just before leaving office, Pres. Theodore Roosevelt, an avid hunter, established Mount Olympus National Monument, in order to preserve the summer range and breeding grounds of dwindling herds of Roosevelt elk (flatteringly named for the president himself in a brilliant piece of prelegislative public relations). In 1938, Pres. Franklin Roosevelt turned the national monument into a national park, and in 1953 the coastal strip was added. Finally, in 1981, the park was declared a World Heritage Park.

Today, Olympic National Park encompasses more than 900,000 acres of mountains and rain forests, glacial lakes, and Pacific shoreline. It was either a fortunate stroke of planning, or fortunate lack of money, that there are no roads that divide the interior of the park. Consequently, large sanctuaries exist here for the elk, deer, eagles, bear, cougars, and other inhabitants and visitors to its interior.

Avoiding the Crowds. Avoiding the crowds in Olympic National Park is not as simple as it would seem. With easy access from both Seattle and Victoria, B.C., Olympic National Park is a magnet for visitors from around the world. However, there are a few options within your control.

The easiest solution is to go in the off-season, especially in the fall. Although the west side of Olympic is often deluged with rain in the fall and winter, the eastern side can actually be fairly dry at the same time. So head east toward **Duckabush** or **Sequim.** Otherwise, strap on your snorkel and try some winter camping in the **Hoh** or the **Queets.**

You might also try getting to the park via the southern route, up the peninsula through Aberdeen. If you choose this route, you can see everything the peninsula offers in a nutshell. Instead of going to the Hoh, try the Queets. Although less traveled, this area affords the same rainforest views as the more popular Hoh. On the east side, try a walk into the interior from Duckabush or Dosewallips. Both jumping-off points are less trafficked than the more northerly areas, and the views as you walk through the

old growth beside the blue-white rivers are as good as any in the park.

Finally, if you absolutely have to come in the summer and don't want to miss the most popular views, such as those on **Hurricane Ridge,** try heading up in the late afternoon when everyone else is on their way down. You're liable to get spectacular views of the sunset over the Strait of Juan de Fuca as the fog rolls in and the deer make their evening pilgrimage to the parking lot at the Hurricane Ridge Visitor Center.

Just the Facts

GETTING THERE & GATEWAYS

The main travel artery for all visitors to Olympic National Park is **U.S. 101.** This northernmost point of the famous coastal highway encircles and only briefly enters the park. Most of the traffic into and out of the park is on the northeastern side, from Vancouver and Seattle.

If you're departing from **Seattle,** you can take either one of the ferries that run daily/hourly from the same downtown Seattle dock. No reservations are needed for the ferries, which cost about $11 for a vehicle and two people one way. The **Seattle–Bainbridge Island Ferry** takes you for a half-hour ride across the Puget Sound before arriving in Bainbridge Island. From there, take Wash. 305 north through Poulsbo to the Hood Canal Floating Bridge, and then Wash. 104 across to U.S. 101. The **Seattle-Bremerton Ferry** arrives in Bremerton after a 45-minute ride. From Bremerton, take Wash. 3 north to the Hood Canal Floating Bridge. The **Edmonds-Kingston Ferry** is a 30-minute ride to Kingston, where you take Wash. 104 24 miles to U.S. 101. In addition, the **Keystone Ferry** shuttles between Whidbey Island and Port Townsend. It's smaller, but in the off-season it can be a good bet for shorter lines.

For all ferry **schedules,** contact the **Washington State Ferries,** Colman

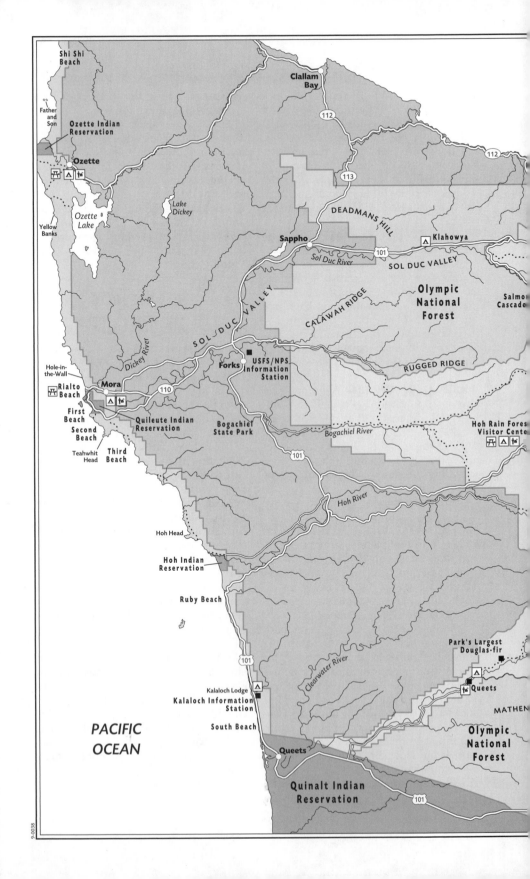

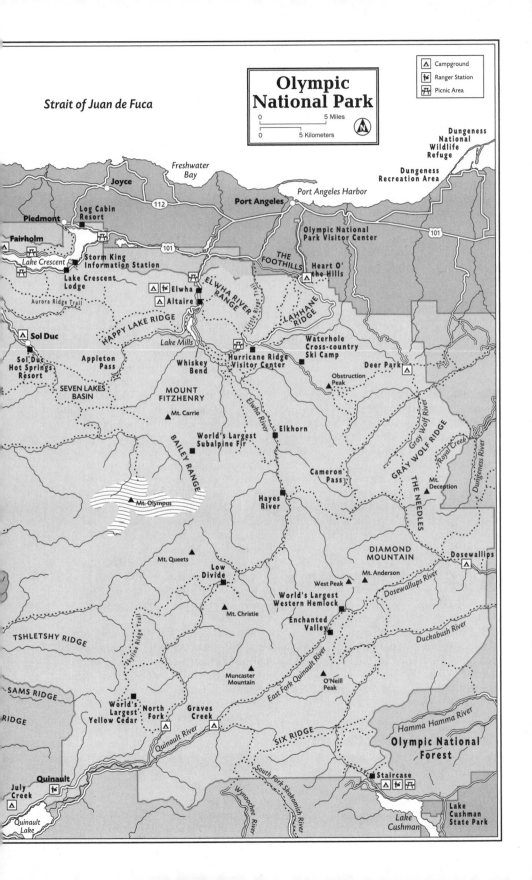

Olympic National Park

▲	Campground
⛺	Ranger Station
⛱	Picnic Area

0 — 5 Miles
0 — 5 Kilometers

Strait of Juan de Fuca

Freshwater Bay

Joyce

Port Angeles Harbor

Port Angeles

Dungeness National Wildlife Refuge

Dungeness Recreation Area

Log Cabin Resort

Piedmont

Fairholm

Lake Crescent

Storm King Information Station

Lake Crescent Lodge

Aurora Ridge Trail

Olympic National Park Visitor Center

THE FOOTHILLS

Heart O' the Hills

Elwha

Altaire

ELWHA RIVER RANGE

Little River Trail

LAHHANE RIDGE

Sol Duc

Sol Duc Hot Springs Resort

Appleton Pass

HAPPY LAKE RIDGE

Lake Mills

Whiskey Bend

Hurricane Ridge Visitor Center

Waterhole Cross-country Ski Camp

Deer Park

Obstruction Peak

SEVEN LAKES BASIN

MOUNT FITZHENRY

Mt. Carrie

World's Largest Subalpine Fir

Elwha River

Elkhorn

Cameron Pass

Gray Wolf River

GRAY WOLF RIDGE

Royal Creek

Dungeness River

BAILEY RANGE

Mt. Olympus

Hayes River

Mt. Deception

THE NEEDLES

Mt. Queets

Low Divide

DIAMOND MOUNTAIN

West Peak

Mt. Anderson

Dosewallips

Mt. Christie

World's Largest Western Hemlock

Enchanted Valley

Dosewallips River

Duckabush River

TSHLETSHY RIDGE

Skyline Ridge Trail

Muncaster Mountain

East Fork Quinault River

O'Neill Peak

SAMS RIDGE

RIDGE

World's Largest Yellow Cedar

North Fork

Graves Creek

Quinault River

SIX RIDGE

Hamma Hamma River

Olympic National Forest

Quinault

July Creek

Quinault Lake

South Fork Skokomish River

Wynoochee River

Staircase

Lake Cushman

Lake Cushman State Park

Dock/Pier 52, 801 Alaskan Way, Seattle, WA 98104 (☎ 800/843-3779 or 206/464-6400; www.wsdot.wa.gov/ferries/current).

If you'd rather drive your car over dry land only, head west from **Tacoma** via Wash. 16 over the Tacoma Narrows Bridge, which connects with the eastern shore of the Kitsap Peninsula just south of Gig Harbor. Drive north on Wash. 16 to Port Orchard and Bremerton. From Bremerton, take Wash. 3 to the Hood Canal Floating Bridge and across to U.S. 101.

To access the park from the south, take I-5 to **Olympia,** where you can connect with U.S. 101 North, or with Wash. 8 West to the other side of the U.S. 101 loop, to access the Pacific Ocean section of the park.

The Nearest Airport. Seattle-Tacoma **International Airport** (☎ 206/431-4444) is located 15 miles south of Seattle on I-5. It's served by most major airlines and car rental companies. **Fairchild International Airport** is located in Port Angeles, site of the park's main visitor center, and is served by **Horizon Air** and **Harbor Airlines,** and **Budget Rent-A-Car.** Toll-free numbers for airlines and car-rental companies are listed in the appendix.

INFORMATION

Contact **Olympic National Park,** 600 E. Park Ave., Port Angeles, WA 98362-6798 (☎ 360/452-0330; www.nps.gov/olym). There are several free publications that provide a good look at the area, including the *North Olympic Peninsula Visitor's Guide,* published by the Peninsula Daily News twice yearly.

VISITOR CENTERS

There are three visitor centers in the park, offering exhibits, maps, guides, and information; plus smaller ranger and information stations that are located at popular trailheads and open only in summer.

The **Olympic National Park Visitor Center** (☎ 360/452-0330), located on the northern end of the park and within close proximity to Port Angeles, is a good jumping-off station before heading into the northwest part of the park. It's a 45-minute drive from there to one of the most popular spots in the park, the **Hurricane Ridge Visitor Center.** Here you'll find beautiful views (free telescopes!) of the Olympic Mountains and alpine meadows blooming with wildflowers each summer. It also has a snack bar, interpretive exhibits, and trails. If you want to avoid the crowds, drive up in the late afternoon, as everyone else is leaving. Wait for sundown, and you might get a beautiful view of the mists coming in, and a visit from some surprisingly tame deer. Those who arrive before 10am will find more elbow room as well.

The **Hoh Rain Forest Visitor Center,** on the west side of the main part of the park, is some 15 miles off a turnoff from U.S. 101. This is an excellent spot for those who want to experience a temperate rain forest, without spending a soaking couple of days hiking. The information center is, like the Hurricane Ridge Observatory, a favorite spot for tourists in the summer season. There are several interpretive trails and the beautiful **Hall of Mosses** nearby, as well as longer trails into the heart of the rain forest. Just remember that this visitor center is in the middle of the rain forest—it gets unbelievably humid when full!

Smaller centers include the **Storm King Information Station,** on Crescent Lake in the northern section of the park, and the **Kalaloch Information Station,** on the south end of the beach section of the park. You can get food and some supplies near the **Sol Duc Ranger Station** at the Hot Springs Resort.

FEES

Entrance into the park for up to a week costs $10 per vehicle, or $5 per individual hiking or biking. There is a $1 per day parking charge at Ozette. A $5 wilderness use fee is charged to camp in the wilderness (for groups up to 12 people) plus $2 per person per night.

Camping in the park campgrounds costs $8 to $12 a night. Dump station use costs $3.

SPECIAL REGULATIONS & WARNINGS

Wilderness use permits, available at the Wilderness Information Center (located just behind the main visitor center in Port Angeles) and at all ranger stations, are required for overnight stays in the backcountry. During the summer, you may also need reservations for certain areas. Call the **Wilderness Information Center** (☎ **360/452-0300**) for information.

When hiking, be prepared for sudden and extreme weather changes.

SEASONS & CLIMATE

The climate of the entire peninsula is best described as varied, of the marine type. In the winter the temperatures stay in the 30s and 40s during the day, and 20s and 30s at night. At the lower elevations, near the water, there is rarely more than 6 inches of accumulated snow per season, and it melts quickly. However, on the upper slopes, the snowfall can become quite heavy.

Spring is the late half of the rainy season, mostly wet, mild, and windy. Temperatures range from 35° to 60°F, with lingering snow flurries in the mountains.

Summer temperatures range from a low of 45°F in the evening to 75° and up to 80°F during the afternoons. In the latter half of the summer and early fall, fog and cloud banks drift into the valleys and remain until midday, burn off, and sometimes return in the evening. Thunderstorms may occur in the evening in the upper elevations.

The fall is moderately cold and blustery, and ushers in the rainy season. Snow begins to fall in the mountains as soon as early autumn. Temperatures range from 30° to 65°F.

Rainfall is varied throughout the Olympic Peninsula, but 76% of the precipitation falls during the 6-month period between October and March, primarily on the Pacific side of the peninsula.

SEASONAL EVENTS

There are seasonal events all over the place on the Olympic Peninsula, if not within the park itself. They include salmon cook-offs; classical, jazz, and bluegrass festivals; boat races; light opera; arts and craft festivals; and many others. For a full list, contact the **Port Angeles Chamber of Commerce Visitor Center,** 121 E. Railroad Ave. (☎ **360/452-2363**), or the **North Olympic Peninsula Visitor & Convention Bureau** (☎ **800/942-4042**).

If You Only Have 1 Day

First things first: Decide in advance what you would like to see. This is a big park, and no roads go completely through it. The roads that do venture inside (and they're major tourist attractions) are generally short and pleasant. It's 18.5 miles from U.S. 101 to the Hoh Visitor Center, and 17 miles to Hurricane Ridge.

If you want to see the **rain forests and the coastal strip,** drive up from Olympia on U.S. 101 through the coastal region, perhaps stopping at the Kalaloch Information Station and Ruby Beach, and then head to the Hoh Rain Forest Visitor Center, from where you can explore further. To see the **glaciers and the alpine meadows** of the east side of the park, start by driving to the Olympic National Park Visitor Center in Port Angeles, and from there head up to Hurricane Ridge, where you can take in a hike, or drive even further into the park.

Exploring the Park by Car

THE RAIN FORESTS & THE COAST

If the rain forests are your destination, your best bet would be to drive west and north from Olympia along the western side of the peninsula. (Or, in reverse, west and south from Port Angeles or Port Townsend.) The first opportunity to see a bit of the rain forest is near the south shore of **Lake Quinault,** at the southern end of the main part of the park. If you plan to stay the night, this area is packed with lodges, motels, and campgrounds. From the ranger station on the south shore, there are several interpretive hikes along the lake. The view of the mountains here is quite spectacular on a sunny day, but save the rest of your day for nature trails or longer hikes in nearby rain forests. Lake Quinault serves as a good hors d'oeuvre more than anything.

Drive north on U.S. 101. At this point, you have an option—you can drive east to the **Queets Ranger Station** in the Queets River Valley for a rugged hike into some of the most beautiful (and remote) rain forests on the peninsula, or keep driving northwest to the **Kalaloch Information Station,** where you can enjoy views of the Pacific from Kalaloch to Ruby Beach. It's a tough call. You might get to see elk in some of the former homestead meadows in the early morning or late afternoon on the 3-mile **Sam's River Loop Trail** in the Queets, but understand, it's the least accessible of the rain forests. The road to Queets is unpaved, but it's still a relatively decent gravel road. Despite the occasional pothole, it's highly navigable by your average light truck or utility vehicle, and fairly navigable by your "beater" car, but occasionally intolerable for your Caddie. Watch out for seasonal closures during the winter and late fall.

After leaving the coastal area at Ruby Beach, continue your northward drive on U.S. 101 to the turnoff for the **Hoh Rain Forest Visitor Center.** It's an 18.5-mile drive from U.S. 101 to the center, with excellent views of the Hoh River along the way. You could also spend a long day hiking from the Hoh Visitor Center Parking Lot 9 miles up to the **Olympus Ranger Station.** In just a few hours, this moderate to heavy hike goes from temperate rain forest to alpine

meadows with stunning views of Mount Olympus. If you're not feeling so ambitious, take the short **Hall of Mosses** or **Spruce Nature trails,** and get ready to head north again, to Sol Duc.

The last leg of our rain forest excursion takes you to one of the most commercially developed areas in the park, **Sol Duc** and the **Sol Duc Hot Springs Resort.** It might be a nice idea, before you head back down the coast to Olympia, or to sleep in your campsite or hotel room, to have a dip in these famous hot springs (open from late spring to early fall). The hot springs experience costs $6.75 to enter, but packages, including a sauna and a massage, can be purchased as well. You also have your choice of comfort levels, anywhere from 70° to 158°F. But be forewarned: There's a resort here, and the springs can be crowded. Still, if you're into luxuriating after a long day hiking, it could be just the thing.

The area has more than hot springs. Try taking the 1-mile hike from the springs through some wonderfully dense forest to **Sol Duc Falls.** Or take the **Mink Lake Trail** through 2.5 miles of uphill grade and dense forest to get a look at one of the many higher altitude lakes that dot the Sol Duc region.

THE EAST SIDE OF THE PARK

Seen the rain forests? You could do a lot worse than spending a day seeing the glaciers and the alpine meadows of the east side of the park. This time, the jumping off point of convenience would probably be **Port Angeles.** First, visit the **Olympic National Park Visitor Center,** to get acquainted with what you're about to see.

As in the rain forest tour, this tour starts off with a choice: Head back through Port Angeles for the **Elwha/Altaire area,** or from the visitor center head to **Hurricane Ridge.** Either way, you're going to be treated to a variety of Olympic experiences.

The Elwha area has a small ranger station beside **Lake Mills** (a reservoir), and further up the road, a very nice observation point for viewing the surrounding hills. In addition, if you don't want to deal with the crowds at Sol Duc, you can hike 2.5 miles from Elwha to the only other hot springs available inside the park. Located on the banks of Boulder Creek, the **Olympic Hot Springs** is not accessible by car, and don't expect amenities or guarantees of sanitation either. In other words, use at your own risk.

Along the way to Hurricane Ridge from Port Angeles, pass the **Heart O' the Hills Ranger Station.** At Hurricane Ridge, one of the most popular spots in the park, there are a number of short interpretive trails, very good for seeing wildflowers, and many larger trails intersect here as well. The visitor center has numerous interpretive exhibits and a snack bar.

Leaving Hurricane Ridge, Port Angeles, or the Elwha area, drive a little farther southeast, and off a turnoff of U.S. 101 is the less crowded **Deer Park Ranger Station,** where you get the same sort of views as Hurricane Ridge without jostling for position. The road to Deer Park is steep and graveled. It's not accessible for RVs and trailers, and prepare to deal with steep inclines, turns, and potholes. In the winter the road may be closed.

Outside Olympic National Park, consider visiting other locations along U.S. 101, such as **Dungeness** or **Sequim Bay** state parks on the northeastern tip of the peninsula, with their beautiful shorelines and views of the strait. As you travel further south, the **Hood Canal** will appear on your left—there are numerous places here to see seals on the rocks on a good day, especially at **Seal Point.**

Organized Tours & Ranger Programs

There are a variety of educational programs offered in Olympic National Park. Visitor centers and ranger stations have exhibits and provide information. Campfire talks, stargazing, and beach walks are just some of the activities available.

You'll find rain forest tours originating from the Hoh and the Quinault ranger stations; alpine wildflower walks from the Hurricane Ridge area; and lakeside and waterfall walks from the Storm King Ranger Station. Contact park headquarters for a seasonal schedule of day and evening events.

Historic & Man-Made Attractions

There aren't many man-made attractions within the park itself, although there are **old homestead sites** scattered throughout the park, such as those found along the **Geyser Loop Trail.** Also, there's an old cabin located behind the Olympic National Park Visitor Center that will leave you wondering how early settlers here managed to maintain their sanity in such a claustrophobic environment.

Day Hikes

There's a vast number of trails in the park, and it seems like they all connect somewhere. Consequently, it's very easy to tie several trails together to create your own, customized route. For a complete listing, write ahead for a free **Olympic National Park map** from the Wilderness Information Center, Olympic National Park, 600 East Park Ave., Port Angeles, WA 98362.

The following is a partial, though representative, list of some of the many wonderful trails within the park. **Backcountry permits** are required for overnight trips. They're available at the Wilderness Information Center (located just behind the main visitor center in Port Angeles) and at all ranger stations. During the summer, you may also need reservations for certain areas. There is a $5 registration fee for wilderness camping for groups up to 12 people, plus $2 per person per night. Call the Wilderness Information Center (☎ **360/452-0300**) for information.

Cape Alava/Sand Point Loop

9.1 mi. RT. Easy. Access: Ozette Ranger Station.

This loop begins with a stroll over a cedar-plank boardwalk through teeming coastal marsh and grasslands. (Careful! Boards are slippery when wet, which is most of the time.) The trail connects to its second leg on a wilderness beach strip of the Pacific shoreline, the westernmost point in the Lower 48. Camping is permitted on the beach, but beware, it's a popular spot in the summer. Continue south 1 mile past the petroglyphs that can be seen from the rocks along the shore next to the high-tide line. Two miles south, the trail connects to the Sand Point leg, which is an easy stroll back to the Ozette Ranger Station. (There's a permit and reservation required here. Call the Wilderness Information Center.)

Hoh River to Queets River

14.7 mi. one way. Easy to moderate. Access: Ruby Beach parking lot.

The beaches here are wide and flat, the surf fishing is good, and with its proximity to U.S. 101, you can expect to see a lot of people here in the summer. This section, compared to the more northern trails, is fairly tame. Destruction Island Overlook is famous for its

> **Warning:** Coastal hiking can be treacherous. Tides can trap you. Never round headlands without knowledge of the tide heights and times. Carry a tide chart. Obtain additional information from the Wilderness Information Center.

whale watching from March to April and November to December.

Sand Point to Rialto Beach

17 mi. one way. Easy to moderate. Access: Ozette Lake Ranger Station from the north or Mora Campground from the south.

This is a coastline famous for its shipwrecks, the memorials of which dot the beach at many points, along with an abandoned mine. Other than that, though, there's not a lot of man-made activity going on. Enjoy the sand and the mist, the forests that come down to land's end, and get ready for the storms that visit here regularly.

Second Beach Trail

0.8 mi. one way. Easy. Access: Second Beach parking area on the La Push road, 14 mi. west of U.S. 101.

Wander through a lovely forest to a sandy beach, with tide pools and sea stacks. There's a long set of stair steps at the end. For a short hike, this is hard to beat.

Third Beach to Hoh River

17 mi. one way. Moderate to strenuous. Access: Third Beach Parking Area, 3 mi. beyond the La Push Rd. left fork.

This trail is not your leisurely stroll. You'll be required to do a bit of inland skirting along old oil company roads to avoid some of the more wicked headlands, and there are some sand ladders (contraptions constructed of cables and wooden slats) just beyond Taylor Point. In addition, there's a slightly treacherous crossing farther south at Goodman Creek. So what's the reward for the intrepid hiker? Toleak Point is located approximately 5 miles down the beach, where there is a sheltered campsite famous for its wildlife. The entire area is well known for its shipwrecks, wildlife, coastal headlands, and stacks. The trail ends at Oil City, north of the Hoh Indian Reservation.

Bogachiel River

Length varies. Easy to moderate in the low-lands, more strenuous further inland. Access: 5 mi. south of Forks, turn left across from Bogachiel State Park onto Undie Rd., and continue 5 mi. to the trailhead.

This hike is as long or short as you want to make it, but it is an equally beautiful cousin to the often crowded Hoh River Trail. The beginning is loaded with rainforest extravaganza—huge Douglas firs, spruce, cedar, and big-leaf maples, including the world's largest silver fir, some 8 miles from the trailhead. Approximately 6 miles into the trail is the Bogachiel Shelter, and 8 miles in is Flapjack Camp, both good backcountry campsites. This is pretty much the end of the flatland; further up, the trail begins to get steep.

Hoh River Valley

Up to 17 mi. one way. Easy to moderate in the lowlands, more strenuous further inland. Access: Hoh Rain Forest Visitor Center.

This is one of the most heavily traveled trails in the park, at least in the lower elevations, and it won't take you long to figure out why. Huge Sitka spruces hung with moss shelter the Roosevelt elk that wander among its lowlands. The first 13 miles, through the massive rain forests and tall grass meadows along the Hoh River Valley bottomlands, are relatively flat. The number of fellow walkers drops off after the first few miles. Happy Four Camp (6 miles in) and Olympus Guard Station (9 miles in) provide excellent camp or turnaround sites. Continue eastward into the hills for the remaining 4 or 5 miles. If you connect with the Hoh Lake Trail, you can eventually find yourself at the edge of the famous Blue Glacier on Mount Olympus, elevation 7,965 feet. Be careful. After July, hiking near the park's glaciers can be dangerous because of snowmelt.

Lake Quinault Loop

4 mi. RT. Easy. Access: Trailheads located at various spots along the loop, including South Shore Rd., Quinault Lodge, Willaby Campground, Quinault Ranger Station, and Falls Creek Campground. All access originates from the south shore of Lake Quinault.

This trail is easily accessible, well maintained, and offers beautiful views. Consequently, it's quite crowded in the summer. Elevation changes are gentle, making this an excellent walk for kids.

The trail wanders about the shore of Lake Quinault, past historic Lake Quinault Lodge as well as the adjacent campgrounds and other lakeside attractions before heading into its most popular section, the Big Tree Grove. Here you can wander among the huge trunks of 500-year-old Douglas firs. Watch for the interpretive signs. In addition, the Big Tree Grove can be accessed via a short, 1-mile loop trail, originating from the Rain Forest Nature Trail Parking Lot.

Maple Glade Rain Forest Trail

0.5 mi. RT. Easy. Access: Across the bridge from the Quinault Ranger Station.

Another beautiful, peaceful little trail with lots of exhibits. Take the kids, or just enjoy it yourself. As you meander, you'll pass through dense trees, open meadows, and an abandoned beaver pond. As usual, keep your eyes peeled for the ever-possible elk sighting.

North Fork of the Quinault

Up to 15 mi. one way. Moderate. Access: End of the North Shore Rd. Alternatively, if a washout has occurred at the trailhead, the trail is accessible from the South Shore Rd. as well.

This is either the end of the Skyline Ridge Trail or the beginning of the North Fork Trail, both of which could conceivably take you 47 miles all the way through the park to Altaire and Elwha on the north side—if you make the right connections and are maniacal enough. The trail is relatively benign for the first dozen miles as it winds its way inward along the river toward its source near Mount Seattle. Campsites are available at Wolf Bar (2.5 miles in), Halfway House (5.3 miles in), and in a gorge in Elip Creek (6.5 miles in). For the last several miles, the trail climbs steeply toward Low Divide, Lake Mary, and Lake Margaret, where you can get beautiful views of Mount Seattle, at an elevation of 6,246 feet. Snow can remain at this elevation until midsummer, so be ready. There's a summer ranger station at Low Divide, and many high-elevation campsites here as well.

Queets River Trail

Up to 16 mi. one way. Moderate to strenuous. Access: Queets River Campground.

This is the trail for the serious rain forest/wilderness lover. Part of its appeal is that it requires a bit of an effort from the average hiker to reach the trail's solitude and quietly majestic scenery. Within 50 yards of your car, you'll be traversing the Queets River. Even on this first of several fords you will have to make across the river, the water can be treacherous if it's up. It's best to visit during the dry season in late summer, or you might be in for more than an atmospheric dunking. Alternatively, you can cross the Sams River to the right of the Queets, connecting and crossing the Queets River farther up. At 2.5 miles, gape in awe at the largest Douglas fir on the planet. After 5 miles of hiking through elk and giant fern territory, you'll arrive at Spruce Bottom, which is a common haunt for steelhead anglers and has several good campsites. The trail reaches ends at Pelton Creek where there are also campsites available.

Sams River Loop Trail

3 mi. RT. Easy to moderate. Access: Queets River Ranger Station.

This short loop parallels both the Sams River and the Queets River, providing a view of some old homestead meadows,

beautiful spruce trees, and perhaps an elk or two in the meadows in the evening.

Lovers Lane Loop

6 mi. RT. Easy to moderate. Access: Next to site 62 in Loop B of the Sol Duc Campground.

This trail extends a loop that begins just pass Sol Duc Falls. Cross the bridge at the falls and continue around on the Lovers Lane Trail, which will return you to the resort/campground area after taking you through beautiful spruce groves and fern glades. Portions of the trail are narrow and rocky and can get muddy until things dry out in midsummer. Occasionally grouse are spotted along the trail.

Mink Lake Trail

5 mi. RT. Moderate. Access: Opposite end of the Sol Duc Resort parking lot from the pools.

This is a long climb up to Mink Lake, where herons are known to pursue an elusive trout or two. In late summer, brilliant buckbean flowers fill the marshy edges of the lake, and huckleberries are abundant.

Deer Lake

8 mi. RT. Moderate. Access: Junction of Sol Duc Falls.

A good choice for those who want to see deer, this trail is a steady climb through beautiful woods to this tree-lined lake. Canada jays await to eat your food, but don't feed them. There are some switchbacks on this trail, and it can get pretty bumpy in spots.

Elwha River Trails

Up to 50 mi. one way. Difficulty varies. Access: Drive just beyond the Elwha Ranger Station to Whiskey Bend Rd. Go past the Glines Canyon Dam, 1.5 mi. up the road. Approximately 2 mi. above the dam is the Whiskey Bend Trailhead, just beyond the Upper Lake Mills Trailhead.

The serious backpacker arranges a pick-up car to be at the Dosewallips or the North Fork ranger districts and heads for a week or so along the trail that was fortuitously blazed for you by the famed 1889 Press Expedition, the expedition that essentially broke this park wide open. For a good distance, the trail follows the intense blue-green of the Elwha River to its source on the sometimes snow-slushy peak at Low Divide (elevation 3,600 ft.), which is also the head of the Quinault River. You can follow the trail blessedly downhill at this point to the North Fork of the Quinault.

What can you expect on such a monumental trip?

Old-growth forests, moist valley flatlands, and gently sloping hills appear around you as you explore the Elwha Valley before you begin your ascent towards the sometimes calf-busting Low Divide. Roosevelt elk, black bears, mountain lions, marmots, or a grouse or two might show up. At Low Divide, you're treated to spectacular views of Mount Seattle to the north and Mount Christie to the south. From here, you begin your descent from alpine heights to the deep, dense rain forests along the Quinault.

Geyser Valley Loop

5 mi. RT. Moderate. Access: Drive just beyond the Elwha Ranger Station to Whiskey Bend Rd. Go past the Glines Canyon Dam, 1.5 mi. up the road. Approximately 2 mi. above the dam is the Whiskey Bend Trailhead, just beyond the Upper Lake Mills Trailhead.

From the Whiskey Bend Trailhead, hike 0.75 mile down the trail to the Eagles Nest Overlook for a view of the meadows that stretch from valley to valley. You may see an elk or black bear. Head back to the trail and proceed 0.5 mile to the Rica Canyon Trail for a view of Goblin's Gate, a rock formation in the Canyon Gorge that might look like a bunch of goblins' heads staring at you, if you stare back hard enough. The trail to Goblin's Gates drops 325 feet on the 0.5-mile walk to the

viewing area. At this point, you can follow a riverside trail for another 0.5 mile to some prime fishing spots, or continue on to the Krause Bottom and Humes Ranch area. The Humes Ranch has been restored, although some of the wood is starting to get moldy. At any one of these points you can return north back to the Whiskey Bend Trail, or continue 0.8 mile northeast past Michael's Cabin, another old homestead.

High Divide Loop

Up to 20 mi. RT. Moderate. Access: Sol Duc Ranger Station.

Like many trails in the park, this one gives you a chance to design your own trail. Take as short or as long a hike as you like. From the Sol Duc Ranger Station Trailhead, climb a relatively easy 0.8 wooded mile to Sol Duc Falls, and keep going. You can take a leg out to the Seven Lakes Basin Area, where you'll find many campsites (crowded in the summer), or toward Appleton Pass, some 14 miles inland. From Appleton Pass, pass nearby Heart Lake, and begin your climb toward Bogachiel Peak (elevation 5,474 ft.), which presents some of the most breathtaking views in the park. On clear summer days, you can enjoy the wildflowers along the slopes of Bogachiel, the view to the south of the glaciers of Mount Olympus, or the brilliant sunsets on the western Pacific horizon. Continue back down toward Sol Duc Trail through the Deer Lake area, and the final leg back to the Sol Duc Trailhead.

Marymere Falls

2.2 mi. RT. Easy. Access: Storm King Ranger Station.

This is one of the most popular hikes in the park. It's easy, well maintained, close to U.S. 101, and has a definite goal: beautiful Marymere Falls. It's a popular trail for kids. The Barnes Creek Trail leads 0.7 mile through beautiful maples and conifers to the Marymere Trail turnoff.

Continue up to the falls, where silvery water drops from a moss-covered outcropping some 100 feet to the basin below.

North Fork of the Sol Duc

2.4 mi. RT. Moderate. Access: North Fork Trailhead, 3.8 mi. down the Sol Duc Rd. away from the resort.

On this trail you climb the ridge between the main and north forks of the river before descending into the North Fork Valley. The trail passes through old-growth forests, before arriving at the deep-green pools of the river. The curious can venture upriver for several more miles.

Sol Duc Falls

1.7 mi. RT. Easy. Access: Sol Duc Ranger Station.

One of the more popular spots on the peninsula, beautiful Sol Duc Falls is viewed from a bridge that spans the canyon just below the falls. On the way, check out the huge hemlocks and Douglas firs, some of which are 300 years old. This trail is wide, graveled, and level, making it great for kids.

Spruce Railroad

8 mi. RT. Easy. Access: 4 mi. from the Fairholm Campground, at the end of the North Shore Rd. along Lake Crescent.

This is the trail you want to take for a leisurely, hot summer afternoon stroll. The trail does nothing but wander gently around the unbelievably blue-green, glacial-fed waters of Crescent Lake, along an old stretch of abandoned railroad. Weather permitting, clamber down the bank and go for a swim, or simply enjoy the views of Mount Storm King. There are two abandoned railroad tunnels (don't go in!) and a much photographed arch bridge at Devil's Point. This flat, wide trail provides easy access to one of the parks most beautiful glacial lakes.

HURRICANE RIDGE AREA

Cirque Rim Trail and Big Meadow Loops

0.5 mi. and 0.25 mi. RT. Easy. Access: Hurricane Ridge Visitor Center parking lot.

These trails provide a wonderful little taste of alpine meadows, deer, and the spring fireworks display of wildflowers, along with excellent views of Port Angeles and the Strait of Juan de Fuca.

Grand Ridge (Obstruction Point to Green Mountain)

11 mi. RT. Moderate. Access: From Hurricane Ridge, turn left onto the dirt road to Obstruction Point, and continue 8.5 mi. to the end of the road.

This is the highest section of trail in the park, a fact you might notice as you gaze out to Victoria, B.C., and the Strait of Juan de Fuca to the north, or to the south, where you'll see the Grand Valley with its string of lakes and the numerous snow-clad peaks of the Olympic interior. There is both a shortage of trees and water on this hike.

From the parking lot, follow the trail to the left. (The right goes to Grand Valley.) In 2 miles you'll find yourself at the breathtaking top of Elk Mountain. Over the next 5.5 miles, you will pass through Roaring Winds Camp (not misnamed), up to Maiden Peak and finally Green Mountain. In late June the air is filled with the smell of Lyle's lupine, which grows amid the loose scree. This is a good turnaround point, unless you want to descend to Deer Park.

High Ridge, Alpine Hills to Klahane Ridge

1 to 8 mi. RT. Easy to moderate. Access: Hurricane Ridge Visitor Center.

You can take the short, paved 1-mile High Ridge Route (which is chock-full of interpretive exhibits) and then return to the parking lot. Or you can proceed along the unpaved portion to Sunrise Ridge, a rocky little backbone of a view point off the High Ridge Trail, providing excellent panoramas of the Strait of Juan de Fuca, Port Angeles, and beautiful alpine glaciers and wildflowers. The rest of the 3.3-mile, somewhat strenuous walk climbs to the top of Klahane Ridge. As numerous signs mention, beware of the deer and marmots here! They're unafraid, and may hassle people who approach them.

Hurricane Hill

2.75 mi. RT. Easy to moderate. Access: 1.5 mi. from the Hurricane Ridge Visitor Center.

This is a popular trail in the summertime, as it is a broad, easy climb along an abandoned work road up to brilliant alpine meadows, with fantastic views of the Strait of Juan de Fuca and Port Angeles to the north.

EASTERN & SOUTHEASTERN SECTION

Main Fork Dosewallips/ Constance Pass

11 mi. one way. Moderate. Access: Dosewallips Campground and Ranger Station.

Take the Main Fork Dosewallips to the north, and you'll find yourself on a moderate climb through old-growth forests for 7.5 miles before the trail flattens out at Constance Pass. There are fields of wildflowers skirting the edge of Mount Constance. The trail ends in another 3.4 miles at Boulder Shelter in Olympic National Forest. You can also catch the Upper Big Quilcene Trail or the Upper Dungeness Trail here.

Main Fork of the Dosewallips

31 mi. RT. Moderate. Access: Dosewallips Ranger Station.

This is a versatile trail. You can catch a lot more of the inland trails from here, including Constance Pass Trail, the Gray Wolf Trail, and the Elwha River Trail. The Dosewallips side of the park sometimes seems like the neglected side—it's not as flashy as a glacial meadow or a rain forest. But the Dosewallips is one of the most beautiful rivers in the country, its jade-green water crashing down among narrow cliffs. And you might skirt some of the crowds.

Staircase Rapids

6.5 mi. RT. Easy to moderate. Access: Staircase Ranger Station.

The Staircase Trail is one of the more popular hikes in the park, and once you get to Staircase Falls, you'll see why. Along the way you'll enjoy the sight of the North Fork Skokomish River's white water rushing through stands of huge cedar trees. After the falls, the trail continues for another 1.5 miles, following in the footsteps of the 1890 O'Neil Expedition that named the area.

Other Sports & Activities

Biking. Almost all trails in the park are closed to mountain bikes. The only exception is the **Spruce Railroad Trail,** which was once a railroad grade that ran along the shore of the lake. It is quite flat and easy for its 4-mile length, and there is an additional 1.5-mile stretch of road past the North Shore Picnic Area. In the summer there are spots where you can get down the banks for a little dip in Lake Crescent. The highlight of the trail is a much photographed arched bridge across a rocky cove. There's also a few **dirt roads** for mountain bikers, extending from paved roads, like the section from Hurricane Ridge to Obstruction Peak.

For road bikers, U.S. 101 can be somewhat treacherous, with eager motorists rubbernecking and all. But if you get through all that, you can find some pleasant rides on any of the roads that poke their way into the park.

Kayaking & Canoeing. Although large and often windy, glacier-carved **Lake Crescent** is a beautiful place to do a little paddling. Lush, green forests rise straight up from the shores of this 624-foot deep lake, giving these waters a fjordlike quality unmatched anywhere on the peninsula. Boat ramps can be found on U.S. 101 at Storm King (near the middle of the lake) and at Fairholm (at the west end of the lake). On East Beach Road, on the lake's northeast shore, there is a private boat ramp at the Log Cabin Resort.

If you launch at Storm King, you can explore around Barnes Point, away from U.S. 101 traffic noise (but in view of the Lake Crescent Lodge). From Fairholm, you can paddle along the north shore, and from the Log Cabin Resort, you can explore the narrow bay that feeds the Lyre River, the lake's outlet stream. When winds blow down this lake, as they often do, the waters can be very dangerous for small boats.

Canoes can be rented at **Fairholm General Store** (☎ **360/928-3325**) at the west end of the lake, or at the **Log Cabin Resort,** 3183 E. Beach Rd. (☎ **360/928-3325**), on the lake's northeast shore.

Ozette Lake, 300 feet deep, nearly 10 miles long, and the third-largest natural lake in Washington, is a fascinating place to explore by sea kayak or canoe. Situated only a mile from the Pacific Ocean, the lake is indented by numerous coves and bays, and surrounds three small islands. Campsites along the shore include the boat-in sites at Erickson's Bay.

The **Swan Bay boat launch,** one of the lake's two, is probably the best choice for paddlers heading out on this large lake. For a leisurely half-day paddle, just explore the shores of this convoluted bay, in the middle of which is Garden Island. For a day-long paddle, try paddling down the lake to Tivoli Island. For an overnighter, head to the lake's western shore and the campsites at Erickson's Bay. From here, you can explore up and down the west shore.

Both Lake Crescent and Ozette Lake are big lakes subject to quick changes of weather and wind. Whitecaps can come up suddenly, and cold waters can lead to hypothermia. Check the weather forecast before leaving, and keep an eye on the sky.

Llama Trips. It's llamas, llamas, llamas within the national park. Try **Wooley Packer Llama Co.,** 171763B Hwy 101, Forks, WA 98331 (☎ **360/374-2243**), which offers trips of up to 7 days within the park; or **Kit's Llamas,** P.O. Box 116, Olalla, WA 98359 (☎ **253/857-5274**), which offers day and extended trips.

Snowshoeing and Cross-Country Skiing. Any of the snow-covered roads leading into the mountains will offer a satisfying winter trek. However, if it's views you seek, then head to **Hurricane Ridge** with the rest of the winter crowd and set out on any of the area's trails. Snowshoe rentals are available at the Hurricane Ridge Lodge.

White-Water Kayaking & Canoeing. Although the Olympic Mountains generate an astounding number of runnable rivers, the best are on the west side of the peninsula and along the southern slopes of the range. However, the east and north sides of the peninsula also offer some good runs. As elsewhere in the Northwest, sweepers, strainers, and logjams are always a problem on the steep, narrow rivers. If you're interested in taking a whitewater kayaking class, or obtaining any other information on local white-water action, contact the **Olympic Outdoor Center,** P.O. Box 2247, Poulsbo, WA 98370 (☎ **360/697-6095**; www.kayakproshop.com), which focuses on sea kayaking and white-water kayaking classes.

White-Water Rafting. White-water rafting, scenic floats, and sea kayaking are offered in and around Olympic National Park. Guided trips are approximately half day, and canoe and kayak rentals are available. Contact **Olympic Raft & Kayak,** 123 Lake Aldwell Road, Port Angeles, WA 98363 (☎ **888/452-1443**; www.northolympic.com/olympicraft). Rates begin at $39 per person for guided trips.

Camping

Campgrounds at Elwha, Heart O' the Hills, Hoh, July Creek, Kalaloch, Mora, Ozette, Queets, and Staircase are open year-round; other campgrounds are open only seasonally, and their exact schedules are subject to change. Campgrounds at higher elevations may be snow-covered (and closed) from early November to late June; seasonal campgrounds at lower elevations may open earlier.

There are no showers or laundry facilities inside the park, though both are available at the Log Cabin Resort.

The park has no RV hookups, and many sites can accommodate RVs of only 21 feet or less. Use of the park's RV dump stations costs $3. RVs and trailers are prohibited at Deer Park and Dosewallips. July Creek's campsites are all hike-ins. However, the Log Cabin Resort, on the north shore of Lake Crescent at the northern edge of the park, offers RV sites with hookups (see below).

NORTH- & EAST-SIDE CAMPGROUNDS

The six campgrounds on the northern edge of the park are some of the busiest in the park due to their proximity to U.S. 101.

Deer Park is the easternmost of these campgrounds (to get there, take Deer Park Road from U.S. 101 east of Port Angeles); at 5,400 feet, it's also the only high-elevation campground in the park. Deer Park is reached by a winding one-way gravel road that will have you wondering how you're ever going to get back down the mountain (thus, RVs and trailers are prohibited). Deer frequent the campground, and hiking trails head out across the ridges and valleys.

Because of its proximity to Hurricane Ridge, **Heart O' the Hills** is especially popular. It's located on Hurricane Ridge Road, 5 miles south of the Olympic National Park Visitor Center. Several trails start at or near the campground.

Two campgrounds are located on Olympic Hot Springs Road, up the Elwha

River, which is popular with kayakers and fly-fishers. **Elwha** is the trailhead for a trail leading up to Hurricane Ridge. **Altaire** has a boat ramp often used by rafters and kayakers. And, yes, there are hot springs, a 2.5-mile hike away.

The only national park campground on Lake Crescent is **Fairholm,** located at the west end of the lake. This campground is popular with power boaters and could be rather noisy. South of this area, nearby **Sol Duc** is set amid impressive stands of old-growth trees, adjacent to the Sol Duc Hot Springs (and the resort there). Not surprisingly, it is often crowded.

Finally, you'll find RV sites with full hookups at the **Log Cabin Resort,** 3183 E. Beach Rd., on the north shore of Lake Crescent (☎ 360/928-3325; fax 360/928-2088). Because there are no hookups at any of the national park campgrounds, this is a good choice for those with RVs, but tent campers aren't allowed. Major credit cards (DISC, MC, V) are accepted, and the resort is open year-round.

SOUTHEAST-SIDE CAMPGROUNDS

At the end of F.S. 2610, which parallels the Dosewallips River and provides access to the Hayden Pass, Anderson Pass, and Lake Constance trails, you'll find **Dosewallips Campground** in a forested setting on the river's banks. RVs and trailers are prohibited.

The remote **Staircase Campground** is located inland from the Hood Canal and is a good base for day hikes or as a starting point for a longer backpacking trip. It's located up the Skokomish River from Lake Cushman on F.S. 24 and is the trailhead for the Six Ridge, Flapjack Lakes, and Anderson Pass trails.

SOUTH- & SOUTHWEST-SIDE CAMPGROUNDS

If you want to say you've camped at the wettest campground in the contiguous U.S., head for **Hoh,** a busy campground near the Hoh Rain Forest Visitor Center.

Queets is more off the beaten track and has good hiking and white-water kayaking nearby. This campground is located 14 miles up the Queets Road (unpaved) from U.S. 101.

Other rain-forest camping options include **July Creek,** a walk-in campground on Quinault Lake's north shore. East of Lake Quinault, **North Fork** and **Graves Creek,** reached only by an unpaved road, provide access to several long-distance hiking trails.

Along the peninsula's west side are several beach campgrounds. One is **Mora,** located on the beautiful Rialto Beach at the mouth of the Quillayute River west of Forks. You can make group reservations (only) here by contacting the ranger station; call the main park number (☎ 360/452-4501) for more information.

The other coastal campground is the remote **Ozette,** on the north shore of Lake Ozette. It's a good choice for kayakers and canoeists, as well as people wanting to day-hike to the beaches on either side of Cape Alava. There is a designated swimming beach on the lake.

Accommodations

INSIDE THE PARK

Kalaloch Lodge

157151 U.S. 101, Forks, WA 98331. ☎ 360/962-2271. Fax 360/962-3391. www.visitkalaloch.com. E-mail: kalaloch@aramark.com. 20 units, 44 cabins. $73–$208 double room; $127–$211 cabin for 2. Lower rates Sun–Thurs, Oct–May. AE, MC, V.

Campground	Elev.	Total Sites	RV Hookups	Dump Station	Toilets
Altaire	450	30	No	No	Yes
Deer Park*	5,400	14	No	No	No
Dosewallips*	1,540	30	No	No	Yes
Elwha	390	41	No	No	Yes
Fairholm	580	88	No	Yes	Yes
Graves Creek	540	30	No	No	Yes
Heart O' the Hills	1,807	105	Yes	No	Yes
Hoh	578	88	No	Yes	Yes
July Creek***	200	29	No	No	Yes
Kalaloch	50	175	No	Yes	Yes
Log Cabin Resort	580	40	Yes	Yes	Yes
Mora**	35	94	No	Yes	Yes
North Fork	7	520	No	No	Yes
Ozette	0	13	No	No	Yes
Queets	290	20	No	No	No
Sol Duc	1,680	82	No	Yes	Yes
South Beach	50	50	No	No	No
Staircase	765	59	No	No	Yes

* Trailer/RVs prohibited.
** Group Reservations Only (must be made directly through the ranger station).

This rustic, cedar-shingled lodge and its cluster of cabins perch on a grassy bluff. Below, the Pacific Ocean thunders against a sandy beach where huge driftwood logs are scattered like so many twigs. The breathtaking setting makes this one of the most popular lodges on the coast, and it's advisable to book rooms at least 4 months in advance (11 months in advance for July, August, and major holidays). The rooms in the old lodge are the least expensive, but the ocean-view bluff cabins are the most popular. The log cabins across the road from the bluff cabins don't have the knockout views. For comfort you can't beat the motel-like rooms in the Sea Crest House. The dining room serves breakfast, lunch, and dinner, and a casual coffee shop serves from the same menu. Dinner prices range from $10 to $18. The lodge also has a general store and gas station.

Lake Crescent Lodge

416 Lake Crescent Rd., Port Angeles, WA 98363-8672. ☎ **360/928-3211.** 52 units, 48 with bathroom. $68 double without bathroom, $102–$120 double with bathroom; $113–$145 cottage. AE, DC, DISC, MC, V.

This historic lodge is located 20 miles west of Port Angeles on the south shore of picturesque Lake Crescent and is the lodging of choice for those wishing to stay on the north side of the park. Wood paneling, hardwood floors, a stone fireplace, and a sunroom make the lobby a popular spot for just sitting and relaxing. The guest rooms in the main building are the oldest and all have shared bathrooms. If you'd like more modern accommodations, there are a number of standard motel-style rooms, but these lack the character of the lodge rooms. If you have your family or some friends along, we recommend reserving a

	Drinking Water	Showers	Fire Pits/ Grills	Laundry	Reserve	Fees	Open
	Yes	No	Yes	No	No	$10	Seasonal
	Yes	No	Yes	No	No	$8	Seasonal
	Yes	No	Yes	No	No	$10	Seasonal
	Yes	No	Yes	No	No	$10	Year-round
	Yes	No	Yes	No	No	$10	Seasonal
	Yes	No	Yes	No	No	$10	Seasonal
	Yes	Yes	No	No	No	$10	Year-round
	Yes	No	Yes	No	No	$10	Year-round
	Yes	No	Yes	No	No	$10	Year-round
	Yes	No	Yes	No	Yes	$12	Year-round
	Yes	Yes	Yes	Yes	Yes	$25	Year-round
	Yes	No	Yes	No	Yes	$10	Year-round
	No	Yes	No	No	No	Free	Seasonal
	Yes	No	Yes	No	No	$10	Seasonal
	No	No	Yes	No	No	$8	Seasonal
	Yes	No	No	No	No	$12	Seasonal
	No	No	Yes	No	No	$8	Seasonal
	Yes	No	Yes	No	No	$10	Year-round

*** Walk-in sites.

cottage. Those with fireplaces are the most comfortable (and are also the only rooms available between October 31 and late April), but the others are nice as well. All but the main lodge rooms have views of either the lake or the mountains. Rowboat rentals are available.

The Lodge Dining Room serves a limited menu of continental cuisine with an emphasis on local seafood. Prices are moderate. A lobby lounge provides a quiet place for an evening drink.

Log Cabin Resort

3183 E. Beach Rd., Port Angeles, WA 98363. ☎ **360/928-3325.** Fax 360/928-2088. www.logcabinresort.net. 24 cabins, 8 with bathroom; 4 motel units; 2 chalet. $49 cabin for 2 without bathroom, $76–$90 cabin for 2 with bathroom; $106 double; $121 chalet. DISC, MC, V. Closed Nov–Mar.

This log-cabin resort on the north shore of Lake Crescent first opened in 1895 and still has buildings that date from the 1920s. The least expensive accommodations are rustic one-room log cabins in which you provide the bedding and share a bathroom a short walk away (basically this is camping without the tent). More comfortable are the 1928 cabins with private bathrooms, some of which also have kitchenettes (you provide the cooking and eating utensils). The lodge rooms and a chalet offer the greatest comfort and best views. The lodge dining room overlooks the lake and specializes in local seafood. The resort also has a general store and RV sites.

Sol Duc Hot Springs Resort

Sol Duc Rd., U.S. 101 (P.O. Box 2169), Port Angeles, WA 98362. ☎ **360/327-3583.** Fax 360/327-3593. www.northolympic.com/solduc. 32 cabins. $92–$112 cabin for 2. RV sites $16. AE, DISC, MC, V. Closed Nov–Mar.

Located at the end of Sol Duc Road, The Sol Duc Hot Springs have for years been a popular family vacation spot. Campers, day-trippers, and resort guests all spend the day soaking and playing in the hot-water sitting pools. The grounds of the resort are grassy and open, but the forest is at arm's reach. The cabins are done in modern motel style and are comfortable if not spacious. There's an excellent restaurant here, as well as a poolside deli, espresso bar, and convenience store. Three hot spring–fed sitting pools are the focal point, and the pools are open to the public for a small fee. Massages are available.

NEAR THE PARK

IN PORT ANGELES

Domaine Madeleine

146 Wildflower Lane, Port Angeles, WA 98362. ☎ **888/811-8376.** Fax 360/457-3037. www.northolympic.com/dm. 5 units. TV TEL. $149–$179 double. Rates include full breakfast. AE, DISC, MC, V.

Located 7 miles east of Port Angeles, this B&B is set at the back of a small pasture and has a very secluded feel. Combine this with the waterfront setting and you have a fabulous weekend hideaway—you may not even bother exploring the park. The guest rooms are in several different buildings that are surrounded by colorful gardens, and all have views of the Strait of Juan de Fuca and the mountains beyond. There are also fireplaces and VCRs in the rooms, and whirlpool tubs in all but one. The breakfasts are superb.

Doubletree Hotel Port Angeles

221 N. Lincoln St., Port Angeles, WA 98362. ☎ **800/222-TREE** or 360/452-9215. Fax 360/452-4734. 190 units. A/C TV TEL. $99–$129 double; $165 suite. Lower rates off-season. AE, DC, DISC, MC, V.

If you're on your way to or from Victoria, there's no more convenient hotel than the Doubletree. Located on the waterfront, it's only steps from the ferry terminal. Most rooms have balconies and large bathrooms, and the more expensive rooms overlook the Strait of Juan de Fuca. There's a seafood restaurant adjacent to the hotel. Laundry/valet service is available, and there's an outdoor pool and hot tub.

The Tudor Inn

1108 S. Oak St., Port Angeles, WA 98362. ☎ **360/452-3138.** Fax 360/452-3138. www.tudorinn.com. E-mail: info@tudorinn.com. 5 units. Summer $85–$125 double; off-season $75–$110 double. AE, DISC, MC, V.

Located in a quiet residential neighborhood 13 blocks from the waterfront, this 1910 Tudor home is surrounded by a large yard and pretty gardens. On the ground floor you'll find a lounge and library, both with fireplaces that get a lot of use. Upstairs there are five rooms furnished with European antiques. Several rooms have good views of the Olympic Mountains.

WEST OF PORT ANGELES

Elwha Ranch Bed & Breakfast

905 Herrick Rd., Port Angeles, WA 98363. ☎ **360/457-6540.** www.northolympic.com/elwharanch. 3 units. $90–$120 double. Rates include full breakfast. No credit cards.

Although it isn't located within the national park, this cedar-log inn, on an 80-acre ranch high above the Elwha River Valley, has a superb view up the valley into the park. Two of the rooms are in the main house, which has a casual Western ranch feel and lots of windows to take in the views. If you're traveling with friends or family, opt for the two-bedroom suite. However, the nicest and most comfortable room here is a sort of modern log cabin outside the front door of the main house. Be sure to get directions to the inn. Fresh pies are a specialty of innkeeper Margaret Mitchell.

IN THE FORKS AREA

Eagle Point Inn

384 Stormin' Norman Rd. (P.O. Box 546), Beaver, WA 98305. ☎ **360/327-3236.** 3 units. $85 double. Rates include full breakfast. No credit cards.

Located 10 miles north of Forks, a short drive from milepost 202 on U.S. 101, this rustic B&B is housed in a log home. Although the inn's 5 acres are surrounded by recently planted forest, the inn itself is in a beautiful parklike setting on the bank of the Sol Duc River. The guest rooms are everything the rooms in a log house should be—rustic, romantic, rugged—yet with antiques, down comforters, and private bathrooms. Out in the yard you'll find a hot tub and a covered barbecue area.

Huckleberry Lodge

1171 Big Pine Way, Forks, WA 98331. ☎ **888/822-6008.** Fax 360/374-5270. E-mail: hucklodg@olypen.com. 6 units. Summer $85–$140 double; call for rates at other times. MC, V.

Although ostensibly a modern hunting and fishing lodge, this place makes a great base of operations for anyone visiting the area. The lodge is down a gravel road on the edge of Forks and is set on 5 wooded acres adjacent to the Calawah River. In the living room, a moose antler table and trophy heads on the walls emphasize the hunting lodge aesthetics. Guest rooms are comfortable; two rooms have the private bathrooms across the hall. For greater privacy, there are three cabin units behind the main house. A full breakfast comes with the lodging, and fishing and hunting adventures can be arranged.

Manitou Lodge

Kilmer Rd. (P.O. Box 600), Forks, WA 98331. ☎ **360/374-6295.** Fax 360/374-7495. www.manitoulodge.com. E-mail: manitou@olypen.com. 6 units. $80–$105 double. Rates include full breakfast. AE, MC, V. Take Wash. 110 west from north of Forks; turn right on Spur 110 (Mora Rd.) and then right on Kilmer Rd.

This secluded B&B is set on 10 forested acres and is only minutes from some of the most beautiful and remote beaches in the Northwest. The largest room in the house is the "Sacajawea," which has a marble fireplace and king-size bed. A separate cabin houses two of the rooms. Guests tend to gravitate to the comfortable living room, where a huge stone fireplace is the center of attention. Breakfasts consist of fruit and a main course, sometimes stuffed French toast or skillet-omelettes. There's also a Northwest arts gallery on the premises.

Miller Tree Inn

654 E. Division St. (P.O. Box 1565), Forks, WA 98331. **☎ 360/374-6806.** Fax 360/374-6807. www.northolympic.com/millertree. E-mail: milltree@ptinet.net. 7 units, 3 with bathroom. Peak $60–$75 double without bathroom, $80–$130 double with bathroom. Winter $50–$65 double without bathroom, $70–$100 double with bathroom. Rates include full breakfast. MC, V.

Located just a few blocks east of downtown Forks, this large B&B is on the edge of the country and is surrounded by large old trees and pastures, with a hot tub on the back deck. There's nothing fussy or pretentious about this place—it's just a comfortable, friendly inn that caters primarily to outdoors enthusiasts and, during the winter months, anglers.

SOUTH OF THE PARK

Lake Quinault Lodge

P.O. Box 7, Quinault, WA 98575. **☎ 800/562-6672** in Washington and Oregon, or 360/288-2900. 94 units. June–Oct $99–$140 double, $190–$220 suite. Sept–May $65–$115 double, $150–$175 suite. AE, MC, V.

Located on the shore of Lake Quinault at the southwest corner of the park, this imposing grande dame of the Olympic Peninsula wears an ageless tranquillity. Huge old firs and cedars shade the rustic lodge, and Adirondack chairs on the deck command a view of the lawn. There are small rooms in the main lodge, plumodern rooms with wicker furniture and little balconies and rooms with fireplaces. The annex rooms are the least attractive, but they do have huge bathtubs. There's an indoor pool and a

whirlpool. Canoe and paddleboat rentals are available, as are rain-forest tours. The dining room is a large, dark place as befits such a lodge, and the menu reflects the bounties of the Olympic Peninsula, especially seafood. The lounge has a big-screen TV.

Dining

INSIDE THE PARK

Restaurant choices inside the park are slim. On the north side, there are dining rooms at **Lake Crescent Lodge** (open late April to late October) and the **Log Cabin Resort** (open Valentine's Day to Christmas), both of which are on the shores of Lake Crescent. On Lake Quinault, try the dining rooms at the **Calash Lodge** and the **Lake Quinault Lodge** (see "Accommodations," above).

One other dining option on Lake Crescent is the **Fairholm General Store & Cafe,** 221121 U.S. 101 (**☎ 360/928-3020**), which is at the west end of the lake and is open between April and October. Although all you'll get here are burgers, sandwiches, and breakfasts, the cafe has a deck with a view of the lake.

IN PORT ANGELES

If you're hit with a craving for something sweet while in town, check out **Bonny's Bakery,** 215 S. Lincoln St. (**☎ 360/457-3585**), which is located in a 1930 fire department building next door to the Port Angeles Library. Both French pastries and American favorites are baked here and soup/salad/quiche lunches are served. For a good cup of fresh-roasted coffee, try **Mombasa Coffee Co. Ltd.,** 113-A W. First St. (**☎ 360/452-3238**).

Bella Italia

117-B E. First St. **☎ 360/457-5442.** Main dishes $7–$16. AE, DISC, MC, V. Mon–Sat 11am–10pm, Sun 2–9pm. ITALIAN.

Located in the basement of a natural foods store in downtown Port Angeles, this restaurant has a rathskeller feel, with heavy wood beams overhead and booths for privacy. The menu, however, is strictly Italian and starts with a basket of delicious bread accompanied by an olive oil, balsamic vinegar, garlic, and herb dipping sauce. Daily specials include fresh local seafood. Also on the menu are local mussels, steamed clams, and smoked salmon fettuccini. There's a good selection of wines and the Italian desserts are excellent. This is a good choice for families, as well as those who want a private fine dining experience.

C'est Si Bon

23 Cedar Park Rd. ☎ **360/452-8888.** Reservations recommended. Main courses $20–$25. AE, DISC, MC, V. Tues–Sun 5–11pm. FRENCH.

Located 3 miles east of town just off U.S. 101, C'est Si Bon is painted a striking combination of turquoise, pink, and purple that gives the restaurant a sort of happy elegance. Inside, the nontraditional paint job gives way to more classic decor—reproductions of European works of art, crystal chandeliers, and old musical instruments used as wall decorations. Most tables have a view of the restaurant's pretty garden. The menu is limited, which just about ensures that each dish has been perfected. In addition to French cuisine, they try some local dishes as well. Desserts are limited, but rich and creamy. When you call for reservations, you might ask them for directions from where you are. As a start, they're on the north side of U.S. 101 just off Buchanan Road, at the top of a hill. Good luck; it's worth the search.

Downriggers

115 E. Railroad Ave. ☎ **360/452-2700.** Reservations recommended. Main courses $10–$26. DISC, MC, V. Mon–Thurs 11:30am–9pm, Fri–Sat 11:30am–10pm, Sun 4–9pm. SEAFOOD.

At the back of the Landing Mall on the second level you'll find this large, casual restaurant, convenient to the ferry landing. Walls of glass provide views of the ferries (so you don't miss yours) and take in some great sunsets. A long menu nearly guarantees that you'll find something you like, but just be sure to try the award-winning clam chowder. The salmon Wellington and a fettuccini made with smoked salmon, prawns, and scallops are just a couple of interesting main dishes.

Toga's International Cuisine

122 W. Lauridsen Blvd. ☎ **360/452-1952.** Reservations recommended. Main dishes $14–$27. MC, V. Tues–Sat from 5pm. INTERNATIONAL/GERMAN.

Located on the west side of Port Angeles, this restaurant is an unexpected treat and serves some very unusual dishes. Chef Toga Hertzog apprenticed in the Black Forest and has brought to his restaurant the traditional Jagerstein style of cooking in which diners cook their own meat or prawns on a hot rock. With 24 hours notice you can also have traditional Swiss cheese fondue or a lighter seafood fondue. To start your meal, you might try the crabmeat Rockefeller or the sampler of house-smoked salmon, scallops, oysters, and prawns. For dessert nothing hits the spot like the Black Forest cake.

IN FORKS

The Smoke House Restaurant

U.S. 101 and La Push Rd. ☎ **360/374-6258.** Main dishes $4–$18. DISC, MC, V. Mon–Thurs 11am–9pm, Fri 11am–10pm, Sat 4–10pm, Sun 4–9pm. AMERICAN.

The name says it all here. This place smokes fish, and their salmon is just about the best we've ever had. It's got a good smoky flavor yet is tender and moist. If you don't feel like sitting down for the smoked salmon dinner, smoked salmon salad, or smoked salmon and cheddar cheese tray appetizer, then consider getting some to go. It's great beach picnic food.

28

PETRIFIED FOREST NATIONAL PARK

by Don Laine and Alex Wells

THE FIRST THING YOU'LL NOTICE AT PETRIFIED FOREST NATIONAL Park are the dozens of logs lying atop hills as if on display, many of them pointing in the same direction. Closer up you can see the colors in the wood—reds, greens, yellows, blues, and purples, all of them rich and moist-looking like wet paint. The colors might tempt you to touch the wood, and if you do you'll find that it isn't wood at all, but cold, hard stone.

About 225 million years ago these petrified trees were enormous conifers growing in a tropical forest. Floods swept them into large rivers, tearing off their branches in the process. Eventually the trees bottomed out in the shallow waters of the floodplain, where silt, mud, and volcanic ash buried them. Because almost no oxygen could reach the entombed trunks, they were slow to decay. Silica from the ash gradually permeated them. The silica replaced or filled the wood's cells, eventually leaving quartz in its place. Minerals such as iron and manganese streaked the quartz with colors. The end result: The wood became precious, lovely rock.

Recognizing the financial value of this rock, early settlers began shipping it out on East Coast–bound trains. When the residents of the Territory of Arizona realized that the "wood" might soon be gone, they petitioned Congress to protect the "forests." Using the Antiquities Act, Pres. Theodore Roosevelt created Petrified Forest National Monument in 1906. It was designated a national park in 1962.

The same sediments that entombed the trees buried other plants and animals, preserving them as fossils as well. Today, erosion has exposed these clays and sandstones, collectively known as the Chinle Formation. With little or no vegetation to hold them in place, these sediments erode quickly and unevenly, forming mesas, buttes, and furrowed, conical badlands, unearthing thousands of fossils, including bones from some of the most remarkable creatures ever to inhabit the earth. In addition to the 225-million-year-old fossils, there is evidence that the Ancestral Puebloans (or Anasazi), ancestors of the modern Pueblo tribes, once occupied this area. Evidence of other human occupation dates from 10,000 years ago.

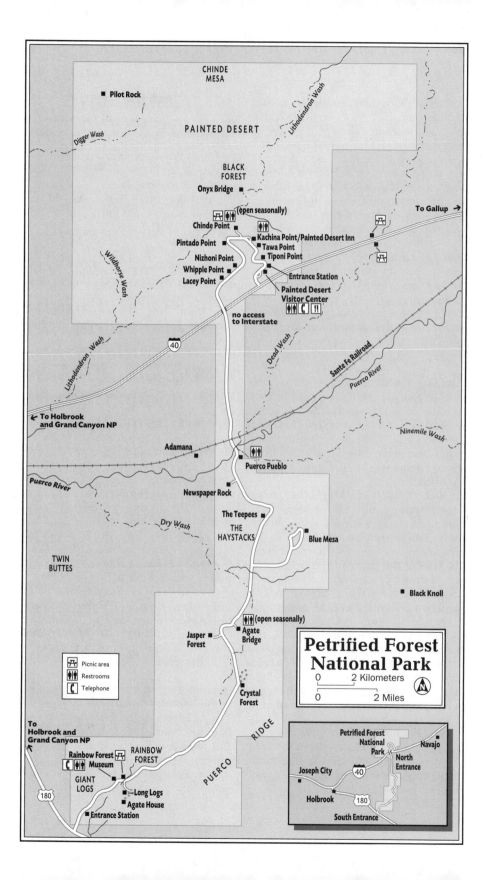

Petrified Forest
National Park

Even without these wonders, it would be worth coming here to see the rich red, gray, and maroon colors of the Painted Desert. Shaped like a tusk (with the wider end near Cameron, Arizona), the desert spans from near Holbrook in the south to the Hopi mesas in the northeast to near the Grand Canyon in the west—far beyond the boundaries of the park. Its seemingly barren landscape is home to a rich diversity of plant and animal life: desert grasses; wildflowers, including Indian paintbrush and globemallow; juniper and other trees; mammals, including pronghorns, cottontails, and porcupines; reptiles, including collared lizards and prairie rattlesnakes; and birds, the most prominent being the raven.

Avoiding the Crowds. About 950,000 people visit the park each year, in part because it is so convenient for cross-country travelers, just a few hundred yards off I-40. Virtually everyone heads down the same 28-mile scenic drive, and the drive's 20 pullouts can get crowded.

Michele M. Hellickson, the park's superintendent, offers three suggestions for avoiding the crowds. First, arrive early. "There aren't many visitors in the first few hours," she says. "It's also before the heat of the day, and the lighting on the rocks is spectacular." Second, stroll away from the parking areas. "Where there are pullouts, there are going to be people," Hellickson says. "But if you park at some of the pullouts and walk the length of the trails, you'll soon be away from the crowds. This will give you a chance to sit and hear the sounds of the desert and maybe get a picture that's different from everyone else's." Third, day-hike into the Painted Desert Wilderness. "That's the instant answer," says Hellickson. "I think it's relatively easy to do in this terrain. It's a landscape that lends itself to going out and exploring, with less fear involved."

Just the Facts

GETTING THERE & GATEWAYS

Petrified Forest National Park is 117 miles east of Flagstaff and 180 miles north of Phoenix. The north entrance is 25 miles east of Holbrook on I-40; the south entrance is 20 miles east of Holbrook on U.S. 180. From Flagstaff, simply take I-40 east.

The Nearest Airport. Flagstaff's **Pulliam Airport** (☎ 520/556-1234) is serviced by **America West Express,** and has rental cars from **Avis, Budget, Hertz,** and **National.** Toll-free reservations numbers are in the appendix.

INFORMATION

Contact **Petrified Forest National Park,** P.O. Box 2217, Petrified Forest National Park, AZ 86028 (☎ **520/524-6228;** www. nps.gov/pefo). The **Petrified Forest Museum Association** (same phone) publishes several excellent books on the park. Written by retired geology professor Sidney Ash, *Petrified Forest: The Story Behind the Scenery* provides a good overview of the human and natural history of the park. Stephen Trimble's colorful book, *Earth Journey: A Road Guide to Petrified Forest,* is almost as good as a guided tour of the park's scenic drive.

For information about area lodging and dining, contact the **Holbrook Chamber of Commerce,** 100 E. Arizona St., Holbrook, AZ 86025 (☎ **800/524-2459** or 520/524-6558; www.arizonaguide. com/holbrook).

VISITOR CENTERS

The park has a visitor center at each end. Both sell books, videos, and park maps, and offer free brochures on the park's geology, flora, and fauna.

The **Painted Desert Visitor Center,** outside the park's North Entrance gate, offers a 20-minute video on the park, which shows on the hour and the half hour. At the South Entrance, the **Rainbow Forest Museum** has displays on the formation of petrified wood, fossilized bones and teeth of ancient animals, and a display of letters from people who stole wood from the park and later regretted it.

FEES & PERMITS

Entrance to the park costs $10 per vehicle, $5 per visitor on foot or bicycle. Backcountry camping permits are free and are issued by the visitor center.

SPECIAL REGULATIONS & WARNINGS

Because an estimated 25,000 pounds of petrified wood are stolen from the park every year, the Park Service has adopted a zero-tolerance policy for visitors who remove even the smallest pieces. Violators are subject to fines starting at $275. If rangers suspect you of removing any wood or other resources, they may detain you and search your car.

There are long stretches between water sources at the park, so fill containers at either visitor center before starting on the scenic drive.

SEASONS & CLIMATE

With an average of just 9.65 inches of precipitation annually, the park couldn't get much drier. Because it averages a lofty 5,400 feet in elevation, however, it's not as hot as many other desert areas. Even in July, daily highs average in the mid-80s, with nightly lows in the low 50s. Of course, the park occasionally heats up—temperatures in the 100s are not unusual in midsummer. The hottest months, July and August, are also the wettest, with afternoon monsoons cutting the morning heat and depositing nearly a third of the yearly precipitation.

These storms continue into early fall, but the weather dries out as it cools. By winter it can get very cold, and snowstorms occasionally close the park. In January, daily highs average 42°F and lows 19°F. Spring tends to be blustery and dry, with daily highs increasing from 54° in March to 80°F in June—the driest month of all, with just 0.33 inch of rainfall.

SEASONAL EVENTS

In March, special events for **Arizona Archeology Month** are scheduled. Call the park office for details.

For 10 days before and after the June 21 **summer solstice,** rangers meet from 8 to 10am daily with visitors at Puerco Pueblo. As the group watches, a shaft of sunlight shines through a natural crack in the rock and gradually moves to the center of a circle carved into the rocks. Archaeologists believe the Ancestral Puebloans used this petroglyph to monitor the seasons.

If You Only Have 1 Day

The obvious way to see the park is to take the 28-mile **scenic drive,** stopping at the pullouts and taking some of the short trails to get close-up views of the petrified wood. With a bit of extra time, you might consider a walk into the **Painted Desert Wilderness.** Combine this with a pre- or posthike picnic at the **Chinde Point Picnic Area.**

Exploring the Park by Car

The direction you choose for the scenic drive depends on which way you're traveling on I-40. If coming from the west, take U.S. 180 east from Holbrook to the park's south entrance, drive through the park, then rejoin I-40 at the park's North Entrance. If coming from the east, do the opposite, driving through the park from the north entrance and exiting on to U.S. 180 in the south. Trails mentioned here are discussed more fully in "Day Hikes," below.

1. If you travel from the south, you'll start at **The Rainbow Forest Museum.** Behind the museum is the **Giant Logs Self-Guided Trail,** the first of several easy trails through the petrified forests.

2. Just past the museum you'll see a spur road to the **Long Logs** and the **Agate House** trailheads. The Agate House Trail, which goes to the right from the parking area, ends at a prehistoric pueblo made of petrified wood. Forking to the left, the Long Logs Trail loops through some of the longest and most spectacular petrified trees in the area.

3. Continuing, you'll come to the **Crystal Forest,** where visitors in the late 1800s discovered ground covered with sparkling bits of petrified wood. At that time, the petrified logs in this area were flecked with quartz and purple amethyst crystals. These crystals attracted gem hunters, some of whom went so far as to dynamite the trees. Although many crystals and the smaller pieces are gone, some very colorful logs remain.

4. Next comes **Jasper Forest,** an overlook from atop a 150-foot-high bluff. This is a great place to observe the various effects of erosion. Looking downhill, you'll notice that large chunks of sandstone and petrified wood have tumbled from the bluff to the desert floor. Soft clay eroded out from under the harder wood and sandstone, undermining it and eventually sending it downhill. Because erosion continues, someday the rocks underfoot will tumble downhill as well.

5. The first thing you'll notice at **Agate Bridge** is the remarkable bridge itself. With each end firmly embedded in sandstone, a petrified log forms a natural bridge across an arroyo that cuts through the ground underneath its midsection. The next thing you'll probably notice is the concrete span that "supports" it. In 1917, workers who wanted to preserve the bridge as a tourist attraction buttressed it with concrete.

6. Next, a 2-mile spur goes to **Blue Mesa.** Like all the badlands in the park, Blue Mesa is made up of soft rocks that are now eroding away by as much as 3 inches a decade—fast enough to change appreciably in the span of a human lifetime. The layers represent different times. The gray and white clay was once part of a floodplain; the sandstone was in streambeds. The Blue Mesa Trail, one of the prettiest walkways in the park, descends from the fourth and last overlook on the spur road.

7. Next comes the turnoff for conical badlands known as the **Teepees.** The base mudstone layer is stained red by iron oxide, the white layer above is sandstone, the darker red layer is siltstone, and the uppermost caprock is clay. The flat rocky surface you see is called **desert pavement,** created when strong winds sweep away the fine sands of the desert floor, exposing small stones and petrified wood fragments.

8. From an overlook 2 miles past the Teepees, you can look down on **Newspaper Rock.** Early inhabitants pecked dozens of petroglyphs into the dark surface of the stone. Among them is an image of the famous humpbacked flute player, Kokopelli. The petroglyphs in this area aren't limited to Newspaper Rock, so be sure to scan the surrounding rocks with your binoculars.

9. With so many petroglyphs around Newspaper Rock, it seems inevitable that a prehistoric dwelling is nearby. Sure enough, a mile down the road is **Puerco Pueblo,** the remains of a 100-room pueblo occupied in the 1100s and again in the 1300s by the Ancestral Puebloans. To see this dwelling, walk the easy 0.5-mile loop trail.

10. The remaining stops between Puerco Pueblo and the Painted Desert Visitor Center are overlooks of the Painted Desert. Each one affords a unique view, but the panorama from the hilltop at **Pintado Point** may be most spectacular. Just past Pintado Point is **Chinde Point,** where you'll find sheltered picnic tables, rest rooms (open seasonally), and another overlook.

11. A quarter of a mile past Chinde Point is the turnoff for **Kachina Point** and the **Painted Desert Inn National Historic Landmark.** Here, you can descend into the desert on the Painted Desert Wilderness Trail, or, if the drop seems a bit imposing, hike to Tawa Point on the Painted Desert Rim Trail. After hiking, be sure to visit the landmark itself, which has displays on the history of the area.

Organized Tours & Ranger Programs

A changing program of guided hikes and talks is presented at various locations throughout the park, with the greatest number during the summer. Check at either visitor center to see what's on tap on a given day.

Historic & Man-Made Attractions

The **Painted Desert Inn,** which overlooks the desert from Kachina Point, once served as a lunch counter and trading post for early travelers on Route 66. After the Park Service purchased the inn from private owners in 1936, workers in the Civilian Conservation Corps (CCC) rebuilt it in the Southwestern style, covering some of the building's original petrified-wood walls with stucco. Inside, they installed oak floors and hand-painted glass ceiling tiles, and added six guest rooms, each with a fireplace. Upon completion in 1940, the 28-room inn became

an immediate hit with travelers. It was closed again, however, during the last years of World War II. After the war, the Fred Harvey Company managed the building, using it as a visitor center and restaurant until 1963, when the new Painted Desert Visitor Center opened.

In 1947, Fred Kabotie, the renowned Hopi artist whose work also graces the Desert Watchtower at the Grand Canyon, painted several murals inside, including one that depicted the annual journey of the Hopi to the sacred Zuni salt mines. Kabotie's murals may have helped save the building, which had severe structural problems caused by expansion and contraction of the clay underneath it. When it was threatened with demolition in the 1960s, preservationists cited the value of Kabotie's art as they called for protecting the building. The Painted Desert Inn was declared a National Historic Landmark in 1987.

Today it houses the **Painted Desert Inn Museum,** which celebrates the area's cultural heritage. Open daily 8am to 4pm, the museum displays American Indian artifacts found in and around the park. Among them is a famous petroglyph of a mountain lion—an image reproduced in contemporary art throughout the Southwest. The building itself is also worth admiring. Several of Kabotie's murals can be seen, and the wood floors and glass ceiling tiles are intact. To the rear of the building, one of the original petrified-wood walls has been exposed. Park crews continue to work on the exterior, but a more significant renovation is on hold, pending an appropriation from Congress.

Day Hikes

Agate House

0.9 mi. RT. Moderate. Access: 0.5 mi. down spur road from Rainbow Forest Museum.

An enjoyable walk takes you to Agate House, a pueblo that archaeologists believe was briefly occupied between A.D. 1100 and 1300. (Archaeologists suspect a brief occupation because very little "trash" was found in the area.) Colorful bits of petrified wood dot the ground on the way to the eight-room pueblo, which sits atop a knoll overlooking a vast expanse of desert. Made from petrified wood and mortar, Agate House must have been one of the prettiest dwellings anywhere in its time—a house of jewels, on a hill. The pueblo's largest room was reconstructed by workers in the '30s. That's how it acquired a window, something the Ancestral Pueblo dwellings never had.

Blue Mesa Trail

1 mi. RT. Moderate to strenuous. Access: Blue Mesa turnoff on scenic drive.

This paved loop trail descends steeply to the floor beneath the blue-, gray-, and white-striped badlands at Blue Mesa—some of the prettiest land in the park. You may notice that it's hard to determine the size of the hills: Because they lack vegetation, there is little to provide a sense of scale. At the bottom, you can observe how the different colors of these hillsides streak and blend where the clay has washed into drainages. Look for small fossils, abundant in the area. The trail has numerous interpretive panels, spaced to give you a chance to catch your breath as you walk.

Crystal Forest Trail

0.8 mi. RT. Moderate. Access: Crystal Forest stop on scenic drive.

This paved trail, which includes a few steep grades, reminds us of why it's important to leave the petrified wood in place. Look carefully and you can see where gem hunters hacked at or even dynamited logs. The wood that's left is still lovely, though, and a few smoky quartz crystals remain. Still, it's hard not to wonder what this area looked like before the scavengers arrived.

Giant Logs Trail

0.4 mi. RT. Easy. Access: Rainbow Forest Museum.

This paved trail loops past some of the park's largest petrified logs, including "Old Faithful," which spans nearly 9 feet at its base. The trail has 11 stops, each corresponding to a page in the guide (free to borrow, 50¢ to keep) available in the museum. At each stop, you'll find out about the trees or the area's geology. Constructed in the '30s by the CCC, the trail has some steps, making access difficult for people in wheelchairs.

Long Logs Trail

0.6 mi. RT. Easy. Access: 0.5 mi. down spur road from Rainbow Forest Museum.

This relatively flat, paved loop will give you an idea of the immensity of the Araucarioxylon trees that grew in this area during the Triassic period. Many of the longest, including one that measures 116 feet, lie alongside the trail on the north end of the loop. You'll see places where these petrified logs protected the softer clay underneath them and prevented it from eroding. The trail also takes you within a few feet of badlands. The different colored layers are caused by mineral deposits in the clay.

Painted Desert Rim Trail

1.2 mi. RT. Easy. Access: Kachina Point stop on scenic drive.

As this cinder trail meanders along the Painted Desert rim between Kachina and Tawa points, it affords stunning views of the desert itself, where gray, pink, and red badlands stand out against the green grasses at their bases. The trail is atop the basalt of the Bidahochi formation, which at 8 million years old, is much younger than most other rocks in the park. This layer has disappeared in many areas of the park but is widespread in other parts of northern Arizona. Here, it provides fertile soil for a diversity of vegetation, including juniper, Mormon tea, sagebrush, and cliffrose.

Painted Desert Wilderness Trail

About 0.5 mi. one way. Moderate to strenuous. Access: Kachina Point.

This trail descends in switchbacks down the face of the badlands below Kachina Point, then follows a wash for a short distance before petering out in the grasslands on the floor of the Painted Desert. You won't find water or shade here, but you will have a chance to experience firsthand the colors and landforms of this desert. Before wandering far, be sure to identify landmarks you can use to retrace your steps. (The Painted Desert Inn is a good one.) If you carry a topographical map and plenty of water and sunscreen, you should have few problems in this desert, which has excellent sight lines and few insurmountable obstacles. Walk on the dry streambeds when possible. Besides being easier, this minimizes the damage to the fragile plant life.

It's worth spending the night here just to watch the sun dip below the red sands of the desert. Before bedding down, you must first obtain a backcountry permit at one of the visitor centers, then walk at least a mile into the 43,000-acre Painted Desert Wilderness, which starts on the other side of Lithodendron Wash. The direction you take from the bottom of the wash will depend on which "use area" you sign up for on your permit. You'll find spots smooth enough for camping near many of the mesas and badlands. (Keep in mind, however, that runoff can create problems during storms.) Don't forget to pack insect repellent; in spite of its dry climate, the park has been known to host an unusually active population of no-see-ums.

Puerco Pueblo Trail

0.5 mi. RT. Easy. Access: Puerco Pueblo.

This relatively flat loop travels around the 100-room Puerco Pueblo. The 30 excavated rooms hint at the floor plan of the buildings—a trapezoid around an outdoor plaza where most of the activity in the community took place. As you walk, you'll observe places where the rooms were one, two, or three deep around the plaza. Where they were two deep, the rooms on the outside may have been used to store crops harvested from the floodplains below. The inside rooms, which opened onto the plaza, were probably used for sleeping or shelter from inclement weather. Three kivas—ceremonial rooms dug into the ground—were located inside the plaza, and one is obvious alongside the trail. Partway around the loop, a short trail leads down to an overlook from which you can see numerous petroglyphs.

Camping

There are no campgrounds within the park boundaries. Backpackers with backcountry permits can stay in the park after it closes for the evening, but they must hike at least 1 mile into the wilderness before setting up camp. For drive-in camping, head to Holbrook, 25 miles west of the park on I-40.

The best thing at the **KOA Campground,** 102 Hermosa Dr., Holbrook, AZ 86025 (☎ 520/524-6689), is the large swimming pool, which shimmers like a mirage on sunny days. The 24 sites and 100 RV hookups themselves are exposed to the sun and wind, as the owners try to grow new trees in an unforgiving landscape. The tent sites, which are grassy, are nicest. The cost is $17.95 for tents, $21.95 for full hookups ($2 less in winter). Reservations are accepted. The campground offers public phones, toilets, drinking water, laundry, showers, and a dump station. It's open year-round. During the high season, campers feast at relatively inexpensive evening cookouts and all-you-can-eat pancake breakfasts.

Located just 3 blocks south of the KOA Campground, **OK RV,** 1576

Roadrunner Rd., Holbrook, AZ 86025, (☎ 520/524-3226), charges a bit less for its 150 hookups. Electric, water, sewer, and cable TV are included in the rates of $15 to $17. There's no pool, though, and the 6 tent sites aren't as plush as at the KOA. OK RV offers public phones, toilets, drinking water, laundry, showers, and a dump station. It's open year-round. Reservations are not accepted.

Accommodations

No accommodations are available inside the park.

NEAR THE PARK

The place to get a bed for the night is Holbrook, 25 miles west of the park. In addition to the fascinating Wigwam Motel, discussed below, Holbrook offers the **Comfort Inn,** 2602 Navajo Blvd. (☎ 520/524-6131), charging $42 to $65 double; **Days Inn,** 2601 Navajo Blvd. (☎ 520/524-6949), charging $39 to $49 double; **Econo Lodge,** 2596 Navajo Blvd., (☎ 520/524-1448), charging $40 to $50 double; **Holiday Inn Express,** 1308 Navajo Blvd. (☎ 520/524-1466), with rates of $50 to $68 double; **Motel 6,** 2514 Navajo Blvd. (☎ 520/524-6101), charging $34 double; **Ramada Limited,** 2608 E. Navajo Blvd. (☎ 520/524-2566), with rates of $40 to $59 double; and **Super 8 Motel,** 1989 Navajo Blvd. (☎ 520/524-2871), charging $55 to $75 double. See the appendix for a list of the national chain toll-free numbers.

Wigwam Motel

811 W. Hopi Dr. (P.O. Box 788), Holbrook, AZ 86025. ☎ **520/524-3048.** E-mail: clewis97@ cybertrails.com. 15 units. A/C TV TEL. $31–$36 double. MC, V. Pets accepted.

Even if you don't stay here, the Wigwam Motel makes for a wonderful photo op. Each of the motel's 15 rooms is inside its own 75-foot-high wood-and-concrete wigwam, built during Route 66's glory days

in the 1940s by the same family that's running it today. The motel's owners have done a good job of preserving this bit of Americana, and also have a small museum on the property containing family items including giant petrified wood slabs, Civil War artifacts, and American Indian items, among others. The wigwams are very clean and well maintained, and each is furnished with the motel's original hand-carved hickory furniture. The only drawbacks are that both the bathrooms and windows are somewhat small by today's standards.

Dining

INSIDE THE PARK

Cougar Café

Next to the Painted Desert Visitor Center. ☎ **520/524-3756.** Breakfast items 80¢–$4.75; lunch and dinner main courses $2.95–$4.50. AE, DC, DISC, MC, V. Summer daily 8am–6pm, winter daily 8am–5pm. CAFETERIA.

The cafe serves hot breakfasts, including eggs and pancakes. At lunch and dinner, Navajo tacos and a variety of sandwiches and burgers are available, as well as daily specials, such as spaghetti and meatballs. *Note:* In addition to the Cougar Cafe, a small fountain serves sandwiches and snacks next to the museum at the park's south entrance.

NEAR THE PARK

Butterfield Stage Co.

609 W. Hopi Dr., Holbrook. ☎ **520/524-3447.** Main courses $9–$18. AE, MC, V. Daily 4–10pm. STEAK/SEAFOOD.

Named for the famous overland stagecoach line that carried the mail from St. Louis to San Francisco in the mid–19th century, this restaurant is owned, surprisingly, by natives of the former Yugoslavia. Tables have historical panels with amusing information to read while waiting for your pepper steak or filet mignon, and there's a soup and salad bar.

Joe and Aggie's

120 W. Hopi, Holbrook. ☎ **520/524-6540.** Lunch and dinner items $2.50–$9.95. DISC, MC, V. Mon–Sat 6am–8pm. AMERICAN/ MEXICAN.

More than 40 years ago, Joe Montano and his wife, Aggie, opened this restaurant, and today you'll still find them at the same Route 66 location, although now a few other family members help out. What you'll find is a friendly, down-home sort of place, with plenty of historic Route 66 charm.

Recommended at breakfast are the chile cheese omelette and the egg burro (scrambled eggs with hash browns and cheese rolled in a flour tortilla). At lunch and dinner you can select from Mexican platters, traditional American dishes, and combinations of both, such as a Mexican hamburger steak with red or green chile. For a sort of Mexican pizza, try the cheese chrisp—a deep fried flour tortilla with melted cheese and toppings such as green chile and taco meat.

Mesa Italiana Restaurant

2318 E. Navajo Blvd., Holbrook. ☎ **520/ 524-6696.** Lunch items $3.50–$8.95; dinner entrees $6.50–$14.95. MC, V. Tues–Sun 11am–9pm. ITALIAN.

Generally regarded as the best restaurant in Holbrook, Mesa Italiana serves traditional Italian dishes, including baked ziti, stuffed shells, lasagna, linguine, and pizza, at reasonable prices. The Italiana Mushrooms (mushrooms stuffed with chicken, spinach, and fresh herbs, all topped with a garlic white-wine sauce) may deceive you into thinking that you've left the land of the green chile hamburger steak. Especially recommended is the Chicken Jerusalem—a chicken breast sautéed with butter, garlic, artichoke hearts, mushrooms, and shrimp, all under a white-wine and lemon sauce.

Picnic & Camping Supplies

Just inside the north entrance to the park you'll find a gas station with a convenience store. In Holbrook, picnic supplies and general foodstuffs are available at **Safeway,** 702 W. Hopi Dr. (☎ **520/ 524-3313**), and **Basha's,** 1519 Navajo Blvd. (☎ **520/524-2607**).

29

POINT REYES NATIONAL SEASHORE

by Eric Peterson

POINT REYES IS A 100-SQUARE-MILE PENINSULA OF DARK FORESTS, wind-sculpted dunes, endless beaches, and plunging sea cliffs. Aside from its beautiful scenery, it also boasts historical treasures that offer a window into California's coastal past,

including lighthouses, turn-of-the-century dairies and ranches, and the site of Sir Francis Drake's 1579 landing, plus a complete replica of a Coast Miwok Indian village.

The national seashore system was created to protect rural and undeveloped stretches of America's coastlines from the pressures of soaring real estate values and increasing population. And nowhere is the success of the system more evident than at Point Reyes. Layers of human history coexist peacefully here with one of the world's most dramatic natural settings. Residents of the surrounding towns—Inverness, Point Reyes Station, and Olema—have steadfastly resisted runaway development. You won't find any strip malls or fast-food joints here—just laid-back coastal towns with cafes and country inns where gentle living prevails. The park, a 71,000-acre hammer-shaped peninsula jutting 10 miles into the Pacific and backed by Tomales Bay, is loaded with wildlife, ranging from tule elk, birds, and bobcats to gray whales, sea lions, and great white sharks.

Though the peninsula's people and wildlife live in harmony above the ground, the situation beneath the soil is much more volatile. The infamous San Andreas Fault separates Point Reyes, the northernmost landmass on the Pacific Plate, from the rest of California, which rests on the North American Plate. Point Reyes is making its way toward Alaska at a rate of about 2 inches per year, but there have been times when it has moved much faster. In 1906, Point Reyes jumped north almost 20 feet in an instant, leveling San Francisco and jolting the rest of the state. The 0.5-mile Earthquake Trail, near the Bear Valley Visitor Center, illustrates this geological drama with a loop through an area torn by the slipping fault. Shattered fences, rifts in the ground, and a barn knocked off its foundation by the quake illustrate that the earth is alive here. If that doesn't convince you, a seismograph in the visitor center will.

Avoiding the Crowds. Though the park is heavily visited, crowds are only a problem

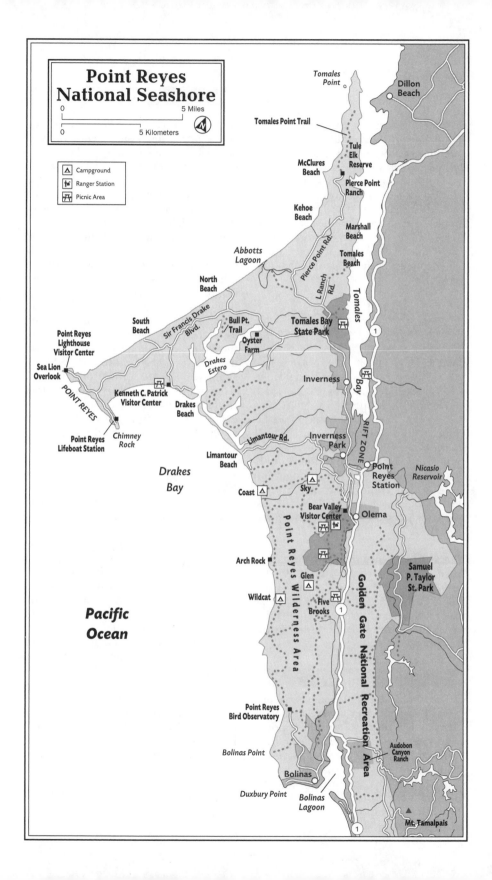

Point Reyes National Seashore

0   5 Miles

0   5 Kilometers

△ Campground

🏠 Ranger Station

🏕 Picnic Area

Tomales Point

Dillon Beach

Tomales Point Trail

Tule Elk Reserve

McClures Beach

Pierce Point Ranch

Kehoe Beach

Marshall Beach

Abbotts Lagoon

Tomales Beach

Pierce Point Rd.

L Ranch Rd.

North Beach

Tomales

South Beach

Sir Francis Drake Blvd.

Bull Pt. Trail

Oyster Farm

Tomales Bay State Park

Bay

Point Reyes Lighthouse Visitor Center

Drakes Estero

Inverness

Sea Lion Overlook

POINT REYES

Kenneth C. Patrick Visitor Center

Drakes Beach

RIFT ZONE

Point Reyes Lifeboat Station

Chimney Rock

Limantour Rd.

Inverness Park

Point Reyes Station

Nicasio Reservoir

Limantour Beach

Drakes Bay

Coast △

Sky △

Bear Valley Visitor Center

Olema

Golden Gate National Recreation Area

Samuel P. Taylor St. Park

Arch Rock

Point Reyes Wilderness Area

Glen △

Pacific Ocean

Wildcat

Five Brooks

Point Reyes Bird Observatory

Bolinas Point

Bolinas

Audobon Canyon Ranch

Duxbury Point

Bolinas Lagoon

▲ Mt. Tamalpais

at a few places and only during certain times. If you visit the lighthouse on a weekend or holiday during whale season (December through March), be prepared for crowds and a wait for the shuttle that operates from Drakes Beach to the lighthouse area. Trails leaving from Bear Valley tend to be more crowded on weekends than others. Try the **Five Brooks** or **Palomarin trailheads** to avoid hordes of backcountry tourists. As a whole, a weekday visitor to Point Reyes will encounter far fewer people than the weekender.

Just the Facts

GETTING THERE & GATEWAYS

Point Reyes is only 30 miles northwest of San Francisco, but it takes at least 90 minutes to reach by car (it's all the small towns, not the topography, that slows you down). The easiest route is via Sir Francis Drake Boulevard from U.S. 101 south of San Rafael; it takes its time getting to Point Reyes, but does so without any detours. For a much longer but more scenic route, take the Stinson Beach/Highway 1 exit off U.S. 101 just south of Sausalito and follow Highway 1 north.

The Nearest Airport. San Francisco International Airport (☎ 650/761-0800), 14 miles south of downtown San Francisco on U.S. 101, is served by all major airlines and car rental companies, whose phone numbers are listed in the appendix.

INFORMATION

Contact **Point Reyes National Seashore,** Point Reyes Station, CA 94956-9799 (☎ 415/663-1092; www.nps.gov/pore). The *Natural History of the Point Reyes Peninsula,* by naturalist Jules G. Evens (Point Reyes National Seashore Association, 1993), is a comprehensive and sometimes anecdotal overview of Point Reyes's natural history.

VISITOR CENTERS

As soon as you arrive at Point Reyes, stop at the **Bear Valley Visitor Center** on Bear Valley Road (look for the small sign posted just north of Olema on Highway 1), and pick up a free trail map, talk with the rangers about your plans, and check out the natural history and cultural displays. It's open daily year-round.

The **Ken Patrick Visitor Center,** located at Drakes Beach, houses a 250-gallon saltwater aquarium and a 16-foot minke whale skeleton, among other exhibits. Open weekends and holidays only (except Christmas) from 10am to 5pm. The **Lighthouse Visitor Center,** located at the most westerly point of the Point Reyes Peninsula, offers information on the lighthouse and life-saving services performed over the 125 years of its use, as well as natural history exhibits on whales, seals, and wildflowers. Hours are from 10am to 5pm. It is closed Tuesday, Wednesday, and Christmas.

FEES

Entrance to the park is free. Hike-in camping is $10 per night.

SPECIAL REGULATIONS & WARNINGS

◆ Dogs and other pets are not permitted on trails, in campgrounds, or on beaches that are seal habitats or bird nesting areas. On other beaches they must be leashed. Check at park visitor centers before taking your dog to a beach to avoid seasonal closures.

◆ Wood fires are prohibited in campgrounds. Use only charcoal, gas stoves, or canned heat. Driftwood fires are permitted only on sandy beaches below the high-tide line, but you must obtain a free permit at a visitor center.

◆ Check the tide tables before walking on the beaches. Rising water can trap you against a cliff with no possibility of escape.

♦ For your safety, sleeping on the beach is prohibited; it can be really dangerous. High tide frequently comes to the base of the cliffs and can trap the unwary.

♦ Do not climb cliffs—they can crumble easily. Your foothold may vanish, leaving you in thin air. Walking or sitting below cliffs is also dangerous due to falling rock.

♦ In wooded areas keep an eye out for poison oak's waxy three-leaf clusters. Also be sure to check for ticks as the Lyme disease–carrying black-legged tick is common here.

♦ The pounding surf and rip currents are treacherous, especially at McClures Beach and Point Reyes Beaches, north and south. Stay away from the water.

♦ Don't disturb any abandoned baby seals or sea lions you may encounter on the beach. The mother may be preoccupied with finding lunch, and she won't come back until you leave. In fact, you could be fined up to $10,000 for your good intentions. However, if a pup looks injured or in danger, call the **Mammal Center** at ☎ 707/465-MAML.

SEASONS & CLIMATE

Weather at Point Reyes is very fickle. The seasons here generally reverse expectations: Summer tends to be cold and foggy until the afternoon (the point itself is the foggiest place on the West Coast), while winter is clear and, if not exactly warm, often more tolerable. But these are generalizations at best—winter storms can rage for weeks and sometimes the summer fog miraculously holds off for days. Spring and fall usually see the best weather (that is, little fog, warm temperatures).

To make matters more frustrating, the clearing of fog often signals the onset of strong winds. So, if you are planning to explore the park on foot, prepare yourself for cool weather, dampness, and wind (*lots* of wind, winds that have reached up to 133 m.p.h., the highest

wind speed recorded on the Pacific Coast). The best plan is to take advantage of variations in local weather by being flexible with your itinerary: Save indoor sightseeing for rainy or foggy days, and hit the beach or go hiking when the sun comes out.

SEASONAL EVENTS

Point Reyes National Seashore hosts an annual **Native American Celebration** every third Saturday in July. American Indian basket-makers, wood- and stone-carvers, singers, and dancers convene at Point Reyes for an annual public celebration at Kule Loklo, an authentic reconstruction of a village of the indigenous Coast Miwok Indian tribe. Classes in traditional crafts and skills are also offered intermittently throughout the year. Call ☎ 415/479-3281 for information.

If You Only Have 1 Day

First, stop at the **Bear Valley Visitor Center** and pick up the free Point Reyes map, which lists all the trails and roads open to cars, bikes, horses, and hikers. While you're here, spend some time at the nearby **Kule Loklo,** an authentic reconstruction of a village of the indigenous Coast Miwok Indian tribe, and **Morgan Horse Ranch,** a good place to see park patrol horses. Afterward, take a short stroll along the **Earthquake Trail,** an informative 0.7-mile walk along the infamous San Andreas Fault, and, time permitting, the 0.7-mile self-guided **Woodpecker Nature Trail.**

By far the most popular, and crowded, attraction at Point Reyes National Seashore is the venerable **Point Reyes Lighthouse,** located at the westernmost tip of Point Reyes. The drive alone on the **Sir Francis Drake Highway** is worth the trip—a 45-minute, 20-mile scenic excursion through rolling, windswept meadows and working dairy ranches (watch out for cows on the road). When the fog burns off, the lighthouse and the headlands provide a fantastic lookout point for spying common mures, basking sea lions, and gray whales as they make their migration along the coast from December through March.

If there's still some time left, the **Point Reyes Bird Observatory**—an ornithological research organization located at the southeast end of the park—is a must for bird-watchers, or you can rent a mountain bike in Olema and pedal the popular **Olema Valley Trail.**

Exploring the Park by Car

The main scenic road in the park is the **Sir Francis Drake Highway** (described above in "If You Only Have 1 Day"). An excellent turnoff on this road is **Mount Vision Road**, which winds its way up to the Mount Vision Overlook for a panoramic view of the entire peninsula.

There are two other major roads within the park. **Pierce Point Road** forks north from the Sir Francis Drake Highway toward Tomales Point, passing Tomales Bay State Park (a popular picnicking area that offers relatively warm and safe waters) and Abbotts Lagoon (a bird-watchers' paradise) before ending at McClures Beach. The other major road is **Limantour Road,** which bisects the park before ending at Limantour Beach, a popular spot for beachcombing, picnicking, and bird watching at nearby Estero de Limantour. Both these roads are primarily used to access trailheads and beaches, but can also double as scenic alternatives to touring Sir Francis Drake Highway.

Organized Tours & Ranger Programs

Rangers lead programs within Point Reyes National Seashore year-round, including wildlife hikes, local history lessons, and habitat restoration. All tours are free, but you'll need to call the **Bear Valley Visitor Center** (☎ 415/663-1092) for up-to-date schedules.

Groups such as the **Golden Gate Audubon Society** (☎ 510/843-2222) and **Oceanic Society Expeditions** (☎ 415/474-3385) run excursions and outings to the park. During whale season the Oceanic Society takes naturalist-led whale-watching boats from the San Francisco Marina to Point Reyes every weekend, weather permitting. The 6-hour trip costs $50 for adults and $48 for kids and senior citizens. No children under 10 are allowed.

Historic & Man-Made Attractions

Kule Loklo is a restored Coast Miwok Indian village which often hosts displays of dancing, basket-making, cooking, and indigenous art. Until recently, **Morgan Horse Ranch** was the only working horse-breeding farm in the National Park System. Although breeding is defunct, the ranch remains a good place to see park patrol horses. Also, there are exhibits here that offer an interpretive glimpse into the area's horse ranching past. Both are located near the **Bear Valley Visitor Center** on Bear Valley Road and are open year-round.

But if you really want to escape the crowds and have some stinky man-made entertainment, head to **Johnson's Oyster Farm** (☎ 415/669-1149), off Sir Francis Drake Boulevard, about 6 miles west of Inverness (open Tuesday to Sunday 8am to 4pm). Located in the park, right on the edge of Drakes Estero (a large saltwater estuary within the Point Reyes Peninsula that produces nearly 20% of California's commercial oyster yield), Johnson's may look and smell like a dump, with its cluster of trailer homes, shacks, and oyster tanks surrounded by huge piles of oyster shells, but those tasty bivalves don't come any fresher or cheaper. The popular modus operandi is 1) to buy a couple of dozen, 2) head for a picnic area along nearby Drakes Beach, 3) fire up the barbecue pit (don't forget the charcoal), 4) split and barbecue the little guys, 5) slather them in Johnson's special sauce, and then 6) slurp 'em down.

Day Hikes

There's a little of everything for hikers here—32,000 acres, crisscrossed by 70 miles of trails, are set aside as wilderness where no motor vehicles or bicycles are allowed. The principal trailheads are Bear Valley, Palomarin, Five Brooks, and Estero. Pick up a free trail map at the visitor center before shoving off.

Abbotts Lagoon Trail

3 mi. RT. Easy. Access: Abbotts Lagoon Trailhead parking area on Pierce Point Rd.

If you're looking for a short, easy trail located well away from the masses, this is the one. After climbing a small ridge, you're led down to Abbotts Lagoon, a popular watering hole for migratory birds.

Bear Valley Trail

8 mi. RT. Easy. Access: Bear Valley Trailhead south of the visitor center parking area.

This well-worn trail leads through wooded hillsides until it reaches the shore at Arch Rock, where Coast Creek splashes into the sea through a "sea tunnel" (actually the arch of Arch Rock). This is your best bet for a beautiful walk through the woods to the beach.

Coast Trail

7 mi. RT. Easy to moderate. Access: Palomarin Trailhead, just off Mesa Rd. at the southern tip of the park.

Recommended by locals, this trek is one of Point Reyes's prettiest. This section of the trail skirts a cliff offering stunning views and then passes several small lakes and meadows before it reaches Alamere Falls, a freshwater stream that cascades down a 40-foot bluff onto Wildcat Beach.
    Easily the longest trail at the national seashore, the Coast Trail continues on for a 15-mile one-way hike along the

coast that is usually done in 2 days, camping a third of the way through at Wildcat Beach. (There's another campground at Santa Maria Beach.) The trail ends at the American Youth Hostel. You'll need a second car, however, to shuttle you back to the trailhead where you began.

Estero Trail

4.5 mi. one way. Easy to moderate. Access: Estero Parking Area.

A favorite with birders, this mellow trail meanders along the edge of Drakes Estero and Limantour Estero (*Estero* is the Spanish word for estuary). The brackish waters here draw flocks of waterfowl and shorebirds as well as many raptors and smaller species. Along the way you cross a dam and a bridge over Home Bay.

Mount Wittenberg Trail

2 mi. one way. Strenuous. Access: Bear Valley Trailhead.

For the Rambo in your group, this huffer-puffer weeds out the weenies due to its steep elevation, peaking at 1,407 feet rather abruptly. Start at the Bear Valley Trailhead, south of the parking area, and turn right on to the Mount Wittenberg Trail after 0.2 mile. The trail up the ridge is steep but rewards hikers with great views back east across the Olema Valley. Instead of turning around directly, if you still have the energy you can loop back along Baldy Trail and take an alternative path such as the Meadow Trail back to Bear Valley Trail, the main route home.

Stewart Trail

9 mi. RT. Moderate. Access: Five Brooks parking area.

This trail to Wildcat beach is one of the few unpaved trails in the park open to mountain bikes and is also quite popular with horseback riders. It's quite steep and not nearly as scenic as most other trails.

Tomales Point Trail

4.5 mi. one way. Easy to moderate. Access: Parking lot at the end of Pierce Point Rd.

This trail gives hikers a tour of the park's rugged shoreline and also passes through an elk reserve, home to the park's 400-strong herd of tule elk. Watch for their V-shaped tracks on the trail. About halfway through, you come to the highest spot on Pierce Point, where on a clear day you can see over the bay to the Sonoma Coast and Mt. Saint Helena to the northeast.

Beaches

The **Great Beach** is one of California's longest. It is also one of the windiest, and home to large and dangerous waves. You can't swim here, but the beachcombing is some of the best in the world. Tide poolers should go to lonely **McClure's Beach** at the end of Pierce Point Road during low tide or hike out to **Chimney Rock,** east of the lighthouse. Swimmers and dog owners will want to stick to **Limantour Beach,** located in the protected lee of Point Reyes. **Kehoe Beach,** in the northwest of the park, is known for its spring wildflower blooms, while **Hearts Desire Beach** at Tomales Bay State Park has the warmest, safest swimming (as well as a $5 per vehicle fee).

Sir Francis Drake reputedly landed the *Pelican* (later rechristened the *Golden Hind*) on the sandy shore of Drakes Bay in June 1579, to replenish supplies and make repairs before sailing home to England. **Drakes Beach** is now home to the Kenneth C. Patrick Visitor Center and **Drakes Beach Cafe** (Thursday to Monday 10am to 6pm; ☎ 415/669-1297), the only food concession in the park, famous for its great oysters. This beach is good for swimming and beach fires.

Other Sports & Activities

Biking. As most ardent Bay Area mountain bikers know, Point Reyes National Seashore has some of the finest mountain-bike trails in the region—narrow dirt paths winding through densely forested knolls and ending with spectacular ocean views. A trail map is a must (available for free at the Bear Valley Visitor Center) since many of the park trails are off-limits to bikes. *Note:* Bicycles are forbidden on the wilderness area trails, and plotting a course exclusively on the bike trails can be tricky, so plan your route well in advance. The Abbotts Lagoon Trail, the Stewart Trail, the Estero Trail, the Olema Valley Trail, and part of the Bear Valley Trail are all open to bikes.

If you didn't bring your own, you can rent a mountain bike at **Building Supply,** a hardware store in Point Reyes Station (☎ 415/663-1737) for about $25 a day.

Bird Watching. During Audubon's annual Christmas bird count, Point Reyes is regularly found to have the largest concentration of diverse bird species in the continental United States—approximately 350. Popular bird-watching spots are Abbotts Lagoon and Estero de Limantour, or you can hang out with the pros at the **Point Reyes Bird Observatory—Palomarin Field Station** (☎ 415/868-0655), one of the few full-time ornithological research stations in the United States, located at the southeast end of the park on Mesa Road. This is where ornithologists keep an eye on approximately 350 feathered species. Admission to the visitor center and nature trail is free, and visitors are welcome to observe the tricky process of catching and banding the birds. (Open May to November, Monday to Saturday, 15 minutes after sunrise to sunset. Banding hours vary, as well as other seasonal hours; call for exact times.)

Horseback Riding. Equestrian activities are very popular at Point Reyes, as all of the trails (save Bear Valley Trail on weekends and holidays) are horse-friendly. A good resource is **Fivebrooks Ranch** (☎ 415/663-1570; www.fivebrooks. com), located at the Fivebrooks Trailhead, 3.5 miles south of Olema on

Highway 1. They offer guided trail rides (horses provided) ranging from $30 for an hour-long ride to $110 for an all-day excursion. Horse boarding is available here.

Kayaking. Kayak trips, including 3-hour sunset outings, 3½-hour full-moon paddles, yoga tours, day trips, and longer excursions, are organized by **Tamal Saka Tomales Bay Kayaking** (☎ 415/663-1743; www.tamalsaka.com; e-mail: info @tamalsaka.com). Instruction, clinics, and boat delivery are available, and all ages and levels are welcome. Prices start at $45 for tours. Rentals begin at $25 for one person, $35 for two. Don't worry: The kayaks are very stable and there are no waves to contend with because you'll be paddling through placid Tomales Bay, a haven for migrating birds and marine mammals. The launching point is located on Highway 1 at the Marshall Boatworks in Marshall, 8 miles north of Point Reyes Station.

Whale Watching. Each year, gray whales (it's the barnacles that make them appear gray) migrate from their winter breeding grounds in the warm waters off the Baja Coast to their summer feeding grounds in Alaska. You can observe them as they undertake this enormous 10,000-mile journey from just about anywhere within Point Reyes National Seashore, though the most popular vantage point is the Point Reyes Lighthouse.

During peak season (December to March), you might see dozens of whales from the lighthouse, and the **Lighthouse Visitor Center** offers great displays on whale migration and maritime history. During this period, the Park Service runs a shuttle from Drakes Beach to the **Point Reyes Lighthouse** (a small fee is charged for adults; children 12 and under are free) where watchers have been known to see as many as 100 whales in a single afternoon. Even if the whales don't materialize, the lighthouse itself, a fabulous old structure teetering high above the sea at the tip of a promontory, is worth a

visit. Two other spots, **Chimney Rock,** to the east of the lighthouse, and **Tomales Point,** at the northern end of the park, offer just as many whales without the crowds.

Camping

Camping within the park is limited to four hike-in camps. **Wildcat Camp,** near Alamere Falls, is a 6.5-mile hike from Bear Valley Trailhead. **Coast Camp** is on an open bluff, 2.3 beach miles west of the Limantour Beach parking lot. These camps near the sea are often foggy and damp, so bring a good tent and sleeping bag. **Sky Camp** (1.7 mi. from Sky Trailhead on Limantour Road) and **Glen Camp** (4.6 mi. from the Bear Valley Trailhead) are set in the woods away from the sea, more protected from the coastal elements.

In all camps, individual sites hold up to eight people and have picnic tables and food lockers. Pit toilets are available. Stays are limited to 4 days; and sites can be reserved up to 3 months in advance by calling ☎ 415/663-8054 Monday to Friday 9am to 2pm.

Just outside the park is the **Olema Ranch Campground** (☎ 415/663-8001), which accommodates tents and RVs, and is close to restaurants and a grocery store. It's located about 0.5 mile north of downtown Olema on Highway 1. Reservations are recommended, and you must be 21 or older to register here.

Accommodations

INSIDE THE PARK

Point Reyes Hostel

Off Limantour Rd., P.O. Box 247, Point Reyes Station, CA 94956. ☎ **415/663-8811.** 44 bunks, 1 private rm. $12 per person. MC, V. Reception hrs. daily 7:30–9:30am and 4:30–9:30pm.

Located deep inside Point Reyes National Seashore, this beautiful old ranch-style complex has 44 dormitory-style accommodations, including one room that's reserved for families (though at least one child must be 5 years old or younger). There are also two common rooms, each warmed by wood-burning stoves during chilly nights, as well as a fully equipped kitchen, barbecue (bring your own charcoal), and patio. If you don't mind sharing your sleeping quarters with strangers, this is a deal that can't be beat. Reservations (and earplugs) are strongly recommended. The maximum stay is 5 nights.

NEAR THE PARK

There are four towns in and around the Point Reyes National Seashore boundary—Olema, Point Reyes Station, Inverness Park, and Inverness—but they are all so close together that it really doesn't matter where you stay, because you'll always be within a stone's throw of the park. While the accommodations in Point Reyes are excellent, they're also expensive, with most rooms averaging $100 per night. Be sure to make your reservation far in advance during the summer and holidays, and dress warm: Point Reyes gets darn chilly at night.

Note: If you're having trouble finding a vacancy in Point Reyes, call the **West Marin Network** (☎ 415/663-9543) for information on available lodgings.

Bear Valley Inn

88 Bear Valley Rd., Olema, CA 94950. ☎ **415/663-1777.** 3 units (call about bathroom arrangements). $80–$135 double. Rates include breakfast. AE, DISC, MC, V.

Ron and JoAnne Nowell's venerable two-story 1899 Victorian has survived everything from a major earthquake to a recent forest fire—which is lucky for you, because you'll be hard pressed to find a better B&B for the price in Point Reyes. Granted, the Bear Valley Inn isn't perfect: The rooms lack private bathrooms on weekends, and the main highway is a tad too close. But it's loaded with Victorian charm, right down to the profusion of flowers and vines outside and comfy chairs fronting a toasty-warm wood stove inside. It's in a great location, too, with a couple of good restaurants only a block away, and the entire national seashore at your doorstep.

Blackthorne Inn

266 Vallejo Ave. (off Sir Francis Drake Blvd., south of Inverness), P.O. Box 712, Inverness, CA 94937. ☎ **415/663-8621.** www. blackthorneinn.com. 5 units. $175–$300 double. Rates include buffet breakfast. MC, V.

This elaborate redwood home, with its octagonal widow's walk, spiral staircase, turrets, and multiple decks, looks more like a superdeluxe tree house than a B&B. The delightful but most expensive unit is the Eagle's Nest, an octagonal room enclosed by glass and topped with a private sundeck with a catwalk leading to the private bathroom. The largest room is the Forest View Studio, virtually a suite with a deck, furnished with wicker and decorated with floral fabrics and

Campground	Total Sites	RV Hookups	Dump Station	Toilets	Drinking Water
Coast Camp	12	No	No	Yes	Yes
Glen Camp	12	No	No	Yes	Yes
Olema Ranch Campground (private)	300	Yes	Yes	Yes	Yes
Sky Camp	12	No	No	Yes	Yes
Wildcat Camp	12	No	No	Yes	Yes

modern lithographs. It can be combined with another studio to accommodate a traveling foursome. The main sitting room in the house features a large stone fireplace, skylight, and stained-glass windows and is surrounded by a huge deck. Guests have use of the hot tub on the top deck.

Manka's Inverness Lodge & Restaurant

P.O. Box 1110, on Argyle St. (off Sir Francis Drake Blvd., 2 blocks north of downtown Inverness), Inverness, CA 94937. ☎ **800/ 58-LODGE** or 415/669-1034. www.mankas. com. 13 units. $145–$415 double. MC, V.

This immediately lovable old hunting lodge is a wonderful place to stay and dine on the coast. Every room resembles the sort of rustic old mountain cabin you read about in Jack London novels, and the restaurant has that perfect balance of countrified charm and polished refinement. In addition to the standard rooms in the main lodge (which are anything but standard with their tree-limb bedsteads, billowy down comforters, and bucolic furnishings), there are two luxuriously appointed cabins adjacent to the inn, and a quartet of smaller, less expensive rooms in the redwood annex.

For the ultimate romantic splurge, inquire about their three secluded guest houses: Grizzly Lodge, Boat House, and Chicken Ranch. The lodge's reputation is built on its restaurant, which dominates the bottom floor (see "Dining," below).

Point Reyes Country Inn & Stables

12050 Hwy. 1 (P.O. Box 501), Point Reyes Station, CA 94956. ☎ **415/663-9696.** Fax 415/ 663-8888. www.ptreyescountryinn.com. E-mail: prci@svn.net. 6 units, 2 studios, 2 cottages. $95–$275 double. $10–$15 per horse. Rates include breakfast. MC, V.

Are you and your horse dreaming of a country getaway to the Point Reyes National Seashore? Then book a room at Point Reyes Country Inn & Stables, a five-bedroom, ranch-style home on 4 acres that offers pastoral accommodations for two- and four-legged guests (horses only). Each room has a private bathroom, either a balcony or a garden, and plenty of hiking and riding trails. The innkeepers have also added two new studios with kitchens above the stables, and rent out two cottages on Tomales Bay equipped with decks, stocked kitchens, fireplaces, and a shared dock.

Dining

The Gray Whale

12781 Sir Francis Drake Blvd., Inverness. ☎ **415/669-1244.** Main courses $5–$10. MC, V. Open summer Sun–Thurs 11am–9pm, Fri–Sat 11am–10pm; winter Sun–Fri 11:30am– 8:30pm, Sat 11am–9pm. ITALIAN.

For more than a decade The Gray Whale cafe has been a popular pit stop for Bay Area residents heading to the lighthouse at Point Reyes. Why? First, it's cheap: Sandwiches such as the roasted eggplant

Showers	Fire Pits/ Grills	Laundry	Public Phone	Reserve	Fees	Open
No	Yes	No	No	Yes	$10	Year-round
No	Yes	No	No	Yes	$10	Year-round
Yes	Yes	Yes	Yes	Yes	$20–$25	Year-round
No	Yes	No	No	Yes	$10	Year-round
No	Yes	No	No	Yes	$10	Year-round

with pesto and mozzarella are only $5, as are most of the salads and pastas. Second, it's good: Favorites are the specialty pizzas, such as the Californian (artichoke hearts, fresh basil, and tomatoes) and the Vegetarian (baked eggplant, roasted onions and romas, broccoli, and piles of freshly grated Parmesan cheese). Veteran hikers and mountain bikers stop by for an espresso, sipped on the small patio overlooking the block-long town of Inverness.

Manka's Inverness Lodge & Restaurant

On Argyle St. (off Sir Francis Drake Blvd., 2 blocks north of downtown Inverness), Inverness. ☎ **415/669-1034.** Fixed-price dinner $42–$48. MC, V. Open Thurs–Mon 6–9pm. AMERICAN.

The specialty of this fine restaurant is game and fish, including oysters from Tomales Bay. The menu changes every night, and might feature pheasant with a Madeira jus, mashed potatoes, and a wild huckleberry jam; black buck antelope chops with sweet corn salsa; or everybody's favorite, pan-seared elk tenderloin.

Station House Cafe

11180 Main St., Point Reyes Station. ☎ **415/663-1515.** Reservations recommended. Breakfast $4.45–$7.50; lunch items $6–$13; dinner main courses $8–$20. DISC, MC, V. Daily 8am–10pm. AMERICAN.

A local favorite, the Station House Cafe is known for its good food and animated atmosphere, particularly when the live music fires up on weekends. For breakfast, try the frittata with asparagus, goat cheese, and olives, which always seems to taste better while sitting outside on the shaded garden patio. Luncheon specials might include two-cheese polenta served with sautéed fresh spinach and grilled garlic-buttered tomatoes. The menu changes every week, but always features locally grown beef and a good selection of fresh fish. For dinner, start with a platter of local oysters and mussels, followed by a braised lamb shank (made with Guinness Stout) or one of their old standbys such as meat loaf with garlic mashed potatoes or fish-and-chips with country fries and coleslaw. Rounding out the menu are homemade chili, steamed clams, and fresh soup made daily. The cafe has an extensive list of fine California wines, plus local and imported beers.

Taqueria La Quinta

11285 Hwy. 1 (at 3rd and Main sts.), Point Reyes Station. ☎ **415/663-8868.** Main courses $4–$6. No credit cards. Wed–Mon 10am–9pm in the summer, 11am–9pm in the winter. MEXICAN.

Fresh, good, fast, and cheap: What more could you ask for? Taqueria La Quinta has been a favorite lunch stop in downtown Point Reyes for years. A huge selection of Mexican American standards is posted above the counter, but those in the know inquire about the seafood specials. Since it's all self-serve, you can skip the tip, but watch out for the salsa—it's *hot.*

30

REDWOOD NATIONAL & STATE PARKS

by Eric Peterson

I T'S IMPOSSIBLE TO EXPLAIN THE FEELING YOU GET IN THE OLD-GROWTH forests of Redwood National and State Parks without resorting to Alice-in-Wonderland comparisons. Like a tropical rain forest, the redwood forest is a multistoried affair, the tall trees being only the

top layer. Everything is big, misty, and primeval; flowering bushes cover the ground, 10-foot-tall ferns line the creeks, and the smells are rich and musty. It's so Jurassic Park that you can't help but half-expect to turn the corner and see a dinosaur.

When Archibald Menzies first noted the botanical existence of the coast redwood in 1794, more than 2 million acres of redwood forest carpeted California and Oregon. By 1965 heavy logging had reduced that to 300,000 acres, and it was obvious something had to be done if any redwoods were to survive. The state created several parks around individual groves in the 1920s, and in 1968 the federal government created Redwood National Park. In 1994, the National Park Service and the California Department of Parks and Recreation signed an agreement to manage the four contiguous redwood parks cooperatively, hence the name Redwood National *and* State Parks.

The 105,516-acre park offers a lesson in ecology. When the park was first created to protect the biggest coast redwoods, logging companies continued to cut much of the surrounding area, sometimes right up to the park boundary. Unfortunately, redwoods in the park began to suffer as the quality of the Redwood Creek drainage declined from upstream logging, so in 1978 the government purchased a major section of the watershed, having learned that you can't preserve individual trees without preserving the ecosystem they depend on.

Unaware that the logging of old-growth redwoods in the region is still a major bone of contention between the government, private landowners, and environmentalists, the trees thrive. They are living links to the Age of Dinosaurs and humble reminders that the era of mankind is but a hiccup in time to the venerable *Sequoia sempervirens.*

Avoiding the Crowds. The parks include three major features—the ocean setting, old-growth forests, and the prairies. Not many people discover the latter. These bald hills (called "prairies," here) offer

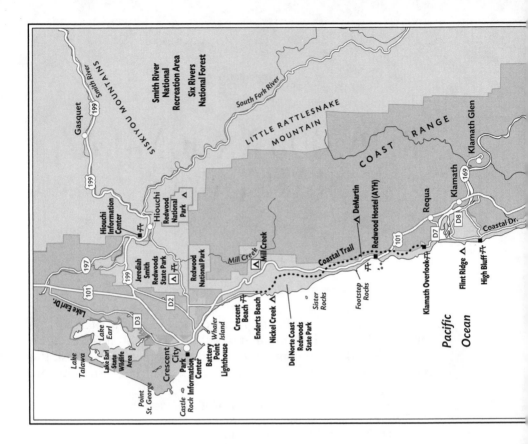

excellent views over the tops of the redwoods and down to the ocean. If you are chilled by the coastal environment and hiking in the shade of the redwoods, they are hot and sunny in the summertime. The prairie region also offers many opportunities to explore the park by either hiking to the historic barns used during the ranching days before the park's establishment, visiting the School House Peak Firelook to check out the view, or hiking to the valley bottom along the Dolason Prairie Trail.

Just the Facts

GETTING THERE & GATEWAYS

The parks are located on a narrow strip near the coast in northern California, about 375 miles north of San Francisco. There are three major routes to the Redwood Coast. U.S. 101 travels up from San Francisco and down from Brookings, Oregon, to traverse much of the length of the parks. U.S. 199 leads from the north of the park to Grants Pass, Oregon, to the northeast. The main route to the east is Calif. 299, which goes from Redding, California, to meet up with U.S. 101 south of the park.

If you're heading from the south, you'll want to stop in Orick. If you're heading from the north (Oregon), you'll want to stop in Crescent City. Why? Because both towns have excellent information centers crammed with useful (and important) information about the Redwood National and State Parks, including free maps.

The Nearest Airports. Arcata-Eureka Airport (no phone; call airline directly) is located in McKinleyville, 28 miles south of the Redwood Information Center near Orick. **Crescent City Airport** (☎ 707/464-7311) is located in Crescent City, at the north end of the park. Both are served by **United Airlines.**

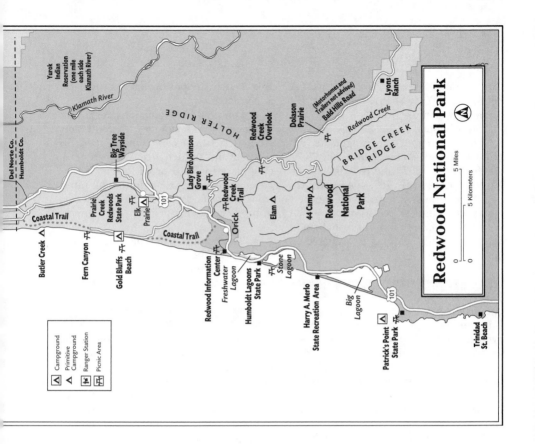

Much further afield, **San Francisco International Airport** (☎ 650/761-0800) is located 14 miles south of downtown San Francisco on U.S. 101. All major **car-rental chains** have offices at San Francisco International Airport; Some rentals are also available at the Eureka-Arcata and Crescent City airports. Airline and car-rental phone numbers are listed in the appendix.

INFORMATION

Contact **Redwood National and State Parks,** 1111 Second St., Crescent City, CA 95531 (☎ 707/464-6101; www.nps.gov/redw). The *Visitor Guide* published each summer describes activities taking place in the parks plus information on the wildlife you're likely to see.

VISITOR CENTERS

The southern gateway to the Redwood National and State Parks is the town of Orick, on U.S. 101. You can't miss it: Just look for the dozens of burl stands alongside the road. Here you'll find the sleek **Redwood Information Center,** P.O. Box 7, Orick, CA 95555 (☎ 707/464-6101, ext. 5265), where you can get a free map and see a variety of exhibits. It's open daily from 9am to 5pm year-round. If you missed the Redwood Information Center, don't worry: About 7 miles further north on U.S. 101 is the **Prairie Creek Visitor Center** (☎ 707/464-6101, ext. 5300), which carries same maps and information. It's open daily from 9am to 5pm in the summer, daily 10am to 2pm in winter.

The northern gateway to the Redwood National and State Parks is Crescent City. This "city" is a real eyesore (at least along U.S. 101), but it's your best bet for a cheap motel, gas, fast food, and outdoor supplies. Before touring the park, pick up a free guide at the **Redwood National and State Parks Headquarters and Information Center,** 1111

2nd St. (at K Street), Crescent City, CA 95531 (☎ 707/464-6101, ext. 5064). It's open daily 8am to 5pm.

If you happen to be arriving via U.S. 199 from Oregon, the rangers at the **Hiouchi Information Station** (☎ 707/464-6101, ext. 5067) and **Jedediah Smith Visitor Center** (☎ 707/464-6101, ext. 5113) can also supply you with the necessary maps and advice. Both are open daily in the summer months from 9am to 5pm and when staffing is available in spring and fall.

FEES & PERMITS

Admission to the national park is free, but to enter any of the three state parks (which contain some of the best redwood groves), you'll have to pay a $5 day-use fee, good at all three.

Camping fees range from $12 to $16 for drive-in sites. Walk-in sites are free, though a backcountry permit is required.

To travel the Tall Trees Trail (see "If You Only Have 1 Day," below) you'll have to get a permit from the Redwood Information Center near Orick (see "Visitor Centers," above).

SPECIAL REGULATIONS & WARNINGS

The north coast used to be one of those places where people left their keys in the ignition in case someone had to move their car. But no more. Lock your car and put valuables in the trunk or take them with you.

♦ **Don't disturb any abandoned baby seals or sea lions** you may encounter on the beach. The mother may be nearby, but will not return until you leave. In fact, you may be fined up to $10,000 for your good intentions. If a pup looks injured or in danger, call the **Mammal Marine Center** at ☎ 707/465-MAML.

♦ On the beach, **be aware of tidal fluctuations.** Swimming is hazardous because of cold water and strong rip currents.

♦ **Watch for poison oak,** particularly in coastal areas.

♦ **Follow park regulations regarding bears** and food storage; all food and scented personal care items should be secured and hidden from view in vehicles, placed in bear-proof lockers (located at each drive-in campsite), or hung from trees. Roosevelt elk are wild and unpredictable; do not approach them on foot.

♦ **Treat water** from natural sources before drinking.

♦ **Tree limbs can fall** during high winds, especially in old-growth forests.

SEASONS & CLIMATE

Frankly, all those huge trees and ferns wouldn't have survived for 1,000 years if it didn't rain a lot here. Count on rain or at least a heavy drizzle during your visit, then get ecstatic when the sun comes out—it can happen anytime. Spring is the best season for wildflowers. Summer is foggy (it's called "the June gloom" but often includes July and August). Fall is the warmest, sunniest (relatively) time of all, and winter isn't bad, though it is cold and wet, and some park facilities are closed. A storm can provide the most introspective time to see the park, since you'll probably be alone. And after a storm passes through, sunny days often follow. On an even brighter note, chances are you won't freeze to death or wither and melt, as the average annual temperature along the Redwood Coast varies only 16°, ranging from a low of 45° to 61°F.

SEASONAL EVENTS

Annual events include an **Earth Day beach cleanup,** the **Smith River cleanup** in May, 4 days of summer seminars with interpretive, ranger-led kayaking tours ($50 per person), the **banana slug derby** in August, and the **Jammin' at Jed concert** in September. Contact the park for exact dates and times. Also, Crescent City holds a **surf contest** in October, and the park holds a **candlelight celebration** through the old growth in December.

If You Only Have 1 Day

First stop at one of the information centers for a free map, which will clue you in to the parks' main attractions.

Next, take the detour along U.S. 101 called the **Newton B. Drury Scenic Parkway,** which passes through dazzling groves of redwoods and elk-filled meadows before leading back onto the highway 8 miles later. Two other spectacular drives are the **Coastal Drive,** which winds through stands of redwoods and offers grand views of the Pacific, and **Howland Hill Road,** an unforgettable journey through an unbelievably beautiful old-growth redwood forest.

The best way to experience the redwoods, however, is on foot. The short **Fern Canyon Trail** leads through a fantastically lush grotto of ferns clinging to 50-foot-high vertical canyon walls. **Lady Bird Johnson Grove Loop** is an easy self-guided tour that loops around a glorious lush grove of mature redwoods. Closer to shore is the **Yurok Loop Nature Trail,** a self-guided trail that gradually climbs to the top of a rugged sea bluff (with wonderful panoramic views of the Pacific). However, the best trail of all is **Boy Scout Tree Trail,** through a lush, cool, damp forest brimming with giant ferns and majestic redwoods.

If you are more of a type A person, take a **Klamath River Jet Boat Tour** (☎ 800/887-JETS or 707/482-7775) up the Klamath River Estuary to view bear, deer, elk, and more along the river banks, or a **kayak tour** around the Klamath River Estuary or other nearby waters.

But the real reason you came here is to see the world's tallest tree, right? To do this you'll first have to get a permit from the Redwood Information Center near Orick to travel the **Tall Trees Trail.** This 4-hour drive/hike expedition is limited to the first 50 permits each day, so get yours early. It's an experience you'll never forget.

Exploring the Park by Car

A number of scenic drives cut through the park. Steep, windy **Bald Hills Road** (located a few miles north of Orick on U.S. 101) will take you back into the Redwood Creek watershed and up to the shoulder of 3,097-foot Schoolhouse Peak. Don't even think of driving a motor home up here or pulling a trailer. A few miles further north is the **Lost Man Creek Trail,** a short, unpaved scenic drive through the redwood forest. The 1.5-mile trip leads past the World Heritage Site dedication area and on to a cascade on Lost Man Creek. Again, anyone with a motor home or pulling a trailer can forget this one.

A don't-miss detour along U.S. 101 is the **Newton B. Drury Scenic Parkway,** which passes through dazzling groves of redwoods and elk-filled meadows before leading back onto the highway 8 miles later. While you're cruising along, take the **Cal-Barrel Road** turnoff, a narrow, packed-gravel road located just north of the Prairie Creek Visitor Center off the Newton B. Drury Scenic Parkway. It offers a spectacular 3-mile tour through an old-growth redwood forest (no trailers or motor homes).

One of the premier coastal drives on the Redwood Coast starts at the mouth of the Klamath River and runs 8 miles south toward Prairie Creek Redwoods State Park. The narrow, partially paved **Coastal Drive** winds through stands of redwoods, with spectacular views of the Pacific and numerous pullouts for picture taking (sea lions and pelicans abound) and short hikes. Keep an eye out for the World War II radar station, disguised as a farmhouse and barn. If you're heading south on U.S. 101, take the Alder Camp Road exit just south of the Klamath River Bridge and follow the signs to the Mouth of Klamath. Northbound travelers should take the Redwood National and State Parks Coastal Drive exit off the Newton B. Drury Scenic Parkway. Campers and cars with trailers are not advised.

The most amazing car-friendly trail in all of the Redwood National and State Parks, however, is the hidden, well-maintained gravel road called **Howland Hill Road** that winds for about 12 miles through Jedediah Smith Redwoods State Park. It's an unforgettable journey through a spectacular old-growth redwood forest—considered by many one of the most beautiful areas in the world. To get there from U.S. 101, keep an eye out for the BP gas station at the south end of Crescent City; just before the station, turn right on Elk Valley Road, and follow it to Howland Hill Road, which will be on your right. After driving through the park, you'll end up at U.S. 199 near the town of Hiouchi, and from there it's a short jaunt west to get back to U.S. 101. Plan at least 2 to 3 hours for the 45-mile round-trip, or all day if you want to do some hiking or mountain biking in the park. Driving a trailer or a motor home is not recommended.

Organized Tours & Ranger Programs

The parks run interpretive programs on subjects ranging from trees to tide pools, legends to landforms, at the Hiouchi and Redwood information centers and in the Crescent Beach area during summer months, as well as year-round at the park headquarters in Crescent City. Park rangers lead campfire programs and numerous other activities throughout the year as well. Call the **Parks Information Service** (☎ 707/464-6101, ext. 5265) for current schedules.

Day Hikes

Regardless of the length of your hike, dress warmly and bring plenty of water and sunscreen.

Big Tree Trail

0.25 mi. RT. Easy. Access: Take the Big Tree turnoff along the Newton B. Drury Scenic Parkway.

For the nonhiker in your group, this is a short paved trail leading to an impressively large tree.

Boy Scout Tree Trail

6 mi. RT. Easy. Access: Ask for directions and a map at the Jedediah Smith Information Center.

After taking this trail through Jedediah Smith Redwoods State Park, you'll understand why an activist like Woody Harrelson would chain himself to the Golden Gate Bridge to protest logging old-growth forests. This is nature primeval, a lush, cool, damp forest brimming with giant ferns and majestic redwoods. It's truly an emotional experience just being here.

Enderts Beach Trail

1.2 mi. RT. Easy. Access: End of Enderts Rd. at the south end of Crescent City (about 3 mi. south on U.S. 101 from downtown, across from the Ocean Way Motel).

This short trail leads down to Enderts Beach. In the summer, free 1½- to 2-hour ranger-guided tide pool and seashore walks are offered when the tides are right. You start at the beach parking lot, descend to the beach, and explore rocky tide pools at its southern end. For specific tour times, call ☎ 707/464-6101, ext. 5064.

Fern Canyon Trail

1.5 mi. RT. Easy. Access: From U.S. 101, take the Davison Rd. exit (at Rolf's Park Cafe), which follows along Gold Bluffs Beach to the Fern Canyon parking lot. Day-use fee is $5. No trailers or motor homes over 24 ft. long.

This short, heavily traveled trail leads to an unbelievably lush grotto of lady, deer, chain, sword, five-finger, and maidenhair ferns clinging to 50-foot-high vertical walls divided by a babbling brook. It's only about a 1.5-mile walk from Gold Bluffs Beach, but be prepared to scramble across the creek several times on your way via small footbridges.

Friendship Ridge, Coastal Loop Trail

7.5 mi. RT. Moderate. Access: Fern Canyon Trailhead on Davison Rd.

This is possibly the most varied and beautiful hike in Redwood National Park. Beginning at the Fern Canyon Trailhead, you'll follow the Coastal Loop Trail north, then veer right and follow the Friendship Ridge Trail. For the next 3 miles you'll walk through a magical fern and redwood forest, then join the West Ridge Trail through old-growth forest to Butler Creek Camp and back south along the Coastal Loop Trail.

Lady Bird Johnson Grove Loop

1 mi. RT. Easy. Access: Lady Bird Johnson Grove. Take the Bald Hills Rd. exit off U.S. 101, 0.5 mi. north of Orick.

Here's a self-guided tour that loops around a glorious lush grove of mature redwoods. It's the site at which the national park was dedicated by Lady Bird Johnson in 1968. The following year it was named for her.

Tall Trees Trail

1.3 mi. one way. Moderate. Access: End of Tall Trees Access Rd., off Bald Hills Rd. Permit required.

To see the world's tallest trees—some 360 feet tall and more than 600 years old—you'll first have to go to the Redwood Information Center near Orick to obtain a free map and permit to drive to the Tall Trees Grove Trailhead. (*Note:* Only 50 permits are issued per day on a first-come, first-served basis.) After driving to the trailhead, you have to walk a steep 1.3 miles down into the grove, but what a small price to see the tallest trees in the world, some reaching 360 feet high. By the way, the average time spent gawking at the world's largest trees is 1 minute 40 seconds, even though the whole expedition takes about 4 hours.

> *Picnickers Alert:* **The Crescent Beach Overlook, along Enderts Road, is one of the prettiest picnic sites on the California coast. Pack a picnic lunch from Good Harvest Cafe (see "Picnic & Camping Supplies," below), park at the Overlook, lay your blanket on the grass, and admire the ocean view atop your personal 500-foot bluff.**

Yurok Loop Nature Trail

1 mi. RT. Easy. Access: 6.5 mi. north of the Klamath River Bridge on U.S. 101 at Lagoon Creek.

This self-guided trail gradually climbs to the top of a rugged sea bluff (with wonderful panoramic views of the Pacific) before looping back to the parking lot. If someone's willing to act as shuttle driver, have him or her meet you at the Requa Trailhead and take the 4-mile coastal trail to the mouth of the Klamath.

Exploring the Backcountry

The long, beautiful **Coastal Trail,** which runs the entire length of the parks' coastal section and as near the ocean as possible, can either be hiked in a day in small segments, or as a great 3- or 4-day trip using several backcountry camps on the route. One of the nicest runs is from Crescent Beach south into the Del Norte Coast Redwoods State Park. A free permit is required if you stay overnight at Butler Creek or along Redwood Creek.

Redwood Creek Trail

16 mi. RT. Moderate to strenuous. Access: End of Redwood Creek access road, off Bald Hills Rd.

This hike is a beauty, passing through Tall Trees Grove (where the tallest trees in the world grow on the banks of Redwood Creek), periodic meadows, new-growth forests, and awesome vantage points overlooking the Grove. You'll camp along the fine sandbars of Redwood Creek. The bridges on Redwood Creek are only installed from May 15 to September 15, and from the end of October to the beginning of April heavy rains make creek crossings extremely dangerous.

Other Sports & Activities

Beaches. The park's beaches vary from long white-sand strands to cobblestone pocket coves. The water temperature is in the high 40s to low 50s year-round, and it's often rough out there. Swimmers and surfers should be prepared for adverse conditions.

Crescent Beach is a long sandy beach just 2 miles south of Crescent City that's popular with beachcombers, surf fishers, and surfers. Just south of Crescent Beach is **Endert's Beach,** a protected spot with a hike-in campground and tide pools at its southern end.

Bicycling. Most of the hiking trails throughout the Redwood National and State Parks are off limits to mountain bikers. However, **Prairie Creek Redwoods State Park** has a fantastic 19-mile mountain-bike trail through dense forest, elk-filled meadows, and glorious mud holes. Parts of it are difficult, though, so beginners should sit this one out. Pick up a 25¢ trail map at the Elk Prairie Campground Ranger Station.

There are a few other mountain-bike loops in the 20-mile range, but they are serious thigh burners and make the one above look easy. These loops are the Holter Ridge Trail and Little Bald Hills. Also, there is mountain biking available on the old U.S. 101, now the Coastal Trail within Del Norte Coast Redwoods State Park.

Fishing. The Redwood Coast's streams are some of the best steelhead trout and salmon breeding habitat in California. Park beaches are good for surf casting but be prepared for heavy wave action. A California fishing license is required, and you should check with rangers about any special closures.

Horseback Trail Rides. A variety of guided trail rides, including lunch and dinner trips, are offered by **Redwood Trails Horseback Riding** (☎ 707/488-3895 or 707/488-2061), located at the Redwood Trails Campground (5 miles south of Orick on U.S. 101). Riders should be at least 5 years old. Call for current rates.

Jet-Boat Tours. Tours aboard a jet-boat take visitors upriver from the Klamath River Estuary to view bear, deer, elk, osprey hawks, otters, and more along the riverbanks. It's about $20 for a 30-mile trip, $28 for a 55-mile lunch or dinner cruise. The prices for children are lower, and free for kids under 4. Tours run May through October. Contact **Klamath River Jet Boat Tours,** Klamath (☎ 800/887-JETS or 707/482-7775).

Campground	Total Sites	RV Hookups	Dump Station	Toilets	Drinking Water
Elk Prairie	75	0	Yes	Yes	Yes
Gold Bluffs Beach	25	0	No	Yes	Yes
Jedediah Smith	106	0	Yes	Yes	Yes
Mill Creek	145	0	Yes	Yes	Yes
Crescent City Redwoods KOA	94	42	Yes	Yes	Yes

Kayaking. An alternative to exploring the waters of Redwood National Park and vicinity in a jet-boat is to take a guided **kayak tour** through Redwood Creek or the Smith River by **Aurora River Adventures.** Offered upon reservation only during spring, a 2-day, class III white water trip costs approximately $200 per person (for a minimum of 4 people) and includes all the requisite kayak gear and food. However, this trip is extremely weather-dependent; the company also offers numerous other trips in northwest California. Contact **Aurora River Adventures** (☎ **800/562-8475** or 530/629-3843).

Whale Watching & Bird Watching. High coastal overlooks (like **Klamath Overlook** and **Crescent Beach Overlook**) make great whale-watching outposts during the December/January southern migration and the March/April return migration. The northern sea cliffs also provide valuable nesting sites for marine birds like auklets, puffins, murres, and cormorants. Birders will also love the park's coastal freshwater lagoons, which are some of the most pristine shorebird and waterfowl habitat left and are chock-full of hundreds of different species.

Wildlife Viewing. One of the most striking aspects of Prairie Creek Redwoods State Park is its herd of **Roosevelt elk,** usually found in the appropriately named Elk Prairie in the southern end of the park. These gigantic beasts can weigh up to 1,000 pounds. The bulls carry huge antlers from spring to fall. Elk are also sometimes found at Gold Bluffs Beach—it's an incredible rush to suddenly come upon them out of the fog or after a turn in the trail. Nearly 100 **black bears** also call the park home but are seldom seen. Unlike those at Yosemite and Yellowstone, these bears are still afraid of people.

Camping

Most drive-in camping is in the state parks. In the southern part of the complex, Prairie Creek Redwoods State Park (☎ **707/464-6101,** ext. 5300), known for its old-growth redwoods and herds of elk, has two drive-in campgrounds. **Elk Prairie Campground,** 5 miles north of Orick on U.S. 101, is near fishing and hiking trails, has a nature center, and offers evening campfire talks. Reservations are available from Parknet (☎ **800/444-7275**). **Gold Bluffs Beach Campground** is 3 miles north of Orick on U.S. 101, then 5 miles west on Davison Road. It's somewhat more primitive and offers trail access.

In the northern part of the complex, the campground at **Jedediah Smith Redwoods State Park** (☎ **707/464-6101,** ext. 5113), along U.S. 199 at Hiouchi, provides easy access to some of the area's biggest and most spectacular redwoods, as well as campsites along the scenic Smith River. Also in the northern section is **Mill Creek Campground,** in Del Norte Coast Redwoods State Park (☎ **707/464-6101,** ext. 5113), located 7 miles south of Crescent City on U.S. 101. It has sites for both RVs and tents, and the walk-in tent

Showers	Fire Pits/ Grills	Laundry	Public Phone	Reserve	Fees	Open
Yes	Yes	No	Yes	Yes	$14–$16	Year-round
Yes	Yes	No	No	No	$14–$16	Year-round
Yes	Yes	No	Yes	No	$12–$16	Year-round
Yes	Yes	No	Yes	Yes	$15–$16	Year-round
Yes	Yes	Yes	Yes	Yes	$20–$25	Feb 15–Dec

sites are nestled among the redwoods. Both Jedediah Smith and Mill Creek take reservations through Parknet (see above for phone).

Those seeking RV hookups and the usual commercial campground amenities will find several choices in Crescent City, including the quiet, well maintained **Crescent City Redwoods KOA,** 4241 U.S. 101 North, Crescent City, CA 95531 (☎ 707/464-5744). Tent sites are among the redwoods, and some RV sites are also shaded. There's a nature trail, farm animals, a recreation room, convenience store with RV supplies, propane, and cable TV hookups. The KOA also has 14 cabins situated among the redwoods; all use the campground bathhouse.

In addition to the developed drive-in campgrounds discussed above, there are five small primitive hike-in campgrounds located in the national park, which require a walk of 0.25 to 0.5 mile. All are free and have fire rings and toilets. Contact park offices (☎ 707/464-6101, ext. 5064) for directions and current information.

There are also campgrounds in the mountains above the park, located along U.S. 199 in the **Smith River Recreation Area** (☎ 707/457-3131). Sites cost $8 to $17 per night and can be reserved by calling ☎ 800/280-2267, where an actual person can help you make decisions.

Accommodations

A number of bed-and-breakfasts and funky roadside motels are available in the surrounding communities of Crescent City, Orick, and Klamath. **The Crescent City/Del Norte Chamber of Commerce** (☎ 800/343-8300) can steer you toward a good match.

If you're bringing along the family or traveling in a group along the Redwood Coast, then consider dropping the motel idea and instead renting a fully furnished home on the ocean or river's edge for as little as $80 a night from **Redwood Coast Vacation Rentals** (☎ 707/465-0150).

Redwood HI–AYH Hostel

14480 U.S. 101 (across from Wilson Creek Beach, about 7 mi. north of Klamath) Klamath, CA 95548. ☎ **707/482-8265.** Fax 707/482-4665. E-mail: redwoodhostel@mail.telis.org. 30 bunks, 1 couples rm. $13–$15 per person. MC, V. Credit cards accepted for payment as well as reservations.

The only lodging actually within the park, this turn-of-the-century settler's ranch was remodeled in 1987 to accommodate 30 guests dormitory-style (bunks and shared bathrooms). The minimal privacy is more than overshadowed by the location—a mere 100 yards from the beach, surrounded by hiking trails leading along the Redwood Coast (the staff leads nature walks and is well versed in local history). One private room that accommodates two is available with advance notice, and the hostel even takes reservations by credit card (strongly recommended in the summer). Showers, common room, redwood deck, country kitchen, dining room, wood stove, and outdoor lockers are included in the nightly rate. Reservations are strongly recommended in summer.

Crescent Beach Motel

1455 Redwood Hwy. S. (2 mi. south of downtown on U.S. 101), Crescent City, CA 95531. ☎ **707/464-5436.** 27 units. TV. Summer $69–$77 double; winter $49–$55 double. AE, DISC, MC, V.

Crescent City has the dubious distinction of being the only city along the coast without a fancy hotel or bed-and-breakfast. There is, however, an armada of cheap motels, the best of which is the Crescent Beach. Near the highway, about 1 mile south of town, this single-story structure is the only local motel set directly on the beach. The newly remodeled and refurbished rooms are clean and simple; most have queen-size beds and all have remote control color TVs with cable. Four of the units face the highway; try to get one of the others, all of which have sliding glass doors opening onto decks and a small lawn area overlooking the bay. One of the city's most popular restaurants, the Beachcomber (see "Dining," below), is next door.

Curly Redwood Lodge

701 Redwood Hwy. S., Crescent City, CA 95531. ☎ **707/464-2137.** Fax 707/464-1655. www.curlyredwoodlodge.com. E-mail: curlyredwood@telis.org. 36 units. TV TEL. Summer $60–$65 double; winter $37–$39 double. AE, DC, MC, V.

This is a blast from the past, the kind of place where you might have stayed as a kid during one of those cross-country vacations in the family station wagon. It was built in 1959 on grasslands across from the town's harbor, and completely trimmed with lumber from a single ancient redwood. Although they're not full of the latest high-tech gadgets, the bedrooms are among the largest and best-soundproofed in town, and certainly the most evocative of a bygone, more innocent age. In winter, about a third of the bedrooms (the ones upstairs) are locked and sealed. Overall, the aura is more akin to Oregon than anything you might imagine in California.

Klamath Inn

451 Requa Rd. (from U.S. 101 take the Requa Rd. exit and follow the signs), Klamath, CA 95548. ☎ **707/482-1425.** 10 units. $59–$95 double. DISC, MC, V.

Established in 1885, the venerable Requa Inn, a two-story charmer located on the banks of the lower Klamath River, offers 10 spacious guest rooms, each modestly decorated with antique furnishings; all with private bathrooms with showers or claw-foot tubs. Four offer views of the lower Klamath River. The inn's main attraction is the cozy parlor downstairs,

where guests bury themselves in the plump armchairs to read beside the wood-burning pellet stove. There are plenty of enticements just outside, including sandy riverside beaches, numerous hiking trails in nearby Redwood National Park, and, of course, fishing. Breakfast is included in the room rate and dinner is served daily (see "Dining," below).

Dining

Beachcomber

1400 U.S. 101, Crescent City. ☎ **707/464-2205.** Reservations recommended. Main courses $6–$15. MC, V. Thurs–Tues 5–9pm. SEAFOOD.

The decor is as predictably nautical as its name implies: rough-cut planking, a scattering of artfully arranged driftwood, fishnets, and buoys dangling above a dimly lit space. The restaurant lies beside the beach, 2 miles south of Crescent City's center. Its fans cite it as one of the two best restaurants in town. The cuisine is a joy to fish lovers who prefer not to mask the flavor of their seafood with complicated sauces. Most of the dishes are grilled over madrone-wood barbecue pits, a technique perfected since the restaurant was established in 1975. Pacific salmon, halibut, lingcod, Pacific snapper, oysters, and steamer clams are house specialties, dishes for which visitors line up, especially on Friday and Saturday nights.

Harbor View Grotto Restaurant & Lounge

150 Starfish Way, Crescent City. ☎ **707/464-3815.** Lunch main courses $4.50–$9; dinner $8–$35. MC, V. Daily 11:30am–10pm. SEAFOOD/STEAKS.

This is the best-established nonchain restaurant in town, specializing in fresh seafood at market prices since 1961. Completely renovated in December 1995, it has pleasant views of the ocean and harbor from both the dining room and lounge. It's capped with a miniature lighthouse inspired by Crescent City's Battery Point Lighthouse. The "light eaters" menu includes a cup of white chowder (made fresh daily) or salad, a main course, and vegetables; hungrier diners can choose from two different cuts of prime rib. Menu items include a seasonal variety of fresh fish from local fishing fleets, such as Pacific snapper or salmon. Crab (in season) or shrimp Louis, as well as crabmeat or shrimp sandwiches, are perennial favorites.

Klamath Inn Restaurant

451 Requa Rd., (from U.S. 101 take the Requa Rd. exit and follow the signs), Klamath. ☎ **707/482-8205.** Main courses $10–$21. DISC, MC, V. Dinner daily 5–9pm. SEAFOOD/ STEAKS.

This simple yet dignified restaurant— one of only two in the greater Klamath area—serves a no-nonsense menu of steak, chicken, and fresh seafood. The grilled salmon and halibut are also good bets, as is the fresh-baked blackberry cobbler with a side of vanilla ice cream. Be sure to request a table overlooking the Klamath River. After dinner, retire to the parlor for an after-dinner drink by the fireplace.

Rolf's Park Café

On U.S. 101 (about 2 mi. north of town), Orick, CA 95555. ☎ **707/488-3841.** Main courses $5–$13 lunch; $9.50–$17.50 dinner. MC, V. Daily 8am–9pm. Possibly closed Dec–Mar, so call ahead. GERMAN.

Rolf Rheinschmidt, a talented chef who has worked around the world, decided it was time to semiretire, so he opened up his own restaurant in the small town of Orick. For 16 years since, he has wowed the Redwood National and State Parks' visitors with his tried-and-true versions of bratwurst, Wiener schnitzel, and crêpes suzette, as well as his specialty, a marinated rack of spring lamb. He also offers more exotic choices such as buffalo, wild boar, and elk steak (if you're truly adventurous, get a combo of all three). Each dinner entree includes lots of extras: hors d'oeuvres, a salad, vegetables, farm-style potatoes, and bread. If you're a big breakfast eater, Rheinschmidt's German Farmer Omelet—an open-faced concoction of ham, bacon, sausage, mushrooms, cheese, potatoes, and pasta, topped with sour cream and salsa and garnished with a strawberry crepe—is guaranteed to fill your tank.

Picnic & Camping Supplies

You can purchase sandwiches and other light fare at the **Good Harvest Cafe,** 700 Northcrest Dr., in Crescent City (☎ **707/465-6028**). They also serve a good hot breakfast, including vegetarian dishes.

Groceries are available in Crescent City at **Safeway,** 475 M St. (☎ **707/465-3353**), and **Ray's Supermarket,** 625 M St. (☎ **707/465-4045**). Or you might try the **Orick Market,** 121175 Hwy. 101 in Orick (☎ **707/488-3225**).

Kmart in Crescent City sells camping supplies.

31

ROCKY MOUNTAIN NATIONAL PARK

by Don and Barbara Laine

SNOW-COVERED PEAKS STAND WATCH OVER LUSH VALLEYS AND SHIM-
mering alpine lakes, creating the perfect image of America's
most dramatic and beautiful landscape: the majestic Rocky
Mountains. Here, the pine- and fir-scented forests are deep, the

air is crisp and pure, and the rugged
mountain peaks reach to grasp the deep-
blue sky.

What makes Rocky Mountain National Park unique, however, is not only its
breathtaking scenery, but also its variety.
In relatively low areas, up to 9,000 feet,
ponderosa pine and juniper cloak the
sunny southern slopes, with Douglas fir
on the cooler northern slopes. The
thirstier blue spruce and lodgepole pine
cling to the banks of streams, along with
occasional groves of aspen. Elk and mule
deer thrive. On higher slopes, forests of
Engelmann spruce and subalpine fir
dominate, interspersed with wide meadows vibrant with wildflowers in spring
and summer. This is also home to
bighorn sheep, which have become a
symbol of the park. Above 11,500 feet the
trees become increasingly gnarled and
stunted, until they disappear altogether
and alpine tundra takes over. Fully one-
third of the park is in this bleak, rocky
world, many of its plants identical to
those found in the Arctic.

Within the park's 415 square miles are
17 mountains above 13,000 feet. Longs
Peak, at 14,255 feet, is the highest.

Trail Ridge Road, which cuts west
through the middle of the park from
Estes Park, then south down its western
boundary to Grand Lake, is one of America's most scenic highways. Climbing to
12,183 feet, it's the highest continuously
paved highway in the United States. The
road is usually open from Memorial Day
into October, depending on snowfall.
The 48-mile drive from Estes Park to
Grand Lake takes about 3 hours, allowing for stops at numerous view points.
Exhibits at the Alpine Visitor Center at
Fall River Pass, 11,796 feet above sea
level, explain life on the alpine tundra.

Fall River Road, the original park
road, leads from Estes Park to the Fall
River Pass via Horseshoe Park Junction.
As you negotiate its gravely switchbacks,
you get a clear idea of what early auto
travel was like in the West. This road, too,
is closed in winter. Among the few paved
roads in the Rockies that lead into a

Tips from a Park Ranger

The diversity of the park and the ease in which visitors can experience its many facets make Rocky Mountain National Park special, says Doug Caldwell, the park's former information officer.

"There are other alpine tundra areas in the United States, but you usually have to do a lot of hard hiking," Caldwell says. "What makes Rocky Mountain National Park unique is that Trail Ridge Road takes you up to the tundra, above tree line, in the comfort of your car; you can see plant and animal communities that if not for this park you would have to go to the Arctic Circle to see."

Those willing and able to hike can see plenty of tundra country, according to Caldwell, who suggests having a friend drop you off at the **Ute Trail** turnout on Trail Ridge Road, and hiking the 6 miles down through Forest Canyon to Upper Beaver Meadows. "This canyon is among the wildest in the park," says Caldwell, "and the hike along its steep side provides spectacular views of the canyon and Longs Peak, the park's tallest mountain."

Hikers who want to work a bit harder will be well rewarded on another of Caldwell's favorites. "One that I really enjoy on the west side of the park is the **East Inlet Trail**," Caldwell says. "Once you get up there a couple of miles, and gain some elevation, you look back toward Grand Lake and think you're in Switzerland."

Longs Peak, at 14,255 feet elevation, is the northernmost of Colorado's famed "fourteeners" (mountains that exceed 14,000 ft.), and it's a popular hike, says Caldwell. "You don't need technical climbing gear once the ice is gone, usually by mid-July," Caldwell says, adding that hikers may have some physical problems with the altitude at first. "It's wise to give yourself a couple of days to acclimate before tackling Longs Peak," Caldwell says. He also recommends that high-elevation hikers drink more fluids, eat regularly, carry energy bars, and take it slow. "Listen to your body," he advises. Another bit of advice he gives backpackers is to discuss their plans with rangers in the park's backcountry office before setting out. "We'd much rather spend time with them beforehand to try to get to know their abilities and expectations and advise them where to go, than be called out on a search-and-rescue mission."

Asked how to avoid the crowds, Caldwell says that since most visitors remain close to the roads, the easiest way to find a bit of solitude even during the park's busiest times is to take off down a hiking trail. "The farther you go up the trail the fewer people you'll encounter." He adds that another sure way to escape humanity is to visit in winter, and explore the park on snowshoes or cross-country skis.

But when would he visit?

"Fall, from September through mid-October, is the best time," he says. "Days are warm and comfortable, nights are cool and crisp, there are fewer people than in summer, and the aspens are changing. You can see hundreds of elk, and watch the bulls bugle as they protect their harems from the other bulls."

high, mountain basin is Bear Lake Road, which is kept open year-round, with occasional half-day closings to clear snow.

Avoiding the Crowds. The park is only fully accessible for half the year, so few people come in the off-season. The very busiest time in the park is from mid-June through mid-August—essentially during school vacation—so just before or just after that period is best. But winter is gaining in popularity too, even though you won't be able to drive the entire Trail Ridge Road, because it is the quietest time, and although the park can be bitterly cold, it is also beautiful. Regardless

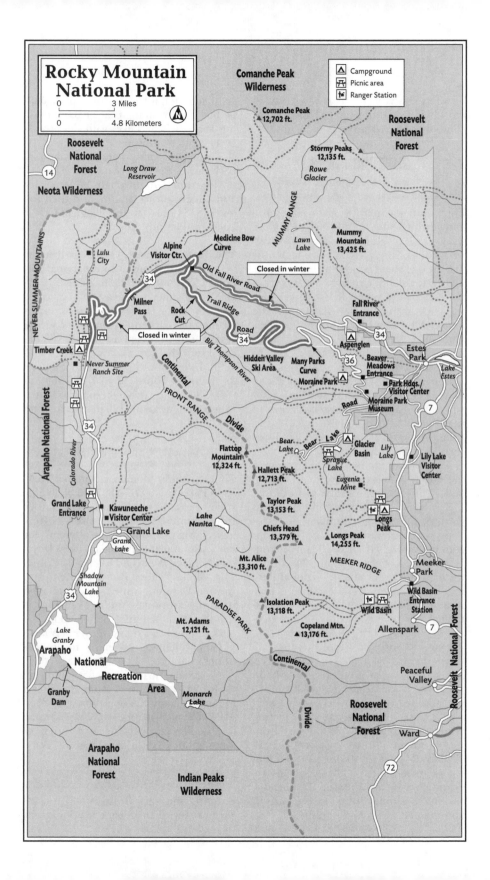

Rocky Mountain National Park

0 _____ 3 Miles
0 _____ 4.8 Kilometers

Campground
Picnic area
Ranger Station

Roosevelt National Forest

Comanche Peak Wilderness

Comanche Peak
12,702 ft.

Roosevelt National Forest

Neota Wilderness

Long Draw Reservoir

Stormy Peaks
12,135 ft.

Rowe Glacier

MUMMY RANGE

Mummy Mountain
13,425 ft.

Lulu City

Alpine Visitor Ctr.

Medicine Bow Curve

Lawn Lake

34

Old Fall River Road

Closed in winter

Milner Pass

Rock Cut

Trail Ridge

Fall River Entrance

Closed in winter

Road

34

Aspenglen

Estes Park

Timber Creek

Never Summer Ranch Site

Big Thompson River

Hidden Valley Ski Area

Many Parks Curve

Moraine Park

36

Beaver Meadows Entrance

Lake Estes

Continental

FRONT RANGE

Divide

Park Hdqs./ Visitor Center

Moraine Park Museum

Road

Colorado River

Bear Lake

Bear Lake

Glacier Basin

Lily Lake

7

Flattop Mountain
12,324 ft.

Hallett Peak
12,713 ft.

Sprague Lake

Eugenia Mine

Lily Lake Visitor Center

Grand Lake Entrance

Kawuneeche Visitor Center

Grand Lake

Lake Nanita

Taylor Peak
13,153 ft.

Chiefs Head
13,579 ft.

Longs Peak
14,255 ft.

Longs Peak

Grand Lake

Mt. Alice
13,310 ft.

MEEKER RIDGE

Meeker Park

Shadow Mountain Lake

34

PARADISE PARK

Isolation Peak
13,118 ft.

Wild Basin

Wild Basin Entrance Station

Allenspark

7

Lake Granby

Arapaho National Recreation Area

Mt. Adams
12,121 ft.

Copeland Mtn.
13,176 ft.

Continental

Roosevelt National Forest

Granby Dam

Monarch Lake

Divide

Peaceful Valley

Ward

Arapaho National Forest

Indian Peaks Wilderness

Roosevelt National Forest

72

NEVER SUMMER MOUNTAINS

Arapaho National Forest

of when you visit, the best way to avoid crowds is by putting on a backpack or climbing onto a horse.

Just the Facts

GETTING THERE & GATEWAYS

Entry into the park is from either the east (through the town of Estes Park) or the west (through Grand Lake). East and west sides of the park are connected by Trail Ridge Road, open during summer and early fall, but closed because of snow the rest of the year. Most visitors enter the park from the Estes Park side. The **Beaver Meadows Entrance,** west of Estes Park via U.S. 36, is the national park's main entrance and the best way to get to the visitor center and headquarters. It is also the most direct route to Trail Ridge Road. U.S. 34 West from Estes Park takes you to the **Fall River Entrance** (north of the Beaver Meadows Entrance), and from there you can access Old Fall River Road or Trail Ridge Road.

Estes Park is about 71 miles northwest of Denver, 44 miles northwest of Boulder, and 42 miles southwest of Fort Collins.

The most direct route from Denver is via U.S. 36 through Boulder. At Estes Park, that highway joins U.S. 34, which runs up the Big Thompson Canyon from I-25 and Loveland, and continues through Rocky Mountain National Park to Grand Lake. An alternative scenic route to Estes Park is Colo. 7, the "Peak-to-Peak Scenic Byway" that transits Central City (Colo. 119), Nederland (Colo. 72), and Allenspark (Colo. 7) under different designations.

Heading south from Estes Park on Colo. 7 you can access two trailheads in the southeast corner of the national park, but there are no connecting roads to the main part of the park from those points. These are **Longs Peak Trailhead**—the turnoff is 9 miles south of Estes Park and the trailhead about another mile; and **Wild Basin Trailhead**—another 3.5 miles south to the turnoff and then 2.2 miles to the trailhead.

In summer, a free national park **shuttle bus** runs from the Glacier Basin parking area to Bear Lake, with departures every 15 to 30 minutes.

Those who want to enter the national park from the west can take U.S. 40 north from I-70 through Winter Park and Tabernash to Granby, and then follow U.S. 34 north to the village of Grand Lake and on into the park.

The Nearest Airport. Visitors arriving by plane fly into **Denver International Airport** (☎ 800/247-2336 or 303/342-2000), 90 miles southeast of the park's east entrances. It's served by most major airlines and car-rental companies, whose reservation numbers are in the appendix. From the airport, travelers can also get to Estes Park with **Estes Park Shuttles & Mountain Tours** (☎ 800/586-5009 or 970/586-5151; www.estesparkco.com), which charges about $20 per person one way.

INFORMATION

Contact **Rocky Mountain National Park,** Estes Park, CO 80517-8397 (☎ 970/586-1206; www.nps.gov/romo). The park's visitor centers (see below) have U.S. Geological Survey topographical maps for sale. Also available is *Hiking Rocky Mountain National Park* (Old Saybrook, Conn.: The Globe Pequot Press) by Kent and Donna Dannen, which gives detailed trail descriptions. You'll also find a wealth of detailed information about the park in *Frommer's Rocky Mountain National Park,* which was written by the authors of this chapter.

A great variety of trip-planning tools can be obtained from the **Rocky Mountain Nature Association** (☎ 800/816-7662 or 970/586-0108; www.rmna.org/bookstore), which sells a variety of maps, guides, books, and videos.

VISITOR CENTERS

Entering the park from Estes Park, it's wise to stop first at **park headquarters,**

U.S. 36 west of Colo. 66 (☎ 970/586-1206). There's a good interpretive exhibit here, including a relief model of the park, an audiovisual program, and a bookstore.

The **Kawuneeche Visitor Center** is at the Grand Lake end of Trail Ridge Road (☎ 970/627-3471). In addition to exhibits on the geology, plants, animals, and human history of the park's west side, there is a small theater where films and video programs are shown. The **Alpine Visitor Center** (open in summer only), at Fall River Pass, has exhibits that explain life on the alpine tundra and a viewing platform from which you are almost certain to see elk. Next door is the Fall River Store, also open only in summer, with a snack bar and gift shop. The **Moraine Park Museum** (open mid-June to mid-September) is located on Bear Lake Road in an historic log building. It has full visitor facilities, in addition to excellent natural-history exhibits that describe the creation of the park's landscape, as well as the plants and animals of the park.

The **Lily Lake Visitor Center** (open June through September only) is located along Colo. 7 about 7 miles south of Estes Park. In addition to information on the national park, it has exhibits and information on activities in the adjacent Roosevelt and Arapaho national forests.

A new visitor center, scheduled to open in late summer 2000 or by summer 2001, will be located on U.S. 34, outside the park, east of the Fall River Entrance Station. Built with private funds, but staffed by park rangers and volunteers from the Rocky Mountain Nature Association, it will contain exhibits on park wildlife and wildlife-watching etiquette, plus a bookstore.

FEES & PERMITS

Park admission costs $10 per vehicle for up to 1 week; $5 for bicyclists and pedestrians. Camping in developed campgrounds costs $16 per night during the summer and $10 in the off-season when the water is turned off, usually from late September to May. Required overnight backcountry permits cost $15 from May through October and are free the rest of the year.

SPECIAL REGULATIONS & WARNINGS

Rocky Mountain National Park's high elevation and extremes of climate and terrain are among its most appealing features, but also its greatest hazards. Hikers should try to give themselves several days to acclimate to the altitude before seriously hitting the trails, and hikers with respiratory or heart problems would do well to discuss their plans with their physicians before leaving home. Hikers also need to be prepared for rapidly changing conditions, including sudden afternoon thunderstorms in July and August. If lightning threatens, stay clear of ridges and other vulnerable high points.

SEASONS & CLIMATE

Even though the park is open year-round, **Trail Ridge Road,** the main east-west thoroughfare through the park, is always closed in winter. It's safest to assume that you will not be able to drive clear across the park from mid-October until Memorial Day—even into June it's possible that the road will be closed for hours or even a day or more by snow. That's not to say that intrepid travelers can't enjoy the park in winter. All park entrances are open, trails are open to snowshoers and cross-country skiers, and roads to a number of good view points and trailheads are plowed. Snowmobiling is also permitted, but only on the west side of the park, accessible from Grand Lake. Those with the proper skills and equipment can cross-country ski into the high country, although they need to be aware of storm and avalanche dangers and should always check with rangers before setting out.

Weather is a key factor that will affect your trip to the park in any season. In summer, temperatures typically climb into the 70s during the day and drop into the 40s at night, but because of the park's high elevation—and range of elevations—you'll find that temperatures vary greatly. The higher into the mountains you go the cooler it gets. Rangers say that for every 1,000 feet in elevation gain, the climate changes the equivalent of traveling 600 miles north. Tree line in the park—the elevation at which trees can no longer grow—varies, but is at about 11,500 feet.

Winters usually see high temperatures in the 20s and 30s and lows from 10° below zero to 20° above. Spring and fall temperatures can vary greatly from pleasantly warm to bitterly cold and snowy. For this reason, spring and fall are when you need to be flexible and adjust your itinerary to suit current conditions. Particularly at higher elevations, windchill factors can be extreme, and hypothermia can be a problem at any time, even in summer, when afternoon thunderstorms sometimes occur without warning, causing temperatures to drop dramatically and suddenly.

SEASONAL EVENTS

The **elk rutting season** in September and October brings hundreds of elk to the lower elevations, where you can often hear the macho bulls bugle and watch them trying to keep other bulls away from their females.

If You Only Have 1 Day

This park simply begs for an extended visit—4 to 7 days would be ideal—but it offers wonderful experiences for visitors who have only a short amount of time, or who are not able or willing to hike.

Those arriving in summer or early fall with only 1 day to see the park will want to stop at one of the visitor centers, and then drive the fantastically scenic **Trail Ridge Road,** described below. Stop at the view points and take the half-hour walk

along the **Tundra World Nature Trail** to get a close-up view of the plants, animals, and terrain of the tundra. Those returning to the east or west sides will have time for little else, since it takes about 3 hours each way for the 48-mile drive, but those passing through the park on their way to somewhere else might want to take another short hike.

Exploring the Park by Car

Although Rocky Mountain National Park is generally considered the domain of hikers and climbers, ideal for those who want to leave the crowds behind and head into the backcountry, it's surprisingly easy to enjoy this park thoroughly without working up a sweat. For that we thank **Trail Ridge Road,** built in 1932 and undoubtedly one of America's most scenic highways, providing expansive and sometimes dizzying views in all directions. This remarkable 48-mile road rises to over 12,000 feet in elevation and crosses the Continental Divide. Along the way it offers spectacular vistas of snowcapped peaks, deep forests, and meadows of wildflowers full of browsing bighorn sheep, elk, and deer. Allow at least 3 hours for the drive, and consider a short walk or hike from one of the many vista points.

To get a close-up look at the tundra, pull off Trail Ridge Road into the **Rock Cut Parking Area** (elevation 12,110 ft.), about halfway along the scenic drive. You'll have splendid views of glacially carved peaks along the Continental Divide, and on the 0.5-mile **Tundra Nature Trail** you'll find signs identifying and discussing the hardy plants and animals that inhabit this region.

Trail Ridge Road is closed by winter snows. In recent years it has usually been clear by late May and closed again between mid- and late October. But even well into June, the road can be closed for snow for hours or even days at a time.

There are two other roads within the park. **Old Fall River Road,** 9 miles long and unpaved, is one way uphill only. It's usually open from July 4 through mid-October. **Bear Lake Road** is the access road to Bear Lake and is open year-round.

Organized Tours & Ranger Programs

Campfire talks and other programs are offered between June and September. Activities vary from talks on the park's wildlife and geology to photo walks, fly-fishing, and orienteering programs. At night, rangers periodically lead night-sky programs using the park's computerized telescopes, and also give nightly talks during the elk's rutting season. Winter visitors will find a variety of activities, including moonlight hikes and snowshoe and cross-country ski trips. Check at visitor centers for current schedules.

Several companies offer van tours into the park, including **Estes Park Shuttles & Mountain Tours** (☎ 800/586-5009 or 970/586-5151; www.estesparkco.com), which provides 2- and 3-hour guided trips each summer, starting in either Estes Park or Denver. Call for rates.

Historic & Man-Made Attractions

Remnants from the area's mining and ranching days of the late 1800s and early 1900s still persist in the park. Hikers will encounter the ruins of several historic cabins on the Lulu City and Eugenia Mine trails (see "Day Hikes," below). The **Moraine Park Museum** on Bear Lake Road contains exhibits mainly on natural history, but the building itself—a log structure built as a social center in 1923—is listed on the National Register of Historic Places. A 0.5-mile walk from Trail Ridge Road on the west side of the park stands **Never Summer Ranch,** a preserved dude ranch dating from the 1920s. It was started as a cattle ranch by

Denver saloon owner John Holzworth after Prohibition began, but Holzworth soon discovered that it was more pleasant and profitable to take in paying guests (at $11 per week including room, meals, and a horse) than to do the hard work of actual ranching. The ranch buildings contain many of their original furnishings.

Day Hikes

The park contains more than 350 miles of hiking trails, ranging from short, easy walks to extremely strenuous and difficult hikes that require climbing skills. Trail difficulty can also vary by time of year—the higher elevations usually have snow until at least mid-July. Many of the park's trails, such as Longs Peak, can be done either as day hikes or overnight backpacking trips. Hikers are strongly advised to discuss their plans with park rangers before setting out. The following are some favorites; there are many more.

SHORTER TRAILS

Alberta Falls Trail

0.6 mi. one way. Easy. Access: Glacier Gorge parking area.

With an elevation change of only 160 feet, this is an easy and scenic walk along Glacier Creek to pretty Alberta Falls. Along the sunny trail you'll see beaver dams and an abundance of golden-mantled ground squirrels.

Bierstadt Lake Trail

1.4 mi. one way. Moderate. Access: North side of Bear Lake Rd., 6.4 mi. from Beaver Meadows.

This trail climbs 566 feet through an open forest of aspen to Bierstadt Lake. From there you'll find good views of Longs Peak from the northwest side of the lake. This trail also connects with several other trails, including one that leads to Bear Lake.

Eugenia Mine Trail

1.4 mi. one way. Moderate. Access: Longs Peak Ranger Station.

This walk to an abandoned mine follows the Longs Peak Trail for about 0.5 mile and then forks off to the right, heading through groves of aspens and then evergreens before arriving at the site of the mine, where you'll see hillside tailings, the remnants of a cabin, and abandoned mine equipment. The trail has an elevation gain of 508 feet.

Emerald Lake Trail

1.8 mi. one way. Easy to moderate. Access: Bear Lake.

This trail offers spectacular scenery on its route past Nymph and Dream lakes to its destination of Emerald Lake. The 0.5-mile hike to Nymph Lake is easy, climbing 225 feet; then the trail is rated moderate to Dream Lake (another 0.6 mile) and Emerald Lake (another 0.7 mile), which is 605 feet higher than the starting point at Bear Lake. In addition to the mountain lakes, you'll see the surrounding mountains, which are especially pretty when reflected in the surface of Nymph Lake, or towering over Dream Lake. In summer there's an abundance of wildflowers along the path between Nymph and Dream lakes.

Gem Lake Trail

2 mi. one way. Moderate. Access: Trailhead on Devil's Gulch Rd., north of Estes Park.

This is a relatively low-elevation trail, starting at only 7,740 feet, but has an elevation change of 1,090 feet. It offers good views of the town of Estes Park and Longs Peak, and delivers hikers to a pretty lake.

Mills Lake Trail

2.5 mi. one way. Moderate. Access: Glacier Gorge Junction.

This trail leads to a picturesque mountain lake, nestled in a valley among towering mountain peaks. Among the best spots in the park for photographing dramatic Longs Peak (the best lighting is usually in late afternoon or early evening), this is also the perfect place for a picnic. The trail has an elevation change of about 700 feet.

Ouzel Falls Trail

2.7 mi. one way. Moderate. Access: Wild Basin Ranger Station.

This hike climbs about 950 feet and crosses Cony Creek on two bridges before delivering you to a picture-perfect waterfall, among the park's prettiest. The trail passes through areas that were burned in a 1978 fire—usually good spots to see wildlife—and also offers fine views of Longs Peak and Mount Meeker.

Tundra World Nature Trail

0.5-mi. loop. Easy. Access: Near Rock Cut parking area on Trail Ridge Rd.

This wheelchair-accessible nature trail has exhibits identifying various tundra plants and animals, and describing how they have adapted to the harsh tundra environment.

LONGER TRAILS

East Inlet Trail

6.9 mi. one way. Moderate to strenuous. Access: West portal of Adam's Tunnel, southeast of the town of Grand Lake.

This trail is an easy walk the first 0.3 mile to scenic Adams Falls. It then wanders along some marshy areas, crosses several streams, and then, becoming more strenuous, climbs sharply in elevation to Lone Pine Lake, about 5.5 miles from the trailhead. It is another 1.4 miles, partly through a subalpine forest, to Lake Verna. The trail continues after the lake, but it is not maintained. Total elevation gain to Lake Verna is 1,809 feet.

East Longs Peak Trail

8 mi. one way. Strenuous. Access: Longs Peak Ranger Station.

Recommended only for experienced mountain hikers and climbers in top physical condition, this trail climbs 4,855 feet along steep ledges and through a narrows to the top of 14,255-foot Longs Peak, the highest point in the park. The trek takes most hikers about 15 hours to complete and can be done in 1 or 2 days. Those planning a 1-day hike should consider starting out extremely early, so they will be well off the peak before the summer afternoon thunderstorms arrive. For a 2-day hike, go 5 or 6 miles the first day, stay at a designated backcountry campsite, and complete the trip the following day. Those making the hike in early summer (usually up until mid-July) should be prepared for icy conditions.

Lawn Lake Trail

6.2 mi. one way. Strenuous. Access: Trailhead on Fall River Rd.

This hike, with an elevation gain of 2,249 feet, follows the Roaring River through terrain dotted with ponderosa pine. Along the way you can see all too plainly the damage done by a massive flood that occurred when the Lawn Lake Dam broke in 1982, killing three campers. At higher elevations there are scenic views of Mummy Mountain.

Lulu City Trail

3.7 mi. one way. Moderate. Access: Colorado River Trailhead near the western boundary of the park.

This trail gains just 350 feet in elevation, as it winds along the river floodplain, through lush vegetation, past an 1880s mine and several mining cabins, and then along an old stage route into a subalpine forest before arriving at Lulu City. Founded in 1879 by prospectors hoping to strike gold and silver, it was abandoned within 10 years, and little remains today except for the ruins of a few cabins.

Timber Lake Trail

4.8 mi. one way. Strenuous. Access: East side of Trail Ridge Rd., 9.6 mi. north of the Grand Lake Entrance.

You'll work hard on this hike but be amply rewarded with views of timberline lakes and alpine tundra. With an elevation change of 2,060 feet, this hike takes you through a forest of lodgepole pines, follows a creek lined with subalpine wildflowers, and then arrives at the lake, surrounded by rocks, tundra, snow, and a few trees.

Ute Trail

6 mi. one way. Moderate. Access: Ute Trail turnout on Trail Ridge Rd.

An excellent way to see the tundra, this moderate hike is really fairly easy if you can get a ride to the top from a friend and walk down the 3,300-foot descent. The hike down the side of a canyon provides great views.

Exploring the Backcountry

There are numerous opportunities in the park for backpacking and technical climbing, and hikers and climbers will generally find that the further they go into the backcountry, the fewer humans they will see. Some of the day hikes discussed above can also be done as overnight hikes; for example, the East Longs Peak Trail, which takes most people about 15 hours round-trip, is often completed over 2 days. Hikers can also combine various shorter trails to produce loops that can keep them in the park's backcountry for up to a week.

The park has well over 100 small **backcountry campsites,** which must be reserved. Backpackers should carry portable stoves, since wood fires are permitted at only a few sites with metal fire rings. In addition to the designated backcountry campsites, there are two dozen cross-country zones, in some of the least accessible sections of the park, which are recommended only for those with good map and compass skills.

The park's **Backcountry Office** should be the first stop for those planning backpacking trips. Rangers there know the trails and camping areas well and are happy to advise hikers on the best choices for their abilities and expectations. Backcountry permits are required for all overnight hikes. Technical climbers who expect to be out overnight usually set up a bivouac, a temporary, open-air encampment that is normally at or near the base of a route or on the face of a climb. Designated bivouac zones have been established; permits are required.

Backcountry and bivouac permits are obtained at park headquarters and ranger stations. They cost $15 from May through October but are free from November through April. For information call ☎ 970/586-1242. Only seven campers are allowed in any backcountry campsite at the same time, and there are also limits for some bivouac areas. In addition, there is a 7-night backcountry camping and bivouac limit from June to September, with no more than 3 nights in any one spot. Tents are not permitted in the backcountry in summer, or in bivouac zones at any time.

Other Sports & Activities

In addition to the businesses discussed below, **Colorado Wilderness Sports,** 358 E. Elkhorn Ave. (☎ 800/504-6642 or 970/586-6548), has an indoor climbing gym and offers fly-fishing and climbing instruction and guided trips both in and near the national park, plus a kids' outdoor adventure program in half- and full-day sessions (call for details).

Biking. As in most national parks, bikes are not permitted off established roads, and here bicyclists will in most cases be sharing roadways with motor vehicles along narrow roads with 5% to 7% grades. However, bikers still enjoy the challenge and scenery. One popular 16-mile ride is the **Horseshoe Park/Estes Park Loop,** which goes from Estes Park west on U.S. 34 past Aspenglen Campground and the park's Fall River Entrance, and then back east at the Deer Ridge Junction, following U.S. 36 through the Beaver Meadows Entrance. There are plenty of beautiful mountain views. A free park brochure provides information on safety, regulations, and suggested routes.

Tours, rentals, and repairs are available at **Colorado Bicycling Adventures,** 184 E. Elkhorn Ave., Estes Park (☎ 800/607-8765 or 970/586-4241; www.coloradobicycling.com). Rentals are $5 to $7 for 1 hour, $15 to $25 for a half day, and $21 to $40 for a full day, depending on type of bike, with discounts for multi-day rentals. They also have child carriers, car racks, and locks. The company offers both road trips in the national park (downhill on paved roads), for around $50 to $70, and off-road mountain-bike tours outside the park for experienced riders for about $50 per person.

Climbing & Mountaineering. Colorado Mountain School, P.O. Box 1846, Estes Park, CO 80517 (☎ 970/586-5758; fax 970/586-5798; www.cmschool.com; e-mail: cmschool@cmschool.com), is a year-round guide service and a national park–sanctioned technical rock climbing and mountaineering school (including ice climbing and ski mountaineering) that caters to all ages and abilities. The most popular climb is **Longs Peak** (the highest mountain in the park). It can be ascended by novice climbers in good physical condition via the "Keyhole," but its north and east faces are for experts only. Colorado Mountain School offers both half- and full-day excursions, with rates per person ranging from $75 to $300. The school offers instructional courses in all aspects of climbing, lasting up to 2 weeks, and guided expeditions around the world. It also operates a small store and offers lodging in a hostel-type setting (see "Accommodations," below).

Educational Programs. The Rocky Mountain Nature Association, Rocky Mountain National Park, Estes Park, CO 80517 (☎ 800/816-7662 or 970/586-0108), offers a wide variety of seminars and workshops, ranging from half-day to several days. Subjects vary but might include songbirds, flower identification, edible and medicinal herbs, painting, wildlife photography, tracking park animals, astronomy, human history, and edible mushrooms. Programs are scheduled year-round, although most are held in the summer. Rates range from $25 to $60 for half- and full-day programs, and $65 to $175 for multiday programs.

Fishing. Four species of **trout** are fished in the park: brown, rainbow, brook, and cutthroat. Anglers must get a state fishing license and are only permitted to use artificial lures or flies. A number of lakes and streams, including Bear Lake, are closed to fishing; a list of open and closed waters plus regulations and other information are available in a free park brochure.

Horseback Riding. Many of the national park's trails are open to those on horseback, and several outfitters provide guided rides, both within and outside the park, usually from spring through fall. Typical prices are $20 for a 1-hour ride, $35 for 2 hours, $45 for 3 hours, $55 for a half day, and $80 for a full day. Highly recommended are the **Sombrero Ranch Stables'** breakfast and supper rides. The breakfast ride includes a 2-hour ride and all-you-can eat full breakfast for $35, and the supper ride includes a 2-hour ride and a steak dinner for $40. Sombrero has stables on the east side of the park opposite Lake Estes Dam, at 1895 Big Thompson Hwy. (U.S. 34) (☎ 970/586-4577). The company also offers horseback rides on the west side of the park in the Grand Lake area (☎ 970/627-3514).

Hi **Country Stables** operates two stables inside the park, with similar rides and rates: **Glacier Creek Stables** (☎ 970/586-3244) and **Moraine Park Stables** (☎ 970/586-2327). **National Park Village Stables** at the Fall River Entrance of the national park on U.S. 34 (☎ 970/586-5269) and the **Cowpoke Corner Corral,** at Glacier Lodge, 3 miles west of town, 2166 Colo. 66 (☎ 970/586-5890), both offer similar rides and rates from May through September.

Skiing & Snowshoeing. A growing number of people have been discovering the joys of exploring the park on cross-country skis and snowshoes, which are conveniently available for rent at area sporting goods stores (see "Picnic & Camping Supplies," below).

If you're headed into the backcountry for cross-country skiing or snowshoeing, stop by park headquarters for maps, information on where the snow is best, and a free backcountry permit if you plan to stay out overnight. Keep in mind that trails are not groomed. On winter weekends, rangers often lead guided snowshoe walks on the east side of the park and guided cross-country ski trips on the west side, starting in February. Participants must supply their own equipment.

Popular winter recreation areas include Bear Lake, south of the Beaver Meadows Entrance. A lesser-known part of the park is Wild Basin, which is south of the park's east entrances, off Colo. 7 about a mile north of the community of Allenspark. A 2-mile road, closed to motor vehicles for the last mile in winter, winds through a subalpine forest to the Wild Basin Trailhead, which follows a creek to a waterfall, a rustic bridge, and eventually to another waterfall. Total distance to the second falls is 2.7 miles. Chances are good for spotting birds along the trail, such as Clark's nutcrackers, Steller's jays, and the American dipper. On winter weekends, the Colorado Mountain Club often opens a warming hut at the Wild Basin Ranger Station.

Guided **snowshoe tours** in the park are offered by **Colorado Bicycling**

Especially for Kids

The park offers a variety of special hikes and programs for children, including an especially popular trip to the park's beaver ponds. A ranger-led program for kids from 6 to 12 years old, called **"A Child's View,"** concentrates on the park's geology and wildlife through hands-on activities. The park's **Junior Ranger Program** lets kids earn badges by completing activities that teach them about the park's plants and animals and environmental concerns. Most of the kids activities are scheduled during the summer; check on schedules at any park visitor center.

Adventures (see "Biking," above, or www.coloradosnowshoe.com) starting at $25 per person, including snowshoe rental.

Snowmobiling. Several areas on the park's west side are open to snowmobiles, including all of **Trail Ridge Road** to the west of Milner Pass. There is also a snowmobile trail that leads from the park into the adjacent Arapaho National Forest. Snowmobilers are required to register at the Kawuneeche Visitor Center, near Grand Lake. You can rent snowmobiles from **Grand Lake Snowmobile** (☎ 970/627-8304), located at Elk Creek Campground (see "Camping," below). Cost, including snowmobile, fuel, suits, and helmets, is $40 for one person for 2 hours, $55 for two people for 2 hours, $126 for one person for 8 hours, and $140 for two people for 8 hours.

Wildlife Viewing & Bird Watching. Rocky Mountain National Park is a premier wildlife-viewing area, especially in fall, winter, and spring. Look for large herds of elk in meadows and on mountainsides. During the fall rutting season a group of park volunteers called the **Rocky Mountain National Park Elk Bugle Corps** are stationed at elk-viewing areas in the evenings to help people get the best views while not disturbing the animals—elk are often just 30 or 40 feet away.

Park visitors also often see mule deer, beavers, coyotes, and river otters. Watch for moose among the willows on the west side of the park. In the forests there is an abundance of songbirds and small mammals; particularly plentiful are gray and Steller's jays, Clark's nutcrackers, chipmunks, and golden-mantled ground squirrels. You also have a good chance of seeing bighorn sheep, marmots, pikas, and ptarmigan along Trail Ridge Road. For detailed and current wildlife-viewing information, stop by one of the park's visitor centers and check on the many interpretive programs, such as bird walks. Local wildlife-watching suggestions can be heard on radio at 1610AM.

Camping

INSIDE THE PARK

The park has five campgrounds with a total of 589 sites, with nearly half at Moraine Park. Moraine Park and Glacier Basin require reservations Memorial Day through early September. For reservations call ☎ 800/365-2267, or make reservations through the park's Web site. In summer, arrive early if you hope to snare one of the first-come, first-served campsites. Campsites cost $16 per night during the summer; $10 in the off-season when water is turned off. No showers or RV hookups are available. Camping is limited to 3 days at Longs Peak and 7 days at other campgrounds.

NEAR THE PARK

THE EAST SIDE

Choices on the east side include the **Estes Park KOA,** 1 mile east of Estes Park on U.S. 34, at 2051 Big Thompson Ave.,

Estes Park, CO 80517 (☎ **800/562-1887** for reservations, or 970/586-2888). Scenically located across the street from Lake Estes and within walking distance of the Big Thompson River, this KOA lacks a swimming pool, but makes up for it with cable TV hookups, a basketball court, and a game room. It also sells LP gas. In addition to the campsites, there are 16 cabins ($44 to $52 double) and five tepees ($32 double). There are fire pits in the tent and cabin areas, but not at RV sites.

The **National Park Resort,** 3501 Fall River Rd., Estes Park, CO 80517 (☎ **970/586-4563**), is a wooded campground on the border of the park, just across the street from the park's new Gateway Visitor Center. It can accommodate both tents and RVs; all sites have at least water and electricity, while full hookups include electricity, water, sewer, and cable TV. A coin-operated laundry is nearby. Cabins, available year-round, cost $90 to $150.

The most luxurious camping is at **Spruce Lake R.V. Park,** U.S. 36 and Mary's Lake Road (P.O. Box 2497), Estes Park, CO 80517 (☎ **970/586-2889**), located about a mile west of the intersection of U.S. 34 and Business U.S. 36. Here you'll be pampered with miniature golf, a heated swimming pool, a large playground, stocked private fishing lake (fee), large sites, cable TV hookups, and numerous scheduled activities such as ice cream socials. Ground tents are not permitted.

There are links to Web sites for the above and other commercial campgrounds at **www.estesparkresort.com**.

There are two **Roosevelt National Forest** campgrounds within easy driving distance of the park's east entrances: **Olive Ridge,** 14.5 miles south of Estes Park along Colo. 7, not far from Allenspark, has pleasant, shady, well-spaced sites, picnic tables, and an amphitheater. A less-developed campground, for those who carry their own drinking water and don't want picnic tables, is **Meeker Park,** about 12 miles south of Estes Park on

Colo. 7. Both campgrounds have vault toilets.

In Estes Park, a **Forest Service Information Center** is located at 161 Second St. (☎ **970/586-3440**); it's open daily in summer, and has limited hours for several days a week in winter, depending on staff and volunteer availability. For year-round information, contact the **Boulder Ranger District** (☎ **303/444-6600**). Forest information is also available at the national park's **Lily Lake Visitor Center** (see "Visitor Centers" above).

For reservations (Olive Ridge Campground only) contact the National Recreation Reservation Service (☎ **877/444-6777;** www.reserveusa.com). There is a nonrefundable $8.65 fee per reservation in addition to campground fees.

THE WEST SIDE

Covering more than 36,000 acres along the western edge of Rocky Mountain National Park in Arapaho National Forest, the **Arapaho National Recreation Area** contains excellent fishing lakes (several with boat ramps) and opportunities for hiking, mountain biking, cross-country skiing, snowshoeing, snowmobiling, hunting, and camping in a mountain forest.

The recreation area's campgrounds offer shaded campsites plus the usual picnic tables and fire pits. These include its most developed, **Stillwater Campground,** located off U.S. 34 on the west bank of Lake Granby, about 6 miles south of the community of Grand Lake. Stillwater has showers plus water and electric hookups, available only in summer; a limited number of sites are open in winter, although water is then turned off.

Also located in the Arapaho National Recreation Area, south of Grand Lake, are **Green Ridge Campground** (about 4 miles south on U.S. 34 and then 1 mile south on County Road 66); and **Willow Creek** (about 9 miles south on U.S. 34 and then about 4 miles west on County Road 40). All three are located on lakes with fishing and boat ramps. For information, contact the **Arapaho National Recreation Area office** (☎ 970/887-4100). Campsite reservations (Stillwater and Green Ridge only) are available from the **National Recreation Reservation Service** (☎ 887/444-6777; www.reserveusa.com). There is a nonrefundable $8.65 fee per reservation in addition to campground fees.

There are also several commercial campgrounds in the community of Grand Lake, just outside the national park's west entrance. They all combine modern conveniences with a forest-camping feel. **Elk Creek Campground,** P.O. Box 549, Grand Lake, CO 80447 (☎ 800/355-2733 or 970/627-8502), is located on Golf Course Road, off U.S. 34 on the north side of the village. It has tent and RV sites in a wooded setting, a pond with license-free trout fishing (there is a

per fish charge), a playground, a game room, and a convenience store. There are also 10 log cabins ($39 double).

Accommodations

There is no lodging or dining inside the park.

NEAR THE PARK

ESTES PARK AREA (EAST SIDE OF THE NATIONAL PARK)

For help finding accommodations in and around Estes Park, contact the **Estes Park Chamber Resort Association,** 500 Big Thompson Ave., Estes Park, CO 80517 (☎ 800/443-7837 or 970/586-4431; fax 970/586-6336; www.estesparkresort.com).

Among national chains here are **Best Western Lake Estes Resort,** 1650 Big

Campground	Elev.	Total Sites	RV Hookups	Dump Station	Toilets
Inside the Park					
Aspenglen	8,230	54	0	No	Yes
Glacier Basin	8,600	150	0	Yes	Yes
Longs Peak	9,400	26	0	No	Yes
Moraine Park	8,150	247	0	Yes	Yes
Timber Creek	8,900	100	0	Yes	Yes
Near the Park's East Side					
Estes Park KOA	7,500	62	40	Yes	Yes
Meeker Park	8,600	29	0	No	Yes
National Park Resort	8,200	100	100	Yes	Yes
Olive Ridge	8,350	56	0	No	Yes
Spruce Lake RV Park	7,622	110	110	Yes	Yes
Near the Park's West Side					
Elk Creek	8,500	48	33	Yes	Yes
Green Ridge	8,360	77	0	Yes	Yes
Stillwater	8,300	129	20	Yes	Yes
Willow Creek	8,130	35	0	No	Yes

* Fees are winter/summer.

Thompson Ave. (U.S. 34), Estes Park, CO 80517 (☎ **800/292-8439** or 970/586-3386), with rates of $120 to $130 for two people from mid-June to mid-September, and $50 to $85 double the rest of the year; **Comfort Inn,** 1450 Big Thompson Ave., U.S. 34, (P.O. Box 393), Estes Park, CO 80517 (☎ **970/586-2358**), with rates for two of $89 to $169 mid-May through September and $52 to $131 at other times (closed November to March); and **Holiday Inn,** U.S. 36 and Colo. 7 (P.O. Box 1468), Estes Park, CO 80517 (☎ **970/586-2332**), charging $81 to $132 double in summer, $63 to $89 at other times.

Allenspark Lodge Bed & Breakfast

Colo. 7 Business Loop (P.O. Box 247), Allenspark, CO 80510. ☎ **303/747-2552.** Fax 303/747-0151. 13 units (6 with bath-

room). $65–$135 double. Rates include breakfast. AE, DISC, MC, V.

This three-story lodge, built in 1933 of hand-hewn ponderosa pine logs, boasts a large native stone fireplace. Located 16 miles south of Estes Park, in a tiny village at the southeast corner of the national park, all rooms offer mountain views and original handmade 1930s pine furniture. Guests share the large sunroom, the stone fireplace in the Great Room, books in the library, and videos, puzzles, and games in the recreation room. There's also a hot tub, conference rooms, an espresso coffee shop, and a wine and beer bar.

Alpine Trail Ridge Inn

927 Moraine Ave. (P.O. Box 3959), Estes Park, CO 80517. ☎ **800/233-5023** or 970/586-4585. Fax 970/586-6249. www.

Drinking Water	Showers	Fire Pits/ Grills	Laundry	Public Phone	Reserve	Fees*	Open
Yes	No	Yes	No	Yes	No	$16	May–Sept
Yes	No	Yes	No	Yes	Yes	$16	June–Sept
Yes	No	Yes	No	No	No	$10–$16	Year-round
Yes	No	Yes	No	Yes	Yes	$10–$16	Year-round
Yes	No	Yes	No	Yes	No	$10–$16	Year-round
Yes	Yes	No	Yes	Yes	Yes	$22–$30	Mid-Apr to late Oct
No	No	Yes	No	No	No	$6	Memorial Day to Labor Day
Yes	Yes	Yes	No	Yes	Yes	$25–$27	May–Sept
Yes	No	Yes	No	No	Yes	$12	Mid-May to Oct
Yes	Yes	No	Yes	Yes	Yes	$21–$33	Apr–Oct 15
Yes	Yes	Yes	Yes	Yes	Yes	$18–$22	May–Nov
Yes	No	Yes	No	Yes	Yes	$12	May–Oct
Yes	Yes	Yes	No	Yes	Yes	$12–$17	Year-round
Yes	No	Yes	No	No	No	$10	May–Oct

alpinetrailridgeinn.com. E-mail: alpine@alpinetrailridgeinn.com. 48 units. TV TEL. First 3 weeks May and mid-Sept to mid-Oct $48–$79; late May to mid-June and mid-Aug to mid-Sept $59–$90; mid-June to mid-Aug plus holidays and special events $76–$106. AE, CB, DC, DISC, MC, V. Closed mid-Oct to Apr.

The Alpine offers a variety of accommodations. Seven units have shower only, the rest have tub/shower combos, and all have a refrigerator, plus table and upholstered chairs. Largest are the balcony units, with beamed cathedral ceilings, private balconies, and either two queen beds or one king. The modern American decor is underlined with scenic or nature prints on the white walls. Standard units are fairly spacious and quite comfortable, with different combinations of king, queen, double, and twin beds. Even the smallest economy unit doesn't feel cramped, boasting a cabinlike decor, with knotty pine and white stucco walls; but the views aren't quite as good as the standard and balcony units. Two family units are available.

Complimentary hot beverages are available in the mornings, and the on-site Sundeck Restaurant serves three meals daily. There's a heated outdoor pool, patio with picnic table, and the trailhead for a 0.75-mile walking trail to the park's visitor center is adjacent to the motel. The owners are knowledgeable hikers, who enthusiastically help with guests' hiking plans.

Aspen Lodge at Estes Park

6120 Colo. 7, Longs Peak Rte., Estes Park, CO 80517. ☎ **800/332-6867** from outside Colorado (reservations only), or 970/586-8133. Fax 970/586-8133. www.aspenlodge.com. E-mail: aspen@aspenlodge.com. 59 units. June–Aug: 2-day minimum, packages include 3 meals, children's program, entertainment, and recreation (horseback riding extra). 2 days shared rm $300 each adult, $180 each child 3–12 years, children under 3 free; single adult $380. 3 days shared rm $450 each adult, $270 each child 3–12 years, children under 3 free; single adult $580. 7 days shared rm $930 each adult, $610 each child 3–12 years, children under 3 free; single adult $1,345. Sept–May $79–$129 double per night for lodge rooms or 1-rm cabins, including full breakfast. Holiday rates higher. Call for 2- and 3-rm cabin rates. AE, DISC, DC, MC, V.

Among Colorado's top dude ranches, Aspen Lodge is a full-service western-style resort, offering horseback riding, tennis, hiking, mountain biking, fishing, cross-country skiing, ice-skating, snowshoeing, and a myriad of other activities. Guests stay in the handsome log lodge, with a commanding stone fireplace in the lobby, or in cozy one-, two-, or three-room cabins nestled among the aspens. All lodge rooms have balconies, and most rooms and cabins have splendid views of Longs Peak, the national park's tallest mountain. Trails on the lodge's 82 acres of grounds lead directly into the national park. Guests can also enjoy an outdoor heated swimming pool and hot tub, racquetball, a weight room, sauna, various activities, and a restaurant that serves three meals daily

Baldpate Inn

4900 S. Colo. 7 (P.O. Box 4445), Estes Park, CO 80517. ☎ **970/586-6151.** www.baldpateinn.com. 12 units (2 with full bathroom, 1 with half bathroom), 3 cabins (all with full bathroom). $85–$140 double. Rates include full breakfast. DISC, MC, V. Closed Nov–Apr.

Built in 1917, the Baldpate was named for the novel *Seven Keys to Baldpate*, a murder mystery in which each of seven visitors believes he or she possesses the only key to the hotel. In 1996 the Baldpate was added to the National Register of Historic Places. Guests today can watch several movie versions of the story, read the book, and add their keys to the inn's collection of more than 20,000.

The inn is located 7 miles south of Estes Park, at an elevation of 9,000 feet. It offers several prime areas for relaxation: the comfortable lobby, with an impressive fireplace; the library, with a VCR and free use of the inn's video collection; the covered front porch; and the sunny open deck, at the site of the inn's former dance hall, where big bands led by Tommy Dorsey and Lawrence Welk once performed. The early 20th-century–style rooms are each unique, with handmade quilts on the beds. An excellent soup-and-salad buffet is served for lunch and dinner daily during summer. The inn is completely smoke free.

Boulder Brook on Fall River

1900 Fall River Rd., Estes Park, CO 80517. ☎ **800/238-0910** or 970/586-0910. Fax 970/586-8067. www.estes-park.com/ boulderbrook. 16 units. TV TEL. $89–$199 double 1-bedroom suite; $129–$229 double spa suite. Rates vary by season. AE, DISC, MC, V.

It would be hard to find a more beautiful setting for lodging. Surrounded by tall pines, all suites face the Fall River, have private riverfront decks, and full or partial kitchens. One-bedroom suites offer king beds, window seats, two TVs, fireplaces, and bathrooms with oversized whirlpool tub and shower combinations. Spa suites contain two-person spas, fireplaces, sitting rooms with cathedral ceilings, and king beds. There's also a year-round outdoor hot tub. Movie buffs will love the VCRs in every suite and the extensive movie library. The inn is popular with those celebrating wedding anniversaries and other events, and special occasion packages are available year-round.

Colorado Mountain School

351 Moraine Ave. (P.O. Box 1846), Estes Park, CO 80517. ☎ 970/586-5758. Fax 970/586-5798. www.cmschool.com. E-mail: cmschool@ cmschool.com. 18 dormitory beds. Per bed, summer $20; off-season $17. AE, DISC, MC, V. Open year-round, but office hours are 8am–5pm, until 6pm in summer.

This is lodging at its simplest: coed dormitory-style rooms furnished in light woods that are clean and well maintained, with bunk beds, lockable private storage, and showers (no tubs). See also "Climbing & Mountaineering," above.

The Eagle Manor— A Bed and Breakfast Place

441 Chiquita Lane (P.O. Box 1013), Estes Park, CO 80517. ☎ **888/603-3578** (reservations) or 970/586-8482. Fax 970/586-1748. www. eaglemanor.com. E-mail: eaglemanor@aol.com. TV TEL. 4 units. Late May to late Sept and holidays $135 double; rest of year $125 double. Rates include full breakfast. AE, DISC, MC, V.

This gracious Tudor-style carriage house and manor was built in 1917. In the 1960s a large living room, indoor swimming pool/garden room, and additional living quarters—where your congenial host, Mike Smith, lives—were added. The Great Room is the connecting link, with seductive and enveloping leather-covered overstuffed chairs and sofas. There's a gas-fired fireplace as well as a wood-burning fireplace, big-screen TV, antique billiards table, and a sauna and outdoor hot tub.

Rooms are spacious and comfortable. Three have queen-sized beds and the fourth has two twins. Breakfast includes eggs, breakfast meat, cereals, and breads. Special dietary needs can be accommodated with advance notice. The decor is a coordinated mixture of styles that works well: antiques, primitives, Mike's collection of kerosene hurricane lamps, old Navajo rugs, and massive wood bedroom furniture in classic styles.

Estes Park Center/ YMCA of the Rockies

2515 Tunnel Rd., Estes Park, CO 80511-2550. ☎ 970/586-3341, or from Denver direct 303/448-1616. 530 units (450 with bathroom), 205 cabins. Lodge rooms summer $48–$92, winter $36–$69; cabin year-round $53–$223. No credit cards. Pets accepted in cabins only.

Extremely popular, this resort is an ideal place to get away from it all or to use as home base while exploring the Estes Park area. The spacious mountain cabins have two to four bedrooms (accommodating up to 10), complete kitchens, and telephones. Some have fireplaces.

Lodge units are basic but perfectly adequate. YMCA membership is required (available at a nominal charge). The center occupies 860 wooded acres, and offers hiking, horseback riding, miniature golf, a heated swimming pool and children's pool, fishing, biking (rentals available), three tennis courts, and cross-country skiing. There's also a self-service laundry.

Romantic RiverSong Inn

Lower Broadview Dr. off Mary's Lake Rd. (P.O. Box 1910), Estes Park, CO 80517. ☎ 970/586-4666. Fax 970/577-0699. www. romanticriversong.com. 9 units. $150–$275 double. Rates include full breakfast. MC, V.

A 1920 Craftsman mansion on the Big Thompson River, this elegant bed-and-breakfast is at the end of a country lane, the first right off Mary's Lake Road after it branches off U.S. 36 south. Its grounds include 27 forested acres with hiking trails and a trout pond, as well as abundant wildlife. The cozy bedrooms are decorated with a blend of antique and modern country furniture; some have ornate brass beds and claw-foot tubs, several have jetted tubs for two, and all have fireplaces. Smoking is not permitted. Gourmet candlelight dinners are available by advance arrangement for the romantically inclined; wedding and elopement packages are available, including a wedding ceremony by a mail-order minister.

Stanley Hotel & Conference Center

333 Wonderview Ave. (P.O. Box 1767), Estes Park, CO 80517. ☎ 800/976-1377 or 970/586-3371. Fax 970/586-3673. www. grandheritage.com. 133 units. TV TEL. Late May to mid-Oct $169–$209 double, $269–$299 suite; mid-Oct to late May $139–$179 double, $219–$249 suite. AE, DISC, MC, V.

Freelan O. Stanley, coinventor of the Stanley Steam Car, began construction of this elegant, white-pillared hotel in 1906, and opened the doors in June 1909. The equal of European resorts of the time, it was constructed into solid rock and was entirely electric—including the kitchen. Stanley built a hydroelectric plant to generate the necessary power, at the same time providing power to Estes Park. He also built a water system from the mountains so the hotel, and incidentally the town, would have running water.

The hotel and grounds are listed on the National Register of Historic Places, and the entire building, both guest rooms and public areas, was remodeled in 1997. As often happens in historic hotels, each room differs in size and shape, offering a variety of views of Longs Peak, Lake Estes, and surrounding hillsides. Furnishings are in keeping with the building's Georgian architecture, with 1920s-era mahogany pieces—some original and many reproductions. Amenities include a heated outdoor pool, tennis and volleyball courts, sundeck, and access to a nearby health club. And of course there's a vintage Stanley Steamer in the lobby. Restaurants serve three meals daily, and there's a bar, a gift shop, and small museum.

GRAND LAKE AREA (WEST SIDE OF THE NATIONAL PARK)

For a complete listing of lodging and dining choices in the Grand Lake Area, contact the **Grand Lake Area Chamber of Commerce,** P.O. Box 57, Grand Lake, CO 80447 (☎ 800/531-1019 or 970/627-3372 for the chamber, 970/627-3402 for the visitor center; fax 970/627-8007; www.grandlakecolorado.com).

Daven Haven Lodge

604 Marina Dr. (P.O. Box 1528), Grand Lake, CO 80447. ☎ 970/627-8144. Fax 970/627-5098. www.grandlakecolorado.com/lodging/dh/home.htm. E-mail: davenhaven@rkymtnhi.com. 16 cabins. TV. $78–$185; off-season midweek discounts available. DISC, MC, V. 3-night minimum required on reservations from mid-June through Labor Day, plus holidays.

Set among pine trees about 1 block from the lake, this group of cabins offers secluded and quiet lodging in a mountain resort-type setting. The cabins vary in size, sleeping from two to nine people; each has its own picnic table and six have stone fireplaces. Decor and furnishings vary, but most have attractive light wood walls and both solid wood and upholstered furniture. You'll also find a heated outdoor swimming pool, a volleyball court, horseshoes, a bonfire pit, and a barbecue area. The Back Street Steakhouse (see "Where to Eat," below) serves dinner in summer.

Driftwood Lodge

12255 U.S. 34 (P.O. Box 609), Grand Lake, CO 80447. ☎ and fax **970/627-3654.** www.rkymtnhi.com/driftwood. E-mail: jsig@rkymtnhi.com. 17 units. TV TEL. Summer $60–$75 double, $95 suite; lower rates in winter. DISC, MC, V.

Located 3 miles south of town, this comfortable and well-maintained motel offers basic rooms plus suites. It has a swimming pool, sauna, whirlpool, and a playground.

E.G.'s Garden Grill & Country Inn

1000 Grand Ave. (P.O. Box 1618), Grand Lake, CO 80447. ☎ **970/627-8404.** Fax 970/627-0118. www.egscountryinn.com. E-mail: egs@rkymthi.com. 3 units. TV TEL. $145–$195 double. Rates include full breakfast. AE, DISC, MC, V.

Opened in spring 1999, this luxury country inn is located in downtown Grand Lake on the third floor of a 1910 building. The three spacious, well-appointed rooms are individually decorated with an eclectic mix of new, old, and antique furnishings. Each room has a gas fireplace, combination TV/VCR, two phones, and data ports. Two units have king-sized beds and jetted tubs; one room has a queen bed with an old-fashioned footed tub, plus a shower. Views of the lake and national park are great. Room service for lunch and dinner is available, since E.G.'s Garden Grill is downstairs (see "Dining," below). All rooms are no-smoking.

Grand Lake Lodge

15500 U.S. 34 (P.O. Box 569), Grand Lake, CO 80447. ☎ **970/627-3967.** Fax 970/627-9495. www.grandlakelodge.com. 56 units. $70–$160 double. Minimum stays apply to some units, and during some holidays. AE, DISC, MC, V. Closed mid-Sept to May. Take U.S. 34 north 0.5 mi. from Grand Lake (or 0.5 mi. south of the park entrance) and turn east (watch for their sign) onto the entrance road.

At an elevation of 8,769 feet, Grand lake Lodge claims to have Colorado's "favorite front porch," affording panoramic views of Grand Lake—both the town and the lake—and the surrounding mountains. Established in 1921, the Lodge has been owned and operated by three generations of the Ted L. James family since 1953, offering excellent service and food in a delightful rustic setting. Sleeping quarters are in cabins scattered among the pines beyond the Main Lodge. Decor and furnishings vary, but most have Southwest-style bed coverings and upholstery, and walls of wood-grain paneling. Units range from single rooms (that sleep two) in a duplex cabin, to two rooms with fully equipped kitchenettes and either gas heat or electric baseboard heating and a Franklin stove (these units sleep four to six). There's a large outdoor heated pool, hot tub, decks, playground, picnic area with grills, riding stables, volleyball, horseshoes, and hiking trails; recreation room and laundry facilities; gift shop, bar, and restaurant.

The Inn at Grand Lake

1103 Grand Ave. (P.O. Box 1590), Grand Lake, CO 80447. ☎ **800/722-2585** or 970/627-9234. 17 units. Summer $60–$70 double; lower rates in winter. AE, DISC, MC, V.

This restored historic building, constructed about 1881, was originally

Grand Lake's courthouse and jail. Now the inn offers comfortable, modern lodging with rustic western-style furnishings and a genuine Old West feel. Rooms have a variety of bed combinations, and several sleep up to six. Some rooms have refrigerators and microwaves. About half have shower-tub combinations, and the rest have showers only. The inn is located in the center of town, about a half block from the lake.

Dining

NEAR THE PARK

ESTES PARK AREA (EAST SIDE OF THE NATIONAL PARK)

The Dunraven Inn

2470 Colo. 66. ☎ **970/586-6409.** Reservations highly recommended. Main courses $8–$27. AE, DISC, MC, V. Sun–Thurs 5–10pm, Fri–Sat 5–11pm; closed slightly earlier in winter. ITALIAN.

The eclectic decorations here include various images of the *Mona Lisa,* from a mustachioed lady to opera posters, plus autographed dollar bills posted in the lounge area. House specialties are scampi, linguine with clam sauce, veal parmigiana, chicken cacciatore, and Dunraven Italiano, which is a charbroiled sirloin steak in a sauce of green, red, and yellow peppers, with black olives, mushrooms, and tomatoes. Fresh fish is served most evenings, and vegetarian plates are also available. There's a good wine list, and a separate smokers' room leaves the main dining room entirely smoke-free.

Estes Park Brewery

470 Prospect Village Dr. ☎ **970/586-5421.** Main courses $5–$8. AE, DC, DISC, MC, V. Summer daily 11am–10pm; closes earlier in winter. AMERICAN.

Pizzas, burgers, sandwiches—including meatball and grilled turkey—and bratwurst made with the brewery's own beer are the fare here. Vegetarians can order a veggie burger and a variety of salads. The brewery specializes in Belgian-style ales and also produces an excellent India pale ale. Even children are welcome in the tasting room, where they can sample the brewery's own root beer and cream soda—on tap, of course. There are also video games and pool tables.

Grumpy Gringo

1560 Big Thompson Ave. (U.S. 34). ☎ **970/586-7705.** Main courses $4.95–$11.95. AE, DISC, MC, V. Daily 11am–10pm summer, 11am–8pm the rest of the year. Closed last week of Jan and first week of Feb. On U.S. 34, 1 mi. east of the junction of U.S. Hwy. 34 and 36. MEXICAN.

This classy restaurant has private booths, white-washed plaster walls, green plants and bright poppies for a splash of color, and a few choice sculptures. And although the food is excellent and portions are large, the prices are surprisingly low. The most popular item is the burrito—and there are several varieties; the enchilada olé is three huge enchiladas; and the fajitas—either chicken or beef—are delicious. There are six sauces to choose from, each homemade, and rated mild to hot. Burgers and sandwiches are also offered. The house specialty drink is the Gringo Margarita—made with Cuervo gold from an original (and secret) recipe.

Timberline Family Restaurant.

451 S. St. Vrain Ave. ☎ **970/586-9840.** Reservations not accepted in summer. Sun breakfast and lunch $4.75–$12; dinner $10–$16. AE, DISC, MC, V. Summer, Sun 10am–2pm, Sun–Thurs 4–9pm, Fri–Sat 4–10pm; slightly shorter hours rest of year. AMERICAN.

The pleasant, light-pine paneled dining room has a mountain lodge feel, complete with a stone fireplace. Original local and regional artwork and three-dimensional petroglyphlike figures decorate the walls. The emphasis, though, is on friendly service and good home-style food. Dinner favorites include the Rocky Mountain trout, coconut shrimp, and charbroiled steaks. Lighter items include the Timberline salad—fresh field greens tossed with walnuts and Parmesan cheese and topped with mandarin orange slices and a sliced pear half. It's well worth saving a bit of appetite for the homemade desserts, such as double chocolate Boston cream pie. The entire property is no-smoking.

GRAND LAKE AREA (WEST SIDE OF THE NATIONAL PARK)

Back-Street Steakhouse

In the Daven Haven Lodge, 604 Marina Dr. ☎ **970/627-8144.** Reservations recommended in summer and on winter weekends. Main courses $14–$23. DISC, MC, V. Summer and Christmas holidays Sun–Fri 5–9pm, Sat 5–10pm; winter Wed–Sat 5–9pm. Closed Nov and Apr. STEAKS.

This cozy, country inn–like restaurant offers fine dining in a down-home atmosphere. Steaks—from the 8-ounce filet mignon to the 20-ounce porterhouse—are all USDA choice beef, cooked to perfection. The house specialty, Jack Daniel's pork chops (breaded, baked, and served with a creamy Jack Daniel's mushroom sauce), was featured in the November 1997 issue of *Bon Appétit.* Also on the menu are pasta, chicken, and fish dishes, plus slow-roasted prime rib.

Chuck Hole Cafe

1131 Grand Ave. ☎ **970/627-3509.** Main courses $2–$6. DISC, MC, V. Memorial Day to Labor Day 6:30am–3pm; shorter hours rest of year. AMERICAN.

This small cafe, decorated with historic photos and prints, has a very Western feel. It serves traditional breakfasts such as omelettes and pancakes, and quick lunches including burgers and sandwiches.

E.G.'s Garden Grill

1000 Grand Ave. ☎ **970/627-8404.** Main courses $7–$11.50 at lunch; $8–$25 at dinner. AE, DISC, MC, V. Summer daily 11am–10pm; call for winter hours. NEW AMERICAN/ SOUTHWESTERN.

The large stone fireplace, trellised ceiling, and spacious outdoor beer garden give this restaurant a warm and comfortable atmosphere. The menu offers innovative variations on traditional American dishes, often with a Southwestern flair. Although the menu changes seasonally, house specialties usually include items such as mustard catfish with jalapeño tartar sauce and jicama slaw, shrimp enchiladas, and baby back ribs with E.G.'s homemade barbecue sauce. There are also pizza, sandwiches, soups and salads, daily seafood specials, plus a fairly extensive wine list.

Picnic & Camping Supplies

Just 0.75 mile from the main east entrance to the park, **Country Supermarket** is located at 900 Moraine Ave. in Estes Park (☎ 970/586-2702). The store has a good stock of groceries, a deli and ATM, and firewood.

Those looking for camping and outdoor sports supplies should stop at **Outdoor World,** downtown at 156 E. Elkhorn Ave. (☎ 970/586-2114), which sells and rents a wide variety of equipment. Another good choice is **Colorado Wilderness Sports,** 358 E. Elkhorn Ave. (☎ 800/ 504-6642 or 970/586-6548), which offers sales and rentals and an indoor climbing gym.

In Grand Lake, the **Mountain Food Market,** 400 Grand Ave. (☎ 970/627-3470), and the **Circle D,** 701 Grand Ave. (☎ 970/627-3210), have good selections of groceries and picnic supplies.

32

SAGUARO NATIONAL PARK

by Don and Barbara Laine

THE STATELY SAGUARO CACTUS, SYMBOL OF THE AMERICAN SOUTH-west, is the king here, dominating the entire landscape. One of America's few national parks dedicated to protecting one specific plant, Saguaro National Park also preserves an impressive area of Sonoran Desert. Saguaros are plants with personalities. They often look human, standing tall and proud, their arms reaching toward the sky or pointing the way. Though some achieve heights of 50 feet and weigh up to 8 tons, saguaros grow slowly. It usually takes them 15 years to reach 1 foot in height, and they don't flower or produce fruit until they're about 30. They take about 100 years to reach a height of 25 feet. Their maximum life span is about 200 years.

One of the hottest and driest parts of North America, the Sonoran Desert also, somewhat ironically, has an amazing variety of life, more than any other of the continent's deserts. Although the saguaro towers above the landscape, and is consequently the first thing we notice here, this desert is home to dozens of other cacti, grasses, shrubs, flowers, and trees, as well as several hundred species of birds, mammals, and reptiles. Many of them are uniquely adapted to the demanding environment of this dry land. For instance, javelinas, those odd-looking piglike animals, have mouths so tough they can bite through prickly pear cactus pads in search of moisture; and kangaroo rats never need to drink—they extract all the water they need from seeds.

The park is composed of two separated sections. The Tucson Mountain District, also called Saguaro West, covers 32 square miles of Sonoran Desert west of the city of Tucson; while the Rincon Mountain District, also called Saguaro East, covers 104 square miles of saguaro forest, desert, foothills, and mountain terrain on the east side of Tucson. The two sections are about 30 miles apart.

Both districts have scenic drives and trails, with good wildlife viewing and bird watching. When the rain cooperates at the right time of year, there are also spectacular shows of wildflowers and cactus blooms.

Avoiding the Crowds. Annual visitation is about 3.3 million people, with Saguaro West receiving the greater number. The park's busiest time is from Christmas through Easter. Those wanting to avoid crowds should visit at other times, although all visitors who plan on hiking will want to avoid summer's extreme heat. Fall through mid-December can offer the best of both worlds: fewer crowds and lower temperatures.

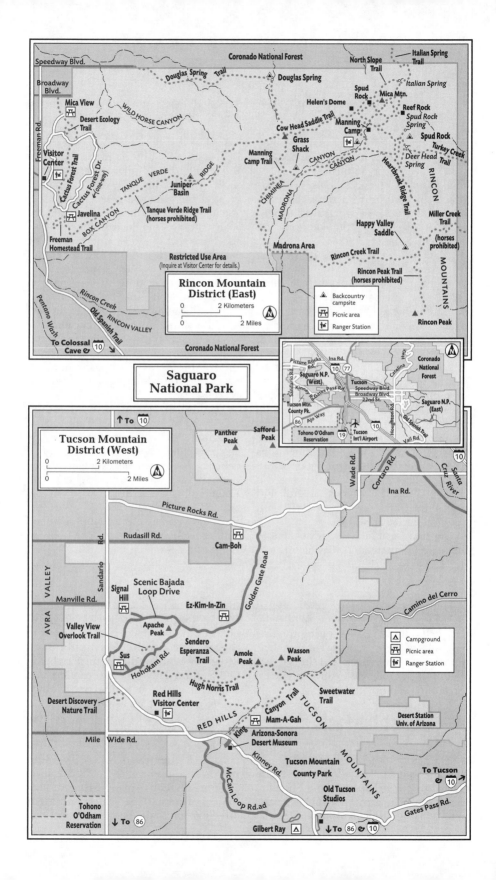

Saguaro National Park

Rincon Mountain District (East)

Speedway Blvd.

Broadway Blvd.

Coronado National Forest

Douglas Spring Trail

North Slope Trail

Italian Spring Trail

Douglas Spring

Italian Spring

Spud Rock

Mica Mtn.

Helen's Dome

Reef Rock

Spud Rock Spring

Mica View

Desert Ecology Trail

WILD HORSE CANYON

Cow Head Saddle Trail

Manning Camp

Spud Rock

Freeman Rd.

Visitor Center

Cactus Forest Trail

Cactus Forest Dr. (one-way)

TANQUE VERDE RIDGE

Juniper Basin

Grass Shack

Manning Camp Trail

CHIMINEA CANYON

MADRONA CANYON

Deer Head Spring

Turkey Creek Trail

RINCON MOUNTAINS

Javelina

Tanque Verde Ridge Trail (horses prohibited)

Happy Valley Saddle

Miller Creek Trail (horses prohibited)

Freeman Homestead Trail

BOX CANYON

Madrona Area

Rincon Creek Trail

Restricted Use Area
(Inquire at Visitor Center for details.)

Rincon Peak Trail (horses prohibited)

Rincon Peak

Rincon Creek

RINCON VALLEY

Old Spanish Trail

Pantano Wash

To Colossal Cave

10

Coronado National Forest

▲	Backcountry campsite
⊞	Picnic area
⌂	Ranger Station

0 ——— 2 Kilometers
0 ——— 2 Miles

Picture Rocks Rd.

Ina Rd.

10 77

Saguaro N.P. (West)

Sandario Rd.

Kinney Rd.

Gates Pass Rd.

Catalina Hwy

Coronado National Forest

Tucson

Speedway Blvd.
Broadway Blvd.
22nd St.

Saguaro N.P. (East)

Tucson Mtn. County Pk.

86 Ajo Way

Tohono O'Odham Reservation

19 Tucson Int'l Airport

Houghton Rd.

Old Spanish Trail

Vail Rd.

Tucson Mountain District (West)

0 ——— 2 Kilometers
0 ——— 2 Miles

↑ To 10

Panther Peak

Safford Peak

Wade Rd.

Cortaro Rd.

Santa Cruz River

10

Picture Rocks Rd.

Ina Rd.

Rudasill Rd.

Sandario Rd.

Cam-Boh

AVRA VALLEY

Manville Rd.

Signal Hill

Scenic Bajada Loop Drive

Ez-Kim-In-Zin

Golden Gate Road

Camino del Cerro

Valley View Overlook Trail

Apache Peak

Sendero Esperanza Trail

Amole Peak

Wasson Peak

Sus

Hohokam Rd.

Hugh Norris Trail

Sweetwater Trail

TUCSON MOUNTAINS

Desert Discovery Nature Trail

Red Hills Visitor Center

Canyon Trail

Mam-A-Gah

Desert Station Univ. of Arizona

Mile Wide Rd.

RED HILLS

King

Arizona-Sonora Desert Museum

Kinney Rd.

Tucson Mountain County Park

Old Tucson Studios

To Tucson

10

McCain Loop Rd.ad

Gates Pass Rd.

Tohono O'Odham Reservation

↓ To 86

Gilbert Ray

↓ To 86 & 10

△	Campground
⊞	Picnic area
⌂	Ranger Station

Tips from a Park Ranger

For those who have not experienced the Southwest's deserts, and particularly the Sonoran Desert of southern Arizona, Saguaro National Park can be an unusual experience, according to Tom Danton, the park's chief of interpretation.

"Many visitors are petrified," he says. "It's essential they stop at the visitor center to learn about the park before going out into it." The park environment, with its extreme heat and forests of saguaro, is alien to most people's experiences. Visitors can be even more frightened, Danton says, when they learn there are rattlesnakes, Gila monsters, and other poisonous creatures.

Among his suggestions for enjoying Saguaro West are hiking the 5.5-mile Hugh Norris Trail. "Within 30 minutes you feel like you're on the top of the world," he says. "You get a tremendous sense of accomplishment." For those with less ambition or time, he suggests the short Valley View Overlook Trail and the Desert Discovery Nature Trail, both also in the western district.

On the east side, he suggests the easy Freeman Homestead Trail, which passes by the site of a historic homestead, and the challenging Tanque Verde Ridge Trail, which, he says, is "steep and rugged, but gives you great views of Tucson and the mountains." To really be alone, he recommends trying some of the backcountry trails, where you'll be hiking from desert up into forests of Douglas fir and ponderosa pine.

The prettiest time at the park is spring, when the wildflowers and cacti are in bloom; but Danton himself would visit in midwinter, because the weather is best for hiking. In winter there are also a large number of interpretive programs, such as moonlight walks, and you seldom see any poisonous reptiles.

Danton says that one problem for visitors going to Saguaro East is the lack of parking, even at the visitor center. He suggests that those with recreational vehicles use a smaller vehicle in the park, if they have one, or check with rangers about where to park their big rigs. There are pullouts just inside the Cactus Forest Drive where motor homes can be parked when there's no room in the parking lot.

The other way to avoid crowds, even at the busiest times, is to hike. While the park gets a lot of visitors during the first 3 months of the year, many confine their activities to scenic drives and short walks. Within 15 minutes you can easily leave the crowds behind.

Just the Facts

GETTING THERE & GATEWAYS

Saguaro National Park is located in southern Arizona near **Tucson,** about 116 miles southeast of Phoenix. There are two parts to the park: the **Rincon Mountain District** (Saguaro East) and the **Tucson Mountain District (Saguaro West),** each about 15 miles from downtown Tucson. To get to Saguaro East from Tucson, head east on Broadway Boulevard and turn right on Old Spanish Trail, which meanders in a southeast direction to the park. Watch for signs for the park as you go.

To get to Saguaro West from Tucson, go west on Speedway Boulevard, which first becomes Gates Pass Road and then ends at Kinney Road, where you turn right and continue to the park entrance.

From Phoenix, follow I-10 southeast toward Tucson and watch for signs directing you to the park.

The Nearest Airport. Located 6 miles south of downtown, **Tucson International Airport** (☎ **520/573-8000**) is served by most major airlines and all major car-rental agencies, whose toll-free numbers are in the appendix.

INFORMATION

Contact the **Superintendent, Saguaro National Park,** 3693 South Old Spanish Trail, Tucson, AZ 85730-5699 (☎ **520/ 733-5153** for the east side, 505/733-5158 for the west side; fax 520/733-5183; www. nps.gov/sagu). For information on other area attractions and services, contact the **Tucson Convention and Visitors Bureau,** 130 S. Scott Ave., Tucson, AZ 85701 (☎ **800/638-8350** or 520/624-1817; www.visittucson.org).

Those particularly interested in the plants, animals, and geology of the park can get additional information from two books, both titled *Saguaro National Monument.* The larger, more detailed one was written by Napier Shelton and published by the National Park Service in 1985. The shorter version was written by Doris Evans and published in 1993 by the Southwest Parks and Monuments Association.

VISITOR CENTERS

The park has two visitor centers, one in each district. On the west side of the park, in the Tucson Mountain District, the **Red Hills Visitor Center** contains a museum, an information desk, and a bookstore. The museum offers exhibits on desert life and a 15-minute slide program on the uniqueness and importance of deserts.

On the park's east side, in the Rincon Mountain District, the **visitor center** has similar facilities on a somewhat smaller scale. There's an excellent 15-minute video on the flora and fauna of the park, plus exhibits on saguaro and the world's deserts. Both visitor centers are open daily year-round except Christmas.

FEES

Entry into the east district costs $4 per private vehicle, or $2 per person on foot or bike. Entry into the west district is free.

SPECIAL REGULATIONS & WARNINGS

Extreme heat, cactus spines, and poisonous reptiles are the main safety hazards here. Temperatures that soar to 115°F in summer make hiking not only uncomfortable but often dangerous. Those who insist on hiking in the hot months can minimize the dangers by starting very early in the day, perhaps by 4am, and getting off the trails by noon. Hikers should carry plenty of water and drink it even if they do not feel thirsty.

Cactus spines can be very painful, as anyone who's inadvertently backed into one while trying to line up a photo can tell you. The bites of rattlesnakes, Gila monsters, and various types of scorpions are poisonous. Park rangers recommend that you always look before putting your hands or feet under rocks or in other hidden spots, and that you use a flashlight at night to help avoid unwanted encounters. Weather-related dangers include lightning (stay off exposed ridges during thunderstorms) and flash floods (avoid drainages during rain).

SEASONS & CLIMATE

Summers are hot and winters comfortable, so the best time to visit, especially for hikers, is between October and April. Summer high temperatures are routinely between 100° and 115°F, with lows generally in the 70s. Visitors should also beware of the occasional torrential thunderstorms in July, August, and September, which bring dangers from lightning and flash floods.

During winter, high temperatures are usually in the 60s and low 70s, with lows dropping into the upper 30s and 40s. Occasionally it snows, but it's almost always light and melts quickly. Winters are also known for periodic gentle rains, but most of the time it's sunny.

The best wildflower displays are from mid-March through mid-April. Cacti bloom a bit later—some kinds flower from mid-April through September, although the saguaro usually bloom from late April through June.

If You Only Have 1 Day

Because Saguaro National Park is com-posed of two separate sections, visitors should ideally spend at least a day or two at each district, starting with the visitor centers, then the short interpretive walks, and finally a serious hike or two. Those with only a day can either see a bit of each district or choose to explore one of them more thoroughly.

To see both sections of the park in 1 day, start in the **Tucson Mountain District** at the impressive new **Red Hills Visitor Center,** where you can examine the exhibits and try to get a handle on life in the Sonoran Desert. Check the bulletin board for the schedule of ranger-led activities; if your timing is right you can join a short guided walk on the **Cactus Garden Trail,** just outside the visitor cen-ter, which serves as an excellent intro-duction to the park. You can also take this short walk on your own. Then drive the 9-mile **Bajada Loop Drive** through a thick stand of saguaro, taking time for a short hike along the **Valley View Over-look Trail.** Those interested in early American Indians will want to take a slight detour off the Bajada Loop Drive to ponder the rock art on the **Signal Hill Petroglyph Trail.**

By now it should be lunchtime, so you can stop in one of the picnic areas if you happened to bring food, or at a restau-rant in Tucson as you drive through on your way to the **Rincon Mountain Dis-trict.** Stop at the visitor center as you enter the park—by now you may have a

few questions for the rangers, such as, "What were those two big eyes staring out at me from a hole in that old saguaro?" (probably an elf owl). Then head out onto the 8-mile **Cactus Forest Drive** for an easy close-up look at a for-est of saguaro. About a third of the way into the drive the road crosses the **Cactus Forest hiking trail,** where you can get out of your vehicle, stretch your legs, and walk a short way into the saguaro forest. If time remains, pull off at the Javelina Picnic Area access road and take a walk along the **Freeman Homestead Trail,** which offers good scenic views and a look at the remains of an old homestead.

Exploring the Park by Car

Each section of the park has its own scenic drive. Before you set out on one, consider buying one of the inexpensive booklets discussing the park's terrain and vegetation at the visitor centers. The 9-mile **Bajada Loop Drive** in the western section begins at the Red Hills Visitor Center and proceeds through a dense forest of saguaro cacti, offering scenic views. There are pullouts where you can get out of your vehicle for a close-up view of the saguaro, and a trailhead for the very worthwhile **Valley View Overlook Trail** (see "Day Hikes," below). Because 6 miles of the loop is gravel, those driving low-clearance vehicles or towing trailers should check on current conditions before starting.

In the eastern section of the park, the **Cactus Forest Drive** is a somewhat hilly and twisting 8-mile loop that wanders through a forest of saguaro. This one-way road is paved, and also provides access to picnic areas, several hiking trails, and short walks.

Organized Tours & Ranger Programs

Ranger-led guided walks, hikes, and talks take place year-round, although most occur from December through April. Activities vary, but might include an easy cactus or bird identification walk, a 4-mile hike through the desert, a video program on desert life, or slide shows on wildflowers or bats. Check at the visitor centers for schedules.

Historic & Man-Made Attractions

Both sections of the park contain impressive **rock art** believed to have been created by the Hohokam people, who lived here from about A.D. 700 to 1500. The best and easiest place to see rock art is on the Signal Hill Petroglyphs Trail in the Tucson Mountain District. These petroglyphs (a type of rock carving) usually depict figures of humans and animals plus many abstract designs, such as wavy lines and combinations of circles and spirals.

The park also contains reminders of the miners and settlers who arrived in the late 1800s. The remains of the **Gould Mine,** active in the early 1900s, can be seen along the Sendero Esperanza Trail, in the Tucson Mountain District. In the Rincon Mountain District you can see what's left of an **adobe house** built in 1929 on the Freeman Homestead Trail, and several **lime kilns,** built in about 1880, along the Cactus Garden Trail. See "Day Hikes," below.

Day Hikes

Desert hiking can be a killer, literally. Those planning to do any serious hiking at Saguaro National Park are strongly advised to talk with rangers about their plans before setting out, and then to carry at least a gallon of water per day per person. Rangers do not recommend hiking at all in the summer, when temperatures frequently reach a scorching 115°F. Because some of the longer trails are difficult to follow, hikers are advised to carry good topographic maps, available at the visitor centers.

TUCSON MOUNTAIN DISTRICT (SAGUARO WEST)

SHORTER TRAILS

Cactus Garden Trail

0.15 mi. RT. Easy. Access: Red Hills Visitor Center.

A level nature walk just outside the visitor center, this wheelchair-accessible trail is a good introduction to the park and the Sonoran Desert environment. Interpretive signs identify a variety of desert plants.

Desert Discovery Nature Trail

0.5 mi. RT. Easy. Access: Kinney Rd., 1 mi. northwest of the Red Hills Visitor Center.

This mostly level wheelchair-accessible trail has signs describing the plants, animals, and ecology of the Sonoran Desert. It also provides panoramic views of the Tucson Mountains.

Signal Hill Petroglyphs Trail

0.25 mi. RT. Easy. Access: North of Signal Hill picnic area, off Golden Gate Rd., 5 mi. northwest of the Red Hills Visitor Center.

This trail zigzags up the side of a small hill to an area containing dozens of examples of American Indian rock art, believed to have been left by the Hohokam people between 500 and 1,300 years ago (see "Historic & Man-Made Attractions," above).

Valley View Overlook Trail

1.5 mi. RT. Easy. Access: Bajada Loop Dr., 3.5 mi. north of the Red Hills Visitor Center.

Built by the Civilian Conservation Corps in the 1930s, this trail passes through cactus forests and two washes before climbing to a ridge for splendid views of the surrounding desert and mountains.

LONGER TRAILS

Hugh Norris Trail

4.9 mi. one way. Strenuous. Access: Bajada Loop Dr., 2.5 mi. north of the Red Hills Visitor Center.

The longest and most difficult in the park's Tucson Mountain District, this trail begins with a series of switchbacks that lead to a ridge overlooking a huge forest of saguaro cactus. From there it offers good panoramic views and passes old mines and intriguing rock formations. The trail climbs another series of switchbacks before finally making its way to the top of Wasson Peak, at 4,687 feet, from which you generally have spectacular views of Tucson and the surrounding mountains. The trail has a total elevation gain of 2,087 feet.

King Canyon Trail

3.5 mi. one way. Moderate to strenuous. Access: On Kinney Rd., directly across from the Arizona-Sonora Desert Museum, about 2 mi. southwest of the Red Hills Visitor Center.

This trail combines with the last 0.3 mile of the Hugh Norris Trail to take you from 2,800 feet elevation to the top of Wasson Peak, at 4,687 feet, the highest point in the Tucson Mountains. Along the trail are petroglyphs believed to have been created by the Hohokam people, some open mine shafts that you'll want to avoid, and panoramic views once you get to the higher elevations. The trail is rocky in spots so good hiking boots are recommended.

Sendero Esperanza Trail

3.2 mi. one way. Moderate. Access: Golden Gate Rd., about 6 mi. northeast of the Red Hills Visitor Center.

There are several steep switchbacks as the trail leaves an old mining road and climbs to a ridge, with spectacular views in all directions, before finally dropping to the Mam-A-Gah Picnic Area and a

junction with the King Canyon Trail. Along the way it passes the remains of the Gould Mine, which was enthusiastically but unproductively worked in the early part of the 1900s.

RINCON MOUNTAIN DISTRICT (SAGUARO EAST)

SHORTER TRAILS

Desert Ecology Trail

0.25 mi. RT. Easy. Access: Cactus Forest Dr., east of the Mica View Picnic Area.

Interpretive signs along this paved wheelchair-accessible walkway explain how plants and animals of the Sonoran Desert make the most of the limited amount of water available.

Freeman Homestead Trail

1 mi. RT. Easy. Access: Off Cactus Forest Dr., on the Javelina Picnic Area access road.

This walk through gently rolling desert terrain offers good panoramic views as well as close-up views of saguaro, ocotillo, and other desert plants. Along the way, you'll find several interpretive signs describing desert life and the remains of the Freeman Homestead, a three-room adobe house built by Safford Freeman in 1929. All that's left now is a mound of sand from the adobe bricks and a portion of the foundation.

LONGER TRAILS

Cactus Forest Trail

5 mi. one way. Easy. Access: Near the east end of Broadway Blvd., just east of Freeman Rd.

This sandy, level trail, which can also be accessed from two points on the Cactus Forest Drive, is simply a very pleasant walk though a forest of cactus, primarily saguaro, a variety of other desert plants, such as paloverde and mesquite, as well as large beehive-shaped lime kilns, dating from about 1880.

Douglas Spring Trail

6 mi. one way (to Douglas Spring Campground). Strenuous. Access: East end of Speedway Blvd.

This trail through the foothills of the Rincon Mountains is considered strenuous, starting off fairly level but gradually becoming steeper, and then alternating between steep and flat sections all the way to Douglas Spring Campground. Along the way you'll find lots of cactus, especially prickly pear, and some interesting rock formations. Signs of damage from a devastating 1989 fire can still be seen here, as well as the results of revegetation. The trail continues beyond the campground, providing access to other backcountry trails. You need a backcountry permit to stay overnight at the campground (see "Camping," below).

Tanque Verde Ridge Trail

6.9 mi. one way (to Juniper Basin Campground). Strenuous. Access: Javelina Picnic Area off Cactus Forest Dr.

This trail offers splendid panoramic views as it follows a ridgeline northeast into the wilderness area. You'll see saguaro, cholla, prickly pear, and other cactus for a while, and then piñon, juniper, and some oak as you climb higher into the foothills. The Juniper Basin Campground, at 6,000 feet, is 2,900 feet higher than the trailhead. Although the trail continues, this is a good spot for day hikers to turn around. See "Exploring the Backcountry," below, for information on forging ahead.

Exploring the Backcountry

All the park's backcountry hiking and camping opportunities are in the Rincon Mountain District (the eastern section), which includes the 59,930-acre **Rincon Mountain Wilderness.** Varying considerably in elevation, this area contains both hot desert sprinkled with saguaro and other cacti, and relatively cool forests

Especially for Kids

Kids will enjoy the "Please Touch" table in the **Red Hills Visitor Center.** The park also has several **Junior Ranger Programs,** in which children complete a variety of projects and activities to earn Junior Ranger badges and certificates.

of pine and mixed conifer. The main access routes into the backcountry are the **Douglas Spring Trailhead** and **Tanque Verde Ridge Trailhead,** which are discussed above. From these two trails you can access more than 100 miles of interconnecting trails, as well as the park's six backcountry campgrounds (see "Camping," below). Dirt roads lead to several other trailheads; check with park rangers for directions and current conditions. Rangers strongly suggest that those going into the backcountry carry topographical maps, which can be purchased at either visitor center. A backcountry permit is necessary for camping. Pick up the required (but free) permit at the Rincon Mountain District Visitor Center or by writing to the park.

Other Sports & Activities

Biking. Bikes are permitted on the scenic drives in both districts. In addition, mountain bikes are allowed in the Rincon Mountain District on the section of the Cactus Forest Trail within the loop drive.

Horseback Riding. Horseback riding is permitted on most trails in both districts of the park, although horses are not allowed off-trail. Horses may be kept overnight in the backcountry campgrounds in the Rincon Mountain

District. At Manning Camp there's a corral; at the other backcountry campgrounds, riders should secure horses with a picket rope slung between two trees. Get details from park rangers.

Wildlife Viewing & Bird Watching. Both sections of the park offer abundant opportunities for wildlife and bird watching, although because Saguaro East has a greater range of elevations, and therefore climates, you'll see a larger variety of animals there.

In both sections of the park, look for holes punched in saguaro cacti by Gila woodpeckers and gilded flickers. These finicky birds sometimes make several cavities before settling on one as home for the year. They always punch out a new home when they return the following year. The extra holes are taken over by other desert inhabitants, including cactus wrens, Lucy's warblers, and cute little elf owls.

Among other birds you're likely to see in both sections of the park are black-throated sparrows, brown towhees, verdin, brown-crested flycatchers, Costa's hummingbirds, roadrunners, mourning doves, white-winged doves, Gambel's quail, American kestrels, and red-tailed hawks. In the eastern part of the park you'll also see rufous-crowned sparrows, olive warblers, yellow-rumped warblers, solitary vireos, American robins, pygmy nuthatches, Steller's jays, mountain chickadees, violet-green swallows,

broad-tailed hummingbirds, and Cooper's hawks.

Mammals commonly seen in the park include desert cottontails, Harris ground squirrels, round-tailed ground squirrels, striped skunks, javelina, mule deer, and southern long-nose bats, which pollinate saguaro flowers while feeding on their nectar. You may also spot white-tailed deer in the higher elevations of Saguaro East. Reptiles commonly seen include zebra-tailed and western whiptail lizards, gopher snakes, and king snakes. In the desert and foothill areas, watch out for the many western diamondback rattlesnakes, which are poisonous.

Camping

INSIDE THE PARK

There are no drive-in campgrounds within the national park, but backpackers will find six backcountry campgrounds in the Rincon Mountain Wilderness. All the campgrounds have three sites each except Manning Camp, which has six. Water is available at Manning year-round, but water availability at the other campgrounds is spotty—ask a ranger. Campers who don't want to get sick must treat backcountry water before drinking. Backcountry camping is permitted only in designated campsites. Pick up the required (but free) permit at the Rincon Mountain District Visitor Center or by writing to the park.

Campground	Elev.	Total Sites	RV Hookups	Dump Station	Toilets	Drinking Water
Cactus Country R.V. Resort	3,300	246	246	Yes	Yes	Yes
Catalina State Park	2,700	48	23	Yes	Yes	Yes
Gilbert Ray	2,600	139	133	Yes	Yes	Yes
Molino Basin	4,370	49	0	No	Yes	No
Rose Canyon	7,200	74	0	No	Yes	Yes
Spencer Canyon	8,000	68	0	No	Yes	Yes

Four miles south of the park's Tucson Mountain District is **Gilbert Ray Campground,** just off Kinney Road on McCain Loop Road, operated by the Pima County Parks and Recreation Department (☎ 520/883-4200). It offers an attractive desert mountain environment of saguaro, prickly pear, cholla, mesquite, and paloverde, with well-maintained gravel sites. No wood fires are permitted. RV hookup sites offer electricity only.

Convenient for visitors to the national park's Tucson Mountain District, the campground at **Catalina State Park,** 9 miles north of Tucson on Ariz. 77 (☎ 520/628-5798), has nicely spaced, well-shaded sites, an abundance of rock squirrels, and splendid views of the Santa Catalina Mountains to the southeast.

There are also campgrounds in the Santa Catalina District of the **Coronado National Forest** (☎ 520/749-8700), to the north of the national park's Rincon Mountain District. Located along the Catalina Highway, they include **Molino Basin,** about 18 miles northeast of Tucson, which has virtually no facilities and can accommodate trailers up to 22 feet only; **Rose Canyon,** about 33 miles northeast of Tucson, which offers fishing at Rose Canyon Lake; and **Spencer Canyon,** located near the top of Mount Lemmon about 39 miles northeast of Tucson, which can accommodate trailers up to 18 feet only.

Among commercial campgrounds in the area are **Cactus Country RV Resort,** 10195 S. Houghton Rd. (☎ 800/777-8799), at I-10 Exit 275, which has large spaces, some shade trees, and attractive desert landscaping. All RV sites have full hookups including cable TV. There are only a small number of tent sites. Campers have access to a convenience store with RV supplies and propane, a game room, a playground, shuffleboard, and horseshoes.

Accommodations

There are no accommodations inside the park.

In addition to the lodgings listed below, you'll find dozens of chain motels along I-10, including the **Days Inn Tucson,** 222 S. Freeway (Exit 258; ☎ 520/791-7511), charging $55 to $129 double; **Motel 6—Tucson/Congress Street,** 960 S. Freeway (Exit 258; ☎ 520/628-1339), and **Motel 6—Tucson/22nd Street,** 1222 S. Freeway (Exit 259; ☎ 520/624-2516), both charging $36 to $51 double; and **Super 8—Tucson/Downtown,** 1248 N. Stone St. (Exit 257; ☎ 520/622-6446), charging $47 to $92 double. Among hotels near the airport is the **Best Western Inn at the Airport,** 7060 S. Tucson Blvd. (☎ 800/772-3847 or 520/746-0271), with winter rates from $69 to $139 double, $49 to

Showers	Fire Pits/ Grills	Laundry	Public Phone	Reserve	Fees	Open
Yes	No	Yes	Yes	Yes	$15–$25	Year-round
Yes	Yes	No	Yes	No	$10–$15	Year-round
No	No	No	Yes	No	$7–$11	Year-round
No	Yes	No	No	No	$6	Oct–Apr
No	Yes	No	No	No	$10	Apr–Oct
No	Yes	No	No	No	$10	May–Oct

$89 double at other times; and **Super 8—Tucson/East,** 1990 S. Craycroft Rd. (Exit 265 off I-10; ☎ **520/790-6021**), charging $46 to $90 double. See the appendix for a list of the national chain toll-free numbers.

Bienestar Bed & Breakfast

10490 E. Escalante Rd., Tucson, AZ 85730. ☎ **800/293-0004** or 520/290-1048. Fax 520/290-1367. www.bienestar.com. E-mail: bienestarbandb@hotmail.com. 4 units. A/C TV TEL. $90–$150 double. Rates include full breakfast. AE, DISC, MC, V. Not suitable for children.

Located on the east side of Tucson, about 2 miles from the entrance to the Rincon Mountain District of Saguaro National Park, this hacienda-style home is set amid natural desert landscaping, with a series of short nature trails. The grounds abound with wildlife. You're likely to see a wide variety of birds, including Gambel's quail, Gila woodpeckers, mourning doves, and roadrunners; plus javelina, desert cottontails, coyotes, and maybe even a bobcat.

Innkeepers Diane Strausser and Richard Scanlin provide a refreshingly tranquil lodging. All units have VCRs, refrigerators, robes, hair dryers, and firm beds. The two-room Santa Rita Suite, with red brick and white stucco walls and Southwest decor, can accommodate five, and includes a microwave oven and complete entertainment center. The delightful Casita, a separate one-bedroom unit, is decorated in Mexican motif, with handmade tile and tinwork. Popular as a honeymoon cottage, it boasts a gas fireplace and full kitchen, and a bathroom with shower only (all other units have shower/tub combos). The inn's two smaller units are equally comfortable and attractive, and one contains a king-size bed that can be converted to two twin beds.

Breakfast might include such items as baked apples with caramel sauce, Southwest tamale pie with lime hollandaise sauce, and chorizo apricot compote with brown sugar. Special diets can be accommodated with advance notice. The inn also has a meeting room, a large outside terrace, a swimming pool, and a whirlpool spa. Smoking is not permitted.

Casa Tierra

11155 W. Calle Pima, Tucson, AZ 85743. ☎ **520/578-3058.** Fax 520/578-8848. 4 units. $95–$135 double; $175–$225 suite. Rates include a full vegetarian breakfast. MC, V. Closed mid-July to mid-Aug.

If you've come to Tucson to really be a *part* of the desert, this is an excellent choice. A modern adobe home surrounded by 5 acres of cacti and paloverde, Casa Tierra is on the west side of Saguaro National Park's Tucson Mountain District, and has fabulous views of a saguaro landscape. Guests also enjoy stunning sunsets and views of the mountains to the north. Surrounding a central courtyard with a desert garden and a fountain is a covered seating area where guests congregate. The rooms have queen beds, brick floors, and private patios; the family suite includes two bedrooms, bathroom, dining area, and a library area. There's also an exercise room and a common area with TV, stereo, and games. There's an outdoor whirlpool spa that makes a perfect stargazing spot at night; a telescope is provided!

Doubletree Guest Suites

6555 E. Speedway Blvd., Tucson, AZ 85710. ☎ **800/222-TREE** or 520/721-7100. Fax 520/721-1991. www.dtguestsuites.com. 304 suites. A/C TV TEL. Mid-Sept to mid-Jan $144–$154 double; mid-Jan to mid-May $94–$114 double; mid-May to mid-Sept $75–$85 double. Rates include full breakfast (lower rates without breakfast). AE, DISC, MC, V. Pets accepted ($25 nonrefundable fee).

With surprisingly reasonable rates throughout the year, this all-suite hotel is a good choice for those who want plenty of space. The five-story brick building is arranged around two long garden courtyards, one of which has a large pool and whirlpool. The pool and gardens, along with the full breakfast and evening cocktail hour, are the best reasons for vacationers to stay here. The two-room suites feature contemporary furnishings and all have refrigerators, coffeemakers, hair dryers, and irons and ironing boards (most also have microwaves). The hotel has a restaurant, an exercise room (and access to a nearby health club), room service, and valet/laundry service.

El Adobe Ranch

4630 N. El Adobe Ranch Rd., Tucson, AZ 85745. ☎ **520/743-3525.** Fax 520/297-2080. www.arizonaguide.com/el-adobe-ranch. E-mail: ellen@eladoberanch.com. 5 casitas. Oct–Apr $175 double; May–Sept $110 double. Rates include continental breakfast. AE, MC, V.

Sort of a cross between a bed-and-breakfast and a guest ranch, this unusual lodging offers seclusion amid saguaros and accommodation in contemporary Southwestern-style casitas. Staying here is a bit like having your own modern home down a dirt road out in the desert, with the Tucson Mountain District of Saguaro National Park practically in your backyard. Three casitas—Spanish-style cabins—have their own kitchens, and two have kitchenettes and whirlpool tubs. All have fireplaces in both the living room and the bedroom.

Hotel Congress

311 E. Congress St., Tucson, AZ 85701. ☎ **800/722-8848** or 520/622-8848. Fax 520/792-6366. www.hotcong.com. 40 units. TEL. $35–$75 double. Student discount available. Lower rates for shared hostel rms. AE, MC, V.

Located in the heart of Tucson's downtown arts district, the Hotel Congress once hosted John Dillinger. Today it operates as a youth hostel and budget hotel. Conveniently located near the Greyhound and Amtrak stations, this hotel is especially popular with students and European backpackers. The lobby has been restored to its original Southwestern elegance, and most of the hostel rooms have been recently renovated.

Some bathrooms have tubs only and others have showers only. There's a cyberbar with high-speed Internet access, a popular cafe off the lobby, and an appropriately Western bar. At night the Club Congress is a popular and loud dance club. Guests can pick up free earplugs at the front desk if they want to sleep through the noise.

Smuggler's Inn

6350 E. Speedway Blvd. (at Wilmot), Tucson, AZ 85710. ☎ **800/525-8852** or 520/296-3292. Fax 520/722-3713. E-mail: smugglers@rtd.com. 150 units. A/C TV TEL. Jan–Mar $99–$119 double, $125–$135 suite; Apr–May $89–$119 double, $125 suite; June–Sept $79 double, $89 suite; Oct–Dec $89–$119 double, $99 suite. AE, CB, DC, DISC, MC, V.

Built around an attractive garden and pond, the Smuggler's Inn is a comfortable and economically priced hotel, with neatly trimmed lawns and tall palm trees that provide a tropical look. Guest rooms are spacious, and all have modern furnishings and a balcony or patio. A fairly recent renovation has kept the rooms in good shape. Amenities include coffeemakers and video games on the TVs, a cocktail lounge, golf and health club privileges available, and an outdoor pool, whirlpool, and putting green.

Wayward Winds Lodge

707 W. Miracle Mile, Tucson, AZ 85705. ☎ **800/791-9503** or 520/791-7526. Fax 520/791-9502. 40 units. A/C TV TEL. Mid-Dec to mid-Apr $69–$129 double; mid-Apr to mid-Dec $59–$85. Kitchenettes, mid-Dec to mid-Apr $89–$149 double; mid-Apr to mid-Dec $69–$99. Rates include continental breakfast mid-Dec to mid-Apr. DC, DISC, MC, V. Pets accepted.

Spacious rooms, a delightful large pool, and nicely landscaped grounds make the Wayward Winds a good choice for those seeking a good clean motel room at a reasonable rate. Family owned and operated since it opened in 1958, the motel's well-maintained units have vaulted ceilings with exposed beams, brick and stucco walls, wood furnishings, and Southwest decor. There are nine kitchenette units, plus shuffleboard courts, barbecues, a coin-operated laundry, and covered parking.

Dining

There are no restaurants inside the park.

NEAR THE PARK

Anthony's in the Catalinas

6440 N. Campbell Ave. ☎ **520/299-1771.** Reservations highly recommended. Main courses $7.50–$15 at lunch, $19–$30 at dinner. AE, DC, MC, V. Mon–Fri 11:30am–2:30pm and 5:30–10pm; Sat–Sun 5:30–10pm. SOUTHWESTERN/CONTINENTAL.

If you head north on Campbell Avenue up into the foothills of the Catalinas, you'll come to this modern hacienda-style building overlooking the city. Anthony's exudes Southwestern elegance from the moment you drive under the portico and let the valet park your car. The waiters are smartly attired in tuxedos and the guests are almost as well dressed. Quiet classical music plays in the background, and the lights of the city below twinkle through the windows. In such a rarefied atmosphere you'd expect only the finest meal, and that's what you get. Smoked salmon is a fitting beginning, followed by lamb Wellington, baked in puff pastry with pâté and prosciutto. At 80 pages, the wine list is quite likely the most extensive in the city. The pastry selection may tempt you, but, if it's available, don't miss out on the best part of a meal: the day's soufflé (order early).

El Charro Cafe

311 N. Court Ave. ☎ **520/622-1922.** Reservations recommended for dinner. Main courses $5–$14. AE, CB, DC, DISC, MC, V. Sun–Thurs 11:30am–10pm, Fri–Sat 11:30am–11pm. MEXICAN.

Located in an old stone building in El Presidio Historic District, El Charro claims to be Tucson's oldest family operated Mexican restaurant—it's been serving authentic Tucson-style Mexican food for almost 80 years. A porch has been glassed in for a greenhouselike dining area overlooking the street, and there's also dining downstairs. Look at the roof of El Charro as you approach, and you might see a large metal cage containing beef drying in the sun. This is the main ingredient in *carne seca*, El Charro's well-known specialty, rarely found outside the Tucson area.

Other El Charro branches can be found in the Tucson International Airport (☎ **520/573-8222**) and at 6310 E. Broadway (☎ **520/745-1922**). Adjacent to all locations is the family run Toma!, a colorful bar/cantina, and a gift shop.

Little Anthony's Diner

7010 E. Broadway Blvd. ☎ **520/296-0456.** Burgers and sandwiches $4–$7. MC, V. Mon 11am–9pm, Tues–Thurs 11am–10pm, Fri 11am–11pm, Sat 8am–11pm, Sun 8am–10pm. AMERICAN.

This is a great place for kids, although kids-at-heart will also enjoy the 1950s music and decor. The staff is good with children, and there's a video-game room and a rocket ship outside to ride. How about a Jailhouse Rock Burger or Hound Dog Hot Dog with a tower of onion rings? Daily specials and bottomless soft drinks make feeding the family fairly inexpensive. Beer and wine are also served. Most nights after 5pm there's a DJ along with the dinner.

Pronto

2955 E. Speedway Blvd. ☎ **520/326-9707** (for take-out). $3.50–$10. MC, V. Mon–Thurs 11am–9pm, Fri–Sat 11am–10pm. INTERNATIONAL.

A good example of what can be done to recycle a fast-food establishment, Pronto retains the walk-up counter, but now boasts an international menu and hip decor. Come here for fast, affordable food in an informal setting. You'll discover innovative twists on old standards such as burgers, sandwiches, tacos, salads, pizzas, and pastas—plus more exotic creations such as Mediterranean-style vegetarian dishes and chicken satay. Beer, wine, and espresso are available. Sit at the collage-topped cafe-style tables or get your order to go—Pronto is consistently voted Tucson's best take-out restaurant by readers of a local newspaper.

Scordato's

4405 W. Speedway Blvd. ☎ **520/792-3055.** Reservations highly recommended. Main courses $16–$21. AE, CB, DC, DISC, MC, V. Daily 5–9pm. ITALIAN.

Located near Saguaro West, this restaurant looks a bit like a lost Italian villa searching for the Mediterranean Coast, with saguaros standing next to cypresses out front. Inside, plush carpets, comfortable brocade chairs, and big windows allow diners to enjoy desert views in comfort. Despite the crystal chandeliers and tapestries on the walls, you don't have to dress up for dinner here, where you'll find both families and business types. The menu contains many tempting choices, although it's difficult to move beyond the veal. Veal stresa is a favorite—it's stuffed with prosciutto and mozzarella and then sautéed in marsala and white-wine sauce. There's an extensive wine list.

The Tack Room

7300 E. Vactor Ranch Trail (off Sabino Canyon Rd., about 0.5 mi. north of Tanque Verde Rd.). ☎ **520/722-2800.** Reservations recommended. Main courses $24.50–$34. AE, DC, DISC, MC, V. Daily 6–11pm (closed Mon May to mid-Jan). SOUTHWESTERN/AMERICAN.

The Tack Room is Tucson's most prestigious restaurant, and dining here is a very special experience. Housed in an older Southwestern-style hacienda with an atmosphere of casual elegance, The Tack Room has a bevy of tuxedoed waiters who attend to your every need, with service that is both attentive and discreet. Diners are pampered from the time they sit down and taste the little bites of marinated salads to the moment the last bit of dessert is savored. Particularly tasty are the plump guaymas shrimp subtly seasoned with orange zest and garlic, the perfectly grilled salmon with papaya salsa, and the crisp yet succulent duck. Coffee comes with a condiment tray that includes whipped cream and crumbled Belgian chocolate.

Picnic & Camping Supplies

Although there are no stores within the park's boundaries, you'll find plenty of places to stock up on supplies in the Tucson area. Recommended for basic groceries are the numerous **Safeway** supermarkets, including the one at 7110 N. Oracle Rd., Tucson (☎ **520/575-0949**), which has a deli, bakery, pharmacy, and liquor department, in addition to a good selection of groceries. You'll also find pretty much any food and beverages you need at the area's several **Albertson's Food & Drug Stores,** including the outlet at 6363 E. 22nd St. (☎ **520/571-9091**).

For camping, hiking, backpacking, and mountain-biking gear, as well as tips on outdoor recreation locations, stop at **Summit Hut,** 5045 E. Speedway Blvd., Tucson (☎ **520/325-1554**), open 7 days a week and offering both sales and rentals. Another good bet for supplies and equipment is **Popular Outdoor Outfitters,** 6315 E. Broadway Blvd. (at Wilmot) (☎ **520/290-1644**), also open 7 days a week.

33

SEQUOIA & KINGS CANYON NATIONAL PARKS

by Stacey Wells

I N THE HEART OF THE SIERRA NEVADA, JUST SOUTH OF YOSEMITE, ARE Sequoia and Kings Canyon national parks, home to the largest Giant Sequoia trees in the world and a deep gorge of a canyon that rivals Yosemite Valley. Sequoia and Kings Canyon are separate

parks snuggled next to one another and managed as a single entity. Combined, they outsize Yosemite. Their peaks stretch across 1,350 square miles and include the 14,494-foot Mount Whitney, the tallest point in the continental United States. The parks are also home to the Kaweah Range, a string of dark, beautiful mountains nestled amid the Sierra, and three powerful rivers: the Kings, Kern, and Kaweah. Despite their size, these two parks attract less than half the number of Yosemite's annual visitors, making them an appreciated alternative for those looking to avoid huge crowds.

In fact, visitors from Yosemite might find the contrast shocking. You won't find four dozen ranger-led hikes here, or a shuttle bus with drivers pointing out landmarks like tour guides. There are no special events, nothing aimed at bringing more folks in than would otherwise come just to see the beauty and majesty of the largest living things on earth. None of this is likely to change any time soon. The Park Service here is determined to learn from Yosemite's mistakes

and so are residents in nearby towns. This is nature, not Disneyland. Expect far fewer people, far less to entertain, and far more to explore at your leisure.

The parks owe their existence to a small band of determined conservationists in the mid-1800s. Alarmed by the wholesale destruction of the region's sequoia forests, these farsighted people pushed to make the area a protected park. Finally, Sequoia National Park was created in 1890, along with the tiny General Grant National Park, which was established to protect Grant Grove. But the move was too late to spare the Converse Basin from the profiteers. Once the largest stand of Giant Sequoias in the world, today it's a cemetery of tree stumps, the grave markers of fallen giants.

In 1926, the park was expanded eastward to include the smaller Kern Canyon and Mount Whitney. But rumblings continued over the fate of Kings Canyon itself. For awhile, its future lie as a reservoir. It wasn't until the 1960s that Kings Canyon was finally protected for good. In

1978, Mineral King was added to Sequoia's half of the park and since then, the boundaries have stayed put. The parks have been managed jointly since World War II.

Avoiding the Crowds. Though Sequoia and Kings Canyon national parks are far less visited than nearby Yosemite, it still can get crowded, especially in the summer high season. Luckily, there's a lot of empty space in these parks, so it's relatively easy to find solitude once you leave your car and start walking. To get the most access to the park while avoiding traffic, try to visit before Memorial Day or after Labor Day, keeping in mind that snow can limit access in the high elevations. Fall provides some scenic color often missing from the California landscape. As always, a trip to the backcountry will help avoid the crowds.

You can also try taking one of the dead-end roads into the park. Mineral King, South Fork and, to a lesser extent, Cedar Grove, all lack the through traffic prevalent on the larger highways.

Just the Facts

GETTING THERE & GATEWAYS

There are two main entrances to the parks. Calif. 198 via Visalia and the town of Three Rivers leads to the **Ash Mountain Entrance** in Sequoia National Park. Calif. 180 via Fresno leads straight to the **Big Stump Entrance** near Grant Grove in Kings Canyon National Park. There are also three dead-end entrance roads open only in the summer: the Kings Canyon Highway (a continuation of Calif. 180) to **Cedar Grove** in Kings Canyon National Park, and two smaller roads to **Mineral King** and to **South Fork,** both in the south part of Sequoia National Park.

The parks are roughly equidistant (5 hrs. by car) from both San Francisco and Los Angeles. The Ash Mountain Entrance is 36 miles from Visalia, or

about an hour away. The Big Stump Entrance is 53 miles from Fresno, or about 1½ hours away.

The Nearest Airports. The closest major airport is **Fresno-Yosemite International Airport** (☎ 559/498-4095), 53 miles from the Big Stump Entrance in Kings Canyon. It's served by **America West, American Eagle, Delta Connection, Sky West-Continental United Airlines, United Express, Alaska, Northwest, Mexicana,** and **US Airways,** with direct connections with airports in San Francisco and Los Angeles, and cars from most major rental companies. **Visalia Municipal Airport** (☎ 559/738-3201) is a tiny airstrip 36 miles from the Ash Mountain Entrance that's served by **United Express** (☎ 800/241-6522).

Toll-free reservations numbers for airlines and car rentals are in the appendix.

INFORMATION

Contact **Sequoia & Kings Canyon National Park,** 47050 Generals Hwy., Three Rivers, CA 93271-9651 (☎ 209/565-3341, or 209/565-3134 for a live operator; www.nps.gov/seki).

VISITOR CENTERS

There are three visitor centers in the parks where you can buy books and maps. The biggest is in Sequoia National Park at **Lodgepole** and it's open spring, summer, and fall. It's 4.5 miles north of Giant Forest Village, near a new museum of the sequoias. Lodgepole includes exhibits on geology, wildlife, air quality, and park history. The **Foothills Visitor Center** just inside the Ash Mountain Entrance on Highway 198, is open all year and includes exhibits on the chaparral region's ecosystem. The visitor center in **Grant Grove,** Kings Canyon National Park, includes exhibits on logging and the role of fire in the forests. It's also open year-round.

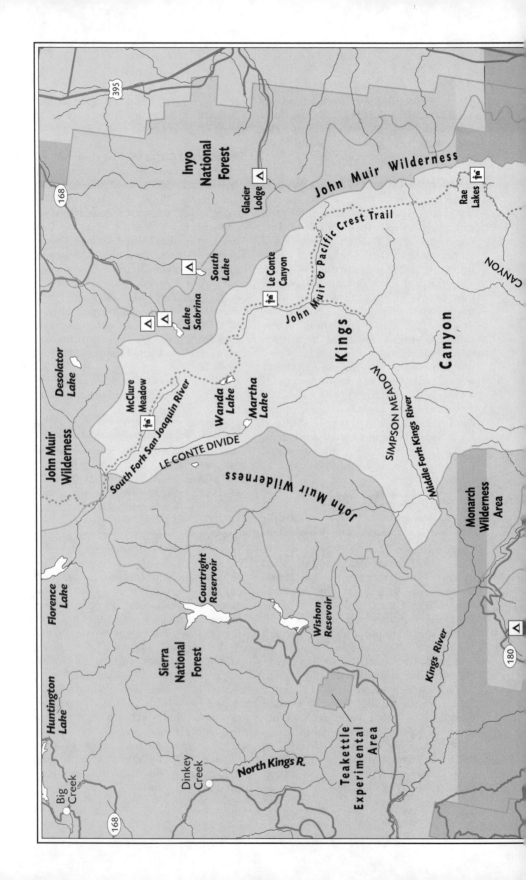

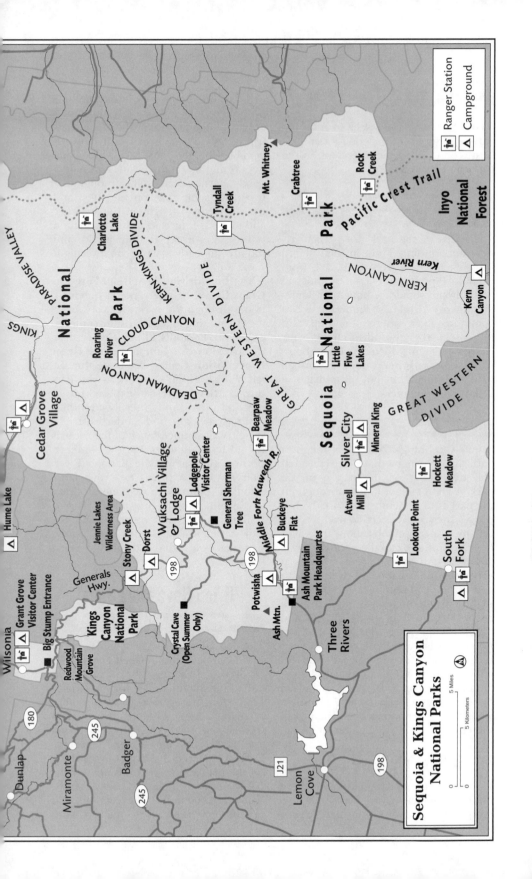

Sequoia & Kings Canyon National Parks

🏚	Ranger Station
▲	Campground

FEES

It costs $10 per car per week to enter the park or $5 for individuals on foot or bike. Cost is $6 to $16 a night to camp in the park campgrounds.

SPECIAL REGULATIONS & WARNINGS

The roads in the park are particularly steep and winding. Those in RVs will find it easiest to come from Calif. 180 from Fresno. Piped water is safe, but all groundwater should be boiled for 3 minutes before drinking. Rattlesnakes are common; look where you step and touch. In the foothills, check your clothes frequently for ticks. Beware also of black bears. When camping, store all food in lockers and put all garbage in bear-proof containers.

SEASONS & CLIMATE

Sequoia and Kings Canyon, for the most part, share a climate that varies considerably depending on the region of the park. A good rule of thumb throughout the park is to remember that the higher you go, the cooler it gets. So pack a parka on any trip that climbs above the valley floor or ventures into the backcountry.

During the summer, temperatures at lower elevations can climb into the 90s and higher, and plummet into the 50s at night. Afternoon temperatures average in the 60s and 70s in spring and fall, and again, evenings are usually cool. Afternoon showers are fairly common year-round. Winter days average in the 40s and 50s, and seldom drop below zero, although much of the land is buried beneath several feet of snow. Remember, a particularly wet winter often leads to an incredibly stunning and powerful spring.

If You Only Have 1 Day

Eighty percent of park visitors come here on day trips—an amazing statistic considering the geography of this place. Three to 4 days will do the park justice, but it is possible to take a short walk through a grove of big trees in one afternoon. Day-trippers should stick to Grant Grove if possible—it's the most accessible. Coming from the south, Giant Forest is a good alternative as well, although the trip takes some time on the steep and narrow Generals Highway. Cedar Grove and Mineral King, two other destination points, are a bit farther afield and require an early start or an overnight stay.

Consider **driving from Giant Forest to Grant Grove,** or vice versa. It's about 2 hours through the park. Get your bearings by starting at a park visitor center—either the **Foothills Visitor Center** near the Ash Mountain Entrance or the **Grant Grove Visitor Center.** You'll see the varied climate within the park as you pass through dense forest to exposed meadows and then through scrubby foothills covered in oaks and underbrush. In spring and summer, much of the route is dotted by wildflowers and the southern portion runs along the Kaweah River. This route also passes near two large stands of Giant Sequoias, one at Grant Grove and the other at Giant Forest. Both have easy trails looping through the majestic stands. At Grant Grove, a footpath passes lengthwise through a fallen sequoia.

If You Have More Time

SEQUOIA NATIONAL PARK

The best-known stand of sequoias in the world can be found in **Giant Forest,** part of Sequoia National Park. Named in 1875 by explorer and environmentalist John Muir, this park consists mostly of huge meadows and a large grove of giant trees. At the northern edge of the grove, you can't miss the **General Sherman Tree,** considered the largest living thing on the planet, although it is neither the tallest nor the widest. It is believed to be between 2,300 and 2,700 years old, *and it's still growing.* Every year, it adds enough new wood to make another 60-foot-tall tree. The tree is part of the 2-mile **Congress Trail,** a foot trail that includes groups of trees with names such as The Senate and The House.

Another interesting stop in Giant Forest is **Tharp's Log,** a cabin named after the first non–Native American settler in the area, Hale Tharp, who grazed cattle among the Giant Sequoias and built a summer cabin in the 1860s from a fallen sequoia hollowed by fire. It is the oldest cabin remaining in the park.

You'll also encounter two kitschy items in the Giant Forest vicinity. **Tunnel Log** is a toppled tree that you can drive *through,* and **Auto Log** is a tree that you can drive *on.*

Nearby **Crescent Meadow** is a pristine clearing dotted with wildflowers and tall grasses. A trail wraps around the meadow. This is also the trailhead for several backcountry hikes.

Also in the area is **Moro Rock,** a large granite dome that offers one of the most spectacular views in the Sierra. From atop the rock, the high-elevation, barren mountains in the Kaweah Range appear dark and ominous. Snow caps the ridgeline throughout the year. While the cliffs appear towering and steep, they are actually smaller than the summit of the Sierra, which is obscured from view. The walk to the top takes visitors up hundreds of stairs and requires about a half hour to get up. At the top is a narrow, fenced plateau with endless views. During a full moon, the mountain peaks shimmer like silver.

South of the Giant Forest is the turnoff for **Crystal Cave,** one of more than 100 caves in the park and one of just two in the area that offer guided tours (Boyden Cavern in the neighboring national forest is the other). The cave is composed of limestone that has turned to marble, and is full of stalactites and stalagmites. To reach the entrance, drive 7 miles down the narrow, winding road (RVs, trailers, and buses are prohibited), and the cave entrance is an additional 15-minute walk down a steep path. The Sequoia Natural History Association conducts 45-minute tours daily between 11am and 4pm from June to Labor Day, and less often in May and late September. Tickets are not sold at the cave, but rather at the Lodgepole and Foothills visitor centers. Cost is $5 for adults, $2.50 for children and seniors with a Golden Eagle Pass, and free for children under age 6. Information is also available by telephone (☎ 209/565-3759). It gets cold underground, so bring a sweater or jacket.

Near the Giant Forest, you will also find a new development, **Wuksachi Village,** which includes a dining room, gift shop, and lodge.

Lodgepole, the most developed area in both parks, lies just northeast of the Giant Forest on the Generals Highway. Here, you'll find the largest visitor center, a large market, several places to eat, the **Walter Fry Nature Center** (see "Especially for Kids," below), a laundry, and a post office.

South of Giant Forest about 16 miles is the region of the park known as the **Foothills.** Located near the Ash Mountain Entrance, the Foothills has a visitor center, several campgrounds, and **Hospital Rock,** a large boulder with ancient pictographs that are believed to have been painted by the Monache Indians, who once lived here. Nearby are about 50 grinding spots once used to smash acorns into flour. A short trail leads down to a beautiful spot along the Kaweah River where the water gushes over rapids into deep, clear pools. Hospital Rock also has a nice picnic area.

Mineral King is a pristine, undeveloped region in the southern part of the park. This high-mountain valley was carved by glaciers and is bordered by the tall peaks of the Great Western Divide. To reach this area, patient drivers must follow the marked highway sign 3 miles outside Sequoia National Park's Ash Mountain Entrance. From the turnoff to Mineral King, it's a 28-mile trip that makes many tight turns and takes 1.5 hours to drive. Trailers, RVs, and buses are not allowed. The road is closed in winter.

The rocky landscape in Mineral King is as colorful as a rainbow—red and orange shales mix with white marble and black metamorphic shale and granite. In winter, this area is prone to avalanches. The most prominent point in the area is **Sawtooth Peak,** which reaches 12,343 feet. Sawtooth and other peaks in this region resemble the Rocky Mountains more than the rest of the Sierra Nevada because they are made of metaphoric rocks. The trails in Mineral King begin at 7,500 feet and climb from there. Park rangers sometimes conduct hikes around here. The best way to experience Mineral King is to stay overnight in one of two nearby campgrounds.

KINGS CANYON NATIONAL PARK

With its rugged canyon, huge river, and desolate backcountry, Kings Canyon is considered a hiker's dream. It consists of Grant Grove and Cedar Grove, as well as portions of the Monarch Wilderness and Jennie Lakes Wilderness. *One other point of note:* Between Grant Grove and Cedar Grove is a stretch of land not in the park, but in Sequoia National Forest instead. This region includes Hume Lake, Boyden Cavern, and several campgrounds.

Grant Grove is the most crowded region in either park. Not only is it located just a few miles from a main entrance, but the area is also a thoroughfare for travelers heading from Giant Forest to the south or Cedar Grove to the east. The grove was designated as General Grant National Park in 1890, and was incorporated when Kings Canyon National Park was formed in 1940.

Here you'll find the towering **General Grant Tree** amid a grove of spectacular Giant Sequoias. The tree was discovered by Joseph Hardin Tomas in 1862 and named 5 years later to honor Ulysses S. Grant. It measures 267.4 feet tall, 107.6 feet around, and is thought to be the world's third-largest living thing, possibly

2,000 years old. This tree has been officially declared "The Nation's Christmas Tree" and is the cornerstone of the park's annual Christmas tree ceremony.

Two and a half miles southwest of the grove is the **Big Stump Trail,** an instructive hike that can be slightly depressing as it winds among the remains of logged sequoias. Since sequoia wood decays slowly, you'll see century-old leftover piles of sawdust that remain from the logging days. Nearby, **Panoramic Point** visitors can stand atop a 7,520-foot ledge and see across a large stretch of the Sierra, and across Kings Canyon. **Grant Grove Village** also has a restaurant, market, gift shop, and visitor center.

Although in the same park, **Cedar Grove** seems a world away. That this region is around today is sheer luck. There were plans to flood Kings Canyon by damming the Kings River. With that future thwarted, the region stood to become another Yosemite, but people fought hard to prevent that fate and eventually everyone agreed that there are better uses for the Sierra than to convert it to a giant parking garage. Even after the park was established, Cedar Grove was excluded due to the controversy over how this region would be developed. It was finally annexed in 1965 and under a master plan for the area, will remain as it is today. One look and you'll see why any other alternative would have been foolish.

Cedar Grove is covered with lush landscape, tumbling waterfalls, and miles upon miles of solitude. Half the fun is driving through **Kings Canyon** as its sheer granite walls close around you and the wild South Fork of the Kings River races by. One mile east of the Cedar Grove Village turnoff is **Canyon View,** where visitors can see the glacially carved U shape of Kings Canyon. Easily accessible nature trails in Cedar Grove include Zumwalt Meadow, Roaring River Falls, and Knapp's Cabin. **Zumwalt Meadow** is dotted with ponderosa pine and has good views of two rock formations, the

Grand Sentinel and **North Dome.** The top of Grand Sentinel is 8,504 feet above sea level while North Dome, which some say resembles Half Dome in Yosemite, towers over the area at 8,717 feet. The mile-long trail around the meadow is one of the prettiest in the park. The best place to access this walk is at a parking lot 4.5 miles east of the turnoff for Cedar Grove Village.

Roaring River Falls is a 5-minute walk from the parking area 3 miles east of the turnoff to the village. Even during summer and dry years, water crashes through a narrow granite chute into a cold, green pool below. During a wet spring, these falls are powerful enough to drench visitors who venture too close. **Knapp's Cabin** can be reached via a short walk from a turnoff 2 miles east of the road to Cedar Grove Village. Here, during the 1920s, Santa Barbara businessman George Knapp commissioned lavish fishing expeditions. This tiny cabin was used to store tons of expensive gear.

Ten miles west of Cedar Grove, in the national forest and back toward Grant Grove, is the entrance to **Boyden Cave,** the only other cave in the area to host tours. Boyden Cave welcomes visitors in summertime only (☎ 209/736-2708). Cost is $7 for adults and children age 14 and up, and $3.50 for children ages 3 to 13. Children under age 3 are admitted free. Tickets can be purchased at the entrance. The cave is open May to October from 11am to 4pm daily.

Cedar Grove also has a small village with a store and gift shop, restaurant, laundry, showers, lodge, and campgrounds. This region of the park is often less crowded than others because it is at the end of the road. It is closed from mid-November to mid-April.

The **Monarch Wilderness** is a 45,000-acre region protected under the 1984 California Wilderness Act. Part of it lies on the grounds of Sequoia National Forest and it adjoins wilderness in Kings Canyon National Park. It's small, tough to reach, and so steep that hikers practically need to be roped in to climb. You're near the wilderness area when you pass Kings Canyon Lodge and Boyden Cave.

The **Jennie Lakes Wilderness** is even smaller at 10,500 acres. Although tiny enough to hike through in a day, it exhibits a variety of wilderness features, including the 10,365-foot Mitchell Peak and several wide, lowland meadows. This region lies between the Generals Highway and Highway 180, east of Grant Grove.

Organized Tours & Ranger Programs

Once again, Sequoia and Kings Canyon national parks are not Yosemite—there aren't a lot of organized activities. Those programs that are offered are seasonal and apt to change at whim. Pick up the park newspaper, *The Sequoia Bark,* or ask at a visitor center for details.

Day Hikes

NEAR GIANT FOREST

Congress Trail

2 mi. RT. Easy. Access: General Sherman Tree, just off the Generals Hwy., 2 mi. northeast of Giant Forest Village.

This self-guided nature walk circles some of Sequoia National Park's most well known and loved giants. The trail is a paved loop with a 200-foot elevation gain. Here you'll find the General Sherman Tree, considered to be the largest living thing on earth. Other Giant Sequoias along this loop include the President, Chief Sequoyah, General Lee, and McKinley trees. The Lincoln tree is nearby. Several groups of trees include The House and The Senate. Try standing in the middle of these small clusters of trees to gain the perspective of an ant at a picnic. The walk is dotted with inviting benches.

Crescent Meadow Loop

1.8 mi. RT. Easy. Access: Crescent Meadow parking area.

The meadow is a large, picturesque clearing dotted with high grass and wildflowers, encircled by a forest of firs and sequoias. The park's oldest cabin (Tharp's Log) is along this route as well. This is a particularly nice hike in early morning and at dusk, when the indirect sunlight allows those with a camera to take the best pictures.

Hazelwood Nature Trail

1 mi. RT. Easy. Access: South side of the Generals Hwy., across from the road to Round Meadow.

Follow the signs for a good, educational walk with exhibits that explain the relationship between trees, fire, and humans while winding among several stands of sequoias.

High Sierra Trail

9 mi. RT. Moderate. Access: Near the rest rooms at the Crescent Meadow parking area.

This is one gateway to the backcountry, but the first few miles also make a great day hike. Along the way are spectacular views of the Kaweah River's middle fork and the Great Western Divide. The trail runs along a south-facing slope and is therefore warm in spring and fall. Get an early start in summer. From the trailhead, cross two wooden bridges over Crescent Creek until you reach a junction. Tharp's Log is to the left, the High Sierra Trail to the right. Hike uphill and a bit further on through the damage done by the Buckeye Fire of 1988, a blaze ignited by a discarded cigarette 3,000 feet below near the Kaweah River. After 0.75 mile you'll reach Eagle View, which offers a picturesque vision of the Great Western Divide. To the south are the craggy Castle Rocks.

Continue on to see Panther Rock, Alta Peak, and Alta Meadow. At 2.75 miles is a sign to the Wolverton Cutoff, a trail used as a stock route between the Wolverton Corrals and the high country. A bit further on is Panther Creek and a small waterfall. At 3.25 miles is another fork of Panther Creek and above is the pink and gray Panther Rock. Follow a few more creeks to reach the last fork of Panther Creek, down a steep, eroded ravine.

Huckleberry Trail

4 mi. RT. Moderate. Access: Hazelwood Nature Trail parking area, 0.3 mi. east of Giant Forest Village on the Generals Hwy.

This is a great hike with a lot of beauty and not a lot of people. It passes through forest and meadow, near a 100-year-old cabin and an old Indian village. The first mile of this hike takes you along the Hazelwood Nature Trail. Head south at each junction until you see a big sign with blue lettering that marks the start of the Huckleberry Trail. You pass a small creek and meadow before reaching a second sign to Huckleberry Meadow. The next mile is steep and there's a cross beneath sequoias, dogwood, and white fir. At the 1.5-mile point is a Squatter's Cabin, built in the 1880s. East of the cabin is a trail junction. Head north (left) up a short hill. At the next junction, veer left along the edges of Circle Meadow for about a quarter mile before you reach another junction. The right is a short detour to Bear's Bathtub, a pair of sequoias hollowed by fire and filled with water. Legend has it that an old mountain guide named Chester Wright once surprised a bear taking a bath here, hence its name. Continue on the trail heading northeast to the Washington Tree, almost as big as the General Sherman Tree, then on to Alta Trail. Turn west (left) to Little Deer Creek. On both sides of the creek are Indian mortar holes. Some of the largest are 3 feet in diameter and their function is unknown. At the next junction, head north (right) to return to the Generals Highway and the last leg of the Huckleberry Trail to the parking area.

Moro Rock

0.25 mi. one way. Moderate. Access: Moro Rock parking area.

This walk climbs 300 feet up 400 steps that twist along this gigantic bolder perched perilously on a ridge top. Take it slow. The view from the top is breathtaking. It stretches to the Great Western Divide, which looks barren and dark, like the end of the world. Mountains are often snowcapped well into summer. During a full moon, the view is even stranger, and more beautiful.

Moro Rock and Soldiers Loop Trail

4.6 mi. RT. Moderate. Access: 30 yd. west of the cafeteria at Giant Forest Village.

This hike cuts cross-country from the village to Moro Rock. Part of the early trail is parallel to a main road, but the trail quickly departs from the traffic and heads through a forest dotted with Giant Sequoias. A carpet of ferns occasionally hides the trail. It pops out at Moro Rock, and then it's just a quick heart-thumper to the top.

Trail of the Sequoias

6 mi. RT. Moderate. Access: The northeast end of the General Sherman Tree parking area.

This trail offers a longer, more remote hike into Giant Forest, away from the crowds and along some of the more scenic points of this plateau. The first quarter mile is along the Congress Trail before heading uphill at Alta Trail. Look for signs that read Trail of the Sequoias. After 1.5 miles, including a 0.5-mile steep climb among Giant Sequoias, is the ridge of the Giant Forest. Here are a variety of specimens, young and old, fallen and sturdy. Notice the shallow root system of fallen trees, and the lightning-blasted tops of others still standing. The trail continues to Log Meadow, past Crescent Meadow and Chimney Tree, a sequoia hollowed by fire. At the junction with Huckleberry Trail, follow the blue and green signs north toward the General Sherman Tree and back to Congress Trail.

Azalea Trail

3 mi. RT. Easy. Access: Grant Grove Visitor Center.

From the visitor center, walk past the amphitheater to the Sunset Campground and cross Calif. 180. The first mile joins the South Boundary Trail as it meanders through Wilsonia and crisscrosses Sequoia Creek in a gentle climb. After 1.5 miles is the third crossing of Sequoia Creek, which may be dry in late summer, but the banks are lush with ferns and brightly colored azaleas. Return the way you came.

Big Stump Trail

1 mi. RT. Easy. Access: Picnic area near the entrance to Grant Grove from Kings Canyon.

This trail meanders through what was once a grove of Giant Sequoias. All that's left today are the old stumps and piles of 100-year-old sawdust. A brochure available at visitor centers (and at the trailhead during the summer) describes the logging that occurred here in the 1880s. To continue onward, see the Hitchcock Meadow Trail described below, which leads to Viola Fall.

Dead Giant Loop

2.25 mi. RT. Easy. Access: The lower end of the General Grant Tree parking area, at a locked gate with a sign that reads "North Grove Loop."

The Dead Giant Loop and the North Grove Loop (described below) share the first 0.75 mile. The trail descends a fire road and after a quarter mile hits a junction. Take the lower trail. After another half mile you'll break off from the North Grove Loop and head south around a lush meadow. It's another quarter mile to a sign that reads "Dead Giant." Turn west to see what's left of this tree. The trail climbs slightly as it circles a knoll and comes to Sequoia Lake Overlook. The lake was formed in 1899 when the Kings River Lumber Company built a dam on Mill Flat Creek. The water was diverted down a flume to the town of Sanger. During logging, millions of board feet of Giant Sequoias were floated down that flume to be finished at a mill in Sanger. The lumber company went bankrupt in a few years and sold the operation to new owners who moved it over to Converse Basin. The lumber company clear-cut Converse Basin, once the world's largest stand of sequoias. Continue around the loop back to the Dead Giant sign, then head back to the parking area.

General Grant Tree Trail

0.5 mi. RT. Easy. Access: Grant Tree parking area 1 mi. northwest of the visitor center.

The walk leads to the huge General Grant Tree, which is also the nation's only living national shrine. Signs help visitors interpret forest features.

Hitchcock Meadow Trail

3.5 mi. RT. Easy. Access: Picnic area near the entrance to Grant Grove from Kings Canyon.

This trail arrives at the pretty Viola Fall. The first half mile mirrors the Big Stump Trail described above. From there, hike another quarter mile to Hitchcock Meadow, a large clearing actually in Sequoia National Forest that is surrounded by sequoia stumps. Notice the small sequoias in this area, these are the descendants of the Giant Sequoias logged in the last century. From here the trail climbs slightly to a ridge, where it reenters Kings Canyon National Park before descending a short series of steep switchbacks to Sequoia Creek. Cross the creek and look for a sign directing you to Viola Falls, a series of short steps that join into one fall when the water level is high. It is very dangerous to venture down the canyon, but above it are several flat places that make great picnic spots.

North Grove Loop

1.2 mi. RT. Easy. Access: Lower end of the General Grant Tree parking area.

The trail follows an abandoned mill road from long ago. It cuts through stands of dogwood, sugar pine, sequoia, and white fir. A large dead sequoia shows evidence of a fire.

Park Ridge Trail

4.7 mi. RT. Easy. Access: Panoramic Point parking area, a 2.5-mi. drive down a steep road from Grant Grove Village.

This hike begins by walking south along the ridge, where views of the valley and peaks dominate. On a clear day, you can see Hume Lake in Sequoia National Forest, the San Joaquin Valley and occasionally, the coast range 100 miles away. Return the same way.

Sunset Trail

6 mi. RT. Moderate to strenuous. Access: Across the road from the Grant Grove Visitor Center.

The hike climbs 1,400 feet past two waterfalls and a lake. After crossing the highway, the trail heads left around a campground. After 1.25 miles, follow the South Boundary Trail toward Viola Falls. You'll reach a paved road where you can head to the right to see the park's original entrance. Return the way you came, or follow the road to the General Grant Tree parking area and walk to the visitor center.

NEAR CEDAR GROVE

Bubbs Creek Trail

8 mi. RT. Moderate to strenuous. Access: East end of the parking area at Road's End.

The trail begins by crossing and recrossing Copper Creek. This site was once an Indian village and shards of obsidian can still be found on the ground. After the first mile you'll enter a swampy area that offers a good place to watch for wildlife. The trail here closes in on the river, where deer and bear drink. At 2 miles, you'll come to a junction. The trail to Paradise Valley heads north (left), while the hike to Bubbs Creek veers right and crosses Bailey Bridge, over the South Fork of the Kings River.

Continue hiking east over four small, wooden bridges that cross Bubbs Creek. The creek was named after John Bubbs, a prospector and rancher who arrived here in 1864. The trail will climb on the creek's north side, throwing in a few steep switchbacks to keep you alert. The switchbacks also provide nice, alternating views of the canyon of Paradise Valley and Cedar Grove. At 3 miles is a large, emerald pool with waterfalls. Far above is a rock formation named the Sphinx by John Muir. At 4 miles you enter Sphinx Creek, a nice place to spend the day or night (with a wilderness permit). There are several campsites nearby. Hike back the way you came or along the Sentinel Trail described below.

Mist Falls

8 mi. RT. Moderate to strenuous. Access: Short-term parking area at Road's End, past Cedar Grove Village and follow the signs.

This is one of the more popular trails leading to the backcountry, but it's also a nice day hike. The first 2 miles are dry, until you reach Bubbs Creek Bridge. Take the fork to the left and head uphill. The first waterfall is not your destination point, although it is a pretty spot to take a break. From here, the trail meanders along the river, through forest and swamp areas before it comes out at the base of Mist Falls, a wide fall that flows generously in spring. There are dozens of great picnic spots here, and along the way up. Return along the same route, or at Bubbs Creek Bridge, cross over and head back on the Sentinel Trail described below. This will add a mile to the hike. From Mist Falls, you can also continue on to Paradise Valley, described below.

Muir's Rock

100 yards RT. Easy. Access: The rock is 100 yd. from the parking area at Road's End, along the trail to Zumwalt Meadow.

OK, so you can't walk too far, don't have time, and so on. Well now there's no excuse. This level, simple, short stroll takes you to one of the most historically significant spots in the park's modern-day history. From this wide, flat rock, John Muir used to deliver impassioned speeches about the Sierra.

Paradise Valley

12 mi. RT. Moderate to strenuous. Access: Short-term parking area at Road's End, past Cedar Grove Village and follow the signs.

This is a great overnight hike because the valley is so pretty and there's much to explore. But it can also be accomplished as an ambitious day hike. Follow the above trail to Mist Falls and then head up 3 miles of switchbacks to Paradise Valley. The valley is 3 miles long, relatively flat, and beautiful. Hike through the valley to connect with the John Muir Trail and the rest of the backcountry, or return the way you came.

River Trail

5.5 mi. RT. Easy. Access: From the Cedar Grove Ranger Station, drive 3.1 mi. to the Roaring River Falls parking area.

The trail hugs the river and can be shortened if you just want to walk to the waterfalls (0.5 mile round-trip), or Zumwalt Meadows (3 miles round-trip; a shorter version is listed below). The waterfalls are 0.25 mile along the trail. The falls are short, but powerful. Do *not* attempt to climb them. Just north of the falls, back toward the parking area, is a sign that reads ZUMWALT MEADOW—ROAD'S END. Take this trail, which initially hugs the highway before breaking off into a beautiful canyon.

At 1.5 miles is the Zumwalt Bridge. If you cross the bridge you'll be a quarter mile from the Zumwalt Meadow parking area. Do not cross the bridge; continue onward up the canyon for another quarter of a mile to Zumwalt Meadow. From here there's a slight incline. In a half mile you'll reach a fork; head uphill. The rest of the hike follows the riverbank, which sports plenty of swimming and fishing holes. After 2.5 miles you'll come to another footbridge. Cross over and it's a short half-mile walk back to the Road's End parking area, where you can try and catch a ride. Otherwise, retrace your steps back to your car.

Sentinel Trail

4.6 mi. RT. Easy. Access: The trailhead mirrors the hikes to Bubbs Creek, Mist Falls, and Paradise Valley described above.

Essentially what this hike does is encircle a small length of the South Fork of the Kings River. After hiking 2 miles on the river's north side, the trail splits and heads north to Mist Falls and Paradise Valley or east across Bailey Bridge toward Bubbs Creek. Follow the eastern trail but instead of hiking on to Bubbs Creek, follow a sign that reads road's end—2.6 miles. This will take you through dense groves of pine and cedars, with occasional views of Grand Sentinel. You'll cross Avalanche Creek before emerging into a huge meadow and returning near the riverbank. At 2 miles, you can see Muir's Pulpit, the huge boulder described above. At 2.25 miles, you'll find a footbridge that points back to the parking area.

Zumwalt Meadows

1.5 mi. RT. Easy. Access: Zumwalt Meadows parking area, 1 mi. west of Road's End, on Calif. 180 past Cedar Grove Village.

Cross the bridge and walk left for 100 yards to a fork. Take the trail that leads right for a bird's-eye view of the meadow before descending 50 feet to the ground below. The trail leads along the meadow's edge, where the fragrance of ponderosa pine, sugar pine, and incense cedar fill the air. The loop around

returns along the banks of the South Fork of the Kings River. Grand Sentinel and North Dome rise in the background.

OTHER HIKES

Cold Springs Nature Trail

2 mi. RT. Easy. Access: Mineral King's Cold Springs Campground, across from the ranger station.

This easy loop illustrates the natural history and beauty of the region. It passes near private cabins that predate the area's addition to Sequoia National Park in 1978. The walk offers views of the Mineral King Valley and surrounding peaks. It can get hot and dry in summer, so carry additional water.

Deer Cove Trail

4 mi. RT. Strenuous. Access: In the Monarch Wilderness, on Calif. 180, about 2.7 mi. west of the Cedar Grove Village turnoff. The parking area is on the north side of the road.

This hike in the Monarch Wilderness, officially maintained by the U.S. Forest Service, starts at 4,400 feet and climbs to 5,600 feet. It follows short, steep switchbacks that climb through bear clover and manzanita. After the first 0.5 mile, it passes above a large spring. Deer Cove Creek is in a steep drainage area at the 2-mile mark. This area is heavily wooded with cedar, fir, and Jeffrey pine. To continue on, see the Wildman Meadow Trail below.

Kings River National Recreation Trail

6–10 mi. RT. Easy to Spring Creek; strenuous to Garlic Meadow Creek. Access: On Calif. 180, 6 mi. below Big Stump Entrance, turn north on F.S. 12S01 (a U.S. Forest Service road), a dirt road marked MCKENZIE HELIPORT, DELILAH LOOKOUT, CAMP 4½. Drive 17.5 mi. to the Kings River. Turn west and drive another 2.5 mi. to Rodgers Crossing. Cross the bridge and turn east, following signs to Kings River Trail. The trailhead is at the east end of a parking lot another 7 mi. ahead, at the road's end.

So it's a long drive, but after hiking in upper Kings Canyon, this is a great place to see what it looks like from the bottom. The views here rival anything in the park, with peaks towering overhead and the river rushing nearby. The hike cuts through the Monarch Wilderness along the belly of Kings Canyon although this trail, too, lies in the national forest, not the park. The trail starts along a dirt road but soon departs and follows the river, which is broad and powerful at this point. The first mile alternates between rapids and great fishing pools. At 1.5 miles is a view up Converse Creek and its rugged canyon.

At 3 miles you'll find Spring Creek, a short but pretty waterfall and good place to rest. You can turn around here for a total hike of 6 miles, or proceed for the 10-mile option. The trail from here ascends the steep Garlic Spur, a ridge that ends suddenly at the ledge of the canyon. The trail above Spring Creek is flecked with obsidian. The nearest source of this rock is the Mono Craters, more than 100 miles to the north. For that reason, many believe this trail was used for trading by the Monache Indians. After the long, steep ascent, the trail heads down to Garlic Meadow Creek. A short way upstream are large pools and wide resting areas. Beyond the creek, the trail is not maintained.

Marble Fork Trail

6 mi. RT. Strenuous. Access: Follow the dirt road at the upper end of Potwisha Campground, which is 3.8 mi. east of the Ash Mountain Entrance. There is a small parking area past campsite no. 16.

This is one of the most scenic hikes in the Foothills area. The walk leads to a deep gorge where the roaring Marble Falls spills in a cascade over multicolored boulders. From the parking area, begin hiking north up the Southern California Edison flume. After crossing the flume

on a wooden bridge, watch for a sign to the trail and head east uphill. The trail crosses some steep switchbacks and near some large poison oak bushes with stems 3 inches wide. Watch out for these bare sticks in late fall and winter.

The trail will begin to flatten out and settle into a slight slope for the rest of the hike up to the waterfalls. Look for large yuccas and California bay along the way. After 2 miles, you can see the waterfalls as the hike cuts through white and gray marble, a belt of the rock that is responsible for seven caves in the park, including Crystal Cave near Giant Forest. Once you reach the falls, it's almost impossible to hike any further and only very experienced hikers should attempt a walk downstream. The marble slabs break very easily. Boulders in the area can get very slick. Be extra careful when water is high. This is a good hike year-round, but can be very hot during summer afternoons.

Potwisha & River's Edge

0.5 mi. RT. Easy. Access: From the Ash Mountain Entrance, take the highway to the Potwisha Campground. At the campground entrance (which will be to your left) turn right down a paved road toward an RV dump station. Take the paved road until it hits a dead-end at a parking area. Continue toward the river on a footpath to open bedrock.

This was once the site of an Indian village known as Potwisha, home to a tribe of Monache Indians. The main village was just about where the dump station is now (another modern-day reminder of the respect shown Native Americans). On the bedrock are mortar holes where the women squatted nearby to grind acorns into meal. From here the trail continues above the river to a sandy beach and a good swimming hole. The trail turns east upstream before the suspension bridge, then northward up a short but steep hill. Near the top of the hill you'll run into Middle Fork Trail. Turn west (left) and hike the short distance back to the parking area.

Wildman Meadow

14 mi. RT. Strenuous. Access: The trailhead for the Deer Cove Trail, with which this trail connects, is in the Monarch Wilderness, on Hwy. 180, about 2.7 mi. west of the Cedar Grove village turnoff. The parking area is on the north side of the road.

This hike through the Monarch Wilderness mirrors the first 2 miles of the hike to Deer Cove. After reaching Deer Cove, it's a steep ascent to 7,500 feet—a 1,900-foot gain in 5 miles. From Deer Cove, hike 3.5 miles to a sandy knoll, from where there is a good view into the rugged canyon drainage area of Grizzly Creek. At 6.5 miles, you'll top the ridge and cross over to the north-facing slope. A quick drop lands you in Wildman Meadow, where a large stock camp occupies the edge of the clearing.

Exploring the Backcountry

Be aware of bears that frequent these regions. In the summer months, mosquitoes and sunburn are real pests. Stay off of high peaks during thunderstorms and don't attempt any climb if it looks as if a storm is rolling in. Exposed peaks are often struck by lightning. And finally, many of these routes are buried under snow in winter.

Backcountry permits are required for all overnight hikes. Make reservations only by mail to the park at least 14 days in advance, but no earlier than March 1. A few permits are available on the day of departure on a first-come, first-served basis.

Note: There are 15 ranger stations in the wilderness of the park. There are seven along the John Muir and Pacific Crest trails. Another seven are in the southern part of the park in the Sequoia backcountry. Most are not staffed from fall to spring. To find which ranger station is closest to your trailhead, consult the park map handed out free at all entrances.

Alta Peak—Alta Meadow

16 mi. RT. Strenuous. Access: From Giant Village, drive about 3 mi. north on the Generals Hwy. and then turn right on the Wolverton Rd. turnoff. Look for the trail at the southeast end of the parking area at Wolverton Creek.

From Wolverton, hike on the Lakes Trail toward the Panther Gap Trail. Head right on the Panther Gap Trail, up through the 8,400-foot gap to Alta Trail. Turn left on Alta Trail, hike past the junction with Seven-Mile Hill Trail and the junction with Alta Peak Trail. Left takes you up Alta Peak, a 2,000-foot ascent in 2 miles that offers spectacular vistas. If climbing isn't your idea of fun, plow straight ahead to Alta Meadow, which also has a nice view and good places to camp.

High Sierra Trail

10 mi. RT. Moderate to strenuous. Access: Take Calif. 198 to Giant Village and proceed to Crescent Meadow Rd. Bear right at the Y, passing the signed parking area for Moro Rock to the road's end and the Crescent Meadow parking area.

This trail is a popular route into the backcountry. Some utilize this as a one-way passage to Mount Whitney. This trail gets a lot of sun, so begin early. From the parking area, head out on a paved trail to the south, over several bridges to a junction. Turn right onto the High Sierra Trail. You will pass Eagle View, the Wolverton Cutoff, and Panther Creek. Hike at least 3 miles before setting up camp.

Jennie Lakes Trail

12 mi. RT. Moderate to strenuous. Access: From Grant Grove, drive about 7 mi. south on the Generals Hwy. to the turnoff for Big Meadows Campground. The trailhead and parking are on the south side of the road next to a ranger station.

This is a nice overnight hike that's not too demanding, and can be further extended into the Jennie Lakes Wilderness Area. From the parking area, cross through the campground and across Big Meadow Creek. From here the trail climbs. At Fox Meadow, there is a wooden trail sign and register for hikers to sign. At the next junction, head right toward Jennie Lakes (left goes toward the Weaver Lake Trail) and up to Poop Out Pass. From here it's a drop down to the Boulder Creek drainage area and on to emerald-green Jennie Lakes. This hike can be combined with a second day hike to Weaver Lake. Just retrace your steps to the Weaver Lake turnoff. Weaver Lake is a relatively warm mountain lake surrounded by blueberry bushes that weigh heavy with fresh fruit in July.

Lakes Trail

12.5 mi. RT. Moderate to strenuous. Access: From Giant Forest, drive north on the Generals Hwy. to the Wolverton parking area. The trailhead is on the left of the parking lot as you enter from the highway.

This trail hikes along a string of tarns, high-mountain lakes created by the scouring action of glaciers thousands of years ago. Heather Lake and Pear Lake are popular destinations along this route. From the trailhead head east, avoiding the Long Meadow Trail. Climb up a moraine ridge and soon you'll be hiking above Wolverton Creek, which darts through small meadows strewn with wildflowers. At a junction with the Panther Gap Trail head left toward Heather Lake. At a second junction you have to choose. To the right is Hump Trail, a steep but always open trail. Left is the Watchtower Trail, which leads along a granite ledge blasted in the rock with dynamite. With the Tokopah Valley far below, this hike is not for those who suffer vertigo. Both trails wind up at Heather Lake. Camping is not allowed here, but is allowed further up the trail at Pear Lake.

Especially for Kids

The **Walter Fry Nature Center** in Sequoia, located at the Lodgepole Campground, is a fun place for children to visit during the summer months. They can look through a microscope, watch water bugs, and generally get entertained, albeit briefly.

Other Sports & Activities

Cross-Country Skiing. Sequoia Ski Touring (☎ 559/565-3435) operates at Wolverton, just north of Giant Forest. They offer rentals, instruction, and trail maps for 35 miles of marked backcountry trails.

Fishing. Easily accessed waters are limited to Kings and Kaweah rivers, and fishing permits are required. High-country lakes have a few nonnative trout.

Kayaking. The Kaweah and Upper Kings rivers inside the parks are not open for boating, but there are companies that run trips just outside the parks. Trips on the Kings are only for the very brave and experienced as it is one of the steepest, wildest rivers in the West.

Snowshoeing. On winter weekends, rangers lead introductory snowshoe hikes in **Grant Grove** and **Giant Forest** (☎ 209/335-2856). Snowshoes are provided, but a $1 donation is requested.

White-Water Rafting. If you want the thrill without the fear, try white-water rafting. **Kaweah White Water Adventures** (☎ 800/229-8658 or 559/561-1000) is a local outfit that runs class III, IV, and V trips for beginners and intermediate paddlers. Trips usually last 5 hours, are run in inflatable kayaks or rafts, and are offered from April through August with costs up to $125 per person. Half the fee is due when you make a reservation, but walk-in bookings are often available, too. **Whitewater Voyages** (☎ 800/ 488-RAFT; www.whitewatervoyages.com) also runs trips down the Kaweah and Kern rivers.

Camping

Twelve of the 14 campsites in the parks are on a first-come, first-served basis and do not accept reservations in advance. Only Lodgepole and Dorst require

advanced reservations, and then only from Memorial Day to mid-October (☎ 800/365-2267). Grant and Cedar Grove group campsites must be made by mail-in reservation. Mail requests to either **Sunset Group Sites** at Grant Grove, or **Canyon View Group Sites** at Cedar Grove, at P.O. Box 926, Kings Canyon National Park, CA 93633.

There is a 14-day camping limit in the park from June 14 to September 14, with a 30-day maximum per year. There is a limit of one vehicle and six people per campsite, except at Potwisha, which allows two vehicles. Group campsites are

Campground	Elev.	Total Sites	RV Hookups	Dump Station	Toilets	Drinking Water
Inside Sequoia National Park						
Atwell Mill	6,650	21	0	No	Yes	Yes
Buckeye Flat	2,800	28	0	No	Yes	Yes
Cold Springs	7,500	40	0	No	Yes	Yes
Dorst	6,700	218	0	Yes	Yes	Yes
Lodgepole	6,700	250	0	Yes	Yes	Yes
Potwisha	2,100	44	0	Yes	Yes	Yes
South Fork	3,650	13	0	No	Yes	No
Inside Kings Canyon National Park						
Azalea	6,600	114	0	Yes	Yes	Yes
Crystal Springs	6,600	66	0	Yes	Yes	Yes
Moraine	4,600	120	0	Yes	Yes	Yes
Sentinel	4,600	83	0	Yes	Yes	Yes
Sheep Creek	4,600	111	0	Yes	Yes	Yes
Sunset	6,600	184	0	Yes	Yes	Yes
Near the Parks						
Big Meadows	7,600	15	0	No	Yes	No
Buck Rock	7,500	5	0	No	Yes	No
Hume Lake	5,200	74	0	No	Yes	Yes
Landslide	5,800	9	0	No	Yes	No
Upper Ten Mile	5,800	10	0	No	Yes	No
Horse Creek	300	80	0	Yes	Yes	Yes
Lemon Cove	300	55	30	Yes	Yes	Yes

available at Dorst, Sunset, and Canyon View. Trailers are permitted at 11 of the 14 campgrounds.

INSIDE SEQUOIA NATIONAL PARK

To get to **Buckeye Flat** (The Foothills, Sequoia National Park; ☎ 209/565-3341) from the Ash Mountain Entrance, drive about 6 miles northeast on the Generals Highway to the Hospital Rock Ranger Station. Then follow signs to the campground, which is several miles down a narrow, windy road. This is a small campground in a park where large campgrounds dominate. It's set along the Middle Fork of the Kaweah River and offers lots of shade and privacy, though it still gets toasty in summer.

Potwisha (The Foothills, Sequoia National Park; ☎ 209/565-3341) is 3 miles northeast of the Ash Mountain Entrance on the Generals Highway. This is one of the smaller campgrounds in the park, located along the Marble Fork of the Kaweah River. Sites are nestled beneath oak trees, but it can get very hot in the summer.

To reach **South Fork** (The Foothills, Sequoia National Park; ☎ 209/565-

Showers	Fire Pits/ Grills	Laundry	Public Phone	Reserve	Fees	Open
No	Yes	No	Yes	No	$8	May–Oct
No	Yes	No	Yes	No	$14	Apr–Oct
No	Yes	No	Yes	No	$8	May–Oct
No	Yes	Yes	Yes	Yes	$16	June–Aug
Yes	Yes	Yes	Yes	Yes	$16	Year-round
No	Yes	No	Yes	No	$14	Year-round
No	Yes	No	Yes	No	$8	Year-round
No	Yes	No	Yes	No	$14	Year-round
Yes	Yes	No	Yes	No	$14	May–Oct
Yes	Yes	Yes	Yes	No	$14	May–Oct
Yes	Yes	Yes	Yes	No	$14	Apr–Oct
Yes	Yes	Yes	Yes	No	$14	June–Sept (as needed)
Yes	Yes	Yes	Yes	No	$14	May–Oct (as needed)
No	Yes	No	Yes	No	Free	June–Oct
No	Yes	No	Yes	No	Free	June–Oct
No	Yes	No	Yes	No	$14	May–Sept
No	Yes	No	Yes	No	$8	May–Oct
No	Yes	No	Yes	No	Free	May–Oct
No	Yes	No	Yes	No	$14	Year-round
Yes	Yes	Yes	Yes	Good idea	$15–$19	Year-round

3341), take Calif. 198 from Visalia to Three Rivers and turn east on South Fork Road, where you then drive 23 miles to the campground. The smallest and most remote campground in the park, South Fork is just inside Sequoia's southwestern border. It is set along the South Fork of the Kaweah River. A ranger station nearby has hiking maps and information.

Atwell Mill (Mineral King, Sequoia National Park; ☎ 209/565-3341) is located on the winding Mineral King Road, 25 miles east of Calif. 198 in Three Rivers. This road is not recommended for trailers or RVs. Mineral King is a beautiful area to stay in, just not easy to get to. This small, pretty campground is located near the East Fork of the Kaweah River, at Atwell Creek.

Cold Springs (Mineral King, Sequoia National Park; ☎ 209/565-3341) is a few miles east of Atwell Mill on the Mineral King Road—it's also not recommended for trailers or RVs. This campground is at an elevation of 7,500 feet, the highest car camping available in the park. It's also a good starting point for many backcountry hikes.

Dorst (Giant Forest, Sequoia National Forest; ☎ 800/365-2267) is 14 miles northwest of Giant Forest on the Generals Highway. This is one of the larger campgrounds in the park and, at 6,700 feet, one of the highest. It's near some nice backcountry trails and Muir Grove. A grocery, dump station, and laundry are nearby. There are also evening ranger programs.

Lodgepole (Giant Forest, Sequoia National Park; ☎ 800/365-2267), 5 miles northeast of Giant Forest Village, is the park's largest campground and one of the most popular. It's pretty, but crowded. In summer, you'll find a grocery, showers, restaurant, laundry, dump station, gift shop, horseback riding facilities, and other amenities. Evening ranger talks are also held here. The campground is near some spectacular big trees and enough backcountry trails to offer some solitude.

INSIDE KINGS CANYON NATIONAL PARK

There are three campgrounds located near Calif. 180 in Grant Grove. All three have evening ranger programs, a grocery, a dump station, horseback riding facilities, and showers nearby. **Azalea** (Grant Grove, Kings Canyon National Park; ☎ 209/565-3341) is one of the nicest large campgrounds in the park. It's set at 6,600 feet, near the privately owned Lake Sequoia (available for sightseeing only). **Crystal Springs** (Grant Grove, Kings Canyon National Park; ☎ 209/565-3341) and **Sunset** (Grant Grove, Kings Canyon National Park; ☎ 209/565-3341) both offer a pretty spot to relax near the big trees.

There are three campgrounds in Cedar Grove, all within a short walk of Cedar Grove Village near Calif. 180. In the village, you'll find a grocery, dump station, and laundry, as well as bike rentals and horseback-riding facilities. **Sentinel** (Cedar Grove, Kings Canyon National Park; ☎ 209/565-3341) fills up fast. If this is full, nearby **Sheep Creek** (Cedar Grove, Kings Canyon National Park; ☎ 209/565-3341) opens to catch the overflow. The third, **Moraine** (Cedar Grove, Kings Canyon National Park; ☎ 209/565-3341) also opens on an as-needed basis. This is the furthest from the crowds and the noise.

INSIDE SEQUOIA NATIONAL FOREST

There are several campgrounds in Sequoia National Forest, roughly between Grant Grove and Cedar Grove. Call ☎ 209/338-2251 for information. **Big Meadows** and **Buck Rock** are located about 5 miles down Big Meadows Road, which is off the Generals Highway. Big Meadows, set at 7,600 feet, is close to trails to the Jennie Lakes Wilderness. Buck Rock, about 2 miles further down the Big Meadows Road, is a good place to go to beat the crowds.

Hume Lake, set on the banks of (appropriately enough) Hume Lake, has fishing spots nearby and is close to a grocery store. To get there from Grant Grove, drive 6 miles northeast on Calif. 180 to Hume Lake Road, then turn south and drive 3 miles to the lake.

To get to **Landslide,** drive south on Hume Lake Road 7 miles around the lake, and then go up Ten Mile Road to the campground. This hidden gem is set along Ten Mile Creek, 2 miles from Hume Lake. **Upper Ten Mile** is another primitive campsite a few miles further along Ten Mile Road.

Accommodations

INSIDE THE PARKS

If you aren't camping, there are just four places to stay inside the park. Two are in Kings Canyon National Park, one is at Wuksachi Village in Sequoia, and the other is in Sequoia's Mineral King. Call ☎ 559/335-5500 to make reservations. This is also the number to call to secure reservations in Sequoia National Forest, the forestland that connects the two parks. Other numbers are listed below.

Cedar Grove Lodge

Calif. 180, Cedar Grove, Kings Canyon National Park. ☎ **559/335-5500.** 18 units. A/C. $85 double. DISC, MC, V. Closed in winter.

The motel offers comfortable rooms on the bank of the Kings River. There are communal decks with river views. Rooms are standard motel fare. Getting here is half the fun. It's a 36-mile drive down a winding highway that provides beautiful vistas along the way.

Grant Grove Lodge

Calif. 180, Grant Grove, Kings Canyon National Park. ☎ **559/335-5500.** 52 units, 9 with private bathroom. $125–$212 lodge double; $35–$85 cabin. DISC, MC, V.

Amenities are scarce at this rustic lodge. Nine cabins have electricity, indoor

plumbing, and private baths. The other 43 are cabins with kerosene lanterns for light, wood-burning stoves for heat, and communal bathrooms. Some are rustic wooden cabins; others are made of canvas. Still, rooms and tents provide comfortable places to stay. Some cabins have outdoor stoves for cooking. There's a new 30-room, modern unit as well.

Silver City Resort

Mineral King, Sequoia National Park. ☎ **559/561-3223,** or 805/528-2730 in winter. www.silvercityresort.com. 14 cabins, 7 with shared bathroom. $70–$200 double. MC, V. Closed Sept–May. Take Hwy. 198 through Three Rivers to the Mineral King turnoff. Silver City is a little more than halfway between Lookout Point and Mineral King.

This place fills up fast. Reservations are accepted in January for the year, so call the winter line listed above. Most of the cabins have kitchens or wood-burning stoves. Less-expensive rooms can sleep two to five people. More expensive units have three bedrooms, private bathrooms, and a living area.

Wuksachi Lodge

Calif. 180 and 198, Sequoia National Park. ☎ **888/252-5757,** or 559/253-2199 from overseas. 102 units. A/C TV. $110–$155 double. MC, V. Rates discounted Oct 12–May 11.

The Wuksachi Village and Lodge are the newest development in the park. The lodge has a dining room, lounge, gift shop and conference rooms. Guest rooms include telephones and data ports. The park plans to add 300 more rooms here in the next five years.

INSIDE SEQUOIA NATIONAL FOREST

Kings Canyon Lodge

Calif. 180, Sequoia National Forest. ☎ **559/335-2405.** 11 units, 2 with shared bathroom. $65–$150 double. MC, V. Sometimes closed in winter. Take Hwy. 180 from Grant Grove toward

Cedar Grove. The lodge is at the halfway point, about 15 mi. from both locations.

Built in the 1930s, this lodge is practically a historic landmark. It's also one of the only places to buy gasoline near the parks and uses double gravity pumps that are worth seeing even if you don't need to fill up. The lodge is a mixture of cabins and rooms. All were built out of knotty pine. Each has either one or two double beds. There is also a bar and grill that serves breakfast, lunch, and family style dinners.

Montecito-Sequoia Lodge

8000 Generals Hwy., Sequoia National Forest. ☎ **800/227-9900,** 800/843-8667, or 559/565-3388. Fax 559/565-3223. 36 units, plus 13 cabins that share a bathhouse. $55–$139, plus $45 for each extra person. Special week-long packages available. Rates include breakfast and dinner. AE, DISC, MC, V. Take Hwy. 180 into the park, turn right at the fork, and drive 8 mi. south to the lodge entrance, turn right, and follow the road about 0.5 mi. to the parking lot.

The Montecito offers comfortable rooms in a well-stocked resort that caters to families with children and large groups. It also does just as well at providing for guests of all ages. The only sizable lodge open all year in the Sequoia/Kings Canyon area, it's located in Sequoia National Forest, between Grant Grove and Lodgepole. Rooms are in four separate buildings. Another 13 individual cabins share a bathhouse. The main building and many private rooms overlook the Kaweah Range. Meals are served buffet style. There is also a bar on the premises. A large lake accommodates sailing and canoeing. During winter, guests can also go cross-country skiing, snowshoeing, and ice-skating.

Stony Creek Lodge

Generals Hwy., Sequoia National Forest. ☎ 559/335-5500 or 559/561-3314. 11 units. $97 double. MC, V. Closed Sept–May. Take the Stony Creek Village exit off the Generals Hwy. between Grant Grove and Giant Village.

This is the plushest place to stay in the Sequoia/Kings Canyon area. Rooms are cozy and large. The lodge itself is in Sequoia National Forest, between Grant Grove and Lodgepole. A restaurant is nearby.

NEAR THE PARKS

Of the two entrances to the parks, Calif. 198 offers the bulk of accommodations. *One important note:* As the highway bisects the town of Three Rivers, its name changes to Sierra Drive. The **Three Rivers Reservation Centre** offers one-stop shopping (☎ 559/561-0410; www.sequoiapark.com) for guests looking for a place to stay in the Three Rivers and Lemon Cove areas. Visalia is another option, and there are a few scattered motels along Highway 180.

Ben Maddox House

601 N. Encina St., Visalia. ☎ **800/401-9800** or 559/739-0721. www.benmaddoxhouse.com. 4 units. TV TEL. $120 double. Rates include breakfast. AE, DISC, MC, V.

The house is set on a Victorian-lined street, 4 blocks from downtown. Large palm trees grace the front yard and the house itself is impressive, with a large, triangular gable. Built of redwood in 1876, the owners of the Ben Maddox House have worked to retain the home's original charm. Rooms are trimmed in dark oak with white oak floors. Furnishings date from the 18th and 19th centuries. Two front rooms have a small porch accessed through French doors. There's a swimming pool and a Jacuzzi.

Best Western Holiday Lodge

40105 Sierra Dr., Three Rivers. ☎ **800/528-1234,** 888/523-1909, or 559/561-4119. Fax 559/561-3427. 54 units (3 with shower only). A/C TV TEL. $59–$99 double. AE, DC, DISC, JCB, MC, V.

Standard motel fare in a nice location. Most rooms look out on the Kaweah River. Rooms come with two double beds, two queens, one king, or one queen. Suites have a separate living area, two televisions, and sleeper sofas. Some rooms have fireplaces. If an agent at the toll-free number says the motel is full, call the front desk directly. Outside there is a pool and children's playground.

Buckeye Tree Lodge

46000 Sierra Dr., Three Rivers. ☎ **559/561-5900**. www.buckeyetree.com. 11 units and 1 cottage (8 with shower only). A/C TV TEL. $59–$160 double. AE, DC, DISC, MC, V.

This lodge looks pretty average from the outside, but its rolling lawns that end at the riverbank are picturesque. This is a relaxing place to stay, with rear porches off of every room. Rooms are standard but come equipped with a refrigerator and VCR. Pets are allowed as well and should be mentioned when making reservations.

Lake Elowin Resort

43840 Dineley Dr., Three Rivers. ☎ **559/561-3460**. Fax 209/561-1300. www.lake-elowin. com. 10 cabins, with showers only. A/C. $61–$92 double. AE, DISC, MC, V. From eastbound Sierra Dr. in Three Rivers, about 2.5 mi. before the park entrance, turn left on Dineley Dr. (the street sign says DINLEY) and drive across a bridge. Bear right, and it's less than 0.5 mi. to the resort's driveway.

Undoubtedly one of the best places to stay in the Sierra, this 70-year-old resort is as a resort should be: a place to get away from it all. No phones, no televisions, rustic but clean cabins nestled under huge trees, all looking out at Lake Elowin, a small body of water above the Kaweah River. Brothers Milton and Dennis Melkonian have owned it for years. Milton purchased it after returning from Southeast Asia with the idea of creating a place to coexist with nature. That was more than 20 years ago, and to hear him talk, there's still much more to do. He is fastidious about his creation. All guests must sign a contract upon check-in saying they'll abide by the rules: no smoking, no littering, no car alarms, no pets, no visitors, and so on. Guests who break the rules are fined $150. But they're easy rules to abide by, more in place to ward off those with an uncooperative attitude. Cabins can accommodate two to six people. Cabin No. 1 sits close to the lake, with a nice view from the kitchen window. It also has a bedroom, ample-size living room, and bath. Cabin No. 3 has recently undergone a substantial renovation that includes a deck and Jacuzzi. Cabin No. 9 includes a picnic table and outdoor barbecue. Cabin No. 10 has a bedroom that sleeps five, a family room, and a dining area. All cabins include linens and towels, kitchen utensils, pots and pans. Some have fireplaces and barbecues. You bring the food, sun block, and good attitude.

Organic Gardens Bed & Breakfast

44095 Dineley Dr., Three Rivers. ☎ **559/561-0916**. www.theworks.com/~eggplant. 2 units. A/C. $115 and $130. Rates include full breakfast. 2-night minimum stay on weekends. MC, V. From eastbound Sierra Dr. in Three Rivers, about 2.5 mi. before the park entrance, turn left on Dineley Dr. (the street sign says DINLEY) and drive across a bridge. Bear right again and drive about a mile. The driveway will be on your left.

This B&B is a tiny jewel tucked into the Sierra. The two large guest rooms are enhanced by the obvious attention to detail that went into their design (for example, both have private entrances and solariums). The tile floors were laid by the innkeepers, rooms are aired out between occupancies, there's a Jacuzzi (guests can request private hours) and photography/looming studio on the premises, as well as an impressive organic garden. Best of all is the hospitality of owners Brenda Stoltzfus and Saundra Sturdevant, who moved here from the Bay Area. Breakfasts are vegetarian and served on the deck, weather permitting. Times are flexible. The menu may include crepes, pumpkin-walnut scones, fried potatoes, homemade bread, homemade granola with yogurt, seasonal fruits, and fresh coffee. Smoking is not allowed.

Sierra Lodge

43175 Sierra Dr., Three Rivers. ☎ **800/ 367-8879** or 559/561-3681. Fax 559/ 561-3264. 22 units (8 with shower only). A/C TV TEL. $58–$150 double. AE, CB, DC, DISC, MC, V.

Built to resemble a Swiss chalet, this is a funky place to stay. Rooms all enter from double sliding-glass doors. They're snug and spotless, some have fireplaces and all have a small refrigerator. The bathtubs are tiny. There are also barbecue areas available for guests. And outside there's a small pool.

The Spalding House

631 N. Encina St., Visalia. ☎ **559/739-7877.** Fax 209/625-0902. 3 units. $85 double. Rates include breakfast. MC, V.

This turn-of-the century Colonial Revival house offers only suites, each with a private bathroom and sitting room. Guests always enjoy the library that contains more than 1,500 books and the music room with its 1923 Steinway grand piano. The owners have restored the entire home themselves, decorating it with Oriental rugs, antiques, and reproductions. Smoking is not allowed.

Dining

INSIDE THE PARKS

Cedar Grove Cafe

Cedar Grove, Kings Canyon National Park. Breakfast and lunch $4–$6, dinner $6–$12. MC, V. Daily 8am–8pm. Closed Oct–May. AMERICAN.

This is a fine place to grab a quick bite. The menu is simple and the prices are affordable by national park standards. Breakfasts include eggs, cereals, fruit, and pastries, and lunch is mostly burgers and sandwiches. Dinner specials change nightly and may include pasta and chicken. There's a nice outdoor seating area near the river.

Grant Grove Restaurant

Grant Grove, Kings Canyon National Park. Breakfast and lunch $4–$6, dinner $8–$20. MC, V. Daily May–Sept 7am–9pm, Oct–Apr 7am–8pm. AMERICAN.

It's nothing fancy or spectacular, but if you're hungry this is the place. It offers a simple menu with something for everyone. Breakfast ranges from omelettes and pancakes to simple cereal or fruit. Lunch offers sandwiches, hot entrees, and an all-you-can-eat buffet. Dinner meals include New York steak, chicken cordon bleu, and nightly specials. There's also a tasty dinner buffet available. Prices are a little steep but lower than most national park restaurants.

Kings Canyon Lodge Bar and Grill

Calif. 180, Sequoia National Forest. ☎ **209/ 335-2405.** Weekend barbecue dinners $6– $12. MC, V. Daily 8am–8pm. Sometimes closed in winter, so call ahead. AMERICAN.

This privately owned place is tucked off the road between Grant Village and Cedar Grove. The restaurant is a short-order fare for breakfast, with burgers, soups, and salads for lunch and dinner. All the food is prepared in a small kitchen and served piping hot. On weekends, try the barbecue dinner special for $12. It includes all the trimmings and is a sort of tradition. The actual dining room here is tiny, and an antique bar occupies the main portion of the lodge. The atmosphere is very kid-friendly around mealtime.

Lodgepole Deli & Pizza

Lodgepole, Sequoia National Park. Menu items $4–$12. MC, V. Daily 8am–8pm. DELI/PIZZA.

One of the few year-round places to grab a quick sandwich, salad, calzone, or pizza. Ice-cream dishes are available.

Stony Creek Restaurant

Generals Hwy., Sequoia National Forest. ☎ **559/565-3909.** Reservations suggested. Breakfast and lunch $5–$10, dinner $8–$22. Daily 7am–3pm and 5–9pm. MC, V. AMERICAN.

This is the nicest restaurant nearby and the closest you'll get to fine dining without traveling to Visalia or Fresno. All three meals are available. Breakfast includes the staples, plus a variety of delicious homemade muffins. Salads and sandwiches are served for lunch, and the dinner specials change nightly.

Wuksachi Dining Room

Wuksachi Village, Sequoia National Park. ☎ **559/565-4070.** $5–$20. MC, V. Daily 6:30am–9:30pm. Lounge open noon–11pm. AMERICAN

The newest restaurant in the park offers respectable dining in a spacious setting. It's better than Denny's but no four-star dining experience. Construction continues in this vicinity so step carefully.

NEAR THE PARKS

Noisy Water Cafe

41775 Sierra Dr., Three Rivers. ☎ **559/561-4517.** Breakfast and lunch $4–$7, dinner $8 and up. AE, MC, V. Daily 6:30am–10pm in summer, 6:30am–9pm in winter. Closed Mon. AMERICAN.

A great place to eat. Prices are reasonable and the food is high quality, but the best part about this cafe is the selection. Breakfasts include a choice of omelettes, pancakes, French toast, steak and eggs, or south-of-the-border specialties. Lunch includes dozens of hot and cold sandwiches. And dinner entrees include fish, pasta, beef, and chicken specialties, plus

vegetarian dishes. The restaurant also has an extensive wine and beer selection. There is a large main dining room and a smaller anteroom with huge windows overlooking the Kaweah River. The service is friendly, fast, and knowledgeable.

Vintage Press

216 N. Willis St., Visalia. ☎ **559/733-3033.** Reservations recommended. Main courses $12–$25. AE, CB, DC, MC, V. Mon–Thurs 11:30am–2pm and 6–10pm, Fri–Sat 11:30am–2pm and 6–11pm. Sun brunch 10am–2pm, dinner 5–9pm. AMERICAN/CONTINENTAL.

This is the best place to eat within 100 miles. The interior was designed to replicate a gin mill in Gold Rush San Francisco. The bar was made by Brunswick of bowling alley fame. This place seats 250 amid a host of antiques and leaded mirrors. The menu features a dozen meat and fish selections, including steak; red snapper with lemon, almonds, and capers; and pork tenderloin with Dijon mustard, red chile, and honey. The menu also includes ambitious daily selections. A piano player entertains in the bar from 5 to 9pm on Thursday to Saturday.

Picnic & Camping Supplies

Markets throughout the park may have that forgotten flashlight, tarp, or lantern mantle—then again, they may not. It's very hit and miss in the parks, but persistence pays off. Some also have limited backcountry equipment, and of course, bear canisters.

The **Cedar Grove Market** is open 7am to 8pm daily from May to September; closed October to April. The **Grant Grove Market** is open 8am to 9pm May to September and 8am to 7pm October to April. The **Lodgepole Market,** which has the widest selection available, is open 8am to 8pm May to September. During the winter in Sequoia, a small variety of goods are available at Wolverton.

34

THEODORE ROOSEVELT NATIONAL PARK

by Jack Olson

NESTLED IN THE NORTH DAKOTA BADLANDS STANDS A PARK NAMED for a president who is remembered as being, among other things, one of America's great conservationists. In western North Dakota, where many of his early experiences formed

his later environmental efforts, Theodore Roosevelt is honored with a national park that bears his name.

When he became president in 1901, Roosevelt pursued his love of natural history by creating the U.S. Forest Service and by signing the 1906 Antiquities Act, under which he proclaimed 18 national monuments. He also obtained congressional approval to establish five national parks and 51 wildlife refuges, as well as set aside millions of acres of land as national forests. As a conservationist, Roosevelt is arguably without equal among American presidents. So it seems appropriate that he is the only president for whom a national park has been named.

Roosevelt first traveled to the North Dakota badlands in 1883. Before returning home to New York, he became interested in the cattle business and joined two other men as partners in the Maltese Cross Ranch. The following year,

Roosevelt returned to North Dakota and established a second open-range ranch, the Elkhorn, which became his principal residence in the area.

During his frequent visits, Roosevelt led the "strenuous life" that he loved. When he wasn't studying botany or herding cattle, he hunted, fished, and enjoyed the camaraderie of fellow Dakotans, some of whom would later form the nucleus of his Rough Riders.

Roosevelt arrived in the badlands soon after the last of the bison herds had been slaughtered, and he spent much time pondering what was being done to the animals and land around him. He carried those thoughts and convictions, born on the Dakota prairie, into his later political life.

Badlands & Buffalo. The colorful moonscape of the North Dakota badlands provides the scenic backdrop for Theodore Roosevelt National Park. Carved over

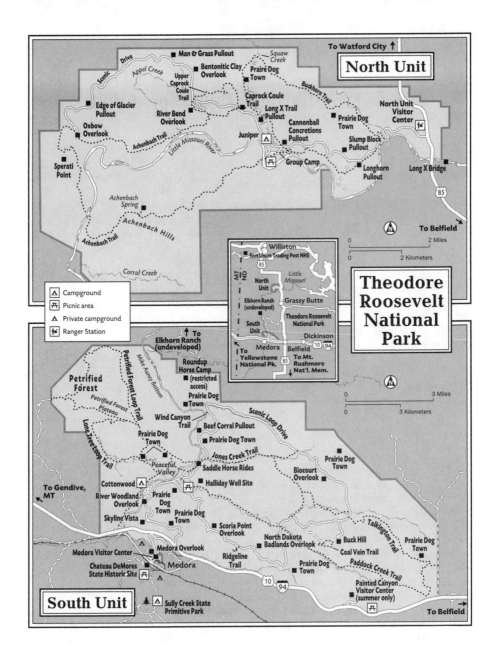

millions of years by the natural forces of the wind and rain, and the tireless waters of the Little Missouri River, this land is home to a variety of animals and plant life.

Some 60 million years ago, streams carried eroded materials eastward from the young Rocky Mountains, then deposited them on a vast lowland, today's Great Plains. During the warm, rainy

Tips from the Chief of Interpretation

After a decade at Theodore Roosevelt National Park, a dozen years with the National Park Service in Alaska, and 6 years in Death Valley, Chief of Interpretation Bruce Kaye has some insights for prospective visitors.

"The best month to be without crowds at Theodore Roosevelt National Park, yet do the things you want to do in view of the weather, is September," Kaye says. "But even at the height of the summer season, most visitors will not be bothered by overcrowding." Kaye adds, "Summertime is not all that busy—you can still go out into the backcountry and not see people; you can even drive one of the loop roads and not be inundated."

He encourages visitors to view Roosevelt's two ranch sites—the Maltese Cross, whose ranch house was relocated to the park in 1959 from the state capital in Bismarck; and the Elkhorn Ranch site, located 35 miles north of Medora. Kaye said visitors should check with rangers before traveling to the Elkhorn site, to ensure that high water will not impede their progress.

While visiting the park, Kaye says travelers should keep their eyes out for a wide variety of wildlife, including bison, elk, wild horses, mules, white-tailed deer, coyotes, antelope, 200 species of birds, and the ever-abundant prairie dog.

Since the park is open every day of the year, Kaye says that hiking, camping, and cross-country skiing are ideal experiences in the off-season.

---

periods that followed, dense vegetation grew, fell into swampy areas, and was later buried by new layers of sediment. Eventually this plant material turned into lignite coal. Some plant life became petrified.

Even as layers of sediment were being deposited, streams were starting to carve through the soft strata, sculpting the infinite variety of buttes, tablelands, and valleys that comprise the badlands today.

As inhospitable and barren as this land looks, it is home to a large variety of creatures and plants. Rainfall supports an abundance of prairie grasses and wildflowers, and more than 200 species of birds have been counted.

Mule deer and white-tailed deer inhabit the park, and prairie dogs have built their tunnel "towns" in the grasslands. Through careful management, some animals that nearly became extinct in the 19th and early 20th centuries are once again thriving on the Great Plains. Bison and elk, for example, were reintroduced into the area in 1956 and 1985, respectively.

The wealth of wildlife that first attracted Theodore Roosevelt and thousands of other avid sports enthusiasts to this area still exists. Bands of wild horses roam in the park's South Unit, just as they did when Roosevelt rode over this land and tended his cattle a century ago.

Avoiding the Crowds. Since the park has 70,000 acres, two spread-out units, and less than a half million visitors per year, avoiding crowds at Theodore Roosevelt National Park is not difficult. In general, you'll see fewer visitors in early morning and evening hours, particularly during the high-visitation months of June, July, and August. Early fall is especially appealing to those seeking a more contemplative experience. But even during the height of the summer season, those enjoying backcountry treks and scenic drives are not likely to encounter throngs of camera-clad vacationers: This national park is just too big, and visitation too low, to make that occur.

Just the Facts

GETTING THERE & GATEWAYS

The park's **South Unit** is located 130 miles west of Bismarck and just north of Medora (Exit 27 on I-94). The **North Unit** is located near Watford City. From I-94, take Exit 42 (Belfield), then you must continue north on U.S. 85 another 50 miles to the North Unit Entrance. The park also includes **Theodore Roosevelt's Elkhorn Ranch,** which is located between the North and South units, but visitors should ask rangers about road conditions before attempting to go there.

The Nearest Airports. About 130 miles east of the park is **Bismarck Municipal Airport** (☎ 701/222-6502), served by **Northwest** and **United Express** airlines plus **Avis** and **Enterprise** car rentals. **Dickinson Airport** (☎ 701/483-1062) is 35 miles from Medora and is served by **United Express.** The toll-free numbers for airlines and car-rental agencies are in the appendix.

INFORMATION

Contact the **Superintendent, Theodore Roosevelt National Park,** P.O. Box 7, Medora, ND 58645 (☎ 701/623-4466 for the South Unit, the main number; or 701/842-2333 for the North Unit; www.nps.gov/thro). The National Park Service has a variety of brochures that explore the park's cultural and natural resources, including a very useful **road log guide,** sold in the visitor center. Also, the Theodore Roosevelt Nature and History Association produces *Frontier Fragments,* an excellent park newspaper. It's updated annually and filled with relevant stories on the park's history, wildlife, interpretive offerings, and visitor services. It also includes a "Kid's Corner," with appropriate activities and articles for youngsters.

> I never would have been president if it had not been for my experiences in North Dakota.
> —Theodore Roosevelt

For information about the area, contact the **Medora Chamber of Commerce**, P.O. Box 186, Medora, ND 58645 (☎ 701/623-4910).

VISITOR CENTERS

The park has three visitor centers. The Medora Visitor Center (for the South Unit) is located just inside the park entrance at Medora and is open daily year-round. The Painted Canyon Visitor Center is about 7 miles east of Medora and open daily from April to mid-November. The North Unit Visitor Center, located at the eastern end of the North Unit, just off U.S. 85, is open daily from Memorial Day through September and weekends and most weekdays the rest of the year.

FEES & PERMITS

Entry into the park for up to 7 days costs $10 per vehicle or $5 per person on foot or bike. Campsites cost $10 per night, plus $1 per horse if you use the group horse-camping site in the South Unit. Group camps cost $2 per person, with a minimum of $20. Backcountry permits are free.

SPECIAL REGULATIONS & WARNINGS

The animals in the park are wild and should be viewed from a safe distance (even the prairie dogs can bite). Watch out for ticks in late spring and early summer. Climbing on the steep, barren slopes of the badlands can be dangerous due to slippery clays and soft sediments that may yield underfoot, so stay on designated trails. Horses are prohibited in campgrounds, picnic areas, and on self-guided nature trails.

SEASONS & CLIMATE

The climate in the badlands can be extreme (bitter cold and snow in the winter and intense heat in the summer), with high or low temperatures and sudden violent storms.

If You Only Have 1 Day

If you only have 1 day, you'll probably want to limit yourself to either the North or South Unit. Since it's more accessible from I-94, and more developed, it's likely you'll choose the South Unit.

If you're coming from the east, stop first at the **Painted Canyon Overlook and Visitor Center** to get a sweeping, panoramic view of the North Dakota badlands, then continue 7 miles west to the **Medora Visitor Center.** Here, you'll be able to view a film and listen to one or more ranger talks. There's also a museum with some of Theodore Roosevelt's personal effects. Be sure to stop in at the **Maltese Cross cabin,** behind the visitor center. Take the 36-mile scenic **driving loop** around the park, stopping at the overlooks (be sure to stop at one of the prairie dog towns), and stop along the way to explore one of the scenic trails.

Exploring the Park by Car

THE SOUTH UNIT

If you're traveling west on I-94, your first introduction to Theodore Roosevelt National Park is the **Painted Canyon Overlook and Visitor Center,** about 7 miles east of Medora. Here, on the upper ridge of the badlands, is an unparalleled panorama of ragged ridges and colorful hues. Watch for wild horses, the descendants of former domestic ranching stock; you might even see bison grazing.

A highlight of the South Unit is a paved 36-mile **scenic loop road** with interpretive signs that explain some of the park's historical and natural phenomena. The scenic drive is best accessed from the Medora Visitor Center by turning right onto the loop in Peaceful Valley. If you've bought the **road log** you'll want to travel counterclockwise around the loop. Descriptions of the shorter interpretive trails are incorporated into the driving tours for the North and South units; for more information on longer hiking opportunities, please see "Exploring the Backcountry," below.

South Unit Scenic Drive. In any season, the South Unit Scenic Drive can take you into some of the most remote areas of North Dakota. When Gen. Alfred Sully traveled through these badlands he described them as "hell with the fires burned out." In reality, they are teeming with wildlife, wildflowers, and bird life. The South Unit is comprised of 46,158 acres, of which 10,510 acres are designated as wilderness.

Scoria Point is the first overlook you'll come to. Strictly speaking, scoria is volcanic in origin, but in the badlands, wherever a seam of coal has caught fire and baked the surrounding sand and clay, it's called scoria. You'll see it from this viewpoint, where the topsoil has been stripped away by erosion and the harder material underneath is exposed.

About a mile farther, you'll come to the **Ridgeline Nature Trail.** If you choose to take this very short (0.6-mile loop) hike, you'll learn more about the badlands and their ecology. This is a moderately easy trail, suitable for most people.

Next is the **North Dakota Badlands Overlook.** The view here is over Paddock Creek, and what you'll see is a bleak, almost lunar landscape. This is because erosion has worn away the top soil, leaving behind only the rocks and harder materials underneath the thin, top layer.

After crossing Paddock Creek, you'll come to the turnoff for the **Coal Vein Trail,** a short (0.8-mile) loop that winds through an area where a fire burned in a coal seam from 1951 through early 1977.

After 25 years, the fire had baked the clay and soil here, changing both the appearance of the terrain and altering the vegetation patterns. Here, you'll be walking around the scoria (the same kind of formations you viewed from a distance at the Scoria Point Overlook earlier). You must drive down a short, unpaved road to reach the trail.

After returning to the main loop road, you'll next come to the turnoff for **Buck Hill.** It's only a short walk to the hill itself from the end of the road. The hill (at 2,855 ft.) has two very different slopes. On the south side, the slopes are hot and dry, and you'll see only shrubs and small plants. On the north side, which is wetter and cooler, you'll see trees.

Several miles farther will bring you to the **Boicourt Overlook,** which affords one of the best views of the badlands in the South Unit.

The next stop is **Wind Canyon Trail.** This is a very short walk up to a ridge, where you'll have a great view of the Little Missouri River, which did much to create the landscape here. Beyond the river, to the west, is the virtually untouched wilderness of the South Unit. Pause here around sunrise to listen for the call of coyotes in the valley below.

After passing the **Beef Corral Pullout** and a **prairie dog town,** which is just beyond on your left, you'll pass the parking lot for the **Jones Creek Trail.** This is one of two trailheads for the Jones Creek Trail on Scenic Loop Drive. (You passed the other one earlier; it was at the parking area between the Boicourt Overlook and the Wind Canyon Trail pullout.) The trail itself is 3.7 miles and leads into the heart of the badlands.

The final stop on the Scenic Loop Drive is in Peaceful Valley, shortly before you reach the intersection where you turned off onto the loop. The **Peaceful Valley Ranch,** which is on the National Historic Register, was established during the heyday of cattle ranching in the 1880s. The tall central section of the ranch house was constructed about 1885. Today, the ranch offers trail rides for a fee from May through the end of September (see "Horseback Riding in the Park," below).

THE NORTH UNIT

Fewer visitors take the time to travel to the park's North Unit, and much of it is not served by paved roads. There are 24,070 acres in the North Unit, of which 19,410 acres are designated as wilderness. Stop at the visitor center at the entrance to the unit, and the rangers will help you plan your time.

North Unit Scenic Drive. The 14-mile scenic drive travels from the entrance station to the **Oxbow Overlook** with plenty of turnouts and interpretive signs along the route. Keep your eyes open for longhorns on the prairie between the entrance and Juniper Campground— these are the same type of cattle raised by ranchers here during Roosevelt's time. At the Oxbow Overlook, you must double back along the same route.

Since less of the North Unit is developed, the thing to do here is to get out of the car at one of the scenic pullouts and take a hike. Whether you go a long or a short distance, you'll be able to see dramatic scenery populated with many bison, elk, and bighorn sheep but few people.

The **Little Mo Nature Trail,** which starts at Juniper Campground, offers a comfortable, leisurely walk through the Little Missouri River bottom. The trail cuts through woodlands near the river as well as badlands formations and gives you two options. The shorter portion of the loop is only 0.7 mile, paved, and wheelchair accessible. But you can also extend your hike by 0.4 mile and take the unpaved portion. If you're more adventurous, you'll see additional formations and cross some wildlife trails that (mostly) bison use.

Just across the road from the Juniper Campground entrance road, stop at the **Cannonball Concretions Pullout.** A short walk reveals the well-named rock formations. Contrasting formations in the area make this stop a photographer's delight.

The **Caprock Coulee Nature Trail,** 1.5 miles west of Squaw Creek Campground, is another easy, self-guiding nature trail that winds through badlands, dry water gulches, across breaks, then finds a welcome interruption in the grassy plains of the park. The total length of the round-trip is 1.6 miles.

If you want to do something more ambitious, combine the self-guiding nature trail with the Upper Caprock Coulee Trail. Together, they run a distance of 4.1 miles (this portion is 3.3 miles). You'll go farther into the wilderness this way; it also brings you back to the trailhead so that you don't have to double back over the same route. Bighorn sheep were introduced into the North Unit in 1996. Be on the lookout for these majestic animals.

It's at this point where the North Unit Scenic Drive is closed for the winter. If you continue, you'll end up at the **Oxbow Overlook,** another sweeping panoramic view of the badlands.

The **Sperati Point Trail** can be accessed from the Oxbow Overlook. This is the spur of the Achenbach Trail that leads to the Oxbow Bend Overlook and makes a less strenuous alternative if you want something shorter than the Achenbach's 16 miles. (The length of this trail is 1.5 miles round-trip.) The trail leads to the narrowest gateway in the badlands. The flow of the Little Missouri River once continued north to Hudson Bay. Blocked during the Ice Age, the river was forced to find a new course and finally broke through the gap between this point and the Achenbach Hills on the other side. The Little Missouri now drains into the Gulf of Mexico via the Missouri-Mississippi system. Take this trail for a taste of prairie country and long, sweeping views.

Exploring the Backcountry

If you wish to explore some of the wilderness the park has to offer, you'll need a free backcountry permit from the Medora or North Unit visitor center to do any overnight camping. You can also explore the backcountry on horseback. If you bring a horse, you must camp either in the backcountry or at the group campsite in the South Unit. You can also board your horse at the Peaceful Valley Ranch (see "Horseback Riding in the Park," below). Your stay in the Theodore Roosevelt National Park backcountry is limited to 14 consecutive days.

Special Regulations. You cannot have a campfire in the backcountry due to the possibility of wildfires, so you must bring a self-contained camp stove. You must pack out what you pack in (no burying of trash). Groups entering the backcountry are limited to 10 persons (or 8 persons with 8 horses). Finally, don't drink the water in the backcountry; there are no safe, approved water sources here.

The mother of all trails in the area is the **Maah Daah Hey Trail,** completed in summer 1999. The Maah Daah Hey is a 120-mile hiking, horseback, and mountain biking trail that traverses through the scenic and rugged North Dakota badlands. The trail passes through the Little Missouri National Grasslands, as well as state and private land, as it connects the North and South Units of Theodore Roosevelt National Park. The north end of the trail begins at the U.S. Forest Service CCC Campground in McKenzie County, located 20 miles south of Watford City off Highway 85. The trail winds its way to its southern terminus at Sully Creek State park in Billings County, south of Medora. Six fenced overnight campsites with hitching posts, vault toilets, and campfire rings have been constructed along the trail.

For more information about this trail, contact the **U.S. Forest Service,** Medora Ranger District, at 161 21st St. W., Dickinson, ND 58601 (☎ **701/225-5151;** www.fs.fed.us/r1/dakotaprairie); or the **McKenzie Ranger District office** at HC02, Box 8, Watford City, ND 58854 (☎ **701/842-2393**).

SOUTH UNIT TRAILS

Petrified Forest Trail

16 mi. RT (from the east). Moderate. Access: You can get on the trail at the parking area at Peaceful Valley at the trail's eastern end; from the west, the trailhead is located at the end of a dirt road outside the park (ask park rangers for directions).

Pieces of petrified wood are scattered throughout this national park, but the greatest concentration can be reached only on foot or horseback along this lengthy trail. The trail leads up along Petrified Forest Plateau. Just don't take any souvenirs.

NORTH UNIT TRAILS

Achenbach Trail

16 mi. RT. Moderate. Access: Juniper Campground.

This route climbs from the river bottomlands up through the Achenbach Hills, drops down to the river again, climbs to the Oxbow Overlook on a spur trail, then returns along the river bottom to the campground. Before departing, ask a ranger about the condition of river crossings. The "spur" trail is the Sperati Point Trail described in "The North Unit," above.

Buckhorn Trail

11 mi. RT. Moderate. Access: From the Caprock Coulee Nature Trail (see "The North Unit," above).

About a mile into this loop, hikers discover a large prairie dog town. Of the five varieties of prairie dogs, only the black-tailed variety inhabits Theodore Roosevelt National Park.

Organized Tours & Ranger Programs

From mid-June to early September, ranger programs, including nature walks and longer hikes, are offered at various locations. If snow conditions permit, rangers may conduct ski tours in winter.

Historic & Man-Made Attractions

There are a variety of historic attractions, both in the national park and nearby.

A **museum** housed in the Medora Visitor Center features personal items that once belonged to Theodore Roosevelt, ranching artifacts, and natural history displays. Tours are conducted (free, about 20 min.) through the **Maltese Cross cabin** from mid-June through Labor Day; if there are no scheduled tours, you can still take a self-guided tour. Roosevelt used this cabin, which was relocated to its new home behind the visitor center after a detailed restoration program.

At the **Elkhorn Ranch site,** where Theodore Roosevelt started his second cattle ranch in the area, no buildings remain (save the foundation stones from the main ranch house). To get there, you must take the dirt road that goes north out of the South Unit (its turnoff is at the top of the Scenic Loop Drive) and drive another 20 miles, but you must cross the river to get to the actual ranch site. Inquire at the Medora Visitor Center about river conditions before attempting this trip. An alternate route accesses the site from the west.

Château DeMores State Historic Site (☎ 701/623-4355), near the town of Medora, is a 27-room château that the Marquis DeMores built for his wife in 1884. The wealthy French nobleman owned a number of businesses in early day Medora, including a slaughterhouse, the chimney of which still dominates the town. The marquis named the town for his wife and persuaded the Northern Pacific Railroad to locate a station there. He was a casual acquaintance of Theodore Roosevelt. Admission costs $5 adults, $2.50 kids 6 to 15. Guided tours of the château are generally offered from late May through September.

Knife River Indian Villages National Historic Site (☎ 701/745-3309), consisting of three villages along the Knife River in North Dakota, was inhabited by the Mandan, Hidatsa, and later the Arikara from the early 1500s to 1860. Located 0.5 mile north of Stanton, North Dakota (via County Road 37), it offers insights into the life of the North Plains Indians. The site is open from 8am to 6pm (Mountain time) daily from Memorial Day through Labor Day, to 4:30pm daily the rest of the year. Admission is free. The exhibits and 15-minute orientation program depict life in the villages before and after Euro-American contact. Earthlodge tours are conducted at 11am, 1pm, and 3pm, June through August. The annual **Northern Plains Indian Culture Fest** is held the last full weekend in July.

Trails, from 0.5 mile to 2 miles in length, lead to three village sites. Other trails meander through prairie and woodland ecosystems. All trails are open during visitor center hours and some are wheelchair accessible. For information, contact the **Superintendent, Knife River Indian Villages NHS,** P.O. Box 9, Stanton, ND 58571 (☎ 701/745-3309; www.nps.gov/knri).

Fort Union Trading Post National Historic Site was, for nearly 4 decades in the early 19th century, known as Fort Union, a bastion of John Jacob Astor's American Fur Company, which dominated the fur trade in the region of modern-day North Dakota, Montana, and Saskatchewan. Now, as then, the focal point of the historic site is Fort Union's Indian Trade House. Here, goods were traded between the fur company and Assiniboines, Crows, Crees, and Lakotas. In this, the farthest reaches of the Missouri River country, the National Park Service and the Fort Union Association have meticulously restored and refurnished the Trade House to its appearance in 1851. The site is located about 2 hours north of Theodore Roosevelt National Park via U.S. 85 at Belfield, North

Dakota; N. Dak. 16 at Beach, North Dakota; or Mont. 16 at Glendive, Montana. The Bourgeois House Visitor Center is open from 8am to 8pm from Memorial Day through Labor Day, from 9am to 5:30pm the remainder of the year. The Indian Trade House is open from 9:45am to 5:45pm daily during the summer only. Ranger tours are offered from noon to 3:30pm daily during the summer, with self-guided tours the remainder of the year.

For scheduled dates of special programs, or for more information, contact the **Superintendent, Fort Union Trading Post NHS,** 15550 Highway 1804, Williston, ND 58801 (☎ 701/572-9083; www.nps.gov/fous).

Horseback Riding in the Park

Many backcountry trails are open to those on horseback, and you can use either your own horse or go on a guided trail ride with a park concessionaire. In the South Unit, contact **Peaceful Valley Ranch,** P.O. Box 608, Medora, ND 58645 (☎ 701/623-4568); winter contact, P.O. Box 108, Hawley, MN 56549 (☎ 218/937-5686). They offer horseback rides from Memorial Day to Labor Day and have regularly scheduled rides lasting from 1½ to 5 hours. Trail rides run daily from 8:30am to evening. A riding lesson is provided with every scheduled ride. An overnight ride to Diamond Bar Bed and Breakfast can be arranged. In the North Unit, the concessionaire is **Little Knife Outfitters,** R.R. 1, Box 116, Stanley, ND 58784 (☎ 800/438-6905 or 701/842-2631).

Camping

Cottonwood Campground in the South Unit and **Juniper Campground** in the North Unit are operated on a first-come, first-served basis. You'll find drinking water, flush toilets, public telephones, and fire grates in both campgrounds, but no showers or RV hookups. Juniper Campground has an RV dump station, but Cottonwood does not. Camping costs $10 per night. Campgrounds are open year-round, but the availability of water is limited during the winter.

Camping for organized groups is available at the Cottonwood Campground in the South Unit and in part of the Juniper Campground in the North Unit. Groups must have a written reservation from the park superintendent.

Riding groups with their own horses should write the superintendent to make arrangements. It's possible to camp with a horse, but only at the Roundup Group Horse Campground in the South Unit; the cost is additional.

Other privately run and Forest Service campgrounds are located near both units of the park, and you can get a list from park offices.

Accommodations & Dining

There are no accommodations or dining facilities in the park, but you will find hotels, motels, bed-and-breakfasts, as well as a variety of modest restaurants in Medora, Belfield, and Beach near the South Unit, and in Watford City near the North Unit. Most are open year-round, but some may close in the winter. Rates are highest in summer.

IN MEDORA

The **AmericInn,** the most luxurious choice, is located at 75 E. River Rd. S., 1 block south of the Medora Community Center (☎ 800/634-3444 or 701/623-4800). It has seasonal rates, ranging in the main tourist season from $60 to $155 double; American Express, Diners Club, Discover, MasterCard, and Visa are accepted.

The **Badlands Motel,** on Pacific Avenue, and the **Rough Riders Motel,** at 301 3rd Ave., both in Medora, charge $45 for a double in the winter, $79 in the summer. They both take American Express, Discover, MasterCard, and Visa. For reservations, call ☎ 800/MEDORA-1 or 701/623-4444; fax 701/623-4494.

Custer's Cottage, located at 156 East River Rd. S. in Medora, is a medium-sized house with two units, one main floor and one basement, with separate private entrances, full kitchens, large living rooms, cable TV, up to four bedrooms, and laundry facilities. It is open year-round by advance reservations (☎ 800/783-6366, PIN 0749, or 701/623-4378; e-mail: custerscottage@juno.com); prices range from $45 to $100, depending on how many bedrooms are used. One group or party per night. Credit cards are not accepted for payment but may be used to reserve a room.

IN BELFIELD

The **Bel-Vu Motel** is located west of U.S. 85 on U.S. 10 (☎ 701/575-4245). A double costs $36 to $40 in the winter, $40 to $45 in the summer; MasterCard and Visa are accepted.

The **Trapper's Inn** is located at I-94 and U.S. 85 North (☎ 800/284-1855 or 701/575-4261). Rates range from $70 to $81 in the peak season; American Express, Diners Club, Discover, MasterCard, and Visa are accepted.

IN BEACH

The **Buckboard Inn** is located at I-94 and N. Dak. 16 South (☎ 888/449-3599; fax 701/872-4794, ext. 127). A double costs $37 to $42 during the summer; American Express, Discover, MasterCard, and Visa are accepted.

IN WATFORD CITY

The **McKenzie Inn** is located on U.S. 85 West (☎ 701/842-3980). The year-round rate is $34 for a double; American Express, Discover, MasterCard, and Visa are accepted.

The **Roosevelt Inn & Suites** is on U.S. 85 West (☎ 701/842-3686). Rates year-round are $40 for a double; American Express, Discover, MasterCard, and Visa are accepted.

35

YELLOWSTONE NATIONAL PARK & LITTLE BIGHORN BATTLEFIELD NATIONAL MONUMENT

by Geoff O'Gara and Jack Olson

HAT OTHER NATIONAL PARK BOASTS SUCH AN ASSORTMENT OF thermal geysers and hot springs that their total exceeds the number found on the rest of the planet? On top of which there's a waterfall that's twice as tall as Niagara Falls. Not to

mention a canyon deep and colorful enough to fall into the "grand" category. Sure, other parks have great hiking trails and beautiful geologic formations, but virtually all of the geology in Yellowstone is reachable by anyone in average shape.

Wildlife? Ever focus your telephoto lens on a wild, untamed grizzly bear? Or a bald eagle? What about a wolf? Thousands of visitors have these experiences here every year.

And the park doesn't appeal solely to the visual senses; you'll smell it, too. By one biologist's estimate, Yellowstone has more than 1,100 species of plants, so when wildflowers cover the meadows in spring, you won't just see them, you'll be overpowered by their fragrances. The mud pots and fumaroles have their own set of odors, though many are less pleasing than a wild lily.

Your ears will be filled with the sounds of geysers noisily spewing forth thousands of gallons of boiling water into the blue Wyoming sky. After sunset, coyotes break the silence of the night with their high-pitched yips.

You can spend weeks hiking its backcountry or fishing its streams, or spend a day or two seeing the park from behind the windshield.

And yes, it's possible to see the highlights of Yellowstone without ever leaving your car. Really. Park roads lead past most of the key attractions and are filled with wildlife commuting from one grazing area to another. There's no doubt you will return home with vivid memories if you take this approach to your visit of the park, but of course there's so much more to see by actually getting out of your vehicle.

And Yellowstone's season is year-round: It's just as active even well after summer, when the park is open for snowmobiling and skiing for 3 months during the winter.

The beauty of Yellowstone's natural architecture comes from its geology. The area experienced three separate volcanic periods beginning 600,000 years ago. During major eruptions, thousands of square miles of landmass were blown skyward, leaving enormous calderas (volcanic depressions). This process repeated itself several times—there is geologic evidence of 27 layers of lava in some areas. The volcanic mountains were subsequently glaciated during the ice ages. The powerful glacial bulldozing caused by the movement of these gigantic blocks of ice shaped the valleys and canyons of the park.

Yellowstone National Park was officially created in 1872, when Pres. Ulysses Grant signed legislation making it the first national park in the world. In the years afterward it suffered from incompetent superintendents and shortages of cash until at last, in 1886, the U.S. Army took possession. In 1916, control of the park was transferred to the newly created National Park Service. Yellowstone became the first park to come under its stewardship.

Avoiding the Crowds. If a few thousand people on the benches in front of Old Faithful is not your idea of a wilderness park experience, then skip Yellowstone's busy summer season, which amounts to July and August. Or, if you can't avoid that time of year, head up the trails away from the roads and car traffic.

While the beautiful seasons between May and mid-June and after Labor Day are no longer the best-kept secret in the Rockies, they are still far less crowded than summer. Just be careful how far you push it. A beautiful Halloween weekend of rustling leaves and bright sun can become a winter wonderland overnight. Come too early in the spring—which is when most of the region's precipitation falls—and you'll be stuck at lower elevations while snowbanks melt on the higher trails. Try June and September, or if you like taking chances, go the first 2 weeks in October. Any earlier or later, and you're on your own—truly on your own, because most of the inns in the park will have shut their doors.

Even if your visit is scheduled during the park's busy months, you can still avoid the crowds: Take short hikes in popular spots at times of day when others are eating. Take a sack lunch—you can buy them at the Hamilton stores—and avoid the lines at restaurants.

Even better, take longer, further walks. About 500 yards from a trailhead, the crowd thins rapidly. Strap on a backpack (be sure and get a backcountry permit) and spend a night in the wilderness. You'll see some of the park's most beautiful landscape, and there won't be a tourist in the picture.

Just the Facts

GETTING THERE & GATEWAYS

To get to Yellowstone from I-90 and **Bozeman,** Montana (91 miles), take U.S. 191 south to its junction with U.S. 287 and head straight through the town of **West Yellowstone** to the park's west entrance.

Billings, Montana, is 129 miles from Yellowstone's Northeast Entrance over Beartooth Pass (closed from October 15 to Memorial Day). It's a 65-mile drive south from I-94 on U.S. 212 to Red Lodge, then 30 miles on the Beartooth Highway to the park.

Cody, Wyoming, is 52 miles to Yellowstone's east entrance, which is closed from November 1 to April 30, via U.S. 14/16/20. To Yellowstone's Northeast Entrance, it's 53 miles via Wyo. 120/296 to the Beartooth Highway (which is closed from October 15 to Memorial Day) intersection, and 14 miles beyond that to the entrance.

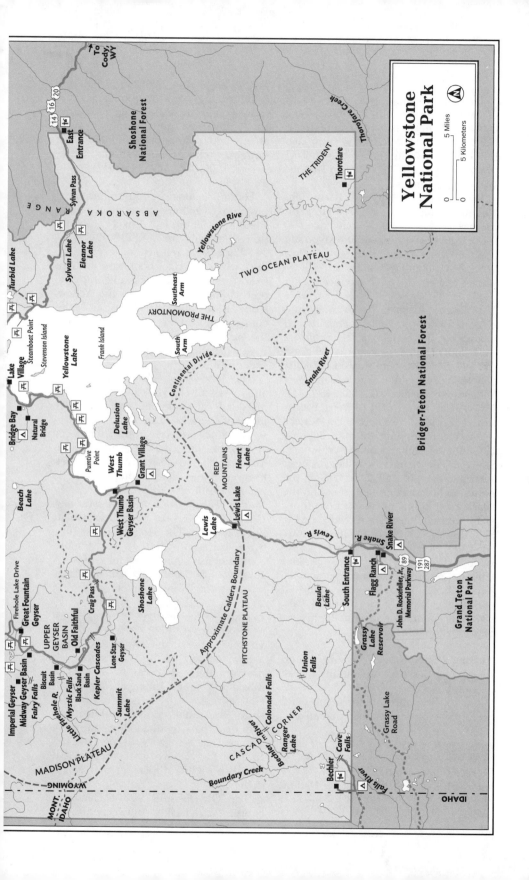

Yellowstone National Park

0 — 5 Miles
0 — 5 Kilometers

To Cody, WY

14 16 20

East Entrance

Shoshone National Forest

Thorofare Creek

ABSAROKA RANGE

Sylvan Pass

Sylvan Lake

Eleanor Lake

Turbid Lake

THE TRIDENT

Thorofare

Yellowstone Rive

TWO OCEAN PLATEAU

Southeast Arm

THE PROMONTORY

Steamboat Point

Stevenson Island

Yellowstone Lake

Frank Island

South Arm

Lake Village

Bridge Bay

Natural Bridge

Delusion Lake

Pumtive Point

Continental Divide

Snake River

Beach Lake

West Thumb

Grant Village

RED MOUNTAINS

Heart Lake

West Thumb Geyser Basin

Bridger-Teton National Forest

Firehole Lake Drive

Great Fountain Geyser

Imperial Geyser

Midway Geyser Basin

Fairy Falls

Biscuit Basin

Little Firehole R.

Mystic Falls

Black Sand Basin

Kepler Cascades

Lone Star Geyser

Summit Lake

UPPER GEYSER BASIN

Old Faithful

Craig Pass

Shoshone Lake

Lewis Lake

Lewis Lake

Lewis R.

Snake R.

Snake River

South Entrance

Flagg Ranch

191 287

89

John D. Rockefeller, Jr. Memorial Parkway

Grand Teton National Park

Grassy Lake Reservoir

Beula Lake

Approximate Caldera Boundary

PITCHSTONE PLATEAU

MADISON PLATEAU

Union Falls

Colonade Falls

CASCADE CORNER

Ranger Lake

Bechler River

Boundary Creek

Cave Falls

Bechler

Falls River

Grassy Lake Road

WYOMING
MONT.
IDAHO

IDAHO

Jackson, Wyoming, is 57 miles south of Yellowstone's South Entrance. Take U.S. 89/191 north through Grand Teton National Park. You can also approach this entrance from the east over Togwotee Pass on U.S. 26/287 from **Dubois,** Wyoming (83 miles).

From **Little Bighorn Battlefield National Monument,** an easy detour on the way to or from Yellowstone, take I-90 south from the monument into Wyoming about 50 miles to Exit 9, and then follow U.S. west about 188 miles to Yellowstone's east entrance (closed in winter).

The Nearest Airports. You can fly into Bozeman's airport, **Gallatin Field,** which provides daily service via Delta, Northwest, and United as well as Horizon (☎ 800/547-9308) and Skywest (☎ 800/453-9417) commuter flights. The **West Yellowstone Airport** (☎ 406/646-7631), U.S. 191, 1 mile north of West Yellowstone, provides commercial air service seasonally, from June through September only, on Delta's commuter service, Skywest. The airport in Billings, **Logan International** (☎ 406/238-3420), is the busiest in Montana and is located on the rimrocks 2 miles north of downtown. Daily intrastate service is provided by **Big Sky Airlines** (☎ 800/237-7788 or 406/245-2300). Regional daily service is provided by Delta, Horizon, Northwest, and United. Cody's **Yellowstone Regional Airport** (☎ 307/587-5096) serves the east entrance of Yellowstone National Park with year-round commercial flights via Skywest and United Express.

Renting a Car. Most of the major auto rental agencies have operations in the gateway cities.

For toll-free numbers for airlines and rental car agencies, see the appendix.

INFORMATION

To receive maps and information before your arrival, contact **Yellowstone National Park,** WY 82190 (☎ 307/344-7381; www.nps.gov/yell).

Information regarding lodging, some campgrounds, tours, boating, and horseback riding in Yellowstone is available from **Yellowstone National Park Lodges,** Yellowstone National Park, WY 82190 (☎ 307/344-7311; www.travelyellowstone.com).

For information regarding educational programs in Yellowstone, contact **Yellowstone Association,** P.O. Box 117, Yellowstone National Park, WY 82190 (☎ 307/344-2293; www.YellowstoneAssociation.org), which operates bookstores in park visitor centers, museums, and information stations, and oversees the **Yellowstone Association Institute** and the courses taught at the old buffalo ranch in the park's northeast corner. They also have a catalog of publications you can order by mail.

The following books are interesting and informative. If you cannot find them in your local bookstore, you can order many of them by mail from the Yellowstone Association (see above). Look for *Yellowstone Trails,* Mark C. Marschall (Yellowstone National Park, Wyo.: The Yellowstone Association) if you're a hiker. If you're traveling with kids, pick up *An Outdoor Family Guide to Yellowstone and Grand Teton National Parks,* Lisa Gollin Evans (Seattle: The Mountaineers, 1001 SW Klickitat Way, 98134). For a more comprehensive guide, look for *Frommer's Yellowstone & Grand Teton National Parks,* by the author of this chapter.

VISITOR CENTERS

There are five major visitor and information centers in the park, and each has something different to offer. The **Albright Visitor Center** at Mammoth Hot Springs, is the largest. It provides visitor information and publications about the park, exhibits depicting park history from prehistory through the creation of the National Park Service, and houses a wildlife display on the second floor.

The **Old Faithful Visitor Center** is another large facility. An excellent short film describing the geysers, *Yellowstone, A Living Sculpture,* is shown throughout the day in an air-conditioned auditorium. Rangers dispense various park publications and post projected geyser eruption times here. An informative seismographic exhibit is an added attraction.

The **Canyon Visitor Center** in Canyon Village, is the place to go for books and an informative display about bison in the park. It's staffed with friendly rangers used to dealing with crowds.

The **Fishing Bridge Visitor Center** near Fishing Bridge on the north shore of Yellowstone Lake, has an excellent wildlife display. You can get information and publications here as well.

The **Grant Village Visitor Center** has information, publications, a slide program, and a fascinating exhibit that examines the effects of fire in Yellowstone.

Other sources of park information are at the Madison Information Station; the Museum of the National Park Ranger and the Norris Geyser Basin Museum, both at Norris; and the West Thumb Information Station.

FEES & PERMITS

A pass to enter Yellowstone is $20 per vehicle for a 7-day period (no matter the number of occupants), and covers both Yellowstone and Grand Teton national parks. Entering on a snowmobile or motorcycle costs $15 for 7 days, and someone who comes in on bicycle, skis, or foot pays $10. If you expect to visit the parks more than once in a year, buy an annual pass for $40.

You must have a backcountry permit for any overnight trip, on foot, horseback or by boat. See "Exploring the Backcountry," below, for more information.

SPECIAL REGULATIONS & WARNINGS

It is unlawful to approach within 100 yards of a bear or within 25 yards of other wildlife. Feeding any wildlife is illegal. Wildlife calls such as elk bugles or other artificial attractants are forbidden.

SEASONS & CLIMATE

For general information on seasons and climate in the area, see "Seasons & Climate," in the Grand Teton National Park chapter. Keep in mind that nearby Grand Teton is actually a bit lower in elevation than Yellowstone, so snows melt later in Yellowstone and temperatures are slightly lower.

ROAD OPENINGS

Scheduling a driving trip to Yellowstone during spring months can be a roll of the dice, since openings can be delayed for weeks, especially at higher altitudes. A heavy snowstorm in October can compel early closure of the park gates. Depending upon weather, most other park roads remain open until the park season ends on the first Sunday in November (the Beartooth Highway between Cooke City and Red Lodge, Montana, closes mid-October). The only road open year-round is the **Mammoth Hot Springs–Cooke City Road.**

Plowing in Yellowstone begins in early March. The first roads open to motor vehicles usually include **Mammoth-Norris, Norris–Canyon, Madison–Old Faithful,** and **West Yellowstone–Madison.** The latter may open by the end of April. If the weather cooperates, the east and south entrances, as well as roads on the east and south sides of the park, will open early in May. Opening of the **Tower-Roosevelt** to **Canyon Junction Road,** however, may be delayed by late season snowfall on Dunraven Pass.

The **Sunlight Basin Road** (which is also called the **Chief Joseph Highway**), connecting the entrance at Cooke City, Montana, with Cody, Wyoming, often opens by early May. The **Beartooth Highway** between Cooke City and Red Lodge, Montana, is generally open by Memorial Day weekend.

The road between **Gardiner and Cooke City, Montana,** remains open year-round to serve the needs of the inhabitants of that small, isolated community. This presents late-season travelers with an opportunity to see the northeast area of the park and some of its abundant wildlife during winter months.

If You Only Have 1 Day

If you'll be coming into Yellowstone one day and leaving the next, here's an itinerary that highlights the best of the best. If you'll be spending the night, try to reserve a room in one of the park hotels—either Old Faithful Inn or the Lake Hotel—and you'll find yourself minutes from all of the major attractions.

The quickest route to the inner road loops of the park is by the west entrance road, so come in that way, stopping perhaps for a stroll along the banks of the **Madison River,** where you can see the forest recovering from the 1988 fires. You'll also spot wildlife: ducks and trumpeter swans on the river, grazing elk and bison. Turn north at Madison Junction to **Norris Geyser Basin,** where there are two boardwalk tours. Take the southern one if you don't feel there's time for both, because there you can wait for the **Echinus Geyser** pool to fill and erupt.

You're now driving the **upper loop,** which goes north to **Mammoth Hot Springs,** east to **Tower-Roosevelt,** south to **Canyon Village,** and west again to Norris, finally returning to Madison Junction, a circuit of about 85 miles. But don't complete the loop—at Canyon, continue south on the southern loop, which will take you to **Fishing Bridge** and **Lake Village,** then by **West Thumb,** west over Craig Pass to **Old Faithful,** and back to the Madison Junction from the south. If you'd done the entire loop, it covers 96 miles. My recommendation: Do one loop the day you enter the park, spend the night, then do the second loop and leave the way you came. If this is part of a longer cross-country trip, you can enter one side of the park and leave the other.

The Upper Loop. The Norris Geyser basin is a major concentration of thermal attractions, including **Porcelain Basin** and the legendary (but dormant) **Steamboat Geyser,** and has a nice **museum.** Mammoth has one of the park's major attractions, the ever-growing terraces of **Mammoth Hot Springs.** In addition to the natural attraction, the Albright Visitor Center provides excellent historical background for everything you'll see in the park. There is a fine old hotel at Mammoth, and lodging just outside the park in Gardiner, too, but we recommend you continue further around the loop on your first day. From Mammoth the route winds through forested areas that lead to the edge of the **Lamar Valley,** a deep, rounded path for the Lamar River that is a major wildlife repository. You could stop for the night at nearby **Roosevelt Lodge,** or continue south to Yellowstone's **Grand Canyon,** one of the most dramatic sights in the park, and on to the Lake Yellowstone Hotel, at the north end of **Yellowstone Lake.**

The Lower Loop. This is a better way to go in our opinion. You'll also see the two largest geyser areas in Yellowstone: **Norris** to the north and the park's signature attraction, **Old Faithful,** to the south. On the eastern side of this route, you'll find the **Grand Canyon of the Yellowstone** and **Hayden Valley,** where you'll find resident herds of buffalo. Farther south, the **Yellowstone Lake** area is a haven for water-lovers: There's fishing, boating, and places for picnicking on the shore of the lake.

Altogether, this circuit is called the **"Grand Loop,"** and takes you through all the major areas of the park except the road between Norris and Canyon Village. If you have 2 days, then do both loops. You could do it in a day—it's only 120 miles long—but you'd scare a lot of other travelers as you sped by.

If You Have More Time

Stretching your visit to several days will give you time to take advantage of everything the park offers. Since the roads in Yellowstone are organized into a series of interconnecting loops, which you can come into from any of the park's five entrances, it doesn't really matter where you begin your tour. To simplify things, we will discuss attractions and activities going clockwise along each section of the **Grand Loop Road,** beginning at **Madison Junction.** But you can enter the loop at any point and pick up our tour as long as you are traveling clockwise. We haven't suggested an optimum amount of time to spend on each leg of the loop since that will depend on your particular interests.

WEST YELLOWSTONE TO NORRIS

Since the largest percentage of visitors to Yellowstone enter at the **West Yellowstone Entrance,** we'll use that as a jumping-off point to begin an extended tour of the park. As you travel the 14 miles from the gate to **Madison Junction,** you will find the **Two Ribbons Trail,** which offers an opportunity to walk through and inspect the effects of the 1988 fire. Park maps don't identify all the observation points and side roads in the area. So now is the time to begin forming the habit of driving off the beaten path, even when you may not know where you're going. Keep a sharp eye peeled for the poorly marked **Riverside turnout** on the Madison River side of the road; it's a paved road on the north side of the highway about 6 miles from the entrance. This back road takes you along a river, removed from most traffic, with a number of turnouts perfectly situated to look for resident swans, enjoy a picnic, or test your fly-fishing ability.

As you continue toward **Madison Junction,** you'll see vivid evidence of the 1988 fire and, odds are, a herd of bison that frequents the area during summer

months. As frightening as the fire was, it had its good points: When temperatures exceeded 500°F, pine seeds were released from fire-adapted pine cones, which has quickened the rebirth cycle. The hundreds of tiny trees making their way through the soil are evidence that this forest is recovering very quickly.

The short **Harlequin Lake Trail** offers an excellent, easy opportunity to explore the area and see various types of waterfowl. An alternative hike, the **Purple Mountain Trail** is more strenuous, but is one of the best in the area. For descriptions of both, see "Day Hikes" below.

Madison Junction marks the confluence of the Gibbon and Firehole Rivers, two famous trout streams, which meet to form the Madison River, one of three which join to form the Missouri. It's also where you'll enter the northern loop toward Norris Junction, along a windy 14-mile section of road that parallels the **Gibbon River.** At **Gibbon Falls,** which is 84 feet tall, you'll see water bursting out of the edge of a caldera in a rocky canyon, the walls of which were hidden from view for several hundred years until being exposed by the fire of 1988. There's a delightful **picnic area** just below the falls, on an open plateau overlooking the Gibbon River. Before arriving at Norris Junction, you'll discover the **Artist Paint Pot Trail** in Gibbon Meadows 4.5 miles south of the Norris Junction, an interesting, worthwhile, and easy half-mile stroll. Across the road from the trailhead is **Elk Park,** where you can expect to see a large resident herd of elk.

NORRIS GEYSER BASIN

Perhaps more than any other area in Yellowstone, this basin is living testimony to the park's unique thermal activity. It changes from year to year as thermal activity and the ravages of wind, rain, and snow create new and different ponds and landscapes. This is the location of one of the park's highest concentration of thermal features, including the most active geysers, with underground water temperatures that reach 459°F.

There are two loop trails here, both mostly level with wheelchair access, to the Porcelain Basin and the Back Basin. If you take in both of them, you'll see most of the area's interesting thermal features. If you're pressed for time, take the shorter, **Porcelain Basin Trail,** a boardwalk that takes only 45 minutes. To me, this area is especially spectacular on summer days when thermal activity takes place on the ground with thunder and lightning storms overhead.

The **Porcelain Basin Trail** is a 0.75-mile round-trip that can be completed in 45 minutes; on it are Black Growler Steam Vent, Ledge Geyser, and the descriptively named Whale's Mouth.

The 1.5-mile **Back Basin Loop** is easily negotiable in 1 hour and passes by **Steamboat Geyser,** which has been known to produce the world's highest and most memorable eruptions. However, these 400-foot waterspouts occur infrequently, so it will take some luck to see one. Conversely, **Echinus Geyser** erupts several times a day.

Among the many highlights of the area is the **Norris Geyser Basin Museum,** a beautiful, single-story stone-and-log building with several excellent exhibits explaining the nature of the area. Also nearby is the **Museum of the National Park Ranger,** which is little more than a room full of artifacts in a small building near the campground (see below). Both museums open in mid- to late May, weather permitting, and are open until September; hours vary by season, but you can expect the museums to be open from 8am to 6pm during the busiest times (roughly Memorial Day to Labor Day, but again weather is a factor).

NORRIS TO MAMMOTH HOT SPRINGS

From Norris Geyser Basin, it's a 21-mile drive north to Mammoth Hot Springs, past the **Twin Lakes,** beautiful, watery jewels surrounded by trees. During the early months of the park year, the water is milky green because of the runoff of ice and snow. This is an excellent place to call timeout and do some bird watching.

This stretch of road, between Norris Junction and Mammoth Hot Springs, presents yet another excellent opportunity to see the effects of the 1988 fire. The large **meadow** on the west (left, if you are traveling north) side of the highway that begins 3 miles from Norris is popular with moose, thanks to water from bogs, marshes, and a creek. As you travel alongside **Obsidian Creek,** you'll notice the smell of sulfur in the air, evidence of thermal vents.

On the east (right, if you are traveling north) side of the road 4 miles from Norris is **Roaring Mountain,** a patch of ground totally devoid of brush and plant life, covered with trees and stumps from the fire. Its bareness is attributed to the fact that, as steam vents developed here, the ground became too hot and acidic, which bleached and crumbled the rock, taking the undergrowth with it. Historians say that the noise from the Roaring Mountain was once so loud that it could be heard as far as 4 miles away; these days it is very quiet.

Just up the road 2 miles is the **Beaver Lake Picnic Area,** an excellent little spot right on Beaver Lake for a snack. It's also a good place to keep an eye out for moose.

As you wend your way a 0.5 mile to Obsidian Cliff, across the road from the picnic area the terrain changes quickly, and you'll find yourself driving through a narrow valley bisected by a beautiful green stream. **Obsidian Cliff** is where ancient peoples of North America gathered to collect obsidian, a hard, black rock that was used to make weapons and implements.

If you didn't stop at Beaver Lake, consider taking time for the 3-minute detour to **Sheepeater Cliffs** (unless you're driving an RV or pulling a trailer). This quiet, secluded spot on the banks of the Gardner River is home to yellow-bellied marmots that live in the rocks, safe from flying predators (like eagles) and coyotes.

Exiting the valley, head north onto a high plateau, where you'll find **Swan Lake,** which is surrounded by Little Quadrant Mountain and Antler Peak to the west, and Bunsen Peak to the north.

At the northernmost edge of the Yellowstone Plateau, you'll begin a descent through **Golden Gate.** This steep, narrow stretch of road was once a stagecoach route constructed of wooden planks anchored to the mountain by a massive rock called the **Pillar of Hercules,** the largest rock in an unmarked pile that sits next to the road.

From the 45th parallel parking area on the North Entrance road north of Mammoth Hot Springs, a short hike leads to the **Boiling River.** Here you can take a dip, during daylight hours, where a hot spring empties into the Gardner River.

MAMMOTH HOT SPRINGS

The large Albright Visitor Center located near park headquarters, has more visitor information and publications than other centers. You'll probably want to stop in here.

This area may offer the best argument for getting off the roads and out of your car. Though it's possible to see most of the wildlife and the major thermal areas from behind car windows, your experience of the park will be multiplied tenfold by the expenditure of a small amount of energy. Most people in average shape are capable of negotiating the trails here, a significant percentage of which are level or only moderately inclined boardwalks. Even the more challenging trails frequently have rest areas where you can catch your wind and stop and absorb the magnificent views.

One of Yellowstone's most unique, beautiful, and fascinating areas are the **Upper** and **Lower terraces.** Strolling among them, you can observe Mother Nature going about the business of mixing and matching heat, water, limestone, and rock fractures to sculpt the area. With the exception of the Grand Canyon of the Yellowstone River, this is the most colorful area of the park; its tapestries of orange, pink, yellow, green, and brown, formed by masses of bacteria and algae, seem to change colors before your eyes.

The mineral-rich hot waters that flow to the surface here do so at an unusually constant rate, roughly 750,000 gallons per day, which results in the deposit of almost 2 tons of limestone on these ever-changing terraces. Contours are constantly undergoing change in the hot springs, as formations are shaped by large quantities of flowing water, the slope of the ground, and trees and rocks that determine the direction of the flow.

On the flip side of the equation, nature has a way of playing tricks on some of her creatures: **Poison Spring** is a sinkhole on the trail, so named because carbon dioxide collects there, often killing creatures who stop for a drink. The **Lower Terrace Interpretive Trail** (see "Day Hikes," below) is one of the best ways to see this area.

After passing **Palette Spring,** where bacteria create a collage of browns, greens, and oranges, you're on your way to **Cleopatra** and **Minerva terraces.** Minerva is a favorite of visitors because of its bright colors and travertine formations, the product of limestone deposits.

The hike up the last 150 feet to the Upper Terrace Loop Drive is slightly steeper, though there are benches at frequent intervals. From here you can see all the terraces and several springs— **Canary Spring** and **New Blue Spring** being the most distinctive—and the red-roofed buildings of **Fort Yellowstone,** which is now the park headquarters.

MAMMOTH HOT SPRINGS TO TOWER JUNCTION

Heading east from Mammoth on the Tower Road, a 6-mile drive will bring you to the **All Person's Fire Trail;** this flat, easy, boardwalk stroll is an excellent opportunity to learn about the environmental effects of the fire.

Two miles later is **Blacktail Plateau Drive,** a 7-mile, one-way dirt road that offers great wildlife-viewing opportunities and a bit more solitude. You'll emerge back onto the Mammoth-Tower Road, about a mile west of the turnoff to the Petrified Tree.

Turn right onto this half-mile-long road that dead-ends at the **Petrified Tree,** a redwood that, while standing, was burned by volcanic ash more than 50 million years ago.

TOWER-ROOSEVELT

Just beyond the Petrified Tree, you'll come to **Tower-Roosevelt,** the most relaxed of the park's villages and a great place to take a break from the more crowded attractions. Even if you aren't going to stay, you might want to take a look at the **Tower Soldier Station,** now the ranger residence at Tower Junction, one of three surviving outposts from the era of U.S. Cavalry management of the park. Also here is **Roosevelt Lodge,** a rustic building that commemorates Pres. Teddy Roosevelt's camping excursion to this area of the park in 1903.

At **Specimen Ridge,** 2.5 miles east of the Tower Junction on the northeast entrance road, you'll find a ridge that entombs one of the world's most extensive fossil forests.

FROM TOWER JUNCTION TO THE GRAND CANYON OF THE YELLOWSTONE

A few minutes' drive from the Tower area is the **Calcite Springs Overlook.** A short loop along a boardwalk leads to the overlook at the rim of **The Narrows,** the narrowest part of the canyon. You can hear the river raging through the canyon some 500 feet below, and look across at the canyon walls comprised of rock spires and bands of columnar basalt. Just downstream is the most prominent feature in the canyon, **Bumpus Butte.**

Continuing south, you will travel through the **Washburn Range,** an area in which the 1988 fire ran especially hot and fast. The terrain changes dramatically as the road climbs, as well as along some major hills toward **Mount Washburn.** There are trailheads for the **Mount Washburn Trail,** one of my favorites, on each side of the summit.

As you approach **Dunraven Pass** (8,859 ft.), keep your eyes peeled for the shy mountain sheep, as this is one of their prime habitats.

One mile further south is the **Washburn Hot Springs Overlook,** which offers sweeping views of the Grand Canyon. On a clear day, you can see 50 to 100 miles south, beyond Yellowstone Lake.

CANYON VILLAGE

You're in for yet another eyeful when you reach the **Grand Canyon** of Yellowstone National Park. Compared to the Grand Canyon of Arizona, the Yellowstone canyon is relatively narrow; however, the steepness of the cliffs, which descend hundreds of feet to the bottom of a gorge where the Yellowstone River flows, are equally impressive. It's also equally colorful, with displays of oranges, reds, yellows, and golds. You won't find thermal vents in Arizona, but you will find them here, a constant reminder of ongoing underground activity.

You should plan on encountering crowds when you reach **Canyon Village.** The **Canyon Visitor Center** is the place to go for books and a bison exhibit.

An auto tour of the canyon follows **North Rim Drive,** a two-lane, one-way road that begins in Canyon Village, to your first stop, **Inspiration Point.** On the way, you'll pass a **glacial boulder** estimated to weigh 500 tons that was deposited by melting ice more than 10,000 years ago.

At Inspiration Point, a moderately strenuous descent down 57 steps takes you to an overlook with views of the Lower Falls and canyon. There are several other view points you can stop at along North Rim Drive before you reconnect with the main Canyon Village–Yellowstone Lake road, which will take you down to South Rim Drive.

For the adventurous, an alternative to driving from one overlook to another is to negotiate the **North Rim Trail,** which is slightly more than 2.25 miles long, beginning at Inspiration Point. Unfortunately, the North Rim Trail is not a loop, so if you take the hike, you'll have to backtrack. The footpath brings you closer to what you want to see, and you won't be fighting for elbow room, as you will at the overlooks that are only accessible to cars.

Whether you drive or walk, you should go down to the **Upper Falls View,** where a 0.25-mile trail leads down from the parking lot to the brink of the **Upper Falls** and an overlook within splashing distance of the rushing river and the waterfall. At this point you won't just hear, you'll feel the power of the river as it begins its course down the canyon.

The **South Rim Drive** leads to several overlooks and better views of the Lower Falls. The most impressive vantage point is from the bottom of **Uncle Tom's Trail,** a steep, 500-foot route to the river's edge that begins at the first South Rim parking lot.

South Rim Road continues to a second, lower parking lot and a trail that leads to **Artist Point.** The view here is astounding, one of my favorites in the park, and is best in the early morning.

CANYON VILLAGE TO FISHING BRIDGE

The road winds through the **Hayden Valley,** which is a vast expanse of beautiful green meadows accented by brown cuts where the soil is eroded along the banks of the Yellowstone River. The valley is now a wide, sprawling area where bison and antelope play and where trumpeter swans, white pelicans, and Canada geese float along the river. This is also a prime habitat for the grizzly, so during early spring months pay close attention to binocular-toting visitors grouped beside the road.

Nature is working at her acidic best at the **Sulphur Caldron** and **Mud Volcano** areas, 12 miles south of the Canyon Junction, which were described by the frontier minister Edwin Stanley as "unsightly, unsavory, and villainous." I think he was right on the money, so you'll not want to miss this area. After all, there's nothing like the sound of burping mud pots.

At **Dragon's Mouth Spring,** turbid water from an underground cavern is propelled by escaping steam and sulfurous gases to an earth-side exit where it colors the earth shades of orange and green. The belching of steam from the cavern and the attendant sound, which is due to the splash of 180°F water against the wall in a subterranean cavern, creates a medieval quality; hence, the name of the spring.

Nearby **Mud Volcano** is an unappetizing mud spring, the product of vigorous activity caused by escaping sulfurous gases and steam. The youngest feature in the area is **Black Dragon's Caldron,** which is often referred to as the demon of the backwoods, and rightly so. The caldron emerged from its subterranean birthplace for the first time in 1948 when it announced its presence by blowing a hole in the landscape, scattering mature trees hundreds of feet in all directions. Since then, continual seismic activity and intermittent earthquakes in the area have caused it to relocate 200 feet south of its original position.

The road across the Yellowstone River at **Fishing Bridge** was once the only eastern exit in the park, the route leading over Sylvan Pass to Cody, Wyoming. The bridge, which was built in 1902, spans the Yellowstone River as it exits Yellowstone Lake, and is another prime spawning area for native trout. The **Fishing Bridge Visitor Center** has a first-rate wildlife display. You'll find an excellent hiking trail, **Elephant Back Loop Trail,** leading off the short strip of highway between Fishing Bridge and the Lake Village area.

YELLOWSTONE LAKE AREA

As if the park didn't have enough record-setting attractions, at 7,773 feet **Yellowstone Lake** is North America's largest high-altitude lake. The lake exhibits its multifaceted personalities daily, ranging from a placid, mirrorlike surface to a cauldron whipped by southerly winds that create 3- to 4-foot waves. Because the lake has the largest population of native cutthroat trout in North America, it makes an ideal fishing spot during the summer.

Lake Village, on the northwest shore of the lake, offers a wide range of amenities, the most prominent of which is the majestic 100-year-old **Lake Yellowstone Hotel,** perhaps the most beautiful structure in the park.

Just south of Lake Village is the **Bridge Bay Marina,** the center of the park's water activities. Here you can arrange for guided fishing trips or small boat rentals, or learn more about the lake during an informative and entertaining 1-hour narrated boat tour. The marina is usually open from mid-June to mid-September.

Though the **Natural Bridge,** near Bridge Bay, is well marked on park maps, it's one of the park's best-kept secrets, and you may end up enjoying it by yourself. The mile-long path down to the bridge, a geologic masterpiece consisting of a massive rock arch 51 feet overhead, spanning Bridge Creek, is an excellent bike route.

The **West Thumb** area along the western shoreline, is the *deepest* part of Yellowstone Lake. Because of its suspiciously craterlike contours, many scientists speculate that this 4-mile-wide, 6-mile-long, water-filled crater was created during volcanic eruptions approximately 125,000 years ago.

The **West Thumb Geyser Basin** is notable for a unique series of geysers. Some are situated right on the shores, some overlook the lake, and some can be seen *beneath* the lake surface. Three of the shoreline geysers, the most famous of which is **Fishing Cone,** are occasionally marooned offshore when the lake level rises. Fortunately, boardwalks surround the area, so it's easy to negotiate. Maps and details on the area are available in the **West Thumb Information Station.**

As you depart the West Thumb area, you are presented with two choices: either to head south toward Grand Teton

National Park or to head west across the **Continental Divide** at Craig Pass, en route to Old Faithful.

GRANT VILLAGE TO THE SOUTH ENTRANCE

In contrast to the forgettable village of Grant is the beautiful 22-mile drive to **Grand Teton** along high mountain passes and **Lewis Lake.** After the lake loses its winter coat of ice, it is a popular spot for early season anglers who are unable to fish streams that are clouded by the spring runoff.

Beyond the lake, the road follows the Lewis River through an alpine area and along the **Pitchstone Plateau,** a pile of lava more than 2,000 feet high and 20 miles wide that was created some 500,000 years ago. A high gorge overlooking the river provides views that are different from, but just as spectacular as, those in other sections of the park.

WEST THUMB TO OLD FAITHFUL

The most interesting phenomenon on the Old Faithful route is **Isa Lake** at Craig Pass. Unlike most lakes and streams in the park, it drains into both eastern and western drainages and ends up in the Pacific Ocean and the Gulf of Mexico. Amazingly, as a consequence of a gyroscopic maneuver, the outlet on the *east* curves *west* and drains to the Pacific, and the outlet on the *west* curves *east* and drains to the Gulf.

Before you reach the Old Faithful geyser area, two additional detours are recommended. Two and one-half miles southeast of Old Faithful is an overlook at the spectacular **Kepler Cascades,** a 150-foot, stair-step waterfall on the Firehole River that is footsteps from the parking lot.

Near that parking lot is the trailhead for the second detour, a 5-mile round-trip to the **Lone Star Geyser** (on the eponymous trail), which erupts every 3 hours, sending steaming water 30 to 50 feet from its 12-foot cone.

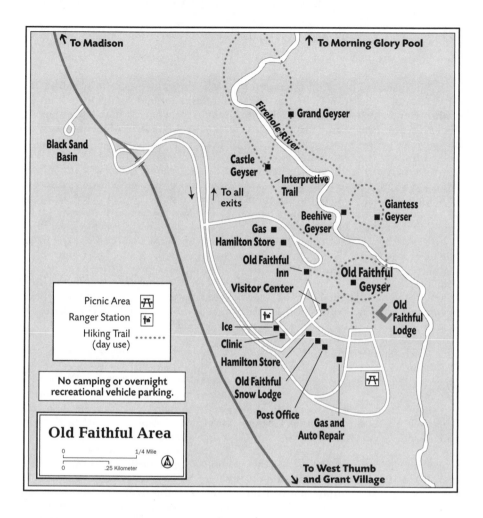

Old Faithful Area

0 —————— 1/4 Mile
0 —————— .25 Kilometer

OLD FAITHFUL GEYSER AREA

Despite the overwhelming sight of the geysers and steam vents that populate the Old Faithful area, I suggest you resist the temptation to explore until you've stopped at the **Old Faithful Visitor Center.** Check the information board for estimated times of geyser eruptions, and plan accordingly.

The Old Faithful area is generally divided into four sections: **Upper Geyser Basin,** which includes Geyser Hill, **Black Sand Basin, Biscuit Basin,** and **Midway Geyser Basin.** All of these areas are connected to the Old Faithful area by paved trails and roads. If time allows, hike the area; it's fairly level, and distances are relatively short. Between the Old Faithful area and Madison Junction, you'll also

find the justifiably famous **Lower Geyser Basin,** including **Fountain Paint Pot** and the trails surrounding it. You can see some of these geysers on Firehole Lake Drive.

Though **Old Faithful** is not the largest or most regular geyser in the park, its image has been seen on everything from postage stamps to whiskey bottles. Like clockwork, the average interval between eruptions is 79 minutes, though it may vary 20 minutes in either direction. A typical eruption lasts $1\frac{1}{2}$ to 5 minutes, during which 3,700 to 8,400 gallons of water are thrust upward to heights of 180 feet. For the best views and photo opportunities of the eruption in the boardwalk area, plan on arriving at least 15 minutes before the scheduled show to assure a first-row view.

An alternative to a seat on the crowded boardwalk is a stroll from the Old Faithful Geyser up the **Observation Point Trail** to an observation area that provides better views of the entire geyser basin. The path up to the observation point is approximately 0.5 mile, and the elevation gain is only 200 feet, so it's an easy 15-minute hike. The view of the eruption of the geyser is more spectacular from here and the crowds less obtrusive.

Accessible by walkways from Old Faithful Village, the **Upper Geyser Basin Loop** is referred to as Geyser Hill on some maps. The 1.3-mile loop trail winds among several thermal attractions. **Anemone Geyser** may offer the best display of the various stages of a typical eruption as the pool fills and overflows, after which bubbles rising to the surface begin throwing water in 10-foot eruptions, a cycle that is repeated every 7 to 10 minutes.

Two other stars of the show in the Upper Geyser Basin are **Castle Geyser** and **Grand Geyser.** Castle Geyser, with the largest cone of any geyser in the park, currently erupts for 20 minutes every 10 to 12 hours, after which a noisy steam phase may continue for half an hour. Grand Geyser, the tallest predictable geyser in the world, usually erupts every 7 to 15 hours with powerful bursts that produce streams of water that may reach 200 feet in height.

The **Riverside Geyser** is situated on the bank of the Firehole River, near **Morning Glory Pool.** One of the most picturesque geysers in the park, its 75-foot column of water creates an arch over the river. **Morning Glory Pool** was named for its likeness to its namesake flower in the 1880s, but has since lost its bloom. Vandals have tossed so much debris into its core over the years that it now suffers from poor circulation and reduced temperatures, which are causing unsightly brown and green bacteria to grow on its surface.

The **Black Sand Basin** is a cluster of especially colorful hot springs and geysers located a mile north of Old Faithful. It is interesting primarily because of its black sand, a derivative of obsidian. **Biscuit Basin,** located 2 miles further up the road, was named for biscuitlike deposits that surrounded colorful **Sapphire Pool** until a 1959 earthquake caused the pool to erupt, sending them skyward. Both the Black Sand Basin and the Biscuit Basin can be viewed from flat, interpretive boardwalks.

The **Midway Geyser Basin** extends for about a mile along the Firehole River. The major attractions here are the **Excelsior Geyser,** the third-largest geyser in the world and once the park's most powerful geyser, and the well-known **Grand Prismatic Spring,** the largest hot spring in Yellowstone, and the second largest in the world.

OLD FAITHFUL TO MADISON JUNCTION

Believe it or not, there are other superb geysers and hot springs on **Firehole Lake Drive,** all viewable without leaving your vehicle, along a 3-mile, one-way road. The turnoff for Firehole Lake Drive is about 8 miles north of Old Faithful area. There are three geysers of particular interest on this road. The largest is **Great Fountain Geyser,** which erupts every 8 to 12 hours, typically spouting water some 100 feet high for periods of 45 to 60 minutes. However, the lucky visitor may see the occasional "superburst" that reaches heights of 200 feet or more.

Estimates are that **White Dome Geyser** has been erupting for hundreds of years. Unfortunately, the age and height of this massive cone are not matched by spectacular eruptions. The vent on top of the cone has been nearly sealed with deposits of "geyserite," so eruptions now reach only 30 feet. However, the cone itself is worth a trip down this road.

Further on, **Pink Cone Geyser** couldn't be closer to the road, since road builders cut into the geyser's mound during construction.

About a half mile north of where Firehole Lake Drive rejoins the Grand Loop Road is the **Fountain Paint Pots** area. This is a very popular spot, so you may be forced to wait for a parking place. All the various types of thermal activity are on display here, so as you stroll along the easy, 0.5-mile boardwalk, you'll be in an area that may have six geysers popping their lids at the same time.

Organized Tours & Ranger Programs

Self-guided car audio tours are a great way to get the most out of a drive through the park in your own vehicle. Just rent an audiocassette player that plugs into your vehicle's cigarette lighter and plays through your FM radio, sit back, and listen as prerecorded messages describe park routes and attractions, and provide historical and environmental information. There's even a section that addresses the interests of younger travelers. The system, which rents for $25 for a full day or $16 for a half day, is available from **Yellowstone National Park Lodges** at all hotel activity desks and is highly recommended.

A number of tour companies offer bus tours of the park originating in gateway communities: **Powder River Coach USA** (☎ 800/527-6316) out of Cody has daylong tours; **Gray Line of Yellowstone** (☎ 800/523-3102) takes travelers around the park from West Yellowstone, as does **Buffalo Bus Lines** (☎ 800/426-7669). If you are looking for specialized guided trips such as photo safaris or snowmobile tours, contact the chambers of the gateway community where you want to begin.

Within the park, the hotel concessionaire, **Yellowstone National Park Lodges** (☎307/344-7311; ynp-lodges.com) has a variety of general and specialized tours. Three different **motor coach tours** are available from all of Yellowstone's villages. For $29 you can explore either the Upper Loop (Norris Geyser Basin, the Grand Canyon of the Yellowstone and Mammoth Hot Springs) or the Lower Basin (Old Faithful, Yellowstone Lake, the Hayden Valley), or, for $33, you can do the whole thing, the Grand Loop. These are full-day tours, with stops at all

the sights and informative talks by the guides. Specialty trips include photo safaris, wildlife trips up the Lamar Valley (try it in winter), and special group charters of the historic yellow "gearjammers" from the 1930s.

At Bridge Bay Marina, 1-hour **Scenicruiser tours** depart throughout the day from June to the end of September for a trip around the northern end of giant Yellowstone Lake. You view the Lake Hotel from the water, and visit Stevenson Island, while a guide fills you in on the history, geology, and biology. Fares are $9 for adults, $5 for children 2 to 12. Guided fishing trips on 22-foot and 34-foot cabin cruisers are also available from Yellowstone National Park Lodge at Bridge Bay, and you can rent smaller outboard and rowboats.

Buses are replaced in the winter by **snowcoach tours.** These are more vans than buses, mounted on tank treads with skis in front for steering. The snowcoach can pick you up at the south or west entrances, or at Mammoth, and take you all over the park. You can spend a night at Old Faithful and then snowcoach up to Mammoth the next night, or do round-trip tours from the gates or wherever you're lodged in the park. One-way trips range from $40 to $44, while round-trips cost $79 to $88.

Ranger-led programs are held throughout the park during the summer, sometimes at campground amphitheaters, some at visitor centers, some on hikes or at key landmarks. It's the best value in the park: free.

Evening campfire programs are presented nightly in the summer at campgrounds at Mammoth Hot Springs, Norris, Madison, Old Faithful, Grant, Bridge Bay, and Canyon, three times weekly at Lewis Lake campground and the Tower Falls Amphitheater. Many of these activities are accessible to travelers with disabilities. There are more tours and evening programs in the **Old Faithful** area than anywhere else in the park. The talks and walks, which can run as long as 1½ hours, usually focus on the geysers, their fragile plumbing, and their role in the Yellowstone ecosystem. Check the park newspaper when you enter the park for a current listing of ranger programs.

Day Hikes

WEST YELLOWSTONE TO MADISON

Artist Paint Pot Trail

0.5 mi. RT. Easy. Access: Gibbon Meadow 4.5 mi. south of Norris Junction.

This interesting and worthwhile stroll along a relatively level path winds through a lodgepole pine forest in Gibbon Meadows, to a mud pot at the top of a hill. This thermal area contains some small geysers, hot pools, and steam vents.

Harlequin Lake Trail

0.5 mi. RT. Easy. Access: West entrance rd. 1.5 mi. west of the Madison Campground.

This is an excellent, easy opportunity to explore the area while winding through the burned forest to a small lake populated by various types of waterfowl.

Purple Mountain Trail

6 mi. RT. Easy. Access: Madison-Norris Rd. 0.25 mi. north of the Madison Junction.

This hike requires more physical exertion as it winds through a burned forest to the top of what many consider only a tall hill, with an elevation gain of 1,400 feet.

Two Ribbons Trail

0.75 mi. RT. Easy. Access: A turnout on the north side of the road 3 mi. east of the west entrance.

Along this trail you'll see a mosaic of blackened, singed, and unburned trees. The scraggly, deformed branches and piles of rock are surrounded by bushes and fresh, bright green tree shoots that are only now emerging from the soil.

NORRIS GEYSER BASIN

Back Basin Loop

1.5 mi. RT. Easy. Access: Norris Geyser Basin.

This level boardwalk is easily negotiable in 1 hour and passes by Steamboat Geyser, which has been known to produce the world's highest and most memorable eruptions. However, these 400-foot waterspouts occur infrequently, so it will take some luck to see one.

Porcelain Basin Trail

0.75 mi. RT. Easy. Access: Norris Geyser Basin.

This short trail, which can be completed in 45 minutes, is on a level boardwalk that, like the Back Basin Loop, is in a concentration of thermal attractions that may change every year.

MAMMOTH HOT SPRINGS AREA

All Person's Fire Trail

0.5 mi. RT. Easy. Access: Tower Rd., 8 mi. east of Mammoth Hot Springs.

This level, easy stroll along a boardwalk presents an excellent opportunity to learn about the effects of the fire on the environment.

Bunsen Peak Trail

4.2 mi. RT. Moderate. Access: Across the road from the Glen Creek Trailhead, 5 mi. south of Mammoth on the Mammoth-Norris Rd.

This trail leads to a short but steep 2.1-mile trip to the 8,564-foot summit, with a 1,300-foot gain in elevation. Park rangers say this is a favorite for watching the sunrise behind Electric Peak, off to the northwest, which glows with a golden hue. At the top of the peak, you will be 3,000 feet above the valley.

Lower Terrace Interpretive Trail

1.5 mi. RT. Easy. Access: South of the village on the road to Norris.

This interpretive trail is one of the best ways to see this area. The trail starts at 6,280 feet and climbs another 300 feet along marginally steep grades, through a bare, rocky, thermal region to a flat alpine area and observation deck at the top, but it's not a difficult climb.

GRAND CANYON OF THE YELLOWSTONE RIVER AREA

Mount Washburn Trail

6 mi. RT. Moderate. Access: At the end of Old Chittenden Rd. and at Dunraven Pass.

The Mount Washburn Trail falls into the "If you can only do one hike, do this one" category. The rises are fairly gradual, and they're interspersed with long, fairly level stretches. At this elevation, however, the best method of attacking the mountain is to pace yourself, which has its own rewards: You have time to appreciate the views to the east of the Absaroka Mountains, south to Yellowstone Lake, and west to the Gallatin Mountains. Odds are good that you'll see mountain sheep, since it's a popular summer grazing area for them, as well as yellow-bellied marmots and the wily red fox. The hike to the summit is an easy 90-minute walk at a steady pace, or 2 hours with breaks. At this elevation, where weather changes quickly, it's always a good idea to bring several layers of clothing. Fortunately, there's a warming hut in the base of the ranger lookout, viewing telescopes, and rest rooms, but, alas, no hot chocolate machine.

North Rim Trail

2 mi. one way. Easy. Access: Inspiration Point.

This trail, which is described more fully in the Grand Canyon section above, has as its primary attractions better views than you'll see from the paved overlooks.

South Rim Trail

3.2 mi. one way. Easy. Access: In the parking lot just beyond South Rim Dr. Bridge.

Like the North Rim Trail, there are more and better views of the canyon and river than you can see from a vehicle, and you're away from the crowds.

Uncle Tom's Trail

500 ft. one way. Moderate. Access: South Rim parking lot.

The short trip is down 328 stairs and paved inclines that lead to the river. The trail is rather steep, but can be negotiated in an hour, though it will be challenging for inexperienced hikers.

YELLOWSTONE LAKE AREA

Elephant Back Loop Trail

2 mi. RT. Easy. Access: Just before the turnoff for the Lake Yellowstone Hotel.

The hike is to an overlook that provides photographers with panoramic views of Yellowstone Lake and its islands, the Absaroka Range, and Pelican Valley.

Storm Point Trail

2 mi. RT. Easy. Access: Directly across from the Pelican Valley Trailhead (on the lake side of the road), 3.5 mi. east of Fishing Bridge.

The Storm Point Trail follows a level path that terminates at a point jutting into the lake with panoramic views. During spring months, this is a popular spot with grizzlies, so the trail may be closed; even when it's open, check with rangers regarding bear activity.

OLD FAITHFUL AREA

Fairy Falls Trail

12 mi. RT. Moderate. Access: Imperial Meadows in Biscuit Basin.

Though considerably longer than the Mystic Falls Trail, the Fairy Falls Trail is equally popular with the park staff because it leads to a taller waterfall. The hike begins at the Imperial Meadows

Trailhead, 1 mile south of the Firehole River Bridge on Fountain Flat Drive. It winds through an area populated by elk along Fairy Creek, then past the Imperial Geyser. From here, it joins Fairy Creek Trail and travels east to the base of the falls. The total gain in elevation is only 100 feet.

Fountain Paint Pot Trail

0.5 mi. RT. Easy. Access: Fountain Paint Pot parking lot.

This area is a very popular attraction, so you may be forced to wait for a parking place. All of the various types of thermal activity strut their stuff here, so as you stroll along the easy 0.5-mile boardwalk you'll be in an area that may have six geysers popping their lids at the same time.

Geyser Hill Basin Loop

1.3 mi. RT. Easy. Access: Old Faithful boardwalk.

One of the most interesting, and easiest, loops in the area, this trail winds around several thermal attractions. Anemone Geyser may offer the best display of the various stages of a typical eruption as the pool fills and overflows. The Lion Group consists of four geysers that are interconnected beneath the surface; and Doublet Pool is especially popular with photographers who are attracted by a complex series of ledges and deep-blue waters. Giantess Geyser is known for its violent eruptions.

Lonestar Geyser Trail

5 mi. RT. Easy. Access: The parking lot opposite Kepler Cascades.

This is another trail that falls into the "Gotta do it" category, and its popularity is its only disadvantage. Despite the probability that you'll be sharing the territory with others, there are several compelling reasons to give it a go. From the trailhead you'll wend your way through a forested area along a trail that parallels

the Firehole River. The payoff for your effort is the arrival at the geyser, though it will not be found in the *Guinness Book of Records*. It sits alone, a vanilla-chocolate ice-cream cone near the middle of a vast meadow partially covered by grass and trees, exposed rock, gravel, and volcanic debris. Surrounding it are small, bubbling geysers and steam vents. The 5-mile hike is easily doable in 2 hours.

Mystic Falls Trail

1.1 mi. one way. Easy. Access: Imperial Meadows in Biscuit Basin.

This is a favorite of park rangers. The trail leads to a waterfall on the Little Firehole River that drops more than 100 feet, one of the steepest in the park. The trail starts at Biscuit Basin, crosses the river, then disappears into the forest. The total distance to the falls is only 1.1 miles; there's a trail to take you to the top.

To make your return more interesting, continue 0.2 mile to the Little Firehole Meadows Trail, which has an overlook that offers a view of Old Faithful in the distance. Best estimates are that the total time for the hike is an easy 2 hours, with an elevation gain of only 460 feet.

Observation Point Trail— Solitary Geyser

2.1 mi. RT. Easy. Access: Old Faithful boardwalk.

This trail leads to an observation area that provides better views of the entire geyser basin. The path up to the observation point is approximately 0.5 mile, and the elevation gain is only 200 feet, so it's an easy 15-minute hike. The view puts the entire Upper Geyser Basin into a different perspective; it is possible to see most of the major geysers, as well as inaccessible steam vents located in the middle of wooded areas. From the top of the boardwalk continue to the Solitary Geyser on a downhill slope that leads past the geyser, through the basin, and back to the inn, which completes the loop.

Exploring the Backcountry

The backcountry season in Yellowstone is brief but glorious: For just 2 or 3 months, the snow melts off, the streams drop to fordable levels, and you can go deep into a domain of free-roaming wildlife, unfenced, untracked by humans, and largely unpatrolled.

You must have a backcountry permit for any overnight trip, on foot, horseback, or by boat, and you can camp only in designated campsites, many of which are equipped with food storage poles to keep wildlife out of your stores. You can pick up a permit for hiking or boating the day before beginning a trip, but if you'll be traveling during peak season, make a reservation in advance. It costs $20 to hold a site, and you can begin making reservations for the upcoming year beginning April 1.

Contact the **Yellowstone Backcountry Office** (P.O. Box 168, Yellowstone National Park, WY 82190) and they'll send you a useful "Backcountry Trip Planner" with a detailed map showing where the campsites are, how to make reservations, and how to prepare. Pick up your permit in the park within 48 hours of your departure, at one of the following visitor ranger stations any day of the week during the summer: Bechler, Canyon, Mammoth, Old Faithful, Tower, West Entrance, Grant Village, Lake, South Entrance, and Bridge Bay.

Backcountry Geysers. If you just can't get your fill of geysers, or if you've had your fill of people, several trails lead to more isolated geysers. The **Shoshone Geyser Basin** and **Heart Lake Geyser Basin** contain active geysers, as do **Ponuntpa Springs** and the **Mudkettles** in the Pelican Valley Area, **Imperial Geyser** in the Firehole area, and the **Highland Hot Springs** on the Mary Mountain Trail. If you head in these directions, be careful about walking on unstable surfaces: A young man died in 1988 when he fell into a superheated pool.

Shoshone Lake. Shoshone Lake is the park's largest backcountry lake and a popular spot for hikers. The shortest route is via the **Delacy Creek Trail,** which begins 8 miles east of Old Faithful on the Old Faithful–West Thumb road. The trail winds 3 miles along Delacy creek through moose country and the edge of the forest at the lake. From here you can head around the lake (a distance of 18 miles) in either direction. Assuming you take a clockwise track, you'll take the **East Shore Trail** to its intersection with **Dogshead Trail,** then head west on the **South Shore Trail** until it intersects with the North Shore Trail and returns to your starting point.

A detour: At the western end of the lake you'll arrive at the 1-mile-long **Shoshone Geyser Basin Trail,** which loops through a number of geysers, hot springs, and meadows that during spring months are ankle-deep in water and mud.

As you travel the lake's loop trail along the **East Shore Trail,** you'll have views of the lake at the top of a 100-foot rise. Then, on the **South Shore Trail,** you'll cross the Lewis Channel, which may have thigh-high water as late as July. Beyond that, the trail is a series of rises that are easily negotiable by the average hiker, passing across shallow Moose Creek and through meadows where you may spot deer or moose early in the morning or evening.

The 7-mile **North Shore Trail** is a mostly level path through a lodgepole-pine forest, though there is one 200-foot-tall ridge. The best views of the lake are from cliffs on this trail. The loop trail is especially popular with overnighters, since there are 26 campsites on the loop.

The Bechler Region. This area is often referred to as the Cascade Corner because it contains a majority of the park's waterfalls. It offers great opportunities to view thermal features. Many backpacking routes cut through this region, including one that leads to Old Faithful on the **Bechler River Trail.**

To begin your hike, drive into the park from Ashton, Idaho, and check in at the Bechler Ranger Station. To reach the ranger station, drive east 17 miles from Ashton on the Cave Falls Road; 3 miles before reaching Cave Falls, you'll find the ranger station turnoff. The ranger station is 1.5 miles down the gravel road.

The **Bechler Meadows Trail** takes you into this southwest corner, rich in waterfalls, cascades, and thermal areas, and rarely visited. About 6 miles into the journey, the trail fords the river several times as it enters Bechler Canyon, where it passes Collonade and Iris Falls. This is a camping trip—you can cover a good 30 miles, depending on what turns you take—best made late in the summer to avoid high water during creek crossings. For a shorter trip, hike 3.5 miles along the **Bechler River Trail** to the **Boundary Creek Trail,** then return to the station via the **Bechler Meadows Trail,** a round-trip of 7 miles.

The most adventurous, and most scenic, route takes you 30 miles from the ranger station to the end of the trail at the **Lonestar Trailhead** near Old Faithful. Beyond Iris Falls, and then Ragged Falls, you'll reach a patrol cabin at Three Rivers Junction at the 13-mile mark, a popular camping area. If you continue towards Old Faithful, you'll intersect the **Shoshone Lake Trail** at the 23.5 mile mark and exit 6.5 miles later.

Thorofare Area. When you enter this section you're venturing into the most remote roadless area in the Lower 48. You can make a round-trip of around 70 miles deep into the wilderness, or shorter hikes, such as a trip from the park's east entrance road to the Yellowstone River inlet on Yellowstone Lake's southeast arm. The remoteness of this country discourages many hikers, so you'll have it mostly to yourself. The tepee rings and lean-tos that you may see are remnants of the presence of Indians, who once used this area as the main highway between Jackson Hole and points north.

The trail follows the eastern shore of Yellowstone Lake and then the Yellowstone River into some of the most remote and beautiful backcountry in the Rockies. It's a lot of miles and climbing, but you'll be rewarded with views of the Upper Yellowstone Valley, Two Oceans Plateau, and abundant wildlife. You'll reach the Park Service's Thorofare Ranger Station at 32 miles, and a few miles further you'll come to Bridger Lake, outside the park, and a gorgeous alpine valley with a ranger station known as Hawk's Rest. Fishers love this area—so do grizzly bears, especially during the cutthroat trout spawning season in early summer. You'll be a good 35 miles from the trailhead at the lake, and even the most capable hikers should consider riding with an outfitter. You can cut the journey shorter by getting a boat shuttle to the mouth of the lake's southwest arm, call ☎ 307/344-7901. Only nonmotorized boats are allowed into the arm to the Yellowstone River outlet (you can canoe in, a wonderful trip in good weather). Or you can come into Thorofare through Bridger-Teton National Forest up the North Fork of the Buffalo Fork to the south (check with the forest's Blackrock Ranger Station).

Aside from grizzlies, the major obstacle to early season trips in the Thorofare is water; you'll encounter knee-deep water at **Beaverdam Creek** and at **Trapper Creek,** as late as July.

The Sportsman Lake Trail. This moderate, 14-mile trail begins near Mammoth Hot Springs and extends west toward U.S. 191 to Sportsman Lake. From the Glen Creek Trailhead 5 miles south of Mammoth Hot Springs, you'll spend 2 miles on the Glen Creek Trail as you traverse a mostly level, wide-open plateau, covered with sagebrush, that is the home of herds of elk and a bear management area. At the **Sepulcher Mountain Trail** at the 3 mile mark, the terrain gets steeper as you continue northwest on the **Sportsman Lake Trail**—the elevation gain is approximately 2,300 feet to the Sepulcher summit (though you don't go to it on this route). The trail eventually enters the forest and descends to a log that is used to cross Gardner River. Then, it's uphill for another 4 miles to **Electric Divide,** another 2,000-foot gain in elevation. From there, the trail descends 2,100 feet in 3 miles to Sportsman Lake. The lake, which sits in a meadow populated by moose and elk, is teeming with cutthroat trout. There are two campsites.

Other Summer Sports & Activities

Biking. Yellowstone's narrow and twisty roads and lack of bike lanes make life difficult for bikers, and off-road opportunities are limited because of the small number of trails on which bikes are allowed. The following trails are available to bikers, but know that you will share the roads with hikers. The **Mt. Washburn trail,** leaving from the Old Chittenden Road, is a strenuous trail that climbs 1,400 feet. The **Lone Star Geyser trail,** accessed at Kepler Cascade near Old Faithful, is an easy 1-hour ride on a user-friendly partly paved road. Near Mammoth Hot Springs, **Bunsen Peak Road** and **Osprey Falls trails** present a combination ride/hike: The first 6 miles travel around Bunsen Peak; getting to the top requires a hike. A hike down to Osprey Falls adds 3 miles to the journey.

Bike rentals are available in the gateway towns West Yellowstone (**Yellowstone Bicycles, ☎ 406/646-7815**) and Jackson (**Hoback Sports, ☎ 307/733-5335;** or **The Edge Sports,** 490 W. Broadway, ☎ **307/734-3916**).

Boating. The best place to enjoy boating in Yellowstone is on **Yellowstone Lake,** which has easy access and beautiful, panoramic views. The lake is also one of the few areas where power boats are allowed. Rowboats and outboard motorboats can be rented at **Bridge Bay Marina** (☎ **307/344-7381**). Motorboats, canoes, and kayaks can be used on **Lewis Lake** as well.

Fishing. Seven varieties of game fish live in the parks: native cutthroat, rainbow, brown, brook and lake trout, grayling, and mountain whitefish. Of the trout, only the cutthroat are native, and they are being pressured in the big lake by the larger lake trout, despite efforts to remove the exotic strains by gill-netting. As a result, you can't keep any pink-meat cutthroat caught in Yellowstone Lake, and you *must* keep any lake trout.

The Yellowstone season typically opens on the Saturday of Memorial Day weekend and ends on the first Sunday in November. The exceptions are Yellowstone Lake's slightly shorter season, and the lake's tributaries, which are closed until July 15 to avoid conflicts between humans and grizzly bears, both of which are attracted to spawning trout.

In June try the **Yellowstone River** downstream of Yellowstone Lake, where the cutthroat trout spawn. In July fish the **Madison River** near the west entrance, and again in late fall for rainbow and some brown trout. In late summer you can try to hook the cutthroats that thin out by September on the **Lamar River** in the park's beautiful northeast corner.

You can fish the **Yellowstone River** below the Grand Canyon by hiking down into **Seven Mile Hole,** a great place to cast (not much vegetation to snag on) for cutthroat trout from July to September, with the best luck around Sulphur Creek.

Other good fishing stretches include the **Gibbon** and **Firehole** rivers, which merge to form the Madison River on the park's west side, and the 3-mile **Lewis River Channel** between Shoshone and Lewis lakes during the fall spawning run of brown trout.

Horseback Riding. People who want to pack their gear on a horse, llama, or mule must get permits to enter the

Yellowstone backcountry, or hire an out-fitter with a permit (see below). Other visitors who want to get in the saddle but not disappear in the wilderness can put themselves in the hands of the concessionaire, **Yellowstone National Park Lodges.** Stables are located at Canyon Village, Roosevelt Lodge, and Mammoth Hot Springs. Roosevelt Lodge also offers **evening rides** from June into September. Choices are 1- and 2-hour guided trail rides daily aboard well-broken, tame animals. Wranglers refer to these as "nose-and-tail" tours, and an experienced rider is likely to find them awfully tame.

If you're looking for a longer, overnight horse-packing experience, contact the park and request a list of approved concessionaires that lead backcountry expeditions. Most offer customized, guided trips, with meals, horses, and camping and riding gear provided. Costs will run from $200 to $400 per day per person, depending on the length of trip and number of people. In Gardiner, at the north entrance to the park, **Wilderness Connection** (☎ 406/848-7287) offers horseback trips in the park for groups of 2 to 10; rates begin at $200 per day for customized, guided hikes and horseback trips, with meals and lodging in tents or nearby hostelries. Coming from the south side of the park, try **Press Stephens, Outfitter** (☎ 307/455-2250).

Winter Sports & Activities

The average snowfall in a Yellowstone winter is nearly 50 inches, creating a beautiful setting for sightseers, and a wonderful resource for outdoor winter recreation. The steaming hot pools and geysers create little islands of warmth and attract not just tourists but wildlife as well. Nearby trees are transformed into "snow ghosts" by frozen thermal vapors. Bison become frosted, shaggy beasts, easily spotted as they take advantage of the more accessible vegetation on the thawed ground. Yellowstone Lake's surface freezes to an average thickness of 3 feet, creating a vast ice sheet that sings and moans as the huge plates of ice shift. But the ice is thinner where hot springs come up on the lake bottom, and you'll see otters surfacing at the breaks in the ice. Waterfalls become astounding pieces of frozen sculpture.

Only two of the park's hostelries, **Mammoth Hot Springs** and the **Old Faithful Snow Lodge,** provide accommodations from December through March, as does **Flagg Ranch,** just outside the park's south entrance. The only road that's open for cars is the **Mammoth Hot Springs–Cooke City Road.** Most visitors these days come into Yellowstone in winter from the west or south by snowcoach or snowmobile.

For additional information on all of the following winter activities and accommodations, as well as snowcoach reservations, contact **Yellowstone National Park Lodges** (☎ 307/344-7311). (For more on snowcoach tours, see "Organized Tours & Ranger Programs," above).

The **Yellowstone Institute** (☎ 307/344-2294) offers winter courses based out of its headquarters at the old Buffalo Ranch in Lamar Valley. Past offerings have included 3-day classes devoted to "Backcountry by Ski," "Yellowstone's Winter World," and "Tracking Yellowstone's Wolves."

Cross-Country Skiing. There are 40 miles of **cross-country trails** in the Old Faithful area, including the popular **Lone Star Geyser Trail,** an 8-mile trail in a remote setting that starts at the Old Faithful Snow Lodge; the **Fern Cascades trail,** which winds for 3 miles through a rolling woodland landscape on a short loop close to the Old Faithful area. In the Mammoth area, try the **Upper Geyser Basin and Biscuit Basin trail,** which some say is the best in Yellowstone, though it may take an entire day to negotiate.

Equipment rentals (about $12 per day), ski instruction ($17 per person for a 2-hour group lesson), ski shuttles to various locations, and guided ski tours are available at the **Old Faithful Snow Lodge** and the **Mammoth Hot Springs Hotel.** A half-day guided excursion (two-person minimum) is around $32 per person; a full day is $69 per person. For groups of three or more, the cost is considerably lower: $21 per person for a half day, $48 per person for a full day.

Ice-Skating. The **Mammoth Skating Rink** is located behind the Mammoth Hot Springs Recreation Center. On a crisp winter's night you can rent a pair of skates ($1 per hour, $4 per day) and glide across the ice while seasonal melodies are broadcast over the PA system. It's cold out there, but there's a warming fire at the rink's edge.

Snowmobiling. Roads that are jammed with cars during the summer fill up with bison and snowmobiles during the winter. In deference to these shaggy road warriors, moderate speed limits are strictly enforced, but this is still an excellent way to sightsee at your own pace. A driver's license is required for rental ($120 for a single rider, $135 per day for two at **Mammoth Hot Springs Hotel** or **Old Faithful Snow Lodge**) and a quick lesson will put even a first-timer at ease. A helmet is included with the snowmobile, and you can rent a clothing package for protection against the bitter cold. **Warming huts** are located at Mammoth, Indian Creek, Canyon, Madison, West Thumb, and Fishing Bridge. They offer snacks, a hot cup of coffee or chocolate, and an excellent opportunity to recover from a chill. *A caution:* Keep an eye on snow conditions. While it's true that snowmobile trails are groomed for travel, when snow cover is scanty, a normally smooth trip can become something akin to riding on a jackhammer. Also, if engine noise is what you came to Yellowstone to escape, this is probably not for you.

Snowmobile rentals are also available in the **gateway communities** of Gardiner and West Yellowstone, Montana, and at Flagg Ranch). Most rental shops accept reservations weeks in advance, so reserving at least a day to 2 weeks ahead of time is a good idea. Plan on making reservations for the week between Christmas and New Year's at least 6 months in advance.

Camping

There are 12 campgrounds in Yellowstone, 5 of them under the efficient management of **Yellowstone National Park Lodges,** the park concessionaire. The other seven are smaller, less expensive, and often less crowded—my personal favorites are Slough Creek, in the Lamar Valley, and Norris, a shady spot by the river near the Norris Geyser Basin. The seven campgrounds still run by the **National Park Service** are at Indian Creek, Lewis Lake, Mammoth, Norris, Pebble Creek, Slough Creek, and Tower Fall. They fill daily on a first-come, first-served basis.

Yellowstone National Park Lodges runs the bigger campgrounds, at Bridge Bay, Canyon, Grant Village, Madison, and Fishing Bridge. **Same-day** and **advance reservations** may be made by calling ☎ **307/344-7311** (TDD 307/344-5395) or by writing to Yellowstone National Park Lodges, P.O. Box 165, Yellowstone National Park, WY 82190. The only campground equipped with RV hookups is at **Fishing Bridge RV Park,** and it accepts hard-sided vehicles only (no tents or tent trailers), with electrical, water, and sewer hookups. Though there are no hookups at the other campgrounds, RVers can be accommodated at any of them.

Camping is allowed only in designated areas and is limited to 14 days between June 15 and Labor Day, and to 30 days the rest of the year. Checkout time for all campgrounds is 10am. Quiet hours are strictly enforced between the hours of 8pm and 8am. No generators, radios, or other loud noises are allowed during these hours. See the chart below for specific amenities and prices at each campground.

INSIDE THE PARK

The **Tower Falls Campground** is near a convenience store, restaurant, and gas station at Roosevelt Lodge and has **forested** sites; it is located 19 miles north of Canyon Village and 18 miles east of Mammoth.

Slough Creek Campground is located in the Lamar Valley, near the northeast entrance, where there are fewer people, good fishing, and the possibility of a wolf howl to stimulate your dreams; however, rest room facilities are in pit toilets.

Canyon Campground fills early in the day, so you have to be prompt to get a slot. This is the only campground where rangers assign sites, rather than letting you seek your own; the camp is in a heavily wooded area. There's a store, restaurants, visitor center, and laundry nearby at Canyon Center.

Fishing Bridge RV Park is somewhat controversial because of its location in an area where bears feed in the spring; only hard-sided camping vehicles are allowed.

Bridge Bay Campground is near the shores of Yellowstone Lake, offering tremendous views, especially at sunrise and sunset. Unfortunately, though surrounded by the forest, the area has been clear-cut, so it offers no privacy, except for the sites around the perimeter, where there is forest. It's close to boat launching facilities and the boat rental operation.

The **Madison** Campground is in a wooded area just south of the river. It has good access to fishing and hiking, and a short drive to the amenities of West Yellowstone.

The **Norris Campgrounds** attractive, wooded sites are in the heart of the park's east side, close to wildlife activity, geothermal areas and the Gibbon River.

Campground	Total Sites	RV Hookups	Dump Station	Toilets	Drinking Water
Inside the Park					
Bridge Bay*	430	No	Yes	Yes	Yes
Canyon*	272	No	Yes	Yes	Yes
Fishing Bridge*†	341	Yes	Yes	Yes	Yes
Grant Village*	425	No	Yes	Yes	Yes
Indian Creek	75	No	No	Yes	Yes
Lewis Lake	85	No	No	Yes	Yes
Madison*	280	No	Yes	Yes	Yes
Mammoth	85	No	No	Yes	Yes
Norris	116	No	No	Yes	Yes
Pebble Creek	36	No	No	Yes	Yes
Slough Creek	29	No	No	Yes	Yes
Tower Fall	32	No	No	Yes	Yes
Near the Park					
Bakers Hole †	72	No	No	Yes	Yes
Lonesomehurst	26	No	No	Yes	Yes
Rainbow Point †	85	No	No	Yes	Yes

* Reserve through Amfac Parks and Resorts.
† Accept hard-sided vehicles only.

NEAR THE PARK

There are three U.S. Forest Service campgrounds in the **West Yellowstone** area, all in the Gallatin National Forest. Bakers Hole and Rainbow Point accommodate RVs only; Lonesomehurst accommodates RVs and tent campers. They are all convenient to the park entrance at West Yellowstone. For reservations, call ☎ **800/280-2267. Bakers Hole,** just 3 miles north of West Yellowstone on U.S. 191, is popular, so reserve early. Only RVs are accepted, but there are no hookups. **Lonesomehurst,** 8 miles west of the park on U.S. 20, then 4 miles north on Hebgen Lake Road, is only one-third the size of Bakers Hole and fills up quickly in summer, so reservations are strongly advised. It has tent and RV sites. **Rainbow Point** is reached by driving 5 miles north of West Yellowstone on U.S. 191, then 3 miles west on Forest Service

Road 610, then north for 2 miles on Forest Service Road 6954. It accommodates only RVs, but there are no hookups.

Accommodations

INSIDE THE PARK

If you're coming at the height of summer, book ahead! Contact **Yellowstone National Park Lodges,** P.O. Box 165, Yellowstone National Park, WY 82190 (☎ **307/344-7311**), for lodging in the park. Accommodations are normally open from early summer to late October. Mammoth Hot Springs and Old Faithful Snow Lodge then reopen for the winter season beginning in mid-December and running through mid-March.

Another option is **Flagg Ranch Resort** (see the "Grand Teton National Park" chapter). Only 2 miles from Yellowstone's South Entrance, it's a convenient

Showers	Fire Pits/ Grills	Laundry	Public Phone	Reserve	Fees	Open
No	Yes	No	Yes	Yes	$15	Late May to Sept
Yes	Yes	Yes	Yes	Yes	$15	June to Sept
Yes	Yes	Yes	Yes	Yes	$26	Late May to Labor Day
Yes	Yes	Yes	Yes	Yes	$15	Late May to Sept
No	Yes	No	No	Yes	$10	June to Sept
No	Yes	No	No	No	$10	Mid-June to Nov
No	Yes	No	Yes	Yes	$15	Late May to Nov
No	Yes	No	Yes	No	$12	Year-round
No	Yes	No	Yes	No	$12	Mid-May to Sept
No	Yes	No	No	No	$10	Mid-June to Sept
No	Yes	No	No	No	$10	Late May to Nov
No	Yes	No	No	No	$10	Mid-May to Late Sept
No	Yes	No	Yes	Yes	$10	Late May to Sept
No	Yes	No	No	Yes	$10	Late May to Sept
No	Yes	No	Yes	Yes	$10	Late May to Sept

jumping-off point for exploring the southern reaches of the park and for snowmobiling in Yellowstone during the winter months.

MAMMOTH HOT SPRINGS AREA

Mammoth's distance from key attractions like Old Faithful and the Grand Canyon of the Yellowstone makes it one of the last places to fill up. Despite that, it's a good base: home to the park's best visitor center, as well as to colorful limestone terraces.

Mammoth Hot Springs Hotel and Cabins

P.O. Box 165, Yellowstone National Park, WY 82190. ☎ **307/344-7311.** Fax 307/344-7456. www.travelyellowstone.com. 98 units, 126 cabins. $48–$83 double; $48–$77 cabin. AE, CB, DC, DISC, MC, V.

This historic building stands below the steaming, stair-stepping terraces of Mammoth Hot Springs, only 5 miles from the north entrance. It began life as a hostelry in 1911, and was replaced by a lodge in 1937. The hotel's dormer windows and wood floors are attractive, and the high-ceilinged lobby is comfortable and relatively quiet. The only high-end accommodations are the suites. Standard rooms and cabins are arranged around three grassy areas, where the resident elk often graze. If you require a tub be sure and request one when you make your reservation; otherwise, you could get a cramped, old-fashioned shower stall. The cabins here are cottage-style buildings, some with private hot tubs and sundecks. A formal dining room and a fast-food restaurant are both located in a separate building; nearby amenities include a medical clinic, grocery store, stables, and a filling station.

CANYON VILLAGE AREA

You may feel, standing at the center of Canyon Village, like you're in a mall parking lot. With one of the park's biggest attractions close by, this is one of the most bustling areas, and the design of the place adds to it. It's certainly a plus, though that the Grand Canyon of the Yellowstone is a short walk from the center of the village.

Canyon Lodge and Cabins

In Canyon Village (P.O. Box 165), Yellowstone National Park, WY 82190. ☎ **307/344-7311.** www.travelyellowstone.com. Open June 4–Sept 12. 37 units, 572 cabins. $105 double; $51–$101 cabin. AE, CB, DC, DISC, MC, V.

This lodge and cabin complex is one of the newer facilities in the park, but it can't escape the retro-1950s California-style atmosphere of Canyon Village. The lodge offers tastefully appointed motel-style accommodations in its three-story building, and in cabins that are scattered throughout the village. The motel units have various sleeping configurations designed to accommodate the needs of singles and families. The cabins are single-story duplex and fourplex structures with private bathrooms. They're nicer than their "rustic" counterparts in other centers, but given the sheer number of units involved, this isn't the place to "get away from it all." The newly opened Dunraven Lodge is tasteful and simple and nicely backed up against forest, away from the traffic of the village.

TOWER-ROOSEVELT AREA

This complex is a cheerful throwback to the early days of car camping in Yellowstone: no big complex of shops and services, not a lot of amenities. It's small, out of the way, and less crowded, which is worth a lot. Hiking trails and the beautiful corridor of the Lamar Valley and River that runs to the northeast entrance are nearby.

Roosevelt Lodge Cabins

P.O. Box 165, Yellowstone National Park, WY 82190. ☎ **307/344-7311** for reservations. 80 cabins (none with private bathroom). $40–$77 cabin. AE, CB, DC, DISC, MC, V.

This is considered the park's family hideaway, a low-key operation with primitive cabins and a lodge restaurant that's more like a big ranch house. It's a good choice for budget-conscious, outdoor types interested in exploring the northeast part of Yellowstone. The bare-bones cabins, Roughriders, are furnished with two simple beds, clean linens, a writing table, and a wood stove. Frontier cabins are slightly higher quality. The lodge is a rugged but charming stone edifice with a long, deep porch outfitted with rockers for relaxing. There's a dining area and a small lounge. Stagecoach rides, horseback trips, and Western trail cookouts give this place a cowboy flavor that many enjoy, and it's a less pushy, crowded scene than other park villages.

LAKE VILLAGE AREA

This resort along the lake is reminiscent of another, less hurried era. The location puts you near the lake's recreational opportunities and hiking trails, and you'll find accommodations in a historic hotel as well as motel and cabin units, and nearby lakeside camping sites. The food at the hotel is as good as any in the park, though low-priced alternatives are in the neighborhood.

Lake Lodge Cabins

On Lake Yellowstone (P.O. Box 165), Yellowstone National Park, WY 82190. ☎ **307/ 344-7311.** www.travelyellowstone.com. Open June 10–Sept 12. 186 cabins. $48–$101 cabin. AE, CB, DC, DISC, MC, V.

These cabins, which surround Lake Lodge, stand near the lake just around the corner north of the hotel. The lodge is an old Western longhouse fronted by a porch and rockers that invite visitors to sit and gaze out across the water. Accommodations are in well-preserved, clean, freestanding cabins near a trout stream that threads through a wooded area. The cabins come in two grades: Western cabins provide electric heat, paneled walls, two double beds, and combination bathrooms, while Frontier cabins are smaller and sparsely furnished, with only one double bed each and small shower-only bathrooms. There's a small bar area and a cafeteria that serves inexpensive meals.

Lake Yellowstone Hotel and Cabins

On the north side of the lake (P.O. Box 165), Yellowstone National Park, WY 82190. ☎ **307/344-7311.** www.travelyellowstone. com. 195 units, 102 cabins. Open May 14– Oct 3. $96–$143 double; $77 cabin. AE, CB, DC, DISC, MC, V.

The ionic columns, dormer windows, and deep porticos of this yellow frame building will carry you back to the Victorian era. The facility was completely restored in the early 1990s, and its better rooms are the park's most comfortable and roomiest. Accommodations are in three- and four-story wings in the hotel, in a motel-style annex, and in cabins. The upper-end rooms here have stenciled walls and traditional spreads on one queen or two double beds. The free-standing cabins, a good, low-priced alternative, are decorated with knotty-pine paneling and furnished with double beds and a writing table. *Note:* If you take a cabin, request a single rather than a duplex, since walls are paper thin.

Only the bar here leaves something to be desired: Guests are served from what looks like a temporary setup by the dining room entrance. The dining room has rattan furniture and is big enough to feed the busloads that arrive at mealtimes. A take-out delicatessen on the first floor serves ordinary finger food at a snail's pace.

GRANT VILLAGE AREA

Though Grant Village is near the south end of beautiful Lake Yellowstone and has a good visitors center, this fairly recent addition to park accommodations lacks character. The village is isolated from other park centers, so guests here are likely to frequent its tiny lounge and eat in one of its two decent restaurants overlooking the lake. Other guest services include a laundry facility, service station, and convenience store.

Grant Village

On the West Thumb of Yellowstone Lake (P.O. Box 165), Yellowstone National Park, WY 82190. ☎ **307/344-7311.** www.travelyellowstone.com. Open May 28–Oct 3. 300 units. $83–$96 double. AE, CB, DC, DISC, MC, V.

The southernmost of the major overnight accommodations in the park, Grant Village was completed in 1984 and seemed from the beginning lackluster. The lodge consists of six ordinary looking, motel-type two-story chalets set back from the water's edge, as well as a reception area and gift shop that are in a separate building near the village entrance. Rooms are tastefully furnished, most outfitted with light wood furniture and track lighting. Nicer, more expensive rooms with lake views have mullioned windows and full bathrooms. Midrange rooms are set farther back from the lake and overlook drab grounds.

OLD FAITHFUL AREA

At the Old Faithful area you'll spend a night in the midst of the largest and most famous geyser basin in the world. The park has removed some of the old building clutter, and does its best to protect the geothermal features and control the crowds. Here you have more choices of rooms, restaurants, and services—including a visitor center, gas station, and Hamilton store—than anywhere else in the park.

Old Faithful Inn

P.O. Box 165, Yellowstone National Park, WY 82190. ☎ **307/344-7311.** Fax 307/344-7456. www.travelyellowstone.com. Open May 1–Oct 17. 359 units. $52–$242 double. AE, CB, DC, DISC, MC, V.

When Robert Ringer designed the Old Faithful Inn almost a century ago, he created the perfect blend of rustic and regal, a grand building that blends beautifully with the native timbers and rock. There are three hotels within viewing distance of the geyser, including a very nice new one, but this is the crown jewel of Yellowstone's man-made wonders. Seven stories tall with dormers peaking from a shingled, steep-sloping roof, it looks like a lodgepole jungle gym inside—and indeed, you can climb the stairs to its internal balconies, and, with permission, ascend to a widow's walk and crow's nest. Only 30 miles from the west entrance and 40 miles from the south entrance, this is the first place visitors think of when they want a bed for the night, so make reservations far ahead during the busy summer months. The dining room is warmed on cool evenings by a fieldstone fireplace. Like other park properties, this lobby also houses a busy fast-food outlet that serves light meals, and there is a bar and a gift shop. Guest rooms are in the main building, and in wings that flank the main lodge. Original rooms are well appointed with conservative fabrics and park-theme art, but may not have private bathrooms; the wing rooms offer better facilities and more privacy.

Old Faithful Lodge Cabins

P.O. Box 165, Yellowstone National Park, WY 82190. ☎ **307/344-7311.** www.travelyellowstone.com. Open May 21–Sept 19. 122 cabins (some without private bathroom). $32–$58 double. AE, CB, DC, DISC, MC, V.

The cabins that once littered the landscape around the world's most famous geyser were hauled off years ago, but those that remain offer an inexpensive lodging option. Rent one of the Budget Cabins, just slightly less flimsy than tents, and you'll get basic beds and sinks, and a sense of what it was like to visit Yellowstone half a century ago. Showers and rest rooms are a short walk away. Next up the scale are the Economy cabins, which have beds, sinks and toilets, but no bathrooms. Frontier Cabins are the best units, adding a private bathroom to other amenities. You're within a short walk of a cafeteria and a snack bar. The lodge has several snack shops and a huge cafeteria dishing up varied fast food. Just off the lobby is one of the largest gift shops in the park and an old gymnasium that occasionally hosts square dancing and movies.

Old Faithful Snow Lodge

Old Faithful, P.O. Box 165, Yellowstone National Park, WY 82190. ☎ **307/344-7311.** Fax 307/344-7456. www.travelyellowstone.com. 100 units, 34 one-bedroom cabins. $121 double; $101 cabin. AE, CB, DC, DISC, MC, V.

If your last visit to Yellowstone included a stay at the Old Faithful Snow Lodge, put the memory out of your mind. The old dormitory-style lodge was torn down in 1998, and this new, award-winning place could aptly be called the *New* Faithful Snow Lodge. The big beam construction and high ceiling in the lobby echo the Old Faithful Inn, and a copper-lined balcony curves above the common area, where guests can relax in wicker furniture. The rooms are spacious and comfortable, and a spacious dining room shares a two-sided fireplace with a lounge.

NEAR THE PARK

See the "Grand Teton National Park" chapter for information about Jackson activities, lodging, and dining.

WEST YELLOWSTONE

West Yellowstone is turning itself into the park's biggest all-season gateway town. It has lots of new motel rooms, but it can still fill up during the peak seasons. **West Yellowstone Central Reservations** (☎ 888/646-7077) handles booking for many of the hotels.

Moderately priced chains (with prices ranging from $70 to $120 double) include the **Marriot Fairfield Inn** (☎ 800/565-6803) at 105 S. Electric and the **Days Inn** (☎ 800/548-9551) at 118 Electric. There are also some Best Western affiliates; the general toll-free number is (☎ 800/528-1234). These include the **Best Western Desert Inn,** 133 Canyon (☎ 406/646-7376); the **Executive Inn,** 236 Dunraven (☎ 406/646-7681); and the **Best Western Weston Inn,** 103 Gibbon (☎ 406/646-7373). Still holding its own is the 88-room **Stagecoach Inn,** 209 Madison (at Dunraven) (☎ 800 842/2882).

Less expensive options (doubles cost $65 to $89) include the **Brandin' Iron Motel,** 201 Canyon (☎ 800/217-4613 or 406/646-9411), and the **City Center Motel,** 214 Madison Ave. (☎ 800/742-0665 or 406/646-7337).

Firehole Ranch

11500 Hebgen Lake Rd., West Yellowstone, MT 59758. ☎ **406/646-7294** in summer, or 307/733-7669 year-round. www.troutvacations.com/lodges/firehole.htm. 10 cabins, each sleeps up to 6. $225–$290 per person per day, double occupancy. Rate includes all meals, airport transfers, and activities (except guided fishing). 4-day minimum stay. No credit cards.

Visitors can take a boat ride to the lodge's location on a mile of private shore along Hebgen Lake, only 16 miles from Yellowstone National Park. The resort is surrounded by thousands of acres of national forest in which guests can ride horses, hike, canoe, and make use of the ranch's mountain bikes. The ranch also offers fishing on Hebgen Lake and in six different streams near the park. Lodging is in 10 cabins, most suitable for two guests. The nicest units have separate living quarters, complete with wood-burning stoves and private bathrooms with tub-shower combinations. There are no television sets on the property, and telephone service is limited. Cocktails are served in a cozy nook before dinner—exquisite meals prepared by a French chef. Breakfast is buffet style, and there are box lunches at midday.

West Yellowstone Conference Hotel Holiday Inn SunSpree Resort

315 Yellowstone Ave., West Yellowstone, MT 59758. ☎ **800/HOLIDAY** or 406/646-7365. www.yellowstone-conf-hotel.com. 123 units. A/C TV TEL. $79–$144 double. Special snowmobile/snowcoach packages available during winter. AE, DISC, MC, V.

From its individual rooms to its restaurant, this big, new resort is West Yellowstone's standout offering. Small conveniences like coffeemakers, plush carpeting, hair dryers, microwaves, a big indoor pool, and laundry service abound. You can arrange fishing and rafting trips, bike and ATV rentals, and chuck wagon cookouts. Snowmobilers who have been rattling around all day can relax in the Jacuzzi in the king spa suites. Rooms are spacious with bright decor, comfortable furniture, and landscape art on the walls. The Iron Horse Saloon serves regional microbrews, and the Oregon Short Line Restaurant features western cuisine. At the center of the restaurant sits the restored railroad club car that brought Victorian gents to Yellowstone a century ago.

GARDINER

This little town has character, and it's where the year-round park employees hang out in the winter. Chain motels include the new **Motel 6** (109 Hellroaring Dr.; ☎ 877/266-8356 or 406/848-7520) and the virtually new **Super 8** on U.S. 89 South (☎ 800/800-8000 or 406/848-7401). Both are open year-round, with high season rates ranging from $80 to $100 double.

Absaroka Lodge

U.S. 89 at the Yellowstone River Bridge. ☎ **800/755-7414** or 406/848-7414. www. yellowstonemotel.com. E-mail: ablodge@aol. com. 41 units. A/C TV TEL. $50–$100. AE, DC, DISC, MC, V.

Every room in this lodge has a balcony, many with nice views of the Yellowstone River. The lodge's riverbank location—with a nice slope of lawn overlooking the river gorge—is just a few blocks from the village center, and the rooms are well appointed with queen-size beds. Suites with kitchenettes cost a little more. The owners have been in business here for decades; but the building is modern and new. Like most other properties in town, the lodge has staff ready and able to assist in arrangements with outfitters for fly-fishing and rafting.

Best Western by Mammoth Hot Springs

U.S. 89, P.O. Box 646, Gardiner, MT 59030. ☎ **800/828-9080** or 406/848-7311. www. bestwestern.com/mammothhotsprings. 85 units. A/C TV TEL. Summer $94–$104 double; winter $57–$67 double. AE, MC, V.

Though 0.5 mile farther south of the center of the town, the Best Western also has nicely furnished rooms with spectacular views, and is adjacent to the Mine, one of the better restaurants. There is also a heated pool, and an adjacent casino. During winter months you can rent cross-country skiing and snowmobile equipment; winter packages are available.

COOKE CITY

If you choose to spend the night in little Cooke City, you have several options, although none of them includes modern facilities, gourmet dining, or valet parking. Rooms at each of the properties listed below are clean and comfortable, but that's about all lodgings in Cooke City offer. A room for the night will be less expensive than in other gateway towns, anywhere from $35 to $80 a night. The **Soda Butte Lodge** (☎ 406/838-2251) is the biggest, newest, and poshest motel in Cooke City, and it includes the good **Prospector Restaurant** and a small casino; or you can go to the cheaper, bare-bones **Alpine Motel** (☎ 406/838-2262), also on Main Street, which accepts pets.

CODY

With some of the showmanship of its founder, William F. "Buffalo Bill" Cody, this town offers more than just a gateway to the east entrance. The night rodeo and the very fine historical center are the big summer attractions.

Buffalo Bill Village Resort: Comfort Inn, Holiday Inn & Buffalo Bill Village Historic Cabins

17th and Sheridan Ave., Cody, WY 82414. ☎ **800/527-5544.** Fax 307-587-2795. E-mail: jblair@wavecom.net. **Comfort Inn:** 75 units. A/C TV TEL. $75–$130 double. **Holiday Inn:** 190 units. A/C TV TEL. $75–$130 double. **Buffalo Bill Village Historic Cabins:** 83 units. TV TEL. $50–$130 double. AE, CB, DC, DISC, MC, V. Buffalo Bill Village is open only May–Sept.

This is not exactly a "resort" but an oddly matched cluster of lodgings with a convenient downtown location. The Holiday and Comfort Inns are similar to their chain brethren elsewhere, but the village of aged cabins provides a rustic exterior with a more Western feel and modern conveniences inside. Family units have two bedrooms. There is also a short "Old West" boardwalk where you can shop for curios or sign up for tours and river trips, an outdoor heated pool, and several restaurants.

Double Diamond X Ranch

3453 Southfork Rd., Cody, WY 82414. ☎ **800/833-RANCH.** Fax 307/587-2708. www.ddxranch.com. E-mail: ddx@cody.wtp.net. 5 cabins, one 7-unit lodge. $1,460 per adult per week, $1,020 per child. MC, V.

There are a number of fine dude and guest ranches outside of Cody up the Wapiti Valley and along the South Fork of the Shoshone River. Here on the South Fork you'll find green horse pastures, volcanic rock spires, a tumbling river, and snow-capped peaks. Guests visit the Double Diamond X to ride, fish, view wildlife, and just kick back. Guests are coddled with bounteous meals, a pool, Jacuzzi, children's programs, and live evening entertainment.

The Irma Hotel

1192 Sheridan Ave., Cody, WY 82414. ☎ **800/745-4762** or 307/587-4221. www.irmahotel.com. E-mail: irma@cody.wtp.net. 40 units. A/C TV TEL. $75–$102 double. AE, DC, DISC, MC, V.

Buffalo Bill did a lot for this part of Wyoming, including building this charming old hotel named after his daughter in the heart of town. Cody hoped to corral tourists who got off the train on their way to Yellowstone, and one of his lures was an elaborate cherry-wood bar, a gift from straitlaced Queen Victoria. You can still hoist a jar on Her Royal Majesty's slab in the Silver Saddle Saloon. Suites are named after local characters from the town's early days: The Irma Suite, on the corner of the building, has a queen-size bed, writing table, a vanity in the bedroom area, a small sitting area with TV, and an old-fashioned bathroom with a tub-shower combination. The large restaurant serves excellent prime rib and a summer breakfast buffet. Every summer night except Monday a gang of mustachioed gunfighters draws crowds as they fire blanks at each other on the porch along 11th Street.

Dining

INSIDE THE PARK

Each of the dining rooms at Mammoth Hot Springs Hotel, Old Faithful Inn, and Lake Yellowstone Hotel has a distinctive ambience, but the cuisine seems less distinct than it did a few years ago—perhaps because they're all managed by one corporate parent (for reservations, contact **Yellowstone National Park Lodges** at ☎ **307/344-7901**). Nevertheless, you should plan a visit to one or more of these big halls. The prices are decent, the atmosphere is festive and just elegant enough that you might want to dress up a bit for dinner—put on socks perhaps, and a shirt with a collar. The prices aren't bad, and the big halls absorb sound well enough that young children are rarely a bother. Reservations are recommended, but not required.

If you're not up for restaurant dining, there is counter-style fast food service at the **Hamilton General Stores** and snacks shops and cafeterias in the villages at Canyon, Mammoth, Grant Village, the Yellowstone Lake Lodge and at Old Faithful.

MAMMOTH HOT SPRINGS

You'll find the **Terrace Grille** at the opposite end of the building in which Mammoth Hot Springs Hotel Dining Room is located. It serves typical restaurant fare in a less formal—and less pricey—dining room, but doesn't take reservations.

Mammoth Hot Springs Hotel

At Mammoth Hot Springs. ☎ **307/344-7901.** www.travelyellowstone.com. Dinner reservations required. Breakfast $2–$6; lunch $6–$9; dinner $8–$21. AE, DC, DISC, MC, V. Summer daily 6:30–10am, 11:30am–2pm, and 5:30–10pm. STEAK/SEAFOOD.

In this big, high-ceilinged dining room, the breakfast buffet features scrambled eggs, French toast, and muffins. Delicious omelettes are served with home fries and toast. Lunch features an array of sandwiches, including teriyaki chicken breast, a grilled vegetarian sandwich, and grilled German bratwurst. Dinner is a bit more substantial, and bears a predictable similarity to its counterparts at other park hotels. The specialty is shrimp and scallops served over linguine and topped with a curry sauce.

CANYON VILLAGE AREA

Arrayed around this busy village parking lot are a casual, soda fountain–style restaurant, a cafeteria, a take-out place, and a conventional dining room.

The **Canyon Glacier Pit Snack Bar,** operated by Hamilton Stores, shares a building with a convenience store and souvenir shop, so it's possible to buy a souvenir ashtray as well as a burger. Seating is on stools in the fashion of a '50s soda fountain, and you can expect to wait up to 30 minutes during peak hours. Breakfast consists of egg dishes, lunch is soup and sandwiches, and dinner is traditional Western food. The snack bar is open from 6:30am to 10pm daily from mid-May to late September.

The **Canyon Lodge Cafeteria** is a fast-food alternative across the parking lot in the Canyon Lodge area. Hours are the same as at the snack bar, and the menu bears some striking similarities—but you may get through the cafeteria line faster than you would get a stool at the soda fountain. The cafeteria is open from June to early September.

Canyon Lodge Dining Room

Reservations required. ☎ **307/344-7901.** Open June to mid-Sept. Breakfast $2–$6; lunch, $5–$7; dinner $12–$17. Open daily in season 6:30–10:30am; 11:30am–2pm; and 5:30–10pm. AC, DC, DISC, MC, V. STEAK/SEAFOOD.

This spacious dining area, with the 1950s feel that infects most of Canyon Village, gets noisy when it fills up. The salad bar is long and loaded, but otherwise the fare is similar to that at other park restaurants. The crowds can be large, but there is a relaxed and unhurried feel to the place that you don't find at some of other busy areas in the park.

TOWER-ROOSEVELT AREA

Roosevelt Lodge

At Tower Junction. ☎ **307-344-7901.** www.travelyellowstone.com. Breakfast $4–$7; lunch $6–$12; dinner $8–$21. AE, CB, DC, DISC, MC, V. Summer daily 7–10am, 11:30am–3pm, and 5–9pm. STEAK/SEAFOOD.

Advertised as family friendly and cowboy style, an alternative to the fancier menus of the big hotels, the food at Roosevelt is pretty unimpressive. Like the aging cabins that take you back to the early days of auto camping, Roosevelt's dining area is simple and spare, a collection of tables that take up one side of the lodge's big lobby. My recommendation: Join Roosevelt's Old West Dinner Cookout, and ride by horse or wagon through the Pleasant Valley to a chuck-wagon dinner that includes cornbread, steak, watermelon, beans, and apple crisp. It's $39 to $50 for an adult, depending on the route of your horseback ride, or $32 if you go by wagon. Children pay less.

YELLOWSTONE LAKE

For the eat-on-the-run traveler, a **deli** in the Lake Yellowstone Hotel serves light fare in an area slightly larger than a broom closet from 11am to 9pm. Just down the road the **Hamilton store** offers three meals in a section of the store that is shared with tourist items; the best bet here is breakfast or a burger. It's open from 7am to 9pm. Inexpensive meals served cafeteria-style are available at the **Yellowstone Lake Lodge and Cabins** from 7am to 8pm.

Lake Yellowstone Hotel

On the north side of the lake. ☎ **307/344-7901.** www.travelyellowstone.com. Dinner reservations required. Breakfast $4–$6; lunch $5–$7; dinner $8–$21. AE, DC, DISC, MC, V. Open mid-May to early Oct. Daily 6:30–10am, 11:30am–2:30pm, and 5:30–10pm. PASTA/STEAK/SEAFOOD.

This is one of most pleasant places to eat in Yellowstone, with a view of the lake stretching south from a big, high-ceilinged dining room that doesn't feel crowded even when it's full. Among the variations here are a generous breakfast buffet with alternatives including a tasty traditional country pan breakfast of bacon, eggs, and home fries; a Southwestern pan breakfast seasoned with chiles and salsa; and huevos rancheros.

There's also a wide selection of fresh fruit, juices, pastries, and cereals. The dinner menu is equally inviting. Appetizers include duck quesadillas and spanikopitas (a tasty Greek pastry stuffed with spinach and cheese), while entrees include breast of duck, fettuccine with smoked salmon, and, of course, several beef dishes.

GRANT VILLAGE

The casual choice here is the **Lake House,** footsteps away from the Grant Village restaurant. It specializes in less expensive fish entrees, as well as burgers and beer. Meals are served from 5:30 to 9pm. No reservations.

Grant Village

At Grant Village. ☎ **307/344-7901.** www.travelyellowstone.com. Dinner reservations required. Open June–Sept. Breakfast $4–$6; lunch $6–$9; dinner $11–$21. AE, CB, DISC, MC, V. Summer daily 6:30–10am, 11:30am–2:30pm, and 5:30–10pm. STEAK/SEAFOOD.

Breakfast and lunch at the Grant Village restaurant are much like the other restaurants in the park, though the chef occasionally surprises diners with interesting items that stray from the norm. Lunch may include panfried trout covered with toasted pecans and lemon butter, Wyoming Cheese steak, and a gourmet burger. The dinner menu ranges from honey-lemon chicken to swordfish with lemon dill butter to blackened prime rib. Quality and ambience here are comparable to the better dining rooms at the major park hotels.

OLD FAITHFUL AREA

For quick and inexpensive, there is the **Old Faithful Inn** cafeteria, which serves lunch and dinner in a fast-food environment; an ice-cream stand in the lobby is your best choice for dessert. The **Hamilton Store** also has a lunch counter.

Old Faithful Inn

Near Old Faithful. ☎ **307/545-4999.** Dinner reservations required. Breakfast buffet $7; lunch $5–$9; dinner $9–$22. AE, DC, DISC, MC, V. Open May to mid-Oct daily 6:30–10am, 11:30am–2:30pm, and 5–10pm. STEAK/ SEAFOOD.

There's nothing wrong with the food here, but it pales beside, or beneath, the gnarled log architecture of this distinguished historic inn. Breakfast is strictly buffet, but there's a lot to choose from. The dinner menu is fairly long, with four cuts of prime rib, fish dishes, roasted Cornish game hen, and pastas including a fettuccini with artichoke hearts, mushrooms, and olives. They also serve a tasty broiled Mexican Caesar salad.

Old Faithful Snow Lodge

Near Old Faithful (east of Inn). ☎ **307/344-7901.** No reservations. Breakfast $4–$7; lunch $5–$9; dinner $9–$16. AE, DC, DISC, MC, V. Open May to mid-Oct and mid-Dec to mid-May daily 6:30–10am, 11:30am–2:30pm, and 5–10pm. STEAK/SEAFOOD.

In the well-designed new snow lodge, a spacious restaurant provides an alternative to the Old Faithful Inn dining room. It's a little quieter, a little less expensive, and a little less formal, which is reflected in a menu heavy on burgers and salads. It still has some park standbys on the menu—teriyaki chicken and London broil—and, again in contrast to the Inn, there is a breakfast menu that goes beyond buffet. It's a huge improvement over the cramped restaurant of the old Snow Lodge.

NEAR THE PARK

WEST YELLOWSTONE

Bullwinkle's Saloon, Gambling and Eatery

19 Madison. ☎ **406/646-7974.** Lunch $5–$8; dinner $9–$24. Summer daily 11am–2am. MC, V. AMERICAN.

Boisterous and noisy crowds, families and fishers, gamblers and goof-offs fill this restaurant, and they leave well fed. Both luncheon and dinner menus are packed with traditional American entrees: burgers and salads for lunch, chicken, ribs, and steaks at dinner. Try the inexpensive and plentiful Bullwinkle's salad (shrimp included).

The Canyon Street Grill

22 Canyon St. ☎ **406/646-7548.** Most dishes $5–$11. Open daily in season 7am–7pm. No credit cards. AMERICAN.

You gotta like a restaurant whose slogan is, "We are not a fast food restaurant. We are a cafe reminiscent of a bygone era when the quality of the food meant more than how fast it could be served." This delightful, 1950s-style spot serves hearty food for breakfast, lunch, and dinner. Hamburgers and chicken sandwiches are popular, accompanied by milk shakes made with hard ice cream. A combo of steak, mashed potatoes, and veggies goes for $10.95.

Elno's Tavern

8955 Gallatin Rd. ☎ **406/646-9344.** Reservations not accepted. Most items $4 and up. No credit cards. Daily noon–8pm. Closed first 2 weeks of Dec. AMERICAN.

Locals snowmobile out from West Yellowstone to Elno's (there's a trail that follows Highway 191) to become their own chefs at the grill here. It's a novel concept, and one that keeps people coming back to this restaurant with a fine view of Hegben Lake. At the counter order your meat—steak, teriyaki chicken, hamburger, or hot dog—and don't be surprised when it arrives raw. Go to the grill, slap it on, and stand around drink in hand shooting the breeze with other patrons until your food is exactly the way you like it. Steaks and chicken come with a baked potato or a garden salad; hamburgers come with potato chips. Snowmobilers can purchase gas and oil here, too.

The Outpost Restaurant

115 Yellowstone Ave. (in the Montana Outpost Mall). ☎ **406/646-7303.** Dinner $6–$15. AE, DISC, MC, V. Daily 6am–11pm. Closed Oct 15–Apr 15. AMERICAN.

This fine restaurant tucked away in a downtown mall is hard for some visitors to find. The beef stew is typical of their family-oriented home cooking. Also available are salmon, steaks, trout, and an excellent salad bar. The opening of new establishments in West Yellowstone has put a dent in this restaurant's business, which may also suffer from the absence of a bar. However, it's a quiet, friendly place to feed a family.

GARDINER

Bear Country Restaurant

232 Park St. ☎ **406/848-7188.** Breakfast $2–$5, lunch $5–$8, dinner $9–$12. AE, DISC, MC, V. 7am–10pm. AMERICAN.

There's nothing fancy about this pleasantly rundown, family-oriented restaurant. Its location across from the park entrance, its early morning hours and its no-nonsense service are among its attractions. The American fare menu is undistinguished, but the portions are generous, and you'll be among locals.

The Chico Inn

Old Chico Rd., Pray, Mont. ☎ **800/HOT-WADA.** Reservations recommended. Main dinner courses $16–$27. AE, DISC. Daily 5:30–10pm summer; Sun–Thurs 6–9pm, Fri–Sat 5:30–10pm winter. CONTINENTAL.

It's 30 miles north of Gardiner, but it's worth the drive for some of the best food in the Rockies, and a chance to visit the bar where Peter Fonda's *Easy Rider* motorcycle is enshrined. You'll want to linger over the food, so consider a night's stay in either the old lodge or the newer additions; you can relax and digest in the hot springs.

The Yellowstone Mine

In the Best Western by Mammoth Hot Springs, Hwy. 89. ☎ **406/848-7336.** Reservations not accepted. Breakfast $4–$6; dinner $11–$22. AE, DISC, MC, V. Daily 6–11am and 5–9pm. AMERICAN.

The low-light old-time mining atmosphere here may not spark your appetite, but the meals come in healthy portions and the prices are reasonable. Steaks and seafood are the restaurant's specialty. There's also a lounge and casino.

CODY

Franca's Italian Dining

1421 Rumsey Ave. ☎ **888/806-5354** or 307/587-5354. Reservations recommended. Main courses $14.50–$26. No credit cards. Wed–Sun 6–10pm. Open May 15–Oct 15. ITALIAN.

Franca Facchetti uses her mother's old-world recipes to cook four-course meals in the sagebrush hills of Wyoming that will transport you to the grapevined hills of northern Italy. Franca's loin of veal in tuna sauce, ravioli, and tortellini are all recommended, but if you get lucky, you'll show up on a night when she cooks fresh salmon stuffed with sole mousse and pistachios. The small restaurant—only 24 can be seated at once—is in a turn-of-the-century home a block off Sheridan Avenue, nicely decorated by Franca's artist-husband. There's also an impressive wine cellar.

La Comida

1385 Sheridan Ave. ☎ **307/587-9556.** E-mail: cajun@wavecom.net. Main dinner courses $5–$11. AE, DISC, MC, V. Daily 11am–10pm. MEXICAN.

The cheerfully lit wood patio of La Comida is a wonderful place to sit outside and watch the passing scene. Favorite dishes include *pechuga* over rice (chicken breast baked in cream with green chiles and

Swiss cheese) and a quesadilla filled with shaved rib-eye steak and green chiles. Like most Mexican fare in this region, the spices are mild, just like the night air on fair summer nights on La Comida's casual porch.

Maxwell's Restaurant

937 Sheridan Ave. ☎ **307/527-7749.** Mon–Sat 11am–9pm. DISC, MC, V. Lunch dishes $7–$10; dinner entrees $8.75–$16.50. ECLECTIC AMERICAN.

A family restaurant in which *family* does not translate to *bland,* Maxwell's has some spicy chicken and pasta dishes to go with its salads, seafood, and beef. The wine list is respectable, and you can order a Philly steak, uncommon in Wyoming. The low-backed booths and varnished wood tables are sometimes packed with boisterous families, raising the noise level and waitress stress, but it's a friendly crowd.

Silver Dollar Bar & Grill

1313 Sheridan Ave. ☎ **307/587-3554.** Reservations not accepted. Most items $5–$8. No credit cards. Grill open Mon–Sat 11am–10pm, Thurs 11am–7pm, Sun noon–10pm. PUB GRUB.

Visitors expect music, loud voices, and hearty food in Wyoming bars, and the Silver Dollar has offered all of these for decades. The building was once the town's post office, and like a post office, it's a good place to mingle with locals. The burgers are touted as Wyoming's best.

Stefan's Restaurant

1367 Sheridan Ave. ☎ **307/587-8511.** Lunch $5–$7, dinner $10–$23. AE, DISC, MC, V. Summer daily 8am–10pm; off-season Mon–Sat 11am–9pm. ECLECTIC.

Stefan is a restless chef, so his menu today is almost completely different from what he began with a few years ago. Among the entree survivors is a local favorite, a filet mignon stuffed with Gorgonzola, sun-dried tomatoes, and portobello mushrooms. The Southwestern interior might lead you to expect an enchilada or two, but you can't tell a restaurant by its decor—you're just as likely to find fish in an avocado and mango sauce. Experimentation has kept Stefan's menu deliciously spry. There are separate lunch and Sunday brunch menus and a "little bites" menu with $3 children's meals.

Picnic & Camping Supplies

Pick up your food and camping supplies at the ubiquitous **Hamilton stores,** which are in all the park villages.

A Nearby National Monument

Even given its importance in American history, Little Bighorn Battlefield will probably not be your primary destination in Montana. But you will find that it is a relatively easy detour on the way west or east if you are passing through this area, and is worth a trip if you are anywhere close by. Most people who visit the battlefield include it in their trip to Grand Teton or Yellowstone National Park. For driving directions from the monument to Yellowstone, see "Getting There & Gateways," above.

LITTLE BIGHORN BATTLEFIELD NATIONAL MONUMENT

Like the Revolutionary War battlefield at Lexington, Massachusetts, and Civil War battlefields at Gettysburg, Pennsylvania, and Appomattox, Virginia, the Little Bighorn Battlefield National Monument in eastern Montana presents visitors with an opportunity to immerse themselves in American history. The battle that occurred here reflected a series of events that began with an unstoppable push westward from the Atlantic seaboard, and which included what some call the unscrupulous behavior of a government, the politics of capitalism, and, ultimately, the final chapter in the traditional lifestyle of the American Indian.

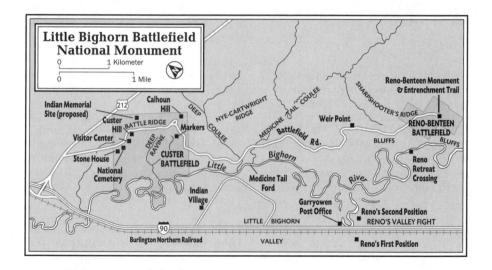

Until 1991, the battlefield was known as the Custer Battlefield in honor of the soldiers who fought there. However, when 20th-century activists protested that the battlefield recognized only one side of what occurred on its dusty soil, Congress changed the name. Since then, a design has been selected and plans have been approved for the construction of a monument commemorating the Indians who fought to defend their homeland. A timetable calls for completion of the monument in 2000.

JUST THE FACTS

When to Go. The national monument is popular, and visitation is busiest in the summer season between Memorial Day and Labor Day. The best advice if you wish to avoid crowds is to avoid these months, or arrive early in the morning or late in the day. This is also good advice because summers in eastern Montana can get very hot and there is no shade on the battlefield.

Getting There. If you are coming from the west, from Billings, Montana, take I-90 east 61 miles to the Little Bighorn Battlefield off-ramp at U.S. 212. If you are coming from the south, from Sheridan, Wyoming, take I-90 north (approximately 70 miles) to the same off-ramp at U.S. 212. If you are coming from the east, from the Black Hills of South Dakota, you will already be on U.S. 212.

The battlefield is 42 miles west of Lame Deer, Montana.

The Nearest Airport. Billings is home to the busiest airport in Montana, **Logan International.** For more information, see "The Nearest Airport" in the Yellowstone section above.

Information & Visitor Center. Contact the Superintendent, Little Bighorn Battlefield National Monument, P.O. Box 39, Crow Agency, MT 59022 (☎ **406/ 638-2621;** www.nps.gov/libi).

At the **Visitor Center** just inside the park entrance, you'll see actual uniforms worn by Custer, read about his life, and view an eerie reenactment of the battles on a small-scale replica of the battlefield.

Park Hours & Fees. The park is open daily from 8am to 9pm from Memorial Day to Labor Day; spring and fall hours are 8am to 6pm; winter hours are 8am to 4:30pm. There is a $6 admission fee per vehicle.

Ranger Programs & A Guided Tour. Hourly **interpretive talks** enable visitors to understand the battle and its participants. Subjects vary during the day, and include discussion of the culture and life of the northern plains tribes that engaged in the battle, army life in the 1870s, weapons and tactics, and the significance of the battle.

For an insider's view, join up with **Apsaalooke Tours,** concessionaire at Little Bighorn Battlefield. Contact them at: Little Big Horn College, P.O. Box 370, Crow Agency, MT 59022. (☎ **406/638-7211,** ext. 23; fax 406/638-2229). This 1-hour bus tour begins at the Visitor Center and proceeds 4.5 miles south to the Reno-Benteen Battlefield, where the Battle of the Little Bighorn actually began. American Indian guides interpret the battle, stopping at key battle sites. There are five tours daily in summer. Cost is $10 for adults, $5 for children, and $8 for seniors.

EXPLORING THE MONUMENT

It's possible to view the entire site in less time than passes during half-time of an NFL football game, but you'll short-change yourself with that approach. Instead, plan to spend enough time to explore the visitor center, listen to interpretive historical talks presented by rangers there, and then tour the site. You'll leave with a greater appreciation for the monument and understanding of the history that led up to the battle.

After stopping at the **visitor center,** drive 4.5 miles to the **Reno-Benteen Monument Entrenchment Trail,** at the end of the monument road, and double back. Interpretive signs at the top of this bluff show the route followed by the armies of Custer, Benteen, and Reno as they approached the area from the south, and the position from which they defended themselves from their Indian attackers.

As you proceed north along the ridge, you'll pass **Custer's Lookout,** the spot from which the general first viewed the Indian village, which was populated by what may have been the largest gathering of Plains Indians in history. This was the spot at which Custer sent for reinforcements, though he continued marching north.

Capt. Thomas Weir led his troops to **Weir Point** in hopes of assisting Custer,

but was immediately discovered by the Indian warriors and forced to retreat to the spot held by Reno.

The **Medicine Trail Ford,** on the ridge, overlooks a spot well below the bluffs in the Medicine Trail Coulee on the Little Bighorn River, where hundreds of warriors who had been sent from the Reno battle pushed across the river in pursuit of Custer and his army.

Further north, the Cheyenne warrior Lame White Man led an attack up **Calhoun Ridge** against a company of the Seventh Cavalry that had charged downhill into the coulee. When Indian resistance overwhelmed the army, troops retreated back up the hill, where they were killed.

As you proceed to the north, you will find detailed descriptions of the events that occurred on the northernmost edges of the ridge, as well as white markers that indicate the places where army troops fell in battle. The bodies of Custer, his brothers Tom and Boston, and nephew Autie Reed, all were found on Custer Hill.

Indian casualties during the rout are estimated at 60 to 100 warriors. Following the battle, which some say began early in the morning and ended within 2 hours, the Indians broke camp in haste and scattered to the north and south. Within a few short years they were all confined to reservations.

The survivors of the Reno-Benteen armies buried the bodies of Custer and his slain army where they fell. In 1881, the graves that could be located were reopened, and the bones reinterred at the base of a memorial shaft found overlooking the battlefield. Custer's remains were eventually reburied at the U.S. Military Academy at West Point in 1877.

There are three **walking trails** within the monument for visitors wishing to explore the battle in greater depth.

The adjacent **National Cemetery,** established in 1879, incorporates a self-guided tour to some of the more significant figures buried there.

36

YOSEMITE NATIONAL PARK

by Stacey Wells

OSEMITE'S SKY-SCRAPING GEOLOGIC FORMATIONS, LUSH MEADOWS, swollen rivers, and spectacular waterfalls make it a destination for travelers from around the world. It's home to three of the world's 10 tallest waterfalls and the largest single piece of exposed granite anywhere, not to mention one of the world's largest trees and the most recognized rock formation.

The greatest thing about all this is that you don't have to be a mountaineer to enjoy the beauty. Yosemite's most popular attractions are accessible to everyone. No matter where you go, you'll see a view worth remembering. In the span of a mile, you can behold the quiet beauty of a forest, walk through a pristine meadow, observe a sunset from a towering granite cliff, hike a half-mile-high waterfall, enjoy a moonlit night as bright as day, climb a rock, and eat a gourmet meal before falling asleep, be it under the stars or in a luxurious four-star hotel.

Yosemite Valley, where 95% of tourists head, is just a small sliver of the park, but it holds the bulk of the region's jaw-dropping features. An estimated 4.1 million people visit here each year. This is the place of record-setting statistics: the highest waterfall in North America and three of the tallest in the world (Upper Yosemite, Sentinel, and Ribbon falls); the biggest and tallest piece of exposed granite (El Capitan); and stands of the Giant Sequoia.

In spite of its beauty, recent years have brought a disquieting sense of foreboding to this wilderness haven. One trip during peak season and you'll understand why. Traffic backs up for miles, trees and branches along the Merced River become clotheslines, and candy wrappers, cigarette butts, and discarded soft drinks litter the valley. Songbirds can barely be heard over the din of voices yelling and hooting. At times like these, New York's Central Park offers more respite. Preserving the wild beauty of the park despite the hordes of visitors is the biggest challenge facing Yosemite today. Big changes are expected in the next 5 years as the Park Service grapples with the best way to permit access without causing more irreparable damage to this natural wonderland.

Visitors should also know that Yosemite is still living with the aftereffects of Mother Nature. Floods and rock slides have recently altered the face of the valley, destroying campgrounds and some trails. While park workers have managed to clean most of the fallen trees, boulders, and rocks out of the heavily populated parts, half of the campsites in the valley are gone for good. The folks who live here now do so with a measure of understanding: They're living at the mercy of Mother Nature.

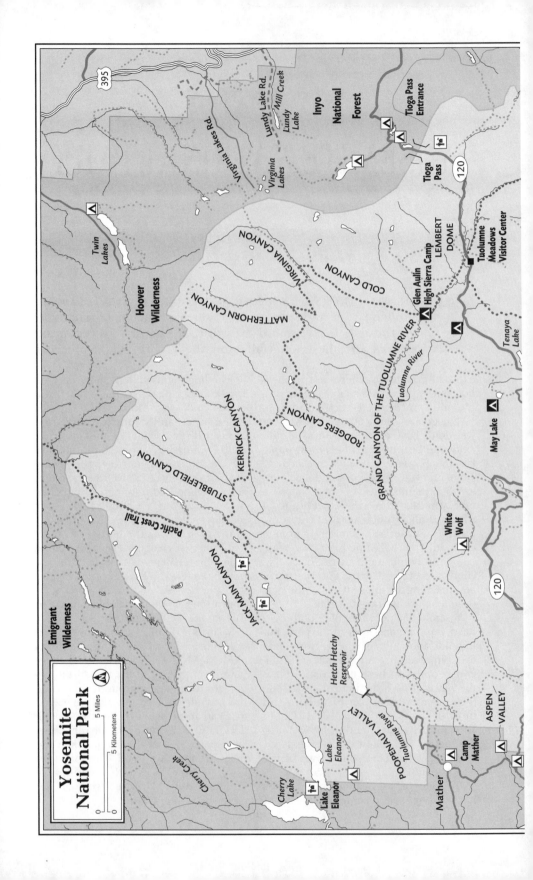

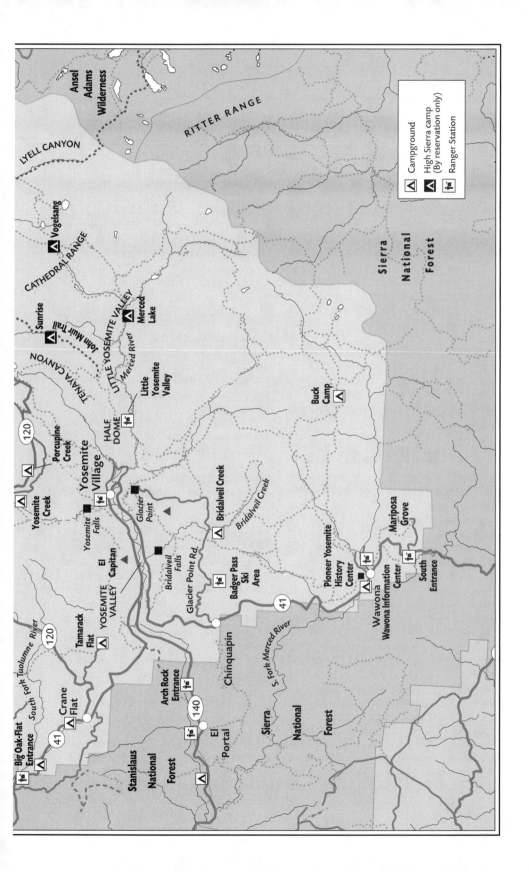

Avoiding the Crowds. In Yosemite, we recommend avoiding holiday weekends in spring and summer if possible—during the busiest times, the park has often had to turn people away due to overcrowding. Until a more elaborate system is in place, the park will continue to close entrances when a certain number of vehicles have been admitted and, in their estimation, a maximum density of visitors has been reached. The campgrounds are usually full from June through August, and expect some crowds in late spring and early fall as well. Winter is a great time to visit Yosemite—not only is the park virtually empty, but there are a number of activities from skiing at Badger Pass to sledding, ice-skating, and snowshoeing. Keep in mind, however, that the high country along Calif. 120 and Tioga Pass Road is inaccessible to vehicles from midfall to early June, depending on snow levels.

Just the Facts

GETTING THERE & GATEWAYS

Yosemite is a 3½-hour drive from San Francisco and a 6-hour drive from Los Angeles. Many roads lead to Yosemite's four entrances. From the west, the **Big Oak Flat Entrance** is 88 miles from Manteca via Calif. 120, and passes through the towns of Groveland, Buck Meadows, and Big Oak Flat. **Arch Rock Entrance** is 75 miles northeast of Merced via Calif. 140, which passes through Mariposa and El Portal. The **south entrance** from Wawona is 64 miles north of Fresno and passes through Oakhurst, Bass Lake, and Fish Camp. From the east, the **Tioga Pass Entrance** is the only option. It is 10 miles west of Lee Vining via Calif. 120.

In an effort to relieve traffic in Yosemite Valley, the National Parks Service will provide shuttles into the park from commuter parking lots along the three highways leading into Yosemite. The program is scheduled to begin in summer 2000.

The Nearest Airports. Fresno-Yosemite International Airport is the nearest major airport, located 90 miles from the south entrance at Wawona (☎ 559/498-4095 from 8am to 8pm daily). It is served by major airlines and has direct connections with airports in San Francisco and Los Angeles. Most of the major car-rental companies can be found in Fresno. The toll-free numbers for airlines and car-rental agencies are in the appendix. **Mariposa Airport** (☎ 209/966-2143) has a tiny airstrip with space for 50 private planes.

INFORMATION

Get general information from **Headquarters, Yosemite National Park,** P.O. Box 577, Yosemite, CA 95387 (☎ 209/372-0200, 900/454-YOSE, or 209/372-4726 for the hearing impaired; www.nps.gov/yose/).

A superb resource is the **Yosemite Area Travelers Information** (☎ 209/723-3153; www.yosemite.com). It's the best Web site for Yosemite information. The **Yosemite Association** publishes books and interpretive information for visitors (☎ 209/379-2646; www.yosemite.org).

VISITOR CENTERS

In the park, the best and biggest visitor center is the **Valley Visitor Center in Yosemite Village** (☎ 209/372-0299), open year-round. The center offers tour information, daily ranger programs, lodging, and restaurants. The rangers here are helpful, insightful, and knowledgeable. Inside, information boards update road conditions and campsite availability, and serve as a message board. Maps, books, and videos can also be purchased. There are several exhibits on the park, its geologic history, and the history of the valley. Nearby is **Yosemite Valley Wilderness Center,** a small room with high country maps, information on necessary equipment, and trail information. A ranger at the desk can answer all your questions, issue permits, and offer advice about the high country. Elsewhere, the **Wawona Information Station** (☎ 209/375-9501) and **Big Oak Flat Information Center** (☎ 209/379-1899) give general park information. In the high country, the **Tuolumne Meadows Visitor Center** (☎ 209/372-0263) is helpful. These centers are closed in winter.

FEES

It costs $20 per car per week to enter the valley, or $10 per person per week if arriving on bike or on foot. It costs $3 to $15 a night to camp in a Yosemite campground. Prices are subject to change without notice.

SPECIAL REGULATIONS & WARNINGS

Under no circumstances should food be left in tents, cabins, or cars. The bear population is healthy and, in some cases, fearless. There are storage lockers and bear-proof containers throughout the park—use them.

Never feed a bear, or any animal for that matter. When animals become dependent on human food, they quit foraging and begin harassing travelers for meals. Most often, this results in the animal's demise, as park rangers take a dim view of troublesome pests, which are quickly put down.

SEASONS & CLIMATE

For general information on the climate of Yosemite, see the "Seasons & Climate" section of the chapter on nearby Sequoia & Kings Canyon national parks. The climate there is very similar to Yosemite's.

The high country in Yosemite receives up to 20 feet of snow, and visitors who plan a winter trip should be well-experienced in winter travel.

SEASONAL EVENTS

January to February: Chefs' Holidays. Yosemite hosts nationally renowned

chefs, who share their secrets with participants. Each session concludes with a banquet in The Ahwahnee Dining Room. Cost is $75 per person, including gratuity but excluding alcohol. Two, 3- and 5-day packages that include overnight accommodations at The Ahwahnee and admission to banquets are available. Call ☎ 559/252-4848 for rates.

November to December: Vintners' Holiday. California's finest winemakers hold tastings in The Ahwahnee Great Lounge. Each session concludes with a Vintners' Banquet. Cost is $80 per person, including gratuities and wine. Two-, 3- and 5-night packages are also available. Call ☎ 559/252-4848 for rates and information.

December 22, 24 & 25: The Bracebridge Dinner. The event transports diners to 17th-century England. Servers wear costumes and the dining room is filled with music, song, and course upon course of delectable dishes. This popular event requires reservations, which are secured by lottery. Applications are available December 1 to January 15 and are due February 15 for the following year. Expect to pay around $200 per person.

December 31: New Year's Eve Dinner. On New Year's Eve, the tenor for the night is set by a swing band and dinner dance. The same reservations system applies here as with the Bracebridge Dinner. The cost is also around $200 per person.

If You Only Have 1 Day

If you're like most visitors to Yosemite, you'll stick to the valley and not stay long. It's ironic, considering the immensity and grandeur of the property, but if you have limited time, don't despair—there's a lot to see and do.

Most important, learn two very important words: *shuttle bus.* Dump your car and pick up a bus schedule; it will quickly become your friend. *Note:* If you don't plan to stay overnight, use the Curry Village day-use parking lot to catch the shuttle. The bus is free, easy, and operates year-round, with fewer stops in winter. For that reason, we've included shuttle bus stop numbers wherever possible throughout the valley sections in this book. Bus stops are well marked and within easy walking distance from all parking lots.

The **Valley Visitor Center** (shuttle bus stop nos. 6 and 9) is your logical starting point. Here, you'll see and hear an orientation on how the valley was created, learn about Yosemite's unique granite landscaping, and gain an appreciation and understanding of the park. More importantly, you can see what there is to see and orient yourself.

If you're not apt to take off on your own, try one of the guided tours (see "Organized Tours & Ranger Programs," below). But if group activities aren't really your bag, try the following sites on your own.

The base of **Lower Yosemite Fall** (stop no. 7) is an easy walk from the parking lot across from Yosemite Lodge. From here, you will be able to see a portion of the magnificent water show. During peak runoff, it's not uncommon to get sprayed by the falls. In winter, a huge snow cone caused by freezing water rises to heights of up to 300 feet at the base of this fall.

Happy Isles (stop no. 16) is another major attraction. Located at the convergence of several inlets, it's the site of the valley's new nature center. This is also the trailhead for Vernal and Nevada falls, two picturesque staircase waterfalls that can be reached on foot.

Next, we recommend a visit to **Mirror Lake** (stop no. 17), a small lake named for its near-perfect reflection of the surrounding scenery. It's slowly filling up with silt and is less dramatic than it used to be, but its shore still offers a beautiful view of Half Dome. This short stroll is well marked.

From there, if you have more time, there's a variety of hikes and activities at your disposal.

If You Have More Time

It's relatively easy to find your way around Yosemite. All road signs are clear and visible. You'll soon realize that everything leads to a one-way road that hugs the valley's perimeter. To get from one side to the other, you can either drive the entire loop or travel one of the few bridges over the Merced River. It is, however, easy to find yourself heading in the wrong direction on the one-way road, so be alert whenever you merge.

In addition to the year-round shuttle bus in Yosemite Valley, Wawona and Tuolumne Meadows offer a similar service during summer months only. Driving in any of these places during peak season—or even off-season in the valley—is a surefire way to miss important sights, get stuck in traffic, and hate your vacation.

YOSEMITE VALLEY

Face it, most people come to Yosemite to see this giant study in shadow and light. In spring, after winter snow begins melting in the high country, waterfalls encircle Yosemite Valley, shimmering like a diamond necklace. Careful observers can watch rock climbers inch up the massive granite face of El Capitan or Half Dome. There are wide, beautiful meadows, towering trees, and the ever-present sound of rushing water in the background.

Yosemite Valley consists of three developed areas. All the hotels, restaurants, and shops can be found in **Yosemite Village, Yosemite Lodge,** and **Curry Village,** and all campgrounds are within walking distance of these places. Curry Village (also called Camp Curry) and Yosemite Lodge offer the bulk of the park's overnight accommodations. Curry Village is near shuttle bus stop nos. 1, 13, and 14. Yosemite Lodge is served by stop no. 8. Both locations have restaurants and a small grocery. The lodge has a large public swimming pool, and Curry Village has an ice rink open in winter.

Yosemite Village is the largest developed region within the valley, and is served by shuttle bus stop nos. 3, 5, 6, 9, and 10. It is home to the park's largest visitor center and headquarters for the National Park Service in Yosemite. The village also has a host of stores and shops, including a grocery, restaurants, and the valley's only medical clinic, dentist, post office, beauty shop, and ATM.

Also, check out the **Yosemite Pioneer Cemetery,** a peaceful graveyard in the shade of tall sequoias with headstones dating from the 1800s. Several notables in Yosemite history are buried here, such as James Lamon, an early settler, known for his apple trees that still bear fruit, who died in 1875.

Next door, you'll find the **Yosemite Museum and Indian Cultural Exhibit.** Both are free and provide a historic picture of the park. The museum entrance is marked by a crowd-pleaser, the cross-section of a **1,000-year-old sequoia** with memorable dates identified on the tree's rings. Look for the signing of the Magna Carta in 1215, the landing of Columbus in the New World, and the Civil War. The ring was cut in 1919 from a tree that fell in the Mariposa Grove south of the valley in Wawona. The Indian Cultural Exhibit explains the life of Native Americans who once lived here, and Native Americans regularly speak or give demonstrations in long-forgotten arts such as basket weaving. Kids get a real kick out of this.

The village of **Ahwahnee** is behind the museum and Indian Cultural Exhibit. The village offers a free, self-guided walking tour accessible from the back door of the visitor center. This exhibit takes visitors through the transformation of the Ahwahneeche, the tribe that inhabited Yosemite Valley until the mid-1850s. The village includes a ceremonial roundhouse that's still in use.

The **Ansel Adams Gallery** is open daily from 9am to 6pm. Prints and cards of photographs are available for purchase. The shop serves as a small gallery for current artisans, some with works for sale.

East of Yosemite Village on a narrow, dead-end road is the majestic old **Ahwahnee Hotel.** Take the shuttle bus to stop no. 4. It's definitely worth a visit for anyone interested in architecture and design.

The **LeConte Memorial Lodge** is an educational center and library at shuttle bus stop no. 12. Built in 1903 in honor of University of California geologist Joseph LeConte, the Tudor-style granite building provide talks free of charge. They are listed in the Yosemite Guide.

One of the park's highlights is **The Mist Trail** to Vernal Fall. The trail itself can be slick and treacherous, but it is a pretty walk up 500 steps to the top of the waterfall. Miniature rainbows dot the trail as mist from the waterfall splashes below and ricochets back onto the trail. This walk is frequently closed in winter due to snow.

At the valley's far east end beyond Curry Village is the **Happy Isles Nature Center** (stop no. 16). The center is closed in the winter. Summer hours are 9am to 5pm daily, with spring and fall hours as posted. This new structure was built after a deadly rock slide damaged the previous quarters. A huge slab of granite high up on a wall behind the building crashed to earth in late 1996 with such force that it created a 120 mile-per-hour gust of wind that flattened about 500 trees. While some of the trees are gone, the remnants of the rock slide remain. Happy Isles serves as the trailhead for some great hikes (see "Day Hikes," below). The nature center offers exhibits and books on the various animal and plant life found in Yosemite. It's a super place for children to explore, and we know a couple of 30-something kids who had a great time here too. This is also the location of the park's Junior and Senior Ranger programs.

NORTH OF THE VALLEY

Hetch Hetchy and Tuolumne Meadows are remarkably different regions on opposite sides of the park. **Hetch Hetchy**

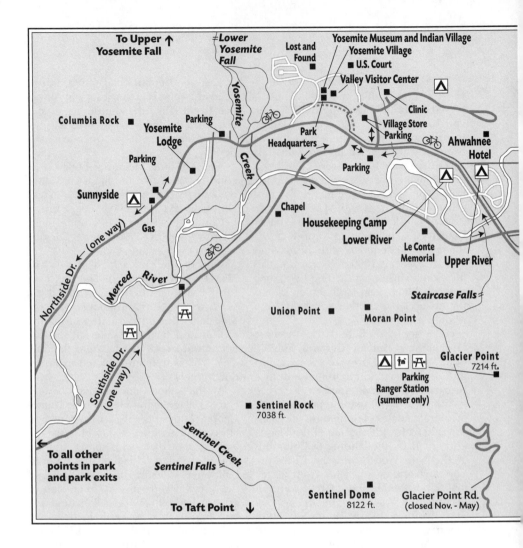

To Upper ↑ Yosemite Fall

≠Lower Yosemite Fall

Lost and Found

Yosemite Museum and Indian Village
Yosemite Village
■ U.S. Court
Valley Visitor Center

Clinic
Village Store
Parking
Ahwahnee Hotel

Columbia Rock ■

Yosemite Lodge

Parking

Park Headquarters ➤

Parking

Yosemite Creek

Parking

Sunnyside

Gas

Chapel

Housekeeping Camp
Lower River
Le Conte Memorial
Upper River

Northside Dr. (one way)

Merced River

Staircase Falls ≠

Union Point ■

Moran Point ■

Southside Dr. (one way)

Glacier Point
7214 ft.

Parking
Ranger Station
(summer only)

To all other points in park and park exits

Sentinel Creek

Sentinel Rock
7038 ft.

Sentinel Falls ≠

Sentinel Dome
8122 ft.

Glacier Point Rd.
(closed Nov. - May)

To Taft Point ↓

is on the park's western border and can be reached by taking the turnoff just outside the park's Big Oak Flat Entrance. **Tuolumne Meadows** is on the park's eastern border, just inside Tioga Pass. Both places are inaccessible by motor vehicle in the winter. In summer, Hetch Hetchy gets hot and Tuolumne Meadows gets crowded.

Hetch Hetchy is home to the park's reviled reservoir, one fought for years by the famed conservationist John Muir. In the end, Muir lost and the dam was built ensuring water for the city of San Francisco. Many believe the loss exhausted Muir and hastened his death in 1914, a

year after a bill was signed to fund the dam project. Construction began in 1919.

South of Hetch Hetchy, inside the park, are two large stands of **Giant Sequoias.** The Merced and Tuolumne groves offer a quiet alternative to the Mariposa Grove of Big Trees in Wawona. The two groves are accessible only on foot. The **Merced Grove** is a 4-mile round-trip walk that begins on Calif. 120 about 4.5 miles beyond the Big Oak Flat Entrance. While the trees don't mirror the majesty of the Mariposa Grove, the solitude here makes this a real treat for hikers. The **Tuolumne**

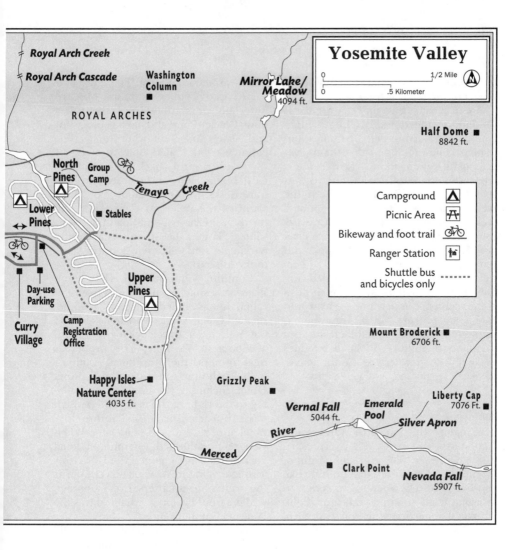

Grove of about 25 trees can be reached by a 1-mile hike (2 hr. round-trip) on a trail located near Crane Flat.

About 1½ hours east along Calif. 120 is Yosemite's **high country.** This primitive region is low on amenities, which makes it a frequent haunt for those who enjoy roughing it—but even couch potatoes will love the beauty up here. Glistening granite domes tower above lush green meadows, cut by silver swaths of streams and lakes. Many of Yosemite's longer hikes begin or pass through here. There are some worthwhile sights for anyone willing to venture away from the valley masses.

A drive toward the high country on Calif. 120, also known as Tioga Road and Tioga Pass Road, offers other breathtaking views of granite landscaping. There are nearby picnic spots at the picturesque Tenaya Lake.

Olmsted Point, located midway between White Wolf and Tuolumne Meadows, offers one of the most spectacular vistas anywhere in the park. Here you can see the enormous walls of the Tenaya Canyon and an endless view all the way to Yosemite Valley. In the distance are Cloud's Rest and the rear of Half Dome. To the east Tenaya Lake glistens like a sapphire. One of the park's larger lakes, Tenaya is easily accessible, but the water is freezing.

About 8 miles east of Tenaya Lake is **Tuolumne Meadows,** a huge high-country flat surrounded by domes and steep granite mountains that themselves offer exhilarating climbs. The meadow is a beautiful place to hike and fish, or just stand and gape. To the north of the meadow is Lembert Dome, at about 2 o'clock, and then working clockwise, Johnson Peak at 7 o'clock, Unicorn Peak and Fairview Dome at 10 o'clock, and Pothole Dome. Up the road is the central region of Tuolumne, a crowded conglomerate of buildings that include a visitor center, campground, canvas tent cabins, and grocery. The real draw here is the scenery and lack of valley crowds. But in July and August, the small confines make it just as intolerable. Continue east to reach Tioga Lake and Tioga Pass.

SOUTH OF THE VALLEY

This region, which includes Wawona and the Mariposa Grove of Big Trees, is densely forested. There are a handful of granite rock formations, but nothing like those found elsewhere. En route to Wawona from Yosemite Valley on Calif. 41, you'll come across several wonderful views of the valley. **Tunnel View,** a turnout just before passing through a long tunnel en route to Wawona, provides one of the park's most recognizable vistas—it was memorialized on film by photographer Ansel Adams. To the right is Bridalveil Fall, opposite El Capitan. Yosemite Falls and Half Dome lie straight ahead.

Between Yosemite Valley and Wawona is Glacier Point Road, the thoroughfare to the spectacular **Glacier Point.** From the parking area 16 miles down the road, it's a short hike to an amazing overlook that provides a view of the glacier-carved granite rock formations all along the valley and beyond. From here, you are eye-level with Half Dome, which looks close enough to reach out and touch. Far below, Yosemite Valley resembles a green-carpeted ant farm. There are also some pretty sights of more obscure waterfalls not visible from the valley floor. Glacier Point also has a geology hut and a new lodge for wintertime cross-country skiers that doubles the rest of the year as a snack shack. To reach Glacier Point, take one of the buses (check at tour desks for information) or drive south of the valley on Calif. 41 to the turnoff for Glacier Point Road (closed in winter). Follow the winding road to the parking lot and walk a few hundred yards to the lookout.

Continue south on Calif. 41 to reach **Wawona,** a small town 30 miles from the valley. It was settled in 1856 by homesteader Galen Clark, who built a rustic way station for travelers en route from Mariposa to Yosemite. The property's next owners, the Washburn brothers, built much of what is today the Wawona Hotel, including the large, white building to the right of the main hotel, which was constructed in 1876. The two-story hotel annex went up 3 years later. When Congress established Yosemite National Park in 1890 and charged the U.S. Army with managing it, Wawona was chosen as the army's headquarters. Every summer, soldiers would camp in what today is the Wawona Campground.

As Yosemite grew in popularity, so did the Wawona Hotel and the town itself. When the Wawona Hotel was added to the park in 1932, Section 35 (the number assigned to the plot in its legal description) was allowed to remain in private ownership. It remains so today, just east of the hotel off of Calif. 41. Unless you're hiking or staying here in a private home or cabin, there is no real reason to venture along the narrow road that leads to the town.

The public Wawona is much more enjoyable. The **Mariposa Grove** is a stand of Giant Sequoias, some of which have been around for 3,000 years. They stretch almost 300 feet tall, are 50 feet in circumference, and weigh an average of 2 million pounds. The 500 trees here are divided into the Upper Grove and Lower

Grove. The easiest way to see the trees is on an open-air tram that runs during summer. The cost is $8 for adults, $7.25 for seniors, $4 for children. Kids under age 4 are free. A family pass costs $24 and admits two adults and kids age 4 to 15. Trams leave every 20 minutes. The trip is narrated by a ranger and lasts about an hour. It's worth hopping out and walking around as often as possible. Just take the next tram back. All of this is also accessible on foot. It's an uphill walk to the groves, 2.5 miles each way.

The **Grizzly Giant** is the largest tree in the grove. At "just" 200 feet it is shorter than some of its neighbors, but its trunk measures more than 30 feet in diameter at the base. A huge limb halfway up measures 6 feet in diameter and is bigger than many of the "young" trees in the grove. Some say that limb is larger than any tree east of the Mississippi.

The **Wawona Tunnel Tree** had a tunnel 10 feet high and 26 feet long cut through it in 1881. Thousands of visitors were photographed driving through the tree before it toppled in winter 1968–69—its death was caused by heavy snowfall. (The tree had been weakened by the tunnel and its shallow root system.) No one saw the tree fall. Another tunnel tree, the California Tree, cut in 1895, still stands near the Grizzly Giant.

The **Mariposa Grove Museum** was the first building built by Galen Clark. During the summer, it displays exhibits and sells books and educational material.

Near the Wawona Hotel are the **Thomas Hill Studio** and **Pioneer Yosemite History Center.** The studio, which keeps sporadic hours that are impossible to pin down but are frequently listed in the park newspaper, the *Yosemite Guide,* is the former work space of noted 19th-century painter Thomas Hill. Hill painted a number of award-winning landscapes, including some recognizable ones of Yosemite.

The Pioneer Center offers a self-guided walking tour of cabins and buildings moved to this site in 1961 from various locations in the park. Each represents a different time in Yosemite's short history. During the summer, the National Park Service interpreters dress in period clothing and act out characters from the park's past. To reach the Pioneer Center, walk across the covered bridge. An entertaining 10-minute stagecoach ride is offered from here for a small fee.

Organized Tours & Ranger Programs

If you're staying in the valley, the Park Service and Yosemite Concession Services present nearly a dozen **evening programs** that explore all aspects of the park's history and culture. In past summers, programs have included a discussion on early expeditions to Yosemite, the park's flora and fauna, and legends of Native Americans who once lived here. Other programs have focused on the courageous ascent of paraplegic Mark Wellman up El Capitan, and the global ecology and major threats to Yosemite's environment.

Inquire about current programs upon check-in at your hotel or at the information booth outside the Valley Visitor Center. While most programs are held in the valley, all major campgrounds in the park offer **campfire programs** throughout the week.

A number of **guided walks** are also available. Check at one of the visitor centers or in the park newspaper for current topics, start times, and locations. Walks may vary from week to week, but you can always count on nature hikes, evening discussions, and the sunrise photography program aimed at replicating some of Ansel Adams's works. Most do not require advance registration—just show up at the appointed time and place. The sunrise photo walk always gets rave reviews from the early risers who venture out at dawn. The living history evening program outside at Yosemite Lodge is great for young and old alike.

Guided backpacking tours range from simple walks to multiday excursions into

Yosemite's backcountry and can be arranged by calling ☎ 209/372-8344. Techniques and skills are taught along the way. Meals are included on longer trips. The instructor-to-student ratio does not exceed 7 to 1. Private trips are available, as is transportation to and from the trailhead. Three-day trips ascend Mount Lyell or hike from Young Lakes to Mount Conness. Four-day excursions travel from Ten Lakes to Tuolumne Meadows, or from Tuolumne Meadows to Yosemite Valley.

A host of **guided bus tours** is also available. You can buy tickets at tour desks at Yosemite Lodge, The Ahwahnee, Curry Village, or beside the Village Store in Yosemite Village. Advance reservations are suggested for all tours, and space can be reserved in person or by calling ☎ 209/372-1240. Double-check at tour desks for updated departure schedules and prices. Most of the tours leave from Yosemite Lodge.

The **Valley Floor Tour** is a great way to get acclimated. It's a 2-hour ride in either an open-air tram or an enclosed motor coach, depending on the weather. The cost is $17 per person, $8.50 for children, and $15 for seniors. Trams depart from Yosemite Village, the Ahwanhee, Yosemite Lodge, and Curry Village every half hour daily (hours vary by season). The trip includes a good selection of photo ops, including El Capitan, Tunnel View, and Half Dome. A guide leads a historical, geological, and informative discussion from a pulpit at the head of the tram. This ride is also available on nights when the moon is full or near full. It's an eerie but beautiful scene. Dress warmly; it can get mighty chilly after the sun goes down, though blankets and hot cocoa are provided. If you take this trip during the day, wear sunscreen.

The **Glacier Point Tour** is a 4-hour scenic bus ride through the valley to Glacier Point. The round-trip cost was $20 for adults, $19.25 for seniors, and $10.25 for children. Buses depart Yosemite Lodge, the Ahwahnee, Yosemite Village, and Curry Village daily at 10am

and 1:30pm. One-way trips are also available for hikers on foot. The cost is $10 for adults and seniors, and $5 for children. One-way fares leave Yosemite Lodge at 8:30am, 10am, and 1:30pm daily. Buses depart Glacier Point at 10am, noon, and 3:30pm. Reservations must be made at least 1 day ahead of time. All Glacier Point buses are available in spring through fall only.

Tours also depart from Yosemite Valley to **Mariposa Grove.** The trip takes 6 hours and costs $34 for adults and $18 for children. Buses depart Yosemite Lodge at 9:30am daily. The trip includes the Big Trees tram tour that winds through the grove and stops for lunch at Wawona (lunch is not provided). You can combine the trip to Glacier Point and Mariposa Grove in an 8-hour bus ride that costs $44.50 for adults and $25 for children. Buses depart Yosemite Lodge at 9:30am daily.

Buses also depart Yosemite Valley for **Tuolumne Meadows,** although they don't allow for much time to explore, unless you arrange to stay overnight. It's an all-day trip, with stops along the way. Cost is $20 for adults and seniors, $10.25 for children. You can also jump off at any point along the way and the fare will be reduced.

Yosemite Sightseeing Tours (☎ 559/877-8687) conducts scheduled as well as customized trips. Costs range from $48 to $58, depending on the season. Tours are operated on small air-conditioned buses with huge picture windows. Sightseeing includes Mariposa Grove, Yosemite Valley, and Glacier Point, and geology, flora, and fauna are pointed out along the way. Stops are scheduled for lunch, shopping, and photo opportunities. Pickup can be arranged from various motels throughout Oakhurst and Bass Lake.

From spring through fall, the **Yosemite Theater** offers inexpensive theatrical and musical programs designed to supplement Park Service programs. Old favorites include a conversation with John Muir, a film on Yosemite's future, and sing-alongs. Inquire at the Valley Visitor Center.

Day Hikes

You'll need a **permit** to camp overnight in the backcountry. Permits are free, but it's a good idea to reserve one in advance during high season, and for that there's a fee of $3. To get one, call ☎ 209/372-0200 or stop by any ranger station or the Valley Wilderness Center. When hiking, make your safety a priority. Trails, especially ones over rock and granite, can be slick. Be especially careful on Mist Trail, where wind and water can make for treacherous conditions. Always carry more than enough water.

INSIDE & NEAR THE VALLEY

Base of Bridalveil Fall

0.5 mi. RT. Easy to moderate. Access: Bridalveil Fall parking area, about 3 mi. west of Yosemite Village. Follow trail markers.

Bridalveil Fall drops 620 feet from top to bottom. In the spring, expect to get wet. This walk is wheelchair accessible with assistance.

Columbia Rock

2 mi. RT. Moderate. Access: Same as Upper Yosemite Fall (see below).

The hike mirrors the beginning ascent of the waterfall trail, but stops at Columbia Rock, 1,000 feet above the valley. There's no valley view from here, but the sights are still impressive. Because it's on the sunny side of the valley, it's also less likely to get an accumulation of snow.

Four-Mile Trail to Glacier Point

9.6 mi. RT. Strenuous. Access: 1.25 mi. from Yosemite Village, at the Four Mile parking area, post V-18, or shuttle bus to stop no. 8 and walk behind the Lodge over the Swinging Bridge to Southeast Dr. The trailhead is 0.25 mi. west.

This trail climbs 3,200 feet and has some terrific views. It ends at Glacier Point,

but if you'd like to extend, it connects with the Panorama Trail at the end. The combined round-trip distance is 14 miles.

Half Dome

16.5 mi. RT. Moderate to strenuous. Access: Happy Isles (stop no. 16).

This long, steep trip climbs 4,900 feet. From Happy Isles, take the John Muir Trail past Vernal and Nevada falls, and through Little Yosemite Valley. Leave the John Muir Trail for the Half Dome Trail and look for a natural spring atop a short spur. This is the last water source on the way up. The last 200 feet up the back of Half Dome require the use of cables. And a strong heart wouldn't hurt. It's possible to cut the length by beginning in Little Yosemite Valley (you'll need a wilderness permit to camp here).

Lower Yosemite Fall

0.5 mi. RT. Easy. Access: Shuttle bus to stop no. 7. Follow the paved path from the Yosemite Fall parking area to the base of this waterfall.

Be prepared to get damp. Lower Yosemite Fall reaches only 320 feet, but it packs the accumulated punch of the entire 2,425-foot waterfall. You can also take this trip from Yosemite Village by following the path from the Valley Visitor Center to the Yosemite Fall parking area. Add another 0.5 mile or 40 minutes each way. This walk is wheelchair accessible with assistance.

Mirror Lake

2.6 mi. RT. Easy. Access: Shuttle bus stop no. 17 or 18 and follow the signs.

A 0.5-mile paved trail climbs about 60 feet along the west side of Tenaya Creek to Mirror Lake, whose still surface reflects the overhanging granite above. A beautiful 3-mile loop around the lake has recently reopened. The trail, which once traversed Tenaya Creek via a picturesque rock footbridge, was washed out in 1997; part of it toppled into the creek bed.

Mist Trail to Vernal Fall

3 mi. RT. Moderate to strenuous. Access: Shuttle bus to stop no. 16; cross Happy Isles Bridge and follow the signs.

This hike begins on the famous 211-mile John Muir Trail to Mount Whitney in Sequoia and Kings Canyon national parks. From the Happy Isles Bridge, the trail climbs 400 feet to the Vernal Fall Bridge, which has a good view of what lies ahead, as well as water and rest rooms. The rest of the climb requires a choice. You can either take a series of switchbacks along the side of the mountain and come out above the fall, or ascend the Mist Trail (our suggestion), which is a steep climb with 500 steps—it's wet, picturesque, and refreshing. Be warned: It's slick and requires cautious steps. Once you reach the top, you can relax on a series of smooth, granite benches before hiking back down.

Onward to Nevada Fall

6.8 mi. RT. Moderate to strenuous. Access: Vernal Fall trailhead.

This trip mirrors the Vernal Fall climb for the first 3 miles. From Vernal Fall, hike to Nevada Fall on either side of the river. Along the south side, you'll walk the John Muir Trail. The north side is the extension of the Mist Trail. Either way, it's a climb. For variety, you can descend on the opposite trail.

Panorama Trail

9 mi. one way. Moderate to strenuous. Access: Glacier Point, at the east end of the parking area.

From Glacier Point, this trail drops 3,200 feet, but somehow it still feels like a climb. At one of the prettiest points, it crosses Illilouette Fall about 1.5 miles from Glacier Point. It continues along the Panorama Cliffs and eventually winds up at Nevada Fall, where it's a straight descent to Yosemite Valley via the Mist or John Muir trails. You can hike this trail in conjunction with the Four-Mile Trail, but it might entail an overnight stop. It's also possible to take the bus to Glacier Point and hike only one way.

Upper Yosemite Fall

7.2 mi. RT. Strenuous. Access: Shuttle bus to stop no. 8. Sunnyside Walk-in Campground, behind Yosemite Lodge.

Climbing 2,700 feet and offering spectacular views from the ledge above, this hike is really not for the faint of heart. Take it slow, rest often, and absorb the scenery as you climb higher and higher above the valley. One mile up, you'll reach Columbia Point, which offers a panoramic view. The rest of the trail dips and climbs, with ample opportunity for cooling off beneath the spray from the fall above. The last quarter mile is a series of torturous, seemingly endless switchbacks that ascend through underbrush before opening at a clearing near the top of the fall. The view from here inspires vertigo. It's a worthwhile walk upstream to see the creek before it takes a 0.5-mile tumble to the valley floor below. You can also stay overnight up here, with proper permits and equipment.

SOUTH OF THE VALLEY

Chilnualna Falls from Bridalveil Fall

18.8 mi. RT. Moderate to strenuous. Access: Calif. 41 to Glacier Point Rd. and turn east to Bridalveil Campground.

The trail goes along gentle grades through forests at first, then turns up toward Turner Meadows. It's a scenic trip without Yosemite's summer crowds. It offers pretty views as the trail wanders near overlooks along the route to the falls.

Chilnualna Falls from Wawona

8 mi. RT. Strenuous. Access: North on Calif. 41. Turn right on Chilnualna Rd., just north of the Merced River's south fork. Stay on this

road until it dead-ends at "The Redwoods," about 1.3 mi.

One of the tallest outside Yosemite Valley, this fall cascades down two chutes. The one at the bottom is narrow and packs a real punch after a wet winter. A series of switchbacks leads to the top fall, and from here you can hike to Bridalveil Campground, or continue on to Chilnualna Lakes. If you plan to hike to the lakes, this is a great place to stay overnight. Remember to pack a swimsuit—there are a few swimming holes at the base of the waterfall.

Grizzly Giant

1.6 mi. RT. Easy. Access: Near the map dispenser at the east end of the Mariposa Grove parking lot.

This is the walking alternative to the tram tour. It's a nice stroll to see an impressive tree and the hike only climbs 400 feet.

The Mariposa Grove

13 mi. RT. Moderate to strenuous. Access: Wawona Store parking area; walk east 0.25 mi. to Forest Dr. The trailhead is on the right.

It sounds long, but in the summer you can use the Wawona shuttle bus service on the return trip. This hike is a nice alternative to the crowded drive to the Mariposa Grove. It climbs through a forest, then ascends the Wawona Dome and Wawona Basin, both of which provide excellent views.

Ostrander Lake

12.8 mi. RT. Moderate to strenuous. Access: Calif. 41 to Glacier Point Rd. and turn east. Trailhead is 1.3 mi. past Bridalveil Campground, on the right-hand side of the road.

The trail begins on an abandoned road before winding through evidence of a forest fire until it reaches Bear Meadow. After crossing Bridalveil Creek, it climbs across several ridges before reaching the lake. The best camping is on the lake's west end. Ostrander Lake is popular in summer and during winter as a cross-country ski spot. The Sierra Club also manages the nearby Ostrander Hut.

Sentinel Dome

2.2 mi. RT. Moderate. Access: Glacier Point Rd. to the Sentinel Dome parking lot.

You'll be able to see Sentinel Dome on your left. At the first fork, bear right. The trail winds through manzanita and pine before beginning its ascent. It's a steep scramble to the top of Sentinel Dome and you have to leave the trail on the north side in order to scramble up. The top offers a 180° panorama of Yosemite Valley.

Taft Point

2.2 mi. Easy. Access: Same as Sentinel Dome trail. At the fork, head left.

The walk to Taft Point is undemanding. It crosses a broad meadow dotted in early summer by wildflowers. Near Taft Point, note the deep chasms in the rock, known as the "fissures." Some of the cracks are 40 feet long, 20 feet wide at the top, and 100 feet deep. The wall of Yosemite Valley actually overhangs the narrow ravine below and if you carefully peer over the cliff, you'll see that your head is on the opposite side of a stream running far beneath you. A small pipe railing further on marks the Taft Point Overlook.

Wawona Meadow Loop

3.5 mi. Easy. Access: Take the paved road through the golf course on the west side of Calif. 41, and walk about 50 yd. to the trail.

This relaxing stroll encircles Wawona Meadow, curving around at its east end and heading back toward the road. It crosses the highway and winds through forest, returning to the Wawona Hotel. Some cars still use this road, so watch out.

Wawona Point

1 mi. Easy. Access: Wawona Tunnel Tree.

Hike back to the north, toward Wawona and follow a spur road at the Galen Clark

Tree. From here you can see the entire Wawona Basin, a view only available to those who venture out on foot.

NORTH OF THE VALLEY

Cathedral Lakes

8 mi. Moderate. Access: West end of Tuolumne Meadows, west of Budd Creek. Take the shuttle bus in summer to avoid parking problems.

These lakes are set in granite bowls cut by glaciers. The peaks and domes around both Lower and Upper Cathedral lakes are worth the hike alone. Lower Cathedral Lake, next to Cathedral Peak, is a good place to stop for a snack before heading up the hill to enjoy the upper lake.

Cloud's Rest

14 mi. Moderate. Access: Calif. 120 to Tenaya Lake. The trailhead begins at a campground parking lot down a closed road that crosses an outlet of the lake.

This hike descends through a wooded area toward Sunrise Lake. Ascend out of Tenaya Canyon and at a junction, bear right (this part of the trail is usually well signed). Your destination is clear, which is a good thing since the trail is sketchy at this point. The last scramble to the top is a little spooky, with sheer drops on each side. Yosemite River is on the right and the Little Yosemite on the left. Bravery is rewarded with spectacular views of the park's granite domes. Overnight stays are rewarded with beautiful sunrises.

Dog Lake

3 mi. Easy. Access: Calif. 120 to the Tuolumne Lodge access road. Pass the Ranger Station and park at a parking lot on the left. Walk north up an embankment and recross the highway to find trail.

This is an easy climb through forests with great views of Mount Dana. Dog Lake is warm, shallow, and great for swimming.

El Capitan (the back way)

14.4 mi. Strenuous. Access: Calif. 120 to the Tamarack Flat Campground. Turn right and follow the road to the east end of the campground, where you'll see an abandoned road.

Trek along the abandoned road to Cascade Creek and then along a roadbed to the North Rim Trail. Prepare for switchbacks. The trail climbs and climbs and climbs to a summit, where it hits a spur trail. Take the spur to the summit to enjoy the views. (The main trail heads to Eagle Peak.) *Be careful:* Punishment for carelessness is a poorly rated, one-way trip to the valley floor.

Elizabeth Lake

6 mi. Moderate. Access: Calif. 120 to the group camping area of Tuolumne Meadows Campground.

This popular day hike attracts a slew of people, which can be a bummer, but it's magnificent nonetheless. Elizabeth Lake glistens like ice. Don't forget your camera and some extra film—the entire route is one long Kodak moment.

Gaylor Lakes

6 mi. Moderate. Access: Calif. 120 to Tioga Pass. Northwest side of the road.

This trail begins with a climb, then descends to the alpine lake. It's a particularly pretty hike in early summer, when the mountainsides are dotted with wildflowers.

Glacier Canyon to Dana Lake

4.6 mi. Moderate to strenuous. Access: Calif. 120 to west side of Tioga Lake, about a mile east of the pass.

This is a less-crowded alternative to the above hike to Mount Dana that doesn't top the mountain, although experienced hikers can. The trail begins at the Ansel

Adams Wilderness and is not maintained, although it is fairly visible. This area is easily damaged so make sure to tread lightly. The route leads through the headway of Glacier Canyon to Dana Lake, which is fed by glaciers. Mount Dana looms large from the lake's shore.

Glen Aulin

10.4 mi. Moderate to strenuous. Access: Calif. 120 toward Tuolumne Meadows, about 1 mi. east of the Tuolumne Meadows Visitor Center and just a few yards east of the bridge over the Tuolumne River. Follow a marked turnoff and take the paved road on your left. The trailhead begins about 0.3 mi. ahead, at a road that turns right and heads up a hill toward the stables.

Start hiking across a flat meadow toward Soda Springs and Glen Aulin. The trail is well marked and signs along the way point out the area's history. This was once the old Tioga Road, which was built in 1883 to serve the Great Sierra Mine in Tioga Pass.

Lembert Dome rises behind you almost 900 feet above the meadow. About 0.4 mile from the trailhead the road forks; head right up a grassy slope. In less than 500 feet is a trail that leaves the road on the right and a steel sign for Glen Aulin. Along the way you'll pass Fairview Dome, Cathedral Peak, and Unicorn Peak. The crashing noise you hear is Tuolumne Falls, a cascade of water that drops down a series of ledges. From here you can see a nearby High Sierra camp. There's also a hikers' camp if you want to spend the night.

Lembert Dome

2.8 mi. Moderate. Access: Parking lot north of Calif. 120 in Tuolumne Meadows at road marker T-32. Follow the nature trail to marker no. 2.

This hike offers a bird's-eye view of Tuolumne Meadows. A well-marked trail leads you to the top, and from there you'll see the peaks that encircle the valley. It's a great place for sunrises and sunsets.

May Lake

2.5 mi. Easy. Access: Calif. 120 east past White Wolf. Turn off at road marker T-21 and drive 2 mi. to the May Lake parking area.

Winding through forests and granite, this picturesque hike offers ample opportunities to fish, but swimming is not allowed. May Lake is in the center of the park and is a good jumping-off point for other high-country hikes. There are numerous peaks surrounding the lake, including the 10,855-foot-high Mount Hoffman. There is a High Sierra camp here as well, and a hikers' camp on the south side of the lake.

Mono Pass

8.5 mi. Moderate to strenuous. Access: South side of Calif. 120 as you enter the park from Lee Vining. Drive about 1.5 mi. from the park entrance to Dana Meadows. Trail begins on an abandoned road alongside Parker Creek Pass.

You'll pass some historic cabin sites, then hike down to Walker Lake, and return via the same route. The hike loops into the Inyo National Forest and the Ansel Adams Wilderness, and climbs to an altitude of 10,600 feet.

Mt. Dana

5.8 mi. Strenuous. Access: Southeast side of Calif. 120 at Tioga Pass.

This climb is an in-your-face reminder that Mount Dana is Yosemite's second-highest peak. The mountain rises 13,053 feet and the trail gains a whopping 3,100 feet in 3 miles. The views at the top are wonderful, once you're able to catch your breath. You can see Mono Lake from the summit. In summer, the wildflowers are beautiful.

North Dome

10 mi. Easy to moderate. Access: Calif. 120 east to the Porcupine Flat Campground, past White Wolf. About 1 mi. after the campground is a sign for Porcupine Creek at a closed road. Park in the designated area.

Walk south down the abandoned road toward the Porcupine Creek Campground. A mile past the campground the trail hits a junction with the Tenaya Creek and Tuolumne Meadows Trail. Pass a junction toward Yosemite Falls and head uphill toward North Dome. The ascent is treacherous due to loose gravel, but from the top you'll catch an all-encompassing view of Yosemite Valley, second only to the view from Half Dome.

Polly Dome Lake

12.5 mi. Easy to moderate. Access: Calif. 120 past White Wolf to Tenaya Lake. Drive about 0.5 mi. to a picnic area midway along the lake. The trailhead is across the road.

This hike is easily the road least traveled. The trip to Polly Dome Lake is a breeze and you'll find nary another traveler in sight. There are several lakes beneath Polly Dome that can accommodate camping. The trail fades in and out so watch for markers. It crosses a rocky area en route, then skirts southeast at a pond. Polly Dome Lake is at the base of Polly Dome, a visual aide to help hikers stay the course.

Soda Springs

1.5 mi. Easy. Access: Either crosswalk just east of the Tuolumne Meadows Visitor Center, or parking lot north of Calif. 120 at road marker T-32. Follow the gravel road around a locked gate.

This trail crosses Tuolumne Meadows, then Tuolumne River on a wooden bridge. It's peaceful and beautiful, the sound of the river gurgling along as it winds slowly through the Tuolumne Meadow. The trail heads to a carbonated spring where you can taste the water, although it gets mixed reviews. For years, the spring was administered and owned by the Sierra Club, which operates the nearby Parsons Lodge, now an activity center. Also nearby is the historic McCauley Cabin, which is now a ranger's residence.

Sunrise Lakes

7–8 mi. Moderate to strenuous. Access: Calif. 120 to Tenaya Lake parking area on the east side of the road near the southwest end of the lake.

Look for a sign that says SUNRISE. Follow the level road to Tenaya Creek. Cross the creek and follow the trail to the right. The hike parallels Tenaya Creek for about 0.25 mile, then moves away through a wooded area and climbs gently up a rocky rise. After a while the trail descends quickly to the outlet of Mildred Lake. You'll be able to see Mount Hoffmann, Tuolumne Peak, and Tenaya Canyon.

At the halfway mark, the trail passes through a hemlock grove and then comes to a junction. Head left. (The trail on the right goes toward Cloud's Rest.) About 0.25 mile from the junction you'll reach Lower Sunrise Lake, tucked into the slope of Sunrise Mountain. The trail climbs past Middle Sunrise Lake and continues upward along a cascading creek coming from Upper Sunrise Lake. From there it follows the lake's shore and opens in less than 0.5 mile onto a wide, bare sandy pass. It's all downhill from here. Before you is the snowcapped Clark Range. The trail then begins its descent, sharply switching back and forth in some places. There is a High Sierra camp and backpackers' camp here as well.

Vogelsang

14.4 mi. Moderate to strenuous. Access: Calif. 120 to Tuolumne Meadows and watch for the signed trailhead for the John Muir Trail and Lyell Fork.

The trail goes south through the woods to a footbridge over the Dana Fork. Cross the bridge and follow the John Muir Trail upstream. Go right at the next fork. The trail crosses the Lyell Fork by footbridge. Take the left fork 200 feet ahead. Continue onward and just before crossing the bridge at Rafferty Creek, you'll reach another junction. Veer right and prepare for switchbacks up a rocky slope. The trail climbs steeply for about a quarter mile then levels off as it darts toward and away from Rafferty Creek for the next 4 miles.

The trail then gradually ascends to Tuolumne Pass, crossing many small creeks and tributaries en route. Two small tarns mark the pass. Just south of the tarns the trail splits. Veer left. (The right fork offers a 2-mile round-trip jaunt to Boothe Lake.) You'll climb to a meadow with great views, and here, at 10,180 feet, reach the highest of Yosemite's High Sierra camps. It's very pretty, with a great location—the base of Fletcher Peak, on the banks of Fletcher Creek and close to Fletcher Lake.

Other Sports & Activities

About the only thing you can't do in Yosemite is surf. In addition to sightseeing, Yosemite is a great place to bike, ski, rock climb, fish, even golf.

Biking. Bikes may be rented by the hour ($5.25) or the day ($20) at Curry Village or Yosemite Lodge. Both shops are open from 8am to 7pm daily in the summer, but the Curry Village shop closes in winter. Hours may vary slightly depending on weather and the season. Information is also available by phone (☎ 209/372-8319). Helmets are required for all riders under age 18 and are provided to riders of all ages free of charge. Cyclists have access to special bikeways, as well as shuttle bus roads and thoroughfares for general traffic. Biking is prohibited on all trails.

Cross-Country Skiing. Excursions are led from Badger Pass and Glacier Point. Information is available by phone (☎ 209/372-8444). Learn to telemark, snow camp, or take an overnight expedition. Skis can be rented at Badger Pass and at the mountain shop in the valley.

Fishing. General information is available from the **California State Department of Fish and Game** (☎ 559/222-3761) or the **U.S. Army Corps of Engineers** (☎ 559/689-3255). **Yosemite Creek Outfitters** leads fly-fishing trips in Yosemite (☎ 209/962-5060). The Groveland-based organization offers everything from 1-day fly-fishing lessons to multiday excursions on horseback or by white-water raft. You can also make custom arrangements.

Golf. Wawona sports a 9-hole golf course designed in 1917 by noted designer Walter G. Fovarque, who laid out many courses in Japan. You can book your tee time by phone (☎ 209/375-6572). There are several other courses just outside the park. The **River Creek Golf Course** (☎ 559/683-3388) is a 9-hole course in the small hamlet of Ahwahnee (not the hotel). And just to add to the confusion, the **Ahwahnee Golf Course** (☎ 559/642-1343) is in Oakhurst.

Horseback Riding. Yosemite offers 2-hour and half-day rides from stables in Yosemite Valley and Wawona spring through fall, weather permitting. In summer, rides also depart from Tuolumne Meadows. Pack animals and private stock may also board at stables. Call ☎ 209/372-8348 for more information or reservations. Prices range from $35 for a few hours to $900 for a 6-day, guided trip into the backcountry. Backcountry trips are available only with advanced reservations from May to September. These lead to Yosemite's High Sierra camps and trips include meals. **Yosemite Trails Pack Station** (☎ 559/683-7611) offers riding just south of Wawona. **Minarets Pack Station** (☎ 559/868-3405) is in the High Sierra and leads day trips to Yosemite and the Ansel Adams Wilderness.

Ice-Skating. The ice rink at **Curry Village** is open from early November to March, weather permitting. One session costs $5 for adults and $4.50 for children. Skate rental is another $2. Session hours are noon to 2:30pm, 3:30 to 6pm, and 7 to 9:30pm daily. The rink also offers

Especially for Kids

Many of the activities listed above have special programs for children, including rock-climbing and ski lessons. In addition, Yosemite offers a **Junior and Senior Ranger program** and special walks and lectures. All are described in chapter 1, under "Tips for Traveling with Kids."

morning sessions from 8:30 to 11am on weekends.

Rafting. A raft rental shop is located at **Curry Village** (☎ 209/372-8341). Daily rental fees are $12.50 for adults, $10.50 for children under 13. Fees include a raft, paddles, mandatory life preservers, and transportation from El Capitan back to Curry Village.

Rock Climbing. No guidebook would be complete without mentioning Yosemite's famous rock-climbing school. The park is considered one of the world's premier playgrounds for experienced climbers and wannabes. The **Yosemite Mountaineering School** (☎ 209/372-8344) provides experienced instruction for beginning, intermediate, and advanced climbers in the valley and Tuolumne Meadows from April through October. Classes last anywhere from a day to a week. Private lessons are also available. All equipment is provided and rates vary according to the class or program.

Skiing. Yosemite's **Badger Pass** is open from Thanksgiving through Easter Sunday (☎ 209/372-8430). There are special programs for kids, including a daylong child care/ski school called Badger Pups that also serves nutritional snacks. Lessons for all levels of skiers are available and prices are reasonable: A

half-day beginners lesson with all equipment and all-day lift ticket runs about $45. *Tip:* You can get a free lift ticket by staying overnight Sunday through Thursday after January 3 (excluding holidays) in one of the accommodations operated by Yosemite Concession Services.

Twenty-two miles from the valley, Badger Pass was established in 1935. It's a small resort with nine runs, four lifts, and a chairlift. It's geared toward intermediate skiers and it can be an excellent place to learn to ski. Its reputation rests squarely on the shoulders of Nic Fiore, a Yosemite ski legend who arrived in the park in 1947 to ski for a season and never left. Fiore became director of the ski school in 1956.

And lest we forget the much-adored, nonconforming snowboarder, you, too are welcome. Yosemite even has boards and boots for rent.

Camping

Campsite reservations in Yosemite are accepted in 1-month blocks beginning on the 15th of each month and can be made up to 5 months in advance. That said, make your reservations as soon following the 15th of the month, 5 months in advance, as you can, especially for sites in the valley. Additional campground information is available by Touch-Tone phone at ☎ 209/372-0200.

To make a reservation to camp in Yosemite National Park, call ☎ 800/436-7275 or on-line at www.reservations.nps.gov. *Note:* Wilderness permits are required for all overnight backpacking trips in the park. No wilderness camping is allowed in the valley.

In Yosemite National Park there is a 7-day camping limit in the valley and Wawona, and a 14-day limit elsewhere, from May 1 to September 15. For the remaining months of the year, there is a 30-day limit. Some campgrounds are closed in winter, so call in advance. Some sites are first-come, first-served. A maximum of six people and two vehicles may stay at each campsite. Check-in, check-out time is 10am. Pets are allowed in some campgrounds.

Now for the bad news: The valley lost half of its roughly 800 campsites during a flood in early 1997. The lost campsites will eventually be replaced further away from the Merced River, but no one's predicting when construction will begin.

Outside the park, campgrounds range from $9 to $11 per night in national forests, and are first-come, first-served. Private campgrounds are also available.

INSIDE THE PARK

Near the beautiful Glacier Point, **Bridalveil Creek** is away from the valley crowds but within a moderate drive to the valley sights. The campground is set along Bridalveil Creek, which flows to Bridalveil Fall, a beauty of a waterfall, especially after a heavy winter or wet spring. The camp can accommodate some pack animals.

Near the Big Trees and away from valley crowds, **Crane Flat** is a large but nice campground with the essential comforts nearby. Yosemite Valley is about 20 miles away. From Buck Meadows, drive 20 miles east on Highway 120 to the campground. **Hodgdon Meadow** is located along North Crane Creek and near the Tuolumne River's south fork. Yosemite Valley is 25 miles away; the Big Trees are 3 miles southeast. From Buck Meadows, drive 13 miles east on Highway 120 to the campground.

Like most campgrounds in Yosemite Valley, **Lower Pines** is wide open with lots of shade but limited privacy. Still, it's a nice place: easy to camp, clean bathrooms, bordered on the north by a nice meadow. Parking is available or take the shuttle bus to stop no. 19.

Beautifully situated beneath a grove of pine trees that offer little privacy but big shade, **North Pines** is also near the river and roughly a mile from Mirror Lake. Parking is available, or take the shuttle bus to stop no. 18. **Porcupine Flat,** near

Yosemite Creek, is another great campground that may have space if you're in a pinch. It's first-come, first-served, with lots of shade, shrubs, and trees. From Tuolumne Meadows, drive 16 miles west on Highway 120. From Yosemite Valley, drive 38 miles east on Highway 120.

Sunnyside Walk-in is situated behind Yosemite Lodge, near the trailhead for Yosemite Falls and near rocks frequently used by beginning rock climbers. This small campground is the most bohemian gathering in the valley, a magnet for hikers and climbers taking off or just returning from trips. Showers can be bought nearby at Camp Curry for about $2. Parking is available about 50 yards away or take the shuttle bus to stop no. 7.

Tamarack Flat, near Big Oak Flat Entrance, is sort of off the beaten path. This little-known campground accessible by car is more secluded than most, which means fewer folks rest their heads here. It's equidistant from the valley and Tuolumne Meadows. From Buck Meadows drive 21 miles east on Highway 120, bear left, and drive 3 miles to the campground entrance on the right. The campground is another 2.5 miles down the road

The biggest campground in Yosemite, and, amazingly, often the least crowded, the high-country **Tuolumne Meadows Campground** makes a good spot from which to head off with a backpack. It's also near the Tuolumne River, hence good for fishing. Showers and a grocery store are nearby. From Yosemite Valley, drive 46 miles east on Highway 120.

Upper Pines is the only valley campground that allows pets and the valley's only campground open in winter. Pets must be on a leash and are allowed only in the campground, not on trails. The property is pretty and shady. This site is closest to the Happy Isle Nature Center, so no seclusion or peace and quiet in the summer. Showers, grocery, laundry, propane gas, rafting, bicycle and ski rentals are nearby. Parking is available or take the shuttle bus to stop No. 15 or 19.

Campground	Elev.	Total Sites	RV Hookups	Dump Station	Toilets	Drinking Water
Bridalveil Creek	7,200	110	0	No	Yes	Yes
Crane Flat	6,200	116	0	No	Yes	Yes
Hodgdon Meadow	4,900	195	0	No	Yes	Yes
Lower Pines	4,000	60	0	Nearby	Yes	Yes
North Pines	4,000	81	0	Nearby	Yes	Yes
Porcupine Flat	8,100	52	0	No	Yes	No
Sunnyside	4,000	35 (tent only)	0	No	Yes	Yes
Tamarack Flat	6,200	52 (tent only)	0	No	Yes	No
Tuolumne Meadows	8,600	304	0	Nearby	Yes	Yes
Upper Pines	4,000	238	0	Yes	Yes	Yes
Wawona	4,000	93	0	Nearby	Yes	Yes
White Wolf	7,900	74	0	No	Yes	Yes
Yosemite Creek	6,200	75 (tent only)	0	No	Yes	No
Near the Park						
Lumsden	1,500	10 (tent only)	0	No	Yes	No
Lumsden Bridge	1,500	9 (tent only)	0	No	Yes	No
Lost Claim	3,100	10	0	No	Yes	Hand-pumped
The Pines	3,200	21	0	No	Yes	Only to Oct
South Fork	1,500	25	0	No	Yes	No
Indian Flat	1,500	35	0	No	Yes	Yes
Jerseydale	5,800	12	0	No	Yes	Yes
Summerdale	5,000	30	0	No	Yes	Yes
Summit Camp	5,800	2 (tent)	0	No	Yes	Yes
Aspen Grove	8,000	58	0	No	Yes	No
Big Bend	7,800	18	0	No	Yes	Yes
Ellery Lake	9,500	13	0	No	Yes	Yes
Junction	9,600	10	0	No	Yes	No
Lee Vining	8,000	129	0	No	Yes	No
Saddlebag Lake	10,000	22	0	No	Yes	Yes
Tioga Lake	9,700	13	0	No	Yes	Yes
Yosemite-Mariposa	2,000	40	30	Yes	Yes	Yes

Wawona Campground doesn't have much seclusion but it's a pretty place to stay beneath towering trees. The campground is near the Mariposa Grove of Giant Sequoias and Wawona. It's also close to the Merced River, which offers some of the better fishing in the park. A grocery store, propane gas, disposal station, and horseback riding facility are nearby. From Wawona, drive 1 mile north of Highway 41 to the campground.

Showers	Fire Pits/ Grills	Laundry	Public Phone	Reserve	Fees	Open
No	Yes	No	Yes	No	$10	June–Oct
No	Yes	No	Yes	Yes	$15	June–Oct
No	Yes	No	Yes	May–Sept	$15	Year-round
Nearby	Yes	Nearby	Yes	Yes	$15	Mar–Oct
Nearby	Yes	Nearby	Yes	Yes	$15	Apr–Sept
No	Yes	No	Yes	No	$6	July–Sept
Nearby	Yes	Nearby	Yes	No	$3	Year-round
No	Yes	No	Yes	No	$6	July–Sept
Nearby	Yes	No	Yes	For half the spaces	$6	June–Sept
Nearby	Yes	Nearby	Yes	Yes	$15	Year-round
No	Yes	No	Yes	May–Sept	$15	Tent Only
Nearby	Yes	No	Yes	No	$10	July–Sept
No	Yes	No	Yes	No	$6	July–Sept
No	Yes	No	Yes	No	Free	Apr–Oct
No	Yes	No	Yes	No	Free	Apr–Oct
No	Yes	No	Yes	No	$8	May–Oct
No	Yes	No	Yes	No	$9	Year-round
No	Yes	No	Yes	No	free	Apr–Nov
No	Yes	No	Yes	No	$9	Year-round
No	Yes	No	Yes	No	free	May–Nov
No	Yes	No	Yes	No	$9	May–Oct
No	Yes	No	Yes	No	free	June–Nov
No	Yes	No	Yes	No	$5	May–Oct
No	Yes	No	Yes	No	$7	May–Oct
No	Yes	No	Yes	No	$7	June–Oct
No	Yes	No	Yes	No	free	June–Oct
No	Yes	No	Yes	No	$5	May–Oct
No	Yes	No	Yes	No	$7	May–Oct
No	Yes	No	Yes	No	$7	June–Oct
Yes	Yes	Yes	Yes	A good idea	$18–$30	Year-round

Secluded in a forest, **White Wolf Campground** is a nice place to stay for several days with easy access to nearby hiking. The trails here lead to several lakes, including Grant Lake and Lukens Lake. There's a dirt road to Harden Lake, and beyond that, a trail to Smith Peak, which overlooks the Hetch Hetchy Reservoir. Mosquitoes are fierce in the summer. The bathrooms can get neglected. Showers available at nearby White Wolf Lodge for $2. A small grocery is nearby. From Buck Meadows, drive 20 miles east on Highway 120, bear left, and drive 15 miles to White Wolf Road and turn left. The road dead-ends at the campground.

Finally, **Yosemite Creek Campground** is a quaint place set along Yosemite Creek if the park is full and you need a place to stay. It's a lesser-known campground where you do everything yourself and for that reason it frequently has space available. From Buck Meadows, drive 30 miles east on Highway 120 to the campground road. It's 5 miles down the road to the campground.

NEAR THE PARK

Yosemite is surrounded by national forests that offer campgrounds comparable to the ones in Yosemite, albeit less crowded. There are also private campgrounds, which will cost you.

To get to the campgrounds in **Stanislaus National Forest** (☎ 209-962-7825), take Calif. 120 from Groveland about 8 miles east (about a mile east of the turn for County Road J20). There you'll find to the right the entrance road for **The Pines,** about 1.5 miles from the Tuolumne River. This campground gets scorching hot here during the summer. If you turn left instead and drive 1 mile, then turn right onto a dirt road and drive 6 more miles, you'll come to **Lumsden,** along the Tuolumne River, on a scenic stretch between the Hetch Hetchy and Don Pedro reservoirs. It's at an elevation of about 1,500 feet and is also very hot in summer. **Lumsden Bridge** is another 1.5 miles down the dirt road. This is a fave of rafters because the location is close to the Tuolumne River's best stretches, which are some of California's most awesome stretches of white water.

West of the park, 7 miles northeast of Mariposa on Calif. 140, is **Yosemite-Mariposa KOA Campground,** 6323 Calif. 140, Mariposa (☎ 209/966-2201), which comes complete with a swimming pool, playground, store, and laundry. This is

another good save if Yosemite is full. The campground is 28 miles from the park entrance and near the Merced River.

Indian Flat, in the Sierra National Forest (☎ 559/683-4665), is 4 miles south of El Portal on Calif. 140, and 24 miles north of Mariposa. This is a pretty place next to the Merced with several good swimming holes.

The **Lee Vining Creek Campgrounds,** 4 to 5 miles west of Lee Vining along Calif. 120, are four campgrounds clustered in a group. They're basically just places to rest your head for a fee. The campgrounds are set along Lee Vining Creek.

Tioga Lake, 10 miles west of Lee Vining on Calif. 120, is located in the Inyo National Forest (☎ 760/872-4240). A pretty camp set at 9,700 feet in the eastern Sierra, it's a good place to stay if Tuolumne Meadows is full.

Accommodations

There are accommodations to fit every budget and every taste in or near Yosemite. Yosemite Valley itself caters to families and offers everything from campgrounds to the opulent Ahwahnee Hotel where every room has a view of the valley's sheer granite greatness. All sites are located at or near shuttle bus stops and have parking nearby. A more narrow scope of choices is available outside the valley but still within the park.

INSIDE THE PARK

Lodging in the park is under the auspices of **Yosemite Concession Services Corp.** Rooms can be reserved up to 366 days in advance (☎ 209/252-4848). Reservations are also accepted by mail at **Yosemite Reservations,** 5410 E. Home Ave., Fresno, CA 93727.

The exception to all of this is Wawona. While YCS operates the Wawona Hotel, there are several dozen private homes that are rented seasonally through **Redwood Guest Cottages** (☎ 209/375-6666).

It's a real hodgepodge and appears fairly hit-and-miss in terms of quality, which may be why these places are seldom mentioned in guidebooks. But it's an option.

The Ahwahnee

Yosemite Valley. ☎ **209/252-4848.** 99 units, 24 cottages. A/C TEL. $229.50 for all regular units and cottages; up to $485 for suites. Lower rates Dec–Jan. CB, DC, DISC, JCB, MC, V. Rates include continental breakfast. Parking available. Shuttle bus: Stop no. 4.

The hotel's accommodations are fit for a king or queen, and it has hosted both. Queen Elizabeth slept here, as did Pres. John F. Kennedy, actor Clint Eastwood, poet Alfred Noyes, and quarterback Steve Young. It's tough to top The Ahwahnee, a six-story rock structure that offers beautiful views from every window. Common rooms on the ground floor contain three fireplaces large enough to stand in, and are furnished with large overstuffed sofas and chairs on which to read or play games. Guest rooms are upstairs, with suites located on the top floor, accessible only by special elevator key. Suites include a bedroom and sitting room. The Sun Suite is a bright pair of rooms in lime and yellow with comfy lounges and floor-to-ceiling French windows that open out onto the valley. Regular rooms offer a choice of two double or one king-size bed, with a couch and snuggly comforters. Rooms have original stencils on the walls dating from 1927, when the hotel was built. There's an outdoor pool, sundecks, nature trails, conference rooms, tour desk, and boutiques. The entire hotel received a $1.5 million renovation in January 1997.

The Ahwahnee offers a fine selection of food, most notably in its spacious dining room (see "Dining," later in this chapter). Prices vary depending on the meal, but be forewarned—it's expensive, but the food is excellent. Reservations are necessary for dinner (☎ 209/372-1489). The hotel also has a lounge with a full bar and limited food service.

Curry Village

Yosemite Valley. ☎ **209/252-4848.** 427 canvas tent-cabins with shared bathroom; about 100 wooden cabins, some with bathroom. $42 per tent-cabin, double occupancy, with additional charge for extra adults or children. Cabin $59.25–$75.25 with bathroom, double occupancy, with an additional charge for extra adults. Lower rates Nov–Mar. CB, DC, DISC, JCB, MC, V. Parking available. Shuttle bus: Stop nos. 1, 13, and 14.

Curry Village is a mass of white canvas tents that dot the valley's south slope. It was founded in 1899 as a cheaper alternative for valley visitors at a mere $2 a day. Today, it's often condemned as a kiddie hellhole, filled in the summer with crying and roughhousing. We found it tolerable and the easiest place to crash. It is also home to a decent pizza parlor with beer by the pitcher and a large-screen TV, a hamburger shack, a general store with the valley's best wine selection (still meager), one grossly overpriced cafeteria, and an ice-cream stand. It has a main tour desk where guests can book events throughout the valley. Canvas tents have wood floors, sleep two to four people, and are equipped with beds, dressers, and an ample supply of wool blankets. Tents have electrical outlets and daily maid service. There's an outdoor swimming pool, sundeck, bike and raft rental, nature trails, and a children's program. In short, convenience usually makes this worth the noisy toddler next door.

Housekeeping Camp

Yosemite Valley. ☎ 209/252-4848. 266 units, all with shared bathrooms and shower facilities. $44.50 per site (up to 4 people; $4 for every extra person). CB, DC, DISC, JCB, MC, V. Open summer only.

This place is funky. It's the closest thing to camping without pitching a tent. The sites are fence-enclosed shanties built on concrete slabs, each with a table, cupboard, electrical outlets, shelves, a mirror, and lights. The sleeping areas have two single-size fold-down bunks and a double bed. The park is slowly eliminating sites at Housekeeping Camp, with the idea of eventually getting the number of units down to 232.

Tuolumne Meadows Lodge

Hwy. 120, Tuolumne Meadows, Yosemite National Park. ☎ **209/252-4848.** 69 canvas tent-cabins, all with shared bathroom and shower house. $44 double, with additional $7.50 per adult or $3.50 per child. CB, DC, DISC, JCB, MC, V. Parking available in an adjacent lot. Closed in winter. From Yosemite Valley, take Hwy. 120 east 55 mi. toward Tioga Pass.

Not a lodge, but another group of canvas tent-cabins. Like White Wolf, these also have wood-burning stoves, tables, and sleep up to four. The crowds get thicker here as this is prime hiking territory. There's also a tiny general store and restaurant, nature trails, and a tour desk.

Wawona Hotel

Hwy. 41, Wawona, Yosemite National Park. ☎ **209/252-4848.** 104 units, 50 with shared bath. $70.75–$97.50 double, with additional charge for extra adults. CB, DC, DISC, JCB, MC, V. From Yosemite Valley, take Hwy. 41 south 27 mi. toward Fresno.

This is a classic Victorian-style hotel comprised of six stately white buildings set near towering trees in a green clearing. Don't be surprised if a horse and buggy rounds the driveway by the fishpond—it's that kind of place. Maybe it's the wide porches, the nearby 9-hole golf course, or the vines of hops cascading from one veranda to the next. The entire place was designated a National Historic Landmark in 1987. Clark Cottage is the oldest building, dating from 1876. The main hotel was built in 1879. Rooms are comfortable and quaint with a choice of a double and a twin, a king, or a double bed (most of the latter share bathrooms). All rooms open onto wide porches and overlook green lawns. Clark

Cottage is the most intimate. The main hotel has the widest porches and plenty of Adirondack chairs, and at night the downstairs sunroom hosts a pianist. Check out the whistling maintenance man who hits every high note in the "Star Spangled Banner" while the American flag is hoisted each morning (leaving many bystanders speechless as more than a few Wawona employees chime in to complete this whistling orchestra). There's a large outdoor pool, sundecks, two outdoor tennis courts, a golf course, nature trails, and conference rooms. An adjacent dining room serves great food and an awesome Sunday brunch. There is also a lounge.

White Wolf Lodge

Hwy. 120, White Wolf, Yosemite National Park. ☎ **209/252-4848.** 24 canvas tent-cabins, with shared bathroom and shower house; 4 cabins. $44–$80 double, with an additional charge of $7.50 per adult and $3.50 per child. CB, DC, DISC, JCB, MC, V. Parking available across a 2-lane road. Closed in winter. From Yosemite Valley, take Hwy. 120 east 33 mi. toward Tioga Pass.

Imagine a smaller, quieter, cleaner Curry Village with larger tents, each equipped with a wood-burning stove. White Wolf Lodge is not a lodge but a cluster of canvas tent-cabins, a few wooden ones out front, and a general store/restaurant. It's located halfway between the valley and the high country, and generally isn't overrun with visitors. It can get crowded but retains a homey feeling. Maybe it's the fact that there's no electricity after 11pm when the generator shuts off. Wood cabins all have a private bathroom and resemble a regular motel room, with neat little porches and chairs out front. Canvas cabins beat the Curry Village style by a mile. Each sleeps four in any combination of twin and double beds. There's a table and the helpful staff will show guests how to work the wood-burning stove. Bathrooms are clean and access is controlled by guests, with the exception of a few midday hours when nearby campers can pay for showers.

Yosemite Lodge

Yosemite Valley. ☎ **209/252-4848.** 249 motel units. $70.50–$107.25 double, with additional charge for extra adults. Lower rates Nov–Mar. CB, DC, DISC, JCB, MC, V. Parking available. Shuttle bus: Stop no. 8.

This is a conglomerate of cabins, regular motel rooms, and suites. Most rooms offer one or two double or king-size beds; some have air-conditioning. They are unremarkable but comfortable and clean. Some look out on Yosemite Falls, and some have patios or terraces with stunning views of Yosemite Falls at sunrise. It's not uncommon to see deer and other wildlife scamper through this area. The complex also contains an overpriced cafeteria, the new Mountain Room Restaurant, which has great views and wonderful desserts, and the Garden Terrace, which serves an awesome salad bar. There is also a lounge, general store, tour desk, large outdoor swimming pool, bike rentals, nature trails, and children's programs.

Yosemite West Cottages

P.O. Box 36, Yosemite National Park. ☎ **209/642-2211.** Various cabins and private homes. TV. $85–$150 and up. Take Hwy. 41 for 12 mi. north of Wawona.

Yosemite West rents private homes and cottages in the park that range in size and accommodate families as well as couples. All cabins have kitchenettes, and the vacation homes have full kitchens. It's just like living in the park. From here it's 10 miles to the valley and 8 miles to Badger Pass.

OUTSIDE THE PARK

If you strike out in the park, or prefer to stay outside, there is a plethora of choices. Each gateway community has built up a strong tourist trade catering to travelers.

ALONG CALIF. 120 (EASTBOUND)

Groveland Hotel

18767 Hwy. 120, Groveland. ☎ **800/273-3314** or 209/962-4000. Fax 209/962-6674. www.groveland.com. 17 units. All with private bathroom, 4 with shower only. A/C TEL. $95–$175 double, $25 for each extra person. Rates include continental breakfast and wine in the evening. AE, CB, DC, DISC, MC, V.

This is a great place to stay. In fact, *Country Inns* magazine named it as one of the nation's top 10 inns in 1997. The rooms are spacious, the hosts are gracious, and there's enough history, good food, and conversation to give travelers pause before heading into Yosemite. Groveland is about as quaint a town as you can get, and Peggy and Grover Mosley have poured their heart into making their hotel an elegant but comfortable place to stay. It is now a historic landmark. The hotel was built in 1849 to house workers constructing the nearby Hetch Hetchy Dam. Most of the rooms are upstairs and many have large spa bathtubs. Most rooms are named after women of the Sierra. One exception is Lyle's Room, named for the hotel's resident ghost. Return patrons swear it's true. Then there's Charlie's Room, named for a hard-driving, tobacco-spitting resident who drove a stagecoach, then started a trucking company. When he died, the townspeople learned he was a she. All rooms are filled with antiques, have thick down comforters, beds you want to jump on, and plush robes. Suites have fireplaces. The hotel also has a great dining room (see "Dining," later in this chapter).

Hotel Charlotte

18736 Hwy. 120, Groveland. ☎ **800/961-7799** or 209/962-6455. 11 units, 3 with shared bathroom, 2 with shower only. $62–$72 double. Rates include continental breakfast. AE, MC, V.

Walking into the Charlotte is like stepping back in time. Built in 1918 by an Italian immigrant of the same name, it's warm, comfortable, and no-nonsense. You'll be greeted in the lobby filled with antiques and red velvet–covered furnishings. The rooms are all upstairs, with twin, double, or queen beds. Several rooms adjoin each other and have connecting bathrooms (perfect for families). Rooms are quaint and have the basics but nothing more; air-conditioning is available in the summer. There is also a common game-television room. The continental breakfast is great—strong coffee, fresh warm muffins, and juices.

Inn at Sugar Pine Ranch

21250 Hwy. 120, Groveland. ☎ **888/800-7823** or 209/962-7823. 12 units, 8 with shower only. A/C. $110–$150 double, $25 for each extra person. Rates include full breakfast. MC, V.

This whitewashed inn is a new addition along the route to Yosemite, but its buildings date from the turn of the century and beyond. It's just outside of Groveland headed toward the park. The main building is an old farmhouse built in 1860. There are also separate cottages. Everything is laid out beneath tall pine trees. Rooms are comfortable and plush; some have balconies, all have nice views. Three cottages have fireplaces and whirlpool baths.

ALONG CALIF. 140

Best Western Yosemite Way Station

4999 Hwy. 140, Mariposa. ☎ **800/528-1234** or 209/966-7545. Fax 209/966-6353. 78 units. A/C TV TEL. $79–$85 double, $10 for each additional person. Rates include continental breakfast. AE, CB, DC, DISC, MC, V.

Typical motel accommodations. Clean and comfortable, but nothing fancy.

There's a pool and Jacuzzi, perfect after a hard day hiking. It is within walking distance of restaurants and shops and is near public transportation to Yosemite.

Cedar Lodge

9966 Hwy. 140, El Portal. ☎ **800/321-5261** or 209/379-2612. Fax 209/379-2712. 206 units, 1 three-bedroom suite with private pool and Jacuzzi. A/C TV TEL. $85–$135 double; $289–$399 suite. AE, MC, V.

Eight miles outside the park, this lodge offers ample-size rooms in a wooded setting. Variety makes this place an attractive option for visitors. It can accommodate every size group, from couples to families and large groups. Conference room seating is available for 250. There are two restaurants and a lounge on the premises, plus VCRs, video rentals, and indoor and outdoor pools. Public buses to the park are available from here.

Comfort Inn

4994 Bullion St., Mariposa. ☎ **800/321-5261** or 209/966-4344. Fax 209/966-4655. 78 units. A/C TV TEL. $79–$85 double; $180–$350 suite. Rates include continental breakfast. AE, CB, DC, DISC, MC, V.

These large, clean motel-style suites are conveniently located within walking distance of restaurants and near public transportation to Yosemite. There's a pool and Jacuzzi.

The Inn at the Mariposa Hotel

5029 Hwy. 140, Mariposa. ☎ **800/317-3244** or 209/966-4676. Fax 209/742-5963. www. yosemitehotel.com. 5 units. A/C TV. $99–$115 double, $20 for each additional person. Rates include full breakfast. Rates 15% lower Nov–Mar. AE, DISC, MC, V.

A former stage stop, this building was converted to a hotel in 1901. It has undergone several renovations since— each in an effort to expand the size of its rooms—without losing its historic charm. Guests enter from a large oak door at street level and climb an interior flight of stairs to the foyer, from which a long hall leads to individual rooms. All the rooms are large with sitting areas. The Marguerite Room has the hotel's original claw-foot bathtub. Della's Room is named after a Native American whose hand-woven baskets hang on the walls. The veranda at the rear of the hotel often serves as a gathering point and breakfast spot. The hotel is close to shopping and restaurants.

Miners Inn

5181 Hwy. 49 N., Mariposa. ☎ **800/321-5261** or 209/742-7777. Fax 209/966-2343. 78 units. A/C TV TEL. $79–$159 double, $6 for each additional person. AE, DC, DISC, MC, V.

A standard motel in a rustic setting that strives to recapture the Old West. Deluxe rooms include spa tubs and fireplaces. There is an on-site restaurant and lounge, pool, and there's nearby public transportation to Yosemite.

Mother Lode Lodge

5052 Hwy. 140, Mariposa. ☎ **800/398-9770** or 209/966-2521. 14 units, including a suite and family unit. TV. $39–$65 double. Lower rates in off-season. Rates include continental breakfast in summer. DISC, MC, V.

Best on the budget. The no-frills rooms here are sparse but clean. Basic rooms have one or two queen-size beds, a small desk, and a mirror. The bathrooms are tiny and the televisions have very few channels. Outside is a pool.

Poppy Hill Bed & Breakfast

5218 Crystal Aire Dr., Mariposa. ☎ **800/58-POPPY** or 209/742-6273. www.yosemite.com. 3 units. A/C. $110 double May–Oct, $100 Nov–Apr; $20 each additional person. Rates include full breakfast. AE, CB, DC, DISC, MC, V. Take Hwy. 140 past Mariposa 3 mi., turn left on Whitlock Rd. and right on Crystal Aire Dr.

This restored country home filled with antiques offers queen-size beds, down

comforters, bathrobes, sitting areas, and scenic views. There's an aboveground pool and Jacuzzi.

Yosemite View Lodge

11136 Hwy. 140, El Portal. ☎ **800/321-5261** or 209/379-2681. Fax 209/379-2704. 158 units. A/C TV TEL. $109–$179 double. MC, V.

Just outside Arch Rock entrance, this lodge offers guests accommodations on the river, which can turn wet and wild during the spring. All rooms have refrigerators and microwaves; some have spa tubs and fireplaces. There are two outdoor pools, three outdoor Jacuzzis. A new restaurant is under construction. Public buses to the park are available.

ALONG HIGHWAY 41

Comfort Inn

40489 Hwy. 41, Oakhurst. ☎ **800/321-5261** or 559/683-8282. Fax 559/658-7030. 116 units. A/C TV TEL. $89–$120 double, $129 suite. Lower rates off-season. Rates include continental breakfast. AE, CB, DC, DISC, MC, V.

This place offers regular motel-style accommodations and large, clean rooms. It's one of the larger motels outside the park that may have that last-minute room you need. There's a pool and Jacuzzi, and it's near the River Creek and Ahwahnee golf courses.

Ducey's on the Lake

Pines Village, N. Shore, Bass Lake (P.O. Box 109, Bass Lake). ☎ **800/350-7463** or 559/642-3902. www.basslake.com. 20 units. A/C TV. $179–$249 double in summer, $59–$199 in winter; $199–$309 suite. CB, DC, DISC, JCB, MC, V. From Hwy. 41, take Rd. 222 to the north shore of Bass Lake.

This historic country inn offers a variety of leisure activities. Guests stay in chalets and rooms that boast Native American decor and comfortable furnishings. Vaulted ceilings and beams were built with trees from the 44-acre property.

Large bathrooms have plush towels and thick bathrobes. All units have terraces and fireplaces, and some have whirlpools. On the grounds are a sundeck, tennis courts, and a jogging track, plus three restaurants and a bar.

Oakhurst Lodge

40302 Hwy. 41, Oakhurst. ☎ **800/655-6343** or 559/683-4417. Fax 559/683-4417, ext. 171. 60 units. A/C TV TEL. $79 double. Lower rates off-season. AE, CB, DC, DISC, MC, V.

This place offers clean rooms with one or two queen-size beds. There's a good selection of cable television channels and all rooms have small refrigerators. The motel is within walking distance of numerous restaurants and adjacent to a nice picnic area. There's an outdoor pool.

Pine Rose Inn

41703 Rd. 222, Oakhurst. ☎ **559/642-2800.** 9 units, 7 with full bathroom, 1 with shower only. A/C TV. $55–$125 in summer, lower rates in winter. Rates include expanded continental breakfast. DISC, MC, V. Take Hwy. 41 through Oakhurst 3 mi. to Rd. 222, turn right, and drive exactly 2 mi. The inn is on your left.

Rooms range from single bedrooms to split-level family cottages nestled in a picturesque canyon. Some rooms have fireplaces and hot tubs. The Garden Room is pretty, with a separate entrance, private bathroom, kitchenette, and nice porch. The family units are spacious. One includes a deep bathtub, slate tile, nice patio, living room, and full kitchen. The Hidden Rose Room is small but romantic. The owners are helpful and unobtrusive and guests benefit from the Rose Pine Inn's off-the-beaten-path location— the accommodations are a bargain. The homemade cinnamon rolls for breakfast are yummy.

Tenaya Lodge

1122 Hwy. 41, Fish Camp. ☎ **800/635-5807** or 209/683-6555. Fax 559/683-0249. 244 units. A/C MINIBAR TV TEL. $109–$259 double. Add $20–$80 for suite. Buffet breakfast $11 per couple. Children stay free in parents' rm. AE, DC, DISC, JCB, MC, V.

Whoever built this place had one foot in the Adirondack Mountains and another in the Southwest. This three- and four-story resort opened in 1990 on 35 acres full of hiking trails. The rest of the lodge includes a gas station and general store. The lobby has an impressive fireplace towering three stories and built of river rock. The staff is nice, helpful, and accommodating. The rooms are ultra-modern with multiple phones and a built-in safe. There's an indoor and outdoor swimming pool, on-site massage specialists, health club, game room, and sleigh and hay rides depending on the season.

Dining

We're not sure much proper "dining" goes on around these parts, but there are a dozen places to please your palate in the valley and a handful in the rest of the park. Some are good, a few are wonderful, and all are overpriced.

Finding great food outside Yosemite isn't impossible, but it'll take some work. More common are the average restaurants and cafes, where you can grab something in a pinch and again, pay more than it's worth. These places are everywhere, particularly along Calif. 140 and Calif. 41. However, there are some good buys, quirky places, and excellent establishments along each route.

IN THE VALLEY

Ahwahnee Dining Room

Ahwahnee Hotel, Yosemite Valley. ☎ **209/ 372-1489.** Dinner reservations required. Breakfast $6–$15, lunch $9–$13, dinner $10–$25. CB, DC, DISC, JCB, MC, V. Daily 7–10:30am, 11:30am–3pm, and 5:30–9pm. Shuttle bus stop no. 4. GOURMET CONTINENTAL.

Dining here takes your breath away. Even if you are a died-in-the-wool, down-to-the-earth, sleep-under-the-stars backpacker, the Ahwahnee Dining Room will not fail to make an impression. This is where the great outdoors meets four-star cuisine. With understated elegance, the cavernous dining room, its cande-labra chandeliers hanging from the 34-foot-tall beamed ceiling, seems intimate once you're seated at a table. Don't be fooled—it seats 450. Now open the menu. How about Salmon Ahwahnee, with Dungeness crab with béarnaise sauce and wild rice. Or rack of lamb with rosemary polenta. Or New York steak buried under a trio of mushrooms and served with herb-roasted potatoes. Don't forget dessert. The crème de bole is to die for. Breakfast includes a mouthwater-ing selection of omelettes, frittatas, and house specialties, such as a thick apple crepe filled with raspberry puree. Lunch sandwiches range from a portobello mushroom sandwich to pasta salad with tomato and fresh mozzarella. The Ahwahnee also has a tremendous wine list. An evening dress code requires men to wear a coat and tie.

Curry Cafeteria

Curry Village. All items $4–$12. CB, DC, DISC, JCB, MC, V. Daily 7–10am and 5:30–8pm. Shuttle bus: Stop nos. 1, 14, and 15. CAFETE-RIA.

Starving? Eat here. Otherwise, go to great lengths to stay away. It's not that the food is bad, but the prices are extreme. While there's something here for everyone—big breakfast, small nibble, you name it—the shell shock of paying $20 for breakfast for two (and meager breakfasts they were) requires advanced preparation. This place is short on atmosphere and long on dollar signs. Yosemite Concession Services, with all its know-how, should be ashamed.

Curry Hamburger Stand

Curry Village. $3–$4.50. No credit cards. Daily 11am–4pm. Closed in winter. Shuttle bus: Stop nos. 1, 14, and 15. BURGERS.

Your basic burger joint. This burger stand also offers chicken sandwiches and outdoor seating. It's a quick place for a quick bite. Try an order of fries—they're huge.

Curry Village Pizza Patio

Curry Village, Yosemite Valley. Pizza $8–$14. CB, DC, DISC, JCB, MC, V. Mon–Fri 5–9pm, Sat–Sun noon–9pm. Shuttle bus: Stop nos. 1, 14, and 15. PIZZA.

Need to watch ESPN? This is the place, but you may have to wait in line. The alternative to the big-screen room is the scenic outdoors with its large umbrellas, table service, and Mother Nature, plus or minus a hundred kids. The lounge also taps a few brews—nothing special but a mix aimed to please. This is a great place to chill after a long day.

Degnan's Deli

Yosemite Village. Sandwiches $4–$5. CB, DC, DISC, JCB, MC, V. Daily 8am–6pm. Shuttle bus: Stop nos. 3, 5, and 10. DELI.

A solid delicatessen with a large selection of sandwiches made to order as well as incidentals. It's half market, half deli. The sandwiches are generous. The line can be long, but it moves quickly. There's also a selection of premade stuff—salads, sandwiches, desserts—in addition to snacks to stuff in a knapsack before head-ing out for the day. Degnan's also has a decent beer and wine selection.

Degnan's Pasta

Yosemite Village. Main courses $4–$7. CB, DC, DISC, JCB, MC, V. Mon–Fri 11am–2pm and 5–8pm, Sat–Sun 11:30am–8pm. Shuttle bus: Stop nos. 3, 5, and 10. PIZZA/PASTA.

Adjacent to Degnan's Deli and Degnan's Pizzeria and Ice Cream (a gastronomic monopoly in Yosemite?), this is one of the valley's newest editions. Formerly the Loft Restaurant, Degnan's Pasta is a good family place. The atmosphere is cheery. There's a central fireplace and high-beamed ceilings. The pasta menu features a variety of pasta sauces that frequently rotate. Hot bread sticks, salads, and desserts are made fresh daily.

Degnan's Pizzeria and Ice Cream

Yosemite Village. Pizza $7–$13. CB, DC, DISC, JCB, MC, V. Daily 11:30am–5:30pm. Shuttle bus: Stop nos. 3, 5, and 10. PIZZA.

Adjacent to Degnan's Deli, this place offers pizza and ice cream. The pizza is definitely not baked in a brick wood-fired oven, but it's pizza. The ice-cream scoops are small, but it's ice cream.

Garden Terrace

Yosemite Lodge. $7.75 flat price, $5.50 for ages 5–15, $1.50 for ages 1–5. CB, DC, JCB, MC, V. Daily 11am–9pm. Shuttle bus: Stop no. 8. SALAD BAR.

This all-you-can-eat soup, salad, and pasta bar may be the best deal in the valley. It includes 30 selections of homemade soups, fresh salads, and baked goods. Pasta selections vary and can range from spaghetti to manicotti. Carved meats are also available for an additional $3.75. A double-pane skylight and windows allow plenty of sunlight.

Mountain Room Restaurant

Yosemite Lodge. Main courses $12–$20. CB, DC, DISC, JCB, MC, V. Daily 6–9pm. Shuttle bus: Stop no. 8. AMERICAN.

The best thing about this restaurant is the view. The food's good, too, but the floor-to-ceiling windows overlooking Yosemite Falls are spectacular. There's not a bad seat in the house. The restaurant opened in 1997 and is a worthy alternative to the pricey Ahwahnee. We spent $55 on dinner for two, including wine. The grilled chicken breast was flavorful and moist, as was the Idaho trout—but watch out for a few bones. Meals come with vegetables and bread. There is a children's menu, entrees for vegetarians, and an amazing dessert tray. The Mountain Room also has a good wine list.

Village Grill

Yosemite Village. Burgers and sandwiches $3–$4.50. No credit cards. Summer only, daily 7:30am–4pm. Shuttle bus: Stop nos. 3, 5, and 10. BURGERS.

Your basic burger joint. The Village Grill also offers chicken sandwiches and outdoor seating. It's a quick place for a quick bite.

Yosemite Lodge Cafeteria

Yosemite Lodge. Main courses $4–$12. CB, DC, DISC, JCB, MC, V. Daily 6:30–10am, 11:30am–2pm, and 5–8:30pm. Shuttle bus: Stop no. 8. CAFETERIA.

Breakfast, lunch, and dinner, but it comes at a price. The food is thoroughly mediocre, but it's convenient. It's also grossly overpriced, but that doesn't seem to bother the hundreds of people who eat here every day. There's enough room here to accommodate a family. Kids love the place.

ELSEWHERE IN THE PARK

Tuolumne Meadows Lodge

Tuolumne Meadows, Hwy. 120. ☎ **209/372-8413.** Reservations required for dinner. Breakfast $2–$6, dinner $4–$16. CB, DC, DISC, JCB, MC, V. Daily 7–9am and 6–8pm. AMERICAN.

One of the two restaurants in Yosemite's high country, the lodge offers something for everyone. The breakfast menu includes eggs, pancakes, fruit, and granola. Dinners always include a beef, chicken, fish, pasta, and vegetarian specialty, all of which change frequently. The quality can swing. The prime rib and New York steak are consistently edible. There's also a children's menu.

Wawona Hotel Dining Room

Wawona, Hwy. 41, Wawona. ☎ **209/375-1425.** Breakfast and lunch $4–$7, dinner $12–$20. CB, DC, DISC, JCB, MC, V. Mon–Sat

7:30–10am, noon–1:30pm, and 5:30–8:30pm; Sun 7:30am–1:30pm (brunch) and 5:30–8:30pm. AMERICAN.

The Wawona dining room mirrors the hotel's ambience—wide open, lots of windows, and sunlight. And the fare is great. For breakfast choose from a variety of items, including the Par Three, a combo of French toast or pancakes, eggs, and bacon or sausage—just what you need before hitting the golf course. Lunch is a buffet that changes seasonally. Dinner is delectable. In addition to some amazing entrees, such as roast duckling with cranberry orange glaze, grilled polenta, and Indian Tom's South Fork Trout, there are amazing appetizers. The stuffed mushroom caps, grilled artichoke, and Gulf shrimp cocktail are sumptuous.

White Wolf Lodge

White Wolf, Hwy. 120. ☎ **209/372-8416.** Reservations required for dinner. Breakfast $4–$7, dinner $10–$17. CB, DC, DISC, JCB, MC, V. Daily 7–9am and 6–8:30pm. AMERICAN.

Breakfast offers a choice of eggs, pancakes, omelettes, or biscuits and gravy. Dinner always includes a beef, chicken, fish, pasta, and vegetarian dish. The actual menu items vary. The portions are large, the staff is wonderful and enthusiastic, but alas, the food is mediocre.

NEAR THE PARK

Branding Iron

640 W. 16th St., Merced. ☎ **209/722-1822.** Reservations suggested. Main courses $13–$20. AE, MC, V. Mon–Fri 11:30am–2pm and 5:30–9pm, Sat–Sun 5:30–9pm. STEAK/SEAFOOD.

Merced's most popular steak house is in the heart of town, beyond big green awnings. The prime rib is a house favorite, but the rest of the menu gets rave reviews as well. Entrees come with soup, salad, vegetables, and potatoes.

Castillo's Mexican Food

4995 5th St., Mariposa. ☎ **209/742-4413.** Reservations recommended in summer. Main courses $8–$15. MC, V. Daily 11am–9pm. From eastbound Hwy. 140, turn right on 5th St. Drive 1 block. The restaurant is on your right. MEXICAN.

Established in 1955, this cheerful, cozy cantina serves breakfast, lunch, and dinner all day. The food is good and portions are plentiful. Entrees come with salad, rice, and beans, and can also be ordered à la carte. The house specialty, the Tostada Compuesta, fills a hungry belly. A children's menu is available. The service is great. Chips, salsa, and guacamole arrived before we'd removed our coats.

Charles Street Dinner House

5043 Hwy. 140, Mariposa. ☎ **209/966-2366.** Reservations recommended in summer. Main courses $15–$50. AE, DISC, MC, V. Tues–Sat 5–9pm. Closed Jan. STEAK/SEAFOOD.

The owner here likes to describe this place as "gourmet." Let's just say it's a hearty place with hearty food and leave it at that. Whatever it is, the Charles Street Dinner House is straight out of the Old West. The huge wagon wheel in the front window makes that clear. Inside is a kitschy compilation of family photos and plastic flowers. The menu covers everything that American food is supposed to be to international travelers. There is a wide selection of steak and seafood dishes, plus nightly specials, and all entrees come with soup, salad, and bread. The food can be mediocre, especially for the prices. It didn't help that the selection of wines and beers was weak. The service was quite good, however.

Groveland Hotel's Victorian Room

18767 Hwy. 120, Groveland. ☎ **800/273-3314** or 209/962-4000. Reservations suggested. Main courses $13–$20. AE, CB, DC, DISC, JCB, MC, V. Daily 6–11pm in summer and 6–8:30pm in winter. CALIFORNIAN.

With the unique combination of four-star food and a one-star dress code, this restaurant offers casual dining at its finest. The menu has something for everyone and is constantly changing to reflect what's fresh and in season. There's a sumptuous rack of lamb marinated in rosemary and garlic, salmon with fresh cucumber and dill, chicken breast with fresh fruit salsa, and more. The menu usually has a fresh seafood and pasta special as well as an innkeeper's special. All entrees are served with soup or salad and fresh warm bread. There's an adjacent bar and what has to be one of the most extensive wine lists in the Sierra. The restaurant is handicapped accessible.

Hotel Charlotte

18736 Hwy. 120, Groveland. ☎ **800/961-7799** or 209/962-7872. Reservations suggested in the summer. Main courses $11–$16. AE, MC, V. Daily 6–10pm in summer and 5–9pm in winter. AMERICAN.

Casual dinners are offered in the small dining room of this quaint hotel. The menu includes mostly meat and fish dishes. Daily specials range from halibut with lemon to barbecued baby back ribs. Vegetarians can choose from pasta primavera or stir-fry. All meals include soup, salad, veggies, potato or rice, and bread. There is also a full bar and a healthy wine list.

Iron Door Saloon and Grill

Hwy. 120, Groveland. ☎ **209/962-6244.** Main courses $4–$14. DISC, MC, V. Daily 11am–9pm. BURGERS.

You'll miss this place if you blink. Groveland is about 3 blocks long and this is the best watering hole in town. It's a funky, fun, comfortable place to hang out for a few hours if (a) you're sick of traffic, (b) you're sick of lines, or (c) you just want to stall before hooking up with your entire family for a weekend getaway in

one of the most crowded places around. The saloon and grill are in adjacent rooms. The bar is stocked with history, from the hunting trophies on the walls to the dollar bills pinned to the ceiling (go ahead, ask). The food is strictly burgers, fries, and shakes, and it's all good. There are 27 burger variations, including buffalo meat and veggie tofu. There are kids' offerings and salads. The milk shakes are dreamy. There's live music most Fridays and Saturdays. *Warning:* Thursday night is family karaoke night, which for some unknown reason compels hordes of teens to take to the stage to sing tunes from the 1970s and 1980s (think *Saturday Night Fever*).

Lenny's

1052 W. Main St., Merced. ☎ **209/722-0350.** Main courses $10–$16. AE, MC, V. Mon–Fri 7am–9:30pm, Sat 7am–10pm, Sun 9am–9pm. ITALIAN.

This popular Merced restaurant serves old-world favorites. Recipes here have been passed down for generations, but the owner has added a few American twists of his own. The lunch buffet, loaded with pastas and at least 15 other dishes, seems the best bargain in town. Dinners are more elaborate, with all sauces and sausages made on the premises. Lenny's also serves 150 kinds of beer and has an espresso bar.

Meadows Ranch Cafe

5024 Hwy. 140, Mariposa. ☎ **209/966-4242.** Reservations recommended on summer weekends. Breakfast $3–$6, lunch $4–$6, dinner $6–$16, pizza $7.95. MC, V. Mon–Sat 7am–10pm in summer, 7am–9pm in winter; Sun 9am–noon. AMERICAN.

A great place for a quick bite or a full meal. The food is wholesome and fresh. The coffee is great. Breakfasts include a variety of egg dishes, omelettes, and breakfast burritos. For lunch pick from a selection of more than two dozen sandwiches on a variety of breads. Dinner includes pizzas, pasta, and a few grilled selections, including grilled lemon herb chicken breast and barbecued beef. The owners recently began a much-anticipated Sunday brunch. The 100-year-old dining room is adjacent to the cafe's new brew pub, where patrons can watch the brewing process.

PJ's Cafe and Pizzeria

18986 Hwy. 120, Groveland. ☎ **209/ 962-7501.** Main courses $3–$7, pizza $5–$15. No credit cards. Daily 7am–8pm.

Best known as a pizzeria and burger house, PJ's serves a hearty breakfast with an eye toward helping patrons lower their fat and cholesterol intake. That being said, you can still order bacon and eggs without getting the evil eye. PJ's also uses only lean ground chuck in its chili, taco meat, and meat sauces, which are available for lunch and dinner. The pizzas are interesting, ranging from a create-your-own to the yummy pesto-chicken-artichoke-tomato combination.

Picnic & Camping Supplies

If you forget something, chances are you'll be able to get it in the valley. But elsewhere in the park it's tough to find equipment. The best place to get supplies and camping equipment in the valley is the **Yosemite Village Store.** The **Yosemite Lodge Gift Shop** and **Curry Village General Store** stock some supplies. The **Mountaineering Shop** at Curry Village sells clothing and equipment for day hikes as well as backcountry excursions.

37

ZION NATIONAL PARK & CEDAR BREAKS NATIONAL MONUMENT

by Don and Barbara Laine

I

T'S NOT HARD TO CONJURE UP A SINGLE DEFINING IMAGE OF MOST national parks, but Zion, a collage of images and secrets, is impossible to pin down. Zion National Park is not simply the towering Great White Throne, the deep Narrows Canyon, or the cascading waterfalls and emerald green pools. There's an entire smorgasbord of experiences and sights here, from massive stone sculptures and monuments to lush forests and rushing rivers.

Today, 150 years after the Mormon settler Isaac Behunin named his homestead here "Little Zion," the park still casts its spell as you gaze upon its sheer multicolored walls of sandstone, explore its narrow canyons, hunt for hanging gardens of wildflowers, or listen to the roar of the churning, tumbling Virgin River. Take time to walk its trails, visit viewpoints at different times of the day to see the changing light, and let the park work its magic.

Because of its extremes in elevation (from 3,700 ft. to almost 9,000 ft.) and climate, Zion harbors a vast array of flora and fauna. Wildlife here includes pocket gophers, mountain lions, hundreds of birds (including golden eagles), and dozens of snakes. As for plants, about 800 native species have been found: cactus, yucca, and mesquite in the hot, dry desert areas; ponderosa pine trees on the high plateaus; and cottonwoods and box elders along the rivers and streams. Watch for the red claret cup cactus, which has spectacular blooms in the spring, and for wildflowers such as the manzanita, with its tiny pink blossoms, and the bright red hummingbird trumpet, sometimes called the "Zion Lily." And don't miss the hanging gardens of plant life clinging to the sides of the sandstone cliffs.

The park means different things to different people: a day hike down a narrow canyon, a rugged climb up the face of a massive stone monument, the red glow of sunset over majestic peaks. To some degree, each of these experiences is possible only because of rocks—their formation, uplifting, shifting, breaking, and eroding. The most important of Zion's nine rock layers in creating its colorful formations is Navajo sandstone, the thickest rock layer in the park, at up to

2,200 feet. Millions of years ago a shallow sea covered the sand dunes here, causing minerals, including lime from the shells of sea creatures, to glue sand particles together to form sandstone. Later, movements in the earth's crust lifted the land, draining away the sea but leaving rivers that gradually carved the soft sandstone into the spectacular shapes we see today.

But where do the marvelous colors of the rocks come from? Essentially, from rust. Most of the rocks at Zion are colored by iron, or hematite (iron oxide), either contained in the original stone or carried into the rocks by groundwater. Although iron often creates red and pink hues, seen in much of Zion's sandstone faces, it can also result in blacks, browns, yellows, and even greens. Sometimes the iron seeps into the rock, coloring it through, but often it just stains the surface in vertical streaks. Rocks are also colored by bacteria that live on their surfaces. The bacteria ingest dust and expel iron, manganese, and other minerals, which stick to the rock and produce a shiny black, brown, or reddish surface called desert varnish.

Avoiding the Crowds. Try to avoid the peak summer months of June, July, and August, when temperatures are hot and Zion receives almost half its annual visitors. The quietest months are December, January, and February, but of course it's cold and you may have to contend with some snow and ice. A good time to visit, if your schedule permits, is in April, May, September, or October, when the weather is still good and the park is less crowded than in the summer.

Once in the park, the best way to avoid crowds is to walk away from them, either on the longer and more strenuous hiking trails or into the backcountry. It's sad but true: Most visitors in Zion never bother to venture far from the main viewpoints, and their loss can be your gain. You can also avoid the hordes by spending time in Kolob Canyons, in the far northwest section of the park; it's spectacular and receives surprisingly little

use, at least in comparison to Zion Canyon.

Just the Facts

GETTING THERE & GATEWAYS

Zion National Park is in the southwestern corner of Utah, 83 miles southwest of Bryce Canyon National Park and 120 miles northwest of the north rim of Grand Canyon National Park in northern Arizona. It's 309 miles south of Salt Lake City, 42 miles northwest of Kanab, and 158 miles northeast of Las Vegas, Nevada. It's composed of two parts: Zion Canyon, the main section of the park, and the less-visited Kolob Canyons, in the park's northwest corner. The closest towns with airport service are St. George (46 miles southwest of the park), and Cedar City (60 miles north).

The easiest way to get to the park is to approach from the west on I-15, which runs north to Salt Lake City and southwest through Arizona to Nevada. From I-15, go east on Utah 9 if approaching from the south, or go south on Utah 17 and then east on Utah 9 if approaching from the north; Utah 9 then continues east to the park's south entrance. The western approach is the easiest route into the park—it's more direct, avoids possible delays at the Zion–Mt. Carmel Tunnel, and delivers you to Springdale, just outside the park's south entrance, where most of the area's lodging and restaurants are located.

The Kolob Canyons section, in the park's northwest corner, is reached on the short Kolob Canyons Road off I-15, Exit 40.

The eastern approach to the park is less direct but far more beautiful. From either the south or the north take U.S. 89 to Utah 9 at Mount Carmel, then go east on Utah 9 for a spectacularly scenic 24-mile drive. However, be aware that this route into the park drops over 2,500 feet in elevation, passes through the mile-long Zion–Mount Carmel Tunnel, and winds down six steep switchbacks.

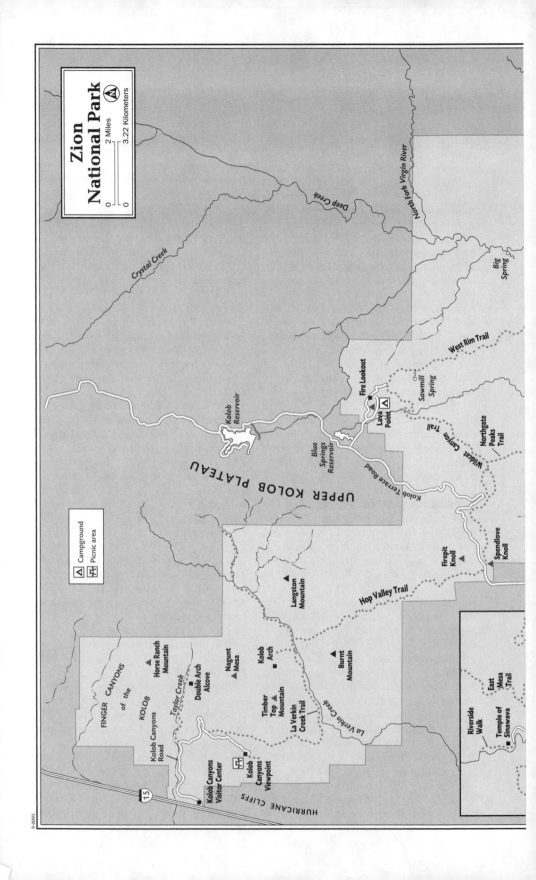

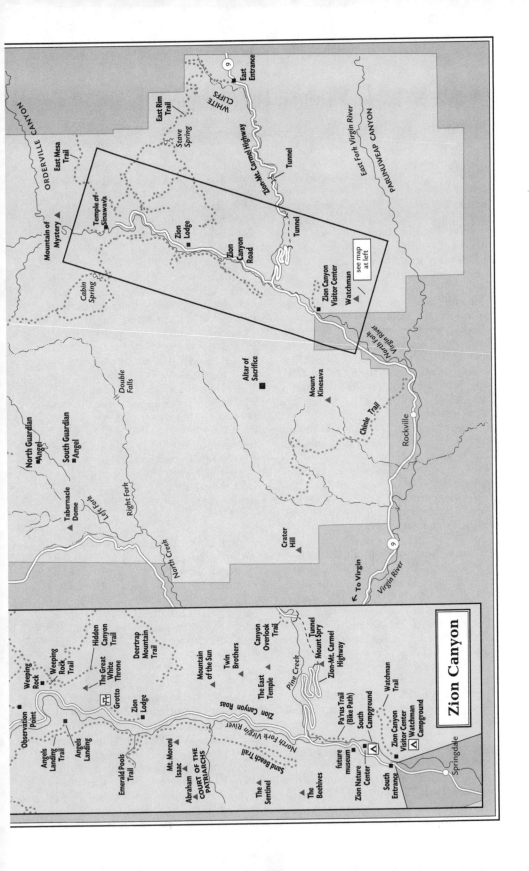

Tips from a Park Ranger

"Overpowering, but also intimate" is how former backcountry ranger Dave Rachlis sees Zion National Park, adding, "These are some of the highest vertical rock walls that some people will ever see." Rachlis explains that the Navajo sandstone that forms Zion's walls is one of the thickest sedimentary formations in the world. It can be seen in the West Temple just behind the visitor center.

Rachlis says that one of the best aspects of the park, from the visitor's point of view, is its trail system. "The park has a sense of grandeur, but then it also has access—you can go up the West Rim Trail or you can go up the East Rim Trail, and you can get into these narrow canyons, and really experience the park pretty easily."

Most visitors to Zion, according to Rachlis, stay only a short time and see only a small part of the park—what's visible from the viewpoints—but he recommends a visit of at least a full day, preferably more. "In 2 or 3 days you can see most of the major regions of the park and get a chance to get out on the trails a bit for day hikes," he says.

Hikers should keep in mind that they can see the park from two perspectives. "You need to decide what experience you want—to climb to a high plateau and gaze down into the canyons; or to descend into a canyon and look up. I think the West Rim Trail is probably our most scenic trail in terms of getting you up onto the plateau where you can look down into the canyons." He also recommends the La Verkin Creek Trail, which leads to Kolob Arch, believed to be the world's largest freestanding arch. "This trail is very intimate, very colorful—the rock is a little more orange to red than it is in the main canyon. It's just a really magnificent area."

A hike through the Narrows is "the ultimate slot canyon experience," according to Rachlis. "You're following a river drainage, wading or swimming in spots. In summer, it's one of the cooler areas of the park."

One mistake that some park visitors make, Rachlis says, is to downplay the dangers of the easy and moderate hiking trails, where most injuries occur. He says that people understand the hazards on difficult trails such as Angels Landing, where you're inching along a knife-edge ridge; but that you also need to be careful on trails with less-obvious dangers. "Sandstone is slippery, and a 20-foot fall can kill you as easily as a 1,000-foot fall," he says.

As for when to visit, Rachlis says the trails can be hot in summer, so the best time for hiking is probably spring and fall—from April through June and from September through November. The park is also less crowded at those times. But he adds that the park has unpredictable weather, so it's best to call to check on current conditions before showing up.

Oversized vehicles are charged $10 to use the tunnel (see "Special Regulations & Warnings," below).

INFORMATION

Contact the **Superintendent, Zion National Park,** Springdale, UT 84767-1099 (☎ 435/772-3256; www.nps.gov/zion). You can purchase books, maps, and videos from the nonprofit **Zion Natural History Association,** Zion National Park, Springdale, UT 84767 (☎ 800/635-3959 or 435/772-3264). Some publications are available in foreign languages, and videos can be purchased in VHS or PAL formats. Look for the colorful and informative *Zion National Park, Towers of Stone,* by J. L. Crawford; the brief, easy-to-understand *An Introduction* to the *Geology of Zion National Park*, by Al Warneke; and *Exploring the Backcountry of Zion National Park: Off-trail Routes*, by Thomas Brereton and James Dunaway. Those planning backcountry hikes should purchase a copy of the association's topographical map. *The Zion Park Map & Guide*, a small free newspaper-format guide, is packed with extremely helpful information.

VISITOR CENTERS

The park has two visitor centers. The **Zion Canyon Visitor Center and Transportation Hub,** near the south entrance, has outdoor exhibits that provide an introduction to the park. Rangers here can answer questions and provide backcountry permits. You can also buy books, maps, videos, postcards, and posters, and pick up free brochures. The **Kolob Canyons Visitor Center,** in the northwest corner of the park off I-15, provides information, permits, books, and maps.

FEES & PERMITS

Entry into the park (for up to 7 days), which includes unlimited use of the shuttle bus, costs $20 per private vehicle, $5 per individual on motorcycle or bicycle, or $4 per individual for those on foot using the pedestrian only entrance. Oversized vehicles (see "Special Regulations & Warnings," below) are charged $10 for use of the Zion–Mt. Carmel Tunnel on the east side of the park.

Permits ($5 per person per night and available at either visitor center) are required for all overnight hikes in the park and all slot canyon routes. Camping costs $10 per night for basic campsites and $14 per night for sites with electric hookups.

SPECIAL REGULATIONS & WARNINGS

The mile-long Zion–Mount Carmel Tunnel was not built for big vehicles. The tunnel is too narrow for two-way traffic involving anything larger than passenger cars and pickup trucks. Therefore, any vehicle over 7 feet, 10 inches wide (including mirrors) or 11 feet, 4 inches tall (including luggage racks) can only pass by driving down the center of the tunnel after all other traffic has been stopped. Large vehicles can accomplish this feat only from 8am to 8pm daily from March to October; during other months arrangements can be made at park entrances or by calling park headquarters. The charge is $10, good for two trips through the tunnel during a 7-day period.

All vehicles over 13 feet, 1 inch tall and certain other particularly large vehicles are prohibited from driving anywhere on the park road between the east entrance and Zion Canyon.

Bicycles are prohibited in the Zion–Mount Carmel Tunnel, the backcountry, and on trails, except the Pa'rus Trail. At the visitor center, backcountry hikers can pick up a free brochure describing close to 20 trails and listing regulations, such as prohibitions against lighting fires and limits on the number of people permitted in various backcountry areas.

SEASONS & CLIMATE

Zion experiences all four seasons, although the winters are mild and rarely bring snow. The best times to come are spring and fall, when the temperatures range from lows in the 40s to pleasant highs in the 80s. Remember that summer daytime highs often soar above 100°F, with lows in the 70s. Do your hiking then in the early morning to avoid both the heat and the frequent afternoon thunderstorms in July and August, which can change a babbling brook into a raging torrent in minutes.

If You Only Have 1 Day

If you only have a day, stop first at the **Zion Canyon Visitor Center** to see the exhibits and look through the free *Zion Park Map & Guide*, which describes the available options. Then hop on the shuttle bus, which hits the major Zion Canyon roadside viewpoints. But, when you get to the **Temple of Sinawava,** instead of just taking a quick look and jumping on the next shuttle, hike the easy 2-mile round-trip **Riverside Walk,** which follows the Virgin River through a narrow canyon past hanging gardens. Then continue the shuttle bus trek back to the lodge (total time: 2 to 4 hours), where you might stop at the gift shop and possibly have lunch in the lodge restaurant.

Near the lodge you'll find the trailhead for the **Emerald Pools.** Especially pleasant on hot days, this easy walk through a forest of oak, maple, fir, and cottonwood trees leads to a waterfall, hanging garden, and the shimmering lower pool. This part of the walk should take about an hour round-trip, but those with a bit more ambition may want to add another hour and another mile to the loop by taking the moderately strenuous hike on a rocky, steeper trail to the upper pool.

If time and energy remain, head back toward the south park entrance and stop at **Watchman Trailhead.** Here, a moderately strenuous, 2-mile, 2-hour round-trip hike takes you to a plateau with beautiful views of several rock formations and the town of Springdale. That evening, try to take in the campground amphitheater program.

Exploring the Park by Car or Shuttle

If you enter the park from the east, along the steep **Zion–Mt. Carmel Highway,** you'll travel 13 miles to the **Zion Canyon Visitor Center,** passing between the White Cliffs and Checkerboard Mesa, a massive sandstone rock formation covered with horizontal and vertical lines that make it look like a huge fishing net. Continuing, you'll pass through a fairyland of fantastically shaped rocks of red, orange, tan, and white, as well as the **Great Arch of Zion,** carved by the forces of erosion high in a stone cliff. At the east end of the Zion–Mt. Carmel Tunnel is the **trailhead parking** for the Canyon Overlook Trail, a relatively easy 1-mile walk to a great viewpoint. After driving through the tunnel you'll traverse a number of long switchbacks as you descend to the canyon floor.

A shuttle bus system, scheduled to begin in spring 2000, has been implemented in the main section of the park to reduce traffic congestion and the resultant problems of pollution, noise, and damage to park resources. The shuttle system consists of **two loops:** one in the town of Springdale and the other along Zion Canyon Road, with the loops connecting at the transit/visitor center just inside the south park entrance. From March through October, access to Zion Canyon Road (above Utah 9) will be limited to shuttle busses, hikers, and bikers. The only exception will be overnight Zion Lodge guests and tour busses connected with the lodge, who will have access as far as the lodge. Shuttle stops are at all the major-use areas in the park, and shuttles will run frequently (about every 6 min. at peak times). In winter, when visitation is lowest, visitors will be permitted to drive the full length of **Zion Canyon Road** in their own vehicles.

The ride through Zion Canyon is impressive by any standards, with massive stone reaching straight up to the heavens, and the North Fork of the Virgin River threading its way through the maze of rocks. In every direction the views are awe-inspiring. Stops along the road provide access to viewpoints and hiking trails.

The first stop is across from the **Court of the Patriarchs,** where a short paved trail leads to an impressive viewpoint. The next stop is **Zion Lodge,** and across the road from the lodge is the trailhead for the **Emerald Pools Trail system.** The Grotto Picnic Area is about 0.5-mile beyond the lodge, and a trail, paralleling Zion Canyon Road, leads from the lodge to the picnic area. Across from the Grotto Picnic Area parking lot is a footbridge that leads to the Emerald Pools, Angels Landing, and West Rim Trails.

Continuing north into Zion Canyon, the road passes the **Great White Throne** on the right and then **Angels Landing** on the left, before the turnoff to the **Weeping Rock Trailhead** parking area. From here the road closely traces the curves of the river, with a couple of stops to allow different views of **the Organ,** which to some resembles a huge pipe organ. Finally the road ends at the **Temple of Sinawava,** where the paved **Riverside Walk** follows the Virgin River toward **the Narrows,** one of the most incredible sights in Zion.

To escape the crowds of Zion Canyon, head to the northwest corner of the park. The **Kolob Canyons Road** runs 5 miles among spectacular red and orange rocks, ending at a high vista. Allow about 45 minutes round-trip, stopping at numbered viewpoints. Be sure to get a copy of the *Kolob Canyons Road Guide* at the Kolob Visitor Center. Here's what you'll pass along the way:

Leaving **Kolob Canyons Visitor Center,** you'll drive along the Hurricane Fault to **Hurricane Cliffs,** a series of tall, gray cliffs composed of limestone, and onward to **Taylor Creek,** where a piñon-juniper forest clings to life on the rocky hillside, providing a home to the bright blue scrub jay. Your next stop is **Horse Ranch Mountain,** which, at 8,726 feet, is the national park's highest point. Passing a series of colorful rock layers, where you might be lucky enough to spot a golden eagle, your next stop is **Box Canyon,** along the South Fork of Taylor Creek, with sheer rock walls soaring over 1,500 feet high. Along this stretch you'll see multicolored layers of rock, pushed upward by tremendous forces from within the earth, followed by a side canyon, with large, arched alcoves boasting delicate curved ceilings. Head on to a view of **Timber Top Mountain,** which has a sagebrush-blanketed desert at its base, but is covered with stately fir and ponderosa pine at its peak. Watch for mule deer on the brushy hillsides, especially between October and March, when they might be spotted just after sunrise or before sunset. From here, continue to **Rockfall Overlook;** a large scar on the mountainside marks the spot where a 1,000-foot chunk of stone crashed to the earth in July 1983, the victim of erosion. And finally, stop to see the canyon walls themselves, colored orange-red by iron oxide and striped black by mineral-laden water running down the cliff faces.

Ranger Programs

Park rangers present a variety of free programs and activities. **Amphitheater programs,** which sometimes include a slide show, take place most evenings at campground amphitheaters. Topics vary, but could include the animals or plants of the park, geology, or something unique to Zion, such as its slot canyons. Rangers also give short talks on similar subjects several times daily at various locations. **Ranger-guided hikes and walks,** which may require reservations, might take you to little-visited areas of the park, or on a trek to see wildflowers, or out at night for a hike under the full moon. Schedules are posted on bulletin boards at the visitor centers and campgrounds.

Historic & Man-Made Attractions

There are no major historic sites in Zion National Park, but there is some evidence of the early peoples who inhabited the area. Lucky hikers with sharp eyes may see potsherds, pieces of ancient stone tools, rock art, and other archaeological objects. Park officials ask that you do not touch these artifacts (skin oils can damage them), but report their location to rangers.

Day Hikes

Zion offers a wide variety of hiking trails, ranging from easy half-hour walks on paved paths to grueling overnight hikes over rocky terrain. Hikers with a fear of heights should be especially careful when choosing trails; many include steep, dizzying, and potentially fatal drop-offs. Water found in streams in the park is not safe to drink. Smoking is prohibited on all trails.

Canyon Overlook

1 mi. RT. Moderate. Access: East side of Zion–Mt. Carmel Tunnel.

This self-guided trail takes you to an overlook with a magnificent view of lower Zion Canyon and Pine Creek Canyon. There are some long drop-offs, and the sandy trail can be slippery, but the fences will reassure nervous walkers. Trail guides are available at the visitor center and at the trailhead.

Emerald Pools Trails

1.2–2.5 mi. RT. Easy to moderate. Access: Across from Zion Lodge.

This can be either an easy 1-hour walk or a moderately strenuous 2-hour hike with steep drop-offs, depending on how much you choose to do. A 0.6-mile paved path leads from the Emerald Pools parking area through a forest of oak, maple, fir, and cottonwood, to several waterfalls, a hanging garden, and the picturesque Lower Emerald Pool.

From here, a steeper, rocky trail (not appropriate for wheelchairs) continues 0.25 mile to Middle Emerald Pool, and then climbs another 0.33 mile past cactus, yucca, and juniper to Upper Emerald Pool, with another waterfall. Total elevation gain is 69 feet to Lower Emerald Pool, 150 feet to the middle pool, and 400 feet from the trailhead to Upper Emerald Pool.

Hidden Canyon Trail

2 mi. RT. Moderate to strenuous. Access: Weeping Rock parking lot.

A particularly scenic hike, this trail climbs 850 feet through a narrow water-carved canyon, ending at the canyon's mouth. Those wanting to extend the hike can go another 0.6 mile to a small natural arch. Hidden Canyon Trail includes long drop-offs, and is not recommended for anyone with a fear of heights.

Pa'rus Trail

3.5 mi. RT. Easy. Access: From either the entrance to Watchman Campground, near the amphitheater parking area, or near the Nature Center at South Campground.

This paved trail (fully accessible to wheelchairs) follows the Virgin River, providing views of the rock formations in lower Zion Canyon. Unlike other park trails, this one is open to bicycles and leashed pets. The elevation gain is only 50 feet.

Riverside Walk and the Gateway to the Narrows

2 mi. RT. Easy. Access: Temple of Sinawava parking lot.

This paved trail follows the Virgin River upstream to the Zion Canyon Narrows, past trailside exhibits and hanging wildflowers in spring and summer. Accessible to those in wheelchairs with some assistance, the trail has an elevation change of only 57 feet. At the Narrows, the pavement ends, and here you have to decide whether to turn around or to continue upstream into the Narrows itself (yes, you will get wet), where the canyon walls are less than feet apart in some areas and more than 1,000 feet high. *Warning:* The bottom of a very narrow slot canyon is definitely not a place you want to be in a rainstorm (common in July and August), when flash floods are a serious threat. Before entering the Narrows, check the weather forecast and discuss your plans with park rangers. Permits are required for longer treks in the Narrows but not for short day hikes (see "The Narrows," below).

Watchman Trail

3 mi. RT. Moderate. Access: Zion Canyon Visitor Center and Transportation Hub.

This moderately strenuous but relatively short hike gets surprisingly light use, possibly because it can be very hot in the middle of the day. Climbing to a plateau near the base of the Watchman formation, it offers splendid views of lower Zion Canyon, Oak Creek Canyon, the Towers of the Virgin, the West Temple formations, and the town of Springdale. The trail takes about 2 hours to complete and has an elevation gain of 368 feet.

Weeping Rock Trail

0.5 mi. RT. Easy to moderate. Access: Weeping Rock parking lot.

This is among the park's shortest and easiest rambles, although it is steep in spots. A self-guiding nature trail, it leads to a rock alcove with a spring and hanging gardens of ferns and wildflowers. Although paved, the trail is relatively steep (gaining 98 ft.) and slippery, and not suitable for wheelchairs.

LONGER TRAILS

Angels Landing Trail

5 mi. RT. Strenuous. Access: Grotto picnic area.

This 4-hour hike is most certainly not for anyone with even a mild fear of heights. The trail climbs 1,488 feet to a summit that offers spectacular views into Zion Canyon. *But be prepared:* The final half mile follows a narrow, knife-edge trail along a steep ridge, where footing can be slippery even under the best of circumstances. Support chains have been set along parts of the trail.

East Rim Trail

8 mi. RT. Strenuous. Access: Weeping Rock parking lot.

This strenuous hike takes all day and climbs over 2,000 feet to Observation Point. But if you can manage it, the incredible views down into the canyon make all the exertion worthwhile. This

trail also gives access to other east rim trails: Cable Mountain and Deertrap Mountain.

Hop Valley Trail

13.4 mi. RT. Moderate to strenuous. Access: Trailhead on Kolob Terrace Rd.

This backcountry trail loses about 1,000 feet as it meanders through sunny fields and past Gambel oak, partly following an old Jeep road and then a stream, before taking you to La Verkin Creek. Some hikers connect with the La Verkin Creek/Kolob Arch Trail to see Kolob Arch.

La Verkin Creek/Kolob Arch Trail

14 mi. RT. Strenuous. Access: Kolob Canyons Rd. at Lee Pass.

Although there are no drop-offs, this backcountry trail is quite strenuous. Descending almost 700 feet, it follows Timber and La Verkin creeks, ending at Kolob Arch, which, at 310 feet long, may be the world's largest freestanding arch.

The Narrows

16 mi. one way. Moderate. Access: Chamberlain's Ranch (outside the park). By permit only.

Hiking The Narrows is not hiking a trail at all, but walking or wading along the bottom of the Virgin River, through a spectacular 1,000-foot-deep chasm that, at a mere 24 feet wide, definitely lives up to its name. Passing fanciful sculptured sandstone arches, hanging gardens, and waterfalls, this moderately strenuous hike is recommended for those in good physical condition who are up to fighting sometimes-strong currents. Those who want a taste of The Narrows can walk and wade in from the end of the Riverside Walk (see above), but more than a short trip will involve a long full- or 2-day trek, which includes arranging a shuttle to the starting point at Chamberlain's Ranch and then transportation from the Temple of Sinawava, where you'll leave the canyon.

The Narrows is subject to flash flooding, and can be very treacherous. Park service officials remind hikers that they are responsible for their own safety, and should check on current water conditions and weather forecasts. This hike is *not* recommended when rain is forecast or threatening. Permits ($5) are required for full-day and overnight hikes, and must be purchased at the visitor center the day before your hike.

Taylor Creek Trail

5.4 mi. RT. Moderate. Access: Kolob Canyons Rd., about 2 mi. from Kolob Canyons Visitor Center.

This is a 4-hour hike along the middle fork of Taylor Creek—you might get your feet wet fording the creek. The trail leads past two historic cabins to Double Arch Alcove, with an elevation gain of 450 feet.

Exploring the Backcountry

There are numerous backpacking opportunities in the park, and a number of the day hikes discussed above are actually more comfortably done in 2 or more days. In addition to the park's established trails and the famous Narrows, there are a number of off-trail routes for those experienced in using topographical maps—get information at the Backcountry Desk in the Zion Canyon Visitor Center. Backcountry permits ($5 per person per night) are required for all overnight hikes in the park and all slot canyon routes.

The difficult **West Rim Trail** climbs over 3,500 feet into the high country, with a viewpoint overlooking the Right Fork of North Creek Canyon (at 12.8 miles) and then continuing to Lava Point. The round-trip distance is 26.6 miles and access is at the Grotto Picnic Area. There are striking views from most points on the trail.

Other Sports & Activities

Biking & Mountain Biking. Although bikes are prohibited on almost all trails, as well as forbidden to travel cross-country within the national park boundaries, Zion is among the West's most bike-friendly parks. The **Pa'rus Trail** runs a little under 2 miles along the Virgin River, from the south park entrance and South Campground to Zion Canyon Road, crossing the river and several creeks, and providing good views of the Watchman, West Temple, the Sentinel, and other lower canyon formations. The trail is paved and open to bicyclists, pedestrians, pets on leashes, and those with strollers or wheelchairs, but is closed to cars.

Starting in summer 2000, the **Zion Canyon Road** beyond its intersection with the Zion–Mt. Carmel Highway will be closed to private motor vehicles, except to motorists with reservations at Zion Lodge. However, the road, formerly called Zion Scenic Drive, will be open to hikers and bicyclists, as well as shuttle buses.

Bicycles can also be ridden on other park roads, though not through the Zion–Mt. Carmel Tunnel.

Although mountain bikes are prohibited on the trails (except the Pa'rus Trail), just outside the park—mostly on Bureau of Land Management and state-owned property—there are numerous rugged Jeep trails that are great for mountain biking, plus more than 100 miles of slickrock cross-country trails and single-track trails. Talk with the knowledgeable staff at **Bike Zion,** 1800 Zion Park Blvd., Springdale (☎ **800/475-4576** or 435/772-3929; www.bikezion.com) about the best trails for your interests and abilities. This full-service bike shop also offers maps, a full range of bikes and accessories, repairs, and rentals ($23 to $35 for a full day, $17 to $27 for a half day). The company can also arrange shuttles for you and your bike. Bike rentals are also available from **Scenic Cycles,** 180 Zion Park Blvd., Springdale (☎ 435/772-2453; www.sceniccycles. com) at similar rates.

Bike Zion offers **guided mountain bike trips** outside the park, starting at $35 for a 2½-hour tour; and a variety of multiday excursions, including some with catered gourmet meals or educational themes.

Horseback Riding. Guided rides in the park are available March through October from **Canyon Trail Rides,** P.O. Box 128, Tropic, UT 84776 (☎ 435/679-8665; www.onpages.com/canyonrides), with ticket sales and information at Zion Lodge. A 1-hour ride along the Virgin River costs $15 and a half-day ride on the Sand Beach Trail costs $40. Riders must weigh no more than 220 pounds, and children must be at least 5 years old for the 1-hour ride and 8 years old for the half-day ride. Reservations are advised.

Rock Climbing. Expert technical rock climbers love the tall sandstone cliffs in Zion Canyon, although rangers warn that much of the rock is loose, or "rotten," and climbing equipment and techniques suitable for granite are often less effective here. Permits (free at this writing) are required for overnight climbs, and because some routes may be closed at times, such as during peregrine falcon nesting from early spring through July, climbers should check at the visitor center before setting out.

Wildlife Viewing & Bird Watching. It's a rare visitor to Zion who doesn't spot a critter of some sort, from mule deer—often seen along roadways and in campgrounds year-round—to the many varieties of lizards seen from spring through fall, including the park's largest lizard, the chuckwalla, which can grow to 20 inches. The ringtail cat, a relative of the raccoon, prowls Zion Canyon at

night, and is not above helping itself to your camping supplies. Along the Virgin River you'll see bank beaver, so named because they live in burrows instead of building dams. The park is also home to coyotes, black-tailed jackrabbits, cottontails, chipmunks, several types of squirrels, voles, skunks, porcupines, gophers, and a variety of bats.

The rare peregrine falcon, among the world's fastest birds, sometimes nests in the Weeping Rock area, where you're also likely to see the American dipper, canyon wren, and white-throated swift. Bald eagles sometimes winter in the park, and you might also see golden eagles. Snakes include the poisonous great basin rattlesnake, usually found only below 8,000 feet elevation, as well as nonpoisonous king snakes and gopher snakes. Tarantulas are often seen in the late summer and fall.

Camping

INSIDE THE PARK

The best places to camp are at one of the **national park campgrounds,** just inside the park's south entrance. Reservations can be made for **Watchman Campground** (☎ 800/365-2267) up to 20 days before arrival, and a reservation charge of $2.50 per site per night will be added to the regular camping fee. Reservations are not accepted for **South Campground,** and it often fills by noon in the summer, so get there early in the day to claim a site.

Both of Zion's main campgrounds have paved roads, well-spaced sites, lots of trees, flush toilets, and that national park atmosphere you came here to enjoy. **Lava Point,** located on the Kolob Terrace, is more primitive (vault toilets), but has a delightful wooded setting. There are no showers in the national park, but the commercial campgrounds listed below offer showers, for a fee, to those camping in the park.

Just outside the park entrances, on both the east and south sides, are commercial campgrounds with all the usual amenities. Keep in mind that the park's visitor center, campgrounds, and most of its developed attractions are closer to the south entrance than the east.

Mukuntuweep RV Park & Campground, about 0.25 mile east of the East Entrance to Zion National Park on Utah 9 (P.O. Box 193, Orderville, UT 84758; ☎ 435/648-2154; www.expressweb.com/ zionpark), has great views of the surrounding rocks. There are some shade trees, grassy tent sites, a fishing pond, a playground, and a game room. Across the street, under the same management, is a store, restaurant (see "Dining," below), curio shop, and gas station. In addition to campsites, there are six log cabins, a hogan, and a tepee, all of which share the campground's bathhouse and cost $25 for two persons.

Just outside the South Entrance to the park is **Zion Canyon Campground,** on Zion Park Boulevard 0.25 mile south of the park's South Entrance, P.O. Box 99, Springdale, UT 84767 (☎ 435/772-3237; fax 435/772-3844). It has tree-shaded sites and grassy tent areas, and although quite crowded in summer, the campground is clean and well maintained. On the premises is a store with groceries, souvenirs, and RV supplies, plus a restaurant.

In addition to the campgrounds discussed here, there is also camping at Cedar Breaks National Monument. See "A Nearby National Monument," below.

Accommodations

Zion Lodge

In Zion National Park. ☎ **435/772-3213.** Fax 435/772-2001. Information and reservations: AmFac Parks & Resorts, 14001 E. Iliff Ave., Suite 600, Aurora, CO 80014. ☎ **303/297-2757.** Fax 303/338-2045. www.amfac.com. 121 units. A/C TEL. $85–$95 double; $95–$105 cabin. AE, DISC, MC, V.

The charming cabins on the forested grounds here offer spectacular views of the park's rock cliffs. Each contains a private porch, a stone (gas-burning) fireplace, two double beds, pine board walls, and log beams. The comfortable motel units are basic, with two queen-size beds and all the usual amenities except televisions. Suites have a king-size bed, a separate sitting room, and refrigerator. At the gift shop you can get everything from postcards and T-shirts to top-quality silver and turquoise American Indian jewelry. The lodge's restaurant (see "Dining," below) serves up wonderful views with its three daily meals.

The properties listed here are either in Springdale, a village of some 350 people at the park's south entrance, or between

Campground	Elev.	Total Sites	RV Hookups	Dump Station	Toilets	Drinking Water
Lava Point	7,900	6	0	No	Yes	No
South	4,000	126	0	Yes	Yes	Yes
Watchman	4,000	231	50+	Yes	Yes	Yes
Mukuntuweep	6,000	150	30	Yes	Yes	Yes
Zion Canyon	3,800	202	102	Yes	Yes	Yes

Springdale and the nearby community of Virgin, to the west.

Best Western Zion Park Inn

1215 Zion Park Blvd., Springdale, UT 84767. ☎ **800/934-7275** or 435/772-3200. Fax 435/772-2449. 120 units. A/C TV TEL. Apr–Oct $88–$94 double, $110–$160 suite and family unit; Nov–Mar $58–$68 double, $85–$125 suite and family unit. AE, DC, DISC, MC, V. Pets accepted for a fee at management discretion.

Rooms in this handsome two-story complex are tastefully appointed in Southwest style, with two double beds, two queens, or one king-size bed. The grounds are beautifully landscaped, with phenomenal views of the area's red rock formations. Facilities include a heated outdoor swimming pool and hot tub, restaurant serving three meals daily, gift shop, convenience store, guest laundry, liquor store, and conference and meeting rooms.

Bumbleberry Inn

97 Bumbleberry Lane, Springdale, UT 84767. ☎ **800/828-1534** or 435/772-3224. Fax 435/772-3947. www.bumbleberry.com. E-mail: bumbleberry@southernutah.com. 47 units. A/C TV TEL. Apr–Oct $62–$77 double; Nov–Mar $49–$62 double. DISC, MC, V.

Set back from the main highway, the Bumbleberry offers large, quiet rooms at a good price. Furnishings are simple but more than adequate, with a desk in addition to a table and two chairs, and prints depicting the area's scenery. Most rooms contain two queen-size beds and tub/shower combinations, although five rooms have one queen bed and shower only. Facilities include indoor racquetball, an arcade, indoor whirlpool tub, heated outdoor pool, and an adjacent restaurant that serves three meals daily.

Canyon Ranch Motel

668 Zion Park Blvd. (P.O. Box 175), Springdale, UT 84767. ☎ **435/772-3357.** Fax 435/772-3057. 21 units. A/C TV. Mar–Oct $58–$78 double; Nov–Feb $44–$54 double. AE, DISC, MC, V. Pets accepted at management discretion.

Consisting of a series of two- and four-unit cottages set back from the highway, this motel has the look of 1930s cabins on the outside while providing modern motel rooms inside. Rooms are either new or newly remodeled, and options include one queen- or king-size bed, two queens, or one queen and one double. Some rooms have showers only, while some have shower/tub combinations. Kitchen units are also available. The units, all with great views of the surrounding rock formations, surround a lawn with trees and picnic tables, and there is also an outdoor heated swimming pool and whirlpool tub.

Canyon Vista
Bed & Breakfast at Zion

2175 Zion Park Blvd. (P.O. Box 351), Springdale, UT 84767. ☎ **435/772-3801.**

Showers	Fire Pits/ Grills	Laundry	Public Phone	Reserve	Fees	Open
No	Yes	No	No	No	Free	May–Oct
No	Yes	No	Yes	No	$10	Apr–Sept
No	Yes	No	Yes	Yes	$10–$14	Year-round
Yes	Yes	Yes	Yes	Yes	$14–$19	Year-round
Yes	Yes	Yes	Yes	Yes	$15–$20	Year-round

www.canyonvista.net. 2 units. A/C TV TEL. $100 double (tax included). Rates include continental breakfast. DISC, MC, V. Pets accepted.

Unusual among bed-and-breakfast inns, Canyon Vista not only allows guests to bring their children and pets, but encourages them! The inn's two spacious studio suites are decorated with country oak furnishings and local artwork, with a modern, Southwest look. Each suite has a king-size bed, queen-size hide-a-bed, and a comfortable living area with a TV/VCR combo (with movie videos) and a stereo. There's a fully equipped kitchenette (complete with coffee, tea, and popcorn), a working desk with a phone with data port, and a bathroom with a shower/tub combo, robes, and a good selection of toiletries. Breakfast, delivered to the room, includes fresh-baked sweet breads, orange juice, granola, fruit, yogurt, hot and cold cereals, and hot beverages. A snack is served each afternoon, including biscuits for pets.

Cliffrose Lodge & Gardens

281 Zion Park Blvd. (P.O. Box 510), Springdale, UT 84767. ☎ **800/243-UTAH** or 435/772-3234. Fax 435/772-3900. www.cliffroselodge.com. 36 units. A/C TV TEL. Summer $88–$145 double. Call for winter rates. AE, DISC, MC, V.

With river frontage and 5 acres of lawns, shade trees, and flower gardens, the Cliffrose offers a beautiful setting just outside the entrance to Zion National Park. The modern, well-kept rooms have all the standard motel appointments, with wood furnishings, floral-print bedspreads, and unusually large bathrooms with shower/tub combinations. On the lawns you'll find comfortable seating, including a lawn swing, plus a playground and large outdoor heated pool. There's also a self-service laundry.

Desert Pearl Inn

707 Zion Park Blvd., Springdale, UT 84767. ☎ **888/828-0898** or 435/772-8888. Fax 435/772-8889. www.desertpearl.com. E-mail: info@desertpearl.com. 61 units. A/C TV TEL. $70–$150 double. AE, DISC, MC, V.

This handsome property offers luxurious and comfortable accommodations with beautiful views of the area's scenery. Spacious rooms, with modern Southwest decor, have either two queen-size beds or one king. Units also have comfortable seating, refrigerators, microwave ovens, wet bars, and bidets. The grounds are nicely landscaped. The inn also has a huge outdoor heated pool and whirlpool.

El Rio Lodge in Zion Canyon

995 Zion Park Blvd. (P.O. Box 204), Springdale, UT 84767. ☎ **888/772-3205** or 435/772-3205. www.elriolodge.qpg.com. E-mail: elrio@infowest.com. 11 units. A/C TV. Summer $47–$52 double, $60 suite; lower in winter. AE, DISC, MC, V. Pets accepted with $10 fee.

A mom-and-pop operation built in the early 1960s, El Rio has five rooms upstairs and five downstairs, all with private bathrooms and tub/shower combos. Although small, the rooms are very clean and comfortable, with simple but attractive decor. The upstairs rooms have two double beds and an outdoor walkway and porch affording terrific views of Zion Canyon. The downstairs rooms have one queen bed each, though rollaways are available. The suite has its own private parking area, refrigerator, extralarge bathroom, and use of the yard, with great views of the rock walls of Zion Canyon. Although there are no phones in the rooms, a public phone is available outside.

Flanigan's Inn

428 Zion Park Blvd. (P.O. Box 100), Springdale, UT 84767. ☎ **800/765-7787** or 435/772-3244. Fax 435/772-3396. 39 units. A/C TV TEL. Mid-Mar to Nov $79–$99 double; Dec to mid-Mar $49–$69 double. Rates include continental breakfast. AE, DISC, MC, V.

A mountain lodge atmosphere pervades this very attractive complex of natural wood and rock, set among trees, lawns, and flowers just outside the entrance to Zion National Park. Parts of the inn date from 1947, but all rooms were completely renovated in the early 1990s, and have Southwest decor with wood furnishings and local art. Some units also have whirlpool tubs and bidets, and one room has a fireplace. Flanigan's has its own nature trail leading to a hilltop vista, a spa, and a heated outdoor swimming pool. Kitchenettes are available, but if you don't want to cook, the on-site restaurant serves dinner, in addition to a continental breakfast for guests only (see "Dining," below).

Harvest House
Bed & Breakfast at Zion

29 Canyon View Dr. (P.O. Box 125), Springdale, UT 84767. ☎ **435/772-3880.** Fax 435/772-3327. www.harvesthouse.net. 4 units. A/C. $80–$100 double. Rates include full breakfast. DISC, MC, V. Children over 6 only.

This Utah territorial–style house, built in 1989, has a cactus garden out front and a garden sitting area in back with a koi (Japanese carp) pond and spectacular views of the national park rock formations. The rooms are furnished with an eclectic mixture of contemporary and wicker items, and decorated with original art and photography. One upstairs room faces west and has grand sunset views, and the other two have private decks facing Zion's impressive rock structures. The suite can accommodate up to five adults. The full, gourmet, yet low-fat, breakfasts are sumptuous, and include fresh baked sweet breads, fresh-squeezed orange juice, granola, fruit, yogurt, and a hot main course that changes daily. Facilities include an outdoor whirlpool.

O'Tooles Bed & Breakfast

980 Zion Park Blvd. (P.O. Box 29), Springdale, UT 84767. ☎ **435/772-3457.** Fax 435/772-3324. www.otooles.com. 5 units (2 with shared bathroom). A/C. Apr–Oct $69–$79 double; $125 suite; lower rates off-season. Rates include full breakfast. DISC, MC, V. Children over 7 welcome.

This lovely two-story bed-and-breakfast, built in 1929, is furnished mostly with antiques, many from the families of owners Rick and Michelle O'Toole. On the first floor there are two cheerful rooms, decorated in early 20th-century style. They share a bathroom (shower only), and each has one double bed and a private sink. Upstairs the large suite takes up the entire floor, and has a vaulted ceiling, a wood-burning stove, a queen-size bed plus a queen futon, and its own kitchen. In addition, the cute Garden Cottage, which was moved here from inside the national park, contains three rooms, two on the main floor and one in the basement. The homemade breakfast generally includes home-baked breads, fresh fruit, and a hot main dish such as an omelette or pancakes.

Snow Family Guest Ranch

633 E. Utah 9 (P.O. Box 790190), Virgin, UT 84779. ☎ **800/308-7669** or 435/635-2500. Fax 435/635-2758. www.snowfamilyranch. com. E-mail: bandb@redrock.net. 10 units. A/C. $85–$105 double. Rates include full breakfast. AE, DISC, MC, V.

This delightful horse ranch is nestled in the shadow of Zion National Park on 12 acres of green pastures, all enclosed in white rail fences. The location is peaceful and quiet, just 12 miles west of the park's south entrance. The rooms have handsome log furnishings, and either one or two queen-size beds, a king, or two twins; most also feature comfortable window seats. Views extend out across the ranch to the red rock mesas and canyons beyond. There is also a living room with piano, a separate TV room with a big-screen TV, and a swimming pool, hot tub, gazebo, and a pond. Guided scenic trail rides are offered for an additional charge.

Dining

INSIDE THE PARK

Zion Lodge

Zion National Park. ☎ **435/772-3213.** Dinner reservations required in the summer. Breakfast $2.95–$5.95; lunch $4.95–$9.95; dinner $8.95–$19.95. AE, DC, DISC, MC, V. Daily 6:30–10am, 11:30am–3pm, and 5:30–9pm. AMERICAN.

A mountain lodge atmosphere prevails here, complete with large windows that look out toward the park's magnificent rock formations. House specialties at dinner include an excellent slow-roasted prime rib au jus, and the very popular Utah red mountain trout. The menu also includes several chicken dishes, such as a skinless chicken breast basted with a spicy Caribbean sauce and served with a red-onion relish. Vegetarians have several choices, such as pasta marissa and black-bean ragout. Ask about the lodge's specialty ice creams and other exotic desserts. At lunch you'll find trout, barbecued pork ribs, burgers, sandwiches, and salads. Breakfasts offer all the usual American selections. The restaurant will pack lunches to go and offers full liquor service.

NEAR THE PARK

All of the following restaurants, except the Zion Mt. Carmel Restaurant, are located in Springdale, just outside the park's south entrance.

Bit & Spur Restaurant & Saloon

1212 Zion Park Blvd., Springdale. ☎ **435/772-3498.** Reservations recommended. Main courses $7–$16.50. MC, V. Mar–Oct 5–10pm (bar open until 1am) and a weekend brunch is offered May–Sept (call for hours); Nov–Feb Thurs–Mon 5–10pm. Closed Christmas holidays. MEXICAN/SOUTHWESTERN.

This may look like an Old West saloon, with its rough wood-and-stone walls and exposed beam ceiling, but it has a family dining room, patio dining, and original oil paintings on the walls. The food here is also a notch or two above what might be expected, closer to what you'd expect in a good Santa Fe restaurant. You'll find generous portions of Mexican standards such as burritos, flautas, chile rellenos, and a traditional chile stew with pork; but you'll also find more exotic creations, such as the *pollo relleno,* grilled breast of chicken stuffed with cilantro pesto and goat cheese and served with pineapple salsa. Highly recommended is the deep-dish chicken enchilada, with scallions, green chiles, and cheese. The Bit & Spur has full liquor service and an extensive wine list.

Flanigan's Inn

428 Zion Park Blvd., Springdale. ☎ **435/772-3244.** Reservations recommended. Main courses $8.95–$18. AE, DISC, MC, V. Mon–Thurs 3–9:30pm, Fri–Sun until 10pm. Call for winter hours. AMERICAN/REGIONAL.

This restaurant makes the most of the area's spectacular scenery with large windows for inside diners plus an outdoor patio. The menu includes items such as wood-fired pizzas, pastas, salads, and Black Angus beef. Especially recommended are the New York steak in a green peppercorn sauce and the grilled spring lamb chops with a demiglacé sauce. Microbrewery draft beers are available, and the wine cellar stocks more than 2,000 bottles.

Reese's Log House Restaurant

2400 Zion Park Blvd., Springdale. ☎ **435/772-3000.** Reservations not accepted. Lunch $4.95–$8.95, dinner $7.95–$21.95. AE, CB, DC, DISC, MC, V. Daily 11:30am–9pm. AMERICAN.

This magnificent log structure—built with logs salvaged from the great 1988 fire in Yellowstone National Park—boasts splendid views from every window. The casual atmosphere is reflected in the high-beamed ceiling, log walls, simple Western decor, solid wood tables, and cushioned chairs. Slate tile from India was used on the floor. There are hot sandwiches for lunch, including burgers, turkey, chicken, fish, and steak; plus cold deli sandwiches, soup, pasta, and salads. The dinner menu includes chicken fried steak, a turkey breast tenderloin steak, several beefsteaks, and the Log House specialty chicken dinner. The building also houses a gift shop, a Western clothing store, and a North American wildlife exhibit. Beer and wine are served.

Zion Mt. Carmel Restaurant

Utah 9, 0.25 mi. east of the east entrance to Zion National Park. ☎ **435/648-2829.** Sandwiches $3.50–$5.50; Mexican dishes $2.95–$7.95. AE, DISC, MC, V. Daily 9am–5pm. AMERICAN/MEXICAN.

This is a down-home coffee shop, with great homemade pies, spicy New Mexican–style Southwest dishes, burgers, sandwiches, shakes, and sundaes. Locals love the green chile beef and bean burrito and the enchilada-style burrito, smothered in chile sauce. The breakfast menu includes the standards: ham and eggs, omelets, pancakes, and French toast. No alcoholic beverages are served.

Zion Park Gift & Deli

666 Zion Park Blvd., Springdale. ☎ **435/772-3843.** $4.30–$8.20. AE, DISC, MC, V. Summer, Mon–Sat 8am–9pm; shorter hours in winter. SANDWICHES.

A good choice for a top quality deli-style sandwich at an economical price, which you eat at one of the cafe-style tables inside, on the outdoor patio, or carry off on your trip into the national park. All baked goods, including the excellent sandwich breads and sub rolls, are made in-house. In typical fast-food restaurant style, you order at the counter and wait as your meal is prepared, with your choice of bread, meats, cheeses, and condiments. It's also a good breakfast stop for those who enjoy fresh-baked cinnamon rolls, muffins, banana nut bread, and similar goodies, with a cup of espresso. Locally made candy and 16 flavors of ice cream and frozen yogurt are also offered. No alcohol is served.

Zion Pizza & Noodle

868 Zion Park Blvd., Springdale. ☎ **435/772-3815.** Reservations not accepted. Main courses $7.95–$11.95. No credit cards. Summer Mon–Thurs 4–10:30pm; Fri–Sun 11:30am–10:30pm. Call for winter hours. PIZZA/PASTA.

Located in a former church with a turquoise steeple, this busy restaurant has small, closely spaced tables and black-and-white photos on the walls. Patrons order at the counter and help themselves at the soft drink beverage bar while waiting for their food to be delivered. The 12-inch pizzas, with lots of chewy crust, are baked in a slate stone oven. You can get exotic combinations, such as the southwestern burrito pizza or barbecue chicken pizza, as well as a basic cheese pizza or add any of more than a dozen extra toppings, from pepperoni to green chiles to pineapple. The noodle side of the menu offers a variety of pastas, such as penne with grilled chicken, broccoli, carrots, fresh cream. Take out and delivery are available. The restaurant serves microbrews and domestic beer.

Picnic & Camping Supplies

You'll find most of the groceries and camping and RV supplies you want in Springdale, just outside the park's south entrance. At **Zion Canyon Campground,** on Zion Park Boulevard 0.5-mile south of the park's south entrance (☎ 435/772-3237), is a store with groceries, souvenirs, and RV supplies, plus a restaurant. In downtown Springdale, the **Zion Park Market,** 855 Zion Park Blvd. (☎ 435/772-3251), stocks a good selection of groceries. On the south end of Springdale on Utah 9 (the opposite side of town from the national park), is the highly recommended **Springdale Fruit Company** (☎ 435/772-3222), which sells fresh organic fruits, vegetables, and juices (try the fruit smoothies), plus trail mix and baked goods. It also has a picnic area. The **Switchback C-Store,** 1149 South Zion Park Blvd. (☎ 435/772-3700), stocks snacks and pastries and contains the local **state liquor store.** Those in need of outdoor equipment, hiking boots, clothing, and the like will find what they need at **Zion Outdoor,** 868 Zion Park Blvd. (☎ 435/772-0630).

Just outside the east entrance to the park there is a small store, gas station, restaurant, curio shop, and campground.

Nearby Entertainment

Virtual nature and live music and theater attract national park visitors to Springdale.

The Grand Circle: A National Park Odyssey, a multimedia production presented on a 24-by-40-foot screen in the outdoor Obert C. Tanner Amphitheater, is an excellent introduction to the national parks and monuments of southern Utah and northern Arizona. Using a state-of-the-art sound and projection system, and with the cliffs of Zion National Park in the background, the 1-hour program gives a brief look at the geology of the area, but devotes most of its time, sounds, and sights to the awe-inspiring scenery. Showings are scheduled at dusk three or four nights each week from late May to early September. Tickets cost $4 for adults, $3 for students and children under 12, and $10 per family.

The amphitheater, located just off Zion Park Boulevard, is also the venue for a variety of **concerts** and other live productions each summer, ranging from the annual Utah Symphony pops concert in late June or early July, to bluegrass, country, and acoustic performances, plus a fun-filled melodrama. Tickets cost about $8. Contact **Dixie College** in St. George (☎ 435/652-7994).

You'll find an even bigger screen—some six stories high by 80 feet wide—at **Zion Canyon Theatre** (☎ 435/772-2400), just outside the south entrance to Zion National Park at 145 Zion Park Blvd. Here you can see the dramatic film *Zion Canyon—Treasure of the Gods* with thrilling scenes of the Zion National Park area, including a hair-raising flash flood through Zion Canyon's Narrows and some dizzying bird's-eye views. Admission costs $7 for adults and $4.50 for children 3 to 11. Shows begin hourly, 364 days a year: April through October from 9am to 9pm, and November through March from 11am to 7pm. The theater complex also contains a tourist information center, ATM, picnic area, gift and souvenir shops, food emporium, and bookstore.

A Nearby National Monument

The area surrounding Zion National Park offers a variety of scenic wonders and recreational opportunities. In addition to other nearby national parks, which are discussed elsewhere in this book, you'll discover one relatively unknown gem, Cedar Breaks National Monument, that looks a lot like a small version of Bryce Canyon National Park.

CEDAR BREAKS NATIONAL MONUMENT

This delightful little park is a wonderful place to spend a few hours or several days, gazing down from the rim into the spectacular natural amphitheater, hiking the trails, and camping among the spruce, firs, and summer wildflowers.

The park forms a natural coliseum, more than 2,000 feet deep and over 3 miles across, filled with stone spires, arches, and columns shaped by the forces of erosion and painted in ever-changing reds, purples, oranges, and ochers. Why the name Cedar Breaks? Well, the pioneers who came here called such badlands "breaks," and they mistook the juniper trees along the cliff bases for cedars.

JUST THE FACTS

When to Go. At over 10,000 feet elevation, it's always pleasantly cool at Cedar Breaks. At night it actually gets downright cold, so take a jacket or sweater, even if the temperature is scorching just down the road in St. George. The monument opens for its short summer season only after the snow melts, usually in late May, and closes in October, unless you happen to have a pair of cross-country skis or a snowmobile, in which case you can visit anytime.

Getting There. Cedar Breaks National Monument is 85 miles north of the main section of Zion National Park. From Zion's south entrance head west on Utah 9, then north on Utah 17 to I-15. Then follow I-15 north to Exit 57 for Cedar City, turn and head east on Utah 14, then north on Utah 148, which goes straight into the monument. From the Kolob Canyons section of Zion, which is off Exit 40 of I-15, it is only 40 miles to Cedar Breaks.

The national monument is 23 miles east of Cedar City, 56 miles west of Bryce Canyon National Park, and 247 miles south of Salt Lake City. If you're coming from Bryce Canyon or other points east, the park is accessible from the town of Panguitch via Utah 143. If you're coming from the north, take the Parowan Exit off I-15 and head south on Utah 143. It's a steep climb from whichever direction you choose, so take care, especially if your vehicle is prone to vapor lock or (like many motor homes) to loss of power on hills.

Information & Visitor Center. One mile from the South Entrance gate is the visitor center, open daily June to late September, with exhibits on the geology, flora, and fauna of Cedar Breaks. You can purchase books and maps there, and ask rangers for help in planning your visit. For information, contact the **Superintendent, Cedar Breaks National Monument,** 2390 W. Utah 56, Suite 11, Cedar City, UT 84720 (☎ **435/586-9451;** www.nps.gov/cebr).

Fees. Admission is $4 per vehicle or $2 per person on foot or bike. Camping costs $10 per night.

Health & Safety Concerns. The high elevation—10,350 feet at the visitor center—is likely to cause shortness of breath and tiredness. Those with heart or respiratory conditions should consult their doctors before making the trip to Cedar Breaks. During thunderstorms you need to avoid overlooks and other high, exposed areas—they're often targets for lightning.

Ranger Programs. During the monument's short summer season, rangers offer nightly **campfire talks** at the campground; **geology talks** at Point Supreme, a viewpoint near the visitor center, every day at 2:30pm and Monday through Friday also at 10am; and **guided hikes** on Saturday and Sunday mornings. A complete schedule is posted at the visitor center and the campground.

EXPLORING CEDAR BREAKS BY CAR

The 5-mile road through Cedar Breaks National Monument offers easy access to the monument's scenic overlooks and trailheads. Allow 30 to 45 minutes to make the drive. Start at the visitor center and nearby **Point Supreme** for a panoramic view of the amphitheater. Then drive north, past the campground and picnic ground turnoff, to **Sunset View** for a closer look at the amphitheater and its colorful canyons. From each of these overlooks you'll be able to see out across Cedar Valley, over the Antelope and Black mountains and into the Escalante Desert.

Continue north to **Chessman Ridge Overlook,** so named because the stone hoodoos directly below the overlook seem like massive chess pieces. Watch for swallows and swifts soaring among the rock formations. Then get back into your car and head north to **Alpine Pond,** to walk among the wildflowers on the self-guided nature trail (see "Hiking," below). Finally, proceed to **North View,** which offers perhaps your best view of the amphitheater and its stately rock statues.

SUMMER SPORTS & ACTIVITIES

Hiking. There are no trails to the bottom of the amphitheater, but the monument does have two high-country trails. The fairly easy 2-mile **Alpine Pond Trail** loop leads to a picturesque forest glade and pond surrounded by wildflowers, and offers panoramic views of the amphitheater along the way. A trail guide is available at the trailhead.

A somewhat more challenging hike, the 4-mile **Spectra Point Trail** (also called the Ramparts Trail) follows the rim more closely than the Alpine Pond Trail. It also takes you through fields of wildflowers and groves of bristlecone pines more than 1,500 years old. You'll need to be especially careful of your footing along the exposed cliff edges.

Wildlife Watching. Because of its relative remoteness, Cedar Breaks is a good place for spotting wildlife. You're likely to see mule deer grazing in the meadows along the road early and late in the day. Marmots make their dens near the rim, and are often seen along the Spectra Point Trail. You'll spot ground squirrels, red squirrels, and chipmunks everywhere. Pikas, related to rabbits, are here too, but it's unlikely you'll see one. They're small, with short ears and stubby tails, and prefer the high, rocky slopes.

Birders should have no trouble spotting the Clark's nutcracker in the campground, with its gray torso and black-and-white wings and tail. The monument is also home to swallows, swifts, blue grouse, and golden eagles.

WINTER SPORTS & ACTIVITIES

The monument is essentially shut down from late October through mid-May, but though the snow-blocked roads will keep cars out, they're perfect for snowmobilers and cross-country skiers, who usually come over from nearby Brian Head Ski Area. Keep in mind, though, that all facilities are closed and the only people you're likely to see will be an occasional park ranger patrolling on a snowmobile.

CAMPING

A 30-site campground in a beautiful high-mountain setting, **Point Supreme,** just north of the visitor center, is open from June to mid-September, with sites available on a first-come, first-served basis. It has rest rooms, drinking water, picnic tables, grills, and an amphitheater for the ranger's evening campfire programs; but there are no showers or RV hookups. Camping fee is $10 per night. Keep in mind that, even in midsummer, temperatures can drop into the 30s at night at this elevation, so bring cool-weather gear.

USEFUL TOLL-FREE NUMBERS & WEB SITES

◆ Airlines ◆

Air Canada
☎ 800/776-3000
www.aircanada.ca

Air Nevada
☎ 888/575-4546

Alaska Airlines
☎ 800/426-0333
www.alaskaair.com

American Airlines
☎ 800/433-7300
www.americanair.com

American Trans Air
☎ 800/435-9282
www.ata.com

America West Airlines
America West Express
☎ 800/235-9292
www.americawest.com

Big Sky Airlines
☎ 800/237-7788

British Airways
☎ 800/247-9297
☎ 0345/222-111 in Britain
www.british-airways.com

Canadian Airlines
  International
☎ 800/426-7000
www.cdnair.ca

Continental Airlines
☎ 800/525-0280
www.flycontinental.com

Delta Air Lines
☎ 800/221-1212
www.delta-air.com

Eagle Canyon Airlines
☎ 800.446-4584

Frontier Airlines
☎ 800.432-1359

Hawaiian Airlines
☎ 800/367-5320
www.hawaiianair.com

Horizon Air
☎ 800/547-9308

Kiwi International
  Air Lines
☎ 800/538-5494

L.A.B Flying Service
☎ 800/426-0543

Mesa Airlines
☎ 800/637-2247

Midway Airlines
☎ 800/446-4392
www.midwayair.com

Midwest Express
☎ 800/452-2022
www.midwestexpress.com

Northwest Airlines
☎ 800/225-2525
www.nwa.com

Scenic Airlines
☎ 800/634-6801

Skywest
☎ 800/453-9417

Sun Country
☎ 800/752-1218

Southwest Airlines
☎ 800/435-9792
www.iflyswa.com

Tower Air
☎ 800/34-TOWER
  (800/348-6937) outside
  New York
☎ 718/553-8500
www.towerair.com

Trans World Airlines
  (TWA)
☎ 800/221-2000
www.twa.com

United Airlines
United Express
☎ 800/241-6522
www.ual.com

US Airways
☎ 800/428-4322
www.usairways.com

Virgin Atlantic Airways
☎ 800/862-8621 in
  continental U.S.
☎ 0293/747-747 in
  Britain
www.fly.virgin.com

◆ Car Rental Agencies ◆

Advantage
☎ 800/777-5500
www.arac.com

Alamo
☎ 800/327-9633
www.goalamo.com

Avis
☎ 800/331-1212 in
   continental U.S.
☎ 800/TRY-AVIS in Canada
www.avis.com

Budget
☎ 800/527-0700
www.budgetrentacar.com

Dollar
☎ 800/800-4000
www.dollarcar.com

Enterprise
☎ 800/325-8007
www.pickenterprise.com

Hertz
☎ 800/654-3131
www.hertz.com

National
☎ 800/CAR-RENT
www.nationalcar.com

Payless
☎ 800/PAYLESS
www.paylesscar.com

Rent-A-Wreck
☎ 800/535-1391
rent-a-wreck.com

Thrifty
☎ 800/367-2277
www.thrifty.com

Index